— SONGWRITERS —

—SONGWRITERS—

A Biographical Dictionary with Discographies

by NIGEL HARRISON

McFarland & Company, Inc., Publishers

Jefferson, North Carolina, and London

British Library Cataloguing-in-Publication data are available

Library of Congress Cataloguing-in-Publication Data

Harrison, Nigel, 1960–
    Songwriters : a biographical dictionary with discographies / by
Nigel Harrison.
       p.   cm.
    Includes bibliographical references and index.
    ISBN 0-7864-0542-2 (library binding : 50# alk. paper) ∞
    1. Popular music — Bio-bibliography — Dictionaries.
2. Composers — Biography — Dictionaries.   3. Lyricists —
Biography — Dictionaries.   4. Popular music — Discography.
I. Title.
ML102.P66H47   1998
782.42164'092'2 — dc21
  [B]   98-11824
                                              CIP
                                              MN

Manufactured in the United States of America

McFarland & Company, Inc., Publishers
  Box 611, Jefferson, North Carolina 28640

For Alison and Marlowe

Acknowledgments

My gratitude is extended to the following individuals and organizations, without whom this project would never have been accomplished:

Corale Amende at the Diamond Music Companies, ASCAP, BMI, Mark Broomer of Activ 8, Linda Calloway, Ian Carr, Jim Cook, Sam Dees, Jim DiGiovanni at F. Sharp Productions, Enid and Gordon Harrison, Michael Harrison at the BBC, Melanie Smith-Howard at Harlan Howard Songs, Tammi Holt at Perspective, Matthew James, Warren James at Night River, Dean Kaufman, Gordon Lightfoot Concerts, Bill Lowery at Lowery Music, Don McLean, Henry Mancini Enterprises, Inc., Todd C. Mayfield at Curtom Records, Paul Meissner for Daryl Hall, Middle Ear, Inc., Mona at HAG, Inc., Lisa Phelps at Leiber and Stoller Productions, Pete Seeger, Karen Simpson at Neil Sedaka Music, Robin Siegel at the Jimmy Webb Music Company, Joe South, Carla Stoelting at Alive Enterprises, Trevor Timmers, Joe Ward, and countless library staff across two continents.

I am also indebted to my wife for her patience and computer skills.

Table of Contents

Music is a moral law. It gives a soul to the universe, wings to the mind, flight to the imagination, a charm to sadness and a gaiety and life to everything. It is the essence of order and leads to all that is good, true and beautiful.

PLATO

Without music life would be a mistake.

NIETZSCHE

Song is the joint art of words and music, two arts under emotional pressure coalescing into a third.

ENCYCLOPÆDIA BRITANNICA

The popular song of the past half-century had the largest impact on American culture of any so-called art form… The popular song is American culture!

IRVING CAESAR

Preface

This book is devoted to over 1000 composers and lyricists of the finest and most popular songs of the nineteenth and twentieth centuries. The musical genres featured range from early folk, minstrel, and parlor songs to mainstream rock and pop. Although not a history of songwriting, the book attempts to recognize collectively everyone responsible for the evolution of the popular song.

Despite being the architects of popular music, songwriters still find that their names appear in the smallest print on sheet music and recordings, a frequent under-recognition that is in direct contrast to their importance. Albert Hammond, a successful songwriter, said in 1989, "The singers are nothing without the songwriters because without the song, what would they sing?"

Popular songwriters first began composing professionally in the late nineteenth century. Before then, songs were seldom published and certainly not written for profit. This encyclopedia is the first comprehensive guide to English-language composers and lyricists who have been published or recorded from the late 1800s to the present day. It provides biographical information and a catalog of each writer's albums and CDs, as well as all compositions that attained a ranking on British or American charts. It reveals the enormous variety of songwriters whose songs have gained popularity or have been influential over the last century. Although most of the entries are of British, American, or Canadian songwriters, a few of other nationalities are included because they were successful in translation or they originally wrote in English.

The inclusion criteria for this encyclopedia have been kept as simple as possible. The work features those individuals or partnerships who have been either commercially or critically successful, as well as those who have not necessarily been successful themselves but who have had an influence on other songwriters or performers. Some generally overlooked songwriters who meet neither of these criteria are also featured, as are a handful whose mere one or two song contributions have been highly significant. Performers such as Willie Nelson and Ray Charles, who have been successful with their own material, are included, whereas the likes of Bonnie Raitt and Joan Baez, who compose relatively little of their overall output and are principally song interpreters, are not. Performers or group members who have not necessarily been successful themselves but have written hit songs for others are listed; however, group members who contribute only the occasional single or album track are not included.

It has never been my intention to condense an entire lifetime of artistic work into a few sentences or a paragraph. Each entry is only a basic overview of a particular songwriter's success and significance. Further information on these individuals may be found in the many books that have been written about popular music in recent years, some of which are listed in this book's bibliography. Liner notes on the listed recordings are also a good source of information. My own extensive research took me to a variety of libraries in Britain and America, and also consisted of intensive listening sessions involving the vast record collections belonging to some ever-patient friends and colleagues. Many publishers, agents, and managers were extremely helpful and forthcoming with discographies and song lists for their artists; some of these entries would have been inconceivable without their assistance. Unfortunately, despite exhaustive efforts, even basic biographical information remains unavailable for some individuals. The many music-related magazines and fanzines that have been published since the late 1960s have made the researcher's job considerably easier in recent times, and information from these sources has been cross-checked whenever possible.

All musical genres that are based around songs are included in this book, and the term "popular music" is taken to mean any musical format that features melodies with words. Musical genres are at best contentious and at worst inaccurate and restricting, but they do serve as a descriptive starting point. It is accepted that the works of many songwriters are often recorded in more than one musical style, and one of the joys of a good song is the different ways in which it can be interpreted. The principal musical categories used are Tin Pan Alley (non-show and film songs spanning the approximate period 1900–1940); C&W (country and western, country rock, hillbilly, and western swing); R&B (rhythm and blues, soul, and funk); rap; music hall; vaudeville; blues (pure blues as opposed to R&B); gospel; jazz; folk; film and stage (songs initially written for movies or theatrical shows); reggae (and ska); pop (a catch-all phrase used to define mainstream popular music); and rock (a heavier, more stylized form of pop that is often performed by electric guitar, drum, and keyboard based groups). Composers of *lieder* and solely instrumental music such as new age, classical, and most jazz are generally excluded, although there are some exceptions, notably film composers who have had their main title themes set to lyrics and sung by groups or vocalists. Essentially, anything that might qualify for or find its way onto the pop, country, or R&B charts is included. The size of each entry relates to an individual's musical significance, degree of commercial success, or volume of recorded output, none of which is necessarily a determination of quality.

The book is arranged alphabetically by last name, except where a songwriter is best known by a single name or nickname (for example, DOCTOR John is followed by Thomas DOLBY). All names beginning with "Mac" or "Mc" read as "Mac"; thus Paddy McAloon precedes Michael MacDonald, and both come before Madonna.

Each entry begins with the name of the songwriter, followed by a birth name (if different), a date and place of birth (and death where applicable), a principal musical genre, the main musical instruments played (if any), a short biographical section, and a list of British and American chart compositions. Next comes a list of original long-playing vinyl albums or compact disks, the titles of which appear in boldface, followed by the year of release, record label, and peak chart positions — e.g. **Born to Run** (1975, Columbia) US#3 UK#17. Noteworthy compilation albums are also listed. The "HIT VERSION" section that follows is an alphabetical list of every known chart version of any songs by that particular songwriter since 1890 (when *Billboard* first compiled a pop chart), naming the artist who recorded it, the year that it entered the chart, and the peak chart position. (Chart positions followed by + denote a disk still rising on the chart when the book went to press.) It should be noted that records are often released on different labels in Europe and America, and that all record labels and dates correspond to first-issue, country-of-origin releases.

Many songs listed in this book were collaborative efforts by two or more people — most often a composer and a lyricist, though the labor was not always so neatly divided. Had each of the collaborators been given an individual entry, it would have been necessary to list many songs two or more times; for instance, every song by Burt Bacharach and Hal David would have been listed first under Bacharach, then again under David. To avoid such duplication, each song is listed under only one individual, who for the purpose of this listing is considered the principal writer. A roman numeral following the title of each collaborative song refers to a co-writer listed at the end of the entry. For example, the first chart composition in Bryan Adams's entry is listed as "*Lonely Nights* [i] (1982)." At the end of Adams's entry the reader finds the list of co-writers, beginning with "[i] Bob Clearmountain." Thus the reader sees that Bob Clearmountain was the co-writer of *Lonely Nights*.

A representative selection of songwriters, musicologists, music industry insiders, and publishers assisted the author in classifying individuals as principal writers and co-writers. In collaborations of composer and lyricist, the composer in every case has been considered the principal writer. For a lyricist who does not have his or her own entry, biographical facts (places and dates of birth and death) are listed in the entry in which that lyricist first appears as a co-writer. That entry can be easily located by looking up the lyricist in the index at the back of the book.

A "see also" reference at the end of an entry indicates that additional work by the songwriter is listed under the entry of a collaborator. For example, at the end of Hal David's entry one finds the notation "*See also under* Burt BACHA-RACH," where David's main body of work is listed.

A few more notes about the arrangement of entries:

Individual song titles are listed in italics, e.g. *All the Things You Are.*

Names or titles that start with numbers appear as if the number is spelled out in full, thus *1,2,3* reads as *One, Two, Three*; *007* as *Double O-Seven*; and *5.15* as *Five-Fifteen.*

Film, show, and book titles appear in quotation marks followed by the year of release, e.g. "The Wizard of Oz" (1939).

American (US) chart positions are those published weekly in the trade magazine *Billboard*, while British (UK) chart positions are those published weekly in the trade magazine *Music Week*.

Recording Industry of America awards are noted directly after the release date of a particular record: p = platinum disk (1 million unit sales), g = gold disk (half a million unit sales). Check the list of abbreviations for other special notations.

It is my hope that every individual who deserves a mention is included somewhere within these pages.

Introduction

As a child, I was fascinated by such songs as *The Sun Has Got His Hat On* and *Summer Holiday*. I still am. Before my teens I rarely knew who sang the songs that I heard on the radio, let alone who composed them, and the disk jockeys of the day certainly never announced who had written a particular number.

Around the age of ten or eleven I discovered the Beatles, a significant musical enlightenment that indirectly led to my enjoyment of many other forms of music. At the same time, I also became obsessed with a strange song about American roads and county lines, things about which I, an English schoolboy, knew nothing. The mysticism of the song, *Wichita Lineman*— even the title was incomprehensible to me at the time — so haunted my psyche that I bought a copy of the single by Glen Campbell. What fascinated me further at the time was the name underneath the song title: Jim Webb. I had never heard of him. Who was this person? Why was his name written in such small letters? I continued to be intrigued by the names under the titles of all the singles that I bought for many years, and even today, upon acquiring a new disk, I immediately look to see who wrote the songs I like the best.

There are independent encyclopedias dedicated to classical, jazz, rock, pop, soul, folk and country music, but none specifically about songwriters. The format of this book took shape after a series of lengthy conversations with other songwriter aficionados, agents, and music industry insiders, all of whom agreed that the tunesmith rarely receives the credit that he or she deserves. Even those composers that are more widely known still seem destined to remain mere footnotes in a particular performer's career, and in far too many cases they remain completely unrecognized outside the music industry. It is hoped that this volume not only results in a re-evaluation of the role of the songwriter throughout the history of popular music, but also proves a useful reference tool for further study into the subject.

Before popular songs became widely available on sheet music and other forms of recorded media, songwriters were seldom even credited with their creations. The great periods of American popular song, from the late 1800s minstrel tradition through the "golden age" of the 1920s, 1930s and 1940s, have already been documented in considerable detail, but what is seldom conveyed is the sheer number of songs that have been successful for individual writers.

The popular song is the most accessible and enduring of all the arts, and before the television era, it was arguably the best loved. Today, despite numerous diversions competing for the spending money of adults and teenagers alike, live and recorded music remains a significant worldwide industry, and quite often, songs enjoy a new lease of life when given a makeover by a new artist. An entire history of British and American culture has been documented in popular song, and despite the frequent changes in the taste of the record-buying public, the advent of the compact disk has ensured that music from previous eras enjoys an even wider availability than ever before.

The first well-known British songwriters were Gilbert and Sullivan, whose comedy operettas enthralled Victorian audiences. America's first major songwriter of lasting significance was the minstrel pioneer Stephen Foster in the late 1800s. Tin Pan Alley was initially a name given to West 28th Street in Manhattan; subsequently it became a generic term for American popular music until the late 1940s. Before Elvis Presley made the recording and performance of a particular number more significant that its actual publication, the success of a song was judged by the amount of sheet music copies it sold. The era is superbly documented in David A. Jansen's book "Tin Pan Alley — The Composers of the Songs, the Performers and Their Times" (Donald I. Fine, Inc., 1988), which reveals that sheet music was marketed just as vigorously during the late 1890s as compact disks are today. Interestingly, Jansen speculates that a publisher had to spend approximately $1,300 to create a hit song in the 1890s; that figure had risen to some $30,000 by the 1950s. Today, record companies claim that it costs somewhere in the region of $300,000 to break a major new act, and that individual hit singles are often loss leaders designed to promote the more profitable album format.

A number of fundamental changes took place in popular music after World War II. Many leading jazz musicians turned their backs on the big band sound and created bebop, which often utilized just the basic melody of popular Tin Pan Alley and show tunes as a backdrop for extensive musical improvisation. This new sound in jazz inspired the next generation of songwriters, such as Jerry Leiber and Mike Stoller, Burt Bacharach, and Donald Fagen, composers who would later introduce the jazz idiom to mainstream R&B, pop, and rock.

By the late 1950s, what had initially been termed "race" music had become rhythm and blues (R&B), which, through such innovators as James Brown, was further fragmented into soul and funk, and later rap. White songwriters such as Leiber and Stoller, and Doc Pomus and Mort Shuman, grew up listening to the blues and R&B, and they in turn created a new type of white pop music that was performed by black artists, merging for the first time the normally separate black and white record markets.

As musical barriers continued to break down, the clean-cut teen idols of the late 1950s were evicted from the pop charts by such up-and-coming stars as Chuck Berry, who had taken straight blues and R&B and turned them into a

newer, wilder, but altogether more accessible sound that became known as rock and roll, a phrase coined by the late disk jockey Alan Freed. When a young former truck driver from Memphis named Elvis Presley arrived on the scene, rock and roll became a youth phenomenon, and its fresh batch of pop stars all required new material to sing, resulting in a veritable explosion of talented young tunesmiths who began plying their wares to publishers, record companies and performers, in much the same way that Tin Pan Alley had plugged its wares half a century before.

The most astute and talented of these individuals became a new breed of songwriter and record maker, with such mavericks as Bert Berns and Phil Spector ultimately writing and producing the recording sessions of their acts. Certain cities become associated with particular sounds: the raw urban blues of Chicago, the classy Motown Sound from Detroit, and the teen-oriented pop formula of New York's Brill Building school of songwriters, which included Neil Sedaka, Barry Mann, Cynthia Weil, Neil Diamond, Ellie Greenwich, and Jeff Barry.

Across the Atlantic, young British musicians absorbed these new sounds, distilled the R&B with the immediacy of the Brill Building pop, and brewed up a fresh, white, blues-based concoction that collectively became known as "beat" music. The "British Invasion" — groups including the Beatles, the Who, the Rolling Stones, Herman's Hermits, and the Kinks — stormed the American charts during the early 1960s, often playing in a watered-down R&B style that rather ironically amounted to selling America back its own musical heritage.

The Beatles themselves were to make musical history many times over, their compositions and approach to recording influencing many other performers to write most of their own material for the first time. They pioneered the experimental nature of pop and were the first group to treat their music with an eye toward posterity, spending considerably longer than the norm in the recording studio perfecting it.

One of the biggest influences on the Beatles was the Brill Building tunesmiths, and it was many of these songwriters who left their cubicles to embark on successful second careers as solo recording artists in the early 1970s. The most successful was Carole King, who achieved unprecedented success with her 24 million–selling album **Tapestry** (1971). This signaled the beginning of the singer-songwriter era, setting the stage for a more introspective breed of writer and performer, including James Taylor, Joni Mitchell, Jackson Browne, and Neil Young. King's momentous success led to a trend whereby performers often gained critical respect only if they recorded their own compositions.

For a while, it looked as if the independent songwriter might be made redundant, but pop and rock parted company during the early 1970s, with unexpected results. Rock become a more "serious" art form, and compositions started clocking in at over ten minutes long, emphasizing musical dexterity, often at the expense of the quality of the actual song being performed. Rock also investigated classical themes as it branched off into such sub-genres as "progressive rock" and "jazz-rock." Pop became more gimmick-laden and faddish, as evidenced by "glam rock," "disco," and more recently, "hip hop" and "dance music." During the late 1970s, as a backlash against the era that had gone before, "punk rock" and "new wave" returned to the 1960s "beat" era concept of young groups with guitars performing often furiously paced, three-minute pop songs.

Contemporary popular songs all remain rooted in folk music, a style developed by "troubadours," human radios of their time who wandered the land playing for the same kind of wages most musicians still earn today. In their travels they either wrote or collected the best-known melodies of the day, tunes now classified as "traditional." The renowned folk instrumentalist Pete Seeger has expressed the opinion that all songwriters who came after Woody Guthrie are plagiarists, but while many perhaps are, there have been distinctive and genuine innovators, including John Lennon and Paul McCartney, Paul Simon, Elvis Costello, Joni Mitchell, and Jimmy Webb.

The most intriguing, most durable, and longest-lasting format of contemporary composition has been the "protest song," a musical heritage that essentially began with Woody Guthrie in the 1930s. Guthrie was a politically oriented folk singer who chronicled his times in words and music, and his style and legacy would later be developed by Bob Dylan and Phil Ochs during the folk protest movement of the 1960s. In the 1970s, protest songs began to mirror the society and culture in which they were written, passing through the slick cynicism of the Eagles' *Hotel California* (1976) into the rather more frustrated hands of 1980s rap artists, who aggressively focused on almost the same issues of poverty, inequality, and injustice that Guthrie had sung about half a century earlier. Modern rapping as a format for social protest can be traced back at least as far as the talking blues style of Dylan, whose rambling monologues and fast-paced wordplay on *Talkin' John Birch Paranoid Blues* was as acerbic and relevant in the 1960s as Public Enemy's *Letter to the New York Post* was in the 1990s. Dylan also redefined the popular song, introducing to it poetic and literary aspirations; his lengthy *Like a Rolling Stone* (1965) turned the standard three-minute pop single into a metaphysical mini-symphony.

The contemporary blues composition can be traced back in recorded form to the wonderful enigma that was Robert Johnson, an illiterate, hobo guitar picker whose truly exceptional songs remain perhaps the most refined examples of the "devil's music" ever recorded.

America's oldest original songwriting style of all, country, has remained its most consistently popular, despite all the changes in musical fashion over the years. Originally known as hillbilly and country and western, country music has become the last preserve of the independent songwriter, still hustling his or her compositions to Nashville publishers in the time-honored tradition. With such rock-oriented country artists as Garth Brooks, Alan Jackson and John Michael Montgomery now selling so many millions of records, country music looks likely to become the only mainstream music left in America.

Popular music fragmented even further during the 1980s, and after a period of highly self-conscious synthesizer acts in the early 1980s, a harder form of rap and gangster rap grew out of the hip-hop street sounds of Los Angeles and

New York. At the same time, R&B, to which rap is related, moved ever closer to the pop mainstream. New labels were constructed to cover other forms of music; folk and traditional became "roots music," and anything not from Britain or America almost inevitably became known as "world music."

Although professional songwriters have survived during every era of popular music since the turn of the century, the late 1980s saw a remarkable return to the concept of songwriter-producer as mentor. In America, where the Hot 100 format requires instantly recognizable, almost production line material, with image becoming more important than content, glossy formula songs have become a lucrative area for back-room songwriters. Many country and R&B artists since the 1980s have relied heavily on songwriter-producers as a source of new material, even when they also compose for themselves, and many bands that normally write all the songs on their albums have increasingly turned to outside songwriters for a decidedly more commercial, chart-oriented track, the former jazz-rock act Chicago being a most obvious example.

Today, new popular songs appear to be in as much demand as they have ever been. One hopes that songwriters will continue to thrive much as they have for over a hundred years, and that the craft of songwriting will be furthered by new, ever more gifted composers.

Abbreviations

\# number
ABC American Broadcasting Company
AK Alaska
AL Alabama
a.m. ante meridiem (before noon)
AR Arkansas
ASCAP American Society of Composers, Authors, and Publishers
AZ Arizona
b. born
BBC British Broadcasting Corporation
BMI Broadcast Music, Inc.
c circa
CA California
C&W country and western
CBE Commander of the Order of the British Empire
CBS Columbia Broadcasting System
CD compact disk
CO Colorado
Co. Company
Corp. Corporation
CT Connecticut
d. died
DC District of Columbia
DE Delaware
Dr. Doctor
e.g. exempli gratia (for example)
EP extended-play (record)
etc. et cetera (and so on)
FL Florida
g Record Industry of America gold sales award
GA Georgia
HI Hawaii
IA Iowa
ID Idaho
i.e. id est (that is)
IL Illinois
IN Indiana

Inc. Incorporated
Jr. Junior
KS Kansas
KY Kentucky
LA Louisiana
LP long-playing micro groove record
Ltd. Limited
MA Massachusetts
MBE Member of the Order of the British Empire
MCA Music Corporation of America
MD Maryland
ME Maine
MGM Metro-Goldwyn-Mayer
MI Michigan
MN Minnesota
MO Missouri
MS Mississippi
MT Montana
NBC National Broadcasting Company
NC North Carolina
ND North Dakota
NE Nebraska
NH New Hampshire
NJ New Jersey
NM New Mexico
NV Nevada
NY New York (state of)
OBE Officer of the Order of the British Empire
oc original cast
OH Ohio
OK Oklahoma
OR Oregon
ost original soundtrack
p Record Industry of America platinum sales award
PA Pennsylvania
PBS Public Broadcasting System

p.m.   post meridiem (after noon)
R&B   rhythm and blues
RAF   Royal Air Force
rc   radio cast
RCA   Record Corporation of America
Rev.   Reverend
RI   Rhode Island
SC   South Carolina
sc   studio cast
SD   South Dakota
Sr.   Senior
st   studio soundtrack
TN   Tennessee
TV   television

tvst   television soundtrack
TX   Texas
UCLA   University of California, Los Angeles
UK   United Kingdom of Great Britain and Northern Ireland
US(A)   United States (of America)
UK   Utah
VA   Virginia
VT   Vermont
WA   Washington
WI   Wisconsin
WV   West Virginia
WY   Wyoming

The Dictionary

1. ACE, Johnny (b. John Marshall Alexander, Jr., June 9, 1929, Memphis, TN; d. December 24, 1954, Houston, TX) R&B keyboard player and vocalist. An influential R&B singer who first performed alongside the blues vocalist Bobby Bland in the group the Beale Streeters, which charted with the singles *My Song* (1952) R&B#1, *Cross My Heart* (1953) R&B#3 and *The Clock* (1953) R&B#1. As Johnny Ace, Alexander became a major solo star, but he also became rock and roll's first casualty, infamously shooting himself backstage while playing Russian roulette. CHART COMPOSITIONS: *Saving My Love for You* (1953) R&B#2, *Please Forgive Me* (1954) R&B#6, *Never Let Me Go* (1954) R&B#9, *Anymore* (1955) R&B#7. ALBUM: **Memorial Album** (1955, Duke). HIT VERSION: *My Song* Aretha Franklin (1968) R&B#10 US#31.

2. ACKLES, David (b. February 20, 1937, Rock Island, IL) Folk guitarist, pianist and vocalist. A singer-songwriter with an inquisitive musical vision, who delicately merged European operetta and theatre with traditional American rural music. Ackles' almost spoken, world weary baritone graced a quartet of highly original albums, the best of which was the conceptual **American Gothic** (1972), which blended folk, country, dixieland, gospel and jazz for a concise examination of the fading American Dream. None of his records sold particularly well, and Ackles quit commercial music in 1974 to concentrate on ballet scores and film scripts, a recent work being the musical "Sister Aimee" (1994). ALBUMS: **David Ackles** (1968), **Subway to the Country** (1970), **American Gothic** (1972, all Elektra) US#167; **Five and Dime** (1973, Columbia). HIT VERSION: *Road to Cairo* Julie Driscoll with Brian Auger (1968) UK#53.

3. ACUFF, Roy Claxton (b. September 15, 1903, Maynardsville; d. November 23, 1992, Nashville, both TN) C&W harmonica player, fiddler and vocalist. A former medicine-show performer and 1930s radio star who became famous for weeping at his own performances. Although Acuff composed a handful of country standards, his major contribution to the popular song was co-founding, with Fred Rose, Nashville's first music publishing company, Acuff-Rose. Acuff charted sixteen country singles between 1944–1974, many of which were recorded with his group the Smoky Mountain Boys, selling over thirty million records. He appeared in such films as "My Darling Clementine" (1943), ran his own Hickory label, and is credited with having discovered Hank Williams. Acuff released over fifty albums, and in his later years became a patriarchal figure in country music. He died of congestive heart disease in 1992. CHART COMPOSITIONS: *Wabash Cannon Ball* (1938) g US#12, *The Prodigal Son* (1944) C&W#4 US#19, *I'll Forgive You, But I Can't Forget* (1944) C&W#3 US#26, *Write Me, Sweetheart* (1943) C&W#6, *Unloved and Unclaimed* [i] (1948) C&W#14. ALBUMS: **The Voice of Country Music** (1965, Capitol); **Once More** (1965), **Hand Clapping Gospel Songs** (1965), **Great Train Songs** (1966, all Hickory); **Roy Acuff Sings Famous Opry Favorites** (1968, London); **Greatest Hits, Volume 1** (1979, Elektra); **Roy Acuff** (1985, Columbia); **Two Different Worlds** (1986, Sundown); **Steamboat Whistle Blues** (1988), **Fly, Birdie, Fly, 1939–1941** (1988, both Rounder); **The Essential Roy Acuff, 1936–1949** (1993, Sony); **King of Country Music** (1993, Rounder). HIT VERSIONS: *Wabash Cannon Ball* Lonnie Donegan on *Lonnie Donegan Showcase LP* (1956) UK#26/Dick Todd & the Appalachian Wildcats as *Big Wheel Cannonball* (1967) C&W#52/Dick Curless as *Big Wheel Cannonball* (1970) C&W#27/Danny Davis (1970) C&W#63 US#131/Boxcar Willie in *Train Medley* (1980) C&W#95/Willie Nelson & Leon Russell (1984) C&W#91. Co-writer: [i] Vito Pellettieri.

4. ADAMS, Bryan (b. Bryan Guy Adams, November 5, 1959, Kingston, Ontario, Canada) Rock guitarist and vocalist. One of the best selling mainstream, melodramatic, rock balladeers of the 1980–1990s. Adams first recorded as a member of the group Sweeney Todd, which released the album **If Wishes Were Horses** (1976), before forming a long-term songwriting partnership with the former Prism drummer Jim Vallance, to compose material for Bachman-Turner Overdrive, Kiss and Bonnie Tyler. Adams embarked on a solo career in the early 1980s, and has seldom been off the charts since, becoming particularly successful with the eight million seller *(Everything I Do) I Do for You* [iv], from the film "Robin Hood: Prince of Thieves" (1990). CHART COMPOSITIONS: *Lonely Nights* [i] (1982) US#84, *Straight from the Heart* [iii] (1983) US#10 UK#51, *Cuts Like a Knife* [vii] (1983) US#15, *This Time* [vii] (1983) US#24 UK#41, *Run to You* [vii] (1984) US#6 UK#11, *Somebody* [vii] (1985) US#11 UK#35, *Heaven* [vii] (1985) p US#1 UK#38, *Summer of '69* [vii] (1985) US#5 UK#42, *One Night Love Affair* [vii] (1985) US#13, *It's Only Love* [vii] with Tina Turner (1985) UK#29, *Christmas Time* [vii] (1985) UK#55, *The Heat of the Night* [vii] (1987) US#6 UK#50, *Hearts on Fire* [vii] (1987) US#26 UK#57, *Victim of Love* [vii] (1987) US#32 UK#68, *(Everything I Do) I Do for You* [iv] (1991) p US#1 UK#1, *Can't Stop This Thing We Started* [v] (1991) g US#2 UK#12, *There Will Never Be Another Tonight* [vi] (1991) US#31 UK#32, *Thought I'd Died and Gone to Heaven* [v] (1992) US#13 UK#8, *All I Want Is You* [v] (1992) UK#22, *Do I Have to Say the Words?* [vi] (1992) US#11 UK#30, *Please Forgive Me* [v] (1993) US#7 UK#2, *All for Love* [iv] with Rod Stewart and Sting (1993) p US#1 UK#2, *Have You Ever Really Loved a Woman?* (1995) US#1 UK#4, *Rock Steady* with Bonnie Raitt (1995) US#73 UK#50, *The Only Thing That Looks Good on Me Is You* (1996) UK#6, *Let's Make a Night to Remember* (1996) UK#10, *Star* (1996) UK#13. ALBUMS: **Bryan Adams** (1981), **You Want It, You Got It** (1982) US#118 UK#78, **Cuts Like a Knife** (1983) p US#8 UK#21, **Reckless** (1984) p US#1 UK#7, **Into the Fire** (1987) p US#7 UK#10, **Waking Up the Neighbours** (1991) p US#6 UK#1, **Live! Live! Live!** (1994) UK#17, **18 'Til I Die** (1996, all A&M) UK#1. COMPILATION: **So Far So Good** (1993, A&M) p US#7 UK#1. HIT VERSIONS: *(All I Know) Feels Like Forever* [ix] Joe Cocker (1992) UK#25, *Back to Paradise* [ii] .38 Special (1987) US#41, *Can't Wait All Night* [vii] Juice Newton (1984) US#66, *Dangerous* [vii] Loverboy (1985) US#65, *(Everything I Do) I Do for You* [iv] Fatima Mansions (1992) UK#7/Q featuring Tony Jackson (1994) UK#47; *Let Me Down Easy* [vii] Roger Daltrey (1985) US#86, *Run to You* [vii] Rage (1992) UK#3, *Teacher, Teacher* [vii] .38 Special (1984) US#25, *When the Night Comes* [viii] Joe Cocker (1989) US#7 UK#61, *Why Must We Wait Until Tonight* [v] Tina Turner (1993) UK#16. Co-writers: [i] Bob Clearmountain, [ii] Giraldo/Jim Vallance, [iii] Eric Kagna, [iv] Michael Kamen/Robert John Lange, [v] Robert John Lange, [vi] Robert John Lange/Jim Vallance,

[vii] Jim Vallance, [viii] Jim Vallance/Diane Warren, [ix] Diane Warren. (*See also under* Rod STEWART.)

5. ADAMS, Stephen (b. Michael Maybrick, 1844, Liverpool; d. 1913, both England) Lyricist, organist and vocalist. A church organist and baritone singer who was also a prolific ballad lyricist. Although much of his work is now forgotten, Adams introduced such pastoral themes as the countryside to the British popular song, and during his lifetime he published nearly one and a half thousand lyrics. He also studied the law and wrote children's books. One of his best known songs is *The Blue Alsatian Mountains*.

6. ADAMSON, Harold (b. December 10, 1906, Greenville, NJ; d. August 17, 1980, Beverly Hills, CA) Film lyricist. A versatile lyricist who collaborated with many of his peers, and continued to write until the mid–1970s. Adamson's songs were featured in such films as "Hold That Ghost" (1941) and "Thousands Cheer" (1944). ALBUMS: **Seven Hills of Rome** ost (1958, RCA); **Minstrel Days** oc (1959, Everest); **Scent of Mystery** ost (1960, Ramrod). HIT VERSIONS: *Aurora* [vi] Andrews Sisters (1941) US#10, *Daybreak* [v] Jimmy Dorsey (1942) US#18/Tommy Dorsey (1942) US#10/Harry James (1942) US#17; *Disco Lucy (I Love Lucy Theme)* [ii] Wilton Place Street Band (1977) R&B#41 US#24, *Ferry Boat Serenade (La Piccinina)* [iv] Andrews Sisters (1940) US#1/Gray Gordon (1940) US#7/Frankie Masters (1940) US#12/Leo Reisman (1940) US#22/ Kay Kyser (1941) US#6; *It's a Wonderful World* [vii] Charlie Barnet (1940) US#8, *Manhattan Serenade* [i] Jimmy Dorsey (1942) US#19/Harry James (1942) US#9/Tommy Dorsey (1943) US#4; *Moonlight Mood* [iii] Connee Boswell (1942) US#22/Kay Kyser (1943) US#13/Glenn Miller (1943) US#11; *On the Trail* [v] Paul Whiteman (1932) US#13/Ray Anthony (1953) US#26; *720 in the Books* [vii] Jan Savitt (1939) US#17, *Woodpecker Song, The* [iv] Andrews Sisters (1940) US#6/Will Glahe (1940) US#12/Glenn Miller (1940) US#1/Kate Smith (1940) US#14. Co-writers: [i] Louis Alter (b. 1902; d. 1980), [ii] Eliot Daniel, [iii] Peter De Rose, [iv] Eldo Di Lazzaro, [v] Ferde Grofe (b. 1892; d. 1972), [vi] Mario Lago/Roberto Roberti, [vii] Jan Savitt/Johnny Watson. (*See also under* Hoagy CARMICHAEL, Walter DONALDSON, Jimmy McHUGH, Burton LANE, Harry WARREN, Victor YOUNG.)

7. ADLER, Richard (b. August 3, 1921, New York, NY) Film and stage composer, producer. A lyricist who frequently teamed up with the composer Jerry Ross for such hits as *Rags to Riches* [iii] (1953). Adler and Ross contributed to many successful shows, including "John Murray Anderson's Almanac Revue" (1953), "The Pajama Game" (1954) and "Damn Yankees" (1955). Adler later wrote both the music and words to the shows "Kwamina" (1961) and "A Mother's Kisses" (1968), which he followed with television and advertising work. In 1974, he directed Sammy Cahn's one-man stage show. ALBUMS: **Damn Yankees** oc (1955, RCA) US#6; **The Pajama Game** ost (1957, Columbia) g US#9; **Damn Yankees** ost (1958, RCA) US#21; **Little Women** ost (1958, Kapp); **Gift of the Magi** ost (1959, United Artists); **Kwamina** oc (1962, Capitol) US#139; **Olympus 7-0000** ost (1966, Command). HIT VERSIONS: *Even Now* [ii] Eddie Fisher (1953) US#7, *Everybody Loves a Lover* [i] Doris Day (1958) US#8 UK#25/Angels (1962) US#103/Shirelles (1963) R&B#15 US#19; *Fini* [iii] Eydie Gorme (1954) US#19, *Heart* [iii] Eddie Fisher (1955) US#6/Four Aces (1955) US#13/Max Bygraves (1957) UK#14/Johnston Brothers (1957) UK#23/Rita Pavone (1966) UK#27; *Hernando's Hideaway* [iii] Archie Bleyer (1954) US#2/Guy Lombardo (1954) US#14/Johnny Ray (1954) US#14 UK#11/Johnston Brothers (1955) UK#1; *Hey, There* [iii] Rosemary Clooney (1955) g US#1 UK#4/Sammy Davis, Jr. (1955) US#16 UK#19/Johnny Ray (1955) US#27 UK#5/Lita Roza (1955) UK#17; *Rags to Riches* [iii] Tony Bennett (1953) g US#1/Billy Ward & the Dominos (1953) R&B#2/David Whitfield (1953) UK#3/Sunny & the Sunglows (1963) R&B#45/Lenny Welch (1966) US#102/Elvis Presley (1971) US#33 UK#9; *Steam Heat* [iii] Patti Page (1954) US#8, *Two Lost Souls* Perry Como & Jaye P. Morgan (1955) US#18, *Whatever Lola Wants* [iii] Dinah Shore (1955) US#12/Sarah Vaughan (1955) US#6/Alma Cogan (1957) UK#26. Co-writers: [i] Robert Allen, [ii] Dan Howell/Jerry Ross, [iii] Jerry Ross (b. March 9, 1926; d. November 11, 1955).

8. AGER, Milton (b. October 6, 1893, Chicago, IL; d. April 6, 1979, Los Angeles, CA) Film and stage composer, pianist and arranger. A self-taught pianist who accompanied vaudeville acts before working as a song-plugger and arranger between 1910–1914. Ager often composed with the lyricist Jack Yellen, the pair first teaming up for the Broadway score "What's in a Name?" (1920), before contributing to the show "Rain or Shine" (1928), which they followed with the films "Honky Tonk" (1929) and "The King of Jazz" (1930). One of their best remembered songs is the Depression-era standard *Happy Days Are Here Again* [viii], which was introduced in the film "Chasing Rainbows" (1930). HIT VERSIONS: *Ain't She Sweet* [ix] Gene Austin (1927) US#4/Johnny Marvin (1927) US#14/Ben Bernie (1927) US#1/Mr. Goon Bones & Mr. Ford (1949) US#14/Winifred Atwell in *Let's Have a Ding Dong* (1955) UK#3/Joe "Mr. Piano" Henderson in *Sing It Again with Joe* (1955) UK#18/Russ Conway in *Even More Party Pops* (1960) UK#27/Mrs. Mills in *Mrs. Mills' Medley* (1961) UK#18/Beatles (1964) US#19 UK#29; *Ain't That a Gran' and Glorious Feeling?* [ix] Johnny Marvin (1927) US#10, *Anything Is Nice if It Comes from Dixie* [iii] American Quartet (1919) US#9, *Auf Wiederseh'n, My Dear* [vi] Jack Denny (1932) US#3/Morton Downey (1932) US#17/Abe Lyman (1932) US#13/Ben Selvin (1932) US#15; *Baghdad* [viii] Paul Specht 1924) US#7, *Bench in the Park, A* [ix] Jive Five (1965) US#106, *Crazy Words–Crazy Tune* [ix] Frank Crumit (1927) US#9/Dorothy Provine (1962) UK#45; *Everything Is Peaches Down in Georgia* [iii] American Quartet (1918) US#18/Prince's Orchestra (1918) US#4; *Forgive Me* [ix] Gene Austin (1927) US#1/Eddie Fisher (1952) US#7/Al Martino (1965) US#61; *Glad Rag Doll* [v] Ruth Etting (1929) US#17/Ted Lewis (1929) US#10/Russ Conway in *Even More Party Pops* (1960) UK#27; *Happy Days Are Here Again* [ix] Benny Meroff (1930) US#1/Leo Reisman (1930) US#3/Ben Selvin (1930) US#1/Winifred Atwell in *Let's Have a Ding Dong* (1955) UK#3; *Hard-Hearted Hannah* [ii] Belle Baker (1924) US#13/Cliff Edwards (1924) US#13/Dolly Kay (1924) US#3; *I Wonder What's Become of Sally?* [ix] Al Jolson (1924) US#1/Ted Lewis (1924) US#7/Van & Schenck (1924) US#24; *I'm Nobody's Baby* [iv] Ruth Etting (1927) US#9/Judy Garland (1940) US#3/Marion Harris (1921) US#3/Ozzie Nelson (1940) US#14/Aileen Stanley (1921) US#11/Bea Wain (1940) US#11; *I'm the Last of the Red Hot Mamas* [ix] Sophie Tucker (1928) US#15, *Is She My Girlfriend?* [ix] Coon-Sanders Orchestra (1928) US#19/Van & Schenck (1928) US#10; *Louisville Lou* [ix] Arthur Gibbs (1923) US#7/Ted Lewis (1923) US#11; *Lovin' Sam (The Sheik of Alabam')* [ix] Nora Bayes (1923) US#4, *Mama Goes Where Papa Goes* [ix] Sam Lanin (1924) US#13, *My Pet* [ix] Paul Ash (1928) US#18, *She Don't Wanna* [ix] Orrin Tucker (1942) US#21, *Trouble in Paradise* [viii] Eddy Duchin (1933) US#18/Glen Gray & the Casablanca Orchestra (1933) US#16; *Trust in Me* [viii] Mildred Bailey (1937) US#37/Wayne King (1937) US#5/Eddie Fisher (1952) US#25/Etta James (1961) R&B#4 US#30; *Who Cares?* [ix] Al Jolson (1923) US#4, *You Can't Pull the Wool Over My Eyes* [vii] Benny Goodman (1936) US#2, *Young Man's Fancy, A* [ii] Art Hickman (1920) US#9/Isham Jones (1920) US#12. Co-writers: [i] John Murray Anderson/Jack Yellen, [ii] Charles Bates/Bob Bigelow/Jack Yellen, [iii] Grant Clarke/George W. Meyer, [iv] Benny Davis/Lester Santley (b. 1894; d. 1983), [v] Dan Dougherty/Jack Yellen, [vi] Al Goodhart/Al Hoffman/Ed G. Nelson, [vii] Charles Newman (b. 1901; d. 1978)/Murray Mencher, [viii] Jean Schwartz/Ned Weaver, [ix] Jack Yellen.

9. AHLERT, Fred E. (b. September 19, 1892; d. October 20, 1953, both New York, NY) Tin Pan Alley composer and arranger. A lawyer who turned to songwriting in the 1920s. After working in music publishing, Ahlert began writing material for vaudeville artists, his first published tune being the foxtrot *Beets and Turnips* [ii] (1915). A much recorded composer of his era, Ahlert's material was featured in such films as "A Guy Named Joe" (1943) and "You Were Meant for Me" (1948). In 1997, James Taylor recorded a delightful version of his *Walkin' My Baby Back Home* [v]. HIT VERSIONS: *I Don't Know Why (I Just Do)* [vi] Benny Krueger (1931) US#8/Kate Smith (1931) US#15/Andrews Sisters (1946) US#17/Linda Scott (1961) US#12/Eden Kane (1962) UK#7/Marty Robbins (1977) C&W#10 US#108; *I'd Love to Fall Asleep and Wake Up in My Mammy's Arms* [iv] Peerless Quartet (1920) US#5, *I'll Follow You* [vi] Paul Whiteman (1932) US#19, *I'll Get By (As Long as I Have You)* [vi] Ruth Etting (1929) US#3/Nick Lucas (1929) US#12/Aileen Stanley (1929) US#18/Harry James (1944) US#1/Ink Spots (1944) R&B#4 US#7/King Sisters (1944) US#12/Connie Francis (1958) UK#19/Shirley Bassey (1961) UK#10; *I'm Gonna Sit Right Down and Write Myself a Letter* [vii] Fats Waller (1935) US#5/Boswell Sisters (1936) US#3/Connee Boswell (1953) US#29/Billy Williams (1957) R&B#9 US#3 UK#22/Palm Beach Band Boys (1966) US#117/Willie Nelson (1981) C&W#26/Barry Manilow (1982) UK#36; *Life Is a Song* [vii] Ruth Etting (1935) US#1/Freddy Martin (1935) US#10; *Love, You Funny Thing* [vi] Louis Armstrong (1932) US#4, *Mean to Me* [vi] Ruth Etting (1929) US#3/Helen Morgan (1929) US#11/Teddy Wilson with Billie Holiday (1937) US#7; *Moon Was Yellow (And the Night Was Young), The* [iii] Bing Crosby (1934) US#13, *Sing an Old-Fashioned Song* Fats Waller (1936) US#13, *There's a Cradle in Caroline* [iv] Frankie Trumbauer (1927) US#10/Gene Austin (1928) US#8; *Walkin' My Baby Back Home* [v] Charleston Chasers (1931) US#15/Lee Morse (1931) US#18/Nick Lucas (1931) US#8/Ted Weems (1931) US#8/Nat "King" Cole (1952) US#8/Johnny Ray (1952) US#4 UK#12; *Where the Blue of the Night (Meets the Gold of the Day)* [i] Russ Columbo (1931) US#13/Bing Crosby (1932) US#4, re-issued (1940) US#27; *With Summer Coming On* [vi] Fred Waring's Pennsylvanians (1932) US#18. Co-writers: [i] Bing Crosby (b. Harry Lillis Crosby, May 2, 1901, Tacoma, WA; d. October 14, 1977, Madrid, Spain)/Roy Turk, [ii] Cliff Hess, [iii] Edgar Leslie, [iv] Sam M. Lewis/Joe Young (b. 1889; d. 1939), [v] Harry Richman (b. Harry Reichman, 1895; d. November 3, 1972)/Roy Turk, [vi] Roy Turk, [vii] Joe Young.

10. AKST, Harry (b. August 15, 1894, New York, NY; d. March 31, 1963, Los Angeles, CA) Film and stage composer, pianist. A successful Tin Pan Alley songwriter, who learned the piano at the age of five and first worked as a song demonstrator for a publishing house, before accompanying the vaudeville performer Nora Bayes. After serving in World War I, Akst became a staff pianist at Irving Berlin's publishing house, shortly after which he achieved his first hits with material that was featured in such shows as "The New Plantation Club Revue" (1923), and the films "On with the Show" (1929), "Palmy Days" (1931), and "Jolson Sings Again" (1949). Akst later toured as Al Jolson's accompanist. HIT VERSIONS: *Am I Blue?* [i] Tom Gerun (1929) US#18/Annette Hanshaw (1929) US#11/Libby Holman (1929) US#4/Ben Selvin (1929) US#17/Nat Shilkret (1929) US#12/Ethel Waters (1929) US#1; *Baby Face* [ii] Jan Garber (1926) US#1/Ipana Troubadors (1926) US#10/Ben Selvin (1926) US#6/"Whispering" Jack Smith (1926) US#6/Sammy Kaye (1948) US#11/Henry King (1948) US#14/Art Mooney (1948) US#3/Jack Smith (1948) US#13/Big Ben Banjo Band in *Let's Get Together Again* (1955) UK#18/Winifred Atwell in *Piano Party* (1959) UK#10/Little Richard (1959) R&B#32 US#41 UK#2/Mrs. Mills in *Mrs. Mills' Medley* (1961) UK#18/Bobby Vee (1961) US#119/Bobby Darin (1962) UK#40/Wing & a Prayer Fife & Drum Corps. (1976) R&B#32 US#14 UK#12; *Dinah* [iii] Cliff Edwards (1926) US#5/Fletcher Henderson (1926) US#13/Revelers (1926) US#4/Ethel Waters (1926) US#2/Ted Lewis (1930) US#8/Bing Crosby (1932) US#1/Mills Brothers (1932) US#1/Boswell Sisters (1935) US#3/Fats Waller (1936) US#7/Sam Donohue (1946) US#9; *Everything's Gonna Be All Right* [ii] Ipana Troubadors (1926) US#14, *I'm the Medicine Man for the Blues* [i] Ted Lewis (1929) US#10, *Smile Will Go a Long, Long, Way, A* [ii] Peerless Quartet (1924) US#13/Ted Weems (1924) US#4. Co-writers: [i] Grant Clarke, [ii] Benny Davis, [iii] Sam M. Lewis/Joe Young. (*See also under* Irving BERLIN, Mann CURTIS, Harry RUBY, Richard WHITING.)

11. ALEXANDER, Arthur (b. May 10, 1940, Florence; June 9, 1993, both AL) R&B vocalist. A raw and gritty blues singer who blended rural country, gospel, soul and pop, whose best work had a vitality comparable to that of Bobby Bland. Although a minor figure on the R&B charts, Alexander was nevertheless a major influence on the British R&B boom of the early 1960s, when his compositions *You Better Move On* and *Anna (Go to Him)* were recorded by the Rolling Stones and the Beatles respectively. Paul McCartney paid him the ultimate compliment in 1987, when he remarked, "We wanted to be like Arthur Alexander." Alexander's father was a semi-professional musician, and he grew up listening to such vocalists as Clyde McPhatter, Jerry Butler and Ben E. King, before cutting sides for the Judd label in 1960. Never a major record seller, Alexander quit the music business in 1976, later saying, "I had so many disappointments about getting paid. The money was always short." His compositions continued to be recorded, one of the finest interpretations being Ry Cooder's version of *Go, Home Girl*. After working as a bus driver for nearly twenty years, Alexander began recording and performing again in 1993, but his triumphant comeback was cut short when he died from a heart attack later that year. A various artists album was recorded in his honor, **Adios Amigo: A Tribute to Arthur Alexander** (1994, Demon). CHART COMPOSITIONS: *Where Have You Been All My Life?* (1962) US#58, *You Better Move On* (1962) US#24, *Anna (Go to Him)* (1962) R&B#10 US#68, *Go, Home Girl* (1963) US#102, *Pretty Girls Everywhere* (1963) US#118, *Everyday I Have to Cry* (1975) US#45, *Sharing the Night Together* (1976) R&B#92. ALBUMS: **You Better Move On** (1962, Dot); **Arthur Alexander** (1972, Warner Brothers); **Live** (1975, Line); **Lonely Just Like Me** (1993, Elektra/Nonesuch). COMPILATIONS: **Alexander the Great** (1962, London); **A Shot of Rhythm and Blues** (1985), **Arthur Alexander** (1989), **Greatest** (1989), **Soldier of Love** (1987, all Ace); **Story of Rock 'n' Roll** (1977, Ariola), **The Ultimate Arthur Alexander** (1993, Razor & Tie). HIT VERSIONS: *You Better Move On* Billy "Crash" Craddock (1971) C&W#10/Tommy Roe (1979) C&W#70/George Jones & Johnny Paycheck (1981) C&W#18.

12. ALLEN, Peter (b. Peter Allen Woolnough, October 2, 1944, Tenterfield, Australia; d. June 18, 1992, San Diego, CA) Pop pianist and vocalist. A cabaret artist who was once married to the actress Liza Minnelli. Allen was considerably more successful with cover versions of his songs than he was as a recording artist. He composed the Quantos airline theme *I Call Australia Home*, before dying of an AIDS-related illness in 1992. CHART COMPOSITION: *Fly Away* [ii] (1981) US#92. ALBUMS: **Peter Allen** (1971), **Tenterfield Saddler** (1972, both Metromedia); **Continental American** (1974), **Taught By Experts** (1976), **It's Time for Peter Allen** (1977), **I Could Have Been a Sailor** (1979) US#171, **Bi–Coastal** (1980, all A&M) US#123; **Not the Boy Next Door** (1983, Arista) US#170; **Legs Diamond** oc (1988), **Making Every Moment Count** (1990, both RCA). COMPILATION: **The Best** (1982, A&M). HIT VERSIONS: *Don't Cry Out Loud* [iii] Elkie Brooks (1978) UK#12/Melissa Manchester (1979) US#10; *Fly Away* [ii] Stevie Woods (1982)

US#84, *I Go to Rio* [i] Pablo Cruise (1979) US#46, *I'd Rather Leave While I'm in Love* [iii] Rita Coolidge (1979) US#38. Co-writers: [i] A. Anderson, [ii] David Foster/Carole Bayer Sager, [iii] Carole Bayer Sager. (*See also under* Burt BACHARACH, Jeff BARRY, Christopher CROSS.)

13. ALLEN, Terry (b. May 7, 1943, Wichita, KA) C&W pianist and vocalist. A country influenced folk and roots artist with a cult following, whose material often embraces subjects seldom approached in popular song. One of the best versions of his compositions was Little Feat's *New Delhi Freight Train*. Allen also composed music for the film "Amerasia" (1986). ALBUMS: **Juarez** (1975), **Lubbock (On Everything)** (1978), **Smokin' the Dummy** (1980), **Bloodlines** (1983), **The Silent Majority** (1993, all Fate); **Human Remains** (1996, Sugar Hill).

14. ALLISON, Mose (b. November 11, 1927, Tippo, MS) Jazz pianist and vocalist. A singer-songwriter in a jazz-blues idiom, who has written such satirical material as *Parchman Farm* and *Tell Me Something*. Allison grew up in the Mississippi delta, where he was influenced by boogie-woogie piano styles. During the 1950s, he became a backing pianist for the jazz saxophonists Gerry Mulligan and Stan Getz, before embarking on a solo career. ALBUMS: **Back Country Suite** (1957), **Local Color** (1958), **Young Man Mose** (1958), **Creek Bank** (1959), **Autumn Song** (1960), **Ramblin' with Mose** (1961), **The Seventh Son-Mose Allison Sings** (1963), **Down Home Piano** (1966), **Mose Allison Plays for Lovers** (1967, all Prestige); **The Transfiguration of Hiram Brown** (1960), **I Love the Life I Live** (1960, both Columbia); **Talk to the Hills** (1962, Epic); **Don't Worry About a Thing** (1962), **Swingin' Machine** (1962), **The Word from Mose** (1964, all Atlantic); **V-8 Ford** (1964, Columbia); **Mose Alive!** (1966) UK#30, **Wild Man on the Loose** (1966), **I've Been Doin' Some Thinkin'** (1968), **Hello There, Universe** (1969), **Western Man** (1971), **Mose in Your Ear** (1972), **That's Jazz** (1976), **Your Mind's on Vacation** (1976, all Atlantic); **Middle Class White Boy** (1982), **Lessons in Living** (1983, both Elektra); **Ever Since the World Ended** (1988, Blue Note); **Tell Me Something: The Songs of Mose Allison** with Georgie Fame, Van Morrison and Ben Sidran (1996, Verve).

15. ALLMAN, Gregg (b. Gregory L. Allman, December 8, 1947, Nashville, TN) Rock organist, guitarist and vocalist. The lead singer in the American blues-rock group the Allman Brothers Band, who has a formidable, world weary, blues soaked voice, and who has composed a small but distinctive catalogue of country-blues influenced, lovelorn, mid-tempo ballads. Allman grew up in Daytona, Florida, with his older brother, the guitarist Duane Allman. They listened to R&B, blues, country, and rock, before playing in a variety of groups during the early 1960s. By 1963, they were performing up to six sets a night in Florida roadhouses as the Allman Joys, before recording two albums as the psychedelic-blues outfit Hourglass, **Hourglass** (1967) and **Power of Love** (1967, both Liberty). By 1968, their group the 31st of February had evolved into the Allman Brothers Band, which developed a formidable live reputation as a mixed race, rock and blues act that specialized in lengthy versions of blues standards that were characterized by an imaginative use of two lead guitarists and two drummers. The group's early recordings featured many of Allman's finest compositions, including *It's Not My Cross to Bear, Every Hungry Woman, Black Hearted Woman, Whipping Post,* and *Dreams.* The Allman Brothers' crowning achievement remains the double in-concert set **Live at Fillmore East** (1971), shortly after which, both Duane and bassist Berry Oakley were killed in unrelated motorbike accidents. Subsequently, the band developed a more laid-back style as the remaining guitarist, Dickey Betts, adopted a casual country influence, best evidenced on **Brothers and Sisters** (1973). During the early 1990s, the group was revitalized after the surprise success of a six album retrospective **Dreams** (1989), and they returned to recording and performing the blend of southern boogie and rocking blues that they had pioneered. CHART COMPOSITIONS: *Ain't Wastin' Time No More* (1972) US#77, *Melissa* (1972) US#86, *Crazy Love* (1979) US#29, *Nevertheless* (1975) US#67. ALBUMS: **The Allman Brothers Band** (1970) US#188, **Idlewild South** (1970, both Atco) US#38; **Live at Fillmore East** (1971) p US#13, **Eat a Peach** (1972) g US#4, **Brothers and Sisters** (1973) g US#1 UK#42, **Win, Lose or Draw** (1975) g US#5, **Wipe the Windows, Check the Oil, Dollar Gas** (1976) US#75, **Enlightened Rogues** (1979, all Capricorn) g US#9; **Reach for the Sky** (1980) US#27, **Brothers of the Road** (1981, both Arista) US#44; **Seven Turns** (1990) US#53, **Shades of Two Worlds** (1991) US#85, **An Evening with the Allman Brothers (First Set)** (1992) US#80, **Where It All Begins** (1994) US#45, **An Evening with the Allman Brothers (Second Set)** (1995, all Epic) US#88. COMPILATIONS: **Early Allman** (1973, Dial) US#171; **Duane and Gregg** (1972, Bold) US#129; **Beginnings** (1973, Atco) g US#25; **The Road Goes on Forever** (1975, Capricorn) US#43 UK#54; **Best of the Allman Brothers** (1981) g US#189, **Dreams** (1989) g US#103, **Live at Ludlow Garage** (1990), **The Fillmore Concerts** (1992), **A**

Decade of Hits (1995, all Polydor) p. Allman has also pursued an intermittent solo career, charting with *Midnight Rider* [i] (1973) US#19. ALBUMS: **Laid Back** (1973) g US#13, **The Gregg Allman Tour** (1974, both Capricorn) US#50; **Two the Hard Way** with Cher (1976, Warner Brothers); **Playin' Up a Storm** (1977, Capricorn) US#42; **I'm No Angel** (1983) g US#30, **Just Before the Bullets Fly** (1988) US#117; **Searching for Simplicity** (1988, all Epic). HIT VERSIONS: *Dreams* Molly Hatchet (1979) US#106, *Midnight Rider* [i] Joe Cocker (1972) US#27/Paul Davidson (1975) UK#10/Willie Nelson (1980) C&W#6. Co-writer: [i] Kim Payne.

16. ALMOND, Marc (b. Peter Marc Almond, July 9, 1956, Southport, England) Pop vocalist. An idiosyncratic, pseudo-torch singer with a cult following, who, alongside keyboard player Dave Ball, first performed as the synthesizer duo Soft Cell. CHART COMPOSITIONS: *Bedsitter* [i] (1981) UK#4, *Say Hello, Wave Goodbye* [i] (1982) UK#3, re-mixed (1991) UK#38; *Torch* [i] (1982) UK#2, *Where the Heart Is* [i] (1982) UK#21, *Numbers/Barriers* [i] (1983) UK#25, *Soul Inside* [i] (1983) UK#16, *Down in the Subway* [i] (1984) UK#24. ALBUMS: **Non-Stop Erotic Cabaret** (1981) US#22 UK#5, **Non-Stop Ecstatic Dancing** (1982) US#57 UK#6, **The Art of Falling Apart** (1982) US#84 UK#5, **This Last Night in Sodom** (1984, all Some Bizarre) UK#12. COMPILATION: **The Singles Album** (1986, Mercury) UK#58. After parting company with Ball in the mid–1980s, Almond formed various short-lived outfits such as Marc and the Mambas, under which names his essentially solo releases were issued. CHART COMPOSITIONS: *The Boy Who Came Back* (1984) UK#52, *You Have* (1984) UK#57, *Stories of Johnny* (1985) UK#23, *Melancholy Rose* (1987) UK#71, *Tears Run Rings* (1988) US#67 UK#26, *Bitter Sweet* (1988) UK#40, *Only the Moment* (1989) UK#45, *A Lover Spurned* (1990) UK#29, *The Desperate Hours* (1990) UK#45, *My Hand Over My Heart* [ii] (1992) UK#33, *What Makes a Man a Man?* (1993) UK#60, *Adored and Explored* (1995) UK#25, *The Idol* (1995) UK#44, *Child Star* (1995) UK#41, *Yesterday Has Gone* (1996) UK#58. ALBUMS: **Untitled** (1982) UK#42, **Torment and Toreros** (1983) UK#28, **Violent Silence** (1984), **Vermin in Ermine** (1984) UK#36, **Stories of Johnny** (1985) UK#22, **Mother Fist and Her Five Daughters** (1987, all Some Bizarre) UK#41; **The Stars We Are** (1988, Parlophone) US#144 UK#41; **Enchanted** (1990) UK#52, **Jacques** (1990), **Tenement Symphony** (1991, all Some Bizarre) UK#39; **12 Years of Tears-Live at the Royal Albert Hall** (1993), **Fantastic Star** (1996, both Mercury) UK#54. COMPILATIONS: **Memorabilia-The Singles** (1991, Some

Bizarre) UK#8; **Treasure Box** (1995, EMI). Co-writers: [i] Dave Ball (b. May 3, 1959, Blackpool, England), [ii] Dave Ball/Norris.

17. AMESBURY, Bill (b. Canada) Rock guitarist, producer and vocalist. A sadly neglected singer-songwriter with a richly timbered baritone, whose highly original second album, **Can You Feel It?** (1976), remains something of a lost classic, with its deft arrangements and stylish mix of soul, country, rock and pop. His outstanding composition was *Harlow*, a florid tribute to the actress Jean Harlow, that was both a clever pastiche of Hollywood's fakery and a middle-aged man's lament on obsessive love. CHART COMPOSITION: *Virginia (Touch Me Like You Do)* (1974) US#59. ALBUMS: **Jus' a Taste of the Kid** (1974, Casablanca); **Can You Feel It?** (1976 Power Exchange).

18. AMOS, Tori (b. Myra Ellen Amos, August 22, 1963, Newton, NC) Pop pianist and vocalist. A child piano scholar from the Baltimore Peabody Conservatory who became a live performer at the age of thirteen. After a brief period in the rock band Y Kant Tori Read, which recorded the album **Y Kant Tori Read** (1988, Atlantic), Amos opted for a solo career, with her quirky, individualistic songs. CHART COMPOSITIONS: *Silent all These Years* (1991) UK#51, re-issued (1992) UK#26; *China* (1992) UK#51, *Winter* (1992) UK#25, *Crucify EP* (1992) UK#15, *Cornflake Girl* (1994) US#111 UK#4, *Pretty Good Year* (1994) UK#7, *God* (1994) US#79 UK#44, *Past the Mission* (1994) UK#31, *Only Saw Today* (1994) UK#48, *Let Love Shine* (1995) UK#31, *Church of Freedom* (1995) UK#54, *Caught a Lite Sneeze* (1996) US#60 UK#20, *Talula* (1996) UK#22, *Hey Jupiter/Professional Widow* (1996) UK#20, *Blue Skies* (1996) UK#26. ALBUMS: **Little Earthquakes** (1992) p US#54 UK#14, **Under the Pink** (1994, both Atlantic) p US#12 UK#1; **Boys for Pele** (1996, East West) g US#2 UK#2; **from the choirgirl hotel** (1998, Atlantic) US#5.

19. ANDERSEN, Eric (b. February 14, 1943, Pittsburgh, PA) Folk guitarist and vocalist. A singer-songwriter who came to prominence in the 1960s New York folk scene. Andersen scored the film "Istanbul" (1988), and has had his songs recorded by Joan Baez, Peter, Paul and Mary, Johnny Cash, and Merrilee Rush. ALBUMS: **Today Is the Highway** (1965), **'Bout Changes and Things** (1966), **'Bout Changes and Things, Take 2** (1967), **More Hits from Tin Can Alley** (1968), **A Country Dream** (1969, all Vanguard); **Avalanche** (1970), **Eric Andersen** (1970, both Warner Brothers); **Blue River** (1972) US#169, **Stage** (1973, both Columbia); **Be**

True to You (1975) US#113, **Sweet Surprise** (1976, both Arista); **Danko/Fjeld/Andersen** (1993, Rykodisc); **Midnight Son** (1994), **Tight in the Night** (1995, both Wind & Sand); **Ghosts Upon the Road** (1989, Cypress); **Stages: The Lost Album** (1991, Columbia). COMPILATIONS: **Best of Eric Andersen** (1971, Vanguard); **The Best Songs** (1977, Arista).

20. ANDERSON, Bill (b. James William Anderson, III, November 1, 1937, Columbia, SC) C&W vocalist. A country songwriter of melodramatic love songs, that are based on simple, catchy melodies with easily digestible lyrics, which gave him nearly eighty country hits between 1958–1987. Anderson grew up in Georgia, and learned the guitar at the age of twelve. After studying journalism at the University of Georgia, he hosted his own local radio show, before working for various Atlanta newspapers as a sportswriter. In his spare time, Anderson began writing songs and playing in the country group the Avondale Playboys. Ray Price was the first major artist to record his material, and topped the chart with *City Lights* (1958). Other singers were also quick to capitalize on the commercial appeal of Anderson's songs during the 1960s. As a solo recording artist, Anderson earned the nickname "Whispering Bill," on account of his singing style. By the 1980s, he had written over one thousand tunes, and often appeared on the Grand Ole Opry. During the 1960s, he hosted his own syndicated television show, and also starred in a handful of films. Anderson became the compare of the television game show "Mr. and Mrs." in the 1980s. CHART COMPOSITIONS: *That's What It's Like to Be Lonesome* (1958) C&W#12, *Ninety-Nine Years* (1959) C&W#13, *Dead or Alive* (1959) C&W#19, *Tip of My Fingers* (1960) C&W#7, *Walk Out Backwards* (1960) C&W#9, *Po' Folks* (1961) C&W#9, *Get a Little Dirt on Your Hands* (1962) C&W#14, *Mama Sang a Song* (1962) C&W#1 US#89, *Still* (1963) C&W#1 C&W#8, *8 X 10* (1963) C&W#2 US#53, *Five Little Fingers* (1964) C&W#5 US#118, *Easy Come-Easy Go* (1964) C&W#14, *Me* (1964) C&W#8, *In Case You Ever Change Your Mind* (1964) C&W#38, *Three A.M.* (1964) C&W#8, *Certain* (1965) C&W#12. *Bright Lights and Country Music* (1965) C&W#11, *Golden Guitar* (1966) C&W#11, *I Love You Drops* (1966) C&W#4, *I Know You're Married (But I Love You Still)** (1966) C&W#29, *I Get the Fever* (1966) C&W#1, *Get While the Gettin's Good* (1967) C&W#5, *No One's Gonna Hurt You Anymore* (1967) C&W#10, *Papa* (1967) C&W#64, *For Loving You** (1967) C&W#1, *Stranger on the Run* (1967) C&W#42, *Wild Weekend* (1968) C&W#2, *Happy State of Mind* (1968) C&W#2, *My Life (Throw It Away If I Want To)* (1969) C&W#1, *But You Know I Love You* (1969) C&W#2, *Love Is a*

Sometime Thing (1970) C&W#5, *Where Have All Our Heroes Gone* (1970) C&W#6 US#93, *Always Remember* (1971) C&W#6 US#111, *Quits* (1971) C&W#3, *Dis-Satisfied* (1971) C&W#4, *All the Lonely Women in the World* (1972) C&W#5, *Don't She Look Good* (1972) C&W#2, *If You Can Live with It (I Can Live Without It)* (1973) C&W#2, *The Corner of My Life* (1973) C&W#2, *World of Make Believe* (1973) C&W#1, *Can I Come Home to You?* (1974) C&W#24, *Every Time I Turn the Radio On* (1974) C&W#7, *I Still Feel the Same About You* (1975) C&W#14, *Country D.J.* (1975) C&W#36, *Sometimes** (1975) C&W#1, *Peanuts and Diamonds* (1976) C&W#10, *That's What Made Me Love You** (1976) C&W#7, *Liars One Believers Zero* (1976) C&W#6, *Head to Toe* (1977) C&W#7, *I Can't Wait Any Longer* [ii] (1978) C&W#4 US#80, *Where Are You Going Billy Boy?** (1977) C&W#18, *I'm Way Ahead of You** (1978) C&W#25, *Double S* (1978) C&W#30, *More Than a Bedroom Thing* (1979) C&W#51, *Make Mine Night Time* (1980) C&W#35, *Get a Little Dirt on Your Hands* with David Allan Coe (1980) C&W#46, *Rock 'n' Roll to Rock of Ages* (1980) C&W#58, *I Want That Feelin' Again* (1980) C&W#83, *Mister Peepers* (1981) C&W#44, *Homebody* (1981) C&W#74, *Whiskey Made Me Stumble (The Devil Made Me Fall)* (1981) C&W#76, *Southern Fried* (1982) C&W#42, *Laid Off* (1982) C&W#82, *Thank You Darling* (1983) C&W#70, *Son of the South/20th Century Fox* (1983) C&W#71, *Your Eyes* (1984) C&W#76, *Wino the Clown* (1985) C&W#58, *Pity Party* (1985) C&W#62, *When You Leave That Way You Can Never Go Back* (1985) C&W#75, *Sheet Music* (1986) C&W#80, *No Ordinary Memory* (1987) C&W#78. ALBUMS: **Bill Anderson Sings Country Heart Songs** (1961), **Still** (1963) US#36, **8 X 10** (1963), **Bill Anderson Sings** (1964), **Bill Anderson Showcase** (1964), **From This Pen** (1965), **Bright Lights and Country Music** (1965), **I Love You Drops** (1966), **Get While the Gettin's Good** (1966), **I Can Do Nothing Alone** (1967), **For Loving You*** (1967), **Wild Weekend** (1968), **Happy State of Mind** (1969), **My Life/But You Know I Love You** (1970), **Bill Anderson Christmas** (1970), **If It's All the Same to You*** (1971), **Love Is a Sometimes Thing** (1971), **Where Have All Our Heroes Gone** (1971), **Always Remember** (1971), **Bill and Jan*** (1972), **Singing His Praise*** (1972), **All the Lonely Women in the World** (1972), **Don't She Look Good** (1973, all Decca), **Bill** (1973), **Whispering Bill Anderson-Can I Come Home to You?** (1974), **Everytime I Turn the Radio On** (1974), **Sometimes*** (1976), **Peanuts and Diamonds and Other Jewels** (1976), **Scorpio** (1976), **Billy Boy and Mary Lou*** (1977), **Love and Other Sad Stories** (1978), **Ladies Choice** (1978), **Whisperin' Bill Anderson** (1979), **Nashville Mirrors** (1980, all MCA);

On the Road with Bill Anderson (1980 Independent); **Bill Anderson Hosts Backstage at the Grand Ole Opry** (1982, RCA); **Southern Fried** (1983, Southern Tracks); **Country Music Heaven** (1992, Whispering). COMPILATIONS: **Greatest Hits** (1967), **The Bill Anderson Story** (1970), **Greatest Hits, Volume 2** (1971, all Decca); **Yesterday, Today and Tomorrow** (1984, Swane); **Golden Greats** (1985, MCA); **Best of Bill Anderson** (1990, Curb); **Greatest Hits** (1996, Varese Vintage). HIT VERSIONS: *But You Know I Love You* Kenny Rogers & the First Edition (1969) US#19/Dolly Parton (1981) C&W#1 US#41; *Cincinnati, Ohio* Connie Smith (1967) C&W#4, *City Lights* Ray Price (1958) C&W#1 US#71/Johnny Bush (1971) C&W#53/Mickey Gilley (1974) C&W#1; *Cold Hard Facts of Life, The* Porter Wagoner (1967) C&W#2, *Double S* Whispering Will as *Double W* (1979) C&W#89, *8 X 10* Ken Dodd (1964) UK#22, *Five Little Fingers* Frankie McBride (1967) UK#7, *Happiness* Ken Dodd (1964) UK#31, *Happy Birthday to Me* Hank Locklin (1961) C&W#7, *How the Other Half Lives* Johnny & Jonie Mosby (1964) C&W#21, *I Can't Remember* Connie Smith (1965) C&W#9 US#130/Stephanie Winslow (1980) C&W#38; *I Don't Love You Anymore* Charlie Louvin (1964) C&W#4, *I Know You're Married (But I Love You Still)* Red Sovine (1970) C&W#52, *I May Never Get to Heaven* Conway Twitty (1979) C&W#1, *I Missed Me* Jim Reeves (1960) C&W#3 US#44, *I Never Once Stopped Loving You* [i] Connie Smith (1970) C&W#5, *I'll Go Down Swinging* Porter Wagoner (1964) C&W#11, *I'm Alright* Lynn Anderson (1970) C&W#20 US#112, *I've Enjoyed as Much of This as I Can Stand* Porter Wagoner (1963) C&W#7, *It Comes and Goes* Burl Ives (1963) US#124, *Lord Knows I'm Drinking, The* Cal Smith (1972) C&W#1 US#64, *Lost in the Feeling* Conway Twitty (1983) C&W#2, *Mama Sang a Song* Walter Brennan (1962) US#38/Stan Kenton (1962) US#32; *My Name Is Mud* James O'Gwynn (1962) C&W#7, *My Whole World Is Falling Down* O.B. McLinton (1973) C&W#36, *No Thanks I Just Had One* Faron Young & Margie Singleton (1964) C&W#40, *Nobody But a Fool (Would Love You)* Connie Smith (1966) C&W#4, *Once a Day* Connie Smith (1964) C&W#1 US#101/Timi Yuro (1966) US#118; *Our Hearts Are Holding Hands* Ernest Tubb & Loretta Lynn (1965) C&W#24, *Pepsi Man* Bobby Mackay (1982) C&W#57, *Quits* Gary Stewart (1977) C&W#26, *Saginaw, Michigan* Lefty Frizzel (1964) C&W#1 US#85, *Sittin' in an All Nite Cafe* Warner Mack (1965) C&W#4, *Sometimes* Johnny Lee (1975) C&W#59, *Still* Karl Denver (1963) UK#13/Ken Dodd (1963) UK#35/Sunrays (1966) US#93; *Still #2* Ben Colder (1963) US#98, *That's What It's Like to Be Lonesome* Ray Price (1959) C&W#7/Carl Smith (1971) C&W#58; *Then and Only Then* Connie Smith (1965) C&W#4 US#116, *Three A.M.* Jim Ed Brown (1969) C&W#29, *Tip of My Fingers, The* Roy Clark (1963) C&W#10 US#45/Eddy Arnold (1966) C&W#3 US#43/Des O'Connor (1970) UK#15/Jean Shepherd (1975) C&W#16/Steve Wariner (1992) C&W#4; *Truck Driving Man* Red Steagall (1976) C&W#29, *Wine* Mel Tillis (1965) C&W#14, *You and Your Sweet Love* Connie Smith (1969) US#6, *Your Eyes* Simon & Verity (1985) C&W#91. With: * Jan Howard, ** Mary Lou Turner. Co-writers: [i] Harlan Howard, [ii] B. Killen. (*See also under* Roger MILLER.)

21. ANDERSON, Brett (b. September 27, 1967, Sussex, England) Pop vocalist, and **BUTLER, Bernard** (b. May 1, 1970, England) Pop guitarist. The founder members of and principal songwriting team in the British glam-rock inspired group Suede, which Anderson left in 1996. CHART COMPOSITIONS: *The Drowners* (1992) UK#49, *Metal Mickey* (1992) UK#17, *Animal Nitrate* (1993) UK#7, *So Young* (1993) UK#22, *Stay Together* (1994) UK#3, *We Are the Pigs* (1994) UK#18, *The Wild Ones* (1994) UK#18, *New Generation* (1995) UK#21, *Trash* (1996) UK#3, *Beautiful Ones* (1996) UK#8. ALBUMS: **Suede** (1993) UK#1, **Dog Man Star** (1994) UK#3, **Coming Up** (1996, all Nude) UK#1. Butler has also recorded with David McAlmont as the duo McAlmont and Butler, charting with *Yes* (1995) UK#8 and *You Do* (1995) UK#17. ALBUM: **The Sound of McAlmont and Butler** (1995, Hut) UK#33.

22. ANDERSON, Ian (b. August 10, 1947, Edinburgh, Scotland) Rock flutist, producer and vocalist. The lead singer and principal songwriter in the folk influenced British progressive rock group Jethro Tull. CHART COMPOSITIONS: *Living in the Past* (1969) UK#3, re-issued (1973) US#11, re-issued (1993) UK#32; *Sweet Dreams* (1969) UK#7, *The Witch's Promise/Teacher* (1970) UK#4, *Hymn 43* (1971) US#91, *Life Is a Long Song* (1971) UK#11, *A Passion Play (Edit #8)* (1973) US#80, *A Passion Play (Edit #10)* (1973) US#105, *Bungle in the Jungle* (1975) US#11, *Minstrel in the Gallery* (1975) US#79, *Locomotive Breath* (1976) US#62, *Ring Out Solstice Bells* (1976) UK#28, *The Whistler* (1977) US#59, *Fallen On Hard Times* (1982) US#108, *Lap of Luxury* (1984) UK#70, *She Said She Was a Dancer* (1986) UK#55, *Rocks on the Road* (1992) UK#47. ALBUMS: **This Was** (1968) US#62 UK#10, **Stand Up** (1969) g US#20 UK#1, **Benefit** (1970) g US#11 UK#3, **Aqualung** (1971, all Island) p US#7 UK#4; **Thick as a Brick** (1972) g US#1 UK#5, **A Passion Play** (1973) g US#1 UK#13, **War Child** (1974) g US#2 UK#14, **Minstrel in the Gallery** (1975) g US#7 UK#20, **Too Old to Rock 'n' Roll, Too Young to Die** (1976) US#14 UK#25, **Songs from the Wood** (1977) g US#8 UK#13, **Heavy Horses** (1978) g US#19 UK#20, **Live: Bursting Out** (1978) g US#21 UK#17, **Stormwatch** (1979) g US#22 UK#27, **"A"** (1980) US#30 UK#25, **Broadsword and the Beast** (1982) US#19 UK#27, **Under Wraps** (1984) US#76 UK#18, **Crest of a Knave** (1987) g US#32 UK#19, **Rock Island** (1989) US#56 UK#18, **Catfish Rising** (1990) US#88 UK#27, **A Little Light Music** (1992) US#150 UK#34, **Roots to Branches** (1995, all Chrysalis) US#114 UK#20. COMPILATIONS: **Living in the Past** (1972) g US#3 UK#8, **M.U.-The Best of Jethro Tull** (1976) p US#13 UK#44, **Repeat-The Best of Jethro Tull, Volume 2** (1977) US#94, **Original Masters** (1985) UK#63, **20 Years of Jethro Tull** (1988) US#97 UK#78, **25th Anniversary Box Set** (1993) **The Other Box Set** (1993, all Chrysalis). Anderson's songs were also recorded by the London Symphony Orchestra as **A Classic Case-The London Symphony Orchestra Plays the Music of Jethro Tull** (1986, RCA) US#93. Although he has essentially become Jethro Tull, hiring and firing backing musicians at whim, Anderson has also recorded as a solo artist. ALBUMS: **Walk into Light** (1983, Chrysalis) UK#78; **Divinities-Twelve Dances with God** (1995, EMI).

23. ANDERSON, John A. (b. December 13, 1954, Apopka, FL) C&W guitarist and vocalist. One of a batch of singer-songwriters who incorporates mainstream rock into his country sound. Anderson learned the guitar at the age of seven, and was a staff writer in Nashville during the early 1970s, before recording for the Ace of Hearts label in 1974. He has charted over forty singles, including many of his own compositions. CHART COMPOSITIONS: *Swingin'* [ii] (1983) g C&W#1 US#43, *Black Sheep* (1983) C&W#1, *Straight Tequila Night* (1991) C&W#1, *Who Got Your Love* [ii] (1991) C&W#67, *Seminole Wind* (1992) C&W#2, *I Wish I Could Have Been There* [iii] (1994) C&W#4, *Long Hard Lesson Learned* [i] (1996) C&W#51+. ALBUMS: **Wild and Blue** (1983) g US#58, **All the People Are Talkin'** (1983) US#163, **I Just Came Home to Count the Memories** (1984), **Eye of a Hurricane** (1985), **Tokyo, Oklahoma** (1986), **Countryfied** (1986, all Warner Brothers); **Blue Skies Again** (1986, MCA); **Seminole Wind** (1992) p US#35, **Solid Ground** (1993) g, **Takin' the Country Back** (1997, all BNA). COMPILATION: **Greatest Hits** (1986, Warner Brothers) g. Co-writers: [i] D. Anderson/M.A. Anderson, [ii] L.A. Delmore, [iii] K. Robbins.

24. ANDERSON, Jon (b. October 25, 1944, Accrington, England) Rock vocalist. The distinctive soprano vocalist, lyricist and founder member of the classical-progressive rock group Yes. CHART COMPOSITIONS: *Your Move* (1971) US#40, *Roundabout* [iii] (1972) US#13, *And You and I (Part II)* (1973) US#42, *Wondrous Stories* (1977) UK#7, *Going for the One* (1977) UK#24, *Don't Kill the Whale* (1978) UK#36, *Owner of a Lonely Heart* [ii] (1983) R&B#69 US#1 UK#28, *It Can Happen* [iii] (1984) US#51, *Brother of Mine** (1989) UK#63, *Lift Me Up* (1991) US#86. ALBUMS: **Yes** (1969), **Time and a Word** (1970) UK#45, **The Yes Album** (1971) g US#40 UK#7, **Fragile** (1971) g US#4 UK#7, **Close to the Edge** (1972) g US#3 UK#4, **Yessongs** (1973) g US#12 UK#7, **Tales from Topographic Oceans** (1973) g US#6 UK#1, **Relayer** (1974) g US#5 UK#4, **Going for the One** (1977) g US#8 UK#1, **Tormato** (1978) p US#10 UK#8, **Yesshows** (1981, all Atlantic) US#43 UK#22; **90125** (1983) p US#5 UK#16, **9012 Live: The Solos** (1985) US#81 UK#44, **Big Generator** (1987, all Atco) p US#15 UK#17; **Anderson, Bruford, Wakeman, Howe** (1989) g US#30 UK#14, **Union** (1991, both Arista) g US#15 UK#7; **History of the Future** (1993), **Talk** (1994) US#33 UK#20, **Keys to Ascension** (1996, all Victory). COMPILATIONS: **Yesterdays** (1975) US#17 UK#27, **Classic Yes** (1982) US#142 (1991, all Atlantic). The group's music was also recorded by the London Philharmonic Orchestra as **The Symphonic Music of Yes** (1993, RCA) US#164. Anderson has also recorded as the duo Jon and Vangelis, charting with *I Hear You Now* [iv] (1980) US#58 UK#8, *I'll Find My Way Home* [iv] (1982) US#51 UK#6, *He Is Sailing* [iv] (1983) UK#61, and *State of Independence* [iv] (1984) UK#67. ALBUMS: **Short Stories** (1980) US#125 UK#4, **The Friends of Mr. Cairo** (1981) US#64 UK#6, **Private Collection** (1983, all Polydor) US#148 UK#22; **Page of Life** (1991, Arista). COMPILATION: **Best of Jon and Vangelis** (1984, Polydor) UK#42. Anderson has also pursued an intermittent solo career, charting with *Some Are Born* (1981) US#109. ALBUMS: **Olias of Sunhillow** (1976) US#47 UK#8, **Song of Seven** (1980) US#143 UK#38, **Animation** (1982, all Atlantic) US#142; **3 Ships** (1985, Elektra) US#166; **In the City of Angels** (1988), **Deseo** (1994, both RCA); **Change We Must** (1994, EMI); **Angels Embrace** (1996), **The Promise Ring** (1997, both Higher Octave). HIT VERSIONS: *State of Independence* [iv] Donna Summer (1982) R&B#31 US#41 UK#14, re-mixed (1996) UK#13/Moodswings & Chrissie Hynde as *Spiritual High (State of Independence)* (1991) UK#66. As: * Anderson, Bruford, Wakeman, Howe. Co-writers: [i] Trevor Horn/Chris Squire (b. March 4, 1948, London, England)/Trevor Rabin, [ii] Steve Howe (b. April 8, 1947, London), [iii] Chris Squire/Trevor Rabin, [iv] Vangelis (b. Evangelos Papathanassiou, March 29, 1943, Volos, Greece).

25. ANDERSON, Laurie (b. Laura Phillips Anderson, June 5, 1947, Chicago, IL) Violinist and performance artist. Initially a sculptor who presented the multi-media, audio-visual show "The Life and Times of Joseph Stalin" (1973) in Brooklyn, before recording conceptual avante-garde albums. In 1995, Anderson published the CD-Rom "Puppet Motel." CHART COMPOSITION: *O Superman* (1981) UK#2. ALBUMS: **Big Science** (1982) US#124 UK#29, **Mister Heartbreak** (1984) US#60 UK#93, **United States Live** (1985) US#192, **Home of the Brave** (1986) US#145, **Strange Angels** (1989) US#171, **Bright Red** (1994) US#195, **The Ugly One with the Jewels and Other Stories** (1995, all Warner Brothers).

26. ANDERSON, Liz (b. Elizabeth Jane Haaby, March 13, 1930, Roseau, MN) C&W vocalist. The mother of the country singer Lynn Anderson, who charted nineteen country hits of her own between 1966-1973. Anderson was most successful as a songwriter for others, before retiring in 1976. HIT VERSIONS: *Fugitive, The* [i] Merle Haggard (1967) C&W#1, *Guess My Eyes Were Bigger Than My Heart* Conway Twitty (1966) C&W#18, *Just Between the Two of Us* Merle Haggard & Bonnie Owens (1964) C&W#28, *(My Friends Are Gonna Be) Strangers* Merle Haggard (1965) C&W#10, *Pick of the Week* Roy Drusky (1964) C&W#13, *Ride, Ride, Ride* Lynn Anderson (1967) C&W#36. Co-writer: [i] Casey Anderson.

27. ANDERSSON, Benny (b. Goran Bror Benny Andersson, February 16, 1946, Stockholm, Sweden) Pop keyboard player and producer, and **ULVAEUS, Bjorn** (b. Bjorn Christian Ulvaeus, April 5, 1945, Gottenburg, Sweden) Pop guitarist and producer. The composers and principal musicians in the Swedish pop group Abba, as which, they created a sound that dominated the European charts during the late 1970s, in much the same way that the Beatles had done a decade earlier. Abba achieved nine British number one singles and eight number one albums, becoming the biggest selling group in recording history, with worldwide sales of nearly one hundred million records. In 1978, Abba were reported as being Sweden's fastest growing corporation. Andersson and Ulvaeus' catchy formula consisted of banal lyrical cliches, pristine vocal arrangements and frequently unforgettable melodies, and their songs often employed the Motown Records and Lennon and McCartney technique of starting with the chorus. Their Scandinavian folk routes were often apparent in their material, and they cleverly utilized such sounds and rhythms as Spanish bullfight choruses, German beer festival drinking-songs, cha-chas, flamenco, and European cabaret. Andersson had initially performed on the Swedish folk circuit in the Hootenanny Singers, while also playing in a skiffle group and a Dixieland influenced jazz outfit. He met Ulvaeus at a party in 1963, shortly after which, they formed a songwriting partnership, their first composition being *Isn't It Easy to Say* (1963). In 1964, Andersson joined Sweden's most popular band, the Hep Stars, and soon became their chief tunesmith, penning such singles as *No Response* and *Sunny Girl*. Two years later, Ulvaeus joined him in the group. ALBUMS: **Mashed Potatoes** (1964), **The Hep Stars** (1966), **Jul Med Hep Stars** (1967), **Songs We Sang** (1967, all Olga); **It's Been a Long Time** (1967, Cupol); **Hep Stars Pa Svenska** (1967, Olga). They left the Hep Stars in 1969 to record an album as Bjorn and Benny, **Lycka** (1970, Polar), and to work for the producer Stig Anderson's Polar Music as in-house songwriters and producers. Having linked up with two female vocalists, Agnetha Falskog and Frida Lyngstad, they began performing as the quartet Bjorn, Benny, Agnetha and Frida, charting in Sweden with *People Need Love*. As Abba, they were successful in Japan with *She's My Kind of Girl*. Andersson and Ulvaeus' first attempt at a Swedish Eurovision Song Contest entry was not successful, although the composition, *Ring Ring* [iii], was a hit throughout Scandinavia, as was Lena Andersen's version of their song *Better to Have Loved*. In 1974, Abba won the contest with their amiable *Waterloo* [i], an inoffensive song that began a formidable hit making career. By 1992, Abba's song catalogue was earning approximately four million dollars a year in publishing and mechanical royalties alone. CHART COMPOSITIONS: *Waterloo* [i] (1974) US#6 UK#1, *Ring Ring* [iii] (1974) UK#32, *Honey, Honey* [i] (1974) US#27, *I Do, I Do, I Do* [i] (1975) US#15 UK#38, *S.O.S.* [i] (1975) US#15 UK#6, *Mamma Mia* [i] (1975) US#32 UK#1, *Fernando* [ii] (1976) US#13 UK#1, *Dancing Queen* [i] (1976) g US#1 UK#1, re-issued (1992) UK#16; *Money Money Money* (1976) US#56 UK#3, *Knowing Me, Knowing You* [i] (1977) US#14 UK#1, *The Name of the Game* [i] (1977) US#12 UK#1, *Take a Chance on Me* (1978) g US#3 UK#1, *Summer Night City* (1978) UK#5, *Chiquitita* [iv] (1979) US#29 UK#2, *Does Your Mother Know?* (1979) US#19 UK#4, *Angel Eyes/Voulez Vous* (1979) UK#3, *Voulez Vous* (1979) US#80, *Angel Eyes* (1979) US#64, *Gimme Gimme Gimme (A Man After Midnight)* (1979) UK#3, *I Have a Dream* (1979) UK#2, *The Winner Takes It All* (1980) US#8 UK#1, *Super Trooper* (1980) US#45 UK#1, *On and On and On* (1981) US#90, *Lay All Your Love on Me* (1981) UK#7, *One of Us* (1983) US#107 UK#3, *When All Is Said and Done* (1982) US#27, *The Visitors* (1982)

US#63, *The Day Before You Came* (1982) UK#32, *Under Attack* (1982) UK#26, *Head Over Heels* (1982) UK#25, *Thank You for the Music* (1983) UK#33. ALBUMS: **Ring Ring** (1973), **Waterloo** (1974) US#145 UK#28, **Abba** (1974) US#174 UK#13, **Arrival** (1976) g US#20 UK#1, **The Album** (1977) p US#14 UK#1, **Voulez Vous** (1979) g US#19 UK#1, **Super Trooper** (1980) g US#17 UK#1, **The Visitors** (1981, all Polar) US#29 UK#1. COMPILATIONS: **Greatest Hits** (1976) p US#48 UK#1, **Greatest Hits, Volume 2** (1979, both Polar) g US#46 UK#1; **The Singles-The First Ten Years** (1982) US#62 UK#1, **Thank You for the Music** (1983, both Epic) UK#17; **Live** (1988, Polydor); **Absolute Abba** (1988, Telstar) UK#70; **Gold-Greatest Hits** (1992) p US#63 UK#1, **More Abba Gold-More Abba Hits** (1993, both Polydor) UK#14. The group split up in 1982, although Andersson and Ulvaeus stayed together as writers, working on the musical "Chess," which was recorded as the albums **Chess** sc (1984, RCA) US#47 UK#10 and **Chess Pieces** sc (1985, Telstar) UK#87. They followed it with the musical "Kristina from Duvemala" (1992). Andersson has also issued a solo album, **Klinga Mina Klockor** (1987, Mono). HIT VERSIONS: *Dancing Queen* [i] Carol Douglas (1977) US#102/Abbacadabra (1992) UK#57; *Day Before You Came, The* Blancmange (1994) UK#22, *Fernando* [ii] (1976) Stars On in *Stars on 45* (1981) US#120 UK#18, *Gimme Gimme Gimme (A Man After Midnight)* Stars On in *Stars on 45* (1981) US#120 UK#18, *Honey, Honey* [i] (1974) Sweet Dreams (1974) US#68, *I Have a Dream* Cristy Lane (1981) C&W#17, *I Know Him So Well* [v] Elaine Paige & Barbara Dickson (1985) UK#1, *Knowing Me, Knowing You* [i] Stars On in *Stars on 45* (1981) US#120 UK#18, *Lay All Your Love On Me* Stars On in *Stars on 45* (1981) US#120 UK#18/Information Society (1989) US#83/Erasure on *Abba-esque* (1992) UK#1 US#85; *On and On and On* Stars On in *Stars on 45* (1981) US#120 UK#18, *One Night in Bangkok* [v] Murray Head (1984) R&B#89 US#3 UK#12, re-entry (1985) UK#74/Robey (1985) US#77; *S.O.S.* [i] Stars On in *Stars on 45* (1981) US#120 UK#18/Erasure on *Abba-esque* (1992) UK#1 US#85; *Summer Night City* Stars On in *Stars on 45* (1981) US#120 UK#18, *Super Trooper* Stars On in *Stars on 45* (1981) US#120 UK#18, *Take a Chance on Me* Erasure on *Abba-esque* (1992) UK#1 US#85, *Voulez Vous* Stars On in *Stars on 45* (1981) US#120 UK#18/Erasure on *Abba-esque* (1992) UK#1 US#85; *Waterloo* [i] Dr. & the Medics (1986) UK#45, *Winner Takes It All, The* Stars On in *Stars on 45* (1981) US#120 UK#18. Co-writers: [i] Stig Anderson, [ii] Stig Anderson/Benny Andersson only, [iii] Stig Anderson/Phil Cody/Neil Sedaka, [iv] Buddy McCluskey, [v] Tim Rice (b. Timothy Miles Bindon Rice, November 10, 1944, Amersham, England).

28. ANDREOLI, Peter (b. New York, NY) Pop composer, and **PONCIA, Vincent** (b. New York, NY) Pop producer and vocalist. Former members of the group the Videls, which charted with their song *Mister Lonely* (1960) US#73, who became staff writers for the publishers Hill and Range. Andreoli and Poncia also charted as the studio groups the Trade Winds, with *New York's a Lonely Town* (1965) US#32 and *Mind Excursion* (1966) US#51, and as Innocence, with *There's Got to Be a Word* (1967) US#34. Andreoli released an eponymous solo album in 1972, while Poncia became a co-writer and producer during the 1970s, capitalizing on the disco boom. ALBUM: **The Anders and Poncia Album** (1969, Warner Brothers). HIT VERSION: *You Gave Me Somebody to Love* [i] Manfred Mann (1966) UK#36. Co-writer: [i] Ross. (*See also under* Melissa MANCHESTER, Leo SAYER, Phil SPECTOR.)

29. ANDREWS, Chris (b. 1942, Romford, England) Pop producer and vocalist. A singer-songwriter who was successful during the 1960s with his own singles, and eight songs that he wrote for the vocalist Sandie Shaw. CHART COMPOSITIONS: *Yesterday Man* (1965) US#94 UK#3, *To Whom It Concerns* (1965) UK#13, *Something on My Mind* (1966) UK#41, *Whatcha Gonna Do Now* (1966) UK#40, *Stop That Girl* (1966) UK#36. ALBUM: **Who Is This Man** (1977, Epic). COMPILATIONS: **20 Golden Pieces** (1987, Bulldog); **Swinging Sixties Hit Man: The Definitive Anthology** (1996, Repertoire). HIT VERSIONS: *First Time, The* Adam Faith (1963) UK#5, *Girl Don't Come* Sandie Shaw (1964) US#42 UK#3, *How Can You Tell* Sandie Shaw (1965) US#131 UK#21, *I'll Stop at Nothing* Sandie Shaw (1965) US#123 UK#4, *If He Tells You* Adam Faith (1964) UK#25, *It's Alright* Adam Faith (1965) US#31, also on B-side of *I Love Being in Love with You* (1964) UK#33; *Long Live Love* Sandie Shaw (1965) US#97 UK#1/Nick Berry (1992) UK#47; *Message Understood* Sandie Shaw (1965) UK#6, *Nothing Comes Easy* Sandie Shaw (1966) UK#14, *Someone's Taken Maria Away* Adam Faith (1965) UK#34, *Tomorrow* Sandie Shaw (1966) UK#9, *We Are in Love* Adam Faith (1964) UK#11/Bobby Byrd (1965) US#120; *You've Changed* Sandie Shaw (1967) UK#18.

30. ANKA, Paul (b. July 30, 1941, Ottawa, Canada) Pop producer and vocalist. One of the first genuine singer-songwriters in popular music, who, although a teen pop idol, was one of the first to compose much of his own material. Over four hundred of Anka's compositions have been recorded by other artists, which have collectively sold over one hundred million records. Anka's father was a Lebanese immigrant who owned and ran a restaurant, and he ac-

tively encouraged his son's show business inclinations. Anka made his first public appearance in 1953, imitating the singer Johnnie Ray, and began writing songs while still in high school, which were initially influenced by the Syrian tunes that his father played. In 1956, Anka headed for Los Angeles, where he supported himself as a movie usher and recorded a single for Modern Records, *Blau Wildesbeeste Fontaine* (1956), which was titled after a city in South Africa. He sung briefly in a vocal trio called the Bobby-Soxers, before, at the age of fifteen, composing a song about his younger brother's babysitter, *Diana*, a plaintiff love ballad that noted how teenage girls grow up quicker than teenage boys. Anka's demo of the song landed him a recording contract with ABC/Paramount in 1957, and a newly recorded version quickly topped the charts around the world, eventually selling over fourteen million copies and attracting three hundred and twenty cover versions. Anka followed his initial success with a further fifty-eight American hits. Two of his finest ballads, *Put Your Head on My Shoulder* and *It Really Doesn't Matter Anymore*, were recorded by the Beach Boys and Buddy Holly respectively. By 1963, Anka had purchased his original ABC/Paramount masters and created his own publishing company. He appeared in such films as "Let's Rock" (1958), "Girls' Town" (1959) and "The Longest Day" (1972), and also composed one of the most lucrative tunes of all time, Johnny Carson's *The Tonight Show Theme* [ii] (1962). One of popular music's most astute artists, Anka would often record a song in up to five different languages during the same session, giving him such simultaneous worldwide hits as the Italian million seller *Ogni Volta* (1964). During the 1960s, Anka became a popular cabaret act, and he also appeared in the Broadway musical "What Makes Sammy Run?" (1964). His ever sagacious eye on the European song market, resulted, in 1969, in his acquisition to the rights of the melody of a French tune entitled *Comme D'Habitude*, to which he wrote new lyrics — As *My Way* [iv], the song was recorded over forty times, and became Frank Sinatra's theme tune. Anka's material was also recorded by Annette as **Annette Sings Anka** (1960, Buena Vista). CHART COMPOSITIONS: *Diana* (1957) R&B#1 US#1 UK#1, *I Love You Baby* (1957) US#97 UK#3, *Tell Me That You Love Me* (1957) US#25, *You Are My Destiny* (1958) R&B#14 US#7 UK#6, *Crazy Love* (1958) US#15 UK#26, *Let the Bells Keep Ringing* (1958) US#18, *Midnight* (1958) US#69 UK#26, *Just Young* (1958) US#80, *The Teen Commandments* with George Hamilton, IV, and Johnny Nash (1958) US#29, *Lonely Boy* (1959) R&B#6 US#1 UK#3, *I Miss You* (1959) US#33, *Put Your Head on My Shoulder* (1959) R&B#12 US#2 UK#7, *It's Time to Cry* (1960) R&B#13 US#4

UK#28, *Puppy Love* (1960) US#2 UK#33, *Adam and Eve* (1960) US#90, *My Home Town* (1960) US#4, *I Love You in the Same Old Way* (1960) US#40, *Summer's Gone* (1960) US#29 UK#11, *The Story of My Life* (1961) US#16, *Don't Say You're Sorry* (1961) US#108, *Tonight My Love Tonight* (1961) US#13, *Dance on Little Girl* (1961) US#10, *Kissin' on the Phone* (1961) US#35, *The Bells at My Wedding* (1961) US#104, *Loveland* (1961) US#110, *Cinderella* (1961) US#70, *Love Me Warm and Tender* (1962) US#12 UK#19, *A Steel Guitar and a Glass of Wine* (1962) US#13 UK#41, *I'll Never Find Another You* (1962) US#106, *I'm Coming Home* (1962) US#94, *Every Night (Without You)* (1962) US#46, *Remember Diana* (1963) US#39, *Hello Jim* (1963) US#97, *Did You Have a Happy Birthday?* (1963) US#89, *My Baby's Comin' Home* (1964) US#113, *Happy* (1969) US#86, *Do I Love You* (1971) US#53, *Jubilation* (1972) US#65, *Let Me Get to Know You* (1974) US#80, *(You're) Having My Baby** (1974) g US#1 UK#6, *One Man Woman/One Woman Man** (1974) US#7, *I Don't Like to Sleep Alone* (1975) US#8, *(I Believe) There's Nothing Stronger Than Our Love** (1975) US#15, *Anytime (I'll Be There)* (1976) US#33, *Happier* (1976) US#60, *My Best Friend's Wife* (1977) US#80, *Everybody Ought to Be in Love* (1977) US#75, *Hold Me 'Til the Morning Comes* [iii] (1983) US#40. ALBUMS: **Paul Anka** (1958), **My Heart Sings** (1959), **Paul Anka Sings His Big 15** (1960) US#4, **Swings for Young Lovers** (1960), **Anka at the Copa** (1960) US#23, **It's Christmas Everywhere** (1960), **Strictly Instrument** (1961), **Paul Anka Sings His Big 15, Volume 2** (1961) US#72, **Paul Anka Sings His Big 15, Volume 3** (1962, all ABC/Paramount); **Young Alive and in Love** (1962) US#61, **Let's Sit This One Out** (1962) US#137, **Our Man Around the World** (1963), **Songs I Wish I'd Written** (1963), **Excitement on Park Avenue-Live at the Waldorf Astoria** (1964), **Strictly Nashville** (1966), **Live** (1967), **Goodnight My Love** (1969) US#101, **Sincerely** (1969), **Life Goes On** (1969) US#194, **Paul Anka '70s** (1970, all RCA); **Paul Anka** (1971) US#188, **Jubilation** (1972, both Buddah) US#192; **Anka** (1974) g US#9, **Feelings** (1975) US#36, **Times Of Your Life** (1975) g US#22, **The Painter** (1976) US#85, **The Music Man** (1977, all United Artists) US#195; **Listen to Your Heart** (1978) US#179, **Headline** (1979), **Both Sides of Love** (1981, all RCA) US#171; **Walk a Fine Line** (1983, Columbia) US#156; **Amigos** (1993). COMPILATIONS: **Diana** (1962, ABC/Paramount); **21 Golden Hits** (1963, RCA) US#65; **Gold** (1974, Sire) US#125; **Italiano** (1987, Crescent); **30th Anniversary Collection** (1991, Rhino); **Zwei Madchen Aua Germany** (1992, Bear Family); **Five Decades** (1993). HIT VERSIONS: *Anytime (I'll Be There)* Frank Sinatra (1975) US#75, *Broken Heart*

and a Pillow Filled with Tears, A Patti Page (1961) US#91, *Can't Get You Out of My Mind* Margaret Whiting (1968) US#124, *Diana* Bobby Rydell (1959) US#98, *Don't Leave Me in the Morning* Odia Coates (1975) US#91, *Everything's Been Changed* 5th Dimension (1973) US#70, *I Confess* New Colony Six (1966) US#80, *I Love You, Baby* Freddie & the Dreamers (1964) UK#19, *I've Been Waiting for You All My Life* Con Hunley (1979) C&W#14, *It Doesn't Matter Anymore* Buddy Holly (1959) US#13 UK#1/ Linda Ronstadt (1975) C&W#54 US#47/R.C. Bannon (1977) C&W#33; *Let Me Try Again* [i] Frank Sinatra (1973) US#63, *Lonely Boy* Donny Osmond (1972) US#13, *Longest Day, The* Mitch Miller (1962) US#109, *My Way (Comme D'Habitude)* [iv] Frank Sinatra (1969) US#27 UK#5, re-entry (1970) UK#18, re-entry (1971) UK#22, re-entry (1972) UK#50/Brook Benton (1970) R&B#25 US#72/ Dorothy Squires (1970) UK#25/Elvis Presley (1977) g C&W#2 US#22 UK#9/Sex Pistols (1978) UK#7/ Shane MacGowan (1996) UK#29; *Puppy Love* Donny Osmond (1972) g US#3 UK#1, *Put Your Head on My Shoulder* Lettermen (1968) US#44/Sunday Sharpe (1975) C&W#48/Leif Garrett (1978) US#58; *She's a Lady* Tom Jones (1971) g R&B#42 US#2 UK#12, *Teddy* Connie Francis (1960) US#17, *This Is Your Song* Don Goodwin (1973) US#86, *While We're Still Young* Wayne Newton (1973) US#107. With: * Odia Coates. Co-writers: [i] Sammy Cahn/Vasori Caraveli/ Michael Jourdan, [ii] Johnny Carson, [iii] David Foster, [iv] Claude Francois/Jacques Ravaux/Gillis Thibout. (*See also under* Burt BACHARACH.)

31. ANT, Adam (b. Stuart Leslie Goddard, November 3, 1954, London, England) Pop vocalist. A punk rocker who, as the leader of the group Adam and the Ants, became one of the most popular British teen acts of the early 1980s. CHART COMPOSITIONS: *Kings of the Wild Frontier* [i] (1980) UK#48, re-issued (1981) UK#2; *Dog Eat Dog* [i] (1980) UK#4, *Antmusic* [i] (1981) UK#2, *Young Parisians* (1981) UK#9, *Zerox* (1981) UK#45, *Cartrouble* (1981) UK#33, *Stand and Deliver* [i] (1981) UK#1, *Prince Charming* [i] (1981) UK#1, *Ant Rap* [i] (1982) UK#3, *Deutscher Girls* (1982) UK#13, *The Antmusic EP* [i] (1982) UK#46. After the group disbanded in 1982, Ant continued as a solo artist before, during the 1990s, concentrating on an acting career. CHART COMPOSITIONS: *Goody Two Shoes* [i] (1982) US#12 UK#1, *Friend or Foe* [i] (1982) UK#9, *Desperate But Not Serious* (1982) US#66 UK#33, *Puss 'n Boots* [i] (1983) UK#5, *Strip* [i] (1983) US#42 UK#41, *Apollo 9* [i] (1984) UK#13, *Vive le Rock* (1985) UK#50, *Room at the Top* (1990) US#17 UK#13, *Can't Set Rules About Love* (1990) UK#47, *Wonderful* [i] (1995) US#39 UK#32, *Gotta*

Be a Sin [i] (1995) UK#48. ALBUMS: **Dirk Wears White Sox** (1979, Do It) UK#16; **Kings of the Wild Frontier** (1981) g US#44 UK#1, **Prince Charming** (1981) US#94 UK#2, **Friend or Foe** (1982) g US#16 UK#5, **Strip** (1983) US#65 UK#20, **Vive le Rock** (1985, all CBS) US#131 UK#42; **Manners and Physique** (1990, MCA) US#57 UK#19; **Wonderful** (1995, EMI) US#151 UK#24. COMPILATIONS: **Ant Music-The Very Best of Adam and the Ants** (1993, Arcade) UK#6; **B-Side Babies** (1995, Epic). Co-writer: [i] Marco Pirroni (b. April 27, 1959, England).

32. ARGENT, Rod (b. Rodney Argent, June 14, 1945, St. Albans, England) Rock keyboard player and producer. A founder member of the British beat group the Zombies, which charted with *She's Not There* (1964) US#2 UK#12, *Tell Her No* (1965) US#6 UK#42, *She's Coming Home* (1965) US#58, *Whenever You're Ready* (1965) US#110, *I Want You Back Again* (1965) US#95, *Time of the Season* (1969) g US#3, and *Imagine the Swan* [i] (1969) US#109. ALBUMS: **The Zombies** (1965, Parrot) US#39; **Odessey and Oracle** (1967, Columbia) US#95. COMPILATION: **Time of the Zombies** (1974, Epic). After the group split up in 1969, he formed the progressive rock group Argent, charting with the single *Hold Your Head Up* [i] (1972) US#5 UK#5. ALBUMS: **Argent** (1970), **Ring of Hands** (1971), **All Together Now** (1972) US#23 UK#13, **In Deep** (1973) US#90 UK#49, **Nexus** (1974) US#149, **Encore-Live in Concert** (1975) US#151, **Circus** (1975, all Epic) US#171; **Counterpoint** (1975, RCA). COMPILATION: **The Argent Anthology: A Collection of Greatest Hits** (1974, Epic). After the exit of its principal composer Russ Ballard, the group folded in 1976, after which, Argent opted for a brief solo career and ran his own keyboard shop in Denmark Street, London. CHART COMPOSITIONS: *Argentine Melody** (1978) UK#14, *Aztec Gold*** (1986) UK#48. ALBUMS: **Moving House** (1978, MCA); **Red House** (1988, RCA). HIT VERSIONS: *She's Not There* Neil MacArthur (1969) UK#34/Road (1969) US#114/Santana (1977) US#27 UK#11; *Tell Her No* Juice Newton (1983) US#27. As: * San Jose featuring Rodriguez Argentina, ** Silsoe. Co-writer: [i] Chris White (b. March 7, 1943, Barnet, England). (*See also under* Russ BALLARD.)

33. ARLEN, Harold (b. Hyman Arluck, February 15, 1905, Buffalo; d. April 23, 1986, New York, both NY) Film and stage composer, pianist, arranger and vocalist. A gifted and widely recorded songwriter, who once confessed, "I wanted to be a singer. Never dreamed of songwriting." Arlen composed many significant film themes that often fea-

tured a subtle use of the blues idiom, as evidenced by *Blues in the Night* [vii], *Stormy Weather* [vii] and *One for My Baby (And One More for the Road)* [vi]. A classically trained pianist, he played in his own teenage jazz and ragtime groups, the Snappy Trio and the Buffalodians, before achieving his first hit with *Get Happy* [vi], from the show "The 9.15 Revue" (1930). In partnership with the lyricist Ted Koehler, Arlen contributed to numerous Cotton Club shows during the 1930s. He composed songs for over twenty-five films, including the Oscar winning score "The Wizard of Oz" (1939), which introduced the standard *Over the Rainbow* [iv], alongside such gems as *We're Off to See the Wizard* [iv]. The entire soundtrack was later recorded by the electronic group Meco as **The Wizard of Oz** (1978, Millennium) US#68. Arlen also collaborated with Ira Gershwin on the often filmed revue "A Star is Born" (1934). CHART COMPOSITIONS: *Little Girl* (1931) US#4, *Stormy Weather* [vi] (1933) US#1, *Let's Fall in Love* [vi] (1934) US#19, *Ill Wind (You're Blowing Me No Good)* [vi] (1934) US#3, *You're a Builder Upper* (1934) US#6. ALBUM: **Arlen Sings Arlen** (1966, Columbia). HIT VERSIONS: *As Long As I Live* [vi] Benny Goodman (1941) US#24, *Between the Devil and the Deep Blue Sea* [vi] Cab Calloway (1931) US#15/Louis Armstrong (1932) US#12/Boswell Sisters (1932) US#13; *Blues in the Night* [vii] Woody Herman (1941) US#1/Artie Shaw (1941) US#10/Cab Calloway (1942) US#8/Benny Goodman (1942) US#20/Jimmie Lunceford (1942) US#4/Dinah Shore (1942) g US#4/Rosemary Clooney (1952) US#17; *Buds Won't Bud* [iv] Tommy Tucker (1940) US#29; *Come Rain or Come Shine* [vii] Helen Forrest & Dick Haymes (1946) US#23/Margaret Whiting (1946) US#17/Ray Charles (1960) US#83, re-issued (1968) US#98; *Ding Dong the Witch Is Dead* [iv] Glenn Miller (1939) US#17, *Evelina* [iv] Frankie Carle (1945) US#16/Bing Crosby (1945) US#9; *Fancy Meeting You (The Evolution Song)* [iv] Russ Morgan (1936) US#20, *For Every Man There's a Woman* [viii] Benny Goodman & Peggy Lee (1948) US#25/Tony Martin (1948) US#30; *Fun to Be Fooled* [iii] Henry King (1934) US#17, *Gal/Man That Got Away, The* [ii] Judy Garland (1954) US#22/Frank Sinatra (1954) US#21; *Get Happy* [vi] Nat Shilkret (1930) US#6/Frankie Trumbauer (1930) US#15; *God's Country* [iv] Vic Damone (1950) US#27/Frank Sinatra (1950) US#25, *Hit the Road to Dreamland* [vii] Freddie Slack (1943) US#16, *Hittin' the Bottle* [vi] Colonial Club Orchestra (1930) US#8, *Hooray for Love* [viii] Tony Martin (1948) US#21/Johnny Mercer (1948) US#25; *I Gotta Right to Sing the Blues* [vi] Louis Armstrong (1933) US#18/Cab Calloway (1933) US#17/Benny Goodman (1934) US#20; *I Love a Parade* [vi] Arden-Ohman Orchestra (1932) US#13, *I Promise You* [vii] Peter Van Steeden (1932) US#13/Kay Kyser (1939)

US#7; *I've Got the World on a String* [vi] Cab Calloway (1932) US#18/Bing Crosby (1933) US#19/ Frank Sinatra (1953) US#14; *Ill Wind (You're Blowing Me No Good)* [vi] Leo Reisman (1934) US#17, *It's Only a Paper Moon* [v] Cliff Edwards (1933) US#13/ Paul Whiteman (1933) US#9/Ella Fitzgerald (1945) R&B#4 US#9/Benny Goodman (1945) US#10; *Kickin' the Gong Around* [vi] Cab Calloway (1931) US#4/Louis Armstrong (1932) US#11; *Let's Fall in Love* [vi] Eddy Duchin (1934) US#1/Fred Rich (1934) US#8/Linda Scott (1963) US#108/Peaches & Herb (1967) US#21; *Let's Take the Long Way Home* [vii] Cab Calloway (1945) US#20/Jo Stafford (1945) US#14; *Lydia, the Tattooed Lady* [iv] Rudy Vallee (1939) US#15, *Minnie the Moocher's Wedding Day* Cab Calloway (1932) US#8, *My Shining Hour* [vii] Glen Gray (1944) US#4, *Napoleon* [iv] Mitch Miller (1954) US#25, *Now I Know* [vi] Eddie Fisher (1967) US#131, *One for My Baby (And One More for the Road)* [vii] Lena Horne (1945) US#12, *Out of This World* [vii] Tommy Dorsey (1945) US#12/Jo Stafford (1945) US#9; *Over the Rainbow* [iv] Larry Clinton (1939) US#10/Bob Crosby (1939) US#2/Judy Garland (1939) US#5/Glenn Miller (1939) US#1/Demensions (1960) US#16/Billy Thorpe & the Aztecs (1965) US#130/ Gary Tanner (1978) US#69/Jerry Lee Lewis (1980) C&W#10/Matchbox (1980) UK#15/Sam Harris (1985) UK#67; *Public Melody Number One* [vi] Louis Armstrong (1937) US#7, *Stormy Weather* [vi] Duke Ellington (1933) US#4/Ted Lewis (1933) US#6/Guy Lombardo (1933) US#2/Ethel Waters (1933) US#1/ Lena Horne (1943) US#21/Magnificent Men (1967) US#133; *Tess' Torch Song* [vi] Ella Mae Morse (1944) US#19; *That Old Black Magic* [vii] Hoarce Heidt (1943) US#11/Glenn Miller (1943) US#1/Freddie Slack (1943) US#10/ Sammy Davis, Jr. (1955) US#13 UK#16/Louis Prima & Keely Smith (1958) R&B#26 US#18/Bobby Rydell (1961) US#21/Softones (1975) R&B#29; *Themes from the Wizard of Oz* [iv] Meco (1978) US#35, *This Time the Dream's on Me* [vii] Woody Herman (1941) US#8/Glenn Miller (1941) US#11; *Tickeration* Cab Calloway (1931) US#8, *Two Blind Loves* [iv] Kenny Baker (1938) US#15, *What's Good About Goodbye?* [viii] Margaret Whiting (1948) US#29, *You're a Builder Upper* [iii] Glen Gray (1934) US#11/Henry King (1934) US#7. Co-writers: [i] Lou Davis (b. 1881; d. 1961), [ii] Ira Gershwin, [iii] Ira Gershwin/E.Y. Harburg, [iv] E.Y. Harburg, [v] E.Y. Harburg/Billy Rose, [vi] Ted Koehler, [vii] Johnny Mercer, [viii] Leo Robin. (*See also under* Jimmy McHUGH.)

34. ARMATRADING, Joan (b. December 9, 1950, St. Kitts, West Indies) Pop guitarist, pianist and vocalist. A British based singer-songwriter who often composes refined love ballads that have mysteriously been neglected by other, more commercially minded vocalists. Armatrading's father was a carpenter who, in 1958, emigrated with his family to Birmingham, England. By 1964, Armatrading had learned the piano and guitar, and had written her first published song, *When I Was Young*, which was recorded by Marianne Faithfull. Armatrading performed on the British folk circuit, and in 1968 she joined the "Hair" National Touring Company, before moving to London and working with Dice, a music and dance troupe. After a couple of unsuccessful solo albums, she hit her stride in 1976 with a folk inflected, Caribbean vocal styled eponymous album, that featured her excellent compositions *Down to Zero* and *Love and Affection*. Armatrading explained her unusual acoustic guitar style in 1980, "I was trying to be all the musicians in a band and my weird tempo changes came from not knowing what I was doing." Nearly all of her best songs are ballads, none more so than *No Love, I Wanna Hold You* and *The Weakness in Me.* CHART COMPOSITIONS: *Love and Affection* (1976) UK#10, *Show Some Emotion* (1978) US#110, *Rosie* (1980) UK#49, *Me Myself I* (1980) UK#21, *All the Way from America* (1980) UK#54, *I'm Lucky* (1981) UK#46, *No Love* (1982) UK#50, *Drop the Pilot* (1983) US#78 UK#11, *Temptation* (1985) UK#65, *More Than One Kind of Love* (1990) UK#75, *Wrapped Around Her* [i] (1992) UK#56. ALBUMS: **Whatever's for Us** (1972, Cube); **Back to the Night** (1975), **Joan Armatrading** (1976) US#67 UK#12, **Show Some Emotion** (1977) US#52 UK#6, **To the Limit** (1978) US#125 UK#13, **Steppin' Out** (1979), **How Cruel** (1980) US#136, **Me Myself I** (1980) US#28 UK#5, **Walk Under Ladders** (1981) US#88 UK#6, **The Key** (1983) US#32 UK#10, **Secret Secrets** (1985) US#73 UK#14, **Sleight of Hand** (1986) US#68 UK#34, **The Shouting Stage** (1988) US#100 UK#28, **Hearts and Flowers** (1990) US#161 UK#29, **Square the Circle** (1992, all A&M) UK#34; **What's Inside** (1995, RCA) UK#48. COMPILATIONS: **Live at Bijou Cafe** (1977), **Track Record** (1983) US#113 UK#18, **Very Best of Joan Armatrading** (1991) UK#9, **Love and Affection** (1997, all A&M). HIT VERSION: *Love and Affection* Sinitta (1990) UK#62. Co-writer: [i] Lyle.

35. ASHFORD, Nickolas (b. May 4, 1942, Fairfield, SC) R&B pianist, producer and vocalist, and **SIMPSON, Valerie** (b. August 26, 1948, Bronx, NY) R&B producer and vocalist. A husband and wife songwriting and production team who were million selling songwriters at Motown Records during the late 1960s, before they pursued a second career as an R&B vocal duo during the 1970s. Ashford and Simpson's extravagant production values developed the Motown pop song away from its initial three minute format, and their soulful, miniature pop symphonies, crammed with catchy hooks, made refreshing pop music, while lyrically they cornered a market in abbreviated, sloganized, slang titles. Simpson also recorded as a solo artist during the early 1970s, charting with *Silly Wasn't I* (1972) R&B#24 US#63, and releasing the albums **Exposed** (1971) US#159 and **Valerie Simpson** (1972, both Tamla) US#162, which were later compiled as **Best of Valerie Simpson** (1992, Motown). Ashford and Simpson first met when Simpson was a seventeen year old singer in the White Baptist Church Choir in Harlem. Their first compositions were gospel based, and in 1964 they recorded three unsuccessful singles as Nick and Valerie for the Glover label, *I'll Find You, Don't You Feel Sorry* and *It Ain't Like That*, before signing a publishing deal with Sceptor Records. The duo also contributed to a number of successful film soundtracks **Come Back Charleston Blue** ost (1972, Atco) US#198; **The Wiz** (1978, MCA) p US#40; **Body Rock** ost (1984, EMI America); and **The Golden Child** ost (1986, Capitol) US#126. CHART COMPOSITIONS: *I'll Find You* (1964) US#117, *(I'd Know You) Anywhere* (1973) R&B#37 US#88, *Have You Ever Tried It* (1974) R&B#77, *Main Line* (1974) R&B#37, *Everybody's Got to Give It Up* (1974) R&B#53, *Bend Me* (1975) R&B#73, *It'll Come, It'll Come, It'll Come* (1976) R&B#96, *Somebody Told Me a Lie* (1976) R&B#5, *Tried, Tested and Found True* (1976) R&B#52, *So So Satisfied* (1977) R&B#27, *Over and Over* (1977) R&B#39, *Send It* (1977) R&B#15, *Don't Cost You Nothing* (1978) R&B#10 US#79, *By Way of Love's Express* (1978) R&B#35, *It Seems to Hang On* (1978) R&B#2 UK#8, *Is It Still Good to Ya* (1978) R&B#12, *Flashback* (1979) R&B#70, *Found a Cure* (1979) R&B#2 US#36, *Nobody Knows* (1979) R&B#19, *Love Don't Make It Right* (1980) R&B#6, *Happy Endings* (1980) R&B#35, *Get Out Your Handkerchief* (1981) R&B#65, *It Shows in the Eyes* (1981) R&B#34, *Street Corner* (1982) R&B#9 US#56, *Love It Away* (1982) R&B#17, *High-Rise* (1983) R&B#17, *It's Much Deeper* (1983) R&B#45, *I'm Not That Tough* (1984) R&B#78, *Solid* (1984) R&B#1 US#12 UK#3, *Outta the World* (1985) R&B#4 US#102, *Babies* (1985) R&B#29 US#102 UK#56, *Count Your Blessings* (1986) R&B#14 US#84. ALBUMS: **Gimme Something Real** (1974) US#156, **I Wanna Be Selfish** (1974) US#195, **Come As You Are** (1976) US#189, **So So Satisfied** (1977) US#180, **Send It** (1977) g US#52, **Is It Still Good to Ya** (1978) g US#20, **Stay Free** (1979) g US#23, **A Musical Affair** (1980) US#38, **In Performance** (1981, all Warner Brothers) US#125; **Street Opera** (1981) US#45, **High-Rise** (1982) US#84, **Solid** (1984) g US#29 UK#42, **Real Love** (1986) US#74,

Love or Physical (1989, all Capitol) US#135. COMPILATIONS: **The Composer Series** (1987, Motown); **Capitol Gold-The Best of Ashford and Simpson** (1993, Capitol). HIT VERSIONS: *Ain't No Mountain High Enough* Marvin Gaye & Tammi Terrell (1967) R&B#3 US#19/Diana Ross (1970) R&B#1 US#1 UK#6/Boystown Gang (1981) UK#46; *Ain't Nothing Like the Real Thing* Marvin Gaye & Tammi Terrell (1968) R&B#1 US#8 UK#34/Aretha Franklin (1974) R&B#6 US#47/Donny & Marie Osmond (1976) US#21/Chris Christian (1982) US#88; *Body Rock* Maria Vidal (1985) US#48 UK#11, *Boss, The* Diana Ross (1979) R&B#12 US#19 UK#40, *Bourgie Bourgie* Gladys Knight & the Pips (1980) R&B#45 UK#32, *California Soul* 5th Dimension (1965) R&B#49 US#25, *Clouds* Chaka Khan (1980) R&B#10 US#103, *Cry Like a Baby* Aretha Franklin (1968) R&B#27 US#119, *Destination: Anywhere* Marvelettes (1968) R&B#28 US#63, also on B-side of *What's Easy for Two Is Hard for One* (1968) US#114; *Didn't You Know (You'd Have to Cry Sometime)* Gladys Knight & the Pips (1969) R&B#11 US#63, *Don't Send Nobody Else* [iii] Ace Spectrum (1974) R&B#20 US#57, *Good Lovin' Ain't Easy to Come By* Marvin Gaye & Tammi Terrell (1969) R&B#11 US#30 UK#26, *Hey Ho What You Do to Me* Guess Who (1965) US#125, *I Don't Need No Doctor* [i] Ray Charles (1966) US#72 R&B#45/Humble Pie (1971) US#73/New Riders of the Purple Sage (1971) US#81; *I Had a Love* Ben E. King (1976) R&B#23, *I Wouldn't Change the Man He Is* Blinky (1969) US#128, *I'm Every Woman* Chaka Khan (1977) R&B#1 US#21 UK#11, re-mixed (1989) UK#8/Whitney Houston (1993) g R&B#5 US#4 UK#4; *I'm Satisfied* Chuck Jackson & Maxine Brown (1966) US#112, *It's My House* Diana Ross (1979) R&B#27 UK#32/Storm (1979) UK#36; *Keep on Lovin' Me Honey* Marvin Gaye & Tammi Terrell (1968) R&B#11 US#24, *Landlord* Gladys Knight & the Pips (1980) R&B#3 US#46, *Let's Go Get Stoned* [i] Ray Charles (1965) US#31, *Never Had It So Good* Ronnie Milsap (1965) R&B#19 US#106, *No One Gets the Prize* Diana Ross (1979) UK#59, *Onion Song, The* Marvin Gaye & Tammi Terrell (1970) R&B#18 US#50 UK#9, *Please Little Angel* Doris Troy (1964) US#128, *Reach Out and Touch (Somebody's Hand)* Diana Ross (1970) R&B#7 US#20 UK#33, *Real Thing, The* Tina Britt (1965) R&B#20 US#102, *Remember Me* Diana Ross (1971) R&B#10 US#16 UK#7/Boystown Gang (1981) UK#46/Sinitta on *The Supreme EP* (1993) UK#49; *Ride-O-Rocket* Brothers Johnson (1978) R&B#45 US#104 UK#50, *Running Out* Four Tops (1975) R&B#13 US#71, *Shoe Shoe Shine* Dynamic Superiors (1974) R&B#16 US#68, *Some Things You Never Get Used To* Supremes (1969) R&B#43 US#30 UK#34, *Stuff Like That* [ii] Quincy Jones (1978)

R&B#1 US#21 UK#34, *Surrender* Diana Ross (1971) R&B#16 US#38 UK#10, *Taste of Bitter Love* Gladys Knight & the Pips (1980) R&B#38 UK#35, *Tear It on Down* Martha & the Vandellas (1972) R&B#37 US#103, *Too Hot to Hold* Major Lance (1965) R&B#32 US#93, *What You Gave Me* Marvin Gaye & Tammi Terrell (1969) R&B#6 US#49/Diana Ross (1971) R&B#86; *Who's Gonna Take the Blame* Smokey Robinson & the Miracles (1970) R&B#9 US#46, *You Ain't Livin' Until You're Lovin'* Marvin Gaye & Tammi Terrell (1968) UK#21, *You're All I Need to Get By* Marvin Gaye & Tammi Terrell (1968) R&B#1 US#7 UK#19/Aretha Franklin (1971) R&B#3 US#19/Tony Orlando & Dawn (1975) US#34/Johnny Mathis & Deniece Williams (1978) R&B#10 US#47 UK#45/Method Man featuring Mary J. Blige in *I'll Be There for You* (1995) US#3 UK#10; *Your Precious Love* Marvin Gaye & Tammi Terrell (1967) R&B#2 US#5/Stephen Bishop & Yvonne Elliman (1980) US#105/Al Jarreau & Randy Crawford (1982) R&B#16 US#102. Co-writers: [i] Joseph Armstead, [ii] Steve Gadd (b. c1945, Rochester, NY)/Eric Gale (b. September 20, 1938, New York, NY)/Quincy Jones (b. 14 March, 1933, Chicago, IL)/Ralph MacDonald/Richard Tee (b. November 24, 1943; d. July 21, 1993, both New York, NY).

36. ATKIN, Pete (b. Cambridge, England) Folk guitarist and vocalist. A singer-songwriter who, with lyricist and future author and television presenter Clive James (b. Sydney, Australia), recorded a series of poetical, sometimes charming, folk based albums. The vocalist Julie Covington also recorded an album of their compositions, **The Beautiful Changes** (1971, Columbia). Atkin later became a BBC radio producer, and returned to live performance in the late 1990s. ALBUMS: **Beware of the Beautiful Stranger** (1970, Fontana); **Driving Through Mythical America** (1971, Philips); **A King at Nightfall** (1973), **The Road of Silk** (1974), **Secret Drinker** (1974), **Live Libel** (1975), **Riders to the World's End** (1976, all RCA). COMPILATIONS: **Master of Revels** (1977), **The Essential Pete Atkin** (1977, both RCA).

37. AUTRY, Gene (b. Orvon Gene Autry, September 29, 1907, Tioga Springs, TX) C&W guitarist and vocalist. A successful and influential country vocalist and actor, who popularized the singing cowboy on television and in over one hundred films. Autry also composed over two hundred songs, often in partnership with Ray Whitley or Fred Rose. He was taught the guitar by his mother, and he first performed in medicine shows while still in high school. Autry was one of the few singing cowboys to actu-

ally ever work as one, and he also played the saxophone with the Fields Brothers Medicine Show. During the 1920s, Autry recorded for a variety of record labels, and performed in vaudeville before becoming a 1930s radio star in the serial "The Phantom Empire." He scored nearly thirty hits between 1944-1951. CHART COMPOSITIONS: *That Silver Haired Daddy of Mine* [ii] (1935) g US#7, *Be Honest with Me* [iii] (1941) US#23, *You'll Be Sorry* [iii] (1942), *I Hang My Head and Cry* (1944) C&W#4, *Tweedle O'Twill* [iii] (1944) US#20, *Here Comes Santa Claus (Down Santa Claus Lane)* [i] (1947) g C&W#5 US#9, re-issued (1948) C&W#4 US#8, re-issued (1950) US#24. ALBUMS: **50th Anniversary** (1979, Republic); **Live from Madison Square Garden** (1982), **Gene Autry Sings South of the Border** (1982), **Twenty Golden Pieces** (1982, all Bulldog); **Gene Autry** (1982, Columbia); **Yellow Rose of Texas** (1986, Bear Family); **Back in the Saddle Again** (1989, Platinum). HIT VERSIONS: *Back in the Saddle Again* Art Kassel (1940) US#24/Sonny James (1976) C&W#14; *Be Honest with Me* [iii] Bing Crosby (1941) US#19/Freddy Martin (1941) US#24/ Kathy Barnes (1975) C&W#92; *Goodbye Little Darlin'* Johnny Cash (1959) C&W#22, *That Silver Haired Daddy of Mine* [ii] Slim Whitman (1980) C&W#69, *Tweedle O'Twill* [iii] Kathy Barnes (1977) C&W#88, *You're the Only Star in My Blue Heaven* Billy Vaughn (1960) US#110/Mike Campbell (1984) C&W#77. Co-writers: [i] Oakley Haldeman, [ii] Jimmy Long, [iii] Fred Rose.

38. AXTON, Hoyt (b. May 25, 1938, Duncan, OK) C&W guitarist, pianist and vocalist. One of the key links between the traditional country-folk songwriting style of Woody Guthrie, and the more rock oriented contemporary sound of Garth Brooks. Axton's warm, down-home voice and working man's wit are best evidenced on his album **Joy to the World** (1971), which features superior versions of many of the hits that he has written for others. Axton grew up in the dust bowl shortly after the depression, his mother being a songwriter whose biggest success was co-composing Elvis Presley's *Heartbreak Hotel*. Axton sang at high school and took piano lessons, and began writing songs during his army service. In the late 1950s, he performed in coffee houses and folk clubs on the west coast, frequently appearing alongside Lightnin' Hopkins and John Lee Hooker, both of whom were to influence his own style. Axton's first recordings were made in Nashville in 1957, where he released the single *Follow the Drinking Gourd*. During the early 1960s, he recorded in a folk and blues style, before achieving his first success as a songwriter when the Kingston Trio recorded his *Greenback Dollar* [ii]. In the late 1970s, Axton branched out into acting, appearing on television shows and in such films as "Black Stallion" (1979) and "E.T." (1982) CHART COMPOSITIONS: *When the Morning Comes* (1974) C&W#10 US#54, *Boney Fingers* (1974) C&W#8, *Nashville/Speed Trap* (1975) C&W#61 US#105, *Lion in Winter* with Linda Ronstadt (1975) C&W#57, *Flash of Fire* (1976) C&W#18, *You're the Hangnail in My Life* (1977) C&W#57, *Little White Moon* (1977) C&W#65, *Della and the Dealer* (1979) C&W#17 UK#48, *A Rusty Old Halo* (1979) C&W#14, *Wild Bull Rider* (1980) C&W#21, *Evangelina* (1980) C&W#37, *Where Did the Money Go?* (1980) C&W#80, *Flo's Yellow Rose* (1981) C&W#78, *The Devil* (1981) C&W#86. ALBUMS: **The Balladeer** (1962), **Thunder 'n' Lightnin'** (1963, both Horizon); **Saturday's Child** (1963), **Hoyt Axton Explodes** (1964, both Vee-Jay); **Hoyt Axton Sings Bessie Smith My Way** (1964, Exodus); **Mr. Greenback Dollar Man** (1965, Surrey); **My Griffin Is Gone** (1969, Columbia); **Joy to the World** (1971), **Country Anthem** (1971, both Capitol); **Less Than the Song** (1973), **Life Machine** (1974), **Southbound** (1975) US#188, **Fearless** (1976, all A&M) US#171; **Snowblind Friend** (1978), **Free Sailin'** (1978, both MCA); **A Rusty Old Halo** (1979), **Where Did the Money Go?** (1980, both Jeremiah); **Down and Out** (1980, both Allegiance); **Everybody's Goin' on the Road** (1981, Youngblood); **Live** (1981, Jeremiah). COMPILATIONS: **Best of Hoyt Axton** (1964, Vee-Jay); **Road Songs** (1977, A&M); **Pistol Packin' Mama** (1982, Jeremiah); **American Originals** (1993, Capitol). HIT VERSIONS: *Greenback Dollar* [ii] Chas McDevitt Shuffle Group (1957) UK#28/ Kingston Trio (1963) US#21; *Joy to the World* Murry Kellum (1971) C&W#26/Three Dog Night (1971) g R&B#46 US#1 UK#24; *Less Than the Song* Patti Page (1975) C&W#67, *Lightnin' Bar Blues* Johnny Holm (1977) C&W#100, *Never Been to Spain* Ronnie Sessions (1972) C&W#36/Three Dog Night (1972) g US#5/Sammi Smith (1975) C&W#75; *No No Song* [i] Ringo Starr (1975) US#3, *Red, White and Blue* Loretta Lynn (1976) C&W#20, *Snowblind Friend* Steppenwolf (1971) US#60, *Southbound* R.C. Bannon (1977) C&W#99, *Sweet Fantasy* Bobby Borchers (1978) C&W#20, *Sweet Misery* Jimmy Dean (1967) C&W#16/Ferlin Husky (1971) C&W#14; *Willie Jean* Sunshine Company (1968) US#111. Co-writers: [i] David Jackson, [ii] Ken Ramsey.

39. AYERS, Kevin (b. August 16, 1945, Herne Bay, England) Rock bassist and vocalist. An eclectic singer-songwriter who co-formed the group the Wilde Flowers in 1963, which, by 1966, had evolved into the jazz influenced progressive rock group the Soft Machine. Ayers' often bizarre songs were recorded on the albums **The Soft Machine** (1968) US#160 and **Volume 2** (1969, both Probe). Ayers left the group in 1969, to reside in Ibiza, from where he has pursued an individualistic but increasingly intermittent solo career. ALBUMS: **Joy of a Toy** (1969), **Shooting at the Moon** (1970), **Whatevershebringswesing** (1972), **Bananmour** (1973, all Harvest); **The Confessions of Dr. Dream** (1974), **June 1st, 1974** with John Cale (1974), **Sweet Deceiver** (1975, all Island); **Odd Ditties** (1976), **Yes We Have No Mananas** (1976), **Rainbow Takeway** (1978), **That's What You Get Babe** (1980, all Harvest); **Diamond Jack and the King of Pain** (1983, Charly); **As Close as You Think** (1986, Illuminated); **Falling Up** (1988, Virgin); **Still Life with a Guitar** (1992, Permanent). COMPILATIONS: **The Kevin Ayers Collection** (1983, See for Miles); **Best of Kevin Ayers** (1989, Harvest); **Kevin Ayers** (1989, Beat Goes On); **Singing the Bruise: The BBC Sessions, 1970–1972** (1996, Band of Joy).

40. AZNAVOUR, Charles (b. Sharmouz Varenagh Aznavourian, May 22, 1924, Paris, France) Pop vocalist. A popular French singer of chansons during the 1950s, and latter day actor, who has also written over five hundred songs. Aznavour's *La Mama* (1964), sold over a million copies in France. Born to Armenian parents, Aznavour's father was a restaurant owner and singer. A child actor and teenage singer, Aznavour performed in Paris nightclubs during World War II, while his songs attracted the attention of both Edith Piaf and Maurice Chevalier, some of which were translated into English. His first major success was as composer of George Ulmer's *J'ai bu (I Have Drunk)* [v] (1942), which he followed with his own European hit *Sur Ma Vie (Believe in Me)* [iv] (1956). CHART COMPOSITIONS: *The Old Fashioned Way* [ii] (1973) UK#38, *She* [iii] (1974) UK#1. ALBUMS: **Aznavour Sings Aznavour, Volume 1** (1972), **Aznavour Sings Aznavour, Volume 2** (1973), **Aznavour Sings Aznavour, Volume 3** (1974) UK#23, **A Tapestry of Dreams** (1974) UK#9, **Je N'ai Pas Vu le Temps Passer** (1979), **Je M'Voyais Deja** (1979), **Il Faut Savoir** (1979), **Qui** (1979), **Reste** (1979), **La Mama** (1979), **Le Temps** (1979), **Non Je N'ai Rien Oublie** (1979), **La Boheme** (1979), **Emmez Moi** (1979), **Comme Ils Disent** (1979), **Visages De L'amour** (1979), **Les Grandes Success** (1979), **Face Au Public** (1979), **Hier Encore** (1979), **Plein Feu Sur Aznavour** (1979), **Paris Au Mois D'aout** (1979), **Best of** (1979, all Barclay); **His Greatest Love Songs** (1980, K-Tel) UK#73; **1980...A L'Olympia** (1981, IMS); **My Christmas Album** (1981, Hallmark); **A Private Christmas** (1982, MAM); **The Charles Aznavour Collection 1** (1982), **The Charles Aznavour Collection 2** (1982, both Barclay); **30 Carats** (1983,

EMI); **In Times to Be** (1983), **The Premiere Danse** (1983), **Amour Toujours** (1984), **Autobiographie** (1988), **Charles Chante Aznavour/Dimey** (1988, all Barclay); **We Were Happy Then** (1988, DRG); **She-The Best of Charles Aznavour** (1996, EMI). HIT VERSIONS: *For Mama* [i] Matt Monroe (1964) UK#36; *She* [iii] Vegas (1992) UK#43, *Yesterday, When I Was Young* [iii] Roy Clark (1969) C&W#9 US#19. Co-writers: [i] Don Black, [ii] George Garvarentz, [iii] Herbert Kretzmer, [iv] Geoffrey Parsons/John Turner, [v] Pierre Roche.

41. Babyface (b. Kenneth Edmonds, April 10, 1959, Indianapolis, IN) R&B multi-instrumentalist, producer and vocalist. The most consistently successful R&B songwriter-producer since the late 1980s. Babyface has worked with such singers as Mariah Carey, and has co-written songs that have sold over twenty-six million singles and seventy-two million albums. Babyface has often collaborated with L.A. Reid, with whom he has written and produced more than twenty R&B number ones. In 1991, the duo set up their own La Face label, and the following year composed most of the songs for the film "Boomerang" (1992). In April 1994, Babyface had seven co-compositions on the Billboard Hot 100 R&B singles chart. He first performed with another regular co-writer Daryl Simmons, in the group Manchild, charting with the single *Especially for You* (1977) R&B#70, from the album **Power and Love** (1977, Chi-Sound) US#154. Babyface subsequently teamed up with Reid in the considerably more successful R&B act the Deele. CHART COMPOSITIONS: *Body Talk* (1983) R&B#3 US#77, *Just My Luck* (1984) R&B#25, *Surrender* (1984) R&B#66, *Material Thangz* (1985) R&B#14 US#101, *Suspicious* (1985) R&B#66, *Can-U-Dance* (1987) R&B#48, *Two Occasions* [i] (1987) R&B#4 US#10, *Shoot 'Em Up Movies* (1988) R&B#10. ALBUMS: **Street Beat** (1984) US#78, **Material Thangz** (1985) US#155, **Eyes of a Stranger** (1988, all Solar) g US#54. COMPILATION: **Best of the Deele** (1996, Deep Beats). His own solo recordings are a commercial blend of electronic keyboard dominated dance music. CHART COMPOSITIONS: *Lovers* (1987) R&B#42, *I Love You, Babe* (1987) R&B#8, *Mary Mack* (1987) R&B#29, *If We Try* (1988) R&B#65, *My Kinda Girl* (1989) US#30, *Whip Appeal* [xi] (1989) US#6, *It's No Crime* [viii] (1989) US#7, *Tender Love* [xi] (1989) US#14, *Give U My Heart* featuring Toni Braxton (1992) R&B#2 US#29, *For the Cool in You* [ii] (1993) R&B#10 US#81, *Never Keeping Secrets* (1993) R&B#3 US#15, *And Our Feelings* [ii] (1994) R&B#8 US#21, *Rock Bottom* (1994) UK#50, *When Can I See You* (1994) g R&B#11 US#4 UK#35, *Someone to Love* with Jon B. (1995) US#10, *This Is for the Lover in You*

(1996) UK#12. ALBUMS: **Lovers** (1987), **Tender Love** (1989, both Solar) p US#14; **For the Cool in You** (1993) p US#16, **Waiting to Exhale** (1995), **The Day** (1996, both Epic). COMPILATION: **A Closer Look** (1997, Epic). HIT VERSIONS: *Always in My Heart* [viii] Tevin Campbell (1994) US#23+, *Another Sad Love Song* [ii] Toni Braxton (1993) g R&B#2 US#7 UK#51, re-issued (1994) UK#15; *Baby-Baby-Baby* [ix] TLC (1992) p R&B#1 US#2 UK#55, *Breathe Again* Toni Braxton (1993) g R&B#4 US#3 UK#2, *Can He Love U Like This* [viii] After 7 (1993) R&B#22 US#103, *Can We Talk* [ii] Tevin Campbell (1993) g R&B#1 US#10, *Can't Stop* [vii] After 7 (1990) R&B#1 US#6 UK#54, *Count on Me* [iv] Whitney Houston & Cece Winans (1996) R&B#8+ US#10+, *Days Like This* Sheena Easton (1989) UK#43, *Dial My Heart* [ix] Boys (1988) US#13 UK#61, *Diggin' on You* TLC (1996) R&B#1 US#5 UK#18, *Don't Be Cruel* [ix] Bobby Brown (1988) g R&B#1 US#8 UK#42, re-issued (1989) UK#13; *End of the Road* [ix] Boyz II Men (1992) R&B#1 US#1 UK#1, *Every Little Step* [vii] Bobby Brown (1989) g R&B#1 US#3 UK#6, *Exhale (Shoop Shoop)* Whitney Houston (1996) p R&B#1 US#2 UK#11, *Fairweather Friend* Johnny Gill (1990) US#28, *Girlfriend* [ix] Pebbles (1987) R&B#1 US#5 UK#8, *Giving You the Benefit* [ix] Pebbles (1990) R&B#1 US#4 UK#73, *Good Enough* [ix] Bobby Brown (1992) R&B#6 US#7 UK#41, *Gotta Learn My Rhythm* [ix] Damian Dame (1992) R&B#20, *Heat of the Moment* After 7 (1989) US#19, *Humpin' Around* [x] Bobby Brown (1992) R&B#1 US#3 UK#19, *I Dream, I Dream* [ix] Jermaine Jackson (1992) R&B#30, *I'll Make Love to You* Boyz II Men (1994) R&B#1 US#1, *I'm Ready* Tevin Campbell (1994) R&B#2 US#9, *I'm Your Baby Tonight* [vii] Whitney Houston (1990) R&B#1 US#1 UK#5, *Knocked Out* [ix] Paula Abdul (1988) US#41 UK#45, re-mixed (1990) UK#21; *Long Way from Home* [viii] Johnny Gill (1993) R&B#42, *Love Shoulda Brought You Home* [iii] Toni Braxton (1992) R&B#2 US#33, *Lover in Me, The* [ix] Sheena Easton (1989) US#2 UK#15, *Miracle* [vii] Whitney Houston (1991) US#9, *My, My, My* [ix] Johnny Gill (1990) US#10, *Not Gon' Cry* Mary J. Bile (1996) g R&B#1 US#2, *Nothin' (That Compares to U)* Jacksons (1989) US#77 UK#33, *On Our Own* [viii] Bobby Brown (1989) p R&B#1 US#2 UK#4, *101* Sheena Easton (1989) UK#54, *Ready or Not* [vii] After 7 (1990) US#7, *Right Down to It* [ix] Damian Dame (1991) R&B#2 US#90, *Rock Steady* [vi] Whispers (1987) R&B#1 US#7 UK#38, *Rock Wit 'Cha* [ii] Bobby Brown (1989) R&B#1 US#7 UK#33, *Roni* Bobby Brown (1989) R&B#1 US#3 UK#21, *Roses Are Red* [i] Mac Band featuring the McCampbell Brothers (1988) R&B#1 UK#8, *Secret Rendezvous* [ix] Karyn White (1989) R&B#1 US#8 UK#22, *Sittin'*

Up in My Room Brandy (1996) g R&B#2 US#2, *Something in Your Eyes* Bell Biv Devoe (1993) R&B#6 US#64, *Superwoman* [ix] Karyn White (1989) g R&B#1 US#8 UK#11, *Sweet November* Troop (1992) R&B#1 US#58, *Til You Do Me Right* After 7 (1995) US#40, *Truly Something Special* [xii] After 7 (1993) R&B#49, *Un-Break My Heart* Toni Braxton (1995) R&B#1 US#1 UK#2; *Way You Love Me, The* [ix] Karyn White (1988) g R&B#1 US#7 UK#42, *Willing to Forgive* [ix] Aretha Franklin (1994) R&B#5 US#26 UK#17, *Word to the Badd!!* [v] Jermaine Jackson (1991) R&B#90 US#78, *You Mean the World to Me* [viii] Toni Braxton (1994) R&B#4 US#7, *You Said, You Said* [ix] Jermaine Jackson (1991) R&B#25. All Babyface/Reid, except: [i] Babyface/Dee/Anthony Johnson only, [ii] Babyface/Daryl Simmons only, [iii] Babyface/Daryl Simmons/B. Watson only, [iv] Whitney Houston/M. Houston, [v] Jermaine Jackson/L. Lopes, [vi] D. Ladd/B. Watson, [vii] Antonio Reid only, [viii] Antonio Reid (b. Mark Antonio Reid, June 7, 1957, Cincinnati, OH)/Daryl Simmons, [ix] Daryl Simmons, [x] Daryl Simmons/Stylz, [xi] P. Smith, [xii] B. Watson. (*See also under* Madonna.)

42. BACHARACH, Burt (b. May 12, 1928, Kansas City, MI) Pop multi-instrumentalist, producer, arranger and vocalist. One of the first songwriters, in collaboration with the lyricist Hal David and the vocalist Dionne Warwick, to create a sophisticated R&B-pop sound for white audiences. Bacharach compositions have topped the British singles chart on six occasions, and his appeal has lasted well into the 1990s, when the British rock group Oasis cited him as one of its influences. Bacharach grew up in New York, where he took piano lessons at school and played in various amateur jazz groups during the 1950s. He studied the cello, drums, piano, music theory and composition at the Music Academy of the West in Santa Barbara, California, where his rhythmic structures were partly influenced by his tutors Henry Cowell and Darius Milhaud. It was Milhaud who once told him, "Never be ashamed to write something that people can remember and whistle." During the 1950s, Bacharach worked as pianist, producer and arranger for a variety of torch singers, eventually becoming Marlene Dietrich's musical director between 1958–1961. He wrote his first hits with the lyricists Bob Hilliard and Mack David, before in 1957, teaming up with the latter's younger brother Hal, for the million sellers *The Story of My Life* [iii] and *Magic Moments* [iii]. Their greatest artistic and commercial success was as writer-producers for the intuitive R&B singer Warwick, who sold over fifteen million copies of their songs in eight years. Bacharach wrote exclusively with Warwick's

vocal versatility in mind, enabling him to abandon the standard thirty-two bar pop song structure, in order to arrange each separate element of the tune as an inherent whole, when the normal practice at the time was to write a song, find a singer, and then select a key and arrangement. Bacharach's shifting time signatures, with their odd meters and abrupt melodic changes, were revolutionary in pop music, no more effortlessly displayed than in *Anyone Who Had a Heart* [iii], which moved through 5/4, 4/4 and 7/8 in a mere handful of bars. Bacharach and David were also successful on Broadway with "Promises, Promises" (1968), which ran for over one thousand performances, and they inevitably composed for films, their finest score being the Oscar winning "Butch Cassidy and the Sundance Kid" (1969), which introduced the million seller *Raindrops Keep Falling on My Head* [iii]. Bacharach, David and Warwick parted company somewhat acrimoniously in 1972, with Bacharach later saying, "There was a ten year period when we weren't even speaking." It was not until 1992 that they were to work together again, causing David to remark, "it was like picking up where we left off." There have been many albums devoted entirely to Bacharach and David songs, the most successful being those by: the Four Seasons, **Big Hits by Burt Bacharach, Hal David and Bob Dylan** (1965, Philips) US#106; **The Anita Kerr Singers Reflect on the Music of Bacharach and David** (1969, Dot) US#162; Christopher Scott, **Switched-On Bacharach** (1969, Decca) US#175; Ed Ames, **The Songs of Bacharach and David** (1971, RCA) US#199; the Renaissance, **Bacharach Baroque** (1971, Ranwood) US#198; **The Dells Sing Dionne Warwick's Greatest Hits** (1973, Cadet) US#162; **Johnny Mathis Sings the Music of Bacharach and Kaempfert** (1974, Columbia) US#169; Strings for Pleasure, **Best of Bacharach** (1979, MFP) UK#49; and **Bacharach and David-They Write the Songs** (1990, Dino) UK#16. Bacharach pursued a solo career during the 1970s, the initial success of which set a trend for somewhat bland, choral arrangements of popular songs by other orchestra leaders, commonly known as easy listening music. During the 1980s, he wrote with his second wife, the lyricist Carole Bayer Sager, and in 1996, his records became popular again in Britain during an easy listening revival on the London nightclub scene. CHART COMPOSITIONS: *Saturday Sunshine* (1963) US#93, *Trains and Boats and Planes* [iii] (1965) UK#4, *I'll Never Fall in Love Again* [iii] (1969) US#93, *All Kinds of People* [iii] (1971) US#116. ALBUMS: **Hit Maker** (1965, London) UK#3; **What's New Pussycat?** ost (1965, United Artists) US#14; **Burt Bacharach Plays His Hits** (1966, Kapp); **Reach Out** (1967, A&M) g US#96 UK#52; **Casino Royale** ost (1967, Colgems)

US#22 UK#35; **Promises, Promises** oc (1968, United Artists) US#95; **Make It Easy on Yourself** (1969) g US#51, **Butch Cassidy and the Sundance Kid** ost (1969) g US#16, **Burt Bacharach** (1971) g US#18, **Living Together** (1973, all A&M) US#181; **Lost Horizon** ost (1973, Bell) US#58 UK#36; **In Concert** (1974, A&M); **The Special Magic of Burt Bacharach and Stan Getz** (1975, Verve); **Futures** (1977); **Woman** (1979, both A&M). COMPILATIONS: **Portrait in Music** (1971) UK#5, **Greatest Hits** (1974, both A&M) US#173. HIT VERSIONS: *Alfie* [iii] Cilla Black (1966) US#95 UK#9/Cher (1967) US#32/Dionne Warwick (1967) R&B#5 US#15/Stevie Wonder (1968) US#66/Delfonics (1973) R&B#88/Everything But the Girl on *Don't Leave Me Behind EP* (1986) UK#72; *Amanda* [iii] Dionne Warwick (1971) US#83, *Another Night* [iii] Dionne Warwick (1967) R&B#47 US#49, *Another Tear Falls* [iii] Walker Brothers (1966) UK#12, *Any Day Now* [v] Chuck Jackson (1962) R&B#2 US#23/Percy Sledge (1969) R&B#35 US#86/Don Gibson (1979) C&W#26/Ronnie Milsap (1982) C&W#1 US#14; *Anyone Who Had a Heart* [iii] Cilla Black (1964) UK#1/Mary May (1964) UK#49/Dionne Warwick (1964) R&B#8 US#8 UK#42; *April Fools, The* [iii] Dionne Warwick (1969) R&B#33 US#37/Aretha Franklin on B-side of *All the King's Horses* (1972) R&B#7 US#26; *Are You There (With Another Girl?)* [iii] Dionne Warwick (1966) R&B#35 US#39/Deacon Blue on *Four Bacharach and David Songs EP* (1988) UK#2; *Baby, It's You* [iv] Shirelles (1961) R&B#3 US#8/Dave Berry (1964) UK#24/Masqueraders (1976) R&B#76/Janie Fricke (1978) C&W#21/Pia Zadora (1980) C&W#55/Stacy Lattisaw & Johnny Gill (1984) R&B#37 US#102/Beatles (1995) US#67 UK#7; *Beginning of Loneliness, The* [iii] Dionne Warwick (1967) R&B#44 US#79, *Blob, The* [iv] Five Blobs (1958) US#33, *Blue on Blue* [iii] Bobby Vinton (1963) US#3, *Casino Royale* [iii] Herb Alpert & the Tijuana Brass (1967) US#27 UK#27, *Do You Know the Way to San Jose* [iii] Dionne Warwick (1968) R&B#23 US#10 UK#8, *Don't Make Me Over* [iii] Dionne Warwick (1962) R&B#5 US#21/Swinging Blue Jeans (1966) US#116 UK#31/Brenda & the Tabulations (1970) R&B#15 US#77/Jennifer Warnes (1979) C&W#84 US#67/Sybil (1989) g US#20 UK#19; *Don't You Believe It* [v] Andy Williams (1962) US#39, *Ever Changing Times* [ii] Siedah Garrett (1987) R&B#44/Aretha Franklin (1992) R&B#19; *Everybody's Out of Town* [iii] B.J. Thomas (1970) US#26, *Finder of Lost Loves* [viii] Dionne Warwick & Glenn Jones (1985) R&B#47, *Green Grass Starts to Grow, The* [iii] Dionne Warwick (1971) US#43, *Here I Am* [iii] Dionne Warwick (1966) US#65, *(Here I Go Again) Looking with My Eyes (Leading with My Heart)* [iii] Dionne Warwick

(1965) US#64, *House Is Not a Home, A* [iii] Dionne Warwick (1964) US#71/Brook Benton (1964) US#75/Charles & Eddie (1993) UK#29; *I Don't Need You Anymore* [ix] Jackie DeShannon (1980) US#86, *I Just Don't Know What to Do with Myself* [iii] Tommy Hunt (1962) US#119/Dusty Springfield (1964) UK#3/Dionne Warwick (1966) R&B#20 US#26/Brook Benton on B-side of *Do Your Own Thing* (1969) US#99/Gary Puckett (1970) US#61; *I Say a Little Prayer* [iii] Dionne Warwick (1967) R&B#8 US#4/Aretha Franklin (1968) g R&B#3 US#10 UK#14/Del Irwin & Mamie Galore (1968) US#114/Sergio Mendes (1968) US#106/Glen Campbell & Anne Murray (1971) C&W#40 US#81/Isaac Hayes & Dionne Warwick (1977) R&B#65; *I Wake Up Cryin'* [iii] Chuck Jackson (1961) R&B#13 US#59, *I'll Never Fall in Love Again* [iii] Bobbie Gentry (1969) UK#1/Dionne Warwick (1970) R&B#17 US#6/Liz Anderson (1972) C&W#56/Deacon Blue on *Four Bacharach and David Songs EP* (1988) UK#2; *I'm a Better Man (For Having Loved You)* [iii] Engelbert Humperdinck (1969) US#38 UK#15, *If We Only Have Love* [iii] Dionne Warwick (1972) US#84, *In the Land of Make Believe* [iii] Dusty Springfield (1969) US#113, *It's Love That Really Counts* [iii] Merseybeats (1963) UK#34, *Keep Away from Other Girls* [v] Helen Shapiro (1962) UK#40, *Let Me Be Lonely* [iii] Dionne Warwick (1968) US#71, *Let Me Go to Him* [iii] Dionne Warwick (1970) R&B#45 US#32, *Lifetime of Loneliness, A* [iii] Jackie DeShannon (1965) US#66, *Living Together, Growing Together* [iii] Tony Bennett (1972) US#111/5th Dimension (1973) US#32; *Long Ago Tomorrow* [iii] B.J. Thomas (1971) US#61, *Look of Love, The* [iii] Dusty Springfield (1967) US#22, also on B-side of *Give Me Time* (1967) UK#24/Sergio Mendes & Brazil '66 (1968) US#4/Isaac Hayes (1971) US#79/Gladys Knight & the Pips (1973) UK#21/Deacon Blue on *Four Bacharach and David Songs EP* (1988) UK#2/T-Empo (1996) UK#71; *Lost Horizon* [iii] Shawn Phillips (1973) US#63, *Love Always* [ix] El Debarge (1986) R&B#7 US#43, *Love of a Boy, The* [iii] Timi Yuro (1962) US#44/Julie Rogers on B-side of *The Wedding* (1964) US#10 UK#3; *Love Power* [viii] Dionne Warwick & Jeffrey Osborne (1987) R&B#5 US#12, *Magic Moments* [iii] Perry Como (1958) US#4 UK#1/Ronnie Hilton (1958) UK#22; *Make It Easy on Yourself* [iii] Jerry Butler (1962) R&B#18 US#20/Walker Brothers (1965) US#16 UK#1/Dionne Warwick (1970) R&B#26 US#37/Johnny Mathis (1972) US#103/Tommy Jennings (1975) C&W#96/Michael Henderson (1982) R&B#68/Ron Banks (1983) US#31; *Make the Music Play* [iii] Dionne Warwick (1963) US#81, *Making Love* [ix] Roberta Flack (1982) R&B#64 US#13, *Man Who Shot Liberty Valance, The* [iii] Gene Pitney (1962) US#4, *Me,*

Japanese Boy, I Love You [iii] Bobby Goldsboro (1964) US#74, *Message to Martha/Michael (Kentucky Bluebird)* [iii] Lou Johnson (1964) US#104 UK#36/Adam Faith (1964) UK#12/Dionne Warwick (1966) R&B#5 US#8/Deacon Blue on *Four Bacharach & David Songs EP* (1988) UK#2; *My Little Red Book* [iii] Love (1966) US#52/Manfred Mann (1965) US#124; *Night Shift* [vii] Quarterflash (1982) US#60, *Odds and Ends (Of a Beautiful Love Affair)* [iii] Dionne Warwick (1968) US#43, *On My Own* [viii] Patti LaBelle & Michael McDonald (1986) g R&B#1 US#1 UK#2, *One Less Bell to Answer* [iii] 5th Dimension (1971) g R&B#4 US#2, *Only Love Can Break a Heart* [iii] Gene Pitney (1962) R&B#16 US#2/Margaret Whiting (1967) US#116/Sonny James (1972) C&W#2/Bobby Vinton (1977) US#99/Dionne Warwick (1977) US#109/Kenny Dale (1979) C&W#7; *Over You* [viii] Ray Parker, Jr. & Natalie Cole (1987) R&B#10 UK#65, *Please Stay* [v] Drifters (1961) R&B#13 US#14, *Promise Her Anything* [iii] Tom Jones (1965) US#74, also B-side of *The Green, Green Grass of Home* (1966) US#11 UK#1; *Promises, Promises* [iii] Lynn Anderson (1968) C&W#4/Dionne Warwick (1968) R&B#47 US#19; *Raindrops Keep Falling on My Head* [iii] B.J. Thomas (1970) g US#1 UK#38/Sacha Distel (1970) UK#10/Bobbie Gentry (1970) UK#40/Barbara Mason (1970) R&B#38 US#112; *Reach Out for Me* [iii] Lou Johnson (1963) US#74/Dionne Warwick (1964) R&B#20 US#20 UK#23/Michael Henderson (1978) R&B#78; *Someone Else's Eyes* [ix] Aretha Franklin (1991) R&B#53, *Story of My Life, The* [iii] Michael Holliday (1958) UK#1/Dave King (1958) UK#20/Marty Robbins (1958) R&B#1 US#15/Alma Cogan (1958) UK#25/Al Downing (1962) US#117; *Sunny Weather Lover* [iii] Dionne Warwick (1993) R&B#114, *That's What Friends Are For* [viii] Dionne Warwick (1985) g R&B#1 US#1 UK#16, *(There's) Always Something There to Remind Me* [iii] Lou Johnson (1964) US#49/Sandie Shaw (1964) US#52 UK#1/Patti LaBelle & the Bluebells (1967) US#125/Dionne Warwick (1968) US#65/R.B. Greaves (1970) R&B#50 US#27/Naked Eyes (1983) US#8 UK#59/Tin Tin featuring Espivitu (1995) UK#14; *(They Long to Be) Close to You* [iii] Carpenters (1970) g US#1 UK#6, re-issued (1990) UK#25/Jerry Butler & Brenda Lee Eager (1972) R&B#6 US#91/B.T. Express (1976) R&B#31 US#82/Tyrone Davis (1977) R&B#33/Gwen Guthrie (1985) R&B#69 UK#25/George Lamond sampled in *Baby I Believe in You* (1992) US#66; *This Empty Place* [iii] Dionne Warwick (1963) R&B#26 US#84, *This Guy/Girl's in Love with You* [iii] Herb Alpert & the Tijuana Brass (1968) g US#1 UK#3/Dionne Warwick (1968) US#7/James Brown & Lyn Collins on B-side of *What My Baby Needs Now* (1972) R&B#17 US#56; *To Wait for Love* [iii] Herb Alpert & the Ti-

juana Brass (1968) US#51/Tom Jones on B-side of *It's Not Unusual* (1965) US#10 UK#1; *Tower of Strength* [v] Gene McDaniels (1961) US#5 UK#49/Gloria Lynne (1961) US#100/Frankie Vaughan (1961) UK#1/Sue Richards (1975) C&W#32/Narvel Felts (1979) C&W#33; *Trains and Boats and Planes* [iii] Billy J. Kramer (1965) US#47 UK#12/Dionne Warwick (1966) R&B#44 US#22; *True Love Never Runs Smooth* [iii] Gene Pitney (1963) US#21, *Twenty Four Hours from Tulsa* [iii] Gene Pitney (1963) US#17 UK#5/Randy Barlow (1977) C&W#18; *Walk on By* [iii] Dionne Warwick (1964) US#6 UK#9/Isaac Hayes (1969) R&B#13 US#30/Gloria Gaynor (1975) US#98/Stranglers (1978) UK#21/Average White Band (1979) R&B#32 US#92 UK#46/D-Train (1982) R&B#42 UK#44/Transvision Vamp on B-side of *Sister Moon* (1988) UK#41/Sybil (1990) US#74 UK#6; *What the World Needs Now (Is Love)* [iii] Jackie DeShannon (1965) R&B#40 US#7/Sweet Inspirations (1968) US#128/Tom Clay (1971) R&B#32 US#8/Lyn Collins on B-side of *Give It Up or Turnit a Loose* (1974) R&B#77/Ron Shaw (1979) C&W#90/Billie Jo Spears (1981) C&W#58; *What's New Pussycat?* [iii] Tom Jones (1965) US#3 UK#11, *Who Gets the Guy?* [iii] Dionne Warwick (1971) R&B#41 US#57, *Who is Gonna to Love Me?* [iii] Dionne Warwick (1968) R&B#43 US#33, *Windows and Doors* [iii] Jackie DeShannon (1966) US#108, *Windows of the World* [iii] Dionne Warwick (1967) R&B#27 US#22, *Wishin' and Hopin'* [iii] Merseybeats (1964) UK#13/Dusty Springfield (1964) US#6; *Wives and Lovers* [iii] Jack Jones (1964) US#14, *You Can Have Him* [iii] Dionne Warwick (1965) US#75 UK#37, *You'll Never Get to Heaven (If You Break My Heart)* [iii] Dionne Warwick (1964) US#34 UK#20/Stylistics (1973) R&B#8 US#23 UK#24. Co-writers: [i] Paul Anka, [ii] Bill Conti/Carol Bayer Sager, [iii] Hal David, [iv] Mac David/Barney Williams, [v] Bob Hilliard, [vi] Peter Allen/Carol Bayer Sager/Christopher Cross, [vii] Ross/Carol Bayer Sager, [viii] Carol Bayer Sager, [ix] Carol Bayer Sager/Bruce Roberts. (*See also under* Christopher CROSS, Neil DIAMOND, Jimmy JAM and Terry LEWIS, Maurice WHITE.)

43. BACHMAN, Randy (b. September 27, 1943, Winnipeg, Canada) Rock guitarist and vocalist. A Canadian songwriter and guitarist who, with the vocalist Burton Cummings, fronted the 1960s group the Guess Who. CHART COMPOSITIONS: *These Eyes* [i] (1969) g US#6, *Undone* (1969) US#22, *Laughing* [i] (1969) g US#10, *No Time* [i] (1969) US#5, *American Woman* (1970) g US#1 UK#19. ALBUMS: **Shakin' All Over** (1965, Quality); **Wheatfield Soul** (1968) US#45, **Canned Wheat Packed By the Guess Who** (1969) US#91, **American**

Woman (1970, all RCA) g US#9. COMPILA-
TIONS: **Best of the Guess Who** (1971) g US#12,
The Greatest of the Guess Who (1977) US#173, **A
Retrospective** (1997, all RCA). Bachman quit the
group in 1970 to form Brave Belt, releasing the albums **Brave Belt** (1971) and **Brave Belt II** (1972,
both Reprise) US#180. The group evolved into the
blue collar rock band Bachman-Turner Overdrive,
which enjoyed a significant chart run during the
mid-1970s. CHART COMPOSITIONS: *Blue Col-
lar* [ii] (1973) US#68, *Let It Ride* [iii] (1974) US#23,
Takin' Care of Business (1974) US#12, *You Ain't Seen
Nothing Yet* (1974) p US#1 UK#2, *Roll on Down the
Highway* [ii] (1975) US#14 UK#22, *Hey You* (1975)
US#21, *Down to the Line* (1976) US#43, *Lookin' Out
for #1* (1976) US#65, ALBUMS: **Bachman-Turner
Overdrive** (1973) g US#70, **Bachman-Turner
Overdrive II** (1974) g US#4, **Not Fragile** (1974) g
US#1 UK#12, **Four Wheel Drive** (1975) g US#5,
Head On (1976, all Mercury) g US#23; **Bachman-
Turner Overdrive** (1984, Compleat) US#191; **Live!-
Live!-Live!** (1986, MCA/Curb). COMPILATION:
Best of B.T.O. (So Far) (1976, Mercury) p US#19.
Bachman left the band in 1976, and re-emerged three
years later in the group Ironhorse, which charted
with *Sweet Lui-Louise* (1979) US#36 UK#60 and
What's Your Hurry Darlin' [iv] (1980) US#89, from
the albums **Ironhorse** (1979) US#153 and **Every-
thing Is Grey** (1980, both Scotti Brothers). Bach-
man has also recorded as a solo artist. ALBUMS:
Axe (1970), **Solo Album** (1975, both RCA); **Survivor** (1978, Polydor); **Any Road** (1993, Sony):
Prairie Town (1996, Koch). HIT VERSIONS: *These
Eyes* [i] Jr. Walker & the All Stars (1969) R&B#3
US#16, *You Ain't Seen Nothing Yet* Figures on a Beach
(1989) US#67. Co-writers: [i] Burton Cummings,
[ii] C. Kelly, [iii] Charles Fred Turner (b. October
16, 1943), [iv] Carl Wilson (b. December 21, 1946,
Hawthorne, CA).

44. BAILEY, Tom (b. January 18, 1957, Halifax, England) Pop keyboard player, producer and
vocalist, and **CURRIE, Alannah** (b. September 20,
1959, Auckland, New Zealand) Pop percussionist
and vocalist. The core members of the once seven
strong British pop group the Thompson Twins.
CHART COMPOSITIONS: *Lies* [i] (1982) US#30
UK#67, *Love on Your Side* [i] (1983) US#45 UK#9,
We Are Detective [i] (1983) UK#7, *Watching* [i] (1983)
UK#33, *Hold Me Now* [i] (1983) UK#4, *Doctor! Doctor!* [i] (1984) US#11 UK#3, *You Take Me Up* [i]
(1984) US#44 UK#2, *Sister of Mercy* [i] (1984)
UK#11, *Lay Your Hands on Me* [i] (1984) US#6
UK#13, *The Gap* (1984) US#69, *Don't Mess with
Doctor Dream* (1985) UK#15, *King for a Day* [i]
(1985) US#8 UK#22, *Nothing in Common* (1986)

US#54, *Get That Love* (1987) US#31 UK#66, *In the
Name of Love* (1988) R&B#69 UK#46, *Sugar Daddy*
(1989) US#28, *Come Inside* (1991) UK#56, *The Saint*
(1992) UK#53. ALBUMS: **A Product of...** (1981),
Set/In the Name of Love (1982, both, Tee) US#148
UK#48; **Quick Step and Side Kick/Side Kicks**
(1983) US#34 UK#2, **Into the Gap** (1984) p US#10
UK#1, **Here's to Future Days** (1985) g US#20
UK#5, **Close to the Bone** (1987, all Arista) US#76
UK#90; **Big Trash** (1989) US#143, **Queer** (1991,
both Warner Brothers). COMPILATIONS: **Great-
est Mixes/The Best of the Thompson Twins** (1988,
Arista) US#175; **Greatest Hits** (1990, Stylus) UK#23.
In 1993, Bailey and Currie recorded an album under
the name Babble, **The Stone** (1993, Reprise). HIT
VERSION: *I Want That Man* Deborah Harry (1989)
UK#13. Co-writer: [i] Joe Leeway (November 15,
1957, London, England).

45. BALIN, Marty (b. Martyn Jerel Buch-
wald, January 30, 1942, Cincinnati, OH) Rock vocalist. A founder member of the 1960s American
folk-psychedelic group the Jefferson Airplane, which
later became Jefferson Starship. A fine ballad singer,
Balin was initially the group's most melodic tune-
smith, composing *It's No Secret* and the haunting
Come Up the Years. CHART COMPOSITIONS:
The Ballad of You and Pooneil [iii] (1967) US#42,
Volunteers [iii] (1969) US#65, *Plastic Fantastic Lover*
(1969) US#133, *Miracles* (1975) g US#1, *With Your
Love* [ii] (1976) US#12, *St. Charles* [i] (1976) US#64.
ALBUMS: **Jefferson Airplane Takes Off** (1966)
US#128, **Surrealistic Pillow** (1967) g US#3, **After
Bathing at Baxters** (1967) US#17, **Crown of Cre-
ation** (1968) g US#6, **Bless Its Pointed Little Head**
(1969) US#17 UK#38, **Volunteers** (1969, all RCA)
g US#13 UK#34; **Dragonfly** (1974) g US#11, **Red
Octopus** (1975) p US#1, **Spitfire** (1976) p US#3
UK#30, **Earth** (1978, all Grunt) p US#5; **Jefferson
Airplane** (1989, Epic) US#85; **Deep Space/Virgin
Sky** (1995, Intersound). COMPILATIONS: **The
Worst of the Jefferson Airplane** (1971, RCA) g
US#12; **Early Flight** (1974) US#110, **Flight Log
(1966–1976)** (1977) g US#37, **Gold** (1979, all
Grunt) g US#20; **2400 Fulton Street-An Anthology** (1987) US#138, **Jefferson Airplane Loves You**
(1992, both RCA); **Journey...Best of Jefferson Airplane** (1996, Camden). Over the years, Balin has
quit and rejoined the band on many occassions. He
also recorded eponymous albums as a member of the
groups **Bodacious D.F.** (1974, RCA), and **KBC
Band** (1986, Arista) US#75, while also working as a
solo artist. ALBUMS: **Balin** (1981) US#35, **Lucky**
(1983, both EMI America) US#165; **Better Generation** (1992, GWE). Co-writers: [i] Jesse Barish/
Craig Chaquico (b. September 26, 1954)/Paul Kanter

(b. March 12, 1941, San Francisco, CA)/Thunderhawk, [ii] Covington/Smith, [iii] Paul Kantner.

46. BALL, Ernest (b. 1856, Ireland; d. July 5, 1927) Film and stage composer, vocalist. One of the most efficacious songwriters of the pre-Tin Pan Alley era, who co-composed the standard *When Irish Eyes Are Smiling* [iii]. Ball's compositions were featured in such shows as "The Heart of Paddy Whack" (1914), and the films "Irish Eyes Are Smiling" (1944) and "Doughboys in Ireland" (1944). CHART COMPOSITION: *Good-bye, Good Luck, God Bless You* (1916) US#8. HIT VERSIONS: *All the World Will Be Jealous of Me* [ii] Henry Burr (1917) US#4/Charles Harrison (1917) US#2; *Dear Little Boy of Mine* [i] Charles Harrison (1918) US#6/Will Oakland (1918) US#7; *In the Garden of My Heart* Frank Stanley & Henry Burr (1909) US#2, *Let the Rest of the World Go By* [i] Lewis James & Charles Hart (1920) US#14/ Elizabeth Spencer (1920) US#2; *Little Bit of Heaven (Shure, They Call It Ireland), A* [i] Charles Harrison (1915) US#2/John McCormack (1915) US#9/George MacFarlane (1915) US#1/John Barnes Wells (1915) US#8; *Love Me and the World Is Mine* [iv] Harry Anthony (1906) US#6/Henry Burr (1906) US#1/Albert Campbell (1906) US#1/Haydn Quartet (1908) US#7; *Mother Machree* [iii] John McCormack (1911) US#1/ Will Oakland (1911) US#1/Chauncey Olcott (1913) US#7/Taylor Trio (1915) US#5; *Till the Sands of the Desert Grow Cold* Donald Chalmers (1912) US#5/ Frank Croxton (1913) US#9/Alan Turner (1913) US#1; *West of the Great Divide* [vi] Henry Burr (1925) US#13, *When Irish Eyes Are Smiling* [iii] Harry MacDonough (1913) US#3/Chauncey Olcott (1913) US#1/John McCormack (1917) US#4; *Will You Love Me in December (As You Do in May)?* [v] Albert Campbell (1906) US#3/Haydn Quartet (1906) US#2. Co-writers: [i] J. Keirn Brennan, [ii] Al Dubin, [iii] Chauncey Olcott (b. 1858, Ireland; d. March 18, 1932)/Rida Johnson Young, [iv] Dave Reed, [v] James J. Walker, [vi] George Whiting.

47. BALLARD, Clint, Jr. Pop composer. A British songwriter who achieved four number one songs, and who advised Decca Records to sign the Kalin Twins in 1958. HIT VERSIONS: *Every Day of My Life* Malcolm Vaughan (1955) UK#5/McGuire Sisters (1956) US#37/Bobby Vinton (1972) US#24; *Game of Love, The* Wayne Fontana & the Mindbenders (1965) US#1 UK#2, *Ginger Bread* [i] Frankie Avalon (1958) US#9 UK#30, *Good Timin'* [ii] Jimmy Jones (1960) US#3 UK#1, *I'm Alive* Hollies (1966) US#103 UK#1/Electric Light Orchestra (1980) US#16 UK#20; *Just a Little Bit Too Late* Wayne Fontana & the Mindbenders (1965) US#45 UK#20, *Little Bitty Girl* [ii] Bobby Rydell (1960) US#19, *One*

of Us (Will Weep Tonight) [ii] Patti Page (1960) US#31, *You're No Good* Betty Everett (1963) US#51/ Dee Dee Warwick (1963) US#117/Swinging Blue Jeans (1964) UK#3/Linda Ronstadt (1975) US#1/ Aswad (1995) UK#35. Co-writers: [i] Hank Hunter, [ii] Fred Tobias.

48. BALLARD, Glen (b. America) Pop producer. The co-writer of over two hundred recorded songs, whose most recent successes have been producing the vocal group Wilson Phillips, and the singer Alanis Morissette, whose debut album **Jagged Little Pill** (1995), has sold over twenty-four million copies worldwide to become the most successful debut album by any artist in popular music. HIT VERSIONS: *All I Need* [iv] Jack Wagner (1985) US#2, *Give It Up* [v] Wilson Phillips (1992) US#30, *Hand in My Pocket* [iii] Alanis Morissette (1995) UK#26, *Head Over Feet* [iii] Alanis Morissette (1996) UK#8, *Hold On* [v] Wilson Phillips (1990) g US#1 UK#6, *I Wonder Why* [vi] Curtis Stigers (1991) US#11, *Ironic* [iii] Alanis Morissette (1996) US#4 UK#11, *It's Gonna Be Special* [ii] Patti Austin (1984) R&B#15 US#82, *Man in the Mirror, The* [i] Michael Jackson (1988) R&B#1 US#1 UK#21, *Perfect* [iii] Alanis Morissette on B-side of *You Oughta Know* [iii] (1995) UK#22, *Release Me* [v] Wilson Phillips (1990) g US#1 UK#36, *You Learn* [iii] Alanis Morissette (1996) UK#24, *You Oughta Know* [iii] Alanis Morissette (1995) UK#22, *You Won't See Me Cry* [v] Wilson Phillips (1992) US#20 UK#18, *You're in Love* [v] Wilson Phillips (1991) US#1 UK#29. Co-writers: [i] Siedah Garrett, [ii] Clifton Magness, [iii] Alanis Morissette (b. Alanis Nadine Morissette, June 1, 1974, Ottawa, Canada), [iv] David Robert Pack/ Clifton Magness, [v] Carnie Wilson (b. April 29, 1968, Los Angeles, CA)/Chynna Phillips (b. February 12, 1968, Los Angeles, CA), [vi] Curtis Stigers (b. 1966, Boise, ID). (*See also under* David FOSTER.)

49. BALLARD, Hank (b. Henry Ballard, November 18, 1936, Detroit, MI) R&B vocalist. A major influence on the development of early R&B, in particular James Brown, who is best known for writing Chubby Checker's million seller *The Twist*, one of only two songs — *White Christmas* being the other — to reach the top of the American charts on two separate occasions. Ballard was raised in Alabama, and worked at the Ford Motor Company, before forming the doo-wop group the Royales in 1953, which soon became the Midnighters. CHART COMPOSITIONS: *Work with Me Annie* (1954) R&B#1 US#22, *Sexy Ways* (1954) R&B#2, *Annie Had a Baby* (1954) R&B#1 US#23, *Annie's Aunt Fannie* (1954) R&B#10, *The Twist* (1959) R&B#16, re-entry (1960) R&B#6 US#28; *Lets Go, Let's Go, Let's Go* (1960) R&B#1 US#6, *Finger Poppin' Time* (1960) R&B#2 US#7, *Do You Know How to Twist?* (1962) US#87. ALBUMS: **Their Greatest Hits** (1954), **The Midnight, Volume 2** (1957, both Federal); **Greatest Juke Box Hits** (1958), **Singin' and Swingin'** (1959), **One and Only** (1960), **Mr. Rhythm and Blues** (1960), **Sing Along** (1961), **Let's Go Again** (1961, all King); **Spotlight on Hank Ballard and the Midnighters** (1961, Parlophone); **Jumpin'** (1962), **Twistin' Fools** (1962), **The 1963 Sound** (1962), **Biggest Hits** (1963, all King); **The Jumpin' Hank Ballard** (1963, London); **Star in Your Eyes** (1964), **Those Lazy Days** (1965), **Glad Songs Sad Songs** (1965), **24 Hits** (1966), **24 Greatest Hits** (1966), **You Can't Keep a Good Man Down** (1969), **20 Hits** (1977, all King); **What You Get When the Gettin' Gets Good** (1985), **Live at the Palais** (1987, both Charly); **Sexy Ways: The Best of Hank Ballard and the Midnighters** (1993, King). HIT VERSIONS: *Dance with Me Henry* [i] Georgia Gibbs (1955) US#1, *Lets Go, Let's Go, Let's Go* Chambers Brothers (1974) R&B#76, *Tore Up* Harmonica Fats (1963) US#103, *Twist, The* Chubby Checker (1960) US#1 UK#5, re-issued (1962) US#1, re-issued (1975) UK#5/Fat Boys with Chubby Checker (1988) US#16 UK#2; *Woman, a Lover, a Friend, A* Jackie Wilson (1960) R&B#4 US#15. Co-writers: [i] Etta James/Johnny Otis.

50. BALLARD, Russ (b. Russell Ballard, October 31, 1947, Waltham Cross, England) Rock guitarist, producer and vocalist. A rock all-rounder, who, during the 1980s, had an ear for radio-friendly, soft-rock hits. After learning the guitar in his teens, in 1963, Ballard became a guitarist with Adam Faith's backing group the Roulettes, which was followed by a brief stint in the act Unit 4+2. Between 1970–1974, Ballard was a member of the British progressive rock group Argent, composing the hits *Tragedy* (1972) US#106 UK#34 and *God Gave Rock and Roll to You* (1973) US#18 UK#49. During the early 1980s, he recorded as a solo artist. CHART COMPOSITIONS: *On the Rebound* (1980) US#58, *Voices* (1984) US#110, *Two Silhouettes* (1984) US#106, *The Fire Still Burns* (1985) US#105. ALBUMS: **Russ Ballard** (1974), **Winning** (1976), **At the Third Stroke** (1978), **Barnet Dogs** (1980) US#187, **Into the Fire** (1981, all Epic); **Russ Ballard** (1984) US#147, **The Fire Still Burns** (1985, both EMI America) US#166. HIT VERSIONS: *Can't Shake Loose* Agnetha Faltskog (1983) UK#63, *Come and Get Your Love* Roger Daltrey (1975) US#68, *Free Me* Roger Daltrey (1980) US#53 UK#39, *God Gave Rock and Roll to You* Kiss (1991) UK#4, *I Did It for Love* Night Ranger (1988) US#75, *I Know There's Something Going On* Frida

(1982) UK#43, *I Surrender* Rainbow (1981) US#105 UK#3, *Liar* Three Dog Night (1971) US#7, *New York Groove* Hello (1975) UK#9/Ace Frehley (1979) US#13; *No More the Fool* Elkie Brooks (1987) UK#5, *Nowhere to Run* Santana (1982) US#66, *Since You Been Gone* Head East (1978) US#46/Cherie & Marie Currie (1979) US#95/Rainbow (1979) US#57 UK#6; *So You Win Again* Hot Chocolate (1977) US#31 UK#1, *Winning* Santana (1981) US#17, *Wrap Your Arms Around Me* Agnetha Faltskog (1983) UK#44, *You Can Do Magic* America (1982) US#8 UK#59. (*See also under* Rod ARGENT.)

51. BANKS, Homer (b. August 2, 1941, Memphis, TN) R&B producer and vocalist. An in-house writer and producer at Stax Records during the 1960s, who often collaborated with Carl Hampton and Raymond Jackson on material that was recorded by many of the best R&B acts of the era, including Sam and Dave, who cut *A Lot of Love*. Banks first sang gospel as a member of the Consolidators in the 1950s, before recording for Liberty Records as a solo artist, and later as Banks and Hampton, charting with *I'm Gonna Have to Tell Her* (1977) R&B#80. HIT VERSIONS: *Be What You Are* [v] Staple Singers (1973) R&B#18 US#66, *I Can't Stand Up for Falling Down* [vi] Elvis Costello (1980) UK#4, *I'll Be the Other Woman* [iv] Soul Children (1974) R&B#3 US#36, *I've Got a Feeling (We'll Be Seeing Each Other Again)* [iv] Al Wilson (1976) R&B#3 US#29, *If Loving You Is Wrong (I Don't Want to Be Right)* [v] Jackie Burns (1972) C&W#71/Luther Ingram (1972) R&B#1 US#3/Millie Jackson (1975) R&B#42 US#42/Barbara Mandrell (1979) C&W#1 US#31/Rod Stewart (1980) UK#23/Rhonda Clark (1992) R&B#26; *If You're Ready (Come Go with Me)* [v] Staple Singers (1973) g R&B#1 US#9 UK#34/Ruby Turner featuring Jonathon Butler (1986) R&B#58 UK#30; *Taxi* [i] J.Blackfoot (1984) R&B#4 US#90 UK#48, *Take Care of Your Homework* [iii] Johnnie Taylor (1969) R&B#2 US#20, *Touch a Hand, Make a Friend* [v] Staple Singers (1974) R&B#3 US#23, *Who's Making Love* [ii] Johnnie Taylor (1968) g R&B#1 US#5/Blues Brothers (1981) US#39; *Woman to Woman* [v] Shirley Brown (1974) R&B#1 US#22/Tammy Wynette (1974) C&W#4/Barbara Mandrell (1978) C&W#4 US#92; *You Says It All* [i] Randy Brown (1979) R&B#47 US#72. Co-writers: [i] Chuck Brooks, [ii] Bettye Crutcher/Don Davis/Raymond Jackson, [iii] Don Davis/Raymond Jackson/Thomas Kelly, [iv] Carl Hampton, [v] Carl Hampton/Raymond Jackson, [vi] Alan Jones.

52. BANNON, R.C. (b. Dan Shipley, May 2, 1945, Dallas, TX) C&W vocalist. A former Washington disc jockey who recorded for Capitol

Records during the early 1970s, before signing to Warner Brothers as a staff writer in 1976. Bannon charted seventeen country hits between 1977–1982, six of which were duets with Louise Mandrell. AL-BUMS: **R.C. Bannon Arrives** (1978), **Inseparable** (1980), **Love Won't Let Us Go** (1981, all Columbia); **Me and My R.C.** (1982), **(You're My) Superwoman (You're My) Incredible Man** (1983, all RCA). COMPILATION: **Best of R.C. Bannon** (1984, RCA). HIT VERSIONS: *One of a Kind Pair of Fools* Barbara Mandrell (1983) C&W#1, *Only One Love in My Life* [i] Ronnie Milsap (1978) C&W#1 US#63, *Save Me* Louise Mandrell (1983) C&W#6, *Too Hot to Sleep* Louise Mandrell (1983) C&W#10, *Women Get Lonely* Charly McClain (1980) C&W#18. Co-writer: [i] John Bettis.

53. BARE, Bobby (b. Robert Joseph Bare, April 7, 1935, Ironton, OH) C&W guitarist and vo-calist. A country singer who charted seventy hits be-tween 1962–1986. Bare first achieved success under the pseudonym Bill Parsons, with the self-composed million seller *The All American Boy* (1959) R&B#16 US#2 UK#22, the publishing rights of which he had sold for fifty dollars shortly before being drafted in 1958. Bare was a musical arranger for Chubby Checker before he commenced a lengthy chart ca-reer under his own name in 1962. During the 1980s, Bare hosted his own television show "Bobby Bare and Friends." CHART COMPOSITIONS: *Shame on Me* (1962) C&W#18 US#23, *500 Miles Away from Home* [i] (1963) C&W#5 US#10, *Have I Stayed Away Too Long?* (1964) C&W#47 US#94, *Times Are Get-tin' Hard* (1965) C&W#30, *Marie Laveau* (1974) C&W#1, *Red-Neck Hippie Romance* (1975) C&W#85. ALBUMS: **Detroit City and Other Hits** (1963) US#119, **500 Miles Away from Home** (1964) US#133, **Lullabys, Legends and Lies** (1974), **Sin-gin' in the Kitchen** (1975), **Tunes for Two** (1975), **Famous Country Hit Makers** (1979), **More Tunes for Two** with Skeeter Davis (1980, all RCA); **Down and Dirty** (1980), **Encore** (1984), **As Is** (1981, all Columbia); **The Mercury Years, 1970–1972** (1987 Bear Family); **Ain't Got Nothing to Lose** (1988, Co-lumbia); **Bobby Bare** (1988, Country Store). HIT VERSION: *Through the Eyes of a Fool* Roy Clark (1964) C&W#31 US#128. Co-writers: [i] Hedy West/Charlie Williams.

54. BARLOW, Gary (b. January 20, 1971, Fradham, England) Pop vocalist. The lead singer and principal songwriter in the manufactured British pop group Take That, which spilt up in 1996. CHART COMPOSITIONS: *Do What U Like* [i] (1991) UK#82, *Promise* [iii] (1991) UK#38, *Once You've Tasted Love* (1992) UK#47, *A Million Love Songs EP* (1992) UK#7, *Why Can't I Wake Up with You?* (1993) UK#2, *Pray* (1993) UK#1, *Babe* (1993) UK#1, *Every-thing Changes* (1994) UK#1, *Love Ain't Here Anymore* (1994) UK#3, *Sure* [ii] (1994) UK#1, *Back for Good* (1995) US#7 UK#1, *Never Forget* (1995) UK#1. AL-BUMS: **Take That and Party** (1992) UK#2, **Every-thing Changes** (1993) UK#1, **Nobody Else** (1995, all RCA) UK#1. COMPILATIONS: **Greatest Hits** (1996, RCA) UK#1; **Nobody Else** (1995, Arista) US#69 UK#26. Barlow embarked on a solo career in 1996, charting with *Forever Love* (1996) UK#1, from the album **Open Road** (1996, RCA) UK#1. Co-writers: [i] Ray Hedges, [ii] Mark Owen (b. Mark Anthony Owen, January 27, 1974, England)/Robbie Williams (b. February 13, 1974, Stoke-on-Trent, England), [iii] Stack.

55. BARRETT, Richard (b. 1936, Philadel-phia, PA) R&B producer and vocalist. A former member of the 1950s group the Valentines, who recorded as a solo artist for a variety of record labels, before masterminding the career of the R&B vocal groups the Chantels and the Three Degrees. HIT VERSIONS: *A.B.C.s of Love, The* [i] Frankie Lymon & the Teenagers (1956) R&B#8 US#77, *I Want You to Be My Girl* [i] Frankie Lymon & the Teenagers (1956) R&B#3 US#13, *Look in My Eyes* Chantels (1961) R&B#6 US#14, *Maybe* Chantels (1958) R&B#2 US#15/Three Degrees (1970) R&B#4 US#29. Co-writer: [i] George Goldner.

56. BARRETT, Syd (b. Roger Keith Barrett, January 6, 1946, Cambridge, England) Rock gui-tarist and vocalist. A highly original songwriter who co-founded the progressive rock group Pink Floyd, which defined the British psychedelic sound of the 1960s with his frequently charming, but decidedly off-beat, drug induced songs. CHART COMPOSI-TIONS: *Arnold Layne* (1967) UK#20, *See Emily Play* (1967) US#134 UK#6. ALBUM: **The Piper at the Gates of Dawn** (1967, Columbia) g UK#6. COM-PILATIONS: **Pink Floyd** (1967, Tower) US#131; **Relics** (1971, Regal-Starline) US#152 UK#32, **Lon-don '66–'67** (1995, See for Miles). Barrett left the group in 1968, and released two enigmatic solo sets before becoming one of rock's most famous recluses. ALBUMS: **The Madcap Laughs** (1970) UK#40, **Barrett** (1970, both Harvest). COMPILATIONS: **The Madcap Laughs/Barrett** (1974, Harvest) US#163; **Opel** (1988, EMI); **The Peel Session** (1995, Strange Fruit); **Crazy Diamond** (1996, EMI). (*See also under* Roger WATERS.)

57. BARRIS, Harry (b. November 24, 1905, New York, NY; d. December 13, 1962, Burbank, CA) Tin Pan Alley composer and pianist. A fourteen year old pianist in Paul Whiteman's vocal group Rhythm Boys (1926), whose first composition was *Mississippi Mud* (1927). Barris' material was included in such films as "The Big Broadcast" (1932). HIT VERSIONS: *From Monday On* Paul Whiteman (1928) US#14, *I Surrender, Dear* [ii] Gus Arnheim (1931) US#3/Earl Burtnett (1931) US#18/Red Norvo (1935) US#20; *It Must Be True* [i] Gus Arnheim (1930) US#4/Earl Burtnett (1930) US#13; *It Was So Beautiful* [iii] Ruth Etting (1932) US#13/Enric Madriguera (1932) US#7/Ozzie Nelson (1932) US#16/ George Olsen (1932) US#14/Harry Richman (1932) US#7; *Lies* [vi] Gene Austin (1931) US#20/Perry Como (1953) US#30; *Little Dutch Mill* [iv] Bing Crosby (1934) US#1/Don Bestor (1934) US#13/Guy Lombardo (1934) US#13; *Wrap Your Troubles in Dreams* [v] Bing Crosby (1931) US#4/Erskine Hawkins (1942) US#23. Co-writers: [i] Gus Arnheim (b. 1897; d. 1955)/Gordon Clifford (b. 1902; d. 1968), [ii] Gordon Clifford, [iii] Arthur Freed, [iv] Ralph Freed (b. May 1, 1907, Vancouver, BC; d. February 13, 1973, Los Angeles, CA), [v] Ted Koehler/Billy Moll (b. 1905; d. 1968), [vi] George Springer. (*See also under* James CAVANAUGH.)

58. BARRY, Jeff (b. April 3, 1939, New York, NY) Pop producer and vocalist. A Brill Building staff songwriter and producer, who first achieved success with the melodramatic *Tell Laura I Love Her* [v]. Barry was remarkably successful in partnership with Ellie Greenwich, first as the studio group the Raindrops, and secondly as a multi-million selling songwriting team. He later worked as a producer at A&M Records. ALBUM: **The Idolmaker** ost (1980, A&M) US#130. HIT VERSIONS: *Bang-Shang-a-Lang* Archies (1968) US#22, *Chip Chip* [iii] Gene McDaniels (1962) US#10/Patsy Sledd (1974) C&W#33; *Feelin' So Good (S.k.o.o.b.y-D.o.o.)* [iv] Archies (1969) US#53, *How'd We Ever Get This Way?* [iv] Andy Kim (1968) US#21, *I Honestly Love You* [i] Olivia Newton-John (1974) g US#1 UK#22, re-issued (1983) UK#52/Staple Singers (1978) R&B#68; *Jingle Jangle* [iv] Archies (1970) g US#10, *Montego Bay* [ii] Bobby Bloom (1970) US#8 UK#3/Freddie Notes & the Rudies (1970) UK#45/Sugar Cane (1978) UK#54/ Amazulu (1986) UK#16; *Rock Me Gently* Andy Kim (1974) g US#1 UK#2, *Sister James* [vi] Nino Tempo & the 5th Avenue Sax (1973) US#53, *Sugar Sugar* [iv] Archies (1969) g US#1 UK#1, re-issued (1978) UK#91/Wilson Pickett (1970) R&B#4 US#25/ Sakkarin (1971) UK#12/Mike Lunsford (1975) C&W#87/Stars On in *Stars on 45* (1981) g US#1 UK#2; *Sunshine* [iv] Archies (1970) US#57, *Tell Laura I Love Her* [v] Ray Peterson (1960) US#7/ Ricky Vallance (1960) UK#1; *Tell Me What He Said* Helen Shapiro (1962) UK#2, *Who's Your Baby* [iv]

Archies (1970) US#40. Co-writers: [i] Peter Allen, [ii] Bobby Bloom, [iii] Cliff Crawford/Arthur Resnick, [iv] Andy Kim (b. Andrew Joachim, Canada), [v] Ben Raleigh, [vi] Nino Tempo. (*See also under* Peter ALLEN, Ellie GREENWICH, Barry MANN.)

59. BARRY, John (b. John Barry Prendergast, March 11, 1933, York, England) Film and stage composer, producer, arranger, trumpeter, and orchestral leader. Britain's greatest living film composer, and a versatile and consistent writer who has successfully merged jazz, classical and contemporary pop into his highly regarded work. Barry has written over eighty film and television scores, and has won five Oscars. He was one of the first to turn the film score into more than just incidental music. Barry studied the piano as a child and listened to Chopin, alongside other classical composers, before leaving school at fifteen to work in his father's chain of film theatres, where he was first exposed to the potency of movie soundtracks. Barry subsequently learned the trumpet and studied music with the minister of York Cathedral, which led to his extensive arranging and compositional skills. He undertook a correspondence course in musical arranging with Bill Russo-Stan Kenton's arranger — before setting himself up as a dance band arranger. When rock and roll turned the music scene upside down in the late 1950s, Barry, easily one of the most talented musicians in Britain at the time, formed the instrumental beat group, the John Barry Seven, which absorbed and imitated the major rock and roll sounds of the day, and backed such singers as Tommy Steele. Between 1960–1963, the group achieved ten British hits, during which time their style developed from the beatnik-pop of *Hit and Miss* to the much copied guitar-led instrumental sound of *The James Bond Theme* [vii]. Barry captured a vitality and energy that became synonymous with the "swinging London" of the early 1960s. He also produced and backed the vocalist Adam Faith between 1959–1962, creating Faith's infamous pizzicato string sound on twelve hit singles. As the altogether more sophisticated John Barry Orchestra, he composed lush and moody orchestral scores while experimenting with musical instruments previously unheard of on pop records, such as the synthesizer and balalaika in *The Persuaders Theme*. Barry's major breakthrough as a film composer came in 1962, when producer Cubby Broccoli, unhappy with the original Monty Norman composed score, employed Barry to write a new soundtrack for the first James Bond film, "Dr. No." Having read neither the book nor seen the rushes, Barry created one of the most influential film scores of the 1960s. Barry worked on a further eleven Bond films, later describing them as, "million dollar Mickey Mouse music." He became one of the first film composers popular enough to see his scores regularly released on album, a sizeable selection of which are more memorable than the films themselves. His ability to further evoke the mood of a film is fully evidenced in his scores for "Zulu" (1964), "The I.P.C.R.E.S.S. File" (1965), "The Quiller Memorandum" (1966), and "The Lion in Winter" (1968). During the late 1980s, Barry battled with a lengthy illness that kept him from the podium until 1991, when he returned with the Oscar winning "Dances with Wolves," the album of which sold an unprecedented million copies. He was the subject of an American PBS special 1992, and his compositions were recorded by the Roland Shaw Orchestra as **Themes from the James Bond Thrillers** (1965) US#38 and **More Themes from the James Bond Thrillers** (1966, both London) US#119. They also feature on the collection **James Bond's Greatest Hits** (1982, Liberty) UK#4. CHART COMPOSITIONS: *Hit and Miss* (1960) UK#10, *Beat for Beatniks* (1960) UK#40, *Never Let Go* (1960) UK#49, *Walk Don't Run* (1960) UK#11, *Cutty Sark* (1962) UK#35, *The James Bond Theme* [vii] (1962) UK#13, *From Russia with Love* (1963) UK#39, *Goldfinger* (1964) US#72, *Midnight Cowboy* (1969) US#116, *The Persuaders* (1971) UK#13. SOUNDTRACK ALBUMS: **Beat Girl** (1960) UK#11, **Never Let Go** (1960, both Columbia); **Dr. No** (1962, United Artists) US#82; **It's All Happening** (1963, Columbia); **Elizabeth Taylor in London** (1963, Colpix); **From Russia with Love** (1964) US#27, **Goldfinger** (1964, both United Artists) US#1 UK#14; **Sophia Loren in Rome** (1964, Columbia); **The Newcomers** (1964, Capitol); **The Man in the Middle** (1964, Stateside); **Zulu** (1964, United Artists); **King Rat** (1965, Fontana); **The Knack and How to Get It** (1965, United Artists); **The I.P.C.R.E.S.S. File** (1965) US#133, **Passion Flower Hotel** oc (1965, both CBS); **Thunderball** (1965, United Artists) US#10; **The Quiller Memorandum** (1966, CBS); **Born Free** (1966, MGM) US#42; **The Chase** (1966, CBS); **Four in the Morning** (1966, Roulette); **The Wrong Box** (1966, Mainstream); **Vendetta** (1966, CBS); **The Whisperers** (1967), **You Only Live Twice** (1967, both United Artists) US#27; **Deadfall** (1968, Stateside); **Petulia** (1968, Warner Brothers); **The Lion in Winter** (1968, CBS) US#182; **Boom!** (1968, MCA); **Midnight Cowboy** (1969) g US#19, **On Her Majesty's Secret Service** (1969, both United Artists) US#103, **The Last Valley** (1970, Probe); **Monte Walsh** (1970, MCA); **Walkabout** (1970, Poo); **Lolita My Love** (1971, Blue Pear); **Diamonds Are Forever** (1971, United Artists) US#74; **Follow Me** (1971, MCA); **They Might Be Giants** (1971, Disc); **Alice's Adventures in Won-**derland (1972, Warner Brothers); **The Glass Menagerie** (1973, Polydor); **Billy** oc (1974, CBS); **The Dove** (1974, ABC); **The Man with the Golden Gun** (1974, United Artists); **The Day of the Locust** (1974, A&M); **King Kong** (1976, Reprise) US#123; **Robin and Marian** (1976, Sherwood); **The Deep** (1977, Casablanca) US#70; **Game of Death** (1978, Tam); **Betsy** (1978, GSF); **Mary Queen of Scots** (1978, MCA); **Starcrash** (1978, Carrere/Durium); **The Black Hole** (1979, Pickwick); **The Story of the Black Hole** (1979, Disneyland); **Moonraker** (1979, United Artists) US#159; **Inside Moves** (1980, Full Moon); **Raise the Titanic** (1980, Disc/7 Seas); **Somewhere in Time** (1980) g US#187, **The Legend of the Lone Ranger** (1981, both MCA); **Frances** (1983), **Body Heat** (1983, both Southern Cross); **The Golden Seal** (1983, Compleat); **High Road to China** (1983, Southern Cross); **Octopussy** (1983, A&M) US#137; **Cotton Club** (1984, Geffen); **Until September** (1984), **Jagged Edge** (1985, both Varese Sarabande); **Out of Africa** (1985, MCA) g US#38 UK#81; **A View to a Kill** (1985, Parlophone) US#38 UK#81; **Howard the Duck** (1986, MCA); **Peggy Sue Got Married** (1986, Varese Sarabande); **The Golden Child** (1986, Capitol) US#126; **The Living Daylights** (1987, Warner Brothers) UK#57; **Dances with Wolves** (1991, Epic) p US#48 UK#45; **Amicalement Votre** (1991, CBS); **Chaplin** (1992, Epic); **Indecent Proposal** (1993, MCA); **My Life** (1994), **The Specialist** (1995, both Epic). NON-SOUNDTRACK ALBUMS: **Stringbeat** (1961, Columbia); **Plays 007** (1964), **John Barry Meets Chad and Jeremy** (1965, both Ember); **The Incredible World of James Bond** (1965, United Artists); **Ready When You Are J.B.** (1967), **Great Movie Sounds of John Barry** (1967), **Greatest Movie Hits** (1967), **The Persuaders** (1971, all CBS) UK#18; **John Barry Revisited** (1975, Ember); **The Concert John Barry** (1976), **Americans** (1977, both Polydor); **The Music of John Barry** (1976, CBS); **Play It Again** (1977), **Very Best of John Barry** (1977, both Polydor); **Best of John Barry** (1979, EMI); **Big Screen Hits** (1981, CBS); **Hit and Miss** (1982, See for Miles); **Film Music of John Barry** (1988, Columbia); **John Barry Themes** (1989, Silva Screen); **Moviola** (1992, Epic); **John Barry 20** (1992, CBS/Sony); **The Ember Years, Volume 1** (1992), **The Ember Years, Volume 2** (1992, both Play It Again); **Best of James Bond-30th Anniversary** (1992) UK#2, **The EMI Years, Volume 1, 1957–1960** (1993), **The EMI Years, Volume 2, 1961** (1993, all EMI), **Moviola II: Action and Adventure** (1995, Epic); **The John Barry Experience** (1997, Carlton). HIT VERSIONS: *All Time High* [viii] Rita Coolidge (1983) US#36 UK#75, *Born Free* [iii] Matt Monroe (1966) US#126/Roger Williams (1966) US#7/Hesitations (1968) R&B#4 US#38; *Diamonds*

Are Forever [iii] Shirley Bassey (1972) US#57, *007 Theme* Soft Cell on B-side of *Soul Inside* (1983) UK#16, *Down Deep Inside* [ix] Donna Summer (1977) UK#5, *From Russia with Love* [i] Matt Monroe (1963) UK#20/Al Caiola (1964) US#120/Village Stompers (1964) US#81; *Goldfinger* [v] Shirley Bassey (1964) US#8 UK#21/Jack La Forge (1964) US#96/Jimmy Smith (1965) US#105/Billy Strange (1965) US#55; *James Bond Theme, The* [vii] Billy Strange (1964) US#135/Selector on B-side of *Three Minute Hero* (1980) UK#16; *King Kong, Theme from* Love Unlimited Orchestra (1977) R&B#15 US#68, *Made You* Adam Faith (1960) UK#5, *Midnight Cowboy* Ferrante & Teicher (1969) US#10/Midnight Cowboy Soundtrack (1980) UK#47; *Music of Goodbye, The* [ii] Al Jarreau & Melissa Manchester (1986) UK#75, *Thunderball* [iii] Tom Jones (1966) US#25 UK#35, *View to a Kill, The* [vi] Duran Duran (1985) g US#1 UK#2, *We Have All the Time in the World* Louis Armstrong (1994) UK#3, re-entry (1995) UK#66; *You Only Live Twice* [iv] Mantovani (1967) US#11/Nancy Sinatra (1967) US#44/Soft Cell on B-side of *Soul Inside* (1983) UK#16. Co-writers: [i] Lionel Bart, [ii] Alan Bergman/Marilyn Bergman, [iii] Don Black, [iv] Leslie Bricusse, [v] Leslie Bricusse/Anthony Newley, [vi] Duran Duran, [vii] credited to Monty Norman only, [viii] Tim Rice, [ix] Donna Summer (b. Adrian Donna Gaines, December 31, 1948, Dorchester, MA). (*See also under* Chrissie HYNDE, Ann and Nancy WILSON.)

60. BARSON, Mike (b. April 21, 1958, London, England) Pop keyboard player. The principal tunesmith, until 1983, in the British pop group Madness, which blended ska and punk with witty visuals and erudite lyrics. CHART COMPOSITIONS: *My Girl* (1980) UK#3, re-issued (1992) UK#27; *Baggy Trousers* [ii] (1980) UK#3, *Embarrassment* [iv] (1980) UK#4, *The Return of the Los Palmas Seven* [i] (1981) UK#7, *Grey Day* (1981) UK#4, *House of Fun* [iv] (1982) UK#1, re-issued (1992) UK#40; *Driving in My Car* (1982) UK#4, *Tomorrow's Just Another Day* [iii] (1983) UK#8, *The Sun and the Rain* (1983) US#72 UK#5. ALBUMS: **One Step Beyond** (1979) US#128 UK#2, **Absolutely** (1980) US#146 UK#2, **Seven** (1981) UK#5, **The Rise and Fall of Madness** (1982) UK#10, **Utter Madness** (1986) UK#29, **Divine Madness** (1992, all Stiff) UK#1. COMPILATION: **Complete Madness** (1982, Stiff) UK#1. HIT VERSION: *My Guy* Tracey Ullman (1984) UK#23. Co-writers: [i] Mark Bedford (b. August 24, 1961, London, England)/Daniel Woodgate (b. October 19, 1960, London, England), [ii] Christopher Foreman (b. August 8, 1958, London, England)/Graham McPherson (b. January 13, 1961, Hastings, England), [iii] Cathal Smyth (b. January 14, 1959, London,

England), [iv] Lee Thompson (b. October 5, 1957, London, England).

61. BART, Lionel (b. Lionel Begleiter, August 1, 1930, London, England) Film and stage composer, vocalist. The co-composer of one of Britain's most successful musicals, "Oliver!" (1960), which ran for over two and half thousand performances before winning six Oscars as a film in 1968. Bart had originally played the washboard in Tommy Steele's 1950s skiffle group the Cavemen. Bart's first stage show was the cockney influenced "Fings Ain't Wot They Used T'Be" (1959), which he followed with "Lock Up Your Daughters" (1959). He achieved his biggest ever success the following year with "Oliver!," which featured four British hit singles and such memorable material as *Food, Glorious Food* and *You've Got to Pick a Pocket or Two*. Unfortunately, Bart was never able to repeat the artistic and commercial success of "Oliver!," and his follow-up "Twang!" (1965), is regarded by many as the worst musical show of the decade. His songs were also featured in such films as "Let's Get Married" (1960). Bart eventually declared himself bankrupt, and by the 1990s was allegedly living on social security in a flat above a shop, remaining philosophical about the fact that in the 1960s it was estimated that he was earning sixteen pounds a minute, "I figured I could spend eight (pounds) per minute. Of course, I was wrong: but, with hindsight I wasn't wrong, because I had a great time doing it." CHART COMPOSITION: *Happy Endings (Give Yourself a Pinch)* (1989) UK#68. ALBUMS: **Bart for Bart's Sake** (1959), **Fings Ain't Wot They Used to Be** oc (1960) UK#5, **Oliver!** oc (1960) UK#4; **Stop the World I Want to Get Off** oc (1961, both Decca) UK#8; **Blitz** oc (1962, HMV) UK#7; **Oliver!** oc (1962, RCA) g US#4; **Lock Up Your Daughters** oc (1963, London); **Man in the Middle** ost (1965, 20th Century Fox); **Oliver!** ost (1968, RCA) g US#20 UK#4; **Isn't This Where We Came in** (1967, Deram); **Optimists** ost (1973, Paramount); **Oliver!** oc (1995, First Night) UK#36. HIT VERSIONS: *As Long As He/She Needs Me* Shirley Bassey (1960) UK#2/Sammy Davis, Jr. (1963) US#59; *Butterfingers* [iv] Tommy Steele (1957) UK#8, *Consider Yourself* Max Bygraves (1960) UK#50, *Do You Mind?* Anthony Newley (1960) UK#1/Andy Williams (1960) US#70; *Easy Going Me* Adam Faith (1961) UK#12, *Fings Ain't Wot They Used T'Be* Max Bygraves (1960) UK#5/Russ Conway (1960) UK#47; *Handful of Songs, A/Water, Water* [iii] Tommy Steele (1957) UK#5, *I'd Do Anything* Mike Preston (1960) UK#23, *Kicking Up the Leaves* Mark Wynter (1960) UK#24, *Little White Bull* [i] Tommy Steele (1959) UK#6, *Living Doll* Cliff Richard (1959) US#30 UK#1/Cliff Richard & the Young Ones (1986) UK#1;

Rock with the Cavemen [iii] Tommy Steele (1956) UK#13, *Tokyo Melody* [ii] Helmut Zacharias (1964) UK#9. Co-writers: [i] Jimmy Bennett/Michael Pratt, [ii] Heinz Hellmer/Helmut Zacharias, [iii] Michael Pratt/Tommy Steele (b. Thomas Hicks, December 17, 1936, London, England), [iv] Tommy Steele. (*See also under* John BARRY.)

62. BARTHOLOMEW, David (b. December 24, 1920, Edgard, LA) R&B trumpeter, bandleader, producer, arranger, and vocalist. A former New Orleans jazz musician who became a producer at Imperial Records during the late 1940s, where he worked with Shirley and Lee and Lloyd Price. During the 1950s, Bartholomew produced and co-wrote many of Fats Domino's biggest hits. He also recorded his own sides, some of which were influential in the development of Jamaican ska music. CHART COMPOSITION: *Country Boy* (1950) R&B#14. ALBUMS: **Fats Domino Presents Dave Bartholomew** (1961), **New Orleans House Party** (1963, both Imperial); **Jump Children** (1984), **The Monkey** (1985, both Pathe Marconi). HIT VERSIONS: *I Hear You Knocking* [i] Fats Domino (1961) US#67, also B-side of *Jambalaya* (1962) US#30/Smiley Lewis (1955) R&B#2/Gale Storm (1955) R&B#15 US#2/Dave Edmunds (1970) UK#1; *I'm Gone* [ii] Shirley & Lee (1952) R&B#2, *One Night* [i] Smiley Lewis (1956) R&B#11/Elvis Presley (1959) R&B#10 US#4 UK#1/Jeannie C. Riley (1972) C&W#57/Roy Head (1976) C&W#51/Dave Clark Five in medley *More Good Old Rock 'n' Roll* (1969) UK#34; *Witchcraft* [i] Elvis Presley (1963) US#32. Co-writers: [i] Pearl King, [ii] Leonard Lee. (*See also under* Fats DOMINO, Lloyd PRICE.)

63. BASKIN, Richard (b. America) Film composer, pianist, producer and vocalist. A seemingly gifted composer who never appeared to match his initial promise. Baskin's finest hour remains the exquisite song-cycle that he composed and recorded with Keith Carradine for the film "Welcome to L.A." (1976), in which his compositions *City of the One Night Stands* and *The Best Temptation of All* expertly examined the self-indulgent and disconnected lifestyle of 1970s Los Angeles. Although his material was recorded by such singers as Barbra Streisand, Baskin's career stalled in the 1980s. ALBUMS: **Nashville** ost (1975, ABC) US#80; **Welcome to L.A.** ost (1976, United Artists). (*See also under* David FOSTER.)

64. BATT, Mike (b. February 6, 1950, Southampton, England) Pop organist, arranger, producer and vocalist. A former 1960s A&R man who became a pop opportunist and creator of the fictional

pop group the Wombles, as a member of which, he performed in a rat-costume on British television. CHART COMPOSITIONS: *The Wombling Song* (1974) UK#4, *Remember You're a Womble* (1974) UK#3, *Banana Rock* (1974) UK#9, *Minuetto Allegretto* (1974) UK#16, *Wombling Merry Christmas* (1974) UK#2, *Wombling White Tie and Tails* (1975) UK#22, *Super Womble* (1975) UK#20, *Let's Womble to the Party Tonight* (1975) UK#34. ALBUMS: **Wombling Songs** (1974) UK#19, **Remember You're a Womble** (1974) UK#18, **Keep on Wombling** (1974, all CBS) UK#17. COMPILATION: **20 Wombling Greats** (1977, Warwick) UK#29. Batt's later solo efforts were often portentous conceptual theatrical works. CHART COMPOSITION: *Summertime City* (1975) UK#4. ALBUMS: **Moog at the Movies** (1973, Discreet); **Schizophrenia** (1977), **Tarot Suite** (1979, both Epic); **Caravans** (1979, CBS); **Waves** (1980), **6 Days in Berlin** (1981), **Zero Zero** (1983, all Epic); **The Hunting of the Snark** (1986, Starblend). HIT VERSIONS: *Ballerina (Prima Donna)* Steve Harley (1983) UK#51, *Bright Eyes* Art Garfunkel (1979) UK#1, *I Feel Like Buddy Holly* Alvin Stardust (1984) UK#7, *Please Don't Fall in Love* Cliff Richard (1983) UK#7, *Soldier's Song* Hollies (1980) UK#58, *Winter's Tale, A* [i] David Essex (1983) UK#2. Co-writer: [i] Tim Rice.

65. BECAUD, Gilbert (b. Francois Silly, 1927, Toulon, France) Pop vocalist. A popular French singer-songwriter of the 1950–1960s, whose sentimental songs were often translated into English to become middle-of-the-road staple repertoire. CHART COMPOSITION: *A Little Love and Understanding (Un Peu D'amour Et D'amitie)* [vii] (1975) UK#10. ALBUMS: **A Little Love and Understanding** (1975, Decca); **Al'Olympia** (1983), **The Gilbert Becaud Collection** (1983), **Disque D'Or, Volume 1** (1983), **Disque D'Or, Volume 2** (1983), **Gilbert Becaud** (1983), **Moi Je Veux Chanter** (1983, all EMI); **Mon Copain** (1988, DRG). HIT VERSIONS: *Day the Rains Came (Le Jour Ou il Pluie Viendra), The* [v] Raymond Lefevre (1958) US#30/Jane Morgan (1958) US#21 UK#1; *If Only I Could Live My Life Again* [i] Jane Morgan (1957) UK#29, *Importance of Your Love, The* [vi] Vince Hill (1968) UK#32, *It Must Be Him (Seul Sur Son Etoile)* [iv] Vicki Carr (1967) US#3 UK#2, *Let It Be Me (Je T'appartiens)* [ii] Arthur Pryscock (1966) US#124/Nino Tempo & April Stevens (1968) US#127/Jill Corey (1957)/Everly Brothers (1959) US#7 UK#13/Sweet Inspirations (1967) R&B#13 US#94/Glen Campbell & Bobbie Gentry (1969) C&W#14 US#36/Willie Nelson (1982) C&W#2 US#40; *What Now My Love (Et Maintenant)* [i] Shirley Bassey (1962) UK#5/Ben E. King (1964) US#102/Herb

Alpert & the Tijuana Brass (1966) US#24/Richard "Groove" Holmes (1966) US#96/Sonny & Cher (1966) US#14 UK#13/Mitch Ryder & the Detroit Wheels (1967) US#30; *With Your Love (Mes Mains)* [iii] Malcom Vaughan (1956) UK#18/Jack Scott (1958) US#28. Co-writers: [i] L. Amade/Pierre Delanoe/Elly Leighton, [ii] Mann Curtis/Pierre Delanoe, [iii] Pierre Delanoe/Geoffrey Parsons/John Turner, [iv] Mack David, [v] Pierre Delanoe/Carl Sigman, [vi] Norman Newell, [vii] Marcel Stellman. (*See also under* Neil DIAMOND.)

66. BECKER, Walter (b. February 20, 1950, New York, NY) Rock guitarist, bassist, producer and vocalist, and **FAGEN, Donald** (b. October 1, 1948, Passaic, NJ) Rock keyboard player, producer and vocalist. Influenced by the music of no less than Charlie Parker and Miles Davis, Becker and Fagen's group Steely Dan elevated the common rock song into a jazz related art form. Their use of chromatic musical relationships and intervals, unique in rock, explored the parameters of the popular song while remaining accessible and commercial. Fagen once said, "Steely Dan's music is dark because that is the shade of good drama." Both were jazz fans who met and teamed up while studying at Bard College in 1967. Before graduating in English Literature, Fagen performed as the Donald Fagen Jazz Trio, and as a member of the college bands the Leather Canary and the Bad Rock Group. During 1969, Becker and Fagen tried to sell what Fagen described as their "cheesy songs" in the Brill Building, New York, but their music was far too esoteric for mainstream pop acts. After working as backing musicians for the vocal group Jay and the Americans, Becker and Fagen scored a low budget movie, "You've Got to Walk It Like You Talk It or You'll Lose That Beat" (1971), before joining the guitarist Denny Dias' group Demian, demos of which later surfaced as the album **The Early Years** (1973). Becker and Fagen's compositions so impressed the independent record producer Gary Katz, that he took them with him as staff writers when he was offered an in-house position at ABC/Dunhill Records in California in 1971, where, after placing some of their songs with the likes of Barbra Streisand, Thomas Jefferson Kaye and John Kay, the duo began rehearsing as the group Steely Dan, after hours in the ABC office complex. The band achieved immediate success with their superlative debut album **Can't Buy a Thrill** (1972), a collection of cryptic, sardonic, obtuse and musically challenging songs that had finely crafted hooks, elegant melodies and superb arrangements. Becker and Fagen's subject matters ranged from perpetual losers, in *Do It Again*, to ambivalent cynicism in *Brooklyn (Owes the Charmer Under Me)*. Throughout their career,

Becker and Fagen avoided the concert hall at every opportunity, preferring instead to spend more and more time in the studio polishing their albums, resulting in their masterwork **Aja** (1977), which featured the half-step reggae shuffle of *Home at Last*, and the mid-tempo, minor-key title track. Becker and Fagen parted company during the early 1980s, with Becker becoming a producer and releasing the intriguing solo set **11 Tracks of Whack** (1994, Giant). Fagen released all of two solo albums in twelve years, before returning to occasional live performances during the late 1980s, and recording as a member of **The New York Rock and Soul Revue Live at the Beacon** (1991, Giant) US#170. In 1993, against all expectations, Becker and Fagen reformed a new Steely Dan for a series of live concerts, which, by 1996, had become a lengthy world tour. Reflecting once again their jazz routes, Fagen had evolved into a big band, orchestral leader in the style of Count Basie and Duke Ellington, leading the group from a portable keyboard. CHART COMPOSITIONS: *Do It Again* (1972) US#6 UK#39, *Reelin' in the Years* (1973) US#11, *Show Biz Kids* (1973) US#61, *My Old School* (1973) US#63, *Rikki Don't Lose That Number* (1974) US#4 UK#58, *Pretzel Logic* (1974) US#57, *Black Friday* (1975) US#37, *Bad Sneakers* (1975) US#103, *Kid Charlemagne* (1978) US#82, *The Fez* [i] (1976) US#59, *Haitian Divorce* (1976) UK#17, *Peg* (1977) US#11, *Deacon Blues* (1978) US#19, *FM (No Static at All)* (1978) US#22 UK#49, *Josie* (1978) US#26, *Hey Nineteen* (1981) R&B#68 US#10, *Time out of Mind* (1981) US#22. ALBUMS: **Can't Buy a Thrill** (1972) p US#17 UK#38, **Countdown to Ecstacy** (1973) g US#35, **Pretzel Logic** (1974) p US#8 UK#37, **Katy Lied** (1975) p US#13 UK#13, **The Royal Scam** (1976) p US#15 UK#11, **Aja** (1977, all ABC) p US#3 UK#5; **Gaucho** (1980, MCA) p US#9 UK#27; **Alive in America** (1995, Giant) US#40 UK#62. COMPILATIONS: **You've Got to Walk It Like You Talk It or You'll Lose That Beat** ost (1971, Spark); **The Early Years** (1973, Aero); **Greatest Hits** (1979, ABC) p US#30 UK#41; **Steely Dan Gold** (1981, MCA) g US#115 UK#44; **Sun Mountain** (1985, Showcase); **Reelin' in the Years-The Best of Steely Dan** (1985) UK#43, **A Decade of Steely Dan** (1985, both MCA) g; **Do It Again-The Very Best of Steely Dan** (1987, Telstar) UK#64; **Remastered-The Best of Steely Dan** (1993) UK#42, **Citizen Steely Dan** (1993, both MCA). HIT VERSIONS: *Do It Again* Club House (1983) R&B#61 US#75 UK#11/Slingshot (1978) R&B#25/Art of Noise with Tom Jones sampled in *The Kiss* (1988) US#31 UK#5; *Don't Let Me In* Sneaker (1982) US#63, *Peg* De La Soul sampled in *Eye Know* (1989) UK#14, *Rikki Don't Lose That Number* Tom Robinson (1984) UK#58. Co-writer: [i] Paul Griffin. (*See also under* Donald FAGEN.)

67. BECKLEY, Gerry (b. September 12, 1952, TX) Pop guitarist and vocalist. One third of the soft-rock, vocal harmony group America, which was formed in 1969. CHART COMPOSITIONS: *I Need You* (1972) US#9, *Daisy Chain* (1975) US#20, *Sister Golden Hair* (1975) US#1. ALBUMS: **America** (1972) p US#1 UK#14, **Homecoming** (1972) g US#9 UK#21, **Hat Trick** (1973) US#28 UK#41, **Holiday** (1974) g US#3, **Hearts** (1975) g US#4, **Hideaway** (1976) g US#11, **Harbor** (1977) US#21, **Live** (1977, all Warner Brothers) US#129; **Silent Letter** (1979) US#110, **Alibi** (1980) US#142, **View from the Ground** (1982) US#41, **Your Move** (1983) US#81, **Perspective** (1984) US#185, **In Concert** (1985, all Capitol); **Hourglass** (1995, American Gramophone). COMPILATIONS: **History/Greatest Hits** (1975, Warner Brothers) p US#11 UK#60; **Encore: More Greatest Hits** (1993, Rhino). (*See also under* Dewey BUNNELL.)

68. BELEW, Carl (b. April 21, 1931, Salina, OK) C&W vocalist. A plumber who became a country singer-songwriter after he gained a regular slot on the "Louisiana Hayride" television show in the 1950s. CHART COMPOSITIONS: *Am I That Easy to Forget* [i] (1959) C&W#9, *Too Much to Lose* (1960) C&W#19, *Hello Out There* (1962) C&W#8 US#120, *In the Middle of a Memory* (1964) C&W#23, *Crystal Chandelier* (1965) C&W#12, *Boston Jail* (1966) C&W#43, *Walking Shadow, Talking Memory* (1966) C&W#64, *Girl Crazy* (1967) C&W#65, *Mary's Little Lamb* (1968) C&W#68, *All I Need Is You* with Betty Jean Robinson (1971) C&W#51, *Welcome Back to My World* (1974) C&W#56. ALBUMS: **Carl Belew** (1960, Decca); **Hello Out There** (1964), **Am I That Easy to Forget** (1968), **Twelve Shades of Belew** (1968, all RCA); **When My Baby Sings His Song** (1972, MCA). HIT VERSIONS: *Am I That Easy to Forget* [i] Skeeter Davis (1960) C&W#11/ Debbie Reynolds (1960) R&B#13 US#25/Little Esther Phillips (1963) US#112/Engelbert Humperdinck (1968) US#18 UK#3/Jim Reeves (1973) C&W#12/ Orion (1980) C&W#60: *Don't Squeeze My Sharmon* Charlie Walker (1967) C&W#8, *Lonely Street* [ii] Andy Williams (1959) R&B#20 US#5/Clarence "Frogman" Henry (1961) UK#42/Tony Booth (1974) C&W#84/Rex Allen, Jr. (1977) C&W#8; *Stop the World (And Let Me Off)* Johnnie & Jack (1958) C&W#7/Waylon Jennings (1965) C&W#16/Susan Raye (1974) C&W#74/Donny King (1976) C&W#91; *That's When I See the Blues (In Your Pretty Brown Eyes)* Jim Reeves (1968) C&W#9, *What's He Doing in My World* Eddy Arnold (1965) C&W#1 US#60. Co-writers: [i] Shelby Singleton/W.S. Stevenson, [ii] Kenny Sowder/W.S. Stevenson.

69. BELL, Thom (b. 1940, Philadelphia, PA) R&B multi-instrumentalist, arranger and producer. A consistently successful R&B songwriter and producer during the 1970s, who created his own sound for a succession of soul vocal groups. Bell's style was influential for many years, and his warm, concise melodies were strong on harmonic structure and always deftly arranged. The son of West Indian immigrants, Bell learned music from the age of eight, mastering the drums and flugelhorn before training as a classical pianist. In high school he befriended Kenny Gamble, with whom he recorded during the 1950s as Kenny and Tommy, and later as Kenny Gamble and the Romeos. As a session player at Cameo Records, Bell toured Britain as Chubby Checker's musical director, and arranged the Showstoppers' hits *Ain't Nothin' But a House Party* and *Eeny Meeny* (1968). His first productions for a soul vocal group were for the Delfonics on the Philly Groove label, where he developed a lush, string laden sound that played against a jerky, rhythmic style. With a significant emphasis on the lead falsetto vocal of William Hart, and playing most of the instruments himself, Bell's dense layers of sound introduced, for the first time on R&B discs, French horns, woodwinds and brass, creating a neo-classical, sweet, soft blend of soul. Bell also worked alongside Gamble for the Mercury label, before joining forces with Gamble and Leon Huff at Philadelphia International Records during the early 1970s. Bell's most important creative writing partnership was with the lyricist Linda Creed, with whom he composed a series of hits for the Stylistics, a vocal group that Bell molded into a more sophisticated Delfonics via the smooth tenor of Russell Thompkin. A lengthy relationship with the Spinners, resulted in a top heavy drum sound that was performed almost exclusively on the hi-hat and toms, over which the group sang close harmony soul. Bell remained an in-demand producer throughout the 1970s. ALBUM: **Bell and James** (1978, A&M) US#31. HIT VERSIONS: *Aiming at Your Heart* Temptations (1981) R&B#36 US#67, *Are You Ready for Love* Elton John (1979) UK#42, *Betcha By Golly Wow* [iii] Stylistics (1971) g R&B#2 US#3 UK#13/Norman Connors (1977) R&B#29 US#102/Band of Gold in *Love Songs Are Back Again* (1984) R&B#62 US#64/Prince (1996) UK#3; *Break Up to Make Up* [iv] Stylistics (1972) g R&B#5 US#5 UK#34/Will Downing (1994) R&B#66; *Break Your Promise* [v] Delfonics (1968) R&B#12 US#35, *Didn't I (Blow Your Mind This Time)* [v] Delfonics (1970) g R&B#3 US#10 UK#22/ Millie Jackson (1980) R&B#49/New Kids on the Block (1989) g US#8 UK#8; *Easy Come, Easy Go* [iii] Spinners (1978) R&B#46, *Ghetto Child* [iii] Spinners (1972) R&B#4 US#29 UK#7, *He Doesn't Really Love You* [v] Delfonics (1968) R&B#33 US#92, *Help Me to Find a Way (To Say I Love You)* Little Anthony & the Imperials (1970) R&B#32 US#92, *His House and Me* Dionne Warwick (1976) R&B#75, *I'll Be Around* [vi] Spinners (1972) g R&B#1 US#3/Terri Wells (1984) R&B#81 UK#17/What Is This (1985) US#62/Rappin' 4-Tay (1995) UK#30; *I'm Coming Home* [iii] Spinners (1974) R&B#3 US#18/Sylistics (1977) R&B#77/Johnny Mathis (1973) R&B#92 US#75; *I'm Doin' Fine Now* [viii] New York City (1973) R&B#14 US#17 UK#20/Pasadenas (1992) UK#4; *I'm Sorry* [v] Delfonics (1968) R&B#15 US#42, *I'm Stone in Love with You* [i] Stylistics (1972) g R&B#4 US#10 UK#29/Johnny Mathis (1975) UK#10; *If You Wanna Do a Dance All Night* [ii] Spinners (1978) R&B#17 US#49, *It's Your Conscience* Deniece Williams (1981) R&B#45, *La La Means I Love You* [v] Delfonics (1968) R&B#2 US#4 UK#19/L.A. Boppers (1981) R&B#77/Tierra (1981) R&B#33 US#72; *Life Is a Song Worth Singing* [iii] Johnny Mathis (1974) R&B#65 US#54, *Living a Little, Laughing a Little* [iii] Spinners (1974) R&B#7 US#37, *Love Don't Love Nobody* [iii] Spinners (1974) R&B#4 US#15/Jean Carne (1981) R&B#35; *Loving You, Losing You* Phyliss Hyman (1977) R&B#32 US#103, *Old Friend* Phyliss Hyman (1986) R&B#14, *Peak-a-Boo* [iii] Stylistics (1972) UK#35, *People Make the World Go Round* [iii] Stylistics (1971) R&B#6 US#25/Mark Dorsey (1994) R&B#65; *Quick, Fast and in a Hurry* [iii] New York City (1973) R&B#19 US#79, *Ready or Not Here I Come (Can't Hide from Love)* [v] Delfonics (1969) R&B#14 US#35 UK#41, *Rock 'n' Roll Baby* [iii] Stylistics (1973) R&B#3 US#14 UK#6, *Rubberband Man, The* [iii] Spinners (1976) g R&B#1 US#2 UK#16, *Somebody Loves You* [v] Delfonics (1969) R&B#41 US#72, *Stop, Look, Listen (To Your Heart)* [iii] Stylistics (1971) R&B#6 US#39/Diana Ross & Marvin Gaye (1974) UK#25; *Trying to Make a Fool Out of Me* [v] Delfonics (1970) R&B#8 US#40, *Waiting* Deniece Williams (1982) R&B#72, *Waiting By the Hotline* Deniece Williams (1982) R&B#29 US#103, *Wake Up Susan* [viii] Spinners (1976) R&B#11 US#56 UK#29, *You Are Everything* [iii] Stylistics (1971) g R&B#10 US#9/Pearls (1973) UK#41/Diana Ross & Marvin Gaye (1974) UK#5/Roberta Flack (1979) R&B#98 US#74/Eloise Laws (1981) R&B#53/Special Generation (1991) R&B#90/Melanie Williams & Joe Roberts (1995) UK#28; *You Make Me Feel Brand New* [iii] Stylistics (1973) g R&B#5 US#2 UK#2/Band of Gold in *Love Songs Are Back Again* (1984) R&B#62 US#64/Roberta Flack (1992) R&B#50; *You've Got Yours and I'll Get Mine* [v] Delfonics (1969) R&B#6 US#40. Co-writers: [i] Anthony Bell/Linda Creed (b. 1949, Philadelphia, PA; d. 1986), [ii] Leroy Bell/Casey James, [iii] Linda Creed, [iv] Linda Creed/Kenny Gamble, [v] William Hart (b. January 17, 1945, Washington, DC), [vi] Phil Hurtt, [vii] Sherman Marshall. (*See also under* Kenny GAMBLE and Leon HUFF.)

70. BELL, William (b. William Yarborough, July 16, 1939, Memphis, TN) R&B vocalist. An R&B performer in the country-soul vein, who composed many songs for a variety of artists during his seven year tenure at Stax Records. Bell won a local talent contest at the age of fourteen, which earned him his first single release, *Alone on a Rainy Night.* He subsequently formed his own vocal group the Del-Rios, and abandoned his medical studies to pursue music when he sang in the Phineas Newborn Band. After serving in the U.S. Army in 1963, Bell signed to Stax, where he became one of the label's earliest in-house writers. He later ran his own WRC, Peachtree and Wilbe labels, but by the mid-1980s, he seemingly drifted into semi-retirement. CHART COMPOSITIONS: *Any Other Way* (1962) US#131, *Share What You Got* [i] (1966) R&B#27, *Everybody Loves a Winner* [ii] (1967) R&B#18 US#95, *Everyday Will Be Like a Holiday* (1968) R&B#33, *A Tribute to a King* [ii] (1968) R&B#16 US#86 UK#31, *Private Number* [ii] with Judy Clay (1968) R&B#17 US#75 UK#8, *Every Man Ought to Have a Woman* (1968) US#115, *I Forgot to Be Your Lover* [ii] (1968) R&B#10 US#45, *I Need You Woman** (1969) US#106, *Happy* [i] (1969) US#129, *Lovin' on Borrowed Time* (1973) R&B#22 US#101, *I've Got to Go on Without You* (1973) R&B#54, *Gettin' What You Want (Losin' What You Got)* (1974) R&B#39, *Trying to Love Two* [iii] (1976) g R&B#1 US#10, *Coming Back for More* (1977) R&B#66, *Easy Comin' Out (Hard Goin' In)* (1977) R&B#30, *Bad Time to Break Up* (1983) R&B#65, *I Don't Want to Wake Up (Feelin' Guilty)* with Janice Bullock (1986) R&B#59, *Headline News* (1986) R&B#65 UK#70. ALBUMS: **Soul of a Bell** (1968), **Bound to Happen** (1969), **Boy Meets Girl*** (1969), **Relating** (1970), **Wow** (1971), **Phases of Reality** (1972, all Stax); **Coming Back for More** (1977) US#63, **It's Time You Took Another Listen** (1979, both Mercury); **Survivor** (1983, Kat Family); **Exposed** (1986, Virgin); **Passion** (1986), **On a Roll** (1989), **Bedtime Stories** (1992, all Wilbe). COMPILATIONS: **Do Right Man** (1984, Charly); **Best of William Bell** (1990), **A Little Something Extra** (1992, both Stax). HIT VERSIONS: *All God's Children Got Soul* [ii] Dorothy Morrison (1969) US#95, *Born Under a Bad Sign* [ii] Albert King (1967) R&B#49, *Everybody Loves a Winner* [ii] Dickey Lee (1982) C&W#56, *I Forgot to Be Your*

Lover [ii] Gene Chandler as *To Be a Lover* (1967) R&B#9 US#94/Billy Idol as *To Be a Lover* (1986) US#6 UK#22; *Private Number* [ii] Jets (1986) R&B#28 US#47, *Trying to Love Two* [iii] Kin Vassy (1983) C&W#80, *You Don't Miss Your Water* King Curtis (1967) US#105. With: * Carla Thomas. Co-writers: [i] Steve Cropper, [ii] Booker T. Jones, [iii] Paul Mitchell.

71. BELLAMY, David (b. September 16, 1950, Derby, FL) C&W guitarist, keyboard player and vocalist. A country composer who charted with the solo single *Nothin' Heavy* (1975) US#77, before forming the soft-rock influenced Bellamy Brothers, which achieved thirty-four country hits between 1976–1988. CHART COMPOSITIONS: *If I Said You Have a Beautiful Body Would You Hold It Against Me* (1979) C&W#1 US#39 UK#3, *Hell Cat* (1976) US#70, *Dancin' Cowboys* (1980) C&W#1, *When I'm Away from You* (1983) C&W#1, *Cowboy Beat* [i] (1992) C&W#23, *Can I Come Home to You* (1992) C&W#70, *Hard Way to Make an Easy Livin'* [ii] (1993) C&W#62, *Rip Off the Knob* (1993) C&W#66, *Not* (1994) C&W#71. ALBUMS: **The Bellamy Brothers** (1976) g US#69 UK#21, **Plain and Fancy** (1977), **Beautiful Friends** (1978), **The Two and Only** (1979), **You Can Get Crazy** (1980), **Sons of the Sun** (1980), **When We Were Boys** (1982), **Strong Weakness** (1982, all Warner Brothers); **Restless** (1984), **Howard and David** (1986), **Country** (1988), **Crazy from the Heart** (1989), **Rebels Without a Clue** (1988, all MCA); **The Latest and Greatest** (1992, Bellamy Brothers). COMPILATIONS: **Best of the Bellamy Brothers** (1985), **Greatest Hits** (1987, both MCA). HIT VERSIONS: *Spiders and Snakes* [iii] Jim Stafford (1974) g C&W#66 US#3 UK#14, *Your Bulldog Drinks Champagne* [iii] Jim Stafford (1975) US#24. Co-writers: [i] John E. Beland, [ii] Howard Bellamy (b. February 2, 1946, Derby, FL)/John E. Beland, [iii] Jim Stafford (b. January 16, 1944, Eloise, FL).

72. BELVIN, Jesse (b. December 15, 1933, San Antonio, TX; d. February 6, 1960, Little Rock, AK) Doo-wop vocalist. An influential R&B singer whose career was cut short when he was killed in a car accident at the age of twenty-nine. Belvin first recorded in a duo with Marvin Philips, as Marvin and Johnny, charting with *Baby Doll* (1953) R&B#9 and *Tick Tock* (1954) R&B#9, before singing in the doo-wop groups the Cliques and the Sharptones. Belvin also achieved four solo hits between 1953–1959, but is best remembered as the composer of the doo-wop standard *Earth Angel (Will You Be Mine)*. CHART COMPOSITIONS: *Dream Girl* (1953) R&B#2, *Goodnight My Love* (1956) R&B#7, *Funny* (1959) R&B#25 US#81. ALBUMS: **Just Jesse Belvin** (1959), **Mr. Easy** (1960, both RCA); **The Casual** (1960), **Unforgettable** (1960, both Crown); **Best** (1966, Camden); **Yesterdays** (1975, RCA); **Memorial Album** (1984, Ace); **Hang Your Tears Out to Dry** (1987, Earth Angel). HIT VERSIONS: *Earth Angel (Will You Be Mine)* Penguins (1955) R&B#1 US#8/Crew Cuts (1955) US#3 UK#4/Gloria Mann (1955) US#18/Tucker Williams (1980) C&W#96/Richard "Dimples" Fields (1981) R&B#81/New Edition (1986) R&B#3 US#21; *Girl of My Dreams* Tony Brent (1958) UK#58, *So Fine* Fiestas (1959) R&B#3 US#11.

73. BENJAMIN, Bennie (b. 1907, America) Pop composer. HIT VERSIONS: *Cancel the Flowers* [ii] Tony Martin (1942) US#22, *Don't Let Me Be Misunderstood* [iii] Animals (1965) US#15 UK#3/Nina Simone (1964) US#131/Santa Esmeralda & Leroy Gomez (1977) US#15 UK#41/Elvis Costello & the Attractions (1986) UK#33/Joe Cocker (1996) UK#53; *Fabulous Character* [v] Sarah Vaughan (1956) US#19, *I Don't Want to Set the World on Fire* [iv] Mitchell Ayres (1941) US#18/Hoarce Heidt (1941) US#1/Ink Spots (1941) US#4/Tommy Tucker (1941) US#4/Fats Domino (1964) US#122/Suzy Bogguss (1987) C&W#68; *Strictly Instrumental* [i] Harry James (1942) US#5. Co-writers: [i] Edgar Battle/Sol Marcus (b. 1912; d. 1976)/Eddie Seiler (b. 1911; d. 1952), [ii] Sol Marcus/Eddie Seiler, [iii] Gloria Caldwell/Sol Marcus, [iv] Eddie Dunham/Sol Marcus/Eddie Seller, [v] Sol Marcus. (*See also under* George David WEISS.)

74. BENTON, Brook (b. Benjamin Franklin Peay, September 19, 1931, Camden, SC; d. April 9, 1988, New York, NY) R&B vocalist. An R&B-pop balladeer with a smooth baritone, who sold over twenty million records during his lifetime. Benton first sang gospel with the Camden Jubilee Singers in the late 1940s, before performing R&B with the Sandmen and singing on publishers demos. He later became a co-writer for such singers as Nat "King" Cole and Clyde McPhatter, before achieving thirty-seven hits of his own between 1959–1978. Benton died of complications from spinal meningitis in 1988. CHART COMPOSITIONS: *It's Just a Matter of Time* [vii] (1959) R&B#1 US#3, *Hurtin' Inside* [i] (1959) R&B#23 US#78, *Endlessly* [vi] (1959) R&B#3 US#12 UK#28, *So Close* [iv] (1959) R&B#5 US#38, *Thank You Pretty Baby* [vi] (1959) R&B#1 US#16, *Kiddio* [vi] (1960) R&B#1 US#7 UK#41, *A Rockin' Good Way (To Mess Around and Fall in Love)* with Dinah Washington (1960) R&B#1 US#7, *Hither and Tither and You* [ii] (1960) US#58, *The Same One* [vi] (1960) R&B#21 US#16, *For My Baby* [vi] (1961)

R&B#2 US#28, *Boll Weevil Song* [vi] (1961) R&B#2 US#2 UK#30, *Revenge* [v] (1962) R&B#2 US#15, *Lie to Me* [viii] (1962) R&B#3 US#13. ALBUMS: **It's Just a Matter of Time** (1959), **Brook Benton** (1959), **Endlessly** (1959), **So Many Ways** (1960), **Two of Us** (1960), **Songs I Love to Sing** (1960), **Dinah Washington and Brook Benton** (1960), **The Boll Weevil Song (And Eleven Other Great Hits)** (1961) US#70, **Sepia** (1961), **If You Believe** (1961), **Singing the Blues-Lie to Me** (1962), **There Goes That Song Again** (1962), **Born to Sing the Blues** (1964, all Mercury); **Laura (What's He Got That I Ain't Got)** (1967, Reprise) US#156; **Do Your Own Thing** (1969) US#189, **Today** (1970) US#27, **Home Style** (1970, all Cotillion) US#199; **The Gospel Truth** (1971), **Something for Everyone** (1973), **That Old Feeling** (1974), **Sings a Love Story** (1975), **Lovin'** (1976), **Mr. Bartender** (1976), **This Is Brook Benton** (1976), **Makin' Love Is Good for You** (1977), **Ebony** (1978), **Sings the Standards** (1984), **Magic Moments** (1985, all RCA). COMPILATIONS: **Golden Hits** (1961) US#82, **Golden Hits, Volume 2** (1963) US#82, **40 Greatest Hits** (1990, all Mercury). HIT VERSIONS: *Endlessly* [vi] Sonny James (1970) C&W#1 US#108/Mavis Staples (1972) US#109/Eddie Middleton (1977) C&W#38; *For My Baby* [vi] Cal Smith (1972) C&W#58, *It's Just a Matter of Time* [vii] Sonny James (1970) C&W#1/Glen Campbell (1985) C&W#7/Randy Travis (1989) C&W#1; *Looking Back* [vii] Nat "King" Cole (1958) US#6/Joe Simon (1968) R&B#42 US#70; *Lover's Question, A* [x] Clyde McPhatter (1958) R&B#1 US#6/Del Reeves (1970) C&W#14/Loggins & Messina (1975) US#89/Jacky Ward (1978) C&W#3; *Rockin' Good Way, A* [iv] Shakin' Stevens & Bonnie Tyler (1984) UK#5, *Think Twice* Jackie Wilson & LaVern Baker (1966) US#93. Co-writers: [i] Cirino Colacrai/Clyde Otis/Teddy Randazzo, [ii] Vin Corso/Chris Towns, [iii] Luchi De Jesus/Clyde Otis, [iv] Luther Dixon/Clyde Otis, [v] Marnie Ewald/Oliver Hall, [vi] Clyde Otis, [vii] Clyde Otis/Belford C. Hendricks, [viii] Margie Singleton, [ix] Chris Towns, [x] Jimmy T. Williams.

75. BERGMAN, Alan, and BERGMAN, Marilyn Film and stage lyricists. A husband and wife lyric writing team who have worked with numerous composers. Johnny Mathis recorded an entire album of their best known material as **How Do You Keep the Music Playing?** (1993, Columbia), and their songs have been featured in such films as "10,000 Bedrooms" (1957), "In the Heat of the Night" (1967), "The Life and Times of Judge Roy Bean" (1972), "Ballroom" (1978), and "Tootsie" (1983). ALBUM: **Tootsie** ost (1983, Warner Brothers) US#144. HIT VERSIONS: *In the Heat of the Night* [ii] Ray Charles (1967) R&B#21 US#33, *It Might Be You* [i] Stephen Bishop (1983) US#25, *Nice 'N' Easy* [iv] Frank Sinatra (1960) UK#15/Charlie Rich (1964) US#131, re-issued (1970) C&W#37; *Yellow Bird* [iii] Arthur Lyman Group (1961) US#25. Co-writers: [i] Dave Grusin (June 26, 1934, Denver, CO), [ii] Quincy Jones, [iii] Norman Luboff, [iv] Lew Spence. (*See also under* Neil DIAMOND, Marvin HAMLISCH, Michel LEGRAND, Kenny LOGGINS.)

76. BERLIN, Irving (b. Israel Baline, May 11, 1888, Temun, Russia; d. September 22, 1989, New York, NY) Film and stage composer, pianist. The master craftsman of the popular song, and the most successful American songwriter of the twentieth century, whose composition *God Bless America* (1939), has become the nation's unofficial second national anthem. Berlin created more standards than any other songwriter, despite being unable to read or write music, and only being capable of playing the piano in the key of F sharp major. His song *White Christmas*, from the film "Holiday Inn" (1942), is the biggest selling record of all time, shifting over seventy million copies, thirty million of which were a single recording by Bing Crosby. Berlin was particularly successful with Broadway scores, including "Alexander's Ragtime Band" (1938), "Annie Get Your Gun" (1946), "Easter Parade" (1948), and "Call Me Madam" (1950). He also wrote for the films "Top Hat" (1935) and "On the Avenue" (1937). Berlin's composition were based in jazz and ragtime, and he excelled at ballads, many of which remain some of the finest, yet simplest ever written. The son of Russian immigrants, Berlin grew up in poverty, before working in his teens as a song-plugger and a singing cafe waiter in 1906. Utilizing only the black notes of the piano keyboard, Berlin began writing his first compositions, and in 1907, published his first song, *Marie from Sunny Italy*, a printing error on the sheet music of which mistakenly credited Baline as Berlin, a name he subsequently adopted. Capable of turning simple phrases into catchy songs, Berlin also created a veritable selection of characters in his one-joke refrains, particular favorites being mother-in-laws and ethnic stereotypes. Throughout his career, he seemed able to gauge what people wanted to hear and buy, and thus composed accordingly. His composition *Alexander's Ragtime Band* (1911), was initially disregarded before it sold two million copies for Emma Carus — the song ultimately changing the course of popular music, as it was the first ever syncopated pop-jazz hit. In 1913, Berlin performed his material in England, and the following year wrote his first musical, "Watch Your Step." He recorded his own tunes for a variety of record labels, and after

World War I, staged revues in his own Music Box Theatre. Berlin sat on the first Board of ASCAP Directors in 1914, and lived to the age of one hundred and one, having copyrighted some nine hundred titles. Of the many albums of his songs, the most successful were Guy Lombardo's **Berlin By Lombardo** (1958, Capitol) US#12; Mantovani's **Waltzes of Irving Berlin** (1956) US#12 and **All-American Showcase** (1960, both London) US#8; Perry Como's **The Best of Irving Berlin's Songs from Mr. President** (1962, RCA) US#90; and **The George Mitchell Minstrels Sing the Irving Berlin Songbook** (1968, Columbia) UK#33. CHART COMPOSITION: *Oh, How That German Could Love!* (1910) US#10. ALBUMS: **Lady Be Good** oc (1924, World); **Flying Down to Rio** ost (1938, Sandy Hook); **Holiday Inn** ost (1942), **This Is the Army** oc (1942), **Blue Skies** ost (1946, all Decca); **Easter Parade** ost (1948, MGM); **Miss Liberty** oc (1949, Columbia); **Call Me Madam** oc (1950, RCA); **Call Me Madam** ost (1951, Mercury); **Ford 50th Anniversary TV Show** tvst (1953), **White Christmas** ost (1954), **There's No Business Like Show Business** (1955, all Decca) US#6; **Annie Get Your Gun** oc (1957, Capitol) US#12; **Sayonara** ost (1957, RCA); **Dance to the Music of Irving Berlin** ost (1959, Vocalion); **Mr. President** oc (1962, Columbia) US#14; **Mister President** sc (1962), **Annie Get Your Gun** oc (1966, both RCA) US#113; **Irving Berlin Revisited** oc (1967), **Annie Get Your Gun/Show Boat** ost (1973) US#184, **Easter Parade/Singin' in the Rain** ost (1973, all MGM) US#185; **Irving Berlin: 100th Anniversary Collection** sc (1988, MCA). HIT VERSIONS: *Abraham* Freddy Martin (1942) US#22, *After the Honeymoon* Walter Van Brunt (1912) US#7, *After You Get What You Want, You Don't Want It* Van & Schenck (1920) US#2, *Alexander's Ragtime Band* Arthur Collins & Byron Harlan (1911) US#1/Billy Murray (1911) US#2/Prince's Orchestra (1912) US#3/Victor Military Band (1912) US#4/Bessie Smith (1927) US#17/Boswell Sisters (1935) US#9/Louis Armstrong (1937) US#12/Boswell Sisters (1938) US#4/Bing Crosby & Connee Boswell (1938) US#1/Ray Noble (1938) US#6/Bing Crosby & Al Jolson (1947) g US#20/Nellie Lutcher (1948) R&B#13/Johnston Brothers in *Join in and Sing Again #3* (1956) UK#24; *All Alone* Cliff Edwards (1925) US#6/Lewis James (1925) US#12/Al Jolson (1925) US#1/Abe Lyman (1925) US#10/John McCormack (1925) US#1/Ben Selvin (1925) US#11/Paul Whiteman (1925) US#1; *All By Myself* Frank Crumit (1921) US#5/Vaughn Deleath (1921) US#13/Benny Krueger (1921) US#6/Ted Lewis (1921) US#1/Ben Selvin (1921) US#14/Aileen Stanley (1921) US#5; *All of My Life* Bing Crosby (1945) US#12/Sammy Kaye (1945) US#10/Three Suns (1945) US#10; *Always* Henry Burr

(1926) US#3/Lewis James (1926) US#12/Vincent Lopez (1926) US#1/Nick Lucas (1926) US#4/George Olsen (1926) US#1/Gordon Jenkins (1944) US#16/Paul Lavalle (1944) US#29/Sammy Kaye (1945) US#10/Guy Lombardo (1945) US#10/Sammy Turner (1959) R&B#2 US#19 UK#26/Patsy Cline (1980) C&W#18; *Any Bonds Today?* Barry Wood (1941) US#21, *Anything You Can Do* Majors (1963) US#117, *Araby* Harry MacDonough (1916) US#3, *At Peace with the World* Lewis James & Franklyn Buar (1926) US#12/Al Jolson (1926) US#3/Isham Jones (1926) US#5; *At the Devil's Ball* Peerless Quartet (1913) US#6, *Back to Back* Glenn Miller (1939) US#8, *Be Careful, It's My Heart* Bing Crosby (1942) US#2/Tommy Dorsey (1942) US#13; *Because I Love You* Henry Burr (1927) US#12, *Begging for Love* Guy Lombardo (1931) US#4, *Better Luck Next Time* Jo Stafford (1948) US#26, *Blue Skies* Vaughn Deleath (1927) US#15/George Olsen (1927) US#2/Vincent Lopez (1927) US#9/Johnny Marvin & Ed Smalle (1927) US#9/Harry Richman (1927) US#13/Ben Selvin (1927) US#1/Johnny Long (1941) US#22/Count Basie (1946) US#8/Benny Goodman (1946) US#9/Winifred Atwell in *Piano Party* (1959) UK#10/Willie Nelson (1978) C&W#1; *Bring Back My Lovin' Man* Ada Jones (1912) US#5, *But Where Are You?* Ozzie Nelson (1936) US#18, *By the Sad Luana Shore* Marguerite Farrell (1916) US#6, *Call Me Up Some Rainy Afternoon* Ada Jones (1910) US#4/Ada Jones & the American Quartet (1910) US#1; *Change Partners* Fred Astaire (1938) US#1/Jimmy Dorsey (1938) US#1/Ozzie Nelson (1938) US#6/Lawrence Welk (1938) US#13; *Cheek to Cheek* Fred Astaire (1935) US#1/Boswell Sisters (1935) US#10/Eddy Duchin (1935) US#2/Guy Lombardo (1935) US#2/Phil Ohman (1935) US#5/Frank Sinatra on *Come Dance with Me LP* (1959) UK#30; *Coquette* Dorsey Brothers Orchestra (1928) US#20/Guy Lombardo (1928) US#6/Rudy Vallee (1929) US#10/Billy Eckstine (1953) US#26; *Count Your Blessings Instead of Sheep* Rosemary Clooney (1954) US#27/Bing Crosby (1954) US#27 UK#11/Eddie Fisher (1955) US#5; *Crinoline Days* Paul Whiteman (1923) US#2, *Dance of the Grizzly Bear* American Quartet (1911) US#9, *Doin' What Comes Natur'lly* Jimmy Dorsey (1946) US#8/Freddy Martin (1946) US#2/Dinah Shore (1946) US#3; *Easter Parade* Leo Reisman & Clifton Webb (1933) US#5/Guy Lombardo (1939) US#11, new version (1947) g US#21/Harry James (1942) g US#11, re-issued (1946) US#23/Bing Crosby (1947) US#22, re-issued (1948) US#22/Liberace (1954) US#26/Freddie Mitchell (1950) R&B#7; *Down in Chattanooga* Arthur Collins & Byron Harlan (1914) US#4, *Everybody Knew But Me* Woody Herman (1946) US#11, *Everybody Step* Ted Lewis (1922) US#3/Paul Whiteman (1922) US#11; *Everybody's*

Doin' It Now Arthur Collins & Byron Harlan (1912) US#2/Peerless Quartet (1912) US#6/Arthur Pryor's Band (1912) US#6; *Fella with an Umbrella, A* Bing Crosby (1948) US#23, *For Your Country and My Country* Frances Alda (1917) US#9/Peerless Quartet (1917) US#5; *Freedom Train, The* Bing Crosby & the Andrews Sisters (1947) US#21, *From Here to Shanghai* Gene Greene & the Peerless Quartet (1917) US#7/Al Jolson (1917) US#4; *Gentlemen Prefer Blondes* Ernest Hare & Billy Jones (1927) US#6, *Girl on the Magazine, The* Harry MacDonough (1916) US#1, *Girl on the Police Gazette, The* Russ Morgan (1937) US#20, *Girl That I Marry, The* Frank Sinatra (1946) US#11/Eddy Howard (1947) US#23; *Girls of My Dreams, The* Cliff Edwards (1920) US#5, *God Bless America* Bing Crosby (1939) US#17/Kate Smith (1939) US#10, re-issued (1940) US#5, re-issued (1942) US#23; *Goodbye, France* Nora Bayes (1919) US#3/Peerless Quartet (1919) US#9; *Hand That Rocked the Cradle Rules My Heart, The* John Steel (1920) US#7, *He Ain't Got Rhythm* Benny Goodman (1937) US#20, *He's a Devil in His Own Home Town* [ii] Eddie Morton (1914) US#8/Billy Murray (1914) US#2; *He's a Rag Picker* Peerless Quartet (1915) US#3, *Heat Wave* Meyer Davis (1933) US#17/Glen Gray (1933) US#10/Ethel Waters (1933) US#7; *Home Again Blues* Frank Crumit (1921) US#10/Original Dixieland Jazz Band (1921) US#2/Aileen Stanley (1921) US#6; *Homesick* Nora Bayes (1923) US#5, *Homework* Jo Stafford (1949) US#11, *How About Me?* Fred Waring's Pennsylvanians (1929) US#14, *How Deep Is the Ocean? (How High Is the Sky?)* Benny Goodman (1945) US#19/Guy Lombardo (1932) US#4/Ethel Merman (1932) US#14/Rudy Vallee (1932) US#7/Paul Whiteman (1932) US#5/Toni Fisher (1960) US#95; *How Many Times?* Ernest Hare & Billy Jones (1926) US#15/Benny Krueger (1926) US#3; *I Can't Do Without You* Fred Waring's Pennsylvanians (1928) US#5, *I Can't Remember* Eddy Duchin (1933) US#15, *I Got the Sun in the Morning* Les Brown (1946) US#10/Artie Shaw (1946) US#17; *I Left My Heart at the Stage Door Canteen* Sammy Kaye (1942) US#3/Charlie Spivak (1942) US#8; *I Love a Piano* Billy Murray (1916) US#1, *I Never Had a Chance* Eddy Duchin (1934) US#3/Glen Gray (1934) US#6; *I Never Knew* Henry Burr & John Meyer (1920) US#12, *I Poured My Heart Into a Song* Jimmy Dorsey (1939) US#13/Artie Shaw (1939) US#4; *I Threw a Kiss in the Ocean* Jimmy Dorsey (1942) US#12/Kate Smith (1942) US#10; *I Used to Be Color Blind* Fred Astaire (1938) US#8, *I Want to Go Back to Michigan (Down on the Farm)* Elida Morris (1914) US#3/Morton Harvey (1915) US#8; *I'd Rather Lead a Band* Fred Astaire (1936) US#12, *I'll See You in C-U-B-A* Jack Kaufman (1920) US#14/Ted Lewis (1920) US#4/Billy Murray (1920) US#3;

I'll Take You Back to Italy Ada Jones & Billy Murray (1918) US#9, *I'm Afraid, Pretty Maid, I'm Afraid* Ada Jones & Walter Van Brunt (1912) US#3, *I'm Getting Tired So I Can Sleep* Jimmy Dorsey (1943) US#19, *I'm Going Back to Dixie* Arthur Collins & Byron Harlan (1912) US#8, *I'm Gonna Pin My Medal on the Girl I Left Behind* Peerless Quartet (1918) US#4, *I'm on My Way Home* "Whispering" Jack Smith (1927) US#13, *I'm Putting All My Eggs in One Basket* Fred Astaire (1936) US#1/Jan Garber (1936) US#14/Guy Lombardo (1936) US#14; *I'm Sorry for Myself* Guy Lombardo (1939) US#7, *I've Got My Captain Working for Me Now* Billy Murray (1919) US#6/Al Jolson (1920) US#1; *I've Got My Love to Keep Me Warm* Glen Gray (1937) US#18/Billie Holiday (1937) US#4/Ray Noble (1937) US#3/Red Norvo (1937) US#11/Les Brown (1949) g US#1/Art Lund (1949) US#22/Mills Brothers (1949) US#9/Starlighters (1949) US#26; *If I Had My Way* Peerless Quaret (1914) US#3/Bunny Berigan (1936) US#19/Glen Gray (1939) US#20; *If You Believe* Johnnie Ray (1955) UK#7, *In My Harem* Walter Van Brunt (1913) US#6, *International Rag, The* Arthur Collins & Byron Harlan (1914) US#3, *Is There Anything Else I Can Do for You?* Ada Jones (1910) US#9, *Isn't This a Lovely Day?* Fred Astaire (1935) US#3/Phil Ohman (1935) US#16; *It All Belongs to Me* Ruth Etting (1927) US#17, *It Only Happens When I Dance with You* Frank Sinatra (1948) US#19, *It's a Lovely Day Today* Doris Day (1951) US#30, *Just a Blue Serge Suit* Vaughn Monroe (1945) US#17, *Just a Little Longer* Fred Rich (1927) US#18/Phil Spitalny (1927) US#14/Rudy Vallee (1930) US#8; *Just One Way to Say I Love You* Perry Como (1949) US#23/Jo Stafford (1949) US#12; *Kate (Have I Come Home Too Early, Too Late?)* Ray Bloch (1947) US#11/Eddy Howard (1947) US#7; *Kiss Me, My Honey, Kiss Me* Elida Morris (1910) US#4/Ada Jones & Billy Murray (1911) US#5; *Lady of the Evening* John Steel (1923) US#4/Paul Whiteman (1923) US#11; *Lazy* Brox Sisters (1924) US#12/Al Jolson (1924) US#4/Blossom Seeley (1924) US#9/Paul Whiteman (1924) US#9; *Learn to Do the Strut* Vincent Lopez (1924) US#9, *Let Me Sing and I'm Happy* Al Jolson (1930) UK#2, *Let Yourself Go* Fred Astaire (1936) US#2, *Let's All Be Americans Now* American Quartet (1917) US#6, *Let's Face the Music and Dance* Fred Astaire (1936) US#5/Ted Fio Rito (1936) US#9/Nat "King" Cole (1994) UK#30; *Let's Have Another Cup of O' Coffee* Fred Waring's Pennsylvanians (1932) US#5, *Let's Start the New Year Right* Bing Crosby (1943) US#18, *Let's Take an Old-Fashioned Walk* Perry Como (1949) US#15/Doris Day (1949) US#17/Frank Sinatra (1949) US#17; *Listening* Grace Moore (1925) US#5, *Little Bungalow* Roger Wolfe Kahn (1926) US#8, *Little Butterfly* John Steel (1924) US#4, *Little Things in Life, The* Ted Wallace (1930) US#11/

Gus Arnheim (1931) US#4; *Louisiana Purchase* Ray Noble (1940) US#26, *Love and the Weather* Jo Stafford (1947) US#25, *Mandy* Shannon Four (1919) US#4/Van & Schenck (1919) US#2/Ben Selvin (1920) US#5; *Marie* Franklyn Bauer (1929) US#15/Nat Shilkret (1929) US#9/Rudy Vallee (1929) US#2/Tommy Dorsey (1937) g US#1, re-issued (1938) US#16/Four Tunes (1953) US#13/Bachelors (1965) US#15 UK#9; *Maybe It's Because I Love You Too Much* Guy Lombardo (1933) US#11/Leo Reisman (1933) US#17/Rudy Vallee (1933) US#6; *Me!* Ben Bernie (1931) US#11, *Minstrel Parade, The* Arthur Collins & Byron Harlan (1915) US#9, *My Bird of Paradise* Peerless Quartet (1915) US#1, *My Walking Stick* Tommy Dorsey (1938) US#8/Ray Noble (1938) US#17; *My Wife's Gone to the Country (Hurrah! Hurrah!)* Arthur Collins & Byron Harlan (1909) US#4/Bob Roberts (1909) US#7; *Night Is Filled with Music, The* Will Hudson (1938) US#11/Hal Kemp (1938) US#13; *No Strings* Fred Astaire (1935) US#9, *Nobody Knows (And Nobody Seems to Care)* Irving & Jack Kaufman (1920) US#4, *Now It Can Be Told* Bing Crosby (1938) US#7/Tommy Dorsey (1938) US#2/Tony Martin (1938) US#13; *Oh, How I Hate to Get Up in the Morning* Arthur Fields (1918) US#1/Irving Kaufman (1918) US#5; *Oh, That Beautiful Rag* [iii] Arthur Collins (1910) US#3, *One O'Clock in the Morning* Walter Van Brunt (1912) US#7, *Ooh! Maybe It's You* Ben Selvin (1927) US#17, *Orange Grove in California, An* John Steel (1924) US#11/Paul Whiteman (1924) US#5; *Pack Up Your Sins (And Go to the Devil)* Emil Coleman (1923) US#13, *Piccolino, The* Fred Astaire (1935) US#10/Ray Noble (1935) US#14; *Play a Simple Melody* Walter Van Brunt & Mary Carson (1915) US#8/Billy Murray & Elsie Baker (1916) US#4/Bing & Gary Crosby (1950) g US#2/Georgia Gibbs & Bob Crosby (1950) US#25/Phil Harris (1950) US#30/Jo Stafford (1950) US#18; *Porcelain Maid* Paul Specht (1923) US#14, *Pretty Girl Is Like a Melody, A* Sam Ash (1919) US#7/John Steel (1919) US#1; *Pullman Porter's Parade, The* Al Jolson (1913) US#5, *Puttin' on the Ritz* Earl Burtnett (1930) US#17/Leo Reisman (1930) US#20/Harry Richman (1930) US#1/Taco (1983) g US#4; *Ragtime Jockey Man, The* Maurice Burkhardt & Peerless Quartet (1912) US#6, *Ragtime Mocking Bird, The* Dolly Connolly (1912) US#7, *Ragtime Violin, The* American Quartet (1912) US#3, *Reaching for the Moon* Ruth Etting (1931) US#6, *Remember* Isham Jones (1925) US#1/Jean Goldkette (1925) US#6/Cliff Edwards (1926) US#10; *Roses of Yesterday* Fred Waring's Pennsylvanians (1928) US#7, *Russian Lullaby* Franklyn Baur (1927) US#12/Jesse Crawford (1927) US#13/Ernie Golden (1927) US#14/Roger Wolfe Kahn (1927) US#1/Revelers (1927) US#17/Bunny Berigan (1938) US#19; *Sadie Salome (Go Home)* Edward M.

Favor (1909) US#8/Bob Roberts (1910) US#5; *San Francisco Bound* Peerless Quartet (1913) US#10, *Say It Isn't So* Connee Boswell (1932) US#10/George Olsen (1932) US#1/Ozzie Nelson (1932) US#8/Rudy Vallee (1932) US#12/Aretha Franklin (1963) US#113; *Say It with Music* Ben Selvin (1921) US#6/Paul Whiteman (1921) US#1/Columbians (1922) US#12/John Steel (1922) US#11; *School House Blues* Brox Sisters (1922) US#11, *Shaking the Blues Away* Ruth Etting (1927) US#4/Paul Whiteman (1927) US#14; *Sisters* Rosemary Clooney & Betty Clooney (1954) US#30, *Sittin' in the Sun (Countin' My Money)* Louis Armstrong (1953) US#30, *Slummin' on Park Avenue* Fletcher Henderson (1937) US#15/Jimmie Lunceford (1937) US#18/Red Norvo (1937) US#8; *Smile and Show Your Dimple* Sam Ash (1918) US#10, *Snooky Ookums* Arthur Collins & Byron Harlan (1913) US#4/Billy Murray (1913) US#4; *So Help Me* Emil Coleman (1934) US#13, *Soft Lights and Sweet Music* Fred Waring's Pennsylvanians (1932) US#8, *Some Sunny Day* Marion Harris (1922) US#3/Paul Whiteman (1922) US#5; *Someone Else May Be There When I'm Gone* Al Jolson (1917) US#2, *Song Is Ended, The* Ruth Etting (1928) US#7/"Whispering" Jack Smith (1928) US#14/Nellie Lutcher (1948) R&B#3 US#23; *Spanish Love* Andrea Sarto (1911) US#9, *Stop, Stop, Stop (Come Over and Love Me Some More)* Elida Morris (1911) US#4, *Sunshine* Nick Lucas (1928) US#12/Paul Whiteman (1928) US#6; *Sweet Italian Love* Byron G. Harlan (1910) US#4/Billy Murray (1910) US#8; *Syncopated Walk, The* Prince's Orchestra (1915) US#9, *Tell Her in the Springtime* Grace Moore (1925) US#8/Paul Whiteman (1925) US#8; *Tell Me, Little Gypsy* Art Hickman (1920) US#2/John Steel (1920) US#3; *That Hula Hula* Charles King & Elizabeth Brice (1916) US#10, *That International Rag* Prince's Orchestra (1914) US#8/Victor Military Band (1914) US#6; *That Mesmerizing Mendelssohn Tune* [ii] Arthur Collins & Byron Harlan (1910) US#2, *That Mysterious Rag* [iii] American Quartet (1912) US#6/Arthur Collins & Albert Campbell (1912) US#5; *That's a Good Girl* Ben Selvin (1927) US#17, *There's a Girl in Havana* [i] Lyric Quartet (1912) US#6, *There's No Business Like Show Business* Bing Crosby, Dick Haymes & Andrews Sisters (1947) US#25, *They Call It Dancing* Paul Whiteman (1922) US#5, *They Say It's Wonderful* Perry Como (1946) US#4/Bing Crosby (1946) US#12/Ethel Merman (1946) US#20/Andy Russell (1946) US#10/Frank Sinatra (1946) US#2; *They Were All Out of Step But Jim* Billy Murray (1918) US#3, *This Is the Army, Mr. Jones* Hoarce Heidt (1943) US#20/Hal McIntyre (1942) US#18, re-entry (1943) US#19; *This Year's Kisses* Shep Fields (1937) US#5/Benny Goodman (1937) US#1/Hal Kemp (1937) US#1/Teddy Wilson with Billie Holiday (1937) US#8; *To My Mammy* Al

Jolson (1930) US#7, *Together, We Two* Vaughn De-leath & Ed Smalle (1928) US#13/Ruth Etting (1928) US#12/Isham Jones (1928) US#5; *Top Hat, White Tie and Tails* Fred Astaire (1935) US#2/Ray Noble (1935) US#4; *Waiting at the End of the Road* Paul Whiteman (1929) US#12, *Waltz of Long Ago* Paul Specht (1924) US#6, *Was There Ever a Pal Like You?* Henry Burr (1920) US#10, *We Saw the Sea* Fred As-taire (1936) US#15, *What Does It Matter Now?* Nat Shilkret (1927) US#10, *What'll I Do?* Henry Burr & Marcia Freer (1924) US#4/Carl Fenton (1924) US#10/Lewis James (1924) US#6/Irving Kaufman (1924) US#11/Vincent Lopez (1924) US#8/Paul Whiteman (1924) US#1/Nat "King" Cole (1948) US#22/Frank Sinatra (1948) US#23/Johnny Tillot-son (1962) US#106; *When I Get Back to the U.S.A.* Billy Murray (1916) US#9, *When I Leave the World Behind* Sam Ash (1915) US#9/Henry Burr (1915) US#5/Russ Conway in *More and More Party Pops* (1959) UK#5; *When I Lost You* Henry Burr (1913) US#1/Manuel Romain (1913) US#2; *When My Baby Smiles at Me* Henry Burr (1920) US#11/Ted Lewis (1920) US#1, re-issued (1938) US#18/Billy Murray & Gladys Rice (1920) US#8; *When My Dreams Come True* Paul Whiteman (1929) US#10, *When That Man Is Dead and Gone* Glenn Miller (1941) US#23, *When the Midnight Choo-Choo Leaves for Alabam'* Arthur Collins & Byron Harlan (1913) US#1/Victor Military Band (1913) US#9; *When Winter Comes* Artie Shaw (1939) US#6, *When You Drop Off at Cairo, Illinois* Billy Murray (1916) US#10, *When You Walked Out, Someone Else Walked Right In* Frank Crumit (1923) US#10/Isham Jones (1923) US#4; *When You're Down in Louisville* Anna Chandler (1916) US#8, *When You're in Town* Henry Burr & Elise Stevenson (1911) US#6, *Where Is the Song of Songs for Me?* Franklyn Baur (1929) US#19, *White Christmas* Bing Crosby (1942) g R&B#1 US#1, re-issued (1943) US#5, re-issued (1944) R&B#9 US#6, re-issued (1945) US#1, re-issued (1947) US#1, re-issued (1948) US#3, re-issued (1949) US#6, re-issued (1950) US#5, re-is-sued (1951) US#13, re-issued (1952) US#13, re-issued (1953) US#21, re-issued (1954) US#21, re-issued (1955) US#7, re-issued (1957) US#34, re-issued (1960) US#26, re-issued (1961) US#12, re-issued (1962) US#38, re-issued (1977) UK#5, re-issued (1985) UK#69/Gordon Jenkins (1942) US#15/ Freddy Martin (1942) US#24, re-issued (1945) US#16/Charlie Spivak (1942) US#12/Frank Sinatra (1944) g US#7, re-issued (1945) US#5, re-issued (1946) US#6/Jo Stafford (1946) US#9/Perry Como (1947) US#23/Eddy Howard (1947) US#21/Ravens (1949) R&B#9/Ernest Tubb (1949) C&W#7/Man-tovani (1952) US#23 UK#6/Drifters (1954) R&B#2 US#80, re-issued (1955) US#5, re-issued (1956) US#12/Pat Boone (1957) UK#29/Freddie Starr

(1975) UK#41/Darts (1980) UK#48/Jim Davidson (1980) UK#52/Keith Harris & Orville (1985) UK#40/Max Bygraves (1989) UK#71; *Who Do You Love, I Hope* Elliot Lawrence (1946) US#6, *With You* Guy Lombardo (1930) US#17, *Woodman, Woodman, Spare That Tree* [i] Bob Roberts (1911) US#2/Bert Williams (1913) US#2; *Yam, The* Fred Astaire (1938) US#10, *You Can't Brush Me Off* Dinah Shore & Dick Todd (1940) US#24, *(You Can't Lose the Blues with) Colors* Rosemary Clooney (1957), *You Forgot to Re-member* Henry Burr (1926) US#5/John McCormack (1926) US#11; *You Keep Coming Back Like a Song* Bing Crosby (1946) US#12/Dinah Shore (1946) US#5/Jo Stafford (1946) US#11; *You'd Be Surprised* All-Star Trio (1920) US#8/Eddie Cantor (1920) US#3/Irving Kaufman (1920) US#8/Orrin Tucker (1940) US#5/Johnnie Ray (1954) US#25; *You're Just in Love* Rosemary Clooney (1951) US#24/Perry Como (1951) US#5/Ethel Merman & Dick Haymes (1951) US#30; *You're Laughing at Me* Wayne King (1937) US#15/Fats Waller (1937) US#4; *You're Lonely and I'm Lonely* Tommy Dorsey (1940) US#9, *You've Got Your Mother's Big Blue Eyes* Marguerite Dunlap (1914) US#2. Co-writers: [i] E. Ray Goetz/Ted Sny-der (d. 1881; d. 1965), [ii] Felix Mendelssohn (b. Feb-ruary 3, 1809, Hamburg; d. November 4, 1847, Leipzig, both Germany), [iii] Ted Snyder.

77. BERNS, Bert

(b. Bertram R. Berns, De-cember 31, 1929; d. December 1, 1967, both New York, NY) R&B-pop producer. An energetic and creative pioneer during rock and roll's formative years, who cunningly merged black R&B and white pop with Cuban tinged melodies, often utilizing dis-tinctive, unconventional, yet strangely effective chord progressions. Berns graduated from song-plugger and record salesman to producer and record label owner during the course of his career, and he was never without a sense of humor in the highly competitive music industry, noting when the Beatles became popular in America during the early 1960s, "These boys have genius. They may be the ruin of us all." Berns occasionally composed under the pseudonyms Bert Russell and Russell Byrd, and much of his best work was created at Atlantic Records for the R&B vocalist Solomon Burke. Berns' enthusiastic and influential career was cut short, when he died at the age of thirty-eight from a heart attack. HIT VER-SIONS: *Am I Grooving You* Freddie Scott (1967) R&B#25 US#71/Z.Z. Hill (1974) R&B#84; *Are You Lonely for Me* Freddie Scott (1966) R&B#1 US#39, *Cry Baby* [v] Garnet Mimms & the Enchanters (1963) g R&B#1 US#4/Janis Joplin (1971) US#42; *Cry to Me* Solomon Burke (1962) R&B#5 US#44/Betty Harris (1963) R&B#10 US#23, re-issued (1969) R&B#44/ Pretty Things (1965) UK#28/Freddie Scott (1967)

R&B#40 US#70/Loleatta Holloway (1975) R&B#10 US#68; *Down in the Valley* Solomon Burke (1962) R&B#20 US#71, *Everybody Needs Somebody to Love* [i] Solomon Burke (1964) US#58/Wilson Pickett (1967) R&B#19 US#29/Blues Brothers (1989) UK#12; *Hang on Sloopy/My Girl Sloopy* [ii] Vibrations (1964) US#26/Little Caesar & the Consuls (1964) US#50/McCoys (1965) g US#1 UK#5/Ramsey Lewis Trio (1965) R&B#6 US#11/Nancy Ames as *Friends and Lovers Forever* (1966) US#123/Lettermen (1970) US#93/Rick Derringer (1975) US#94/Sandpipers (1976) UK#32; *He Ain't Give You None* Freddie Scott (1967) R&B#24 US#100, *He's Just a Playboy* Drifters (1964) US#115, *Heart Be Still* [v] Lorraine Ellison (1967) R&B#43/Carl Graves (1976) R&B#26; *Here Comes the Night* Lulu (1964) UK#50/Them (1965) US#24 UK#2; *I Don't Want to Go on Without You* Moody Blues (1965) UK#33, *I Want Candy* [iii] Strangeloves (1965) US#11/Bow Wow Wow (1982) US#62; *I'll Take Good Care of You* [v] Garnet Mimms & the Enchanters (1966) US#15, *I'm Gonna Run Away from You* Tammi Lynn (1971) UK#4, re-issued (1975) UK#36; *If I Didn't Have a Dime (To Play the Jukebox)* Gene Pitney (1962) US#58, *If You Need Me* Solomon Burke (1963) R&B#2 US#37/Wilson Pickett (1963) R&B#30 US#64; *Killer Joe* Rocky Fellers (1963) US#16, *Little Bit of Soap, A* Jarmels (1961) R&B#7 US#12/Garnet Mimms (1965) US#95/Exciters (1966) US#58/Paul Davis (1970) US#52/Showaddywaddy (1978) UK#5/Nigel Olsson (1979) US#34; *Make Me Your Baby* Barbara Lewis (1965) R&B#9 US#11, *Night Time* Strangeloves (1966) US#30, *One Way Love* [v] Drifters (1964) R&B#56 US#56/Cliff Bennett & the Rebel Rousers (1964) UK#9; *Piece of My Heart* [v] Erma Franklin (1967) R&B#10 US#62, re-issued (1992) UK#9/Big Brother & the Holding Company (1968) US#12/Etta James (1978) R&B#93/Sammy Hagar (1982) US#73/John Hartford (1984) C&W#81/Elkie Brooks on B-side of *We've Got Tonight* (1987) UK#69/Faith Hill (1994) C&W#1 US#116; *Price, The* Solomon Burke (1964) US#57, *Tell Her/Him* Exciters (1963) R&B#5 US#4 UK#46/Billie Davis (1963) UK#10/Drew-Vels (1964) US#90/Patti Drew (1967) R&B#22 US#85/Hello (1974) UK#6/Pia Zadora (1979) C&W#98/Kenny Loggins (1989) US#76; *Time Is on My Side* [v] Moody Blues on B-side of *I Don't Want to Go on Without You* (1965) UK#33/Rolling Stones (1982) UK#62; *Twist and Shout* [iv] Isley Brothers (1962) R&B#2 US#17 UK#42/Brian Poole & the Tremeloes (1963) UK#5/Beatles (1986) US#89, also on B-side of *Back in the U.S.S.R.* (1976) UK#19/D.B.M. on *DiscoBeatlemania* (1977) UK#45/Elton John on B-side of *Cry to Heaven* (1986) UK#47/Salt-N-Peppa (1988) g US#38 UK#19/Chaka Demus & Pers (1992) UK#1; *Twistin' with Linda* Isley Brothers (1962) US#54. Co-writ-ers: [i] Solomon Burke (b. 1936, Philadelphia, PA)/Jerry Wexler (January 10, 1917, New York, NY), [ii] Wes Farrell, [iii] Bob Feldman/Jerry Goldstein/Richard Gottener, [iv] Philip Medley, [v] Jerry Ragovoy.

78. BERNSTEIN, Leonard (b. August 25, 1918, Lawrence, MS; d. October 14, 1990) Pianist, composer, arranger and conductor. Although primarily a classical conductor, Bernstein also scored a number of films, including "On the Waterfront" (1954), and was successful on Broadway with "On the Town" (1944), "Wonderful Town" (1953) and "Candide" (1956). His best known non-classical work remains "West Side Story" (1959), which he co-wrote with the lyricist Stephen Sondheim, and which introduced at least half a dozen pop standards, including *I Feel Pretty* [i]. Bernstein died of a heart attack in 1990. ALBUMS: **Peter Pan** oc (1950, Columbia); **Wonderful Town** oc (1953, Decca); **Land of the Pharaohs** ost (1955, EBFMC); **Candide** oc (1956, Columbia); **Trouble in Tahiti** tvst (1958, MGM); **Wonderful Town** tvst (1958), **West Side Story** oc (1958, both Columbia) g US#5 UK#3; **West Side Story** oc (1960, Philips) UK#14; **Bernstein Plays Brubeck Plays Bernstein** (1960) US#13, **West Side Story** ost (1961) p US#1 UK#1, **On the Town** oc (1961), **Mass (From the Liturgy of the Roman Mass)** (1971) US#53, **Candide** oc (1973, all Columbia); **Candide** oc (1982, New World); **West Side Story** sc (1985) US#70 UK#11, **West Side Story-Highlights** sc (1986, both Deutsche Grammophon) UK#72; **West Side Story** sc (1993, IMG) UK#33. HIT VERSIONS: *America* Nice (1968) UK#21, *Maria* [i] Johnny Mathis (1960) US#100, re-issued (1961) US#88/Roger Williams (1961) US#48/George Chakiris (1962) US#110/P.J. Proby (1965) UK#8; *Somewhere* [i] Tymes (1964) US#19/Brothers Four (1965) US#131/P.J. Proby (1965) US#91 UK#6/Len Barry (1966) US#26/Johnny Nash (1966) R&B#35 US#120/Barbra Streisand (1985) US#43; *Tonight* [i] Ferrante & Teicher (1961) US#8/Jay & the Americans (1961) US#120/Shirley Bassey (1962) UK#21; *West Side Encounter-West Side Story (Medley)* Salsoul Orchestra (1978) R&B#68. Co-writer: [i] Stephen Sondheim.

79. BERRY, Chuck (b. Charles Edward Anderson Berry, October 18, 1926, St. Louis, MI) R&B guitarist and vocalist. One of the principal architects of contemporary pop music, and an influence on nearly every rock guitarist that came after him. Berry has created one of the best known and most recorded song catalogues since the mid-1950s, and his material is as literate and cheeky as it is succinct and humorous. Peppered with irony and charm, Berry's songs feature teenage characters that are perpetually unable to conform to parental rules. His art is his simplicity, from his unforgettable four-bar guitar introductions to his astute observations about the changing American youth culture of the late 1950s and early 1960s. As a teenager, Berry listened to boogie woogie and swing while teaching himself the guitar. In the early 1950s, he worked as a hairdresser while performing at nights in the Johnnie Johnson Trio, a group that evolved into the Chuck Berry Combo. In 1955, Berry signed to Chess Records, where his first session for the label included a version of his own composition *Ida Red*, which, retitled *Maybelline* [i], became a fast, blues based country-rockabilly number, quite unlike anything anybody had ever heard before. Berry was one of the first pop stars to appear in movies, featuring in "You Can't Catch Me" and "Rock, Rock, Rock" (both, 1956). He became the master of the three minute single, none more so than the petulant *Rock and Roll Music*, and *Johnny B. Goode*, which opened with arguably the best known guitar riff in rock, a recording of which is one of the cultural artifacts on the Voyagers I and II spacecraft. A significant influence on the Rolling Stones, the Beatles and the Beach Boys, in 1988, Berry appeared in the autobiographical film "Hail! Hail! Rock and Roll." CHART SINGLES: *Maybelline* [i] (1955) R&B#1 US#5, *Wee Wee Hours* (1955) R&B#10, *Thirty Days (To Come Back Home)* (1955) R&B#8, *No Money Down* (1956) R&B#8, *Roll Over Beethoven* (1956) R&B#2 UK#29, *Too Much Monkey Business* (1956) R&B#4, *Brown-Eyed Handsome Man* (1956) R&B#5, *School Days* (1957) g R&B#1 US#3 UK#24, *Oh Baby Doll* (1957) R&B#12 US#57, *Rock and Roll Music* (1957) R&B#6 US#8, *Sweet Little Sixteen* (1958) g R&B#1 US#2 UK#16, *Beautiful Delilah* (1958) US#81, *Johnny B. Goode* (1958) R&B#2 US#8, *Carol* (1958) R&B#9 US#18, *Sweet Little Rock and Roller* (1958) R&B#13 US#47, *Almost Grown* (1959) R&B#3 US#32, *Anthony Boy* (1959) US#60, *Little Queenie* (1959) US#80, *Jo Jo Gunne* (1959) US#83, *Merry Christmas Baby* (1959) US#71, *Run Rudolph Run* (1959) US#69, reissued (1963) UK#36; *Back in the U.S.A.* (1959) US#16 UK#37, *Broken Arrow* (1960) US#108, *Too Pooped to Pop* (1960) US#18 UK#42, *Let It Rock* (1960) US#64, *Bye Bye Johnny* (1961) US#64, *Jaguar and the Thunderbird* (1961) US#109, *Go Go Go* (1963) UK#38, *Memphis, Tennessee* (1963) US#87, *Let It Rock/Memphis, Tennessee* (1963) UK#6, *Dear Dad* (1963) US#95, *Nadine (Is It You?)* (1964) US#23 UK#27, *No Particular Place to Go* (1964) US#10 UK#3, *You Never Can Tell* (1964) US#14 UK#23, *Little Marie* (1964) US#54, *Promised Land* (1964) US#41 UK#26, *My Ding-a-Ling* (1972) g R&B#42 US#1 UK#1, *Reelin' and Rockin'* (1972) US#27

UK#18. ALBUMS: **Rock, Rock, Rock** (1956), **After School Session** (1957), **One Dozen Berrys** (1958), **Chuck Berry Is on Top** (1959), **Rockin' at the Hops** (1959), **New Juke Box Hits** (1963), **Twist** (1963), **Chuck Berry on Stage** (1963, all Chess) US#29 UK#6; **Chuck and Bo*** (1963, Pye); **Two Great Guitars*** (1964, Checker); **St. Louis to Liverpool** (1964) US#124, **Chuck Berry in London** (1965), **Fresh Berrys** (1966, all Chess); **Chuck Berry in Memphis** (1967), **Live at the Fillmore** (1967), **Concerto in B. Goode** (1969, all Mercury); **Back Home** (1970), **San Francisco Dues** (1971), **The London Chuck Berry Sessions** (1972, all Chess) g US#8; **St. Louis to Frisco to Memphis** (1972, Mercury) US#185; **Bio** (1973) US#175, **Chuck Berry** (1975, both Chess); **Live in Concert** (1978, Magnum); **Rock It** (1979, Atco); **Hail! Hail! Rock 'n' Roll** (1987, Chess); **American Heartbeat** (1994, Virgin). COMPILATIONS: **Chuck Berry** (1963, Pye) UK#12; **More Chuck Berry** (1963) UK#9, **Greatest Hits** (1964, both Chess) US#34; **His Latest and Greatest** (1964) UK#8, **You Never Can Tell** (1964, both Pye) UK#18; **Golden Decade** (1967) US#72, **Golden Decade, Volume 2** (1973) US#110, **Motorvatin'** (1977, all Chess) UK#7; **Poet of Rock 'n' Roll** (1994, Charly). HIT VERSIONS: *Around and Around* David Bowie on B-side of *Drive-in Saturday* (1973) UK#3, *Back in the U.S.A.* Beach Boys as *Surfin' U.S.A.* (1963) g R&B#20 US#3 UK#34, also in *Beach Boys Medley* (1981) US#47/Carmol Taylor (1975) C&W#48/Linda Ronstadt (1978) C&W#41 US#16/Leif Garrett (1977) US#20; *Brown-Eyed Handsome Man* Buddy Holly (1963) US#113 UK#3/Waylon Jennings (1969) C&W#3; *Bye Bye Johnny* Bruce Springsteen on B-side of *I'm on Fire* (1985) US#6, *Carol* Tommy Roe (1969) US#61, *Come On* Rolling Stones (1963) UK#21, *Forty Days* Ronnie Hawkins (1959) US#45, *Johnny B. Goode* Dion (1964) US#71/Surfer Girls as *Draggin' Wagon* (1964) US#134/Buck Owens & His Buckaroos (1969) C&W#1 US#114/Johnnie Winter (1970) US#92/Jimi Hendrix (1972) UK#35/Peter Tosh (1983) US#84 UK#48/Judas Priest (1988) UK#64; *Little Queenie* Bill Black's Combo (1964) US#73/Mel McDaniel as *Let It Roll* (1985) C&W#6; *Let It Rock* Rolling Stones on B-side of *Brown Sugar* (1971) UK#2, *Maybelline* [i] Jim Lowe (1955) R&B#13/Marty Robbins (1955) C&W#9/Johnny Rivers (1964) US#12/George Jones & Johnny Paycheck (1978) C&W#7; *Memphis, Tennessee* Lonnie Mack (1963) R&B#4 US#5 UK#47/Dave Berry (1963) UK#19/Johnny Rivers (1964) US#2/Dave Clark Five in medley *Good Old Rock 'n' Roll* (1969) UK#7/Fred Knoblock (1981) C&W#10 US#102; *Nadine (Is It You)* Coronets (1953) R&B#3/Dells on B-side of *Open Up My Heart* (1970) R&B#5 US#51/Freddy Weller (1979) C&W#40; *Promised*

Land Freddie Weller (1970) C&W#3 US#125/Elvis Presley (1975) US#14 UK#9; *Reelin' and Rockin'* Dave Clark Five (1965) UK#24, also in medley *Good Old Rock 'n' Roll* (1969) UK#7; *Rock and Roll Music* Dave Clark Five in medley *More Good Old Rock 'n' Roll* (1969) UK#34/Frost (1970) US#105/Humble Pie (1975) US#105/Beach Boys (1976) US#5 UK#36; *Roll Over Beethoven* Velaires (1961) US#51/Beatles (1964) US#68, also on *Four By the Beatles EP* (1964) US#92/Jerry Lee Lewis & Linda Gail Lewis (1971) C&W#71/Electric Light Orchestra (1973) US#42 UK#6/Narvel Felts (1982) C&W#64; *School Day (Ring! Ring! Goes the Bell)* Don Lang (1957) UK#26, *Sweet Little Rock and Roller* Showaddywaddy (1979) UK#15, *Sweet Little Sixteen* Jerry Lee Lewis (1962) US#95 UK#38/Dave Clark Five in medley *Good Old Rock 'n' Roll* (1969) UK#7; *Too Much Monkey Business* Freddie Weller (1973) C&W#8/Milli Vanilli on B-side of *Baby, Don't Forget My Number* (1988) US#1 UK#16; *Tulane* Steve Gibbons Band (1977) UK#12; *You Never Can Tell* Emmylou Harris (1977) C&W#6. With: * Bo Diddley. Co-writers: [i] Russ Fratto/Alan Freed (b. December 15, 1922, Johnstown PA: d. January 20, 1965, Palm Springs, FL).

80. BERRY, Jan (b. April 3, 1941, Los Angeles, CA) Pop vocalist. One half, with Dean Torrence (b. March 10, 1940), of the American vocal duo Jan and Dean, which popularized California surf music before the Beach Boys, charting twenty-four singles between 1959–1966. Berry co-wrote many of Jan and Dean's best known hits before suffering brain damage and partial paralysis in a 1966 automobile accident. CHART COMPOSITIONS: *Surf City* [vi] (1963) R&B#3 US#1 UK#26, *Honolulu Luly* [iii] (1963) US#11, *Drag City* [iv] (1964) US#10, *Dead Man's Curve* [ii] (1964) US#8, *The New Girl in School* (1964) US#37, *Ride the Wild Surf* (1964) US#16, *You Really Know How to Hurt a Guy* [i] (1965) US#27. ALBUMS: **Jan and Dean Take Linda Surfin'** (1963) US#71, **Surf City and Other Swingin' Cities** (1963) US#32, **Drag City** (1964) US#22, **Dead Man's Curve/The New Girl in School** (1964) US#80, **The Little Old Lady from Pasadena** (1964) US#40, **Ride the Wild Surf** ost (1964) US#66, **Command Performance/Live in Person** (1965) US#33, **Folk 'n' Roll** (1966) US#145, **Jan and Dean Meet Batman** (1966), **Filet of Soul** (1966)) US#127, **One Summer Night-Live** (1982, all Liberty). COMPILATIONS: **Golden Hits** (1962), **Golden Hits, Volume 2** (1965) US#107, **Drag City** (1966, all Liberty); **The Jan and Dean Story** (1980, K-Tel) UK#67; **Surf City-The Best of Jan and Dean** (1995, EMI); **Teen Suite, 1958–1962** (1995, Varese Sarabande). HIT VERSION: *I Adore Him* [v] Angels (1963) US#25. Co-writers: [i] Roger Christian/Jill

Gibson, [ii] Roger Christian/Artie Kornfeld, [iii] Roger Christian/Spunky, [iv] Roger Christian/Brian Wilson, [v] Artie Kornfeld, [vi] Brian Wilson.

81. BERRY, Richard (b. April 11, 1935, Extension, LA; d. January 23, 1997, Los Angeles, CA) R&B pianist and vocalist. The composer of the rock and roll classic *Louie Louie*, which has been recorded over one thousand two hundred times, and is a song with an entire history of its own, the lyrics of which were once the subject of an investigation by the F.B.I. Berry first performed with the group the Debonairs in the 1940s, which became the Hollywood Bluejays and later the Flairs, before cutting solo sides for the Modern and RPM labels in the late 1950s. As the Pharaohs, Berry scored a regional hit with *Louie Louie* (1956), which, seven years later, became a multi-million seller for the Kingsmen. The influence of the song on the development of rock and roll is inestimable, but it can clearly be heard in the early sounds of groups as diverse as the Rolling Stones and the Clash. ALBUMS: **Richard Berry and the Dreamers** (1963, Crown); **Live from the H.D. Century Restaurant** (1968), **Wild Berry Live** (1968, both Pam); **Get Out of the Car** (1982, Ace); **Louie Louie** (1987, Earth Angel). HIT VERSIONS: *Louie Louie* Kingsmen (1963) US#2 UK#26, re-issued (1966) US#97/Paul Revere & the Raiders (1963) US#103/Sandpipers (1966) US#30/Travis Wammack (1966) US#128/John Belushi (1978) US#89/Motorhead (1978) UK#68/Pretenders (1981) US#110/Fat Boys (1988) US#89 UK#46.

82. BETTIS, John Pop lyricist. A former member, with Richard Carpenter, of the 1960s group Spectrum, who became a highly successful mainstream lyricist in the 1970s. In 1994, Bettis collaborated with Steve Dorff on the musical "Lunch," which was also recorded as **The Stars Sing...** (1994, FLAC). The duo later composed material for the film "Step Lively" (1995). HIT VERSIONS: *As Long as We Got Each Other* [vi] Louise Mandrell & Eric Carmen (1988) C&W#51, *Body Rock* [vii] Maria Vidal (1984) US#48 UK#11, *Can You Stop the Rain* [i] Peabo Bryson (1991) R&B#26, *Crazy for You* [viii] Madonna (1985) US#1 UK#2, re-mixed (1991) UK#2; *Goodbye to Love* [iii] Carpenters (1972) US#7 UK#9, *Heart of the Night* [v] Juice Newton (1982) US#25, *Heartland* [vi] George Strait (1992) C&W#1, *Human Nature* [x] Michael Jackson (1983) R&B#27 US#7, *If You Go Away* [i] NKOTB (1991) UK#9, *Like No Other Night* [ii] .38 Special (1986) US#14, *Love Is a Losing Game* [i] Kirk Whalum (1993) R&B#53, *Once in a While* [vi] Billy Dean (1994) C&W#53, *Only Yesterday* [iii] Carpenters (1975) US#4 UK#7, *Right Here (Human Nature)* [ix] SWV (1993) g

R&B#1 US#2, *Slow Hand* [v] Pointer Sisters (1981) g R&B#7 US#2 UK#10/Del Reeves (1981) C&W#53/ Conway Twitty (1982) C&W#1; *Those Good Old Dreams* [iii] Carpenters (1981) US#63, *Top of the World* [iii] Carpenters (1973) g US#1 UK#5/Lynn Anderson (1973) C&W#2 US#74; *So Hard Livin' Without You* [iv] Airwaves (1978) US#62, *Wild Again* [v] Starship (1988) US#73, *Woman in Me, The* [v] Donna Summer (1983) R&B#30 US#33 UK#62, *Yesterday Once More* [iii] Carpenters (1973) g US#2 UK#2/Moe Bandy (1980) C&W#10/Spinners (1981) R&B#32 US#52/Redd Kross (1994) UK#45. Co-writers: [i] Walter Afanasieff, [ii] Don Barnes/Jeff Carlisi/Jim Vallance, [iii] Richard Carpenter (b. October 15, 1946, New Haven, CT), [iv] K. Charter, [v] Michael Clark, [vi] Stephen Dorff, [vii] Sylvester Levay, [viii] John Lind, [ix] B.A. Morgan/Steve Porcaro (b. September 2, 1957, Hartford, CT), [x] Steve Porcaro. (*See also under* R.C. BANNON, Albert HAMMOND.)

83. BETTS, Richard "Dickey" (b. December 12, 1943, Sarasota, FL) Rock guitarist and vocalist. After the death of Duane Allman, Betts became the key songwriter and lead guitarist in the Allman Brothers Band, his country and bluegrass influenced style significantly altering the direction of the group's sound. He composed its hits *Ramblin' Man* (1973) US#2, *Jessica* (1974) US#65, *Louisiana Lou and Three Card Monty John* (1975) US#67, *Crazy Love* (1979) US#29, *Angeline* [i] (1980) US#58, and *Straight from the Heart* [i] (1981) US#39. Betts has also pursued an intermittent solo career with his groups Great Southern and the Dickey Betts Band. ALBUMS: **Highway Call** (1974, Capricorn) US#19; **Dickey Betts and Great Southern** (1977) US#31, **Atlanta's Burning Down** (1978, both Arista) US#157; **Pattern Disruptive** (1988, Epic) US#187. HIT VERSIONS: *Blue Sky* Joan Baez (1975) US#57, *Ramblin' Man* Jimmy Payne (1973) C&W#79/Gary Stewart (1973) C&W#63; *Your Memory Ain't What It Used to Be* Mickey Gilley (1985) C&W#5. Co-writers: [i] Johnny Cobb/Mike Lawler. (*See also under* Gregg ALLMAN.)

84. BEVERLY, Frankie (b. Philadelphia, PA) R&B keyboard player and vocalist. The principal songwriter and lead vocalist in the soul act Maze, which had evolved from two earlier Beverly groups, the Butlers and Raw Soul. CHART COMPOSITIONS: *While I'm Alone* (1977) R&B#21 US#89, *Lady of Magic* (1977) R&B#13 US#108, *Workin' Together* (1978) R&B#9, *Golden Time of Day/Travelin' Man* (1978) R&B#39, *I Wish You Well* (1978) R&B#61, *Feel That Your Feelin'* (1979) R&B#7 US#67, *Timin'* (1979) R&B#55, *Southern Girl* (1980) R&B#9, *The*

Look in Your Eyes (1980) R&B#29, *Running Away* (1981) R&B#7, *Before I Let Go* (1981) R&B#13, *We Need Love to Live* (1982) R&B#29, *Love Is the Key* (1983) R&B#5 US#80, *Never Let You Down* (1983) R&B#26, *We Are One* (1983) R&B#47, *I Wanna Thank You* (1984) R&B#59, *Back in Stride* (1985) R&B#1 US#88, *Too Many Games* (1985) R&B#5 US#103 UK#36, *I Want to Feel I'm Wanted* (1985) R&B#28, *I Wanna Be with You* (1986) R&B#12 UK#55, *When You Love Someone* (1986) R&B#38, *Joy and Pain* (1989) UK#57, *Laid Back Girl* (1993) R&B#15, *The Morning After* (1993) R&B#19 US#115, *What Goes Up* [i] (1994) R&B#32. ALBUMS: **Maze featuring Frankie Beverly** (1977) g US#52, **Golden Time of Day** (1978) g US#27, **Inspiration** (1979) g US#33, **Joy and Pain** (1980) g US#31, **Live in New Orleans** (1981) g US#34, **We Are One** (1983) US#25 UK#38, **Can't Stop the Love** (1985) g US#45 UK#41, **Live in Los Angeles** (1986, all Capitol) US#92 UK#70; **Silky Soul** (1989) g US#37 UK#43, **Back to Basics** (1993, both Warner Brothers) US#37. HIT VERSIONS: *Joy and Pain* Donna Allen (1989) UK#10/Rob Base & D.J. E-Z Rock (1989) UK#47. Co-writer: [i] A. Beverly.

85. BICKERTON, Wayne Pop producer. Former A&R man and current chairman of the British Performing Rights Society, who achieved considerable success as the co-composer for the 1970s British pop act the Rubettes. HIT VERSIONS: *Don't Do It Baby* [i] Mac & Katie Kissoon (1975) UK#9, *I Can Do It* [i] Rubettes (1975) UK#7, *Juke Box Jive* [i] Rubettes (1974) UK#3, *Like a Butterfly* [i] Mac & Katie Kissoon (1975) UK#18, *Sugar Baby Love* [i] Rubettes (1974) US#37 UK#1, *Sugar Candy Kisses* [i] Mac & Katie Kissoon (1975) UK#3, *Tonight* [i] Rubettes (1974) UK#12, *We Can Do It* [i] Liverpool Football Team (1977) UK#15. Co-writer: [i] Tony Waddington.

86. BISHOP, Stephen (b. 1951, San Diego, CA) Pop guitarist and vocalist. A singer-songwriter who enjoyed a brief period of commercial success in the late 1970s. Bishop learned the guitar at the age of fourteen and played in the 1960s group the Weeds, before working as a staff writer for a variety of publishing houses, where he composed music for such films as "National Lampoon's Animal House" (1978) and "The Blues Brothers" (1980). His material has been recorded by Phoebe Snow, Art Garfunkel, Barbra Streisand, Chaka Khan, and the Four Tops. CHART COMPOSITIONS: *Save It for a Rainy Day* (1977) US#22, *On and On* (1977) US#11, *Everybody Needs Love* (1978) US#32, *Animal House* (1978) US#73, *Send a Little Love My Way. (Like Always)* (1981) US#108, *If Love Takes You Away* (1982)

US#108, *Unfaithfully Yours (Our Love)* (1984) US#87.
ALBUMS: **Careless** (1976) US#34, **Bish** (1978, both
ABC) g US#35; **Red Cab to Manhattan** (1980,
Warner Brothers); **Bowling in Paris** (1989, Atlantic);
Blue Guitars (1996, Foundation). COMPILA-
TION: **Best of Bish** (1991, Rhino). HIT VER-
SIONS: *On and On* Kenny Rankin (1977) US#110/
Aswad (1989) UK#25; *Separate Lives (Theme from
"White Nights")* Phil Collins & Marilyn Martin
(1985) g US#1 UK#4.

87. BLACK, Clint (b. Long Branch, NJ)
C&W guitarist and vocalist. One of the many suc-
cessful rock influenced country artists to emerge in
the 1990s. Black achieved five chart toppers from his
debut album alone. CHART COMPOSITIONS:
Killin' Time [vi] (1989) C&W#1, *Better Man* [vi]
(1989) C&W#1, *Nobody's Home* [vi] (1990) C&W#1,
Where Are You Now [vi] (1991) C&W#1, *This Night-
life* [vi] (1992) C&W#61, *We Tell Ourselves* [vi] (1992)
C&W#2, *Burn One Down* [v] (1992) C&W#4, *A
Bad Goodbye* (1993) C&W#3 US#43, *No Time to
Kill* [vi] (1993) C&W#3, *State of Mind* (1993)
C&W#2 US#102, *Tuckered Out* [vi] (1994) C&W#74,
A Good Run of Bad Luck [vi] (1994) C&W#1, *Half
the Man* [vi] (1994) C&W#9+. ALBUMS: **Killin'
Time** (1989) p US#31, **Put Yourself in My Shoes**
(1990) p US#18, **The Hard Way** (1992) p US#8, **No
Time to Kill** (1993) p US#14, **One Emotion** (1994,
all RCA). ALBUMS: **The Greatest Hits** (1996,
RCA). HIT VERSIONS: *He Would Be Sixteen* [ii]
Michelle Wright (1992) C&W#31, *It's Who You Love*
[i] Don Williams (1992) C&W#73, *My Night to
Howl* [iv] Lorrie Morgan (1994) C&W#31, *You Lie*
[iii] Reba McEntire (1990) C&W#1. Co-writers: [i]
R.M. Bourke/K. Kane, [ii] J. Colucci/A. Roberts,
[iii] B. Fisher/A. Roberts, [iv] R. Giles/A. Roberts,
[v] Frankie Miller/Hayden Nicholas, [vi] Hayden
Nicholas.

88. BLACK, Don (b. June 21, 1938, London, England) Film and stage lyricist. One of
Britain's most consistently successful lyricists. Black
was an usher at the London Palladium before becoming an office boy at the British music paper New
Musical Express in the 1950s. He performed as a
music hall stand-up comic and worked as a Denmark Street song-plugger, before writing his own
lyrics. Black's first recorded song was *April Fool* [vi]
by Matt Monroe (1964), whom he managed for
fifteen years after 1970, and who recorded the album
Matt Monroe Sings Don Black (1990, EMI). Black
has contributed songs to over one hundred films, including a selection of James Bond movies, and has
also worked on such stage musicals as "Maybe That's
Your Problem" (1971), "Billy" (1974) and "Budgie"

(1988). In 1990, Black became vice-president of the
British Academy of Songwriters, Composers and Au-
thors. ALBUM: **Off the Wall** (1992). HIT VER-
SIONS: *Always There* [v] Marti Webb (1986)
UK#13, *Anyone Can Fall in Love* [v] Anita Dobson
(1986) UK#4, *Ben* [vii] Michael Jackson (1972) US#1
UK#7/Marti Webb (1985) UK#5/Toni Warne (1987)
UK#50; *Best of Both Worlds* [iv] Lulu (1968) US#32,
Every Face Tells a Story [i] Olivia Newton-John (1976)
US#55, *I'll Put You Together Again* [viii] Hot Choco-
late (1978) UK#13, *To Sir with Love* [iv] Lulu (1967)
g R&B#9 US#1, also on B-side of *Let's Pretend* (1967)
UK#11/Al Green (1979) R&B#71; *True Grit* [ii] Glen
Campbell (1969) C&W#9 US#35, *Walk Away* [iii]
Matt Monroe (1964) US#23 UK#4. Co-writers: [i]
M. Allison/P. Sills, [ii] Elmer Bernstein (b. 1922),
[iii] Udo Jurgens, [iv] Mark London, [v] Simon
May/Leslie Osborne, [vi] Al Saxon, [vii] Walter
Scharf, [viii] Geoff Stevens (b. October 1, 1934, Lon-
don, England). (*See also under* Charles AZNAVOUR,
John BARRY, John FARRAR, Andrew Lloyd WEB-
BER.)

89. BLACKWELL, Bumps (b. Robert A.
Blackwell, May 23, 1922, Seattle, WA; d. March 9,
1985, Whittier, CA) Pop arranger and producer. A
1940s jazz performer who later studied composition,
before becoming an arranger and producer at Speciality Records in the 1950s. As Arte Rupe's assistant
at the label, Blackwell co-wrote some of the singer
Little Richard's classic material. Blackwell worked as
an A&R man for Mercury Records during the early
1960s, and later became Richard's manager. HIT
VERSIONS: *Girl Can't Help It, The* Little Richard
(1957) R&B#7 US#49 UK#9/Darts (1977) UK#6;
Good Golly Miss Molly [ii] Little Richard (1958)
R&B#4 US#10 UK#8, re-issued (1977) UK#37/
Swinging Blue Jeans (1964) US#43 UK#11/Dave
Clark Five in medley *More Good Old Rock 'n' Roll*
(1969) UK#34; *How Do You Catch a Girl?* Sam the
Sham & the Pharaohs (1967) US#27, *Long Tall Sally*
[i] Little Richard (1956) R&B#1 US#6 UK#3/Pat
Boone (1956) US#8 UK#18/Dave Clark Five in medley *Good Old Rock 'n' Roll* (1969) UK#7; *Ready Teddy*
[ii] Little Richard (1956) R&B#8 US#44, *Rip It Up*
[ii] Little Richard (1956) R&B#1 US#17 UK#30, re-
issued (1977) UK#37. Co-writers: [i] Enotris John-
son/Richard Penniman, [ii] John Marascalco.

90. BLACKWELL, Otis (b. 1931, Brooklyn, NY) R&B pianist and vocalist. An early pioneer
of rock and roll who has written over one thousand
songs, that have collectively sold nearly two hundred
million records. Blackwell released his first single
when still a teenager, *Daddy Rollin' Stone* (1958),
which was later recorded by both Dean Martin and

the Who. In 1955, Blackwell sold six of his compositions to a music publisher for twenty-five dollars a song, two of which became Elvis Presley standards, the five million selling *Don't Be Cruel* [v] and the million selling *Return to Sender* [vi]. Blackwell subsequently wrote hits for numerous artists, sometimes using the pseudonym John Davenport, and during the 1960s he worked in A&R and as an arranger. In 1994, his songs were re-interpreted by a variety of artists on the album **Brace Yourself-A Tribute to Otis Blackwell** (Shanachie). Blackwell's own handful of records are wonderful reminders of how raw rock and roll originally was. ALBUMS: **Singin' the Blues** (1956, Davis); **These Are My Songs** (1977, Inner City); **Otis Blackwell, 1953–1955** (1990, Flyright). HIT VERSIONS: *All Shook Up* [v] Elvis Presley (1957) g R&B#1 C&W#1 US#1 UK#1, also on *The Elvis Medley* (1982) US#71 UK#51/Suzi Quatro (1974) US#85/Orbit featuring Carol Hall (1983) R&B#75/Billy Joel (1992) US#92 UK#27; *Breathless* Jerry Lee Lewis (1958) R&B#3 C&W#4 US#7 UK#8, *Don't Be Cruel* [v] Elvis Presley (1956) R&B#1 C&W#1 US#1 UK#24, re-issued (1971) UK#10, re-issued (1992) UK#42, also in *The Elvis Medley* (1985) US#17 UK#51/Bill Black's Combo (1960) R&B#9 US#11 UK#32/Billy Swan (1975) UK#42/Cheap Trick (1988) US#4/Judds (1987) C&W#10; *Fever* [i] Little Willie John (1956) R&B#1 US#24/Peggy Lee (1958) R&B#5 US#8 UK#5, re-issued (1992) UK#75/Pete Bennett & the Embers (1961) US#105/Alvin Robinson (1964) US#108/Helen Shapiro (1964) UK#38/McCoys (1965) US#7 UK#44/Rita Coolidge (1972) US#76/Swing Out Sister on B-side of *Fooled By a Smile* (1987) UK#43)/Madonna (1993) UK#6; *For My Good Fortune* [vii] Pat Boone (1958) US#21, *Great Balls of Fire* [iii] Jerry Lee Lewis (1957) R&B#3 C&W#1 US#2 UK#1/Tiny Tim (1969) UK#45/Dolly Parton on B-side of *Sweet Summer Lovin'* (1979) C&W#7 US#77; *Handy Man* [iv] Jimmy Jones (1960) R&B#3 US#2 UK#3/Del Shannon (1964) US#22 UK#36/James Taylor (1977) US#4/Joel Hughes (1982) C&W#75; *Hey, Little Girl* [vii] Dee Clark (1959) R&B#2 US#20/Del Shannon (1962) US#38 UK#2; *Just Keep It Up (And See What Happens)* Dee Clark (1959) R&B#9 US#18 UK#26, *Nine Times Out of Ten* [ii] Cliff Richard (1960) UK#3, *One Broken Heart for Sale* [vi] Elvis Presley (1963) R&B#21 US#11 UK#8, *Paralysed* Elvis Presley (1956) US#59 UK#8, *Return to Sender* [vi] Elvis Presley (1962) g R&B#5 US#2 UK#1, *Space Jungle, The* [viii] Adamski (1990) UK#7, *(Such an) Easy Question* [iii] Elvis Presley (1962) US#11, *(You're the) Apple of My Eye* Four Lovers (1956) US#62. Co-writers: [i] Eddie Cooley, [ii] Waldense Hall, [iii] Jack Hammer, [iv] Jimmy Jones, [v] Elvis Presley, [vi] Winifred Scott, [vii] Bobby Stevenson, [viii] Adam Tinley.

91. BLAIKLEY, Alan (b. March 23, 1940, London, England), and **HOWARD, Ken** (b. December 26, 1939, London, England) Both pop producers. Two BBC Television trainees who wrote and produced thirteen consecutive top thirty British hits for the group Dave Dee, Beaky, Mick and Tich during the 1960s. Howard and Blaikley's compositions were some of the more charming and original pop music of the era, strong on melody and humor, and lacking any pretensions. Some of the novel sounds that they introduced to pop discs were the bouzouki and Greek dance on *Bend It*, and the Caribbean rhythms of *Zabadak*. The duo also managed and produced the group the Honeycombs, and were the first British songwriters to write a hit single for Elvis Presley. During the 1970s, they penned various television themes, and worked on a musical, "Mardi Gras" (1976). One of their less successful projects was the conceptual album by Flaming Youth, **Ark 2** (1969, Fontana), a group that eventually became Genesis. In 1985, Howard wrote a British television biography of John Lennon. HIT VERSIONS: *Bend It* Dave Dee, Dozy, Beaky, Mick & Tich (1966) US#110 UK#2, *Boy* Lulu (1968) UK#15, *Don Juan* Dave Dee, Dozy, Beaky, Mick & Tich (1969) UK#23, *From the Underworld* Herd (1967) UK#16, *Have I the Right?* Honeycombs (1964) g US#5 UK#1, *Hideaway* Dave Dee, Dozy, Beaky, Mick & Tich (1966) UK#10, *Hold Tight* Dave Dee, Dozy, Beaky, Mick & Tich (1966) UK#4, *I Don't Want Our Loving to Die* Herd (1968) UK#5, *I've Lost You* Elvis Presley (1970) C&W#57 US#32 UK#9, *Is It Because* Honeycombs (1964) UK#38, *Last Night in Soho* Dave Dee, Dozy, Beaky, Mick & Tich (1967) UK#8, *Legend of Xanadu, The* Dave Dee, Dozy, Beaky, Mick & Tich (1967) US#123 UK#1, *Okay!* Dave Dee, Dozy, Beaky, Mich & Tich (1967) UK#4, *Paradise Lost* Herd (1967) UK#15, *Save Me* Dave Dee, Dozy, Beaky, Mich & Tich (1966) UK#4, *Snake in the Grass* Dave Dee, Dozy, Beaky, Mick & Tich (1969) UK#23, *Something Better Beginning* Honeycombs (1965) UK#39, *Tell Me How You Care* Brian Poole & the Tremeloes on B-side of *Three Bells* (1964) UK#17, *That's the Way* Honeycombs (1965) UK#12, *Touch Me, Touch Me* Dave Dee, Dozy, Beaky, Mich & Tich (1967) UK#13, *Wait for Me Marianne* Marmalade (1968) UK#30, *Wreck of the Antoinette, The* Dave Dee, Dozy, Beaky, Mick & Tich (1967) UK#14, *You Make It Move* Dave Dee, Dozy, Beaky, Mick & Tich (1966) UK#26, *Zabadak* Dave Dee, Dozy, Beaky, Mick & Tich (1967) US#52 UK#3.

92. BLAKE, Eubie (b. James Hubert Blake, February 7, 1883, Baltimore, MD; d. February 12, 1983, New York, NY) Ragtime pianist. One of the first successful black American songwriters, who composed over three hundred songs, many of which were premiered on Broadway during the 1920–1930s. The ragtime revival of the 1950s saw Blake as its foremost exponent. The son of slaves, Blake learned the organ at the age of six and later studied music theory, before, in his teens, performing in Baltimore nightclubs. One of his first published piano rags was *The Chevy Chase* (1914), after which he formed a partnership with the songwriter Noble Sissle, scoring a hit with *It's All Your Fault* [ii] (1915), a song made popular by the singer Sophie Tucker. Blake and Sissle subsequently performed as a vaudeville act the Dixie Duo, and in 1921, wrote the second all-black musical to become successful on Broadway, "Shuffle Along," which ran for nearly five hundred performances, and introduced such songs as the salacious *If You've Never Been Vamped By a Brownskin (You've Never Been Vamped at All)* [ii], *I'm Craving for That Kind of Love* [ii], and the widely recorded *I'm Just Wild About Harry* [ii]. In 1923, the duo filmed a pioneering sound short entitled "Sissle and Blake's Snappy Songs," probably the earliest attempt at a pop music promo, and certainly the first surviving example of what would later become the music video. Their material was also included in such shows as "Andre Charlot's Revue of 1924." Blake recorded solo piano rolls from 1917, and was later backed by an orchestra. He retired in 1946 to study composition, but ultimately pursued a second career as a lecturer and performer. His life was the subject of the Broadway show "Eubie!" (1978), which ran for four hundred and thirty-nine performances. He lived to be a hundred years old, saying in his later years that if he had known how long he was going to live, that he would have taken better care of himself. CHART COMPOSITIONS: *Bandana Days* [ii] (1921) US#8, *Arkansas Blues* [ii] (1922) US#10, *Down-Hearted Blues* [ii] (1923) US#13. ALBUMS: **The Wizard of Ragtime Piano** (1958, 20th Century Fox); **Live Concert** (1987), **Rags to Riches** (1988, both Stash); **The Eighty-Six Years of Eubie Blake** (1969, Columbia). HIT VERSIONS: *Gypsy Blues* [ii] Paul Whiteman (1922) US#4, *I'm Just Wild About Harry* [ii] Vaughn Deleath (1922) US#10/Marion Harris (1922) US#4/Vincent Lopez (1922) US#11/ Ray Miller (1922) US#4/Paul Whiteman (1922) US#4/Big Ben Banjo Band in *Let's Get Together #1* (1954) UK#6; *Love Will Find a Way* [ii] Edwin Dale (1922) US#14/Ben Selvin (1922) US#7; *Memories of You* [i] Louis Armstrong (1930) US#18/Ink Spots (1940) US#29. Co-writers: [i] Andy Razaf, [ii] Noble Sissle.

93. BLAND, James A. (b. October 22, 1854, Flushing, NY; d. May 5, 1911, Philadelphia, PA) Vaudeville performer. The composer of such songs as *Oh! Dem Golden Slippers* (1879), who was a member of the Original Black Diamonds during the 1870s. Bland also performed with the Original Georgia Minstrels, and was the first significant black American songwriter to write about life on the plantations. Although he died in poverty—the first of many blacks coerced into signing away their copyrights—Bland nevertheless made history, when, in 1881, he became the only known black vaudeville artist to perform in front of Queen Victoria, thus popularizing the minstrel tradition in England. HIT VERSIONS: *Carry Me Back to Old Virginny* Len Spencer (1893) US#2/Alma Gluck (1915) US#1; *Hand Me Down My Walking Cane* Paul Tremaine (1930) US#18, *In the Evening by the Moonlight, Dear Louise* Harry MacDonough (1907) US#3/Frank Stanley (1907) US#6/Haydn Quartet (1913) US#2.

94. BLANE, Ralph (b. 1914) Film and stage composer. An occasionally successful composer of such film songs as *The Boy Next Door* [i], from "Meet Me in St. Louis" (1944), *Girls Were Made to Take Care of Boys*, from "One Sunday Afternoon" (1950), and *Love* [i], from "Ziegfeld Follies" (1947). Blane's material was also featured in such shows as "The Girl Rush" (1955). HIT VERSIONS: *Buckle Down, Winsocki* [i] Art Jarrett (1942) US#21, *Have Yourself a Merry Little Christmas* [i] Judy Garland (1944) US#27, *Trolley Song, The* [i] Judy Garland (1944) US#4/King Sisters (1944) US#13/Guy Lombardo (1945) US#19/Vaughn Monroe (1945) US#4/Pied Pipers (1944) US#2. Co-writer: [i] Hugh Martin (b. 1914). (*See also under* Harry WARREN.)

95. BLUE, Barry (b. Barry Green, England) Pop producer and vocalist. A British pop opportunist who scored a run of self-composed hit singles in the early 1970s. CHART COMPOSITIONS: *(Dancing) On a Saturday Night* [i] (1973) UK#2, *Do You Wanna Dance* [iii] (1973) UK#7, *School Love* [i] (1974) UK#11, *Miss Hit and Run* (1974) UK#26, *Hot Shot* (1974) UK#23. Blue also recorded as the studio group Cry Sisco!, charting with *Afro Dizzi Act* (1989) UK#42, re-entry (1990) UK#70. HIT VERSIONS: *All Fall Down* [iv] Five Star (1985) R&B#16 US#65 UK#15, *I Eat Cannibals* [ii] Total Coello (1983) UK#8. Co-writers: [i] Lynsey De Paul, [ii] P. Greedus/R. Nicholson, [iii] Ron Roker/Gerry Shury, [iv] R. Smith. (*See also under* Lynsey DE PAUL.)

96. BLUE, David (b. Stuart David Cohen, February 18, 1941, Pawtucket, RI; d. December 2, 1982, New York, NY) Folk guitarist and vocalist. A singer-songwriter and occasional actor from the Greenwich Village folk scene of the 1960s, who died of a heart attack in 1982, shortly after scoring the

movie "Uncertain Futures." CHART COMPOSI-
TION: *Outlaw Man* (1973) US#94. ALBUMS:
Singer/Songwriter Project (1964), **David Blue**
(1966), **David Blue and the American Patrol** (1967,
all Elektra); **These 23 Days in September** (1968),
Me (1970, both Reprise); **Stories** (1972), **Nice Baby
and the Angel** (1973), **Comin' Back for More**
(1975), **Cupid's Arrow** (1976, all Asylum).

97. BOCK, Jerry (b. Jerrold Lewis Bock,
November 23, 1928, New Haven, CT) Film and
show composer, and **HARNICK, Sheldon** (b. Shel-
don Mayer Harnick, December 27, 1924, Chicago,
IL) Film and show lyricist. A songwriting duo best
known for their show, and subsequent film, "Fiddler
on the Roof" (1964), which introduced such songs
as *Matchmaker, Matchmaker*. ALBUMS: **Mister
Wonderful** oc (1956, Decca); **Fiorello!** oc (1959,
Capitol) US#7; **Fiorello!** sc (1959, RCA), **Body
Beautiful** oc (196?, Blue Pear); **Tenderloin** oc (1961,
Capitol) US#15; **Man in the Moon** oc (1963,
Golden); **She Loves Me** oc (1963, MGM) US#15;
Fiddler on the Roof oc (1964, RCA) p US#7; **Fid-
dler on the Roof** by Cannonball Adderley (1964,
Capitol); **Fiddler on the Roof** oc (1964, London);
To Broadway with Love oc (1964), **The Apple Tree**
oc (1966, both Columbia) US#113; **Fiddler on the
Roof** oc (1967, CBS) UK#4; **Rothschilds** oc (1970,
Columbia); **Fiddler on the Roof** ost (1971, United
Artists) g US#30 UK#26. HIT VERSION: *If I Were
a Rich Man* Topol (1967) UK#9. (*See also under*
George David WEISS.*)

98. BOHANNON, Hamilton (b. March
7, 1942, Newman, GA) R&B drummer, producer
and vocalist. A former Stevie Wonder sideman dur-
ing the mid-1960s, who was a Motown Records band-
leader and arranger before pursuing a solo career with
a series of self-composed disco hits. CHART COM-
POSITIONS: *South African Man* (1974) R&B#78
UK#22, *Foot Stompin' Music* (1975) R&B#39 US#98
UK#23, *Disco Stomp* (1975) R&B#62 UK#6, *Happy
Feeling* (1975) UK#49, *Bohannon's Beat* (1976)
R&B#65, *Bohannon Disco Symphony* (1977) R&B#67,
Let's Start the Dance (1978) R&B#9 US#101 UK#56,
Me and the Gang (1979) R&B#82, *Cut Loose* (1979)
R&B#43, *The Groove Machine* (1979) R&B#60,
Throw Down the Groove (1980) R&B#59, *Dance,
Dance, Dance All Night* (1980) R&B#76, *Don't Be
Ashamed to Call My Name* (1981) R&B#54, *Goin' for
Another One* (1981) R&B#91, *Let's Start to Dance
Again* featuring Dr. Perri Johnson (1981) R&B#41
UK#49, *I've Got the Dance Fever* (1982) R&B#72,
The Party Train (1982) R&B#69, *Wake Up* (1983)
R&B#87. ALBUMS: **Stop and Go** (1973), **Keep on
Dancin'** (1974), **Mighty Bohannon** (1975), **South**

African Man (1975), **Inside Out** (1975, all Dakar);
Dance Your Ass Off (1976), **Phase II** (1977), **Summertime Groove** (1978) US#58, **Too Hot to Hold**
(1979), **Cut Loose** (1979), **Music in the Air** (1980,
all Mercury); **Goin' for Another One** (1981), **Alive**
(1981), **One Step Ahead** (1980, all Phase 2); **Make
Your Body Move** (1983), **Bohannon Drive** (1983,
both Compleat); **Motions** (1984), **Here Comes Bohannon** (1989 both MCA). COMPILATIONS: **Bohannon's Best** (1978, London); **Essential Dance-
floor Artists Series, Volume 3** (1994, Castel).

99. BOLAN, Marc (b. Mark Feld, September 30, 1947, London; d. September 16, 1977, Wim-
bledon, both England) Pop guitarist and vocalist.
One of Britain's best-loved performers of the 1970s,
who, alongside David Bowie and the Sweet, was the
major proponent of "glam rock." A former male
model, Bolan first recorded a handful of unsuccessful solo singles before briefly joining the group John's
Children in 1967, recordings as which were later issued on the album **Smashed Blocked!** (1997, New
Millennium). The following year, Bolan formed the
hippy influenced acoustic duo Tyrannosaurus Rex.
As T-Rex, with the addition of electric instruments
and more band members, Bolan became a permanent
feature of the British pop charts throughout the
1970s, with compositions that verged from the brilliant to the nonsensical. In 1969, his singing style
was described by rock critic Lillian Roxon as, "a high-
pitched vibrato that rattles and wails like a witch
doctor in a jungle horror movie." Bolan died at the
age of thirty when the car in which he was travelling collided with a tree. CHART COMPOSI-
TIONS: *Debora* (1968) UK#34, re-issued (1972)
UK#7; *One Inch Rock* (1968) UK#28, *King of the
Rumbling Spires* (1969) UK#44, *Ride a White Swan*
(1970) US#76 UK#2, *Hot Love* (1971) US#72 UK#1,
Get It On (1971) US#10 UK#1, re-issued (1987)
UK#54; *Jeepster* (1971) UK#2, *Telegram Sam* (1972)
US#67 UK#1, re-issued (1982) UK#69; *Metal Guru*
(1972) UK#1, *Children of the Revolution* (1972)
UK#2, *Solid Gold Easy Action* (1972) UK#3, *Twen-
tieth Century Boy* (1973) UK#3, re-issued (1991)
UK#13; *The Groover* (1973) UK#4, *Truck on (Tyke)*
(1973) UK#12, *Teenage Dream* (1974) UK#13, *Light
of Love* (1974) UK#22, *Zip Gun Boogie* (1974)
UK#41, *New York City* (1975) UK#15, *Dreamy Lady*
(1975) UK#30, *London Boys* (1976) UK#40, *I Love
to Boogie* (1976) UK#13, *Laser Love* (1976) UK#41,
The Soul of My Suit (1977) UK#42, *Return of the
Electric Warrior* EP (1981) UK#50, *You Scare Me to
Death* (1981) UK#51, *Megarex* (1985) UK#72. AL-
BUMS: **My People Were Fair and Had Sky in
Their Hair, But Now They're Content to Wear
Stars on Their Brows** (1968) UK#15, **Prophets,**

Seers and Sages, the Angels of the Ages (1968), Unicorn (1969) UK#12, A Beard of Stars (1970, all Regal Zonophone) UK#21; T-Rex (1970) US#188 UK#13, Electric Warrior (1971, both Fly) US#32 UK#1; The Slider (1972) US#17 UK#4, Tanx (1973) US#102 UK#4, Zinc Alloy and the Hidden Riders of Tomorrow (1974) UK#12, Zip Gun (1974), Futuristic Dragon (1976) UK#50, Dandy in the Underworld (1977, all EMI) UK#26. COMPILATIONS: Best of T-Rex (1971) UK#21, My People Were Fair and Had Sky in Their Hair, But Now They're Content to Wear Stars on Their Brows/ Prophets, Seers and Sages, the Angels of the Ages/ Tyrannosaurus Rex (A Beginning) (1972) US#113 UK#1, Bolan Boogie (1972, all Fly) UK#1; Unicorn/A Beard of Stars (1972, Cube) UK#44; Blackjack (1973), Great Hits (1973, both EMI) UK#32; The Beginning of Doves (1974, Track); Solid Gold (1979, EMI) UK#51; In Concert (1981, Marc) UK#35; You Scare Me to Death (1981, Cherry Red) UK#88; Dance in the Midnight (1983, Marc on Wax) UK#83; Best of the 20th Century Boy (1985, K-Tel) UK#5; The Ultimate Collection (1991, Telstar) UK#4; BBC Radio 1 Live in Concert (1993, Windsong); Left Hand Over-The Alternative Tanx (1995), Recordings, Volume 1: 1972 Part 1 (1995), T-Rex Unchained: Unreleased Recordings, Volume 2: 1972 Part 2 (1995), T-Rex Unchained: Unreleased the Light of Love (1995, all Edsel); The Essential Collection (1995, PolyGram) UK#24; Acoustic Warrior (1996, Telstar); A Wizard, a True Star: Marc Bolan and T-Rex, 1972-1977 (1996, Edsel); The Electric Warrior Sessions (1996, Pilot); Marc Bolan and T-Rex-Live in 1977 (1997), T-Rex Unchained, Volume 7 (1997, both Edsel). HIT VERSIONS: *Children of the Revolution* Baby Ford (1989) UK#53/Unitone Rockers featuring Steel (1993) UK#60; *Get It On* Power Station (1985) US#9, *Jeepster* Polecats (1981) UK#53.

100. **BOLTON, Michael** (b. Michael Bolotin, February 26, 1953, New Haven, CT) Pop vocalist. A multi-million selling R&B influenced singer, who specializes in radio-friendly power ballads that are all performed in a bombastic, over-produced style. Bolton first recorded as a member of the rock band Blackjack, releasing the albums **Blackjack** (1978) US#127 and **Words Apart** (1979, both Shelter). After opting for a solo career, he became a major star in the 1980s. CHART COMPOSITIONS: *Love Me Tonight* [ix] (1979) US#62, *Fools Game* [ii] (1983) US#82, *That's What Love Is All About* [ix] (1987) R&B#62 US#19, *Wait on Love* [iii] (1988) US#79, *Soul Provider* [vi] (1989) US#17, re-issued (1996) UK#35; *How Am I Supposed to Live Without You* [viii] (1989) US#1 UK#3, *How Can We Be Lovers* [iv]

(1990) US#3 UK#10, *Love Is a Wonderful Thing* [vi] (1991) US#4 UK#23, *Steel Bars* [v] (1992) UK#17, *Missing You Now* [i] (1992) US#12 UK#28, *Said I Loved You...But I Lied* [xi] (1993) g US#6 UK#15, *Soul of My Soul* (1994) UK#32, *Completely* [xiv] (1994) US#32 UK#32, *Can I Touch You...There?* (1995) US#27 UK#6. ALBUMS: **Every Day of My Life** (1976, RCA); **Michael Bolton** (1983) g US#89, **Everybody's Crazy** (1985), **The Hunger** (1987) p US#46 UK#44, **Soul Provider** (1989) p US#3 UK#4, **Time, Love and Tenderness** (1991) p US#1 UK#2, **Timeless (The Classics)** (1992) p US#1 UK#3, **The One Thing** (1993, all Columbia) p US#3 UK#4. COMPILATION: **Greatest Hits, 1985–1995** (1995, Columbia) p US#5 UK#2; **The Early Years** (1997, BMG). HIT VERSIONS: *By the Time This Night Is Over* [vii] Kenny G. with Peabo Bryson (1993) R&B#37 US#25, *How Am I Supposed to Live Without You* [viii] Laura Branigan (1983) US#12, *I Found Someone* [xii] Laura Branigan (1986) US#90/Cher (1988) UK#5); *Til Somebody Loves You* [xiii] Henry Lee Summer (1991) US#51. Co-writers: [i] Walter Afanasieff/Diane Warren, [ii] C. Brooks/Mark Mangold, [iii] Jonathan Cain (b. February 26, 1950, Chicago, IL), [iv] Desmond Child/Diane Warren, [v] Bob Dylan, [vi] Andy Goldmark, [vii] Andy Goldmark/Diane Warren, [viii] Douglas James, [ix] Eric Kaz, [x] Bruce Kulick, [xi] R.J. Lange, [xii] Mark Mangold, [xiii] Henry Lee Summer (b. Brazil, IN)/Diane Warren, [xiv] Diane Warren. (*See also under* Paul STANLEY.)

101. **BON JOVI, Jon** (b. John Bongiovi, March 2, 1962, Sayreville, NJ) Rock guitarist, producer and vocalist. The lead singer and principal songwriter in the rock group Bon Jovi, which specializes in radio friendly stadium rock and power ballads. CHART COMPOSITIONS: *Runaway* [iv] (1984) US#39, *Only Lonely* [i] (1985) US#54, *In and Out of Love* (1985) US#69, *Hardest Part Is the Night* (1985) UK#68, *You Give Love a Bad Name* [iv] (1986) p US#1 UK#14, *Livin' on a Prayer* [iv] (1986) US#1 UK#4, *Wanted Dead or Alive* [vii] (1987) US#7 UK#13, *Never Say Never* (1987) UK#21, *Bad Medicine* [iv] (1988) US#1 UK#17, *Born to Be My Baby* [iv] (1988) US#3 UK#22, *I'll Be There for You* [vii] (1989) US#1 UK#18, *Lay Your Hands on Me* [vii] (1989) US#7 UK#18, *Living in Sin* (1989) US#9 UK#35, *Keep the Faith* [iv] (1992) US#29 UK#5, *Bed of Roses* (1993) US#10 UK#13, *In These Arms* [ii] (1993) US#27 UK#9, *I'll Sleep When I'm Dead* [iv] (1993) US#97 UK#17, *I Believe* (1993) UK#11, *Dry Country* (1994) UK#9, *Always* (1994) p US#4 UK#2, *Someday I'll Be Saturday Night* (1995) UK#7, *This Ain't a Love Song* (1995) US#14 UK#6, *Something for the Pain* (1995) US#39 UK#8, *Lie to Me* (1995)

US#88 UK#10, *These Days* (1995) US#4 UK#7, *Hey God* (1996) UK#13. ALBUMS: **Bon Jovi** (1984) US#43 UK#71, **7800 Fahrenheit** (1985) g US#37 UK#28, **Slippery When Wet** (1986) p US#1 UK#6, **New Jersey** (1988) p US#1 UK#1, **Keep the Faith** (1992) p US#5 UK#1, **These Days** (1995) p US#9 UK#1, **These Days Tour Edition** (1996, all Mercury). COMPILATION: **Crossroads-The Best of Bon Jovi** (1994, Jambco) p US#8 UK#1. Bon Jovi has also recorded as a solo artist. CHART COMPOSITIONS: *Blaze of Glory* (1990) US#1 UK#13, *Miracle* (1990) US#12, *Midnight in Chelsea* (1997) UK#4. ALBUMS: **Blaze of Glory/Young Guns II** ost (1990) p US#3 UK#2, **Destination Anywhere** (1997, both Mercury) UK#3. HIT VERSIONS: *Notorious* [iii] Loverboy (1987) US#38, *Sometimes (It's a Bitch)* [v] Stevie Nicks (1991) US#56 UK#40, *We All Sleep Alone* [iv] Cher (1988) US#14 UK#47. Co-writers: [i] David Bryan (b. David Rashbaum, February 7, 1962, NJ), [ii] David Bryan/Richie Sambora (b. July 11, 1959, Sayreville, NJ), [iii] T. Cerney/P. Dean/M. Reno/Richie Sambora, [iv] Desmond Child/Richie Sambora, [v] B. Falcon, [vi] G. Karak, [vii] Richie Sambora.

102. BONO, Sonny (b. Salvatore Bono, February 16, 1935, Detroit, MI; d. January 5, 1998, Sierra Nevada, CA) Pop producer and vocalist. One half of the 1960s husband and wife vocal duo Sonny and Cher. Bono first recorded as Don Christy for a variety of record labels, before working as a producer and backing vocalist for Phil Spector, through whom he met and subsequently teamed up with Cher. Their sloppy, hippie-chic lifestyle was much imitated during the mid-1960s. CHART COMPOSITIONS: *I Got You Babe* (1965) g R&B#19 US#1 UK#1, re-issued (1993) UK#66; *Baby Don't Go* (1965) US#8 UK#11, *Just You* (1965) US#20, *But You're Mine* (1965) US#15 UK#17, *Little Man* (1966) US#21 UK#9, *The Beat Goes On* (1967) US#6 UK#29. ALBUMS: **Look at Us** (1965, Atco) g US#2 UK#7; **Baby Don't Go** (1965, Reprise) US#69; **The Wondrous World of Sonny and Cher** (1966) US#34 UK#15, **In Case You're in Love** (1967) US#45, **Good Times** ost (1967, all Atco) US#73; **Live** (1971) g US#35, **All I Ever Need Is You** (1972, both Kapp) g US#14; **Mama Was a Rock and Roll Singer, Papa Used to Write All Her Songs** (1974) US#132, **Live in Las Vegas, Volume 2** (1973, both MCA) US#175. COMPILATIONS: **Best of Sonny and Cher** (1967) US#23, **The Two of Us** (1972, both Atco) US#122; **Greatest Hits** (1974, MCA) US#146. Sonny and Cher ultimately divorced, after which, Bono scored a couple of solo successes before entering politics when he was elected mayor of Palm Springs in 1988. CHART COMPOSITIONS: *Laugh at Me* (1965)

US#10 UK#9, *The Revolution Kind* (1965) US#70. HIT VERSIONS: *Bang Bang (My Baby Shot Me Down)* Cher (1966) g US#2 UK#3, *Boy Next Door, The* Standells (1965) US#102, *High School Dance* Larry Williams on B-side of *Short Fat Fanny* (1957) R&B#1 US#5, *I Feel Something In the Air* Cher (1966) UK#43, *I Got You Babe* UB40 with Chrissie Hynde (1985) US#28 UK#1/Cher with Beavis & Butt Head (1993) US#108; *Mama (When My Dollies Have Babies)* Cher (1966) US#124, also on B-side of *Behind the Door* (1966) US#97; *Needles and Pins* [i] Jackie DeShannon (1962) US#84/Searchers (1964) US#13 UK#1/Smokie (1977) US#68; *Where Do You Go?* Cher (1965) US#25, *You Better Sit Down Kids* Cher (1967) US#9, *You Bug Me Baby* Larry Williams on B-side of *Bony Maronie* (1957) R&B#4 US#14. Co-writer: [i] Jack Nitzsche.

103. BONOFF, Karla (b. December 27, 1952, Los Angeles, CA) Pop pianist and vocalist. A singer-songwriter, gifted with a strong sense of melody and a finely timbered voice, who appeared on the scene just as the genre was in decline. Bonoff's compositions have appealed to such female vocalists as Linda Ronstadt, Bonnie Raitt and Nicolette Larson. Bonoff trained as a classical pianist before making her debut performance at the age of sixteen at the Troubadour in Los Angeles. While studying at UCLA, she formed the group Bryndle with Kenny Edwards, Andrew Gold and Wendy Waldman, which recorded an unreleased album for A&M Records in 1970, and would not actually release an album until **Bryndle** (1995, Music Masters). Oddly, Bonoff's biggest hit single was not one of her own compositions. CHART COMPOSITIONS: *I Can't Hold On* (1978) US#76, *Baby Don't Go* [i] (1980) US#69, *Please Be the One* (1982) US#63. ALBUMS: **Karla Bonoff** (1977) g US#52, **Restless Nights** (1979) US#31, **Wild Heart of the Young** (1982, all Columbia) US#49; **New World** (1988, Goldcastle). HIT VERSIONS: *All My Life* Linda Ronstadt & Aaron Neville (1990) US#11, *Lose Again* Linda Ronstadt (1977) US#76, *Someone to Lay Down Beside Me* Linda Ronstadt (1977) US#42, *Tell Me Why* Wynonna Judd (1993) C&W#3. Co-writer: [i] Kenny Edwards.

104. BOWIE, David (b. David Robert Hayward Jones, January 8, 1947, London, England) Rock guitarist, saxophonist, producer and vocalist. A much imitated performer who has tried his hand at everything over the years; from British R&B through Carnaby Street cockney-dandy pop, hippie acoustic folk, theatrical rock, white soul, bleak, minimalist and nihilistic electronic soundscapes, and, most recently, modern dance music, drums and bass, and wallpaper production. In his attempt to be jack-of-all-trades, Bowie has rarely pursued any one particular style long enough to master it, and his career is littered with bonafide classics and superficial duds. An inquisitive talent who has been highly influential over the years, there have been at least as many Bowie clones as there have been Bob Dylan ones. Bowie is at his best when wholly original, as evidenced on **Ziggy Stardust and the Spiders from Mars** (1972), **Aladdin Sane** (1973), and his masterpiece **Station to Station** (1976). As a teenager, he listened to rock and roll, the beat poets and jazz, before developing an interest in theatre and mime. During the 1960s, Bowie worked for an advertising agency, while performing and recording with various unsuccessful beat and R&B groups, including the King Bees, the Manish Boys, the Lower Third, the Buzz, and the Kon-Rads. He experimented with movie shorts and stage production, before adopting the stage name David Bowie for a series of unsuccessful singles, many of which parodied Anthony Newley. After a brief foray into television work, a spell in a Buddhist monastery, a short-lived rock band called Feathers, and a tour with Lindsay Kemp's mime troupe in 1969, Bowie signed to the Philips label and scored a hit single with the science fiction epic *Space Oddity*, a metaphorical study of the personal alienation that follows sudden mass popularity. A change of label to RCA resulted in a series of strong but poorly produced albums, alongside some magnificent singles, none more so than *Life on Mars*, which he composed in author William Burroughs' cut-up technique. Many of Bowie's 1970s albums featured a recurring theme of mental illness, a disease that eventually caused his brother Terry to commit suicide. The androgynous image that he assembled for **Ziggy Stardust and the Spiders From Mars** (1972) and **Aladdin Sane** (1973) was a major influence on the British "glam rock"movement of the period. In 1975, Bowie made an enigmatic acting debut, perfectly cast in Nicholas Roeg's film "The Man Who Fell to Earth" (1975). Two collaborations with Brian Eno, the albums **Low** and **Heroes** (both 1977), were intriguing but somewhat mannered investigations of electronic music. His chart oriented **Let's Dance** (1983) was a major success, but **Tonight** the following year, was hopeless beyond measure, and featured an appalling version of the Beach Boys' classic *God Only Knows*. An attempt to immerse himself in the ranks of the rock quartet Tin Machine during the late 1980s was considered an artistic misjudgment, although it did result in renewed chart activity with the singles *Tin Machine* (1989) UK#61, *Under the God* (1989) UK#51, *You Belong in Rock 'n' Roll* [iv] (1991) UK#33, and *Baby Universal* [iv] (1991) UK#48; from the albums **Tin Machine** (1989, EMI

America) US#28 UK#3; **Tin Machine 2** (1991) US#126 UK#23 and **Oy Vey, Baby** (1992, both London). In 1997, Bowie became the first rock star to float himself on the stock market, in a bond issue that raised a considerable sum of money against future royalties on his back catalogue. CHART COMPOSITIONS: *Space Oddity* (1969) US#124 UK#5, re-issued (1973) US#15, re-issued (1975) UK#1; *Changes* (1971) US#66, live version (1974) US#41; *Starman* (1972) US#16 UK#10, *John, I'm Only Dancing* (1972) UK#12, *The Jean Genie* (1972) US#71 UK#2, *Drive-in Saturday* (1973) UK#3, *Life on Mars* (1973) UK#3, *The Laughing Gnome* (1973) UK#6, *Rebel Rebel* (1974) US#64 UK#5, *Rock 'n' Roll Suicide* (1974) UK#22, *Diamond Dogs* (1974) UK#21, *Young Americans* (1975) US#28 UK#18, *Fame* [ii] (1975) g R&B#21 US#1 UK#17, re-mixed (1990) UK#28; *Golden Years* (1975) US#10 UK#8, *TVC15* (1976) US#64 UK#33, *Sound and Vision* (1977) US#69 UK#3, *Heroes* (1977) US#35 UK#24, *Beauty and the Beast* (1978) UK#39, *Breaking Glass EP* (1978) UK#54, *Boys Keep Swinging* (1979) UK#7, *D.J.* (1979) US#106 UK#29, *John, I'm Only Dancing (1975)/John, I'm Only Dancing* (1972) (1979) UK#12, *Ashes to Ashes* (1980) US#101 UK#1, *Fashion* (1980) US#70 UK#5, *Scary Monsters (And Super Creeps)* (1981) UK#20, *Up the Hill Backwards* (1981) UK#32, *Under Pressure* [iii] with Queen (1981) US#29 UK#1, *Cat People (Putting out Fire)* [vi] (1982) US#67 UK#26, *Let's Dance* (1983) g R&B#14 US#1 UK#1, *China Girl* [vii] (1983) US#10 UK#2, *Modern Love* (1983) US#14 UK#2, *Without You* (1983) UK#73, *Blue Jean* (1984) US#8 UK#6, *Tonight* (1984) US#53 UK#53, *This Is Not America* [v] with the Pat Metheny Group (1985) US#32 UK#14, *Loving the Alien* (1985) UK#19, *Absolute Beginners* (1986) UK#2, *Underground* (1986) UK#21, *When the Wind Blows* (1986) UK#44, *Day In-Day Out* (1987) US#21 UK#17, *Time Will Crawl* (1987) UK#33, *Never Let Me Down* (1987) US#27 UK#34, *Real Cool World* (1992) UK#53, *Jump They Say* (1993) UK#9, *Black Tie White Noise* with Al B. Sure! (1993) UK#36, *Miracle Goodnight* (1993) UK#40, *The Buddha of Suburbia* with Lenny Kravitz (1993) UK#35, *The Heart's Filthy Lesson* (1995) US#92 UK#35, *Strangers When We Meet/The Man Who Sold the World* (live) (1995) UK#39, *Hallo Spaceboy* (1996) UK#12. ALBUMS: **David Bowie** (1969, Deram); **The Man Who Sold the World** (1970) US#105 UK#26, **Hunky Dory** (1971) US#93 UK#3, **Ziggy Stardust and the Spiders from Mars** (1972) g US#75 UK#5, **Aladdin Sane** (1973) g US#17 UK#1, **Pin Ups** (1973) US#23 UK#1, **Diamond Dogs** (1974) g US#5 UK#1, **David Live** (1974) g US#8 UK#2, **Young Americans** (1975) g US#9 UK#2, **Station to Station** (1976) g US#3 UK#5, **Low** (1977) US#11 UK#2, **Heroes** (1977)

US#35 UK#3, **Stage** (1978) US#44 UK#5, **David Bowie Narrates Serge Prokofiev's Peter and the Wolf** with Eugene Ormandy and the Philadelphia Orchestra (1978) US#136, **Lodger** (1979) US#20 UK#4, **Scary Monsters and Super Creeps** (1980) US#12 UK#1, **Ziggy Stardust-The Motion Picture** (1983, all RCA) US#89 UK#17; **Let's Dance** (1983) p US#4 UK#1, **Tonight** (1984) p US#11 UK#1, **Labyrinth** ost (1986, all EMI America) US#68 UK#38; **When the Wind Blows** ost (1986, Virgin); **Never Let Me Down** (1987, EMI America) g US#34 UK#6; **Black Tie White Noise** (1993, Savage) US#39 UK#1; **The Buddha of Suburbia** tvst (1993, Arista); **1. Outside** (1995, Virgin) US#21 UK#8; **Earthling** (1997, RCA) UK#6. COMPILATIONS: **Space Oddity** (1972, RCA) US#16 UK#17; **Images, 1966–1967** (1973, London) US#144; **Changesonebowie** (1976) p US#10 UK#2, **Christiane F.** ost (1981, both RCA) US#135; **Very Best of David Bowie** (1981, K-Tel) UK#3; **Changestwobowie** (1982) US#68 UK#24, **Rare** (1983) UK#34, **Golden Years** (1983) US#99 UK#33, **Fame and Fashion** (1984, all RCA) US#147 UK#40; **Love You Till Tuesday** (1984, Deram) UK#53; **Sound and Vision** (1989, Rykodisk) g US#97; **Changesbowie** (1990, EMI) p US#39 UK#1; **The Manish Boys/Davy Jones** (1992, See for Miles); **The Singles Collection, 1969–1993** (1993, EMI) UK#9; **Santa Monica '72** (1994) UK#74, **RarestOneBowie** (1995, both Trident). HIT VERSIONS: *All the Young Dudes* Mott the Hoople (1972) US#37 UK#3/Skids on B-side of *Working for the Yankee Dollar* (1979) UK#20/Bruce Dickinson (1990) UK#23; *Chant of the Ever-Circling Skeletal Family* Wedding Present on B-side of *Loveslave* (1992) UK#17, *John, I'm Only Dancing* Polecats (1981) UK#35, *Man Who Sold the World, The* Lulu (1974) UK#3, *Oh, You Pretty Things* Peter Noone (1974) UK#12, *Rebel Rebel* DNA sampled in *Rebel Woman* (1991) UK#42, *Under Pressure* [iii] Vanilla Ice sampled in *Ice Ice Baby* (1990) US#1 UK#1, *Ziggy Stardust* Bauhaus (1982) UK#15. Cowriters: [i] Carlos Alomar, [ii] Carlos Alomar/John Lennon, [iii] John Deacon/Brian May/Freddie Mercury/Roger Taylor, [iv] Reeves Gabrels, [v] Lyle Mays (b. November 27, 1953, Wausaukee, WI)/Pat Metheny (b. August 12, 1954, Kansas City, MO), [vi] Giorgio Moroder, [vii] Iggy Pop.

105. BOYCE, Tommy (b. September 29, 1944, Charlottesville, VA; d. November 24, 1994, Nashville, TN). Pop producer and vocalist. The writer, frequently in partnership with Bobby Hart, of over three hundred songs that have collectively sold over forty-two million records. Boyce achieved his first hits when Fats Domino and Curtis Lee recorded his compositions, and during the early 1960s, he pursued a solo career before forming a songwriting and performing partnership with Hart in 1967. The duo's most lucrative success was as songwriters for the manufactured pop group the Monkees, for which they composed *The Monkees Theme* [iii]. In 1975, Boyce and Hart toured with two of the Monkees as "The Golden Great Hits of the Monkees Show-The Guys Who Wrote 'Em and the Guys Who Sang 'Em," but they parted company in the 1970s, whereupon Boyce worked as a record producer in Britain for the Darts. Boyce committed suicide in 1994. CHART COMPOSITIONS: *Along Came Linda* (1962) US#118, *Sunday, the Day Before Monday** (1966) US#132, *Out and About* [iii]* (1967) US#39, *Sometimes She's a Little Girl* [iii]* (1967) US#110, *I Wonder What She's Doing Tonite?* [iii] (1968) US#8, *Goodbye Baby (I Don't Want To See You Cry)* [iii]* (1968) US#53, *Alice Long (You're Still My Favorite Girlfriend)* [iii]* (1968) US#27, *We're all Going to the Same Place* [iii]* (1968) US#123, *L.U.V. (Let Us Vote)* [iii]* (1969) US#111. ALBUMS: **Two Fold Talent** (1967, Camden); **Test Patterns*** (1967) US#200, **I Wonder What She's Doing Tonite?*** (1968) US#109, **Which One's Boyce and Which One's Hart?*** (1968), **It's all Happening on the Inside*** (1968), **L.U.V.*** (1969, all A&M); **Blowin' Away** as Christopher Cloud (1973, Chelsea); **Dolenz, Jones, Boyce and Hart**** (1975, Capitol); **Concert in Japan**** (1996, Varese Sarabande). HIT VERSIONS: *Action* Freddy Cannon (1965) US#13, *Be My Guest* Fats Domino (1959) R&B#2 US#8, *Beverly Jean* Curtis Lee on B-side of *Under the Moon of Love* [iv] (1961) US#46, *Come a Little Bit Closer* [ii] Jay & the Americans (1964) US#3/Trini Lopez (1969) US#121/Johnny Duncan & Janie Fricke (1977) C&W#4; *Gee, I Wish You Were Here* Curtis Lee on B-side of *Pretty Little Angel Eyes* [iv] (1961) US#7 UK#47, *Green Grass* [i] Gary Lewis & the Playboys (1966) US#8, *(I'm Not Your) Stepping Stone* [iii] Sex Pistols (1980) UK#21, *In the Night* Freddy Cannon (1965) US#132, *Last Train to Clarksville* [iii] Monkees (1966) g US#1 UK#1, also on *The Monkees EP* [iii] (1990) UK#33 re-issued (1989) UK#62/Ed Bruce (1967) C&W#69; *Let Me Show You Where It's At* Freddy Cannon (1965) US#127, *Pretty Little Angel Eyes* [iv] Curtis Lee (1961) US#7 UK#47/Showaddywaddy (1978) UK#5; *She* Del Shannon (1967) US#131/Tommy James & the Shondells (1970) US#23; *Tear Drop City* [iii] Monkees (1969) US#56, *Under the Moon of Love* [iv] Curtis Lee (1961) US#46/Showaddywaddy (1976) UK#1; *Valleri* [iii] Monkees (1968) g US#3 UK#12. With: * Bobby Hart, ** Mickey Dolenz, David Jones and Bobby Hart. Cowriters: [i] Roger Atkins, [ii] Wes Farrell/Bobby Hart, [iii] Bobby Hart, [iv] Curtis Lee (b. October 28, 1941, Yuma, AZ).

106. BOYLAN, Terence (b. America) Rock guitarist and vocalist. A singer-songwriter who, with his elder brother, the producer John Boylan, debuted as a member of the show cast of **The Appletree Theatre** oc (1968, Verve Forecast), before releasing three solo sets, the best of which was the mellifluous **Terence Boylan** (1977), a distinguished selection of low-key, melancholic songs that were fascinating vignettes of American life, lost love and failed aspirations. Unfortunately, Boylan's Jackson Browne-styled introspection failed to find a wider audience, and nothing has been heard from him since 1980. ALBUMS: **Alias Boona** (1969, Verve Forecast); **Terence Boylan** (1977) US#181, **Suzy** (1980, both Elektra). HIT VERSION: *Shake It* Ian Matthews (1978) US#13.

107. BRADDOCK, Bobby (b. August 5, 1940, Lakeland, FL) C&W guitarist, pianist and vocalist. A witty and commercial country songwriter who played in various bands before moving to Nashville in 1964, where he first worked as a pianist for Marty Robbins. CHART COMPOSITIONS: *I Know How to Do It* (1967) C&W#74, *The Girls in Country Music* (1969) C&W#62, *Between the Lines* (1979) C&W#58, *Nag, Nag, Nag* (1980) C&W#87. ALBUMS: **Bobby Braddock** (1967, MGM); **Between the Lines** (1979), **Love Bomb** (1982, both Elektra); **Hardpore Cornography** (1983, RCA). HIT VERSIONS: *Come on In* Sonny James (1976) C&W#8/Jerry Lee Lewis (1978) C&W#10/Bobby Hood (1978) C&W#91/Oak Ridge Boys (1979) US#3; *Did You Ever?* Charlie Louvin & Melba Montgomery (1971) C&W#26/Nancy Sinatra & Lee Hazlewood (1971) UK#2; *D.I.V.O.R.C.E.* [iv] Tammy Wynette (1968) C&W#1 US#63, re-issued (1975) UK#12/Billy Connolly (1975) UK#1; *Fakin' Love* T.G. Sheppard & Karen Brooks (1983) C&W#1, *Georgia in a Jug* Johnny Paycheck (1978) C&W#17, *Golden Ring* George Jones & Tammy Wynette (1976) C&W#1, *Happy Hour, The* Tony Booth (1974) C&W#49/Snuff (1982) C&W#71; *He Stopped Loving Her Today* George Jones (1980) C&W#1, *He's a Good Ole Boy* [i] Arlene Harden (1968) C&W#32/Chely Wright (1994) C&W#58+; *I Don't Remember Loving You* [i] John Conlee (1983) C&W#10, *I Feel Like Loving You Again* T.G. Sheppard (1981) C&W#1, *Nothing Ever Hurt Me (Half as Much as Losing You)* George Jones (1973) C&W#7, *Old Flames Have New Names* [ii] Mark Chestnutt (1992) C&W#5, *Ruthless* Statler Brothers (1967) C&W#10, *Silent Partners* Frizzell & West (1984) C&W#20, *Somebody Ought to Tell Him That She's Gone* Ogden Harless (1987) C&W#84, *Something to Brag About* Charlie Louvin & Melba Montgomery (1970) C&W#18/Mary Kay Place & Willie Nelson (1978) C&W#9; *They Call It Making Love* Tammy Wynette (1979) C&W#6,

Thinkin' of a Rendezvous Johnny Duncan (1976) C&W#1, *Time Marches On* Tracy Lawrence (1996) C&W#32+, *Unwed Fathers* [iii] Tammy Wynette (1983) C&W#63/Gail Davies (1985) C&W#56; *(We're Not the) Jet Set* George Jones & Tammy Wynette (1974) C&W#15, *While You're Dancin'* Marty Robbins (1966) C&W#21, *Womanhood* Tammy Wynette (1978) C&W#3, *Would You Catch a Falling Star* John Anderson (1982) C&W#6, *You Can't Have Your Kate and Edith Too* Statler Brothers (1967) C&W#10. Co-writers: [i] Harlan Howard, [ii] Ralph Van Hoy, [iii] John Prine, [iv] Curly Putman. (*See also under* Sonny CURTIS.)

108. BRADY, Paul (b. May 19, 1947, Strabane, County Tyrone, Northern Ireland) Folk-rock multi-instrumentalist and vocalist. A singer-songwriter whose best work has often been within the Irish folk idiom. Brady learned the piano and guitar while still at school, and during his summer vacations performed in the pubs and clubs of Donegal. After stints in various Dublin rock bands such as the Kult and Rockhouse, he performed with the folk group the Johnstons. ALBUMS: **The Johnstons** (1967), **Give a Damn** (1968), **The Barleycorn** (1969), **Bitter Green** (1970), **Colors of the Dawn** (1971, all Transatlantic). COMPILATION: **The Transatlantic Years** (1993, Demon). Between 1972–1973, Brady resided in America, and after a brief period as a member of the folk group Planxty, he recorded a series of highly regarded folk collaborations, including a set of traditional Irish songs with Andy Irvine. Brady then began blending his native folk with pop and rock, creating songs that attracted the attention of Santana and Tina Turner. In 1980, Brady achieved a number one in Eire with *Crazy Dreams*. CHART COMPOSITION: *The World Is What You Make It* (1996) UK#67. ALBUMS: **Andy Irvine and Paul Brady** (1976, Mulligan); **The High Part of the Road** with Tommy Peoples (1977, Shanachie); **Welcome Here Kind Stranger** (1978, Mulligan); **Hard Station** (1982), **True for You** (1983, both 21 Records); **Full Moon** (1984, Demon); **Molloy Brady Peoples** with Matt Molloy & Tommy Peoples (1986, Mulligan); **Back to the Centre** (1986, Phonogram); **Primitive Dance** (1987, Mercury); **The Green Crow Craws-The Words and Music of Sean O'Casey** with John Kavanagh (1988, EMI); **Trick or Treat** (1991) UK#62, **Spirits Colliding** (1995, both Fontana). COMPILATION: **Songs and Crazy Dreams** (1992, Fontana). HIT VERSION: *Not the Only One* Bonnie Raitt (1992) US#34.

109. BRAGG, Billy (b. Steven William Bragg, December 20, 1957, Barking, England) Pop guitarist and vocalist. A politically oriented singer-songwriter in the protest tradition, who started his career as a member of the punk rock outfit Riff Raff. CHART COMPOSITIONS: *Between the Wars EP* (1985) UK#15, *Days Like These* (1986) UK#43, *Levi Stubbs' Tears* (1986) UK#29, *Greetings to the New Brunette* (1986) UK#58, *Waiting for the Great Leap Forward* (1988) UK#52, *Sexuality* (1991) UK#27, *You Woke Up My Neighbourhood* [i] (1991) UK#54, *Accident Waiting to Happen EP* (1992) UK#33, *Upfield* (1996) UK#46. ALBUMS: **Life's a Riot with Spy Vs. Spy** (1984, Utility) UK#30; **Brewing Up with Billy Bragg** (1984) UK#16, **Talking with the Tax-man About Poetry** (1986) UK#8, **Back to Basics** (1987) UK#37, **Workers Playtime** (1988) all Go! Disks) US#198 UK#17; **The Internationale** (1990, Utility) UK#34; **Don't Try This at Home** (1991, Go! Disks) UK#8; **William Bloke** (1996, Cooking Vinyl). HIT VERSIONS: *New England, A* Kirsty MacColl (1985) UK#7, *Won't Talk About It* [ii] Beats International (1990) UK#9. Co-writers: [i] Buck, [ii] Norman Cook.

110. BREL, Jacques (b. April 8, 1929, Schaerbeck, Belgium; d. October 9, 1978, Bobigny, France) Folk pianist, guitarist and vocalist. The modern day heir to the Parisian music hall of Jacques Offenbach, Brel merged Flemish folk and Argentinean tangos with traditional French music, to create a wholly individual style of songwriting and performance. When he died of cancer in 1978, Brel was already recognized as a songwriting genius of extreme passion, and he remains an influential force in music on artists such as Tom Waits. Brel cast himself as a happy-go-lucky fellow, constantly in search of pleasure, and the characters in his songs frequently embraced life with little care for tomorrow. His mastery of rhythm added genuine excitement to his performances, and songs such as *Next* became hits for such rock groups as the Sensational Alex Harvey Band, although they seldom work as well outside their original language. Intense imagery and dark humor were used by Brel to make accurate social observations. He was a prolific tunesmith, originally influenced by Bertolt Brecht and Kurt Weil, whose recurring subjects were the classic European themes of love, lust, madness, suicide, death and despair, all of which he dispatched with great drama and bravado. At the age of fifteen, Brel learned the guitar and began writing songs while working in his father's factory. After his military service in 1953, he moved to Paris, France, where he became a singer in the cafes, clubs and music halls of the Pigalle district. Brel later became the subject of a New York theatrical show, "Jacques Brel Is Alive and Well and Living in Paris" (1968), and during the late 1960s, the American songwriter Mort Shuman translated some

of his best songs into English, after which they began attracting the attention of such singers as Shirley Bassey, David Bowie and Ray Charles. Scott Walker proved Brel's finest English language interpreter, recording magnificent versions of *Jacky* [iii], *Mathilde* [iii], *Amsterdam* [iii], and *The Girls and the Dogs. Le Moribund (The Dying Man)* was translated by Rod McKuen as the six million selling *Seasons in the Sun* [ii]. Many of Brel's albums were only ever released in Europe, and during the last years of his life he lived as something of a recluse in France and Polynesia, surfacing briefly in 1977 with the two million selling **Brel.** ALBUMS: **American Debut** (1957, SMP); **The Poetic World of Jacques Brel** (1957, Philips); **Le Plat Pays** (1965), **Le Chansaon Des Vieux Amants** (1965), **Amsterdam** (1965), **Vesoul** (1965), **La Fanette** (1966), **Les Vieux** (1966), **Ces Gens La** (1966), **Ne Me Quitte Pas** (1966, all Barclay); **A L'Olympia** (1968, Fontana); **Personally** (1975, Barclay); **Grand Jacques, 1955, Volume 1** (1976), **Quand on a Qui, 1957, Volume 2** (1976), **Au Printemps, 1958, Volume 3** (1976), **La Valse a Mille, Volume 4** (1976), **Les Bourgeois, 1961, Volume 5** (1976, all Phonogram); **Brel** (1976, Barclay); **Greatest Hits, Volume 1** (1977), **Greatest Hits, Volume 2** (1977, both Impact); **J'arrive** (1979), **La Chanson Francaise** (1979, both Barclay); **Music for the Millions** (1983, Philips); **Les Marquis** (1984, Phonogram); **Ses Plus Grandes Chansons** (1984, Philips); **Brel Alive in Paris** (1986, Vanguard); **Jacques Brel** (1986), **Master Series** (1988, both Philips); **Jaures-The Best of Jacques Brel, Volume 1** (1992), **Orly-The Best of Jacques Brel, Volume 2** (1992), **Quinze Ans D'Amour** (1992, all Polygram); **Jacques Brel, 1954–1962** (1992, Barclay). HIT VERSIONS: *Amsterdam* [iii] David Bowie on B-side of *Sorrow* (1973) UK#3, *Chanson De Jacky, La (Jacky/Jackie)* [iii] Scott Walker (1967) UK#22/Marc Almond (1991) UK#17; *Moribond, Le (Seasons in the Sun)* [ii] Kingston Trio on B-side of *If You Don't Look Around* (1964) US#123/Terry Jacks (1974) g US#1 UK#1/Bobby Wright (1974) C&W#24; *Ne Me Quitte Pas (If You Go Away)* [ii] Damita Jo (1967) US#68/Terry Jacks (1974) US#68 UK#8; *Quand on a Que L'amour (If We Only Have Love)* [iii] Dionne Warwick (1972) US#84. English lyrics by: [i] Eric Blau/Mort Shuman, [ii] Rod McKuen, [iii] Mort Shuman.

111. BRICUSSE, Leslie (b. January 29, 1931, London, England) Film and stage composer, producer. A British hit songwriter for the singer Max Bygraves, who preceded the rock and roll era of the late 1950s. Bricusse first began writing in the 1950s for the Cambridge Footlights Revue, before appearing in his own West End show "An Evening with

Beatrice Lillie" (1954). His first musical was "Lady at the Wheel" (1958), after which he formed a song-writing partnership with the singer Anthony Newley, creating the musicals "Stop the World, I Want to Get Off!" (1961) and "The Roar of the Greasepaint, the Smell of the Crowd" (1965). Bricusse is best remembered for scoring the film "Doctor Doolittle" (1967), which featured the Oscar winning theme song *Talk to the Animals*. His later musicals included "Beyond the Rainbow" (1978). ALBUMS: **Stop the World, I Want to Get Off!** oc (1962, London) US#3; **Fool Britannia** sc (1963, Parlophone); **Pickwick** oc (1963, Philips) UK#12; **The Roar of the Greasepaint, the Smell of the Crowd** oc (1965) US#54, **The Roar of the Greasepaint, the Smell of the Crowd** sc (1965, both RCA); **Stop the World, I Want to Get Off!** ost (1966, Warner Brothers); **Doctor Doolittle** ost (1967, 20th Century) g US#55; **Salt and Pepper** ost (1968, United Artists); **Goodbye, Mr. Chips** ost (1969, MGM) US#164; **Scrooge** (1970, Columbia) US#95; **The Good Old Bad Old Days!** oc (1971, AEI); **Willy Wonka and the Chocolate Factory** (1971, Paramount); **Victor/Victoria** ost (1982, MGM); **Hook** ost (1992, Epic) US#182. HIT VERSIONS: *Candy Man* [ii] Sammy Davis, Jr. (1971) g US#1, *Can You Read My Mind* [iv] Maureen McGovern (1979) US#52, *Gonna Build a Mountain* [ii] Matt Monro (1961) UK#44/Sammy Davis, Jr. (1962) UK#26; *If I Ruled the World* [iii] Tony Bennett (1965) US#34 UK#40/Harry Secombe (1963) UK#18/Sammy Davis, Jr. (1965) US#135; *My Kind of Girl* Matt Monro (1961) US#18 UK#5/Frank Sinatra (1963) UK#35; *Out of Town* [i] Max Bygraves (1956) UK#18/Dickie Valentine on *All Star Hit Parade EP* (1956) UK#2; *What Kind of Fool Am I?* [ii] Anthony Newley (1961) UK#36/Vic Damone (1962) US#131/Sammy Davis, Jr. (1962) US#17 UK#26/Robert Goulet (1962) US#89/Shirley Bassey (1963) UK#47; *Who Can I Turn To?* [ii] Tony Bennett (1964) US#33/Dionne Warwick (1965) R&B#36 US#62. Co-writers: [i] Robin Beaumomnt, [ii] Anthony Newley (b. September 24, 1931, London, England), [iii] Cyril Ornadel, [iv] John Williams. (*See also under* John BARRY, Henry MANCINI.)

112. BRISTOL, Johnny (b. Morgantown, NC) R&B pianist, producer and vocalist. A successful songwriter-producer at Motown Records during the second half of the 1960s, who also had a series of solo hits in the 1970s. Bristol first sang with Jackie Beavers as Johnny and Jackie, recording sides for the Tri-Phil label, one of which was the future Supremes' million seller *Someday We'll Be Together* [i]. When Tri-Phil was taken over by Motown in 1967, Bristol became an assistant producer and co-writer alongside Harvey Fuqua, where his stylish, in-

tense and dramatic ballads were recorded by a variety of Motown acts. Bristol's most consistent run of hits were those that he composed for Junior Walker and the All Stars, Motown's most genuine R&B act on account of Walker's rough, bluesy voice and raw saxophone sound, which perfectly suited Bristol's southern-blues compositions. During the 1970s, Bristol worked as a producer at Columbia Records, but after being rejected as a vocalist by the label, he signed to MGM and scored a million seller with *Hang on in There Baby* (1974). CHART COMPOSITIONS: *Hang on in There Baby* (1974) g R&B#2 US#8 UK#3, new version with Alton McClain (1980) R&B#73; *You and I* (1974) R&B#20 US#48, *Leave My World* (1975) R&B#23 US#104, *Love Takes Tears* (1975) R&B#72, *Do It to My Mind* (1976) R&B#5 US#50, *You Turned Me on to Love* (1977) R&B#36 US#106, *I Sho Like Groovin' with Ya* (1977) R&B#47, *Waiting on Love* (1978) R&B#27, *Love No Longer Has a Hold on Me* (1981) R&B#75. ALBUMS: **Hang on in There Baby** (1974) US#82 UK#12, **Feeling the Magic** (1975, both MGM); **Bristol's Creme** (1976) US#154, **Strangers** (1978, both Atlantic); **Free to Be Me** (1981, Handshake). COMPILATION: **Best of Johnny Bristol** (1978, Polydor). HIT VERSIONS: *Check It Out* Tavares (1974) R&B#5 US#35, *Daddy Could Swear, I Declare* [iii] Gladys Knight & the Pips (1973) R&B#2 US#19, *Do You See My Love (For You Growing)* [iv] Junior Walker & the All Stars (1970) R&B#3 US#32, *Gotta Hold on to This Feeling* [ix] Junior Walker & the All Stars (1970) R&B#3 US#21, *Hang on in There Baby* Curiosity (Killed the Cat) (1992) UK#3, *I Can't Believe You Love Me* Tammi Terrell (1966) R&B#27 US#72, *I Don't Want to Do Wrong* [viii] Gladys Knight & the Pips (1971) R&B#2 US#17, *I'm Still a Struggling Man* Edwin Starr (1969) R&B#27 US#80, *I've Lost Everything I've Ever Loved* David Ruffin (1969) R&B#11 US#58, *If I Could Build My Whole World Around You* [iii] Marvin Gaye & Tammi Terrell (1968) R&B#2 US#10 UK#41, *It's All Over But the Shouting* Bob Luman (1969) C&W#65, *It's Been a Long, Long Time* Elgins (1967) R&B#35 US#92, *La La Peace Song* [xii] O.C. Smith (1974) US#62/Al Wilson (1974) R&B#19 US#30; *Love Me for a Reason* [ii] Osmonds (1974) US#10 UK#1/Boyzone (1994) UK#2; *My Whole World Ended the Moment You Left Me* [vi] David Ruffin (1969) R&B#2 US#9, *Pucker Up, Buttercup* [iv] Junior Walker & the All Stars (1967) R&B#11 US#31, *Someday We'll Be Together* [i] Diana Ross & the Supremes (1969) g R&B#1 US#1 UK#13/Bill Anderson & Jan Howard (1970) C&W#4; *Take Me Girl, I'm Ready* [xiii] Junior Walker & the All Stars (1971) R&B#18 US#50 UK#16, *That's How Love Goes* Jermaine Jackson (1972) R&B#23 US#46, *That's the Sound That*

Lonely Makes [v] Tavares (1974) R&B#10 US#70, *These Things Will Keep Me Loving You* Velvettes (1966) R&B#43 US#135, re-issued (1971) UK#34; *Touch Me Baby (Reaching Out for Your Love)* Tamiko Jones (1975) R&B#12 US#62, *Twenty-Five Miles* [vii] Edwin Starr (1969) R&B#6 US#6, *Walk in the Night* [xi] Junior Walker & the All Stars (1972) R&B#10 US#46 UK#16/Paul Hardcastle (1988) UK#54; *We've Come Too Far to End It Now* Smokey Robinson & the Miracles (1972) R&B#9 US#46, *What Does It Take (To Win Your Love)?* [iii] Junior Walker & the All Stars (1969) R&B#1 US#4 UK#13/Motherlode (1969) US#111/Garland Jeffreys (1983) US#107/ Kenny G. (1986) R&B#15 UK#64; *What Is a Man* Four Tops (1969) US#35 UK#16. Co-writers: [i] Robert Beavers/Harvey Fuqua, [ii] Wade Brown, Jr./David Jones, Jr., [iii] Vernon Bullock/Harvey Fuqua, [iv] Danny Coggins/Harvey Fuqua, [v] James Dean/Jim Glover, [vi] Harvey Fuqua/Jimmy Roach/Pam Sawyer, [vii] Harvey Fuqua/Edwin Starr (b. Charles Hatcher, January 21, 1942, Nashville, TN), [viii] William Guest/Walter Jones/Gladys Knight (b. May 28, 1944, Atlanta, AL)/Merald Knight, Jr./Catherine Shaffner, [ix] Joe Hinton/Pam Sawyer, [x] Gladys Knight/Merald Knight, Jr., [xi] Marilyn McLeod, [xii] L. Martin, [xiii] Pam Sawyer/Laverne Ware.

113. BROOKER, Gary (b. May 29, 1945, Southend, England) Rock pianist and vocalist. The principal songwriter and lead singer in the classical and R&B influenced British progressive rock group Procol Harum. Brooker worked almost exclusively with the enigmatic lyricist Keith Reid. He had originally been a member of the 1960s R&B group the Paramounts, recordings by which were anthologized on **Whiter Shades of R&B** (1983, Edsel). Procol Harum was formed in 1967, and immediately became successful with the six million selling *A Whiter Shade of Pale* [i], which was a psychedelic adaptation of Johann Sebastian Bach's *Suite #3 in D Major*. The somewhat untypical song became something of a millstone for the band over the years, but despite constant personnel changes, Procol Harum developed as a forceful and interesting rock group during the 1970s, turning in at least one classic album, the magisterial **Grand Hotel** (1973). CHART COMPOSITIONS: *A Whiter Shade of Pale* [i] (1967) R&B#22 US#5 UK#1, re-issued (1972) UK#13; *Homburg* [i] (1967) US#34 UK#6, *Quite Rightly So* [i] (1968) UK#50, *A Salty Dog* [i] (1969) UK#44, *Conquistador* [i] (1972) UK#22, *Grand Hotel* [i] (1973) US#117, *Pandora's Box* [i] (1975) UK#16. ALBUMS: **Procol Harum** (1967) US#47, **Shine on Brightly** (1968) US#24, **A Salty Dog** (1969) US#32 UK#27, **Home** (1970, all Regal Zonophone) US#34

UK#49; **Broken Barricades** (1971) US#32 UK#41, **In Concert with the Edmonton Symphony Orchestra** (1972) g US#5 UK#48, **Grand Hotel** (1973) US#21, **Exotic Birds and Fruit** (1974) US#86, **Procol's Ninth** (1975) US#52 UK#41, **Something Magic** (1977, all Chrysalis) US#147; **The Prodigal Stranger** (1991, Zoo). COMPILATIONS: **A Whiter Shade of Pale/A Salty Dog** (1972, Fly) UK#26; **Best of Procol Harum** (1973, A&M) US#131; **Portfolio** (1988, Chrysalis). Between group activities, Brooker flirted with a solo career and composed the ballet score "Delta" (1991). ALBUMS: **No More Fear of Flying** (1979, Chrysalis); **Lead Me to the Water** (1982), **Echoes in the Night** (1986, both Mercury). HIT VERSIONS: *Salty Dog, A* [i] Marc Almond on B-side of *A Woman's Story* (1984) UK#41, *Whiter Shade of Pale, A* [i] Munich Machine (1978) UK#42/ Hagar, Schon, Aaronson, Shrieve (1984) US#94/ Annie Lennox (1995) UK#16. Co-writer: [i] Keith Reid (b. October 10, 1946, England).

114. BROOKS, Garth (b. Troyal Garth Brooks, February 7, 1962, Yukon, OK) C&W guitarist and vocalist. The biggest selling artist in the history of country music, whose combined record sales stand at over fifty million and rising. Brooks is the country singer who has taken the genre out of the medium sized venues and into the stadium rock league. His music is actually nearer to rock than it is to country, and he is at the vanguard of a new generation of artists that exclusively dominate American country radio. Brooks' first trio of albums have sold over twenty million copies, while **The Hits** (1994), at over seven million copies sold, is the biggest selling compilation in country music history. The son of the singer Colleen Carroll, who recorded for Capitol Records in 1954, Brooks is a shrewd, populist, but undoubtedly talented and committed artist, who, despite his popularity, is unlikely to have the long term effect on the genre that either Hank Williams or Jimmie Rodgers had. CHART COMPOSITIONS: *Much Too Young (To Feel This Damn Good)* (1989) C&W#8, *If Tomorrow Never Comes* [v] (1989) C&W#1, *Unanswered Prayers* [iii] (1990) C&W#1, *Two of a Kind* (1991) C&W#1, *The Thunder Rolls* [i] (1991) C&W#1, *What She's Doing Now* [i] (1992) C&W#1, *Papa Loved Mama* [xi] (1992) C&W#3, *The River* [ix] (1992) C&W#1, *We Shall Be Free* [vii] (1992) C&W#12, *Somewhere Other Than the Night* [v] (1992) C&W#1, *The Old Man's Back in Town* [iv] (1992) C&W#48, *That Summer* [ii] (1993) C&W#1, *Ain't Going Down (Til the Sun Comes Up)* [vi] (1993) C&W#1 UK#13, *Standing Outside the Fire* [xii] (1993) C&W#71, re-issued (1994) UK#28; *She's Every Woman* (1995) UK#55, *The Beaches of Cheyenne* [viii] (1996) C&W#1, *It's Midnight Cinderella* [vi]

(1996) C&W#67+. ALBUMS: **Garth Brooks** (1989) p US#13, **No Fences** (1990) p US#3, **Ropin' the Wind** (1991, all Capitol) p US#1 UK#41; **Beyond the Season** (1992) p US#2, **The Chase** (1992) p US#1, **In Pieces** (1993, all Liberty) p US#1 UK#2; **Fresh Horses** (1995) p US#2 UK#22, **The Limited Series** (1998, both Capitol) p US#1. COMPILATION: **The Hits** (1994, Liberty) p US#1 UK#54. HIT VERSIONS: *Like We Never Had a Broken Heart* [i] Trisha Yearwood (1991) C&W#4, *Walk Outside the Lines* [x] Marshall Tucker Band (1993) C&W#71. Co-writers: [i] Pat Alger, [ii] Pat Alger/S. Mahl, [iii] Pat Alger/L. Bastain, [iv] L. Bastian/R. Taylor, [v] Kent Blazy, [vi] Kent Blazy/Kim Williams, [vii] Stephanie Davis, [viii] B. Kennedy/D. Roberts, [ix] Victoria Shaw, [x] C. Stefl, [xi] Kim Williams, [xii] J. Yates.

115. BROOKS, Shelton (b. May 4, 1886, Amesburg, Canada; d. September 6, 1975, Los Angeles, CA) Pianist and vaudeville performer. A Tin Pan Alley composer who first performed as a ragtime pianist, before creating his own vaudeville act. Brooks' first songwriting success was with Sophie Tucker's two million selling version of *Some of These Days* (1910). In his later years, Brooks performed on radio and in films. HIT VERSIONS: *All Night Long* Ada Jones & Billy Murray (1913) US#7, *Darktown Strutters' Ball, The* Original Dixieland Jazz Band (1917) US#2/Six Brown Brothers (1917) US#10/Arthur Collins & Byron Harlan (1918) US#1/Jaudas' Society Orchestra (1918) US#9/Ted Lewis (1927) US#12/Alan Dale & Connie Haines (1948) US#29/Lou Monte (1954) US#7/Big Ben Banjo Band in *Let's Get Together #1* (1954) UK#6/Joe Brown & the Bruvvers (1960) UK#34; *Some of These Days* American Quartete (1911) US#3/Sophie Tucker (1911) US#2/Original Dixieland Jazz Band (1923) US#5/Sophie Tucker with Ted Lewis (1927) US#1/Bing Crosby (1932) US#16/Johnston Brothers in *Join in and Sing Again* (1955) UK#9/Russ Conway in *More Party Pops* (1958) UK#10.

116. BROWN, Charles (b. 1922, Texas City, TX) Blues pianist and vocalist. An influential baritone balladeer who linked the blues to crooning, a path that the genre has seldom meandered since. Brown initially trained as a chemist, before turning to music and performing in the trio the Three Blazers with the guitarist Johnny Moore. The group charted with *Drifting Blues* (1946) R&B#2 and *Merry Christmas Baby* (1947) R&B#3, re-issued (1948) R&B#8, re-issued (1949) R&B#9. As the Charles Brown Trio, he continued to be successful throughout the 1940s. Brown was still performing in the late 1980s, alongside the singer Bonnie Raitt, and as a member of the New York Rock and Soul Revue.

CHART COMPOSITIONS: *Get Yourself Another Fool* (1949) R&B#4, *Long Time* (1949) R&B#9, *It's Nothing* (1949) R&B#13, *Trouble Blues* (1949) R&B#1, *In the Evening When the Sun Goes Down* (1949) R&B#4, *Homesick Blues* (1949) R&B#5, *Black Night* (1951) R&B#1, *Please Come Home for Christmas* [i] (1961) R&B#21 US#76, re-issued (1962) US#108. ALBUMS: **Mood Music** (1954, Aladdin); **Driftin' Blues** (1957, Score); **Charles Brown Sings Xmas Songs** (1961, King); **Million Sellers** (1961, Imperial); **Charles Brown Will Grip Your Heart** (1964, King); **Ballads My Way** (1965, Mainstream); **Legend** (1970, Bluesway); **Blues and Brown** (1972, Jewel); **Boss of the Blues** (1974, Mainstream); **Charles Brown** (1975, Bulldog); **Sunnyland** (1979, Route 66); **Great Rhythm and Blues, Volume 2** (1982, Bulldog); **Race Track Blues** (1987, Route 66); **I'm Gonna Push on** (1987, Stockholm); **One More for the Road** (1987, Demon); **All My Life** (1991, Rounder); **Someone to Love** (1992, Bullseye), **These Blues** (1995, Verve); **Honey Dripper** (1996, Verve/Gitanes). HIT VERSIONS: *Drifting Blues* Bobby Bland (1968) US#96, *Please Come Home for Christmas* [i] Eagles (1978) US#18/Bon Jovi (1994) UK#7, re-entry (1995) UK#46. Co-writer: [i] Gene Redd.

117. BROWN, Errol (b. November 12, 1948, Kingston, Jamaica, West Indies) Pop vocalist. The lead singer and principal songwriter in the group Hot Chocolate, one of the most pecuniary and commercially successful British singles acts of the 1970s. Brown's ability to emulate any current pop trend gave the band an unbroken fourteen year chart run between 1970–1984. CHART COMPOSITIONS: *Love Is Life* [ii] (1970) UK#6, *You Could Have Been a Lady* (1971) UK#22, *I Believe (In Love)* [ii] (1971) UK#23, *Brother Louie* [ii] (1973) UK#7, *Rumors* (1973) UK#44, *Emma* [ii] (1974) US#8 UK#3, *Cheri Babe* (1974) UK#31, *Disco Queen* [ii] (1974) R&B#40 US#28 UK#11, *A Child's Prayer* (1975) UK#7, *You Sexy Thing* [ii] (1975) g R&B#6 US#3 UK#2, re-mixed (1987) UK#10; *Don't Stop It Now* (1976) R&B#43 US#42 UK#11, *Man to Man* (1976) UK#14, *Heaven Is in the Back Seat of My Cadillac* (1976) UK#25, *Put Your Love in Me* (1977) UK#10, *Everyone's a Winner* (1978) g R&B#7 US#6 UK#12, re-mixed (1987) UK#69; *Mindless Boogie* (1979) UK#46, *Going Through the Motions* (1979) R&B#43 US53 UK#53, *Are You Getting Enough of What Makes You Happy* (1980) UK#17, *Love Me to Sleep* (1980) UK#50, *You'll Never Be So Wrong* (1981) UK#52, *Girl Crazy* (1982) UK#7, *It Started with a Kiss* (1982) UK#5, re-issued (1993) UK#36; *Chances* (1982) UK#32, *Are You Getting Enough Happiness* (1982) R&B#50 US#65, *What Kind of Boy You Looking For (Girl)* (1983) UK#10, *Tears on the Telephone* (1983)

UK#37, *I Gave You My Heart (Didn't I)* (1983)
UK#13. ALBUMS: **Cicero Park** (1974) US#55, **Hot Chocolate** (1975) US#41 UK#34, **Man to Man** (1976) US#172 UK#32, **Every 1's a Winner** (1978) US#31 UK#30, **Going Through the Motions** (1979) US#112, **Class** (1980), **Mystery** (1982) UK#24, **Love Shot** (1983, all Rak). COMPILATIONS: **14 Greatest Hits** (1976, Rak) UK#6; **20 Hottest Hits** (1979) UK#3, **Very Best of Hot Chocolate** (1987) UK#1, **Their Greatest Hits** (1993, all EMI) UK#1. After Hot Chocolate broke up, Brown attempted a brief solo career in the late 1980s. CHART COMPOSITIONS: *Personal Touch* (1987) UK#25, *Body Rockin'* (1987) UK#51. ALBUMS: **That's How Love Is** (1988, WEA); **Secret Rendezvous** (1992, East West). HIT VERSIONS: *Bet Yer Life I Do* Herman's Hermits (1970) UK#22, *Brother Louie* [ii] Stories (1973) g R&B#22 US#1/Quireboys (1993) UK#31; *Lady Barbara* [i] Herman's Hermits (1970) UK#13, *Think About Your Children* Mary Hopkin (1970) US#87 UK#19, re-entry (1971) UK#46. Co-writers: [i] Giancarlo Bigazzi/Tony Wilson (b. October 8, 1947, Trinidad, West Indies), [ii] Tony Wilson.

118. BROWN, James (b. James Joe Brown, Jr., May 3, 1933, Barnwell, SC) R&B organist, producer and vocalist. After Ray Charles, James Brown is the single most important figure in the history of R&B music. He has charted over one hundred R&B singles since 1956, seventeen of which reached number one, and in much the same way that Miles Davis revolutionized jazz by frequently dispensing with the old in order to introduce the new, Brown did the same for R&B, and both he and Charles can be credited with the birth of modern soul music. The feelings and concerns in Brown's songs can be traced back to the original delta blues singers, themes to which Brown later added self-awareness and statements of black pride, as on *I Don't Want Nobody to Give Me Nothing (Open the Door, I'll Get It Myself)*. Through Brown, street corner doo-wop ultimately developed into rap, and he was also one of the first artists to integrate black and white concert audiences. Of the many performers that he has influenced, Sly Stone, George Clinton and Prince owe him the greatest debt. Born into poverty in a one-room shack, Brown was raised by an aunt and led a solitary childhood. He made his first music at the age of five on a harmonica given to him by his father, but after a four year stretch of hard prison labor for teenage criminal behavior, Brown became a shoeshine boy in Augusta, Georgia. In the early 1950s, he learned the drums and organ, while singing with the Gospel Starlighters and the Swanees, before forming an R&B group with Bobby Byrd called the Avons. The group eventually became the Flames, and performed in a

style that was heavily influenced by Little Richard. As the Famous Flames, the band cut a demo of Brown's first song, *Please, Please, Please*, which secured the group a record deal and became Brown's first million seller. After 1959, Brown began touring his infamous soul revue show, a modern form of old time vaudeville which played all over America, sometimes managing up to three hundred and fifty-one one-nighters a year, shows that Brown would often close by leaving the stage with a suitcase, already enroute to the next town. By 1963, Brown was clearly the most original and exciting artist in black music, heralding the genre's golden era and opening the way for such song stylists as Otis Redding, Solomon Burke and Wilson Pickett. *Prisoner of Love* (1963) evidenced a newer, more pleading and dramatic ballad style, while Brown's gospel routes showed up in the oddest places, such as his version of the standard *These Foolish Things*. A dispute with his record company in 1963 resulted in Brown undertaking a personal recording strike, safe in the knowledge that he could rely on his concert performances to earn a living. His record label swiftly capitulated, and the incident won him the right to release future disks of his own choosing, resulting in *Out of Sight* (1964), which featured a hypnotic backbeat over which Brown squealed and shouted phrases that soon became hip street terminology in the ghettos and black inner city neighborhoods. The song was a musical revolution, and introduced a new style of dance music that became known as funk. *Don't Be a Drop-Out* (1966) and the anti-drug *King Heroin* (1972), were two of the earliest black pop disks to openly voice social concerns, while *Cold Sweat* (1967), once again took R&B in a new direction by introducing syncopated rhythms in conjunction with tight, between-the-beat drumming, heavily accented by spacious bass lines. Brown subsequently ran his own People label, upon which he acted as a mentor, writer and producer, and, like Miles Davis, he continually surrounded himself with accomplished young musicians in a seemingly restless exploration of new territory, always dispensing with a style as soon as he had mastered it. Compositions such as *(It's Not the Express) It's the J.B.s Monaurail* created grooves that influenced the sound of R&B disks for over a decade, while *Body Heat* and *Papa Don't Take No Mess* initiated the disco sound of the 1980s. When hip hop and rap artists borrowed obsessively from Brown in the late 1980s, he soon became the most sampled artist in music history. Always a volatile personality, in December 1988, Brown was sentenced to six years in a South Carolina prison on a number of charges. He was paroled in February 1991, whereupon he immediately resumed his recording career. CHART SINGLES: *Please, Please, Please* (1956) R&B#5 US#105, re-issued (1964) US#95; *Try Me* (1959) R&B#1 US#48, instrumental version (1965) US#63; *I Want You So Bad* (1959) R&B#20, *I'll Go Crazy* (1959) R&B#15, re-issued (1966) R&B#38 US#73; *You've Got the Power* (1960) R&B#14 US#86, *This Old Heart* (1960) R&B#20 US#79, *The Bells* (1960) US#68, *Hold It* (1961) US#109, *Bewildered* (1961) US#40, *I Don't Mind* (1961) R&B#4 US#47, *Baby, You're Right* [xi] (1961) R&B#2 US#49, *Just You and Me, Darling* (1961) R&B#17, *Lost Someone* (1961) R&B#2 US#48, *Shout and Shimmy* (1962) R&B#16 US#61, *Mashed Potatoes U.S.A.* (1962) R&B#21 US#82, *Three Hearts in a Tangle* (1962) R&B#18 US#93, *Like a Baby* (1963) R&B#24, *Signed, Sealed and Delivered* (1963) US#77, *Oh Baby Don't You Weep* (1964) US#23, *Caledonia* (1964) US#95, *The Things I Used to Do* (1964) US#99, *In the Wee Small Hours (Of the Nite)* (1964) US#125, *Again* (1964) US#107, *How Long Darling* (1964) US#134, *So Long* (1964) US#132, *Maybe the Last Time* (1964) US#107, *Have Mercy Baby* (1964) US#92, *Devil's Hideaway* (1965) US#114, *Papa's Got a Brand New Bag* (1965) g R&B#1 US#8 UK#25, instrumental version (1965) US#42; *I Got You (I Feel Good)* (1965) g R&B#1 US#36 UK#29, re-issued (1988) UK#52, re-mixed (1992) UK#72; *Ain't That a Groove* (1966) US#42, *It's a Man's, Man's, Man's World* [ix] (1966) g R&B#1 US#8 UK#13, *New Breed (Part 1) (The Boo-Ga-Loo)* (1966) US#102, *Money Won't Change You* (1966) R&B#11 US#53, *Don't Be a Drop-Out* (1966) R&B#4 US#50, *Bring It Up* [vi] (1967) R&B#7 US#29, *Think* with Vicki Anderson (1967) US#100, re-issued (1973) R&B#37 US#80; *Let Yourself Go* (1967) R&B#5 US#46, *Cold Sweat* [iv] (1967) g R&B#1 US#7, *Get It Together* [v] (1967) R&B#11 US#40, *I Can't Stand Myself (When You Touch Me)* (1968) R&B#4 US#28, *There Was a Time* (1968) R&B#3 US#36, *You've Got to Change Your Mind* with Bobby Byrd (1968) R&B#47 US#102, *I Got the Feelin'* (1968) g R&B#1 US#6, *Licking Stick, Licking Stick* [iii] (1968) R&B#2 US#14, *America Is My Home* [viii] (1968) R&B#13 US#52, *Shhhhhhh (For a Little While)* (1968) US#104, *I Guess I'll Have to Cry, Cry, Cry* (1968) R&B#15 US#55, *Say It Loud-I'm Black and I'm Proud* [iv] (1968) g R&B#1 US#10, *Goodbye My Love* (1968) R&B#9 US#31, *Give It Up or Turnit a Loose* (1969) R&B#1 US#15, *Soul Pride* (1969) R&B#33 US#117, *I Don't Want Nobody To Give Me Nothin' (Open the Door I'll Get It Myself)* (1969) R&B#3 US#20, *The Popcorn* instrumental version (1969) R&B#11 US#30, *Mother Popcorn (You Got to Have a Mother For Me)* [iv] (1969) g R&B#1 US#11, *Lowdown Popcorn* (1969) R&B#16 US#41, *World* (1969) R&B#8 US#37, *Let a Man Come in and Do the Popcorn (Part 1)* (1969) R&B#2 US#21, *Let a Man Come in and Do the Popcorn (Part 2)* (1969) R&B#6 US#40, *Ain't It Funky Now* (1969) R&B#3 US#24, *It's a New Day* (1970) R&B#3 US#32, *Funky Drummer* (1970) R&B#20 US#51, *Brother Rapp* (1970) R&B#2 US#32, *Get Up I Feel Like Being a Sex Machine* (1970) g R&B#2 US#15 UK#32, re-issued (1985) UK#47, re-issued (1986) UK#46, re-issued (1991) UK#69; *Super Bad* (1970) g R&B#1 US#13, *Get Up, Get into It, Get Involved* (1971) R&B#4 US#34, *Soul Power* (1971) R&B#3 US#29, *Spinning Wheel* (1971) US#90, *I Cried* (1971) R&B#15 US#50, *Escape-ism* (1971) R&B#6 US#35, *Hot Pants (She Got to Use What She Got to Get What She Wants)* (1971) g R&B#1 US#15, *Make It Funky* (1971) R&B#1 US#22, *My Part (Make It Funky Part 3)* (1971) US#68, *I'm a Greedy Man* (1971) R&B#7 US#35, *Hey America* (1971) US#47, *Talking Loud and Saying Nothing* (1972) R&B#1 US#27, *King Heroin* (1972) R&B#6 US#40, *There It Is* (1972) R&B#4 US#43, *Honky Tonk* (1972) R&B#7 US#44, *Get on the Good Foot* [vii] (1972) g R&B#1 US#18, *I Got a Bag of My Own* (1972) R&B#3 US#44, *What My Baby Needs Now Is a Little More Lovin'* with Lyn Collins (1972) R&B#17 US#56, *I Got Ants in My Pants (And I Want to Dance)* (1973) R&B#4 US#27, *Down and Out in New York City* (1973) R&B#13 US#50, *Sexy, Sexy, Sexy* (1973) R&B#6 US#50, *Stoned to the Bone* (1973) R&B#4 US#58, *The Payback* [x] (1974) g R&B#1 US#26, *My Thang* (1974) R&B#1 US#29, *Papa Don't Take No Mess* [xii] (1974) R&B#1 US#31, *Funky President (People It's Bad)/Cold Blooded* (1974) R&B#4 US#44, *Reality* [xiii] (1975) R&B#19 US#80, *Sex Machine (Part 1)* (1975) R&B#16 US#61, *Hustle!!! (Dead on It)* (1975) R&B#11, *Superbad, Superslick* (1975) R&B#28, *Hot (I Need to Be Loved, Loved, Loved)* (1975) R&B#31, *Get Up Offa That Thing* (1976) R&B#4 US#45 UK#22, *I Refuse to Lose* (1976) R&B#47, *Bodyheat* (1977) R&B#13 US#88 UK#36, *Kiss in '77* (1977) R&B#35, *Give Me Some Skin* (1977) R&B#20, *If You Don't Give a Doggone About It* (1977) R&B#45, *Eyesight* (1978) R&B#38, *The Spank* (1978) R&B#26, *For Goodness Sakes, Look at Those Cakes* (1978) R&B#52, *It's Too Funky in Here* (1979) R&B#15, *Star Generation* (1979) R&B#63, *Regrets* (1980) R&B#63, *Rapp Payback (Where Iz Moses?)* (1981) R&B#46 UK#39, *Stay with Me* (1981) R&B#80, *Bring It On, Bring It On* (1983) R&B#73 UK#45, *Unity* with Afrika Bambaataa (1984) R&B#87 UK#49, *Froggy Mix* (1985) UK#50, *She's the One* (1988) UK#45, *The Payback Mix* (1988) UK#12, *I'm Real* (1988) R&B#2 UK#31. ALBUMS: **Please, Please, Please** (1959), **Try Me** (1959), **Think** (1960), **The Amazing James Brown** (1961), **James Brown Presents His Band/Night Train** (1961), **Shout and Shimmy** (1962), **JB and His Famous Flames Tour the U.S.A.** (1962), **Live at the Apollo** (1963) g US#2, **Prisoner of Love** (1963) US#73,

Pure Dynamite-Live at the Royal (1964, all King) US#10; **Showtime** (1964) US#61, **Grits and Soul** (1964) US#124, **James Brown Sings Out of Sight** (1964, all Smash); **Papa's Got a Brand New Bag** (1965, King) US#26; **JB Plays JB Today and Yesterday** (1966, Smash) US#42; **I Got You (I Feel Good)** (1966) US#36, **Mighty Instrumentals** (1966, both King); **JB Plays New Breed (The Boog-Ga-Loo)** (1966, Smash) US#101; **It's a Man's, Man's, Man's World** (1966) US#90, **Christmas Songs** (1966, both King); **Handful of Soul** (1966) US#135, **The James Brown Show** (1967, both Smash); **Raw Soul** (1967) US#88, **Live at the Garden** (1967, both King) US#41; **JB Plays the Real Thing** (1967, Smash) US#164; **Cold Sweat** (1967, King) US#35; **JB Presents His Show of Tomorrow** (1968), **I Can't Stand Myself (When You Touch Me)** (1968) US#17, **I Got the Feelin'** (1968) US#135, **JB Plays Nothing But Soul** (1968) US#150, **Live at the Apollo, Volume 2** (1968) US#32, **Thinking About Willie John and a Few Nice Things** (1968), **A Soulful Christmas** (1968), **Say It Loud I'm Black and I'm Proud** (1969) US#53, **Gettin' Down to It** (1969) US#99, **James Brown Plays and Directs the Popcorn** (1969) US#40, **It's a Mother** (1969) US#26, **Ain't It Funky** (1970) US#43, **Soul on Top** (1970) US#125, **It's a New Day So Let a Man Come In** (1970) US#121, **Sex Machine** (1970) US#29, **Hey America** (1970), **Super Bad** (1971) US#61, **Sho Is Funky Down Here** (1971, all King) US#137; **Hot Pants** (1971) US#22, **Revolution of the Mind-Live at the Apollo, Volume 3** (1971) US#39, **There It Is** (1972) US#60, **Get on the Good Foot** (1972) US#68, **Black Caesar** ost (1973) US#31, **Slaughter's Big Rip-Off** ost (1973) US#92, **The Payback** (1974) g US#34, **Hell** (1974) US#35, **Reality** (1975) US#56, **Sex Machine Today** (1975) US#103, **Everybody's Doin' the Hustle and Dead on the Double Bump** (1975) US#193, **Hot** (1976), **Get Up Off That Thing** (1976), US#147, **Bodyheat** (1976) US#126, **Mutha's Nature** (1977), **Jam 1980s** (1978) US#121, **Take a Look at Those Cakes** (1979), **The Original Disco Man** (1979) US#152, **People** (1980), **Hot on the One** (1980, all Polydor) US#170; **Soul Syndrome** (1980, TK); **Nonstop!** (1981, Polydor); **Live in New York** (1981, Audio Fidelity); **Bring It On** (1983, Churchill/Augusta Sound); **Gravity** (1986) US#156 UK#85, **I'm Real** (1988, both Scotti Brothers) US#96 UK#27; **James Brown and Friends** (1988, Polydor); **Love Overdue** (1991), **Universal James** (1993, both Scotti Brothers). COMPILATIONS: **The Unbeatable James Brown/16 Hits** (1964, King); **JB Sings Out of Sight** (1968, Smash); **Soul Classics** (1972) US#83, **Soul Classics, Volume 2** (1973, both Polydor); **Live and Lowdown at the Apollo, Volume 1** (1980) US#163, **The Federal Years, Part 1** (1984), **The Federal Years, Part 2** (1984, all Solid Smoke); **Ain't That a Groove-The JB Story, 1966–1969** (1984), **Doing It to Death-The JB Story, 1970–1973** (1984), **Dead on the Heavy Funk-The JB Story, 1974–1976** (1985), **The CD of JB-Sex Machine and Other Soul Classics** (1985), **In the Jungle Groove** (1986, all Polydor); **Best of James Brown-The Godfather of Soul** (1987, K-Tel) UK#17; **CD of JB II-Cold Sweat and Other Soul Classics** (1987), **Sex Machine-The Very Best of James Brown** (1991) UK#19, **Star Time** (1991, all Polydor); **Live in New York** (1991, Enteleky); **Live at Chastain Park** (1992, Instant); **Love Power Peace-Live at the Olympia, Paris, 1971** (1992), **Soul Pride-The Instrumentals** (1993), **All Time Greatest Hits** (1993), **Funky President-Very Best of James Brown, Volume 2** (1993, all Polydor). HIT VERSIONS: *Baby, Baby, Baby* Bobby Byrd & Anna King (1964) R&B#52, *Breakin' Bread* Fred & the New J.B.s (1974) R&B#80, *Cold Sweat* [iv] Mongo Santamaria (1968) R&B#49, *Control (People Go Where We Send You)* First Family (1974) R&B#81, *Damn Right I am Somebody* Fred Wesley & the J.B.s (1974) R&B#32, *Do the Mashed Potato* Nathan Kendrick & the Swans (1963) R&B#8 US#84, *Doing It to Death* Fred Wesley & the J.B.s (1973) g R&B#1 US#22, *Escape-ism* TLC sampled in *Ain't 2 Proud 2 Beg* (1992) p R&B#1 US#6 UK#13, *From the Love Side* Hank Ballard & the Midnight Lighters (1972) R&B#43, *Gimme Me Some More* J.B.s (1971) R&B#11 US#67, *Hot Pants, I'm Coming, I'm Coming* Bobby Byrd (1971) R&B#34 US#85, *How Long Can I Keep It Up?* Lyn Collins (1973) R&B#45, *I Know You Got Soul* Bobby Byrd (1971) R&B#30 US#11, *I Need Help (I Can't Do It Alone)* Bobby Byrd (1970) R&B#14 US#69, *I'll Go Crazy* Buckinghams (1966) US#112, *If You Don't Get It the First Time, Back It Up and Try Again* Fred Wesley & the J.B.s (1973) R&B#24 US#104, *It's a Man's, Man's, Man's World* [ix] Irma Thomas as *It's a Man's-Woman's World* (1966) US#119/ Bobby Womack featuring Tracy (1995) UK#73; *It's My Thing (You Can't Tell Me Who to Sock It To)* Marva Whitney (1969) R&B#19 US#82, *(It's Not the Express) It's the J.B.s* Monaurail Fred & the J.B.s (1975) R&B#63, *Keep on Doin' What You're Doin'* Bobby Byrd (1972) R&B#40 US#88, *Mama Feelgood (The Female Preacher)* Lyn Collins (1973) R&B#37, *Me and My Baby Got Our Own Thing Going* Lyn Collins (1972) US#86, *Mistadobalina* [i] Del Tha Funkee Homosapian (1992) R&B#55, *Paarty* Maceo & the Macks (1973) R&B#24 US#71, *Papa Don't Take No Mess* [xii] Mary J. Blige sampled in *You Don't Have to Worry* (1993) US#63 UK#36, *Papa's Got a Brand New Bag* Otis Redding (1968) R&B#10 US#21/Silent Underdog as *Papa's Got a Brand New Pig Bag* (1985) R&B#69/Keith Sweat sampled in *Keep It Comin'* (1992) US#17; *Pass the Peas* J.B.s (1972) R&B#29 US#95, *Please, Please, Please* 5 Royales (1960) US#114, *Rock Me Again and Again and Again and Again and Again and Again and Again* Lyn Collins (1974) R&B#53, *Same Beat* Fred Wesley & the J.B.s (1973) R&B#26, *Soul Power '74* Maceo & the Macks (1974) R&B#20 US#109, *Take Me Just as I Am* Lyn Collins (1973) R&B#35, *There Was a Time* Dapps featuring Alfred Ellis (1968) US#103, *They Want EFX* Das EFX (1992) g US#25, *Things Got to Get Better (Get Together)* Marva Whitney (1969) R&B#22 US#110, *Think (About It)* Lyn Collins (1972) R&B#9 US#66/Patra featuring Lyn Collins (1993) R&B#89 R&B#105. Co-writers: [i] Charles A. Bobbitt/Del/Ice Cube (b. O'Shea Jackson)/Fred A. Wesley, [ii] Charles A. Bobbitt/Susaye Coton/Fred A. Wesley, [iii] Bobby Byrd/Alfred Ellis, [iv] Alfred Ellis, [v] Alfred Ellis/Buddy Hobgood, [vi] Nat Jones, [vii] Joe Mims/Fred Wesley, [viii] Hayward Moore, [ix] Betty Jean Newsome, [x] John Starks/Fred A. Wesley, [xi] Joe Tex, [xii] Fred A. Wesley, [xiii] G. & S. Wesley.

119. BROWN, Lew (b. Louis Brownstein, December 10, 1893, Odessa, Russia; d. February 5, 1958, New York, NY) Film and stage lyricist, producer. One third of the highly successful songwriting partnership Buddy DeSylva, Lew Brown and Ray Henderson, who wrote his first songs in collaboration with Albert Von Tilzer, and was initially successful with *Give Me the Girl (And Leave the Rest to Me)* (1917). Brown's compositions were included in the shows "George White's Scandals of 1923," "Gay Paree" (1925) and "Yokel Boy" (1939), and he also worked in Hollywood, where he contributed to the films "Animal Crackers" (1930), "A Night in Casablanca" (1946) and "Stand Up and Cheer" (1934). HIT VERSIONS: *Beer Barrel Polk, The* [xi] Andrews Sisters (1939) US#4/Will Glahe (1939) g US#1/Eddie DeLange (1939) US#13/Winifred Atwell in *Make It a Party* (1956) UK#7/Bobby Vinton (1975) US#33; *Comes Love* [x] Larry Clinton (1939) US#7/Eddy Duchin (1939) US#14/Artie Shaw (1939) US#4; *Don't Sit Under the Apple Tree (With Anyone Else But Me)* [x] Andrews Sisters (1942) US#16/Glenn Miller (1942) US#1; *I Came Here to Talk for Joe* [x] Sammy Kaye (1942) US#8, *I'd Climb the Highest Mountain (If I Knew I'd Find You)* [iii] Art Grahman (1926) US#11/Al Jolson (1926) US#7; *I'm Telling the Birds, Telling the Bees (How I Love You)* [vi] Cliff Edwards (1927) US#7/Wendell Hall (1927) US#13; *Last Night on the Back Porch* [ix] Ernest Hare & Billy Jones (1924) US#11/Paul Whiteman (1924) US#3; *Oh, Ma, Ma (The Butcher Boy)* [ii] George Hall (1938) US#13/Dick Robertson (1938) US#7/Rudy Vallee (1938) US#5; *Shine* [v] California Ramblers (1924)

US#10/Louis Armstrong (1932) US#17/Bing Crosby & Mills Brothers (1932) US#7/Frankie Laine (1948) US#9; *Then I'll Be Happy* [iv] "Whispering" Jack Smith (1926) US#9, *When It's Night Time in Italy, It's Wednesday Over Here* [viii] Lew Holtz (1924) US#9, *Where the Lazy Daisies Grow* [vi] Cliff Edwards (1924) US#14/Jean Goldkette (1924) US#12. Co-writers: [i] Nat Bonx/Moe Jaffe, [ii] Paolo Citorello/Rudy Vallee (b. Herbert Pryor Vallee, July 28, 1901, Island Pont, VT), [iii] Sidney Clare (b. 1892; d. 1972)/Antonin Dvorak (b. September 8, 1841, Nelahozeves; d. May 1, 1904, Prague, both Austria-Hungary), [iv] Sidney Clare/Cliff Friend, [v] Ford Dabney (b. 1883; d. 1958)/Cecil Mack (b. Richard Cecil McPherson, (b. 1883; d. 1944), [vi] Cliff Friend, [vii] Jay Gorney (b. Daniel Jayson, December 12, 1896, Bialystok, Russia), [viii] James Kendis (b. 1883; d. 1946), [ix] Carl Schraubstader, [x] Sammy H. Stept/Charles Tobias, [xi] Wladimir Timm/Jaromir Vejvoda. (*See also under* Buddy DESYLVA, Lew BROWN and Ray HENDERSON, Sammy FAIN, Albert VON TILZER, Harry WARREN.)

120. BROWN, Nacio Herb (b. Ignacio Herbert Brown, February 22, 1896, Deming, NM; d. September 28, 1964, San Francisco, CA) Film and stage composer, pianist. One of the songwriting pioneers of early film musicals, Brown was a former tailor and vaudeville pianist who first wrote songs for a hobby with Arthur Freed. The duo eventually collaborated on MGM's first screen musical "The Broadway Melody" (1929), which they followed with many other MGM successes after 1928, including "The Hollywood Revue" (1929), which introduced *Singin' in the Rain* [iv], a song that became the title of a film musical itself in 1952. Brown and Freed also composed material for "The Pagan" (1929), "Hollywood" (1933), "A Night at the Opera" (1935), "Babes in Arms" (1939), and "Greenwich Village" (1944). ALBUMS: **Pagan Love Song** ost (1950), **Singin' in the Rain** ost (1952), **Singin' in the Rain/Easter Parade** ost (1973, all MGM) US#185: **Singin' in the Rain** oc (1983, Rain). HIT VERSIONS: *All I Do Is Dream of You* [iv] Henry Busse (1934) US#9/Jan Garber (1934) US#1/Freddy Martin (1934) US#11/Johnnie Ray (1953) US#27; *Alone* [iv] Al Donohue (1936) US#11/Tommy Dorsey (1936) US#1/Hal Kemp (1936) US#9; *Avalon Town* [i] Gus Arnheim (1929) US#6/Clicquot Club Eskimos (1929) US#13; *Beautiful Girl* [iv] Bing Crosby (1933) US#11, *Broadway Melody, The* [iv] Charles King (1929) US#10/Ben Selvin (1929) US#3/Nat Shilkret (1929) US#13; *Broadway Rhythm* [iv] Guy Lombardo (1935) US#9, *Bundle of Old Love Letters* [iv] Paul Whiteman (1930) US#10, *Chant of the Jungle* [iv] Paul Specht (1929) US#13/Roy Ingraham

(1930) US#1/Nat Shilkret (1930) US#3; *Doll Dance, The* Earl Burtnett (1927) US#12/Nat Shilkret (1927) US#6; *Eadie Was a Lady* [iii] Ethel Merman (1933) US#8/Paul Whiteman (1933) US#17; *Good Morning* [iv] Abe Lyman (1939) US#10, *Hold Your Man* [iv] Don Bestor (1933) US#10/Gertrude Niesen (1933) US#14; *I'm Feeling Like a Million* [iv] Jan Garber (1937) US#19, *I've Got a Feelin' You're Foolin'* [iv] Dorsey Brothers Orchestra (1935) US#3/Eddy Duchin (1935) US#9; *Love Songs of the Nile* [iv] Leo Reisman (1933) US#7, *Moon Is Low* [iv] George Olsen (1930) US#7, *New Moon Is Over My Shoulder* [iv] Johnny Green (1934) US#9, *On a Sunday Afternoon* [iv] Edward M. Favor (1902) US#2/James Aldrich Libbey (1902) US#3/Harry MacDonough (1902) US#5/J.W. Myers (1902) US#1; *Our Big Love Scene* [iv] Leo Reisman (1934) US#17, *Pagan Love Song, The* [iv] Columbians (1929) US#5/Bob Haring (1929) US#1/Nat Shilkret (1929) US#3; *Paradise* [ii] Russ Columbo (1932) US#18/Bing Crosby (1932) US#7/Guy Lombardo (1932) US#1/Leo Reisman (1932) US#1/April Stevens & Nino Tempo (1963) US#126/Frank Ifield (1965) UK#26; *Should I?* [iv] Arden-Ohman Orchestra (1930) US#3/Four Aces (1952) US#9/Chad & Jeremy (1965) US#128; *Singin' in the Rain* [iv] Gus Arnheim (1929) US#9/Earl Burtnett (1929) US#4/Cliff Edwards (1929) US#1/Sheila & B. Devotion (1978) UK#11; *Temptation* [iv] Bing Crosby (1934) US#3/Ted Fio Rito (1934) US#15/Ferde Grofe (1934) US#19/Artie Shaw (1944) US#21/Perry Como (1945) US#15, re-issued (1946) US#21/Red Ingle (1947) US#1/Billy Eckstine (1949) R&B#7/Roger Williams (1960) US#56/Everly Brothers (1961) US#27 UK#1; *We'll Make Hay While the Sun Shines* [iv] Bing Crosby (1934) US#8, *Wedding of the Painted Doll, The* [iv] Earl Burtnett (1929) US#10/Charles King (1929) US#8/Leo Reisman (1929) US#1; *When Buddha Smiles* [v] Eddie Wilkins (1922) US#15/Paul Whiteman (1922) US#2; *You and I* [iv] Bing Crosby (1941) US#5/Tommy Dorsey (1941) US#11/Glenn Miller (1941) US#1; *You Are My Lucky Star* [iv] Louis Armstrong (1935) US#6/Tommy Dorsey with Eleanor Powell (1935) US#10/Dorsey Brothers Orchestra (1935) US#2/Eddy Duchin (1935) US#1; *You Stepped Out of a Dream* [vi] Tony Martin & Kay Kyser (1941) US#22, *You Were Meant For Me* [iv] Connee Boswell (1948) US#19/Gordon MacRae (1948) US#22/Ben Selvin (1929) US#13/Nat Shilkret (1929) US#2; *You're an Old Smoothie* [iii] Paul Whiteman (1933) US#11, *Yours and Mine* [iv] Ben Selvin (1931) US#14/Hudson-De-Lange Orchestra (1937) US#11/Teddy Wilson with Billie Holiday (1937) US#16. Co-writers: [i] Grant Clarke, [ii] Gordon Clifford (b. 1902; d. 1968), [iii] Buddy De Sylva/Richard A. Whiting, [iv] Arthur Freed, [v] Arthur Freed/King Zany, [vi] Gus Khan.

121. BROWN, Oscar, Jr. (b. October 10, 1926, Chicago, IL) R&B vocalist. A composer of acutely observed, witty and sometimes political R&B material. Brown often wrote lyrics to existing jazz tunes, including Bobby Timmons' *Dat Dere*, Miles Davis' *All Blues*, Clark Terry's *One Foot in the Gutter*, and Nina Simone's *Forbidden Fruit*. Brown also worked with the drummer Max Roach on the jazz classic **We Insist! Freedom Now Suite** (1960, Candid), before composing the stage musical "Kicks and Company" (1961). CHART COMPOSITION: *The Lone Ranger* (1974) R&B#27 US#69. ALBUMS: **Sin and Soul** (1960), **Between Heaven and Hell** (1961), **Tells It Like It Is** (1962), **Live at the Cellar Door** (1964, all Columbia); **Movin' On** (1970, Atlantic). HIT VERSIONS: *Snake, The* Al Wilson (1968) R&B#32 US#27, *Work Song* [i] Herb Alpert (1966) US#18. Co-writer: [i] Vernon Duke.

122. BROWN, Pete (b. December 25, 1940, London, England) Rock lyricist. An avante-garde, counter-culture poet who became the rock group Cream's principal lyricist, and wrote such material as *Theme for an Imaginary Western* for the heavy rock act Mountain. ALBUMS: **Jazz Poetry Group** (1966), **A Meal You Can Shake Hands With** (1969), **Mantlepiece*** (1969), **Thousands on a Raft** (1970), **Things May Come and Things May Go, But the Art School Dance Goes on Forever**** (1972, all Harvest); **Not Forgotten Association** (1973, Deram); **My Last Band**** (1977, Harvest); **Party in the Rain** (1982, Discs International); **Before Singing Lessons, 1969–1977** (1987, Harvest); **The Land That Cream Forgot** with Phil Ryan (1997, Viceroy). As: * Battered Ornaments, ** Piblokto. (*See also under* Jack BRUCE.)

123. BROWNE, Jackson (b. October 9, 1948, Heidelberg, West Germany) Rock guitarist, pianist and vocalist. A lyrical and melodic singer-songwriter whose intense studies of human relationships have constantly displayed a mastery of making specific personal emotions seem somehow universal. Browne was born to American parents on army service in Europe, and from 1951 he was raised in California, where, as a teenager he performed on the folk circuit. His self-titled debut album in 1972, was an assured collection of folk based material that depicted the general theme of a young person starting out in life. **For Everyman** (1973), introduced the slide guitarist and fiddle player David Lindley, whose contributions became an integral part of Browne's sound for many years, peaking on the moody **Late for the Sky** (1974), the title track of which is one of the most perceptive first-person narratives ever written about the breakdown of a relationship. **The Pretender**

(1976), was a particular highlight in Browne's career, while **Running on Empty** (1978), successfully documented the experiences of a touring band with material recorded on stage, in motel rooms and during rehearsals. After a series of less intense and more mainstream rock albums during the 1990s, Browne returned to scintillating form following the break-up of his relationship with the actress Daryl Hannah, resulting in the album **I'm Alive** (1993), a stark portrayal of failed aspirations, abandoned expectations and obsessive love. CHART COMPOSITIONS: *Doctor My Eyes* (1972) US#8, *Rock Me on the Water* (1972) US#48, *Red Neck Friend* (1973) US#85, *Here Come Those Tears Again* [i] (1977) US#23, *The Pretender* (1977) US#58, *Running on Empty* (1978) US#11, *You Love the Thunder* (1978) US#109, *Boulevard* (1980) US#19, *That Girl Could Sing* (1980) US#22, *Hold On, Hold Out* (1981) US#103, *Somebody's Baby* [ii] (1982) US#7, *Lawyers in Love* (1983) US#13, *Tender Is the Night* [iii] (1983) US#25, *For a Rocker* (1984) US#45, *For America* (1986) US#30, *In the Shape of a Heart* (1986) US#70 UK#66, *I'm Alive* (1993) US#118, *Everywhere I Go* (1994) UK#67. ALBUMS: **Jackson Browne** (1972) g US#53, **For Everyman** (1973) p US#43, **Late for the Sky** (1974) p US#14, **The Pretender** (1976) p US#5 UK#26, **Running on Empty** (1978) p US#5 UK#28, **Hold Out** (1980) p US#1 UK#44, **Lawyers in Love** (1983) g US#8 UK#37, **Lives in the Balance** (1986, all Asylum) g US#23 UK#36; **World in Motion** (1989) US#45 UK#39, **I'm Alive** (1993) US#40 UK#35, **Looking East** (1996, all Elektra) US#36 UK#47. HIT VERSIONS: *Doctor My Eyes* Jackson Five (1973) UK#9, *For a Dancer* Prelude (1975) US#63, *Rock Me on the Water* Linda Ronstadt (1972) US#85, *You Love the Thunder* Hank Williams, Jr. (1978) C&W#76. Co-writers: [i] Nancy Farnsworth, [ii] Danny Kortchmar, [iii] Danny Kortchmar/Russell Kunkel. (*See also under* Don HENLEY.)

124. BRUCE, Ed (b. William Edwin Bruce, Jr., December 29, 1940, Keiser, AK) C&W vocalist. A rockabilly singer who recorded for the Sun label during the late 1950s, and who also wrote early sides for Johnny Cash, Charlie Rich and Jerry Lee Lewis. After working as a used car salesman due to his lack of musical success, Bruce became a Nashville session singer-songwriter in the late 1960s, charting thirty-five country hits between 1967–1986. He also co-starred in the television series "Maverick" (1981). CHART COMPOSITIONS: *Mamas, Don't Let Your Babies Grow Up to Be Cowboys* [i] (1975) C&W#15, *When I Die, Just Let Me Go to Texas* (1977) C&W#52, *The Man That Turned My Mama On* (1978) C&W#70, *You're the Best Break This Old Heart Ever Had* (1981) C&W#1. ALBUMS: **Shades**

of **Ed Bruce** (1969, Monument); **Mama's Don't Let Your Babies Grow Up to Be Cowboys** (1976, United Artists); **The Tennessean** (1978, Epic); **Last Train to Clarksville** (1982), **I Write It Down** (1982), **You're Not Leaving Here Tonight** (1983), **Tell 'Em I've Gone Crazy** (1984), **Homecoming** (1985), **Next Things** (1986, all RCA); **Ed Bruce** (1986), **One to One** (1986 both MCA). COMPILATION: **Best of Ed Bruce** (1986, MCA); **Rock Boppin' Baby** (1986, Bear Family). HIT VERSIONS: *Mamas, Don't Let Your Babies Grow Up to Be Cowboys* [i] Waylon Jennings & Willie Nelson (1978) C&W#1 US#42/Gibson-Miller Band (1994) C&W#49; *Man That Turned My Mama On, The* Tanya Tucker (1974) C&W#4, *Northeast Arkansas Mississippi County Bootlegger* Kenny Price (1970) C&W#17, *Restless* Crystal Gayle (1974) C&W#39, *Save Your Kisses* Tommy Roe on B-side of *Sheila* (1962) g R&B#6 US#1 UK#3, *See the Big Man Cry* Charlie Louvin (1964) C&W#7/Bobby Wayne Loftis (1976) C&W#85; *Working Man's Prayer* Tex Ritter (1967) C&W#59. Co-writer: [i] Patsy Bruce.

125. BRUCE, Jack (b. John Asher, May 14, 1943, Glasgow, Scotland) Rock bassist and vocalist. The bassist in the seminal 1960s blues-rock group Cream, who co-composed the hits *Wrapping Paper* [i] (1966) UK#34, *I Feel Free* [i] (1967) US#116 UK#11, *Anyone for Tennis* [i] (1968) US#64 UK#40, and *White Room* [i] (1968) US#6, re-issued (1969) UK#28. Bruce studied at the Royal Scottish Academy of Music and played in various blues and R&B bands during his teens, before performing with the Graham Bond Organization and John Mayall's Bluesbreakers. He also recorded as a brief member of Manfred Mann, featuring on the album **Mann Made Hits** (1966, HMV) UK#11. Bruce subsequently recorded as a member of the trio West, Bruce and Laing, releasing the albums **Why Dontcha** (1972) US#26, **Whatever Turns You On** (1973) US#87 and **Live 'N' Kickin'** (1974, all Windfall) US#165. He has also recorded as a solo artist in a jazz-fusion and rock and blues style. ALBUMS: **Songs for a Tailor** (1969) UK#6, **Things We Like** (1970), **Harmony Row** (1971, all Polydor); **Out of the Storm** (1974) US#160, **How's Tricks** (1977, both RSO) US#153; **I've Always Wanted to Do This** (1980, Epic) US#182; **Truce** (1982, Chrysalis) US#109; **Automatic** (1987), **A Question of Time** (1989, both Epic); **Somethingelse** (1993), **Around the Next Dream*** (1994, Virgin); **Cities of the Heart** (1994), **Moon Jack** (1995, all CMP); **Live at the BBC** (1995, Windsong). COMPILATION: **At His Best** (1974, RSO); **Greatest Hits** (1980, Polydor); **The Jack Bruce Collector's Edition** (1996, CMP). HIT VERSIONS: *I Feel Free* [i] Belinda

Carlisle (1988) US#88 UK#11. As: * BBM. Co-writer: [i] Pete Brown.

126. BRYANT, Boudleaux (b. February 13, 1920, Shellman, GA; d. June 30, 1987) C&W multi-instrumentalist, and BRYANT, Felice (b. Felice Scaduto, August 7, 1925, Milwaukee, WI) C&W lyricist.

It has been estimated that the Bryant's wrote over six thousand songs, at least one thousand of which were recorded, collectively selling over three hundred million records. Their old-world immigrant view of fading American values, homespun language, wry humor and quaint nostalgia, turned many of their bluegrass influenced country-pop songs into contemporary standards, leaving few country artists that have not recorded at least one of their compositions. Boudleaux was born of part-Native American heritage into a musical family, and he learned the violin at the age of five. In 1938, he played one season with the Atlanta Philharmonic Orchestra, before turning to the country fiddle and learning the guitar, bass and sousaphone. Bryant toured America in various bluegrass groups during the 1940s, at which time some of his instrumental compositions were recorded by the Pine Ridge Boys and the Hank Penny Band. Felice was the daughter of Italian immigrants, and she sang Italian folk songs from an early age. The pair met in 1945 and married within a matter of days, a union that lasted until Boudleaux's death in 1987. During the initial years of their marriage, Boudleaux continued to earn his living as a musician, and Felice wrote poetry in her spare time. Once they began writing songs together, they composed over eighty before they were able to find a publisher. Of their early days, Boudleaux later commented, "We sent songs out all over the world for a couple of years without any results except rejections and unopened returns." Their first hit was with *Country Boy* [i] by Little Jimmy Dickens (1949), after which they moved to Nashville and wrote *The Richest Man in the World* [i] for Eddy Arnold. Throughout the 1950s, the Bryant's were seldom without a song on the country charts, and they soon formed the first of many publishing companies, which eventually became House of Bryant. Their *Bye Bye Love* [i] was rejected by thirty Nashville artists until it became a multi-million seller for the Everly Brothers, which initiated a lengthy and successful songwriter-artist partnership. Recordings of Boudleaux's 1961 instrumental *Mexico* have collectively sold over six million copies, and his impassioned *Rocky Top* has become a bluegrass standard. After Boudleaux's death, Felice continued to write songs in his memory. ALBUM: **All I Have to Do Is Dream** (1980, DB). HIT VERSIONS: *All I Have to Do Is Dream* Everly Brothers (1958) g C&W#1 R&B#1 US#1 UK#1, re-entry (1961) US#96/Glen Campbell & Bobbie Gentry (1970) C&W#6 US#27 UK#3/Nitty Gritty Dirt Band (1975) C&W#79 US#66/Nancy Montgomery (1981) C&W#85/Phil Everly & Cliff Richard (1994) UK#14, re-entry (1995) UK#58; *All the Time* Kitty Wells (1959) C&W#18/Jack Greene (1967) C&W#1/Eddy Arnold (1976) C&W#22; *Always It's You* [i] Everly Brothers (1960) US#56, *Baby Me, Baby* [i] Johnny Duncan (1968) C&W#67/Roger Miller (1977) C&W#68; *Back Up Buddy* [i] Carl Smith (1954) C&W#2, *Baltimore* Sonny James (1964) C&W#6 US#134, *Before the Ring on Your Finger Turns Green* [i] Dottie West (1966) C&W#22, *Before You Go* Buck Owens (1965) C&W#1 US#83, *Bird Dog* [i] Everly Brothers (1958) g C&W#1 R&B#1 US#1 UK#1/Bellamy Brothers (1978) C&W#86; *Blame It on the Moonlight* Johnny Wright (1965) C&W#28, *Blue Boy* Jim Reeves (1958) C&W#2 US#45, *Brand New Heartache, A* [i] Everly Brothers (1960) US#109, *Bye Bye Love* [i] Everly Brothers (1957) g C&W#1 R&B#5 US#2 UK#6/Webb Pierce (1957) C&W#7 US#73/Barbara Fairchild & Billy Walker (1980) C&W#70/Philippe Wynee (1983) R&B#33; *Christmas Can't Be Far Away* Eddy Arnold (1955) C&W#12, *Come a Little Closer* Johnny Duncan & Janie Fricke (1978) C&W#4, *Come Live with Me* [i] Roy Clark (1973) C&W#1 US#82, *Country Boy* [i] Little Jimmie Dickens (1949) C&W#7 R&B#7/Ricky Skaggs (1985) C&W#1; *Daddy Bluegrass* Stoney Edwards (1974) C&W#85, *Devoted to You* [i] Everly Brothers (1958) C&W#7 R&B#2 US#10/Carly Simon & James Taylor (1978) C&W#33 US#36; *Family Reunion* Oak Ridge Boys (1976) C&W#83, *Gee, But I'm Lonesome* Ron Holden (1960) US#106, *Georgia Pineywoods* Osborne Brothers (1971) C&W#37, *Have a Good Time* [i] Tony Bennett (1952) US#16/Sue Thompson (1962) US#31; *Hawkeye* Frankie Laine (1955) UK#7, *Hey Joe* Carl Smith (1953) C&W#1/Kitty Wells (1953) C&W#8/Frankie Laine (1953) g US#11 UK#1/Joe Stampley & Moe Brandy (1981) C&W#10; *Hey Sheriff* Rusty & Doug (1958) C&W#22, *Hole in My Pocket* Ricky Van Shelton (1989) C&W#3, *How's the World Treating You?* Eddy Arnold (1953) C&W#4/Louvin Brothers (1961) C&W#26; *I Believe in Love* Bonnie Guitar (1968) C&W#10/Stonewall Jackson (1968) C&W#31; *I Can Hear Kentucky Calling Me* Chet Atkins (1980) C&W#83/Osbourne Brothers (1980) C&W#75; *I Love to Dance with Annie* Ernest Ashforth (1964) C&W#4, *I'd Rather Stay Home* Kitty Wells on B-side of *Searching* (1956) C&W#3, *I've Been Thinking* Eddy Arnold (1955) C&W#2, *I've Never Been Loved* Leroy Van Dyke (1967) C&W#66, *In the Middle of the Night* Mel Tillis (1983) C&W#10/Canyon (1988) C&W#54; *It Takes You* Bob Luman (1972) C&W#21, *It's a Lovely, Lovely*

World Carl Smith (1952) C&W#5/Gail Davies (1981) C&W#5; *Johnny My Love (Grandma's Diary)* Wilma Lee & Stoney Cooper (1960) C&W#17, *Just in Case* Ronnie Milsap (1976) C&W#4/Forester Sisters (1986) C&W#1; *Just Wait Till I Get You Alone* Carl Smith (1953) C&W#7, *Let's Think About Living* Bob Luman (1960) C&W#9 US#7 UK#6, *Like Strangers* Everly Brothers (1960) US#22 UK#11/Gail Davies (1980) C&W#21; *Lizzie Lou* Osborne Brothers (1973) C&W#66, *Lonely Heart* Cedar Creek (1983) C&W#81/Tammy Wynette (1984) C&W#40; *Love Hurts* Nazareth (1975) US#8, also on *Hot Tracks EP* (1977) UK#15/Jim Capaldi (1975) US#97 UK#4/ Cher (1991) UK#43/Peter Polycarpou (1993) UK#26; *Love Is Just a Sometimes Thing* Bill Anderson (1970) C&W#5, *Love, Love, Love* Webb Pierce (1955) C&W#1/Sandy Posey (1978) C&W#26: *Love Me Now* Anita Carter (1967) C&W#61/Ronnie Mc-Dowell (1979) C&W#26; *Love of My Life* Everly Brothers (1958) US#40, *Mexico* Bob Moore & His Orchestra (1961) R&B#22 US#7/Backtrack featuring John Hunt (1985) C&W#94; *Midnight* Red Foley (1953) C&W#1, *Million Years or So, A* Eddy Arnold (1963) C&W#13, *Moontan* Jeris Ross (1973) C&W#58, *Muddy Bottom* Osborne Brothers (1971) C&W#62, *My Baby's Gone* Louvin Brothers (1959) C&W#9/Jeanne Pruett (1975) C&W#77/Kendalls (1984) C&W#15/Sawyer Brown (1988) C&W#11; *My Last Date (With You)* Floyd Cramer (1960) C&W#2 US#11/Skeeter Davis (1961) C&W#5 UK#26; *My Mind Hangs on to You* Billy Walker (1973) C&W#34, *Nightmare* Faron Young (1963) C&W#14, *No Place Like Home on Christmas* Randy Travis (1987) C&W#2, *Oh No* Browns (1964) C&W#42, *Once Upon a Time* Bobby Blue (1986) C&W#80, *Our Honeymoon* Carl Smith (1952) C&W#6, *Out Behind the Barn* Little Jimmy Dickens (1954) C&W#9, *Penny Arcade* Roy Orbison (1969) US#133/Christy Lane (1978) C&W#7; *Please* Narvel Felts (1978) C&W#34, *Poor Jenny* [i] Everly Brothers (1959) g US#22 UK#14, *Problems* [i] Everly Brothers (1958) g C&W#17 US#2 UK#6, *Raining in My Heart* [i] Buddy Holly (1958) US#88, also on B-side of *It Doesn't Matter Anymore* (1959) US#13 UK#1/Ray Price (1969) C&W#14/Leo Sayer (1978) C&W#63 US#47 UK#21; *Richest Man in the World, The* [i] Eddie Arnold (1955) C&W#10 US#99, *Rocky Top* Osbourne Brothers (1968) C&W#33/Lynn Anderson (1970) C&W#17; *She Wears My Ring* [i] Ray Price (1968) C&W#6/Soloman King (1968) US#117 UK#3; *So How Come (No One Loves Me)* Don Gibson (1962) C&W#22, *Someone Like You* Emmylou Harris (1985) C&W#26, *Something's Missing (It's You)* Jackie Burns (1969) C&W#60, *Sweet Deceiver* Christy Lane (1977) C&W#53, *Take a Message to Mary* Everly Brothers (1959) g US#16 UK#20/Don

Cherry (1968) C&W#71; *Take Me as I Am (Or Let Me Go)* Ray Price (1968) C&W#8/Mack White (1976) C&W#34/Bobby Bare (1981) C&W#28; *Take My Love* Joy Ford (1979) C&W#97, *Tennessee Hound Dog* Osborne Brothers (1969) C&W#28, *This Orchid Means Goodbye* Carl Smith (1953) C&W#4, *Until My Dreams Come True* Jack Greene (1969) C&W#1, *Wake Me Up* Louise Mandrell (1980) C&W#63, *Wake Up Little Susie* [i] Everly Brothers (1957) g C&W#1 R&B#1 US#1 UK#2/Simon & Garfunkel (1982) US#27; *We Could* Charley Pride (1974) C&W#3, *Wheels* Restless Heart (1988) C&W#1, *Willie Can* [i] Beverly Sisters (1956) UK#23/ Alma Cogan (1956) UK#13; *With Love* Rex Allen Jr. (1978) C&W#10. Co-writer: [i] Felice Bryant.

127. BUCKINGHAM, Lindsey (b. October 3, 1947, Palo Alto, CA) Rock guitarist, producer and vocalist. After recording an album with the vocalist Stevie Nicks, **Buckingham Nicks** (1971, Polydor), the pair were invited to join, and subsequently revitalized the fortunes of, the Anglo-American group Fleetwood Mac. Buckingham composed the band's hits *Go Your Own Way* (1977) US#10 UK#38, *Tusk* (1979) US#8 UK#6, *Oh Diane* (1983) UK#9, *Big Love* (1987) US#5 UK#9, and *Family Man* [i] (1988) US#90 UK#54. In 1988, he left to pursue a solo career, but by 1997, he was recording with a reformed Fleetwood Mac. CHART SINGLES: *Trouble* (1982) US#9 UK#31, *Holiday Road* (1983) US#82, *Go Insane* (1984) US#23, *Slow Dancing* (1984) US#106. ALBUMS: **Law and Order** (1981, Asylum) US#32; **Go Insane** (1984, Elektra) US#45; **Out of the Cradle** (1992, Reprise) US#128 UK#51. HIT VERSION: *Never Going Back Again* Mac Wiseman (1978) C&W#78. Co-writer: [i] R. Dashut. (*See also under* Christine McVIE.)

128. BUCKLEY, Tim (b. Timothy Charles Buckley III, February 14, 1947, Washington, DC; d. June 29, 1975, Santa Monica, CA) Rock guitarist and vocalist. A pioneer and musical visionary who endeavored to merge folk, jazz, R&B and rock. Buckley is best remembered for his remarkable vocal range, all of three octaves, from baritone through countertenor to falsetto, which received praise from such unlikely sources as Jacques Brel and Paul Robeson. Popular music has had more disciplined singers than Buckley, but few have explored the possibilities of the human voice in quite the same way that he did. After learning the banjo and twelve-string guitar, Buckley performed in various country groups during the 1960s, before forming a trio with the lyricist Larry Beckett and bassist Jim Fielder. Regular solo slots at the Troubadour and the Boss Club, soon resulted in a record deal, and in 1966, he issued an electric-folk influenced debut album. The often alluring **Goodbye and Hello** (1967), is frequently cited as his best work, but although a commercial peak, it was not his artistic one. Buckley's intense and magnetic performance style was perfectly captured on the posthumously released **Dream Letter–Live in London, 1968**, while **Happy Sad** (1969), which was recorded without a drummer, was an acoustic folk and jazz amalgam of startling originality. By **Lorca** (1970), Buckley was leaving behind his already small audience and venturing into the realms of free-form jazz, about which he said at the time, "When I did **Blue Afternoon** I had just about finished writing set songs." On **Starsailor** (1971), Buckley dispensed with the basic restrictions of song structure altogether. Recorded at furious tempos in 5/4 and 10/4 time signatures, **Starsailor** created a primal cacophony of sound over which Buckley explored the full range of his voice in a manner reminiscent of the opera singer Cathy Berberian. Inevitably, the album was a commercial failure, and Buckley, disenchanted with the music business, worked for a while as a yellow cab driver, later saying, "I didn't record, because I was repeating myself." In 1972, he returned with **Greetings from L.A.**, a blend of white R&B and energetic rock that explored the seedy side of inner city street life, which he described as, "Full-out blues type barrelhouse rock." Two further albums followed, but at the age of twenty-eight, Buckley's considerable talent was squandered when he died from an unintended heroin overdose. In the same month, twenty-two years later, Buckley's son, the highly regarded singer-songwriter Jeff Buckley, drowned in the Mississippi. ALBUMS: **Tim Buckley** (1966), **Goodbye and Hello** (1967) US#171, **Happy Sad** (1969, all Elektra) US#81; **Blue Afternoon** (1970, Straight) US#192; **Lorca** (1970, Elektra), **Starsailor** (1971, Straight); **Greetings from L.A.** (1972, Warner Brothers); **Sefronia** (1973), **Look at the Fool** (1974, both Discreet). COMPILATIONS: **Best of Tim Buckley** (1983, Rhino); **Dream Letter–Live in London, 1968** (1990, Fiend); **The Peel Sessions** (1991, Strange Fruit); **Live at the Troubadour, 1969** (1994, Bizarre/Demon); **Honeyman: Recorded Live, 1973** (1995, Edsel). HIT VERSION: *Song to the Siren* This Mortal Coil (1983) UK#66.

129. BUFFETT, Jimmy (b. December 25, 1946, Mobile, AL). Rock guitarist and vocalist. A singer-songwriter who, to drunken eastern seaboard sailors, is what Tom Waits once was to Los Angeles down and outs. Buffett us a quirky individualist who, although not the Ernest Hemingway of rock that he would probably like to be, does offer an intriguing slant on American-Caribbean music from his Florida base, with wry nautical imagery and deft wordplay.

Buffett studied journalism at Auburn University in Alabama, and later at the University of Southern Mississippi, before working as a writer for Billboard magazine. With aspirations of becoming a country singer, he relocated to Nashville in 1968 and recorded for the Barnaby label. In 1972, Buffett settled in Key West, Florida, where he lived on a fifty foot ketch and performed in local clubs and bars. Drawing on his locale for much of his songwriting inspiration, he continues to write story songs about characters and events that owe more to Mark Twain than they do to real life. Buffett has written a children's book and a novel, and also runs a restaurant and a clothing store, and edits his own fanzine, "Coconut Telegraph." CHART COMPOSITIONS: *The Great Filling Station Holdup* (1973) C&W#58, *Come Monday* (1974) C&W#58 US#30, *Saxophones* (1974) US#105, *Pencil Thin Mustache* (1974) US#101, *A Pirate Looks at Forty* (1975) US#101, *Door Number Three* (1975) C&W#88 US#102, *Margaritaville* (1977) C&W#13 US#8, *Changes in Latitudes, Changes in Attitudes* (1977) C&W#24 US#37, *Cheeseburger in Paradise* (1978) US#32, *Livingston Saturday Night* (1978) C&W#91 US#52 UK#37, *Manana* (1978) US#84, *Fins* [i] (1979) US#35, *Volcano* [ii] (1980) US#66, *Survive* [iii] (1980) US#77, *When the Wild Life Betrays Me* (1984) C&W#42, *Bigger Than the Both of Us* (1984) C&W#58, *Who's the Blonde Stranger?* (1985) C&W#37, *Gypsies in the Palace* (1985) C&W#56, *If the Phone Doesn't Ring It's Me* (1985) C&W#16, *Please Bypass This Heart* (1986) C&W#50. ALBUMS: **Down to Earth** (1972, Barnaby); **A White Sports Coat and a Pink Crustacean** (1973), **Living and Dying in 3/4 Time** (1974) US#176, **A1A** (1975, both Dunhill) US#25; **Havana Dreamin'** (1976, ABC) US#65; **High Cumberland Jubilee** (1976, Barnaby); **Changes in Latitudes, Changes in Attitudes** (1977) p US#12, **Son of a Son of a Sailor** (1978) p US#10, **You Had to Be There** (1978, all ABC) g US#72; **Volcano** (1979) g US#14, **Coconut Telegraph** (1981) US#30, **Somewhere Over China** (1982) US#31, **One Particular Harbor** (1983) US#59, **Riddles in the Sand** (1987) US#87, **Last Mango in Paris** (1985) US#53, **Floridays** (1985) US#66, **Hot Water** (1988) US#46, **Off to See the Lizard** (1989) US#57, **Feeding Frenzy** (1990, all MCA) g US#68; **Before the Beach** (1993) US#169, **Fruitcakes** (1994) p US#5, **Baromterer Soup** (1995) g US#6, **Xmas Island/Fear** (1996, all Margaritaville). COMPILATIONS: **Songs You Know By Heart–Greatest Hits** (1985, MCA) p US#100; **Boats, Beaches, Bars and Ballads** (1992, Margaritaville) p US#68. Co-writers: [i] Barry Chance/Tom Corcoran/Deborah McColl, [ii] H. Dailey/K. Sykes, [iii] Mike Uttley. (*See also under* Jerry Jeff WALKER.)

130. BUNNELL, Dewey (b. January 19, 1951, Yorkshire, England) Rock guitarist and vocalist. One of a trio of songwriters in the soft-rock group America, who wrote the hits *A Horse with No Name* (1972) g US#1 UK#3, *Tin Man* (1973) US#4, *Amber Cascades* (1976) US#75, and *The Border* [i] (1983) US#33. Co-writer: [i] Russ Ballard. (*See also under* Gerry BECKLEY.)

131. BURKE, Johnny (b. October 3, 1908, Antioch, CA; d. February 25, 1964, New York, NY) Film and stage lyricist. The regular lyricist for the composer Jimmy Van Heusen, who is best remembered for having written the words to Erroll Garner's jazz standard *Misty* [ii]. Although principally a lyricist, Burke did compose some of his songs in their entirety. ALBUMS: **Donnybrook!** oc (1961, Kapp) US#58; **Accentuate the Positive** sc (1962), **But Beautiful/The Emperor Waltz** sc (1962), **Only Forever/Road to Bali** sc (1962), **Road Begins/Star Maker** sc (1962), **Sunshine Cake** sc (1962), **Swinging on a Star** ost (1962), Zing a Little Zong (1962, all Decca). HIT VERSIONS: *Annie Doesn't Live Here Anymore* [vi] Guy Lombardo (1933) US#2, *Beat of My Heart, The* [v] Ben Pollack (1934) US#2, *Charming Little Faker* [iv] Frankie Masters (1940) US#12, *It's Dark on Observatory Hill* [v] Dorsey Brothers Orchestra (1935) US#16, *Misty* [ii] Erroll Garner Trio (1954) US#30/Johnny Mathis (1959) R&B#10 US#12 UK#12/Sarah Vaughan (1959) US#106/Lloyd Price (1963) R&B#11 US#21/Vibrations (1965) R&B#26 US#63/Richard "Groove" Holmes (1966) R&B#12 US#44/Ray Stevens (1975) C&W#3 US#14 UK#2; *Scatter-Brain* [i] Benny Goodman (1939) US#9/Freddy Martin (1939) US#4/Frankie Masters (1939) US#1; *What's New?* [iii] Bing Crosby (1939) US#2/Bob Crosby (1939) US#10/Benny Goodman (1939) US#7/Hal Kemp (1939) US#11/Linda Ronstadt (1983) US#53; *Wild Horses* Ray Anthony (1953) US#28/Perry Como (1953) US#6. Co-writers: [i] Carl Bean/Keene Kahn/Frankie Masters, [ii] Erroll Louis Garner (b. June 15, 1921, Pittsburgh, PA; d. January 2, 1977, Los Angeles, CA), [iii] Bob Haggart, [iv] Keene Kahn/Frankie Masters, [v] Harold Spina, [vi] Harold Spina/Joe Young. (*See also under* Sammy CAHN, Arthur JOHNSTON, Jimmy MONACO, Jimmy VAN HEUSEN.)

132. BURKE, Joseph (b. March 18, 1884, Philadelphia; d. June 9, 1950, Upper Darby, both PA) Film and stage composer, pianist. A successful composer and collaborator whose first song was *Down Honolulu Way* (1916), and who achieved his first hit with the million selling *Oh, How I Miss You Tonight* [iii] (1924). Burke worked in Hollywood from the late 1920s, where he composed much of the score for "Gold Diggers of Broadway" (1929). During the 1930s, he formed a successful partnership with the lyricist Edgar Leslie. HIT VERSIONS: *At a Perfume Counter (On the Rue De La Paix)* [v] Blue Barron (1938) US#13/Jimmy Dorsey (1938) US#9; *By the River of the Roses* [viii] Woody Herman (1944) US#12, *Carolina Moon* [ii] Gene Austin (1929) US#1/Ben Selvin (1929) US#5/Nat Shilkret (1929) US#15/Sammy Kaye (1938) US#15/Connie Francis (1958) US#17 UK#1; *Dancing with Tears in My Eyes* [iv] Ruth Etting (1930) US#10/Regent Club Orchestra (1930) US#2/Ben Selvin (1930) US#5/Nat Shilkret (1930) US#1/Mantovani (1952) US#26; *Dream Mother* [vi] Gene Austin (1929) US#12, *For You* [iv] John Boles (1930) US#9/Joe Green (1931) US#13/Rick Nelson (1964) US#6 UK#14; *Getting Some Fun Out of Life* [v] Billie Holiday (1937) US#10, *In a Little Gipsy Tearoom* [v] Bob Crosby (1935) US#1/Jan Garber (1935) US#2/Russ Morgan (1935) US#10/Louis Prima (1935) US#4; *It Looks Like Rain in Cherry Blossom Lane* [v] Shep Fields (1937) US#6/Guy Lombardo (1937) US#1; *Kiss Waltz, The* [iv] Ben Bernie (1930) US#18/George Olsen (1930) US#6; *Little Bit Independent, A* [v] Fats Waller (1935) US#1/Freddy Martin (1935) US#3/Bob Crosby (1936) US#8; *(Love Is Like a) Ramblin' Rose* [vii] Perry Como (1948) US#18/Bing Crosby (1948) US#18/Gordon MacRae (1948) US#27/Ted Taylor (1965) US#132; *Many Happy Returns of the Day* [iv] Bing Crosby (1931) US#3/Ipana Troubadours (1931) US#16; *Midnight Blue* [v] Henry Allen (1936) US#15/Russ Morgan (1936) US#12; *Moon Over Miami* [v] Connee Boswell (1935) US#19/Eddy Duchin (1936) US#1/Jan Garber (1936) US#5/Art Karle (1936) US#14; *Oh, How I Miss You Tonight* [iii] Benson Orchestra of Chicago (1925) US#6/Lewis James (1925) US#7/Irving Kaufman (1925) US#11/Ben Selvin (1925) US#1; *On Treasure Island* [v] Bing Crosby (1935) US#8/Tommy Dorsey (1935) US#1/Little Jack Little (1935) US#4/Joe Moss (1935) US#8/Teddy Wilson (1935) US#16; *Pagan Moon* [i] Ted Black (1932) US#19, *Painting the Clouds with Sunshine* [iv] Jean Goldkette (1929) US#6/Sammy Fain (1929) US#19/Nick Lucas (1929) US#2; *Robins and Roses* [v] Bing Crosby (1936) US#2/Orvilee Knapp (1936) US#11; *Who Wouldn't Be Blue?* [ii] Ted Weems (1928) US#20, *Yearning (Just for You)* [ii] Gene Austin (1925) US#3/Harry Reser's Orchestra (1925) US#9/Tommy Dorsey (1938) US#3. Co-writers: [i] Alfred Bryan (b. 1871; d. 1958)/Al Dubin, [ii] Benny Davis, [iii] Benny Davis/Mark Fisher, [iv] Al Dubin, [v] Edgar Leslie, [vi] Al Lewis/Al Sherman, [vii] Joseph McCarthy, Jr., [viii] Marty Symes. (*See also under* Charles and Nick KENNY, Charles TOBIAS.)

133. BURNETT, T-Bone (b. Joseph Henry Burnett, 1948, St. Louis, MI) Rock guitarist, producer and vocalist. A country and R&B influenced singer-songwriter and session player who, like John Hiatt, continues to threaten to break big but never does. Burnett was a member of the Alpha Band in the late 1970s, which recorded the albums **Alpha Band** (1977), **Spark in the Dark** (1977) and **Statue Makers of Hollywood** (1978, all Arista). After the group broke up he returned to session and production work. ALBUMS: **The B-52 Band and the Fabulous Skylarks** (1972, Uni); **Truth Decay** (1980, Takoma); **Proof Through the Night** (1983, Warner Brothers) US#188; **Behind the Trap Door** (1984, Demon); **T-Bone Burnett** (1986, MCA); **The Talking Animals** (1988), **The Criminal Under My Own Hat** (1992, both Columbia). HIT VERSION: *Will the Wolf Survive* [i] Los Lobos (1985) US#78. Co-writer: [i] Steve Berlin (b. 1957, Philadelphia, PA).

134. BURNETTE, Dorsey (b. December 28, 1932, Memphis, TN; d. August 19, 1979, Canoga Park, CA) C&W bassist and vocalist. A 1950s rockabilly singer who performed in his younger brother's group the Johnny Burnette Trio, before achieving success as a country songwriter. Burnette first recorded as a member of the Rock 'n' Roll Trio on the Coral label during the 1950s, but had greater chart action in the 1960s when he began writing for other artists. As a solo performer, Burnette tallied up fifteen country hits between 1972–1979. He died of a heart attack in 1979. CHART COMPOSITIONS: *Tall Oak Tree* (1960) US#23, *Hey Little One* (1960) US#48, *Big Rock Candy Mountain* (1960) US#102, *The Ghost of Billy Malloo* (1960) US#103, *Feminine Touch* (1961) US#117. ALBUMS: **Here and Now** (1968), **Dorsey Burnette** (1968, both Capitol); **Things I Treasure** (1977, Calliope); **The Legendary Rock 'n' Roll Trio** (1984, Charly); **Tall Oak Tree** (1987, Era); **Dorsey Burnette, Volumes 1 and 2** (1987, Hollywood); **Complete Recordings** (1988, Bear Family). HIT VERSIONS: *Believe What You Say* [i] Ricky Nelson (1957) R&B#6 US#8, *Here Comes That Feeling* [ii] Brenda Lee (1962) US#89 UK#5, *It's Late* Ricky Nelson (1959) R&B#30 US#9 UK#3/Shakin' Stevens (1983) UK#11; *Just a Little Too Much* Ricky Nelson (1959) US#9 UK#11, *Lonely Corner* Rick Nelson (1964) US#113, *Long Vacation, A* Rick Nelson (1963) US#120, *Magnificent Sanctuary Band* Roy Clark (1971) C&W#39, *Time and Time Again* Brenda Lee (1966) US#126, *Waitin' in School* [i] Ricky Nelson (1957) US#18. Co-writers: [i] Johnny Burnette (b. March 25, 1934, Memphis, TN; d. August 1, 1964, Clear Lake, CA), [ii] Joe Osborne.

135. BUSH, Kate (b. July 30, 1958, Bexleyheath, England) Rock pianist and vocalist. An idiosyncratic singer-songwriter, who, like Joan Armatrading, retains a sizeable and loyal following for her highly personal material. Bush learned the piano and began writing songs at the age of thirteen, and in 1973, while still at school, she recorded a song demo that, with the assistance of Pink Floyd's guitarist Dave Gilmour, secured her a long-term recording contract with EMI Records. Before releasing any recordings, Bush attended voice, mime and dance classes, and performed live as the K.T. Bush Band. Her self-confident debut album **The Kick Inside** (1978), was the first of many resounding successes, and included what remains her best known song, *Wuthering Heights*. Bush's music is characterized by highly dramatic concepts, which she sings in a little girl soprano that verges from the quaint and eccentric to the overly Thespian. She was one of the first artists to imaginatively exploit the potential of the pop video, while her album **Hounds of Love** (1985), embraced influences as diverse as folk music and Lord Alfred Tennyson's poem "The Holy Grail." By *Running Up the Hill*, like Peter Gabriel and Paul Simon, Bush was writing songs that were solely based on rhythms. CHART COMPOSITIONS: *Wuthering Heights* (1978) US#108 UK#1, *The Man with the Child in His Eyes* (1978) US#85 UK#6, *Hammer Horror* (1978) UK#44, *Wow* (1979) UK#14, *Kate Bush on Stage EP* (1979) UK#10, *Breathing* (1980) UK#16, *Babooshka* (1980) UK#5, *Army Dreamers* (1980) UK#16, *December Will Be Magic Again* (1980) UK#29, *Sat in Your Lap* (1981) UK#11, *The Dreaming* (1982) UK#48, *Running Up the Hill* (1985) US#30 UK#3, *Cloudbusting* (1985) UK#20, *Hounds of Love* (1986) UK#18, *The Big Sky* (1986) UK#37, *Experiment IV* (1986) UK#23, *The Sensual World* (1989) UK#12, *This Woman's Work* (1989) UK#25, *Love and Anger* (1989) UK#38, *Rubberband Girl* (1993) US#88 UK#12, *Moments of Pleasure* (1993) UK#26, *The Red Shoes* (1994) UK#21, *The Man I Love* (1994) UK#27, *And So Is Love* (1994) UK#26. ALBUMS: **The Kick Inside** (1978) UK#3, **Lionheart** (1978) UK#6, **Never Forever** (1980) UK#1, **The Dreaming** (1982) US#157 UK#3, **Hounds of Love** (1985) US#30 UK#1, **The Sensual World** (1989) g US#43 UK#2, **The Red Shoes** (1993, all EMI) US#28 UK#2. COMPILATIONS: **Kate Bush on Stage** (1983), **Kate Bush** (1983) US#148, **The Singles File Box Set** (1984), **The Whole Story** (1987) US#76 UK#1, **This Woman's Work** (1990, all EMI). HIT VERSION: *Something Good* [i] Utah Saints (1992) US#98 UK#4. Co-writer: [i] J. Willis.

136. BYRNE, David (b. May 14, 1952,

Dumbarton, Scotland) Rock guitarist, vocalist and producer. The idiosyncratic leader, lyricist and principal songwriter in the group Talking Heads. Byrne first performed as a member of the Artistics in 1970, which evolved into Talking Heads, one of America's most literate and exploratory groups of the postpunk era. CHART COMPOSITIONS: *Psycho Killer* [iii] (1978) US#92, *Life During Wartime* (1979) US#80, *Once in a Lifetime* [i] (1981) US#103 UK#14, live version (1986) US#91; *Houses in Motion* (1981) UK#50, *Burning Down the House* [ii] (1983) US#9, *This Must Be the Place (Naive Melody)* [ii] (1984) US#62 UK#51, *And She Was* [ii] (1985) US#54 UK#17, *Road to Nowhere* [ii] (1985) US#105 UK#6, *Wild Wild Life* (1986) US#25 UK#43, *Blind* (1988) UK#59, *Lifetime Piling Up* [ii] (1992) UK#50. ALBUMS: **Talking Heads '77** (1977) US#97 UK#60, **More Songs About Buildings and Food** (1978) g US#29 UK#21, **Fear of Music** (1979) g US#21 UK#33, **Remain in Light** (1980) g US#19 UK#33, **The Name of This Band Is Talking Heads** (1982) US#31, **Speaking in Tongues** (1983) g US#15 UK#21, **Stop Making Sense** ost (1984) p US#41 UK#37, **Little Creatures** (1985) p US#20 UK#10, **True Stories** ost (1986) g US#17 UK#7, **Naked** (1988, all Sire) g US#19 UK#3. COMPILATION: **Popular Favorites, 1976–1992: Sand in the Vaseline** (1992, Sire) US#158 UK#7. After Talking Heads split up in 1991, Byrne pursued a solo career that has thus far embraced writing for opera, television and film. ALBUMS: **My Life in the Bush of Ghosts** with Brian Eno (1981) US#44 UK#29, **The Catherine Wheel** ost (1981, both Sire) US#104; **Music for the Knee Plays** oc (1985, ECM) US#141; **Rei Momo** (1989, Luka Bop) US#71 UK#52; **The Last Emperor** ost with Ryuichi Sakamoto (1988, Virgin) US#152; **Uh-Oh** (1992, Sire) US#125 UK#26; **David Byrne** (1994, Warner Brothers) US#139 UK#44; **Blue in the Face** ost (1995), **Feelings** (1997, both Luka Bop/Warner Brothers). HIT VERSION: *Slippery People* [ii] Staple Singers (1984) R&B#22 US#109. Co-writers: [i] Brian Eno (May 15, 1948, Woodbridge, England)/Chris Frantz (Charlton Christopher Frantz, May 8, 1951, Fort Campbell, KY)/Jerry Harrison (b. Jeremiah Harrison, February 21, 1949, Milwaukee, WI)/Tina Weymouth (b. Martina Weymouth, November 22, 1950, Coronado, CA), [ii] Chris Frantz/Jerry Harrison/Tina Weymouth, [iii] Chris Frantz/Tina Weymouth.

137. CAESAR, Irving (b. Isadore Caesar, July 4, 1895; d. December 17, 1996, both New York, NY) Film and stage lyricist. The writer of over one thousand songs, including the lyrics of *Tea for Two*, who still retained a Brill Building office in the 1990s. Caesar first worked with George Gershwin, before

collaborating with many other composers of the era. A flamboyant character, Caesar once presented himself in a one-man show. He lived to be one hundred and one years old. ALBUMS: **No, No Nanette** oc (1971, Columbia) US#61. HIT VERSIONS: *I Love Her-She Loves Me (I'm Her He-She's My She)* [i] Eddie Cantor (1922) US#3, *Is It True What They Say About Dixie?* [iv] Willie Bryant (1936) US#14/Jimmy Dorsey (1936) US#1/Ozzie Nelson (1936) US#4; *It Goes Like This (That Funny Melody)* [iii] Johnny Johnson (1929) US#20, *Just a Gigolo* [ii] Ben Bernie (1931) US#3/Bing Crosby (1931) US#12/Ted Lewis (1931) US#1/Leo Reisman (1931) US#15/Jaye P. Morgan (1953) US#22/David Lee Roth (1985); *Lady, Play Your Mandolin* [v] Havana Novelty Orchestra (1931) US#10/Nick Lucas (1931) US#5; *My Blackbirds Are Bluebirds Now* [iii] Ruth Etting (1929) US#9, *Oh Susanna, Dust Off the Old Pianna* [iv] Wendell Hall & Shannon Four (1924) US#8. Co-writers: [i] Eddie Cantor (b. Eddie Israel Iskowitz, January 31, 1892, New York, NY; d. October 10, 1964), [ii] Leanello Cassucci, [iii] Cliff Friend, [iv] Sammy Lerner/Gerald Marks (b. 1900, New York, NY; d. January 27, 1997, New York, NY), [v] Oscar Levant. (*See also under* George GERSHWIN, Joseph MEYER, Vincent YOUMANS.)

138. CAHN, Sammy (b. Samuel Cohen, June 18, 1913, New York, NY; d. January 15, 1993, Los Angeles, CA) Film and stage lyricist, vocalist. One of the most successful and influential lyricists of the twentieth century, whose words chronicled the swing era and the post-war optimism of American society. Cahn's forte was mid and uptempo ballads, and many of his and Jimmy Van Heusen's collaborations were recorded by Frank Sinatra. Cahn grew up in poverty in a New York tenement, and was a teenage violinist before forming a 1930s songwriting partnership with the pianist Saul Chaplin. The duo's first successes were *Rhythm Is Our Business* [iii] (1935) and the Yiddish folk song adaptation *Bei Mir Bist du Schoen* [v] (1938). Cahn was a major success in Hollywood, where he and Jule Styne contributed to such films as "Romance on the High Seas" (1948), and the Oscar winning "Three Coins in the Fountain" (1953). He also composed for Broadway, and worked on the musicals "Skyscraper" (1965) and "Walking Happy" (1966). During the 1960s, Cahn performed his own material as a one-man show. He died of heart failure in 1993. ALBUMS: **It Happened in Brooklyn** ost (1947, Hollywood Soundstage); **Two's Company** oc (1952, RCA); **Our Town** tvst (1956, Capitol); **High Button Shoes** ost (1958, RCA); **Anything Goes** ost (1956, Decca); **Pardners** ost (1956, Capitol); **Written on the Wind** ost (1956, Decca); **Ten Thousand Bedrooms** ost (1957), **Some Came**

Running ost (1958, both Capitol); **Say One for Me** ost (1959, Columbia); **This Earth Is Mine** ost (1959, Decca); **World of Susie Wong** ost (1960), **Les Poupees De Paris** oc (1962, both RCA); **Road to Hong Kong** ost (1962, Liberty); **Robin and the 7 Hoods** ost (1964, Reprise) US#56; **Skyscraper** oc (1966) US#128, **Walking Happy** oc (1966, Capitol); **Words and Music** (1974, RCA); **A Touch of Class** ost (1974, Philips) UK#32; **An Evening with Sammy Cahn** (1978, Laureate); **An Evening with Johnny Mercer, Alan Jay Lerner and Sammy Cahn** (1979, Book of the Month); **Heidi's Song** (1982, K-Tel). HIT VERSIONS: *Be My Love* [i] Ray Anthony (1951) US#13/Billy Eckstine (1951) US#26/Mario Lanza (1951) g US#1; *Because You're Mine* [i] Nat "King" Cole (1952) US#16 UK#6/Mario Lanza (1952) US#7 UK#3; *Bei Mir Bist du Schoen* [v] Andrews Sisters (1938) US#1, also in *The Star Sisters Medley* (1983) US#107/Jerry Blaine (1938) US#7/Benny Goodman (1938) US#4/Guy Lombardo (1938) US#2/Russ Morgan (1938) US#3/Kate Smith (1938) US#15; *Best of Everything, The* [xii] Johnny Mathis (1959) US#62 UK#30, *Day By Day* [xv] Les Brown (1946) US#15/Bing Crosby & Mel Torme (1946) US#15/Frank Sinatra (1946) US#5/Jo Stafford (1946) US#8/Four Freshmen (1956) US#42; *Dedicated to You* [vii] Ella Fitzgerald & Mills Brothers (1937) US#19/Andy Kirk (1937) US#11; *Gal with the Yaller Shoes, The* [i] Michael Holliday (1956) UK#13, *Go to Sleep, Go to Sleep, Go to Sleep* [xiv] Mary Martin & Arthur Godfrey (1950) US#8, *Hey, Jealous Lover* [xvi] Frank Sinatra (1956) US#3, *I Should Care* [xv] Tommy Dorsey (1945) US#11/Jimmy Dorsey (1945) US#13/Frank Sinatra (1945) US#8/Martha Tilton (1945) US#10/Ralph Flanagan (1952) US#4/ Jeff Chandler (1954) US#21/Frank Ifield (1964) UK#33/Gloria Lynne (1964) R&B#64; *I'll Never Stop Loving You* [i] Doris Day (1956) UK#17, *(If I Had) Rhythm in My Nursery Rhymes* [vi] Tommy Dorsey (1936) US#10, *If It's the Last Thing I Do* [iii] Tommy Dorsey (1937) US#4/Thelma Houston (1977) R&B#12 US#47; *Indiscretion* [xvii] Jo Stafford & Liberace (1954) US#30, *It's a Woman's World* [xi] Four Aces (1954) US#11, *Joseph, Joseph* [ii] Andrews Sisters (1938) US#18, *Please Be Kind* [iii] Bob Crosby (1938) US#12/Benny Goodman (1938) US#14/Red Norvo (1938) US#1; *'Posin'* [iii] Tommy Dorsey (1937) US#6/Jimmie Lunceford (1937) US#9; *Rhythm Is Our Business* [x] Jimmie Lunceford (1935) US#1/Wingy Manone (1935) US#20; *Same Old Saturday Night* [xiii] Frank Sinatra (1955) US#13, *Serenade* [i] Mario Lanza (1955) UK#15, re-entry (1956) UK#25/Slim Whitman (1956) UK#8; *Somebody Up There Likes Me* [ix] Perry Como (1956) US#18, *Teach Me Tonight* [viii] Janet Brace (1954) US#23/Helen Grayco (1954) US#29/Jo Stafford (1954) US#15/

Dinah Washington (1954) R&B#4 US#23/De Castro Sisters (1955) US#2 UK#20/George Maharis (1962) US#25/Al Jarreau (1982) R&B#51 US#70; *Until the Real Thing Comes Along* [iv] Jan Garber (1936) US#10/Erskine Hawkins (1936) US#20/Andy Kirk (1936) US#1/Fats Waller (1936) US#3/Ink Spots (1941) US#24/Ernie K-Doe (1967) R&B#48. Cowriters: [i] Nicholas Brodszky, [ii] Nellie Casman/Saul Chaplin/Sam Steinberg, [iii] Saul Chaplin, [iv] Saul Chaplin/L.E. Freeman/Mann Holiner, [v] Saul Chaplin/Jacob Jacobs/Sholom Secunda, [vi] Saul Chaplin/Jimmie Lunceford (b. June 6, 1902, Fulton, MO; d. July 13, 1957, Seaside, OR)/Don Raye, [vii] Saul Chaplin/Hy Zaret, [viii] Gene De Paul, [ix] Bronislau Kaper (b. 1902; d. 1983), [x] Saul Kaplan/Jimmie Lunceford, [xi] Cyril Mockridge, [xii] Alfred Newman (b. 1901; d. 1970), [xiii] Frank Reardon, [xiv] Fred Spielman, [xv] Axel Stordahl (b. 1913; d. August 30, 1963)/Paul Weston, [xvi] Kay Twomey/Bee Walker, [xvii] Paul Weston. (*See also under* Paul ANKA, Sammy FAIN, Burton LANE, Jule STYNE, Jimmy VAN HEUSEN, Harry WARREN.)

139. CALDWELL, Toy (b. 1947; d. February 25, 1993, Spartanburg, SC) Rock guitarist and vocalist. A founder member and chief songwriter in the country influenced southern boogie group the Marshall Tucker Band. CHART COMPOSITIONS: *Can't You See* (1973) US#108, re-issued (1977) US#75; *Searchin' for a Rainbow* (1976) C&W#82 US#104, *Long Hard Ride* (1976) C&W#63, *Heard It in a Love Song* (1977) C&W#51 US#14, *A Place I've Never Been* (1983) C&W#62, *This Time I Believe* (1981) US#106. ALBUMS: **The Marshall Tucker Band** (1973) g US#29, **A New Life** (1974) g US#37, **Where We All Belong** (1974) g US#54, **Searchin' for a Rainbow** (1975) g US#15, **Long Hard Ride** (1976) US#32, **Carolina Dreams** (1977) p US#23, **Together Forever** (1978, all Capricorn) g US#22; **Running Like the Wind** (1979) US#30, **Tenth** (1980) US#32, **Dedicated** (1981) US#53, **Tuckerized** (1982, all Warner Brothers) US#95. COMPILATIONS: **Greatest Hits** (1978, Capricorn) g US#67; **Best of the Marshall Tucker Band** (1995, ERA). Caldwell left the band in 1985 for a solo career, releasing the album **Toy Caldwell** (1991, Cabin Fever). HIT VERSION: *Can't You See* Waylon Jennings (1976) C&W#4 US#97.

140. CALE, J.J. (b. Jean Jacques Cale, December 5, 1938, Tulsa, OK) Rock guitarist and vocalist. A session player turned solo artist whose potent guitar style and often finely crafted albums, expertly blend elements of traditional American music with R&B, jazz and rock. Cale's songs have also been recorded by such artists as Eric Clapton, Poco and Lynyrd Skynyrd. Cale learned the guitar at school and grew up listening to hillbilly and blues music, before becoming a Nashville session player during the 1950s. In 1965, he released a handful of poor selling solo singles on Liberty Records, and later contributed to the Leathercoated Minds' psychedelic album **A Trip Down Sunset Strip** (1969, Viva). After building his own recording studio in Oklahoma, Cale began recording the way that he wanted to, and issued a series of albums that laconically embraced most elements of two hundred years of Americana. In 1994, after the release of only his eleventh album in over two decades, Cale said, "I'm still in business, even if I never got up in the big time. But that's a kind of blessing, I thought I'd be selling shoes by now." CHART COMPOSITIONS: *Crazy Mama* (1972) US#22, *After Midnight* (1972) US#42, *Lies* (1972) US#42, *Hey Baby* (1976) US#96. ALBUMS: **Naturally** (1972) US#51, **Really** (1973) US#92, **Okie** (1974) US#128, **Troubadour** (1976) US#84 UK#53, **5** (1979, all Shelter) US#136 UK#40; **Shades** (1981, MCA) US#110 UK#44; **Grasshopper** (1982) US#149 UK#36, **8** (1983, both Mercury) UK#47; **Travelog** (1989) US#131, **10** (1993, both Silvertone) UK#58; **Closer to You** (1994, Virgin); **Guitar Man** (1996, Delabel/Virgin); **Strummin' on the Porch** (1996, Pinnacle). COMPILATIONS: **Special Edition** (1984, Mercury); **Anthology** (1993, PolyGram); **Very Best of J.J. Cale** (1997), **Anyway the Wind Blows: The Anthology** (1997, both Mercury). HIT VERSIONS: *After Midnight* Eric Clapton (1970) US#18/Maggie Bell (1974) US#97; *Cocaine* Eric Clapton on B-side of *Tulsa Time* (1980) US#30, *Sensitive Kind* Santana (1981) US#56.

141. CALLANDER, Pete (b. October 10, 1939, Hampshire, England) Pop producer. A former 1960s song-plugger who is best known for his writing and production partnership with Mitch Murray. Callander has also adapted various continental songs into English. HIT VERSIONS: *All My Love* [i] Cliff Richard (1967) UK#6, *Daddy, Don't You Walk So Fast* [v] Daniel Boone (1971) UK#17/Wayne Newton (1972) US#4; *Don't Answer Me* [vi] Cilla Black (1966) UK#6, *Fool am I, A* [iii] Cilla Black (1966) UK#13, *Give Me Time* Dusty Springfield (1967) US#76 UK#24, *Monsieur Dupont* [ii] Sandie Shaw (1969) UK#6, *Suddenly You Love Me* [iv] Tremeloes (1968) US#44 UK#6, *Walkin' Tall* Adam Faith (1963) UK#23. Co-writers: [i] Monti Arduni, [ii] Christian Bruhn, [iii] F. Carravesi, [iv] Daniele Pace/Mario Panzeri/Lorenzo Pilat, [v] Geoff Stevens, [vi] B. Zambrini/L. Enriques. (*See also under* Mitch MURRAY, Les REED.)

142. CALLIER, Terry (b. 1951, Chicago,

IL) R&B vocalist. A singer whose much sought after recordings for the Cadet label were distinctive mergers of soul, folk and jazz. Callier's composition *Dancing Girl* was a masterpiece, comparable in many ways to Tim Buckley's epic *Goodbye and Hello*. The vocalist Jerry Butler has also recorded some of Callier's songs. CHART COMPOSITION: *Sign of the Times* (1979) R&B#78. ALBUMS: **The New Folk Sound of Terry Callier** (1965, Prestige); **Occasional Rain** (1972), **What Color Is Love** (1974), **I Just Can't Help Myself** (1975, all Cadet); **Fire on Ice** (1978), **Turn on Your Love** (1979, both Elektra); **Timepeace** (1998, Talkin' Loud/Verve). COMPILATION: **Best of Terry Callier** (1995, Demon).

143. CAMPBELL, Junior (b. William Campbell, Jr., May 31, 1947, Glasgow, Scotland) Pop guitarist, keyboard player and vocalist. As a member of the British pop group Marmalade, Campbell co-wrote three of its hits, *Reflections of My Life* [i] (1969) g US#10 UK#3, *Rainbow* [i] (1970) US#51 UK#3, and *My Little One* (1971) UK#15. He also performed on the albums **There's a Lot of It About** (1969, CBS) and **Reflections of My Life** (1970, Columbia) US#71. Campbell left the band in 1971 to study at the Royal College of Music, and to pursue a briefly successful solo career. CHART SINGLES: *Hallelujah Freedom* (1972) UK#10, *Sweet Illusion* (1972) UK#15. ALBUM: **Second Time Around** (1974, Deram). Co-writer: [i] Thomas McAleese.

144. CAPALDI, Jim (b. August 24, 1944, Evesham, England) Rock drummer and vocalist. A co-founding member of the British rock group Traffic. Capaldi has also pursued a sporadically successful solo career. CHART COMPOSITIONS: *Eve* (1972) US#91, *It's All Up to You* (1974) US#110 UK#27, *It's Alright* (1975) US#55, *That's Love* (1983) US#28, *Living on the Edge* (1983) US#75, *I'll Keep Holding On* (1984) US#106. ALBUMS: **Oh How We Danced** (1972) US#82, **Whale Meat Again** (1974) US#191, **Short Cut Draw Blood** (1975, all Island) US#193; **Fierce Heart** (1983, Atlantic) US#91; **Some Come Running** (1989, Island) US#183. HIT VERSION: *Love Will Keep Us Alive* [i] Eagles (1996) UK#52. Co-writers: [i] Paul Carrack/Pete Vale. (*See also under* Steve WINWOOD.)

145. Captain Beefheart (b. Don Van Vliet, January 15, 1941, Glendale, CA) Rock vocalist. An ex-child television star who created Captain Beefheart and His Magic Band in 1964, a group affectionately remembered for its bizarre and eccentric mix of R&B and rock. Beefheart retired to become a painter and sculptor in 1986. ALBUMS: **Safe as Milk** (1967, Buddah); **Strictly Personal** (1968, Blue Thumb); **Trout Mask Replica** (1969) UK#21, **Lick**

My Decals Off, Baby (1971, both Straight) UK#20; **Mirror Man** (1971, Buddah) UK#49; **The Spotlight Kid** (1972) US#131 UK#44, **Clear Spot** (1973, both Reprise) US#191; **Unconditionally Guaranteed** (1974) US#192, **Blue Jeans and Moonbeams** (1974, both Mercury); **Bongo Fury** with Frank Zappa (1975, Discreet) US#66; **Shiny Beast** (1978), **Bat Chain Puller** (1978, both Warner Brothers); **Doc at the Radar Station** (1980), **Ice Cream Crow** (1982, both Virgin) UK#90. COMPILATIONS: **The Legendary A&M Sessions** (1986, A&M); **Zig Zag Wanderer-The Best of Captain Beefheart** (1996, Hill).

146. **CAREY, Mariah** (b. March 27, 1970, New York, NY) Pop vocalist. An artist who is very much a pop product of the 1990s, and one, who, like Michael Bolton and Whitney Houston, is a chief proponent of somewhat sterile, over-produced pop-soul. Carey's forte is melodramatic, often histrionic ballads, which, by 1995, had sold over fifty-five million records and given her eleven number one singles. Carey is the daughter of Patricia Carey, a former New York City Opera singer. CHART COMPOSITIONS: *Vision of Love* [vii] (1990) g US#1 UK#9, *Love Takes Time* [vii] (1990) g US#1 UK#37, *Someday* [vii] (1991) g US#1 UK#38, *I Don't Wanna Cry* [x] (1991) g US#1, *There's Got to Be a Way* [ix] (1991) UK#54, *Emotions* [v] (1991) g R&B#1 US#1 UK#17, *Can't Let Go* [i] (1992) R&B#2 US#2 UK#20, *Make It Happen* [v] (1992) R&B#7 US#5 UK#17, *Dreamlover* [viii] (1993) p R&B#2 US#1 UK#9, *Hero* [i] (1993) p R&B#5 US#1 UK#7, *Never Forget You* [iv] (1994) g R&B#7 US#3 UK#1, *Anytime You Need a Friend* [i] (1994) R&B#22 US#12 UK#8, *All I Want for Christmas Is You* (1994) UK#2, *Fantasy* (1995) p US#1 UK#4, *One Sweet Day* [i] with Boyz II Men (1996) p R&B#2 US#1 UK#6, *Open Arms* (1996) UK#4, *Always Be My Baby* [vi] (1996) R&B#3 US#1. ALBUMS: **Mariah Carey** (1990) p US#1 UK#6, **Emotions** (1991) p US#4 UK#4, **MTV Unplugged** (1992) p US#3 UK#3, **Music Box** (1993) p US#1 UK#1, **Merry Christmas** (1994) p US#3 UK#32, **Daydream** (1995, all Columbia) p US#1 UK#1. HIT VERSION: *Someone to Hold* [iii] Trey Lorenz (1992) R&B#5 UK#65. Co-writers: [i] Walter Afanasieff, [ii] Walter Afanasieff/M. McCary/N. Morris/S. Stockman, [iii] Walter Afanasieff/Trey Lorenz (b. January 19, 1969, Florence, SC), [iv] Babyface, [v] Robert Clivilles/David Cole, [vi] J. Dupree/Jimmy Harris III/Terry Lewis/M. Seal, [vii] Bob Murguiles, [viii] David Porter, [ix] Wake, [x] Michael Narada Walden.

147. **CARMEN, Eric** (b. August 11, 1949, Cleveland, OH) Pop multi-instrumentalist and vocalist. A classically trained musician who founded the American pop group the Raspberries in 1970, and penned all their hits. CHART COMPOSITIONS: *Go All the Way* (1972) g US#5, *I Wanna Be with You* (1973) US#16, *Let's Pretend* (1973) US#35, *Tonight* (1973) US#69, *I'm a Rocker* (1973) US#94, *Overnight Sensation (Hit Record)* (1974) US#18. ALBUMS: **The Raspberries** (1972) US#51, **Fresh** (1972) US#36, **Side 3** (1973) US#128, **Starting Over** (1974, all Capitol) US#143. COMPILATION: **Raspberries' Best featuring Eric Carmen** (1976, Capitol) US#138. Carmen went solo in 1975, eventually selling over fifteen million records worldwide. His songs have been recorded by such artists as Franki Valli and Olivia Newton-John. CHART COMPOSITIONS: *All By Myself* (1976) US#2 UK#12, *Never Gonna Fall in Love Again* (1976) US#11, *Sunrise* (1976) US#34, *She Did It* (1977) US#23, *Boats Against the Current* (1977) US#88, *Change of Heart* (1978) US#19, *It Hurts Too Much* (1980) US#75, *I Wanna Hear It from Your Lips* [i] (1985) US#35, *I'm Through with Love* (1985) US#87, *Make Me Lose Control* [i] (1988, US#3). ALBUMS: **Eric Carmen** (1976) g US#21 UK#58, **Boats Against the Current** (1977) US#45, **Change of Heart** (1978) US#137, **Tonight You're Mine** (1980, all Arista) US#160; **Eric Carmen** (1985, Geffen) US#128. COMPILATION: **Best of Eric Carmen** (1988, Arista) US#59. HIT VERSIONS: *Almost Paradise…Love* [i] Mike Reno & Ann Wilson (1984) US#7, *Hey Deannie* Shaun Cassidy (1977) g US#7, *Let's Hear It for the Boy* [i] Deniece Williams (1984) g R&B#1 US#1 UK#2, *Never Gonna Fall in Love Again* Dana (1976) UK#31, *I Need You* Euclid Beach Band (1979) US#81, *She Did It* Michael Damian (1981) US#69, *That's Rock 'n' Roll* Shaun Cassidy (1977) g US#3. Co-writer: [i] Dean Pitchford.

148. **CARMICHAEL, Hoagy** (b. Hoagland Howard Carmichael, November 22, 1899, Bloomington, IN; d. December 27, 1981, Palm Springs, CA) Film and stage composer, pianist and vocalist. One of the truly great songwriters of America's golden age of song, and the composer of the classic *Georgia on My Mind* [vii]. Carmichael avoided the conventional Tin Pan Alley style of the era and composed such masterpieces as *Stardust* [xiii], the most recorded popular song ever. His art was a unique blend of jazz and blues, that featured strong elements of nostalgia and down-home Americana. Carmichael recorded numerous sides for a variety of labels, and appeared in fourteen films, often as a witty lounge pianist, as in "The Best Years of Our Lives" (1946). Carmichael's mother was a professional pianist who taught him the instrument, and as his taste for jazz developed, he performed at high school dances. In 1925, he made his first recordings for the

Gennett label. After graduating in law in 1929, he began composing tunes for such artists as Frankie Trumbauer and Paul Whiteman, his first major hit being *Riverboat Shuffle* [xii] by the Wolverines (1929). Carmichael collaborated with a variety of lyricists, and contributed to such Broadway shows as "The Show Is On" (1936). His many film works include "Anything Goes" (1936), "Thanks for the Memory" (1938), "Sing You Sinners" (1938), "To Have and Have Not" (1944), and "Here Comes the Groom" (1951), which introduced his and Johnny Mercer's Oscar winning *In the Cool, Cool, Cool of the Evening* [xii]. Through 1940–1960, Carmichael made many radio and television appearances. CHART COMPOSITIONS: *Lazy River* [iii] (1932) US#19, *Rockin' Chair* (1932) US#14, *Two Sleepy People* [x] with Ella Logan (1938) US#13, *Hong Kong Blues* (1945) US#6, *Doctor, Lawyer, Indian Chief* [xvii] (1946) US#18, *Ole Buttermilk Sky* [iv] (1946) US#2, *Huggin' and Chalkin'* (1946) US#1, *The Old Piano Roll Blues* (1950) US#11. ALBUMS: **Hoagy Sings Carmichael** (1956, Pacific Jazz); **The Stardust Road** (1960, RCA); **Curtis Hitch and Hoagy Carmichael*** (1979, Fountain); **Hoagy** (1982, RCA); **Hoagy Carmichael, 1951** (1982, Interstate); **16 Classic Tracks** (1982), **Ballads for Dancing** (1986, both MCA); **Hoagy Carmichael 1944–1945, V-Disc Sessions** (1986, Totem); **Indian Summer, 1923–1928*** (1987, Retrieval); **Hoagy Carmichael Songbook** (1988, Connoisseur). HIT VERSIONS: *Ballad in Blue* [viii] Benny Goodman (1935) US#9, *Blue Orchids* Bob Crosby (1939) US#8/Benny Goodman (1939) US#7/Glenn Miller (1939) US#1; *Bubble Loo, Bubble Loo* [xvii] Peggy Lee (1948) US#23, *Can't Get Indiana Off My Mind* [vi] Bing Crosby (1940) US#8, *Doctor, Lawyer, Indian Chief* [xvii] Les Brown (1946) US#6/Betty Hutton (1946) US#1; *Georgia on My Mind* [vii] Frankie Trumbauer (1931) US#10/Mildred Bailey (1932) US#19/Gene Krupa (1941) US#17/Ray Charles (1960) R&B#3 US#1 UK#20/Righteous Brothers (1966) US#62/Wes Montgomery (1968) US#91/Willie Nelson (1978) C&W#1 US#84/Michael Bolton (1990) US#36; *Heart and Soul* [x] Larry Clinton (1938) US#1/Al Donohue (1938) US#16/Eddy Duchin (1938) US#12/Four Aces (1942) US#11/Cleftones (1961) R&B#10 US#18/Jan & Dean (1961) US#25 UK#24/Incredibles (1967) R&B#45 US#122; *Hong Kong Blues* Tommy Dorsey (1945) US#8, *I Get Along Without You Very Well* [xiv] Jimmy Dorsey (1939) US#9/Red Norvo (1939) US#3; *In the Cool, Cool, Cool of the Evening* [xi] Bing Crosby & Jane Wyman (1951) US#11/Frankie Laine & Jo Stafford (1951) US#17; *Ivy* Dick Haymes (1947) US#19/Jo Stafford (1947) US#13/Vic Damone; *Lamplighter's Serenade, The* [xvii] Bing Crosby (1942) US#23, *Lazy Bones* [xi] Mildred Bailey (1933) US#9//Ted Lewis

(1933) US#1/Don Redman (1933) US#4/Jonathon King (1971) UK#23; *Lazy River* [iii] Mills Brothers (1952) US#19/Art Mooney (1952) US#29/Bobby Darin (1961) US#14 UK#12; *Little Old Lady* [i] Shep Fields (1937) US#8/Abe Lyman (1937) US#2; *My Resistance Is Low* [ii] Orrin Tucker (1940) US#14/Robin Sarstedt (1976) UK#3; *Nearness of You, The* [xvi] Glenn Miller (1940) US#5/Bob Manning (1953) US#16; *Old Man Harlem* [xv] Dorsey Brothers Orchestra (1933) US#20, *Old Music Master, The* [xi] Paul Whiteman (1943) US#19, *Ole Buttermilk Sky* [iv] Connee Boswell (1946) US#14/Helen Carroll (1946) US#7/Kay Kyser (1946) US#1/Danny O'Neil (1946) US#12/Paul Weston (1946) US#2/Bill Black's Combo (1961) US#25; *Ooh! What You Said* [xi] Glenn Miller (1940) US#13, *Riverboat Shuffle* [xii] Benson Orchestra of Chicago (1925) US#15/Isham Jones (1925) US#5/Frank Trumbauer (1927) US#16/Red Nichols (1928) US#14; *Rockin' Chair* Mills Brothers (1932) US#4/Mildred Bailey (1937) US#13/Fats Domino (1951) R&B#9; *Skylark* [xi] Bing Crosby (1942) US#14/Harry James (1942) US#11/Glenn Miller (1942) US#7/Dinah Shore (1942) US#5/Michael Holliday (1960) UK#39/Linda Ronstadt (1984) US#101; *Small Fry* [x] Mildred Bailey (1938) US#9/Bing Crosby & Johnny Mercer (1938) US#3; *Stardust* [xiii] Irving Mills (1930) US#20/Louis Armstrong (1931) US#16/Bing Crosby (1931) US#5/Isham Jones (1931) US#1/Wayne King (1931) US#17/Lee Sims (1931) US#20/Jimmie Lunceford (1935) US#10/Tommy Dorsey (1936) US#8, re-issued (1941) US#7, re-issued (1943) US#23/Benny Goodman (1936) US#2/Sammy Kaye (1939) US#16/Glenn Miller (1941) US#20/Artie Shaw (1941) US#2/Baron Elliott (1943) US#18/Nat "King" Cole (1957) UK#24/Billy Ward & His Dominos (1957) R&B#5 US#12 UK#13, re-entry (1958) UK#26/Ella Fitzgerald as *Stardust Bossa Nova* (1962) US#126/Frank Sinatra (1962) US#98/Nino Tempo & April Stevens (1964) US#32; *Two Sleepy People* [x] Bob Crosby (1938) US#11/Sammy Kaye (1938) US#6/Kay Kyser (1938) US#7/Fats Waller (1938) US#1/Lawrence Welk (1938) US#13/Bob Hope & Shirley Ross (1939) US#15; *Vagabond Dreams* [ix] Glenn Miller (1940) US#16, *Washboard Blues* [v] Red Nichols (1927) US#13/Paul Whiteman (1928) US#17; *Watermelon Weather* [xvii] Bing Crosby & Peggy Lee (1952) US#28/Perry Como & Eddie Fisher (1952) US#19; *We're the Couple in the Castle* [x] Glenn Miller (1942) US#24. With: * Curtis Hitch. Co-writers: [i] Stanley Adams (b. 1907), [ii] Harold Adamson, [iii] Sidney Arodin, [iv] Jack Brooks (b. 1912; d. 1971), [v] Fred B. Callahan/Irving Mills, [vi] Robert De Leon, [vii] Stuart Gorrell, [viii] Irving Kahal, [ix] Jack Lawrence, [x] Frank Loesser, [xi] Johnny Mercer, [xii] Irving Mills/Mitchell Parish/Dick Voynow,

[xiii] Mitchell Parish, [xiv] Jane Brown Thompson, [xv] Rudy Vallee, [xvi] Ned Washington, [xvii] Paul Francis Webster.

149. CARNES, Kim (b. July 20, 1946, Pasadena, CA) Pop pianist and vocalist. A vocalist in the 1960s group the New Christy Minstrels — where she met her future husband and co-writer Dave Ellingson — who enjoyed solo success during the 1980s. Carnes and Ellingson composed Kenny Rogers' entire album **Gideon** (1979, Liberty) US#12, and in 1992, she worked on the musical "Tycoon." CHART COMPOSITIONS: *You're a Part of Me* with Gene Cotton (1978) C&W#99 US#36, *It Hurts So Bad* (1979) US#56, *Draw of the Cards* [i] (1981) US#28 UK#49, *Mistaken Identity* (1981) US#60, *Voyeur* [iv] (1982) US#29 UK#68, *Does It Make You Remember* [ii] (1982) US#36, *You Make My Heart Beat Faster (And That's All That Matters)* [iii] (1983) US#54, *Invitation to Dance* [iii] (1985) US#68, *Crazy in the Night (Barking at Airplanes)* (1985) US#15, *Abadabandango* [iv] (1985) US#67, *Divided Hearts* [v] (1986) US#79, *Make No Mistake, He's Mine* with Barbra Streisand (1985) US#51, *Speed of the Sound of Loneliness* (1988) C&W#70, *Crazy in Love* (1988) C&W#68. ALBUMS: **Rest on Me** (1974, Amos); **Kim Carnes** (1975), **Sailin'** (1977, both A&M); **St. Vincent's Court** (1979), **Romance Dance** (1980) US#57, **Mistaken Identity** (1981) p US#1 UK#26, **Voyeur** (1982) US#49, **Cafe Racers** (1983) US#97, **Barking at Airplanes** (1985) US#48, **Light House** (1986, all EMI America) US#116; **View from the House** (1988, MCA); **Checkin' Out the Ghosts** (1995, Teichiku). COMPILATION: **Gypsy Honeymoon** (1995, EMI America). HIT VERSIONS: *Don't Fall in Love With a Dreamer* [ii] Kenny Rogers (1979) C&W#3 US#4, *Heart Won't Lie, The* [vi] Reba McEntire & Vince Gill (1993) C&W#1, *Love the World Away* Kenny Rogers (1980) US#14, *Make No Mistake, He's Mine* Ronnie Milsap & Kenny Rogers (1987) C&W#1, *You're a Part of Me* Susan Jacks (1975) US#90/Charlie McLain (1979) C&W#20/ Danny White & Linda Nail (1983) C&W#85. Co-writers: [i] B. Como/Dave Ellingson/V. Garay, [ii] Dave Ellingson, [iii] Dave Ellingson/P. Fairweather/ M. Page, [iv] Dave Ellingson/D. Hitchings, [v] Dave Ellingson/K. Kurasch/Donna Terri Weiss, [vi] Donna Terri Weiss.

150. CARPENTER, Mary-Chapin (b. January 21, 1958, Princeton, NJ) C&W guitarist and vocalist. A folk influenced country singer-songwriter. CHART COMPOSITIONS: *Down at the Twist and Shout* (1991) C&W#1, *Going Out Tonight* [i] (1991) C&W#14, *I Feel Lucky* [ii] (1992) C&W#4, *Not Too Much to Ask* [ii] (1992) C&W#27, *The Hard Way* (1993) C&W#11, *He Thinks He'll Keep Her* [ii] (1993) C&W#2 UK#71, *I Take My Chances* [ii] (1994) C&W#2, *One Cool Remove* with Shawn Colvin (1995) UK#40, *Shut Up and Kiss Me* (1995) UK#35. ALBUMS: **Hometown Girl** (1987), **State of the Heart** (1989) g US#183, **Shooting Straight in the Dark** (1991) p US#70, **Come On, Come On** (1992) p US#31, **Stones in the Road** (1994, all Columbia) p US#10 UK#26. HIT VERSION: *Girls with Guitars* Wynonna Judd (1994) C&W#13+. Co-writers: [i] John Edward Jennings, [ii] Don Schlitz.

151. CARR, Michael (b. Maurice Cohen, 1904, Leeds; d. September 16, 1968, London, both England) Film and stage composer, pianist. A versatile composer who was the only British songwriter to successfully imitate American cowboy ballads. Carr lived in Ireland before residing in the United States between 1924–1930, where he held a number of jobs, including that of Montana cowhand, where he first heard the cowboy songs of the west. Upon returning to England, Carr composed songs for such shows as "London Rhapsody" (1937). A five year alliance with the lyricist Jimmy Kennedy resulted in *South of the Border* [iv] (1939), which was recorded by over one hundred artists, and the World War I standard, *We're Gonna Hang out the Washing on the Siegfried Line* [iv] (1939). Carr also composed the popular songs *The General's Fast Asleep* [iv], *Getting Around and About* [iii], *Girl with the Dreamy Eyes* [x], *The Wheel of the Wagon Is Broken* [i] (all 1935); *The Sunset Trail* [iv], *Did Your Mother Come from Ireland* [iv] (both 1936); *Cowboy, Little Boy That Santa Forgot* [ii] (both 1937); *Merrily We Roll Along* [xii] (1939), *A Handsome Territorial* [iv] (1939), *A Pair of Silver Wings* [vi], and *The First Lullaby* [v] (both 1941). During the 1950–1960s, he wrote for television, including the themes *Man of Mystery* (1960) and *Kon-Tiki* (1961). HIT VERSIONS: *Bandit, The* [viii] Percy Faith (1954) US#25/Johnston Brothers (1954) US#26/Tex Ritter (1954) US#30; *Cinderella, Stay in My Arms* [iv] Guy Lombardo (1939) US#3/Glenn Miller (1939) US#16/Jack Teagarden (1939) US#19; *Dinner for One, Please, James* Hal Kemp (1936) US#13/Ray Noble (1936) US#7; *He Wears a Pair of Silver Wings* [vi] Kay Kyser (1942) US#1/Dinah Shore (1942) US#16; *Kon-Tiki* Shadows (1961) UK#1, *Lonely Ballerina* [v] Mantovani (1955) UK#16, *Man of Mystery* Shadows (1960) UK#5, *Misty Islands of the Highlands* [iv] Jan Garber (1936) US#10, *Ole Faithful* [iv] Gene Autry (1935) US#10, *One-Two-Three O'Leary* [vii] Des O'Connor (1968) UK#4, *South of the Border* [iv] Gene Autry (1939) US#12/Shep Fields (1939) US#1/Guy Lombardo (1939) US#8/Tony Martin (1939) US#16/Ambrose (1940) US#8/Frank Sinatra (1953) US#18/Clay

Baker (1987) C&W#91; *Two Bouquets* [iv] Guy Lombardo (1938) US#13, *White Horses* [ix] Jackie Lee (1968) UK#10. Co-writers: [i] Eton Box/Desmond Cox, [ii] Tommie Connor/Jimmy Leach, [iii] Lewis Ilda, [iv] Jimmy Kennedy, [v] Lambrecht, [vi] Eric Maschwitz, [vii] Barry Mason, [viii] Alfredo Ricardo De Nascimento/John Turner, [ix] Ben Nisbet, [x] Eddie Pola, [xi] Jack Popplewell, [xii] Raymond Wallace.

152. **CARROLL, Jim** (b. 1950, New York, NY) Rock vocalist. A published novelist and poet who recorded two albums in the early 1980s. CHART COMPOSITION: *People Who Died* (1980) US#103. ALBUMS: **Catholic Boy** (1980) US#73, **Dry Dreams** (1982, both Atco) US#156.

153. **CARSON, Wayne** (b. Wayne Carson Thompson, Denver, CO) C&W vocalist. A country tinged singer-songwriter, whose best known song is the Box Tops' million seller *The Letter* (1967). CHART COMPOSITIONS: *Barstool Mountain* (1976) C&W#82, *Bugle Ann* (1977) C&W#99, *1 Yr. 2 Mo. 11 Days* (1983) C&W#61. HIT VERSIONS: *I Met Her in Church* Box Tops (1968) US#37, *Letter, The* Box Tops (1967) g R&B#30 US#1 UK#5/ Mindbenders (1967) UK#42/Arbors (1969) US#20/ Joe Cocker (1970) US#7 UK#39/Sammi Smith (1979) C&W#27/Amii Stewart (1980) UK#39/Ronnie Reno (1983) C&W#83; *No Love at All* Lynn Anderson (1970) C&W#15/B.J. Thomas (1971) US#16/ Jan Gray (1980) C&W#80; *Somebody Like Me* Eddy Arnold (1966) C&W#1 US#53, *Soul Deep* Box Tops (1969) US#18 UK#22/Eddy Arnold (1970) C&W#22/ Guy Shannon (1973) C&W#63/Gary "U.S." Bonds (1982) UK#59; *Whiskey Trip* Gary Stewart (1978) C&W#16.

154. **CARTER, John** (b. John Shakespeare, 1942, Birmingham, England), and **LEWIS, Ken** (b. James Hawker, 1942, Birmingham, England) Both pop producers and vocalists. Two former session singers who co-founded the British vocal group the Ivey League, for which they composed the hits *Funny How Love Can Be* (1965) UK#8, *That's Why I'm Crying* (1965) UK#22, *Tossing and Turning* (1965) US#83 UK#3, and *Willow Tree* (1966) UK#50. ALBUM: **This Is the Ivey League** (1965, Piccadilly). COMPILATIONS: **Sounds of the Ivey League** (1967), **Tomorrow Is Another Day** (1969, both Marble Arch); **Best of the Ivey League** (1988, PRT). Carter and Lewis left the group in 1966, and recorded as the Flowerpot Men, charting with *Let's Go to San Francisco* (1967) UK#4, from the album **Let's Go to San Francisco** (1986, Teldec). Carter was later successful as the vocal studio group First Class, imitat-

ing the Beach Boys on the hit *Beach Baby* (1974) US#4 UK#13. HIT VERSIONS: *Knock, Knock, Who's There?* Mary Hopkin (1972) UK#2/Orlons (1964) US#64; *My Sentimental Friend* [i] Herman's Hermits (1969) UK#2, *Peek-a-Boo* [i] New Vaudeville Band (1967) US#72 UK#7, *Semi-Detached, Suburban Mr. James* Manfred Mann (1967) UK#2, *Sunshine Girl* [i] Herman's Hermits (1968) UK#8. All compositions John Carter/Ken Lewis, except: [i] John Carter/Geoff Stevens.

155. **CASEY, Howard Wayne** (b. January 31, 1951, Hialeah, FL) R&B-pop keyboard player, producer and vocalist. The key member of K.C. and the Sunshine Junkanoo Band in 1973, a group whose sparse, disco-samba rhythms later influenced Gloria Estefan's Miami Sound Machine. Casey first worked in a record store, before becoming a recording studio assistant for Tone Distributors in Florida, where he acquired his production, keyboard and engineering skills and teamed up with the studio engineer Richard Finch. As K.C. and the Sunshine Band, the duo composed a series of multi-million selling disco hits during the 1970s, which, alongside the Bee Gees, epitomized the white disco sound of the period. Casey and Finch worked the rich vein of their winning formula until it ran dry, and by the 1980s, they were the only remaining members of the group, playing all the instruments between themselves. The pair were also successful with a series of songs and productions for the falsetto vocalist George McCrae. Casey spent much of 1982 recovering from a near fatal car accident, and returned to the chart later that year with a surprise British number one, *Give It Up*. CHART COMPOSITIONS: *Blow Your Whistle* [v] (1974) R&B#27, *Sound Your Funky Horn* [v] (1974) R&B#21 UK#17, *I'm a Pushover* [v] (1975) R&B#57, *Get Down Tonight* [v] (1975) g R&B#1 US#1 UK#21, *Shotgun Shuffle* [v] (1975) R&B#25 US#88, *That's the Way (I Like It)* [v] (1975) g R&B#1 US#1 UK#4, re-mixed (1991) UK#59; *Rock Your Baby* [v] (1976) R&B#70, *Queen of Clubs* [iii] (1974) R&B#25 US#66 UK#7, *I'm So Crazy ('Bout You)* [v] (1975) UK#34, *(Shake, Shake, Shake) Shake Your Booty* [v] (1976) g R&B#1 US#1 UK#22, *I Like to Do It* [v] (1976) R&B#4 US#37, *I'm Your Boogie Man* [v] (1976) g R&B#3 US#1 UK#41, *Keep It Comin' Love* [v] (1976) R&B#1 US#2 UK#31, *Wrap Your Arms Around Me* [v] (1976) R&B#24 US#48, *Boogie Shoes* [v] (1976) R&B#29 US#35 UK#34, *Black Water Gold* (1978) R&B#75, *Do You Feel Alright* [v] (1978) R&B#62 US#63, *Who Do Ya Love* [v] (1978) R&B#88 US#68, *Do You Wanna Go Party* [v] (1979) R&B#8 US#50, *Please Don't Go* [v] (1979) g US#1 UK#3, *Give It Up* [ii] (1982) US#18 UK#1, *(You Said) You'd Gimme Some*

More (1982) UK#41, *Don't Run (Come Back to Me)* (1983) US#103, *Are You Ready* (1984) US#104. ALBUMS: **Do It Good** (1974), **The Sound of Sunshine** (1975) US#131, **K.C. and the Sunshine Band** (1975) US#4 UK#26, **Part 3** (1976) US#13, **Who Do Ya (Love)** (1978) US#36, **Do You Wanna Go Party** (1979, all TK) US#50; **The Painter** (1981), **Space Cadet** (1981), **All in a Night's Work** (1982, all Epic) US#46; **K.C. Ten** (1984, Meca) US#93; **Oh Yeah** (1993, ZYX); **Get Down Live** (1995, Intersound). COMPILATIONS: **Greatest Hits** (1980, TK) US#132 UK#10; **Greatest Hits** (1983, Epic); **Best of K.C. and the Sunshine Band** (1991, Rhino). HIT VERSIONS: *Connected* [iii] Stereo M.C.s (1993) US#20, *Dance Across the Floor* Jimmy "Bo" Horne (1978) R&B#8 US#38, *Gimme Some* [v] Brendon (1977) UK#14, *Honey I* [v] George McCrae (1975) R&B#18 US#65 UK#33, *I Ain't Lyin'* [v] George McCrae (1975) R&B#31 UK#12, *I Can't Leave You Alone* [v] George McCrae (1974) R&B#10 US#50 UK#9, *I Get Lifted* [v] George McCrae (1974) R&B#8 US#37/Sweet Music (1976) R&B#69; *I Want You Around Me* George McCrae (1979) R&B#91, *I Was Made for Dancing* Leif Garrett (1978) US#10, *It's Been So Long* [v] George McCrae (1974) UK#4, *Kiss Me (The Way I Like It)* [v] George McRae (1977) R&B#57 US#110, *Let's Dance* [v] George McCrae (1978) R&B#93, *Look at You* [v] George McCrae (1975) R&B#31 US#95, *Please Don't Go* [v] Double You? (1992) UK#41/K.W.S. (1992) g US#6 UK#1; *Rock Your Baby* [v] George McRae (1974) g R&B#1 US#1 UK#1/Baby Roots as *Rock Me Baby* (1992) UK#71/K.W.S. (1992) UK#10; *Sing a Happy Song* [v] George McCrae (1975) UK#38, *That's the Way (I Like It)* [v] Dead or Alive (1984) UK#22, *What Makes You Happy* TLC sampled in *Hat 2 Da Back* (1993) US#30, *Where Is the Love* [iv] Betty Wright (1975) R&B#15 US#96 UK#25, *You Can Have It All* [v] George McCrae (1974) UK#23, *You Get Me Hot* Jimmy "Bo" Horne (1979) R&B#18 US#101. Co-writers: [i] R. Birch/Richard Finch (b. January 25, 1954, Indianapolis, IN)/N. Hallan, [ii] Deborah Carter, [iii] Willie Clark, [iv] Willie Clarke/Richard Finch, [v] Richard Finch.

156. CASH, Johnny (b. Johnny R. Cash, February 26, 1932, Kingsland, AK) C&W guitarist and vocalist. One of the most influential country music performers of all time, who blended the blues, gospel and rural American hillbilly into a style uniquely his own. Cash has achieved fourteen number one singles from over one hundred and thirty chart entries, and has released nearly eighty albums of original material. His vocal style was much imitated by male country singers for many years. A quarter-blood Cherokee Indian, Cash grew up in the rural backwoods, where his father was a cotton farmer. He learnt the guitar at the age of twelve, and wrote his first songs in his teens. Cash held various jobs before being stationed in Europe with the U.S. Air Force during the early 1950s, where he formed the country group the Landsberg Barbarians, which performed in German nightclubs. After returning to America, Cash became a disc jockey in Memphis, and published his first song, *Hey, Porter*. In 1954, he joined the Tennessee Three, which, renamed Johnny Cash and the Tennessee Two, gained a recording contract with Sun Records, where *Cry, Cry, Cry* (1955) became his first hit. The release of his debut album, **Johnny Cash with His Hot and Blue Guitar** (1957), turned him into an influential country-rockabilly singer, and after signing to Columbia Records in 1958, Cash became one of the first country artists to be successfully marketed at a mainstream pop audience. Between 1969–1971, he hosted his own television show, and continued to record regularly throughout the 1980s, sometimes collaborating with his fellow country artists Waylon Jennings, Kris Kristofferson and Willie Nelson as the group Highwayman. Despite having sold upwards of fifty million records for Columbia, Cash was dropped by the label in 1987. After unsuccessfully attempting to update his sound at Mercury Records, Cash signed to the American label in 1994, where he recorded his finest album since the 1960s, the all-acoustic **American Recordings**. CHART COMPOSITIONS: *Cry, Cry, Cry* (1955) C&W#14, *So Doggone Lonesome* (1956) C&W#4, *Folsom Prison Blues* (1956) C&W#4, live version (1968) C&W#1 US#32; *I Walk the Line/Get Rhythm* (1956) C&W#2 US#17, *There You Go* (1956) C&W#1, *Train of Love* (1957) C&W#7, *Next in Line* (1957) C&W#9 US#99, *Home of the Blues* (1957) C&W#3 US#88, *Give My Love to Rose* (1957) C&W#13, *Big River* (1958) C&W#4, re-issued (1970) C&W#41; *Come in Stranger* (1958) C&W#6 US#66, *You're the Nearest Thing to Heaven* (1958) C&W#5, *All Over Again* (1958) C&W#4 US#38, *What Do I Care* (1958) C&W#7 US#52, *Don't Take Your Guns to Town* (1959) C&W#1 US#32, *It's Just About Time* (1959) C&W#30 US#47, *Luther Played the Boogie* (1959) C&W#8, *Thanks a Lot* (1959) C&W#12, *You Dreamer You* (1959) C&W#13, *Katy Too* (1959) C&W#11 US#66, *I Got Stripes* (1959) C&W#4 US#43, *Five Feet High and Rising* (1959) C&W#14 US#76, *Straight A's in Love* (1960) C&W#16 US#84, *Seasons of My Heart* (1960) C&W#10 US#110, *Smiling Bill McCall* (1960) C&W#13, *Second Honeymoon* (1960) C&W#15 US#79, *Mean Eyed Cat* (1960) C&W#30, *Down the Street to Number 301* (1960) C&W#85, *The Story of a Broken Heart* (1960) US#107, *Honkey-Tonk Girl* (1960) US#92, *Tennessee Flat-Top Box* (1961)

C&W#11 US#84, *The Big Battle* (1962) C&W#24, *The Matador* (1963) C&W#2 US#44, *Understand Your Man* (1964) C&W#1 US#35, *The Sons of Katie Elder* (1965) C&W#10 US#119, *Happy to Be with You* (1965) C&W#9, *Boa Constrictor* (1966) C&W#39 US#107, *You Beat All I Ever Saw* (1966) C&W#20, *The Wind Changes* (1967) C&W#60, *Get Rhythm* (1969) C&W#23 US#60, *See Ruby Fall* (1969) C&W#4 US#50, *What Is Truth* (1970) C&W#3 US#19 UK#21, *Flesh and Blood* (1970) C&W#1 US#54, *The Man in Black* (1971) C&W#3 US#58, *Singing in Vietnam Talking Blues* (1971) C&W#18 US#124, *Papa Was a Good Man* (1971) C&W#16 US#104, *No Need to Worry*** (1971) C&W#15, *Children* (1973) C&W#30, *Allegheny*** (1973) C&W#69, *Pick the Wildwood Flower* with Maybelle Carter (1973) C&W#34, *Orleans Parish Prison* (1974) C&W#52, *Ragged Old Flag* (1974) C&W#31, *Look at Them Beans* (1975) C&W#17, *Strawberry Cake* (1976) C&W#54, *Sold Out of Flagpoles* (1976) C&W#29, *It's All Over* (1976) C&W#41, *Lady* (1977) C&W#46, *After the Ball* (1977) C&W#32, *Gone Girl* (1978) C&W#44, *It'll Be Her* (1978) C&W#89, *I Will Rock and Roll with You* (1979) C&W#21, *I'll Say It's True* (1979) C&W#42, *Bull Rider* (1980) C&W#66, *Song of the Patriot* (1980) C&W#54, *Cold Lonesome Morning* (1980) C&W#53, *The Last Time* (1980) C&W#85, *Without Love* (1981) C&W#78, *The General Lee* (1982) C&W#26, *Georgia on a Fast Train* (1982) C&W#55, *I'm Ragged But I'm Right* (1983) C&W#75, *That's the Truth* (1984) C&W#84, *The Chicken in the Black* (1984) C&W#45, *I Will Dance with You* with Karen Brooks (1985) C&W#45, *The Night Hank Williams Came to Town* (1987) C&W#43, *W. Lee O'Daniel (And the Light Crust Dough Boys)* (1987) C&W#72, *That Old Wheel* with Hank Williams, Jr. (1988) C&W#21, *Ballad of a Teenage Queen* with Rosanne Cash and the Everly Brothers (1989) C&W#45. ALBUMS: **Johnny Cash with His Hot and Blue Guitar** (1957), **Songs That Made Him Famous** (1958, both Sun); **The Fabulous Johnny Cash** (1959) US#19, **Hymns By Johnny Cash** (1959), **Songs of Our Soil** (1959, all Columbia); **Johnny Cash Sings Hank Williams** (1960, Sun); **Now There Was a Song** (1960), **Ride This Train** (1960), **Hymns from the Heart** (1962), **Sound of Johnny Cash** (1962), **Blood, Sweat and Tears** (1963) US#80, **Christmas Spirit** (1963), **Keep on the Sunnyside** (1964), **I Walk the Line** (1964) g US#53, **Bitter Tears-Ballads of the American Indian** (1964) US#47, **Orange Blossom Special** (1965) US#49, **Johnny Cash Sings the Ballads of the True West** (1965), **The Sons of Katie Elder** ost (1965), **Mean as Hell** (1966), **Everybody Loves a Nut** (1966) US#88 UK#28, **Happiness Is You** (1966), **Carryin' On**** (1967) US#194, **Old Golden Throat**

(1968) US#37, **From Sea to Shining Sea** (1968) US#40, **Johnny Cash at Folsom Prison** (1968) US#13 UK#8, **The Holy Land** (1968) US#54, **More Old Golden Throat** (1969), **Jackson** (1969), **Johnny Cash at San Quentin** (1969) p US#1 UK#2, **Hello, I'm Johnny Cash** (1969) g US#6 UK#6, **Walls of a Prison** (1970), **The Johnny Cash Show** (1970) g US#44 UK#18, **I Walk the Line** ost (1970) US#176, **Little Fauss and Big Halsy** ost (1970), **Man in Black** (1971) US#56 UK#18, **Give My Love to Rose** (1972), **A Thing Called Love** (1972) US#112 UK#8, **America: A 200 Year Salute in Story and Song** (1972) US#176, **Christmas and the Cash Family** (1972), **Sunday Morning Coming Down** (1972), **Any Old Wind That Blows** (1973) US#188, **The Gospel Road** ost (1973), **Johnny Cash and His Woman** (1973), **Five Feet and Rising** (1974, all Columbia); **Johnny Cash at Osteraker Prison** (1974, CBS); **The Junkie and the Juicehead Minus Me** (1974), **Ragged Flag** (1974), **John R. Cash** (1974), **Children's Album** (1975), **Look at Them Beans** (1975), **Previous Memories** (1976), **Destination Victoria Station** (1976, all Columbia); **Johnny Cash in Sweden** (1976, CBS); **Strawberry Cake** (1976), **One Piece at a Time** (1976) US#185 UK#49, **The Last Gunfighter Ballad** (1976), **The Rambler** (1977), **I Would Like to See You Again** (1978), **Gone Girl** (1978), **Itchy Feet** (1978) UK##36, **Silver** (1979, all Columbia); **A Believer Sings the Truth** (1979, Cachet); **Rockabilly Blues** (1980), **The Baron** (1981), **The Survivors** (1982), **Adventures of Johnny Cash** (1982), **Johnny 99** (1983), **Rainbow** (1985), **Highwayman** (i.e. Highwayman*) (1985) US#92, **Heroes** with Waylon Jennings (1986, all Columbia); **Class of '55** with Jerry Lee Lewis, Roy Orbison and Carl Perkins (1986, Smash) US#87; **J.C. Is Coming to Town** (1987), **Water from the Wells of Home** (1988, both Mercury); **Highwayman 2*** (1990, Columbia) US#79; **The Mystery of Life** (1990), **Boom Chicka Boom** (1992, both Mercury); **American Recordings** (1994, American) US#110; **The Road Goes on Forever*** (1995, Liberty); **Unchained** (1996, American). COMPILATIONS: **Ring of Fire-The Best of Johnny Cash** (1963) g US#26, **Greatest Hits, Volume 1** (1967, both Columbia) p US#82 UK#23; **Original Golden Hits, Volume 1** (1969) US#95, **Original Golden Hits, Volume 2** (1969, both Sun) US#98; **Johnny Cash** (1969, Harmony) US#186; **Story Songs of Trains and Rivers** (1969, Sun) US#197, **Get Rhythm** (1969) US#164, **Showtime** (1969) US#181, **The Singing Story Teller** (1969, all Sun) US#186; **The World of Johnny Cash** (1970) g US#54 UK#5, **His Greatest Hits, Volume 2** (1971, both Columbia) g US#94; **Johnny Cash** (1971, Hallmark) UK#43; **Star Portrait** (1972, CBS) UK#16; **Original Golden Hits,**

Volume 3 (1972, Sun); **Best of Johnny Cash** (1976, CBS) UK#48; **Unissued Johnny Cash** (1978, Bear Family); **Foot Tappin' Greats** (1978, CBS) UK#36; **Greatest Hits, Volume 3** (1979, Columbia); **Complete Million Dollar Quartet** with Jerry Lee Lewis, Carl Perkins and Elvis Presley (1988, Charly); **Columbia Records, 1958–1986** (1987), **The Essential Johnny Cash, 1965–1983** (1992), **The Johnny Cash Portrait** (1994) p, **The Man in Black-The Definitive Collection** (1994, Columbia) UK#15; **Live in the Ring of Fire** (1995, Summit). HIT VERSIONS: *Big Foot* Brother Smith (1976) US#57, *Cry, Cry, Cry* Highway 101 (1988) C&W#1, *Folsom Prison Blues* Don Bowman (1968) C&W#74, *I Still Miss Someone* [ii] Lester Flatt & Earl Scruggs (1965) C&W#43/Don King (1981) C&W#38, *She's Mighty Gone* [i] Johnny Darrell (1966) C&W#72, *Tennessee Flat Top Box* Roseanne Cash (1988) C&W#1. As: * Highwayman with Waylon Jennings, Kris Kristofferson and Willie Nelson. With: ** June Carter. Co-writers: [i] June Carter, [ii] Rosanne Cash, Jr., [iii] Roy Orbison.

157. CAVALIERE, Felix (b. November 29, 1944, Pelham, NY) Pop keyboard player, producer and vocalist. Alongside Eddie Brigati, the principal songwriter and vocalist in the R&B, latin and jazz influenced vocal group the Young Rascals, which later became the Rascals. CHART COMPOSITIONS: *You Better Run* [i] (1966) US#20, *Come on Up* (1966) US#43, *I've Been Lonely Too Long* (1967) R&B#33 US#16, *Groovin'* [i] (1967) g R&B#3 US#1 UK#8, *A Girl Like You* [i] (1967) US#10 UK#37, *How Can I Be Sure?* [i] (1967) US#4, *It's Wonderful* [i] (1968) US#20, *A Beautiful Morning* [i] (1968) g R&B#36 US#3, *People Got to Be Free* [i] (1968) g R&B#14 US#1, *A Ray of Hope* [i] (1968) R&B#36 US#24, *Heaven* [i] (1969) US#39, *See* (1969) US#27, *Carry Me Back* (1969) US#26, *Hold On* (1970) US#51, *Glory Glory* (1970) US#58, *Love Me* (1971) US#95, *Right On* (1971) US#119. ALBUMS: **The Young Rascals** (1966) g US#15, **Collections** (1967) g US#14, **Groovin'** (1967) g US#4, **Once Upon a Dream** (1968) US#9, **Freedom Suite** (1969) US#17, **See** (1970) US#45, **Search and Nearness** (1971, all Atlantic) US#198; **Peaceful World** (1971) US#122, **The Island of Real** (1972, both Columbia) US#180. COMPILATIONS: **Time Peace/Greatest Hits** (1968, Atlantic) g US#1; **Anthology, 1965–1972** (1992, Rhino). After the Rascals split up, Cavaliere recorded as a solo artist and occasionally worked as a producer. CHART COMPOSITIONS: *Only a Lonely Heart Sees* [iii] (1980) US#36, *Good to Have Love Back* (1980) US#105. ALBUMS: **Felix Cavaliere** (1974), **Destiny** (1975, both Bearsville); **Treasure** (1976), **Castles in the Air** (1980, both Epic); **Dreams in Motion** (1994, Karambalage). HIT

VERSIONS: *Girl Like You, A* [i] Nigel Olsson (1976) US#107, *Groovin'* [i] Wilson Pickett (1978) R&B#94/War (1985) R&B#79/UB40 (1991) US#90/Pato Banton (1996) UK#14; *Helluva* [ii] Brotherhood Creed (1992) R&B#13 US#67, *How Can I Be Sure?* [i] Dusty Springfield (1970) UK#37/David Cassidy (1972) US#25 UK#1; *People Gotta Be Free* 5th Dimension (1970) US#60, *You Better Run* [i] Pat Benatar (1980) US#20. Co-writers: [i] Eddie Brigati (b. October 22, 1946, Garfield, NJ), [ii] Eddie Brigati/S. McDuffie, [iii] J. Tran.

158. CAVANAUGH, James (b. America) Film and stage composer. A composer whose songs were featured in such films as "The King of Jazz" (1930) and "Garden of the Moon" (1938), alongside the show "These Foolish Things." HIT VERSIONS: *Buffalo Billy* [iv] Roberta Quinlan (1950) US#22, *Christmas in Killarney* [iv] Percy Faith (1950) US#28, *Crosstown* [iii] Glenn Miller (1940) US#9, *(Did You Ever Get) That Feeling in the Moonlight* [ix] Perry Como (1945) US#9/Russ Morgan (1946) US#17; *Gaucho Serenade, The* [iii] Eddy Duchin (1940) US#17/Glenn Miller (1940) US#8/Dick Todd (1940) US#4; *Goody Goodbye* [vii] Dolly Dawn (1939) US#9/Ted Weems (1940) US#15; *Little on the Lonely Side, A* [v] Frankie Carle (1945) US#4/Guy Lombardo (1945) US#5/Phil Moore Four (1945) US#22; *Man with the Mandolin, The* [iv] Hoarce Heidt (1939) US#2/Wayne King (1939) US#6/Glenn Miller (1939) US#1; *Mississippi Mud* [i] Frankie Trumbauer (1928) US#18/Paul Whiteman (1928) US#6; *Roving Kind, The* [viii] Rex Allen (1951) US#20/Guy Mitchell (1951) US#4/Weavers (1951) US#11; *Umbrella Man, The* [vi] Kay Kyser (1939) US#1/Johnny Messner (1939) US#12; *You're Nobody 'Til Somebody Loves You* [ii] Russ Morgan (1946) US#14/Dean Martin (1965) US#25/Ray Price (1986) C&W#60. Co-writers: [i] Harry Barris, [ii] Russ Morgan (b. 1904; d. August 8, 1965)/Larry Stock, [iii] John Redmond/Nat Simon, [iv] John Redmond/Frank Weldon, [v] Dick Robertson/Frank Weldon, [vi] Vincent Rose/Larry Stock, [vii] Nat Simon, [viii] Arnold Stanton, [ix] Larry Stock/Ira Schuster.

159. CAVE, Nick (b. Nicholas Edward Cave, September 22, 1957, Wangaratta, Australia) Rock guitarist and vocalist. A gothic and literary influenced singer-songwriter, who is also a published poet and author. Cave first recorded with the Australian group Boys Next Door, releasing the albums **Door Door** (1978, Mushroom) and **Hee Haw** (1978, Missing Link). The group subsequently became the Birthday Party when Cave re-located to London, England, performing a raw blend of punk and rock on the albums **The Birthday Party** (1979), **Prayers**

on Fire (1981), **The Tuff Monks** (1982), and **Junk-yard** (1982, all 4AD) UK#73. In 1982, Cave formed a new backing group, the Bad Seeds, which has featured on most of his subsequent solo recordings. CHART COMPOSITIONS: *Straight to You/Jack the Ripper* (1992) UK#68, *Do You Love Me* (1994) UK#68, *Where the Wild Roses Grow* (1995) UK#11, *Henry Lee* with P.J. Harvey (1995) UK#36. ALBUMS: **From Her to Eternity** (1984) UK#40, **Honeymoon in Red** with Lydia Lunch (1984), **The First Born Is Dead** (1985) UK#53, **Kicking Against the Pricks** (1986) UK#89, **Tender Prey** (1988) UK#67, **The Good Son** (1990) UK#47, **Henry's Dream** (1992) UK#29, **Live Seeds** (1993) UK#67, **Let Love In** (1994) UK#12, **Murder Ballads** (1996) UK#8, **The Boatman's Call** (1997, all Mute) UK#22.

160. **CETERA, Peter** (b. September 13, 1944, Chicago, IL) Rock bassist and vocalist. A founder member of, and lead vocalist in, the jazz-rock group Chicago, which became increasingly mainstream during the 1980s. During his tenure with the band, Cetera composed the hits *Feelin' Stronger Every Day* [viii] (1973) US#10, *Wishing You Were Here* (1974) US#11, *If You Leave Me Now* (1976) g US#1 UK#1, *Baby What a Big Surprise* (1977) US#4, *No Tell Lover* [vii] (1979) US#14, *Gone Long Time* (1979) US#73, *Hard to Say I'm Sorry* [i] (1982) US#1 UK#4, *Love Me Tomorrow* [i] (1982) US#22, *Stay the Night* [i] (1984) US#16, *You're the Inspiration* [i] (1985) US#3 UK#14, and *Along Comes a Woman* [iv] (1985) US#14. Cetera left Chicago in 1985 for a solo career. CHART COMPOSITIONS: *The Glory of Love (Theme from Karate Kid II)* [ii] (1986) US#1 UK#3, *Big Mistake* [iii] (1987) US#61, *One Good Woman* [vi] (1988) US#4, *Best of Times* [vi] (1988) US#59, *Restless Heart* [v] (1992) US#35, *Even a Fool Can See* [iv] (1993) US#68. ALBUMS: **Peter Cetera** (1981, Full Moon) US#143; **Solitude/Solitaire** (1986, Warner Brothers) g US#23 UK#56; **One More Story** (1988, Full Moon) US#58; **World Falling Down** (1992, Warner Brothers) US#163; **One Clear Voice** (1995, River North). COMPILATION: **Greatest Hits** (1997, Warner Brothers). HIT VERSIONS: *If You Leave Me Now* Upside Down (1996) UK#27. Co-writers: [i] David Foster, [ii] David Foster/Diana Nini, [iii] Galpin, [iv] Mark Goldenberg, [v] A. Hill, [vi] Patrick Leonard, [vii] Lee Loughname/Daniel Seraphine, [viii] James Pankow. (*See also under* Robert LAMM.)

161. **CHAPIN, Harry** (b. Harold Foster Chapin, December 7, 1942, New York; d. July 16, 1981, Long Island, both NY) Folk guitarist and vocalist. A singer-songwriter in the folk-protest tradition, whose literate, narrative songs often featured complicated plots and a sophisticated inner dialogue. *She Is Always Seventeen* and *Better Place to Be*, are both examples of his accurately sketched character studies. An original and entertaining performer, Chapin made several ambitious attempts to mix folk music with theatrical and big band arrangements, and his best known composition is the million selling *Cat's in the Cradle* [i], a succinct tale of American fatherhood. Chapin first sang in the Brooklyn Heights Boys Choir and attended the U.S. Air Force Academy, where he became a pilot before studying at Cornell University. His father was a swing-era jazz drummer, and both his brothers were musicians. In his early twenties, he formed the family group the Chapin Brothers, which performed on the Greenwich Village folk circuit and released the album **The Chapin Brothers** (1966, Rockland). In 1969, Chapin made a documentary film about boxing, "Legendary Champions," before embarking on a musical career. His most precise and focused set was **Short Stories** (1974), which included *W.O.L.D.*, a mid-life crisis tale about a jaded disc jockey. Chapin also composed the Broadway musicals "The Night That Made America Famous" (1974) and "Chapin" (1977), and wrote the theme to the children's television series "Make a Wish." In 1975, he co-founded the charity project World Hunger Year. Chapin died in an automobile accident in 1981. CHART COMPOSITIONS: *Taxi* (1972) US#24, *Sunday Morning Sunshine* (1972) US#75, *Better Place to Be* (1973) US#118, re-issued (1976) US#86; *Cat's in the Cradle* [i] (1974) g US#1, *W.O.L.D.* (1974) US#36 UK#34, *I Wanna Learn a Love Song* (1975) US#44, *Sequel* (1980) US#23, *Story of a Life* (1981) US#105. ALBUMS: **Heads and Tails** (1971) US#60, **Sniper and Other Love Songs** (1972) US#160, **Short Stories** (1973) US#61, **Verities and Balderdash** (1974) g US#4, **Portrait Gallery** (1975) US#53, **Greatest Stories Live** (1976) g US#48, **On the Road to Kingdom Come** (1976) US#87, **Dance Band on the Titanic** (1977) US#58, **Living Room Suite** (1978) US#133, **Legends of the Lost and Found** (1979, all Elektra) US#163; **Sequel** (1980, Boardwalk) US#58. COMPILATIONS: **Anthology** (1985, Elektra); **The Last Protest Singer** (1989, Sequel); **Gold Medal Collection** (1991, Elektra). HIT VERSIONS: *Cat's in the Cradle* [i] Compton Brothers (1975) C&W#97/Ugly Kid Joe (1993) US#6 UK#7/Ricky Skaggs (1996) C&W#60+; *Circles* New Seekers (1972) UK#4. Co-writer: [i] Sandra Chapin.

162. **CHAPMAN, Mike** (b. May 16, 1947, Brisbane, Australia), Pop producer, and **CHINN, Nicky** (b. April 13, 1946, Bristol, England) Pop lyricist. The predominant British songwriting and production team of the 1970s, who scored over fifty hit

singles with a series of instantly identifiable pop songs of the most mercantile kind. Chinn and Chapman's astute exploitation of the frivolous teenage singles buyer, rewarded them with eleven million sellers. During 1973, at the peak of the "glam rock" era, Chinn and Chapman charted nine top three singles, all recorded by a series of barely competent musical groups that were little more than novelty acts in Marvel Comics costumes. Chapman had immigrated to England from Australia in 1967, where he met the budding lyricist Chinn, who was working as a waiter at Tramp, the 1960s socialite London nightclub, and who had already co-written a number of tunes for the film "There's a Girl in My Soup" (1970). They formed a songwriting and production partnership, charting with their very first effort, the Sweet's *Funny Funny* [ii] (1971), which set the tone, style and format for much of their future output. The duo worked almost exclusively for Mickie Most's Rak Records, where, Chapman said, "We were told we were a factory." Their uncanny ability to fashion hit material in a variety of musical styles, resulted in the soft-rock of Smokie and the mock-rockabilly of Mud. In 1978, Chinn and Chapman left Rak to form their own Dreamland label, before they too parted company at the turn of the decade. Chapman subsequently moved to Los Angeles, California, where he became an independent producer for such groups as Blondie and the Knack. HIT VERSIONS: *Alexander Graham Bell* [ii] Sweet (1971) UK#33, *Ballroom Blitz, The* [ii] Sweet (1973) US#5 UK#2/ Tia Carrere (1992) UK#26; *Best, The* [vii] Tina Turner (1989) US#15 UK#5, *Better Be Good to Me* [iv] Tina Turner (1984) R&B#6 US#5 UK#45, *Blockbuster* [ii] Sweet (1973) US#73 UK#1, *Boy Oh Boy* [ii] Racey (1979) UK#22, *Can the Can* [ii] Suzi Quatro (1975) US#56 UK#1, *Cat Crept In, The* [ii] Mud (1974) UK#2, *Close My Eyes Forever* Lita Ford (1988) US#8 UK#47, *Co Co* [ii] Sweet (1971) US#91 UK#2, *Crazy* [ii] Mud (1973) UK#12, *Daytona Demon* [ii] Suzi Quatro (1973) UK#14, *Devil Gate Drive* [ii] Suzi Quatro (1974) UK#1, *Doctorin' the Tardis* [vi] Timelords (1988) UK#1, *Don't Play Your Rock 'N' Roll to Me* [ii] Smokie (1975) UK#8, *DynaMite* [ii] Mud (1973) UK#4, *48 Crash* [ii] Suzi Quatro (1973) UK#3, *Funny Funny* [ii] Sweet (1971 45 (RCA) UK#13, *Hands Tied* Scandal featuring Patty Smyth (1984) US#41, *Heart and Soul* [ii] Exile (1981) US#102, re-issued (1983) US#8 UK#61/Huey Lewis & the News (1983) US#8 UK#61; *Heart of Stone* [ii] Suzi Quatro (1982) UK#60, *Hellraiser* [ii] Sweet (1973) UK#2, *How Could This Go Wrong* [iii] Exile (1979) US#88 UK#67, *Hypnosis* [ii] Mud (1973) UK#16, *I Engineer* [viii] Animotion (1986) US#76, *I'll Meet You at Midnight* [ii] Smokie (1976) UK#11, *I've Never Been in Love Before* [ii] Suzi Quatro (1979)

US#56 UK#44, *If You Can't Give Me Love* [ii] Suzi Quatro (1979) US#45 UK#4, *If You Think You Know How to Love Me* [ii] Smokie (1975) US#96, *It's, It's the Sweet Mix* [ii] Sweet (1985) UK#45, *It's Your Life* [ii] Smokie (1977) UK#5, *Kara Kara* [ii] New World (1971) UK#17, *Kiss You All Over* [ii] Broadway (1978) R&B#92/Exile (1978) g US#1 UK#6/Jim Mundy & Terri Melton (1979) C&W#87; *Lay Back in the Arms of Someone* [ii] Smokie (1977) UK#12/Randy Barlow (1979) C&W#13/Savoy Brown (1981) US#107; *Lay Your Love on Me* [ii] Racey (1978) UK#3, *Lipstick* [ii] Suzi Quatro (1980) US#51, *Little Willy* [ii] Sweet (1972) g US#3 UK#4, *Living Next Door to Alice* [ii] Smokie (1976) US#25 UK#5, new version featuring Roy "Chubby" Brown (1995) UK#3/Johnny Carver (1977) C&W#29; *Lonely This Christmas* [ii] Mud (1974) UK#1, re-entry (1974) UK#61; *Love Is a Battlefield* [vii] Pat Benatar (1983) US#5 UK#49, re-issued (1985) UK#17; *Love Touch* [i] Rod Stewart (1986) US#6 UK#27, *Mama's Boy* [ii] Suzi Quatro (1979) UK#34, *Mickey* [ii] Toni Basil (1982) g US#1 UK#7/"Weird" Al Yankovic as *Ricky* (1983) US#63; *Moonshine Sally* [ii] Mud (1975) UK#10, *Oh Carol* [ii] Smokie (1978) UK#5, *One Night* [ii] Mud (1975) UK#32, *Part of Me That Needs You Most, The* [ii] Jay Black (1980) US#98, *Pleasure and Pain* [vii] Divinyls (1986) US#76, *Poppa Joe* [ii] Sweet (1972) UK#11, *Race Is On, The* [ii] Suzi Quatro (1978) UK#43, *Rocket* [ii] Mud (1974) UK#6/Wedding Present on B-side of *Flying Saucer* (1992) UK#22; *Secrets That You Keep, The* [ii] Mud (1975) UK#3, *She's in Love with You* [ii] Suzi Quatro (1979) US#41 UK#11, *Sister Jane* [ii] New World (1972) UK#9, *Six Teens, The* [ii] Sweet (1974) UK#9, *Some Girls* [ii] Racey (1979) UK#2, *Something's Been Making Me Blue* [ii] Smokie (1976) UK#17, *Stumblin' In* [ii] Suzi Quatro & Chris Norman (1979) US#4 UK#41/Chantilly (1982) C&W#43; *Tear Me Apart* [ii] Suzi Quatro (1977) UK#27, *Teenage Rampage* [ii] Sweet (1974) UK#2, *Tiger Feet* [ii] Mud (1974) UK#1, *Tom Tom Turnaround* [ii] New World (1971) UK#6, *Too Big* [ii] Suzi Quatro (1974) UK#14, *Touch Too Much, A* [ii] Arrows (1974) UK#8, *Truth, The* [vi] Tami Show (1991) US#29, *Try It On* [ii] Exile (1977) US#97, *Wig-Wam Bam* [ii] Sweet (1972) UK#4/Damian (1989) UK#49; *Wild One, The* [ii] Suzi Quatro (1974) UK#7, *You Thrill Me* [ii] Exile (1978) US#40, *Your Mama Won't Like Me* [ii] Suzi Quatro (1975) UK#31. Co-writers: [i] Gene Black/Holly Knight, [ii] Nicky Chinn, [iii] Nicky Chinn/Gary Glitter (b. Paul Gadd, May 8, 1940, Banbury, England)/Ron Grainger, [iv] Nicky Chinn/Holly Knight, [v] Nicky Chinn/J.P. Pennington, [vi] T. Gawenda/M. Jiaras/Massey/Massey, [vii] Holly Knight, [viii] Holly Knight/Bernie Taupin. (*See also under* Holly KNIGHT.)

163. CHAPMAN, Roger (b. April 8, 1944, Leicester, England) Rock vocalist, and **WHITNEY, Charlie** (b. June 24, 1944, Skipton, England) Rock guitarist. The songwriting team behind the British progressive rock group Family. CHART COMPOSITIONS: *No Mule's Fool* (1969) UK#29, *Strange Band EP* (1970) UK#11, *In My Own Time* (1971) UK#4, *Burlesque* (1972) UK#15, *Music* (1977) R&B#70. ALBUMS: **Music in a Doll's House** (1968) UK#35, **Family Entertainment** (1969) UK#6, **A Song for Me** (1970) UK#4, **Anyway** (1970) UK#7, **Old Songs, New Songs** (1971), **Fearless** (1971) US#177 UK#14, **Bandstand** (1972, all Reprise) US#183 UK#13; **It's Only a Movie** (1973, Raft) UK#30. COMPILATIONS: **Best of Family** (1974, Reprise); **In Concert** (1971, BBC). After the band split up in 1974, Chapman and Whitney remained together as the group Streetwalkers. ALBUMS: **Chapman Whitney Streetwalkers** (1974, Reprise); **Downtown Flyers** (1975), **Red Card** (1976) UK#16, **Vicious But Fair** (1977), **Live** (1977, all Vertigo). Since the late 1970s, Chapman has also recorded as a solo artist. ALBUMS: **Chappo** (1979, Arista); **Live in Hamburg** with Shortlist (1979, Acrobat); **The Shadow Knows** (1984, RCA); **Kiss My Soul** (1996, Essential).

164. CHAPMAN, Tracy (b. 1964, Cleveland, OH). Folk guitarist and vocalist. A singer-songwriter in the protest tradition, who heralded a brief resurgence of interest in the genre during the late 1980s. Chapman began writing songs at the age of eight, and took anthropology and African studies at college in Medford, Massachusetts, where she played in an African drum ensemble and began performing as a soloist. By 1986, Chapman was a regular on the Boston folk circuit. Two years later, a televised live appearance at Nelson Mandela's Seventieth Birthday Party gave her an instant and unprecedented new audience, and shortly afterwards her eponymous debut album topped the British and American charts, eventually selling nearly ten million copies. Although she clearly benefited from being in the right place at the right time, Chapman's simple tunes and uncluttered arrangements proved a refreshing change to much of the technical, impersonal and over-produced music that was otherwise popular at the time. After a period when her career looked to be on an irreversible downward trend, Chapman bounced back with a top three single in 1996. CHART COMPOSITIONS: *Fast Car* (1988) US#20 UK#5, *Talkin' 'Bout a Revolution* (1988) US#75, *Baby Can I Hold You* (1988) US#48, *Crossroads* (1989) US#90 UK#61, *Give Me One Reason* (1996) US#3+. ALBUMS: **Tracy Chapman** (1988) p US#1 UK#1, **Crossroads** (1989) p US#2

UK#1, **Matters of the Heart** (1992) US#53 UK#19, **New Beginning** (1995, all Elektra) p US#3 UK#47.

165. CHARLES, Bobby (b. Robert Charles Guidry, 1939, Abbeville, LA) R&B vocalist. An early pioneer of a particular blend of country, R&B and cajun, who recorded for Chess Records in the mid-1950s. Charles is best known as the composer of the rock and roll classic *See You Later, Alligator*. CHART COMPOSITIONS: *See You Later, Alligator* (1956) R&B#14, *Time Will Tell* (1956) R&B#11. ALBUMS: **Bobby Charles** (1972, Bearsville); **Bobby Charles** (1983, Chess); **Clean Water** (1987, Zensor); **Chess Masters** (1988, Chess); **Small Town Talk** (1988, See for Miles); **Wish You Were Here Right Now** (1995, Stony Plain). HIT VERSIONS: *But I Do* Clarence "Frogman" Henry (1961) R&B#9 US#4 UK#3, *See You Later, Alligator* Bill Haley & His Comets (1956) R&B#7 US#6 UK#7/Winifred Atwell in *Let's Rock 'n' Roll* (1957) UK#48; *Walkin' to New Orleans* Fats Domino (1960) R&B#2 US#6 UK#19.

166. CHARLES, Hughie (b. July 24, 1907, Manchester; d. October 6, 1995, Heathfield, both England) Pop pianist and impresario. One of the most amiable talent scouts and songwriters of the 1930s. Charles first worked as a Tin Pan Alley song-plugger before collaborating with a variety of composers on over fifty hit songs for British big bands. He pioneered the early career of the vocalist Shirley Bassey, recorded a number of solo sides for the Decca label, and presented the first all-black musical in London. Dame Vera Lynne described Charles as, "one of the old school, when lyrics were lyrics." Among his many popular songs of the day were *Blue Skies Are Round the Corner* [iii], *I Shall Always Remember You Smiling* [iii] and *There'll Always Be an England* [iii] (all 1939); *I Shall Be Waiting* [i] (1940), *By Candlelight* [ii] (1942), *There's a Land of Begin Again* [iii] and *Where the Waters Are Blue* [ii] (1942). HIT VERSIONS: *I Won't Tell a Soul (That I Love You)* [iii] Roy Fox (1938) US#16/Andy Kirk (1938) US#1/Lawrence Welk (1938) US#8; *Russian Rose* [ii] Johnny Long (1942) US#21, *Silver Wings in the Moonlight* [ii] Freddie Slack (1944) US#19, *We'll Meet Again* [iii] Kay Kyser (1941) US#24/Guy Lombardo (1941) US#24/Benny Goodman (1942) US#16/Vera Lynne (1954) US#29. Co-writers: [i] Joe Irwin/Ross Parker, [ii] Sonny Miller, [iii] Ross Parker.

167. CHARLES, Ray (b. Ray Charles Robinson, September 23, 1930, Albany, GA) R&B pianist, organist and vocalist. The most influential and significant R&B artist in the history of the genre. Charles took his gospel roots and mixed it with country, southern blues, jazz and pop, thus creating a completely new sound that was to cross all musical boundaries. According to the record producer Tom Dowd, "Charles took gospel music and added the devil's words." Blind at the age of seven from glaucoma, Charles overcame his handicap to study classical piano at the State School for Deaf and Blind Children. He performed as a member of the Maxim Trio in the late 1940s, which was also known as the McSon Trio. Initially influenced by Nat "King" Cole, Charles formed his own group in 1954, and began a career which has resulted in nearly one hundred chart singles. During the 1960s, Charles recorded for his own Tangerine imprint through ABC Records, and he has also penned television commercials and sung film themes. An entire album of his material was recorded as **Bobby Darin Sings Ray Charles** (1962, Atco) US#96. CHART COMPOSITIONS: *Baby, Let Me Hold Your Hand* (1951) R&B#5, *It Should've Been Me* (1954) R&B#5, *Don't You Know* (1954) R&B#10, *I've Got a Woman* [iv] (1955) R&B#1, live version (1965) US#79; *Come Back* (1955) R&B#4, *This Little Girl of Mine* (1955) R&B#9, *Hallelujah, I Love Her So* (1956) R&B#5, *What I'd Say* (1959) R&B#1 US#6, *But on the Other Hand Baby* [iii] (1962) R&B#10 US#72, *I Chose to Sing the Blues* [i] (1966) R&B#22 US#32, *Understanding* [i] (1968) R&B#13 US#46, *If It Wasn't for Bad Luck* [ii] with Jimmy Lewis (1969) R&B#21 US#77, *I Can Make It Through the Days (But Oh Those Nights)* (1973) R&B#21 US#81. ALBUMS: **The Great Ray Charles** (1957), **At Newport** (1958), **Soul Brother** (1959), **The Genius of Ray Charles** (1960) US#17, **In Person** (1960, all Atlantic) US#13; **The Genius Hits the Road** (1960) US#9, **Dedicated to You** (1961, both ABC/Paramount) US#11; **Genius + Soul = Jazz** (1961, Impulse) US#4; **What I'd Say** (1961) US#20, **The Genius After Hours** (1961, both Atlantic) US#49; **Ray Charles and Betty Carter** (1961, ABC/Paramount) US#52; **The Genius Sings the Blues** (1961) US#73, **Do the Twist** (1962, both Atlantic) US#11; **Modern Sounds in Country and Western Music** (1962) g US#1 UK#6, **Modern Sounds in Country and Western Music, Volume 2** (1962) g US#2 UK#15, **Ingredients in a Recipe for Soul** (1963) US#2, **Sweet and Sour Tears** (1964) US#9, **Have a Smile with Me** (1964) US#36, **Live in Concert** (1965) US#80, **Country and Western Meets Rhythm and Blues** (1965) US#116, **Crying Time** (1966, all ABC/Paramount) US#15; **Ray's Moods** (1966) US#52, **A Man and His Soul** (1967, both ABC) g US#77); **Ray Charles Invites You to Listen** (1967) US#76, **I'm All Yours-Baby!** (1969) US#167, **Doing His Thing** (1970, all ABC/TRC) US#172; **My Kind of Jazz** (1970, Tangerine) US#155; **Love Country Style** (1970) US#192, **Volcanic Action of My Soul** (1971) US#52, **A Message**

from the People (1972, US#52), **Through the Eyes of Love** (1972, all ABC/TRC) US#186; **Live** (1973, Atlantic) US#182; **Come Live with Me** (1974), **Renaissance** (1975, both Crossover) US#175; **Porgy and Bess** with Cleo Laine (1976, RCA) US#138; **True to Life** (1977, Atlantic) US#78; **Wish You Were Here Tonight** (1983), **Friendship** (1985) US#75, **The Spirit of Christmas** (1985, all Columbia); **My World** (1993, Warner Brothers) US#145; **Strong Love Affair** (1996, Qwest). COMPILATIONS: **The Ray Charles Story** (1962, Atlantic) US#14; **Greatest Hits** (1962, ABC/Paramount) US#5, **Greatest Hits** (1963, HMV) UK#16; **A Portrait of Ray Charles** (1968, ABC/TRC) US#51; **Greatest Hits, Volume 2** (1968, Stateside) UK#24; **A 25th Anniversary in Show Business Salute to Ray Charles** (1971, ABC) US#152; **Heart to Heart-20 Hot Hits** (1980, London) UK#29; **The Collection** (1990, Arcade) UK#36; **The Birth of Soul-The Complete Atlantic R&B Recordings, 1952–1959** (1991, Atlantic); **The Living Legend** (1993, Arcade) UK#48. HIT VERSIONS: *Hallelujah, I Love Her So* George Jones & Brenda Lee (1984) C&W#15, *I've Got a Woman* [iv] Jimmy McGriff (1962) R&B#5 US#20/Rick Nelson (1963) US#49; *Sweet Sixteen Bars* Earl Grant (1962) R&B#9 US#55, *This Little Girl of Mine* Everly Brothers (1958) US#26, *What I'd Say* Bobby Darin (1962) US#24/Kenny Burrell & Jimmy Smith (1963) US#113/Elvis Presley (1964) US#21. Co-writers: [i] Jimmy Holiday, [ii] Jimmy Lewis, [iii] Percy Mayfield, [iv] Renald Richard.

168. CHEVALIER, Albert (b. March 21, 1861, London; d. July 11, 1923, both England) Vaudeville performer and vocalist. The composer and singer of many popular cockney songs that were regular features in Victorian music halls. Chevalier's compositions include *The Future Mrs. Awkins, Knocked 'Em in the Old Kent Road* and *My Old Dutch* (all late 1800s). He also recorded sides for HMV Records in 1911.

169. CHILD, Desmond (b. John Charles Barrett, Jr., October 28, 1953, Miami, FL) Rock vocalist and producer. A record producer and songwriter who recorded as a solo artist before writing hits for such groups as Bon Jovi. CHART COMPOSITIONS: *Our Love Is Insane* (1979) R&B#95 US#51, *You're the Story of My Life* [iii] (1991) US#74. ALBUM: **Desmond Child and Rouge** (1979, Capitol) US#157. HIT VERSIONS: *Calling It Love* [i] Animotion (1989) US#53, *I Hate Myself for Loving You* [ii] Joan Jett & the Blackhearts (1988) US#8 UK#46, *If You Were a Woman (And I Was a Man)* Bonnie Tyler (1986) US#77, *Just Like Jesse James* [iii] Cher (1989) US#8, *Little Liar* [ii] Joan Jett & the

Blackhearts (1988) US#19, *Save Up All Your Tears* [iii] Cher (1991) US#37 UK#37. Co-writers: [i] A. Fig, [ii] Joan Jett (b. September 22, 1960, Philadelphia, PA), [iii] Diane Warren. (*See also under* Michael BOLTON, Jon BON JOVI, Alice COOPER, Paul STANLEY, John WAITE.)

170. CHILTERN, Alex (b. December 28, 1950, Memphis, TN) Rock guitarist and vocalist. A founder member of the 1960s pop group the Box Tops, who featured on the group's albums **The Letter/Neon Rainbow** (1967) US#87, **Cry Like a Baby** (1968) US#59, **Dimensions** (1969) US#77, and **Super Hits** (1968, all Bell) US#45. Chiltern quit the band in 1970 to form the influential Big Star, with which he recorded his best material, including his evocative commentary on teenage yearning, *September Gurls*. ALBUMS: **#1 Record** (1972), **Radio City** (1974, both Stax); **Third Album** (1978, Aura). Since the 1980s, Chiltern has survived as a cult solo artist and producer. ALBUMS: **One Day in New York** (1977, Ork); **Like Flies on Sherbet** (1980, Aura); **Bach's Bottom** (1981), **Live in London** (1983, both Line); **Document** (1986, Aura); **Lost Decade** (1986, Fan Club); **Stuff** (1986), **High Priest** (1987, both New Rose); **Columbia: Live at Missouri University, 4/25/93** (1993, Zoo); **1969** (1996, Ardent).

171. CHURCHILL, Frank (b. 1901; d. 1942, both America) Film composer. An imaginative Disney Studios staff composer, who wrote such songs as *Baby Mine* [iii] and *Dumbo* [iii] from the film "Dumbo" (1942), alongside *Love Is a Song* [i] from "Bambi" (1942). ALBUMS: **Bambi** sc (1954, RCA); **Bambi** ost (1957), **Dumbo** ost (1959, **Three Little Pigs** ost (1961, all Disneyland): **Snow White and the Seven Dwarfs** oc (1979, Buena Vista); **Snow White and the Seven Dwarfs** ost (1980, Disneyland). HIT VERSIONS: *Heigh-Ho (The Dwarf's Marching Song)* [i] Hoarce Heidt (1938) US#12/Seven Dwarfs (1938) US#3; *One Song* [i] Artie Shaw (1938) US#15, *Some Day My Prince Will Come* [i] Adrienne Casillotti (1938) US#10, *Whistle While You Work* [i] Shep Fields (1938) US#5/Seven Dwarfs (1938) US#2; *Who's Afraid of the Big Bad Wolf?* [ii] Ben Bernie (1933) US#8/Don Bestor (1933) US#2/Victor Young (1933) US#3. Co-writers: [i] Larry Morey (b. 1905; d. 1971), [ii] Ann Ronell, [iii] Ned Washington.

172. CLAPTON, Eric, O.B.E. (b. Eric Patrick Clapton, March 30, 1945, Ripley, England). Blues-rock guitarist and vocalist. One of the most authoritative electric guitarists since the late 1960s, who continues to explore the blues medium within the context of the popular song. Clapton played a significant role in bringing the music of the Delta blues artists to a wider audience, and unlike some of his contemporaries, he has never failed to credit the composers of the material that he records. Raised by his grandparents, who gave him his first guitar at the age of seventeen, Clapton grew up listening to the blues, R&B and the music of Blind Lemon Jefferson, Sonny Boy Williamson, Buddy Guy, Chuck Berry and Robert Johnson. He attended the Kingston College of Art during the early 1960s, where he studied stained glass design, but his heart lay in music, so in the evenings he busked and jammed with local bands. Clapton played with the R&B groups the Roosters and Casey Jones and the Engineers, before joining the Yardbirds in 1963, a loud, electric blues group that would eventually lead to the heavy rock of Led Zeppelin. Clapton's work with the Yardbirds was collected on the albums **Five Live Yardbirds** (1964, Columbia); **The Yardbirds with Sonny Boy Williamson** (1964, Fontana); **For Your Love** (1965) US#96, **Having a Rave Up with the Yardbirds** (1965) US#53, **Greatest Hits** (1967) US#28, **The Yardbirds featuring Performances By Jeff Beck, Eric Clapton and Jimmy Page** (1970, all Epic) US#155; **Smokestack Lightning, Volume 1** (1991), **Blues, Backtracks and Shapes of Things, Volume 2** (1991, both Sony). In 1965, while still the idealistic blues purist, Clapton quit the Yardbirds to join John Mayall's Bluesbreakers, which was the most authentic white blues act on the British R&B scene. The Bluesbreakers recorded Clapton's earliest composition, the instrumental *Bernard Jenkins*, but after one album **The Blues Breakers** (1966, Decca) UK#6, Clapton was off again to form, with Jack Bruce and Ginger Baker, the blues-rock trio Cream, the band that catapulted him to stardom. CHART COMPOSITIONS: *Sunshine of Your Love* [i] (1968) g US#5 UK#25, *Badge* [iii] (1969) US#60 UK#18, re-issued (1972) UK#42. ALBUMS: **Fresh Cream** (1967) g US#39 UK#6, **Disraeli Gears** (1967, both Reaction) p US#4 UK#5; **Wheels of Fire** (1968) g US#1 UK#3, **Goodbye** (1969) g US#2 UK#1, **Live Cream** (1970) US#15 UK#4, **Live Cream, Volume 2** (1972, all Polydor) US#27 UK#15. COMPILATIONS: **Wheels of Fire** (1968) UK#7, **Best of Cream** (1969) g US#3 UK#6, **Heavy Cream** (1972, all Polydor) UK#135; **Strange Brew-The Very Best of Cream** (1983, RSO) p; **Those Were the Days** (1997, Polydor). The group's material was also recorded by the Rubber Band as **The Cream Songbook** (1969, GRT) US#135. Clapton's next venture was the short-lived Blind Faith, a group collaboration with Steve Winwood that toured once and released the album **Blind Faith** (1969, Polydor) p US#1 UK#1. Clapton shied away from superstardom for much of the 1970s, preferring to sideline for such artists as Delaney and Bonnie, and contributing to the album **Delaney and Bonnie on Tour with Eric Clapton** (1970, Atco) US#29 UK#39. Clapton's eponymous solo debut, was an absorbing mixture of low-key country-blues, that introduced some of his best known compositions, including *Let It Rain*. Clapton's finest project during this period was his collaboration with the guitarists Duane Allman and Bobby Whitlock, as Derek and the Dominos, which recorded the Clapton gems *Keep on Growing, Anyday* and the rock classic *Layla* [ii]. CHART COMPOSITIONS: *Bell Bottom Blues* (1970) US#78, *Layla* [ii] (1972) US#10 UK#7, re-issued (1982) UK#4; *Why Does Love Got to Be So Bad?* (1973) US#120. ALBUMS: **Layla and Other Assorted Love Songs** (1970, Polydor) g US#16; **In Concert** (1973, RSO) g US#20 UK#36. COMPILATION: **The Layla Sessions-20th Anniversary Edition** (1990, Polydor) US#157. After battling a drug dependency during the early 1970s, Clapton returned with the impressive **461 Ocean Boulevard** (1974), after which he played down his guitar soloing, and, heavily influenced by J.J. Cale, concentrated on a more laid-back sound. By the early 1980s, Clapton had a successful sideline in film soundtracks, contributing to **The Color of Money** (1986, MCA) US#81; **Lethal Weapon** (1987), **Lethal Weapon 2** (1989, both Warner Brothers) US#164; **Homeboy** (1989, Virgin); **Lethal Weapon 3** (1992) US#101, and **Rush** (1992, both Reprise) g US#24. A series of personal tragedies in the early 1990s influenced his return to the blues, a direct result of the loss of his close friend, the guitarist Stevie Ray Vaughan, and three members of his entourage in a helicopter crash. Their deaths were shortly followed by that of his young son Conor, who fell from a New York City apartment window in March 1991. In 1992, Clapton performed an almost acoustic set of material for the MTV television series "Unplugged," which, when it was released as an album, became the biggest seller of his solo career, shifting over seven million copies in America. Over-laden with Grammy awards for the album in 1993, Clapton remarked, "I was convinced that this wasn't worth releasing." In 1995, Clapton was awarded an Order of the British Empire medal. CHART COMPOSITIONS: *Let It Rain* (1971) US#48, *Hello Old Friend* (1976) US#24, *Lay Down Sally* [vi] (1978) g C&W#26 US#3 UK#39, *Wonderful Tonight* (1978) US#16, live version (1992) UK#30; *Watch Out for Lucy* (1978) US#40, *Blues Power* [vii] live version (1980) US#76, *I Can't Stand It* (1981) US#10, *Another Ticket* (1981) US#78, *The Shape You're In* (1983) UK#75, *See What Love Can Do* (1985) US#89, *Edge of Darkness* (1986) UK#65, *Tearing Us Apart* with Tina Turner (1987) UK#56, *Bad Love* (1990) US#88 UK#25, *No Alibis* (1990)

UK#53, *Tears in Heaven* [iv] (1992) p US#2 UK#5, *Layla* [ii] live version (1992) US#12 UK#45, *It's Probably Me* [v] with Sting (1993) UK#30, *Motherless Child* (arrangement only) (1994) UK#63, *Change the World* (1996) UK#18. ALBUMS: **Eric Clapton** (1970, Polydor) US#13 UK#17; **Rainbow Concert** (1973) US#18, **461 Ocean Boulevard** (1974) g US#1 UK#3, **There's One in Every Crowd** (1975) US#21 UK#15, **EC Was Here** (1975) US#20 UK#14, **No Reason to Cry** (1976) US#15 UK#8, **Slowhand** (1977) p US#2 UK#23, **Backless** (1978) p US#8 UK#18, **Just One Night** (1980) g US#2 UK#3, **Another Ticket** (1981, all RSO) g US#7 UK#18; **Money and Cigarettes** (1983) US#16 UK#13, **Behind the Sun** (1985) g US#34 UK#8, **August** (1986) g US#37 UK#3, **Journey Man** (1989) p US#16 UK#2, **24 Nights** (1991) g US#38 UK#17, **Unplugged** (1992) p US#1 UK#2, **From the Cradle** (1994) US#1 UK#1, **Pilgrim** (1998, all Duck). COMPILATIONS: **History of Eric Clapton** (1972) g US#6 UK#20, **At His Best** (1972, both Polydor) US#87, **Clapton** (1973) US#67, **Timepieces-The Best of Eric Clapton** (1982, both RSO) p US#101 UK#20; **Backtrackin'** (1984, Starblend) UK#29; **Timepieces-Live in the Seventies** (1985, RSO); **The Cream of Eric Clapton** (1987) g US#80 UK#3, **Crossroads** (1988) p US#34, **Best of Eric Clapton** (1993) UK#25; **Crossroads 2-Live in the Seventies** (1996, all Polydor) US#137. HIT VERSIONS: *Comin' Home* Delaney & Bonnie (1972) US#84 UK#16, *Lay Down Sally* [vi] Jack Paris (1978) C&W#86/Red Sovine (1978) C&W#70. Co-writers: [i] Peter Brown/Jack Bruce, [ii] James Beck Gordon, [iii] George Harrison, [iv] Will Jennings, [v] Michael Kamen/Sting, [vi] Marcia Levy (b. June 21, 1954, Detroit, IL)/George Terry, [vii] Leon Russell. (*See also under* Jack BRUCE.)

173. CLARK, Dave (b. December 15, 1942, London, England) Pop drummer. The mastermind behind the hugely successful British beat group the Dave Clark Five. The astute Clark retained the rights to his group's music, and later created the west end musical "Time" (1986), the songs from which were issued as **Dave Clark's "Time"** (1985, EMI) UK#21. CHART COMPOSITIONS: *Glad All Over* [ii] (1964) US#6 UK#1, re-issued (1993) UK#37; *Bits and Pieces* [ii] (1964) US#4 UK#2, *Can't You See That She's Mine* [ii] (1964) US#4 UK#10, *Because* [ii] (1964) US#3, *Any Way You Want It* [ii] (1964) US#14 UK#25, *Everybody Knows (I Still Love You)* [i] (1964) US#15 UK#37, *Come Home* [i] (1965) US#14 UK#16, *Catch Us if You Can* [i] (1965) US#4 UK#5, *Please Tell Me Why* [ii] (1966) US#28, *Try Too Hard* [ii] (1966) US#12. ALBUMS: **A Session with the Dave Clark Five** (1964, Columbia) UK#3; **Glad All Over** (1964) g US#3, **The Dave Clark Five Return!** (1964)

US#5, **American Tour** (1964) US#11, **Coast to Coast** (1965) US#6, **Weekend in London** (1965, all Epic) US#24; **Catch Us if You Can** (1965, Columbia) UK#8; **Having a Wild Weekend** (1965) US#15, **Greatest Hits** (1966) US#9, **Try Too Hard** (1966) US#77, **Satisfied with You** (1966) US#127, **More Greatest Hits** (1966) US#103, **5 By 5** (1967) US#119, **You Got What It Takes** (1967, all Epic) US#149; **25 Thumping Great Hits** (1978, Polydor) UK#7; **History of the Dave Clark Five** (1993, Hollywood) US#127; **Glad All Over Again** (1993, EMI) UK#28. HIT VERSIONS: *Glad All Over* [ii] Captain Sensible (1983) UK#6/Crystal Palace (1990) UK#50. Co-writers: [i] Leonard Davidson (b. May 30, 1944, Enfield, England), [ii] Mike Smith (b. December 12, 1943, London, England).

174. CLARK, Gary (b. Dundee, Scotland) Pop guitarist and vocalist. The lead singer and principal composer in the group Danny Wilson, which never matched the initial promise of its often stunning debut album. Clark's classy, baleful pop songs blended intelligence with panache, and drew on influences that ranged from Steely Dan to Tin Pan Alley. He had first sung in the church choir before forming Clark's Commandos, a group, that by the 1980s, had evolved into Danny Wilson. CHART COMPOSITIONS: *Mary's Prayer* (1987) UK#42, re-issued (1988) US#23 UK#3; *Never Gonna Be the Same* (1989) UK#69, *The Second Summer of Love* (1989) UK#23. ALBUMS: **Meet Danny Wilson** (1987) US#79 UK#65, **Bebopmoptop** (1989, both Virgin) UK#24. COMPILATION: **Sweet Danny Wilson** (1991, Virgin) UK#54. The group split up in 1989, after which Clark embarked on what would appear to be a stalled solo career. CHART SINGLE: *We Sail on Stormy Waters* (1993) UK#34. ALBUM: **Ten Short Songs About Love** (1993, Circa) UK#25.

175. CLARK, Gene (b. Harold Eugene Clark, November 17, 1941, Tipton, MO; d. May 24, 1991) Pop guitarist and vocalist. An original member, alongside Roger McGuinn, Chris Hillman and David Crosby, of the innovative 1960s group the Byrds. Clark frequently sang lead during his tenure with the band, and was their most prolific tunesmith, penning the hits *I'll Feel a Whole Lot Better* (1965) US#103, *Set You Free This Time* (1965) US#79 and *Full Circle* (1973) US#109. By 1967, Clark's performance and songwriting royalties were accumulating at an estimated one thousand dollars a day, but he quit the Byrds to form his own Gene Clark Group, before joining the Flying Burrito Brothers in 1968 for the albums **Close Up the Honky Tonks** (1974, A&M) and **Honky Tonk Heaven** (1975, Ariola). Clark re-united with McGuinn and Hillman in 1973,

releasing the albums **The Byrds** (1973, Asylum) US#20 UK#31; **McGuinn, Clark and Hillman** (1979) US#30 and **City** (1980, both Capitol) US#136. The highlight of his sporadic solo career was the sadly neglected **No Other** (1974). Clark died of a heart attack in 1991. ALBUMS: **Gene Clark with the Gosdin Brothers** (1967, Columbia); **Gene Clark** (1969, Together); **Fantastic Expedition*** (1969), **Through the Morning*** (1969), **White Light** (1971, all A&M); **Roadmaster** (1973, Ariola); **No Other** (1974, Asylum) US#144; **Gene Clark and Doug Dillard*** (1975), **Kansas City Southern*** (1975, both Ariola); **Early L.A. Sessions** (1975), **Collector's Classics** (1976, both Columbia); **Two Sides to Every Story** (1977, RSO); **Firebyrd** (1987, Takoma); **So Rebellious a Lover** with Carla Olson (1987, Demon). COMPILATION: **Flying High** (1997). With: * Doug Dillard. (*See also under* Roger McGUINN.)

176. CLARK, Guy (b. Guy Charles Clark, November 6, 1941, Beaumont, TX). C&W guitarist and vocalist. A folk and country influenced singer-songwriter, who is a highly regarded tunesmith despite continually indifferent record sales. Clark learned the guitar by playing along to Mexican songs, and spent his teenage years in the small town of Monahans, Texas, where he lived in a rundown hotel before working as an art director at a Houston television station during the 1960s. After a period making musical instruments at the Dopera Brothers dobro factory, Clark began performing at nights in the bars and coffee houses of Houston, Austin and Dallas. In the 1970s, his songs attracted the attention of other artists, resulting in *Heartbroke* being recorded by Ricky Scaggs and Rodney Crowell, and *New Cut Road* by Bobby Bare. The weathered charm of Clark's debut album, **Old Number One** (1976), remains his most satisfying work, but he has continued to record his tales of isolation, individualism and ordinary lives, whenever he has been able to acquire a record contract, but he seems destined to remain forever a cult artist. CHART COMPOSITIONS: *Fools for Each Other* (1979) C&W#96, *The Partner Nobody Chose* (1981) C&W#38, *Homegrown Tomatoes* (1983) C&W#42. ALBUMS: **Old Number One** (1976), **Texas Cookin'** (1977, both RCA); **Guy Clark** (1978), **South Coast of Texas** (1980), **Better Days** (1983, all Warner Brothers); **Old Friends** (1988, Sugarhill); **Hold That Plane** (1989, Start); **Boats to Build** (1992), **Dublin Blues** (1995, both Asylum); **Keepers: A Live Recording** (1997, Sugarhill). COMPILATIONS: **Best of Guy Clark** (1982), **Greatest Hits** (1983), **Essentials** (1996, all RCA). HIT VERSIONS: *Desperados Waiting for a Train* Highwayman (1985) C&W#15, *L.A. Freeway* Jerry Jeff Walker (1977) US#98, *Last Gunfighter Bal-*

lad, The Johnny Cash (1977) C&W#38, Texas 1947 Johnny Cash (1975) C&W#35.

177. CLARKE, Grant (b. 1891; d. 1931, both America) Film and stage lyricist. HIT VERSIONS: *He'd Have to Get Under-Get Out and Get Under (To Fix Up His Automobile)* [i] Billy Murray (1914) US#2, *Ragtime Cowboy Joe* [ii] Bob Roberts (192) US#1/Pinky Tomlin (1939) US#14/Eddy Howard (1947) C&W#5 US#16/Jo Stafford (1949) US#10/Chipmunks (1959) R&B#29 US#16 UK#11; *Rosie (Make It Rosy for Me)* [iii] Carl Fenton (1921) US#7; *Weary River* [iv] Gene Austin (1929) US#5/ Rudy Vallee (1929) US#2. Co-writers: [i] Maurice Abrahams (b. 1883; d. 1931), [ii] Maurice Abrahams/ Lewis Muir, [iii] J.L. Merkur, [iv] Louis Silver. (*See also under* Harry AKST, Walter DONALDSON, Fred FISHER, Lou HANDMAN, James F. HANLEY, George W. MEYER, Jimmy MONACO, Lewis MUIR, Harry WARREN.)

178. CLARKE, Vince (b. July 3, 1960, Basildon, England) Pop keyboard player and producer. The most consistently successful synthesizer based songwriter since the early 1980s. Clarke first performed in the group Depeche Mode, penning the hits *Dreaming of Me* (1981) UK#57, *New Life* (1981) UK#11 and *Just Can't Get Enough* (1981) UK#8, and featuring on the albums **Speak and Spell** (1981) US#192 UK#10, **The Singles 1981–1985** (1985, both Mute) UK#6; **Catching Up with Depeche Mode** (1987, Sire) US#113. He left the band in 1982 to form a duo Yazoo, with the vocalist Alison Moyet. CHART COMPOSITIONS: *Only You* (1982) US#67 UK#2, *Don't Go* (1982) UK#3, *Situation* [ii] (1982) R&B#31 US#73, re-mixed (1990) UK#14; *The Other Side of Love* [ii] (1982) UK#13. ALBUMS: **Upstairs at Eric's** (1982) p US#92 UK#2, **You and Me Both** (1983, both Mute) US#69 UK#2. As the group the Assembly, Clarke charted with the single *Never Never* (1983) UK#4, before forming another duo, Erasure, with the vocalist Andy Bell. CHART COMPOSITIONS: *Who Needs Love Like That* [i] (1985) UK#55, re-mixed (1992) UK#10; *Heavenly Action* [i] (1985) UK#100, *Oh L'Amour* [i] (1986) UK#85, *Sometimes* [i] (1986) UK#2, *It Doesn't Have to Be* [i] (1987) UK#12, *Victim of Love* [i] (1987) UK#7, *Ship of Fools* [i] (1988) UK#6, *Chains of Love* [i] (1988) US#12 UK#11, *A Little Respect* [i] (1988) US#14 UK#4, *Crackers International EP* [i] (1988) UK#2, *Stop!* [i] (1989) US#97, *Drama!* [i] (1989) UK#4, *You Surround Me* [i] (1989) UK#15, *Blue Savannah* [i] (1990) UK#3, *Star* [i] (1990) UK#11, *Chorus* [i] (1991) US#83 UK#3, *Love to Hate You* [i] (1991) UK#4, *Am I Right? EP* [i] (1991) UK#15, re-mixed (1992) UK#22; *Breath of Life* [i] (1992) UK#8,

Always [i] (1994) US#20 UK#4, *Run to the Sun* [i] (1994) UK#6, *I Love Saturday* [i] (1994) UK#20, *Stay with Me* [i] (1995) UK#15, *Fingers and Thumbs (Cold Summer's Day)* [i] (1995) UK#20. ALBUMS: **Wonderland** (1986) UK#71, **The Circus** (1987) US#190 UK#6, **Two Ring Circus** (1987) US#186 UK#6, **The Innocents** (1988) p US#49 UK#1, **Crackers International** (1989) US#73, **Wild!** (1989) US#57 UK#1, **Abba-esque** (1992) US#85, **I Say, I Say, I Say** (1994) US#18 UK#1, **Erasure** (1995) US#82 UK#14, **Cowboy** (1997, all Mute) UK#10. COMPILATION: **Pop-The First 20 Hits** (1992, Mute) US#93 UK#1. HIT VERSIONS: *Erasure-ish (A Little Respect/Stop!)* [i] Bjorn Again (1992) UK#25, *Oh L'Amour* [i] Dollar (1988) UK#7, *Only You* Flying Pickets (1983) UK#1. Co-writers: [i] Andrew Bell (b. April 25, 1964, Peterborough, England), [ii] Alison Moyet (b. June 18, 1961, Basildon, England).

179. CLEMENT, Jack (b. Jack Henderson Clement, April 5, 1931, Memphis, TN) C&W multi-instrumentalist and producer. A former bluegrass musician and record label owner, who was particularly successful as a country producer and writer at Sun Records during the late 1950s. Clement also recorded a series of solo records, and is credited with having discovered the country singer Charley Pride. CHART COMPOSITIONS: *We Must Believe in Magic/When I Dream* (1978) C&W#86, *All I Want to Do in Life* (1978) C&W#84. ALBUM: **All I Want to Do in Life** (1978, Elektra). HIT VERSIONS: *Ballad of a Teenage Queen* Johnny Cash (1958) C&W#1 US#14, *Everybody Loves a Nut* Johnny Cash (1966) C&W#17 US#96, *Girl I Used to Know, A* George Jones (1962) C&W#3, *Guess Things Happen That Way* Johnny Cash (1958) C&W#1 US#11, *It'll Be Me* Cliff Richard (1962) UK#2, *Miller's Cave* Hank Snow (1960) C&W#9 US#101/Bobby Bare (1964) C&W#4 US#33; *One on the Right Is on the Left, The* Johnny Cash (1966) C&W#2 US#46, *We Must Believe in Magic* Johnny Cash (1983) C&W#84, *What I've Got in Mind* Billie Jo Spears (1976) C&W#5.

180. CLIFF, Jimmy (b. James Chambers, 1948, St. Catherine, Jamaica) Reggae vocalist. A reggae singer-songwriter who enjoyed considerable Jamaican success during the early 1960s, with such self-penned material as *Dearest Beverley* and *Hurricane Hattie*. In 1965, Cliff re-located to England, where he became known for his lead role in the film "The Harder They Come" (1972), for which he composed the title theme and the much covered gospel-soul classic *Many Rivers to Cross*. The best of the many versions that have been recorded of his songs is Bruce Springsteen's rendition of *Trapped*. CHART COM-

POSITIONS: *Wonderful World, Beautiful People* (1969) US#25 UK#6, *Vietnam* (1970) UK#46, *Come into My Life* (1970) US#89, *Special* (1982) R&B#76, *Reggae Night* (1983) R&B#89, *We Are All One* (1984) R&B#75, *Peace* (1992) R&B#96, *Breakout* (1992) R&B#81, *Oneness* (1992) R&B#119. ALBUMS: **Hard Road** (1967, Island); **Jimmy Cliff** (1969, Trojan); **Can't Get Enough** (1969, Veep); **Wonderful World** (1970), **Another Cycle** (1971), **The Harder They Come** ost (1972, all Island) US#140; **Sense of Direction** (1973, Sire); **Struggling Man** (1974, Island); **House of Exile** (1974, EMI); **Unlimited** (1974), **Music Maker** (1974), **Follow My Mind** (1975, all Reprise) US#195; **Brave Warrior** (1975, EMI); **Live in Concert** (1976, Reprise); **Give Thanx** (1978, Columbia); **I Am the Living** (1980), **Give the People What They Want** (1981, both MCA); **Special** (1982) US#186, **The Power and the Glory** (1983), **Cliff Hangar** (1985), **Hanging Fire** (1988, all Columbia); **Images** (1989, Cliff); **Breakout** (1992, JRS). COMPILATIONS: **Pop Chronik, Volume 9** (1975), **Best of Jimmy Cliff** (1975, both Island); **Oh Jamaica** (1976, EMI); **Reggae Greats** (1985, Island); **Fundamental Reggae** (1987, See for Miles). HIT VERSIONS: *Harder They Come, The* Rocker's Revenge (1983) UK#30/Madness (1992) UK#44; *Let Your Yeah Be Yeah* Pioneers (1971) UK#5/Ali Campbell (1995) UK#25; *Many Rivers to Cross* Nilsson (1974) US#109/UB40 (1983) UK#16; *You Can Get It if You Really Want* Desmond Dekker (1970) US#103 UK#2, *Sitting in Limbo* [i] Don Brown (1978) US#76. Cowriter: [i] Bright/Plummer.

181. CLIMIE, Simon (b. April 7, 1960, London, England) Pop vocalist. A songwriter who, with Rob Fisher, recorded as the duo Climie Fisher. CHART COMPOSITIONS: *Love Changes (Everything)* (1987) UK#67, re-mixed (1988) US#23 UK#2; *Rise to the Occasion* [i] (1988) UK#10, *This Is Me* (1988) UK#22, *I Won't Bleed for You* (1988) UK#35, *Love Like a River* (1988) UK#22, *Facts of Love* (1989) UK#50. ALBUMS: **Everything** (1988) US#126 UK#14, **Coming in for the Kill** (1989, both EMI) UK#35. Climie also charted with the solo single *Soul Inspiration* [iv] (1992) UK#60. HIT VERSIONS: *I Knew You Were Waiting (For Me)* [iii] Aretha Franklin & George Michael (1987) R&B#5 US#1 UK#1, *Invincible (Theme from the Legend of Billie Jean)* [ii] Pat Benatar (1985) US#10 UK#53, *My Heart Can't Tell You No* [iii] Rod Stewart (1988) US#4 UK#49, *Room to Move* [i] Animotion (1989) US#9. Co-writers: [i] Rob Fisher/Dennis Morgan, [ii] Holly Knight, [iii] Dennis Morgan, [iv] Thomas.

182. CLINTON, George (b. July 22, 1940, Kannapolis, NC) R&B vocalist and producer. An original R&B performer who, initially influenced by Sly Stone, went on to create an entire R&B-funk-rock philosophy and lifestyle, with an increasingly bizarre series of groups, which were, in turn, a major source of inspiration for Prince. Clinton first sang in the doo-wop act the Parliaments, charting with the singles *(I Wanna) Testify* [x] (1967) R&B#3 US#20, *All Your Goodies Are Gone (The Loser's Seat)* (1967) R&B#21 US#80 and *A New Day Begins* (1969) R&B#44, which released the album **Osmium** (1970, Invictus). By the early 1970s, the group had evolved into the psychedelic disco-funk of Parliament. CHART COMPOSITIONS: *The Breakdown* (1971) R&B#30 US#107, *Up for the Down Stroke* [iv] (1974) R&B#10 US#63, *Testify* [x] (1974) R&B#77, *Chocolate City* [vii] (1975) R&B#24 US#94, *Ride On* (1975) R&B#64, *P. Funk (Wants to Get Funked Up)* (1976) R&B#33, *Tear the Roof Off the Sucker (Give Up the Funk)* [i] (1976) g R&B#5 US#15, *Star Child* (1976) R&B#26, *Do That Stuff* (1976) R&B#22, *Dr. Funkenstein* (1977) R&B#43 US#102, *Fantasy Is a Reality* (1977) R&B#54, *Bop Gun (Endangered Species)* (1977) R&B#14 US#102, *Flash Light* [vii] (1978) g R&B#1 US#16, *Funkentelechy* (1978) R&B#27, *Aqua Boogie (A Psychoalphadiscobetabio-aquadoloop)* [vii] (1979) R&B#1 US#89, *Rumpofsteelskin* (1979) R&B#63, *Party People* (1979) R&B#39, *Theme from the Black Hole* (1980) R&B#8, *The Big Bang Theory* (1980) R&B#50, *Agony of DeFeet* (1980) R&B#7. ALBUMS: **Up for the Down Stroke** (1974), **Chocolate City** (1975) US#91, **Mothership Connection** (1976) p US#13, **The Clones of Dr. Funkenstein** (1976) g US#20, **Parliament Live/P. Funk Earth Tour** (1977) g US#29, **Funkentelchy Vs. The Placebo Syndrome** (1977) p US#13, **Motor-Booty Affair** (1978) g US#23, **Gloryhallastoopid (Or Pin the Tail on the Funky)** (1979) g US#44, **Trombipulation** (1981, all Casablanca) US#61. As Funkadelic, Clinton's increasingly wry but drug oriented wit was taken a step nearer to madness. CHART COMPOSITIONS: *Music for My Mother* (1969) R&B#50, *I'll Bet You* (1969) R&B#22 US#68, *I Got a Thing, You Got a Thing, Everybody's Got a Thing* (1970) R&B#30 US#80, *I Wanna Know if It's Good to You?* (1970) R&B#27 US#81, *You and Your Folks, Me and My Folks* (1971) R&B#42 US#91, *Can You Get to That* (1971) R&B#44 US#93, *Joyful Process* (1972) R&B#38, *Loose Booty* (1973) R&B#49 US#118, *On the Verge of Getting It On* (1974) R&B#27, *Red Hot Mama* (1975) R&B#73, *Let's Take It to the Stage* (1976) R&B#89, *Better By the Pound* [vi] (1975) US#99, *Undisco Kidd* (1976) R&B#30 US#102, *Comin' Round the Mountain* (1977) R&B#54, *Smokey* (1977) R&B#96, *One Nation Under a Groove* [ix] (1978) g R&B#1 US#28 UK#9, *Cholly (Funk Getting Ready to Roll!)* (1979) R&B#43, *(Not Just)*

Knee Deep (1979) R&B#1 US#77, *Uncle Jam* (1979) R&B#53, *The Electric Spanking of War Babies* (1981) R&B#60. ALBUMS: **Funkadelic** (1970) US#126, **Free Your Mind and Your Ass Will Follow** (1970) US#92, **Maggot Brain** (1971) US#108, **America Eats Its Young** (1972) US#123, **Cosmic Slop** (1973) US#112, **Standing on the Verge of Getting It On** (1974) US#163, **Greatest Hits** (1974), **Let's Take It to the Stage** (1975) US#102, **Tales of Kidd Funkadelic** (1976, all Westbound) US#103; **Hardcore Jollies** (1976) US#96, **One Nation Under a Groove** (1978) p US#16 UK#56, **Uncle Jam Wants You** (1979) g US#18, **The Electric Spanking of War Babies** (1981, all Warner Brothers) US#105; **Live** (1996, Westbound). Clinton also recorded as the Brides of Funkenstein, charting with the singles *Disco to Go* (1978) R&B#7 US#101, *Amorous* (1979) R&B#76 and *Never Buy Texas from a Cowboy (Part 1)* (1980) R&B#67, from the albums **Funk or Walk** (1978) US#70 and **Never Buy Texas from a Cowboy** (1980, both Atlantic) US#93. He has also recorded as the P. Funk All-Stars, scoring hits with *Hydraulic Pump* (1982) R&B#66, *One of Those Summers* (1982) R&B#77 and *Generator Pop* (1983) R&B#62. The road to excess did not lead to wisdom for Clinton, and in 1981 he filed for bankruptcy. No longer able to afford the cast of thousands or the elaborate stage sets, Clinton has recorded as a solo artist since 1982. CHART COMPOSITIONS: *Cosmic Slop* (1973) US#102, *Loopzilla* (1982) R&B#19 UK#57, *Atomic Dog* (1983) R&B#1 US#101, *Get Dressed* (1983) R&B#73, *Nubian Nut* (1983) R&B#15, *Last Dance* (1984) R&B#26, *Quickie* (1984) R&B#72, *Double Oh-Oh* (1985) R&B#32 US#101, *Bullet Proof* (1985) R&B#69, *Do Fries Go with That Shake* (1986) R&B#13 UK#57, *Hey Good Lookin'* (1986) R&B#41, *Paint the White House Black* [ii] (1993) R&B#62 US#106, *Martial Law (Hey Man... Smell My Finger)* [iii] (1993) R&B#70. ALBUMS: **The George Clinton Band Arrives** (1975, ABC); **Computer Games** (1982) US#40, **You Shouldn't-Nuf Bit Fish** (1984) US#102, **Some of My Best Jokes Are Friends** (1985) US#163, **R&B Skeletons in the Closet** (1986), all Capitol) US#81; **The Mothership Connection Live from Houston, Texas** (1986), **Cinderella Theory** (1989), **Hey Man...Smell My Finger** (1993, both Paisley Park) US#145; **Parliament/Funkadelic/P. Funk All-Stars/Dope Dogs** (1995, Hot Hands); **The Music of Red Shoe Diaries** (1995, Wienerworld); **Mortal Kombat** ost (1996, TVT); **The Awesome Power of a Fully Operational Mothership** (1996), **T.A.P.O.A.F.O.M.** (1996, both 550/Epic). COMPILATIONS: **Terra Off the Roof** (1993, Mercury); **A Fifth of Funk** (1995, Castle); **Greatest Funkin' Hits** (1996, Capitol). HIT VERSIONS: *Ain't Nobody Better* [xi] Yo-Yo (1991) R&B#30, *Knee*

Deep De La Soul sampled in *Me, Myself and I* [viii] (1989) g R&B#1 US#34 UK#22, *One Nation Under a Groove* [ix] Ice Cube sampled in *Bop Gun (One Nation)* (1994) R&B#45+ US#55+, *Return of the Crazy One* [v] Digital Underground (1993) R&B#77, *Up for the Down Stroke* [iv] Fred Wesley & the Horny Horns (1977) R&B#93. Co-writers: [i] Jerome Brailey/William Collins (b. October 26, 1951, Cincinnati, OH), [ii] W. Bryant III/Berry Gordy, Jr./Barrett Strong/Norman Whitfield, [iii] W. Bryant III/K. Gordy, [iv] William Collins/C. Haskens/Bernie Worrell (b. April 19, 1944, Long Beach, NJ), [v] William Collins/E. Humphrey/J. Jackson/G. Jacobs/Bernie Worrell, [vi] William Collins/Bernie Worrell, [vii] G. Cook, [viii] De La Soul/Paul Huston/Philippe Wynn, [ix] Walter Morrison/Gary Shider, [x] Deron Taylor, [xi] H. Wolinsky/P. Wynn/Yo-Yo.

183. COBAIN, Kurt (b. February 20, 1967, Aberdeen; d. April 5, 1994, Seattle, both WA) Rock guitarist and vocalist. The songwriter and guitarist who formed the influential band Nirvana, which fused punk and rock into a sound that became known as "grunge." Cobain's song *Smells Like Teen Spirit* [i] is one of the true classics of the 1990s. Mentally and emotionally troubled since his parents divorce in 1975, Cobain committed a much publicized suicide in 1994. CHART COMPOSITIONS: *Smells Like Teen Spirit* [i] (1991) p US#6 UK#7, *Come as You Are* [i] (1992) US#32 UK#9, *Lithium* [i] (1992) US#64 UK#11, *In Bloom* [i] (1992) UK#28, *Oh, the Guilt* [i] (1993) UK#12, *Heart Shaped Box* [i] (1993) UK#5, *All Apologies/Rape Me* [i] (1993) UK#32. ALBUMS: **Bleach** (1989, Sub Pop) p US#89 UK#33; **Nevermind** (1991) p US#1 UK#18, **Incesticide** (1993) p US#39 UK#14, **In Utero** (1993) US#1 UK#1, **MTV Unplugged in New York** (1994) p US#1 UK#1, **From the Muddy Banks of the Wishkah** (1996, all DGC) US#1 UK#4. COMPILATION: **The Nevermind and In Utero Singles** (1995, DGC). HIT VERSION: *Smells Like Teen Spirit* [i] "Weird" Al Yankovic as *Smells Like Nirvana* (1992) US#35 UK#58/Abigail (1994) UK#29. Co-writers: [i] Dave Grohl (b. January 14, 1969, USA)/Kris Novoselic (b. May 16, 1965, Croatia, Yugoslavia).

184. COCHRAN, Eddie (b. Ray Edward Cochran, October 3, 1938, Albert Lea, MN; d. April 17, 1960, near Bath, England) Rockabilly guitarist and vocalist. An influential rockabilly artist who initially sang in the Cochran Brothers duo, alongside the unrelated Hank Cochran. He was killed in an automobile accident at the age of twenty-one. CHART COMPOSITIONS: *Summertime Blues* [i] (1957)

R&B#11 US#8 UK#18, *C'mon Everybody* [i] (1959) US#35 UK#6, re-issued (1988) UK#14; *Somethin' Else* [ii] (1959) US#58 UK#22; *Three Steps to Heaven* (1960) US#108 UK#1. ALBUMS: **Singing to My Baby** (1960) UK#19, **Memorial Album** (1963, both London) UK#11; **Cherished Memories** (1963) UK#15, **My Way** (1964), **Very Best of Eddie Cochran** (1970, all Liberty) UK#34; **The Eddie Cochran Singles Album** (1979, United Artists) UK#39; **20th Anniversary Album** (1980), **C'mon Everybody** (1988, Liberty) UK#53; **Eddie and Hank** with Hank Cochran (1991, Rockstar). HIT VERSIONS: *C'mon Everybody* [i] Sex Pistols (1979) UK#3, *Summertime Blues* [i] Blue Cheer (1968) US#14/Who (1970) US#27 UK#38/Jim Mundy (1977) C&W#70/Alan Jackson (1995) C&W#1 US#104+; *Three Steps to Heaven* Showaddywaddy (1975) UK#2. Co-writers: [i] Jerry Capeheart, [ii] Sharron Sheeley. (*See also under* Hank COCHRAN.)

185. COCHRAN, Hank (b. Garland Perry, August 2, 1935, Isola, MS) C&W guitarist and vocalist. A country singer-songwriter who has won seventy-five BMI songwriting awards. Cochran was raised in an orphanage in Tennessee, and after working the oil fields of New Mexico he moved to California, where he learned the guitar and began writing songs. In 1953, he adopted his stage name as one half of a duo with the rockabilly singer Eddie Cochran, performing and recording as the Cochran Brothers. As he hustled his songs in Nashville, Cochran befriended fellow struggling songwriter Willie Nelson, with whom he would co-write many of his first songs while working as a song plugger for Pamper Music. Cochran's own records have tended to act as song sources for other artists. CHART COMPOSITIONS: *Sally Was a Good Old Girl* [ii] (1962) C&W#20, *I'd Fight the World* (1962) C&W#23, *A Good Country Song* (1963) C&W#25, *Willie* with Merle Haggard (1978) C&W#91, *Ain't Life Hell* [iv] with Willie Nelson (1978) C&W#77, *A Little Bitty Tear* (1980) C&W#57. ALBUMS: **The Heart of Hank** (1968, Monument); **With a Little Help from His Friends** (1978, Capitol); **Make the World Go Away** (1980, Elektra); **Eddie and Hank** with Eddie Cochran (1991, Rockstar). HIT VERSIONS: *A-11* Johnny Paycheck (1965) C&W#26, *All of Me Belongs to You* Dick Curless (1967) C&W#28, *Can I Sleep in Your Arms* Jeannie Seely (1973) C&W#6, *Chair, The* Marty Robbins (1971) C&W#7 US#121/George Strait (1985) C&W#1; *Don't Touch Me* Wilma Burgess (1966) C&W#12/Jeannie Seely (1966) C&W#2 US#85/Brenda Joyce (1979) C&W#96/Jerry Naylor & Kelli Warren (1979) C&W#69; *Don't You Ever Get Tired of Hurting Me?* Ray Price (1966) C&W#11/Connie Cato (1977)

C&W#92/Willie Nelson & Ray Price (1981) C&W#11/Ronnie Milsap (1988) C&W#1; *Funny Way of Laughin'* Burl Ives (1962) C&W#9 US#10 UK#29, *Go on Home* Patti Page (1962) C&W#13 US#42), *I Fall to Pieces* [ii] Patsy Cline (1961) C&W#1 US#12, re-mixed (1981) C&W#61/Diana Trask (1969) C&W#37 US#114/Mary K. Miller (1977) C&W#89/Patsy Cline & Jim Reeves (1982) C&W#54/Aaron Neville & Trisha Yearwood (1994) C&W#72; *I Know an Ending When It Comes* B.J. Wright (1981) C&W#81, *I Want to Go with You* Eddy Arnold (1966) C&W#1 US#36 UK#46, *I'd Fight the World* [ii] Jim Reeves (1974) C&W#19, *I'm Not Leaving (I'm Just Getting Out of Your Way)* Ray Price (1985) C&W#81, *It's Not Love (But It's Not Bad)* [iii] Merle Haggard (1972) C&W#1, *It's Only Love* Jeannie Seely (1966) C&W#15, *Little Bits and Pieces* Jim Stafford (1984) C&W#67, *Little Bitty Tear, A* Burl Ives (1962) C&W#2 US#9 UK#9, *Little Unfair, A* [ii] Lefty Frizzell (1965) C&W#36, *Make the World Go Away* Ray Price (1963) C&W#2 US#100/Eddy Arnold (1965) C&W#1 US#6 UK#8/Donny & Marie Osmond (1975) C&W#71 US#44 UK#18/Charly McClain (1977) C&W#73; *Ocean Front Property* George Strait (1987) C&W#1, *Right in the Wrong Direction* Liz Lyndell (1981) C&W#85, *Set 'Em Up Joe* Vern Gosdin (1988) C&W#1, *She's/He's Got You* Patsy Cline (1961) C&W#1 US#14 UK#43/Loretta Lynn (1977) C&W#1/Don McLean (1978) C&W#73; *That's All That Matters* Ray Price (1964) C&W#34/Mickey Gilley (1980) C&W#1; *Those Eyes* Anthony Armstrong Jones (1986) C&W#74, *Undo the Right* [iv] Johnny Bush (1968) C&W#10, *Way to Survive, A* Ray Price (1966) C&W#7, *We Never Touch at All* Merle Haggard (1988) C&W#22, *When You Need a Laugh* Patsy Cline (1964) C&W#47, *Who Do I Know in Dallas?* Kenny Price (1969) C&W#64, *Why Can't He Be You* Loretta Lynn (1977) C&W#7, *Wish I Didn't Have to Miss You* Jack Greene & Jeannie Seely (1970) C&W#2, *Would These Arms Be in Your Way* Keith Whitley (1987) C&W#36, *Years from Now* [i] Dr. Hook (1980) US#51 UK#47, *You Comb Her Hair Every Morning* [ii] George Jones (1963) C&W#5, also on B-side of *Ain't It Funny What a Fool Will Do* (1963) US#124/Del Reeves (1975) C&W#92; *You Just Hurt My Last Feeling* Sammi Smith (1985) C&W#76, *You Wouldn't Know Love (If It Looked You in the Eye)* Ray Price (1970) C&W#8. Co-writers: [i] Roger Cook, [ii] Harlan Howard, [iii] G. Martin, [iv] Willie Nelson. (*See also under* Willie NELSON.)

186. COCKBURN, Bruce (b. May 27, 1945, Ottawa, Canada) Pop guitarist and vocalist. A folk and country based singer-songwriter who has gradually moved more into the pop mainstream. CHART COMPOSITIONS: *Wondering Where the*

Lions Are (1980) US#21, *If I Had a Rocket Launcher* (1985) US#88. ALBUMS: **Bruce Cockburn** (1970), **High Winds White Sky** (1971), **Sunwheel Dance** (1972), **Night Vision** (1973), **Hard Dancing** (1973), **Salt, Sun and Time** (1974), **Joy Will Find a Way** (1975), **In the Falling Dark** (1976), **Circles in the Stream** (1977), **Further Adventures of Bruce Cockburn** (1978, all True North); **Dancing in the Dragon's Jaws** (1980) US#45, **Humans** (1980) US#81, **Selected Hits from 1980 Tour** (1980), **Bruce Cockburn/Resume** (1981) US#174, **Inner City Front** (1981, all Millenium); **Stealing Fire** (1984, Gold Mountain) US#74; **Trouble with Normal** (1985, True North); **World of Wonders** (1986, MCA) US#143; **Rumors of Glory** (1986, FM); **Big Circumstance** (1989, Gold Castle) US#182; **Waiting for a Miracle** (1987, FM); **Nothing But a Burning Light** (1992), **Christmas** (1993), **Dart to the Heart** (1994, all Columbia) US#176; **The Charity of Night** (1996, Rykodisc).

187. COCKER, Jarvis (b. Sheffield, England) Pop vocalist. The lead singer and individualistic songwriter in the British indie group Pulp, which first performed as Arabacus Pulp in the early 1980s. CHART COMPOSITIONS: *Lip Gloss* (1993) UK#50, *Do You Remember the First Time?* (1994) UK#33, re-entry (1996) UK#73; *The Sisters EP* (1994) UK#19, *Common People* (1995) UK#2, *Mis-Shapes/Sorted for Es and Wizz* (1995) UK#2, *Disco 2,000* (1995) UK#7, *Something Changed* (1996) UK#10. ALBUMS: **It** (1994, Cartel); **Freaks** (1987), **Separations** (1993, both Fire); **Pulpintro-The Gift Recordings** (1993), **His 'N' Hers** (1994) UK#9, **Different Class** (1995) UK#1, **Countdown, 1992–1983** (1996, all Island) UK#10. COMPILATIONS: **Masters of the Universe-Pulp on Fire, 1985–1986** (1994, Fire).

188. COE, David Allan (b. September 6, 1939, Akron, OH) C&W guitarist and vocalist. Country music's most genuine "outlaw," who spent some two decades in and out of reform school and prison before becoming a performer. The songs that Coe composed while incarcerated obtained his first recording contract in 1967. He ultimately placed over thirty of his R&B influenced country-blues singles on the charts during the 1970–1980s. CHART COMPOSITIONS: *(If I Could Climb) The Walls of the Bottle* (1974) C&W#80, *Would You Be My Lady* (1975) C&W#91, *Longhaired Redneck* (1975) C&W#17, *Willie, Waylon and Me* (1976) C&W#25, *The Ride* (1983) C&W#4, *Need a Little Time Off for Bad Behavior* (1987) C&W#38, *Tanya Montana* (1987) C&W#62. ALBUMS: **Penitentiary Blues** (1968), **Requiem for a Harlequin** (1969. both SSS); **Mys-**terious Rhinestone Cowboy** (1974), **Once Upon a Rhyme** (1974), **Long Haired Redneck** (1976), **Rides Again** (1977), **Tattoo** (1977), **Family Album** (1978), **Human Emotions** (1978), **Spectrum Seven** (1979), **Nothing Sacred** (1979), **Compass Point** (1980), **I've Got Something to Say** (1980), **Invictus** (1981), **Encore** (1981), **Tennessee Whiskey** (1981), **D.A.C.** (1982), **Castles in the Sand** (1983), **Hello in There** (1983) US#179, **Just Divorced** (1984), **Unchained** (1986), **Matter of Life and Death** (1987, all Columbia). COMPILATIONS: **Greatest Hits** (1978) g, **For The Record-The First 10 Years** (1985), **I Love Country** (1987, all Columbia). HIT VERSIONS: *Loneliness in Lucy's Eyes (The Life Sue Ellen Is Living)*, *The* Johnny Lee (1986) C&W#56, *Take This Job and Shove It* Johnny Paycheck (1977) C&W#1, *Would You Lay with Me (In a Field of Stone)* Tanya Tucker (1974) C&W#1 US#46.

189. COHAN, George M. (b. George Michael Cohan, July 3, 1878, Providence, RI; d. November 5, 1942, New York, NY) Film and stage composer, producer and vocalist. The single most important force in Broadway musicals during the early 1900s, who created twenty-two musicals. Cohan's *Over There* is one of only a handful of songs to reach number one with four different versions. America's most patriotic tunesmith, Cohan always claimed to have been born on the fourth of July. He dominated his own productions in all their aspects, published over five hundred songs, and was the creator of the first true American Broadway musical, "Little Johnny Jones" (1903), which was revived in 1987. Cohan's other successes were "Forty-Five Minutes from Broadway" (1906), "George Washington, Jr." (1906), "Fifty Miles from Boston" (1908), "Little Nelly Kelly" (1922), and "Ah! Wilderness" (1933). A child vaudeville performer who began writing songs in his teens, Cohan was to reign supreme on Broadway for fifteen years, his life becoming the subject matter of the film "Yankee Doodle Dandy" (1942). The singer Billy Murray recorded nearly all of Cohan's songs. During the 1920s, Cohan worked as an actor, although his one brush with Hollywood, "The Phantom President" (1932), resulted in his statement, "I'd rather go to Leavenworth Prison than work in Hollywood again." CHART COMPOSITIONS: *Life's a Funny Proposition, After All* (1911) US#5, *The Small-Town Gal* (1911) US#8. ALBUMS: **Yankee Doodle Dandee** ost (1942, Curtain Calls); **Show Biz (From Vaude to Video)** oc (1954), **Mister Broadway** tst (1957), **Great Personalities of Broadway** sc (1963, all RCA); **George M!** oc (1968, Columbia) US#161. HIT VERSIONS: *Forty-Five Minutes from Broadway* Billy Murray (1906) US#3, *Give My Regards to Broadway* S.H. Dudley (1905)

US#4/Billy Murray (1905) US#1; *Harrigan* Edward Meker (1907) US#8/Billy Murray (1907) US#1; *If I'm Goin' to Die, I'm Goin' to Have Some Fun* Arthur Collins (1907) US#3, *Mary's a Grand Old Name* Bing Crosby (1943) US#20, *Nellie Kelly I Love You* American Quartete (1923) US#7/Prince's Orchestra (1923) US#9; *Over There* American Quartete (1917) UK#1/Nora Bayes (1917) US#1/Billy Murray (1917) US#5/Peerless Quartet (1917) US#1/Enrico Caruso (1918) US#1/Prince's Orchestra (1918) US#6; *Popularity* Vess Ossman (1907) US#6, *So Long, Mary* Ada Jones (1906) US#2/Corrine Morgan (1906) US#1; *When a Fellow's on the Level with a Girl Who's on the Square* Billy Murray (1909) US#6, *When We Are M-A-Double-R-I-E-D* Ada Jones & Billy Murray (1908) US#1, *Yankee Doodle Boy* Billy Murray (1905) US#1/Fred Waring's Pennsylvanians (1943) US#21; *You Remind Me of My Mother* Henry Burr (1923) US#9, *You're a Grand Old Flag* Billy Murray (1906) US#1/Arthur Pryor's Band (1906) US#3/Prince's Orchestra (1917) US#7.

190. COHEN, Leonard (b. Leonard Norman Cohen, September 21, 1934, Montreal, Canada) Rock guitarist and vocalist. A singer who was once described as the grocer of despair. Lacking either a great voice or a significant guitar technique, Cohen has nevertheless crafted songs of startling beauty and poetic originality, that are frequently accurate observations on the human condition. An almost existential songwriter, Cohen has a clear sense of irony and a masterful understanding of the absurd, and he has defined the songwriting process as, "a desperate kind of activity." He first performed in the 1950s country group the Buckskin Boys, before graduating from university and publishing three volumes of poetry and two novels. After turning to songwriting and live performance, his material began attracting the attention of other singers when Judy Collins recorded his epic *Suzanne*. Cohen was the subject of a Canadian television documentary, "Ladies and Gentleman...Mr. Leonard Cohen" (1967), after which, he signed to Columbia Records and released **The Songs of Leonard Cohen** (1968), initially a slow seller that ultimately sold over ten million copies worldwide. The album became the benchmark for every singer-songwriter that was to follow, with its melancholic and nihilistic love songs. Despite the quality of much of his later work, Cohen would never recapture the magic and stark beauty of *Suzanne, The Stranger Song, Sisters of Mercy*, and *Hey, That's No Way to Say Goodbye*. Robert Altman later employed Cohen's material to excellent effect in the film "McCabe and Mrs. Miller" (1974). After scoring and appearing in a Canadian movie "The

Ernie Game" (1968), Cohen released the impressive **Songs from a Room** (1968), from which, *Bird on a Wire* became one of his most covered songs. Cohen's backing singer from this period, Jennifer Warnes, was later to record a memorable collection of his compositions as **Famous Blue Raincoat** (1987, Cypress) US#72 UK#33. Such is the influence of Leonard Cohen, that two various artists collections of material have been recorded, **I'm Your Fan** (1991, East West) UK#16 and **Tower of Song: The Songs of Leonard Cohen** (1995, A&M) US#198. Cohen introduced electronic instruments to his sound in the late 1980s. ALBUMS: **Songs of Leonard Cohen** (1968) g US#83 UK#13, **Songs from a Room** (1969) US#63 UK#2, **Songs of Love and Hate** (1971) US#145 UK#4, **Live Songs** (1973) US#156, **New Skin for the Old Ceremony** (1974, all Columbia) UK#24; **Death of a Ladies' Man** (1977, Warner Brothers) UK#35; **Recent Songs** (1979), **Various Positions** (1985, both Columbia) UK#52; **Cohen in Warsaw** (1985, Akamickie); **I'm Your Man** (1988) UK#48, **The Future** (1992) UK#36, **Cohen Live** (1994, all Columbia) UK#35. COMPILATION: **Greatest Hits** (1977, Columbia) UK#99. HIT VERSIONS: *Ain't No Cure for Love* Jennifer Warnes (1987) C&W#86, *Bird on a Wire* Neville Brothers (1990) UK#72, *First We Take Manhattan* Jennifer Warnes (1974) UK#74, *Hey, That's No Way to Say Goodbye* Vogues (1970) US#101, *Lover, Lover, Lover* Ian McCulloch (1992) UK#47, *So Long, Marianne* Brian Hyland (1971) US#120, *Suzanne* Noel Harrison (1967) US#56.

191. COHN, Marc (b. Cleveland, OH) Rock guitarist, pianist and vocalist. A folk and R&B influenced singer-songwriter, who first played in the group the Supreme Court, before appearing in the show "Starlight Express." Cohn began recording as a solo performer in the early 1990s. CHART COMPOSITIONS: *Walking in Memphis* (1991) US#13 UK#22, *Silver Thunderbird* (1991) US#63 UK#54, *True Companion* (1992) US#80, *Walk Through the World* (1993) US#76 UK#37. ALBUMS: **Marc Cohn** (1991) g US#38 UK#27, **The Rainy Season** (1993, both Atlantic) US#63 UK#24. HIT VERSION: *Walking in Memphis* Cher (1995) US#11.

192. COLE, Bob (b. Robert Cole, July 1, 1868, Athens, GA; d. August 2, 1911, Catskills, NY) Vaudeville performer. A pioneer black composer and lyricist, who had been a comedian and stage manager before becoming a playwright, songwriter and vaudeville performer. Cole formed a partnership with the lyricist and performer Billy Johnson in order to create his first production "A Trip to Coontown" (1898), one of the first theatrical successes to be entirely written and conceived by black artists. In 1900, Cole formed a second partnership with the brothers John Rosamond Johnson and James Weldon Johnson, composing the popular songs *My Castle on the Nile* [i] (1901) and *Oh! Didn't He Ramble* [i] (1902). They also contributed to the productions of "The Belle of Bridgeport" (1900), "The Sleeping Beauty and the Beast" (1901), "The Little Duchess" (1901), and "Sally in Our Alley" (1902), and also wrote the complete Broadway musicals "Humpty Dumpty" (1904), "In Newport" (1904), "The Shoo-Fly Regiment" (1907), and "The Red Moon" (1909), before concentrating solely on vaudeville from 1910. Cole drowned in 1911. HIT VERSIONS: *Under the Bamboo Tree* [i] Arthur Collins (1902) US#1/Arthur Collins & Byron Harlan (1903) US#4; *Who Do You Love?* [i] Arthur Collins & Byron Harlan (1908) US#10. Co-writers: [i] James Weldon Johnson (b. 1871, Jacksonville, FL; d. June 26, 1938, Wiscasset, ME)/John Rosamond Johnson (b. 1873, Jacksonville, FL; d. November 11, 1954, New York, NY).

193. COLE, Lloyd (b. January 31, 1961, Buxton, England) Pop guitarist and vocalist. The lead singer and songwriter in the group Lloyd Cole and the Commotions. CHART COMPOSITIONS: *Perfect Skin* (1984) UK#26, *Forest Fire* (1984) UK#41, *Rattlesnakes* (1984) UK#65, *Brand New Friend* (1985) UK#19, *Lost Weekend* (1985) UK#17, *Cut Me Down* (1986) UK#38, *My Bag* (1987) UK#46, *Jennifer She Said* (1988) UK#31, *From the Hip EP* (1988) UK#59. ALBUMS: **Rattlesnakes** (1984) UK#13, **Easy Pieces** (1985) UK#5, **Mainstream** (1987, all Polydor) UK#2. COMPILATION: **1984–1989** (1989, Polydor). After the group split up in 1989, Cole continued to record as a solo artist. CHART COMPOSITIONS: *No Blue Skies* (1990) UK#42, *Don't Look Back* (1990) UK#59, *She's a Girl and I'm a Man* [i] (1991) UK#55, *So You'd Like to Save the World* (1993) UK#72, *Like Lovers Do* (1995) UK#24, *Sentimental Fool* (1995) UK#73. ALBUMS: **Lloyd Cole** (1990, Polydor) UK#11; **Don't Get Weird on Me, Babe** (1991) UK#21, **Bad Vibes** (1993) UK#38, **Love Story** (1995, all Fontana) UK#27. HIT VERSION: *Are You Ready to Be Heartbroken* Sandi Shaw (1986) UK#68. Co-writer: [i] Quine.

194. COLEMAN, Cy (b. Seymour Kaufman, June 14, 1929, Bronx, NY) Film and stage composer, pianist. The last in the line of traditional Broadway composers, who is a consistently original, melodic, humorous and dramatic composer with an often unique approach to the medium. Coleman's clever use of meter and engaging melodies, ensured that many of his songs remained popular long after the closing of the show in which they appeared. The

production "Hey, Look Me Over" (1981), was a celebration of the enduring quality of his work. From the age of four, Coleman could repeat on the piano tunes that he had heard on the radio, and after taking lessons on the instrument, he gave his first public recital two years later. Coleman studied at the New York College of Music, and worked as a nightclub pianist in Manhattan before forming his own supper club trio in 1947. During the 1940s, he also composed the television theme tunes to "The Dupont Hour," "Date in Manhattan" and "The Katie Smith Show." During the 1950s, he began writing with the lyricist Joseph A. McCarthy, one of many collaborators that he would partner throughout his career. In 1952, Frank Sinatra recorded Coleman's *Why Try to Change Me Now*, and his song *Tin Pan Alley* was used in the theatrical production "John Murray Anderson's Almanac." Nat "King" Cole recorded his composition *I'm Gonna Laugh You Right Out of My Life*, and Tony Bennett his *The Autumn Song*. After scoring the 1950s radio show "Art Ford's Village Party," and contributing to the theatrical release "Compulsion" (1957), Coleman penned *You Fascinate Me* for the show "Demi-Dozen," *The Tempo of the Times* for the nightclub revue "Medium Rare," and *The Playboy Theme* for the television series "Playboy Penthouse Party." In 1957, he teamed up for five years with the lyricist Carolyn Leigh, writing over twenty songs for two Broadway musicals, "Wildcat" (1960) and "Little Me" (1962). The pair also wrote for the film "Father Goose" (1964). Coleman's next partner was the lyricist Dorothy Fields, with whom he wrote the Broadway hit "Sweet Charity" (1966). Further Coleman successes, "Seesaw" (1973), "I Love My Wife" (1977), and the operatic "On the Twentieth Century" (1978), were interrupted by only one genuine flop, "Home Again" (1979), after which, he recovered triumphantly with "Barnum" (1980), an old fashioned musical based on the life of the impresario and charlatan Phineas Taylor Barnum. "Barnum" featured a variety of musical styles that were somewhat revolutionary for Broadway, including ragtime marches and a return to 1930s styled Tin Pan Alley pop songs, alongside deliberately corny, sentimental ballads. A prolific composer, Coleman also scored the film soundtracks "Walk Don't Run" (1966), "The Heartbreak Kid" (1972) and "Garbo Talks" (1984). During the 1970s, he wrote and co-produced the Shirley MacLaine television spectacular "Gypsy in My Soul," and recorded a handful of light, jazz influenced solo albums. In 1990, Coleman wrote a show that lamented Raymond Chandler's Los Angeles of the 1940s, "City of Angels," which he followed with "The Will Rogers Follies" (1991), a pastiche of the Ziegfeld Follies style. His songs have been recorded on two jazz vocal collections; Jackie and Roy's **The Music of Cy Coleman** (1984, Discovery), and Mark Murphy's **The Songs of Dorothy Fields and Cy Coleman** (1977, Audiophile). In 1994, Coleman became a writer vice-president on the board of ASCAP. ALBUMS: **Jamaica** (1958, Jubilee); **Wildcat** oc (1960, Columbia); **Wildcat** sc (1961, Kapp); **Wildcat** sc (1961) US#6, **Little Me** oc (1962, both RCA) US#44; **The Troublemaker** oc (1964, Ava); **Art of Love** oc (1965, Capitol); **Little Me** ost (1965, Pye); **Father Goose** oc (1965), **If My Friends Could See Me Now** (1966), **Sweet Charity** oc (1966) US#92, **Opening Night at the Palace-Sweet Charity** (1966), **Age Of Rock** (1967, all Columbia); **Sweet Charity** oc (1969, EMI); **Sweet Charity** ost (1969, Decca) US#72; **The Heartbreak Kid** oc (1972, Columbia); **See Saw** oc (1973, Buddah); **The Party's on Me** (1976, RCA); **I Love My Wife** oc (1977, Atlantic); **Hellzappopin'** oc (1977, Hellzappopin'); **On the Twentieth Century** oc (1978), **Barnum** oc (1980, both Columbia); **Barnum** (1981, Rhapsody); **Comin' Home** (1988, DRG); **City of Angels** oc (1990), **The Will Rogers Follies-A Life in Revue** oc (1992, both Columbia). HIT VERSIONS: *Big Spender* [i] Shirley Bassey (1967) UK#21, *Firefly* [ii] Tony Bennett (1958) US#20, *Hey, Look Me Over* [ii] Pete King Chorale & Orchestra (1961) US#108, *I'm Gonna Laugh You Right Out of My Life* Nat "King" Cole (1957) US#57, *If My Friends Could See Me Now* [i] Linda Clifford (1978) R&B#68 US#54 UK#50, *Pass Me By* Peggy Lee (1965) US#93, *Real Live Girl* Steve Alaimo (1965) US#77, *Rhythm of Life* [i] Sammy Davis, Jr. (1969) US#124, *Where Am I Going?* Barbra Streisand (1968) US#94, *Witchcraft* [ii] Frank Sinatra (1958) US#6 UK#12/Robert Palmer (1992) UK#50. Co-writers: [i] Dorothy Fields, [ii] Carolyn Leigh (b. 1926; d. 1983).

195. COLLINS, Charles (b. England) A British Victorian music hall composer, who penned the Henry Champion gems *Boiled Beef and Carrots* [ii] (1909) and *Any Old Iron* [i] (1911). Collins also co-wrote the popular *Why Am I Always the Bridesmaid*. HIT VERSION: *Any Old Iron* [i] Peter Sellers (1957) UK#17. Co-writers: [i] Fred Terry/E.A. Sheppard, [ii] Fred Murray. (*See also under* Fred W. LEIGH.)

196. COLLINS, Phil (b. Philip David Charles Collins, January 31, 1951, London, England) Rock drummer, producer and vocalist. A former child actor who became one of the most successful mainstream rock and pop artists of the 1980–1990s. Collins first recorded as a member of the group Flaming Youth, which recorded the album **Ark 2** (1969, Fontana). In 1970, he joined Peter Gabriel's

progressive rock band Genesis as drummer, which, by 1997, had sold nearly one hundred million records. When Gabriel quit Genesis in 1975, Collins stepped out from behind his drum kit to become their lead vocalist, and his more commercial approach considerably widened their audience appeal. Collins officially left the group in 1996. CHART COMPOSITIONS: *Spot the Pigeon EP* [ii] (1977) UK#14, *Follow You, Follow Me* [ii] (1978) US#23 UK#7, *Turn It on Again* [ii] (1980) US#58 UK#8, *Duchess* [ii] (1980) UK#46, *Misunderstanding* [ii] (1980) US#14 UK#42, *Abacab* [ii] (1981) US#26 UK#9, *Keep It Dark* [ii] (1981) UK#33, *No Reply at All* [ii] (1981) US#29, *Man on the Corner* [ii] (1982) US#40 UK#41, *3x3 EP* [ii] (1982) UK#10, *Paperlate* [ii] (1982) US#32, *Mama* [ii] (1983) US#73 UK#4, *That's All* [ii] (1983) US#6 UK#16, *Illegal Alien* [ii] (1984) US#44 UK#46, *Taking It All Too Hard* [ii] (1984) US#50, *Invisible Touch* [ii] (1986) US#1 UK#15, live version (1992) UK#7; *In Too Deep* [ii] (1986) US#3 UK#19, *Throwing It All Away* [ii] (1986) US#4 UK#22, *Land of Confusion* [ii] (1987) US#4 UK#14, *Tonight, Tonight* [ii] (1987) US#3 UK#18, *No Son of Mine* [ii] (1991) US#12 UK#6, *I Can't Dance* [ii] (1992) UK#7, *Hold on My Heart* [ii] (1992) US#12, *Jesus He Knows Me* [ii] (1992) US#23 UK#20, *Never a Time* [ii] (1993) US#21, *Tell Me Why* [ii] (1993) UK#40. ALBUMS: **A Trick of the Tail** (1976) g US#31 UK#3, **Wind and Wuthering** (1976) g US#26 UK#7, **Seconds Out** (1977) US#47 UK#4, **And Then There Were Three** (1978) p US#14 UK#3, **Duke** (1980) p US#11 UK#1, **Abacab** (1981) p US#7 UK#1, **Three Sides Live** (1982) g US#10 UK#2, **Genesis** (1983) p US#9 UK#1, **Invisible Touch** (1986, all Charisma) p US#3 UK#1; **We Can't Dance** (1991) p US#4 UK#1, **The Way We Walk, Volume I: The Shorts** (1992) g US#35 UK#3, **The Way We Walk, Volume II: The Longs** (1993, all Virgin) US#20 UK#1. During the 1980s, Collins also moonlighted with the jazz-rock outfit Brand X, featuring on the group's albums **Unorthodox Behaviour** (1976) US#191, **Moroccan Roll** (1977) US#125 UK#37, **Live Stock** (1977), **Product** (1979) US#165, **Do They Hurt** (1980, all Charisma): **Is There Anything About?** (1982, CBS) UK#93; and **Live at the Roxy, L.A. 1979** (1996, Zok). Since 1981, Collins has recorded as an immensely successful solo artist. He also featured on the soundtrack albums **Against All Odds** (1984) UK#29 and **Buster** (1988, both Virgin) g US#54 UK#2. CHART COMPOSITIONS: *In the Air Tonight* (1981) US#19 UK#2, re-issued (1984) US#102; *I Missed Again* (1981) US#19 UK#14, *If Leaving Me Is Easy* (1981) UK#17, *Thru These Walls* (1982) UK#56, *I Don't Care Anymore* (1983) US#39, *Don't Let Him Steal Your Heart Away* (1983) UK#45, *I Can't Believe It's True* (1983) US#79, *Against All*

Odds (Take a Look at Me Now) (1984) p US#1 UK#2, *Easy Lover* [i] with Philip Bailey (1984) p R&B#3 US#2 UK#1, *Sussudio* (1985) p R&B#8 US#1 UK#12, *One More Night* (1985) p R&B#80 US#1 UK#4, *Take Me Home* (1985) US#7 UK#19, *Don't Lose My Number* (1985) US#4, *Two Hearts* [iv] (1988) g US#1 UK#6, *Another Day in Paradise* (1989) US#1 UK#2, *I Wish It Would Rain* (1990) US#3 UK#7, *Something Happened (On the Way to Heaven)* [v] (1990) US#4 UK#15, *Do You Remember?* (1990) US#4, live version (1990) UK#57; *That's Just the Way It Is* (1990) UK#26, *Hang in Long Enough* (1990) US#23 UK#34, *Who Said I Would* (1991) US#73, *Hero* [iii] with David Crosby (1993) US#44 UK#56, *Both Sides of the Story* (1993) US#25 UK#7, *Everyday* (1994) US#24 UK#15, *We Wait and Wonder* (1994) US#125 UK#45, *Dance into the Light* (1996) UK#9, *It's in Your Eyes* (1996) UK#30. ALBUMS: **Face Value** (1981) p US#7 UK#1, **Hello, I Must Be Going** (1982) p US#8 UK#2, **No Jacket Required** (1985) p US#1 UK#1, **But Seriously** (1989) p US#1 UK#1, **Serious… Hits Live!** (1991) p US#11 UK#2, **Both Sides** (1993, all Virgin) p US#13 UK#1; **Dance into the Light** (1996, East West). Co-writers: [i] Philip Bailey (b. May 8, 1951, Denver, CO)/Nathan East, [ii] Anthony Banks (b. March 1927, 1950, East Heathly, England)/Mike Rutherford, [iii] David Crosby, [iv] Lamont Dozier, [v] D. Stuermer. (*See also under* Lamont DOZIER, Peter GABRIEL.)

197. COLLINS, Tommy (b. Leonard Raymond Snipes, September 28, 1930, Bethany, OK) C&W guitarist and vocalist. A former disc jockey and U.S. Marine who became Buck Owens' lead guitarist, before charting thirteen country hits of his own between 1954–1968. Collins was a church minster for three years from 1961. Owens later recorded some of Collins' songs as **Buck Owens Sings Tommy Collins** (1968, Capitol). CHART COMPOSITIONS: *You Better Not Do That* (1954) C&W#2, *Whatcha Gonna Do* (1954) C&W#4, *Untied* (1955) C&W#10, *It Tickles* (1955) C&W#5. ALBUMS: **This Is Tommy Collins** (1955), **Words and Music Country Style** (1956), **Light of the Lord** (1959, all Capitol); **Let's Live a Little** (1966, Tower); **The Dynamic Tommy Collins** (1967, Columbia); **Country Souvenir** (1981, G&W). HIT VERSIONS: *Carolyn* Merle Haggard (1971) C&W#1 US#58, *If You Ain't Lovin' (You Ain't Livin')* Faron Young (1955) C&W#2/George Strait (1988) C&W#1; *Roots of My Raising, The* Merle Haggard (1976) C&W#1, *Sam Hill* Merle Haggard (1964) C&W#45/Claude King (1964) C&W#11; *You Got-Ta Have a License* Porter Wagoner (1970) C&W#41.

198. COLTER, Jessi (b. Miriam Johnson, May 25, 1947, Phoenix, AZ) C&W vocalist. A church pianist who sang backing vocals for her first husband, the guitarist Duane Eddy, during the early 1960s. Colter later formed a writing and performing duet with her second husband, Waylon Jennings, and her songs have been recorded by the singers Eddy Arnold, Dottie West and Don Gibson. Colter charted thirteen solo country hits between 1975–1981, and was a featured artist on country's first million selling album, **The Outlaws** (1976, RCA) p US#10. Since 1985, she has recorded only gospel music. CHART COMPOSITIONS: *I'm Not Lisa* (1975) C&W#1 US#4, *What's Happened to Blue Eyes?* (1975) C&W#5 US#57. ALBUMS: **A Country Star Is Born** (1966, RCA); **I'm Jessi Colter** (1975) US#50, **Jessi** (1976) US#109, **Diamond in the Rough** (1976) US#79, **Miriam** (1977), **That's the Way a Cowboy Rocks and Rolls** (1978), **Ridin' Shotgun** (1982, all Capitol); **Leather and Lace** with Waylon Jennings (1981, RCA) g US#43.

199. CONFREY, Zez (b. Edward Elzear Confrey, April 3, Peru, IL; d. November 22, 1972, Lakewood, NJ) Ragtime pianist and arranger. A graduate of the prestigious Chicago Musical College, who later worked as a song demonstrator for a publishing company. During his World War I U.S. Navy service, Confrey performed as part of a touring show "Leave It to the Sailors," before becoming an arranger and pianist for the piano roll company QRS, where he recorded over one hundred rolls. Confrey composed some hundred novelty rags, including the much recorded *Stumbling* (1922), which was the first successful pop song to use the time signature 3/4. He also wrote the infamous *Sittin' on a Log* [i]. CHART COMPOSITIONS: *Kitten on the Keys* (1921) US#5, new version (1922) US#5; *Dizzy Fingers* (1927) US#18. HIT VERSIONS: *Nickel in the Slot* Wingy Malone (1936) US#14, *Stumbling* Broadway Dance Orchestra (1922) US#15/Frank Crumit (1922) US#6/Ray Miller (1922) US#7/Billy Murray (1922) US#4/Paul Whiteman (1922) US#1. Co-writer: [i] Byron Gay (b. 1886; d. 1945).

200. CONLEE, John (b. August 11, 1946, Versailles, KY) C&W guitarist and vocalist. A mortician and newsreader who worked as a disc jockey before becoming an R&B influenced country performer during the mid-1970s. Conlee has charted over thirty country singles, including seven number ones. CHART COMPOSITIONS: *Rose Colored Glasses* [i] (1978) C&W#5, *Backside of Thirty* (1979) C&W#1. ALBUMS: **Rose Colored Glasses** (1979), **Busted** (1986), **Songs for the Working Man** (1986, all MCA); **Harmony** (1987, Columbia). COMPILATIONS: **Greatest Hits** (1983) g US#166, **Greatest Hits, Volume 2** (1986, both MCA). Co-writer: [i] Glenn Barber.

201. CONLEY, Earl Thomas (b. October 17, 1941, Portsmouth, OH) C&W vocalist. A prolific singer-songwriter, who has topped the country chart on seventeen occasions. Conley served in the U.S. Army and held various day jobs before singing in a variety of gospel groups. He began songwriting in 1968, and recorded his first solo sides in the early 1970s. CHART COMPOSITIONS: *I Have Loved You Girl (But Not Like This Before)* (1975) C&W#87, new version (1983) C&W#2; *It's the Bible Against the Bottle (In the Battle for Daddy's Soul)* (1975) C&W#87, *High and Wild* (1976) C&W#67, *Queen of New Orleans* (1976) C&W#77, *Dreamin's All I Do* (1979) C&W#32, *Middle-Age Madness* (1979) C&W#41, *Stranded on a Dead End Street* (1979) C&W#26, *Silent Treatment* (1980) C&W#7, *Fire and Smoke* (1981) C&W#1, *Tell Me Why* (1981) C&W#10, *After the Love Slips Away/Smokey Mountain Memories* (1982) C&W#16, *Heavenly Bodies* (1982) C&W#8, *Somewhere Between Right and Wrong* (1982) C&W#1, *Your Love's on the Line* (1983) C&W#1, *Don't Make It Easy for Me* (1984) C&W#1, *Angel in Disguise* (1984) C&W#1, *Chance of Lovin' You* (1984) C&W#1, *All Tangled Up in Love* with Gus Hardin (1984) C&W#8, *Honor Bound* (1985) C&W#1, *Love Don't Care (Whose Heart It Breaks)* (1985) C&W#1, *Nobody Falls Like a Fool* (1985) C&W#1, *Once in a Blue Moon* (1986) C&W#1, *Too Many Times* with Anita Pointer (1986) C&W#2, *I Can't Win for Losin' You* (1986) C&W#1, *That Was a Close One* (1987) C&W#1, *Right from the Start* (1987) C&W#1, *What She Is (Is a Woman in Love)* (1988) C&W#1, *We Believe in Happy Endings* with Emmylou Harris (1988) C&W#1, *What I'd Say* (1989) C&W#1, *Love Out Loud* (1989) C&W#1, *Hard Days and Honky Tonk Nights* [ii] (1992) C&W#36. ALBUMS: **Blue Pearl** (1981, Sunbird); **Somewhere Between Right and Wrong** (1982), **Don't Make It Easy for Me** (1983), **Treadin' Water** (1984), **Too Many Times** (1986), **The Heart of It All** (1988, all RCA). COMPILATION: **Greatest Hits** (1985, RCA). g. HIT VERSIONS: *Smokey Mountain Memories* Mel Street (1975) C&W#13, *This Time I've Hurt Her More Than She Loves Me* [i] Conway Twitty (1975) C&W#1/Neal McCoy (1991) C&W#62. Co-writers: [i] M. Larkin, [ii] Randy Scruggs.

202. CONNOR, Tommie (b. Thomas P. Connor, November 16, 1904, London, England) Film and stage lyricist. A British composer during the 1930–1940s, who claims to have written "a song a day." Connor's best known songs are the eleven million selling *I Saw Mommy Kissing Santa Claus*, and *Lili Marlene* [vi] (1944), for which he wrote the English lyrics. His other big successes were *My Home Town* by Little Mary Hagan (1932), *It's My Mother's Birthday Today* [vii] by Arthur Tracy (1935), *I May Be Poor But I'm Honest* [vii] by Sam Brown and Elsie Carlisle (1935), *I Once Had a Heart Margarita* [viii] by Turner Layton (1937), *The Biggest Aspidistra in the World* [iv] by Gracie Fields (1938), *Down in the Glen* [iii] by Joseph Locke (1949), *Hang on the Bell Nellie* [ii] by Lou Preager (1949), and *The Rose I Bring You* [x] Lee Lawrence (1950). Between 1933–1977, Connor contributed lyrics to a variety of films and musical revues, sometimes in partnership with the composer Michael Carr. HIT VERSIONS: *Chestnut Tree, The* [v] Hal Kemp (1939) US#12, *Give Her My Love* [i] Johnston Brothers (1957) UK#27, *Homing Waltz, The* [x] Vera Lynn (1952) UK#9, *I Saw Mommy Kissing Santa Claus* Jimmy Boyd (1952) C&W#7 US#1 UK#3/Molly Bee (1953) US#19/Beverly Sisters (1953) UK#6/Billy Cotton & His Band (1953) UK#11/Spike Jones (1953) US#4; *Lili Marlene* [vi] Perry Como (1944) US#13, *Never Do a Tango with an Eskimo* Alma Cogan (1955) UK#6, *Till the Lights of London Shine Again* [ix] Bob Chester (1941) US#26, *Wedding of Lili Marlene, The* [x] Andrews Sisters (1949) US#20, *Who's Taking You Home Tonight* [xi] Winifred Atwell in *Let's Have a Ding Dong* (1955) UK#3. Co-writers: [i] Leslie Baguley/Michael Reine, [ii] Clive Erard/Ross Parker, [iii] Harry Gordon, [iv] William G. Haines/Jimmy Harper, [v] Jimmy Kennedy/Hamilton Kennedy, [vi] Hans Leip/Norbert Schultze, [vii] Eddie Lisbona, [viii] Eddie Lisbona/J. Schmitz, [ix] Eddie Pola, [x] Michael Reine, [xi] Manning Sherwin. (*See also under* Michael CARR.)

203. CONRAD, Con (b. Conrad K. Dober, June 18, 1891, New York, NY; d. September 28, 1938, Van Nuys, CA) Film and show composer, pianist. A Vanity Street Theatre pianist in New York, who teamed up with Jay Whidden to compose his first successful songs. During the early 1920s, Conrad often collaborated with Billy Rose, and from 1929, he worked at the 20th Century–Fox film studios in Hollywood, where he became the winner of the first ever Oscar for Best Song, from the film "The Continental" (1934). His compositions were featured in such shows as "The Midnight Rounders of 1921," and the films "Fox Movietone Follies of 1929," "The Gay Divorcee" (1934), "Here's to Romance" (1935), and "The Champagne Waltz" (1937). HIT VERSIONS: *Barney Google* [x] Ernest Hare & Billy Jones (1923) US#2/Georgie Price (1923) US#12; *Big City Blues* [vii] Annette Hanshaw (1929) US#10, *Breakaway, The* [vii] Arnold Johnson (1929) US#20, *Champagne Waltz, The* [v] Glen Gray (1934) US#7, *Continental (You Kiss While You're Dancing), The* [ix] Jolly Coburn (1934) US#2/Lud Gluskin (1934)

US#6/Leo Reisman (1934) US#1/Maureen McGovern (1976) UK#16; *Down in Dear Old New Orleans* [xii] Arthur Collins & Byron Harlan (1908) US#5, *Here's to Romance* [ix] Enric Madriguera (1935) US#5, *Honey, I'm in Love with You* [vi] Paul Whiteman (1925) US#4/Louise Massey (1943) US#19; *Lonesome and Sorry* [iii] Ruth Etting (1926) US#3/Jean Goldkette (1926) US#14; *Ma! He's Making Eyes at Me* [ii] Ted Lewis (1922) US#7/Dick Robertson (1940) US#12/Johnny Otis Show (1957) UK#2/Mrs. Mills in *Mrs. Mills' Medley* (1961) UK#18/Lena Zavaroni (1974) UK#10; *Margie* [iv] Gene Rodemich (1920) US#7/Eddie Cantor (1921) US#1/Frank Crumit (1921) US#7/Ted Lewis (1921) US#4/Original Dixieland Jazz Band (1921) US#9/Claude Hopkins (1934) US#5/Don Redman (1939) US#15/Big Ben Banjo Band in *Let's Get Together Again* (1955) UK#18; *Midnight in Paris* [ix] Richard Hayes (1953) US#24, *Oh! Frenchy* Arthur Fields (1918) US#8, *Palesteena* [xi] Eddie Cantor (1921) US#5/Frank Crumit (1921) US#11/Original Dixieland Jazz Band (1921) US#3; *Singin' the Blues* [viii] Aileen Stanley (1921) US#12/Frankie Trumbauer (1927) US#9/Connee Boswell (1953) US#27; *You Call It Madness (But I Call It Love)* [ii] Smith Ballew (1931) US#12/Russ Columbo (1931) US#5/Nat "King" Cole (1946) US#10/Billy Eckstine (1946) R&B#3 US#13; *You've Got to See Mama Ev'ry Night (Or You Can't See Mama at All)* [x] Dolly Kay (1923) US#5/Billy Murray & Aileen Stanley (1923) US#11/Mammie Smith (1923) US#13/Sophie Tucker (1923) US#6. Co-writers: [i] Sidney Clare (b. 1892; d. 1972), [ii] Russ Columbo/Gladys Du Bois/Paul Gregory, [iii] Benny Davis, [iv] Benny Davis/J. Russell Robinson, [v] Milton Drake/Ben Oakland, [vi] William Friedlander, [vii] Archie Gottler (b. 1896; d. 1959)/Sidney Mitchell, [viii] Sam Lewis/J. Russel Robinson/Joe Young, [ix] Herb Magidson, [x] Billy Rose, [xi] J. Russell Robinson, [xii] Jay Whidden (b. 1886; d. 1968). (*See also under* Buddy DESYLVA.)

204. COOK, Roger (b. Roger James Cook, August 19, 1941, Bristol, England) Pop guitarist, producer and vocalist. A songwriter whose forte has been imitating American R&B, as evidenced by his contribution to the revived fortunes of the vocal group the Drifters during the 1970s. Cook's songs dominated the British charts during the late 1960s and early 1970s, his *I Was Kaiser Bill's Batman* [v] selling over three million copies, and his Coca Cola commercial *I'd Like to Teach the World to Sing* [i] selling over five million. He first performed in the teenage group the Kestrels, before forming the short-lived vocal duo David and Jonathan with fellow composer Roger Greenaway, charting with their compositions *Lovers of the World Unite* [v] (1966) UK#7 and *Speak*

Her Name [v] (1966) US#109. ALBUMS: **Michele** (1966, Capitol); **David and Jonathan** (1967, Columbia). COMPILATIONS: **Lovers of the World Unite** (1984, See for Miles); **Very Best of David and Jonathan** (1987, C5). Although he failed to garner any interest as a solo performer, Cook discovered his niche as writer, producer and musician on numerous bubblegum hits over two decades. His most successful group venture was Blue Mink, which charted with *Melting Pot* [v] (1969) UK#3, *Banner Man* [vi] (1971) UK#3, *Stay with Me* (1972) UK#11, re-entry (1973) UK#43; and *Randy* [vi] (1973) UK#9. ALBUMS: **Our World** (1970), **Melting Pot** (1970), **Real Mink** (1971, all Philips); **Live at the Talk of the Town** (1972), **A Time of Change** (1972, both Regal Zonophone); **Blue Mink** (1973, MCA); **Only When I Laugh** (1973), **Fruity** (1973, both EMI). COMPILATIONS: **Best of Blue Mink** (1973, Philips); **Best of Blue Mink** (1974, EMI); **Hit Making World of Blue Mink** (1975, Decca); **Attention** (1975, Phonogram); **Hit Making Sound** (1977, Gull); **The Blue Mink Collection** (1987, Action Replay); **Best of Blue Mink** (1993, Music Club). During the 1980s, Cook plied his trade in Nashville, where he collaborated with such songwriters as Hank Cochran and John Prine. ALBUMS: **Study** (1970, Columbia); **Meanwhile Back at the World** (1972), **Minstrel in Flight** (1973, both Regal Zonophone); **Alright** (1976, Polydor). HIT VERSIONS: *Blame It on the Pony Express* [ix] Johnny Johnson & the Bandwagon (1970) UK#7, *Can I Take You Home Little Girl* [v] Drifters (1975) UK#10, *Conversations* [viii] Cilla Black (1969) UK#7, *Doctor's Orders* [xii] Carol Douglas (1974) US#11/Sunny (1974) UK#7; *Down on the Beach Tonight* [ix] Drifters (1974) UK#7, *Every Nite's a Saturday Night with You* Drifters (1976) UK#29, *Freedom Come, Freedom Go* [vii] Fortunes (1971) US#72 UK#6, *Gasoline Alley Bred* [ix] Hollies (1970) UK#14, also on *Holliedaze (A Medley)* (1981) UK#28, *Going Down (On the Road to L.A.)* Terry Black & Laurel Wood (1972) US#57, *Good Times, Better Times* [viii] Cliff Richard (1969) UK#12, *Hello Summertime* [i] Bobby Goldsboro (1974) C&W#79 UK#14, *Here Comes that Rainy Day Feeling Again* [ix] Fortunes (1971) US#15/Connie Cato (1976) C&W#80; *Home Lovin' Man* [ix] Andy Williams (1970) UK#7, *I Believe in You* [xiii] Don Williams (1980) C&W#1 US#24, *I Was Kaiser Bill's Batman* [v] Whistling Jack Smith (1967) US#20 UK#5/Wurzels as *Farmer Bill's Cowman* (1977) UK#32, *I'd Like to Teach the World to Sing* [i] Hillside Singers (1971) US#13/New Seekers (1971) g US#7 UK#1; *I've Got You on My Mind* [v] White Plains (1970) UK#17, *It Oughta Sell a Million* [v] Lyn Paul (1975) UK#37, *It's Gonna Be a Cold Christmas* [v] Dana (1975) UK#4, *It's Like We Never Said Good-*

bye [xii] Crystal Gayle (1980) C&W#1 US#63, *Keepin' Power* Crystal Gayle (1983) C&W#49, *Kissin' in the Back Row of the Movies* [ix] Drifters (1974) R&B#83 UK#2, *Last Night I Didn't Get to Sleep at All* [xiv] 5th Dimension (1972) R&B#28 US#8, *Like Sister, Like Brother* [xii] Drifters (1973) UK#7, *Livin' in These Troubled Times* Crystal Gayle (1982) C&W#9, *Long Cool Woman (In a Black Dress)* [iii] Hollies (1972) US#2 UK#32, *Love Games* [xiv] Drifters (1975) UK#33, *Love Is on a Roll* Don Williams (1983) C&W#1, *(Love Me) Love the Life I Lead* [xiv] Fantastics (1972) US#86, *Miracles* Don Williams (1981) C&W#4, *My Baby Loves Lovin'* [v] White Plains (1970) US#13 UK#9/Joe Jeffrey Group (1970) US#115; *Say You'll Stay Until Tomorrow* [vi] Tom Jones (1977) C&W#1 US#15 UK#40, *7-6-5-4-3-2-1 (Blow Your Whistle)* Gary Toms Empire (1975) R&B#5 US#46/Rimshots (1975) UK#26; *Side Show* Chanter Sisters (1976) UK#43, *Softly Whispering I Love You* [v] Congregation (1971) US#29 UK#4/Paul Young (1991) UK#21; *Something Old, Something New* [ix] Fantastics (1971) US#102 UK#9, *Something Tells Me (Something's Gonna Happen Tonight)* [v] Cilla Black (1971) UK#3, *Something's Gotten Hold of My Heart* [v] Gene Pitney (1967) UK#5/Marc Almond & Gene Pitney (1989) UK#1; *Speak Her Name* Walter Jackson (1967) R&B#22 US#89, *Storm in a Teacup* [v] Fortunes (1972) UK#7, *Street Called Hope, A* [v] Gene Pitney (1970) UK#37, *Sunny Honey Girl* [iv] Cliff Richard (1971) UK#19, *Talking in Your Sleep* [xv] Crystal Gayle (1978) C&W#1 US#18 UK#11, *This Golden Ring* [v] Fortunes (1966) US#82 UK#15, *Too Much Love* [v] Don Williams (1992) C&W#72, *Way It Used to Be, The* [ii] Engelbert Humperdinck (1969) US#42 UK#3, *Way of Life, A* [v] Family Dogg (1969) UK#6, *What's Your Name, What's Your Number* [xvi] Andrea True Connection (1978) US#56, *You Just Might See Me Cry* [v] Our Kid (1976) UK#2, *You're More Than a Number in My Little Red Book* [ix] Drifters (1976) UK#5, *You've Got Your Troubles* [v] Fortunes (1965) US#7 UK#2/Nancy Wilson (1966) R&B#48/Jack Blanchard & Misty Morgan (1970) C&W#27. Co-writers: [i] William Backer/Roquel Davis/Roger Greenaway (b. August 23, 1938, Bristol, England), [ii] Franco Cassano/Corrado Conti/Roger Greenaway, [iii] Allan Clark/Roger Greenaway, [iv] John Goodison/Roger Greenaway/Tony Hiller, [v] Roger Greenaway, [vi] Roger Greenaway/Herbie Flowers, [vii] Roger Greenaway/Albert Hammond/Mike Hazlewood, [viii] Roger Greenaway/Jerry Lordan, [ix] Roger Greenaway/Tony MacAulay, [x] Roger Greenaway/John MacLeod, [xi] Roger Greenaway/Barry Mason, [xii] Roger Greenaway/Geoff Stephens, [xiii] S. Hogin, [xiv] Tony MacAuley, [xv] John Prine, [xvi] Bobby Woods. (*See also under* Hank COCHRAN.)

205. COOKE, Sam (b. Samuel Cook, January 2, 1931, Clarksdale, MS; d. December 11, 1964, Los Angeles, CA) R&B producer and vocalist. One of the most important R&B artists in the history of the genre, who charted thirty-five singles between 1957–1965. Cooke's pure, simple and passionately driven music was deceptively crafted, and he was one of the first black R&B songwriters to call for social change and self-development in pop songs, his *A Change Is Gonna Come*, being a cornerstone ballad in the R&B catalog, which introduced ideas and concepts that would become traditional features of Rap music. Cooke's melismatic tenor vocal had been developed during the gospel singing of his youth, he later became the first black artist to introduce secular music to the rhythms of rock and roll, pioneering a pop-gospel journey that was later completed by Otis Redding, Bobby Womack, Marvin Gaye, the Staples Singers, the Winans and the Sounds of Blackness. Cooke's verve and self-confidence, although ultimately his own downfall, forged a path for subsequent black artists, as he initially faced stiff opposition when he crossed over from gospel to pop. Cooke also broke new ground as a black artist by creating his own SAR record company and taking control of his business interests. During his relatively short lifetime, Cooke composed over one hundred and twenty tunes, about which his philosophy was simple, "A song should have a lilting memory." Cooke grew up in Chicago, Illinois, one of eight children, where his father was a church minister. At the age of nine he sang gospel with his brothers as the Singing Children, and later with the Highway Q.C.s and the Pilgrim Fathers. In 1950 he joined the legendary Soul Stirrers, his first recording with the group being *Jesus Gave Me Water*, the group's best work being collected on the albums **Strength, Power and Love** (1960), **Heritage, Volume 1** (1960), **Heritage, Volume 2** (1960, all Jewel); **Heaven Is My Home** (1992, C5); and **Jesus Gave Me Water** (1993, Ace). Cooke's first solo single was *Loveable* (1957), which he released under the pseudonym Dale Cook, and his first major hit was the innovative pop-soul ballad *You Send Me*. He was shot dead at the Hacienda Motel in Los Angeles in 1964, the result of a seemingly avoidable and sordid incident with a female partner who was not his wife. His compositions were later recorded by the vocal group the Supremes as **We Remember Sam Cooke** (1965, Motown) US#75. CHART COMPOSITIONS: *You Send Me* (1957) g R&B#1 US#1 UK#29, *I'll Come Running Back to You* (1957) R&B#1 US#18, *Desire Me* (1958) R&B#17 US#47, *You Were Made for Me* (1958) R&B#7 US#39, *Lonely Island* (1958) R&B#10 US#26, *Win Your Love for Me* (1958) R&B#4 US#22, *Love You Most of All* (1958) R&B#12 US#26,

Everybody Loves to Cha Cha Cha (1959) R&B#2 US#31, *Only Sixteen* (1959) R&B#13 US#28 UK#23, *Summertime (Part 2)* (1959) US#106, *There I've Said It Again* (1959) R&B#25 US#81, *No One (Can Ever Take Your Place)* (1960) US#103, *Teenage Sonata* (1960) R&B#22 US#50, *Wonderful World* [i] (1960) R&B#2 US#12 UK#27, re-issued (1986) UK#2; *Chain Gang* (1960) g R&B#2 US#2 UK#9, *Sad Mood* (1960) R&B#23 US#29, *That's It I Quit I'm Movin' On* (1961) R&B#25 US#31, *Cupid* (1961) R&B#20 US#17 UK#7, *Feel It* (1961) US#56, *Twistin' the Night Away* (1962) g R&B#1 US#9 UK#6, *Bring It on Home to Me* (1962) R&B#2 US#13, *Having a Party* (1962) R&B#4 US#17, *Nothing Can Change This Love* (1962) R&B#2 US#12, *Somebody Have Mercy* (1962) R&B#3 US#70, *Send Me Some Loving* (1963) R&B#2 US#13, *Another Saturday Night* (1963) R&B#1 US#10 UK#23, re-issued (1986) UK#75; *Love Will Find a Way* (1963) US#105, *(Ain't That) Good News* (1964) US#11, *Good Times* (1964) US#11, *That's Where It's At* (1964) US#93, *Cousin of Mine* (1964) R&B#40 US#31, *Shake* (1965) R&B#2 US#7, *A Change Is Gonna Come* (1965) R&B#9 US#31, *(Somebody) Ease My Troublin' Mind'* (1965) US#115, *It's Got the World Shakin'* (1965) R&B#15 US#41, *Sugar Dumpling* (1965) R&B#18 US#32, *When a Boy Falls in Love* (1965) US#52, *Let's Go Steady Again* (1966) US#97. ALBUMS: **Sam Cooke** (1958, Keen) US#16; **Cooke's Tour** (1960), **Hits of the '50s** (1960), **My Kind of Blues** (1961), **Twistin' the Night Away** (1962) US#72, **Mr. Soul** (1963) US#92, **Night Beat** (1963) US#62, **Ain't That Good News** (1964) US#34, **Sam Cooke at the Copa** (1964, all RCA) US#29. COMPILATIONS: **Best of Sam Cooke** (1962, RCA) US#22; **The Gospel Soul of Sam Cooke** (1964), **Two Sides of Sam Cooke** (1964, both Specialty); **Shake** (1965, RCA) US#44; **The Gospel Soul of Sam Cooke, Volume 2** (1965, Specialty); **Best of Sam Cooke, Volume 2** (1965) US#128, **Try a Little Love** (1965, both RCA) US#120; **The Original Soul Stirrers** (1966, Specialty); **The Wonderful World of Sam Cooke** (1966, Keen); **Sam Cooke Sings Billie Holiday** (1976), **Live at the Harlem Square Club, 1963** (1985) US#134, **The Man and His Music** (1985, all RCA) US#175 UK#8; **Sam Cooke and the Soul Stirrers-In the Beginning** (1991, Ace). HIT VERSIONS: *Another Saturday Night* Buddy Alan (1975) C&W#88/Cat Stevens (1975) US#6 UK#19/Jimmy Buffett (1993) C&W#74; *Bring It on Home to Me* Animals (1965) US#32 UK#7/Eddie Floyd (1968) R&B#4 US#17/Lou Rawls (1970) R&B#45 US#96/Rod Stewart (1974) UK#7/Mickey Gilley (1976) C&W#1 US#101; *Chain Gang* [iii] Freddie Hart (1959) C&W#17/Jackie Wilson & Count Basie (1968) R&B#37 US#84/Jim Croce (1975) US#63/

Michael Martin Murphy (1979) C&W#93/Bobby Lee Springfield (1987) C&W#66; *Change Is Gonna Come, A* 5th Dimension in *The Declaration Medley* (1969) US#60/Brenton Wood (1969) US#131; *Cupid* Johnny Nash (1969) US#39/Johnny Rivers (1965) US#76/Dawn (1976) US#22/Spinners (1980) R&B#5 US#4 UK#4; *Having a Party* Ovations (1973) R&B#7 US#56/Pointer Sisters (1977) R&B#62/Norma Jean (1978) R&B#83/Luther Vandross (1982) R&B#3 US#55/Rod Stewart (1993) US#36; *I'll Come Running Back to You* Roy Hamilton (1962) US#105, *I'm Gonna Forget About You* Bobby Womack (1969) R&B#30, *Laughing and Clowning* Ray Charles (1970) R&B#18 US#98, *Nobody Loves Me Like You* Flamingos (1960) R&B#23 US#30, *Only Sixteen* Craig Douglas (1959) UK#1/Al Saxon (1959) UK#24/Dr. Hook (1976) g C&W#55 US#6; *Over You* Aaron Neville (1960) R&B#21 US#111. *Rome Wasn't Built in a Day* Johnny Taylor (1962) US#112/Hank Snow (1969) C&W#26; *Shake* British Walkers (1967) US#106/Otis Redding (1967) R&B#16 US#47; *Soothe Me* Sims Twins (1961) R&B#4 US#42/Sam & Dave (1967) R&B#16 US#56 UK#35; *Sweet Soul Music* [ii] Arthur Conley (1967) g R&B#2 US#2 UK#7; *Twistin' the Night Away* Ricky Dee & the Embers as *Work Out (Part 1)* (1962) US#103/Rod Stewart (1973) US#59, new version (1987) US#80/Divine (1985) UK#47; *Wonderful World* [i] Herman's Hermits (1965) US#4 UK#7/Johnny Nash (1976) R&B#66 US#103/Art Garfunkel (1978) US#17; *You Send Me* Theresa Brewer (1957) US#8/Aretha Franklin (1968) R&B#28 US#56/Ponderosa Twins & One (1971) R&B#12 US#78/Rod Stewart (1974) UK#7/Manhattans (1985) R&B#20 US#81. Co-writers: [i] Lou Adler/Herb Alpert (b. March 31, 1935, Los Angeles, CA), [ii] Arthur Conley (b. April 1, 1946, Atlanta GA)/Otis Redding, [iii] Charles Cooke.

206. COOPER, Alice (b Vincent Damon Furnier, February 4, 1948, Detroit, MI) Rock vocalist. A theatrical rock artist who rose to prominence in the early 1970s with a gothic rock style that he has maintained ever since. Raised in Phoenix, Arizona, Cooper played in the bands the Earwigs, the Spiders and the Nazz, before forming the group Alice Cooper in 1966. By the mid-1970s, Cooper was performing as a solo artist. CHART COMPOSITIONS: *Eighteen* [iii] (1971) US#21, *Caught in a Dream* (1971) US#94, *Under My Wheels* (1972) US#59, *Be My Lover* (1972) US#49, *School's Out* [i] (1972) US#7 UK#1, *Elected* [ii] (1972) US#26 UK#4, *No More Mr. Nice Guy* [i] (1973) US#25 UK#10, *Billion Dollar Babies* [i] (1973) US#57, *Teenage Lament '74* [viii] (1974) US#48 UK#12, *Only Women Bleed* [x] (1975) US#12, *Department of Youth* [vi] (1975) US#67, *Welcome to My Nightmare* [x] (1975) US#45,

I Never Cry [x] (1976) p US#12, *(No More) Love at Your Convenience* (1977) UK#44, *You and Me* [x] (1977) US#9, *How Are You Gonna See Me Now?* [ix] (1978) US#12 UK#61, *For Britain Only/Under My Wheels* (1982) UK#66, *He's Back (The Man in the Mask)* (1986) UK#61, *Freedom* (1988) UK#50, *Bed of Nails* (1989) UK#38, *House of Fire* (1989) US#56 UK#65, *Only My Heart Talkin'* (1990) US#89, *Poison* [iv] (1989) g US#7 UK#2, *Hey Stoopid* (1991) US#78 UK#21, *Love's a Loaded Gun* [vii] (1991) UK#38, *Feed My Frankenstein* [v] (1992) UK#27, *Lost in America* (1994) UK#22, *It's Me* (1994) UK#34. ALBUMS: **Pretties for You** (1969) US#193, **Easy Action** (1970, both Straight); **Love It to Death** (1971) g US#35 UK#28, **Killer** (1971) p US#21 UK#27, **School's Out** (1972) p US#2 UK#4, **Billion Dollar Babies** (1973) p US#1 UK#1, **Muscle of Love** (1973, all Warner Brothers) g US#10 UK#34; **Welcome to My Nightmare** (1975, Atlantic) p US#5 UK#19; **Alice Cooper Goes to Hell** (1976) g US#27 UK#23, **Lace and Whiskey** (1977) US#42 UK#33, **The Alice Cooper Show** (1977) US#131, **From the Inside** (1978) US#60 UK#68, **Flush the Fashion** (1980) US#60 UK#56, **Special Forces** (1981) US#125 UK#96, **Zipper Catches the Skin** (1982), **Dada** (1983, all Warner Brothers) UK#93; **Constrictor** (1986) US#59 UK#59, **Raise Your Fist and Yell** (1987, both MCA) US#73 UK#48; **Trash** (1989) p US#20 UK#2, **Hey Stoopid** (1991) US#47 UK#4, **The Last Temptation of Alice Cooper** (1994) US#68 UK#6, **Classiks** (1995, all Epic); **A Fistful of Alice Cooper** (1997, EMI). COMPILATION: **Greatest Hits** (1974, Warner Brothers) g US#8. HIT VERSIONS: *Elected* [ii] Mr. Bean & Smear Campaign (1992) UK#9, *No More Mr. Nice Guy* [i] Megadeath (1990) UK#13, *Only Women Bleed* [x] Julie Covington (1977) UK#12, *School's Out* [i] Krokus (1986) US#67. Co-writers: [i] Michael Bruce (b. March 16, 1948), [ii] Michael Bruce/Glen Buxton (b. November 10, 1947, Akron, OH)/Dennis Dunaway (b. December 9, 1948, Cottage Grove, OR), [iii] Michael Bruce/Glen Buxton/Dennis Dunaway/Neal Smith, [iv] Desmond Child/John McCurry, [v] Coler/Zodiac Mindwarp/Richardson, [vi] Bob Ezrin/Dick Wagner, [vii] Pepe/Ponti, [viii] Neal Smith (b. September 23, 1947, Akron, OH), [ix] Bernie Taupin/Dick Wagner, [x] Dick Wagner.

207. COOTS, John Frederick (b. May 2, 1897, Brooklyn; d. April 8, 1985, New York, both NY) Film and stage composer. A tunesmith whose best known song is the four million selling *Santa Claus Is Comin' to Town* [iv] (1934). Coots first worked in Tin Pan Alley as a stock clerk and piano demonstrator, before achieving a hit with *Doin' the Raccoon* [vi] (1928). His compositions were featured

in such shows as "The Shopworn Angel" (1929), and the film "Bernadine" (1957). HIT VERSIONS: *Beautiful Lady in Blue, A* [vii] Jan Garber (1936) US#1/Ray Noble (1936) US#13; *Doin' the Raccoon* [vi] George Olsen (1928) US#5, *For All We Know* [vii] Isham Jones (1934) US#16/Hal Kemp (1934) US#3/Caslons (1962) US#120/Dinah Washington (1962) US#88/Esther Phillips (1976) R&B#98; *I Still Get a Thrill (Thinking of You)* [i] Guy Lombardo (1930) US#5/Lee Morse (1930) US#20/Ozzie Nelson (1930) US#8/Ted Weems (1930) US#18; *Love Letters in the Sand* [v] Ted Black (1931) US#6/Pat Boone (1957) R&B#12 US#1 UK#2/Vince Hill (1967) UK#23/Tom T. Hall (1986) C&W#78; *Precious Little Thing Called Love, A* [iii] Ipana Troubadors (1929) US#12/Johnny Marvin & Ed Smalle (1929) US#16/George Olsen (1929) US#1; *Santa Claus Is Comin' to Town* [iv] George Hall (1934) US#12/Bing Crosby & the Andrews Sisters (1947) US#22/Four Seasons (1962) US#23/Jackson Five (1972) UK#43/Carpenters (1975) UK#37/Elvis Presley (1980) UK#41/Bruce Springsteen (1985) UK#9/Bjorn Again (1992) UK#55; *Until Today* [ii] Nat Brandwynne (1936) US#14/Fletcher Henderson (1936) US#11; *You Go to My Head* [iv] Larry Clinton (1938) US#3/Glen Gray (1938) US#9/Teddy Wilson with Billie Holiday (1938) US#20/Bryan Ferry (1975) UK#33. Co-writers: [i] Benny Davis, [ii] Benny Davis/Oscar Levant, [iii] Lou Davis, [iv] Haven Gillespie, [v] Charles Kenny/Nick Kenny, [vi] Ray Klages, [vii] Sam M. Lewis.

208. COPE, Julian (b. October 21, 1957, Bargoed, Wales) Rock guitarist and vocalist. The lead singer of the psychedelic influenced 1970s British group the Teardrop Explodes. CHART COMPOSITIONS: *When I Dream* (1980) UK#47, *Reward* (1981) UK#6, *Treason (It's Just a Story)* [i] (1981) UK#18, *Passionate Friend* [ii] (1981) UK#25, *Colors Fly Away* (1981) UK#54, *Tiny Children* (1982) UK#44, *You Disappear from View* (1983) UK#41. ALBUMS: **Kilimanjaro** (1980) US#156 UK#24, **Wilder** (1981, both Mercury) US#176 UK#29; **Everybody Wants to Shag the Teardrop Explodes** (1990, Fontana) UK#72; **Piano** (1990, Zoo); **Live in Concert** (1990, Windsong). Since 1983, Cope has pursued a prolific solo career with an increasingly bizarre blend of German rock influenced new age psychedelia. CHART COMPOSITIONS: *Sunshine Playroom* (1984) UK#64, *The Greatness and Perfection of Love* (1984, UK#52), *World Shut Your Mouth* (1986) US#84 UK#19, re-issued (1992) UK#44; *Trampoline* (1986) UK#31, *Eve's Volcano (Covered in Sin)* (1987) UK#41, *Charlotte Ann* (1988) UK#35, *China Doll* (1989) UK#53, *Beautiful Love* (1991) UK#32, *Easy Easy Rider* (1991) UK#51, *Head* (1991) UK#57,

Fear Loves This Place EP (1992) UK#42, *Try, Try, Try* (1995) UK#24, *I Come from Another Planet Baby* (1996) UK#34, *Planetary Sit-In (Every Girl Has Your Name)* (1996) UK#34. ALBUMS: **World Shut Your Mouth** (1984) UK#40, **Fried** (1984, both Mercury) UK#87; **Julian Cope** (1987) US#109, **Saint Julian** (1987) US#105 UK#11, **My Nation Underground** (1988) US#155 UK#42, **Shellington** (1990), **Peggy Suicide** (1991) UK#23, **Jehovah Kill** (1992, all Island) UK#20; **Shellington 2** (1993, Def American); **Autogeddon** (1994) UK#16, **Julian Cope Presents 20 Mothers** (1995) UK#20, **Interpreter** (1996, all Echo). COMPILATIONS: **Floored Genius-The Best of Julian Cope** (1992) UK#22, **The Followers of Saint Julian** (1997, both Island). HIT VERSION: *Trampoline* Deacon Blue on B-side of *Wages Day* (1989) UK#18. Co-writers: [i] Ian McCulloch (b. May 5, 1959, Liverpool, England), [ii] Julie McCulloch.

209. Corporation, The The collective pen-name for the Motown Records songwriting and production team, Berry Gordy, Jr., Fonso Mizell, Freddie Perren, and Deke Richards. (*See also under* Berry GORDY, Jr.)

210. COSLOW, Sam (b. December 27, 1902; d. 1982, both New York, NY) Film and stage composer. A Tin Pan Alley composer and lyricist who frequently collaborated with Arthur Johnston. Coslow's songs were included in the films "Too Much Harmony" (1933), "College Scandal" (1935), "It's Love Again" (1936), "Carnegie Hall" (1946), and "Copacabana" (1947). He later co-founded his own publishing company. HIT VERSIONS: *Bebe* [vii] Billy Jones (1923) US#8, *Beware My Heart* Margaret Whiting (1947) US#21, *Good Mornin'* Frank Dailey (1937) US#20/Dick Robertson (1937) US#20; *Hello, Swanee, Hello!* [ii] Ben Bernie (1927) US#6/Fred Waring's Pennsylvanians (1927) US#12; *In the Middle of a Kiss* Hal Kemp (1935) US#2, *Je Vous Aime* Andy Russell (1947) US#22, *Little White Gardenia, A* Hal Kemp (1935) US#10, *New Moon and an Old Serenade, A* [i] Tommy Dorsey (1939) US#5, *Sing, You Sinners* [v] High Hatters (1930) US#10/Smith Ballew (1930) US#18; *Tomorrow Night* [iv] Lonnie Johnson (1948) R&B#1 US#19, *True Confession* [vi] Russ Morgan (1937) US#13/Larry Clinton (1938) US#3/Sammy Kaye (1938) US#11; *Turn Off the Moon* Mal Hallet (1937) US#19, *Was It a Dream?* [iii] Jan Garber (1928) US#10/Fred Waring's Pennsylvanians (1928) US#11. Co-writers: [i] Martin Block/Abner Silver, [ii] Addy Britt, [iii] Addy Britt/Larry Spier, [iv] Will Grosz, [v] Frank Harling, [vi] Frederick Hollander, [vii] Abner Silver. (*See also under* Sammy FAIN, Arthur JOHNSTON, Ralph RAINGER, Sig-

mund ROMBERG, Jimmy VAN HEUSEN, Richard WHITING.)

211. COSTELLO, Elvis (b. Declan P.A. McManus, August 25, 1955, London, England) Rock guitarist and vocalist. A witty and perceptive songwriter who started out as an uptight, neurotic, 1970s punk stylist, and became a sophisticated and inventive commentator on British life during the 1980-1990s. Costello appears to have inherited the mantel of Ray Davies, and is a master of adroit character sketches, mid-line alliteration and memorable couplets. The son of a bandleader, Costello began writing songs in his teens, while working as a computer operator and, as D.P. Costello, performing music in his spare time. He was briefly a member of the group Flip City, and was turned down as a solo artist by all the major labels, signing to the small independent Stiff Records in 1977. Blending elements of punk and reggae with a traditional British pop song structure that stretched back to music hall traditions, Costello, often backed by his tight band the Attractions, released a series of cocky and confident records. His songwriting matured rapidly, taking in R&B and country influences on increasingly droll material, and later works have included a collaboration with the Brodsky String Quartet, **The Juliet Letters** (1992), and the composition of an entire album of material in a weekend for the singer Wendy James, **Now Ain't the Time for Your Tears** (1993, MCA) UK#43. CHART COMPOSITIONS: *Watching the Detectives* (1977) US#108 UK#15, *(I Don't Want to Go To) Chelsea* (1977) UK#16, *Pump It Up* (1978) UK#24, *Radio Radio* (1978) UK#29, *Oliver's Army* (1979) UK#2, *Accidents Will Happen* (1979) US#101 UK#28, *High Fidelity* (1980) UK#30, *New Amsterdam* (1980) UK#36, *Clubland* (1980) UK#60, *I'm Your Toy* (1982) UK#51, *Man Out of Time* (1982) UK#58, *You Little Fool* (1982) UK#52, *Party Party* (1982) UK#48, *Pills and Soap* (1983) UK#16, *Everyday I Write the Book* (1983) US#36 UK#28, *Let Them All Talk* (1983) UK#59, *Peace in Our Time* (1984) UK#48, *I Wanna Be Loved/Turning the Town Red* (1984) UK#25, *The Only Flame in Town* (1984) US#56 UK#71, *Green Shirt* (1985) UK#71, re-entry (1985) UK#68; *Tokyo Storm Warning* (1986) UK#73, *Veronica* [i] (1989) US#19 UK#31, *Baby Plays Around EP* (1989) UK#65, *The Other Side of Summer* (1991) UK#43, *Sulky Girl* (1994) UK#22, *13 Steps Lead Down* (1994) US#111 UK#59, *London's Brilliant Parade EP* (1994) UK#48, *King of America* (1995) UK#71, *It's Time* (1996) UK#58. ALBUMS: **My Aim Is True** (1977, Stiff) p US#32 UK#14; **This Year's Model** (1978) g US#30 UK#4, **Armed Forces** (1979, both Radar) g US#10 UK#2; **Get Happy** (1980) US#11 UK#2, **Trust** (1981) US#28 UK#9, **Almost Blue** (1981) US#50 UK#7,

Imperial Bedroom (1982) US#30 UK#6, **Punch the Clock** (1983) US#24 UK#3, **Goodbye Cruel World** (1984) US#35 UK#10, **King of America** (1986, all F.Beat) US#39 UK#11; **Blood and Chocolate** (1986, Imp) US#84 UK#16; **Spike** (1989) g US#32 UK#5, **Mighty Like a Rose** (1991) US#55 UK#5, **GBH** ost (1992), **The Juliet Letters** (1992) US#125 UK#18, **Brutal Youth** (1994) US#34 UK#2, **Kojak Variety** (1995) US#102 UK#21, **Deep Dead Blue** with Bill Frisell (1995, all Warner Brothers); **Original Music from the Channel 4 Series Jake's Progress** tvst with Richard Harvey (1996, Demon); **All This Useless Beauty** (1996, Warner Brothers) US#53. COMPI-LATIONS: **Live at the El Mocambo** (1977), **Taking Liberties** (1980) US#28, **10 Bloody Mary's and 10 How's Your Father's** (1980, all Columbia); **Best of Elvis Costello and the Attractions-The Man** (1985, Telstar) g US#116 UK#8; **Out of Our Idiot** (1987), **Girls Girls Girls** (1989) UK#67, **2 1/2 Years** (1993), **Very Best of Elvis Costello and the Attractions** (1994, all Demon) UK#57; **For the First Time in America** with Steve Nieve (1997, Warner Brothers). HIT VERSIONS: *Alison* Everything But the Girl on *Covers EP* (1992) UK#13, *Back on My Feet* Paul McCartney on B-side of *Once Upon a Long Ago* (1987) UK#10, *Girls Talk* Dave Edmunds (1979) US#65, *I Love You When You Sleep* Tracie (1984) UK#59, *Shipbuilding* Robert Wyatt (1983) UK#35. Co-writer: [i] Paul McCartney. (*See also under* Paul McCARTNEY.)

212. COTTEN, Elizabeth "Libba" (b. 1893, near Chapel Hill, NC; d. June 29, 1982, Syracuse, NY) Folk guitarist and vocalist. An influential folk guitar stylist who began her musical career at the age of sixty. Cotten originally worked in a department store in Washington, DC, where she had the good fortune to find a lost little girl, Peggy Seeger, the sister of the folk singers Mike and Pete Seeger. Cotten was subsequently hired by Peggy's grateful mother as a domestic, and it was in the Seeger family home that she was encouraged to perform folk music. After a song that she had written as a twelve year old, *Freight Train*, became a worldwide hit for Rusty Draper in 1957, Cotten began performing in public, making her one of the latest starters in musical history. ALBUMS: **Negro Folksongs** (1967), **Elizabeth Cotten, Volume 2: Shake Sugaree** (1967), **When I'm Gone** (1968), **Live** (1985, all Folkways). HIT VERSIONS: *Freight Train* Beverly Sisters on *All Star Hit Parade #2 EP* (1957) UK#15/Rusty Draper (1957) US#6/Charles McDevitt Skiffle Group (1957) US#40 UK#5/Duane Eddy (1970) US#110/Jim & Jesse (1971) C&W#41).

213. COULTER, Phil (b. Londonderry,

Northern Ireland) Pop producer and pianist, and **MARTIN, Bill** (b. England) Pop producer. A songwriting and production team that was responsible for many of the hits by the groups Bay City Rollers and Kenny during the 1970s. Coulter has also worked closely with the Irish folk act the Dubliners, which recorded his political material *The Molly Maguires* and *Free the People*. During the 1980s, Coulter concentrated on creating lush orchestral works. AL-BUMS: **Classic Tranquility** (1983, Panther); **Sea of Tranquillity** (1984) UK#46, **Phil Coulter's Ireland** (1985, both K-Tel) UK#86. HIT VERSIONS: *All of Me Loves All of You* Bay City Rollers (1974) UK#1, *Baby I Love You, O.K.* Kenny (1975) UK#12, *Back Home* England World Cup Squad (1970) UK#1, *Bump, The* Kenny (1974) UK#3, *Congratulations* Cliff Richard (1968) US#99 UK#1, *Fancy Pants* Kenny (1975) UK#4, *Forever and Ever* Slik (1976) UK#1, *Heart of Stone* Kenny (1973) UK#11, *I Will Love You (Ev'ry Time When We Are Gone)* Fureys (1982) UK#54, *Julie Ann* Kenny (1975) UK#10, *My Boy* [i] Richard Harris (1971) US#41/Elvis Presley (1974) US#20 UK#5; *Puppet on a String* Sandie Shaw (1967) UK#1, *Remember (Sha La La)* Bay City Rollers (1974) UK#6, *Saturday Night* Bay City Rollers (1976) g US#1, *Shang-a-Lang* Bay City Rollers (1974) UK#2, *Summerlove Sensation* Bay City Rollers (1974) UK#3, *Surround Yourself with Sorrow* Cilla Black (1969) UK#3, *Thanks* Bill Anderson (1975) C&W#24, *Tonight in Tokyo* Sandie Shaw (1967) UK#21. Co-writers: [i] Jean Bourtayre/Claude Francois.

214. COUSINS, Dave (b. England) Folk guitarist and vocalist. A founder member of the British folk-rock group the Strawbs. CHART COM-POSITIONS: *Lay Down* (1972) UK#12, *Shine on Silver Sun* (1973) UK#34. ALBUMS: **The Strawbs** (1969), **Dragonfly** (1970), **Just a Collection of Antiques and Curios** (1970) UK#27, **From the Witchwood** (1971) UK#39, **Grave New World** (1972) US#191 UK#11, **Bursting at the Seams** (1973) US#121 UK#2, **Hero and Heroine** (1974) US#94 UK#35, **Ghosts** (1975) US#47, **Nomadness** (1975, all A&M) US#147; **Deep Cuts** (1976) US#144, **Burning for You** (1977, both Oyster) US#175; **Deadlines** (1978, Arista); **Don't Say Goodbye** (1987, Strawbs); **Heartbreak Hill** (1995, Witchwood). COMPILATIONS: **All Our Own Work*** (1973, Hallmark); **By Choice** (1974), **Best of the Strawbs** (1978, both A&M); **Sandy and the Strawbs*** (1991, Hannibal); **Preserves Uncanned** (1992, RGO); **A Choice Selection of Strawbs** (1992, A&M); **Greatest Hits Live** (1993, RGO). Cousins currently works in local radio in Devon, having recorded briefly as a solo artist, his under-rated debut album featuring the stunning *Blue Angel*. ALBUMS: **Two Weeks Last**

Summer (1972, A&M); **Old School Songs** (1980, Old School). With: * Sandy Denny.

215. COVAY, Don (b. March, 1938, Orangeburg, SC) R&B vocalist. The R&B singer responsible for influencing many aspects of Mick Jagger's vocal style, and the master of the R&B cheating song. Covay first sang gospel in the group the Cherry Keys, before joining the Rainbows in the early 1950s. He recorded for Pilgrim Records in 1956, and as Pretty Boy for Atlantic the following year. As Don Covay and the Goodtimers, he released a succession of highly charged hits during the 1960s. CHART COMPOSITIONS: *Pony Time* [i] (1961) US#60, *Mercy, Mercy, Mercy* [iii] (1964) US#35, *Take This Hurt Off Me* (1964) US#97, *Please Do Something* (1965) R&B#21, *See Saw* [ii] (1965) R&B#5 US#44, *Watching the Late, Late Show* (1966) US#101, *Somebody's Got to Love You* (1966) US#127, *Shingalong '67* (1967) R&B#50 US#133, *Soul Meeting** (1968) R&B#34 US#91, *Black Woman* (1970) R&B#43, *I Was Checkin' Out, She Was Checkin' In* (1973) R&B#6, *Somebody's Been Enjoying My Home* (1973) R&B#63, *It's Better to Have (And Don't Need)* [iv] (1974) R&B#21 US#63 UK#29, *Rumble in the Jungle* (1975) R&B#83, *Badd Boy* (1980) R&B#74. ALBUMS: **Mercy** (1964, Rosemart); **See Saw** (1966), **House of Blue Lights** (1969, both Atlantic); **Different Strokes** (1970, Janus); **Superdude 1** (1973), **Hot Blood** (1975, both Mercury); **Travelin' in Heavy Traffic** (1976, Philadelphia); **Country Funk** (1970, Polydor). COMPILATIONS: **Sweet Thang** (1987, Topline); **Checkin' in with Don Covay** (1989), **The Definitive Don Covay** (1995, Razor & Tie). HIT VERSIONS: *Chain of Fools* Aretha Franklin (1968) g US#2 UK#43, *I Don't Know What You've Got But It's Got Me (Part 1)* Little Richard (1965) R&B#12 US#92, *I'm Hanging Up My Heart for You* Solomon Burke (1962) R&B#15 US#85, *Letter Full of Tears* Billy Fury (1962) UK#32/Gladys Knight & the Pips (1961) R&B#3 US#19; *Long Tall Shorty* Tommy Tucker (1964) US#96, *Mercy, Mercy, Mercy* [iii] Marlena Shaw (1967) R&B#33 US#58/Johnny "Guitar" Watson & Larry Williams (1967) R&B#23 US#96/Phoebe Snow (1981) US#52; *Pony Time* [i] Chubby Checker (1961) R&B#1 US#1 UK#27, *See Saw* [ii] Aretha Franklin (1968) g R&B#9 US#14, *Sookie, Sookie* [ii] Roy Thompson (1967) R&B#43, *Tonight's the Night* Solomon Burke (1965) R&B#2 US#28, *You Got It* Etta James (1968) US#113, *You Can Run (But You Can't Hide)* Jerry Butler (1962) R&B#23 US#63. As: * Soul Clan. Co-writers: [i] J. Berry, [ii] Steve Cropper, [iii] R. Miller, [iv] Ernie Watts. (*See also under* Peter WOLF.)

216. COWARD, Sir Noel (b. Noel Pierce Coward, December 16, 1899, Teddington, England; d. March 26, 1973, Port Maria, Jamaica) Film and stage composer, pianist and vocalist. One of the most distinguished composers, performers and characters of the twentieth century, whose prolific songwriting skill was never restricted by his ability to play the piano in only three keys. The English equivalent to America's Cole Porter, Coward's acerbic wit and fey, ineffable charm, was fully in evidence in nearly everything he created, as he was also a playwright, author and actor. Coward received no formal musical training, and first appeared on stage at the age of twelve. His first published composition was *Parisian Pierrot*, from the show "London Calling" (1923), after which he worked on musicals that introduced such hits as Alice Delysia's *Poor Little Rich Girl* [i], from the revue "On with the Dance" (1925). Coward's first Broadway success was "This Year of Grace" (1928), which featured the songs *Dance Little Lady* and *A Room with a View*. Other shows for which he is remembered, include "Words and Music" (1932), "Conversation Piece" (1934), "Tonight at 8.30" (1936), "Operetee" (1938), and "Set to Music" (1939). During the 1930s, Coward composed such satirical classics as *I Went to a Marvelous Party, The Stately Homes of England, Mrs. Worthington, Mad About the Boy*, and *Mad Dogs and Englishmen*, all of which displayed a Gilbert and Sullivan influence. Coward entertained troops during World War II, and like many fellow artists of the time, he stoked the allied propaganda machine with such Blitz material as *London Pride*. Some of his parodies were often taken literally, none more so than the wonderfully adroit *Don't Let's Be Beastly to the Germans*. He also won an Oscar for best song with *In Which We Serve* (1944). Coward recorded many sides for HMV Records, but by the 1950s, he had become something of a man out of time, which only added a new edge to such material as *There Are Bad Times Just Around the Corner* (1952). As his songwriting output declined, Coward concentrated on film roles, while remaining a popular nightclub attraction. In 1972, he was the subject of the show "Cowardly Custard." ALBUMS: **Set to Music** oc (1939, JJC); **Bittersweet** oc (1951), **Conversation Piece** oc (1951, both World); **After the Ball** oc (1954, AMR); **Together with Music** tvst (1955, DRG); **Tonight at 8:30** oc (1955, RCA); **At Las Vegas** (1956, Columbia) US#14; **Sail Away** oc (1961, Capitol) US#36; **Bittersweet** sc (1961, Angel); **The Girl Who Came to Supper** oc (1964, Columbia) US#33; **Cowardly Custard** oc (1972, RCA); **Oh Coward!** oc (1972, Bell); **Sail Away** oc (1972, Stanyan); **A Talent to Amuse** (1973, Parlophone); **The Master** (1978, Retrospect); **Noel Coward and Gertrude Lawrence** (1979, Evergreen); **Noel Cow-**

ard Reading (1971, Caedmon); **Noel Coward Sings His Score** (1979, DRG); **The Revues** (1984), **The Master featuring Gertrude Lawrence** (1985), **Great Shows** (1986, all Retrospect); **Together with Music** with Mary Martin (1988, DRG); **Bitter Suite** (1989, That's Entertainment); **Noel Coward Double Bill** (1988, BBC); **The Compact Coward** (1989, EMI). HIT VERSIONS: *Dance, Little Lady* Roger Wolfe Kahn (1929) US#18, *I'll Follow My Secret Heart* Ray Noble (1934) US#8, *I'll See You Again* Leo Reisman (1930) US#10, *Mad About the Boy* Ray Noble (1935) US#19; *Poor Little Rich Girl* [i] Gertrude Lawrence (1926) US#11, *Room with a View, A* Ben Selvin (1929) US#10. Co-writer: [i] Philip Braham.

217. **CRANE, Jimmy** (b. 1910), and **JA-COBS, Al** (b. 1903) Pop composers. HIT VER-SIONS: *Every Day of My Life* Malcolm Vaughan (1955) UK#5/McGuire Sisters (1956) US#37/Bobby Vinton (1972) US#24; *Hurt* Roy Hamilton (1954) R&B#8/Manhattans (1975) R&B#10 US#97 UK#4/ Timi Yuro (1961) R&B#22 US#4/Connie Cato (1975) C&W#14/Juice Newton (1985) C&W#1; *I Need You Now* Eddie Fisher (1954) g US#1 UK#19, *If I Give My Heart to You* [i] Connee Boswell (1954) US#10/ Doris Day (1954) US#3 UK#4/Denise Lor (1954) US#8/Joan Regan (1954) UK#3/Dinah Shore (1954) US#28/Charlie Kunz in *Piano Medley #114* (1954) UK#20/Wright Brothers (1954) US#25/Margo Smith (1979) C&W#10. Co-writer: [i] Jimmy Brewster.

218. **CRAVEN, Beverly** (b. England) Pop pianist and vocalist. CHART COMPOSITIONS: *Promise Me* (1991) UK#3, *Holding On* (1991) UK#32, *Woman to Woman* (1991) UK#40, *Memories* (1991) UK#68, *Love Scenes* (1993) UK#34, *Mollie's Song* (1993) UK#61. ALBUMS: **Beverly Craven** (1991, Columbia) UK#3; **Love Scenes** (1993, Epic) UK#4.

219. **CREATORE, Luigi** (b. New York, NY), and **PERETTI, Hugo** (b. 1918, New York, NY; d. May 1, 1986, Englewood, NJ) Pop producers. A songwriting, production and record label owning partnership best known for their work with the R&B vocal group the Stylistics. Peretti started in music as an arranger and trumpeter in Broadway show bands. In the late 1940s, the duo recorded as Hugo and Luigi, and during the 1950s they purchased the Roulette label, after which they began to write and produce an estimated fifty million selling records. They worked with Sam Cooke at RCA Records until 1963, and later at Avco Records, where they produced the Stylistics. One of Creatore and Peretti's biggest hits was *The Lion Sleeps Tonight* by the Tokens (1961), which they adapted from an African folk

tune *Wimoweh*, first discovered in the 1950s by Pete Seeger. ALBUMS: **The Cascading Voices of the Hugo and Luigi Chorus** (1963) US#14, **Let's Fall in Love** (1963) US#125, **Maggie Flynn** oc (1969, all RCA) US#185. HIT VERSIONS: *Bimbombey* [i] Jimmie Rodgers (1958) US#11, *Can't Give You Any-thing (But My Love)* [ii] Stylistics (1975) R&B#18 US#51 UK#1, *Can't Help Falling in Love* [ii] Elvis Presley (1961) g US#2 UK#1/Andy Williams (1970) UK#3/Softones (1973) R&B#56/UB40 (1993) p US#1 UK#1/Stylistics (1976) R&B#52 UK#4/Corey Hart (1986) US#24/Lick the Tins (1986) UK#42; *Crazy Otto Rag, The* [v] Johnny Maddox & the Rhythmasters (1955) US#2/Stargazers (1955) UK#18; *Experience Unnecessary* [iv] Sarah Vaughan (1955) US#14, *Funky Weekend* [ii] Stylistics (1975) R&B#23 US#76 UK#10, *Heavy Fallin' Out* Stylistics (1974) R&B#4 US#41, *Let's Put It All Together* [ii] Stylistics (1974) R&B#8 US#18 UK#9, *Lion Sleeps Tonight, The* (arrangement only) Tokens (1961) g R&B#7 US#1 UK#11/Karl Denver (1962) UK#4/Robert John (1972) g US#3/Tight Fit (1982) UK#1; *Na Na Is the Saddest Word* [ii] Stylistics (1975) UK#5, *Secretly* Jimmie Rodgers (1958) US#3, *Sing Baby Sing* [ii] Stylistics (1975) UK#3, *Sixteen Bars* Stylistics (1976) UK#7, *Star on a TV Show* [ii] Stylistics (1975) R&B#13 US#47 UK#12, *Thank You Baby* Stylistics (1975) R&B#7 US#70, *Walkin' Miracle, A* [iii] Lim-mie & the Family Cookin' (1974) UK#6/Essex (1963) R&B#11 US#12; *Wild in the Country* [ii] Elvis Pres-ley (1961) US#26 UK#4, *You Are Beautiful* [ii] Styl-istics (1976) R&B#17 US#79. Co-writers: [i] Mack David, [ii] George David Weiss, [iii] Adam Levy/ George David Weiss, [iv] Gladys Shelley, [v] Edward R. White/Mack Wolfson.

220. **CREME, Lol** (b. Lawrence Creme, September 19, 1947, Manchester, England) Pop guitarist, producer and vocalist, and **GODFREY, Kevin** (b. October 7, 1945, Manchester, England) Pop drummer, producer and vocalist. A songwriting and production team who first linked up in the group Hotlegs, which charted with the single *Neanderthal Man* [i] (1970) US#22 UK#2, and released the albums **Thinks: School Stinks** (1970) and **Songs** (1971, both Philips). In 1971, Godley and Creme formed 10 c.c. with Graham Gouldman and Eric Stewart, as members of which, they composed the hits *Donna* (1972) UK#2, *The Dean and I* (1973) UK#10, *Silly Love* (1974) UK#24, and *Life Is a Mine-strone* [i] (1975) US#104 UK#7. ALBUMS: **10 c.c.** (1973) UK#36, **Sheet Music** (1974, both UK) US#81 UK#9; **The Original Soundtrack** (1975) US#15 UK#4, **How Dare You?** (1976, both Mercury) US#47 UK#5. COMPILATIONS: **Greatest Hits** (1975, Decca) US#161 UK#9; **Greatest Hits, 1972-**

1978 (1979, Mercury) US#188 UK#5. In 1976, Godley and Creme left the group to perform as a duo, but during the 1980s, their music career took a back seat as they became pioneering pop video producers. CHART COMPOSITIONS: *Under Your Thumb* (1981) UK#3, *Wedding Bells* (1981) UK#7, *Cry* (1985) US#16 UK#19, re-entry (1986) UK#66. ALBUMS: **Consequences** (1977) UK#52, **L** (1978) UK#47, **Freeze Frame** (1979, all Mercury); **Ismism** (1981) UK#29, **Birds of Prey** (1983), **Goodbye Mr. Blue Sky** (1988), **One World One Voice** (1990, all Polydor) UK#27. COMPILATIONS: **Music from Consequences** (1979, Mercury); **The History Mix, Volume 1** (1985, Polydor) US#37; **Changing Faces: The Very Best of 10 c.c. and Godley and Creme** (1987, ProTV) UK#4. Co-writer: [i] Eric Stewart. (*See also under* Graham GOULDMAN.)

221. CRENSHAW, Marshall (b. 1954, Detroit, IL) Pop guitarist and vocalist. A former cast member of the 1970s show "Beatlemania," who records in a commercial rockabilly style. CHART COMPOSITIONS: *Someday, Someway* (1982) US#36, *There She Goes Again* (1982) US#110, *Whenever You're on My Mind* (1983) US#103. ALBUMS: **Marshall Crenshaw** (1982) US#50, **Field Day** (1983) US#52, **Downtown** (1985), **Mary Jane and 9 Others** (1987, all Warner Brothers); **My Truck Is My Home** (1995, Razor & Tie); **Miracle of Science** (1996, Grapevine). HIT VERSIONS: *Follow You Down/Til I Hear from You* [i] Gin Blossoms (1996) US#9, *My Favourite Waste of Time* Owen Paul (1986) UK#3/Bette Midler (1983) US#78; *Someday, Someway* Robert Gordon (1981) US#76, *Whatever Way the Wind Blows* Kelly Willis (1993) C&W#72. Co-writers: [i] S. Johnson/B. Leen/P. Rhodes/J. Valenzuela/R. Wilson.

222. CREWE, Bob (b. November 12, 1937, Newark, NJ) Pop producer and orchestrator. A successful music business entrepreneur with a talent for opportunist, and occasionally classic, pop melodies. Crewe first tasted chart success in 1958, when he teamed up with Bob Gaudio in the group the Royal Teens for the hit *Short Shorts*. After working as an independent producer in New York, Crewe ran his own Topix label. In 1959, he discovered the vocalist Franki Valli. Three years later, Crewe, Gaudio and Valli issued a version of *Bermuda* as the Four Seasons, which, although not a hit, sufficiently encouraged them to carefully assimilate the studio techniques on a batch of current hit records, which they succinctly incorporated into a version of Gaudio's *Sherry*, which sold over two million copies. The Four Seasons became one of the biggest pop acts in the world, and Crewe and Gaudio's metronomic, half-

step, foot stomping beats and melodramatic lyrics, became a trademark sound. Crewe continued to work with Valli throughout the 1970s, penning the much recorded *Can't Take My Eyes Off You* [v]. Crewe headed several of his own recording and publishing companies during the 1960s, and also hosted the television show "The Bob Crewe Generation," the national exposure of which led to a series of solo hits. He later produced Mitch Ryder and the Detroit Wheels, and was responsible for Disco Tex and the Sex-O-Lettes' hideous series of 1970s disco hits. During the 1980s, Crewe wrote and produced for Peabo Bryson and Roberta Flack. CHART COMPOSITIONS: *Sweetie Pie* (1959) US#111, *After the Ball* (1967) US#126, *Miniskirts in Moscow* (1967) US#129, *Birds of Britain* (1967) US#89, *Street Talk* [ii] (1976) US#56. ALBUMS: **Music to Watch Girls By** (1967) US#100, **Barbarella** ost (1968, both DynoVoice) US#183; **Street Talk** (1976), **Motivation** (1977, both Elektra). HIT VERSIONS: *Across the Street* Lenny O'Henry (1964) US#98, *Big Boys Don't Cry* [v] Four Seasons (1962) R&B#1 US#1 UK#13/David Carroll as *Big Girls Don't Cry Limbo* (1962) US#102; *Bye Bye Baby (Baby Bye Bye)* [v] Four Seasons (1962) US#12/Symbols (1967) UK#44/Bay City Rollers (1975) UK#1 US#1; *California Nights* Lesley Gore (1967) US#16, *Can't Take My Eyes Off You* [v] Lettermen (1967) US#7/Franki Valli (1967) US#2/Andy Williams (1968) UK#5/Nancy Wilson (1969) R&B#27 US#52/Gerri Granger (1975) US#108/Boystown Gang (1982) UK#4/Pet Shop Boys on B-side of *Where the Streets Have No Name* (1991) US#72 UK#4; *Daddy Cool-The Girl Can't Help It* [viii] Darts (1977) UK#6, *Dancin' Kid* [vii] Disco Tex & the Sex-O-Lettes (1976) R&B#99 US#60, *Get Dancin'* [vii] Disco Tex & the Sex-O-Lettes (1974) R&B#32 US#10 UK#8, *Girl Come Running* [v] Four Seasons (1965) US#30, *Girl I'll Never Know (Angels Never Fly This Low)* Franki Valli (1975) US#52, *Hollywood Hot* [ii] Eleventh Hour (1975) US#55, *I Make a Fool of Myself* [v] Franki Valli (1967) US#18, *I Wanna Dance Wit 'Choo (Doo Dat Dance)* [ix] Disco Tex & the Sex-O-Lettes (1975) R&B#33 US#23 UK#6, *Jam Band* Disco Tex & the Sex-O-Lettes (1975) US#80, *La Dee Dah* [viii] Billy & Lillie (1958) R&B#6 US#9, *Lady Marmalade* [vii] LaBelle (1975) g R&B#1 US#1 UK#17/All Saints (1998) UK#1; *Let's Hang On (To What We Got)* [vi] Four Seasons (1965) US#3 UK#4/Barry Manilow (1982) US#32 UK#12; *Lucky Ladybug* Billy & Laurie (1958) US#14, *My Eyes Adored You* [vii] Frankie Valli (1974) US#1 UK#5/Marty Mitchell (1976) C&W#87; *Proud One, The* [v] Franki Valli (1966) US#68/Osmonds (1975) US#8 UK#5; *Rag Doll* [v] Four Seasons (1964) g US#1 UK#2, *Ronnie* [v] Four Seasons (1964) US#6, *Save It for Me* [v] Four Seasons (1964) US#10, *Silence Is Golden* [v] Tremeloes (1967) US#11 UK#1, *Silhouettes* [viii] Diamonds (1957) US#10/Rays (1957) R&B#3 US#3/Herman's Hermits (1965) US#5 UK#3; *So Good* [vii] Eleventh Hour (1974) US#94, *Sock It to Me, Baby* [i] Mitch Ryder & the Detroit Wheels (1967) US#6, *Summer and Sandy* Lesley Gore (1967) US#65, *Sun Ain't Gonna Shine Anymore, The* [v] Frankie Valli (1965) US#128/Walker Brothers (1966) US#13 UK#1/Fuzzy Bunnies (1968) US#115/Nielsen-Pearson (1981) US#56/Cher (1996) UK#26; *Swearin' to God* [ix] Franki Valli (1975) R&B#31 US#6 UK#31, *Tallahassee Lassie* Freddie Cannon (1959) R&B#13 US#6 UK#17/Tommy Steele (1959) UK#16; *To Give (The Reason I Live)* Frankie Valli (1967) US#29, *Toy Soldier* Four Seasons (1965) US#64, *Walk Like a Man* [v] Four Seasons (1963) R&B#3 US#1 UK#12/Divine (1985) UK#23/Mary Jane Girls (1986) R&B#91 US#41; *You're Gonna Hurt Yourself* [iii] Franki Valli (1966) US#39, *You're Looking Like Love to Me* [iv] Peabo Bryson & Roberta Flack (1983) R&B#41 US#58, *You're Ready Now* [v] Frankie Valli (1966) US#112 UK#11. Co-writers: [i] L. Russell Brown, [ii] C. Bullens, [iii] Charles Calello, [iv] R. Corbetta/Bob Gaudio, [v] Bob Gaudio, [vi] Bob Gaudio/Sandy Linzer/Denny Randell, [vii] Kenny Nolan (b. Kenny Nolan Helfman), [viii] A. Picariello/Frank C. Slay, Jr., [ix] Denny Randell. (*See also under* Bob GAUDIO.)

223. CROCE, Jim (b. James Joseph Croce, January 10, 1943, Philadelphia, PA; d. September 20, 1973, LA) Folk guitarist and vocalist. The last of the first wave of folk related singer-songwriters, who perceptively observed the tribulations of ordinary lives. Blessed with a world weary voice and a working-man's down-home image, Croce captured the American notion of the road as a means of escape long before the arrival of Bruce Springsteen. Croce learned the accordion at the age of six, and studied at Villanova University in the early 1960s, where he developed an interest in folk music. He listened to ragtime, dixieland and country, and also ran the campus radio station, where he met his future producer, Tommy West. Croce held various day jobs while he honed his performance skills in coffee houses and bars, and after linking up with the acoustic guitarist Maury Muehleisen, he landed a recording contract with ABC Records in 1972, where he turned in a trio of albums that featured strong love ballads and up-beat character songs. In 1973, when clearly on the verge of becoming a major star, both Croce and Muehleisen were killed in a plane crash enroute to a gig in Texas. During a television documentary about Croce's life, his co-producer Terry Cashman commented, "I've always had

the feeling that we were cheated when Jim was killed." CHART COMPOSITIONS: *You Don't Mess Around with Jim* (1972) US#8, *Operator (That's Not the Way It Feels)* (1972) US#17, *One Less Set of Footprints* (1973) US#37, *Bad, Bad Leroy Brown* (1973) g US#1, *Time in a Bottle* (1973) g US#1, *It Doesn't Have to Be That Way* (1974) US#64, *I'll Have to Say I Love You in a Song* (1974) C&W#68 US#9, *Workin' at the Car Wash Blues* (1974) US#32, *Mississippi Lady* (1976) US#110. ALBUMS: **Approaching Day** with Ingrid Croce (1965, Capitol); **You Don't Mess Around with Jim** (1972) g US#1, **Life and Times** (1973) g US#7, **I Got a Name** (1973, all ABC) g US#2. COMPILATIONS: **Photographs and Memories** (1974, ABC) p US#2; **The Faces I've Been** (1975) US#87, **Time in a Bottle-Jim Croce's Greatest Love Songs** (1977, both Lifesong) US#170; **Live-The Final Tour** (1990, Saga); **The 50th Anniversary Collection** (1992, Saja/Atlantic). HIT VERSIONS: *Bad, Bad Leroy Brown* Anthony Armstrong Jones (1973) C&W#33/Frank Sinatra (1974) US#83; *Lover's Cross* Melanie (1974) US#109, *Workin' at the Car Wash Blues* Tony Booth (1974) C&W#27/Jerry Reed (1980) C&W#36; *You Don't Mess Around with Jim* Bobby Bond (1972) C&W#66.

224. CRONIN, Kevin (b. October 6, 1951, Evanston, IL) Rock guitarist and vocalist. The lead vocalist and principal songwriter in the multi-million selling rock group R.E.O. Speedwagon. CHART COMPOSITIONS: *Roll with the Changes* (1978) US#58, *Time for Me to Fly* (1980) US#56, re-issued (1980) US#77; *Keep on Loving You* (1980) p US#1 UK#7, *Don't Let Him Go* (1981) US#24, *Keep the Fire Burnin'* (1982) US#7, *Sweet Time* (1982) US#26, *Can't Fight This Feeling* (1985) p R&B#89 US#1 UK#16, *Live Every Moment* (1985) US#34, *That Ain't Love* (1987) US#16, *In My Dreams* [ii] (1987) US#19, *Here with Me* [i] (1988) US#20. ALBUMS: **R.E.O. T.W.O.** (1972), **R.E.O.** (1976) US#159, **Live/You Get What You Play For** (1977) p US#72, **You Can Tune a Piano, But You Can't Tuna Fish** (1978) p US#29, **Nine Lives** (1979) g US#33, **Hi Infidelity** (1981) p US#1 UK#6, **Good Trouble** (1982) p US#7 UK#29, **Wheels Are Turnin'** (1985) p US#7, **Life as We Know It** (1987) g US#28, **The Earth, a Small Man, His Dog and a Chicken** (1990, all Epic) US#129; **Building the Bridge** (1996, Essential). COMPILATIONS: **A Decade of Rock 'n' Roll, 1970 to 1980** (1980) p US#55, **The Hits** (1988, both Epic) p US#61. Co-writers: [i] R. Braun, [ii] Tom Kelly.

225. CROPPER, Steve (b. October 21, 1941, Willow Springs, MO) Rock guitarist and producer. An influential country-blues guitar stylist who played on many Stax and Atlantic hits during the 1960s. Cropper elevated the role of the unknown session player to that of fully credited sideman, and he was also Otis Redding's main co-writer. Cropper's inventive, blues based R&B-country guitar riffs were equalled only by Chuck Berry's during the 1960s. After studying engineering at Memphis State University, Cropper worked in a grocery store while learning the guitar and listening to rural blues and country music. He played in various R&B bands before forming the Royal Spades, which became the Mar-Keys, and scored a million seller with *Last Night* (1961) R&B#2 US#3. After quitting college, Cropper toured extensively with the group before becoming a member of the Stax in-house band alongside the organist Booker T. Jones. The group, Booker T. and the MG's, became the most famous session band in the world, its first hit single being little more than an after-hours studio jam titled *Behave Yourself* [ii] (1962), which was promptly flipped by many radio stations for the altogether more dynamic B-side, the million selling *Green Onions* [iii]. CHART COMPOSITIONS: *Green Onions* [iii] (1962) g R&B#1 US#3, re-issued (1979) UK#7; *Chinese Checkers* [iii] (1962) US#78, *Jellybread* [iii] (1962) US#82, *Mo' Onions* [iii] (1964) US#97, *Soul Dressing* [ii] (1964) US#95, *Tic Tac Toe* [ii] (1964) US#109, *Bootleg* [ii] (1965) R&B#10 US#58, *My Sweet Potato* [ii] (1966) R&B#18 US#85, *Booker-Loo* [ii] (1966) R&B#37, *Slim Jenkins' Place* [ii] (1967) US#70, *Hip Hug-Her* [ii] (1967) R&B#6 US#37, *Soul Limbo* [ii] (1968) R&B#7 US#17 UK#30, *Time Is Tight* [ii] (1969) R&B#7 US#6 UK#4, *Melting Pot* [ii] (1971) R&B#21 US#45, *Sugarcane* [ii] (1973) R&B#67. ALBUMS: **Green Onions** (1962) US#33 UK#11, **Soul Dressing** (1964), **Hip Hug-Her** (1967) US#35, **Back to Back** (1967) US#98, **Doin' Our Thing** (1968) US#176, **Uptight** ost (1968) US#98, **Soul Limbo** (1968) US#127, **The Booker T. Set** (1969) US#53, **McLemore Avenue** (1970) US#107 UK#70, **Melting Pot** (1971) US#43, **Memphis Sound** (1975), **Union Extended** (1976, all Stax); **That's the Way It Should Be** (1994, Columbia). COMPILATIONS: **Best of Booker T. and the MG's** (1968, Atlantic) US#167; **Greatest Hits** (1970, Stax) US#132; **And Now** (1992, Rhino). After leaving Stax in 1970, Cropper opened his own TMI studio, where he worked with artists ranging from Rod Stewart to Jose Feliciano. During the 1980s, he starred alongside John Belushi and Dan Ackroyd in the movie "The Blues Brothers," and subsequently played in the Blues Brothers touring band, featuring on the albums **Briefcase Full of Blues** (1978) p US#1, **The Blues Brothers** (1980) g US#13, **Made in America** (1980) US#49, and **Best of the Blues**

Brothers (1982, all Atlantic) US#143. Cropper has also infrequently recorded as a solo artist. ALBUMS: **Jammed Together** with Albert King and Pop Staples (1969) US#171, **With a Little Help from My Friends** (1970, both Stax); **Playin' My Thang** (1981), **Night After Night** (1982, both MCA). HIT VERSIONS: *Don't Fight It* [iv] Wilson Pickett (1965) R&B#4 US#53 UK#29, *Green Onions* [iii] Dick Hyman (1969) US#109, *Hole in the Wall* Packers (1965) R&B#5 US#43, *I Want Someone* Mad Lads (1966) R&B#10 US#74, *In the Midnight Hour* [iv] Wilson Pickett (1965) R&B#1 US#21 UK#12, new version (1988) UK#62/Little Mac & the Boss Sounds (1965) R&B#37/Kit & the Outlaws (1967) US#131/Messengers (1967) US#116/Wanted (1967) US#118/Mirettes (1968) R&B#18 US#45/Cross Country (1973) US#30/Samantha Sang (1979) US#88/Roxy Music (1980) US#106/Razzy Bailey (1984) C&W#14; *Knucklehead* Bar-Kays (1967) R&B#28 US#76, *Ninety-Nine and a Half Won't Do* [iv] Wilson Pickett (1966) R&B#13 US#53/Trammps (1976) R&B#76 US#105; *Puff of Smoke* Roy Head (1971) US#96, *634 5789* [iv] Wilson Picket (1966) R&B#1 US#13 UK#36/Jimmie Peters (1978) C&W#75/Johnny Van Zandt Band (1980) US#105/Marlow Tackett (1982) C&W#54; *Union Man* [i] Cate Brothers (1976) R&B#96 US#24. Co-writers: [i] Earl Cate/Ernie Cate, [ii] Donald V. Dunn (b. November 24, 1941, Memphis, TN)/Al Jackson (b. November 27, 1935, Memphis, TN)/Booker T. Jones, [iii] Al Jackson/Booker T. Jones/Lewis Steinberg (b. September 13, 1933, Memphis, TN), [iv] Wilson Pickett (b. March 19. 1941, Prattville, AL). (*See also under* William BELL, Don COVAY, Eddie FLOYD, Booker T. JONES, Otis REDDING.)

226. CROSBY, David (b. David Van Cortland, August 14, 1941, Los Angeles, CA) Rock guitarist and vocalist. One of the finest harmony singers in popular music, Crosby was a member of two of the most influential groups of the 1960s, the Byrds and Crosby, Stills and Nash. Originally a singer in Les Baxter's Balladeers, Crosby co-founded the Byrds in 1964. After composing the hit *Lady Friend* (1967) US#82, he quit when his composition *Triad* was rejected by the group, although it was later recorded by Jefferson Airplane. In 1969, just in time to perform at the Woodstock festival, Crosby formed a harmony trio with Stephen Stills and Graham Nash. ALBUMS: **Crosby, Stills and Nash** (1969) g US#6 UK#25, **Deja Vu**** (1970) p US#1 UK#5, **4 Way Street**** (1971) p US#1 UK#5, **CSN** (1977) p US#2 UK#23, **American Dream**** (1988) p US#16, **Daylight Again** (1982) p US#8, **Allies** (1983) US#43, **Live It Up** (1990) US#57, **After the Storm** (1994, all Atlantic) US#98. COMPILATIONS: **So Far****

(1974) p US#1 UK#25, **Replay** (1981) US#122, **CSN**** (1992, all Atlantic) g US#109. Crosby has recorded as a solo artist, but he spent much of the 1980s fighting a drug dependency, which ultimately earned him a period in jail, that he says saved his life. CHART COMPOSITIONS: *Music Is Love* (1971) US#95, *Carry Me** (1975) US#52, *Spotlight** (1976) US#109, *Hero* [i] with Phil Collins (1993) US#44 UK#56. ALBUMS: **If I Could Only Remember My Name** (1971) g US#12 UK#12, **Graham Nash/David Crosby*** (1972, both Atlantic) g US#4; **Wind on the Water*** (1975) g US#6, **Whistling Down the Wire*** (1976) g US#26, **Live*** (1977, all ABC) US#52; **Oh, Yes I Can** (1989, A&M) US#104; **Thousand Roads** (1993) US#133, **It's All Coming Back to Me Now** (1995, both Atlantic). COMPILATION: **Best of Graham Nash and David Crosby*** (1978, ABC) US#150. With: * Graham Nash, ** Neil Young. Co-writer: [i] Phil Collins. (*See also under* Gene CLARK, Chris HILLMAN, Roger McGUINN, Graham NASH, Stephen STILLS, Neil YOUNG.)

227. CROSS, Christopher (b. Christopher Geppert, May 3, 1951, San Antonio, TX) Pop guitarist, producer and vocalist. A singer-songwriter whose meteoric rise to fame was as fast going down as it was coming up. The son of a professional musician, Cross learned the drums and guitar in his teens before joining the group Flash in 1971. Two years later, Cross began writing songs and cutting demos, which resulted in his four million selling eponymous debut album in 1980. He won an Oscar in 1981 for his film tune *Arthur's Theme (Best That You Can Do)* [i], but by his album **Rendezvous** (1992), his recordings were only being released in Japan. CHART COMPOSITIONS: *Ride Like the Wind* (1980) US#2 UK#69, *Sailing* (1980) US#1 UK#48, *Never Be the Same* (1980) US#15, *Say You'll Be Mine* (1981) US#20, *Arthur's Theme (Best That You Can Do)* [i] (1981) g US#1 UK#56, re-issued (1982) UK#7; *All Right* (1983) US#12 UK#51, *No Time for Talk* (1983) US#33, *Think of Laura* (1983) US#9, *A Chance for Heaven* [ii] (1983) US#76, *Charm the Snake* [iii] (1988) US#68. ALBUMS: **Christopher Cross** (1980) p US#6 UK#14, **Another Page** (1983) g US#11 UK#4, **Every Turn of the World** (1985, all Warner Brothers) US#127; **Back of My Mind** (1988, Reprise); **Rendezvous** (1992, Ariola); **Window** (1995, Rhythm Safari). COMPILATION: **Best of Christopher Cross** (1996, Warner Brothers). HIT VERSIONS: *Ride Like the Wind* Saxon (1988) UK#52/ East Side Beat (1991) UK#3. Co-writers: [i] Peter Allen/Burt Bacharach/Carol Bayer Sager, [ii] Burt Bacharach/Carol Bayer Sager, [iii] Michael Omartian.

228. CROWELL, Rodney (b. August 7,

1950, Houston, TX) C&W guitarist, producer and vocalist. A country singer-songwriter with a roots feel and a fine tenor, very much influenced by Roy Orbison. After starting out as a schoolboy drummer, Crowell played in a high school band the Arbitrators in 1965, before learning the guitar and moving to Nashville, where, in 1972 he became a staff writer for Jerry Reed. In 1975, Crowell joined Emmylou Harris' backing group the Hot Band, as a member of which he became one of her regular tunesmiths. He left in 1978 for a solo career, and in 1979 married Johnny Cash's daughter Roseanne Cash, for, and with whom, he wrote and produced a series of country hits. Crowell has described songwriting as, "my form of keeping a journal." CHART COMPOSITIONS: *Ashes By Now* (1980) C&W#78 US#37, *Stars on the Water* (1981) C&W#30 US#105, *Victim or a Fool* (1982) C&W#34, *When I'm Free Again* (1986) C&W#38, *She Loves the Jerk* (1987) C&W#71, *Looking for You* (1987) C&W#59, *It's Such a Small World* with Roseanne Cash (1988) C&W#1, *I Couldn't Leave You If I Tried* (1988) C&W#1, *She's Crazy for Leavin'* (1988) C&W#1, *After All This Time* (1989) C&W#1, *Above and Beyond* (1989) C&W#1, *Lovin' All Night* (1993) C&W#10, *What Kind of Love* [i] (1993) C&W#22, *Let the Picture Paint Itself* (1994) C&W#60. ALBUMS: **Ain't Living Long Like This** (1978), **But What Will the Neighbors Think** (1980) US#155, **Rodney Crowell** (1981, all Warner Brothers) US#105; **Street Language** (1986) US#177, **Keys to the Highway** (1988) US#180, **Diamonds and Dirt** (1989), **Life Is Messy** (1992, all Columbia) US#155; **Jewel of the South** (1995), **Let the Picture Paint Itself** (1994, both MCA). COMPILATIONS: **Best of Rodney Crowell** (1983), **The Rodney Crowell Collection** (1989, both Warner Brothers); **Greatest Hits** (1993, Columbia). HIT VERSIONS: *Ain't No Money* Roseanne Cash (1982) C&W#4, *American Dream, An* [iii] Nitty Gritty Dirt Band (1980) C&W#58 US#13, *Angel Eyes* Willie Willoughby (1984) C&W#82, *Couldn't Do Nothing Right* Roseanne Cash (1980) C&W#15, *Even Cowgirls Get the Blues* La Costa (1978) C&W#79/Lynn Anderson (1980) C&W#26/Johnny Cash & Waylon Jennings (1986) C&W#35; *I Ain't Living Long Like This* Waylon Jennings (1980) C&W#1, *I Don't Have to Crawl* Emmylou Harris (1981) C&W#44 US#106, *Leaving Louisiana in the Broad Daylight* Oak Ridge Boys (1979) C&W#1, *No Memories Hangin' 'Round* Rosanne Cash & Bobby Bare (1979) C&W#17, *Shame on the Moon* Bob Seger (1983) C&W#15 US#2, *Somewhere Tonight* [i] Highway 101 (1987) C&W#1, *Take Me, Take Me* Roseanne Cash (1980) C&W#25, *Til I Gain Control Again* Bobby Bare (1979) C&W#42/Crystal Gayle (1982) C&W#1. Co-writers: [i] Harlan Howard, [ii] Will Jennings/Roy Orbison, [iii] Bob McDill.

229. CRUDUP, Arthur "Big Boy" (b. August 24, 1905, Forest, MI; d. March 28, 1974, Nassawadox, VA) R&B guitarist and vocalist. A 1940s R&B artist who was a significant influence on the early style of Elvis Presley. Crudup first sang gospel in church, and later with the Harmonizing Four, before relocating to Chicago in 1934, where he became a blues singer. In 1939, he recorded for the Bluebird label, and from 1941 for RCA Victor. Crudup also recorded as Elmore Jones and Percy Crudup, before retiring from music in 1954 to become a potato farmer, although he made several comebacks during the 1960s. In 1973, he was the subject of the television biography "Arthur Crudup: Born in the Blues." His compositions have been recorded by B.B. King, Brownie McGhee and Eric Clapton. Crudup died in 1974 from a heart attack. CHART COMPOSITIONS: *Rock Me, Mama* (1945) R&B#3, *Who's Been Foolin' You* (1945) R&B#5, *Keep Your Arms Around Me* (1945) R&B#3, *So Glad You're Mine* (1946) R&B#3, *Ethel Mae* (1946) R&B#4, *I'm Gonna Dig Myself a Hole* (1951) R&B#9. ALBUMS: **Arthur Big Boy Crudup** (1961, Fire); **Look on Yonder's Wall** (1968, Delmark); **Mean Ole Frisco** (1969, Trip); **Crudup's Mood** (1970, Delmark); **The Father of Rock 'n' Roll** (1971, RCA); **Roebuck Man** (1973, Liberty); **That's All Right, Mama** (1976, DJM); **Harpin' on It** (1977, Polydor); **Big Boy Crudup and Lightnin' Hopkins** (1982), **Star Bootlegger** (1983), **I'm in the Mood** (1983, all Krazy Kat); **Crudup's Rockin'** (1985, RCA); **Shout Sister Shout** (1987, Bullwhip); **Give Me a 32-20** (1988, Crown Prince); **That's All Right, Mama** (1992, Bluebird). HIT VERSIONS: *That's All Right, Mama* Marty Robbins (1955) C&W#7/Slade (1977) UK#32; *My Baby Left Me* Elvis Presley (1956) C&W#13 US#31, also on B-side of *I Want You, I Need You, I Love You* (1956) R&B#3 US#1 UK#14/ Dave Berry (1964) UK#13/Slade (1977) UK#32.

230. CUMMINGS, Burton (b. December 31, 1947, Winnipeg, Canada) Rock keyboard player and vocalist. The lyricist and lead singer in the Canadian group the Guess Who, in which he often co-composed with Randy Bachman. CHART COMPOSITIONS: *Share the Land* (1970) US#10, *Rain Dance* [iii] (1971) US#19, *Star Baby* (1974) US#39, *Clap for the Wolfman* [ii] (1974) US#6. ALBUMS: **Wheatfield Soul** (1968) US#45, **Canned Wheat Packed By the Guess Who** (1969) US#91, **American Woman** (1970) g US#9, **Share the Land** (1970) g US#14, **So Long, Bannatyne** (1971) US#52, **Rockin'** (1972) US#79, **Live at the Paramount (Seattle)** (1972) US#39, **Artificial Paradise** (1973) US#112, **#10** (1973) US#155, **Road Food** (1974) US#60, **Flavors** (1975) US#48, **Power in the Music**

(1975, all RCA) US#87. COMPILATIONS: **Best of the Guess Who** (1971) g US#12, **The Greatest of the Guess Who** (1977) US#173, **Best of the Guess Who, Volume II** (1974, all RCA) US#186. In 1975, Cummings embarked on an initially successful solo career. CHART COMPOSITIONS: *Stand Tall* g (1977) US#10, *I'm Scared* (1977) US#61, *My Own Way to Rock* (1977) US#74, *Takes a Fool to Love a Fool* (1979) C&W#33, *You Saved My Soul* (1981) US#37. ALBUMS: **Burton Cummings** (1976) US#30, **My Own Way to Rock** (1977, both Portrait) US#51; **Woman in Love** (1980, Epic); **Up Close and Alone** (1996, MCA). HIT VERSION: *Who Listens to the Radio* [i] Sports (1979) US#45. Co-writers: [i] Pendlebury, [ii] Bill Wallace/Kurt Winter, [iii] Kurt Winter. (*See also under* Randy BACHMAN.)

231. CURRIE, Justin (b. December 11, 1964, Glasgow, Scotland) Pop bassist and vocalist. The lead singer and principal songwriter in the British group Del Amitri. CHART COMPOSITIONS: *Kiss This Thing Goodbye* (1989) US#35 UK#43, *Nothing Ever Happens* (1990) UK#11, *Move Away Jimmy Blue* (1990) UK#36, *Spit in the Rain* (1990) UK#21, *Always the Last to Know* (1992) US#30 UK#13, *Be My Downfall* (1992) UK#30, *Just Like a Man* (1992) UK#25, *When You Were Young* (1993) UK#20, *Here and Now* (1995) UK#25, *Driving with Brakes On* (1995) UK#18, *Roll to Me* (1995) US#10 UK#22, *Tell Her This* (1995) US#32. ALBUMS: **Del Amitri** (1985, Big Star); **Waking Hours** (1990) US#95 UK#6, **Change Everything** (1992) US#178 UK#2, **Twisted** (1995) US#170 UK#3, **Some Other Suckers Parade** (1997, all A&M).

232. CURTIS, Ian (b. July 15, 1956; d. May 17, 1980, both Macclesfield, England) Rock vocalist. The angst-laden lyricist in the highly regarded British indie group Joy Division. Curtis, in all probability suffered from manic depression, and he committed suicide in 1980. COMPOSITIONS: *Love Will Tear Us Apart* (1980) UK#13, re-mixed (1995) UK#19; *Atmosphere* (1988) UK#34. ALBUMS: **Unknown Pleasures** (1979) UK#71, **Closer** (1980) UK#6, **Still** (1981, all Factory) UK#5; **The Peel Sessions** (1986, Strange Fruit); **1977–1980, Substance** (1988, Factory) US#146 UK#7; **Permanent: Joy Division, 1995** (1995, London) UK#16.

233. CURTIS, Mann Pop lyricist. A pop journeyman who often translated European hits for the British and American markets. HIT VERSIONS: *Anema E Core* [i] Eddie Fisher (1954) US#21, *Choo'n Gum* [iv] Teresa Brewer (1950) US#17, *Fooled* [v] Perry Como (1955) US#20, *I Like It* [iv] Jane Turzy (1951) US#20, *Jones Boy, The* [iv]

Mills Brothers (1954) US#15, *Mais Oui* [ii] Bob Beckham (1960) US#105/King Brothers (1960) UK#16; *My Dreams Are Getting Better All the Time* [iv] Les Brown (1945) US#1/Johnny Long (1945) US#3/Phil Moore Four (1945) US#3; *Play Me Hearts and Flowers (I Wanna Cry)* [iii] Johnny Desmond (1955) US#6, *Pretty Kitty Blue Eyes* [iv] Merry Macs (1944) US#7, *Whole World Is Singing My Song, The* [iv] Les Brown (1946) US#6/Jimmy Dorsey (1946) US#12. Co-writers: [i] Harry Akst/Salve d'Esposito, [ii] Carlo Donida/Pinchi, [iii] Sanford Green, [iv] Vic Mizzy, [v] Doris Tauber. (*See also under* Gilbert BECAUD, Bobby DARIN, Al HOFFMAN.)

234. CURTIS, Sonny (b. May 9, 1937, Meadow, TX) C&W guitarist and vocalist. The composer of a handful of pop classics, and an original member of the legendary Crickets, who has remained a sideman on the fringes of country music for over thirty years. Curtis learned the guitar and fiddle in his teens, and listened avidly to music on the radio. In 1956, he joined Buddy Holly and the Two Tunes, which recorded a single as Buddy Holly and the Three Tunes, *Blue Days, Black Nights*. During his time with Holly, Curtis played on the original sessions for the album **That'll Be the Day** (1958, Decca) UK#5. He later joined Slim Whitman's backing band, and performed in the "Phillip Morris Country Music Show." After Holly's death, Curtis rejoined the Crickets for a handful of British hits between 1960–1964, including his compositions *When You Ask About Love* [i] (1960) UK#27 and *My Little Girl* (1963) US#134 UK#17. ALBUMS: **In Style with the Crickets** (1960, Coral) UK#13; **Bobby Vee Meets the Crickets** (1962) US#42 UK#2, **Just for Fun** ost (1963), **The Crickets-A Collection** (1965, all Liberty); **Rockin' '50s Rock 'n' Roll** (1971, Barnaby); **Rock Reflections** (1971, Sunset); **Bubblegum, Pop, Ballads and Boogie** (1973, Philips); **Remnants** (1973), **A Long Way from Lubbock** (1974, both Mercury); **The Sound of the Crickets** (1975, Brunswick); **The Complete Crickets** (1984, Charly); **The Crickets Style** (1980, See for Miles); **Three Piece** (1988, Rollercoaster); **Rock 'n' Roll Masters** (1988), **The Liberty Years** (1991, both EMI); **Too Much Monday Morning** (1997, Carlton). Curtis has also recorded as a solo artist since the early 1950s. CHART COMPOSITIONS: *The Best Way to Hold a Girl* (1953) US#28, *My Way of Life* (1966) C&W#49 US#134, *I Wanna Go Bummin' Around* (1967) C&W#50, *Atlanta, Georgia, Stray* (1968) C&W#36 US#120, *The Straight Life* (1968) C&W#45, *The Cowboy Singer* (1979) C&W#77, *Do You Remember Roll Over Beethoven* (1980) C&W#86, *The Real Buddy Holly Story* (1980) C&W#38, *Love*

Is All Around (1980) C&W#29, *Good Ol' Girls* (1981) C&W#15, *Married Women* (1981) C&W#33, *Now I've Got a Heart of Gold* (1986) C&W#69. ALBUMS: **Beatles Hits-Flamenco Style** (1965, Imperial); **First of Sonny Curtis** (1968), **Sonny Curtis** (1969, both Viva); **Sonny Curtis** (1979), **Love Is All Around** (1980, both Elektra); **Spectrum** (1987, Colt); **Rollin'** (1989, Elektra); **No Stranger to the Rain** (1990, Ritz). HIT VERSIONS: *Atlanta, Georgia, Stray* Kenny Price (1969) C&W#62, *Fool Never Learns, A* Andy Williams (1964) US#13 UK#40, *I Fought the Law* Bobby Fuller Four (1966) US#9 UK#33/Sam Neely (1975) C&W#61 US#54/Hank Williams, Jr., (1978) C&W#15/Clash (1988) UK#29, also on *The Cost of Living EP* (1979) UK#22/Nitty Gritty Dirt Band (1992) C&W#66; *I Think I'm in Love* Keith Stegall (1986) C&W#36, *I'm No Stranger to the Rain* Keith Whitely (1989) C&W#1, *I've Been Looking* Nitty Gritty Dirt Band (1988) C&W#2, *Lights of L.A.* Shaun Nielsen (1980) C&W#88, *Love's Made a Fool of You* Bobby Fuller Four (1965) US#26, *More Than I Can Say* [i] Leo Sayer (1980) US#2 UK#2, *Reminiscing* Buddy Holly (1962) UK#17/Linda Nail (1983) C&W#80; *Someday* Webb Pierce (1957) C&W#12, *Straight Life, The* Bobby Goldsboro (1968) US#36, *Tennessee* Jimmy Martin (1968) C&W#72/Ray Sanders (1978) C&W#91; *Together Alone* [ii] Ogden Harless (1988) C&W#92, *Walk Right Back* Everly Brothers (1961) US#7 UK#1/LaWanda Lindsey (1977) C&W#76/Anne Murray (1978) C&W#4 US#103; *When You Ask About Love* [i] Matchbox (1980) UK#4. Co-writers: [i] Jerry Allison, [ii] Bobby Braddock.

235. DAFFAN, Ted (b. Theron Eugene Daffan, September 21, 1912, Beauregarde Parish, LA) C&W guitarist and vocalist. One of the few honky tonk guitarists to introduce elements of jazz to country music. During the 1940s, Daffan ran an electronic repair shop in Texas, and also played in the swing bands the Blue Ridge Playboys and the Texans. CHART COMPOSITIONS: *No Letter Today* (1944) C&W#2 US#9, *Born to Lose* (1944) C&W#3 US#19, *Look Who's Talkin'* (1944) C&W#4, *Time Won't Heal My Broken Heart* (1945) C&W#6, *You're Breaking My Heart* (1945) C&W#5, *Shadow of My Heart* (1945) C&W#5, *Headin' Down the Wrong Highway* (1945) C&W#2, *Shut the Gate* (1946) C&W#5. HIT VERSIONS: *I'm a Fool to Care* Les Paul & Mary Ford (1954) US#6/Joe Berry (1961) US#24 UK#41/Donny King (1975) C&W#72/Marcia Ball (1978) C&W#91; *I've Got Five Dollars and It's Saturday Night* Faron Young (1956) C&W#4/George & Gene (1965) C&W#16; *Last Ride, The* Hank Snow (1959) C&W#3, *No Letter Today* Ray Charles (1963) US#105, also on B-side of *Take These*

Chains from My Heart (1963) R&B#7 US#8; *Tangled Mind* Hank Snow (1957) C&W#4.

236. DALTON, Lacy J. (b. Jill Byrem, October 13, 1948, Bloomsbury, PA) C&W vocalist. A folk and rock singer who turned to country during the 1980s, and scored over 20 hits between 1979–1988. CHART COMPOSITIONS: *Crazy Blue Eyes* (1979) C&W#17, *Hard Times* (1980) C&W#7, *Takin' It Easy* (1981) C&W#2, *16th Avenue* (1982) C&W#7. ALBUMS: **Lacy J. Dalton** (1979), **Takin' It Easy** (1981), **Can't Run Away from Your Heart** (1985), **Highway Diner** (1986), **Blue-Eyed Blues** (1987, all Columbia). COMPILATION: **Best of Lacy J. Dalton** (1992, Columbia).

237. DALY, Gary (b. May 5, 1962, Kirkby, England) Pop vocalist, and **LUNDON, Eddie** (b. June 9, 1962, Kirkby, England) Pop guitarist. The songwriting partnership behind the group China Crisis, which enjoyed a run of chart success during the 1980s. CHART COMPOSITIONS: *African and White* (1982) UK#45, *Christian* (1983) UK#12, *Tragedy and Mystery* (1983) UK#46, *Working with Fire and Steel* (1983) UK#48, *Wishful Thinking* (1984) UK#9, *Hanna Hanna* (1984) UK#44, *Black Man Ray* (1985) UK#14, *King in a Catholic Style* (1985) UK#19, *You Did Cut Me* (1985) UK#54, *Arizona Sky* (1986) UK#47, *Best-Kept Secret* (1987) UK#36. ALBUMS: **Difficult Shapes and Passive Rhythms** (1983) UK#21, **Working with Fire and Steel-Possible Pop Songs, Volume 2** (1983) UK#20, **Flaunt the Imperfection** (1985) US#171 UK#9, **What Price Paradise?** (1986) US#114 UK#63, **Diary of a Hollow Horse** (1989, all Virgin) UK#58; **Warped By Success** (1994, Stardumb); **Acoustically Yours** (1995, Telegraph). COMPILATION: **The China Crisis Collection** (1990, Virgin) UK#32; **Wishful Thinking** (1997).

238. DAMMERS, Jerry (b. Gerald Dankin, May 22, 1954, India) Pop keyboard player and producer. A founder member, with the vocalist Terry Hall, of the British ska group the Specials, which was influenced by the Jamaican sound systems and punk rock. In 1979, Dammers created his own 2-Tone label in order to record his group. CHART COMPOSITIONS: *Gangsters* (1979) UK#6, *Too Much Too Young* (1980) UK#1, *Stereotype* [ii] (1980) UK#6, *Do Nothing* [i] (1981) UK#4, *Ghost Town* (1981) UK#1, *Racist Friend* (1983) UK#60, *Nelson Mandela* (1984) UK#9, *What I Like Most About You Is Your Girlfriend* (1984) UK#51. ALBUMS: **The Specials** (1979) US#84 UK#4, **More Specials** (1980) US#98 UK#5, **Dance Craze** ost (1981) UK#5, **In the Studio** (1984, all 2-Tone) UK#34. COMPILA-TIONS: **The Specials Singles** (1991, 2-Tone) UK#10; **Live-Too Much Young** (1992, Receiver); **Live at the Moonlight Club** (1992, Dover). Co-writers: [i] Lynval Golding (b. July 7, 1952, St. Catherine's, Jamaica), [ii] Neville Staples (b. April 11, 1956, Christiana, Jamaica).

239. DANDO, Evan (b. March 4, 1967, Boston, MA) Rock guitarist and vocalist. The principal songwriter and lead singer in the American indie group the Lemonheads. CHART COMPOSITIONS: *It's a Shame About Ray* (1992) UK#70, reissued (1993) UK#31; *Confetti* (1993) UK#44, *It's About Time* (1993) US#56, *Big Gay Heart* (1994) UK#55. ALBUMS: **Hate Your Friends** (1987), **Creator** (1988), **Lick** (1989, all Taang!); **Lovey** (1990), **It's a Shame About Ray** (1992) US#68 UK#33, **Come on Feel the Lemonheads** (1993, both Atlantic) US#56 UK#5.

240. D'ARBY, Terence Trent (b. March 15, 1962, New York, NY) Pop vocalist. An R&B influenced singer-songwriter, who first sang in the funk group Touch, before recording as a solo artist. CHART COMPOSITIONS: *If You Let Me Stay* (1987) R&B#19 US#68 UK#7, *Wishing Well* [i] (1987) R&B#1 US#1 UK#4, *Dance Little Sister* (1987) US#30 UK#20, *Sign Your Name* (1988) R&B#2 US#4 UK#2, *To Know Someone Deeply Is to Know Someone Softly* (1990) UK#55, *Do You Love Me Like You Say?* (1993) R&B#120 UK#14, *Delicate* (1993) US#74 UK#14, *She Kissed Me* (1993) UK#16, *Let Her Down Easy* (1993) US#111 UK#18, *Holding on to You* (1995) UK#20, *Vibrator* (1995) UK#57. ALBUMS: **Introducing the Hardline According to Terence Trent D'Arby** (1987) p US#4 UK#1, **Neither Fish nor Flesh** (1989) US#61 UK#12, **Symphony or Damn: Exploring the Tension Inside the Sweetness** (1993) US#119 UK#4, **Terence Trent D'Arby's Vibrator** (1995, all Columbia) US#178 UK#11. Co-writer: [i] Shaun Oliver.

241. DARIN, Bobby (b. Walden Robert Cassotto, May 14, 1936, New York, NY; d. December 20, 1973, Los Angeles, CA) Pop multi-instrumentalist and vocalist. A versatile singer and actor who was one of the few 1950s teen idols to remain successful during the rock and roll era. Darin was a regular chart artist for much of his career, and wrote a considerable amount of his own material, before dying after heart surgery at the age of thirty-seven. CHART COMPOSITIONS: *Splish Splash* [iii] (1958) C&W#14 R&B#1 US#3 UK#18, *Early in the Morning/Now We're One* (1958) R&B#8 US#24, *Queen of the Hop* [ii] (1958) R&B#6 US#9 UK#24, *Dream Lover* (1959) R&B#4 US#2 UK#1, *I'll Be*

There (1960) US#79, *Multiplication* (1961) US#30 UK#5, *Things* (1962) US#3 UK#2, *You're the Reason I'm Living* (1963) R&B#9 US#3, *18 Yellow Roses* (1963) R&B#28 US#10, *Long Line Rider* (1969) US#79. ALBUMS: **That's All** (1959) US#7 UK#15, **This Is Bobby Darin** (1960) US#6 UK#4, **At the Copa** (1960) US#9, **Love Swings** (1961) US#92, **Twist with Bobby Darin** (1962) US#48, **Bobby Darin Sings Ray Charles** (1962, all Atco) US#96; **Oh! Look at Me Now** (1962) US#100, **You're the Reason I'm Living** (1963) US#43, **18 Yellow Roses** (1963) US#98, **From Hello Dolly to Goodbye Charlie** (1964) US#107, **Venice Blue** (1965, all Capitol) US#132; **If I Were a Carpenter** (1967, Atlantic) US#142; **Born Walden Robert Cassotto** (1969, Direction). COMPILATIONS: **The Bobby Darin Story** (1961) US#18, **Things and Other Things** (1962, both Atco) US#45; **The Legend of Bobby Darin-His Greatest Hits** (1985, Stylus) UK#39; **As Long as I'm Singing-The Bobby Darin Collection** (1995, Rhino). HIT VERSIONS: *Dream Lover* Paris Sisters (1964) US#91/Billy "Crash" Craddock (1971) C&W#5/Glen Campbell & Tanya Tucker (1980) C&W#59; *Early in the Morning* Rinky-Dinks (1958) US#24/Buddy Holly (1958) US#32 UK#17/Mac Curtis (1970) C&W#35; *I'll Be There* Gerry & the Pacemakers (1965) US#14 UK#15/Cissy Houston (1970) R&B#45 US#125; *Sing a Simple Song of Freedom* Tim Hardin (1969) US#50/Spirit of Us (1970) US#106; *Splish Splash* [iii] Charlie Drake (1958) UK#7, *Things* Buddy Alan (1972) C&W#49/Ronnie Dove (1975) C&W#25/Anne Murray (1976) C&W#22 US#89, *This Little Girl's Gone Rockin'* [i] Ruth Brown (1958) US#24, *You Just Don't Know* Mary K. Miller (1977) C&W#54, *You're the Reason I'm Living* Lamar Morris (1971) C&W#59/Price Mitchell (1976) C&W#75. Co-writers: [i] Mann Curtis, [ii] Woody Harris, [iii] Jean Murray.

242. DARNELL, August (b. Thomas August Darnell Browder, August 12, 1950, Montreal, Canada) Pop vocalist and producer. An individualistic performer who enjoyed chart success during the early 1980s with his group Kid Creole and the Coconuts. Darnell grew up in the Bronx, New York, where he formed such groups as the Strangers and the In-Laws, before joining the esoteric Dr. Buzzard's Original Savannah Band, which charted with *Se Si Bon* (1976) R&B#31 US#27. ALBUMS: **Dr. Buzzard's Original Savannah Band** (1976) g US#22, **Dr. Buzzard's Original Savannah Band Meets King Penett** (1978, both RCA) US#36; **James Monroe High School Presents DBOSB Goes to Washington** (1980, Elektra). In 1980, Darnell formed Kid Creole and the Coconuts, blending sharp suits, 1940s big band stylings and Caribbean rhythms

for a series of novelty hits. CHART COMPOSITIONS: *I'm a Wonderful Thing (Baby)* [ii] (1982) R&B#44 UK#4, *Stool Pigeon* (1982) UK#7, *Annie, I'm Not Your Daddy* (1982) UK#2, *Christmas at B'Dilly Bay EP* (1982) UK#29, *There's Something Wrong with Paradise* (1983) UK#35, *(Welcome to) The Lifeboat Party* (1983) UK#49, *My Male Curiosity* (1984) US#110. ALBUMS: **Off the Coast of Me** (1980), **Tropical Gangsters** (1982) UK#3, **Fresh Fruit in Foreign Places** (1982, all Sire) US#180 UK#99; **Doppelganger** (1983, Island) UK#21; **In Praise of Older Women...and Other Crimes** (1985), **I, Too, Have Seen the Woods** (1987, both Sire). COMPILATIONS: **Wise Guy** (1982, Sire) US#145; **Cre-Ole** (1984, Island) UK#21. HIT VERSIONS: *There But for the Grace of God Go I* [i] Machine (1979) R&B#91 US#77. Co-writers: [i] K. Nance, [ii] Peter Schott.

243. DAVENPORT, Cow Cow (b. Charles Davenport, April 26, 1895, Anniston, AL; d. December 1956, Cleveland, OH) Pop pianist and vocalist. A pioneer of boogie woogie who toured with a carnival troupe in the early 1910s, before recording for a variety of record labels. ALBUM: **Cow Cow Davenport, 1925–1930** (1979, Magpie). HIT VERSIONS: *Cow Cow Blues* Bob Crosby (1941) US#23/Freddie Slack & Ella Mae Morse as *Cow Cow Boogie* (1942) US#9/Ella Fitzgerald & the Ink Spots (1944) R&B#1 US#10; *You Rascal You* Louis Armstrong (1931) US#13/Cab Calloway (1931) US#13/Red Nichols (1931) US#17/Mills Brothers (1932) US#3.

244. DAVID, Hal (b. May 25, 1921, New York, NY) Pop lyricist and producer. A versatile and evocative lyricist, best known for his work with Burt Bacharach, who once admitted to having agonized over a single line for several weeks. The younger brother of the late Mack David, Hal first began writing lyrics while serving in the U.S. Army, scoring his first success with *Four Winds and Seven Seas* [viii] by Sammy Kaye (1949). HIT VERSIONS: *American Beauty Rose* [i] Eddy Howard (1950) US#21/Frank Sinatra (1950) US#26; *Bell Bottom Blues* [ii] Alma Cogan (1954) UK#4/Teresa Brewer (1954) US#17; *Broken-Hearted Melody* [iv] Sarah Vaughan (1959) R&B#5 US#7 UK#7, *Four Winds and the Seven Seas* [viii] Vic Damone (1949) US#16/Herb Jeffries (1949) US#18/Sammy Kaye (1949) US#3/Guy Lombardo (1949) US#19/Mel Torme (1949) US#10; *I Never Said I Love You* [vi] Orsa Lia (1979) US#84, *It Only Took a Minute* [v] Joe Brown (1962) UK#6, *It Was Almost Like a Song* [vi] Ronnie Milsap (1977) C&W#1 US#16, *Johnny Get Angry* [iv] Carol Deane (1962) UK#32/Joanie Sommers (1962) US#7; *Johnny Zero*

[vii] Song Spinners (1943) US#4, *No Regrets* [iii] Shirley Bassey (1965) UK#39, *You'll Answer to Me* [iv] Patti Page (1961) US#46/Cleo Laine (1961) UK#5. Co-writers: [i] Arthur Altman/Redd Evans, [ii] Leon Carr, [iii] Charles Dumont/Michel Vaucaire, [iv] Sherman Edwards, [v] Mort Garson, [vi] Archie Jordan, [vii] Vee Lawnhurst, [viii] Don Rodney. (*See also under* Burt BACHARACH, Albert HAMMOND, Lee POCKRISS.)

245. DAVID, Mack (b. July 5, 1912, New York, NY; d. December 30, 1993, Rancho Mirage, CA) Pop lyricist. The older brother of the lyricist Hal David, who collaborated with dozens of composers after the 1950s. Although principally a lyricist, David also composed some of his songs in their entirety. At the time of his death from a heart attack in 1993, he had co-written over one thousand songs, including the television themes "77 Sunset Strip," "Hawaiian Eye" and "Surfside 6." HIT VERSIONS: *At the Candlelight Cafe* Gordon MacRae (1948) US#20/Dinah Shore (1947) US#24; *Bird Man, The* [i] Highwaymen (1962) UK#64, *Cherry Pink and Apple Blossom White* Eddie Calvert (1955) UK#1/ Alan Dale (1955) US#14/Perez Prado (1955) US#1 UK#1/Modern Romance (1982) UK#15/Joe Cain & the Red Parrot Orchestra in *Perez Prado-Tito Puente Latin Medley* (1983) R&B#69; *Diamond Head* [xiv] Ventures (1965) US#70, *Falling Leaves* [iii] Glenn Miller (1940) US#9, *Hush, Hush, Sweet Charlotte* [iv] Patti Page (1965) US#8, *I Don't Care If the Sun Don't Shine* Patti Page (1950) US#8/Elvis Presley (1956) US#74 UK#23; *It Only Hurts for a Little While* [xii] Ames Brothers (1956) US#11/Margo Smith (1978) C&W#1; *La Vie En Rose* [viii] Louis Armstrong (1950) US#28/Bing Crosby (1950) US#13/Ralph Flanagan (1950) US#27/Tony Martin (1950) US#9/ Edith Piaf (1950) US#23/Paul Weston (1950) US#12/ Victor Young (1950) US#27; *Moon Love* [vii] Mildred Bailey (1939) US#14/Al Donohue (1939) US#7/Glenn Miller (1939) US#1/Paul Whiteman (1939) US#8; *My Own True Love (Tara's Theme)* [xiii] Johnny Desmond (1954) US#23/Leroy Holmes (1954) US#21/Jimmy Clanton (1959) US#33/Duprees (1962) US#13/Rose of Romance Orchestra (1982) UK#71; *On the Isle of May* [vi] Connee Boswell (1940) US#3/Dick Jurgens (1940) US#13; *Singing Hills, The* [xi] Bing Crosby (1940) US#3/Dick Todd (1940) US#16/Slim Whitman (1954) C&W#4; *Sinner Kissed an Angel, A* [v] Tommy Dorsey (1941) US#15/Harry James (1941) US#15; *Sunflower* Jack Fulton (1949) US#12/Jack Kilty (1949) US#28/Ray McKinley (1949) US#19/Russ Morgan (1949) US#5/Jack Smith (1949) US#13/Frank Sinatra (1949) US#14; *Sweet Eloise* [x] Glenn Miller (1942) US#7, *Take Me* [ii] Jimmy Dorsey (1942) US#7/Tommy

Dorsey (1942) US#5/Benny Goodman (1942) US#10; *Walk on the Wild Side* [i] Jimmy Smith (1962) R&B#4 US#21. Co-writers: [i] Elmer Bernstein, [ii] Rube Bloom, [iii] Frankie Carle, [iv] Frank DeVol, [v] Ray Joseph, [vi] Andre Kostelanetz (b. December 23, 1901, St. Petersburg, Russia; d. January 13, 1980), [vii] Andre Kostelanetz/Peter Tchaikovsky, [viii] R.S. Louiguy, [ix] R.S. Louiguy/Jacques Larue, [x] Jack Morgan, [xi] Mammy Mysels/Dick Sanford, [xii] Fred Spielman, [xiii] Max Steiner, [xiv] Hugo Winterhalter. (*See also under* Burt BACHARACH, Gilbert BECAUD, Luigi CREATORE and Hugo PERETTI, Al HOFFMAN, Alex KRAMER, Jerry LIVINGSTON, Johnny MERCER, Harry WARREN.)

246. DAVIES, Ray (b. Raymond Douglas Davies, June 21, 1944, London, England) Rock guitarist and vocalist. The lead singer and principal songwriter in the Kinks, one of the most influential British bands of the 1960s, for which Davies has composed material that wryly examines certain fundamental aspects of contemporary British life, while conjuring up elegant memories of a Great Britain long-past, with images of afternoon tea, grim industrial towns and failed social housing experiments. A world in which Davies' hapless characters desperately seek their own identities in the face of monolithic corporations and bureaucracies. His understanding of the English classes, in particular the homogeny of the public school system, and his bucolic pastiches of an idyllic village life filled with loveable eccentrics, are without precedent. A veracious commentator about his times, Davies cornered the market in failed nostalgia, stating that, "My ongoing theme is about control of the masses by the media." The son of a gardener who grew up in the suburbs of Muswell Hill, London, Davies taught himself the guitar at the age of thirteen and listened to such blues artists as Big Bill Broonzy. After working briefly in an architectural office, he attended art school, where he played in the R&B group the Dave Hunt Band. In 1963, he formed the Ravens with his brother, the guitarist Dave Davies, which, at the behest of their manager Larry Page, became the Kinks, because, "it only had five letters and it fitted on the billboards." Whereas the Beatles and the Rolling Stones looked to America for their musical influences, the Kinks remained whole-heartedly British, although they did achieve their first hit with a re-fashioned blues riff *You Really Got Me* (1964), a song that was the progenitor of both heavy metal and punk rock. By *Set Me Free* (1965), Davies' song-writing had already moved away from simple riffs, his ambiguous *See My Friend* being based on an Indian chant, and the delightful *Dedicated Follower of*

Fashion being performed in a ham-vaudeville style. The chromatic *Sunny Afternoon* (1966), chronicled the fate of a bankrupt member of the British upper class, and was the song that took rock and roll as close to the spirit of Noel Coward as it ever would go. The albums **The Kinks Are the Village Green Preservation Society** (1968) and **Arthur or the Decline and Fall of the British Empire** (1969), were droll inquisitions of English customs and manners. Throughout the 1970s, Davies continued to compose brilliantly constructed pop songs, including *Lola*, the tale of a mendacious transvestite, *Sitting in My Hotel, Celluloid Heroes, Misfits*, and *Sitting in the Midday Sun*. In 1985, he recorded the television soundtrack **Return to Waterloo** ost (Arista). CHART COMPOSITIONS: *You Really Got Me* (1964) g US#7 UK#1, re-issued (1983) UK#47; *All Day and All of Night* (1964) US#7 UK#2, *Tired of Waiting for You* (1965) g US#6 UK#1, *Everybody's Gonna Be Happy* (1965) UK#17, *Set Me Free* (1965) US#23 UK#9, *See My Friend* (1965) US#111 UK#10, *Who'll Be the Next in Line* (1965) US#34, *Til the End of the Day* (1965) US#50 UK#8, *A Well Respected Man* (1966) US#13, *Dedicated Follower of Fashion* (1966) US#36 UK#4, *Sunny Afternoon* (1966) US#14 UK#1, *Dead End Street* (1966) US#73 UK#5, *Waterloo Sunset* (1967) UK#2, *Mr. Pleasant* (1967) US#80, *Autumn Almanac* (1967) UK#3, *Wonder Boy* (1968) UK#36, *Days* (1968) UK#12, *Plastic Man* (1969) UK#31, *Victoria* (1970) US#62 UK#33, *Lola* (1970) US#9 UK#2, *Ape Man* (1970) US#45 UK#5, *Supersonic Rocket Ship* (1972) US#111 UK#16, *20th Century Man* (1972) US#106, *One of the Survivors* (1973) US#108, *Sleepwalker* (1977) US#48, *A Rock 'n' Roll Fantasy* (1978) US#30, *(I Wish I Could Fly Like) Superman* (1979) US#41, *Better Things* (1981) US#46 UK#46, *Destroyer* (1981) US#85, *Come Dancing* (1983) US#6 UK#12, *Don't Forget to Dance* (1983) US#29 UK#58, *Think Visual* (1986) US#81. ALBUMS: **The Kinks** (1964) UK#3, **Kinda Kinks** (1965) US#60 UK#3, **The Kinks Kontroversy** (1965) US#95 UK#9, **Face to Face** (1966) US#135 UK#12, **Live at Kelvin Hall** (1968) US#162, **Something Else By the Kinks** (1966) US#153 UK#35, **The Kinks Are the Village Green Preservation Society** (1968), **Arthur or the Decline and Fall of the British Empire** (1969) US#105, **Lola Versus Powerman and the Moneygoround, Part 1** (1970) US#35, **Percy** ost (1970, all Pye); **Muswell Hillbillies** (1972) US#100, **Everybody's in Showbiz** (1972) US#70, **Preservation Act 1** (1973) US#177, **Preservation Act 2** (1974) US#114, **Soap Opera** (1975) US#51, **Schoolboys in Disgrace** (1975, all RCA) US#45; **Sleepwalker** (1977) US#21, **Misfits** (1978) US#40, **Low Budget** (1979) g US#11, **One for the Road** (1980) g US#14, **Give the People What They Want** (1981) g US#15, **State Of Confusion** (1983) US#12, **Word of Mouth** (1984, all Arista) US#57; **Think Visual** (1986) US#81, **Live-The Road** (1988) US#110, **UK Jive** (1991, all London) US#122; **Phobia** (1993, Columbia) US#166; **To the Bone** (1994, Konk/Grapevine). COMPILATIONS: **You Really Got Me** (1964) US#29, **Kinks-Size** (1965) US#13, **Kinks Kinkdom** (1965) US#47, **Greatest Hits** (1966, all Reprise) g US#9; **Well Respected Kinks** (1966) UK#5, **Sunny Afternoon** (1967, both Marble Arch) UK#9; **A Golden Hour of the Kinks** (1971, Golden Hour) UK#21; **The Kink Kronikles** (1972, Reprise) US#94; **A Golden Hour of the Kinks, Volume 2** (1973, Golden Hour); **The Great Lost Kinks Album** (1973, Reprise) US#145; **Celluloid Heroes-The Kinks' Greatest** (1976, RCA) US#144; **20 Golden Greats** (1978, Ronco) UK#19; **Second Time Around** (1980, RCA) US#177; **Dead End Street-The Kinks Greatest Hits** (1983, PRT) UK#96; **Come Dancing with the Kinks-The Best of the Kinks, 1977-1986** (1986, Arista) US#159; **The Ultimate Collection** (1989, Castle) UK#35; **The EP Collection** (1990, See For Miles); **The Definitive Collection** (1993, Polygram) UK#18. HIT VERSIONS: *All Day and All of Night* Stranglers (1988) UK#7, *Dandy* Herman's Hermits (1966) US#5, *David Watts* Jam (1978) UK#25, *Days* Kirsty MacColl (1989) UK#12, *Death of a Clown* [i] Dave Davies (1966) UK#3, *House in the Country, A* Pretty Things (1966) UK#50, *I Go to Sleep* Pretenders (1981) UK#7, *Lola* Andy Taylor (1990) UK#60, *Something Better Beginning* Honeycombs (1965) UK#39, *Stop Your Sobbing* Pretenders (1980) US#65 UK#34, *Sunny Afternoon* Cathy Dennis on B-side of *Waterloo Sunset* (1997) UK#11, *Susannah's Still Alive* Dave Davies (1967) UK#20, *This Strange Effect* Dave Berry (1965) UK#37, *Waterloo Sunset* Cathy Dennis (1997) UK#11, *You Don't Have to Walk in the Rain* Turtles (1969) US#51, *You Really Got Me* Van Halen (1978) US#36. Co-writer: [i] Dave Davies (b. February 3, 1947, London, England).

247. DAVIS, Benny (b. 1895; d. 1979) Film and stage lyricist. A Tin Pan Alley lyricist, whose songs were featured in such shows as "Cotton Club Parade" (1936), and the film "Bring Your Smile Along" (1955). HIT VERSIONS: *Don't Break the Heart That Loves You* [v] Connie Francis (1962) US#1/Margo Smith (1977) C&W#1 US#104; *Driftwood* [ii] Paul Whiteman (1924) US#5, *Goodbye Broadway, Hello France* [i] American Quartet (1917) US#1/Peerless Quartet (1917) US#5; *I'm Gonna Meet My Sweetie Now* [iv] Jean Goldkette (1927) US#20, *There Must Be a Reason* [v] Charlie Kunz in *Piano Medley #114* (1954) UK#20, *Whose Heart Are You Breaking Tonight?* [v] Connie Francis (1964) US#43.

Co-writers: [i] Billy Baskette/Francis Resiner, [ii] Dohl Davis/Abe Lyman, [iii] Carl Fischer, [iv] Jesse Greer, [v] Ted Murray. (*See also under* Milton AGER, Harry AKST, Joe BURKE, Con CONRAD, John F. COOTS, Abe SILVER.)

248. DAVIS, Mac (b. January 21, 1941, Lubbock, TX) C&W guitarist and vocalist. A country singer-songwriter whose niche was light, innocuous and highly commercial melodies, many of which were recorded by other artists. Davis is the composer of some five hundred songs, of which there are over one hundred and fifty recordings, his *I Believe in Music* being the most popular, having been recorded more than fifty times. Davis first sang as a boy in his local church choir, and grew up listening to Elvis Presley, Jerry Lee Lewis, Jerry Reed and Carl Perkins. He learned the blues harp, congas and guitar, before playing in such high school bands as the Zots. Davis attended university in Atlanta, Georgia, and held various day jobs while performing in local clubs and studio groups. Stating that, "I conned my way into a job as a promotion man for Vee-Jay Records," in 1965, he moved to Hollywood to work in music publishing, where he plugged his song demos relentlessly until Elvis Presley achieved a million seller with *In the Ghetto.* As one of the then hottest songwriters in country music, Davis himself became a regular on the pop and country charts. During the 1970s, he also hosted his own television variety show on NBC, and later starred in the film "North Dallas Forty" (1979). CHART COMPOSITIONS: *Whoever Finds This I Love You* (1970) C&W#43 US#53, *I'll Paint You a Song* (1970) C&W#68 US#110, *I Believe in Music* (1970) US#117, *Baby Don't Get Hooked on Me* (1972) g C&W#26 US#1 UK#29, *Dream Me Home* (1973) C&W#47 US#73, *Your Side of the Bed* (1973) C&W#36 US#88, *Kiss and Make It Better* (1973) C&W#29 US#105, *One Hell of a Woman* [i] (1974) US#11, *Stop and Smell the Roses* [ii] (1974) C&W#40 US#9, *Burnin' Thing* [i] (1975) C&W#31 US#53, *I Still Love You (You Still Love Me)* (1975) US#81, *Every Now and Then* (1976) C&W#34, *Picking Up the Pieces of My Life* (1977) C&W#42, *Music in My Life* (1978) C&W#92, *It's Hard to Be Humble* (1980) C&W#10 US#43, *Let's Keep It That Way* (1980) C&W#10, *Texas in My Rear View Mirror* (1980) C&W#9 US#51, *Hooked on Music* (1981) C&W#2 US#102, *You're My Bestest Friend* (1981) C&W#5, *Rodeo Clown* (1982) C&W#37, *The Beer Drinkin' Song* (1982) C&W#58, *Lying Here Lying* (1982) C&W#62, *Most of All* (1984) C&W#41, *Caroline's Still in Georgia* (1984) C&W#76, *I Never Made Love ('Til I Made Love With You)* (1985) C&W#10, *I Feel the Country Callin' Me* (1985) C&W#34, *Sexy Young Girl* (1986) C&W#46, *Somewhere in America* (1986)

C&W#65. ALBUMS: **Song Painter** (1970) US#182, **I Believe in Music** (1971) US#160, **Baby Don't Get Hooked on Me** (1972) p US#11, **Mac Davis** (1973) US#120, **Stop and Smell the Roses** (1974) g US#13, **All the Love in the World** (1975) g US#21, **Burnin' Thing** (1975) US#64, **Forever Lovers** (1976) US#156, **Thunder in the Afternoon** (1977), **Picking Up the Pieces of My Life** (1977), **Fantasy** (1978, all Columbia); **It's Hard to Be Humble** (1980) g US#69, **Texas in My Rear View Mirror** (1981) US#67, **Midnight Crazy** (1981) US#174, **Forty '82** (1982), **Soft Talk** (1984, all Casablanca); **Till I Made It with You** (1986, MCA). COMPILATIONS: **Greatest Hits** (1979, Columbia); **20 Golden Greats** (1984, Astan); **Vol XC/Losers** (1990, Allegro). HIT VERSIONS: *Daddy's Little Man* O.C. Smith (1969) R&B#9 US#34, *Don't Cry Daddy* Elvis Presley (1970) g C&W#13 US#6 UK#8, *Everything a Man Could Ever Need* Glen Campbell (1970) C&W#5 US#52 UK#32, *Friend, Lover, Woman, Wife* Claude King (1969) C&W#18/O.C. Smith (1969) R&B#25 US#47; *I Believe in Music* Marian Love (1971) US#111/Gallery (1972) US#22; *In the Ghetto* Elvis Presley (1968) g C&W#60 US#3 UK#2/Dolly Parton (1969) C&W#50/Candi Staton (1972) R&B#12 US#48/Beats International (1991) UK#44; *Little Less Conversation, A* Elvis Presley (1968) US#69, *Lonesomest Lonesome, The* Ray Price (1972) C&W#2/Pat Daisy (1973) C&W#49; *Memories* [iii] Elvis Presley (1969) C&W#56 US#35, *Please Be Gentle* Amy (1979) C&W#76, *Poor Little Pearl* Billy Joe Royal (1971) US#111, *Something's Burning* Kenny Rogers & the First Edition (1970) US#11 UK#8/Candi Staton (1973) R&B#83/Kathy Barnes (1977) C&W#81; *Stop and Smell The Roses* [ii] Henson Cargill (1974) C&W#29, *Texas State of Mind* David Frizell & Shelly West (1981) C&W#9, *Watching Scotty Grow* Bobby Goldsboro (1971) C&W#7 US#11. Co-writers: [i] Mark James, [ii] Doc Severinsen, [iii] Billy Strange.

249. DAVIS, Paul (b. April 21, 1948, Meridian, MI) C&W guitarist, producer and vocalist. A singer-songwriter in a country style with a notable tenor. CHART COMPOSITIONS: *Can't You* (1970) US#118, *I Just Wanna Keep It Together* (1970) US#51, *Boogie Woogie Man* (1973) US#68, *Ride 'Em Cowboy* (1975) C&W#47 US#23, *Keep Our Love Alive* (1975) US#90, *Thinking of You* (1975) US#45, *Superstar* (1976) US#35, *I Go Crazy* (1978) US#7, *Sweet Life* [i] (1978) C&W#85 US#17, new version with Marie Osmond (1988) C&W#47; *Do Right* (1980) US#23, *Cry Just a Little Bit* (1980) US#78, *Cool Night* (1982) US#11, *'65 Love Affair* (1982) US#6. ALBUMS: **Little Bit of Soap** (1972), **Paul Davis** (1974), **Ride 'Em Cowboy** (1975) US#148,

Southern Tracks and Fantasies (1976), **Singer of Sad Songs-Teller of Tales** (1978) US#82, **Paul Davis** (1980, all Bang) US#173; **Cool Night** (1981, Arista) US#52. HIT VERSIONS: *All the Way* Brick (1980) R&B#38 US#106, *Bop* [ii] Dan Seals (1985) C&W#1 US#42, *Down to My Last Teardrop* Tanya Tucker (1991) C&W#3, *Revolution in My Soul* Reivers (1970) US#112, *Ride 'Em Cowboy* David Allan Coe (1984) C&W#48/Juice Newton (1984) C&W#32. Co-writers: [i] Susan Collins, [ii] J. Kimball.

250. DEAN, Jimmy (b. Seth Ward, August 10, 1928, Plainview, TX) C&W guitarist, pianist and vocalist. An early country-pop crossover artist who charted twenty-six singles between 1953–1983. After serving in the U.S. Air Force, Dean formed the group the Texas Wildcats in 1948. He hosted his own television series between 1957–1958, and is the only known pop singer to retire from music to run a sausage business. CHART COMPOSITIONS: *Big Bad John* (1961) g C&W#1 US#1 UK#2, *Dear Ivan* (1962) C&W#9 US#24, *Little Black Book* (1962) C&W#10 US#8 UK#33, *I.O.U.* [i] (1976) g US#9 US#35, re-issued (1977) C&W#90, re-issued (1983) C&W#77. ALBUMS: **Big Bad John and Other Fabulous Songs and Tales** (1961) US#23, **Portrait of Jimmy Dean** (1962) US#144, **Jimmy Dean's Hour of Prayer** (1964, all Columbia); **Speaker of the House** (1967), **These Hands** (1972, both RCA); **I.O.U.** (1976, Casino); **His Top Hits** (1986, Timeless). Co-writer: [i] Lawrence Harkes, Jr.

251. DE BURGH, Chris (b. Christopher Davison, October 15, 1948, Argentina) Pop guitarist and vocalist. A British based singer-songwriter who is best known for his syrupy million seller *The Lady in Red*. CHART COMPOSITIONS: *The Traveller* (1980) US#106, *Don't Pay the Ferryman* (1982) US#34 UK#48, *Ship to Shore* (1983) US#71, *High on Emotion* (1984) US#44, *The Lady in Red* (1986) US#3 UK#1, *Fatal Hesitation* (1986) UK#44, *A Spaceman Came Travelling/ The Ballroom of Romance* (1987) UK#40, *The Simple Truth (A Child Is Born)* (1988) UK#55, re-issued (1991) UK#36; *Missing You* (1988) UK#3, *Tender Hands* (1989) UK#43, *This Waiting Heart* (1989) UK#59, *Separate Tables* (1992) UK#30, *Blonde Hair Blue Jeans* (1994) UK#51, *The Snows of New York* (1995) UK#60. ALBUMS: **Far Beyond the Castle Walls** (1975), **Spanish Train and Other Stories** (1975) UK#78, **At the End of a Perfect Day** (1977), **Crusader** (1979) UK#72, **Eastern Wind** (1980), **The Getaway** (1982) US#43 UK#30, **Man on the Line** (1984) US#69 UK#11, **Into the Light** (1986) g US#25 UK#2, **Flying Colours** (1988) UK#1, **High on Emotion-Live from Dublin** (1990)

UK#15, **Power of Ten** (1992) UK#3, **This Way Up** (1994) UK#5, **Beautiful Dreams** (1995, all A&M) UK#33. COMPILATIONS: **Best Moves** (1981) UK#65, **Very Best of Chris De Burgh** (1985) UK#6, **From a Spark to a Flame-The Very Best of Chris De Burgh** (1989, all A&M) UK#4.

252. DEES, Sam (b. Sam L. Dees, 1945, Birmingham, AL) R&B vocalist. A gospel influenced soul balladeer in a tradition stretching back to Sam Cooke. Dees' compositions have been recorded by Z.Z. Hill, Clarence Carter, Regina Belle, and Whitney Houston. He began composing as a child, winning a songwriting contest at the age of nine, before, in 1959, fronting the vocal group the Bossanovians. By the late 1960s, Dees was releasing often brilliant solo singles on a variety of small labels, and his woefully small catalogue of albums contain some of the finest R&B music ever recorded. In 1986, Dees formed his own Pen Pad label and released the beautiful ballad *After All*. CHART COMPOSITIONS: *Just Out of Reach* (1973) R&B#58, *So Tied Up* (1973) R&B#59, *Worn Out Broken Heart* (1974) R&B#15, *The Show Must Go On* (1975) R&B#76, *Storybook Children* (1976) R&B#84, *Say Yeah* (1978) R&B#89. ALBUMS: **The Show Must Go On** (1975), **Soul Deep** (1976, both Atlantic); **Secret Admirer** (1986, Pen Pad); **Second to None** (1995, Kent). HIT VERSIONS: *After Loving You* Jean Wells (1967) R&B#31/ Rockie Robbins (1980) R&B#59; *All in the Name of Love* Atlantic Starr (1987) R&B#51, *Cry to Me* [i] Loleatta Holloway (1975) R&B#10 US#68, *Extra, Extra* Ralph Carter (1976) R&B#59, *Hang Tough* Rockie Robbins (1980) R&B#70, *I Betcha Didn't Know That* Frederick Knight (1975) R&B#27/K.C. & the Sunshine Band (1979) R&B#25; *I Like to Party* Alpaca Phase III (1974) R&B#80, *It's Gonna Take All Our Love* Gladys Knight & the Pips (1988) R&B#29 US#39, *Life* Betty Wright (1976) R&B#64, *Love All the Hurt Away* Aretha Franklin & George Benson (1981) R&B#6 US#46 UK#49, *Lover for Life* Mission (1988) R&B#64, *More More More* Atlantic Starr (1984) R&B#11, *My Time* Gladys Knight & the Pips (1985) R&B#16 US#102, *One in a Million You* Larry Graham & Dionne Warwick (1980) g R&B#1 US#9, *Play Time* Controllers (1988) R&B#69, *Prove It* Lea Roberts (1969) R&B#39, *Right in the Middle (Of Falling in Love)* Solaris (1980) R&B#92/Bettye LaVette (1982) R&B#35 US#103; *Run to Me* Candi Staton (1976) R&B#26, *Save the Overtime (For Me)* [ii] Gladys Knight & the Pips (1983) R&B#1 US#66, *Second Chance* Z.Z. Hill (1972) R&B#39, *Send for Me* [iii] Atlantic Starr (1981) R&B#16/Gerald Alston (1993) R&B#40; *Special Occasion* Dorothy Moore (1978) R&B#30/Millie Jackson (1982) R&B#51; *Stop This Merry Go Round* Bill Brandon (1972) R&B#33/

John Edwards (1973) R&B#45; *Vanishing Love* John Edwards (1975) R&B#60/Chi-Lites (1977) R&B#95; *What a Way to Put It* Willie Clayton (1984) R&B#84, *Where Did We Go Wrong* L.T.D. (1980) R&B#7/ Manhattans (1986) R&B#42; *Who Are You Gonna Love* Rozetta Johnson (1971) R&B#45, *Woman's Way, A* Rozetta Johnson (1970) R&B#39 US#94, *Worn Out Broken Heart* Loleatta Holloway (1977) R&B#25, *(You're My) Aphrodisiac* Dennis Edwards (1984) R&B#15, *You've Been a Part of Me* Wee Gee (1978) R&B#86. Co-writers: [i] D. Camon, [ii] J. Gallo/Brenda Knight/Gladys Knight/R. Smith, [iii] R. Kersey.

253. DEKKER, Desmond (b. Desmond Dacres, July 16, 1941, Kingston, Jamaica) Reggae vocalist. One of the most influential and successful ska and rock-steady artists of the 1960s. Dekker achieved twenty number ones in Jamaica, before becoming the first Jamaican to top the British charts. CHART COMPOSITIONS: *007 (Shanty Town)* (1967) US#14 UK#14, *The Israelites* [i] (1969) US#9 UK#1, re-issued (1975) UK#10; *It Miek* [i] (1969) UK#7, *Picney Girl* (1970) UK#42, *Sing a Little Song* (1975) UK#16. ALBUMS: **This Is Desmond Dekker** (1969, Trojan) UK#27); **Israelites** (1969, Uni) US#153; **Black and Dekker** (1980), **Compass Point** (1981, both Stiff). COMPILATIONS: **Sweet 16 Hits** (1984), **Original Reggae Hit Sound** (1985, both Trojan); **20 Golden Pieces** (1987, President); **Greatest Hits** (1988, Mainline); **Original Live and Rare** (1987, Trojan); **Rockin' Steady-The Best of Desmond Dekker** (1993, Rhino). HIT VERSIONS: *Israelites, The* [i] Chops-EMC + Extensive (1992) UK#60. Co-writer: [i] Leslie Kong (b. 1933, Jamaica; d. 1971).

254. DE LANGE, Edward (b. 1904; d. 1949, both America) Film and stage lyricist. A Tin Pan Alley lyricist, whose material was included in such films as "Along the Navajo Trail" (1946). HIT VERSIONS: *Along the Navajo Trail* [iii] Bing Crosby & the Andrews Sisters (1945) US#2/Gene Krupa (1945) US#7/Dinah Shore (1945) US#7; *And So Do I* [vi] Jimmy Dorsey (1940) US#25, *Haunting Me* [vi] Eddy Duchin (1935) US#14, *If I'm Lucky* [vi] Perry Como (1948) US#19, *Just as Though You Were Here* [i] Ink Spots (1942) R&B#10, *String of Pearls, A* [i] Glenn Miller (1941) US#1, re-issued (1944) US#27/Benny Goodman (1942) US#15; *Velvet Moon* [vi] Harry James (1943) R&B#5 US#2, *Who Threw the Whiskey in the Well?* [ii] Lucky Millinder (1945) US#7. Co-writers: [i] John Benson Brooks, [ii] John Benson Brooks/Lucky Millinder, [iii] Dick Charles/Larry Marks, [iv] Jerry Gray, [v] Paul Mann/Stephan Weiss, [vi] Joseph Myrow. (*See also under* Sammy STEPT.)

255. DELMORE, Alton (b. December 25, 1908, Elkmont; d. June 8, 1964, Huntsville, both AL) C&W guitarist and fiddle player. A prolific country tunesmith who composed over one thousand songs. During the 1920s, Delmore performed with his brother Rabon as the country blues and boogie duo the Delmore Brothers. CHART COMPOSITIONS: *Freight Train Boogie* (1946) C&W#2, *Blues, Stay Away from Me* (1949) C&W#1, *Pan American Boogie* (1950) C&W#7. ALBUMS: **16 All-Time Favorites** (1963, King); **The Delmore Brothers** (1971, County); **Best of the Delmore Brothers** (1987, Gusto); **When They Let the Hammer Fall** with Wayne Raney (1984, Bear Family). HIT VERSIONS: *Beautiful Brown Eyes* [i] Rosemary Clooney (1951) US#11/Jimmy Wakley (1951) C&W#5 US#12; *Blues, Stay Away from Me* Eddie Crosby (1949) C&W#7/Owen Bradley Quintet (1950) C&W#7 US#11; *Freight Train Boogie* Red Foley (1947) C&W#5. Co-writer: [i] Arthur Smith.

256. DENNY, Sandy (b. Alexandra Elene MacLean Denny, January 6, 1948; d. April 21, 1978, both London, England) Folk guitarist, pianist and vocalist. Britain's finest ever female folk singer, who composed an oddly haunting catalogue of traditionally influenced material. Denny first came to prominence as a member of the group the Strawbs, recordings from this period later being released as **All Our Own Work (1968 Recordings)** (1973, Hallmark). In 1969, she joined the folk-rock group Fairport Convention, with which she recorded such classics as *Who Knows Where the Time Goes.* ALBUMS: **What We Did on Our Holidays** (1969), **Unhalfbricking** (1969) UK#12, **Liege and Lief** (1970) UK#17, **Rosie** (1973), **Live (A Moveable Feast)** (1974), **Rising for the Moon** (1975, all Island) US#143 UK#52. COMPILATIONS: **History of Fairport Convention** (1972, Island); **Chronicles** (1976, A&M); **Heyday** (1987, Hannibal); **The Airing Cupboard Tapes, 1971–1974** (1981, Woodworm). Denny left in 1970 to front her own group Fotheringay, and later pursue a solo career, recording material that ranged from her own gems, such as *Listen, Listen* and *One Way Donkey Ride,* to 1930–1940s Tin Pan Alley songs. She died of a brain hemorrhage after falling down stairs at her home. Many of her compositions were recorded by Vikki Clayton as **It Suits Me Well** (1994, Terrapin Trucking). ALBUMS: **Fotheringay**** (1970) UK#18, **North Star Grassman and the Ravens** (1971) UK#31, **Sandy** (1972), **Rock On*** (1972), **Like an Old Fashioned Waltz** (1973) US#197, **Rendezvous** (1977, all Island). COMPILATIONS: **The Original Sandy Denny** (1978, Mooncrest); **Who Knows Where the Time Goes** (1986), **Best of Sandy Denny** (1987, both Hannibal/Island); **The BBC Sessions, 1971–1973** (1997, Strange Fruit). As: * The Bunch, ** Fotheringay.

257. DENVER, John (b. John Henry Deutschendorf, Jr., December 31, 1943, Roswell, NM; d. 1997) Pop guitarist and vocalist. The creator of at least five pop-folk classics, *Leaving on a Jet Plane*, *Take Me Home Country Roads* [i], *Rocky Mountain High*, *Sunshine on My Shoulders*, and *Annie's Song*. The son of a U.S. Air Force pilot, Denver grew up in Aspen, Colorado, an environment that would provide much inspiration for his music. He took guitar lessons as a boy and studied to become an architect, but dropped out of college in 1964 to join the folk group the Chad Mitchell Trio, which was forced to change its name to Denver, Boise and Johnson after Mitchell's departure in 1968. Denver featured on the albums **That's the Way It's Gonna Be** and **Violets of Dawn** (both 1965, Mercury). He began recording as a solo artist in 1969, and by **Rocky Mountain High** (1972), he had become one of America's best selling singer-songwriters. The enormity of his success took a heavy toll on the quality of his songwriting, and in his attempt to become an all-round entertainer, he made vacuous television specials and appeared on "The Muppet Show," instead of honing his compositional skills. By 1986, Denver had turned exclusively to country music, and in 1994, he became the first American to perform in Vietnam since the Vietnam war. He died in a plane crash in 1997. CHART COMPOSITIONS: *Take Me Home Country Roads* (1971) g C&W#50 US#2, *My Sweet Lady* (1971) US#32, *Friends with You* (1971) US#47, *Everyday* (1972) US#81, *Goodbye Again* (1972) US#88, *Hard Life Hard Times (Prisoners)* (1972) US#103, *Rocky Mountain High* (1973) US#9, *I'd Rather Be a Cowboy* (1973) US#62, *Farewell Andromeda* (1973) US#89, *Sunshine on My Shoulders* [ii] (1974) g C&W#42 US#1, *Annie's Song* (1974) g C&W#9 US#1 UK#1, *Back Home Again* (1974) g C&W#1 US#5, *Sweet Surrender* (1975) C&W#7 US#13, *I'm Sorry* (1975) g C&W#1 US#1, *Calypso* (1975) US#2, *Fly Away* (1976) C&W#12 US#13, *Looking for Space* (1976) C&W#30 US#29, *It Makes Me Giggle* (1976) C&W#70 US#60, *Like a Sad Song* (1976) C&W#34 US#36, *My Sweet Lady* (1977) C&W#62 US#32, *How Can I Leave You Again* (1978) C&W#22 US#44, *It Amazes Me* (1978) C&W#72 US#59, *I Want to Live* (1978) US#55, *Downhill Stuff* (1979) C&W#64 US#106, *What's on Your Mind/Sweet Melinda* (1979) C&W#47 US#107, *Autograph* (1980) C&W#84 US#52, *Dancing with the Mountains* (1980) US#97, *Perhaps Love* with Placido Domingo (1982) US#59 UK#46, *Shanghai Breezes* (1982) US#31, *Seasons of the Heart* (1982) US#78, *Wild Montana Skies* with Emmylou Harris (1983) C&W#14, *Love Again* with

Sylvie Vartan (1984) US#85, *Dreamland Express* (1985) C&W#9, *Along for the Ride ('56 T-Bird)* (1986) C&W#57, *Country Girl in Paris* (1988) C&W#96. ALBUMS: **Rhymes and Reasons** (1969) US#148 UK#21, **Take Me to Tomorrow** (1970) US#197, **Whose Garden Was This** (1971), **Poems, Prayers and Promises** (1971) g US#15 UK#19, **Aerie** (1972) g US#7, **Rocky Mountain High** (1972) g US#4, **Farewell Andromeda** (1973) g US#16, **Back Home Again** (1974, all RCA) g US#1 UK#3; **Sunshine** ost (1974, MCA) US#34 UK#47; **An Evening with John Denver** (1975) g US#2 UK#31, **Windsong** (1975) g US#1 UK#14, **Rocky Mountain Christmas** (1975) g US#14, **Live in London** (1976) UK#2, **Spirit** (1976) p US#7 UK#9, **I Want to Live** (1977) p US#45 UK#25, **John Denver** (1978) g US#25 UK#68, **A Christmas Together** with the Muppets (1979) p US#26, **Autograph** (1980) US#39, **Some Days Are Like Diamonds** (1981) g US#32, **Seasons of the Heart** (1982) g US#39, **It's About Time** (1983) US#61 UK#90, **Dreamland Express** (1985) US#90, **One World** (1986, all RCA); **Higher Ground** (1988) US#185, **Different Directions** (1991), **The Flower That Shattered the Stone** (1992, all Windstar); **Wildlife Concert** (1995, Legacy) US#104. COMPILATIONS: **Greatest Hits** (1974) g US#1, **Best of John Denver** (1974, both RCA) UK#7; **Beginnings** (1974, Mercury); **John Denver Gift Pack** (1975) g US#138, **Greatest Hits, Volume 2** (1977) p US#6, **Best of John Denver, Volume 2** (1977, all RCA) UK#9; **The Collection** (1984, Telstar) UK#20; **Greatest Hits, Volume 3** (1985 RCA); **The Rocky Mountain Collection** (1996, Rhino); **Christmas Like a Lullaby** (1996, RCA). HIT VERSIONS: *Annie's Song* James Galway (1978) UK#3, *Leaving on a Jet Plane* Peter, Paul & Mary (1967) g US#1 UK#2/Kendalls (1970) C&W#52; *My Sweet Lady* Cliff DeYoung (1974) US#17, *Take Me Home Country Roads* [i] Olivia Newton-John (1973) US#13 UK#15. Co-writers: [i] Bill Danoff/Taffy Nivert, [ii] Dick Kniss/Mike Taylor.

258. DE PAUL, Lynsey (b. Lynsey Rubin, 1951, England) Pop pianist and vocalist. The performer of a series of novelty hits during the 1970s. CHART COMPOSITIONS: *Sugar Me* [i] (1972) UK#5, *Won't Somebody Dance with Me* (1973) UK#14, *Ooh I Do* (1974) UK#25, *No Honestly* (1974) UK#7, *My Man and Me* (1975) UK#40, *Rock Bottom* [ii] with Mike Moran (1977) UK#19. ALBUMS: **Lynsey Sings** (1972, MAM); **No Honestly** (1977, Hallmark); **Tigers and Fireflies** (1979, Polydor); **Just a Little Time** (1997, Music De Luxe). COMPILATION: **Best of Lynsey De Paul** (1996, BMG). Co-writers: [i] Barry Blue, [ii] Mike Moran. (*See also under* Barry BLUE, Roger COOK.)

259. DE ROSE, Peter (b. 1900; d. 1953) Tin Pan Alley pianist and composer. HIT VERSIONS: *Muddy Water* [i] Ben Bernie (1927) US#5/ Harry Richman (1927) US#10/Paul Whiteman (1927) US#11. Co-writers: [i] Henry Richman/Jo Trent. (*See also under* Harold ADAMSON, Billy HILL, Mitchell PARISH.)

260. DE SHANNON, Jackie (b. Sharon Myers, August 21, 1944, Hazel, KY) Pop vocalist. A singer-songwriter whose biggest hits were songs that she wrote for others. De Shannon grew up in Chicago, Illinois, where she made her radio debut at the age of eleven. After singing in two 1960s groups, the Nomads and the Nighthawks, she recorded singles as Sherry Lee Myers for the Glenn label, before becoming a member of Hale and the Hushabyes. As Jackie De Shannon, she signed to Imperial Records in the early 1960s as a writer and performer, where her soft, country-soul voice coupled a wise selection of material that gave her twenty-five chart entries between 1962–1969. De Shannon also appeared on numerous television shows, and cameoed in the films "Hide and Seek" (1963) and "Surf Party" (1964). In 1990, she was one of the panelists for the UCLA class "Women in Songwriting." HIT VERSIONS: *The Prince* (1962) US#108, *Faded Love* (1963) US#97, *When You Walk in the Room* (1964) US#99, *Come and Get Me* (1966) US#83, *Come on Down (From the Top of That Hill)* (1966) US#121, *Put a Little Love in Your Heart* [i] (1969) g US#4, *Love Will Find a Way* (1969) US#40, *Brighton Hill* (1970) US#82, *It's So Nice* (1970) US#84, *Vanilla Olay* (1972) US#76, *Paradise* (1972) US#110, *Don't Let the Flame Burn Out* (1977) US#68. ALBUMS: **Jackie De Shannon** (1963, Liberty); **This Is Jackie De Shannon** (1964), **You Won't Forget Me** (1964), **In the Wind** (1964, all Imperial); **Breakin' It Up on the Beatles Tour** (1965, Liberty); **Are You Ready for This** (1965), **New Image** (1965), **For You** (1965), **Me About You** (1965), **What the World Needs Now** (1965), **Laurel Canyon** (1966), **Put a Little Love in Your Heart** (1969) US#81, **To Be Free** (1971, all Imperial); **Songs** (1971, Capitol); **Jackie** (1972) US#196, **Your Baby Is a Lady** (1974, all Atlantic); **New Arrangement** (1975, Columbia); **You're the Only Dancer** (1977, Amherst); **Sky High** (1985, Auditrax). COMPILATIONS: **Lonely Girl** (1968, Sunset); **Best of Jackie De Shannon** (1992, Rhino); **Very Best of Jackie De Shannon** (1992, EMI America); **What the World Needs Now-The Definitive Collection** (1994, EMI). HIT VERSIONS: *Bad Water* Raeletts (1971) R&B#40 US#58, *Bette Davis Eyes* [iii] Kim Carnes (1981) US#1 UK#10, *Break Away* [ii] Tracy Ullman (1983) US#70 UK#4/Gail Davies (1985) C&W#15; *Come and Stay with Me* Marianne Faithful (1965)

US#26 UK#4, *Dum Dum* Brenda Lee (1961) US#4 UK#22, *He's Sure to Remember Me* Brenda Lee (1964) US#135, also on B-side of *When You Loved Me* (1964) US#47; *(He's) The Great Imposter* Fleetwoods (1961) US#30, *Heart in Hand* [ii] Brenda Lee (1962) US#15, *Put a Little Love in Your Heart* [i] Dave Clark Five (1969) UK#31/Susan Raye (1970) C&W#30/Annie Lennox & Al Green (1988) US#8 UK#28; *When You Walk in the Room* Searchers (1964) US#35 UK#3/ Child (1978) UK#38/Stephanie Winslow (1981) C&W#29/Paul Carrack (1988) US#90/Pam Tillis (1994) C&W#61+/Status Quo (1995) UK#34; *You Should Have Been There* Fleetwoods (1963) US#114. Co-writers: [i] Randy Meyers/Jimmy Holiday, [ii] Sharon Sheeley, [iii] Donna Weiss.

261. DE SYLVA, Buddy (b. George Gard De Sylva, January 27, 1895, New York, NY; d. July 11, 1950, Los Angeles, CA) Film and stage lyricist, producer. The son of a vaudeville performer who was himself a child performer, before Al Jolson developed a fondness for his lyrics and had them set to music. De Sylva enjoyed a highly successful songwriting partnership with Ray Henderson and Lew Brown, which he dissolved in 1930 in order to produce his own Broadway shows. De Sylva was also one of the co-founders of Capitol Records. His songs were featured in the films "Rose of Washington Square" (1939), "The Jolson Story" (1946), "With a Song in My Heart" (1952), and "The Eddie Duchin Story" (1956), and such shows as "Bombo" (1922). HIT VERSIONS: *April Showers* [xii] Arthur Fields (1922) US#12/Ernest Hare (1922) US#9/Charles Harrison (1922) US#11/Al Jolson (1922) g US#1, reissued (1947) US#15/Paul Whiteman (1922) US#2/ Guy Lombardo (1947) US#9/Big Ben Banjo Band in *Let's Get Together #1* (1954) UK#6; *Avalon* [viii] Art Hickman (1921) US#11/Al Jolson (1921) US#2; *California Here I Come* [vii] California Ramblers (1924) US#10/Al Jolson (1924) US#1/Georgie Price (1924) US#7/Claude Hopkins (1933) US#17/Johnston Brothers in *Join in and Sing Again* (1955) UK#9/ Freddy Cannon (1960) UK#33/Mrs. Mills in *Mrs. Mills' Medley* (1961) UK#18; *Cross Your Heart* [ii] Vaughn Deleath & Ed Smalle (1926) US#12/Roger Wolf Kahn (1926) US#8; *Gentlemen Prefer Blondes* [ii] Ernest Hare & Billy Jones (1927) US#6, *Hello, 'Tucky* [iv] Al Jolson (1925) US#5, *I'll Say She Does* [vi] All-Star Trio (1919) US#6/Al Jolson (1919) US#1/Wilbur Sweatman's Original Jazz Band (1919) US#4; *If You Knew Susie* [x] Eddie Cantor (1925) US#1/Cliff Edwards (1925) US#5/Ernest Hare & Billy Jones (1925) US#7/Jack Shilkret (1925) US#8/Winifred Atwell in *Let's Have a Party* (1953) UK#2; *Just a Cottage Small* [iii] Franklyn Baur (1926) US#9/John McCormack (1926) US#4; *Memory Lane*

[i] Paul Specht (1924) US#8/Fred Waring's Pennsylvanians (1924) US#1; *'N' Everything* [vi] Al Jolson (1918) US#2, *Save Your Sorrow (For Tomorrow)* [xi] Shannon Four (1925) US#7/Ray Miller (1925) US#12/Gene Austin (1926) US#13; *When Day Is Done* [ix] Harry Archer (1927) US#14/Art Kahn (1927) US#18/Nat Shilkret (1927) US#8/Paul Whiteman (1927) US#2; *Yoo Hoo* [v] Al Jolson (1922) US#4, *You Ain't Heard Nothin' Yet* [vi] Al Jolson (1920) US#3. Co-writers: [i] Con Conrad/Larry Spier, [ii] Lewis E. Gensler, [iii] James F. Hanley, [iv] James F. Hanley/Joseph Meyer, [v] Al Jolson, [vi] Al Jolson/Gus Kahn, [vii] Al Jolson/Joseph Meyer, [viii] Al Jolson/Vincent Rose, [ix] Robert Katscher, [x] Joseph Meyer, [xi] Al Sherman, [xii] Louis Silvers. (*See also under* Buddy DE SYLVA, Ray HENDERSON and Lew BROWN, Walter DONALDSON, George GERSHWIN, Victor HERBERT, Jerome KERN, Joseph MEYER, Richard A. WHITING, Vincent YOUMANS.)

262. DE SYLVA, Buddy, BROWN, Lew, and HENDERSON, Ray Film and stage composers. A formidable songwriting trio that was formed in 1925 to undertake a commission to write the songs for the show "George White's Scandals of 1925." They wrote a further ten musical comedies, including the film "Sunnyside Up" (1929), and in 1926, created their own publishing house to oversee the collection of the royalties on songs such as the million seller *Sonny Boy* [i] (1929), which was written on demand for Al Jolson as a corny joke. Their material was featured in such shows as "Good News" (1928), "Artists and Models" (1928) and "Follow Through" (1929), alongside the films "Painting the Clouds with Sunshine" (1951) and "A Star Is Born" (1954). The last Broadway show on which they worked together was "Flying High" (1930), and they were later the subject of the film biography "The Best Things in Life Are Free" (1956). After De Sylva dissolved the partnership in 1930, Henderson and Brown continued to work together, their "George White's Scandals of 1931" becoming the first show to be issued on a twelve inch disc, when it was recorded by Bing Crosby and the Boswell Sisters (Brunswick, 1931). ALBUMS: **Good News** ost (1950, MGM); **The Best Things in Life Are Free** ost (1956, Capitol); **The Best Things in Life Are Free** ost (1958, Liberty); **Good News** oc (1974, Private); **Good News** oc (1974, Signature). HIT VERSIONS: *Best Things in Life Are Free, The* Frank Black (1927) US#16/George Olsen (1927) US#3/Ink Spots (1948) R&B#10/Dinah Shore (1948) US#18/Jo Stafford (1948) US#21; *Birth of the Blues, The* Revelers (1926) US#11/Harry Richman (1926) US#4/Paul Whiteman (1926) US#1/Frank Sinatra (1952) US#19; *Black Bottom* Johnny

Hamp (1926) US#3, *Broken Hearted* Arden-Ohman Orchestra (1927) US#14/Nick Lucas (1927) US#10/Aileen Stanley (1927) US#17/Paul Whiteman (1927) US#3; *Button Up Your Overcoat* Ruth Etting (1929) US#15/Helen Kane (1929) US#3/Fred Waring's Pennsylvanians (1929) US#11/Paul Whiteman (1929) US#5; *Come to Me* High Hatters (1931) US#15/Jaques Renard (1931) US#16; *For Old Times' Sake* Annette Hanshaw (1928) US#10, *Good News* George Olsen (1927) US#6/Fred Rich (1927) US#15; *Here I Am-Broken Hearted* Johnnie Ray (1952) US#8, *I'm on the Crest of a Wave* George Olsen (1928) US#15/Harry Richman (1928) US#19/Paul Whiteman (1928) US#6; *If I Had a Talking Picture of You* Earl Burtnett (1929) US#9/Paul Whiteman (1929) US#7/Johnny Hamp (1930) US#5; *It All Depends on You* Ben Bernie (1927) US#17/Ruth Etting (1927) US#8/Paul Whiteman (1927) US#2; *Just a Memory* Franklyn Baur (1927) US#15/Vincent Lopez (1927) US#11/Paul Whiteman (1927) US#3; *Little Pal* [i] Gene Austin (1929) US#7/Al Jolson (1929) US#1/Paul Whiteman (1929) US#9; *Lucky Day* George Olsen (1926) US#5/Revelers (1926) US#10; *Lucky in Love* George Olsen (1927) US#9, *My Lucky Star* Fred Waring's Pennsylvanians (1929) US#11/Paul Whiteman (1929) US#4; *My Sin* Belle Baker (1929) US#19/Ben Selvin (1929) US#2/Fred Waring's Pennsylvanians (1929) US#7/Julia Lee (1947) US#25/Georgia Gibbs (1954) US#21; *Old Fashioned Girl, An* Paul Whiteman (1922) US#7, *So Blue* Vincent Lopez (1926) US#13/Nick Lucas (1927) US#13/Paul Whiteman (1927) US#5; *Song I Love, The* Fred Waring's Pennsylvanians (1929) US#9, *Sonny Boy* [i] Ruth Etting (1928) US#6/Jan Garber (1928) US#14/Al Jolson (1928) g US#1/Gene Austin (1929) US#12/Andrews Sisters (1941) US#22; *Sunny Side Up* Earl Burtnett (1929) US#9/Johnny Hamp (1929) US#10; *Thank Your Father* Al Goodman (1930) US#17, *Together* Cliff Edwards (1928) US#10/Nick Lucas (1928) US#12/Paul Whiteman (1928) US#1/Helen Forest & Dick Haymes (1944) US#3/Guy Lombardo (1944) US#7/Dinah Shore (1944) US#19/Connie Francis (1961) US#6 UK#6/P.J. Proby (1964) US#117 UK#8; *Turn on the Heat* Earl Burtnett (1929) US#7, *Varsity Drag, The* Cass Hagan (1927) US#15/George Olsen (1927) US#4; *Why Can't You?* [i] Al Jolson (1929) US#4, *You Try Somebody Else (We'll Be Back Together Again)* Guy Lombardo (1931) US#8, *You're the Cream in My Coffee* Ruth Etting (1929) US#15/Ben Selvin (1929) US#2/Ted Weems (1929) US#7. Co-writer: [i] Al Jolson. (*See also under* Lew BROWN, Buddy DE SYLVA, Ray HENDERSON.)

263. DEVILLE, Mink (b. Willy Boray, 1953, New York, NY) Rock guitarist and vocalist. An R&B and punk influenced singer-songwriter.

ALBUMS: **Mink DeVille** (1977) US#186, **Return to Magenta** (1978) US#126, **La Chat Bleu** (1980) US#163, **Savoir Faire** (1981, all Capitol); **Coup De Grace** (1981) US#161; **Where Angels Fear to Tread** (1984), **Sportin' Life** (1986, all Atlantic); **Loup Garou** (1996, East West). HIT VERSIONS: *I Must Be Dreaming* Giuffria (1986) US#52.

264. DEXTER, Al (b. Clarence Albert Poindexter, May 4, 1902, Troup; d. January 28, 1984, Lake Dallas, both TX) C&W guitarist, violinist and vocalist. A country singer-songwriter who achieved seven number ones from sixteen hits between 1944–1948. His best known song is the Bing Crosby favorite *Pistol Packin' Mama*. CHART COMPOSITIONS: *Pistol Packin' Mama* (1942) g C&W#1 R&B#5 US#1, *Rosalita* (1944) C&W#1 US#29, *Too Late to Worry, Too Blue to Cry* (1944) C&W#1 US#23, *Guitar Polka* (1946) C&W#1 US#16. HIT VERSIONS: *Pistol Packin' Mama* Bing Crosby & the Andrews Sisters (1943) g C&W#1 R&B#3 US#2/ Gene Vincent (1960) UK#15/Slade on *Slade Live at Reading '80 EP* (1980) UK#44; *Too Late to Worry, Too Blue to Cry* Texas Jim Lewis (1944) C&W#3/Ronnie Milsap (1975) C&W#6 US#101.

265. DE YOUNG, Dennis (b. February 18, 1947, Chicago, IL) Rock keyboard player and vocalist. The lead singer and main songwriter in the quasi-classical rock group Styx, which sold over fourteen million albums in America. CHART COMPOSITIONS: *Best Thing* (1972) US#82, *Lady* (1975) US#6, *You Need Love* (1975) US#88, *Lorelei* (1976) US#27, *Mademoiselle* [i] (1976) US#36, *Come Sail Away* (1977) US#8, *Babe* (1979) p US#1 UK#6, *Why Me* (1979) US#26, *Borrowed Time* [i] (1980) US#64, *The Best of Times* (1981) US#3 UK#42, *Nothing Ever Goes as Planned* (1981) US#54, *Mr. Roboto* (1983) p US#3, *Don't Let It End* (1983) US#6 UK#56, *High Time* (1983) US#48, *Music Time* (1984) US#40, *Love Is the Ritual* (1990) US#80, *Show Me the Way* (1991) US#3. ALBUMS: **Styx I** (1972), **Styx II** (1973) g US#20, **The Serpent Is Rising** (1974) US#192, **Man of Miracles** (1974, all Wooden Nickel) US#154; **Equinox** (1976) g US#58, **Crystal Ball** (1976) g US#66, **The Grand Illusion** (1978) p US#6, **Pieces of Eight** (1978) p US#6, **Cornerstone** (1979) p US#2 UK#36, **Paradise Theatre** (1981) p US#1 UK#8, **Kilroy Was Here** (1983) p US#3 UK#67, **Caught in the Act-Live** (1984) US#31 UK#44, **End of the Century** (1990, all A&M) US#63. COMPILATIONS: **Best of Styx** (1980, RCA) g; **Greatest Hits** (1995, A&M) US#138. In 1993, De Young played Pontius Pilate in a Broadway production of "Jesus Christ Superstar." He has also recorded as a solo artist. CHART COMPOSI-

TIONS: *Desert Moon* (1984) US#10, *Call Me* (1986) US#54, *This Is the Time* (1986) US#93. ALBUMS: **Desert Moon** (1985) US#29, **Back to the World** (1986) US#108, **Boomchild** (1988), **10 on Broadway** (1995, all A&M). Co-writers: [i] Tommy Shaw (b. September 11, 1950, Montgomery, AL), [ii] James Young (b. November 14, 1948, Chicago, IL).

266. DIAMOND, Neil (b. January 24, 1941, Brooklyn, NY) Pop guitarist, producer and vocalist. One of the most popular live and recording artists in the world, who has sold over forty million records and charted nearly sixty hit singles. Originally a struggling Brill Building tunesmith, Diamond tried long and hard to become a hit songwriter, and as a composer who writes from the guitar, his distinctly folk approach ultimately contributed to a very distinctive sound. Diamond is also a consummate showman, with an audience that sticks with him through any musical fashion. His songs have been recorded by artists that range in styles from hard rock to reggae. Diamond learned the guitar at the age of fourteen, and wrote his first song, *Hear Them Bells*, in 1956. As one half of the duo Neil and Jack, he performed on the folk circuit, releasing two unsuccessful singles on the Duel label, *You Are My Love at Last* (1960) and *I'm Afraid* (1961). In 1961, he became a staff writer at Sunbeam Music in New York's Brill Building, later saying, "I never really chose songwriting, it just absorbed me." After an unsuccessful single for Columbia Records, *Clown Time* (1962), Diamond moved to Roosevelt Music, which resulted in a Pat Boone recording of *Ten Lonely Guys*, followed by two songs for the Rocky Fellers, *Santa Claus* and *We Got Love*. In 1964, determined to make it as a songwriter, Diamond rented a small office above the Birdland jazz club in New York, where he lived and composed. Only one song from this period was ever recorded, *That New Boy in Town* by Jan Tazzy. Many of these early compositions were gathered together on the various artists collection **The Neil Diamond Songbook** (1992, Connoisseur). A short period at Jerry Leiber and Mike Stoller's Trio Music Publishing, led to a publishing contract at Ellie Greenwich and Jeff Barry's Tallyrand Music, which in turn, secured him a record deal with the fledgling Bang label in 1966. Diamond's tenacity finally paid off when Jay and the Americans charted with his song *Sunday and Me* (1965), and the Monkees sold five million copies of his *I'm a Believer* (1966). Diamond's first single for his new label was *Solitary Man*, a melodic, introspective and self-effacing song which, for a 1960s pop record, featured an unusual trombone arrangement. Diamond spoke fondly of the composition in 1992, "That's my all-time favorite record…because it was my first chart record." Dia-

mond rapidly developed as a recording artist, and began to incorporate elements of country and gospel into his sound. In the early 1970s, he concentrated on heavily orchestrated, dramatic ballads, and in 1982, starred in the second remake of "The Jazz Singer." Diamond once commented on his early struggles, "People don't generally notice whether you're talented or not until after you've made it." CHART COMPOSITIONS: *Solitary Man* (1966) US#55, re-issued (1970) US#21; *Cherry, Cherry* (1966) US#6, live version (1973) US#31; *I Got the Feeling (Oh No No)* (1966) US#16, *You Got to Me* (1967) US#18, *Girl You'll Be a Woman Soon* (1967) US#10, *Thank the Lord for the Nighttime* (1967) US#13, *Kentucky Woman* (1967) US#22, *New Orleans* (1968) US#51, *Red, Red Wine* (1968) US#62, *Brooklyn Roads* (1968) US#58, *Two-Bit Manchild* (1968) US#66, *Sunday Sun* (1968) US#68, *Brother Love's Traveling Salvation Show* (1969) US#22, *Sweet Caroline* (1969) g US#4 UK#8, *Holly Holy* (1969) g US#6, *Shilo* (1970) US#24, *Soolaimon* (1970) US#30, *Cracklin' Rose* (1970) g US#1 UK#3, *Do It* (1970) US#36, *I Am...I Said* (1971) US#4 UK#4, *Done Too Soon* (1971) US#65, *I'm a Believer* (1971) US#51, *Stones* (1971) US#14, *Song Sung Blue* (1972) g US#1 UK#14, *Play Me* (1972) US#11, *Walk on Water* (1972) US#17, *Long Way Home* (1973) US#91, *Be* (1973) US#34, *Skybird* (1974) US#75, *Longfellow Serenade* (1974) US#5, *I've Been This Way Before* (1975) US#34, *If You Know What I Mean* (1976) US#11 UK#35, *Don't Think...Feel* (1976) US#43, *Beautiful Noise* (1976) UK#13, *Desiree* (1977) US#16 UK#39, *You Don't Bring Me Flowers* [iv] with Barbra Streisand (1978) g C&W#70 US#1 UK#5, *Forever in Blue Jeans* [iii] (1979) C&W#73 US#20 UK#16, *Say Maybe* (1979) US#55, *September Morn* [ii] (1980) US#17, *Love on the Rocks* [ii] (1980) g US#2 UK#17, *Hello Again* [vii] (1981) US#6 UK#51, *America* (1981) US#8, *Yesterday's Songs* (1982) US#11, *On the Way to the Sky* [viii] (1982) US#27, *Be Mine Tonight* (1982) US#35, *Heartlight* [i] (1982) US#5 UK#47, *I'm Alive* [v] (1983) US#35, *Front Page Story* [i] (1983) US#65, *Turn Around* [i] (1984) US#62, *Headed for the Future* [vi] (1986) US#53. ALBUMS: **The Feel of Neil Diamond** (1966) US#137, **Just for You** (1967, both Bang) US#80; **Velvet Gloves and Spit** (1968), **Brother Love's Traveling Salvation Show** (1969) g US#82, **Touching Me Touching You** (1969) g US#30, **Gold** (1970) p US#10 UK#23, **Tap Root Manuscript** (1970) p US#13 UK#19, **Stones** (1971) g US#11 UK#18, **Moods** (1972, all Uni) p US#5 UK#7; **Hot August Night** (1972, MCA) p US#5 UK#32; **Jonathan Livingston Seagull** (1973) p US#2 UK#35, **Serenade** (1974) p US#3 UK#11, **Beautiful Noise** (1976) p US#4 UK#10, **Love at the Greek** (1977) p US#8 UK#3, **I'm Glad You're Here**

with Me Tonight (1977) p US#6 UK#16, **You Don't Bring Me Flowers** (1978) p US#4 UK#15, **September Morn** (1979, all Columbia) p US#10 UK#14; **The Jazz Singer** ost (1980, Capitol) p US#3 UK#10; **On the Way to the Sky** (1981) p US#17 UK#39, **Heartlight** (1983) p US#9 UK#43, **Primitive** (1984) g US#35 US#7, **Headed for the Future** (1986) p US#20 UK#36, **Hot August Night 2** (1987) g US#59 UK#74, **The Best Years of Our Lives** (1988) p US#46 UK#42, **Lovescape** (1991) US#44 UK#36, **The Christmas Album** (1992) p US#8 UK#50, **Up on the Roof-The Songs from the Brill Building** (1993) g US#28 UK#28, **Live in America** (1994) US#93, **The Christmas Album, Volume II** (1994) US#51, **Tennessee Moon** (1996, all Columbia) g US#14 UK#12. COMPILATIONS: **Greatest Hits** (1968) US#100, **Shilo** (1970) US#52, **Do It** (1971) US#100, **Double Gold** (1972, all Bang) US#36; **Rainbow** (1973) g US#35 UK#39, **His 12 Greatest Hits** (1974) p US#29 UK#13, **And the Singer Sings His Songs** (1976) US#102, **20 Golden Greats** (1978) UK#2, **Love Songs** (1981, all MCA) g US#43; **His 12 Greatest Hits, Volume 2** (1982) p US#48 UK#32; **Classics-The Early Years** (1983, both Columbia) p US#171; **Very Best of Neil Diamond** (1983, K-Tel) UK#33; **The Greatest Hits, 1966–1992** (1992, Columbia) p US#90 UK#1; **20 Golden Greats** (1992, MCA) UK#48; **The Ultimate Collection** (1996, Sony) UK#5. HIT VERSIONS: *And the Grass Won't Pay No Mind* Mark Lindsay (1970) US#44, *Boat That I Row, The* Lulu (1967) US#115 UK#6, also on B-side of *To Sir with Love* (1967) US#1; *Holly Holy* Junior Walker & the All Stars (1971) R&B#33 US#75, *I Am...I Said* Bill Phillips (1972) C&W#66, *I Got the Feelin' (Oh No, No)* Cliff Richard (1967) UK#26, *I'm a Believer* Monkees (1966) g US#1 UK#4/Tommy Overstreet (1974) C&W#9/Robert Wyatt (1974) UK#29/EMF & Reeves & Mortimer (1995) UK#3; *Just Another Guy* Cliff Richard on B-side of *The Minute You're Gone* (1965) UK#1, *Kentucky Woman* Deep Purple (1969) US#38/Randy Barlow (1977) C&W#26; *Let Me Take You in My Arms Again* James Darren (1978) C&W#53, *Little Bit Me, a Little Bit You, A* Monkees (1967) g US#2 UK#3, *Red, Red Wine* Jimmy James & the Vagabonds (1969) US#127/Vic Dana (1970) US#72/Roy Drusky (1971) C&W#17/UB40 (1983) UK#1 US#34, re-entry (1988) g US#1; *Solitary Man* T.G. Sheppard (1976) C&W#14 US#100, *Sunday and Me* Jay & the Americans (1965) US#18, *Sunflower* Glen Campbell (1977) C&W#4 US#39, *Sweet Caroline* Bobby Womack (1972) R&B#16 US#51/Anthony Armstrong Jones (1970) C&W#40; *Ten Lonely Guys* Pat Boone (1962) US#45, *You Don't Bring Me Flowers* [iv] Jim Ed Brown & Helen Cornelius (1978) C&W#10. Co-writers: [i] Burt Bacharach/Carole

Bayer Sager, [ii] Gilbert Becaud, [iii] Winchell Bennett, [iv] Alan Bergman/Marilyn Bergman, [v] David Foster, [vi] Tom Hensley/Alan Lindgren, [vii] Alan Lindgren, [viii] Carole Bayer Sager.

267. DIDDLEY, Bo (b. Otha Ellas Bates, December 30, 1928, McComb, MI) R&B guitarist and vocalist. A former semi-professional boxer who became a major influence on the development of rock and roll. Diddley's compositions were later widely recorded by such artists as Eric Clapton and Creedence Clearwater Revival. After learning the guitar in his teens and studying the violin, Diddley moved to Chicago in 1934, to play in the blues groups the Hipsters and the Langley Avenue Jive Cats. During the 1950s, Diddley built himself a strong live reputation and signed to Chess Records, where he achieved his first hit with the unforgettable self-paean *Bo Diddley*. His best known song is the anthemic *Who Do You Love*, an archetypal two-chord shuffle that was built around a much copied guitar riff. CHART COMPOSITIONS: *Bo Diddley/I'm a Man* (1955) R&B#1, *Diddley Daddy* (1955) R&B#11, *Pretty Thing* (1956) R&B#4 US#34, *I'm Sorry* (1959) R&B#17, *Crackin' Up* (1959) R&B#14 US#62, *Say Man* (1959) R&B#3 US#20, *Say Man, Back Again* (1959) R&B#23 US#106, *Road Runner* (1960) R&B#20 UK#75, *Crawdad* (1960) US#111, *Hey Good Lookin'* (1965) UK#39, *Ooh Baby* (1967) R&B#17 US#88. ALBUMS: **Have Guitar Will Travel** (1961), **In the Spotlight** (1961), **Bo Diddley Is a Lover** (1962), **Bo Diddley Is a Gunslinger** (1962) UK#20, **Bo Diddley Is a Twister** (1962), **Bo Diddley** (1962) US#117 UK#11, **Bo Diddley and Company** (1962), **Surfin' with Bo Diddley** (1963), **Road Runner** (1963), **16 All-Time Hits** (1963, all Checker); **Bo Diddley Rides Again** (1963) UK#19, **Bo Diddley's Beach Party** (1964, both Pye) UK#13; **Two Great Guitars** with Chuck Berry (1964), **The Super Super Blues Band** (1968, both Checker); **London Sessions** (1972, Chess); **Live at the Ritz** (1987, Victory); **Breakin' Through the Sound Barrier** (1989, Triple); **The EP Collection** (1991, SFM); **The Chess Years** (1993, Charly); **This Should Not Be** (1993), **The Mighty Bo Diddley** (1995), **A Man Amongst Men** (1996, Code Blue/Atlantic); **Rare and Well Done** (1997, Chess). HIT VERSIONS: *Bo Diddley* Ronnie Hawkins (1963) US#117, *I'm a Man* Yardbirds (1965) US#17, *Little Girl* Troggs (1968) UK#37, *Mona* Craig McLachlan & Check 1–2 (1990) UK#2, *Oh Yeah* Shadows of the Night (1966) US#39, *Who Do You Love* Woolies (1967) US#95/ Quicksilver Messenger Service (1969) US#91/Juicy Lucy (1970) UK#14/Tom Rush (1971) US#105/ Pointer Sisters (1979) US#106. (*See also under* Muddy WATERS.)

268. DIETZ, Howard (b. September 8, 1896; d. July 30, 1983, both New York, NY) Film and stage lyricist. A director of publicity at MGM films, who collaborated with the composers Jerome Kern and George Gershwin, before teaming up with Arthur Schwartz in 1927. Dietz was a director of ASCAP for two years from 1959, and in 1980, he was the subject of the television special "Song By Song By Howard Dietz." (*See also under* Vernon DUKE, Jerome KERN, George GERSHWIN, Jimmy McHUGH, Ralph RAINGER, Arthur SCHWARTZ.)

269. DIFFORD, Chris (b. November 4, 1954, London, England), and **TILLBROOK, Glenn** (b. August 31, 1957, London, England) Both pop guitarists and vocalists. A songwriting partnership who met through a music paper advertisement in 1974, before forming the group Squeeze with the keyboard player Jools Holland. CHART COMPOSITIONS: *Take Me I'm Yours* (1978) UK#19, *Bang Bang* (1978) UK#49, *Goodbye Girl* (1978) UK#63, *Cool for Cats* (1979) UK#2, re-issued (1992) UK#62; *Up the Junction* (1979) UK#2, *Slap and Tickle* (1979) UK#24, *Another Nail in My Heart* (1980) UK#17, *Pulling Muscles (From a Shell)* (1980) UK#44, *Is That Love* (1981) US#49 UK#35, *Tempted* (1981) US#49 UK#41, *Labelled with Love* (1981) UK#4, *Black Coffee in Bed* (1982) US#103 UK#51, *Annie Get Your Gun* (1982) UK#43, *The Last Time Forever* (1987) UK#45, *Hourglass* (1987) US#15 UK#17, *Trust Me to Open My Mouth* (1987) UK#72, *853 5937* (1987) US#32, *Third Rail* (1993) UK#39, *Some Fantastic Place* (1993) UK#73, *This Summer* (1995) UK#36, remixed (1996) UK#32; *Electric Trains* (1995) UK#44, *Heaven Knows* (1996) UK#27. ALBUMS: **Squeeze** (1978), **Cool for Cats** (1979) UK#45, **Argy Bargy** (1980) US#71 UK#32, **East Side Story** (1981) US#44 UK#19, **Sweets from a Stranger** (1982) US#32 UK#37, **Cosi Fan Tutti Frutti** (1985) US#57 UK#31, **Babylon and On** (1987) US#36 UK#14, **Frank** (1989, all A&M) US#113 UK#58; **A Round and a Bout** (1990, IRS) US#163 UK#50; **Play** (1991, Reprise) UK#41; **Some Fantastic Place** (1993) US#182 UK#26, **Ridiculous** (1995, both A&M) UK#50. COMPILATIONS: **Squeeze** (1979), **Singles-45s and Under** (1982) p US#47 UK#3, **Greatest Hits** (1992) UK#6, **Excess Moderation** (1996, all A&M). In the early 1980s, Difford and Tillbrook wrote the musical "Labelled with Love," and composed material for other artists, including Helen Shapiro, Billy Bremner and Paul Young. They also recorded as a duo, charting with *Love's Crashing Waves* (1984) UK#57, from the album **Difford and Tillbrook** (1984, A&M) US#55 UK#47. HIT VERSIONS: *One Good Reason* [i] Paul Carrack (1988)

US#28, *Tempted* Sting on B-side of *Mad About You* (1991) UK#56. All compositions Difford/Tillbrook, except [i] Paul Carrack/Chris Difford.

270. DIXON, Luther Pop producer. A songwriter-producer whose composition *Boys* [xi] was recorded by the Beatles on their debut album. In 1959, Dixon co-founded the record label Sceptor. HIT VERSIONS: *Big Boss Man* [xi] Jimmy Reed (1961) R&B#13 US#78/Charlie Rich (1963) US#108/ Gene Chandler as *Soul Hootenanny* (1964) US#92/ Elvis Presley (1967) US#38/Pretty Things on B-side of *Rosalyn* (1964) UK#41/B.B. King (1985) R&B#62; *Hundred Pounds of Clay, A* [ii] Craig Douglas (1961) UK#9/Gene McDaniels (1961) R&B#11 US#3; *I Don't Want to Cry* [viii] Chuck Jackson (1961) R&B#5 US#36/Ruby Winters (1969) R&B#15 US#97/Ronnie Dyson (1970) R&B#9 US#50; *I Love You 1,000 Times* [iv] Platters (1966) R&B#6 US#31, *Mama Said* [i] Shirelles (1961) R&B#2 US#4, *Sixteen Candles* [ix] Crests (1959) R&B#4 US#2/Jerry Lee Lewis (1986) C&W#61; *Soldier Boy* [v] Four Fellows (1955) R&B#4/Shirelles (1962) R&B#3 US#1 UK#23; *Soul Serenade* [x] King Curtis (1964) US#51/Willie Mitchell (1968) R&B#10 US#23 UK#43/Jimmy Castor Bunch (1973) R&B#72; *Tonight's the Night* Shirelles (1960) R&B#14 US#39, *Why Baby Why?* [vi] Pat Boone (1957) US#5 UK#17, *With This Ring* [vii] Platters (1967) R&B#12 US#14. Co-writers: [i] Willie Dennson, [ii] Bob Elgin/Kay Rogers, [iii] Wes Farrell, [iv] Inez Foxx (b. September 9, 1942, Greensboro, NC), [v] Florence Green, [vi] Larry Harrison, [vii] Tony Hester/Richard Wylie, [viii] Charles Jackson (b. July 22, 1937, Latta, SC), [ix] Allison R. Khent, [x] Curtis Ousley, [xi] Al Smith.

271. DIXON, Willie (b. July 1, 1915, Vicksburg, MS; d. January 29, 1992, Glendale, CA) Blues guitarist, bassist, producer and vocalist. A blues pioneer who blended an inner city blues sound with rural country, and became a cornerstone at Chess Records during the 1950s, contributing to nearly every significant disk on the label between 1952–1956, including many of Chuck Berry's earliest hits. Dixon was also the most significant blues songwriter of the period, penning over five hundred tunes that often featured scintillating guitar riffs and spun boastful tales of sexual prowess, illicit love and extreme bad luck. According to the Chess house-pianist, Jimmie Johnson, Dixon wrote a song "for just about everybody." One of fourteen siblings, Dixon commented in his autobiography, "We were damned lucky to have a thing to eat." After mastering both the guitar and acoustic bass, he began writing songs. In Chicago, he was marginally successful as a professional boxer, before returning to music in 1937,

when he joined the group the Five Breezes. After being incarcerated as a conscientious objector during World War II, Dixon formed his group the Big Three Trio, shortly after which he became a bassist, arranger, producer and songwriter at Chess. During the 1960s, his songs were introduced to an entirely new audience when they were recorded by the million selling white rock acts Cream, the Rolling Stones, Fleetwood Mac, Led Zeppelin, the Allman Brothers Band, the J. Geils Band, John Mayall's Bluesbreakers, and the Doors. Dixon released records on his own ARC label in the 1950s, and in 1985, issued the single *It Don't Make Sense That You Can't Make Peace*. CHART COMPOSITION: *Walking the Blues* (1955) R&B#6. ALBUMS: **Willie's Blues** (1959, Prestige/Bluesville); **Memphis Slim and Willie Dixon*** (1959), **At the Village Gate*** (1960, both Folkways); **The Blues Every Which Way*** (1960, Verve): **Live at the Trois Mailletz*** (1962, Polydor); **I Am the Blues** (1969, Columbia); **Loaded with the Blues***** (1969, MPS); **Peace** (1971, Yambo); **Catalyst** (1973, Ovation); **Maestro Willie Dixon and His Chicago Blues Band** (1973, Spivey); **What's Happening to My Blues** (1976, Ovation); **Mighty Earthquake and Hurricane** (1984), **Live-Backstage Access** (1985, both Pausa); **I Feel Like Steppin' Out**** (1985, Dr. Horse); **Hidden Charms** (1988, Bug); **The Big Three Trio, Volume 2**** (1990, Dr. Horse); **The Big Three Trio**** (1991, Columbia). COMPILATION: **The Chess Box** (1989, Chess). HIT VERSIONS: *Back Door Man* Derek (1968) US#59/Blues Band on *The Blues Band EP* (1980) UK#68; *Big Boat (Somebody Tell That Woman)* Peter, Paul & Mary (1963) US#93, *Close to You* Muddy Waters (1958) R&B#9, *Diddy Wah Diddy* Blues Band on *The Blues Band EP* (1980) UK#68, *Don't Go No Farther* Muddy Waters (1956) R&B#9, *Doncha' Think It's Time* [i] Elvis Presley (1958) US#15, *Evil (Going On)* Howlin' Wolf (1969) R&B#43, *Help Me* Sonny Boy Williamson (1963) R&B#24, *Hold Me, Baby* Amos Milburn (1949) R&B#2, *I Can't Quit You, Baby* Otis Rush (1956) R&B#6, *I Just Want to Make Love to You* Rolling Stones on B-side of *Tell Me* (1964) US#24/Foghat (1972) US#83, live version (1977) US#33; *I'm Ready* Muddy Waters (1954) R&B#4, *I'm Your Hoochie Coochie Man* Muddy Waters (1954) R&B#3/Dion (1964) US#113/Jimmy Smith (1966) R&B#49 US#94; *Just Make Love to Me* Muddy Waters (1954) R&B#4, *Little Red Rooster* Margie Day (1951) R&B#5/Griffin Brothers (1951) R&B#5/Sam Cooke (1963) R&B#7 US#11/Rolling Stones (1964) UK#1; *My Babe* Little Walter (1955) R&B#1, re-issued (1960) US#106/Righteous Brothers (1963) US#75, re-issued (1965) US#101/Willie Mitchell (1969) R&B#37 US#115/Earl Richards (1975) C&W#91;

Oh Baby Little Walter (1954) R&B#8, *Spoonful* Etta James & Harvey Fuqua (1960) R&B#12 US#78, *24 Hours* Eddie Boyd (1953) R&B#3, *Walkin' the Blues* Jack Dupree & Mr. Bear (1955) R&B#6, *Wang Dang Doodle* Koko Taylor (1966) R&B#4 US#58/Pointer Sisters (1974) R&B#24 US#61; *You Can't Judge a Book By Its Cover* Bo Diddley (1962) R&B#21 US#48/Troy Seals (1974) C&W#78. With: * Memphis Slim. As: ** the Big Three Trio, *** the Chicago Blues All-Stars. Co-writer: [i] Clyde Otis.

272. Doctor John (b. Malcom "Mac" John Rebennack, November 21, 1941, New Orleans, LA) R&B pianist and vocalist. A 1950s session pianist who became a highly regarded solo performer with his unique blend of New Orleans patois, R&B, creole and voodoo mystic-psychedelia. Influenced by the New Orleans style of Professor Longhair, Dr. John was himself an influence on Tom Waits with his 1950s Night Tripper act. After first recording with Ronnie Baron as Drits and Dravy, Dr. John embarked on successful solo career in the 1970s. CHART COMPOSITIONS: *Wash, Mama, Wash* (1970) US#108, *Right Place Wrong Time* (1973) R&B#19 US#9, *Such a Night* (1973) R&B#76 US#42, *(Everybody Wanna Get Rich) Rite Away* (1974) US#92, *Jet Set* (1984) R&B#80. ALBUMS: **Gris Gris** (1968), **Babylon** (1969), **Remedies** (1970), **Dr. John-The Night Tripper (The Sun, Moon and Herbs)** (1971) US#184, **Dr. John's Gumbo** (1972) US#112, **In the Right Place** (1973, all Atco) US#24; **Triumvirate** with Mike Bloomfield and John Paul Hammond (1973, Columbia) US#105; **Desitively Bonnaroo** (1974, Atco) US#105; **Hollywood Be Thy Name** (1975, United Artists); **Cut Me While I'm Hot** (1976, DJM); **City Lights** (1978, A&M); **Tango Palace** (1981), **Love Potion** (1981, both Horizon); **Dr. John Plays Mac Rebennack** (1981, Clean Cuts); **The Brightest Smile in Town** (1982, Demon); **Take Me Back to New Orleans** (1982, Black Lion); **In a Sentimental Mood** (1988, Warner Brothers) US#142; **On a Mardi Gras** (1991, Great Southern); **Goin' Back to New Orleans** (1992, Warner Brothers); **Television** (1995, GRP); **Afterglow** (1995, Blue Thumb). COMPILATIONS: **I Been Hoodood** (1984, Edsel); **Very Best of Dr. John** (1995, Rhino). HIT VERSIONS: *Losing Battle, A* Johnny Adams (1962) R&B#27, *More and More* [i] Carly Simon (1975) US#94, *Walk on Gilded Splinters* Marsha Hunt (1969) UK#46. Co-writer: [i] A. Robinson. (*See also under* Doc POMUS and Mort SHUMAN.)

273. DOLBY, Thomas (b. Thomas Morgan Robertson, October 14, 1958, Cairo, Egypt) Pop keyboard player and producer. After performing in Bruce Woolley and the Camera Club, Dolby became a successful synthesizer based solo artist and producer. CHART COMPOSITIONS: *Europa and the Pirate Twins* (1981) UK#48, re-issued (1983) US#67; *Windpower* (1982) UK#31, *She Blinded Me with Science* [i] (1982) UK#49, re-issued (1983) R&B#49 US#5 UK#56; *Hyperactive* (1984) US#62 UK#17, *Airhead* (1988) UK#53, *Close But No Cigar* (1992) UK#22, *I Love You Goodbye* (1992) UK#36, *Silk Pajamas* (1992) UK#62. ALBUMS: **The Golden Age of Wireless** (1982, Venice in Peril) UK#65; **Blinded By Science** (1983, Harvest) US#20; **The Flat Earth** (1984, Parlophone) US#35 UK#14; **Aliens Ate My Buick** (1988, Manhattan) US#70 UK#30; **Astronauts and Heretics** (1992, Virgin) UK#35; **Cyberia** (1994). COMPILATION: **Best of Thomas Dolby** (1995, Capitol). HIT VERSION: *New Toy* Lene Lovich (1981) UK#53. Co-writer: [i] Joe Kerr.

274. DOMINO, Fats (b. Antoine Domino, February 26, 1928, New Orleans, LA) R&B pianist and vocalist. One of the most important and influential R&B artists, who achieved sales of over sixty-five million records and sixty-three chart hits between 1950–1964. The dynamics of his rocking sound is best evidenced on his million seller *The Fat Man* [i] (1949). Domino was also in part responsible for the development of ska and reggae, when his discs were heard on American radio by young Jamaicans during the 1950s. A direct descendent of the Fats Waller and Albert Ammons school of boogie-woogie, Domino first performed in public at the age of ten, before working as a session player for the singer Lloyd Price, and appearing in the film "Shake, Rattle and Roll" (1956). CHART COMPOSITIONS: *The Fat Man* [i] (1950) R&B#2, *Goin' Home* (1952) g R&B#1 US#30, *Goin' to the River* (1953) g R&B#2 US#24, *Ain't That a Shame* [i] (1955) R&B#1 US#10, re-issued (1957) UK#23; *All By Myself* (1955) R&B#1, *Poor Me* [i] (1955) R&B#1, *Bo Weevil* [i] (1956) R&B#5 US#35, *I'm in Love Again* [i] (1956) R&B#1 US#3 UK#12, *Blue Monday* [i] (1956) R&B#1 US#5 UK#23, *I'm Walkin'* [i] (1957) R&B#1 US#4 UK#19, *Valley of Tears* [i] (1957) R&B#2 US#6, *It's You I Love* [i] (1957) US#22, *Whole Lotta Loving* [i] (1958) R&B#2 US#6, *I'm Ready* [ii] (1959) R&B#7 US#16, *I Want to Walk You Home* (1959) R&B#1 US#8, *I'm Gonna Be a Wheel Someday* [i] (1959) R&B#22 US#17, *Don't Come Knockin'* (1960) R&B#28 US#21, *Three Nights a Week* (1960) R&B#8 US#15, *My Girl Josephine* [i] (1960) R&B#7 US#14, *Let the Four Winds Blow* [i] (1961) R&B#2 US#15. ALBUMS: **Rock and Rollin' with Fats Domino** (1956) US#17, **Fats Domino-Rock and Rollin'** (1956) US#18, **This Is Fats Domino** (1957) US#19, **Million Sellers By Fats Domino** (1962, all Imperial) US#113; **Here**

Comes Fats Domino (1963, ABC/Paramount) US#130; **Fats on Fire** (1964), **Fats Domino '65** (1965), **Live in Las Vegas** (1965. both Mercury); **Fats Is Back** (1968, Reprise) US#189; **Very Best of Fats Domino** (1970, Liberty) UK#56; **Sleeping on the Job** (1979, Sonet); **They Call Me the Fat Man** (1991, EMI); **The Imperial Singles, Volume 1** (1996), **The Imperial Singles, Volume 2: 1953–1956** (1997, both Ace). HIT VERSIONS: *Ain't That a Shame* [i] Pat Boone (1955) R&B#14 US#2 UK#7/Four Seasons (1963) US#22 UK#38/Hank Williams, Jr. (1971) C&W#7/Cheap Trick (1979) US#35; *Blue Monday* [i] James Davis (1963) US#113, *Goin' to the River* Chuck Willis (1953) R&B#4, *I'm in Love Again* [i] Fontane Sisters (1956) US#38, *I'm Walkin'* [i] Rick Nelson (1957) R&B#10 US#17/Doug Kershaw (1977) C&W#96; *My Girl Josephine* [i] Jerry Jaye (1967) US#29, *Whole Lotta Loving* [i] Lois Johnson & Hank Williams, Jr. (1972) C&W#22. Co-writers: [i] Dave Bartholomew, [ii] Sylvester Bradford/Al Lewis.

275. DONALDSON, Walter (b. February 15, 1891, Brooklyn, NY; d. July 15, 1947, Santa Monica, CA) Film and stage composer, pianist. A former song-plugger who became a prolific Tin Pan Alley songwriter. Donaldson's first hit was with *Back Home in Tennessee* [vii] (1915), one of three of his songs to sell a combined total of over eight million copies. He had initially taught himself the piano in order to write songs for a school show, but during World War I, he was stationed with fellow songwriter Irving Berlin, for whose publishing company he later became employed for ten years. One of the million sellers he wrote in his new found position was Al Jolson's *My Mammy* [x] (1919). Donaldson's earliest Broadway contributions were to the shows "Sweetheart Time" (1926), "Whoopee" (1928) and "Ziegfeld Follies of 1927." His most prolific partnership was with the lyricist Gus Kahn, with whom he worked in Hollywood during the 1930s, contributing to the films "Kid Millions" (1934), "Here Comes the Band" (1935), "Follow the Boys" (1944), "The Dolly Sisters" (1945), "April Showers" (1948), "Jolson Sings Again" (1949), and "I'll See You in My Dreams" (1952). In 1928, Donaldson formed his own publishing company. HIT VERSIONS: *At Sundown (When Love Is Calling Me Home)* Arden-Ohman Orchestra (1927) US#12/Franklyn Baur (1927) US#19/George Olsen (1927) US#1; *Earful of Music, An* [ix] Ethel Merman (1935) US#11, *Back Home in Tennessee* [vii] Prince's Orchestra (1916) US#5, *Because My Baby Don't Mean Maybe Now* Ruth Etting (1928) US#10, *Beside a Babbling Brook* [ix] Marion Harris (1923) US#7, *Carolina in the Morning* [ix] American Quartet (1923) US#8/Marion Harris (1923) US#4/

Van & Schenck (1923) US#1/Paul Whiteman (1923) US#5/Danny Winchell (1952) US#30; *Changes* Paul Whiteman (1928) US#4, *Clouds* [ix] Benny Goodman (1935) US#16/Ray Noble (1935) US#5; *Could Be* [xii] Johnny Messner (1939) US#3, *Cuckoo in the Clock* [vii] Kay Kyser (1939) US#5, *Daughter of Rosie O'Grady, The* [ii] Lewis James (1918) US#3, *Did I Remember?* [i] Tommy Dorsey (1936) US#7/Shep Fields (1936) US#1; *Earful of Music, An* [ix] Ethel Merman (1935) US#11, *Georgia* [viii] Carl Fenton (1922) US#6/Peerless Quartet (1922) US#9/Paul Whiteman (1922) US#5; *Give Me My Mammy* [iii] Al Jolson (1922) US#2, *Hello, Beautiful* Wayne King (1931) US#16, *How Ya Gonna Keep 'Em Down on the Farm (After They've Seen Paree)* [x] Nora Bayes (1919) US#2/Arthur Fields (1919) US#7/Byron G. Harlan (1919) US#9; *I Wonder Where My Baby Is Tonight?* [ix] Henry Burr & Billy Murray (1926) US#7/Winifred Atwell in *Let's Have Another Party* (1954) UK#1; *I'm Bringing a Red, Red Rose* [ix] Ruth Etting (1929) US#15, *I've Had My Moments* [ix] Eddy Duchin (1934) US#4, *It's Been So Long* [i] Bunny Berigan (1936) US#18/Benny Goodman (1936) US#1/Freddy Martin (1936) US#8; *Just Like a Melody Out of the Sky* Gene Austin (1928) US#5/Cliff Edwards (1928) US#14/Paul Whiteman (1928) US#15; *Lazy Lou'isiana Moon* Chuck Bullock (1930) US#20/Guy Lombardo (1930) US#10; *Let It Rain, Let It Pour* [vi] Gene Austin (1925) US#6/Ben Selvin (1925) US#13/Nat Shilkret (1925) US#10; *Let's Talk About My Sweetie* [ix] Ruth Etting (1926) US#14, *Little White Lies* Earl Burtnett (1930) US#4/Ted Wallace (1930) US#3/Fred Waring's Pennsylvanians (1930) US#1/Dick Haymes (1948) g US#2/Dinah Shore (1948) US#11/Kenjolairs (1962) US#116; *Love Me or Leave Me* [ix] Ruth Etting (1929) US#2/Benny Goodman (1934) US#16, re-issued (1936) US#4/Sammy Davis, Jr. (1955) US#20 UK#8/Doris Day (1955) US#20/Lena Horne (1955) US#19; *Makin' Whoopee* [ix] Ben Bernie (1929) US#16/Eddie Cantor (1929) US#2/Paul Whiteman (1929) US#8/Ray Charles (1965) R&B#14 US#46 UK#42; *My Baby Just Cares for Me* [ix] Ted Weems (1930) US#30/Hi-Los (1954) US#29/Nina Simone (1987) UK#5; *My Best Girl* Cliff Edwards (1925) US#15/Isham Jones (1925) US#4/Nick Lucas (1925) US#4; *My Blue Heaven* [xii] Gene Austin (1927) g US#1/Paul Whiteman (1927) US#1/Seger Ellis (1928) US#17/Nick Lucas (1928) US#7/Don Voorhees (1928) US#9/Sammy Kaye (1939) US#17/Fats Domino (1956) R&B#5 US#21/Joe "Mr. Piano" Henderson in *Sing It Again with Joe* (1955) UK#18/Dave Clark Five in medley *More Good Old Rock 'n' Roll* (1969) UK#34; *My Buddy* [ix] Henry Burr (1922) US#1/Ben Bernie (1923) US#11/Ernest Hare (1923) US#5/Sammy Kaye (1942) US#23/Eddie Harris (1961) US#114; *My*

Little Bimbo Down on the Bamboo Isle [iv] Frank Crumit (1920) US#6, *My Mammy* [x] Isham Jones (1921) US#11/Peerless Quartet (1921) US#4/Aileen Stanley (1921) US#8/Paul Whiteman (1921) US#1/Yerkes Jazarimba Orchestra (1921) US#8/Al Jolson (1928) g US#2, re-issued (1947) US#18/Big Ben Banjo Band in *Let's Get Together Again* (1955) UK#18/Happenings (1967) US#13 UK#34; *My Mom* Kate Smith (1932) US#10, *My Ohio Home* [ix] Nick Lucas (1928) US#4, *Okay Toots* [ix] Eddie Cantor (1934) US#19, *On the Gin-Gin-Ginny Shore* Ray Miller (1922) US#8, *Roamin' to Wyomin'* California Ramblers (1924) US#10, *Sam, the Old Accordion Man* Ruth Etting (1927) US#5, *Sleepy Head* Ford & Glenn (1926) US#5, *Sweet Indiana Home* Marion Harris (1922) US#5/Aileen Stanley (1922) US#2; *Sweet Jennie Lee!* Isham Jones (1930) US#10, *That Certain Party* [ix] Ernest Hare & Billy Jones (1926) US#9/Ted Lewis (1926) US#8/Dean Martin & Jerry Lewis (1948) US#22/Benny Strong (1948) US#9; *There Ain't No Maybe in My Baby's Eyes* [v] "Whispering" Jack Smith (1927) US#3, *(What Can I Say) After I Say I'm Sorry* [xi] Will Bradley (1940) US#26, *When My Ship Comes In* [ix] Henry Burr & Albert Campbell (1915) US#4, *Where'd You Get Those Eyes?* Vaughn Deleath (1926) US#10/Ted Lewis (1926) US#3; *Yes Sir, That's My Baby* [ix] Gene Austin (1925) US#1/Ben Bernie (1925) US#5/Ace Brigode (1925) US#10/Coon-Sanders Orchestra (1925) US#11/Blossom Seeley (1925) US#2/Big Ben Banjo Band in *Let's Get Together #1* (1954) UK#6/Johnston Brothers in *Join in and Sing Again* (1955) UK#9/Winifred Atwell in *Make It a Party* (1956) UK#7/Sensations (1956) R&B#15/Russ Conway in *More Party Pops* (1958) UK#10/Rick Nelson (1960) US#18/Baja Marimba Band (1968) US#109; *You* [i] Jimmy Dorsey (1936) US#5/Tommy Dorsey (1936) US#1/Freddy Martin (1936) US#11/Sammy Kaye (1952) US#28; *You're Driving Me Crazy! (What Did I Do?)* Guy Lombardo (1930) US#1/Nick Lucas (1931) US#7/Rudy Vallee (1931) US#3/Buddy Greco (1953) US#26/Temperance Seven (1961) UK#1; *You've Got Everything* [ix] Jan Garber (1933) US#10. Co-writers: [i] Harold Adamson, [ii] Monty C. Brice, [iii] Buddy De Sylva, [iv] Grant Clarke, [v] Ray Egan/Gus Kahn, [vi] Cliff Friend, [vii] William Jerome, [viii] Howard Johnson, [ix] Gus Kahn, [x] Sam M. Lewis/Joe Young, [xi] Abe Lyman, [xii] George Whiting. (*See also under* Johnny MERCER.)

276. Donovan (b. Donovan Phillip Leitch, February 10, 1946, Glasgow, Scotland) Pop guitarist and vocalist. A singer-songwriter of wispy folk romanticism and hippie ideologies, who was frequently compared to Bob Dylan, despite being nothing like him. Donovan also scored and appeared in the films

"The Pied Piper" and "Brother Sun, Sister Moon" (both 1972). CHART COMPOSITIONS: *Catch the Wind* (1965) US#23 UK#4, *Colors* (1965) US#61 UK#4, *Turquoise* (1965) UK#30, *Sunshine Superman* (1966) g US#1 UK#2, *Mellow Yellow* (1966) g US#2 UK#8, *Epistle to Dippy* (1967) US#19, *There Is a Mountain* (1967) US#11 UK#8, *Wear Your Love Like Heaven* (1967) US#23, *Summer Day Reflection Song* (1967) US#135, *Jennifer Juniper* (1968) US#26 UK#5, new version with Singing Corner (1990) UK#68; *Hurdy Gurdy Man* (1968) US#5 UK#4, *Lalena* (1968) US#33, *Atlantis* (1968) US#7 UK#23, *To Susan on the West Coast Waiting* (1969) US#35, *Barabajagal (Love Is Hot)* (1969) US#36 UK#12, *Riki Tiki Tavi* (1970) US#55, *Celia of the Seals* (1971) US#84, *I Like You* (1973) US#66. ALBUMS: **What's Bin Did and What's Bin Hid** (1965) UK#3, **Catch the Wind** (1965) US#30, **Fairy Tale** (1965) US#85 UK#20, **Mellow Yellow** (1967) US#14, **A Gift from a Flower to a Garden** (1968) g US#19 UK#13, **Wear Your Love Like Heaven** (1968) US#60, **For Little Ones** (1968) US#185, **In Concert** (1968) US#18, **The Hurdy Gurdy Man** (1968) US#20, **Barabajagal** (1969, all Pye) US#23; **Open Road** (1970) US#16 UK#30, **HMS Donovan** (1971, both Dawn); **Cosmic Wheels** (1973, Epic) US#25 UK#15; **Live in Japan** (1973, Sony); **Essence to Essence** (1974) US#174, **7-Tease** (1974) US#135, **Slow Down World** (1975, all Epic) US#174; **Donovan** (1977, Rak); **Love Is the Only Feeling** (1980) **Neutronic** (1980, both RCA); **Lady of the Stars** (1983, Allegiance); **Rising** (1990); **Sutras** (1996, American). COMPILATIONS: **The Real Donovan** (1966, Hickory) US#96; **Sunshine Superman** (1967, Pye) US#11 UK#25; **Universal Soldier** (1967, Marble Arch) UK#5; **Like It Is, Was and Evermore Shall Be** (1968) US#177, **Greatest Hits** (1969) p US#4, **Best of Donovan** (1969, all Hickory) US#144; **Donovan P. Leitch** (1970, Janus) US#128; **Troubadour-The Definitive Collection, 1964–1976** (1994, Epic). HIT VERSIONS: *Catch the Wind* Kathy Barnes (1977) C&W#50, *Museum* Herman's Hermits (1967) US#39, *Sunny Goodge Street* Tom Northcott (1967) US#123, *Sunshine Superman* Willie Bobo (1966) US#107, *Universal Soldier, The* Glen Campbell (1965) US#45, *Walkin'* C.C.S. (1971) UK#7.

277. DORSET, Ray (b. March 21, 1946, Ashford, England) Pop guitarist and vocalist. The lead singer and principal songwriter in the skiffle influenced Mungo Jerry. Dorset first recorded in the group Good Earth, releasing the albums **It's Hard Rock and All That** and **Swinging London** (both 1968, Saga), before penning Mungo Jerry's first hit, the charming *In the Summertime*, which sold over twenty-three million copies worldwide and topped the charts in some twenty countries. Dorset achieved two further number one compositions, with Mungo Jerry's *Baby Jump*, and Kelly Marie's *Feels Like I'm in Love* (1980). CHART COMPOSITIONS: *In the Summertime* (1970) US#3 UK#1, *Baby Jump* (1971) UK#1, *Lady Rose* (1971) UK#5, *You Don't Have to Be in the Army to Fight the War* (1971) UK#13, *Open Up* (1972) UK#21, *Wild Love* (1973) UK#32, *Long Legged Woman Dressed in Black* (1974) UK#13. ALBUMS: **Mungo Jerry** (1970) US#64 UK#14, **Electronically Tested** (1971) UK#13, **You Don't Have to Be in the Army** (1971), **Boot Power** (1972, all Dawn); **Impala Saga** (1976), **Lovin' in the Alleys, Fightin' in the Streets** (1977), **Ray Dorset and Mungo Jerry** (1978, all Polydor). COMPILATIONS: **Greatest Hits** (1973, Dawn); **Golden Hour of Mungo Jerry** (1974, Golden Hour); **All the Hits Plus More** (1990, Prestige). During the 1980s, Dorset composed television themes, ran his own Saraja label, and recorded two solo albums, **Cold Blue Excursion** (1972, Dawn) and **A Case for the Blues** with Peter Green (1986, Nightflite). HIT VERSION: *Feels Like I'm in Love* Kelly Marie (1980) UK#1.

278. DOZIER, Lamont (b. June 16, 1941, Detroit, MI) R&B producer and vocalist. A songwriter who has co-written seventy-two American top ten singles, and who is best known as one third of the songwriting and production team Holland-Dozier-Holland. Dozier made his first recordings as a teenager in the group the Romeos for the Fox label, and achieved a local solo hit with *Fine, Baby, Fine*, before joining the Voice Masters. In 1958 he recorded as Lamont Anthony, and signed to Motown Records in 1962, where he teamed up with the Holland brothers. Since the mid-1970s, Dozier has also recorded as a solo artist. CHART COMPOSITIONS: *Let Me Start Tonight* (1974) R&B#4 US#87, *All Cried Out* (1975) R&B#41 US#101, *Can't Get Off Until the Feeling Stops* (1976) R&B#89, *Shout About It* (1982) R&B#61. ALBUMS: **Out Here on My Own** (1973) US#136, **Black Bach** (1975, both ABC) US#186; **Love and Beauty** (1975, Invictus); **Right Here** (1976), **Peddlin' Music on the Side** (1977), **Bittersweet** (1979), **Boogie Business** (1979, all Warner Brothers); **Working on You** (1981, ARC); **Bigger Than Life** (1983, Demon); **Lamont** (1981, A&M); **Inside Seduction** (1991, Atlantic). HIT VERSIONS: *Going Back to My Roots* Odyssey (1981) R&B#68 UK#4/FPI Project (1989) UK#9; *Invisible* Alison Moyet (1984) US#45 UK#21, *Loco in Acapulco* [i] Four Tops (1988) UK#7, *To Be Reborn* Boy George (1987) UK#13, *Without You* Peabo Bryson & Regina Belle (1988) R&B#14 US#89. Co-writer: [i] Phil Collins. (*See also under* Phil COLLINS, Debbie GIBSON, Brian HOLLAND, Lamont DOZIER and Edward HOLLAND, Mick HUCKNALL.)

279. DRAKE, Ervin (b. America) Film and stage lyricist. A lyricist who also composed such classics as Frank Sinatra's *It Was a Very Good Year* (1961). Drake's songs were featured in the films "Bathing Beauty" (1944) and "Rome Adventure" (1961). ALBUMS: **What Makes Sammy Run?** oc (1964, Columbia) US#28. HIT VERSIONS: *Al Di La* [iv] Emilio Pericoli (1962) US#6 UK#30/Ray Charles Singers (1964) US#29; *Beloved Be Faithful* [viii] Russ Morgan (1950) US#28, *Castle Rock* [vii] Fontane Sisters (1951) US#27/Johnny Hodges (1951) R&B#4 US#28/Frank Sinatra & Harry James (1951) US#8; *Come to the Mardi Gras* [iii] Freddy Martin (1947) US#16, *Good Morning Heartache* [v] Diana Ross (1973) R&B#20 US#34, *Hay-foot, Strawfoot* [vi] Duke Ellington (1942) R&B#10, *It Was a Very Good Year* Frank Sinatra (1961) US#28, *Meet Mister Callaghan* [ix] Carmen Cavallaro (1952) US#28/Harry Grove Trio (1952) US#11/Mitch Miller (1952) US#23/Les Paul (1952) US#5; *My Friend* [viii] Eddie Fisher (1954) US#15/Frankie Laine (1954) UK#3; *Perdido* [vi] Duke Ellington (1943) US#21, *Rickerty Rickshaw Man, The* Eddy Howard (1946) US#6, *Sonata* [ii] Perry Como (1947) US#9/Jo Stafford (1947) US#10; *Tico Tico* [i] Andrews Sisters (1944) US#24/Charles Wolcott (1944) US#18/Ethel Smith (1945) US#14. Co-writers: [i] Zeguinha Abreu/Aloysio Oliveira, [ii] Alex Alstone/Jimmy Shirl, [iii] Max Bulhoes/Milton De Oliveira/Jimmy Shirl, [iv] Carlo Donida, [v] Dan Fisher/Irene Higginbotham, [vi] Harry J. Lengsfelder/Juan Tizol, [vii] Al Sears/Jimmy Shirl, [viii] Jimmy Shirl, [ix] Jimmy Shirl/Eric Spear.

280. DRAKE, Nick (b. Nicholas Rodney Drake, June 19, 1948, Burma; d. November 25, 1974, Tamworth-in-Arden, England) Folk guitarist, pianist and vocalist. A singer-songwriter whose small body of recorded work is a remarkable testimony to the poetic possibilities of the popular song. Drake explored the melancholic side of British folk music in a manner akin to an American Delta blues player. Drake learned the guitar in his teens, but before attending Cambridge University, the incurably romantic teenager spent an idyllic summer in Aix-en-Provence, France, where he listened to the then new music of Van Morrison, Tim Buckley, John Hartford, and Tim Hardin, alongside such French classical composers as Delibes, influences that Drake would incorporate into an intriguing blend of English folk mixed with European classical romanticism. Drake's stunning debut album, **Five Leaves Left** (1969), was a cycle of songs so fragile that they were nearer to the literature of Henri Alain-Fournier and Marcel Proust than they were to pop music. After dropping out of university and moving to London, Drake rented a bedsit in Hampstead, where he wrote much of his follow-up **Bryter Later** (1970), a series of perceptive and objective self-examinations that balanced humor and self-pity against the backdrop of late 1960s London life. The album was a unique dissemination of the frailties of psyche and character, often written in the third person, as it seemed that for Drake, music had become the sole means by which he could communicate his ideas and emotions. Although the record failed to sell, its producer, Joe Boyd, described it as the one perfect album that he (Boyd) has ever produced. Dismayed by his lack of commercial success, Drake headed to Paris in 1971, purportedly to write songs for Francoise Hardy, although it is not known if any were ever recorded. By the time Drake returned to London the following year he was clearly suffering from manic depression, and only Robert Johnson's 1930s blues recordings are as desperately troubled as Drake's final album, **Pink Moon** (1972), a short, cathartic and stark portrait of a man on the very brink of despair. The album is one of the most painful, nihilistic, yet strangely enchanting song cycles ever commercially released. After checking himself into a psychiatric hospital for five weeks, Drake moved back to live at his parents home, where he died in 1974 from an overdose of prescribed anti-depressants. ALBUMS: **Five Leaves Left** (1969), **Bryter Later** (1970), **Pink Moon** (1972, all Island). COMPILATIONS: **Fruit Tree** (1979, Island); **Time of No Reply** (1987, Hannibal); **The Complete Home Recordings** (1996, Boyds Music).

281. DRESSER, Paul (b. Paul Dreiser, April 21, 1857, Terra Haute, IN; d. January 30, 1906, New York, NY) Film composer and vocalist. The older brother of the novelist Theodore Dreiser, who, although dying in absolute poverty, was one of Tin Pan Alley's first and most successful sentimental ballad composers and publishers. Although Dresser's music sounds nostalgic in retrospect, it should be remembered that it was nostalgic when he wrote it, his forte being ballad portrayals of a long-gone rural America. Dresser ran away from home at the age of sixteen to work in medicine shows and minstrel troupes, after which he performed in vaudeville, before publishing his first song, *Wide Wings* (1884), and his first hit, *The Letter That Never Came* (1886). Dresser's compositions were also featured in such films as "My Gal Sal" (1942) and "Wait Till the Sun Shines Nellie" (1952). He became a music publisher in 1900, but his Howley, Dresser and Company went bankrupt in 1904. HIT VERSIONS: *Just Tell Them That You Saw Me* J.W. Myers (1895) US#1/George J. Gaskin (1896) US#2; *My Gal Sal* Byron G. Harlan (1907) US#1/Columbia Stellar Quartet (1921) US#11/Burl Ives (1965) US#122; *On the Banks of the Wabash*

George J. Gaskin (1897) US#1/Roger Harding (1898) US#3/Steve Porter (1898) US#1/Harry MacDonough & the American Quartet (1913) US#5.

282. DUBIN, Al (b. June 10, 1891, Zurich, Switzerland; d. February 11, 1945, New York, NY) Film and stage lyricist. A composer for sound film in its formative years, who was also Harry Warren's principal lyricist. Dubin was initially a lawyer whose parents had emigrated to America when he was two years old. During the 1900s, he worked as a singing waiter in Philadelphia, and after World War I, he plied his trade on Tin Pan Alley. His first success was with *A Cup of Coffee, a Sandwich and You* [vi], from the show "The Charlot Revue of 1926," which he followed with contributions to such films as "Santa Fe Trail" (1941). HIT VERSIONS: *Along the Santa Fe Trail* [ii] Bing Crosby (1941) US#4/Dick Jurgens (1941) US#6/Sammy Kaye (1941) US#9/Glenn Miller (1941) US#7; *Anniversary Waltz, The* [iii] Bing Crosby (1941) US#24/Anita Harris (1968) US#21; *Crooning* [i] Benson Orchestra of Chicago (1921) US#7, *Cup of Coffee, a Sandwich and You, A* [vi] Gertrude Lawrence & Jack Buchanan (1926) US#5, *Just a Girl That Men Forget* [iv] Henry Burr (1923) US#3/Lewis James (1924) US#12; *Tiptoe Through the Tulips* [vi] Roy Fox (1929) US#18/Jean Goldkette (1929) US#5/Nick Lucas (1929) US#1/Johnny Marvin (1929) US#11/Russ Conway in *More and More Party Pops* (1959) UK#5/Tiny Tim (1968) US#17; *Where Was I?* [v] Charlie Barnet (1940) US#1/Sammy Kaye (1940) US#11/Jan Savitt (1940) US#14. Cowriters: [i] William F. Caesar/Herbert Weise, [ii] Edwina Coolidge/Will Grosz, [iii] Dave Franklin, [iv] Joe Garren/Fred Rath, [v] W. Franke Harling, [vi] Joseph Meyer/Billy Rose. (*See also under* Ernest BALL, Joseph BURKE, Sammy FAIN, Victor HERBERT, Burton LANE, Jimmy McHUGH, Harry WARREN, Allie WRUBEL.)

283. DUKE, Vernon (b. Vladimir Dukelsky, October 10, 1903, Parafianovo, Russia; d. January 16, 1969, Santa Monica, CA) Film and stage composer. A fairly sophisticated composer who was classically trained at the Kiev Conservatory of Music, Russia. Duke fled his homeland after the 1917 revolution, initially settling in England, where he composed for the productions "Yvonne" (1926) and "The Yellow Mask" (1928). In 1929, Duke emigrated to America, basing himself in New York, where he worked with the lyricist Yip Harburg on the Broadway shows "Walk a Little Faster" (1932), "The Ziegfeld Follies" (1934), "Cabin in the Sky" (1940), and "Sadie Thompson" (1944). Duke also collaborated with the poet Ogden Nash on the revue "Two's Company" (1952), and with Ira Gershwin on "The

Ziegfeld Follies of 1936." His compositions were also featured in a number of films, including "Cabin in the Sky" (1942), "Thumbs Up" (1954), "April in Paris" (1953), and "Paris Holiday" (1958). Some of Duke's more sophisticated tunes have since become jazz standards. HIT VERSIONS: *April in Paris* [iv] Henry King (1934) US#14/Freddy Martin (1934) US#5/Count Basie (1956) R&B#8 US#28; *Autumn in New York* Frank Sinatra (1949) US#27, *Cabin in the Sky* [v] Benny Goodman (1943) US#19, *I Can't Get Started* [ii] Hal Kemp (1936) US#14/Bunny Berigan (1938) US#10; *I Am Only Human, After All* [iii] Colonial Club Orchestra (1930) US#8, *Takin' a Chance on Love* [i] Benny Goodman (1943) R&B#10 US#1/Sammy Kaye (1943) US#13; *What Is There to Say?* [iv] Emil Coleman (1934) US#12. Co-writers: [i] Ted Feter/John Latouche, [ii] Ira Gershwin, [iii] Ira Gershwin/E.Y. Harburg, [iv] E.Y. Harburg, [v] John Latouche. (*See also under* Oscar BROWN, Jr.)

284. DURY, Ian (b. May 12, 1942, Upminster, England) Pop vocalist. A polio victim from the age of seven, who overcame his handicap to become a singer in the pub-rock group Kilburn and the High Roads, which released the album **Handsome** (1974, Dawn). In the late 1970s, he formed Ian Dury and the Blockheads, a group of accomplished musicians who blended elements of punk, R&B and British music hall on a series of highly original recordings. CHART COMPOSITIONS: *What a Waste* (1978) UK#9, *Hit Me with Your Rhythm Stick* [i] (1979) UK#1, re-mixed (1985) UK#55, re-mixed (1991) UK#73; *Reasons to Be Cheerful (Part 3)* [ii] (1979) UK#3. ALBUMS: **New Boots and Panties** (1978) US#168 UK#5, **Do It Yourself** (1979) US#126 UK#2, **Laughter** (1980, all Stiff) US#159 UK#48. COMPILATIONS: **Juke Box Duries** (1981), **Sex and Drugs and Rock and Roll** (1987, both Stiff); **Reasons to Be Cheerful** (1996, Repertoire). Dury later recorded as a solo artist, before concentrating on an acting career. He also co-wrote the musical "Apples" (1989). CHART COMPOSITIONS: *I Want to Be Straight* (1980) UK#22, *Superman's Big Sister* (1980) UK#51, *Profoundly in Love with Pandora* (1985) UK#45. ALBUMS: **Lord Upminster** (1981) UK#53, **4,000 Weeks Holiday** (1984, both Polydor) UK#54; **Apples** oc (1989, WEA); **The Bus Driver's Prayer and Other Short Stories** (1992, Demon). Co-writers: [i] Charles Jankel, [ii] Charles Jankel/Davey Payne.

285. DYLAN, Bob (b. Robert Allan Zimmerman, May 24, 1941, Duluth, MN) Folk guitarist, pianist, harmonica player and vocalist. The single most important singer-songwriter after Woody Guthrie. Dylan is a widely recorded and highly influential tunesmith, whose transformation of the three minute pop song changed the course of popular music, while his lazy, laconic vocal style has been much imitated. Dylan performs his music with a casualness that deliberately detracts from his serious intent. His witty development of the talking blues style into a more rhythmic story-telling, with its incisive social observations, created, although seldom acknowledged as such, one of the earliest forms of rap. Dylan's use of meter and language in popular song was revolutionary, and, like the improvisational nature of jazz, his quick, one or two-take approach to recording was the nearest that pop music has ever come to genuine spontaneity. Dylan grew up listening to folk and blues music, learning the guitar in his teens and playing in several groups, later saying, "I was never gonna be anything else…I was twelve years old, and that was all I wanted to do. Play my guitar." After dropping out of university in 1960, he headed to New York, where he met his ailing idol Woody Guthrie, and performed on the Greenwich Village folk scene. Dylan was rejected as a staff songwriter by various publishing houses before he secured his first publishing deal with Leeds Music. During a brief visit to England to inspect the thriving British folk scene of the early 1960s, he was influenced by the premier folk artist Martin Carthy. Dylan signed to Columbia Records in 1961, and released an eponymous debut album that was an authoritative selection of folk, country and blues standards. He followed it with **The Freewheelin' Bob Dylan** (1963), an album that in many ways was the birth of contemporary songwriting, with its remarkable depth and clarity and introduction of topics hitherto unheard of on pop discs. As Dylan the folk interpreter became Dylan the folk innovator, he perfected the protest song and introduced a new poetry to pop with such material as *Masters of War, A Hard Rain's Gonna Fall, Don't Think Twice, It's Alright, Girl from the North Country, Blowin' in the Wind*, and the anti-racist *Oxford Town*. **The Times They Are a-Changin'** and **Another Side of Bob Dylan** (both 1964), contained the work of a songwriting genius, but like all great initiators, Dylan dispensed with a style just as soon as he had mastered it, and he quickly outgrew his folk roots to explore a lyrical world of mystical imagery. **Bringing It All Back Home** (1965), controversially merged folk with electric rock, and was followed by the equally daring **Highway 61 Revisited**, which contained Biblical allegories in the flamenco sounding *Desolation Row*. **Blonde on Blonde** (1966), was a masterpiece of country-blues and ragtime, of which Dylan later said, "The closest I ever got to the sound I hear in my mind was on individual bands on the **Blonde on Blonde** album." An inconsistent period during the early 1970s was halted by **Blood on the Tracks**

(1975), which once again captured him at his most incisive, poetic and melodic on such vignettes as *Tangled Up in Blue*, and the bitter, acrimonious *Idiot Wind*. As the Rolling Thunder Revue, Dylan toured America with a vast entourage, and also made the rambling, incoherent but intriguing movie "Renaldo and Clara" (1975). A flirtation with born-again Christianity resulted in an inspired R&B influenced album, **Slow Train Running** (1979). During the late 1980s, Dylan participated in the Traveling Wilburys group project, charting with the singles *Handle with Care* [ii] (1988) US#45 UK#21, *End of the Line* [ii] (1988) US#63 UK#52 and *Nobody's Child* [ii] (1990) UK#44, from the albums **The Traveling Wilburys, Volume 1** (1988) p US#3 UK#16 and **The Traveling Wilburys, Volume 3** (1990, both Wilbury) p US#11 UK#14. In 1991, Columbia released a massive collection of previously unreleased material and alternative takes, **The Bootleg Series, Volumes 1-3** (1991), which proved a significant insight into the development of Dylan's music from its earliest days. The boxed set proved that with the idiosyncratic Dylan, it is often what he did not release at the time, or the version that dissatisfied him at the last moment, where the paucity of his musical vision is revealed none more so than on the magnificent outtake *Blind Willie McTell*. Allegedly suffering from writer's block throughout the 1990s, Dylan re-discovered his roots on two albums of traditional folk and country-blues standards, **Good as I Been to You** and **World Gone Crazy**, both of which hinted at some of his own sources and inspirations, and also indicated just how much he had achieved with three chords and an acoustic guitar. Of the many recordings of his songs, the most successful albums have been: Joan Baez, **Any Day Now** (1969, Vanguard) g US#30; Barbara Dickson, **Don't Think Twice, It's Alright** (1992) US#32; the Four Seasons, **Big Hits By Burt Bacharach and Bob Dylan** (1965, Philips) US#106; **I Shall Be Released-The Songs of Bob Dylan** (1989, Start) UK#13; and **30th Anniversary Concert Celebration** (1993) g US#40. Dylan once said of his songwriting, "All the words have already been used: it's just how we put them together." CHART COMPOSITIONS: *The Times They Are a-Changin'* (1965) UK#9, *Subterranean Homesick Blues* (1965) US#39 UK#9, *Maggie's Farm* (1965) UK#22, *Like a Rolling Stone* (1965) US#2 UK#4, *Positively 4th Street* (1965) US#7 UK#8, *Can You Please Crawl Out Your Window* (1966) US#58 UK#17, *One of Us Must Know (Sooner or Later)* (1966) US#119 UK#33, *Rainy Day Woman #12 and #35* (1966) US#2 UK#7, *I Want You* (1966) US#20 UK#16, *Just Like a Woman* (1966) US#33, *Leopard-Skin Pillbox Hat* (1967) US#81, *I Threw It All Away* (1969) US#85 UK#30, *Lay Lady Lay* (1969) US#7 UK#5, *Tonight I'll Be Staying Here*

with You (1969) US#50, *Wigwam* (1970) US#41, *Watching the River Flow* (1970) US#41 UK#24, *George Jackson* (1971) US#33, *Knockin' on Heavens Door* (1973) US#12 UK#14, *On a Night Like This* (1974) US#44, *Something There Is About You* (1974) US#107, *Most Likely You'll Go Your Way and I'll Go Mine* (1974) US#66, *Hurricane* [iii] (1975) US#33 UK#43, *Mozambique* [iii] (1975) US#54, *Tangled Up in Blue* (1975) US#31, *Rita May/Stuck Inside of Mobile with the Memphis Blues Again* (1977) US#110, *Baby Stop Crying* (1978) UK#13, *Is Your Love in Vain* (1978) UK#56, *Gotta Serve Somebody* (1979) US#24, *Sweetheart Like You* (1979) US#55, *Union Sundown* (1983) UK#90, *Tight Connection to My Heart (Has Anybody Seen My Love)* (1985) US#103, *Dignity* (1995) UK#33. ALBUMS: **Bob Dylan** (1962) g UK#13, **The Freewheelin' Bob Dylan** (1963) g US#22 UK#1, **The Times They Are a-Changin'** (1964) US#20 UK#4, **Another Side of Bob Dylan** (1964) US#43 UK#8, **Bringing It All Back Home** (1965) g US#6 UK#1, **Highway 61 Revisited** (1965) g US#2 UK#4, **Blonde on Blonde** (1966) g US#9 UK#3, **John Wesley Harding** (1968) g US#2 UK#1, **Nashville Skyline** (1969) p US#3 UK#1, **Self Portrait** (1970) g US#4 UK#1, **New Morning** (1970) g US#7 UK#1, **Pat Garrett and Billy the Kid** ost (1973) US#16 UK#29, **Dylan** (1973, all Columbia) g US#17; **Planet Waves*** (1974) g US#1 UK#7, **Before the Flood*** (1975, both Asylum) g US#3 UK#8; **Blood on the Tracks** (1975) p US#1 UK#4, **The Basement Tapes*** (1975) US#7 UK#8, **Desire** (1976) p US#1 UK#3, **Hard Rain** (1976) g US#17 UK#3, **Street Legal** (1978) g US#11 UK#2, **Bob Dylan at Budokan** (1978) US#13 UK#4, **Slow Train Coming** (1979) p US#3 UK#2, **Saved** (1980) US#24 UK#3, **Shot of Love** (1981) US#33 UK#6, **Infidels** (1983) g US#20 UK#9, **Real Live** (1984) US#115 UK#54, **Empire Burlesque** (1985) US#33 UK#11, **Knocked Out Loaded** (1986) US#53 UK#35, **Down in the Groove** (1988) US#61 UK#32, **Dylan and the Dead** with the Grateful Dead (1989) g US#37 UK#38, **Oh Mercy** (1989) US#30 UK#6, **Under the Red Sky** (1990) US#38 UK#13, **Good as I Been to You** (1992) US#51 UK#18, **World Gone Wrong** (1993) US#70 UK#35, **Unplugged** (1995) US#23 UK#10, **Time Out of Mind** (1997, all Columbia). COMPILATIONS: **Bob Dylan's Greatest Hits** (1967, Columbia) p US#10; **Greatest Hits** (1967, CBS) UK#6; **Greatest Hits, Volume 2** (1971, Columbia) p US#14; **More Bob Dylan Greatest Hits** (1972, CBS) UK#12; **Biograph** (1985) p US#33, **The Bootleg Series, Volumes 1–3 (Rare and Unreleased, 1961–1991)** (1991) US#49 UK#32, **Greatest Hits, Volume 3** (1995) US#126, **Best of Bob Dylan** (1997, all Columbia) UK#6. HIT VERSIONS: *All Along the Watchtower* Jimi Hendrix

(1968) US#20 UK#5, re-issued (1990) UK#52; *All I Really Want to Do* Byrds (1965) US#40 UK#4/Cher (1965) US#15 UK#9; *Ballad of a Thin Man* Grass Roots (1965) US#121, *Blowin' in the Wind* Peter, Paul & Mary (1963) g US#2 UK#13/Stan Getz (1964) US#110/Stevie Wonder (1966) R&B#1 US#9 UK#36/Edwin Hawkins Singers (1969) US#109; *Don't Think Twice, It's All Right* Peter, Paul & Mary (1963) US#9/Wonder Who (1965) US#12/Doc & Merle Watson (1978) C&W#88; *Emotionally Yours* O'Jays (1991) g R&B#2, *Farewell, Angelina* Joan Baez (1965) UK#35, re-entry (1966) UK#49; *Go 'Way Little Boy* Lone Justice on B-side of *Sweet, Sweet Baby (I'm Falling)* (1985) US#73, *Hard Rain's a-Gonna Fall, A* Leon Russell (1971) US#105/Bryan Ferry (1978) UK#10; *I Don't Believe You (She Acts Like We Never Have Met)* Lloyd Cole & the Commotions on B-side of *Jennifer She Said* (1988) UK#31, *I Shall Be Released* Tremeloes (1968) UK#29/Box Tops (1969) US#67/Rick Nelson (1970) US#102/Freddie Scott (1970) R&B#40/Tom Robinson Band on B-side of *2-4-6-8 Motorway* (1977) UK#5; *I'll Be Your Baby Tonight* Glen Garrison (1968) C&W#48/Burl Ives (1968) US#133/Ray Stevens (1970) US#112/Judy Rodman (1987) C&W#5/Robert Palmer & UB40 (1990) UK#6; *If Not for You* Olivia Newton-John (1971) US#25 UK#7/Bobby Wright (1973) C&W#75; *If You Gotta Go, Go Now (Or Else You Gotta Stay All Night)* Manfred Mann (1965) UK#2/Fairport Convention as *Si Tu Dois Partir* (1969) UK#21; *It Ain't Me Babe* Johnny Cash (1964) US#58 UK#28/Turtles (1965) US#8; *It Takes a Lot to Laugh, It Takes a Train to Cry* Leon Russell (1971) US#105, *It's All Over Now Baby Blue* Joan Baez (1965) US#22/Milltown Brothers (1993) UK#48; *Just Like a Woman* Manfred Mann (1966) US#101 UK#10, *Knockin' on Heavens Door* Eric Clapton (1975) UK#38/Guns 'n' Roses (1992) UK#2/Dunblane School (1996) UK#1; *Lay Lady Lay* Byrds (1969) US#132/Ferrante & Teicher (1970) US#99/Isley Brothers (1971) R&B#29 US#71/Jim Bean (1988) C&W#96; *Like a Rolling Stone* Flatt & Scruggs (1968) C&W#58 US#125/Phil Flowers & the Flowershop (1969) US#104/Rolling Stones (1995) UK#12; *Lo and Behold* Marjoe (1972) US#109, *Love Is Just a Four Letter Word* Joan Baez (1969) US#86, *Love Minus Zero/No Limit* Eddie Hodges (1965) US#134/Turley Richards (1970) US#84; *Maggie's Farm* Solomon Burke on B-side of *Tonight's the Night* (1965) R&B#2 US#28/Blues Band on *The Blues Band EP* (1980) UK#68/Specials (1980) UK#4/Tin Machine (1989) UK#48; *Mighty Quinn (Quinn the Eskimo), The* Manfred Mann (1968) US#10 UK#1, *Mr. Tambourine Man* Byrds (1965) g US#1 UK#1, *My Back Pages* Byrds (1967) US#30, *One Too Many Mornings* Beau Brummels (1966) US#95, *Please, Mrs. Henry* Manfred Mann's Earthband (1971) US#108,

She Belongs to Me Rick Nelson (1969) US#33, *This Wheel's on Fire* [i] Julie Driscoll with Brian Auger & the Trinity (1968) US#106 UK#5/Siouxsie & the Banshees (1980) UK#14; *Times They Are a-Changin', The* Peter, Paul & Mary (1964) UK#44/Peter Antell (1965) US#135/Ian Campbell Folk Group (1965) UK#42; *Too Much of Nothing* Peter, Paul & Mary (1967) US#35; *When the Ship Comes In* Peter, Paul & Mary (1965) US#91, *With God on Our Side* Neville Brothers (1989) UK#47; *You Ain't Goin' Nowhere* Byrds (1968) US#74 UK#45, *You Angel You* Manfred Mann (1979) US#58 UK#54. With: * the Band. Co-writers: [i] Rick Danko (b. December 9, 1943, Simcoe, Canada), [ii] George Harrison/Jeff Lynne/Roy Orbison/Tom Petty, [iii] Jacques Levy. (*See also under* Michael BOLTON, Tom PETTY.)

286. EARLE, Steve (b. January 17, 1955, Fort Monroe, VA) C&W guitarist and vocalist. A former Nashville staff songwriter who became one of many new country artists in the 1980s to bridge the gap between country and rock. Earle's songs have also been recorded by Connie Smith, Carl Perkins and Waylon Jennings. CHART COMPOSITIONS: *Nothin' But You* (1983) C&W#70, *What'll You Do About Me?* (1984) C&W#76, *Hillbilly Highway* (1986) C&W#37, *Guitar Town* (1986) C&W#7, *Someday* (1986) C&W#28, *Goodbye's All We've Got Left* (1987) C&W#8, *Nowhere Road* (1987) C&W#20, *Sweet Little '66* (1987) C&W#37, *Six Days on the Road* (1988) C&W#29, *Copperhead Road* (1988) UK#45, *Johnny Come Lately* (1988) UK#75. ALBUMS: **Guitar Town** (1986) US#89, **Exit O** (1987, both MCA) US#90 UK#77; **Copperhead Road** (1988, Uni) US#56 UK#44; **The Hard Way** (1990) US#100 UK#22, **We Ain't Never Satisfied** (1991, both MCA); **BBC Radio 1 Live in Concert** (1992, Windsong); **Shut Up and Die Like an Aviator** (1992, MCA) UK#62; **Train a-Comin'** (1995, Winter Harvest); **I Feel Alright** (1996, WB) US#106 UK#44. COMPILATIONS: **Steve Earle: Early Tracks** (1986, Epic); **The Essential Steve Earle** (1993), **Fearless Heart** (1996, both MCA).

287. EBB, Fred Film and stage lyricist, and **KANDER, John** (b. March 18, 1927, Kansas City, MO) Film and stage composer. A songwriting team best known for their one thousand performance plus Broadway show "Cabaret" (1967). Ebb and Kander first worked together in 1962, when their songs were recorded by Barbra Streisand. They were also covered by Liza Minnelli on the albums **Liza with a "Z"** (1972) US#19, and **Live at the Wintergarden** (1974, both Columbia) US#150. Ebb and Kander wrote separately for television during the 1970s. ALBUMS: **Family Affair** oc (1962, United Artists); **Flora, the**

Red Menace oc (1965, RCA) US#111; **Cabaret** oc (1967) US#37, **Cabaret** sc (1966, both Columbia); **Go Fly a Kite** oc (1966, General Electric); **Happy Time** oc (1968, RCA); **Zorba** oc (1969, Capitol) US#177; **70 Girls, 70** oc (1971, Columbia); **Cabaret** ost (1972, ABC) g US#25 UK#13; **Chicago** oc (1975) US#73; **Funny Lady** ost (1975); **Lucky Lady** oc (1976, all Arista); **Act** oc (1977, DRG); **New York, New York** ost (1977, United Artists) US#50; **An Evening with Fred Ebb and John Kander** oc (1978, Laureate); **Woman of the Year** oc (1981, Arista) US#196; **Rink** oc (1984, Polydor); **Flora, the Red Menace** oc (1989, TER). HIT VERSIONS: *Cabaret* Louis Armstrong (1968) UK#1, *My Coloring Book* Kitty Kallen (1963) US#18/Sandy Stewart (1963) US#20; *New York, New York* Gerard Kenny (1978) UK#43/Frank Sinatra (1980) US#32.

288. EDWARDS, Bernard (b. October 31, 1952, Greenville, NC; d. May 18, 1996, Tokyo, Japan) R&B bassist and producer, and **RODGERS, Nile** (b. September 19, 1952, New York, NY) R&B guitarist, producer and vocalist. The core musicians in the group Chic, which enjoyed enormous success during the 1970s with some of the classiest dance music of the era. Edwards and Rodgers' compositions were always executed with a blase precision, and their chord structures were nearer to jazz than they were to funk. Edwards began his musical career as a saxophonist, and said that the only reason he became a bassist was because, "the bass player who was in the band got drafted." Rodgers grew up listening to jazz, rock and blues, and played in a number of groups, including the folk act New World Rising. He also worked on the television series "Sesame Street," and played guitar in the Apollo Theatre house band. The pair met in 1970, when they formed the Big Apple Band with the drummer Tony Thompson. In 1977, they recorded several self-produced demos that led to a record contract with Atlantic. Chic's tight, sophisticated groove became the epitome of the then in-vogue disco sound, and their composition *Le Freak* was a four million seller. Their self-deprecating lyrics and clever ironies were often mistaken for surface level banalities, but they both became in-demand producers with artists who all hoped for a liberal sprinkling of the magic dust to revive their careers, which, in the cases of Sister Sledge and David Bowie, worked wonders. Chic finally broke up in 1983, although a brief reformation took place in 1992. CHART COMPOSITIONS: *Dance, Dance, Dance (Yowsah, Yowsah, Yowsah)* [ii] (1978) g R&B#6 US#6 UK#6, *Everybody Dance* (1978) R&B#12 US#38 UK#9, *Le Freak* (1979) p R&B#1 US#1 UK#7, re-mixed as *Jack Le Freak* (1987) UK#19; *I Want Your Love* (1979) g

R&B#5 US#7 UK#4, *Good Times* (1979) g R&B#1 US#1 UK#5, *My Forbidden Lover* (1979) R&B#33 US#43 UK#15, *My Feet Keep Dancing* (1979) R&B#42 US#101 UK#21, *Rebels Are We* (1980) R&B#8 US#61, *Real People* (1980) R&B#51 US#79, *Stage Fright* (1981) R&B#34 US#105, *Soup for One* (1982) R&B#14 US#80, *Hangin'* (1982) R&B#48 US#64, *Give Me the Lovin'* (1983) R&B#57, *Megachic-Chic Medley* (1990) UK#58, *Chic Mystique* [iv] (1992) R&B#49 UK#48. ALBUMS: **Chic** (1978) g US#27, **C'est Chic** (1979) p US#4 UK#2, **Risque** (1979) p US#5 UK#29, **Real People** (1980) US#30, **Take It Off** (1982) US#124, **Tongue in Chic** (1982) US#173, **Believer** (1983, all Atlantic); **Chic-ism** (1992, Warner Brothers). COMPILATIONS: **Les Grands Plus Grands Succes De Chic-Chic's Greatest Hits** (1979) US#88, **Best of Chic** (1979, both Atlantic) UK#30; **Soup for One** ost (1982, Mirage) US#168; **Freak Out** with Sister Sledge (1987, Telstar) UK#72; **Megachic** (1990, WEA). Edwards and Rodgers both recorded as solo artists during the 1980s: Rodgers charting with the solo single *Let's Go Out Tonight* (1985) R&B#35 US#88, and releasing the albums **Adventures in the Land of the Good Groove** (1983, Mirage) and **B Movie Matinee** (1983, Warner Brothers), and Edwards recording the album **Glad to Be Here** (1983, Warner Brothers). Edwards died on tour in Japan in 1996 of pneumonia. HIT VERSIONS: *Backfired* Deborah Harry (1981) R&B#71 US#43 UK#32, *Coming to America* [i] System (1988) US#91, *Good Times* Sugarhill Gang sampled in *Rapper's Delight* (1979) R&B#4 US#36 UK#3, re-mixed (1989) UK#58, also on *Calibre Cuts* (1980) UK#75/Club House (1983) UK#59/Soul II Soul sampled in *Keep on Moving* (1989) US#11 UK#5; *Got to Love Somebody Today* Sister Sledge (1979) R&B#6 US#64 UK#34, *He's the Greatest Dancer* Sister Sledge (1979) R&B#1 US#9 UK#6, *High Society* Norma Jean (1979) R&B#19, *I'm Coming Out* Diana Ross (1980) R&B#6 US#5 UK#13, re-mixed (1994) UK#36; *Jam Was Moving, The* Deborah Harry (1981) US#82, *Let's Go on Vacation* Sister Sledge (1980) R&B#63, *Lost in Music* Sister Sledge (1979) R&B#35 UK#17, re-mixed (1984) UK#4, re-mixed (1993) UK#14; *My Old Piano* Diana Ross (1980) US#109 UK#5, *Reach Your Peak* Sister Sledge (1980) R&B#21 US#101, *Saturday* Norma Jean (1978) R&B#15, *Serious Kinda Girl* [iii] Christopher Max (1989) US#75, *Spacer* Sheila & B. Devotion (1980) R&B#28 UK#18, *Thinking of You* Sister Sledge (1984) UK#11, re-mixed (1993) UK#17/Maureen (1990) UK#11; *Upside Down* Diana Ross (1980) g R&B#1 US#1 UK#2, *We Are Family* Sister Sledge (1979) g R&B#1 US#2 UK#8, re-mixed (1984) UK#33, re-mixed (1993) UK#5, also on *Calibre Cuts* (1980) UK#75; *Why* Carly Simon (1982) US#74

UK#10. All compositions Edwards/Rodgers, except: [i] N. Huang/Nile Rodgers, [ii] Bernard Edwards/ Kenny Lehman/Nile Rodgers, [iii] Christopher Max/ Nile Rodgers, [iv] Bernard Edwards/Princesa/Nile Rodgers. (*See also under* Robert PALMER.)

289. EDWARDS, Gus (b. August 18, 1879, Hohensaliza, Germany; d. November 7, 1945, Los Angeles, CA) Stage and film composer, vocalist. A Tin Pan Alley composer whose songs were featured in such films as "Hollywood Revue" (1929). Edwards emigrated to America with his parents at the age of eight, where he quickly developed a love of vaudeville. As a teenager he sung in the group the Newsboy Quintet, and his first published song was *All I Want Is My Black Baby Back* (1898). He went on to collaborate on many big hits of the period, including the three million selling *School Days* [ii] (1907). In 1905, Edwards formed his own publishing company. HIT VERSIONS: *I Just Can't Make My Eyes Behave* [ii] Ada Jones (1907) US#1, *In My Merry Oldsmobile* [i] Arthur Collins & Byron Harlan (1905) US#7/Billy Murray (1905) US#1; *Orange Blossom Time* [iii] Cliff Edwards (1929) US#20, *Tammany* [i] Arthur Collins & Byron Harlan (1905) US#2/S.H. Dudley (1905) US#4/Billy Murray (1905) US#7/ Arthur Pryor's Band (1905) US#5; *School Days* [ii] Byron G. Harlan (1907) US#1/Albert Campbell (1908) US#3; *Sunbonnet Sue* [ii] Haydn Quartet (1908) US#1/Byron G. Harlan (1908) US#4. Co-writers: [i] Vincent Bryan, [ii] Will D. Cobb (b. 1876; d. 1930), [iii] Joe Goodwin. (*See also under* Edward MADDEN.)

290. EDWARDS, Jackie (b. Wilfred Jackie Edwards, Kingston, Jamaica) Reggae vocalist. A regular Jamaican chart artist throughout the late 1950s and early 1960s, who, in 1964, signed to the British label Island, and released a series of highly regarded gospel-reggae albums. Edwards later recorded for the Third World and Starlight labels, but his greatest success was with the three songs that he composed for the Spencer Davis Group. ALBUMS: **The Most of Wilfred Jackie Edwards** (1964), **Stand Up for Jesus** (1964), **Come on Home** (1965), **By Demand** (1966), **Pledging My Love** (1966), **Premature Golden Sands** (1967), **Put Your Tears Away** (1969, all Island); **Let It Be Me** (1970, Direction); **I Do Love You** (1972, Trojan); **Do You Believe in Love** (1976, Klik); **Before the Next Teardrop** (1977), **Let's Fall in Love** (1978), **Come to Me Softly** (1978, all Third World); **The Original Cool Ruler** (1983, Vista). COMPILATION: **Best of Jackie Edwards** (1966, Island). HIT VERSIONS: *Keep on Running* Spencer Davis Group (1966) US#76 UK#1, *Somebody Help Me* Spencer Davis Group (1966) UK#1, re-

issued (1967) US#47; *When I Come Home* Spencer Davis Group (1966) UK#12.

291. EDWARDS, Jonathan (b. July 28, 1946, MN) C&W guitarist and vocalist. A country influenced singer-songwriter who first performed in the 1960s bluegrass group Sugar Creek, before achieving chart success as a solo artist. CHART COMPOSITIONS: *Sunshine* (1971) g US#4, *Train of Glory/Everybody Knows Her* (1972) US#101, *Stop and Start It All Again* (1973) US#112, *We Need to Be Locked Away* (1988) C&W#64, *Look What We Made (When We Made Love)* (1988) C&W#56. ALBUMS: **Jonathan Edwards** (1971, Capricorn) US#42; **Honky-Tonk Stardust Cowboy** (1972) US#167, **Have a Good Time** (1973), **Lucky Day** (1974, all Atco); **Rockin' Chair** (1976, Reprise); **Sailboat** (1977, Warner Brothers); **The Natural Thing** (1989, Curb/MCA). HIT VERSIONS: *Honky-Tonk Stardust Cowboy* Bill Rice (1971) C&W#51, *Sunshine* Juice Newton (1980) C&W#35.

292. EGAN, Raymond (b. 1890; d. 1952, both America) Film and stage lyricist. A frequent collaborator with Richard Whiting and Walter Donaldson, whose songs were featured in such films as "Blondie of the Follies" (1932). HIT VERSIONS: *I Never Knew (I Cold Love Anybody Like I'm Loving You)* [ii] Paul Whiteman (1921) US#7, *Three on a Match* [i] Paul Whiteman (1932) US#3. Co-writers: [i] Ted Fiorito, [ii] Roy Marsh/Tom Pitts. (*See also under* Walter DONALDSON, Richard WHITING.)

293. ELLINGTON, Duke (b. Edward Kennedy Ellington, April 29, 1899, Washington, DC; d. May 24, 1974, New York, NY) Jazz pianist, band and orchestra leader, arranger. A musical genius who was the most versatile and prolific composer in American popular music. Ellington was a leading exponent of big-band jazz, and easily the genre's most influential composer. The total number of Ellington compositions is not known, but he wrote at least two thousand works, many of his shorter pieces later having words set to them by a variety of lyricists. He lived almost permanently on the road, residing in hotel rooms and later in his own Pullman train carriage, where he composed popular standards, film scores, symphonic suites, tone poems, and shows tunes for "Cabin in the Sky" (1940) and "Ballad of Baby Doe" (1956). After studying the piano from the age of seven, Ellington graduated in music from Wilberforce University, after which he performed as a night club pianist. He began writing tunes in his teens, and by 1925, was recording with his first band the Washingtonians, with which he debuted his theme tune *East St. Louis Toodle-oo* [xv].

In 1924, Ellington scored the show "Chocolate Kiddies," and the following year became a bandleader. He was responsible for discovering or recruiting some of the finest jazz musicians in the world, and by insisting at all times on such caliber players, his enormous recorded output has become a benchmark by which other bandleaders have been judged. Ellington's manager, Irving Mills, had lyrics added to many of his tunes, for which he often took co-publishing credits despite making no musical contribution whatsoever. A regular slot at the Cotton Club in New York during the late 1920s, cemented Ellington's reputation. Many of his best tunes were composed in collaboration with the arranger Billy Strayhorn, who joined Ellington in 1940. Ellington's most visionary work was his musical history of black Americans, "Black, Brown and Beige: Tone Poem to the American Negro" (1943). The critic James Lincoln Collier aptly described him as the master chef of music, but Ellington's significance in the world of jazz has often meant that his contribution to the art of the popular song has been overlooked. The finest all-round series of Ellington song interpretations are to be found on **Ella Fitzgerald Sings the Duke Ellington Songbook, Volumes 1 and 2** (1957, Verve). He died in 1974, having written none of his music down, and leaving only a recorded legacy in place of a will. CHART COMPOSITIONS: *East St. Louis Toodle-oo* [xv] (1927) US#10, new version (1937) US#16; *Black and Tan Fantasy* [xv] (1928) US#15, *Creole Love Call* (1928) US#19, *The Mooche* [xvi] (1929) US#16, *Ring Dem Bells* [xvi] (1930) US#17, *Mood Indigo* [ii] (1931) US#3, *Rockin' in Rhythm* [iii] (1931) US#19, *Creole Rhapsody* (1931) US#18, new version (1932) US#19; *It Don't Mean a Thing (If It Ain't Got That Swing)* [xvi] (1932) US#6, *Blue Ramble* (1932) US#16, *Drop Me Off at Harlem* [xiii] (1933) US#17, *Sophisticated Lady* [xviii] (1933) US#3, *I'm Satisfied* [xx] (1933) US#11, *Daybreak Express* (1934) US#20, *Solitude* [v] (1935) US#2, *Saddest Tale* (1934) US#9, *Merry-Go-Round* (1935) US#6, *In a Sentimental Mood* [xiv] (1935) US#14, *Accent on Youth* (1935) US#6, *Cotton* (1935) US#4, *Clarinet Lament* [i] (1936) US#12, *Echoes of Harlem* (1936) US#19, *Yearning for Love* [xviii] (1936) US#16, *Jazz Lips* (1936) US#20, *Scattin' at the Kit-Kat* [xvi] (1937) US#9, *Caravan* [xix] (1937) US#4, *Azure* (1937) US#13, *Harmony in Harlem* [xi] (1938) US#15, *If You Were in My Place (What Would You Do?)* [xvii] (1938) US#10, *I Let a Song Go Out of My Heart* [xvii] (1938) US#1, *The Gal from Joe's* [xvi] (1938) US#20, *Prelude to a Kiss* [x] (1938) US#18, *Ko Ko* (1940) US#25, *Sepia Panorama* (1940) US#24, *I Got It Bad and That Ain't Good* [xxii] (1942) US#13, *Don't Get Around Much Anymore* [xxi] (1943) R&B#1 US#8, *Bojangles (A Portrait of Bill Robinson)* (1943) US#19, *Senti-mental Lady* (1943) R&B#1 US#19, *Do Nothin' Till You Hear from Me* [xxi] (1944) R&B#1 US#10, *Main Stem* (1944) R&B#1 US#23, *I Don't Mind* (1944) R&B#9, *I'm Beginning to See the Light* [ix] (1945) R&B#4 US#6, *Don't You Know I Care* [iv] (1945) R&B#10, *I Ain't Got Nothin' But the Blues* [viii] (1945) R&B#4, *Satin Doll* [xiv] (1953) US#27, *Boo-Dah* (1953) US#30, *Skin Deep* (1954) UK#7. SELECTED ALBUMS: **In Hollywood on the Air** (1933, Max); **Mood Ellington** (1949), **Liberian Suite** (1947), **Masterpieces By Ellington** (1950, all Columbia); **Ellingtonia, Volume 1** (1950), **Ellingtonia, Volume 2** (1950, both Brunswick); **Duke Ellington, Volume 1** (1951), **Duke Ellington, Volume 2** (1950), **Duke Ellington, Volume 3** (1951, all Jazz Panorama); **Ellington Uptown** (1951, Columbia); **Duke Ellington** (1951), **This Is Duke Ellington and His Orchestra** (1952, both RCA); **Premiered By Ellington** (1953, Capitol); **Duke Ellington** (1953, Allegro); **Duke Ellington Plays the Blues** (1953), **Seattle Concert** (1954), **Ellington's Greatest** (1954, all RCA); **Duke Ellington Plays** (1954, Allegro); **The Music of Duke Ellington** (1954, Columbia); **Early Ellington** (1954, Brunswick); **Ellington Plays Ellington** (1954), **The Duke Plays Ellington** (1954), **Ellington '55** (1954), **Dance to the Duke** (1955, all Capitol); **Duke and His Men** (1955, RCA); **Duke's Mixture** (1955), **Blue Light** (1955), **Here's the Duke** (1956), **American Jazz Festival at Newport** (1956) US#14, **Al Hibbler with the Duke** (1956, all Columbia); **Historically Speaking, the Duke** (1956), **Duke Ellington Presents** (1956, both Bethlehem); **Birth of Big Band Jazz** (1956, Riverside); **Ellington Showcase** (1956, Capitol); **A Drum Is a Woman** (1957), **Such Sweet Thunder** (1957, both Columbia); **In a Mellotone** (1957), **Duke Ellington at His Very Best** (1958, both RCA); **Ellington Indigos** (1958), **Black, Brown and Beige** (1958), **The Cosmic Scene** (1958, all Columbia); **Duke Ellington and His Orchestra** (1958, Rondo-lette); **Duke Ellington, Volume 1-In the Beginning** (1958), **Duke Ellington, Volume 2-Hot in Harlem** (1959), **Duke Ellington, Volume 3-Rockin' in Rhythm** (1959, all Decca); **Ellington Moods** (1959, SeSac); **Duke Ellington at the Cotton Club** (1959, Camden); **Back to Back** (1959), **Side By Side** both with Johnny Hodges (1959, both Verve); **Anatomy of a Murder** ost (1959), **Swinging Suites By Edward E. & Edward G.** (1960, all Columbia); **Newport '58** (1959), **Duke Ellington at the Bal Masque** (1959), **Duke Ellington Jazz Party** (1959), **Festival Season** (1959), **Blues in Orbit** (1960), **The Nut Cracker Suite** (1960) UK#11, **Piano in the Background** (1960), **Peer Gynt Suite/Suite Thursday** (1961, all Columbia); **The Indispensable Duke Ellington** (1961, RCA); **Louis Armstrong and**

Duke Ellington (1961, Roulette); **Best of Duke Ellington** (1961, Capitol); **Paris Blues** ost (1961), **Money Jungle** (1962, both United Artists); **Duke Ellington with John Coltrane** (1962, Impulse); **First Time** with Count Basie (1962), **All American** (1962), **Midnight in Paris** (1962, all Columbia); **Afro Bossa** (1962, Reprise); **The Great Reunion** with Louis Armstrong (1963, Roulette); **Great Times!** (1963, Riverside); **Piano in the Foreground** (1963), **The Ellington Era, Volume 1** (1963), **The Ellington Era, Volume 2** (1964, all Columbia); **The Symphonic Ellington** (1964), **Hits of the '60s** (1964), **Ellington '65: Hits of the '60s/This Time By Ellington** (1964, all Reprise) US#133; **Daybreak Express** (1964), **Jumpin' Punkins** (1965), **Johnny Come Lately** (1965), **Pretty Woman** (1965), **Flaming Youth** (1965, all RCA); **Mary Poppins** (1965), **Ellington '66** (1965), **Will Big Bands Ever Come Back?** (1965), **Concert in the Virgin Islands** (1965), **Ellington's Greatest Hits** (1966, all Reprise); **The Duke at Tanglewood** (1966) US#145, **The Popular Duke Ellington** (1966), **Concert of Sacred Music** (1966), **Far East Suite** (1967, all RCA); **Soul Call** (1967), **Francis A. and Edward K.** (1968, both Reprise) US#78; **Duke Ellington Meets Coleman Hawkins** (1968, Impulse); **Second Sacred Concert** (1968, Prestige); **And His Mother Called Him Bill** (1968, RCA); **The Complete Duke Ellington, 1948–1952** (1990, CBS); **The Blanton-Webster Years** (1990, RCA Bluebird); **Live at the Blue Note** (1994, Roulette). HIT VERSIONS: *Black and Tan Fantasy* [xv] Jimmie Lunceford (1935) US#19, *Caravan* [xix] Barney Bigard (1937) US#20/Billy Eckstine (1949) R&B#14 US#27/Esquire Boys (1953) US#27/Ralph Marterie (1953) g US#6/Santo & Johnny (1960) US#48/Duane Eddy (1961) UK#42; *Do Nothin' Till You Hear from Me* [xxi] Woody Herman (1944) R&B#4 US#7/Stan Kenton (1944) R&B#8 US#10; *Don't Get Around Much Anymore* [xxi] Glen Gray (1943) US#7/Ink Spots (1943) R&B#1 US#2; *Gal from Joe's, The* [xvi] Charlie Barnet (1939) US#13, *Happy-Go-Lucky Local* Buddy Morrow as *Night Train* (1952) US#27, *I Didn't Know About You (Sentimental Lady)* [xxi] Count Basie (1945) US#21, *I Got It Bad and That Ain't Good* [xxii] Benny Goodman (1942) US#25, *I Let a Song Go Out of My Heart* [xvii] Mildred Bailey (1938) US#8/Connee Boswell (1938) US#5/Benny Goodman (1938) US#1/Hot Lips Page (1938) US#9; *I'm Beginning to See the Light* [ix] Ella Fitzgerald & the Ink Spots (1945) US#5/Harry James (1945) US#1; *In a Sentimental Mood* [xiii] Benny Goodman (1936) US#13/Mills Blue Rhythm Band (1936) US#19; *It Don't Mean a Thing (If It Ain't Got That Swing)* [xv] Mills Brothers (1932) US#7, *Just a-Sittin' and a-Rockin'* [vii] Delta Rhythm Boys (1946) R&B#3 US#17/Stan

Kenton (1946) US#16; *Just Squeeze Me* [vi] Paul Weston (1947) US#21/Four Aces (1952) US#20; *Merry-Go-Round* Mills Blue Rhythm Band (1936) US#15, *Mood Indigo* [ii] Jimmie Lunceford (1934) US#19/Four Freshmen (1954) US#24/Norman Petty Trio (1954) US#14; *Prelude to a Kiss* [x] Johnny Hodges (1938) US#13, *Satin Doll* [xiv] Billy Maxted & His Manhattan Jazz Band (1961) US#117, *Solitude* [v] Mills Blue Rhythm Band (1935) US#8, *Sophisticated Lady* [xviii] Glen Gray (1933) US#4/Don Redman (1933) US#19/Billy Eckstine (1948) US#24. Cowriters: [i] Albany Bigard, [ii] Albany Bigard/Irving Mills (b. January 16, 1884, New York, NY; d. April 21, 1985, Palm Springs, CA), [iii] Harry Carney/Irving Mills, [iv] Mack David, [v] Eddie De Lange/Irving Mills, [vi] Lee Gaines, [vii] Lee Gaines/Billy Strayhorn, [viii] Don George, [ix] Don George/Harry James (b. March 15, 1916, Albany, GA; d. July 5, 1983)/Johnny Hodges (b. July 25, 1907, Cambridge, MA; d. May 11, 1970, New York, NY), [x] Irving Gordon/Irving Mills, [xi] Johnny Hodges/Irving Mills, [xii] Nick Kenny, [xiii] Manny Kurtz/Irving Mills, [xiv] Johnny Mercer, [xv] Bubber Miley (b. James Wesley, April 3, 1903, Aiken, SC; d. May 20, 1932, New York, NY), [xvi] Irving Mills, [xvii] Irving Mills/Henry Nemo, [xviii] Irving Mills/Mitchell Parish, [xix] Irving Mills/Juan Tizol, [xx] Mitchell Parish, [xxi] Bob Russell, [xxii] Paul Francis Webster.

294. ELLIS, Vivian, C.B.E. (b. October 29, 1904; d. June 19, 1996, both London, England) Stage composer and pianist. A composer and author whose work is evidence of a considerably more sentimental, innocent and unsophisticated era. Born into a family of classical musicians and composers, Ellis studied the piano under Dame Myra Hess when still a boy. He later furthered his musical studies at the Royal Academy in London, after writing his first composition at the age of eight. Ellis worked as a song-plugger for Chappell Music for twenty-eight years, and in his teens, contributed songs to such West End revues as "The Curate's Egg" and "Still Dancing," before achieving his first major success with *Spread a Little Happiness*, from "Mr. Cinders" (1928). During the 1930s, he worked in partnership with the impresario Charles B. Cochran, writing the scores to "Cochran's 1930 Revue," "Follow a Star," "Little Tommy Tucker," "Folly to Be Wise," "The Song of the Drum," and "Stand Up and Sing" (all 1931). Ellis' later successes included "Streamline," "Jill Darling" (both 1934); "Hide and Seek" (1937), "The Fleet's Lit Up," "Running Riot," and "Under Your Hat" (all 1938). He ultimately contributed to forty West End musicals and revues, and a partnership with the author A.P. Herbert resulted in the works "Big Ben" (1946), "Bless the Bride" (1947), "Tough at the Top" (1949), "And So to Bed" (1951), "Listen to the Wind" (1954), and "The Water Gypsies" (1955). When his songwriting success diminished, Ellis turned to writing books. In 1955 he became director of the Performing Rights Society, of which he was elected president in 1983, the same year that saw "Mr. Cinders" revived in London. In 1984, Ellis was appointed a Commander of the Order of the British Empire. A collection of his best known songs was recorded as **Spread a Little Happiness** (1996, Happ). HIT VERSIONS: *I'm on a See-saw* [i] Ambrose (1935) US#3, *Spread a Little Happiness* Sting (1982) UK#16. Co-writer: [i] Desmond Carter.

295. ERTEGUN, Ahmet (b. July 31, 1923, Constantinople, Turkey) R&B producer. The co-founder in 1947, with his brother Nesuhi Ertegun, of the record label Atlantic. During the 1940s, Ertegun had issued jazz instrumentals on the Quality and Jubilee labels, before finding success as a songwriter, record producer and arranger. HIT VERSIONS: *Chains of Love* [v] Big Joe Turner (1951) R&B#2 US#30/Pat Boone (1956) US#20; *Don't Play That Song (You Lied)* [iv] Ben E. King (1962) R&B#2 US#11/Aretha Franklin (1970) g R&B#1 US#11 UK#13; *Don't You Know I Love You* Clovers (1951) R&B#1, *Fool, Fool, Fool* Clovers (1951) R&B#1, *Good Lovin'* [iii] Clovers (1953) R&B#2, *Honey Love* Drifters (1954) R&B#1 US#21, *Little Mama* [i] Clovers (1954) R&B#4, *Lovey Dovey* [ii] Clovers (1954) R&B#2/Bunny Paul (1954) US#24/Clyde MacPhatter (1959) R&B#12 US#49/Buddy Knox (1961) US#25/Otis Redding & Carla Thomas (1968) R&B#21 US#60. Co-writers: [i] Willis Carroll/Carmen Taylor/Jerry Wexler, [ii] Memphis Curtis, [iii] Leroy Kirkland/Jesse Stone/Danny Taylor, [iv] Betty Nelson, [v] Van Wells. (*See also under* Steve MILLER.)

296. ESSEX, David (b. David Albert Cook, July 23, 1947, London, England) Pop vocalist. A durable mainstream singer and actor who started out as a drummer. Essex released numerous flop singles for a variety of labels during the 1960s, before playing Jesus Christ in the 1970s London cast of "Godspell." He starred in the film "That'll Be the Day" (1973), the same year in which he began a lengthy hit recording career. CHART COMPOSITIONS: *Rock On* (1973) g US#5 UK#3, *Lamplight* (1973) US#71 UK#7, *America* (1974) US#101 UK#32, *Gonna Make You a Star* (1974) US#105 UK#1, *Stardust* (1974) UK#7, *Rollin' Stone* (1975) UK#5, *Hold Me Close* (1975) UK#1, *If I Could* (1977) UK#13, *City Lights* (1977) UK#24, *Coming Home* (1977) UK#24, *Cool Out Tonight* (1977) UK#23, *Brave New World*

(1978) UK#55, *Imperial Wizard* (1979) UK#32, *Silver Dream Racer* (1980) UK#4, *Hot Love* (1980) UK#57, *Me and My Girl (Night Clubbing)* (1982) UK#13, *Tahiti* [i] (1983) UK#8, *You're in My Heart* (1983) UK#59, *Falling Angel's Riding* (1985) UK#29. ALBUMS: **Rock On** (1973) US#22 UK#7, **David Essex** (1974) UK#2, **All the Fun of the Fair** (1975) UK#3, **On Tour** (1977) UK#51, **Out on the Street** (1977) UK#31, **Gold and Ivory** (1977, all CBS) UK#29; **Imperial Wizard** (1979) UK#12, **Hot Love** (1980) UK#75, **Be-Bop the Future** (1981), **Stage-Struck** (1982) UK#31, **Mutiny** (1983) UK#39, **The Whisper** (1983) UK#67, **This One's for You** (1985, all Mercury); **Centre Stage** (1986, K-Tel) UK#82; **Touching the Ghost** (1989, Lamplight); **Cover Shot** (1993) UK#3, **Back to Back** (1994, both PolyGram TV) UK#33; **Living in England** (1996, Cleveland International); **Missing You** (1996) UK#26, **A Night at the Movies** (1997, both PolyGram TV) UK#21. COMPILATIONS: **The David Essex Album** (1978, CBS) UK#29, **Very Best of David Essex** (1983, TVR) UK#37; **The David Essex Collection** (1990, Castle); **His Greatest Hits** (1991, Mercury) UK#13. HIT VERSION: *Rock On* Michael Damian (1989) g US#1. Co-writer: [i] Richard Crane.

297. ESTEFAN, Gloria (b. Gloria Fajardo, December 1, 1957, Havana, Cuba) Pop producer and vocalist. The lead singer and principal songwriter in the Latin and disco influenced group Miami Sound Machine, which, by the early 1990s, was dumped for a solo career. CHART COMPOSITIONS: *Words Get in the Way* (1986) US#5, *Rhythm Is Gonna Get You* [iii] (1987) US#5 UK#16, *Can't Stay Away from You* (1988) US#6 UK#7, *One, Two, Three* [iii] (1988) UK#9, *Anything for You* (1988) US#1 UK#10, *Don't Wanna Lose You* (1989) US#1 UK#6, *Oye Mi Canto (Hear My Voice)* (1989) US#48 UK#16, *Cuts Both Ways* (1990) US#44 UK#49, *Coming Out of the Dark* [ii] (1991) US#1 UK#25, *Live for Loving You* [i] (1991) US#22 UK#33, *Always Tomorrow* (1992) US#81 UK#24, *Christmas Through Your Eyes* [v] (1992) UK#8, re-issued (1993) US#43; *Go Away* (1993) US#103 UK#13, *Mi Tierra* (1993) UK#36, *If We Were Lovers* (1993) UK#40, *Montuno* (1993) UK#55, *Reach* [v] (1996) US#58+ UK#15, *You'll Be Mine (Party Time)* (1996) UK#18, *I'm Not Giving You Up* (1996) UK#28. ALBUMS: **Renacer** (1976, Audio Latino); **Eyes of Innocence** (1984, Columbia); **Primitive Love** (1986) p US#23, **Let It Loose** (1987) p US#6, **Cuts Both Ways** (1989) p US#8 UK#1, **Exitos De Gloria Estefan** (1990), **Into the Light** (1991) p US#5 UK#2, **Mi Tierra** (1993) US#27 UK#11, **Christmas Through Your Eyes** (1993) US#43, **Hold Me, Thrill Me, Kiss Me** (1994) UK#5, **Abriendo Puertas** (1995) US#67 UK#70, **Destiny** (1996, all Epic) UK#12.

COMPILATIONS: **Anything for You** (1989) UK#1, **Greatest Hits** (1992, both Epic) p US#15 UK#2. Co-writers: [i] Emilio Estefan (b. March 4, 1953, Havana, Cuba)/Diane Warren, [ii] Emilio Estefan/Joe Secada, [iii] Enrique E. Garcia (b. 1958, Cuba), [iv] Miguel A. Morejon, [v] Diane Warren.

298. ESTES, Sleepy John (b. John Adam Estes, January 25, 1899, Ripley; d. June 5, 1977, Brownsville, both TN) Blues guitarist and vocalist. A charming blues vocalist, who composed much of his own material in a reportage style, long before Phil Ochs or Tom T. Hall. Blind in one eye from birth, and totally blind at the age of fifty, Estes performed throughout the south during the 1920s while recording sides for the Victor, Decca and Bluebird labels. In keeping with the great blues legend, Estes disappeared between 1940–1950, returning in 1962 with a series of recordings for Delmark Records. Two of his best songs were introduced to contemporary listeners by Ry Cooder, who recorded *President Kennedy* and *Goin' to Brownsville*. ALBUMS: **The Legend of Sleepy John Estes** (1961, Delmark); **Portraits in Blues, Volume 10** (1964, Storyville); **Broke and Hungry** (1964), **Brownsville Blues** (1965), **In Europe** (1966), **Electric Sleep** (1966, all Delmark): **1929/1940** (1967, Folkways); **Down South Blues** (1974, MCA); **The Blues of Sleepy John Estes I** (1982, Swaggie); **1929–1930 Sessions** (1986, Roots); **The Blues of Sleepy John Estes II** (1988, Swaggie); **Live in Austria, 1966** with John and Yank Rachell (1988), **Southern Blues, 1974** with Hammie Nixon (1988, both Wolf); **Someday Baby** (1996, IGO).

299. EVANS, Paul (b. March 5, 1938, New York, NY) Pop vocalist. A country influenced novelty songwriter, whose straight ballad *Roses Are Red (My Love)* [iii], sold over three million copies for Bobby Vinton in 1962. CHART COMPOSITIONS: *Happy Go Lucky Me* [i] (1960) US#10, *Brigade of Broken Hearts* (1960) US#81, *Hello, This Is Joanie (The Telephone Answering Machine Song)* (1976) C&W#57 UK#6, *Disneyland Daddy* (1979) C&W#81, *One Night Led to Two* (1980) C&W#80. ALBUMS: **Paul Evans Sings the Fabulous Teens** (1987, Skyline); **The Fabulous Teens and Beyond** (1996, Ace). HIT SONGS: *I Gotta Know* [iv] Elvis Presley (1960) US#20, *Johnny Will* Pat Boone (1960) UK#4, re-issued (1962) US#35; *Next Step Is Love, The* [ii] Elvis Presley (1970) US#32, *Roses Are Red (My Love)* [i] Ronnie Carroll (1962) UK#3/Bobby Vinton (1962) g R&B#5 US#1 UK#15, re-issued (1990) UK#71; *When* [iii] Kalin Twins (1958) R&B#1 C&W#13 US#5 UK#1/Showaddywaddy (1975) UK#3. Co-writers: [i] Al Byron, [ii] Paul Parnes, [iii] Jack Reardon, [iv] Matt Williams.

300. EVANS, Ray (b. February 4, 1915, Salamanca, NY) Film and stage composer. A regular collaborator with the lyricist Jay Livingston at Paramount Pictures during the mid-1940s, whose best known song is the ballad *Mona Lisa* [ii] (1950). Evans and Livingston wrote material for such films as "The Stork Club" (1945), "Golden Earrings" (1947), "The Paleface" (1947), "Copper Canyon," "Fancy Pants" (both 1950), "The Lemon Drop Kid" (1951), "The Man Who Knew Too Much" (1956), and "Tammy and the Bachelor" (1957). Their songs were also featured in the musical "Oh Captain!" (1958), and they also composed the television themes to "Bonanza" and "Mr. Lucky." Some of Evans' best melodies have become jazz standards. ALBUMS: **Aaron Slick from Punkin Crick** ost (1952, RCA); **Red Garters** ost (1954, Columbia); **Satins and Spurs** ost (1954, Capitol); **Tammy and the Bachelor** ost (1957, Coral); **The James Dean Story** ost (1957, Capitol); **Bonanza!** ost (1958, MGM); **Oh Captain!** ost (1958, Houseboat** ost (1958, both Columbia); **No Man Can Tame Me** ost (1959, Empire); **All Hands on Deck** ost (1961, Dot); **Let It Ride** ost (1961, RCA); **Oscar** ost (1966, Columbia); **This Property Is Condemned** ost (1966, Verve); **Torn Curtain** ost (1966, Decca); **What Did You Do in the War, Daddy?** ost (1966, RCA); **Warning Shot** ost (1967, Liberty). HIT VERSIONS: *Angel* [iii] Johnny Tillotson (1964) US#51, *Another Time, Another Place* [ii] Patti Page (1958) US#20, *As I Love You* [ii] Shirley Bassey (1958) UK#1, *Bonanza!* [ii] Johnny Cash (1962) US#94, *Buttons and Bows* [ii] Gene Autry (1948) g C&W#6 US#17/Dinning Sisters (1948) US#5/Betty Garrett (1948) US#8/Evelyn Knight (1948) US#14/Betty Jane Rhodes (1948) US#9/Dinah Shore (1948) g US#1/Browns (1962) US#104; *Dime and a Dollar, A* [ii] Guy Mitchell (1954) UK#8, *G'bye Now* [i] Hoarce Heidt (1941) US#2/Woody Herman (1941) US#10/Vaughn Monroe (1941) US#12; *I'll Always Love You* [ii] Dean Martin (1950) US#11/Martha Tilton (1950) US#23; *Mona Lisa* [ii] Nat "King" Cole (1950) g R&B#1 US#1/Dennis Day (1950) US#29/Harry James (1950) US#14/Ralph Flanagan (1950) US#16/Art Lund (1950) US#14/Moon Mullican (1950) C&W#4/Charlie Spivak (1950) US#16/Jimmy Wakely (1950) C&W#10/Victor Young (1950) US#7/Carl Mann (1959) R&B#24 US#25/Conway Twitty (1955) UK#5 US#29/Willie Nelson (1981) C&W#11; *Que Sera, Sera* [ii] Doris Day (1956) US#2/Geno Washington & the Ram Jam Band (1966) UK#43; *Silver Bells* [ii] Bing Crosby & Carol Richards (1953) US#20; *Streets of Laredo, The* [ii] Johnny Cash (1965) US#124, *Tammy* [ii] Ames Brothers (1957) US#5/Debbie Reynolds (1957) US#1 UK#2; *To Each His Own* [ii] Eddy Howard (1946) g US#1/Ink Spots (1946) g R&B#3 US#1/Freddy Martin (1946) US#1/Tony Martin (1946) g US#4/Modernaires & Paula Kelly (1946) US#3/Platters (1960) US#21. Co-writers: [i] Chic Johnson/Jay Livingston (b. Jay Harold Livingston, March 28, 1915, McDonald, PA)/Ole Olsen, [ii] Jay Livingston, [iii] Jay Livingston/Max Steiner. (*See also under* Henry MANCINI, Victor YOUNG.)

301. EVANS, Tolchard (b. Sydney Evans, 1901; d. March 12, 1978, both London, England) Tin Pan Alley pianist and conductor. One of Britain's earliest professional songwriters, who composed over one thousand songs. Evans learned the piano in his teens, before performing in various bands while working at a Denmark Street music publisher. In 1919 he published the song *Candlelight*, but did not score his first hit until *Barcelona* (1926), after which he cleverly mimicked American Tin Pan Alley tunes on such compositions as *A Message from Missouri*, a style he manipulated in order to present England in a similar, more romantic light, particularly with his ballads *Dreamy Devon* and *Sunset Down in Somerset* (both 1930). Evans went on to present his own BBC radio show "Tuneful Twenties," and was a band conductor from 1925. His 1930s material had a surprisingly popular revival during the 1950s, as did his own recording of *The Singing Piano* (1959). HIT VERSIONS: *Barcelona* Ben Selvin (1926) US#3, *Ev'rywhere* [iii] David Whitfield (1955) UK#3, *I'll Find You* [iv] David Whitfield (1957) UK#27, *If* [i] Perry Como (1951) g US#1/Vic Damone (1951) US#28/Billy Eckstine (1951) US#10/Jan Garber (1951) US#26/Ink Spots (1951) US#23/Guy Lombardo (1951) US#20/Dean Martin (1951) US#14/Jo Stafford (1951) US#8/Timi Yuro (1964) US#120/Al Hirt (1969) US#116; *Lady of Spain* [ii] Ray Noble (1931) US#5, re-issued (1949) US#19/Eddie Fisher (1952) g US#6/Les Paul (1952) US#8/Ray Stevens (1976) US#108; *Let's All Sing Like the Birdies Sing* [i] Ben Bernie (1933) US#18/Tweets (1981) UK#44; *My September Love* [iv] Joan Regan on *All Star Hit Parade EP* (1956) UK#2/David Whitfield (1956) UK#25; *Unless* [i] Eddie Fisher (1951) US#17/Gordon Jenkins (1951) US#30/Guy Mitchell (1951) US#17. Co-writers: [i] Stanley J. Damerell/Robert Hargreaves, [ii] Stanley J. Damerell/Robert Hargreaves/Harry Tilsley, [iii] Larry Kahn, [iv] Richard Mullan.

302. EVERLY, Don (b. Isaac Donald Everly, February 1, 1937, Brownie, KY), and **EVERLY, Phil** (b. January 19, 1939, Chicago, IL) Both pop guitarists and vocalists. Two brothers born of folk singing parents, who first sang in high school and later performed and recorded as the country influenced vocal duo the Everly Brothers. Although many of their hits were written by others, the Everly Brothers did compose some of their best known songs. CHART COMPOSITIONS: *(Til) I Kissed You* [i] (1959) C&W#8 R&B#22 US#4 UK#2, *Cathy's Clown* [iii] (1960) R&B#1 US#1 UK#1, *When Will I Be Loved?* [ii] (1960) US#8 UK#4, *So Sad (To Watch Good Love Go Bad)* [i] (1960) R&B#16 US#7 UK#5, *Gone, Gone, Gone* [iii] (1964) US#31 UK#36, *The Price of Love* [iii] (1965) US#104 UK#2. ALBUMS: **The Everly Brothers** (1958) US#16, **Songs Our Daddy Taught Us** (1958, both Cadence); **It's Everly Time** (1960, Warner Brothers) US#9 UK#2; **The Fabulous Style of the Everly Brothers** (1960, Cadence) US#23 UK#4; **A Date with the Everly Brothers** (1961) US#9 UK#3, **Both Sides of an Evening** (1961), **Instant Party** (1962) UK#20, **Golden Hits of the Everly Brothers** (1962) US#35, **Christmas with the Everly Brothers and the Boys Town Choir** (1962), **The Everly Brothers Sing Great Country Hits** (1963), **Very Best of the Everly Brothers** (1964) g, **Gone, Gone, Gone** (1965), **Rock 'n' Soul** (1965), **Beat Soul** (1965) US#141, **In Our Image** (1966), **Two Yanks in England** (1966), **Hit Sound of the Everly Brothers** (1967), **The Everly Brothers Sing** (1967), **Roots** (1968), **Show** (1970, all Warner Brothers); **Original Greatest Hits** (1970, Barnaby) US#180 UK#7; **Stories We Could Tell** (1972), **Pass the Chicken and Listen** (1973, both RCA); **Very Best of the Everly Brothers** (1974) UK#43, **Walk Right Back with the Everly Brothers** (1975, both Warner Brothers) UK#10; **Living Legends** (1977, Warwick) UK#12; **The New Album** (1977, Warner Brothers); **Love Hurts** (1983, K-Tel) UK#31; **Reunion Concert** (1984, Passport) US#162 UK#47; **EB '84/The Everly Brothers** (1984) US#38 UK#36, **Born Yesterday** (1986, both Mercury) US#83; **Some Hearts** (1988), **Golden Years of the Everly Brothers-Their 24 Greatest Hits** (1993, Warner Brothers) UK#26. Don also charted a series of solo country hits, and one day felt compelled to write a marvelous summation of his later career, *I'm Tired of Singing My Songs in Las Vegas* [i]. ALBUMS: **Don Everly** (1971), **Sunset Towers** (1974, both Ode); **Brother Juke Box** (1977, Hickory). Phil has also recorded as a solo artist. ALBUMS: **Star Spangled Springer** (1973, RCA); **Phil's Diner/There's Nothing Too Good for My Baby** (1975), **Mystic Line** (1975, both Pye); **Living Alone** (1982, Elektra); **Phil Everly** (1983, Capitol) UK#61. HIT VERSIONS: *Better Than Now* [iii] DeWayne Orender (1978) C&W#92, *Cathy's Clown* [iii] Springer Brothers (1981) C&W#89/Tricia Johns (1981) C&W#57; *Gee, But It's Lonely* [ii] Pat Boone (1958) US#31 UK#30, *(Girls, Girls, Girls) Made to Love* [ii] Eddie Hodges (1962) US#14, *It's All Over* [iii] Cliff Richard (1967) UK#9, *Lover Goodbye* [ii] Tanya Tucker

(1979) US#103, also on B-side of *I'm the Singer, You're the Song* (1979) C&W#18; *Price of Love, The* [iii] Bryan Ferry (1989) UK#49, *So Sad (To Watch Good Love Go Bad)* [i] Lois Johnson & Hank Williams, Jr. (1970) C&W#12/Connie Smith (1976) C&W#31/Steve Wariner (1978) C&W#76/Emmylou Harris (1983) C&W#28; *Thou Shalt Not Steal* [i] Kitty Wells (1954) C&W#14, *(Til) I Kissed You* [i] Connie Smith (1976) C&W#10, *When Will I Be Loved?* [ii] Linda Ronstadt (1975) US#2. Composers: [i] Don Everly, [ii] Phil Everly, [iii] Don & Phil Everly.

303. FAGEN, Donald The lead singer in the group Steely Dan, who went on to release the princely sum of two solo albums in twelve years. CHART COMPOSITIONS: *I.G.Y.* (1982) R&B#54 US#26, *Century's End* [i] (1988) US#83, *Tomorrow's Girls* (1993) US#121 UK#46. ALBUMS: **The Nightfly** (1981, Warner Brothers) g US#11 UK#44; **Kamakiriad** (1993, Reprise) g US#10 UK#3. Co-writer: [i] Tom Meher. (*See also under* Walter BECKER.)

304. FAIN, Sammy (b. Samuel Feinberg, June 17, 1902, New York, NY; d. December 6, 1989, Los Angeles, CA) Film and stage composer, pianist. One of Hollywood's most consistently successful composers, who was a self-taught musician and vaudeville performer, before he became a publishing house staff pianist in New York. Fain's first published song was *Nobody Knows What a Redhead Mama Can Do* [iv] (1925), after which, he formed a lengthy partnership with the lyricist Irving Kahal, writing for such films as "It's a Great Life," "The Big Pond" (both 1930); "Footlight Parade" (1933), "Vogues of 1938," "I'll Be Seeing You" (1944), and "April Love" (1957). Fain and Kahal also worked on Broadway, and were particularly successful with the shows "Everybody's Welcome" (1931), "Hellzapoppin" (1938) and "George White's Scandals of 1939." Fain later composed such memorable film material as *The Second Star to the Right* [ii] from "Peter Pan." He also won Oscars for *Secret Love* [x] from "Calamity Jane" (1953), and for the title theme of "Love Is a Many Splendored Thing" (1955). ALBUMS: **Flahooley** ost (1951, Capitol); **Calamity Jane** ost (1953, Columbia); **3 Sailors and a Girl** ost (1954, Capitol); **Ankles Aweigh** ost (1955, Decca); **Love Is a Many Splendored Thing (And All-Time Motion Picture Theme Favorites)** ost (1956, Mercury); **April Love** ost (1957, Dot); **Gift of Love** ost (1958, Columbia); **Mardi Gras** ost (1958, Bell); **Marjorie Morningstar** ost (1958, RCA); **Big Circus** ost (1959, Todd); **Imitation of Life** ost (1959, Decca); **Christine** ost (1960, Columbia); **Tender Is the Night** ost (1962, 20th Century Fox); **New Kind of Love** ost (1963,

Mercury); **If He Hollers, Let Him Go** ost (1968, Tower); **Lady in Cement** ost (1968, 20th Century Fox). HIT VERSIONS: *April Love* [x] Pat Boone (1957) US#1 UK#7, *Are You Having Any Fun?* [xi] Tommy Dorsey (1939) US#6, *Black Hills of Dakota, The* [x] Doris Day (1954) UK#7, *By a Waterfall* [vi] Guy Lombardo (1933) US#6/Leo Reisman (1933) US#6/Rudy Vallee (1933) US#15; *Certain Smile, A* [x] Johnny Mathis (1958) US#14 UK#4, *Dear Hearts and Gentle People* [v] Gordon MacRae (1949) US#19/Bing Crosby (1950) g US#2/Dennis Day (1950) US#14/Ralph Flanagan (1950) US#24/Dinah Shore (1950) US#2/Benny Strong (1950) US#19; *Dickey-Bird Song, The* [iii] Larry Clinton (1948) US#22/Freddy Martin (1948) US#5; *Ev'ry Day* [vi] Victor Young (1935) US#7, *Face to Face* [ii] Gordon MacRae (1954) US#30, *Happy in Love* [xi] Dick Jurgens (1942) US#19, *I Can Dream, Can't I?* [vi] Tommy Dorsey (1938) US#5/Andrews Sisters (1950) g US#1/Toni Arden (1950) US#7/Tex Beneke (1950) US#12; *I Speak to the Stars* Doris Day (1954) US#16, *I'll Be Seeing You (Anyway)* [vi] Bing Crosby (1944) US#1/Tommy Dorsey (1944) US#4/Five Stains (1960) US#79/Frank Sinatra (1961) US#58/Leon Raines (1983) C&W#79; *Let a Smile Be Your Umbrella* [ix] Roger Wolfe Kahn (1928) US#6/Sam Lanin (1928) US#12; *Little Love Can Go a Long, Long Way, A* [x] Dream Weavers (1956) US#33, *Love Is a Many Splendored Thing* [x] Don Cornell (1955) US#26/Four Aces (1955) US#1; *Love Is Never Out of Season* [i] Ozzie Nelson (1937) US#14, *Man on Fire* [x] Frankie Vaughn (1957) UK#6, *Secret Love* [x] Ray Anthony (1954) US#29/Doris Day (1954) g US#1 UK#1/Tommy Edwards (1954) US#28/Slim Whitman (1954) C&W#2/Ahmad Jamal (1958) R&B#18/Kathy Kirby (1963) UK#4/Billy Stewart (1966) R&B#11 US#29/Tony Booth (1973) C&W#47/Freddy Fender (1975) C&W#1 US#20; *That Old Feeling* [i] Shep Fields (1937) US#1/Jan Garber (1937) US#10; *Very Precious Love, A* [x] Ames Brothers (1958) US#23/Doris Day (1958) UK#16/Hernando (1959) US#103; *Was That the Human Thing to Do?* [xii] Boswell Sisters (1932) US#7/Benny Krueger (1932) US#18/Bert Lown (1932) US#6; *Wedding Bells Are Breaking Up That Old Gang of Mine* [viii] Gene Austin (1929) US#8/Steve Gibson (1948) US#21/Four Aces (1954) US#22; *When I Take My Sugar to Tea* [vi] Boswell Sisters (1931) US#6, *When Tomorrow Comes* [vi] Freddy Martin (1934) US#12, *Wildest Gal in Town, The* [xi] Billy Eckstine (1947) US#22, *You Brought a New Kind of Love to Me* [vii] Maurice Chevalier (1930) US#12/High Hatters (1930) US#13/Paul Whiteman (1930) US#3/Helen Ward (1953) US#30/Frank Sinatra on *Songs for Swinging Lovers LP* (1956) UK#12; *Your Mother and Mine* [ii] Paul Whiteman (1929) US#16. Co-writers: [i] Lew Brown, [ii]

Sammy Cahn, [iii] Howard Dietz, [iv] Al Dubin, [v] Bob Hilliard, [vi] Irving Kahal, [vii] Irving Kahal/ Pierre Norman, [viii] Irving Kahal/Willie Raskin, [ix] Irving Kahal/Francis Wheeler, [x] Paul Francis Webster, [xi] Jack Yellen, [xii] Joe Young.

305. FARGO, Donna (b. Yvonne Vaughan, November 10, 1949, Mount Airy, NC) C&W vocalist. A former teacher who charted thirty-seven country singles between 1972–1987, including many of her own songs. Fargo has suffered from multiple sclerosis since 1978, and subsequently has recorded very infrequently. CHART COMPOSITIONS: *Happiest Girl in the Whole U.S.A.* (1972) g C&W#1 US#11, *Funnyface* (1972) g C&W#1 US#5, *Superman* (1973) C&W#1, *You Were Always There* (1973) C&W#1, *Little Girl Gone* (1973) C&W#2, *I'll Try a Little Bit Harder* (1974) C&W#6, *U.S. of A.* (1974) C&W#9 US#86, *It Do Feel Good* (1975) C&W#7 US#98, *Don't Be Angry* (1976) C&W#3. ALBUMS: **The Happiest Girl in the Whole U.S.A.** (1972) g US#47, **My Second Album** (1973) US#104, **All About a Feeling** (1974), **Miss Donna Fargo** (1975), **Whatever I Say Means I Love You** (1976, all Dot); **On the Move** (1977), **Dark Eyed Lady** (1978), **Just for You** (1979), **Fargo** (1981), **Shame on Me** (1978, all Warner Brothers); **Brotherly Love** (1981, MCA).

306. FARIAN, Frank (b. 1942, Germany) Pop producer. A former singer who became a successful music business svengali, masterminding the careers of the fifty million selling disco act Boney M, and later the vocal duo Milli Vanilli. HIT VERSIONS: *Baby Don't Forget My Number* [ii] Milli Vanilli (1989) g US#1 UK#16, *Boney M Megamix* Boney M (1992) UK#7, *Brown Girl in the Ring* (arrangement only) Boney M (1978) UK#2, re-mixed (1993) UK#38; *Daddy Cool* [viii] Boney M (1977) US#65 UK#6, *Girl I'm Gonna Miss You* [i] Milli Vanilli (1989) US#1 UK#2, *Gotta Go Home* [v] Boney M (1979) UK#12, *Hooray, Hooray, It's a Holi Holiday* [vi] Boney M (1979) UK#3, *Ma Baker* [vii] Boney M (1977) US#96 UK#2, *Mary's Boy Child/Oh My Lord* [iv] Boney M (1978) US#85 UK#1, *Megamix* Boney M (1988) UK#52, *Rasputin* [vii] Boney M (1978) UK#2, *Rivers of Babylon, The* [iii] Boney M (1978) US#30 UK#1, *When a Child Is Born* [v] Johnny Mathis (1976) UK#1/Johnny Mathis & Gladys Knight (1981) UK#74. Co-writers: [i] Bischof/Fallenstein/Kawohl, [ii] Dalton/Nail/Reuter, [iii] Brent Dowe/Trevor Mc-Naughton/George Reyam, [iv] Hairston/J. Lorin, [v] Heinz Huth/Fred Jay, [vi] Fred Jay, [vii] Fred Jay/George Reyam, [viii] George Reyam.

307. FARINA, Richard (b. 1937, New York, NY; d. April 30, 1966, Carmel, CA) Folk multi-instrumentalist and vocalist, and **FARINA, Mimi** (b. Mimi Baez, April 30, 1945) Folk vocalist. A rustic husband and wife pop-folk duo who were popular in the 1960s. Richard's first two albums were recorded as a solo artist, **Dick Farina and Eric Von Schmidt** (1963, Folklore) and **Singer/Songwriter Project** (1964, Elektra). Richard was killed in a motorcycle accident shortly before the publication of his novel "Been Down So Long It Looks Like Up to Me" (1966), after which, Mimi recorded with Tom Jans. ALBUMS: **Celebration For a Grey Day** (1965), **Reflections in a Crystal Wind** (1966), **Memories** (1969, all Vanguard). COMPILATION: **Best of Richard and Mimi Farina** (1970, Vanguard). HIT VERSIONS: *Pack Up Your Sorrows* [i] Joan Baez (1966) UK#50, *Hard Lovin' Loser* Judy Collins (1967) US#90. Co-writer: [i] Pauline Marden. (*See also under* Tom JANS.)

308. FARNER, Mark (b. September 29, 1948, Flint, MI) Rock guitarist and vocalist. A member of the 1960s act Terry Knight and the Pack, who co-founded the 1970s rock group Grand Funk Railroad, which sold over twenty million records. CHART COMPOSITIONS: *Heartbreaker* (1970) US#72, *Walk Like a Man* [i] (1973) US#19, *Shinin' On* [i] (1974) US#11, *Bad Time* (1975) US#4, *Sally* (1976) US#69. ALBUMS: **On Time** (1969) g US#27, **Grand Funk** (1970) p US#11, **Closer to Home** (1970) p US#6, **Live Album** (1971) p US#5, **Survival** (1971) p US#6, **E Pluribus Funk** (1972) p US#29, **Phoenix** (1972) g US#7, **We're an American Band** (1973) p US#2, **Shinin' On** (1974) g US#5, **All the Girls in the World Beware** (1975) g US#10, **Caught in the Act** (1975) US#21, **Born to Die** (1975, all Capitol) US#47; **Good Singin' Good Playin'** (1976, MCA); **Grand Funk Lives** (1981) US#149, **What's Funk?** (1983, both Full Moon). COMPILATIONS: **Mark, Don and Mel, 1969–1971** (1972, Capitol) g US#17; **Mark, Don and Terry, 1966–1967** (1972, Abkco) US#192; **Grand Funk Hits** (1976, Capitol) US#126. The group split up in 1977, and Farner embarked on a solo career, becoming, in 1981, a born-again Christian. ALBUMS: **Mark Farner** (1977), **No Frills** (1978, both Atlantic); **Just Another Injustice** (1988), **Wake Up** (1990), **Some Kind of Wonderful** (1991, all Frontline). Co-writer: [i] Don Brewer (b. September 3, 1948, Flint, MI).

309. FARRAR, John (b. Australia) Pop guitarist and producer. A bassist who initially recorded with Hank Marvin and Bruce Welch, releasing the albums **Marvin, Welch and Farrar** (1971) UK#30, **Second Opinion** (1971, both Regal Zonophone) and **Hank Marvin and John Farrar** (1973, EMI). He was also briefly a member of the Shadows, featuring on **Rocking with Curly Leads** (1973) UK#45, **Specs Appeal** (1975) UK#30 and **Live at the Paris Olympia** (1975, all EMI). From the mid-1970s, Farrar wrote, produced and composed for the singer Olivia Newton-John, and in 1996, he and Tim Rice composed the British musical "Heathcliff." HIT VERSIONS: *Don't Stop Believin'* Olivia Newton-John (1976) C&W#14 US#33, *Grease Megamix, The* [ii] Olivia Newton-John & John Travolta (1991) UK#5, *Have You Never Been Mellow* Olivia Newton-John (1975) g C&W#3 US#1 UK#37, *Hopelessly Devoted to You* Olivia Newton-John (1978) g C&W#20 US#3/Sonia (1994) UK#61; *Landslide* Olivia Newton-John (1982) US#52, *Little More Love, A* Olivia Newton-John (1978) g C&W#94 US#3 UK#4, *Magic* Olivia Newton-John (1980) g US#1, *Make a Move on Me* [iv] Olivia Newton-John (1982) US#5, *Sam* [i] Olivia Newton-John C&W#40 US#20 UK#6, *Something Better to Do* Olivia Newton-John (1975) C&W#19 US#13, *Suddenly* Olivia Newton-John & Cliff Richard (1980) US#20 UK#15, *Tied Up* [iii] Olivia Newton-John (1983) US#38, *You're the One That I Want* Olivia Newton-John & John Travolta (1978) p US#1 UK#1/Hylda Baker & Arthur Mullard (1978) UK#22/Debbie Gibson & Craig McLachlan (1993) UK#13. Co-writers: [i] Don Black/Hank Marvin, [ii] Casey/Jacobs, [iii] Lee Ritenour (b. November 11, 1952, Los Angeles, CA), [iv] Tom Snow.

310. FARRELL, Wes (b. 1940, New York, NY; d. 1996) Pop producer and arranger. A music business entrepreneur who built up his own publishing empire after first writing in New York's Brill Building during the 1960s. In the early 1970s, Farrell ran his own Chelsea and Roxbury labels, and co-wrote much of the music for the television series "The Partridge Family." HIT VERSIONS: *Come on Down to My Boat* [vi] Every Mother's Son (1967) US#6, *Could It Be Forever* [vii] David Cassidy (1972) US#37 UK#2/Gemini (1996) UK#38; *Doesn't Somebody Want to Be Wanted?* [iii] Partridge Family (1971) g US#6, *Friend and Lover* Partridge Family (1973) US#99, *Happy Summer Days* [i] Ronnie Dove (1966) US#27, *I Can't Stop* [vi] Osmonds (1971) US#96, *I'll Make All Your Dreams Come True* [ix] Ronnie Dove (1965) US#21, *I'll Meet You Halfway* [v] Partridge Family (1971) US#9, *Let's Lock the Door* [ii] Jay & the Americans (1965) US#11, *Look What You've Done* [viii] Pozo-Seco Singers (1967) US#32, *Our Favorite Melodies* [iv] Craig Douglas (1962) UK#9. Co-writers: [i] Ritchie Adams/Larry Kusik, [ii] Roy Alfred, [iii] Mike Appel/Jimmy Cretcos, [iv] Bob Elgin/Kay Rogers, [v] Gerry Goffin, [vi] Jerry Goldstein, [vii] Danny

Janssen, [viii] Bob Johnston, [ix] Bernice Ross. (*See also under* Bert BERNS, Luther DIXON.)

311. FELDER, Alan (b. Philadelphia, PA) Pop producer. A successful songwriter-producer of pop based R&B material during the 1970s. HIT VERSIONS: *Armed and Extremely Dangerous* [v] First Choice (1973) R&B#11 US#28 UK#16, *Doctor Love* [vi] First Choice (1977) R&B#23 US#41, *Dreamin'* [vi] Loleatta Holloway (1977) US#72, *He's a Friend* [iii] Eddie Kendricks (1976) R&B#2 US#36, *Hold Back the Night* [i] Trammps (1976) R&B#10 US#35 UK#5/Graham Parker on *The Pink Parker EP* (1977) UK#24; *Newsy Neighbors* [v] First Choice (1974) R&B#35 US#97, *Player, The* [v] First Choice (1974) R&B#7 US#70, *Risin' to the Top* Keni Burke (1982) R&B#63, *Smarty Pants* [v] First Choice (1973) R&B#25 US#56 UK#9, *Stop to Start* [iv] Blue Magic (1973) R&B#14 US#74, *Ten Percent* [ii] Double Exposure (1976) R&B#63 US#54, *Touch and Go* [v] Ecstasy, Passion and Pain (1976) R&B#71 US#98, *We're on the Right Track* [v] South Shore Commission (1976) R&B#30 US#94. Co-writers: [i] Ron Baker/Norman Harris/E. Young, [ii] T.G. Conway, [iii] T.G. Conway/B. Gray, [iv] J. Grant, [v] Norman Harris, [vi] Norman Harris/R. Tyson. (*See also under* Bunny SIGLER.)

312. FELLER, Dick (b. January 2, 1943, Bronaugh, MS) C&W guitarist and vocalist. A 1960s Nashville session musician who played behind Mel Tillis, Warner Mack and Skeeter Davis, before becoming a singer-songwriter in the 1970s. CHART COMPOSITIONS: *Biff, the Friendly Purple Bear* (1973) C&W#22 US#101, *Makin' the Best of a Bad Situation* (1974) C&W#11 US#85, *The Credit Card Song* (1974) C&W#10 US#105, *Uncle Hiram and the Homemade Beer* (1975) C&W#49. ALBUMS: **Dick Feller Wrote...** (1973, United Artists); **No Words on Me** (1974, Asylum); **Some Days Are Diamonds** (1975, Elektra); **Live** (1983, Audiograph). HIT VERSIONS: *Any Old Wind That Blows* Johnny Cash (1972) C&W#3, *High Rollin'* Jerry Reed on B-side of *(I Love You) What Can I Say* (1978) C&W#10, *(I Love You) What Can I Say* Jerry Reed (1978) C&W#10, *(I'm Just a) Redneck in a Rock and Roll Bar* Jerry Reed on B-side of *East Bound and Down* (1977) C&W#2 US#103, *Lord, Mr. Ford* Jerry Reed (1973) C&W#1 US#68, *Room for a Boy...Never Used, A* Ferlin Husky (1974) C&W#60, *Some Days Are Like Diamonds* John Denver (1981) C&W#10 US#36, *(Who Was the Man Who Put) The Line in the Gasoline* Jimmy Reed (1979) C&W#40. (*See also under* Jerry REED.)

313. FERRY, Bryan (b. September 26, 1945, Washington, England) Rock pianist and vocalist.

The highly stylized lead singer and chief songwriter in the art influenced rock group Roxy Music. CHART COMPOSITIONS: *Virginia Plain* (1972) UK#4, re-issued (1977) UK#11; *Pyjamarama* (1973) UK#10, *Street Life* (1973) UK#9, *All I Want Is You* (1974) UK#12, *Love Is the Drug* [i] (1975) US#30 UK#2, re-mixed (1996) UK#33; *Both Ends Burning* (1975) UK#25, *Trash* (1979) UK#40, *Dance Away* (1979) US#44 UK#2, *Angel Eyes* [i] (1979) UK#4, *Over You* [ii] (1980) US#80 UK#5, *Oh Yeah (On the Radio)* (1980) US#102 UK#5, *The Same Old Scene* (1980) UK#12, *More Than This* (1982) US#102 UK#6, *Avalon* (1982) UK#13, *Take a Chance with Me* (1982) US#104 UK#26. ALBUMS: **Roxy Music** (1972) UK#10, **For Your Pleasure** (1973) US#193 UK#10, **Stranded** (1973) US#186 UK#1, **Country Life** (1974) US#37 UK#3, **Siren** (1975) US#50 UK#6, **Viva! Roxy Music** (1976, all Island) US#81 UK#6; **Manifesto** (1979) US#23 UK#7, **Flesh and Blood** (1980, both Polydor) US#35 UK#1; **Avalon** (1982) p US#53 UK#1, **Musique/The High Road** (1983) US#67 UK#26, **Heart Still Beating** (1990, all EG). COMPILATIONS: **Greatest Hits** (1977, Polydor) UK#20; **The Atlantic Years, 1973–1980** (1983, Atlantic) UK#23; **Street Life-20 Great Hits** (1986, EG) UK#1; **The Thrill of It All** (1995), **More Than This-Best of Roxy Music and Bryan Ferry** (1995, Virgin) UK#15. Before the group broke up in the early 1980s, Ferry had already developed a concurrent solo career, initially interpreting standards and lesser known contemporary material, before composing his own hits. CHART COMPOSITIONS: *This Is Tomorrow* (1977) UK#9, *Tokyo Joe* (1977) UK#15, *Sign of the Times* (1978) UK#37, *Slave to Love* (1985) US#109 UK#10, *Don't Stop the Dance* (1985) UK#21, *Windswept* (1985) UK#46, *Is Your Love Strong Enough?* (1986) UK#22, *The Right Stuff* (1987) UK#37, *Kiss and Tell* (1988) US#31, *Your Painted Smile* (1994) UK#52, *Mamouna* (1995) UK#57. ALBUMS: **These Foolish Things** (1973) UK#5, **Another Time, Another Place** (1974) UK#4, **Let's Stick Together** (1976, all Island) US#160 UK#19; **In Your Mind** (1977) US#126 UK#5, **The Bride Stripped Bare** (1978, both Polydor) US#159 UK#13; **Boys and Girls** (1985, EG) US#65 UK#1; **Bete Noire** (1987) US#63 UK#9, **Taxi** (1993) US#79 UK#2, **Mamouna** (1994, all Virgin) US#94 UK#11. COMPILATION: **The Ultimate Collection** (1988, EG) UK#6. Co-writers: [i] Andrew MacKay (b. July 23, 1946, London, England), [ii] Phil Manzanera (b. Philip Targett-Adams, January 31, 1951, London, England).

314. FIELDS, Dorothy (b. July 15, 1905, Allenhurst, NJ; d. March 28, 1974, New York, NY) Film and stage lyricist. A successful lyricist who en-

joyed a fifty year career co-composing mainly ballad material for Broadway and Hollywood. Fields also collaborated with Albert Hague on the show "Redhead" (1959). ALBUM: **Redhead** oc (1959, RCA) US#47. (*See also under* Cy COLEMAN, Jerome KERN, Jimmy McHUGH, Arthur SCHWARTZ.)

315. FINDON, Benjamin (b. England) Pop producer. A mainstream songwriter-producer who worked at GTO and Jive Records during the 1970s. HIT VERSIONS: *Atmosphere* [v] Russ Abbot (1984) UK#7, *Attention to Me* [iv] Nolans (1981) UK#9, *Chosen Few, The* Dooleys (1979) UK#7, *Don't Make Waves* [iv] Nolans (1980) UK#12, *Gotta Pull Myself Together* [iv] Nolans (1980) UK#9, *I'm in the Mood for Dancing* [iv] Nolans (1979) UK#3, *Love of My Life* [iii] Dooleys (1977) UK#9, *Love Really Hurts Without You* [i] Alex Brown (1976) R&B#65/Billy Ocean (1976) US#22 UK#2; *Red Light Spells Danger* [i] Billy Ocean (1977) UK#2, *Rose Has to Die, A* Dooleys (1978) UK#11, *Stop Me (If You've Heard It All Before)* [ii] Billy Ocean (1976) UK#12, *Think I'm Gonna Fall in Love with You* [iii] Dooleys (1977) UK#13, *Wanted* [iv] Dooleys (1979) UK#3. Co-writers: [i] Les Charles, [ii] Les Charles/Michael Myers, [iii] Michael Myers, [iv] Mike Myers/Robert Puzey, [v] Stephen Rodway/Eddie Tucker.

316. FINN, Neil (b. May 27, 1958, Te Awamutu, New Zealand) Pop pianist and vocalist. A founder member, with his brother Tim Finn, of the group Split Enz, who composed the band's hits *I Got You* (1980) US#40 UK#12 and *History Never Repeats* (1981) UK#63, and featured on the albums **True Colors** (1980) US#40 UK#42 and **Time and Tide** (1982, both A&M) UK#71. Finn left Split Enz in 1985 to form the considerably more successful Crowded House. CHART COMPOSITIONS: *Don't Dream It's Over* (1987) US#2 UK#27, re-issued (1996) UK#25; *Something So Strong* [ii] (1987) US#7, *World Where You Live* (1987) US#65, *Better Be Home Soon* (1988) US#42, *Chocolate Cake* (1991) UK#69, *Fall at Your Feet* (1991) UK#17, *Weather with You* [i] (1992) UK#7, *Four Seasons in One Day* [i] (1991) UK#26, *It's Only Natural* [i] (1991) UK#24, *Distant Sun* [i] (1993) UK#19, *Nails in My Feet* [i] (1993) UK#22, *Locked Out* [i] (1994) UK#12, *Fingers of Love* [i] (1994) UK#25, *Pineapple Head* [i] (1994) UK#27, *Instinct* (1996) UK#12, *Not the Girl You Think You Are* (1996) UK#20. ALBUMS: **Crowded House** (1986) p US#12, **Temple of Low Men** (1988) US#40, **Woodface** (1991) US#83 UK#6, **Together Alone** (1992, all Capitol) US#73 UK#4. COMPILATION: **Recurring Dream-The Very Best of Crowded House** (1996, Capitol) UK#1. After Crowded House split up in 1996, the Finn brothers recorded as the duo Finn, charting with *Suffer Never* [i] (1995) UK#29 and *Angel's Heap* [i] (1995) UK#41, from the album **Finn** (1995, Parlophone) UK#15. HIT VERSIONS: *Don't Dream It's Over* Paul Young (1991) UK#20. Co-writers: [i] Tim Finn, [ii] M. Froom. (*See also under* Tim FINN.)

317. FINN, Tim (b. June 25, 1954, New Zealand) Pop guitarist and vocalist. A founder member, with his brother Neil Finn, of the group Split Enz. ALBUMS: **Mental Notes** (1975, Mushroom); **Second Thoughts** (1976), **Dizrbythmia** (1977, both Chrysalis); **Frenzy** (1978, Mushroom); **True Colours** (1979, A&M) US#40 UK#42; **Beginning of the Enz** (1980, Chrysalis); **Waiata** (1981) US#45, **Time and Tide** (1982) US#53, **Conflicting Emotions** (1984) US#137, **See Ya Round** (1985, all A&M). COMPILATIONS: **History Never Repeats Itself (The Best of Split Enz)** (1993), **Odz and Endz** (1993), **Rear Enz** (1993, all A&M). Tim briefly joined Neil's group Crowded House in 1991, featuring on the album **Woodface** (1991, Capitol) US#83 UK#6, before recording as a solo artist. CHART COMPOSITIONS: *Persuasion* (1993) UK#43, *Hit the Ground Running* (1993) UK#50. ALBUMS: **Escapade** (1983, A&M) US#161; **Big Canoe** (1985, Virgin); **Before and After** (1993, Capitol) UK#29. He has also recorded an album as member of the group A.L.T., **Attitude** (1995). (*See also under* Neil FINN.)

318. FISHER, Fred (b. September 30, 1875, Cologne, Germany; d. January 14, 1942, New York, NY) Film and show composer, pianist. A songwriter best remembered for composing a considerable series of songs with foreign cities or countries for titles. Fisher emigrated to America in 1900, where he became a saloon pianist in Chicago, before achieving a three million seller with his composition *If the Man in the Moon Were a Coon* (1907). Further million sellers followed, including *Peg O' My Heart* [iii] (1913), which topped the chart in four different versions. Fisher's songs were included in such shows as "The Ziegfeld Follies of 1913" and "Afgar" (1919), but from 1929 he worked in Hollywood, contributing to the films "So This Is College" (1929), "Their Own Desire" (1930) and "The Story of Vernon and Irene Castle" (1939). HIT VERSIONS: *Any Little Girl That's a Nice Little Girl Is the Right Little Girl for Me* American Quartet (1910) US#5/Ada Jones (1911) US#8; *Blue Is the Night* Ipana Troubadors (1930) US#14, *Chicago (That Toddlin' Town)* Bar Harbour Society Orchestra (1922) US#13/Ben Selvin (1922) US#5/Frank Sinatra (1957) US#84 UK#25; *Come, Josephine, in My Flying Machine* [iii] Blanche Ring (1911) US#1/Ada Jones, Billy Murray & the American Quartet (1911) US#1/Harry Tally (1911)

US#7; *Daddy, You've Been a Mother to Me* Henry Burr (1920) US#9/Lewis James (1920) US#12; *Dardanella* [ii] Henry Burr & Albert Campbell (1920) US#12/Prince's Orchestra (1920) US#5/Harry Raderman's Jazz Orchestra (1920) US#9/Ben Selvin (1920) g US#1/Acker Bilk (1962) US#105; *Dardanella Blues* [viii] Billy Murray (1920) US#9/Ed Smalle (1920) US#9; *Fifty Million Frenchmen Can't Be Wrong* [viii] Sophie Tucker (1927) US#13, *Happy Days and Lonely Nights* [ix] Ruth Etting (1928) US#9/Ben Selvin (1929) US#13/Fontane Sisters (1954) US#18/Suzy Miller (1955) UK#14/Ruby Murray (1955) UK#6/Frankie Vaughan (1955) UK#12/Russ Conway in *Even More Party Pops* (1960) UK#27; *I Found a Rose in the Devil's Garden* [vii] Sam Ash (1921) US#8/Sterling Trio (1921) US#5; *I Want to Go to Tokyo* Prince's Orchestra (1915) US#9, *I'd Rather Be Blue Over You (Than Be Happy with Somebody Else)* [ix] Fanny Brice (1929) US#16, *I'm All Dressed Up with a Broken Heart* [x] Ted Lewis (1931) US#7, *I'm on My Way to Mandalay* Henry Burr, Albert Campbell & Will Oakland (1914) US#1, *If the Man in the Moon Were a Coon* Ada Jones (1907) US#3, *In the Land O' Yamo Yamo* Van & Schenck (1918) US#2, *Ireland Must Be Heaven, for My Mother Came from There* [vi] Charles Harrison (1916) US#1, *Peg O' My Heart* [iii] Henry Burr (1913) US#2/Charles Harrison (1913) US#1/Walter Van Brunt (1914) US#7/Buddy Clark (1947) US#1/Clark Dennis (1947) US#8/Harmonicats (1947) g US#1/Art Lund (1947) US#4/Three Suns (1947) US#1/Ted Weems (1947) US#4; *Siam* American Quartet (1916) US#9, *There's a Broken Heart for Every Light on Broadway* Elsie Baker (1916) US#6, *There's a Little Bit of Bad in Every Good Little Girl* [iv] Billy Murray (1916) US#4, *When It's Moonlight on the Alamo* Peerless Quartet (1914) US#4, *When It's Nightime in Italy* Lew Holtz (1924) US#9, *Whispering Grass* [v] Erskine Hawkins (1940) US#13/Ink Spots (1940) US#10/Windsor Davis & Don Estelle (1975) UK#1; *You Can't Get Along with 'Em or Without 'Em* Anna Chandler (1916) US#5, *Your Feet's Too Big* [i] Fats Waller (1939) US#15. Co-writers: [i] Ada Benson/Ink Spots, [ii] Johnny S. Black/Felix Bernard, [iii] Alfred Bryan, [iv] Grant Clarke, [v] Doris Fisher, [vi] Howard Johnson/Joseph McCarthy, [vii] Willie Raskin (b. 1896; d. 1942), [viii] Willie Raskin/Billy Rose, [ix] Billy Rose, [x] Harold Stern/Stella Unger.

319. FLETCHER, Guy (b. April 23, 1944, St. Albans, England) Pop composer. A songwriter whose compositions were recorded by artists ranging from Ray Charles to Elvis Presley. HIT VERSIONS: *By the Devil* Blue Mink (1973) US#26, *Dedication* [i] Bay City Rollers (1977) US#60, *Fallen Angel* Franki Valli (1976) US#36 UK#11, *I Can't Tell* *the Bottom from the Top* [i] Hollies (1970) US#82 UK#7, *Power to All Our Friends* [i] Cliff Richard (1973) US#109 UK#4, *Sing a Song of Freedom* [i] Cliff Richard (1971) UK#13, *With the Eyes of a Child* [i] Cliff Richard (1969) UK#20. Co-writer: [i] Doug Flett (b. October 13, 1935, Sydney, Australia).

320. FLOYD, Eddie (b. June 25, 1935, Montgomery, AL) R&B vocalist. An artist whose music epitomized the vitality of the Stax Records' sound of the 1960s, and the co-composer one of the most famous songs of the decade *Knock on Wood* [i] (1966), which has been recorded over sixty times. Floyd was first successful as a singer, alongside Wilson Pickett, in the doo-wop group the Falcons, which charted three R&B singles between 1956–1962. In 1962, Floyd became a writer and producer at the Safice label, before signing to Stax for a solo recording career. His songs continue to be recorded by such artists as Ry Cooder, Bruce Springsteen and Eric Clapton. CHART COMPOSITIONS: *Knock on Wood* [i] (1966) R&B#1 US#28 UK#19, *Raise Your Hand* [i] (1967) R&B#16 US#79 UK#42, *Don't Rock the Boat* (1967) US#98, *Love Is a Doggone Thing* [i] (1967) R&B#30 US#97, *Things Get Better* [i] (1967) UK#31, *On a Saturday Night* [i] (1967) R&B#22 US#92, *I've Never Found Me a Girl (To Love Me Like You Do)* [ii] (1968) R&B#2 US#40, *Big Bird* [ii] (1968) US#132, *I've Got to Have Your Love* [i] (1969) R&B#50 US#102, *Don't Tell Your Mama (Where You've Been)* (1969) R&B#18 US#73, *Never Never Let You Go* with Mavis Staples (1969) US#125, *Why Is the Wine Sweeter* (1969) R&B#30 US#98, *California Girl* (1970) R&B#11 US#45, *The Best Years of My Life* (1970) R&B#29 US#118, *Blood Is Thicker Than Water* (1971) R&B#33, *Yum Yum Yum (I Want Some)* (1972) R&B#49 US#122, *Baby Lay Your Head Down/Check Me Out* (1973) R&B#50, *Soul Street* (1974) R&B#65, *We Should Really Be in Love* with Dorothy Moore (1977) R&B#74. ALBUMS: **Knock on Wood** (1967) UK#36, **Never Found a Girl** (1968), **Rare Stamps** (1969), **You've Got to Have Eddie** (1969), **California Girl** (1970), **Down to Earth** (1971), **Baby Lay Your Head Down** (1973), **Soul Street** (1974, all Stax); **Think About It** (1974, Atco), **Experience** (1977, Malaco); **Try Me** (1985, Easy Street); **Flashback** (1988, Ichiban-Wilbe). COMPILATIONS: **Chronicle** (1978), **Knock on Wood-The Best of Eddie Floyd** (1988, both Stax). HIT VERSIONS: *I've Never Found Me a Boy (To Love Me Like You Do)* [ii] Esther Phillips (1972) R&B#17 US#106, *Knock on Wood* [i] Otis Redding & Carla Thomas (1967) R&B#8 US#30 UK#35/David Bowie (1974) UK#10/Ami Stewart (1979) g R&B#6 US#1 UK#6, re-mixed (1985) UK#7/Razzy Bailey (1984) C&W#29; *Someone Is Watching*

Solomon Burke (1965) R&B#24 US#89, *Stop, Look What You're Doing* Carla Thomas (1965) R&B#30 US#92, *You Don't Know What You Mean to Me* [i] Sam & Dave (1968) R&B#20 US#48. Co-writers: [i] Steve Cropper, [ii] Alvertis Isbell/Booker T. Jones. (*See also under* William BELL.)

321. FOGELBERG, Dan (b. Daniel Grayling Fogelberg, August 13, 1951, Peoria, IL). Pop guitarist, pianist and vocalist. A country and folk influenced singer-songwriter who was a major star during the 1970–1980s, ultimately selling over fifteen million albums. Fogelberg learned the piano and guitar as a teenager, after which he began writing songs. He studied art at the University of Illinois, while performing folk music in the coffee bars near campus. After graduation, he moved to California, where he toured as a backing artist before signing to the Full Moon label in 1973, for which he recorded mellow, country tinged music with nostalgic Americana lyrics. Fogelberg's material was also recorded by his backing band Fools Gold, on their album **Fools Gold** (1976, Morning Sky) US#100. CHART COMPOSITIONS: *Part of the Plan* (1974) US#31, *Power of Gold* (1978) US#24, *Longer* (1980) g C&W#85 US#2 UK#59, *Heart Hotels* (1980) US#21, *Same Old Lang Syne* (1981) US#9, *Hard to Say* (1981) US#7, *Leader of the Band* (1981) US#9, *Run for the Roses* (1981) US#18, *Missing You* (1981) US#23, *Make Love Stay* (1982) US#29, *The Language of Love* (1984) US#13, *Believe in Me* (1984) US#48, *Go Down Easy* [i] (1985) C&W#56 US#85, *Down the Mountain Pass* (1985) C&W#33, *She Don't Look Back* (1987) US#84. ALBUMS: **Home Free** (1973, Columbia) g; **Souvenirs** (1975) p US#17, **Captured Angel** (1975) p US#23, **Nether Lands** (1977) p US#13, **Twin Sons of Different Mothers*** (1978) p US#8, **Phoenix** (1980) p US#3 UK#42, **The Innocent Age** (1981) p US#6, **Windows and Walls** (1984) g US#15, **High Country Snows** (1985) US#30, **Exiles** (1987) US#48, **The Wild Places** (1990) US#103, **Live Greetings from the West** (1991), **River of Souls** (1993, all Full Moon) US#164; **No Resemblance Whatsoever*** (1995, Giant). COMPILATION: **Greatest Hits** (1982, Full Moon) p US#15; **Portrait** (1997). With: * Tim Weisberg (b. 1943, Los Angeles, CA). Co-writer: [i] M. Lewis.

322. FOGERTY, John (b. John Cameron Fogerty, May 28, 1945, Berkeley, CA) Rock multi-instrumentalist and vocalist. The composer of songs rich in rural American imagery, that often champion the individual over the system. With his group Creedence Clearwater Revival, Fogerty created a rough, rocking R&B sound that was to influence both Bruce Springsteen and Bob Seger. Fogerty learned the guitar, piano, tenor saxophone, drums, dobro and harmonica in his teens, and performed in various 1960s bands before forming the Golliwogs, which released the album **The Golliwogs** (1965, Fantasy). After Fogerty was drafted into the U.S. Army, little was heard from the Golliwogs until 1967, when they re-emerged as Creedence Clearwater Revival, performing Fogerty originals and R&B covers to become one of America's best selling acts, with such classics as Fogerty's million selling ode to a Mississippi steamboat *Proud Mary* (1969), of which, within a year, there were thirty-five cover versions. The group's albums were consistent multi-million sellers until Fogerty mistakenly bowed to band democracy, and allowed inferior material by the other members to appear on the substandard **Mardi Gras** (1972), subsequent to which, the group broke up. CHART COMPOSITIONS: *Proud Mary* (1969) g US#2 UK#8, *Bad Moon Rising* (1969) g US#2 UK#1, re-issued (1992) UK#71; *Lodi* (1969) US#52, *Green River* (1969) US#2 UK#19, *Commotion* (1969) US#30, *Down on the Corner* (1970) g US#3 UK#31, *Fortunate Son* (1970) g US#14, *Travelin' Band* 1970 g US#2 UK#8, *Who'll Stop the Rain* (1970) US#13, *Up Around the Bend* (1970) g US#4 UK#3, *Run Through the Jungle* (1970) US#48, *Lookin' Out My Back Door* (1970) g US#2, *Long as I Can See the Light* (1970) US#57 UK#20, *Have You Ever Seen the Rain* (1971) g US#9 UK#36, *Hey Tonight* (1971) US#90, *Sweet Hitchhiker* (1972) g US#6 UK#36, *Someday Never Comes* (1972) US#25. ALBUMS: **Creedence Clearwater Revival** (1968) p US#52, **Bayou Country** (1969) p US#7 UK#62, **Green River** (1969) p US#1 UK#20, **Willie and the Poor Boys** (1970) p US#3 UK#10, **Cosmo's Factory** (1970) p US#1 UK#1, **Pendulum** (1971) p US#5 UK#23, **Mardi Gras** (1972, all Fantasy) g US#12. COMPILATIONS: **Creedence Gold** (1973) p US#15, **More Creedence Gold** (1973) US#61, **Live in Europe** (1973) US#143, **Chronicle-20 Greatest Hits** (1976) p US#100, **Greatest Hits** (1979) US#35, **Live in Germany** (1975), **Live at the Royal Albert Hall, 1970** (1981), **The Concert** (1981, all Fantasy) US#62; **The Creedence Collection** (1985, Impression) UK#68. Fogerty took a low-key approach to his first solo project, recording as a one-man bluegrass outfit the Blue Ridge Rangers, which he followed with an eponymous set upon which he played all the instruments. After withdrawing his 1976 album **Hoodoo** before it was issued, Fogerty quit music for nearly a decade to live on his ranch in Oregon, from which he has occasionally resurfaced with an R&B influenced rock set. CHART COMPOSITIONS: *Rockin' All Over the World* (1975) US#27, *Almost Saturday Night* (1975) US#78, *You Got the Magic* (1976) US#87, *The Old Man Down the Road* (1985) US#10,

Big Train (From Memphis) (1985) C&W#38, *Rock 'n' Roll Girls* (1985) US#20, *Centerfield* (1985) US#44, *Eye of the Zombie* (1986) US#81. ALBUMS: **The Blue Ridge Rangers** (1973, Fantasy) US#47; **John Fogerty** (1975, Asylum) US#78; **Centerfield** (1985) p US#1 UK#48, **Eye of the Zombie** (1986) g US#26; **Blue Moon Swamp** (1997, all Warner Brothers). HIT VERSIONS: *Almost Saturday Night* Dave Edmunds (1981) US#54 UK#58/Burrito Brothers (1984) C&W#49; *Born on the Bayou* Short-Kuts (1969) US#109, *Down on the Corner* Jerry Reed (1983) C&W#13, *Fortunate Son* Bob Seger on B-side of *American Storm* (1986) US#13, *Have You Ever Seen the Rain* Pam Hobbs (1981) C&W#85/Bonnie Tyler (1983) UK#47; *Lodi* Buddy Alan (1969) C&W#23/ Al Wilson (1969) US#67; *Lookin' Out My Back Door* Buddy Alan (1971) C&W#37; *Proud Mary* Solomon Burke (1969) R&B#15 US#45/Sonny Charles & the Checkmates (1969) US#69/Anthony Armstrong Jones (1969) C&W#22/Ike & Tina Turner (1971) g R&B#5 US#4/Brush Arbor (1972) C&W#56; *Rockin' All Over the World* Status Quo (1977) UK#3, also recorded as *Running All Over the World* (1988) UK#17; *Up Around the Bend* Hanoi Rocks (1984) UK#61.

323. FORBERT, Steve (b. 1955, Meridian, MS) Pop guitarist and vocalist. A former busker and truck driver whose folk influenced debut album showed a potential that has yet to be realized. CHART COMPOSITIONS: *Romeo's Tune* (1979) US#11, *Say Goodbye to Little Joe* (1979) US#85. ALBUMS: **Alive on Arrival** (1978) US#82 UK#56, **Jack Rabbit Slim** (1979) US#20 UK#54, **Little Stevie Orbit** (1980) US#70, **Steve Forbert** (1982, all Nemperor) US#159; **Streets of This Town** (1990, Geffen); **Mission of the Crossroad Palms** (1995, Giant); **In Concert** (1996, BMG); **Rocking Horse Head** (1996, Revolution). COMPILATION: **What Kind of Guy?-The Best of Steve Forbert** (1994, Nemperor).

324. FORDHAM, Julie (b. August 10, 1962, Portsmouth, England) Pop vocalist. A singer-songwriter, who first performed as a backing singer in the group the Wilsations. CHART SINGLES: *Happy Ever After* (1988) UK#27, *Where Does the Time Go* (1989) UK#41, *I Thought It Was You* (1991) UK#64, re-mixed (1992) UK#45; *Love Moves (In Mysterious Ways)* (1992) UK#19, *Different Time, Different Place* (1994) UK#41, *I Can't Help Myself* (1994) UK#62. ALBUMS: **Julia Fordham** (1988) US#118 UK#20, **Porcelain** (1989) US#74 UK#13, **Swept** (1991) UK#33, **Falling Forward** (1994, all Circa) UK#21; **East West** (1997, Capitol).

325. FORREST, George (b. July 31, 1915, Brooklyn, NY), and **WRIGHT, Robert B.** (b. September 25, 1914, Daytona Beach, FL) Both film and stage composers. A songwriting team who worked exclusively together, frequently adopting classics for Broadway. Forrest and Wright's best known songs are those that they wrote for the show "Kismet" (1955). They also contributed to the shows "Song of Norway" (1954) and "Kean" (1961), and the film "Rainbow 'Round My Shoulder" (1952). ALBUMS: **Song of Norway** oc (1949, Decca); **Song of Norway** oc (1958), **Kean** oc (1961, both Columbia) US#80; **Anya** oc (1965, United Artists); **Song of Norway** ost (1970, ABC). HIT VERSIONS: *Baubles, Bangles and Beads* [i] Peggy Lee (1953) US#30/Kirby Stone Four (1958) US#25/Frank Sinatra on *Come Dance with Me LP* (1959) UK#30/George Shearing (1962) UK#49; *It's a Blue World* Tony Martin (1940) US#2/Glenn Miller (1940) US#14/Four Freshmen (1952) US#30; *Jersey Bounce* Jimmy Dorsey (1942) US#9/Shep Fields (1942) US#15/Benny Goodman (1942) US#1; *Pink Champagne* Joe Liggins (1950) US#30, *Strange Music* James Melton (1945) US#21, *Stranger in Paradise* Gordon MacRae (1953) US#29/Tony Bennett (1954) g US#2 UK#1/Eddie Calvert (1955) UK#14/Don Cornell (1955) UK#19/Bing Crosby (1955) UK#17/Four Aces (1954) US#3 UK#6/Tony Martin (1954) US#10 UK#6. Co-writer: [i] Alexander Porphyrevich Borodin (b. September 12, 1833; d. February 27, 1887, both St. Petersburg, Russia). (*See also under* Rudolph FRIML.)

326. FOSTER, Dave (b. Victoria, British Columbia, Canada) Pop keyboard player and producer. One of America's most successful arranger-songwriters since the mid-1980s. Foster was initially a member of the group Attitudes, charting with *Sweet Summer Music* (1976) R&B#43 US#94, and releasing the albums **Attitudes** (1975) and **Good News** (1977, both Dark Horse). He has also recorded as a solo artist. CHART COMPOSITIONS: *Love Theme from St. Elmo's Fire* (1985) US#15, *The Best of Me* [xiii] with Olivia Newton-John (1986) US#80, *Winter Games* (1988) US#85. ALBUMS: **St. Elmo's Fire** ost (1985) g US#21, **David Foster** (1986) US#195, **The Symphony Sessions** (1988, all Atlantic) US#111; **The Christmas Album** (1993, Interscope) US#48. HIT VERSIONS: *After the Love Has Gone* [v] Earth, Wind & Fire (1979) g R&B#2 US#2 UK#4, *Best of Me, The* [xiii] Cliff Richard (1989) UK#2, *Don't Want to Wait Anymore* [xviii] Tubes (1981) US#35 UK#60, *Friends in Love* [v] Dionne Warwick & Johnny Mathis (1982) R&B#22 US#38, *I Have Nothing* [xvii] Whitney Houston (1993) UK#3, *Lady of My Heart, The* [i] Jack Wagner (1985) US#76, *Lonely Won't Leave Me Alone* [ix] Glenn Medeiros

(1987) US#67, *Now and Forever (You and Me)* [viii] Anne Murray (1986) C&W#1 US#92, *St. Elmo's Fire (Man in Motion)* [xvi] John Parr (1985) p US#1 UK#6, *Secret of My Success, The* [iii] Night Ranger (1987) US#64, *She's a Beauty* [xiv] Tubes (1983) US#10, *Through the Fire* [xi] Chaka Khan (1985) R&B#15 US#60, *Tonight, Tonight* [vi] Bill Champlin (1981) US#55, *Too Young* [x] Jack Wagner (1985) US#52, *Twist of Fate* Olivia Newton-John (1983) US#5 UK#57, *What About Me?* [xv] Kenny Rogers, Kim Carnes & James Ingram (1984) C&W#70 US#15, *Who's Holding Donna Now?* [vii] DeBarge (1985) R&B#2 US#6, *Why You Treat Me So Bad* [xii] Club Nouveau (1987) US#39, *Will You Still Love Me?* [ii] Chicago (1986) US#3, *You're the Only Love* [iv] Paul Hyde & Payolas (1985) US#84. Co-writers: [i] Glen Ballard/Jay Grayden, [ii] Richard Baskin/T. Keane, [iii] J. Blades/T. Keane/Michael Landau, [iv] Brock/Paul Hyde/M. Nelson, [v] Bill Champlin/Jay Grayden, [vi] Bill Champlin/R. Kennedy, [vii] Randy Goodrum/Jay Grayden, [viii] Randy Goodrum/Jim Vallance, [ix] J. Jackson/T. Keane/K. Wakefield, [x] Jay Grayden/S. Kipner/Donny Osmond (b. Donald Osmond, December 9, 1957, Ogden, UT), [xi] T. Keane/Cynthia Weil, [xii] J. King/T. McElroy, [xiii] Jeremy Lubbox/Richard Marx, [xiv] Steve Lukather (b. October 21, 1957, Los Angeles, CA)/Fee Waybill (b. John Waldo, September 17, 1950, Omaha, NE), [xv] Richard Marx/Kenny Rogers (b. Kenneth Donald Rogers, August 21, 1938, Houston, TX), [xvi] John Parr (b. Nottingham, England), [xvii] Linda Thompson, [xviii] Rick Anderson (b. August 1, 1947, St. Paul, MN)/Michael Cotton (b. January 25, 1950, Kansas City, MO)/Prairie Prince (b. May 7, 1950, Charlotte, NC)/Roger Steen (b. March 30, 1950, USA)/Fee Waybill/Vince Welnick (b. February 21, 1951, Phoenix, AZ). (*See also under* Peter ALLEN, Paul ANKA, Peter CETERA, Neil DIAMOND, Al JARREAU, Kenny LOGGINS, Madonna, David PAICH, Boz SCAGGS, Maurice WHITE.)

327. FOSTER, Stephen (b. July 4, 1826, Lawrenceville, PA; d. January 13, 1864, New York, NY) Folk pianist and vocalist. Arguably the very place where popular songwriting began, Foster was the first to earn a living as a tunesmith. Essentially a white folk writer, Foster also utilized black American traditions in his music, if sometimes patronizingly, and was the first to capture any elements of black culture in American music. Foster's compositions were popular just as Thomas Edison's cylinders came into use. His influential tunes have been recorded by artists as diverse as James Taylor and Bing Crosby. Foster founded the concept of a chorus in popular songs. A self-taught pianist, his first published work (of more than 200) was *Open Thy*

Lattice Love (1844). His melodies include: *Old Uncle Ned* (1849), *Massa's in de Cold, Cold Ground* (1852), *Old Dog Tray* (1853), *Jeannie with the Light Brown Hair* (1854), and *Beautiful Dreamer* (1864). HIT VERSIONS: *Camptown Races (Gwine to Run All Night), The* Billy Murray (1911) US#9, *Oh! Susannah* Wendell Hall & the Shannon Four (1924) US#8, *Old Folks at Home (Swanee River), The* Len Spencer (1892) US#1/Vess Ossman (1900) US#2/Haydn Quartet (1904) US#6/Louise Homer (1905) US#4/ Alma Gluck (1915) US#3/Taylor Trio (1916) US#4/ Oscar Seagle with the Columbia Stellar Quartette (1919) US#8/Jimmie Lunceford (1936) US#19/Bunny Berigan (1937) US#18; *My Old Kentucky Home* Edison Male Quartette (1898) US#1/Haydn Quartet (1903) US#2/Harry MacDonough (1906) US#3/ Geraldine Farrar (1910) US#5/Alama Gluck (1916) US#3/Columbia Stellar Quartette (1918) US#9/Lucy Gates (1918) US#9; *Old Black Joe* Peerless Quartet (1908) US#10/Mills Brothers (1940) US#30; *Come Where My Love Lies Dreaming* Peerless Quartet (1908) US#4.

328. FOX, Charles (b. America) Pop pianist and producer. A successful television and film theme writer since contributing to the soundtrack of "Barbarella" (1968), Fox's television work has included "The ABC Monday Night Football Theme," "ABC's Wide World of Sports Theme" and "The Aloha Paradise Theme." During the 1970s, in collaboration with the lyricist Norman Gimbel, Fox produced and composed for the singer Lori Lieberman, whose self-titled debut album in 1972 featured two fine ballads that were later interpreted by Roberta Flack, *And the Feeling's Good* [i], and the BMI four million radio performance classic *Killing Me Softly with His Song* [ii], the latter being composed after Gimbel and Fox had attended a Don McLean concert. CHART COMPOSITIONS: *Seasons* [ii] (1981) US#75. ALBUMS: **Barbarella** ost (1968, DynoVoice) US#183; **Goodbye Columbus** ost (1969, Warner Brothers) US#99; **Love American Style** ost (1969), **Pufnstuf** ost (1970, both Capitol); **Star Spangled Girl** ost (1971, Bell); **The Harrad Experiment** ost (1972, Capitol); **The Laughing Policeman** ost (1973, Shady Brook); **The Other Side of the Mountain** ost (1975, MCA); **The Duchess and the Dirtwater Fox** ost (1976, 20th Century); **Two Minute Warning** ost (1976, Centurion); **Victory at Entebbe** ost (1976), **Seals and Crofts Sing Songs from the Original Soundtrack "One on One"** ost (1977, both Warner Brothers) US#118; **Foul Play** ost (1978, Arista) US#102; **Our Winning Season** ost (1978, Epic); **The Last Married Couple in America** ost (1980, Warner Brothers); **9 to 5** ost (1980, 20th Century) US#77; **Oh God!, Book II** ost (1980, Fox); **Seasons** (1981,

RCA); **Six Pack** ost (1982, Allegiance); **Zapped** ost (1982, Regency); **Strange Brew** ost (1989, Mercury). HIT VERSIONS: *Deeply* [i] Anson Williams (1977) US#93, *Different Worlds* [i] Maureen McGovern (1979) US#16, *Goodbye Columbus* Association (1969) US#80, *Happy Days* [i] Pratt & McLain (1976) US#5 UK#31, *I Got a Name* [i] Jim Croce (1973) US#10, *Killing Me Softly with Her/His Song* [i] Roberta Flack (1973) g R&B#2 US#1 UK#6/Al B. Sure! (1988) US#80/Fugees (1996) UK#1; *Making Our Dreams Come True (Theme from Laverne and Shirley)* [i] Cyndi Greco (1976) US#25, *Ready to Take a Chance Again* [i] Barry Manilow (1978) US#11, *Together* O.C. Smith (1976) R&B#62. Co-writers: [i] Norman Gimble, [ii] Ed Newmark. (*See also under* Paul WILLIAMS.)

329. FRAME, Roddy (b. January 29, 1964, East Kilbride, Scotland). Pop guitarist and vocalist. A singer-songwriter who records under the group name Aztec Camera. Frame first performed in the 1970s band Neutral Blue, before forming Aztec Camera in 1980, which released two singles on the independent Postcard label in 1981, one of which was the startling *Just Like Gold/ We Could Send Letters*. The group's debut album **High Land, Hard Rain** (1982), was a mixture of English folk music and British new wave, and featured such strong material as *Oblivious* and *Walk Out to Winter*. CHART COMPOSITIONS: *Oblivious* (1983) UK#18, *Walk Out to Winter* (1983) UK#64, *All I Need Is Everything* (1984) UK#34, *How Men Are* (1987) UK#25, *Somewhere in My Heart* (1987) UK#3, *Working in a Gold Mine* (1987) UK#31, *Deep Wide and Tall* (1987) UK#55, *The Crying Scene* (1990) UK#70, *Good Morning Britain* (1990) UK#19, *Spanish Horses* (1992) UK#52, *Dream Sweet Dreams* (1992) UK#67. ALBUMS: **High Land, Hard Rain** (1982, Rough Trade) US#129 UK#22; **Knife** (1984) US#175 UK#14, **Love** (1987) US#193 UK#10, **Stray** (1990) UK#22, **Dreamland** (1993) UK#21, **Frestonia** (1995, all WEA). COMPILATIONS: **Aztec Camera** (1985, Sire) US#181; **Retrospect** (1993, Sire/Reprise); **New, Live and Rare** (1995, WEA); **Live on the Test** (1994, Windsong). HIT VERSION: *Good Morning Britain* Big Audio Dynamite (1990) UK#19.

330. FRAMPTON, Peter (b. April 22, 1950, Beckenham, England) Rock guitarist and vocalist. One of the best selling artists of the 1970s, whose double live set **Frampton Comes Alive** (1976), sold over ten million copies. Frampton started out as a member of the 1960s British band the Herd, which released the album **Paradise Lost** (1968, Fontana) UK#38, before he formed Humble Pie with Steve Marriott in 1969, in order to perform a heavy blend of blues and R&B. ALBUMS: **As Safe as Yesterday Is** (1969) UK#32, **Town and Country** (1969, both Immediate); **Humble Pie** (1970), **Rock On** (1971) US#118, **Performance-Rockin' the Fillmore** (1972) g US#21 UK#32, **Lost and Found** (1972, all A&M) US#37. Frampton quit Humble Pie in 1972 for a solo career. CHART COMPOSITIONS: *Show Me the Way* (1976) US#6 UK#10, *Baby, I Love Your Way* (1976) US#12 UK#43, *Do You Feel Like We Do?* [i] (1976) US#10 UK#39, *I'm in You* (1977) US#2 UK#41, *Tried to Love* (1978) US#41, *I Can't Stand It No More* (1979) US#14, *Lying* (1983) US#74. ALBUMS: **Winds of Change** (1972) US#177, **Frampton's Camel** (1973) US#110, **Somethin's Happening** (1974) US#25, **Frampton** (1975) g US#32, **Frampton Comes Alive** (1976) p US#1 UK#6, **I'm in You** (1977) p US#2 UK#19, **Where I Should Be** (1979) g US#19, **Breaking All the Rules** (1981) US#47, **The Art of Control** (1982, all A&M) US#174; **Premonition** (1983) US#80, **When All the Pieces Fit** (1989, both Atlantic) US#152; **Peter Frampton** (1994, Relativity); **Frampton Comes Alive II** (1995, IRS). COMPILATIONS: **Classics** (1987), **Shine On-A Collection** (1992, both A&M). HIT VERSIONS: *Baby, I Love Your Way* Walter Jackson (1977) US#19/Will to Power (1988) US#1/Big Mountain (1994) g US#6. Co-writers: [i] Michael Gallagher/John Sidmos. (*See also under* Steve MARRIOTT.)

331. FRANK, Jackson C. (b. 1943, Buffalo, NY) Folk guitarist and vocalist. An introspective singer-songwriter who was a significant influence on the British folk scene during the 1960s, and is best known for his composition *Blues Run the Game*, which was recorded by Sandy Denny and Bert Jansch. Frank's tragic personal life is fully detailed in the liner notes to the 1996 compact disk re-issue of his solitary, but intriguing album, **Jackson C. Frank** (1965, Columbia).

332. FRANKS, Michael (b. September 18, 1944, La Jolla, CA) Rock-jazz vocalist. A singer-songwriter with a mannered, jazz tinged style that echoes the work of the jazz-vocal group Lambert, Hendricks and Ross, who has sold over five million albums. Franks grew up in San Diego, California, where he developed an interest in folk and rock music while still at high school. During the early 1970s, he taught undergraduate music courses at UCLA and Berkeley, and scored two movies, "Count Your Bullets" and "Zandy's Bride" (both 1971). Around the same time, his compositions were recorded by Sonny Terry and Brownie McGhee, and Jackie and Roy. Most of Franks' albums ruminate on the sunny climes of his native California, although **Sleeping Gypsy** (1977), was a more adventurous effort that explored the Latin rhythms of Antonio Carlos Jobim. **Burchfield Nines** (1978), was his first album in a series of song cycles based around the work of painters. CHART COMPOSITION: *Popsicle Toes* (1976) US#43. ALBUMS: **Count Your Bullets** ost (1972, Metromedia); **Michael Franks** (1973, Brut); **The Art of Tea** (1975, Reprise) g US#131; **Sleeping Gypsy** (1977) US#119, **Burchfield Nines** (1978) US#90, **Tiger in the Rain** (1979) US#68, **One Bad Habit** (1980) US#83, **Live** (1980), **Objects of Desire** (1982) US#45, **Passion Fruit** (1983) US#141, **Skin Dive** (1985) US#137, **The Camera Never Lies** (1987, all Warner Brothers) US#147; **Blue Pacific** (1990) US#121, **Dragonfly Summer** (1993, both Reprise). COMPILATION: **Previously Unavailable** (1983, John Hammond).

333. FRAZIER, Dallas (b. October 27, 1939, Spiro, OK) C&W guitarist and vocalist. A successful backroom songwriter of country, pop and novelty material since the early 1960s, whose best known song is *Alley Oop*. By the age of twelve, Frazier was performing and touring with the country singer Ferlin Husky, and during the 1950-1960s he became a solo artist. His songs were also recorded as **George Jones Sings the Songs of Dallas Frazier** (1968, Stateside). CHART COMPOSITIONS: *Just a Little Bit of You* (1966) US#108, *Everybody Oughta Sing a Song* (1967) C&W#28, *The Sunshine of My World* (1968) C&W#43, *I Hope I Like Mexico Blues* (1968) C&W#59, *The Conspiracy of Homer Jones* (1969) C&W#63 US#120, *California Cotton Fields* (1969) C&W#45, *The Birthmark Henry Thompson Talks About* (1970) C&W#45, *Big Mable Murphy* (1971) C&W#43, *North Carolina* (1972) C&W#42. ALBUMS: **Elvira** (1967, Capitol); **Singing My Songs** (1970), **My Baby Packed Up and Left Me** (1971, both RCA). HIT VERSIONS: *Ain't Love a Good Thing* Connie Smith (1974) C&W#10, *All I Have to Offer You Is Me* Charley Pride (1969) C&W#1 US#91, *Alley Oop* Hollywood Argyles (1960) R&B#3 US#1 UK#24/Dante & the Evergreens (1960) US#15/Dyna-Sores (1960) US#59; *Beneath Still Waters* Dana Trask (1970) C&W#38 US#114/Emmylou Harris (1980) C&W#1; *Big Mable Murphy* Sue Thompson (1975) C&W#50, *Did We Have to Come This Far (To Say Goodbye)* Wayne Kemp (1971) C&W#72/Donna Fargo (1982) C&W#80; *Elvira* Rodney Crowell (1978) C&W#95/Oak Ridge Boys (1981) p C&W#1 US#5; *I Can't Believe That You've Stopped Loving Me* Charley Pride (1970) C&W#1 US#71, *I'm a People* George Jones (1966) C&W#6, *(I'm So) Afraid of Losing You Again* Charley Pride (1969) C&W#1 US#74, *If My Heart Had Windows* George Jones (1967) C&W#7/Amy Wooley

(1982) C&W#51/Patty Loveless (1988) C&W#10; *Johnny One Time* Willie Nelson (1968) C&W#36/ Brenda Lee (1969) C&W#50 US#41/Jesseca James (1976) C&W#87; *Just for What I Am* Connie Smith (1972) C&W#5, *Man in the Little White Suit, The* Charlie Walker (1966) C&W#37, *Mohair Sam* Charlie Rich (1965) US#21, *Money Greases the Wheels* Ferlin Husky (1965) C&W#48, *Rainbow in Daddy's Eyes, The* Sammi Smith (1974) C&W#16, *Say It's Not You* George Jones (1968) C&W#8, *Son of Hickory Holler's Tramp, The* O.C. Smith (1968) R&B#32 US#40 UK#2/Johnny Darrell (1967) C&W#22/ Johnny Russell (1976) C&W#32; *Then Who Am I* Charley Pride (1975) C&W#1, *There Goes My Everything* Jack Greene (1966) C&W#1 US#65/Don Cherry (1967) US#113/Engelbert Humperdinck (1967) US#20 UK#2/Elvis Presley (1971) C&W#9 US#21, re-issued (1982) UK#6; *Timber, I'm Falling* Ferlin Husky (1964) C&W#13, *Touching Home* Jerry Lee Lewis (1971) C&W#3, *True Love Travels on a Gravel Road* Duane Dee (1969) C&W#58, *Walk Softly on the Bridges* Rodney Lay (1986) C&W#79/ Mel Street (1973) C&W#11; *What's Your Mama's Name* [i] Tanya Tucker (1973) C&W#1 US#68, *Where Did They Go, Lord* Elvis Presley (1971) C&W#55 US#33, *Will You Visit Me on Sundays* Charlie Louvin (1968) C&W#20. Co-writer: [i] Bob Montgomery.

334. FREED, Arthur (b. Arthur Grossman, September 9, 1894, Charleston, SC; d. April 12, 1973, Hollywood, CA) Film and stage lyricist, producer. Although better known as an MGM producer of film musicals, Freed also wrote the lyrics to compositions by a variety of composers, which appeared in such films as "Cocoanut Grove" (1938) and "Strike Up the Band" (1940). HIT VERSIONS: *I Cried for You* [i] Columbians (1923) US#14/Benny Krueger (1923) US#2/Bunny Berigan (1938) US#13/Bing Crosby (1939) US#13/Glen Gray (1939) US#6/Harry James (1942) US#19/Ricky Stevens (1961) UK#34; *Our Love Affair* [ii] Tommy Dorsey (1940) US#5/ Dick Jurgens (1940) US#10/Glenn Miller (1940) US#8; *You Leave Me Breathless* [iii] Tommy Dorsey (1938) US#4/Ozzie Nelson (1938) US#11. Co-writers: [i] Gus Arnheim/Abe Lyman, [ii] Roger Edens, [iii] Frederick Hollander. (*See also under* Harry BARRIS, Herb Nacio BROWN, Al HOFFMAN, Harry WOODS.)

335. FREY, Glenn (b. November 6, 1948, Detroit, IL) Rock guitarist and vocalist. The co-founder of the country influenced rock group the Eagles, in which Frey and Don Henley became the main songwriting team. After the demise of the band, Frey recorded as a solo artist, forming a new writing partnership with Jack Tempchin. CHART COMPOSITIONS: *I Found Somebody* [i] (1982) US#31, *The One You Love* [i] (1982) US#15, *All Those Lies* (1982) US#41, *Sexy Girl* [i] (1984) US#20, *The Allnighter* [i] (1984) US#54, *Smugglers Blues* [i] (1985) US#12 UK#22, *You Belong to the City* [i] (1985) US#2, *True Love* [i] (1988) US#13, *Livin' Right* [i] (1989) US#90, *I've Got Mine* [i] (1992) US#91, *Love in the 21st Century* [i] (1993) US#112. ALBUMS: **No Fun Aloud** (1982, Asylum) g US#32; **The Allnighter** (1984) g US#22, **Soul Searchin'** (1988) US#36, **Live** (1995, all MCA). COMPILATIONS: **Miami Vice** tvst (1985) p US#1 UK#11, **Solo Collection** (1995, both MCA). Co-writer: [i] Jack Tempchin. (*See also under* Jackson BROWNE, Don HENLEY.)

336. FRIEDMAN, Kinky (b. Richard Friedman, October 31, 1944, Rio Duckworth, TX) C&W vocalist. A satirical country performer and published author, who first recorded with the group King Arthur and the Carrots in 1966, before forming the Texas Jewboys. CHART COMPOSITION: *Sold American* (1973) C&W#69. ALBUMS: **Sold American** (1973, Vanguard); **Kinky Friedman** (1975, ABC) US#132; **Lasso from El Passo** (1976, Epic); **Old Testaments and New Revelations** (1993, Fruit of the Tune 777).

337. FRIEND, Clifford (b. 1893; d. 1974, both America) Film and stage composer. A consistently successful songwriter whose compositions were featured in such films as "Moonlight and Cactus" (1936). HIT VERSIONS: *Concert in the Park* [i] Jan Garber (1939) US#6/Kay Kyser (1939) US#10; *Give Me a Night in June* Ipana Troubadors (1927) US#8/Johnny Marvin (1928) US#18; *Hello Bluebird* Vincent Lopez (1927) US#3/Nick Lucas (1927) US#9; *I Must See Annie Tonight* [ii] Guy Lombardo (1938) US#2/Benny Goodman (1939) US#13, *June Night* [i] Ted Lewis (1924) US#2/Fred Waring's Pennsylvanians (1924) US#7; *Lovesick Blues* [iv] Red Kirk (1949) C&W#14/Hank Williams (1949) C&W#1 US#24/Sonny James (1957) C&W#15/Frank Ifield (1962) UK#1/Sonny Curtis (1957) C&W#78/Drifting Cowboys (1978) C&W#97; *Mama Loves Papa, Papa Loves Mama* [i] Isham Jones (1924) US#8, *Merry-Go-Round Broke Down, The* [ii] Eddy Duchin (1937) US#2/Shep Fields (1937) US#1/Jimmie Lunceford (1937) US#7/Russ Morgan (1937) US#1/ Dick Robertson (1937) US#12; *Sweetest Music This Side of Heaven, The* [iii] Guy Lombardo (1934) US#20, *There's Yes! Yes! in Your Eyes* [v] Paul Whiteman (1924) US#5/Carmen Cavarallo (1949) US#29/ Eddy Howard (1949) US#21; *Wah-Hoo!* Top Hatters (1936) US#15/Paul Whiteman (1936) US#9; *When*

My Dreamboat Comes Home [ii] Henry Allen (1937) US#10/Shep Fields (1937) US#10/Guy Lombardo (1937) US#3/Kay Starr (1937) US#18/Fats Domino (1956) R&B#2 US#14; *You Can't Stop Me from Dreaming* [ii] Guy Lombardo (1937) US#17/Ozzie Nelson (1937) US#5/Dick Robertson (1937) US#11/Teddy Wilson (1937) US#1. Co-writers: [i] Abel Baer (b. 1893; d. 1976), [ii] Dave Franklin, [iii] Carmen Lombardo, [iv] Irving Mills, [v] Joseph Santly. (*See also under* Lew BROWN, Irving CAESAR, Walter DONALDSON.)

338. FRIML, Rudolf (b. Charles Rudolf Friml, December 7, 1879, Prague, Austria-Hungary [now Czech Republic]; d. November 12, 1972, Los Angeles, CA) Film and stage composer, pianist. One of Broadway's finest songwriters in the operetta tradition, whose compositions added considerable depth to such shows as "The Vagabond King" (1927). As a teenager, Friml studied composition at the Prague Conservatory under Anton Dvorak, and in 1904, he premiered his "Piano Concerto in B Major." In 1906, Friml emigrated to America, where he pursued a concert career before achieving success with the Broadway show "The Firefly" (1912), after which he linked up with the lyricist Otto Harbach for the shows "Katinka" (1917), "Sometime" (1918) and "Rose Marie" (1924). Friml's best known songs include *Giannia Mia* [iii] from the film "Firefly" (1912), and *Allah's Holiday* [iii] (1917) and *Dear Love My Love* from the film "June Love" (1921). Neal Hefti and His Orchestra recorded an entire album of Friml compositions as **The Music of Rudolf Friml** (1955, X) US#8, as did Mantovani on **The Music of Rudolf Friml** (1955, London) US#13 and **All-American Showcase** (1960, London) US#8. ALBUMS: **Rose Marie** sc (1950, Columbia); **Firefly** sc (1951), **Vagabond King** sc (1951, both RCA); **Rose Marie** oc (1952, World); **Rose Marie** ost (1952, RCA); **Rose Marie** ost (1954, MGM); **Vagabond King** sc (1956, Decca); **Vagabond King** ost (1956, RCA), **The Three Musketeers** ost (1972, Monmouth Evergreen). HIT VERSIONS: *Donkey Serenade, The* [i] Allan Jones (1938) US#8, *Indian Love Call, The* [ii] Leo Reisman (1925) US#6/Paul Whiteman (1925) US#3/Nelson Eddy & Jeanette MacDonald (1937) g US#8/Artie Shaw (1938) US#6/Slim Whitman (1952) C&W#2 US#9 UK#7/Karl Denver (1963) UK#32/Ray Stevens (1975) C&W#38 US#68 UK#34; *Love Me Tonight* [iv] Bing Crosby (1932) US#4/George Olsen (1932) US#14; *Only a Rose* [iv] Carolyn Thompson (1926) US#7/Bette McLaurin (1953) US#25; *Rose-Marie* [ii] Jess Crawford (1925) US#15/John McCormack (1925) US#5/Lambert Murphy (1924) US#14/Paul Whiteman (1925) US#3/Slim Whitman (1954) C&W#4 US#22 UK#1; *Some*

Day [iv] Tony Martin (1952) US#24/Frankie Laine (1954) US#14; *Something Seems Tingle-Ingling* [iii] Walter Van Brunt (1914) US#5, *Song of the Vagabonds, The* [iv] Dennis King (1926) US#5/Vincent Lopez (1926) US#9; *Sympathy* Helen Clark & Walter Van Brunt (1913) US#1, *When a Maid Comes Knocking at Your Door* [iii] Olive Kline (1913) US#5. Co-writers: [i] George Forrest/Herbert Stothart (b. September 11, 1885, Milwaukee, WI; d. February 1, 1949, Los Angeles, CA)/Robert B. Wright, [ii] Oscar Hammerstein, II/Otto Harbach, [iii] Otto Harbach, [iv] Brian Hooker.

339. FRISHBERG, David L. (b. March 23, 1933, St. Paul, MN) Jazz pianist and vocalist. A little known jazz based composer of wry and somewhat nostalgic Americana. Frishberg performed as a solo pianist during the 1950s, and also ran his own jingle company, before recording with a variety of jazz artists, including Gene Krupa. He was a resident pianist in New York during the 1960s, and his best known composition is *Peel Me a Grape*, which was recorded by Dick Haymes and Fran Jeffries (1962). Frishberg's material has more recently been interpreted by Al Jarreau and Anita O'Day. ALBUMS: **Oklahoma Toad** (1968, CTI); **Solo and Trio** (1975, Seeds); **Getting Some Fun Out of Life** (1977), **You're a Lucky Guy** (1978, both Concord); **The Dave Frishberg Songbook** (1981), **The Dave Frishberg Songbook, Volume 2** (1982, both Omnisound); **Live at Vine Street** (1984), **Can't Take You Anywhere** (1987, both Fantasy).

340. FRIZZELL, Lefty (b. William Orville Frizzell, March 31, 1928, Coriscana, TX; d. July 19, 1975, Nashville, TN) C&W guitarist and vocalist. One of the most influential country and honky tonk artists of the 1950s, whose music was the direct link between Jimmie Rodgers and Merle Haggard. After a failed boxing career, Frizzell turned to music in the 1950s, eventually signing to Columbia Records and charting thirty-nine hits between 1950–1975. Willie Nelson recorded the definitive set of his compositions, **To Lefty from Willie** (1976, Columbia) US#91. Frizell was a Grand Ole Opry star from 1952 until his death from a stroke in 1975. CHART COMPOSITIONS: *If You've Got the Money, Honey, I've Got the Time* (1950) C&W#1, *I Love You a Thousand Ways* (1950) C&W#1, *Look What Thoughts Will Do* (1951) C&W#4, *Shine, Shave, Shower* (1951) C&W#7, *I Want to Be with You Always* (1951) C&W#1 US#29, *Always Late (With Your Kisses)* (1951) C&W#1, *Mom and Dad's Waltz* (1951) C&W#2, *Travelin' Blues* (1951) C&W#6, *Give Me More, More, More (Of Your Kisses)* (1951) C&W#1, *How Long Will It Take (To Stop Loving You)* (1952)

C&W#7, *Don't Stay Away ('Till Love Grows Cold)* (1952) C&W#2, *Forever* (1952) C&W#6, *I'm an Old, Old Man (Tryin' to Live While I Can)* (1952) C&W#3, *(Honey, Baby, Hurry!) Bring Your Sweet Self Back to Me* (1953) C&W#8, *Run 'Em Off* (1954) C&W#8, *I Love You Mostly* (1955) C&W#11, *The Long Black Veil* (1959) C&W#6. ALBUMS: **The Songs of Jimmie Rodgers** (1952), **The One and Only Lefty Frizzell** (1964), **Saginaw, Michigan** (1964), **The Sad Side of Love** (1966, all Columbia); **The Classic Style** (1975, ABC); **Lefty Frizzell** (1982), **The Legend Lives On** (1983, both Columbia); **20 Greatest Hits** (1982, CSP-Gusto); **His Life, His Music** (1984, Bear Family); **Honky Tonkin'** (1986, Flyright); **The Legendary Last Sessions** (1986, MCA); **Lefty Frizzell Goes to Nashville** (1988), **Treasures Untold** (1988, Rounder); **Twenty Golden Hits** (1988, Gusto). HIT VERSIONS: *Always Late (With Your Kisses)* Jo-el Sonnier (1976) C&W#99/Leona Williams (1981) C&W#84/Dwight Yoakam (1988) C&W#9; *Bandy the Rodeo Clown* Moe Bandy (1975) C&W#7, *I Love You a Thousand Ways* Hawkshaw Hawkins (1951) C&W#8/Willie Nelson (1977) C&W#9/John Anderson (1981) C&W#54; *If You've Got the Money, Honey, I've Got the Time* Willie Nelson (1976) C&W#1, *Long Black Veil, The* Sammi Smith (1974) C&W#26, *Mom and Dad's Waltz* Patti Page (1961) C&W#21 US#58, *That's the Way Love Goes* [i] Johnny Rodriguez (1974) C&W#1/Merle Haggard (1983) C&W#1. Co-writer: [i] S.D. Shafer.

341. FROMHOLZ, Steven (b. June 8, 1945, Temple, TX) C&W guitarist and vocalist. A country singer-songwriter who has had more success with cover versions of his material than with his own recordings. ALBUMS: **Frommox** (1969, Probe); **A Rumor in My Own Time** (1976), **Frolicking in the Myth** (1977), **Music from Outlaw Blues** ost (1977, all Capitol); **Jus' Playin' Along** (1978, Lone Star); **Live** (1979), **Frommox 2** (1982, both Felicity). HIT VERSION: *I'd Have to Be Crazy* Willie Nelson (1976) C&W#11.

342. FRY, Martin (b. March 9, 1958, Manchester, England) Pop vocalist. A founder member of, and lyricist in, the once fashionable, soul influenced pop group ABC, which was never able to match or repeat the critical and commercial success of its debut album. CHART COMPOSITIONS: *Tears Are Not Enough* [i] (1981) UK#19, *Poison Arrow* [i] (1982) US#25 UK#6, *The Look of Love* [i] (1982) US#18 UK#4, re-mixed (1990) UK#68; *All of My Heart* [i] (1982) UK#5, *That Was Then But This Is Now* [ii] (1983) US#89 UK#18, *S.O.S.* [ii] (1984) UK#39, *(How to Be a) Millionaire* [ii] (1984) US#20

UK#49, *Be Near Me* [ii] (1985) US#9 UK#26, *Vanity Kills* [ii] (1985) US#91 UK#70, *Ocean Blue* [ii] (1986) UK#51, *When Smokey Sings* [ii] (1987) US#5 UK#11, *The Night You Murdered Love* [ii] (1987) UK#31, *King Without a Crown* [ii] (1987) UK#44, *One Better World* [ii] (1989) UK#32, *The Real Thing* [ii] (1989) UK#68, *Love Conquers All* [ii] (1991) UK#47, *Say It* [ii] (1991) UK#42. ALBUMS: **The Lexicon of Love** (1982) g US#24 UK#1, **Beauty Stab** (1983) US#69 UK#12, **How to Be a Zillionaire** (1985) US#30 UK#28, **Alphabet City** (1987) US#48 UK#7, **Up** (1989, all Neutron) UK#58; **Abracadabra** (1991, Parlophone) UK#50; **Skyscrapping** (1997, Deconstruction). COMPILATIONS: **Absolutely** (1990) UK#7, **The Re-mix Collection** (1995, both Neutron). Co-writers: [i] David Palmer (b. May 29, 1961, Chesterfield, England)/Stephen Singleton (b. April 17, 1959, Sheffield, England)/Mark White (b. April 1, 1961, Sheffield, England), [ii] Mark White.

343. FULLER, Jerry (b. Jerrell Lee Fuller, Fort Worth, TX) Pop producer and vocalist. A vocalist turned songwriter who produced the 1960s group Gary Puckett and the Union Gap. CHART COMPOSITIONS: *Salt on the Wound* (1979) C&W#98, *Lines* (1979) C&W#90. ALBUM: **Teenage Love** (1960, Lin). HIT VERSIONS: *If I Were You* [i] Toby Beau (1980) US#70/Lulu (1981) US#44; *It's Up to You* Rick Nelson (1963) R&B#24 US#6 UK#22, *Lady Willpower* Gary Puckett & the Union Gap (1968) g US#2 UK#5, *Over You* Gary Puckett & the Union Gap (1968) g US#7, *Show and Tell* Al Wilson (1973) g R&B#10 US#1, *That's All She Wrote* Ray Price (1976) C&W#34, *Travelin' Man* Rick Nelson (1961) g US#1/Jacky Ward (1982) C&W#32; *To Make a Long Story Short* Ray Price (1976) C&W#41, *Touch and Go* Al Wilson (1974) R&B#23 US#57, *Young Girl* Gary Puckett & the Union Gap (1968) g US#2 UK#1, re-issued (1974) UK#6/Tommy Overstreet (1976) C&W#29; *Young World* Rick Nelson (1962) US#5 UK#19. Co-writer: [i] J. Hobbs.

344. FULLER, Jesse (b. March 12, 1896, Jonesboro, GA; d. January 29, 1976, Oakland, CA) Folk multi-instrumentalist and vocalist. A former film extra who wrote blues influenced skiffle songs. Fuller was essentially a one-man band in the black minstrel tradition, and he performed as such throughout the 1950s. His most recorded song was *San Francisco Bay Blues*. ALBUMS: **Jesse Fuller** (1955, Cavalier); **Folk Songs** (1958), **Spirituals and Blues: The Lone Cat** (1958), **San Francisco Bay Blues** (1969, all Good Time Jazz); **San Francisco**

345. FUQUA, Harvey (b. July 27, 1924, Louisville, KY) R&B producer and vocalist. An A&R man and songwriter at Chess Records during the 1950s, who went on to form his own Tri-Phi label, where he first worked with the singer Johnny Bristol. Fuqua was also a member of the doo-wop group the Moonglows, which charted with the singles *Sincerely* [i] (1955) R&B#1 US#20, re-recorded (1972) R&B#43; and *Most of All* [i] (1955) R&B#5. ALBUMS: **The Moonglows** (1972, Chess); **Look, It's the Moonglows** (1987, Vogue); **Their Greatest Sides** (1980, Chess). Fuqua subsequently became a producer at Motown Records, where he sang uncredited lead vocal on the Spinners' hit *That's What Girls Are Made For* [ii] (1961), before, in partnership with Johnny Bristol, masterminding the sound of Junior Walker and the All Stars. During the 1970s, Fuqua ran his own Milk and Honey label, and co-produced the disco act Sylvester. He also recorded as a solo artist. CHART COMPOSITION: *Any Way You Wanta* (1963) US#131. HIT VERSIONS: *Most of All* [i] Don Cornell (1955) US#14, *Sincerely* [i] McGuirre Sisters (1955) US#1 UK#14/Tokens (1961) US#120/Paul Anka (1969) US#80/Kitty Wells (1972) C&W#72/Forester Sisters (1989) C&W#8; *That's What Girls Are Made For* [ii] Spinners (1961) R&B#5 US#27. Co-writers: [i] Alan Freed, [ii] Gwen Gordy. (*See also under* Johnny BRISTOL.)

346. FURBER, Douglas (b. England) Film and stage lyricist. A British songwriter whose compositions were featured in the show "Andre Charlot's Revue of 1924," and the films "The Bells of St. Mary's," and "The Ziegfeld Follies" (both 1946). ALBUM: **Me and My Gal** oc (1981, MCA). HIT VERSIONS: *Bells of St. Mary's, The* [i] Frances Alda (1920) US#7/Bing Crosby (1946) US#21; *Limehouse Blues* [ii] Carl Fenton (1924) US#14/Paul Whiteman (1924) US#4/Duke Ellington (1931) US#13/Glen Gray (1934) US#20. Co-writers: [i] A. Emmett Adams, [ii] Philip Braham.

347. GABRIEL, Peter (b. May 13, 1950, Cobham, England) Rock producer and vocalist. A frequently experimental artist, who often explores the notion of songs as pure rhythm. Gabriel, like David Byrne, has also recorded and promoted ethnic music by artists from countries not normally listened to by rock audiences. A member of the theatrical, progressive rock group Genesis until 1975, he composed their first major hit, *I Know What I Like (In Your Wardrobe)* (1974) UK#21. ALBUMS: **From Genesis to Revelation** (1967, Decca) US#170; **Trespass** (1970) UK#98, **Nursery Cryme** (1971) UK#39, **Foxtrot** (1972) UK#12, **Genesis Live** (1973) US#105 UK#9, **Selling England By the Pound**

(1973) g US#70 UK#3, **The Lamb Lies Down on Broadway** (1974, all Charisma) g US#41 UK#10. After leaving the group, Gabriel worked with complex electronics and native rhythms on a series of albums that were all titled **Peter Gabriel**. During the late 1980s, he worked as a producer and ran his own Realworld label, before, in 1994, exploring the potential of multi-media with the release of his CD-ROM "Xplora 1: Peter Gabriel's Secret World." Gabriel, alongside Todd Rundgren, will probably be one of the first artists to leave conventional album making behind him. CHART COMPOSITIONS: *Solsbury Hill* (1977) US#68 UK#13, live version (1983) US#84; *Games Without Frontiers* (1980) US#48 UK#4, *No Self Control* (1980) UK#33, *Biko* (1980) UK#38, live version (1987) UK#49; *I Don't Remember* (1980) US#107, re-issued (1983) UK#62; *Shock the Monkey* (1982) R&B#64 US#29 UK#58, *Walk Through the Fire* (1984) UK#69, *Sledgehammer* (1986) p R&B#61 US#1 UK#4, *In Your Eyes* (1986) US#26, re-issued (1989) US#41; *Don't Give Up* with Kate Bush (1986) US#72 UK#9, *Big Time* (1987) US#8 UK#13, *Red Rain* (1987) UK#46, *Shaking the Tree* with Yousso N'Dour (1989) UK#61, *Solsbury Hill/Shaking the Tree* (1991) UK#57, *Digging in the Dirt* (1992) US#52 UK#24, *Steam* (1993) US#32 UK#10, *Blood of Eden* (1993) UK#43, *Kiss That Frog* (1993) UK#46, *Because of You* (1994) UK#24, *Lovetown* (1994) UK#49, *SW Live EP* (1994) UK#39. ALBUMS: **Peter Gabriel** (1977) US#38 UK#7, **Peter Gabriel** (1978) US#45 UK#10, **Peter Gabriel** (1980) US#22 UK#1, **Peter Gabriel** (1982) g US#28 UK#6, **Peter Gabriel Plays Live** (1983) g US#44 UK#8, **Birdy** ost (1985) US#162 UK#51, **So** (1986, all Charisma) p US#2 UK#1; **Passion-Music for the Last Temptation of Christ** ost (1989, Virgin) US#60 UK#29; **Us** (1992) p US#2 UK#2, **Secret World Live** (1994, both Realworld) US#23 UK#10. COMPILATION: **Shaking the Tree-Sixteen Golden Greats** (1991, Virgin) g US#48 UK#11. (*See also under* Tom ROBINSON.)

348. GAILLARD, Slim (b. Bulee Gaillard, January 4, 1916, Santa Clara, Cuba; d. February 26, 1991, London, England) Jazz pianist, guitarist and vocalist. One half, with Slam Stewart, of the 1930s duo Slim and Slam, in which Gaillard explored and invented his own jive language with such songs as *Vout Oreenie*. His wit was all too frequently misinterpreted, none more so than his song *Yep Roc Heresay*, which was attacked for promoting narcotics when in fact it was the menu from a middle eastern restaurant. Gaillard also appeared in such films as "Hellzappopin" (1941), and throughout his career was a general raconteur and individualist supreme. CHART COMPOSITIONS: *The Flat Foot Floogee*

[iii] (1938) US#2, *Tutti Frutti* [i] (1938) US#3, *Cement Mixer (Put-Ti, Put-Ti)* [ii] (1946) R&B#5 US#21. ALBUMS: **Opera in Vout** (1946, Disc); **Slim Gaillard Rides Again** (1950, Dot); **Cement Mixer** (195?, Folkways); **Anytime, Anyplace, Anywhere** (1982, Hep). COMPILATIONS: **Slim and Slam, Volume 1** (1980), **Slim and Slam, Volume 2** (1980), **Slim and Slam, Volume 3** (1988, all Tax); **The Legendary McVouty** (1982, Hep); **Laughing in Rhythm-The Best of the Verve Years** (1990, Verve). HIT VERSIONS: *Cement Mixer (Put-Ti, Put-Ti)* [ii] Charlie Barnet (1946) US#13/Jimmie Lunceford (1946) US#13/Hal McIntyre (1946) US#18/Alvino Rey (1946) US#5; *Down By the Station* [ii] Tommy Dorsey (1949) US#11/Guy Lombardo (1949) US#20, *Flat Foot Floogee, The* [iii] Benny Goodman (1938) US#18/Wingy Malone (1938) US#18/Mills Brothers (1938) US#20. As: * Slim & Slam. Co-writers: [i] Doris Fisher, [ii] Lee Ricks, [iii] Bud Green/Slam Stewart.

349. GALLAGHER, Noel (b. May 29, 1967, Manchester, England) Pop guitarist and vocalist. The lead guitarist, songwriter and sometime vocalist in the heavily Beatles influenced British group Oasis, which, by the late 1990s, had sold over eighteen million albums. CHART COMPOSITIONS: *Supersonic* (1994) UK#31, re-entry (1995) UK#44, re-entry (1996) UK#47; *Shakermaker* (1994) UK#11, re-entry (1995) UK#52, re-entry (1996) UK#48; *Live Forever* (1994) UK#10, re-entry (1995) UK#50, re-entry (1996) UK#42; *Cigarettes and Alcohol* (1994) UK#7, re-entry (1995) UK#53, re-entry (1996) UK#38; *Whatever* (1994) UK#3, re-entry (1995) UK#48, re-entry (1996) UK#34; *Some Might Say* (1995) UK#1, re-entry (1996) UK#40; *Roll with It* (1995) UK#2, re-entry (1996) UK#55; *Wonderwall* (1996) US#8 UK#2, *Wibbling Rivalry* (1995) UK#52, *Don't Look Back in Anger* (1996) UK#1, *D'You Know What I Mean?* (1997) UK#1. ALBUMS: **Definitely, Maybe** (1994) g US#58 UK#1, **(What's the Story) Morning Glory** (1995) p US#4 UK#1, **Be Here Now** (1997, all Creation) p UK#1. COMPILATIONS: **(What's the Story) Morning Glory Singles Box** (1996) UK#54, **Definitely Maybe Singles Box** (1996, both Creation) UK#53. HIT VERSIONS: *Wonderwall* Mike Flowers Pops (1995) UK#2, re-entry (1996) UK#52/De-Code featuring Beverli Skeete (1996) UK#69.

350. GALLOP, Sammy (b. 1915; d. 1971, both America) Tin Pan Alley lyricist. HIT VERSIONS: *Autumn Serenade* [ix] Harry James (1945) US#16, *Count Every Star* [iv] Ray Anthony (1950) US#4/Dick Haymes & Artie Shaw (1950) US#10/Hugo Winterhalter (1950) US#10; *Elmer's Tune* [ii]

Dick Jurgens (1941) US#8/Glenn Miller (1941) US#1/Del Wood (1953) US#24; *Forgive My Heart* [v] Nat "King" Cole (1955) US#13, *Holiday for Strings* [x] Jimmy Dorsey (1944) US#13/David Rose (1944) US#2/Red Waring's Pennsylvanians (1944) US#14/Spike Jones (1945) US#10; *Maybe You'll Be There* [iii] Gordon Jenkins (1948) g US#3, *My Lady Loves to Dance* [viii] Julius La Rosa (1953) US#21, *Night Lights* Nat "King" Cole (1956) US#11, *Outside of Heaven* [v] Eddie Fisher (1952) US#8 UK#1/Margaret Whiting (1952) US#22; *Shoo-Fly Pie and Apple Pan Dowdy* [xi] Stan Kenton (1946) g US#6/Guy Lombardo (1946) US#6/Dinah Shore (1946) US#6; *Somewhere Along the Way* [i] Nat "King" Cole (1952) US#8 UK#3, *That's the Moon My Son* [ix] Andrews Sisters (1942) US#18, *That's You* [vi] Nat "King" Cole (1960) US#101 UK#10, *There Must Be a Way* [vii] Joni James (1959) US#33 UK#24/Frankie Vaughan (1967) UK#7. Co-writers: [i] Kurt Adams, [ii] Elmer Albrecht/Dick Jurgens, [iii] Rube Bloom, [iv] Bruno Coquatrix, [v] Chester Conn, [vi] Chester Conn/Nelson Riddle (b. June 1, 1921, Oradell, NJ; d. October 6, 1985), [vii] Robert Cook/David Saxon, [viii] Milton De Lugg, [ix] Peter De Rose, [x] David Rose (b. June 15, 1910, London, England), [xi] Guy Woods.

351. GAMBLE, Kenny (b. August 11, 1943, Philadelphia, PA), and **HUFF, Leon A.** (b. 1942, Camden, NJ) R&B producers, pianists and vocalists. The most successful writer-producers of the disco era, who produced twenty-one number one singles and created over three hundred gold and platinum selling records. Gamble and Huff's Philadelphia International label became a veritable hit production line, creating the "Philly Sound," which consisted of solid disco rhythms, heavy electric piano chordings, silky strings and precise horn arrangements, over which they introduced doo-wop vocal styles on material that ranged from love ballads to black politics and social commentary. Gamble said of their writing process in 1976, "We write a lot of titles down and we just start talking and put a tape recorder on and playing 'till we come up with something that sounds original to us." Like Jerry Leiber and Mike Stoller before them, Gamble and Huff's songwriting, arranging and production techniques ultimately became one unifying process. Huff taught himself the piano in his teens and became a boogie woogie session player on east coast R&B records, before graduating to uncredited sideman, session player and co-producer at Cameo Records during the early 1960s. Gamble worked in a hospital before forming, in 1964, Kenny Gamble and the Romeos, a group that featured Thom Bell on keyboards. That year, Gamble and Huff struck up an acquaintance in the elevator of a publishing house, where they discovered a mutual interest in R&B. They first played together on Candy and the Kisses' single *The 81* (1964), after which, said Huff in 1992, "We got to talking about songwriting, so we made plans to meet over at my house 'cause I had a piano. One weekend we must have wrote about seven or ten songs." Huff subsequently replaced Bell in the Romeos, after which the duo wrote and produced for a variety of short-lived record labels. Their work with the vocal group the Intruders resulted in the local hit *All the Time*, which they followed with a series of soul ballads, including the million seller *Cowboys to Girls*. By the late 1960s, Gamble and Huff had become consistent hitmakers and virtual house producers at Sigma Sound Studios in Philadelphia. Some of their finest early work was with the vocalist Jerry Butler for the Mercury label, after which they established Philadelphia International Records in 1971, cutting most of their discs with a house band called MFSB, which they had originally recorded as the Family on one of their earlier labels. Gamble once said of his songwriting, "It's a gift that you have and if you don't use your gift, it will be taken away from you." Huff has also recorded as a solo artist, charting with *Tight Money* (1980) R&B#68, and *I Ain't Jivin' I'm Jammin'* (1981) R&B#57, from the album **Here to Create Music** (1980). HIT VERSIONS: *Are You Happy?* [ii] Jerry Butler (1968) R&B#9 US#39, *At the Top of the Stairs* Formations (1967) US#83, *Baby I'm Lonely* Intruders (1967) R&B#28 US#70, *Back Stabbers* [xii] O'Jays (1972) g R&B#1 US#3 UK#14, *Be Truthful to Me* Billy Paul (1974) R&B#37, *Brand New Me* [i] Dusty Springfield (1968) US#24/Jerry Butler (1969) US#109/Aretha Franklin on B-side of *Bridge Over Troubled Water* (1971) g R&B#1 US#6; *Branded Bad* O'Jays (1969) R&B#41, *Bring the Family Back* Billy Paul (1979) R&B#90 UK#51, *City of Brotherly Love* Soul Survivors (1974) R&B#75, *Close the Door* Teddy Pendergrass (1978) g R&B#1 US#25 UK#41/Donald Harrison (1994) R&B#110; *Come Go with Me* Christopher Williams (1993) R&B#74, *Cowboys to Girls* Intruders (1968) g R&B#1 US#6, *Dance Turned into a Romance* Jones Girls (1980) R&B#77, *Darlin' Darlin' Baby (Sweet Tender Love)* O'Jays (1976) R&B#1 US#72 UK#24, *Deeper in Love with You* O'Jays (1970) R&B#21 US#64, *Determination* Ebonys (1971) R&B#46, *Devil with an Angel's Smile* Intruders (1966) R&B#29, *Dirty Ol' Man* Three Degrees (1973) R&B#58, *Do It Any Way You Wanna* [x] People's Choice (1975) g R&B#1 US#11 UK#36, *Don't Leave Me This Way* [viii] Thelma Houston (1976) R&B#1 US#1 UK#13/Harold Melvin & the Blue Notes (1976) UK#5/Communards (1986) US#40 UK#1; *Don't Let It Go to Your Head* Brand New Heavies (1992) UK#24, *Don't Let Love Hang You Up*

Jerry Butler (1969) R&B#12 US#44, *Drowning in the Sea of Love* Joe Simon (1971) g R&B#3 US#11, *81, The* Candy & the Kisses (1964) US#51, *Enjoy Yourself* Jacksons (1976) g R&B#2 US#6 UK#42, *Explosion in Your Soul* Soul Survivors (1967) R&B#45 US#33, *Expressway to Your Heart* Soul Survivors (1967) R&B#3 US#4/Margo Thunder (1974) R&B#25; *Family Reunion* O'Jays (1976) R&B#45, *50/50 Love* [xiv] Brotherhood Creed (1992) R&B#91, *For the Love of Money* [xii] O'Jays (1974) g R&B#3 US#9/Bulletboys (1989) US#78/Marky Mark & the Funky Bunch sampled in *I Need Money* (1992) US#61; *Forever Mine* O'Jays (1979) R&B#4 US#28, *Gang War (Don't Make No Sense)* Corner Boys (1967) R&B#46, *Gee I'm Sorry, Baby* Sapphires on B-side of *Gotta Have Your Love* (1965) R&B#33 US#77, *(Get Me Back on Time) Engine #9* Wilson Pickett (1970) R&B#3 US#14/Midnight Starr (1987) R&B#11 UK#64; *Get Your Love Back* Three Degrees (1974) UK#34, *Girl, Don't Let It Get You Down* O'Jays (1980) R&B#3 US#55, *Girl You're Too Young* Archie Bell & the Drells (1969) R&B#13 US#59, *Give Her a Transplant* Intruders (1969) R&B#23 US#104, *Give the People What They Want* O'Jays (1975) R&B#1 US#45, *Goin' Places* Jacksons (1977) R&B#8 US#52 UK#26, *Got to See If I Can Get Mommy (To Come Back Home)* Jerry Butler (1970) R&B#21 US#62, *Groovy People* Lou Rawls (1976) R&B#19 US#64, *Here I Go Again* Archie Bell & the Drells (1970) US#112 1972 UK#16, *Hey, Western Union Man* [iv] Jerry Butler (1968) R&B#1 US#16, *Hope That We Can Be Together Soon* Harold Melvin & the Blue Notes with Sharon Paige (1975) R&B#1 US#42, *I Bet He Don't Love You (Like I Do)* Intruders (1971) R&B#20 US#92, *I Can't Live Without Your Love* Teddy Pendergrass (1981) R&B#10 US#103, *I Could Write a Book* Jerry Butler (1970) R&B#15 US#46, *I Don't Love You Anymore* Teddy Pendergrass (1977) R&B#5 US#41, *I Just Can't Stop Dancing* Archie Bell & the Drells (1968) R&B#5 US#9, *I Just Love the Man* Jones Girls (1980) R&B#9, *I Likes to Do It* People's Choice (1971) R&B#9 US#38 UK#36, *I Love Music* O'Jays (1976) g R&B#1 US#5 UK#13, re-issued (1978) UK#36/Rozalla (1992) US#89; *I Love My Baby* Archie Bell & the Drells (1969) R&B#40 US#94, *I Miss You* Harold Melvin & the Blue Notes (1972) R&B#7 US#58, *I Wanna Know Your Name* Intruders (1973) R&B#9 US#60, *I Want My Baby Back* Teddy Pendergrass (1984) R&B#61, *I Want to Know Your Name* Walter & Scotty (1993) R&B#28, *I Wish You Belonged to Me* Lou Rawls (1987) R&B#28, *I'll Always Love My Mama* Intruders (1973) R&B#6 US#36 UK#32, *I'm Always Thinking About You* [xi] Teddy Pendergrass (1994) R&B#90, *I'm Girl Scoutin'* Intruders (1971) R&B#16 US#88, *I'm Gonna Make You Love Me* [v] Dee Dee Warwick (1966) R&B#13

US#88/Aesop's Fables (1968) US#123/Madeline Bell (1968) R&B#32 US#26/Supremes & the Temptations (1969) R&B#2 US#2 UK#3; *(I'm Just Thinking About) Cooling Out* Jerry Butler (1978) R&B#14, *If Only You Knew* [vi] Patti LaBelle (1983) US#46, *If You Don't Know Me By Now* Harold Melvin & the Blue Notes (1972) g R&B#1 US#3 UK#9/Jean Carn (1982) R&B#49/Simply Red (1989) g US#1 UK#2; *Impossible Mission (Mission Impossible)* Soul Survivors (1968) US#68, *It's Forever* [x] Ebonys (1973) R&B#14 US#68, *Jam, Jam, Jam* People's Choice (1978) UK#40, *Let Me Be Good to You* Lou Rawls (1979) R&B#11, *Let Me Make Love to You* O'Jays (1975) R&B#10 US#75, *Let the Good Times Roll and Feel So Good* Bunny Sigler (1965) R&B#20 US#22, *Let's Clean Up the Ghetto* Philadelphia International All Stars (1977) R&B#4 US#91 UK#34, *Let's Groove* Archie Bell & the Drells (1976) R&B#7, *Let's Make a Baby* Billy Paul (1976) R&B#18 US#83 UK#30, *Let's Make a Promise* Peaches & Herb (1968) R&B#34 US#75, *Livin' for the Weekend* [viii] O'Jays (1976) R&B#1 US#20, *Living All Alone* Phyliss Hyman (1986) R&B#12, *Living in Confusion* [iii] Phyliss Hyman (1991) R&B#9, *Lollipop* Intruders (1969) R&B#22 US#101, *Long Lost Love* Three Degrees (1975) UK#40, *Looky Looky (Look at Me Girl)* O'Jays (1970) R&B#17 US#98, *Lost* Jerry Butler (1968) R&B#15 US#62, *Love I Lost, The* Harold Melvin & the Blue Notes (1973) g R&B#1 US#7 UK#21/West End featuring Sybil (1993) US#90 UK#3; *Love in Them There Hills* Vibrations (1968) R&B#38 US#93, *(Love Is Like a) Baseball Game* Intruders (1968) R&B#4 US#26, *Love Is the Message* MFSB (1974) R&B#42 US#85, *Love That's Real, A* Intruders (1967) R&B#35 US#82, *Love Train* O'Jays (1973) g R&B#1 US#1 UK#9/Bunny Sigler (1974) R&B#28; *Love Will Rain on You* Archie Bell & the Drells (1968) R&B#25, *Me and Mrs. Jones* [vii] Billy Paul (1972) g R&B#1 US#1 UK#12/Dramatics (1975) R&B#4 US#47/Freddie Jackson (1992) R&B#32 UK#32; *Me Tarzan, You Jane* Intruders (1969) R&B#41, *Message in Our Music* O'Jays (1976) R&B#1 US#49, *Mixed-Up, Shook-Up Girl* Patty & the Emblems (1964) US#37, *Moody Woman* [iii] Jerry Butler (1969) R&B#3 US#24, *My Balloon's Going Up* Archie Bell & the Drells (1969) R&B#36 US#87, *Mysteries of the World* MFSB (1975) UK#41, *Never Give You Up (Never Gonna Give You Up)* [iv] Jerry Butler (1968) R&B#4 US#20, *Nice Girl Like You, A* Intruders (1974) R&B#21, *992 Arguments* O'Jays (1973) R&B#13 US#57, *Nine Times Out of Ten* Teddy Pendergrass (1982) R&B#31, *Now I'm a Woman* Nancy Wilson (1971) R&B#41 US#93, *Now That We Found Love* Third World (1979) R&B#9 US#47 UK#10/Heavy D. & the Boyz (1991) g US#12 UK#2; *Nursery Rhymes* [ix] People's Choice (1975) R&B#22 US#93, *Oh My Love* [viii] Dells (1992)

R&B#81, *One Life to Live* Lou Rawls (1977) R&B#32, *One Night Affair* O'Jays (1969) R&B#15 US#68, *Only the Strong Survive* [iv] Jerry Butler (1968) g R&B#1 US#4/Billy Paul (1977) R&B#68 UK#33/D.J. Krush (1996) UK#71; *Only You* Teddy Pendergrass (1978) R&B#22 US#106 UK#41, *Pool of Bad Luck* Joe Simon (1972) R&B#13 US#42, *Pop Goes the Weasel* 3rd Bass (1991) US#29 UK#64, *Power of Love* Joe Simon (1972) g R&B#2 US#11/Martha Reeves (1976) R&B#27 US#76; *Pray for Me* Intruders (1971) R&B#25 US#105, *Put Our Heads Together* [xv] O'Jays (1986) R&B#35 UK#45, *Put Your Hands Together* O'Jays (1973) R&B#2 US#10/D-Mob (1990) UK#7; *Satisfaction Guaranteed (Or Get Your Love Back)* [vii] Harold Melvin & the Blue Notes (1974) R&B#6 US#58 UK#32, *See You When I Get There* Lou Rawls (1977) R&B#8 US#66, *Sexy* MFSB (1975) R&B#2 US#37, *Show You the Way to Go* Jacksons (1977) R&B#6 US#28 UK#1/Danni Minogue (1992) UK#30; *Sing a Happy Song* O'Jays (1979) R&B#7 US#102 UK#39, *Sit Down and Talk to Me* Lou Rawls (1979) R&B#26, *Slow Drag* Intruders (1968) R&B#12 US#54, *Slow Motion* Johnny Williams (1972) R&B#12 US#78, *Smoke Signals* Electric Indian on B-side of *Keem-O-Sabe* (1969) R&B#46 US#16, *Sound of Philadelphia (Theme from Soul Train), The* MFSB (1974) g R&B#1 US#1 UK#22, *Stairway to Heaven* Pure Soul (1996) R&B#18 US#79, *Step Off* Grandmaster Flash, Melle Mel & the Furious Five (1985) R&B#48 UK#8, *Sunshine* O'Jays (1975) R&B#17 US#48, *Take Good Care of Yourself* Three Degrees (1975) R&B#64 UK#9, *Tender Is the Love We Knew* Intruders (1970) R&B#25 US#119, *Thanks for Saving My Life* Billy Paul (1974) R&B#9 US#37 UK#33, *(There's Gonna Be) A Showdown* Archie Bell & the Drells (1969) R&B#6 US#21, reissued (1973) UK#35; *This Is My Love Song* Intruders (1970) R&B#22 US#85, *This Song Will Last Forever* Lou Rawls (1977) R&B#74, *Tighten Up* Archie Bell & the Drells (1968) g R&B#1 US#1, *Time to Get Down* O'Jays (1973) R&B#2 US#33, *T.L.C. (Tender Lovin' Care)* MFSB (1975) R&B#54, *Today* Intruders (1967) US#128, *Together* Intruders (1967) R&B#28 US#48/Tiera (1980) R&B#9 US#18; *Turn Off the Lights* Teddy Pendergrass (1979) US#48, *United (We'll Be)* Intruders (1966) R&B#14 US#78/Music Makers (1967) R&B#48 US#78/Peaches & Herb (1968) R&B#11 US#46; *Used Ta Be My Girl* MFSB (1978) R&B#94/O'Jays (1978) g R&B#1 US#4 UK#12; *What's the Use of Breaking Up?* [iii] Jerry Butler (1969) R&B#4 US#20, *When Love Is New* Arthur Pryscock (1976) R&B#10 US#64, *When Will I See You Again* Three Degrees (1975) g R&B#4 US#2 UK#1/Brother Beyond (1989) UK#43/Sheila Ferguson (1994) UK#60; *Win, Place or Show (She's a Winner)* Intruders (1974) R&B#12 UK#14, *Work on Me* O'Jays (1977) R&B#7, *World Without Music, A* Archie Bell & the Drells (1969) R&B#46 US#90, *Year of Decision, The* Three Degrees (1974) R&B#74 UK#13/Wah on B-side of *Hope (I Wish You'd Believe Me)* (1983) UK#37; *Yesterday I Had the Blues* Harold Melvin & the Blue Notes (1972) R&B#12 US#63, *You Gonna Make Me Love Somebody Else* Jones Girls (1979) g R&B#5 US#38, *You'll Never Find Another Love Like Mine* Lou Rawls (1976) g R&B#1 US#2 UK#10/Stanley Turrentine (1976) R&B#68; *You're My Blessing* Lou Rawls (1980) US#77, *You're My Latest, My Greatest Inspiration* Teddy Pendergrass (1981) R&B#4 US#43, *You're the One* Three Degrees (1970) US#19 US#77, *You're the Reason Why* Ebonys (1971) R&B#10 US#51, *Zip, The* MFSB (1975) R&B#72 US#91. Co-writers: [i] Theresa Bell, [ii] Theresa Bell/Jerry Butler (b. December 8, 1939, Sunflower, MS)/Kenny Gamble only, [iii] T. Burrus/Kenny Gamble/Phyliss Hyman only, [iv] Jerry Butler, [v] Kenny Gamble/Jerry Ross/Jerry Williams only, [vi] Kenny Gamble/Dexter Wansell only, [vii] Don Gilbert, [viii] Cary Gilbert, [ix] Cary Gilbert/Leon Huff only, [x] Leon Huff only, [xi] Leon Huff/S. Huff only, [xii] Leon Huff/Gene McFadden/John Whitehead only, [xiii] Anthony Jackson, [xiv] S. McDuffie/A. Arce, [xv] Danny Poku/Charles Scarlet/George Stennet. (*See also under* Thom BELL.)

352. GANNON, Kim (b. 1900; d. 1974, both America) Film lyricist. A lyricist who worked with a variety of composers, on songs that were included in such films as "Always in My Heart," "Now Voyager" (both 1942) and "A Night in Casablanca" (1946). ALBUMS: **Seventeen** ost (1951, RCA); **Johnny Appleseed** ost (1964, Disneyland). HIT VERSIONS: *Always in My Heart* [iii] Kenny Baker (1942) US#14/Jimmy Dorsey (1942) US#16/Glenn Miller (1942) US#10; *Autumn Nocturne* [iv] Claude Thornhill (1941) US#16, *Croce Di Oro* Joan Regan (1955), *Dreamer's Holiday, A* [viii] Buddy Clark (1949) US#12/Gordon Jenkins (1949) US#26/Ray Anthony (1950) US#11/Perry Como (1950) US#3; *Five O'Clock Whistle* [ii] Erskine Hawkins (1940) US#15/Glenn Miller (1940) US#5/Ella Fitzgerald (1941) US#9; *I Understand* [viii] Jimmy Dorsey (1941) US#11, *I Want to Be Wanted* [vi] Brenda Lee (1960) US#1 UK#31, *It Can't Be Wrong* [vii] Dick Haymes (1943) US#1/Allen Miller (1943) US#3; *Moonlight Cocktail* [v] Glenn Miller (1942) US#1, *Under Paris Skies* [i] Mitch Miller (1953) US#26. Co-writers: [i] Hubert Giraud, [ii] Gene Irwin/Josef Myrow, [iii] Ernesto Lecuona, [iv] Joseph Myrow, [v] C. Luckeyth Roberts, [vi] Pino Spotti, [vii] Max Steiner, [viii] Mable Wayne. (*See also under* Buck RAM.)

353. GARCIA, Jerry (b. Jerome John Garcia, August 1, 1942, San Francisco; d. August 9, 1995, Forest Knolls, both CA) Rock guitarist, banjo player and vocalist. The son of a 1930s big band leader who, until his death from a heart attack in 1995, was the focal point of the Grateful Dead, a rock group that had become an institution by the 1980s, and the biggest grossing live act in America. In partnership with the lyricist Robert Hunter, Garcia wrote much of the Dead's original material, although the songs themselves were essentially only a framework for lengthy improvisational live work-outs. Garcia's fluid, jazz inflected guitar soloing, and the all-encompassing Americana of his compositions, which touched on folk, country, rock, bluegrass, R&B and the blues, were the product of a lifestyle dedicated entirely to the performing of music. Initially a hippie, counter-culture, psychedelic band, the Grateful Dead developed into a self-run industry, with a massive, devoted following, the nature of which is unlikely ever to be repeated in rock music again. The Dead were the first to keep in daily contact with their worldwide fan base through the Internet, and although they ceased to mean very much commercially outside of America after the 1960s, the kind of following that they attracted, which was totally unrestricted by age barriers, could only be equated with that of a top league European soccer team. Many of Garcia and Hunter's best known compositions were radically re-interpreted by a diverse selection of artists on **Deadicated** (1992, Arista) US#24. Since Garcia's death, there has been a systematic release schedule of live material from a seemingly endless vault, as it is believed that nearly every, if not all, of the group's live performances have been committed by fans to tape, a systematic self-bootlegging process that was sanctioned by the band. CHART COMPOSITIONS: *Uncle John's Band* [i] (1970) US#69, *Truckin'* [i] (1971) US#64, *Sugar Magnolia* [i] (1973) US#91, *Alabama Getaway* [i] (1980) US#68, *Touch of Grey* [i] (1987) US#9. ALBUMS: **The Grateful Dead** (1967) g US#73, **Anthem of the Sun** (1968) US#87, **Aoxomoxoa** (1969) US#73, **Live/Dead** (1970) US#64, **Workingman's Dead** (1970) p US#27 UK#69, **American Beauty** (1970) p US#30, **Grateful Dead** (1971) US#25, **Europe '72** (1973) g US#24, **History of the Grateful Dead, Volume I (Bear's Choice)** (1973, all Warner Brothers) US#60; **Wake of the Flood** (1973) US#18, **The Grateful Dead from the Mars Hotel** (1974) US#16 UK#47, **Blues for Allah** (1975) US#12 UK#45, **Steal Your Face** (1976, all Grateful Dead) US#56 UK#42; **Terrapin Station** (1977) g US#28 UK#30, **Shakedown Street** (1978) g US#41, **Go to Heaven** (1980) US#23, **Reckoning** (1981) US#43, **Dead Set** (1981) US#29, **In the Dark** (1987, all Arista) p US#6 UK#57; **Dylan and the Dead** with Bob Dylan (1989,

Columbia) US#37 UK#38; **Built to Last** (1989) g US#27, **Without a Net** (1990, both Arista) g US#43; **One from the Vault** (1991) US#106, **Inrafrared Roses** (1991), **Two from the Vault** (1992) US#119, **Dick's Picks, Volume 1** (1993), **Dick's Picks, Volume 2** (1995), **Dick's Picks, Volume 3** (1995), **Hundred Year Hall** (1995) US#26, **Dick's Picks, Volume 4** (1996), **Dick's Picks, Volume 5** (1996), **Dick's Picks, Volume 6** (1996, all Grateful Dead); **Dozin' at the Nick** (1996, Arista); **Dick's Picks, Volume 7** (1997), **Fallout from the Phil Zone** (1997), **Dick's Picks, Volume 8** (1997, all Grateful Dead). COMPILATIONS: **Vintage Dead** (1970) US#127, **Historic Dead** (1971, both Sunflower) US#154; **Best of the Grateful Dead/Skeletons from the Closet** (1974) p US#75, **What a Long Strange Trip It's Been: The Best of the Grateful Dead** (1977, both Warner Brothers) US#121; **Gray Folded** (1994), **Transitive-Axis** (1994, both Swell/Artifact); **The Arista Years** (1996, Arista). Garcia also found time to record an album with the bluegrass group New Riders of the Purple Sage, **New Riders of the Purple Sage** (1971, Columbia) US#39, and to work as a solo artist, charting with the single *Sugaree* [i] (1972) US#94. ALBUMS: **Hooteroll** with Howard Wales (1971, Douglas); **Garcia** (1972, Warner Brothers) US#35; **Live at Keystone*** (1973, Fantasy); **Garcia** (1974) US#49, **Reflections** (1975) US#42; **Old and in the Way**** (1975, all Round) US#99; **Cats Under the Stars** (1977) US#114, **Run for the Roses** (1982, both Arista) US#100; **Keystone Encores, Volume I*** (1988), **Keystone Encores, Volume 2*** (1988, both Fantasy); **Almost Acoustic** (1989, Grateful Dead); **Jerry Garcia Band** (1991, Arista) US#97; **Not for Kids Only**** (1993), **Shady Grove**** (1996, both Acoustic); **How Sweet It Is** (1997), **Blue Incantation** with Sanjay Mishra (1997, both Rykodisc). With: * Merle Saunders, ** David Grisman. Co-composer [i] Robert Hunter.

354. GARTSIDE, Green (b. Green Strohmeyer-Gartside, June 22, 1956, Cardiff, Wales) Pop keyboard player and vocalist. A sweet, falsetto styled vocalist, whose group Scritti Politti merged synthesizer pop with R&B and reggae. CHART COMPOSITIONS: *The Sweetest Girl* (1981) UK#64, *Faithless* (1982) UK#56, *Asylums in Jerusalem/Jacques Derrida* (1982) UK#43, *Wood Beez (Pray Like Aretha Franklin)* (1984) US#91 UK#10, *Absolute* (1984) UK#17, *Hypnotise* (1984) UK#68, *The Word Girl* [i] (1985) UK#6, *The Perfect Way* [i] (1985) R&B#85 US#11, *Oh Patti (Don't Feel Sorry for Lover Boy)* (1988) UK#13, *First Boy in This Town (Lovesick)* (1988) UK#63, *Boom! There She Was* [i] (1988) US#53 UK#55, *She's a Woman* (1991) UK#20, *Take Me in Your Arms and Love Me* (1991) UK#47. ALBUMS:

Songs to Remember (1982, Rough Trade) UK#12; **Cupid and Psyche '85** (1985) US#50 UK#5, **Provision** (1988, both Virgin) US#113 UK#8. HIT VERSIONS: *Love of a Lifetime* Chaka Khan (1986) US#53 UK#52, *Sweetest Girl, The* Madness (1986) US#64 UK#35. Co-writer: [i] David Gamson.

355. GATES, David (b. December 11, 1940, Tulsa, OK) Pop guitarist, producer and vocalist. The lead vocalist and principal songwriter in the soft-rock group Bread, which created some of the most carefully crafted mainstream pop of the 1970s. Gates' father was a band director and his mother a piano teacher, and he took violin and piano lessons from an early age. After performing in a high school band with Leon Russell, Gates released the unsuccessful solo single *Swinging Baby Doll* (1958), before becoming an uncredited 1960s session player. After writing the bubblegum hit *Popsicles and Icicles* for the Murmaids (1964), he moved to Los Angeles, where he performed at the Crossbow Club in the San Fernando Valley and worked as a producer and songwriter. In 1969, with bassist Rob Royer and guitarist James Griffin, Gates formed Bread, which became Elektra Record's first non-folk signing. Their eponymous debut album was heavily indebted to the Beatles, but they soon found their own sound with a series of carefully arranged singles that featured unfussy production values and tight vocal harmonies. CHART COMPOSITIONS: *Make It with You* (1970) g US#1 UK#5, *It Don't Matter to Me* (1969) US#10, *Let Your Love Go* (1971) US#28, *If* (1971) US#4, *Mother Freedom* (1971) US#37, *Baby, I'm a Want You* (1971) US#4 UK#14, *Everything I Own* (1972) US#5 UK#32, *Diary* (1972) US#15, *The Guitar Man* (1972) US#11 UK#16, *Aubrey* (1973) US#11, *Lost Without Your Love* (1976) US#9 UK#27, *Hooked on You* (1977) US#60. ALBUMS: **Bread** (1969) US#127, **On the Waters** (1970) g US#12 UK#34, **Manna** (1971) g US#21, **Baby, I'm a Want You** (1972) g US#3 UK#9, **Guitar Man** (1972) g US#18, **Lost Without Your Love** (1977, all Elektra) g US#26 UK#17. COMPILATIONS: **Best of Bread** (1972) g US#2 UK#7, **Best of Bread, Volume 2** (1974) g US#32 UK#48, **Sound of Bread** (1977, all Elektra) UK#1, **Very Best of Bread** (1987, Telstar) UK#84; **Anthology of Bread** (1985, Elektra) p; **Retrospective** (1996, Rhino); **Essentials** (1997, Warner ESP/Jive) UK#10. Jack Jones recorded many of Gates' compositions on the album **Bread Winners** (1972, RCA) UK#7. After the group broke up, Gates recorded as a solo artist, but he soon lapsed into inactivity and withdrew from music to run his ranch in Northern California, saying, in 1989, "Sometimes it's better to be grateful and stay the heck out of the limelight when your best work is behind you." A

1991 venture with Billy Swan in the group Black Tie was not successful. CHART COMPOSITIONS: *Sail Around the World* (1973) US#50, *Never Let Her Go* (1975) US#29, *The Goodbye Girl* (1978) US#15, *Took the Last Train* (1978) US#30 UK#50, *Where Does the Lovin' Go* (1980) US#46, *Take Me Now* (1981) US#62. ALBUMS: **First** (1973) US#107, **Never Let Her Go** (1975) US#102 UK#32, **The Goodbye Girl** (1977) US#165 UK#28, **Falling in Love Again** (1980, all Elektra); **Take Me Now** (1981, Arista); **Blue Frontier** as the Remingtons (1992, BMG); **Love Is Always Seventeen** (1994, Discovery); **It Is Well** (1997). HIT VERSIONS: *Baby, I'm a Want You* Stephanie Winslow (1980) C&W#35, *Been Too Long on the Road* Mark Lindsay (1971) US#98, *Don't Shut Me Out* Underground Sunshine (1969) US#102, *Everything I Own* Kendalls (1972) C&W#66/Ken Boothe (1974) UK#1/Joe Stampley (1976) C&W#12/Boy George (1987) UK#1; *Heartbreak Ahead* Murmaids (1964) US#116, *Hold Tight* Vicki Sue Robinson (1977) R&B#91 US#67, *If* Telly Savalas (1975) UK#1/Yin & Yan (1975) UK#25/John Alford (1996) UK#24; *Lost Without Your Love* Jacqui Brooks (1984) US#105, *Make It with You* Ralfi Pagan (1971) R&B#32 US#104/Whispers (1977) R&B#10 US#94/Pasadenas (1992) UK#20/Let Loose (1996) UK#7; *Part-Time Love* Gladys Knight & the Pips (1975) R&B#4 US#22 UK#30, *Popsicles and Icicles* Murmaids (1963) US#3, *You'll Be Needing Me Baby* Nino Tempo & April Stevens (1967) US#133. (*See also under* Billy SWAN.)

356. GATLIN, Larry (b. May 2, 1948, Seminole, TX) C&W guitarist and vocalist. A country singer-songwriter who has enjoyed considerable success as a songwriter for others. During the 1960s, Gatlin performed with his siblings as the Gatlin Brothers, before becoming a songwriter for the vocalist Dottie West. Gatlin was also a backing musician for Tammy Wynette, before charting over forty hits of his own. He hosted his own television special in 1981. CHART COMPOSITIONS: *Sweet Becky Walker* (1973) C&W#40, *Bitter They Are Harder They Fall* (1974) C&W#45, *Delta Dirt* (1974) US#14 US#84, *Let's Turn the Lights On* (1974) C&W#14, *All the Gold in California* (1979) US#1. ALBUMS: **The Pilgrim** (1972), **Rain-Rainbow** (1974), **Broken Lady** (1976), **High Time** (1976), **Love Is Just a Game** (1978) US#175, **Oh! Brother** (1978, all Monument) US#140; **Straight Ahead** (1980) g US#102, **Help Yourself** (1981) US#118, **Not Guilty** (1981, all Columbia) US#184; **Houston to Denver** (1984), **Pure 'n' Simple** (1988), **Larry Gatlin and the Gatlin Brothers** (1989, all MCA); **Adios** (1992, Liberty). COMPILATIONS: **Greatest Hits** (1978, Monument) g US#171; **Greatest Hits Encore** (1992, Lib-

erty). HIT VERSIONS: *Help Me* Elvis Presley (1974) C&W#6 US#17/Ray Price (1977) C&W#38; *I Just Can't Get Her Out of My Mind* Johnny Rodriguez (1975) C&W#1.

357. GAUDIO, Bob (b. Robert Gaudio, November 17, 1942, Bronx, NY) Pop keyboard player, producer and vocalist. A former member of the group the Royal Teens, which charted with the single *Short Shorts* [i] (1958) R&B#2 US#3, who, with Bob Crewe, masterminded the career of the Four Seasons, a group that has sold over eighty-five million records. CHART COMPOSITIONS: *Sherry* (1962) g R&B#1 US#1 UK#8, *Marlena* [iii] (1963) US#36, *New Mexican Rose* [iii] (1963) US#36, *Dawn (Go Away)* [vi] (1964) US#3, *Big Man in Town* (1964) US#20, *Beggin'* [iv] (1967) US#16, *Something's on Her Mind* [v] (1969) US#98, *Idaho* [v] (1969) US#95, *The Night* [viii] (1975) UK#7, *Who Loves You* [vii] (1975) US#3 UK#6, *December '63 (Oh, What a Night)* [vii] (1976) US#1 UK#1, re-mixed (1994) US#14; *Silver Star* [vii] (1976) US#38 UK#3, *Rhapsody* [vii] (1977) UK#37, *Down the Hall* [vii] (1977) US#65 UK#34, *Spend the Night in Love* [vii] (1980) US#91. ALBUMS: **Sherry and Eleven Others** (1962) US#6 UK#20, **The Four Seasons Greetings** (1962), **Big Girls Don't Cry and Twelve Others** (1963) US#8, **Ain't That a Shame and Eleven Others** (1963, all Vee-Jay) US#47; **Born to Wander** (1964) US#84, **Dawn (Go Away) and 11 Other Great Songs** (1964) US#25, **Rag Doll** (1964) US#7, **The Four Seasons Entertain You** (1965, all Philips) US#77; **On Stage with the Four Seasons** (1965, Vee-Jay); **Big Hits By Burt Bacharach, Hal David and Bob Dylan** (1966) US#106, **Working My Way Back to You** (1966) US#50, **The Genuine Imitation Life Gazette** (1969) US#85, **Half and Half** (1970, all Philips) US#190; **Chameleon** (1972, Mowest); **Who Loves You** (1975) US#38 UK#12, **Helicon** (1977, both Warner Brothers) US#168; **Streetfighter** (1985, MCA/Curb); **Hope and Glory** (1992, Curb). COMPILATIONS: **Golden Hits of the Four Seasons** (1963) US#15, **Stay and Other Great Hits** (1964) US#100, **More Golden Hits By the Four Seasons** (1964) US#105, **The Beatles Vs. The Four Seasons** (1964, all Vee-Jay) US#142; **The Four Seasons Gold Vault of Hits** (1966) g US#10, **2nd Vault of Golden Hits** (1967) US#22, **Lookin' Back** (1967) US#107, **New Gold Hits** (1967) US#37, **Edizione D'Oro (The Four Seasons Gold Edition-29 Gold Hits)** (1969) g US#37 UK#11, **The Big Ones** (1971, all Philips) UK##37; **The Four Seasons Story** (1976, Private Stock) US#51 UK#20; **Greatest Hits** (1976, K-Tel) UK#4; **The 20 Greatest Hits** (1988, Telstar) UK#38; **25th Anniversary Collection** (1988, Rhino); **Very Best of Frankie Valli and the**

Four Seasons (1992, PolyGram) UK#7. In 1969, Gaudio ran his own Gazette label, and also co-wrote and produced Frank Sinatra's concept album **Watertown** (1970, Reprise) US#101 UK#14. During the 1970s, he worked with Neil Diamond and Barbra Streisand. HIT VERSIONS: *Beggin'* [iv] Timebox (1968) UK#38, *Fancy Dancer* [ii] Frankie Valli (1979) US#77, *I Would Be in Love (Anyway)* [v] Frank Sinatra (1970) US#88, *Sherry* Robert John (1980) US#70, *Short Shorts* [i] Salsoul Orchestra (1977) US#106. Co-writers: [i] Tom Austin/Bill Crandall/Bill Dalton, [ii] Brown, [iii] Charlie Calello, [iv] Peggy Farina, [v] Jake Holmes, [vi] Sandy Linzer, [vii] Judy Parker, [viii] Al Ruzicka. (*See also under* Bob CREWE.)

358. GAY, Noel (b. Richard Moxon Armitage, July 15, 1898, Wakefield; d. March 3, 1954, London, both England) Film and stage composer, pianist and arranger. The composer of over fifteen musicals, who, in 1937, achieved Britain's longest running show "Me and My Girl," which introduced the much recorded *The Lambeth Walk* [v]. Gay was a teenage organist at Wakefield Cathedral in Yorkshire, after which he studied at the Royal College of Music, before going up to Cambridge University, where he composed his first songs for the university dance band and wrote musical comedy for the stage. Gay contributed to the shows "The Charlot Revue of 1926" and "Clowns in Clover" (1927), before scoring his first major hit with *The King's Horses (And the King's Men)* [vi] from "Folly to Be Wise" (1931). A corny but immensely popular songwriter, Gay's general outlook was perhaps best captured in his delightful number *The Sun Has Got His Hat On* [i] (1932). During the 1930s, he worked on the productions of "She Couldn't Say No" (1932), "Jack O' Diamonds" (1935) and "The Little Dog Laughed" (1939), and such films as "The Camels Are Coming" (1934), "Okay for Sound" (1936) and "Me and Marlborough" (1937). After the 1940s, Gay suffered from increasing deafness, and subsequently wrote less music. Some of his biggest hits of the time were *Ali Baba's Camel* (1931), *All for a Shilling a Day* [vii] (1935), *All Over the Place* (1941), *The Fleet's in Port Again* (1936), *Hey Little Hen* (1941), *'Round the Marble Arch* [i] (1932), *I Took My Harp to a Party* [ii] (1934), *There's Something About a Soldier* (1935), *Let's Have a Tiddley at the Milk Bar* (1936), and *My Thanks to You* [viii] (1950). ALBUMS: **Me and My Girl** oc (1981, MCA); **Me and My Girl** oc (1986, EMI). HIT VERSIONS: *King's Horses (And the King's Men), The* [vi] Ben Bernie (1931) US#7, *Lambeth Walk, The* [v] Al Donohue (1938) US#7/Duke Ellington (1938) US#7/Russ Morgan (1938) US#4; *Leaning on the Lamp Post* Herman's Hermits (1966)

US#9, *Things Are Looking Up* Fred Astaire (1937) US#19. Co-writers: [i] Ralph Butler, [ii] Desmond Carter, [iii] Frank Eyton, [iv] Douglas Furber, [v] Douglas Furber/Arthur Rose, [vi] Harry Graham, [vii] Clifford Grey, [viii] Norman Newell.

359. GAYDEN, Mac (b. MacGavock Gayden, 1946, TN) C&W guitarist, banjo player and vocalist. A country session player who was a member of the group Area Code 615, which released the albums **Area Code 615** (1969) US#191 and **A Trip to the Country** (1970, both Polydor). Gayden also recorded as a solo artist and co-composed a handful of pop classics, many of which, including *My Rainbow Valley* [i], were recorded by the R&B singer Robert Knight. ALBUMS: **MacGavock Gayden** (1973, EMI); **Skyboat** (1976), **Hymn to the Street** (1976, both ABC). HIT VERSIONS: *Everlasting Love* [i] Robert Knight (1967) R&B#14 US#13 UK#40, re-issued (1974) UK#19/Love Affair (1968) UK#1/Carl Carlton (1974) R&B#11 US#6/Rufus & Chaka Khan (1977) R&B#17/Narvel Felts (1979) C&W#14/Louise Mandrell (1979) C&W#69/Rex Smith & Rachel Sweet (1981) US#32 UK#35/Sandra (1988) UK#45/Gloria Estefan (1995) US#27 UK#19; *It's Alright* Bobby Bare (1965) C&W#7, *Morning Glory* [i] James & Bobby Purify (1976) UK#27. Co-writer: [i] James "Buzz" Cason.

360. GAYE, Marvin (b. Marvin Pentz Gay, Jr., April 2, 1939, Washington, DC; d. April 1, 1984, Los Angeles, CA) R&B vocalist. One of the most gifted vocalists in the history of black music, whose pitch and phrasing was effortless, and whose recorded achievements include a handful of the most important and influential R&B albums ever made. The least superficial of any soul performer, Gaye had a desperate desire to communicate through his music, and was responsible for a unique style that has inspired nearly every soul balladeer since, none more so than Luther Vandross. Gaye charted over sixty singles between 1962–1985, and, in partnership with Mary Wells, Kim Weston, Tammi Terrell, and Diana Ross, proved himself the master of the boy-girl duet. The son of a church minister, Gaye had an authoritative and religious upbringing. He first sang doo-wop as a teenager in the 1950s vocal group the D.C. Tones, and later the Rainbows, which released the single *Mary Lee* on the Red Robin label. His first composition was entitled *Barbara*, the melody of which he based on the theme tune to the Perry Mason television series. The Rainbows became the Marquees, which recorded four singles and the album **The Marquees** (1960, OKeh), before he joined Harvey and the Moonglows in 1965, in which he met Harvey Fuqua. When Fuqua's Tri-Phi label became part of the Motown Records empire, Fuqua and Gaye re-located to Detroit, where Gaye became a session drummer for the Miracles, the Spinners and Stevie Wonder, and a backing vocalist for the Marvelettes. In 1961 he married Anna Gordy, the sister of label boss Berry Gordy, Jr. A record contract with the Tamla imprint initially proved frustrating, as the company attempted to promote him as a new Nat "King" Cole. Considerably more interested in recording songs that would place him on the charts, Gaye later commented, "Motown wasn't about art. It was about hits." By 1963, he had toughened up his sound, to record some of Motown's most memorable material. Of the early hits that he composed, Gaye once said, "All these songs were naturals, it was like they wrote themselves." As good as his 1960s discs were, nothing about them indicated what was to come next. In 1971, having gained greater artist control over his output, Gaye revolutionized soul music with the release of the album **What's Going On**, which Motown was at first reluctant to issue at all. Gaye abandoned the restrictive Motown formula of three minute songs, and instead conjured up a thematic series of inter-related compositions that, while not a "concept" album as such, worked brilliantly as a substantive whole. Songs were sequenced without gaps, and were so immaculately paced that a tension was built throughout the album until the closing cut. **What's Going On** ruminated on black politics, racial equality, the environment and poverty, and was sung with a spirituality rarely captured on record. Gaye's humanistic pleas made the album a powerful and timeless document, and the track *Inner City Blues* [xii], voiced themes that would later become central to rap music. Two years later, Gaye's attention shifted from world issues to those of a more personal nature, when he released **Let's Get It On**, a short, sophisticated investigation of passion and eroticism. Although later recordings never reached the heights of these two albums, Gaye still came up with the occasional classic, including the hypnotic *(Sexual) Healing* [iii], a blend of electro-soul that was a precursor to the next trend in R&B music. A strangely self-destructive individual, Gaye became increasingly dependent upon drugs, and his heavy cocaine use resulted in a personal financial mess that, by 1984, found him living back in his parents' house. His last public performance was singing *The Star Spangled Banner* at the 1984 National Basketball Association All Star Game. After a rumored suicide attempt in March, 1984, Gaye was shot dead by his father at their home the following month. CHART COMPOSITIONS: *Stubborn Kind of Fellow* [vii] (1962) R&B#8 US#46, *Hitch Hike* [xiii] (1963) R&B#12 US#30, *Pride and Joy* [xiv] (1963) R&B#2 US#10, *Pretty Little Baby* [vii] (1965) R&B#16 US#25, *If*

This World Were Mine with Tammi Terrell (1968) R&B#27 US#68, *What's Going On* [ii] (1971) R&B#1 US#2, *Mercy Mercy Me (The Ecology)* (1971) R&B#1 US#4, *Inner City Blues* [xii] (1971) R&B#1 US#9, *Save the Children* [ii] (1971) UK#41, *You're the Man* (1972) R&B#7 US#50, *Trouble Man* (1972) R&B#4 US#7, *Let's Get It On* [xv] (1973) R&B#1 US#1 UK#31, *Come Get to This* (1973) R&B#3 US#21, *You Sure Love to Ball* (1974) R&B#13 US#50, *Distant Lover* [viii] (1974) R&B#12 US#28, *After the Dance* [xvi] (1976) R&B#14 US#74, *Got to Give It Up* (1977) R&B#1 US#1 UK#7, *A Funky Space Reincarnation* (1979) R&B#23 US#106, *Ego Tripping Out* (1979) R&B#17, *Praise* (1981) R&B#18 US#101, *Heavy Love Affair* (1981) R&B#61, *(Sexual) Healing* [iii] (1982) g R&B#1 US#3 UK#4, *'Til Tomorrow* (1983) R&B#31, *Joy* (1983) R&B#78, *Sanctified Lady* (1985) R&B#2 US#101 UK#51, *It's Madness* (1985) R&B#55. ALBUMS: **The Soulful Moods of Marvin Gaye** (1960), **That Stubborn Kind of Fellow** (1963), **Live on Stage** (1963), **When I'm Alone I Cry** (1964), **Together** with Mary Wells (1964) US#42, **How Sweet It Is (To Be Loved By You)** (1964) US#128, **Hello Broadway** (1964), **A Tribute to the Great Nat "King" Cole** (1965), **Takes Two** with Kim Weston (1967), **United*** (1967) US#69, **You're All I Need*** (1968) US#60, **In the Groove** (1968) US#63, **M.P.G.** (1969) US#33, **Easy*** (1969) US#184, **That's the Way Love Is** (1969) US#189, **What's Going On** (1971) g US#6, **Trouble Man** ost (1972) US#14, **Let's Get It On** (1973, all Tamla) US#2 UK#39; **Diana and Marvin** with Diana Ross (1973, Motown) US#26; **Live** (1974) US#8, **I Want You** (1976) US#4 UK#22, **Live at the London Palladium** (1977) US#3, **Here, My Dear** (1979) US#26, **In Our Lifetime** (1981, all Tamla) US#32 UK#48; **Midnight Love** (1982, Columbia) p US#7 UK#10. COMPILATIONS: **Greatest Hits** (1964) p US#72, **The Moods of Marvin Gaye** (1966) US#118, **Greatest Hits, Volume 2** (1966) US#178 UK#40, **Marvin Gaye and His Girls** (1969) US#183, **Super Hits** (1970) US#117, **Marvin Gaye and Tammi Terrell's Greatest Hits** (1970, all Tamla) US#171 UK#60; **Anthology** (1974, Motown) US#61; **Marvin Gaye's Greatest Hits** (1976, Tamla) US#44; **Best of Marvin Gaye** (1976) UK#56, **Every Great Motown Hit of Marvin Gaye** (1983, both Motown) US#80; **Greatest Hits** (1983, Telstar) UK#13; **Dream of a Lifetime** (1985) UK#46, **Romantically Yours** (1985, both Columbia); **Motown Remembers Marvin Gaye** (1986, Tamla) US#193; **Love Songs** with Smokey Robinson (1988, Telstar) UK#69, **A Musical Testament** (1988, Motown); **Love Songs** (1990, Telstar) UK#39; **Last Concert Tour** (1991, Giant); **Seek and You Shall Find: More of the Best** (1994, Rhino); **Very Best of Marvin Gaye** (1994)

UK#3, **The Master (1961–1984)** (1995), **Vulnerable** (1997, all Motown). HIT VERSIONS: *After the Dance* [xvi] Fourplay featuring El DeBarge (1991) R&B#55, *Baby I'm for Real* [v] Originals (1969) R&B#1 US#14/Esther Phillips (1972) R&B#38/Hamilton Bohannon (1980) R&B#54/After 7 (1992) R&B#9 US#55; *Beechwood 4-5789* [vii] Marvelettes (1962) R&B#7 US#17/Carpenters (1982) US#74; *Bells, The* [vi] Originals (1970) R&B#4 US#12/Color Me Badd (1994) R&B#73; *Come Get to This* Joe Simon (1976) R&B#22 US#102, *Dancing in the Street* [xi] Martha & the Vandellas (1964) g US#2 UK#28, re-issued (1969) UK#4; Mamas & Papas (1966) US#73/Ramsey Lewis (1967) US#84/Dovells (1974) US#105/Donald Byrd (1976) R&B#95/Boney M (1979) R&B#75 US#103/Hodges, James & Smith (1979) R&B#85/Teri De Sario with K.C. (1980) US#66/Tight Fit in *Back to the Sixties* (1981) UK#38/Van Halen (1982) US#38/David Bowie & Mick Jagger (1985) US#7 UK#1/Matt Bianco (1986) UK#64; *Get My Hands on Some Lovin'* Artistics (1964) US#118, *Got to Give It Up* David Sanborn (1994) R&B#125, *If This World Were Mine* Cheryl Lynn & Luther Vandross (1982) R&B#4 US#101, *Inner City Blues* [xii] Grover Washington, Jr. (1972) R&B#42 US#120/Gary (1994) R&B#112/Angela Winbush (1994) R&B#49; *Mercy, Mercy Me (The Ecology)* Robert Palmer (1991) US#16 UK#9; *(Sexual) Healing* [iii] Eleanor Grant (1983) R&B#71, *Six Feet Deep* [iv] Geto Boys (1993) R&B#37 US#40, *We Can Make It Baby* Originals (1970) R&B#20 US#74, *Welcome to the Ghetto* [x] Spice 1 (1992) R&B#39, *What's Going On* [ii] Cyndi Lauper (1987) US#12 UK#57/Speech in *Like Marvin Gaye Said (What's Going On)* (1996) UK#35; *When Did You Stop Loving Me, When Did I Stop Loving You* Daryl Hall in *Stop Loving You, Stop Loving Me* (1994) UK#30, *Wherever I Lay My Hat (That's My Home)* [xvii] Paul Young (1983) US#70 UK#1, *Wholy Holy* Aretha Franklin (1972) R&B#49 US#81. With: * Tammi Terrell. Co-writers: [i] Renaldo Benson (b. 1937, Detroit, IL), [ii] Renaldo Benson/Alfred Cleveland, [iii] Odell Brown, [iv] M. Burnette/B. Jordan/Lionel Richie, [v] Anna Gaye, [vi] Anna Gaye/Berry Gordy, Jr./Elgie Stover, [vii] Berry Gordy, Jr./William Stevenson, [viii] Susaye Greene/G. Fuqua, [ix] Dave Hamilton/Clarence Paul, [x] Jimmy Harris/Terry Lewis/Spice 1, [xi] Ivy Hunter/William Stevenson, [xii] James Nyx, [xiii] William Stevenson, [xiv] William Stevenson/Norman Whitfield, [xv] Edward Townshend, [xvi] Leon Ware, [xvii] Norman Whitfield.

361. GELD, Gary, and **UDELL, Peter** Both film and show composers. ALBUMS: **Looking for Love** ost (1964, MGM); **Purlie** oc (1970,

Ampex) US#138; **Shenandoah** oc (1974, RCA); **Angel** oc (1978, Angel). HIT VERSIONS: *Ain't Gonna Wash for a Week* Brook Brothers (1961) UK#13, *Ginny Come Lately* Brian Hyland (1962) US#21 UK#5, *Hurting Each Other* Carpenters (1972) g US#2, *Let Me Belong to You* Brian Hyland (1961) US#20, *Save Your Heart for Me* Gary Lewis & the Playboys (1965) US#2, *Sealed with a Kiss* Brian Hyland (1962) g US#3 UK#3, re-issued (1975) UK#7/Gary Lewis & the Playboys (1968) US#19/Toys (1968) R&B#43 US#112/Bobby Vinton (1972) US#19; *Warmed Over Kisses (Left Over Love)* Brian Hyland (1962) US#25 UK#28.

362. GELDOF, Bob (b. Robert Frederick Zenon Geldof, October 5, 1954, Dun Laoghaire, Eire) Pop vocalist. A former music journalist who formed and fronted the pop-punk group the Boomtown Rats in 1976. CHART COMPOSITIONS: *Looking After #1* (1977) UK#11, *Mary of the Fourth Form* (1977) UK#15, *She's So Modern* [i] (1978) UK#12, *Like Clockwork* (1978) UK#6, *Rat Trap* (1978) UK#1, *I Don't Like Mondays* (1979) US#73 UK#1, re-issued (1994) UK#38; *Diamond Smiles* (1979) UK#13, *Someone's Looking at You* (1980) UK#4, *Banana Republic* (1980) UK#3, *Elephant's Graveyard (Guilty)* (1981) UK#26, *Never in a Million Years* (1981) UK#62, *House on Fire* (1982) UK#24, *Tonight* (1984) UK#73, *Drag Me Down* (1984) UK#50. ALBUMS: **The Boomtown Rats** (1977) UK#18, **A Tonic for the Troops** (1978) US#112 UK#8, **The Fine Art of Surfacing** (1979, all Ensign) US#103 UK#7; **Mondo Bongo** (1981) US#116 UK#6, **V Deep** (1982, both Mercury) UK#64; **In the Long Grass** (1984, Ensign). COMPILATIONS: **Loudmouth-The Best of the Boomtown Rats and Bob Geldof** (1994, Vertigo) UK#10. After the group split up in 1982, Geldof concentrated on acting before, as a member of the all-star studio group Band Aid, co-writing the multi-million selling Ethiopian famine relief disk *Do They Know It's Christmas?* [ii] (1984) US#13 UK#1, re-issued (1985) UK#3. Geldof's Live Aid concert the following year, was the Woodstock of the 1980s, and it rekindled the benefit concept of live shows and recordings, for which he was awarded an honorary knighthood. During the late 1980s, Geldof pursued a solo recording career, but much of the 1990s was spent running his own television company. CHART COMPOSITIONS: *This Is the World Calling* (1986) US#82 UK#25, *Love Like a Rocket* (1987) UK#61, *The Great Song of Indifference* (1990) UK#15, *Crazy* (1994) UK#65. ALBUMS: **Deep in the Heart of Nowhere** (1986) US#130 UK#79, **The Vegetarians of Love** (1990, both Mercury) UK#21; **The Happy Club** (1993, Polydor). HIT VERSIONS: *Do They Know*

It's Christmas? [ii] Band Aid II (1989) UK#1. Co-writers: [i] Johnnie Fingers (b. John Moylett, September 10, 1956, Eire), [ii] Midge Ure.

363. GENTRY, Teddy (b. Teddy Wayne Gentry, January 22, 1952, Fort Payne, AL) C&W bassist and vocalist, and **OWEN, Randy** (b. Randy Yeull Owen, December 13, 1949, Fort Payne, AL) C&W guitarist and vocalist. Two cousins who are the principle songwriting team in the mainstream country act Alabama, which has sold over fifty million records and scored an unsurpassed thirty number one singles. Gentry and Owen first performed as members of 1960s groups the Singing Owens, the Sand Mountain Chicken Pluckers and Young Country, before forming Alabama in 1977. CHART COMPOSITIONS: *My Home's in Alabama* (1980) C&W#17, *Feel So Right* (1981) C&W#1 US#20, *Lady Down on Love* (1983) C&W#1 US#76, *Tar Top* (1987) C&W#7. ALBUMS: **My Home's in Alabama** (1980) p US#71, **Feels So Right** (1981) p US#16, **Mountain Music** (1982) p US#14, **The Closer You Get** (1983) p US#10, **Roll On** (1984) p US#21, **40 Hour Week** (1985) p US#28, **Christmas** (1985) p US#75, **The Touch** (1986) p US#42, **Just Us** (1987) g US#55, **Live** (1988) g US#76, **Southern Star** (1989) p US#62, **Pass It on Down** (1990) p US#57, **American Pride** (1992, all RCA) p US#46; **Cheap Seats** (1993) g US#76, **Read My Mind** (1995), **In Pictures** (1995, all MCA) g US#100. COMPILATIONS: **Greatest Hits** (1986) p US#24, **Greatest Hits II** (1991, both RCA) p US#72; **Greatest Hits III** (1995, MCA) p US#57.

364. GEORGE, Lowell (b. April 13, 1945, Los Angeles, CA; d. June 29, 1979, Washington, DC) Rock guitarist, producer and vocalist. The founder member of the rock group Little Feat, which paid scant attention to any one particular musical genre, and in so doing merged rock, country, R&B and jazz into a unique hybrid. George's taste for the offbeat and the bizarre, resulted in songs that frequently bristled with charm and humor. After first studying the flute he turned to the guitar, and in 1965 formed his first band, the Factory, their recordings later being collected on the album **Lightning Rod Man** (1993, Edsel). George also played with the Standells and the group the Fraternity of Man, featuring on the latter's album **Get It On** (1968, ABC). After a brief period in Frank Zappa's the Mothers of Invention, George formed Little Feat for a glorious self-titled debut album that sold miserably, despite containing such gems as *Willin'*. ALBUMS: **Little Feat** (1972), **Sailin' Shoes** (1972), **Dixie Chicken** (1973), **Feats Don't Fail Me Now** (1974) g US#36, **The Last Record Album** (1975) US#36 UK#36,

Time Loves a Hero (1977) g US#34 UK#8, **Waiting for Columbus** (1978) p US#18 UK#43, **Down on the Farm** (1979, all Warner Brothers) US#29 UK#46. COMPILATIONS: **Hoy-Hoy!** (1981) US#39 UK#76, **As Time Goes By** (1986, both Warner Brothers). George recorded one solo album **Thanks I'll Eat It Here** (1979, Warner Brothers) US#71 UK#71, before dying after a concert from a massive coronary. HIT VERSION: *Dixie Chicken* [i] Garth Brooks (1993) C&W#73. Co-writer: [i] M. Kibbee.

365. GERSHWIN, George (b. Jacob Gershvin, September 26, 1898, Brooklyn, NY; d. July 11, 1937, Beverly Hills, CA) Film and stage composer, pianist and vocalist. A musical genius and one of the true masters of the art of the popular song, who was influenced by jazz and ragtime. Gershwin was the first composer to introduce genuine quality and swing to jazz vocal recordings, and he penned not only dozens of standards, but also composed the symphonic suites "Rhapsody in Blue" (1924), "Concerto in F" (1925) and "An American in Paris" (1928), alongside the black operetta masterpiece "Porgy and Bess" (1935), a work that was later radically re-interpreted in its entirety by the jazz musicians Miles Davis and Gil Evans. Many of Gershwin's finest songs had lyrics that were written by his elder brother Ira. He learned classical piano as a teenager, and worked as a song-plugger while accompanying such vaudeville singers as Nora Bayes during the 1910s. Gershwin's first composition, *The Real American Folk Song*, was sung by Bayes in 1918, and his first major hit was the multi-million selling *Swanee* [i] by Al Jolson, which was introduced in the show "Sinbad" (1919). Between 1920–1924, Gershwin composed for the annual revue "George White's Scandals." The Gershwin's first self-composed musical was "Half Past Eight" (1919), which they followed with the urbane and sophisticated "Lady, Be Good" (1924). Other shows with which Gershwin was associated include: "Tip-Toes" (1925), "Oh, Kay!" (1926), "Funny Face" (1927), "Rosalie" (1928), "Show Girl" (1929), "Strike Up the Band," "Girl Crazy" (both 1930); and "Of Thee I Sing" (1931). The Gershwin's also composed for films, including "A Damsel in Distress," "Shall We Dance" (both 1937) and "The Goldwyn Follies" (1938). Their compositions have been recorded on many occasions, the most successful being: **Sarah Vaughan Sings George Gershwin** (1957, Mercury) US#14; Leonard Bernstein and the New York Philharmonic, **Gershwin: An American in Paris/Rhapsody in Blue** (1959, Columbia) g; Leontyne Price, **Great Scenes from Gershwin's Porgy and Bess** (1963, RCA) US#66; Roger Williams, **10th Anniversary/Limited Edition Plays Gershwin**

(1964, Kapp) US#108; Ray Charles and Cleo Laine, **Porgy and Bess** (1976, RCA) US#138; Dave Grusin, **The Gershwin Collection** (1991, GRP) US#170; and Larry Adler, **The Glory of Gershwin** (1994) UK#2. Arguably the best interpreter of Gershwin was Ella Fitzgerald, of whom Ira once said, "I never knew how good our songs were until I heard Ella Fitzgerald sing them." Fitzgerald's recordings were issued as **Ella Fitzgerald Sings Gershwin** (1960, Brunswick) UK#13; **Ella Fitzgerald Sings Gershwin, Volume 5** (1960, HMV) UK#18; and **Ella Fitzgerald Sings the George and Ira Gershwin Song Books** (1964, Verve) US#111. Gershwin died at the age of thirty-nine of a brain tumor. CHART COMPOSITIONS: *Rhapsody in Blue* (1924) US#3, new version, both with Paul Whiteman (1927) US#7; *Someone to Watch Over Me* [vi] (1927) US#17, *An American in Paris* (1929) US#7. ALBUMS: **Girl Crazy** ost (1943, Decca); **Funny Face** oc (195?), **Lady, Be Good** oc (195?), **Tip-Toes** oc (195?, all World); **An American in Paris** ost (1951, MGM); **Porgy and Bess** sc (1951, RCA); **Girl Crazy** sc (1952, Columbia); **Of Thee I Sing** oc (1952, Capitol); **Young at Heart** ost (1954, Columbia); **Three for the Show** ost (1955, Mercury); **Funny Face** ost (1957, Verve); **Oh, Kay!** sc (1957), **Porgy and Bess** sc (1959, both Columbia) g US#8 UK#7; **Oh, Kay!** oc (1960, 20th Century Fox); **George Gershwin** (1960, Ember); **Porgy and Bess** sc (1962, CBS) UK#14; **When the Boys Meet the Girls** st (1965, MGM); **Of Thee I Sing** tvst (1972, Columbia); **Blue Monday** sc (1976, Vox Turnabout); **Manhattan** ost (1979, Columbia) US#94; **My One and Only** oc (1983, Atlantic); **The Two Sides of George Gershwin** (1983, Halcyon); **Crazy for You** oc (1992, Angel) US#165; **Gershwin Plays Gershwin-The Piano Rolls** (1994, Elektra Nonesuch) US#193. HIT VERSIONS: *Bidin'' My Time* [vi] Foursome (1931) US#9, *But Not for Me* [vi] Harry James (1942) US#12, *Clap Yo' Hands* [vi] Roger Wolfe Kahn (1927) US#9/"Whispering" Jack Smith (1927) US#15; *Concerto in F* Paul Whiteman (1929) US#10, *Cossack Love Song* [ix] Ipana Troubadors (1926) US#10, *Daybreak* [vi] Jimmy Dorsey (1942) US#18/Tommy Dorsey (1942) US#10/Harry James (1942) US#17; *Delishious* [vi] Nat Shilkret (1932) US#8, *Do-Do-Do* [vi] George Olsen (1927) US#5/Gertrude Lawrence (1927) US#8; *Do It Again* [iii] Paul Whiteman (1922) US#1, *Embraceable You* [vi] Red Nichols (1929) US#2/Jimmy Dorsey (1941) US#23; *Fascinating Rhythm* [vi] Cliff Edwards (1925) US#6/Sam Lanin (1925) US#13; *Fidgety Feet* [vi] Fletcher Henderson (1927) US#17, *Foggy Day, A* [vi] Fred Astaire (1937) US#3/Bob Crosby (1938) US#16; *For You, For Me, For Evermore* [vi] Judy Garland & Dick Haymes (1947) US#19, *Funny Face* [vi] Arden-Ohman Orchestra (1928) US#14, *I Got Plenty O'*

Nuttin' [viii] Leo Reisman (1935) US#5, *I Got Rhythm* [vi] Red Nichols (1931) US#17/Ethel Waters (1931) US#17/Louis Armstrong (1932) US#17/Happenings (1967) US#3 UK#28; *I Loves You, Porgy* [viii] Nina Simone (1959) R&B#2 US#18, *I'll Build a Stairway to Paradise* [iv] Carl Fenton (1922) US#12/Ben Selvin (1923) US#8/Paul Whiteman (1923) US#1; *I've Got a Crush on You* [vi] Joe Sullivan (1940) US#24/Frank Sinatra (1948) US#21; *(I've Got) Beginner's Luck* [vi] Fred Astaire (1937) US#13, *It Ain't Necessarily So* [vi] Leo Reisman (1935) US#16/Bing Crosby (1936) US#18/Bronski Beat (1985) UK#16; *Let's Call the Whole Thing Off* [vi] Fred Astaire (1937) US#5/Eddy Duchin (1937) US#20/Shep Fields (1937) US#16; *Liza (All the Clouds Roll Away)* [vii] Al Jolson (1929) US#9, *Looking for a Boy* [vi] Arden-Ohman Orchestra (1926) US#12; *Love Is Here to Stay* [vi] Larry Clinton (1938) US#15/Red Norvo (1938) US#16; *Love Walked In* [vi] Louis Armstrong (1938) US#19/Kenny Baker (1938) US#14/Jimmy Dorsey (1938) US#7/Jan Garber (1938) US#7/Sammy Kaye (1938) US#1/Hilltoppers (1953) US#8/Dinah Washington (1960) R&B#16 US#30; *Man I Love, The* [vi] Marion Harris (1928) US#4/Fred Rich (1928) US#19/Sophie Tucker (1928) US#11/Paul Whiteman (1928) US#15/Benny Goodman (1937) US#20; *Maybe* [vi] Nat Shilkret (1927) US#12, *Mine* [vi] Emil Coleman (1933) US#12, *My One and Only* [vi] Jane Green (1928) US#14/Fred Astaire (1929) US#18; *Nice Work if You Can Get It* [vi] Shep Fields (1937) US#8/Teddy Wilson & Billie Holiday (1937) US#20/Andrews Sisters (1938) US#12/Fred Astaire (1938) US#1/Maxine Sullivan (1938) US#10; *Of Thee I Sing* [vi] Ben Selvin (1932) US#8, *Oh! Lady Be Good* [vi] Cliff Edwards (1925) US#13/Carl Fenton (1925) US#9/Paul Whiteman (1925) US#2/Abe Lyman (1932) US#10/Ben Selvin (1932) US#8; *Rhapsody in Blue* Glenn Miller (1943) R&B#6 US#13/Deodato (1973) R&B#42 US#41/Walter Murphy (1977) US#102; *Shall We Dance?* [vi] Fred Astaire (1937) US#3, *S' Wonderful* [vi] Frank Crumit (1928) US#5/Ipana Troubadors (1928) US#12; *Somebody Loves Me* [iii] Ray Miller (1924) US#4/Paul Whiteman (1924) US#1/Cliff Edwards (1925) US#11/Marion Harris (1925) US#7/Four Lads (1952) US#22; *Someone to Watch Over Me* [vi] Gertrude Lawrence (1927) US#2/George Olsen (1927) US#3; *Song of the Flame* [x] Ipana Troubadors (1926) US#9/Vincent Lopez (1926) US#5/Victor Light Opera Co. (1926) US#13; *Strike Up the Band* [vi] Arden-Ohman Orchestra (1930) US#12/Red Nichols (1930) US#7; *Summertime* [vi] Billie Holiday (1936) US#12/Al Martino (1960) UK#49/Marcels (1961) US#78 UK#46/Rick Nelson (1962) US#89/Billy Stewart (1966) R&B#7 US#10 UK#39/Fun Boy Three (1982) UK#18; *Swanee* [i] All-Star Trio (1920) US#11/Al Jolson (1920) g US#1/Peerless Quartet (1920) US#11/Big Ben Banjo Band in *Let's Get Together #1* (1954) UK#6/Mrs. Mills in *Mrs. Mills' Medley* (1961) UK#18; *Sweet and Lowdown* [vi] Harry Archer (1926) US#10, *That Certain Feeling* [vi] Paul Whiteman (1926) US#5, *They All Laughed* [vi] Fred Astaire (1937) US#6, *They Can't Take That Away from Me* [vi] Fred Astaire (1937) US#1/Tommy Dorsey (1937) US#11/Billie Holiday (1937) US#12/Ozzie Nelson (1937) US#6; *Things Are Looking Up* [vi] Fred Astaire (1937) US#19, *Waiting for the Sun to Come Out* [v] Lambert Murphy (1921) US#8, *Yankee Doodle Blues* [ii] Billy Murray & Ed Smalle (1923) US#10. Co-writers: [i] Irving Caesar, [ii] Irving Caesar/Buddy De Sylva, [iii] Buddy De Sylva, [iv] Buddy De Sylva/Ira Gershwin, [v] Arthur Francis, [vi] Ira Gershwin, [vii] Ira Gershwin/Gus Kahn, [viii] Ira Gershwin/Du Bose Heyward, [ix] Otto Harbach/Oscar Hammerstein, II, [x] Otto Harbach/Oscar Hammerstein, II/Herbert Stothart, [xi] Du Bose Heyward, II/Herbert Stothart.

366. GERSHWIN, Ira (b. Israel Gershvin, December 6, 1896, New York, NY; d. August 17, 1983, Los Angeles, CA) Film and stage lyricist. Fascinated by words and drawing in his youth, Ira became his brother George's principal lyricist with his witty, refined and debonnaire wordplay. Ira's first major success was his collaboration with Vincent Youmans on the Broadway show "Two Little Girls in Blue" (1921). (*See also under* Harold ARLEN, Vernon DUKE, George GERSHWIN, Jerome KERN, Cole PORTER, Harry WARREN, Kurt WEILL, Vincent YOUMANS.)

367. GESSLE, Per (b. February 12, 1959, Halmstad, Sweden) Pop guitarist and vocalist. One half, with vocalist Marie Frederiksson, of the pop duo Roxette, Sweden's most successful group after Abba, which by 1993, had sold over twenty-one million albums and twelve million singles. CHART COMPOSITIONS: *The Look* (1989) g US#1 UK#7, re-mixed (1995) UK#28; *Dressed for Success* (1989) US#14 UK#48, re-issued (1990) UK#18; *Listen to Your Heart* [i] (1989) US#1 UK#62, *Dangerous* (1989) US#2, *Listen to Your Heart* [i]/*Dangerous* (1990) UK#6, *It Must Have Been Love* (1990) US#1 UK#3, re-issued (1993) UK#10; *Joyride* (1991) US#1 UK#4, *Fading Like a Flower (Every Time You Leave)* (1991) US#2 UK#12, *The Big L* (1991) UK#21, *Spending My Time* [i] (1991) US#32 UK#22, *Church of Your Heart* (1992) US#36 UK#21, *How Do You Do!* (1992) US#58 UK#13, *Queen of Rain* [i] (1992) UK#28, *Almost Unreal* (1993) US#94 UK#7, *Sleeping in My Car* (1994) US#50, *Fireworks* (1994) UK#30, *Run to You* (1994) UK#27, *Vulnerable* (1995) UK#44, *You Don't*

Understand Me (1996) UK#42, *June Afternoon* (1996) UK#52. ALBUMS: **Pearls of Passion** (1986), **Look Sharp** (1988) p US#23 UK#4, **Joyride** (1991) p US#12 UK#2, **Tourism** (1992, all EMI) US#117 UK#2. COMPILATION: **Don't Bore Us, Get to the Chorus!-Greatest Hits** (1995) UK#5. Gessle has also recorded as a solo artist. ALBUM: **The World According to Per Gessle** (1997, EMI). Co-writer: [i] Persson.

368. GIBB, Barry (b. Barry Alan Crompton Gibb, September 1, 1946, Douglas, Isle of Man) Pop guitarist, producer and vocalist. The principal songwriter, often in partnership with his twin brothers Robin and Maurice, in the vocal group the Bee Gees, which, by 1993, had sold over one hundred million records. The trio first performed at a Manchester theatre in 1955, before the Gibb family emigrated to Australia in 1958, where the teenagers became the Gibbs and the BGs before settling on the name the Bee Gees, as which they held a residency at a Brisbane club and another singing between speedway races. Their first composition was *Let Me Love You* [vii], which was recorded by Tommy Steele, and their first hit was as writers of Col Joyce's Australian number one *Starlight of Love* [vii]. During the early 1960s the Bee Gees recorded for the Festival and Leedon labels, and charted eleven Australian hits on Spin Records, with *Spicks and Specks* reaching number one. Gibb also became a songwriter and producer for such Australian singers as Robbie Burns. In 1967, after three Australian album releases, the brothers returned to England, where, influenced by the Beatles, they perfected their three part harmonies and scored the first of many million sellers with *New York Mining Disaster 1941* [viii]. During the mid-1970s the group worked with the veteran R&B producer Arif Mardin, on a highly polished disco sound for the soul tinged million seller **Main Course** (1975). The Gibb's biggest success was writing a collection of compositions for the 1977 dance movie "Saturday Night Fever," the soundtrack to which sold over thirty million copies and featured four Bee Gees million selling number one singles. The group has had many peaks and troughs since the late 1970s, but they always seem to up-date their sound and bounce back with a major worldwide hit every few years. CHART COMPOSITIONS: *New York Mining Disaster 1941* [viii] (1967) g US#14 UK#12, *To Love Somebody* [vii] (1967) US#17 UK#41, *Massachusetts* [viii] (1967) US#11 UK#1, *Holiday* [viii] (1967) US#16, *World* [viii] (1967) UK#19, *I Can't See Nobody* (1967) US#128, *Words* [viii] (1968) US#15 UK#8, *Jumbo* (1968) US#57 UK#25, *The Singer Sang His Song* (1968) US#116, *I've Got to Get a Message to You* [viii] (1968) US#8 UK#1, *I Started a Joke*

(1968) US#6, *The First of May* [viii] (1969) US#37 UK#6, *Tomorrow, Tomorrow* (1969) US#73 UK#23, *Don't Forget to Remember* [v] (1969) US#73 UK#2, *I.O.I.O.* (1970) US#94 UK#49, *If I Only Had My Mind on Something Else* (1970) US#91, *Lonely Days* [viii] (1970) g US#3 UK#33, *How Can You Mend a Broken Heart* [vii] (1971) g US#1, *Don't Wanna Live Inside Myself* (1971) US#53, *My World* [vii] (1972) US#16 UK#16, *Run to Me* [viii] (1972) US#16 UK#9, *Alive* (1972) US#34, *Saw a New Morning* (1973) US#94, *Wouldn't I Be Someone* (1973) US#115, *Mr. Natural* (1974) US#93, *Charade* (1974) US#103, *Jive Talking* [viii] (1975) g US#1 UK#5, *Nights on Broadway* [viii] (1975) US#7, *Fanny (Be Tender with My Love)* (1976) US#12, *You Should Be Dancing* (1976) g R&B#4 US#1 UK#5, *Love So Right* [viii] (1976) g R&B#37 US#3 UK#41, *Boogie Child* [viii] (1977) R&B#31 US#12, *Edge of the Universe* [vii] (1977) US#26, *How Deep Is Your Love* [viii] (1977) g US#1 UK#3, *Stayin' Alive* [viii] (1978) p R&B#4 US#1 UK#4, *Night Fever* [viii] (1978) p R&B#8 US#1 UK#1, *Too Much Heaven* [viii] (1978) p R&B#10 US#1 UK#3, *Rest Your Love on Me* [viii] (1978) C&W#39, *Tragedy* [viii] (1979) p R&B#44 US#1 UK#1, *Love You Inside Out* [viii] (1979) g R&B#57 US#1 UK#13, *Spirits (Having Flown)* [viii] (1980) UK#16, *He's a Liar* [viii] (1980) US#30, *Living Eyes* [viii] (1980) US#45, *The Woman in You* [viii] (1983) R&B#77 US#24, *Someone Belonging to Someone* [viii] (1983) US#49 UK#49, *You Win Again* [viii] (1987) US#75 UK#1, *E.S.P.* [viii] (1987) UK#51, *Ordinary Lives* [viii] (1989) UK#54, *One* [viii] (1989) US#7 UK#71, *Secret Love* [viii] (1991) UK#5, *Paying the Price of Love* [viii] (1993) US#74 UK#23, *For Whom the Bell Tolls* [viii] (1993) US#109 UK#4, *How to Fall in Love Part 1* [viii] (1994) UK#30, *I Could Not Love You More* (1997) UK#14. ALBUMS: **The Bee Gees Sing and Play 14 Barry Gibb Songs** (1965), **Monday's Rain** (1966), **Turn Around and Look at Us** (1967, both Leedon); **The Bee Gees' First** (1967) US#7 UK#8, **Horizontal** (1968) US#12 UK#16, **Idea** (1968) US#17 UK#4, **Odessa** (1969) US#20 UK#10, **Cucumber Castle** (1970) US#94 UK#57, **Two Years On** (1970) US#32, **Marley Purt Drive** (1970), **Trafalgar** (1971) US#34, **To Whom It May Concern** (1972, all Polydor) US#35; **Life in a Tin Can** (1973) US#69, **Mr. Natural** (1974) US#178, **Main Course** (1975) g US#14, **Children of the World** (1976) p US#8, **Saturday Night Fever** ost (1977) p US#1 UK#1, **Here at Last-The Bee Gees Live** (1977) p US#8, **Spirits (Having Flown)** (1979) p US#1 UK#1, **Living Eyes** (1980) US#41 UK#73, **Stayin' Alive** ost (1983, all RSO) p US#6 UK#14; **E.S.P.** (1987) US#96 UK#5, **One** (1989) US#68 UK#29, **High Civilisation** (1991, all Warner Brothers) UK#24; **Size Isn't Everything** (1993) US#153

UK#23, **Still Waters** (1997, both Polydor) UK#2. COMPILATIONS: **Rare, Precious and Beautiful** (1968) US#99, **Rare, Precious and Beautiful, Volume 2** (1968, both Polydor) US#100; **Kitty Can** (1968), **Collectors Item** (1968, both RSO); **Rare, Precious and Beautiful, Volume 3** (1969), **Best of the Bee Gees** (1969, both Polydor) g US#9 UK#7; **Best of the Bee Gees, Volume 2** (1973) US#98, **Bee Gees' Gold, Volume 1** (1976) g US#50, **Bee Gees' Greatest** (1979, all RSO) p US#1 UK#6; **Very Best of the Bee Gees** (1990, Polydor) UK#8; **Tomorrow the World** (1992, Thunderbolt). Gibb also co-composed and co-produced much of Barbra Streisand's twenty million selling album **Guilty** (1980), Dionne Warwick's **Heartbreaker** (1982), and further works by Kenny Rogers and Diana Ross. He also wrote and produced many of his younger brother Andy Gibb's chart successes, and recorded as a solo artist during the early 1980s. CHART COMPOSITIONS: *Guilty* [viii]* (1980) g US#3 UK#34, *What Kind of Fool* [ii]* (1980) US#10, *Shine Shine* [i] (1984) US#37. ALBUMS: **Now Voyager** (1984) US#72 UK#8, **Hawks** ost (1988, both Polydor). HIT VERSIONS: *Ain't Nothin' Gonna Keep Me from You* Teri De Sario (1978) US#43 UK#52, *All the Love in the World* [viii] Dionne Warwick (1982) US#101 UK#10, *An Everlasting Love* Andy Gibb (1978) g US#5 UK#10, *Chain Reaction* [viii] Diana Ross (1985) R&B#85 US#95 UK#1, re-mixed (1985) US#66, re-issued (1993) UK#20; *Come on Over* [vii] Olivia Newton-John (1976) US#23, *Desire* [viii] Andy Gibb (1980) R&B#49 US#4, *Don't Forget to Remember* [v] Skeeter Davis (1973) C&W#44, *Eaten Alive* [vi] Diana Ross (1985) R&B#10 US#77 UK#71, *Emotion* [vii] Samantha Sang (1977) p R&B#42 US#3 UK#11, *Evening Star* Kenny Rogers (1984) C&W#11, *Experience* Diana Ross (1985) UK#47, *Eyes That See in the Dark* [v] Kenny Rogers (1983) C&W#30 US#79 UK#61, *Grease* Franki Valli (1978) p R&B#40 US#1 UK#3/John Travolta & Olivia Newton-John in *The Grease Megamix* (1991) UK#3, also in *The Grease Dream Mix* (1991) UK#47; *Heart (Stop Beating in Time)* [viii] Leo Sayer (1982) UK#22, *Heartbreaker* [viii] Dionne Warwick (1982) R&B#14 US#10 UK#2, *How Can You Mend a Broken Heart* Duane Dee (1971) C&W#36/Spoonbread (1972) R&B#33; *How Deep Is Your Love* [viii] Take That (1996) UK#1, *I Can't Help It* Andy Gibb & Olivia Newton-John (1980) US#12, *I Just Want to Be Your Everything* [iii] Andy Gibb (1977) g R&B#19 US#1 UK#26/Connie Smith (1977) C&W#14; *If I Can't Have You* [viii] Yvonne Elliman (1978) g R&B#60 US#1 UK#4/Kim Wilde (1993) UK#12; *Islands in the Stream* [viii] Kenny Rogers & Dolly Parton (1983) p C&W#1 US#1 UK#7, *Jive Talking* [viii] Rufus featuring Chaka Khan (1976) R&B#35/Boogie Box High

(1987) UK#7; *(Love Is) Thicker Than Water* [iii] Andy Gibb (1977) g US#1, *Love Me* [vii] Yvonne Elliman (1977) US#68, *Marley Purt Drive* Jose Feliciano (1969) US#70, *Massachusetts* [viii] Tommy Roe (1979) C&W#77, *More Than a Woman* [viii] Tavares (1978) R&B#36 US#32 UK#7, *Night Fever* [viii] Carol Douglas (1978) US#106 UK#66/Mixmasters (1991) UK#23; *Nights on Broadway* [viii] Candi Staton (1977) R&B#16 US#102 UK#6, *Only One Woman* [viii] Marbles (1968) UK#5/Nigel Olsson (1975) US#91; *(Our Love) Don't Throw It All Away* [ix] Andy Gibb (1978) g US#9 UK#32, *Promises* Barbra Streisand (1980) US#48, *Rest Your Love on Me* Conway Twitty (1981) C&W#1, *Shadow Dancing* [iv] Andy Gibb (1978) g R&B#11 US#1 UK#42, *Stayin' Alive* [viii] Richard Ace (1978) UK#66/N-Trance (1996) US#62; *Sweetheart* Engelbert Humperdinck (1970) US#47 UK#20, *Take the Short Way Home* [ii] Dionne Warwick (1982) R&B#43 US#41, *This Woman* [ii] Kenny Rogers (1983) US#23, *Time Is Time* [iii] Andy Gibb (1981) US#15, *To Love Somebody* [vii] Sweet Inspirations (1968) R&B#30 US#74/Narvel Felts (1977) C&W#22/Hank Williams, Jr. (1979) C&W#49/Jimmy Sommerville (1991) UK#8/Michael Bolton (1992) US#12 UK#16; *Turn of the Century* Cyrkle (1967) US#112, *Walls Fell Down, The* Marbles (1969) UK#28, *Warm Ride* [viii] Rare Earth (1978) US#39, *Woman in Love* [vii] Barbra Streisand (1980) g US#1 UK#1, *Words* [viii] Rita Coolidge (1977) UK#25/Susan Allanson (1979) C&W#8/Boyzone (1996) UK#1; *You Stepped into My Life* [viii] Melba Moore (1978) R&B#17 US#47/ Wayne Newton (1979) US#90; *Yours* [viii] Dionne Warwick (1982) UK#66. With: * Barbra Streisand. Co-writers: [i] G. Bitzer/Maurice Gibb (b. December 22, 1949, Douglas, Isle of Man), [ii] Albhy Galuten, [iii] Andy Gibb (b. March 5, 1958, Chorlton-Cum-Hardy, England), [iv] Andy Gibb/Maurice Gibb (b. December 22, 1949, Douglas, Isle of Man)/Robin Gibb, [v] Maurice Gibb, [vi] Maurice Gibb/Mick Jackson, [vii] Robin Gibb, [viii] Maurice Gibb/Robin Gibb, [ix] Blue Weaver.

369. GIBSON, Debbie (b. August 31, 1970, Long Island, NY) Pop pianist and vocalist. A childhood musical prodigy who began writing songs at the age of six, and signed her first record contract while still in high school. CHART COMPOSITIONS: *Only in My Dreams* (1987) US#4 UK#54, re-issued (1988) UK#11; *Shake Your Love* (1987) US#4 UK#7, *Out of the Blue* (1988) US#3 UK#19, *Foolish Beat* (1988) US#1 UK#9, *Staying Together* (1988) US#22 UK#53, *Lost in Your Eyes* (1989) US#1 UK#34, *Electric Youth* (1989) US#11 UK#14, *No More Rhyme* (1989) US#17, *We Could Be Together* (1989) US#71 UK#22, *Anything Is Possible* [i] (1990) US#26

UK#51, *Losin' Myself* [iii] (1993) US#86, *Shock Your Mama* (1993) UK#74. ALBUMS: **Out of the Blue** (1987) p US#7 UK#28, **Electric Youth** (1989) p US#1 UK#8, **Anything Is Possible** (1990) g US#41 UK#69, **Body and Soul** (1993, all Atlantic) US#109; **Think with Your Heart** (1995, SBK). COMPILATION: **Greatest Hits** (1995, Atlantic). HIT VERSION: *Jukebox in My Mind* [ii] Alabama (1990) C&W#1. Co-writers: [i] Lamont Dozier, [ii] E. Rogers, [iii] E. Rogers/C. Sturken.

370. GIBSON, Don (b. Donald Eugene Gibson, April 3, 1928, Shelby, NC) C&W guitarist and vocalist. A country performer who specialized in melancholic love songs, and, as on *Give Myself a Party*, ironic self-pity. Gibson's brand of pathos resulted in over eighty country hits between 1956–1980, and he was a major influence on Roy Orbison. By the age of fourteen, Gibson was performing on local radio shows and in clubs, and in 1952, he became a regular on the radio program "Barn Dance." Many unsuccessful years as a honky tonk singer finally paid off for Gibson when he scored his first hits in the late 1950s, his much recorded *I Can't Stop Lovin' You* having exceeded four million radio plays in America. CHART COMPOSITIONS: *Sweet Dreams* (1956) C&W#9, new version (1960) C&W#6 US#93; *Oh, Lonesome Me* (1958) C&W#1 US#7, *I Can't Stop Lovin' You* (1958) C&W#7 US#81, *Blue, Blue Day* (1958) C&W#1 US#20, *Give Myself a Party* (1958) C&W#5 US#46, *Look Who's Blue* (1958) C&W#8 US#58, *Who Cares* (1959) C&W#3 US#43, *A Stranger to Me* (1959) C&W#27, *Lonesome Old House* (1959) C&W#11 US#71, *Don't Tell Me Your Troubles* (1959) C&W#5 US#85, *Big Hearted Me* (1960) C&W#29, *Just One Time* (1960) C&W#2 US#29, *Far, Far Away* (1960) C&W#11 US#72, new version (1972) C&W#5; *What About Me* (1961) C&W#22 US#100, *Sea of Heartbreak* (1961) C&W#2 US#21 UK#14, *Lonesome Number One* (1961) C&W#2 US#59 UK#47, *The World Is Waiting for the Sunrise* (1961) US#108, *What About Me* (1961) US#100, *I Can Mend Your Broken Heart* (1962) C&W#5 US#105, *Head Over Heels in Love with You* (1963) C&W#12, *Anything New Gets Old (Except My Love for You)* (1963) C&W#22, *'Cause I Believe in You* (1964) C&W#23, *Again* (1965) C&W#19, *Watch Where You're Going* (1965) C&W#10, *A Born Loser* (1966) C&W#12, *(Yes) I'm Hurting* (1966) C&W#6, *All My Love* (1967) C&W#23, *Ashes of Love* (1968) C&W#37, *Good Morning Dear* (1968) C&W#71, *It's a Long, Long Way to Georgia* (1968) C&W#12, *Ever Changing Mind* (1968) C&W#30, *Rings of Gold*** (1969) C&W#2, *Solitary* (1969) C&W#28, *I Will Always* (1969) C&W#21, *There's a Story Goin' Round*** (1969)

C&W#7, *Don't Take All Your Loving* (1970) C&W#17, *A Perfect Mountain* (1970) C&W#16, *Someway* (1970) C&W#37, *Guess Away the Blues* (1971) C&W#19, *(I Heard That) Lonesome Whistle* (1971) C&W#29, *The Two of Us Together** (1971) C&W#50, *Country Green* (1971) C&W#5, *Did You Ever Think** (1972) C&W#71, *I Think They Call It Love** (1972) C&W#37, *Woman (Sensuous Woman)* (1972) C&W#1, *Is This the Best I'm Gonna Feel* (1972) C&W#11, *'Cause I Love You** (1972) C&W#64, *If You're Goin" Girl* (1973) C&W#26, *Go with Me** (1973) C&W#52, *Touch the Morning* (1973) C&W#6, *Warm Love* (1973) C&W#53, *That's What I'll Do* (1973) C&W#30, *Snap Your Fingers* (1973) C&W#12, *Bring Back Your Love to Me* (1974) C&W#9, *Good Old Fashioned Love** (1974) C&W#31, *I'll Sing for You* (1975) C&W#27, *(There She Goes) I Wish Her Well* (1975) C&W#24, *Don't Stop Loving Me* (1975) C&W#43, *Oh, How Love Changes** (1975) C&W#36, *I Don't Think I'll Ever (Get Over You)* (1976) C&W#76, *You Got to Stop Hurting Me Darling* (1976) C&W#79, *Doing My Time* (1976) C&W#39, *I'm All Wrapped Up in You* (1976) C&W#23, *Fan the Flame Feed the Fire* (1977) C&W#30, *The Fool* (1978) C&W#22, *Because* (1978) C&W#61, *Forever One at a Time* (1979) C&W#37, *Sweet Sensuous Sensations* (1980) C&W#42, *Love Fires* (1980) C&W#80. ALBUMS: **Oh, Lonesome Me** (1958), **Songs By Don Gibson** (1958), **The Gibson Boy** (1959), **No One Stands Alone** (1960), **Girls, Guitars and Gibson** (1961), **Some Favorites of Mine** (1962), **I Wrote a Song** (1963) US#134, **God Walks These Hills** (1964), **King of Country Soul** (1966), **Dottie and Don*** (1969, all RCA); **Look Who's Blue** (1978, ABC/Hickory). COMPILATIONS: **All Time Country Gold** (1970), **Best of Don Gibson** (1970, both RCA); **Very Best of Don Gibson** (1974, Hickory); **Famous Country Music Makers** (1978, RCA); **Country Number One** (1980, Warwick) UK#13; **20 of the Best** (1982, RCA); **Rockin," Rollin" Gibson** (1984, Bear Family); **Greatest Hits** (1984, RCA); **You Win Again** (1985, Sundown); **Don Gibson and Los Indios Tajaras** (1986), **Early Years** (1986, both Bear Family); **The Collection** (1987, Castle); **A Legend in My Time** (1987, Bear Family); **Greatest Hits** (1992, Woodford); **Don Gibson Sings Country Favorites** (1991, Pickwick); **Country Spotlight** (1992, DOM); **18 Greatest Hits** (1992, Collectibles). HIT VERSIONS: *Blue, Blue Day* Wilburn Brothers (1961) C&W#14, *Don't Tell Me Your Troubles* Kenny Price (1973) C&W#53, *Give Myself a Party* Rosemary Clooney (1961) US#108/Jeannie C. Riley (1972) C&W#12; *Heartbreak Avenue* Carl Smith (1970) C&W#35, *I Can't Stop Lovin' You* Kitty Wells (1958) C&W#3/Tommy Zang (1960) US#108/Ray Charles (1962) g R&B#1 US#1 UK#1/Count Basie (1963)

US#87/Tom Jones (1970) US#25/Conway Twitty (1972) C&W#1/Sammi Smith (1977) C&W#27/Mary K. Miller (1978) C&W#28; *(I'd Be) A Legend in My Time* Sammy Davis, Jr. (1973) US#116/Ronnie Milsap (1975) C&W#1; *If It Don't Come Easy* Tanya Tucker (1988) C&W#1, *Just One Time* Connie Smith (1971) C&W#2 US#119/Tompall & the Glaser Brothers (1981) C&W#17; *Oh, Lonesome Me* Bob Luman (1960) US#105/Johnny Cash (1961) C&W#13 US#93/Craig Douglas (1962) UK#15/Bobbi Martin (1966) C&W#64 US#134/Stonewall Jackson (1970) C&W#63/Loggins & Messina (1975) C&W#92, also on B-side of *A Lover's Question* (1975) US#89; *Oh, Such a Stranger* Frank Ifield (1967) C&W#68, *Sweet Dreams* Faron Young (1956) C&W#2/Dave Sampson (1960) UK#29/Patsy Cline (1963) C&W#5 US#44/Tommy McLain (1966) UK#49/Roy Buchanan (1973) UK#40/Reba McEntire (1979) C&W#19/ Elvis Costello (1981) UK#42; *There's a Big Wheel* Wilma Lee & Stoney Cooper (1959) C&W#3, *Wasted Words* Ray Price (1956) C&W#4. With: * Sue Thompson, ** Dottie West.

371. GIFT, Roland (b. May 28, 1962, Birmingham, England) Pop saxophonist and vocalist. The lead vocalist in the group Fine Young Cannibals. Gift has concentrated more on his acting career since the early 1990s. CHART COMPOSITIONS: *Johnny Come Home* [i] (1985) UK#8, re-issued (1986) US#76; *Blue* [i] (1985) UK#41, *Funny How Love Is* [i] (1986) UK#58, *She Drives Me Crazy* [i] (1989) US#1 UK#5, *Good Thing* [i] (1989) US#1 UK#7, *Don't Look Back* [i] (1989) US#11 UK#34, *I'm Not the Man I Used to Be* [i] (1989) US#54 UK#20, *I'm Not Satisfied* (1990) US#90 UK#46. ALBUMS: **Fine Young Cannibals** (1985) US#49 UK#11, **The Raw and the Cooked** (1989, both London) p US#1 UK#1. COMPILATIONS: **FYC: The Raw and the Remixed** (1992) UK#61, **Finest** (1996, both London) UK#10. Co-writer: [i] David Steele (b. September 8, 1960, Isle of Wight).

372. GILBERT, L. Wolfe (b. 1886, America; d. 1970) Film and stage composer. A newspaper columnist who became a Tin Pan Alley composer, and contributed songs to such shows as "Hullo Ragtime" (1912), "Push and Go" (1914) and "The Fabulous Dorseys" (1941). Gilbert's compositions were also featured in the film "The Story of Vernon and Irene Castle" (1938). HIT VERSIONS: *By Heck* [viii] Byron G. Harlan & Will Robbins (1915) US#6, *Camp Meeting Band* [xi] Arthur Collins & Byron Harlan (1914) US#9, *Chiquita* [xv] Paul Whiteman (1928) US#4, *Dance-O-Mania* [v] Ben Selvin (1920) US#14, *Don't Wake Me Up (Let Me Dream)* [iv] Howard Lanin (1926) US#10/Vincent Lopez (1925)

US#9; *Down Yonder* Ernest Hare & Billy Jones (1921) US#5/Peerless Quartet (1921) US#9/Gid Tanner (1934) US#10/Champ Butler (1951) US#17/Joe "Fingers" Carr (1951) US#14/Lawrence "Piano Roll" Cook (1951) US#22/Freddy Martin (1951) US#15/Frank Petty Trio (1951) US#26/Ethel Smith (1951) US#16/Del Wood (1951) g Johnny & the Hurricanes (1960) UK#8; *Green Eyes* [x] Xavier Cugat (1941) US#16/Jimmy Dorsey (1941) g US#1/Tony Pastor (1941) US#21; *Here Comes My Daddy Now (Oh Pop-Oh Pop-Oh Pop)* [xi] Arthur Collins & Byron Harlan (1913) US#6, *Hitchy-Koo* [i] American Quartet (1913) US#5, I Miss My Swiss *(My Swiss Miss Misses Me)* [ii] Ernest Hare & Billy Jones (1925) US#3/Paul Whiteman (1925) US#6; *Jeannine (I Dream of Lilac Time)* [xii] Gene Austin (1928) US#1/Ben Selvin (1928) US#6/Nat Shilkret (1928) US#2/John McCormack (1929) US#15; *Lucky Lindy* [ii] Vernon Dalhart (1927) US#11, *Mama Don't Want No Peas, an' Rice, an' Coconut Oil* [ix] Count Basie (1938) US#17, *Mama Inez* [vii] Maurice Chevalier (1931) US#18, *Marta (Rambling Rose of the Wildwood)* [xiii] Arthur Tracy (1932) US#19/Tony Martin (1950) US#15/Bachelors (1967) UK#20, *My Mother's Eyes* [ii] George Jessel (1929) US#8, *O Katharina!* [vi] Carl Fenton (1925) US#13/Ted Lewis (1925) US#1/Vincent Lopez (1925) US#5; *Peanut Vendor, The* [xiv] Louis Armstrong (1931) US#15, re-issued (1941) US#25/Don Azpiazu (1931) US#1/California Ramblers (1931) US#5/Red Nichols (1931) US#5; *Ragging the Baby to Sleep* [xi] Al Jolson (1912) US#1, *Ramona* [xv] Gene Austin (1928) g US#1/Ruth Etting (1928) US#10/Scrappy Lambert (1928) US#18/Paul Whiteman (1928) US#1/Gaylords (1953) US#12/Bachelors (1964) UK#4/Billy Walker (1968) C&W#8; *Waiting for the Robert E. Lee* [xi] Arthur Collins & Byron Harlan (1912) US#3/Dolly Connolly (1912) US#4/Heidelberg Quintet (1912) US#1; *When You're Somebody Else* [iii] Seger Ellis (1928) US#4/Louis Armstrong (1929) US#15/Ted Wallace (1930) US#17. Co-writers: [i] Maurice Abrahams/Lewis Muir, [ii] Abel Baer, [iii] Abel Baer/Ruth Etting (b. November 23, 1907, David City, NE; d. September 24, 1978), [iv] Abel Baer/Mabel Wayne, [v] Joe Cooper, [vi] Richard Fall, [vii] Eliseo Grenet, [viii] S.R. Henry, [ix] Charles Lofthouse, [x] Milo Menendez/Adolfo Utrera, [xi] Lewis Muir (b. Louis Frank Meuer, May 30, 1883; d. December 3, 1915, both New York, NY], [xii] Nat Shilkret, [xiii] Moises Simons, [xiv] Moises Simons/Marion Sunshine, [xv] Mabel Wayne.

373. GILBERT, Sir William Schwenck
(b. November 18, 1836, London; d. May 29, 1911, Harrow, both England) Stage composer, and **SULLIVAN, Sir Arthur Seymour** (b. May 13, 1842; d. November 21, 1900, both London, England) stage

lyricist. One of popular music's first songwriting partnerships, who specialized in comic operetta. Gilbert and Sullivan were the most important influence on the development of the popular song in Victorian England, pre-dating such revered American composers as Richard Rodgers and Lorenz Hart by nearly a century. Gilbert wrote bitingly satirical and immensely witty lyrics, which were set to Sullivan's dramatic melodies. Their first successful show was the legal spoof "Trial By Jury" (1875), which they followed with "H.M.S. Pinafore" (1878), "The Pirates of Penzance" (1879), "Patience" (1881), "Iolanthe" (1882), "Princess Ida" (1884), "The Mikado" (1885), "Ruddigore" (1887), "The Yeoman of the Guard" (1888), "The Gondoliers" (1889), "Utopia Limited" (1893), and "The Grand Duke" (1896). By 1881, Gilbert and Sullivan's works were being performed at the Savoy Theatre in London, which had been opened solely to stage their thinly disguised attacks on bureaucrats and politicians. Some of their most popular compositions were *The Lost Chord* (1877), *Farewell My Own* (1878), *Three Little Maids* (1885), *Tit Willow* (1885), and *Take a Pair of Sparkling Eyes* (1888). Their songs were recorded by Stanley Holloway and Joyce Grenfell on the album **The Bab Ballads and Cautionary Verses** (1988, Caedmon). ALBUMS: **The Sorcerer** oc (1959), **The Pirates of Penzance** oc (1968, both Decca); **The World of Gilbert and Sullivan, Volumes 1, 2 and 3** (1969, all WOL); **H.M.S. Pinafore** oc (1974, EMI); **Sullivan Highlights** (1976, Classics for Pleasure); **D'Oyly Carte, 1875–1975** (1979), **Iolanthe** oc (1979), **Patience** oc (1979), **Princess Ida** oc (1979), **Savoy Opera** (1979), **The Yeoman of the Guard/Ballet Suite** (1979, all Decca); **The Pirates of Penzance** oc (1981, Elektra) US#178; **The Pirate Movie** ost (1982, Polydor) US#166; **Gilbert and Sullivan Duets** (1983, HMV); **Gilbert and Sullivan Spectacular** (1983, Spot); **The Yeoman of the Guard/The Gondoliers** oc (1983, Ditto); **The Gondoliers/Ruddigore** oc (1984, PRT); **A Gilbert and Sullivan Gala** (1985), **Gilbert and Sullivan Favorites** (1985), **More Gilbert and Sullivan Favorites** (1985, all HMV); **The Sorcerer** oc (1987, Savoy); **Sullivan Overtures** (1987, Classics for Pleasure); **Best of Gilbert and Sullivan** (1988, EMI); **The Gondoliers** oc (1988), **H.M.S. Pinafore/Trial By Jury** oc (1988, both Angel); **H.M.S. Pinafore/Yeoman of the Guard** oc (1988, HMV); **Iolanthe** oc (1988, Angel); **Iolanthe/Patience** oc (1988), **The Mikado** oc (1988, both HMV); **The Pirates of Penzance** oc (1988), **Ruddigore** oc (1988, both Angel); **Ruddigore/The Pirates of Penzance** oc (1988, HMV); **The Yeoman of the Guard** oc (1988, Angel); **Heyday of Gilbert and Sullivan** (1989, HMV); **The Mikado** oc (1989, TER); **Patience** oc (1988, Angel);

Sullivan Overtures (1988, Nimbus); **The Mikado** tvst (1989, Silva Screen). HIT VERSIONS: *Gems from the Pirates of Penzance* Victor Light Opera Co. (1911) US#10, *How Can I Love Without Her* Christopher Atkins (1982) US#71.

374. GILKYSON, Terry (b. Hamilton Henry Gilkyson, 1919, Phoenixville, PA) Pop vocalist. A pop composer who penned the delightful theme *The Bare Necessities*, from the film "Jungle Book" (1967). Gilkyson made a number of recordings with his group the Easy Riders, but was considerably more successful as a songwriter for others. CHART COMPOSITION: *Marianne* [i] (1957) US#4. ALBUMS: **Golden Minutes of Folk Music** (1953, Brunswick); **Rollin'** (1961), **Remember the Alamo** (1961, both London); **Moon Spinners** ost (1964, Buena Vista); **The Aristocats** ost (1971, Disneyland). HIT VERSIONS: *Bare Necessities, The* UK Mixmasters (1991) UK#14, *Cry of the Wild Goose, The* Tennessee Ernie Ford (1950) C&W#2 US#15/ Frankie Laine (1950) g US#1/Baja Marimba Band (1967) US#113; *Day of Jubilo, The* Guy Mitchell (1952) US#26, *Girl in the Wood, The* [ii] Frankie Laine (1951) US#23, *Green Fields* [i] Brothers Four (1960) US#2 UK#40/Vogues (1969) US#92; *Love Is a Golden Ring* [i] Frankie Laine (1957) US#10, *Marianne* [i] Hilltoppers (1957) US#3 UK#20, *Memories Are Made of This* [i] Dave King (1956) UK#5/Dean Martin (1956) US#1 UK#1/Gale Storm (195) US#5/Val Doonican (1967) UK#11/Gene & Debbe (1969) US#114/Tommy O'Day (1978) C&W#82; *Mister Tap-Toe* [i] Doris Day (1953) US#10, *Rock of Gibraltar* Frankie Laine (1952) US#20, *Tell Me a Story* Frankie Laine & Jimmy Boyd (1953) US#4 UK#5, *Where the Wind Blows* Frankie Laine (1953) UK#2. Co-writers: [i] Richard Dehr/ Frank Miller, [ii] Neal Gilkyson/Stewart Gilkyson.

375. GILL, Vince (b. April 5, 1957, Norman, OK) C&W guitarist and vocalist. One of the few country stars of the 1990s whose music is still routed in past genres and traditions. Gill first performed bluegrass in high school as a member of the groups Mountain Smoke, the Bluegrass Alliance and Sundance. Between 1979–1983 he was the lead vocalist in the country-rock act Pure Prairie League, charting with the single *I'm Almost Ready* (1980) C&W# US#34, and featuring on the albums **Firin' Up** (1980) US#37 and **Something in the Night** (1981, both Casablanca) US#72. Gill has recorded as a solo artist since 1984. CHART COMPOSITIONS: *Victim of Life's Circumstances* (1984) C&W#40, *Oh, Carolina* (1984) C&W#38, *Turn Me Loose* (1984) C&W#39, *True Love* (1985) C&W#32, *If It Weren't for Him* (1985) C&W#10, *Oklahoma Borderline*

(1985) C&W#9, *With You* (1986) C&W#33, *Cinderella* (1987) C&W#5, *Let's Do Something* (1987) C&W#16, *Everybody's Sweetheart* (1988) C&W#11, *The Radio* (1988) C&W#39, *Oklahoma Swing* with Reba McEntire (1990) C&W#13, *When I Call Your Name* with Patty Loveless (1990) C&W#2, *Never Knew Lonely* (1990) C&W#3, *Liza Jane* [vi] (1991) C&W#40+, *Look at Us* [i] (1991) C&W#5, *Take Your Memory with You* (1992) C&W#2, *I Still Believe in You* [iv] (1992) C&W#1, *Don't Let Our Love Start Slippin' Away* [vii] (1992) C&W#1, *No Future in the Past* (1993) C&W#12, *One More Last Chance* [v] (1993) C&W#1, *Tryin' to Get Over You* (1994) C&W#1 US#88, *Whenever You Come Around* [vii] (1994) C&W#2 US#72, *What the Cowgirls Do* [vi] (1994) C&W#18+, *High Lonesome Sound* (1996) C&W#35+. ALBUMS: **Vince Gill** (1985, RCA); **When I Call Your Name** (1989) p US#67, **Pocketful of Gold** (1991) p US#37, **I Still Believe in You** (1992) p US#10, **Let There Be Peace on Earth** (1993) g US#14, **When Love Finds You** (1994) p US#6, **Souvenirs** (1995) p US#11, **High Lonesome Sound** (1996, all MCA). COMPILATIONS: **Best of Vince Gill** (1994), **The Essential Vince Gill** (1996, both RCA). HIT VERSION: *Here We Are* [ii] Alabama (1991) C&W#20. Co-writers: [i] M.D. Barnes, [ii] B.N. Chapman, [iii] C. Jackson, [iv] John B. Jarvis, [v] Gary Nicholson, [vi] R. Nielsen, [vii] Pete Wasner.

376. GILLESPIE, Haven (b. 1888; d. 1975) Pop lyricist. HIT VERSIONS: *Drifting and Dreaming (Sweet Paradise)* [i] George Olsen (1926) US#3, *Kiss* [iii] Dean Martin (1953) UK#5, *Old Master Painter, The* [iv] Phil Harris (1950) US#10/ Richard Hayes (1950) US#2/Dick Haymes (1940) US#4/Snooky Lanson (1950) US#12/Peggy Lee & Mel Torme (1950) US#9/Frank Sinatra (1950) US#13; *That Lucky Old Sun* [iv] Louis Armstrong (1949) R&B#14 US#19/Frankie Laine (1949) g US#1/Herb Lance & the Classics (1949) R&B#6 US#19/Bob Houston (1949) US#27/Vaughn Monroe (1949) US#6/Frank Sinatra (1949) US#16/Sarah Vaughan (1949) US#14/Velvets (1961) UK#46/Ray Charles (1964) US#20/Solomon Burke (1969) US#129/Nat Stuckey (1978) C&W#66; *You're in Kentucky as Sure as You're Born* [ii] Jan Garber (1924) US#10/Isham Jones (1924) US#7. Co-writers: [i] Loyal Curtis/ Erwin Schmidt/Egbert Van Alstyne, [ii] George Little/Larry Shay, [iii] Lionel Newman, [iv] Beasley Smith. (*See also under* John F. COOTS, Pete WENDLING, Richard A. WHITING, Victor YOUNG.)

377. GILMORE, Jimmie Dale (b. Austin, TX) C&W guitarist and vocalist. A former member of the group the Flatlanders, whose material has been recorded by such artists as Joe Ely. CHART COMPOSITION: *White Freight Liner Blues* (1988) C&W#72. ALBUMS: **Fair and Square** (1987), **Jimmie Dale Gilmore** (1989, both Demon); **Two Roads** with Butch Hancock (1990, Virgin); **After Awhile** (1991), **Spinning Around the Sun** (1993), **Braver Newer World** (1996, all Elektra). (*See also under* Butch HANCOCK.)

378. GIMBEL, Norman (b. America) Pop lyricist. A versatile lyricist whose most productive partnership was with the composer Charles Fox. Gimble also won a best original song Oscar for *It Goes Like It Goes*, from the film "Norma Rae" (1980). ALBUMS: **Whoop-Up!** oc (1958, MGM); **Washington Behind Closed Doors** tvst (1977, ABC). HIT VERSIONS: *Canadian Sunset* [viii] Hugo Winterhalter & Eddie Heywood (1956) R&B#7 US#2/Andy Williams (1956) US#7/Etta Jones (1961) US#91/Sounds Orchestral (1965) US#76; *Good Friend* [ii] Mary MacGregor (1979) US#39, *I Will Follow Him* [i] Little Peggy March (1963) R&B#1 US#1, *Land of Dreams* [viii] Hugo Winterhalter (1954) US#28, *Only Love* [vi] Nana Mouskouri (1986) UK#2, *Pa-Paya Mama* [v] Perry Como (1953) US#11, *Ricochet (Rick-O-Shay)* [iv] Teresa Brewer (1953) US#2/Joan Regan (1953) UK#8; *Summer Samba (So Nice)* [x] Walter Wanderly (1966) US#26, *Sway* [ix] Eileen Barton (1954) US#21/Dean Martin (1954) US#15 UK#6/Bobby Rydell (1960) US#14 UK#12; *Tennessee Wig-Walk, The* [iii] Bonnie Lou (1954) UK#4. Co-writers: [i] Arthur Altman/Del Roma/J.W. Stole, [ii] Elmer Bernstein, [iii] Larry Coleman, [iv] Larry Coleman/Joe Darion, [v] Larry Coleman/George Sandler, [vi] Vladimir Cosma, [vii] Pablo Beltran Ruiz, [viii] Eddie Heywood, [ix] Pablo Beltran Ruiz, [x] Macros Valle/Paulo Sergio Valle. (*See also under* Charles FOX, Antonio Carlos JOBIM, Michel LEGRAND.)

379. GLENN, Garry (b. Detroit, IL) R&B keyboard player, producer and vocalist. A former gospel choir director whose songs have been interpreted by Philip Bailey, the Dramatics and Eddie Kendricks. Glenn recorded as a solo artist during the 1980s. CHART COMPOSITIONS: *Do You Have to Go* (1987) R&B#37, *Feels Good to Feel Good* featuring Sheila Hutchinson (1987) R&B#37. ALBUM: **Garry Glenn** (1980, PPL). HIT VERSIONS: *Caught Up in the Rapture* [i] Anita Baker (1986) R&B#6 US#37 UK#51, *Flame of Love* Jean Carne (1986) R&B#21, *Heaven in Your Arms* R.J.'s Latest Arrival (1986) R&B#12, *Spread Love* Al Hudson & the Soul Partners (1978) R&B#75. Co-writer: [i] Dianne Quander.

380. GODDARD, Geoff (b. England) Pop vocalist. A singer who recorded for HMV Records during the early 1960s, but who was only ever successful as a songwriter in collaboration with the influential producer Joe Meek. HIT VERSIONS: *Country Boy* Heinz (1963) UK#26, *Don't You Think It's Time* [i] Mike Berry (1963) UK#6, *Johnny Remember Me* John Leyton (1961) UK#1/Meteors (1983) UK#66; *Just Like Eddie* Heinz (1963) UK#5, *Lonely City* John Leyton (1962) UK#14, *Son This Is She* John Leyton (1961) UK#15, *Tribute to Buddy Holly* Mike Berry (1961) UK#24, *Wild Wind* John Leyton (1961) UK#2. Co-writer: [i] Joe Meek (b. Robert Meek, 1929, Newent, England; d. February 3, 1967, London, England).

381. GOFFIN, Gerry (b. February 11, 1939, Queens, NY) Pop lyricist and vocalist. One of the Brill Building's most successful lyricists, who wrote most of his biggest hits in partnership with Carole King. ALBUM: **It Ain't Exactly Entertainment** (1973, Adelphi). HIT VERSIONS: *I've Got to Use My Imagination* [i] Gladys Knight & the Pips (1973) g R&B#1 US#4, *Yes I Will* [ii] Hollies (1965) UK#9. Co-writers: [i] Barry Goldberg, [ii] Russ Titleman. (*See also under* Wes FARRELL, Jack KELLER, Carole KING, Barry MANN, Michael MASSER.)

382. GOLD, Andrew (b. August 2, 1951, Burbank, CA). Pop multi-instrumentalist and vocalist. A singer-songwriter whose father was the film composer Ernest Gold. At the age of thirteen, Gold learned the piano, guitar and drums, before playing in the high school bands the Doberman, the Herd and the Wails. In 1964, he released an unsuccessful solo single *All the Little Girls*, and in 1969, he formed the group Bryndle with Kenny Edwards and Karla Bonoff. After performing as a member of the Rangers, between 1973–1974, Gold toured as a backing musician for the vocalist Linda Ronstadt. As a producer and musician he also worked with Rita Coolidge, Art Garfunkel and Carly Simon. During the mid-1970s Gold recorded as a solo artist, but after the failure of his marriage to the singer Nicolette Larson in 1980, he moved to England and formed the group Common Knowledge with Graham Gouldman, which, renamed Wax, charted with *Get Loose* [ii] (1981) R&B#79, *Right Between the Eyes* [ii] (1986) US#43 UK#36 and *Bridge to Your Heart* [ii] (1987) UK#12. ALBUMS: **Magnetic Heaven** (1986) US#101, **American English** (1987, both RCA) UK#59. COMPILATION: **The Wax Files** (1997, For Your Love). In the mid-1980s, Gold abandoned his solo career and returned to session work. CHART COMPOSITIONS: *That's Why I Love You* [i] (1976) US#68, *Lonely Boy* (1977) US#7 UK#11, *Never Let*

Her Slip Away (1978) US#67 UK#5, *How Can This Be Love* (1978) UK#19, *Thank You for Being a Friend* (1978) US#25 UK#42. ALBUMS: **Andrew Gold** (1975) US#190, **What's Wrong with This Picture?** (1976) US#95, **All This and Heaven Too** (1978) US#81 UK#31, **Whirlwind** (1980, all Asylum). COMPILATION: **Never Let Her Slip Away-14 Classic Tracks** (1993, Elektra). HIT VERSIONS: *Never Let Her Slip Away* Trevor Walters (1984) UK#73/Undercover (1992) UK#5. Co-writers: [i] G. Garfin, [ii] Graham Gouldman. (*See also under* Karla BONOFF.)

383. GOLDSBORO, Bobby (b. January 18, 1941, Marianna, FL) Pop guitarist and vocalist. A former backing guitarist for Roy Orbison who became a successful pop and country influenced solo performer. Goldsboro's biggest hit was a ten million selling version of Bobby Russell's composition *Honey* (1968). Between 1972–1975, Goldsboro hosted his own syndicated television show. CHART COMPOSITIONS: *Molly* (1962) US#70, *See the Funny Little Clown* (1964) US#9, *Whenever He Holds You* (1964) US#39, *I Don't Know You Anymore* (1964) US#105, *Little Things* (1965) US#13, *If You Wait for Love* (1965) US#75, *If You've Got a Heart* (1965) US#60, *Broomstick Cowboy* (1965) US#53, *Take Your Love* (1966) US#114, *It's Too Late* (1966) US#23, *Voodoo Woman* (1965) US#27, *It Hurts Me* (1966) US#70, *I Know You Better Than That* (1966) US#56, *Goodbye to All You Women* (1967) US#102, *JoJo's Place* (1967) US#111, *Pledge of Love* (1967) US#118, *Autumn of My Life* (1968) US#19, *Glad She's a Woman* (1969) C&W#49 US#61, *I'm a Drifter* (1969) C&W#22 US#46, *Muddy Mississippi Line* (1969) C&W#15 US#53, *Mornin', Mornin'* (1969) C&W#56 US#78, *Can You Feel It* (1970) US#53, *It's Gonna Change* (1970) US#108, *Come Back Home* (1971) US#69, *Danny Is a Mirror to Me* (1971) US#107, *With Pen in Hand* (1972) US#94, *Summer (The First Time)* (1973) C&W#100 US#21 UK#9, *Brand New Kind of Love* (1973) US#116, *Marlena* (1974) C&W#52, *I Believe the South Is Gonna Rise Again* (1974) C&W#62, *A Butterfly for Bucky* (1976) C&W#22 US#101, *The Cowboy and the Lady* (1977) C&W#85, *Me and the Elephants* (1977) C&W#82 US#104. ALBUMS: **Honey** (1968) g US#5, **Word Pictures featuring Autumn of My Life** (1968) US#116, **Today** (1969) US#60, **Muddy Mississippi Line** (1970) US#139, **We Gotta Start Lovin'** (1971) US#120, **Come Back Home** (1971) US#142, **Summer (The First Time)** (1973, all United Artists) US#150; **Goldsboro** (1977, Epic); **Roundup Saloon** (1982, Curb). COMPILATIONS: **Solid Goldsboro-Greatest Hits** (1967) US#165, **Greatest Hits** (1970) US#103, **10th Anniversary Album** (1974, all United Artists) US#174;

Very Best of Bobby Goldsboro (1989, C5). HIT VERSIONS: *Cowboy and the Lady, The* Patsy Sledd (1976) C&W#90/Tommy Cash (1977) C&W#63/ John Denver (1981) C&W#50 US#66; *Little Things* Dave Berry (1965) UK#5/Tennessee Express (1981) C&W#75; *See the Funny Little Clown* Billie Jo Spears (1974) C&W#80, *Whenever She Holds You* Patty Duke (1966) US#64, *With Pen in Hand* Johnny Darrell (1968) C&W#3 US#126/Billy Vera (1968) US#43/Vikki Carr (1969) US#35/Dorothy Moore (1978) R&B#12 US#101.

384. GOODHART, Al (b. America) Film and stage composer. A Tin Pan Alley composer whose songs were included in the film "Johnny Douglas" (1943) and the show "Hi-De-Hi" (1943). HIT VERSIONS: *Johnny Doughboy Found a Rose in Ireland* [i] Kenny Baker (1942) US#11/Sammy Kaye (1942) US#13/Kay Kyser (1942) US#2/Guy Lombardo (1942) US#9/Freddy Martin (1942) US#11/ Tommy Tucker (1942) US#13; *Serenade of the Bells* [ii] Jo Stafford (1947) US#6/Sammy Kaye (1948) US#3/Kay Kyser (1948) US#13. Co-writers: [i] Kay Twomey, [ii] Kay Twomey/Al Urbano. (*See also under* Milton AGER, Al HOFFMAN, George W. MEYER.)

385. GOODMAN, Steve (b. July 25, 1948, Chicago, IL; d. September 20, 1984) Folk guitarist and vocalist. A folk story teller in a traditional style, whose career was cut short when he died of leukemia at the age of thirty-six. Goodman's best known song is the much recorded *City of New Orleans*. He had studied political science at the University of Illinois in 1964, before writing jingles for radio commercials and performing solo in folk clubs. His recordings for the Buddah label featured elements of folk, blues, ragtime and jazz, but his Asylum releases were decidedly more commercial. CHART COMPOSITION: *City of New Orleans* (1972) US#113. ALBUMS: **Steve Goodman** (1971), **Somebody Else's Troubles** (1973, both Buddah); **Jessie's Jig and Other Favorites** (1975) US#144, **Words We Can Dance To** (1976) US#175, **Say It in Private** (1977), **High and Outside** (1979), **Hotspot** (1980, all Asylum); **Gathering at the Earl of Old Town** (1980, Mountain Railroad); **Artistic Hair** (1983), **Affordable Art** (1983), **Santa Ana Winds** (1984), **Unfinished Business** (1984, all Red Pajamas). COMPILATIONS: **The Essential Steve Goodman** (1975, Buddah); **Best of the Asylum Years, Volume 1** (1985), **Best of the Asylum Years, Volume 2** (1985), **My Second Prime** (1991, all Red Pajamas). HIT VERSIONS: *City of New Orleans* Arlo Guthrie (1972) US#18/Sammi Smith (1973) C&W#44/Willie Nelson (1984) C&W#1; *You Never Even Called Me By My Name* David Allan Coe (1975) C&W#8.

386. GORDON, Mack (b. Morris Gittler, June 21, 1904, Warsaw, Poland; d. March 1, 1959, New York, NY) Film and stage lyricist. An American immigrant who became a successful lyricist, and occassional composer during the 1930s. After singing soprano in a minstrel show, Gordon turned to songwriting, and contributed to such films as "Song of the Islands" (1942) and "Wabash Avenue" (1950). HIT VERSIONS: *In an Old Dutch Garden* [ii] Eddy Duchin (1940) US#15/Dick Jurgens (1940) US#3/ Glenn Miller (1940) US#8; *Kokomo, Indiana* [iii] Vaughn Monroe (1947) US#10, *Lookie, Lookie, Here Comes Cookie* Glen Gray (1935) US#7, *Mam'selle* [i] Dennis Day (1947) US#8/Ray Dorey (1947) US#7/ Dick Haymes (1947) US#3/Frankie Laine (1947) US#14/Art Lund (1947) US#1/Pied Pipers (1947) US#3/Frank Sinatra (1947) US#1; *On the Boardwalk in Atlantic City* [iii] Charioteers (1946) US#12/Dick Haymes (1947) US#21; *Sing Me a Song of the Islands* [iv] Bing Crosby (1942) US#22, *This Is the Beginning of the End* Don Cornell (1952) US#20, *You Do It* [iii] Bing Crosby (1947) US#8/Vic Damone (1947) US#7/Vaughn Monroe (1947) US#5/Dinah Shore (1947) US#4/Margaret Whiting (1947) US#5; *You Make Me Feel So Young* [iii] Dick Haymes (1946) US#21. Co-writers: [i] Edmund Goulding, [ii] Will Grosz, [iii] Joseph Myrow, [iv] Harry Owens. (*See also under* Ray HENDERSON, Harry REVEL, Jimmy VAN HEUSEN, Harry WARREN, Vincent YOUMANS.)

387. GORDY, Berry, Jr. (b. November 28, 1929, Detroit, MI) R&B producer and arranger. A high school drop out, who, on January 12, 1959, borrowed eight hundred dollars from his family credit union and founded Motown Records, which became the most successful black owned record company in the world, and was sold by Berry to MCA Records in 1988 for a reported eighty million dollars. Gordy was initially an aspiring songwriter, who had sufficient vision and determination to create an entirely new style of black pop music, which later became known as the "Motown Sound." Gordy worked for the Ford Motor Company before running an unsuccessful record shop with his friend Marv Johnson. In 1957, he began writing songs and producing such singles as *Ooh Shucks* by the Five Stars. Jackie Wilson recorded a handful of Gordy's earliest songs, including the million seller *Lonely Teardrops* [v] (1958), after which, Gordy decided to form his own record label. One of his earliest discs was *I Need You* by the Rayber Voices, which he licensed to a local label for distribution. In order to publish his tunes, Gordy formed the company Jobette, which became one of the most widely recorded song catalogues in the world. HIT VERSIONS: *ABC* [xiii] Jackson Five (1970) R&B#1 US#1 UK#8, *All I Could Do Was Cry* Etta James (1960) R&B#2 US#35, *Bye Bye Baby* Mary Wells (1960) R&B#8 US#60, *Can You Do It* Contours (1964) US#41, *Come to Me* [xii] Marv Johnson (1959) R&B#6 US#30, *Darling Dear* Smokey Robinson & the Miracles (1970) US#100, *Do You Love Me* Contours (1962) R&B#1 US#3, reissued (1988) US#11/Dave Clark Five (1963) US#11 UK#3/Andy Fraser (1983) US#82; *Dream Come True* Temptations (1962) R&B#22, *Get It Together* [xiii] Jackson Five (1973) R&B#2 US#28, *Good Thing Going, A* [xiii] Sugar Minott (1981) UK#4, *Happy Days* Marv Johnson (1960) R&B#7 US#58, *I Love the Way You Love Me* [xi] Marv Johnson (1960) R&B#2 US#9 UK#35, *I Want You Back* [xiii] Jackson Five (1969) R&B#1 US#1 UK#2, re-mixed (1988) UK#8/Graham Parker & the Rumour (1979) US#103; *I'll Be Satisfied* [v] Jackie Wilson (1959) R&B#6 US#20/Don Adams (1973) C&W#91/ Shakin' Stevens (1982) UK#10; *I'll Be There* [viii] Jackson Five (1970) R&B#1 US#1 UK#4/Cissy Houston (1970) R&B#45 US#125/Mariah Carey (1992) R&B#11 US#1 UK#2; *I'm Living in Shame* [vii] Diana Ross & the Supremes (1969) R&B#8 US#10 UK#14, *I'm So Glad I Fell for You* David Ruffin (1969) R&B#18 US#53, *Let Me Go the Right Way* Supremes (1962) R&B#26 US#90, *Lonely Teardrops* [v] Jackie Wilson (1958) g R&B#1 US#7/ Rose Maddox (1963) C&W#18/Brian Hyland (1971) US#54/Narvel Felts (1976) C&W#5 UK#62; *Love You Save, The* [xiii] Jackson Five (1970) R&B#1 US#1 UK#7, *Mama's Pearl* [xiii] Jackson Five (1971) R&B#2 US#2, *Maybe Tomorrow* [xiii] Jackson Five (1971) R&B#3 US#20, *Merry-Go-Round* Marv Johnson (1961) R&B#26 US#61, *Money (That's What I Want)* [ii] Barrett Strong (1960) R&B#2 US#23/ Bern Elliot & the Fenmen (1963) UK#14/Kingsmen (1964) US#16/Junior Walker & the All Stars (1966) R&B#35 US#52/Flying Lizards (1979) US#50 UK#5/Backbeat Band (1994) UK#48; *No Matter What Sign You Are* [vi] Supremes (1969) R&B#16 US#31 UK#37, *O.P.P.* [iii] Naughty By Nature (1991) p R&B#5 US#6; *Power* [i] Temptations (1980) R&B#11 US#43, *Reet Petite* [iv] Jackie Wilson (1957) US#62 UK#6, re-issued (1986) UK#1/Darts (1979) UK#52; *Shake Sherrie* Contours (1963) R&B#21 US#43/Harvey Russell & the Rogues (1966) US#131; *Sugar Daddy* [xiii] Jackson Five (1971) R&B#3 US#10, *Talk That Talk* Jackie Wilson (1959) R&B#3 US#34, *That's Why (I Love You So)* [v] Jackie Wilson (1959) R&B#2 US#13, *To Be Loved* [v] Jackie Wilson (1958) R&B#7 US#23 UK#23/Malcom Vaughan (1958) UK#14/Lenny Welch (1970) US#110/ Peggy Sue (1978) C&W#85/Michael Henderson (1979) R&B#62; *Try It Baby* Marvin Gaye (1964) US#15, *We Have Love* Jackie Wilson (1957) US#93,

You Ain't Gonna Find Cornell Blakely (1961) US#116, *You Better Know It* Jackie Wilson (1959) R&B#1 US#37, *You Got What It Takes* [ix] Marv Johnson (1959) R&B#2 US#10 UK#5/Johnny Kidd & the Pirates (1960) UK#25/Joe Tex (1965) US#51/Dave Clark Five (1967) US#7 UK#28; *You've Made Me So Very Happy* [x] Brenda Holloway (1967) R&B#40 US#39/Blood, Sweat & Tears (1969) g R&B#46 US#2/Lou Rawls (1970) R&B#32 US#95. Co-writers: [i] Angelo Bond/J. Mayer, [ii] Janie Bradford, [iii] V. Brown/A. Criss/K. Gisa, [iv] Tyran Carlo, [v] Tyran Carlo/Gwen Gordy, [vi] Henry Cosby, [vii] Henry Cosby/Pam Sawyer/R. Dean Taylor/Frank Wilson, [viii] Hal Davis/Willie Hutch (b. Willie McKinley Hutchinson, 1946, Los Angeles, CA)/Bobby West, [ix] Raquel Davis/Gwen Gordy, [x] Brenda Holloway (b. June 21, 1946, Atascadero, CA)/Patrice Holloway/Frank Wilson, [xi] Mikal John, [xii] Marv Johnson (b. October 15, 1938, Detroit, MI), [xiii] Al Mizell/Freddie Perren/Deke Richards. (*See also under* George CLINTON, Marvin GAYE, Smokey ROBINSON.)

388. GORE, Martin L. (b. July 23, 1961, Basildon, England) Pop drummer. A founder member of the British synthesizer group Depeche Mode. CHART COMPOSITIONS: *See You* (1982) UK#6, *The Meaning of Love* (1982) UK#12, *Leave in Silence* (1981) UK#18, *Get the Balance Right* (1983) UK#13, *Everything Counts* (1983) UK#6, live version (1989) UK#22; *Love in Itself* (1983) UK#21, *People Are People* (1984) US#13 UK#4, *Master and Servant* (1984) US#87 UK#9, *Somebody/Blasphemous* (1984) UK#16, *Shake the Disease* (1985) UK#18, *It's Called a Heart* (1985) UK#18, *Stripped* (1986) UK#15, *A Question of Lust* (1985) UK#28, *A Question of Time* (1986) UK#17, *Strangelove* (1987) US#76 UK#16, re-mixed (1988) US#50; *Never Let Me Down* (1987) US#63 UK#22, *Behind the Wheel* (1988) US#61 UK#21, *Little 15* (1988) UK#60, *Personal Jesus* (1989) US#28 UK#13, *Enjoy the Silence* (1990) US#8 UK#6, *Policy of Truth* (1990) US#15 UK#16, *World in My Eyes* (1990) US#52 UK#17, *I Feel You* (1993) US#37 UK#8, *Walking in My Shoes* (1993) US#69 UK#14, *Condemnation EP* (1993) UK#9, *In Your Room* (1994) UK#8. ALBUMS: **Speak and Spell** (1981) US#192 UK#10, **A Broken Frame** (1982) US#177 UK#8, **Construction Time Again** (1983) UK#6, **People Are People** (1984) g US#71, **Some Great Reward** (1984) US#51 UK#5, **Black Celebration** (1986) g US#90 UK#4, **Music for the Masses** (1987) p US#35 UK#10, **101** ost (1989) g US#45, **Violator** (1990) p US#7 UK#2, **Songs of Faith and Devotion** (1993) US#1 UK#1, **Songs of Love and Devotion-Live** (1993) US#193, **Ultra** (1997, all Mute). COMPILATIONS: **The Singles, 1981–1985** (1985,

Mute) UK#6; **Catching Up with Depeche Mode** (1987, Sire) g US#113. Gore also recorded an album as a solo artist, **Counterfeit E.P.** (1989, Mute) US#156 UK#51.

389. GOULDMAN, Graham (b. May 10, 1946, Manchester, England) Pop guitarist, keyboard player, producer, and vocalist. A founder member of the group 10 c.c., who had started his career as a 1960s hit songwriter when his song *Susan's Tuba* (1969) became a million seller in France for Freddie and the Dreamers. Gouldman subsequently performed as a member of Wayne Fontana and the Mindbenders, where he met the guitarist Eric Stewart, with whom he formed the groups Hotlegs, and later 10 c.c. CHART COMPOSITIONS: *Rubber Bullets* [iv] (1973) US#73 UK#1, *The Wall Street Shuffle* [iv] (1974) US#103 UK#10, *I'm Not in Love* [iv] (1975) US#2 UK#1, new version (1995) UK#29; *I'm Mandy, Fly Me* [i] (1976) US#60 UK#6, *Art for Art's Sake* [iv] (1976) US#83 UK#5, *The Things We Do for Love* [iv] (1977) US#5 UK#6, *Good Morning Judge* [iv] (1977) US#69 UK#5, *People in Love* [iv] (1977) US#40, *Dreadlock Holiday* [iv] (1978) US#44 UK#1, *For You and I* [iv] (1979) US#85, *Run Away* [iv] (1982) UK#50. ALBUMS: **10 c.c.** (1973) UK#36, **Sheet Music** (1974, both UK) US#81 UK#9; **The Original Soundtrack** (1975) US#15 UK#4, **How Dare You?** (1976) US#47 UK#5, **Deceptive Bends** (1977) US#31 UK#3, **Live and Let Live** (1977) US#146 UK#14, **Bloody Tourists** (1978) US#69 UK#3, **Look Hear?** (1980) US#180 UK#35, **Windows in the Jungle** (1983, all Mercury) UK#70; **Meanwhile** (1992), **Mirror Mirror** (1995, both Avex); **In Concert** (1996, King Biscuit). COMPILATIONS: **Greatest Hits** (1975, Decca) US#161 UK#9; **Greatest Hits, 1972–1978** (1979) US#188 UK#5, **The Changing Faces of 10 c.c. and Godley and Creme** (1987) UK#4, **The Things We Do for Love** (1995, all Mercury). Gouldman has also recorded as a solo artist, and with Andrew Gold in the group Wax. CHART COMPOSITION: *Sunburn* (1979) UK#52. ALBUMS: **The Graham Gouldman Thing** (1967, RCA); **Sunburn** ost (1980, Warwick) UK#45; **Animalympics** ost (1980). HIT VERSIONS: *Behind the Door* Cher (1966) US#97, *Bus Stop* Hollies (1966) US#5 UK#5, *East, West* Herman's Hermits (1966) US#27 UK#37, *Evil Hearted You* Yardbirds (1965) UK#3, *For Your Love* Yardbirds (1965) US#6 UK#3/Chilly (1979) US#108; *Heart Full of Soul* Yardbirds (1965) US#9 UK#2, *I'm Not in Love* [iv] Dee Dee Sharp Gamble (1976) R&B#62/Richie Havens (1976) US#102/Will to Power (1990) UK#50; *Listen People* Herman's Hermits (1966) g US#3, also on B-side of *You Won't Be Leaving* (1966) UK#20; *Look Through Any Window* [iii] Hollies

(1965) US#32 UK#4, *No Milk Today* Herman's Hermits (1966) UK#7, *Pamela, Pamela* Wayne Fontana (1966) UK#11, *Sausalito (Is the Place to Go)* Ohio Express (1969) US#86; *Tallyman* Jeff Beck (1967) UK#30. Co-writers: [i] Lol Creme, [ii] Lol Creme/Kevin Godley/Eric Stewart (b. January 20, 1945, Manchester, England), [iii] Charles Silverman, [iv] Eric Stewart. (*See also under* Lol CREME and Kevin GODLEY, Andrew GOLD.)

390. GRAMM, Lou (b. Lou Grammatico, May 2, 1950, Rochester, NY) Rock vocalist. The lead vocalist in the Anglo-American rock group Foreigner. Gramm has also recorded as a solo artist. CHART COMPOSITIONS: *Midnight Blue* [ii] (1987) US#5, *Ready or Not* [ii] (1987) US#54, *Just Between You and Me* [i] (1990) US#6, *True Blue Love* (1990) US#40. ALBUMS: **Ready or Not** (1987) US#27, **Long Hard Look** (1989, both Atlantic) US#85. Co-writers: [i] Holly Knight, [ii] B. Turgon. (*See also under* Mick JONES.)

391. GRANT, Amy (b. November 25, 1960, Augusta, GA) Pop vocalist. An immensely popular contemporary Christian artist, who records in a mainstream pop style and has sold over fifteen million records. CHART COMPOSITIONS: *Wise Up* (1985) US#66, *Find a Way* [vi] (1985) US#29, *Lead Me On* [iv] (1988) US#96, *Baby Baby* [vii] (1991) US#1, *Every Heartbeat* [iii] (1991) US#2, *That's What Love Is For* [v] (1991) US#7, *Good for Me* [ii] (1992) US#8, *I Will Remember You* [i] (1992) US#20, *Lucky One* [vii] (1994) US#18 UK#60, *Say You'll Be Mine* (1994) UK#41, *House of Love* with Vince Gill (1995) US#37 UK#46. ALBUMS: **Amy Grant** (1976), **My Father's Eyes** (1979) g, **Never Alone** (1980), **In Concert I** (1981), **In Concert II** (1981), **Age to Age** (1982) p, **A Christmas Album** (1983, all Myrrh) g; **Straight Ahead** (1985) g US#133, **Unguarded** (1985, both A&M) p US#35; **The Animal's Christmas** with Art Garfunkel (1986, Columbia); **Lead Me On** (1988) g US#71, **Heart in Motion** (1991) p US#10 UK#25, **Home for the Holidays** (1992) p US#2, **House of Love** (1994, all A&M) p US#13. COMPILATION: **The Collection** (1986, A&M) p US#66. HIT VERSION: *Place in This World, A* [iv] Michael W. Smith (1991) US#6. Co-writers: [i] Gary Chapman/K. Thomas, [ii] W. Kirkpatrick/Jay Gruska/Tom Snow, [iii] W. Kirkpatrick/C. Peacock, [iv] W. Kirkpatrick/Michael W. Smith (b. Kenova, WV), [v] M. Miller/Michael Omartian, [vi] Michael W. Smith, [vii] K. Thomas.

392. GRANT, Eddie (b. Edmund Montague Grant, March 5, 1948, Plaisance, Guyana, West Indies) Pop multi-instrumentalist, producer and vo-

calist. A pop-reggae artist who emigrated to England in 1960, where he formed the ska and R&B influenced group the Equals. CHART COMPOSITIONS: *I Get So Excited* (1968) UK#44, *Baby Come Back* (1968) UK#1, *Viva Bobby Joe* (1969) UK#6, *Black Skinned Blue Eyed Boys* (1971) UK#9. ALBUMS: **Unequalled Equals** (1967) UK#10, **Equals Explosion** (1968, both President) UK#32. COMPILATIONS: **Best of the Equals** (1968, President); **Profile** (1983, Teldec); **20 Greatest Hits** (1984, Astan); **Greatest Hits** (1988, Premier). In 1971, Grant quit the group for a solo career, later forming and recording on his own Ice label. Grant's song *Police on My Back* was recorded by the punk group the Clash. CHART COMPOSITIONS: *Living on the Front Line* (1979) UK#11, *Walking on Sunshine* (1979) R&B#86, re-issued (1989) UK#63; *Do You Feel My Love* (1980) UK#8, *Can't Get Enough of You* (1981) UK#13, *I Love You, Yes I Love You* (1981) UK#37, *I Don't Wanna Dance* (1982) UK#1, re-issued (1983) US#53; *Electric Avenue* (1983) g R&B#18 US#2 UK#2, *Living on the Frontline/Do You Feel My Love* (1983) UK#47, *War Party* (1983) UK#42, *Till I Can't Take Love No More* (1983) UK#42, *Romancing the Stone* (1984) R&B#68 US#26 UK#52, *Gimme Hope Jo'anna* (1988) UK#7. ALBUMS: **Club Ska** (1966); **Eddy Grant** (1975, Torpedo); **Message Man** (1977), **Walking on Sunshine** (1979), **Love in Exile** (1980), **Can't Get Enough** (1981) UK#39, **Killer on the Rampage** (1982, all Ice) g US#10 UK#7; **Going for Broke** (1984, Portrait) US#64; **Live at the Notting Hill Carnival** (1984), **Born Tuff** (1986), **File Under Rock** (1988, all Blue Wave); **Restless World** (1990, Parlophone); **Paintings of the Soul** (1992), **Soca Baptism** (1995, both Pinnacle). COMPILATIONS: **All the Hits: The Killer at His Best** (1984, K-Tel) UK#23; **Walking on Sunshine (The Best of Eddie Grant)** (1989, Parlophone) UK#20; **Greatest Hits** (1996, EMI). HIT VERSIONS: *Baby Come Back* Pato Banton with UB40 (1994) UK#1, *Walking on Sunshine* Bill Summers & Summers Heat (1980) R&B#57/Rocker's Revenge (1982) R&B#63 UK#4/Krush (1992) UK#71.

393. GREEN, Al (b. Al Greene, April 13, 1946, Forest City, AR). R&B vocalist. A blues and gospel influenced soul balladeer, who has sold over thirty million records. During the late 1950s, Green sang in a gospel quartet with his brothers, and in 1964 he formed the group Al Green and the Creations, which recorded for the local Zodiac label. In 1967, he performed as Al Green and the Soul Mates, achieving a hit single with a version of *Back Up Train*. After signing to producer Willie Mitchell's Hi Records, Green cut a series of influential hits, backed by the infamous Memphis recording studio house band, which included the metronomic drummer, Al Jackson. During the 1970s, Green achieved an un-broken run of seven million selling singles. In 1976, he purchased the Full Gospel Tabernacle in Memphis and appointed himself minister, after which, he recorded more gospel oriented material, none better than his compositions *King of All* and *Belle* [i]. Green gradually returned to recording mainstream pop music during the late 1980s. CHART COMPOSITIONS: *You Say It* (1970) R&B#28, *Right Now Right Now* (1970) R&B#23, *Driving Wheel* (1971) R&B#46 US#115, *Tired of Being Alone* (1971) g R&B#7 US#11 UK#4, *Let's Stay Together* [iv] (1971) g R&B#1 US#1 UK#7, *Look What You Done for Me* [iv] (1972) g R&B#2 US#4 UK#44, *I'm Still in Love with You* [iv] (1972) g R&B#1 US#3 UK#35, *Guilty* (1972) R&B#29 US#69, *You Ought to Be with Me* (1972) g R&B#1 US#3, *Hot Wire* (1973) US#71, *Call Me (Come Back Home)* (1973) g R&B#2 US#10, *Here I Am (Come and Take Me)* [ii] (1973) g R&B#2 US#10, *Livin' for You* [v] (1973) R&B#1 US#19, *Let's Get Married* (1974) R&B#3 US#32, *Sha-La-La (Make Me Happy)* (1974) g R&B#2 US#7 UK#20, *L-O-V-E (Love)* [iii] (1975) R&B#1 US#13 UK#24, *Oh Me, Oh My (Dreams in My Arms)* [iii] (1975) R&B#7 US#48, *Full of Fire* [iii] (1975) R&B#1 US#28, *Let It Shine* (1976) R&B#16, *Keep Me Cryin'* [v] (1976) R&B#4 US#37, *I Tried to Tell Myself* (1977) R&B#26 US#101, *Love and Happiness* (1977) R&B#92 US#104, *Belle* [i] (1977) R&B#9 US#83, *I Feel Good* (1978) R&B#36 US#103, *Wait Here* (1979) R&B#58, *Everything's Gonna Be Alright* (1987) R&B#22, *Love Is a Beautiful Thing* (1993) UK#56. ALBUMS: **Back Up Train** (1967, Hot Line); **Green Is Blues** (1971) US#19, **Al Green Gets Next to You** (1971) US#58, **Let's Stay Together** (1972) g US#8, **I'm Still in Love with You** (1972) g US#4, **Call Me** (1973) g US#10, **Livin' for You** (1973) g US#24, **Al Green Explores Your Mind** (1974) g US#15, **Al Green Is Love** (1975) US#28, **Full of Fire** (1976) US#59, **Have a Good Time** (1976) US#93, **The Belle Album** (1977) US#103, **Truth 'n' Time** (1978), **Tokyo Live** (1981, all Hi); **Highway to Heaven** (1981, Myrrh); **Higher Plane** (1982), **Trust in God** (1981, both Hi); **Precious Lord** (1982, Word); **The Lord Will Make a Way** (1982), **I'll Rise Again** (1983, both Myrrh); **He Is the Light** (1985), **Soul Survivor** (1987) US#131, **Going Away** (1988), **I Get Joy** (1989, all A&M); **You Say It** (1990, Hi); **Love Is Reality** (1992), **White Christmas** (1992, both Word); **Don't Look Back** (1993, RCA). COMPILATIONS: **Al Green** (1972, Bell) US#162; **Greatest Hits** (1975) US#17 UK#18, **Greatest Hits, Volume 2** (1977, both Hi) US#134; **Hi Life-The Best of Al Green** (1988, K-Tel) UK#34; **Love Ritual** (1978, Hi); **Al** (1992, Beechwood) UK#41; **Your Heart's in Good Hands** (1995), **Great-est Hits** (1996, both MCA) US#169; **A Deep Shade of Green** (1997, Demon). HIT VERSIONS: *Here I Am (Come and Take Me)* [ii] UB40 (1990) US#7 UK#46, *I'm Still in Love with You* [iv] Meli'sa Morgan (1992) R&B#9, *Jim Dandy Got Married* LaVern Baker (1957) R&B#7 US#76, *Let's Stay Together* [iv] Isaac Hayes (1972) R&B#25 US#48/Margie Joseph (1973) R&B#43/Bobby M. & Jean Carn (1983) R&B#74 UK#53/Tina Turner (1984) R&B#3 US#26 UK#6/Pasadenas (1992) UK#22; *Love and Happiness* [ii] Earnest Jackson (1973) R&B#22 US#58/David Sanborn (1985) R&B#66 US#103/Kawz (1996) R&B#80+; *Take Me to the River* [ii] Syl Johnson (1975) R&B#7 US#48/Talking Heads (1978) US#26; *Tired of Being Alone* Right Choice (1988) R&B#13/Texas (1992) UK#19. Co-writers: [i] R. Fairfax/F. Jordan, [ii] Mabon Hodges, [iii] Mabon Hodges/Willie Mitchell (b. 1928, Ashland, TN), [iv] Al Jackson, Jr./Willie Mitchell, [v] Willie Mitchell.

394. GREEN, Peter (b. Peter Greenbaum, October 29, 1946, London, England) Rock guitarist and vocalist. A blues guitarist who left John Mayall's Bluesbreakers in 1967 to co-found the group Fleetwood Mac. Sadly, Green has suffered from severe health problems since the 1970s, and has produced little work of merit since his sparkling series of compositions during the late 1960s, one of which, *Black Magic Woman*, received a BMI two million airplay award. CHART COMPOSITIONS: *Black Magic Woman* (1968) UK#37, *Albatross* (1969) US#104 UK#1, re-issued (1973) UK#2; *Man of the World* (1969) UK#2, *Oh Well* (1969) US#55 UK#2, *The Green Manalishi (With the Two-Prong Crown)* (1970) UK#10. ALBUMS: **Fleetwood Mac** (1968) US#198 UK#4, **Mr. Wonderful/English Rose** (1968) UK#10 US#184, **Pious Bird of Good Omen** (1969, all Blue Horizon) UK#18; **Then Play On** (1969) US#109 UK#6, **Penguin** (1973, both Reprise) US#49. COMPILATIONS: **Blues Jam at Chess** (1969), **Fleetwood Mac in Chicago** (1971, both Blue Horizon) US#118; **Black Magic Woman** (1971, Epic) US#143; **Greatest Hits** (1972, CBS) US#70; **Vintage Years** (1975, Sire) US#138; **Live at the BBC** (1995, Essential) UK#48. Green has also recorded sporadically as a solo artist. ALBUMS: **The End of the Game** (1970); **In the Skies** (1979, Creole) UK#32; **Little Dreamer** (1980, PVK) US#186 UK#34; **A Case for the Blues** with Ray Dorset (1986, Nightflite); **Farewell Concert** (1996); **Splinter Group** (1997, Snapper). HIT VERSIONS: *Black Magic Woman* Santana (1971) US#4, *Oh Well* Rockets (1979) US#30/*Oh Well* (1989) UK#28.

395. GREENBAUM, Norman (b. November 20, 1942, Malden, MA) Pop guitarist and vocalist. During the 1960s, Greenbaum was a member of the psychedelic, 1920s styled jug group, Dr. West's Medicine Show and Junk Band, which charted with *The Eggplant That Ate Chicago* (1966) US#52, from the album **The Eggplant That Ate Chicago** (1969, Gregar). As a solo artist, Greenbaum is best known for his multi-million selling, gospel influenced psychedelic number, *Spirit in the Sky* [i]. CHART COMPOSITION: *Spirit in the Sky* [i] (1970) g US#3 UK#1, *Canned Ham* (1970) US#46. ALBUMS: **Spirit in the Sky** (1970) US#23, **Back Home Again** (1972), **Petaluma** (1973, all Reprise). HIT VERSION: *Spirit in the Sky* [i] Dr. & the Medics (1986) US#69 UK#1. Co-writer: [i] Erik Jacobsen.

396. GREENFIELD, Howard Pop lyricist. A Brill Building lyricist during the 1960s, who regularly composed with Neil Sedaka, and charted with the solo single, *The Invasion* with Bill Buchanan (1964) US#120. HIT VERSIONS: *Back to School Again* [iv] Four Tops (1982) US#71 UK#62, *Charms* [iii] Bobby Vee (1963) US#13, *Foolish Little Girl* [iii] Shirelles (1963) R&B#9 US#4, *I Was Looking for Someone to Love* [ii] Leif Garrett (1980) US#78, *It Hurts to Be in Love* [iii] Gene Pitney (1964) US#42, *Two Less Lonely People in the World* [i] Air Supply (1983) US#38. Co-writers: [i] Ken Hirsch, [ii] Michael Lloyd, [iii] Helen Miller, [iv] Louis St. Louis. (*See also under* Jack KELLER, Neil SEDAKA.)

397. GREENWICH, Ellie (b. October 23, 1940, Long Island, NY) Pop pianist, producer and vocalist. One of the most talented and celebrated of all the Brill Building's songwriters, whose songs have collectively sold over twenty million records. Greenwich first composed and performed as Ellie Gay while working as a teacher. In 1959, she formed a professional and personal relationship with her future husband Jeff Barry, recording the singles *Cha-Cha Charming* and *Red Corvette* as Ellie Gee and the Jets, before becoming the studio concoction the Raindrops in 1963, which charted with *The Kind of Boy You Can't Forget* [i] (1963) R&B#27 US#17, *What a Guy* [i] (1963) R&B#25 US#41 and *Let's Go Together* [i] (1964) US#109, and released the album **The Raindrops** (1963, Jubilee). Greenwich also sung on promotional tapes by other composers, earning herself the nickname "the demo queen of New York." As staff composers and producers at Jerry Leiber and Mike Stoller's Red Bird label, Greenwich and Barry charted with their first ten releases. Their tunes were described as teen-poetry and adolescent anguish, on account of their dramatic, tear-drenched style. Although their marriage quickly disintegrated, the producer Phil Spector encouraged them to continue

writing together, which resulted in nine further hits during a six month period, the most memorable of all being Ike and Tina Turner's lavish *River Deep, Mountain High* [iii] (1966). Of her Brill Building days, Greenwich later said, "We'd write songs in the elevators, or while we were eating next door at Jack Dempsey's...My original dream in music was to make a hundred dollars a week." Greenwich also recorded as a solo artist, and ran her own companies Jingle Habitat and Pineywood Productions, for which she wrote radio and television adverts throughout the 1970s. In 1985, she starred alongside Darlene Love in the Broadway musical "Leader of the Pack." CHART COMPOSITIONS: *I Want You to Be My Baby* (1967) US#83, *Maybe I Know* [i] (1973) US#122. ALBUMS: **Ellie Composes, Produces and Sings** (1967, United Artists); **Let It Be Written, Let It Be Sung** (1973, Verve); **Leader of the Pack** ost (1985, Elektra). HIT VERSIONS: *All Grown Up* [i] Crystals (1964) US#98, *Baby, I Love You* [iii] Ronettes (1964) US#24 UK#11/Andy Kim (1969) US#9/Ramones (1980) US#24 UK#8; *Be My Baby* [iii] Ronettes (1963) R&B#4 US#2 UK#4/Andy Kim (1970) US#17/Cissy Houston (1971) R&B#31 US#92/Jody Miller (1972) C&W#15/Dave Edmunds (1973) US#8/Ramones (1980) UK#8/Eddie Money in *Take Me Home Tonight* (1986) US#4; *Chapel of Love* [iii] Dixie Cups (1964) g US#1 UK#22/Bette Midler on B-side of *Friends* (1972) US#40; *Da Doo Ron Ron* [iii] Crystals (1963) g R&B#5 US#3 UK#5, re-issued (1974) UK#34/Ian Matthews (1972) US#96/Shaun Cassidy (1977) g US#1; *Do Wah Diddy Diddy* [i] Exciters (1964) US#78/Manfred Mann (1964) US#1 UK#1/Blues Band on *The Blues Band EP* (1980) UK#68; *Don't Ever Leave Me* [i] Connie Francis (1964) US#42, *Fine, Fine Boy, A* [i] Darlene Love (1963) US#53, *Gettin' Together* [i] Tommy James & the Shondells (1967) US#18, *Give Us Your Blessing* [i] Shangri-Las (1965) US#29, *Hanky Panky* [i] Tommy James & the Shondells (1966) g R&B#39 US#1 UK#38/Neil Diamond on B-side of *Do It* (1970) US#36; *He's Got the Power* [i] Exciters (1963) US#57, *Hold on Baby* [i] Sam Hawkins (1965) R&B#10 US#133, *I Can Hear Music* [iii] Ronettes (1966) US#100/Beach Boys (1969) US#24 UK#10/Larry Lurex (1973) US#115; *I Wanna Love Him So Bad* [i] Jelly Beans (1964) US#9, *I Want You to Be My Baby/Boy* [i] Exciters (1965) US#98/Billie Davis (1968) UK#33; *I Wonder* [i] Crystals (1964) UK#36, *I'll Take You Where the Music's Playing* [i] Drifters (1965) US#51, *Keep It Confidential* [iv] Nona Hendryx (1983) R&B#22 US#91, *Leader of the Pack* [ii] Shangri-Las (1965) g US#1 UK#11, re-issued (1972) UK#3, re-issued (1976) UK#7/UTFO (1985) R&B#32/Twisted Sister (1986) US#53 UK#47/Joan Collins Fan Club (1988) UK#60; *Little Bell* [i] Dixie Cups (1965)

US#51, *Little Boy* [i] Crystals (1964) US#92, *Look of Love* [i] Lesley Gore (1965) US#27, *Look What You've Done to My Heart* Marilyn McCoo & Billy Davis, Jr. (1977) R&B#27 US#51, *Maybe I Know* [i] Lesley Gore (1964) US#14 UK#20, *Not Too Young to Get Married* [i] Bob B. Soxx & the Blue Jeans (1963) US#63, *People Say* [i] Dixie Cups (1964) US#12, *River Deep, Mountain High* [iii] Ike & Tina Turner (1966) US#88 UK#3, re-issued (1969) US#112 UK#33/Eric Burdon & the Animals on B-side of *White Houses* (1968) US#87/Deep Purple (1968) US#53/Supremes & the Four Tops (1971) R&B#7 US#14 UK#11/Erasure on B-side of *Ship of Fools* (1988) UK#6; *Sunshine After the Rain* Elkie Brooks (1977) UK#10, *Then He Kissed Me* [iii] Crystals (1963) R&B#8 US#6 UK#2/Beach Boys as *Then I Kissed Her* (1967) UK#4/Gary Glitter (1981) UK#39; *(Today I Met) The Boy I'm Gonna Marry* [i] Darlene Love (1963) US#39, *Wait "Til My Bobby Gets Home* [i] Darlene Love (1963) US#26, *Why Do Lovers Break Each Others Hearts* [v] Bob B. Soxx & the Blue Jeans (1963) US#38/Showaddywaddy (1980) UK#22; *You Don't Know What You're Missing ('Til It's Gone)* [i] Exciters (1969) R&B#49, *You Should Have Seen the Way He Looked at Me* [i] Dixie Cups (1964) US#39. Co-writers: [i] Jeff Barry, [ii] Jeff Barry/George Morton, [iii] Jeff Barry/Phil Spector, [iv] Ellen Foley/J. Kent, [v] Tony Powers/Phil Spector.

398. GREY, Clifford (b. January 5, 1887, Birmingham; d. September 25, 1941, Ipswich, both England) Film and stage lyricist. A lyricist and former actor who collaborated with many of his songwriting contemporaries. Grey's compositions were included in the shows "The Bing Boys Are Here" (1916), "The Bing Boys on Broadway" (1917) and "The Three Musketeers" (1928). HIT VERSIONS: *Another Little Drink Wouldn't Do Us Any Harm* [i] Winifred Atwell in *Let's Have Another Party* (1954) UK#1, *Got a Date with an Angel* [iii] Debroy Somers Band (1932) US#13/Hal Kemp (1934) US#16; *If You Were the Only Girl in the World* [i] Perry Como (1946) US#14/Johnston Brothers in *Join in and Sing Again #3* (1956) UK#24/Russ Conway in *More Party Pops* (1958) UK#10, also in *More and More Party Pops* (1959) UK#5; *Rogue Song, The* [iv] Lawrence Tibbett (1930) US#18, *Valencia* [ii] Jesse Crawford (1926) US#14/Ross Gorman (1926) US#12/Revelers (1926) US#5/Ben Selvin (1926) US#3/Paul Whiteman (1926) US#1/Tony Martin (1950) US#18; *When I'm Looking at You* [iv] Lawrence Tibbett (1930) US#12. Co-writers: [i] Nat D. Ayer, [ii] Lucien Boyer/Jacques Charles/Jose Padilla, [iii] Sonny Miller/Joseph Tunbridge/Jack Waller, [iv] Herbert Stothart. (*See also under* Noel GAY, Victor SCHERTZINGER, Vincent YOUMANS.)

399. GRIFF, Ray (b. April 22, 1940, Vancouver, BC, Canada) Pop pianist, drummer and vocalist. A drummer in the Winfield Amateurs, who formed the group Blue Echoes, before becoming a Nashville songwriter during the 1960s. Griff charted twenty-four solo hits between 1967–1986. CHART COMPOSITIONS: *Your Lily White Hands* (1967) C&W#49, *The Sugar from My Candy* (1968) C&W#50, *The Mornin' After Baby Let Me Down* (1971) C&W#14, *The Last of the Winfield Amateurs* (1976) C&W#27. ALBUMS: **A Ray of Sunshine** (1968), **Expressions** (1975), **Songs for Everyone** (1976, all Dot); **The Last of the Winfield Amateurs** (1977, Capitol); **Canada** (1979, Boot). HIT VERSIONS: *Baby, The* Wilma Burgess (1966) C&W#7/Tennessee Ernie Ford & Andra Willis (1975) C&W#63/Kieran Kane (1981) C&W#80; *Canadian Pacific* George Hamilton, IV (1969) C&W#25, *It Couldn't Have Been Any Better* Johnny Duncan (1977) C&W#1, *Step Aside* Faron Young (1971) C&W#6, *Where Love Begins* Gene Watson (1975) C&W#5, *Who's Gonna Play This Old Piano* Jerry Lee Lewis (1972) C&W#14.

400. GRIFFITH, Nancy (b. July 6, 1953, Seguin, TX) C&W guitarist and vocalist. A country, folk and pop influenced singer-songwriter, who has described her music as "folkabilly." A former teacher, Griffith performed in bars and roadhouses before moving to Nashville, where she played music and wrote novels. Her songs have been recorded by Emmylou Harris and Lynn Anderson, and arguably her finest composition is the contemporary folk classic *It's a Hard Life*. CHART COMPOSITIONS: *Once in a Very Blue Moon* (1986) C&W#85, *Lone Star State of Mind* (1987) C&W#36, *Trouble in the Fields* (1987) C&W#57, *Cold Hearts/Closed Mind* (1987) C&W#64, *I Knew Love* (1988) C&W#37, *Anyone Can Be Somebody's Fool* (1988) C&W#64. ALBUMS: **There's a Light Beyond These Woods** (1978, BF Deal); **Poet in My Window** (1982, Featherbed); **Once in a Very Blue Moon** (1984), **The Last of the True Believers** (1985, both Rounder); **Lone Star State of Mind** (1987), **Little Love Affairs** (1988) UK#78, **One Fair Summer Evening** (1988), **Storms** (1989) US#99 UK#38, **Late Night Grande Hotel** (1991) US#185 UK#40, **Other Voices, Other Rooms** (1993) US#54 UK#18, **Flyer** (1994, all MCA) US#48 UK#20; **Blue Roses from the Moons** (1997, Elektra). COMPILATION: **Best of Nanci Griffith** (1993, MCA) UK#27. HIT VERSIONS: *Listen to the Radio* Kathy Mattea (1993) C&W#64, *Love at the Five and Dime* Kathy Mattea (1986) C&W#3, *Outbound Plane* [i] Suzy Bogguss (1992) C&W#9. Co-writer: [i] Tom Russell.

401. GUTHRIE, Arlo (b. July 10, 1947, Coney Island, NY) Folk guitarist and vocalist. The son of Woody Guthrie and friend of Pete Seeger, who grew up immersed in the folk tradition and learned the guitar at the age of six. Guthrie converted to Catholicism in 1977. CHART COMPOSITION: *Alice's Rock 'n' Roll Restaurant* (1967) US#97. ALBUMS: **Alice's Restaurant** (1967) US#17 UK#44, **Arlo** (1968, both Reprise) US#107; **Alice's Restaurant** ost (1969, UA) US#63; **Running Down the Road** (1969) US#54, **Washington County** (1970) US#33, **Hobo's Lullaby** (1972) US#52, **Last of the Brooklyn Cowboys** (1973) US#87, **Arlo Guthrie** (1974) US#165, **Together in Concert** with Pete Seeger (1975) US#181, **Amigo** (1976, all Reprise) US#133; **One Night** (1978), **Outlasting the Blues** (1979), **Power of Love** (1981, all Warner Brothers) US#184. COMPILATION: **Best of Arlo Guthrie** (1977, Reprise). HIT VERSION: *Alice's Restaurant Massacre* Garry Sherman (1969) US#112.

402. GUTHRIE, Woody (b. Woodrow Wilson Guthrie, July 14, 1912, Okemah, OK; d. October 3, 1967, New York, NY). Folk guitarist, harmonica player and vocalist. The most influential composer of American folk ballads ever, who, alongside Leadbelly, was the founding father of both the folk protest and the singer-songwriter movements. Many of Guthrie's over one thousand compositions have become American standards, including *Oklahoma Hills, Vigilante Man, I Ain't Got No Home, Deportee (Plane Wreck at Los Gatos), Hobo's Lullaby, Bourgeois Blues, Going to the Zoo, Philadelphia Lawyer, Reuben James, Pastures of Plenty, Dusty Old Dust, There's a Better World a-Comin',* and *Pretty Boy Floyd.* He first learned music from an uncle, and from the age of sixteen traveled and worked around the country. During the 1930s he lived as a hobo, a period of his life that he documented in the songs that collectively became known as the Dust Bowl Ballads. From 1939, Guthrie resided in New York, where he involved himself in the trade-union movement, and although America has since taken him to heart as the patriot that he was, it should never be forgotten that Guthrie's outspoken views and political material was often received with hostility and radio bans. By the time he made his first recordings for the Library of Congress in 1940, he had over a decade's worth of compositions to draw upon. Guthrie spent the last fifteen years of his life hospitalized with Huntington's Chorea, from which he eventually died. Guthrie was a significant influence on Bob Dylan, and nearly every singer-songwriter that followed. His songs were recorded by a variety of artists on the albums **Tribute to Woody Guthrie, Part 1** (1968, Columbia) US#183; **Tribute to Woody Guthrie, Part 2** (1970, Warner Brothers) US#189; and **Folkways-A Vision Shared** (1988, Columbia) US#70. ALBUMS: **More Songs By Guthrie** (1955, Melodisc); **Bound for Glory** (1958, Folkways); **Library of Congress Recordings** (1960, Elektra); **Dust Bowl Ballads** (1964, Folkways); **Woody Guthrie** (1965, Xtra); **This Land Is Your Land** (1967, Folkways); **Poor Boy and Songs to Grow On** (1968, Xtra); **Woody Guthrie** (1968, Ember); **The Greatest Songs of Woody Guthrie** (1972, Vanguard); **A Legendary Performer** (1977, RCA); **Columbia River Collection** (1988, Topic); **Struggle/Woody Guthrie Sings Folksongs of Leadbelly** (1988, Folkways); **Very Best of Woody Guthrie** (1992, Music Club); **Long Ways to Travel, 1944–1949** (1994, Smithsonian/Folkways). HIT VERSIONS: *Do-Re-Mi* Lee Dorsey (1962) R&B#22 US#27, *Dust Pneumonia Blues* Mungo Jerry on B-side of *In the Summertime* (1970) US#3 UK#1, *Gamblin' Man* Lonnie Donegan (1957) UK#1, *Grand Coulee Dam* Lonnie Donegan (1958) UK#6, *Gypsy Davy* Arlo Guthrie (1973) US#105, *So Long (It's Been Good to Know Ya)* Ralph Marterie (1951) US#26/Weavers (1951) US#4/Paul Weston (1951) US#21; *This Land Is Your Land* New Christy Minstrels (1962) US#93/Ketty Lester (1962) US#97; *Worried Man, A* Kingston Trio (1959) US#20.

403. HAGGARD, Merle (b. Merle Ronald Haggard, April 6, 1937, Bakersfield, CA) C&W guitarist and vocalist. One of the most influential and successful artists in country music, who has charted over one hundred hit singles, including thirty-eight number ones. Haggard amalgamated the music of his early heroes, Bob Wills, Lefty Frizzell and Jimmie Rodgers, and created a country-folk style of his own, which in turn was much imitated by later performers. A tunesmith who writes about ordinary people with dignity and humility, Haggard once said of his songwriting methods, "Something just comes to mind and I go from there…Sometimes I'll just be picking or strumming, and one note will lead to another." He has also approached subjects seldom sung about in country music, such as his defence of interracial romance in *Irma Jackson*, and his ironic questioning of the intolerance of patriotism in the frequently misunderstood *Okie from Muskogee*. His plaintiff ballad *Today I Started Loving You Again* [iv], has been recorded nearly four hundred times. Haggard's life is the stuff of country legends, beginning with his birth in a converted boxcar to a fiddle playing father who had been a dust bowl refugee working on the railroads. Haggard grew up listening to country music on the radio. He ran away from home in 1951, leading a life of teenage rebellion that eventually resulted in a three year incarceration for burglary in San Quentin during the late 1950s. While

in prison, Haggard played in the warden's country band, where he discovered his future vocation, later saying of his imprisonment, "I'm not so sure it works like that very often, but I'm the one guy the prison system straightened out." After his release, Haggard held various jobs and drifted throughout California performing in clubs and bars, before he became Wynn Stewart's bassist. Haggard's first recordings were for the small Tally label in the early 1960s, and from the outset, the authenticity of his compositions gave him a wide appeal, as he blended country blues with elements of western swing and white gospel, and documented the changing times through the eyes of working people, from itinerant fruit pickers to railroad workers. Explaining his extensive variety of recording styles over the years, Haggard once said, "All my life, I've been interested in not just the music, but where the music came from, how it came to be, and where those who found it actually found it."
CHART COMPOSITIONS: *I'm Gonna Break Every Heart I Can* (1965) C&W#42, *Swinging Doors* (1966) C&W#5, *The Bottle Let Me Down* (1966) C&W#3, *Someone Told My Story* (1966) C&W#32, *I Threw Away the Roses* (1967) C&W#2, *Branded Man* (1967) C&W#1, *Sing Me Back Home* (1967) C&W#1, *The Legend of Bonnie and Clyde* [iii] (1968) C&W#1, *Mama Tried* (1968) C&W#1, *I Take a Lot of Pride in What I Am* (1968) C&W#3, *Hungry Eyes* (1969) C&W#1, *Workin' Man Blues* (1969) C&W#1, *Okie from Muskogee* (1969) C&W#1 US#41, *The Fightin' Side of Me* (1970) C&W#1 US#92, *Street Singer* (1970) C&W#9 US#124, *Jesus Take a Hold* (1970) C&W#3 US#107, *I Can't Be Myself* (1970) C&W#3 US#106, *Someday We'll Look Back* (1971) C&W#2 US#119, *Daddy Frank (The Guitar Man)* (1971) C&W#1, *Grandma Harp/Turnin' Off a Memory* (1972) C&W#1, *I Wonder If They Ever Think of Me* (1972) C&W#1, *The Emptiest Arms in the World* (1973) C&W#3, *Everybody's Had the Blues* (1973) C&W#1 US#73, *If We Make It Through December* (1973) C&W#1 US#28, *Things Aren't Funny Anymore* (1974) C&W#1, *Old Man from the Mountain* (1974) C&W#1, *Always Wanting You* (1975) C&W#1, *Movin' On* (1975) C&W#1, *It's All in the Movies* [ii] (1975) C&W#1, *Ramblin' Fever* (1977) C&W#2, *A Working Man Can't Get Nowhere Today* (1977) C&W#16, *From Graceland to the Promised Land* (1977) C&W#4 US#58, *Running Kind/Making Believe* (1978) C&W#12, *It's Been a Great Afternoon/Love Me When You Can* (1978) C&W#2, *The Way It Was in '51* (1978) C&W#82, *The Bull and the Beaver*** (1978) C&W#8, *Red Bandanna* (1979) C&W#4, *My Own Kind of Hat* (1979) C&W#4, *I Think I'll Just Stay Here and Drink* (1980) C&W#1, *Leonard* (1981) C&W#9, *I Can't Hold Myself in Line* with Johnny Paycheck (1981) C&W#41, *Rainbow*

Stew (1981) C&W#4, *My Favorite Memory* (1981) C&W#1, *Big City* [iii] (1982) C&W#1, *Dealing with the Devil* (1982) C&W#49, *Are the Good Times Really Over (I Wish a Buck Was Still Silver)* (1982) C&W#2, *Going Where the Lonely Go* (1982) C&W#1, *You Take Me for Granted* (1983) C&W#1, *We're Strangers Again* [viii]*** (1983) C&W#42, *What Am I Gonna Do (With the Rest of My Life)* (1983) C&W#3, *Reasons to Quit** (1983) C&W#6, *Someday When Things Are Good* (1984) C&W#1, *Let's Chase Each Other Around the Room* [vii] (1984) C&W#1, *A Place to Fall Apart* [v] with Janie Fricke (1984) C&W#1, *Make-Up and Faded Blue Jeans* (1985) C&W#55, *Kern River* (1985) C&W#10, *Amber Waves of Grain* (1985) C&W#36, *I Had a Beautiful Time* (1986) C&W#5, *Twinkle Twinkle Lucky Star* (1987) C&W#1, *Chill Factor* (1988) C&W#9. ALBUMS: **Strangers** (1965), **Just Between the Two of Us**** (1966), **Swinging Doors** (1966), **I'm a Lonesome Fugitive** (1967) US#165, **Branded Man** (1967) US#167, **Sing Me Back Home** (1968), **The Legend of Bonnie and Clyde** (1968), **Mama Tried** (1968), **Pride in What I Am** (1969) US#189, **Same Train, Different Time** (1969) US#67, **A Portrait of Merle Haggard** (1969) US#99, **Okie from Muskogee** (1969) p US#46, **Introducing My Friends-The Strangers** (1970), **The Fightin' Side of Me** (1970) g US#68, **A Tribute to the Best Damn Fiddle Player in the World, or My Salute to Bob Wills** (1970) US#58, **Hag** (1971) US#66, **Someday We'll Look Back** (1971) US#108, **The Land of Many Churches** (1972), **Let Me Tell You About a Song** (1972) US#166, **It's Not Love (But It's Not Bad)** (1972), **Totally Instrumental, with One Exception** (1973), **I Love Dixie Blues So I Recorded Live in New Orleans** (1973) US#126, **Merle Haggard's Christmas Present** (1973), **If We Make It Through December** (1974) US#190, **Merle Haggard Presents His 30th Album** (1974), **Keep Movin' On** (1975) US#129, **It's All in the Movies** (1976), **My Love Affair with Trains** (1976), **The Roots of My Raising** (1976), **A Working Man Can't Get Nowhere Today** (1977, all Capitol); **Ramblin' Fever** (1977), **My Farewell to Elvis** (1977) US#133, **I'm Always on a Mountain When I Fall** (1978), **Serving 190 Proof** (1979), **The Way I Am** (1980), **Back to the Barrooms** (1980, all MCA); **Bronco Billy** ost (1980, Elektra) US#123; **Rainbow Stew/ Live at Anaheim Stadium** (1981), **Songs for the Mama That Tried** (1981, both MCA); **Big City** (1981) g US#161, **A Taste of Yesterday's Wine** with George Jones (1982) US#123, **Going Where the Lonely Go** (1982), **Poncho and Lefty*** (1982, all Epic) p US#37; **Heart to Heart*** (1983, Mercury); **That's the Way Love Goes** (1983), **The Epic Collection-Live** (1983), **It's All in the Game** (1984),

Kern River (1985), **Out Among the Stars** (1986), **Amber Waves of Grain** (1986), **A Friend in California** (1986), **Seashores of Old Mexico*** (1987), **Walking the Line** (1987), **Chill Factor** (1987), **5:01 Blues** (1989, all Epic); **Blue Jungle** (1990), **All Night Long** (1991), **Merle Haggard 1994** (1994), **Merle Haggard 1996** (1996, all Curb). COMPILATIONS: **Best of Merle Haggard** (1968) g, **Close-Up** (1969) US#140, **Best of the Best of Merle Haggard** (1972) p US#137, **Songs I'll Always Sing** (1977), **The Way It Was in '51** (1978, all Capitol); **Going Home for Christmas** (1982, Epic); **Greatest Hits** (1982, MCA); **His Epic Hits/The First Eleven** (1984, Epic) g; **Best of the Early Years** (1991, Curb); **18 Rare Classics** (1992, Collectibles); **Untamed Hawk** (1995, Bear Family); **Down Every Road** (1996, Capitol); **Poet of the Common Man** (1997, Curb/Hit). HIT VERSIONS: *After Loving You* Eddy Arnold (1962) C&W#7 US#112/Melissa Kay (1988) C&W#79; *Alice in Dallas (Sweet Texas)* Wyvon Alexander (1982) C&W#69, *All of Me Belongs to You* Dick Curless (1967) C&W#28/Hank Cochran (1970) C&W#70; *Branded Man* Sierra (1984) C&W#70, *Don't Give Up on Me* Jerry Wallace (1973) C&W#3/Stoney Edwards (1976) C&W#90/Eddy Arnold (1982) C&W#73; *Everybody's Had the Blues* Maury Finney (1977) C&W#85, *House of Memories* Dick Curless (1967) C&W#72, *I Always Get Lucky with You* [i] George Jones (1983) C&W#1, *I Haven't Learned a Thing* Porter Wagoner (1977) C&W#76, *I Take a Lot of Pride in What I Am* Dean Martin (1969) US#75, *I Wonder What She'll Think About Me Leaving* Conway Twitty (1971) C&W#4 US#112, *I'd Rather Be Gone* Hank Williams, Jr. (1969) C&W#4, *I'm Gonna Hang Up My Gloves* Charlie Walker (1966) C&W#65, *If You've Got Time* Red Steagall (1973) C&W#41, *Irma Jackson* Tony Booth (1970) C&W#67, *Love and Honor* Kenny Serratt (1973) C&W#70, *Shoulder to Cry On, A* Charley Pride (1973) C&W#1 US#101, *Silver Wings* Hagers (1970) C&W#59, *Somewhere Down the Line* Younger Brothers (1983) C&W#50/T.G. Sheppard (1984) C&W#3; *Sunny Side of My Life, The* Roger Miller (1972) C&W#63, *Swinging Doors* Del Reeves (1981) C&W#67, *Today I Started Loving You Again* [v] Al Martino (1969) C&W#69 US#86/Charlie McCoy (1972) C&W#16/Bettye Swann (1972) R&B#26 US#46/Kenny Rogers (1973) C&W#69/Sammi Smith (1975) C&W#9/Bobby Bland (1976) R&B#34 US#103/Arthur Pryscock (1979) C&W#74/Emmylou Harris (1986) C&W#43; *We're Strangers Again* [vii] Randy Travis & Tammy Wynette (1991) C&W#49, *When I Turn Twenty-One* Buddy Alan (1968) C&W#54, *White Line Fever* Buddy Alan (1972) C&W#68/Flying Burrito Brothers (1980) C&W#95; *Yesterday's News (Just Hit Home Today)*

Johnny Paycheck (1981) C&W#57. With: * Willie Nelson, ** Bonnie Owens, *** Leona Williams. Co-writers: [i] G. Chich/E. Powers/T. Whitson, [ii] K. Haggard, [iii] Dean Holloway, [iv] Bonnie Owens (b. October 1, 1932, Blanchard, OK), [v] Buck Owens, [vi] E. Powers/Willie Nelson, [viii] E. Powers/S. Rodgers, [viii] Leona Williams (b. Leona Belle Helton, January 7, 1943, Vienna, MO).

404. HALL, Daryl (b. Daryl Franklin Hohl, October 11, 1949, Pottstown, PA) Pop guitarist, pianist, producer and vocalist. The lead singer and principal songwriter in the pop duo Daryl Hall and John Oates, which achieved nineteen gold and platinum discs with a blend of pop, rock and soul. Initially session musicians and backing singers in Philadelphia, Hall and Oates first joined forces as members of the group Gulliver, releasing the album **Gulliver** (1968, Elektra), before they left to form Hall and Oates. CHART COMPOSITIONS: *She's Gone* [x] (1974) US#60, re-issued (1976) R&B#93 US#7 UK#42; *Sara Smile* [x] (1975) g R&B#23 US#4, *Do What You Want, Be What You Are* [x] (1976) R&B#23 US#39, *Rich Girl* (1976) g R&B#64 US#1, *It's Uncanny* (1977) US#80, *Why Do Lovers Break Each Others Hearts?* [v] (1977) US#73, *It's a Laugh* (1978) US#20, *I Don't Wanna Lose You* (1978) US#42, *Wait for Me* (1979) US#18, *Running from Paradise* (1979) UK#41, *Kiss on My List* [i] (1980) g US#1 UK#33, *You Make My Dreams* [vi] (1981) US#5, *Private Eyes* [iii] (1981) g US#1 UK#32, *Who Said the World Was Fair* (1980) US#110, *I Can't Go for That* [vi] (1981) g R&B#1 US#1 UK#8, *Did It in a Minute* [ii] (1981) US#9, *Your Imagination* (1981) R&B#45 US#33, *Maneater* [vi] (1982) g R&B#78 US#1 UK#6, *One on One* (1982) R&B#8 US#7 UK#63, *Say It Isn't So* (1983) R&B#45 US#2 UK#69, *Adult Education* [vi] (1983) R&B#50 US#8 UK#63, *Out of Touch* [x] (1984) R&B#24 US#1 UK#48, re-mixed (1985) UK#62; *Method of Modern Love* [i] (1984) R&B#21 US#5 UK#21, *Some Things Are Better Left Unsaid* [viii] (1984) R&B#85 US#18, *Possession Obsession* [vi] (1984) R&B#69 US#30, *Everything Your Little Heart Desires* (1988) R&B#40 US#3, *Missed Opportunity* [vi] (1988) US#29, *Downtown Life* [iv] (1988) US#31, *So Close* (1990) US#11 UK#69. ALBUMS: **Whole Oates** (1972), **Abandoned Luncheonette** (1974) g US#33, **War Babies** (1974, all Atlantic) US#86; **Daryl Hall and John Oates** (1975) g US#17 UK#56, **Bigger Than the Both of Us** (1976) g US#13 UK#25, **Beauty on a Back Street** (1977) g US#30 UK#40, **Live Time** (1978) US#42, **Along the Red Ledge** (1978) g US#27, **X-Static** (1979) US#33, **Voices** (1980) p US#17, **Private Eyes** (1981) p US#5 UK#8, **H2O** (1982) p US#3 UK#24, **Big Bam Boom** (1984) p

US#5 UK#28, **Live at the Apollo with David Ruffin and Eddie Kendricks** (1985, all RCA) g US#21 UK#32; **Ooh Yeah!** (1988) p US#24 UK#52, **Change of Season** (1990, both Arista) US#61. COMPILATIONS: **No Goodbyes** (1977, Atlantic) US#92; **Past Times Behind** (1977, Chelsea); **Rock 'n' Soul, Part 1** (1983, RCA) p US#7 UK#16; **Best of Daryl Hall and John Oates-Looking Back** (1991, Arista) UK#9. Since the late 1980s, Hall has recorded with varying degrees of success as a solo artist. CHART COMPOSITIONS: *Dreamtime* [vii] (1986) US#5 UK#28, *Foolish Pride* (1986) R&B#91 US#33, *Someone Like You* (1986) US#57, *I'm in a Philly Mood* [ix] (1993) US#82 UK#52, *Stop Loving Me, Stop Loving You* (1994) UK#30, *Help Me Find a Way to Your Heart* (1993) UK#70, *Gloryland* (1993) UK#36. ALBUMS: **Sacred Songs** (1980) US#58, **Three Hearts in the Happy Ending Machine** (1986, both RCA) US#29 UK#26; **Soul Alone** (1993, Epic) US#177 UK#57. HIT VERSIONS: *Do What You Want to Do* Dramatics (1978) R&B#56, *Every Time You Go Away* Paul Young (1985) US#1 UK#4, *I Can't Go for That* [vi] De La Soul sampled in *Say No Go* (1989) UK#18/Above the Law sampled in *V.S.O.P.* (1993) R&B#97; *She's Gone* [x] Lou Rawls (1974) R&B#81/Tavares (1974) R&B#1 US#50; *Swept Away* [v] Diana Ross (1984) R&B#3 US#19. Co-writers: [i] Janna Allen, [ii] Janna Allen/Sara Allen, [iii] Janna Allen/Sara Allen/Warren Pash, [iv] Sara Allen/R. Iantosca/John Oates (b. April 7, 1949, New York, NY), [v] Sara Allen, [vi] Sara Allen/John Oates, [vii] John Beeby, [viii] Bob Clearmountain/John Oates, [ix] A. Gorrie/P.L. Moreland/V.J. Smith, [x] John Oates. (*See also under* Mick JAGGER.)

405. HALL, John (b. 1948, Baltimore, MD) Rock guitarist and vocalist. A former session player who co-founded the soft-rock group Orleans in 1972. CHART COMPOSITIONS: *Let There Be Music* [ii] (1975) US#55, *Dance with Me* [i] (1975) US#6, *Still the One* [i] (1976) US#5, *Reach* [i] (1977) US#51. ALBUMS: **Orleans** (1973, ABC); **Let There Be Music** (1975) US#33; **Waking and Dreaming** (1976, both Asylum) US#30; **Forever** (1979, Infinity); **One of a Kind** (1982, Radio); **Grown Up Children** (1986, MCA). COMPILATION: **Before the Dance** (1977, ABC). After parting company with Orleans, he formed the John Hall Band. CHART COMPOSITIONS: *Crazy* [iii] (1981) US#42, *You Sure Fooled Me* (1982) US#109, *Love Me Again* (1983) US#64. ALBUMS: **All of the Above** (1981) US#158, **Search Party** (1983, both EMI America) US#147. HIT VERSIONS: *Ms. Grace* [i] Tymes (1974) R&B#75 US#91 UK#1, *Still the One* [i] Bill Anderson (1977) C&W#11/Thrasher Brothers (1982) C&W#60; *What*

You Do to Me Carl Wilson (1983) US#72. Co-writers: [i] Johanna Hall, [ii] L. Hoppen, [iii] B. Leinbach/E. Parker.

406. HALL, Terry (b. March 19, 1959, Coventry, England) Pop vocalist. The lead singer in the British ska group the Specials, who left in 1981 to form the Fun Boy Three. CHART COMPOSITIONS: *The Lunatics (Have Taken Over the Asylum)* [i] (1981) UK#20, *The Telephone Always Rings* [i] (1982) UK#17, *The More I See (The Less I Believe)* [i] (1983) UK#68, *The Tunnel of Love* [i] (1983) UK#10, *Our Lips Are Sealed* [iii] (1983) UK#7. ALBUMS: **Fun Boy Three** (1982) UK#7, **Waiting** (1983, both Chrysalis) US#104 UK#14; **Live on the Test** (1994, Windsong). COMPILATION: **Really Saying Something-The Best of the Fun Boy Three** (1997, Chrysalis). In 1984, Hall formed a further new group, the Color Field. CHART COMPOSITIONS: *The Color Field* (1984) UK#43, *Take* (1984) UK#70, *Thinking of You* [ii] (1985) UK#12, *Castles in the Air* (1985) UK#51. ALBUMS: **Virgins and Philistines** (1985) UK#12, **Deception** (1987, both Chrysalis) UK#95. He also recorded with Dave Stewart in the group Vegas, releasing the album **Vegas** (1993, RCA), before pursuing a solo career. CHART COMPOSITIONS: *Missing* (1989) UK#75, *Forever J* (1994) UK#67, *Sense* (1994) UK#54, *Chasing a Rainbow* (1995) UK#62. ALBUMS: **Ultra Modern Nursery Rhymes** (1989, Chrysalis); **Home** (1994, Anxious); **Laugh** (1997, Southsea). COMPILATION: **Terry Hall: The Collection** (1993, Chrysalis). Co-writers: [i] Lynval Golding (b. July 24, 1954, Coventry, England)/Neville Staples (b. Coventry, England), [ii] Toby Lyons, [iii] Jane Weidlin. (*See also under* Jerry DAMMERS.)

407. HALL, Tom T. (b. Thomas Hall, May 25, 1936, Olive Hill, KY) C&W guitarist and vocalist. A country singer-songwriter who specializes in tales of minor woes and everyday worries, drawing on characters from the seemingly sleepy, small towns of America, that only make the news when they are the subject of a disaster or seedy event. Hall once cited the novelist Ernest Hemingway as being a major influence on his work, and has described his songwriting as a search for, "A sort of undiscovered constant something." His records feature a minimum of musical backing, and are sung in a familiar, country baritone. The son of a church minister, Hall grew up listening to Ernest Tubb's "Nashville Radio Show," and first played homemade instruments, before, at the age of eight, acquiring his first guitar. He worked in a garment factory before, between 1952–1954, performing as a member of the Kentucky Travelers, whose local radio spot led to Hall penning advertising jingles for the show's sponsors. During his U.S. Army service in 1957, Hall was stationed in Germany, where he became an armed forces disc jockey and began singing and writing songs to entertain fellow soldiers. After his discharge in 1961, he returned to America and ran a grocery store, before touring extensively as a member of the Technicians. He signed his first publishing contract in 1964, for which he received the traditional fifty dollars a week against future royalties. His material was recorded by Burl Ives, Jimmy C. Newman and Stonewall Jackson, before *Harper Valley P.T.A.* became a million seller for Jeannie C. Riley in 1968. Of the success of *Harper Valley P.T.A.*, Hall said in his autobiography, "It was like walking down the street and suddenly bending over and finding a million dollars." In 1970, he created his own publishing company Hallnote, and became the television host on "Pop Goes Country." CHART COMPOSITIONS: *I Washed My Face in the Morning Dew* (1967) C&W#30, *The World the Way I Want It* (1968) C&W#66, *Ain't Got the Time* (1968) C&W#68, *The Ballad of Forty Dollars* (1968) C&W#4, *Strawberry Farms* (1969) C&W#40, *Homecoming* (1969) C&W#5, *A Week in a County Jail* (1969) C&W#1, *Shoeshine Man* (1970) C&W#8, *Salute to a Switchblade* (1970) C&W#8, *Day Drinkin'* with Dave Dudley (1970) C&W#23, *One Hundred Children* (1970) C&W#14, *Ode to a Half Pound of Ground Round* (1971) C&W#21, *The Year That Clayton Delaney Died* (1971) C&W#1 US#42, *Me and Jesus* (1972) C&W#8 US#98, *The Monkey That Became President* (1972) C&W#11, *More Than John Henry* (1972) C&W#26, *Old Dogs, Children and Watermelon Wine* (1972) C&W#1, *Hello We're Lonely* with Patti Page (1972) C&W#14, *Ravishing Ruby* (1973) C&W#3, *Watergate Blues/Spokane Motel Blues* (1973) C&W#16 US#101, *I Love* (1973) C&W#1 US#12, *That Song Is Driving Me Crazy* (1974) C&W#2 US#63, *Country Is* (1974) C&W#1, *I Care* (1974) C&W#1 US#55, *Sneaky Snake* (1974) C&W#69, *Deal* (1975) C&W#8, *I Like Beer* (1975) C&W#4, *Faster Horses (The Cowboy and the Poet)* (1976) C&W#1, *Negatory Romance* (1976) C&W#24, *Fox on the Run* (1976) C&W#9, *Your Man Loves You Honey* (1977) C&W#4, *May the Force Be with You Always* (1977) C&W#13, *I Wish I Loved Somebody Else* (1978) C&W#13, *What Have You Got to Lose* (1978) C&W#9, *The Son of Clayton Delaney* (1979) C&W#14, *There Is a Miracle in You* (1979) C&W#20, *You Show Me Your Heart (And I'll Show You Mine)* (1979) C&W#11, *The Old Side of Town/Jesus on the Radio (Daddy on the Phone)* (1980) C&W#9, *Soldier of Fortune* (1980) C&W#51, *Back When Gas Was Thirty Cents a Gallon* (1980) C&W#36, *The All New Me* (1981) C&W#41, *There Ain't No Country Music on This Jukebox* with Earl Scruggs

(1982) C&W#77, *Everything from Jesus to Jack Daniels* (1983) C&W#42, *Famous in Missouri* (1984) C&W#81, *A Bar with No Beer* (1985) C&W#40, *Down in the Florida Keys* (1985) C&W#42, *Susie's Beauty Shop* (1986) C&W#52, *Down at the Mall* (1986) C&W#65. ALBUMS: **Country Is** (1969), **Homecoming** (1970), **In Search of a Song** (1971) US#137, **I Witness Life** (1971), **One Hundred Children** (1972), **The Rhymer and Other Five and Dimers** (1973) US#181, **For the People in the Last Hard Town** (1974) US#149, **Songs of the Hollow** (1975) US#180, **Faster Horses** (1976), **The Magnificent Music Machine** (1976), **Tom T. Hall** (1977), **We All Got Together** (1978), **Tom T. Hall the Storyteller** (1978, all Mercury); **The Places I've Done Time** (1979, AHL); **Natural Dreams** (1984, Mercury); **In Concert** (1986, RCA); **World Class Country** (1985, Range). COMPILATIONS: **Greatest Hits, Volume 1** (1980), **Greatest Hits, Volume 2** (1981), **Greatest Hits, Volume 3** (1982, all Mercury). HIT VERSIONS: *Artificial Rose* Jimmy C. Newman (1965) C&W#8, *Back in Circulation* Jimmy C. Newman (1965) C&W#13, *Back Pocket Money* Jimmy C. Newman (1966) C&W#10, *City of the Angels* Jimmy C. Newman (1965) C&W#37, *Do It to Someone You Love* Norro Wilson (1970) C&W#20, *George and the North Woods* Dave Dudley (1969) C&W#10, *Greenwich Village Folk Song Salesman* Jim & Jesse (1968) C&W#49, *Harper Valley P.T.A.* Ben Colder (1968) C&W#24 US#67/King Curtis (1968) US#93/Bobbi Martin (1968) US#114/Jeannie C. Riley (1968) g C&W#1 US#1 UK#12; *Hello, Vietnam* Johnny Wright (1965) C&W#1, *I'm Not Ready Yet* Blue Boys (1968) C&W#58/George Jones (1980) C&W#2; *If I Ever Fall in Love (With a Honky Tonk Girl)* Faron Young (1970) C&W#4, *Louisiana Saturday Night* [i] Jimmy C. Newman (1967) C&W#24/Mel McDaniel (1981) C&W#7; *Love Is the Foundation* Loretta Lynn (1973) C&W#1, *Mad* Dave Dudley (1964) C&W#6, *Margie's at the Lincoln Park Inn* Bobby Bare (1969) C&W#4, *Pamela Brown* Jud Strunk (1975) C&W#88, *There Ain't No Easy Run* Dave Dudley (1968) C&W#10, *What We're Fighting For* Dave Dudley (1965) C&W#4, *You Always Come Back (To Hurting Me)* [ii] Johnny Rodriguez (1973) C&W#1 US#86. Co-writers: [i] Jimmy C. Newman (b. August 2, 1927, Big Mamou, LA), [ii] Johnny Rodriguez (b. Juan Rodriguez, December 10, 1951, Sabinal, TX).

408. HAMBLEN, Stuart (b. Carl Stuart Hamblen, October 20, 1908, Kellerville, TX; d. March 8, 1989) C&W vocalist. A gospel influenced singing cowboy who was also a film star. Hamblen died in 1989 from a brain tumor. CHART COMPOSITIONS: *But I'll Go Chasin' Women* (1949) C&W#3, *(Remember Me) I'm the One Who Loves You*

(1950) C&W#2, *It's No Secret (What Love Can Do)* (1951) C&W#8, *This Ole House* (1954) C&W#2 US#26. ALBUMS: **It Is No Secret** (1954), **In the Garden** (1958, both RCA); **I Believe** (1960, Columbia); **This Old House Has Got to Go** (1965, Kapp); **Cowboy Church** (1974, Word); **A Man and His Music** (1975, Lamb and Lion). HIT VERSIONS: *Go on By* Alma Cogan (1955) UK#16, *It's No Secret (What Love Can Do)* Bill Kenny (1951) US#18/Jo Stafford (1951) US#15; *Open Up Your Heart* Bing Crosby (1953) US#22/Cowboy Church Sunday School (1955) US#8/Joan Regan (1955) UK#19; *(Remember Me) I'm the One Who Loves You* Ernest Tubb (1950) C&W#5/Dean Martin (1965) US#32; *This Ole House* Billie Anthony (1954) UK#4/Rosemary Clooney (1954) UK#1/Winifred Atwell in *Let's Have a Ball* (1957) UK#4/Wilma Lee & Stoney Cooper (1960) C&W#16/Shakin' Stevens (1981) UK#1.

409. HAMLISCH, Marvin (b. Marvin Frederick Hamlisch, June 2, 1944, New York, NY). Film and stage pianist, producer. The son of an accordion player, who, at the age of four, was discovered to have perfect pitch. After becoming the youngest student ever to study at Juilliard, Hamlisch became a Broadway rehearsal pianist during the 1960s, before, in 1964, arranging the show "Fade Out-Fade In." A 1968 party given by the film director Sam Spiegal resulted in Hamlisch's first film score, "The Swimmer," which he followed with numerous Hollywood soundtracks during the 1970s, including "Save the Tiger" (1973) and "Starting Over" (1979). Hamlisch also scored the Broadway show "Minnie's Boys" (1970), and worked as the straight-man and pianist for the comedian Groucho Marx, before arranging for the vocalists Liza Minnelli, Ann-Margaret and Joel Gray. He won Oscars for his arrangements of Scott Joplin's piano rags and waltzes in the film "The Sting" (1974), and for Barbra Streisand's million selling title theme to "The Way We Were" (1974), about which Hamlisch said, "I had to beg her to sing it." In 1975, he worked on the television movies "Hot L. Baltimore," "Beacon Hill" and "Good Morning America." Hamlisch's greatest success was with the show "A Chorus Line" (1976), co-written with the lyricist Edward Kleban, which opened off-Broadway but soon graduated to Broadway itself. Until 1997, when surpassed by Andrew Lloyd Webber's "Cats," "A Chorus Line" was the longest running Broadway musical. Hamlisch was also successful with "They're Playing Our Song" (1979), "The Goodbye Girl" (1993) and "Smile" (1986). In 1986, he became a music teacher at Julliard. CHART COMPOSITION: *The Entertainer* (arrangement only) (1974) g US#3 UK#25. ALBUMS: **The Swimmer** ost (1968, Columbia); **Take**

the **Money and Run** ost (1969, Command); **The April Fools** ost (1969, Columbia); **Bananas** ost (1971), **The World's Greatest Athlete** ost (1973, both Centurion); **The Entertainer** ost (1974) US#170, **The Sting** ost (1974, both MCA) g US#1 UK#7; **The Way We Were** ost (1974) g US#20, **A Chorus Line** oc (1975, both Columbia) g US#98; **The Prisoner of Second Avenue** ost (1975, Polydor); **The Spy Who Loved Me** ost (1977, United Artists) US#40; **Kotch** ost (1978, Columbia); **The Champ** ost (1979, Planet); **Chapter Two** ost (1979, Disc); **Ice Castles** ost (1979, Arista) US#174; **They're Playing Our Song** oc (1979, Casablanca) US#167; **Ordinary People** ost (1980, Planet); **They're Playing Our Song** oc (19780, Chopper); **The Devil and Max Devlin** ost (1981, Disc); **Pennies From Heaven** ost (1981), **I Ought to Be in Pictures** ost (1982, both Warner Brothers); **Sophie's Choice** ost (1982, Southern Cross); **The Goodbye Girl** oc (1993, Columbia); **A Streetcar Named Desire** ost (1984, Allegiance); **A Chorus Line-The Movie** ost (1985, Casablanca) US#77; **D.A.R.Y.L.** ost (1985, Asylum). HIT VERSIONS: *Break It to Me Gently* [ii] Aretha Franklin (1977) R&B#1 US#85, *California Nights* [iii] Lesley Gore (1967) US#16, *If You Remember Me* [ii] Chris Thompson (1979) US#17 UK#42, *Nobody Does It Better* [ii] Carly Simon (1977) US#2 UK#7, *One Hello* [ii] Randy Crawford (1982) UK#48, *Somewhere I Belong* Teddy Pendergrass (1985) R&B#76, *Sunshine, Lollipops and Rainbows* Lesley Gore (1965) US#13, *Through the Eyes of Love (Theme from Ice Castles)* [ii] Melissa Manchester (1979) US#76, *Too Little, Too Late* Brenda Lee (1966) US#123, *Way We Were, The* [i] Barbra Streisand (1974) g US#1 UK#31/Gladys Knight & the Pips (1975) R&B#6 US#11 UK#4/Manhattans (1979) R&B#33. Co-writers: [i] Alan Bergman/Marilyn Bergman, [ii] Carole Bayer Sager, [iii] Howard Liebling.

410. HAMMERSTEIN, Oscar, II (b. Oscar Greely Glendenning Hammerstein, July 12, 1895, New York, NY; d. August 23, 1960, Doylestown, PA) Film and stage lyricist. The lyricist of six musicals that each ran over four hundred and fifty performances. Hammerstein was born into a musical and theatrical family, but studied law before becoming a stage manager in 1917. He first co-wrote the operettas "Tickle Me" (1920) and "Wildflower" (1923) with Otto Harbach and Herbert Stothart, "Rose Marie" (1924) with Rudolf Friml, "The Desert Song" (1926) with Sigmund Romberg, and "Song of the Flame" (1925) with Harbach and George Gershwin, before forming a partnership with Jerome Kern for "Sunny" (1925), "Sweet Adelaine" (1929), "Music in the Air" (1932), "The Three Sisters" (1934), and "Very Warm for May" (1939), the last of which introduced the jazz standard *All the Things You Are* [ii]. Kern and Hammerstein's finest creation was undoubtedly "Show Boat" (1927), which was later filmed on three occasions, and introduced such classics as *Ol' Man River* [ii], *Bill* [ii] and *Can't Help Loving Dat Man* [ii]. It was a show that re-defined Broadway, essentially ending the operetta tradition and introducing the theatrical and musical play. During the 1930s, Hammerstein wrote for the Hollywood musicals "Viennese Nights" (1930), "The Night Is Young" (1935) and "High, Wide and Handsome" (1937), but he also continued on Broadway with "Carmen Jones" (1954), before becoming Richard Rodgers' second lyricist and co-producer. Hammerstein died of cancer in 1960. HIT VERSIONS: *Dawn* [i] Nat Shilkret (1928) US#16, *I'll Take Romance* [iii] Rudy Vallee (1938) US#19. Co-writers: [i] Otto Harbach/Robert Stolz/Herbert Stothart (b. September 11 1885, Milwaukee, WI; d. February 1, 1949, Los Angeles, CA), [ii] Jerome Kern, [iii] Ben Oakland (b. 1970; d. 1979). (*See also under* Rudolf FRIML, George GERSHWIN, Jerome KERN, Richard RODGERS and Oscar HAMMERSTEIN, II, Sigmund ROMBERG, Harry RUBY, Arthur SCHWARTZ.)

411. HAMMOND, Albert (b. May 18, 1942, London, England) Pop guitarist and vocalist. A singer-songwriter who turned to writing for others when his solo career floundered in the late 1970s. Hammond grew up in Gibraltar, and developed an interest in music during his teens, after which he briefly performed as a member of the 1960s group the Magic Lanterns. In 1966 he formed a songwriting partnership with the lyricist Mike Hazelwood, and in 1972, he emigrated to America, where he enjoyed a short solo career with a series of classy pop singles. Hammond returned to England during the 1980s. CHART COMPOSITIONS: *Down By the River* [ix] (1972) US#91, *It Never Rains in Southern California* [ix] (1972) g US#5, *The Peacemaker* [ix] (1973) US#80, *If You Gotta Break Another Heart* [ix] (1973) US#63, *The Free Electric Band* [ix] (1973) US#48 UK#19, *Half a Million Miles from Home* [ix] (1973) US#87, *I'm a Train* [ix] (1974) US#31, *Air Disaster* [ix] (1974) US#81, *99 Miles from L.A.* [iv] (1975) US#91. ALBUMS: **It Never Rains in Southern California** (1972) US#77, **The Free Electric Band** (1973) US#193, **Albert Hammond** (1974, all MUMS); **99 Miles from L.A.** (1975), **When I Need You** (1977, both Epic); **Your World and My World** (1980, CBS); **Mi Album De Recuerdos** (1980, Epic); **Somewhere in America** (1982, Columbia). COMPILATIONS: **Greatest Hits** (1977, Embassy); **Very Best of Albert Hammond** (1994, Columbia). HIT VERSIONS: *Air That I Breathe, The* [ix] Hollies

(1974) g US#6 UK#2, re-issued (1988) UK#60, also in *Holliedaze (A Medley)* (1981) UK#28/Rex Allen, Jr. (1983) C&W#37; *Be Tender with Me Baby* Tina Turner (1989) UK#28, *Blow the House Down* [xiii] Living in a Box (1989) UK#10, *Couldn't Say Goodbye* [xiv] Tom Jones (1991) UK#51, *Don't Turn Around* [xiv] Tina Turner on B-side of *Typically Male* (1986) US#2 UK#33/Luther Ingram (1987) R&B#55/Aswad (1988) R&B#45 UK#1/Neil Diamond (1992) US#19/ Ace of Base (1994) US#4 UK#5; *Gimme Dat Ding* [vii] Pipkins (1970) US#9 UK#6, *Give a Little Love* [xiv] Aswad (1988) UK#11, *Good Morning Freedom* [ix] Blue Mink (1969) UK#10/Daybreak (1970) US#96; *Here I Go Again (Fallin' in Love Again)* [vi] Frannie Golde (1979) US#76, *I Don't Wanna Lose You* [xi] Tina Turner (1989) UK#8, *I Don't Want to Live Without Your Love* [xiv] Chicago (1988) US#3, *I Need to Be in Love* [ii] Carpenters (1976) US#25 UK#36, *It Isn't, It Wasn't, It Ain't Never Gonna Be* [xiv] Aretha Franklin & Whitney Houston (1989) US#41, *It Never Rains in Southern California* [ix] Tony! Toni! Tone! (1991) US#34 UK#69, *Little Arrows* [ix] Leapy Lee (1969) US#16 UK#2, *Lonely Is the Night* [xiv] Air Supply (1986) US#76, *Love Thing* [x] Tina Turner (1992) UK#29, *Make Me an Island* [ix] Joe Dolan (1969) UK#3, *Names, Tags, Numbers, Labels* [ix] Association (1973) US#91, *Nothing's Gonna Stop Us Now* [xiv] Starship (1986) g US#1 UK#1, *One Moment in Time* [i] Whitney Houston (1988) US#5 UK#1, *Other Side of the Sun, The* Janis Ian (1980) UK#44, *Room in Your Heart* [iii] Living in a Box (1989) UK#5, *Through the Storm* [xiv] Aretha Franklin & Elton John (1989) US#16 UK#41, *To All the Girls I've Loved Before* [iv] Julio Iglesias & Willie Nelson (1984) g C&W#1 US#5 UK#17, *Way of the World, The* [xi] Tina Turner (1991) UK#13, *When I Need You* [xii] Leo Sayer (1979) g R&B#94 US#1 UK#1, re-issued (1993) UK#65/Lois Johnson (1978) C&W#63; *When You Tell Me That You Love Me* [i] Diana Ross (1991) R&B#37 UK#2, *You're Such a Good Looking Woman* [ix] Joe Dolan (1970) UK#17. Co-writers: [i] John Bettis, [ii] John Bettis/Richard Carpenter, [iii] Richard Darbyshire/Marcus Vere, [iv] Hal David, [vi] Frannie Golde, [vii] Roger Greenaway, [viii] Roger Greenaway/Mike Hazlewood, [ix] Mike Hazlewood, [x] Holly Knight, [xi] Graham Lyle, [xii] Carole Bayer Sager, [xiii] Marcus Vere, [xiv] Dianne Warren. (*See also under* Leo SAYER.)

412. HANCOCK, Butch (b. George Hancock, July 12, 1945, Lubbock, TX) C&W guitarist and vocalist. A rugged song individualist who mixes traditional country with Woody Guthrie styled story telling, making him one of the few remaining country artists still influenced by folk roots. Hancock's compositions, like those of Townes Van Zandt, have proven more successful when recorded in a commercial style by other artists. His father was a farmer and published author, and he grew up on a farm in rural Texas. In 1970, he formed the group the Flatlanders with Joe Ely and Jimmie Dale Gilmore, which recorded the solitary album **One More Road** (1970, Charly), which remained unreleased for a decade. After living in an abandoned jailhouse in Clarendon, Texas, between 1973–1975, Hancock relocated to Austin, where he became a permanent fixture on the alternative country music scene. In 1978, he established his own Rainlight label and issued a series of albums that were only available by mail order from his farm. The Rainlight sets feature some of the most authentic country music of recent times, as evidenced by the delightful *West Texas Waltz*. **No Two Alike** (1991), was a one hundred and forty song collection of fourteen one-hour tape cassettes, which captured six nights of live performances at the Cactus Cafe in Austin. ALBUMS: **West Texas Waltzes and Dust Blown Tractor Tunes** (1978), **The Wind's Dominion** (1979), **Diamond Hill** (1980), **1981: A Spare Odyssey** (1981), **Fire Water (Seeks It's Own Level)** (1981), **Yella Rose*** (1985), **Spit and Slide (Apocalypse Now Pay Later)** (1986), **Cause of the Cactus*** (1987, all Rainlight); **Two Roads** with Jimmie Dale Gilmore (1990, CLE); **No Two Alike** (1991, Rainlight); **Own the Way Over Here** (1993, Sugar Hill); **Eats Away the Night** (1994, Glitterhouse). COMPILATION: **Own and Own** (1989, Demon). With: * Marce Lacoutre.

413. HANDMAN, Lou (b. September, 10, 1894, New York; December 9, 1956, Flushing, both NY) Tin Pan Alley composer. A piano accompanist turned song demonstrator, who became a songwriter in the early 1920s. One of Handman's most recorded songs was *I Can't Get the One I Want* (1934). HIT VERSIONS: *Are You Lonesome Tonight?* [i] Henry Burr (1927) US#4/Vaughn Deleath (1927) US#4/Blue Barron (1950) US#19/Elvis Presley (1960) g R&B#3 US#1 UK#1, re-issued (1977) UK#46, live version (1982) UK#25, re-issued (1991) UK#68; *Blue (And Broken Hearted)* [i] Marion Harris (1923) US#7, *Bye Bye Baby* [ii] Charlie Barnet (1936) US#16/Fats Waller (1936) US#4; *Is My Baby Blue Tonight?* [i] Lawrence Welk (1944) US#13, *Me and the Moon* [ii] Bing Crosby (1936) US#9/Hal Kemp (1936) US#8; *Puddin' Head Jones* Rudy Vallee (1934) US#13, *Was It Rain?* [ii] Frances Langford (1937) US#11. Co-writers: [i] Grant Clarke/Edgar Leslie, [ii] Walter Hirsch, [iii] William Tracey, [iv] Roy Turk.

414. HANDY, W.C. (b. William Christopher Handy, November 16, 1873, Florence, AL; d.

March 28, 1958, New York, NY) Jazz cornetist and bandleader. Although it is debatable whether Handy actually wrote all the songs that he copyrighted in his lifetime, there is no doubt that he did compose *St. Louis Blues*, the most recorded tune of the twentieth century, the copyright to which he sold for fifty dollars. Handy was an influential songwriter who was probably the first to utilize flattened thirds and sevenths in his compositions, thus leading the blues to jazz. Born into extreme rural poverty, he studied the organ and music theory before performing as a cornetist in brass bands. He directed Mahara's Minstrels between 1896–1903, and in 1908, co-founded his first music publishing company. Handy's first published composition was *Memphis Blues* [ii] (1912), after which he went on to compose such jazz standards as *Beale Street Blues*. Handy was blinded by an accident in 1943. His songs were recorded by Louis Armstrong and Nat "King" Cole on the album **St. Louis Blues** ost (1958, Capitol) US#18. CHART COMPOSITIONS: *Livery Stable Blues* (1918) US#7, *St. Louis Blues* (1923) US#9. HIT VERSIONS: *Aunt Hagar's Blues* [i] Ted Lewis (1923) US#7, re-issued (1930) US#6; *Beale Street Blues* Earl Fuller (1917) US#8/Prince's Orchestra (1917) US#5/Marion Harris (1921) US#5/Alberta Hunter (1927) US#16/Joe Venturi (1932) US#20/Guy Lombardo (1942) US#20; *Careless Love Blues* [iii] Bessie Smith (1925) US#5, *Memphis Blues* [ii] Victor Military Band (1914) US#9/Prince's Orchestra (1914) US#4/Arthur Collins & Byron Harlan (1915) US#8/Ted Lewis (1927) US#9/Harry James (1944) US#15; *St. Louis Blues* Prince's Orchestra (1916) US#4/Al Bernard (1919) US#9/Marion Harris (1920) US#1/Original Dixieland Jazz Band (1921) US#3/Bessie Smith (1925) US#3/Louis Armstrong (1930) US#11/Cab Calloway (1930) US#16, re-issued (1943) US#18/Rudy Vallee (1930) US#15/Mills Brothers (1932) US#2/Boswell Sisters (1935) US#15/Benny Goodman (1936) US#20/Guy Lombardo (1939) US#11/Billy Eckstine (1953) US#24/Cousins (1961) US#110; *Yellow Dog Blues* Joseph C. Smith's Orchestra (1920) US#4/Ben Pollack (1929) US#20/Ted Lewis (1930) US#4. Co-writers: [i] J. Tim Brymm, [ii] Martha Koenig/Spencer Williams, [iii] Spencer Williams.

415. HANLEY, James Frederick (b. February 17, 1892, Rensalaer, IN; d. February 8, 1942, Douglaston, NY) Film and stage composer. A graduate of the Chicago Musical College, who composed his first hit with Ballard MacDonald, *The Ragtime Volunteers Are Off to War* [vi] (1917). Hanley's songs appeared in such shows as "Ziegfeld Midnight Frolic" (1921), "Ziegfeld Follies of 1921" and "Honeymoon Lane" (1926). HIT VERSIONS: *Breeze (Blow My Baby Back to Me)* [v] American Quartet

(1919) US#10, *Gee, But I Hate to Go Home Alone* [iv] Billy Jones (1922) US#8, *Half a Moon* [iii] Johnny Marvin (1927) US#12, *Indiana* [vi] Conway's Band (1917) US#8/Original Dixieland Jazz Band (1917) US#8/Red Nichols (1929) US#19/Freddy Cannon (1960) UK#42; *Little White House (At the End of Honeymoon Lane), The* [ii] Irving Kaufman (1927) US#6/Johnny Marvin (1927) US#3/Fred Waring's Pennsylvanians (1927) US#11; *Rose of Washington Square* [vi] Henry Burr (1920) US#5/Kentucky Serenaders (1920) US#3/Benny Goodman (1939) US#10; *Second Hand Rose* [i] Ted Lewis (1921) US#2/Fanny Brice (1922) US#3/Barbra Streisand (1966) US#32 UK#14; *Zing! Went the Strings of My Heart* Judy Garland (1943) US#22. Co-writers: [i] Grant Clarke, [ii] Eddie Dowling, [iii] Eddie Dowling/Herbert Reynolds, [iv] Joe Goodwin, [v] Joe Goodwin/Ballard MacDonald, [vi] Ballard MacDonald. (*See also under* Buddy DE SYLVA.)

416. HARBACH, Otto (b. Otto Abels Hauerbach, August 18, 1873, Salt Lake City, UT; d. January 24, 1963, New York, NY) Film and stage lyricist, musical director. A journalist and professor of English who achieved musical success with the shows "The Three Twins" (1908) and "Madame Sherry" (1910). Harbach's songs were also featured in the films "Presenting Lily Mars" (1943) and "On Moonlight Bay" (1951). Between 1950–1953, he was the president of ASCAP. HIT VERSIONS: *Cuddle Up a Little Closer* [ii] Ada Jones & Billy Murray (1908) US#1/Dick Jurgens (1942) US#24/Kay Armen (1943) US#19/Joe "Mr. Piano" Henderson in *Sing It with Joe* (1955) UK#14; *Every Little Movement (Has a Meaning All Its Own)* [ii] Henry Burr & Elise Stevenson (1910) US#6/Harry MacDonough & Lucy Isabelle (1910) US#1/Victor Light Opera Co. (1911) US#6; *Love Nest* [i] Art Hickman (1920) US#1/Joseph C. Smith's Orchestra (1920) US#6/John Steel (1920) US#1. Co-writers: [i] Louis Hirsch, [ii] Karl Hoschna (b. August 16, 1877, Bohemia; d. December 22, 1911, New York, NY). (*See also under* Rudolf FRIML, George GERSHWIN, Oscar HAMMERSTEIN, II, Jerome KERN, Sigmund ROMBERG, Vincent YOUMANS.)

417. HARBURG, E.Y. "Yip" (b. Isidore Hochberg, April 8, 1898, New York, NY; d. March 5, 1981, Los Angeles, CA) Film and stage lyricist. The creator of a pantheon of wry, yet often compassionate songs, none better than the Depression-era classic *Brother, Can You Spare a Dime?* [i], which was introduced in the musical "Americana" (1932). Born into poverty, Harburg achieved exceptional academic qualifications and befriended the fellow lyricist Ira Gershwin. During the 1930s, he collabo-

rated with Vernon Duke on the musicals "The Garrick Gaieties of 1930" and "Walk a Little Faster" (1932), and in the mid-1930s, he frequently worked in Hollywood, where, with Harold Arlen, he composed the score to "The Wizard of Oz" (1939). Harburg's last significant partnership was with Burton Lane, writing the Broadway hit "Finian's Rainbow" (1947). He died in an automobile accident in 1981. ALBUMS: **The Happiest Girl in the World** oc (1961, Columbia) US#84. HIT VERSIONS: *Brother, Can You Spare a Dime?* [i] Bing Crosby (1932) US#1/Rudy Vallee (1932) US#1; *I'm Yours* [ii] Ben Bernie (1930) US#16/Bert Lown (1930) US#3; *What Wouldn't I Do for That Man?* [i] Ruth Etting (1929) US#9. Co-writers: [i] Jay Gorney, [ii] Johnny Green. (*See also under* Harold ARLEN, Vernon DUKE, Burton LANE.)

418. HARDIN, Tim (b. December 23, 1941, Eugene, OR; d. December 29, 1980, Los Angeles, CA) Folk guitarist, harmonica player, pianist and vocalist. One of the 1960s finest world-weary folk and blues singers, who penned some of the most personal, intense and distinguished songs of the era, many of which were hits for artists other than himself. Hardin's first two albums **Tim Hardin 1** (1966) and **Tim Hardin 2** (1967), remain pinnacles of contemporary folk music, but his subsequent work never matched his early potency, and during the early 1970s, heroin and alcohol abuse gradually eroded his talent. Hardin died from a drug overdose in 1980, the tragic conclusion to a strangely troubled and desperately private life. CHART COMPOSITION: *How Can We Hang on to a Dream* (1967) UK#50. ALBUMS: **Tim Hardin 1** (1966), **Tim Hardin 2** (1967), **Tim Hardin 3-Live in Concert** (1968), **Tim Hardin 4** (1969, all Verve/Folkways); **Suite for Susan Moore and Damian** (1970) US#129, **Bird on a Wire** (1970) US#189, **Painted Head** (1972, all Columbia); **Nine** (1974, Antilles). COMPILATIONS: **This is Tim Hardin** (1967, Atco); **Best of Tim Hardin** (1970, Verve); **The Homecoming Concert** (1980, Line); **Unforgiven** (1980, SFS); **State of Grace** (1981, Columbia); **The Memorial Album** (1991, PD); **Hang on to a Dream-The Verve Recordings** (1994, Polydor). HIT VERSIONS: *If I Were a Carpenter* Bobby Darin (1966) US#8 UK#9/Four Tops (1968) R&B#17 US#20 UK#7/Johnny Cash & June Carter (1970) US#36/Bob Seger (1972) US#76/Leon Russell (1975) US#73/Robert Plant (1993) UK#63; *Lady Came from Baltimore, The* Bobby Darin (1967) US#62/Johnny Cash (1974) C&W#14; *Reason to Believe* Suzi Jane Hokum (1969) C&W#75/Rod Stewart (1971) UK#19, also on B-side of *Maggie May* (1971) g US#1 UK#1, live version (1993) US#19 UK#51.

419. HARGROVE, Linda (b. February 3, 1950, Tallahassee, FL) C&W guitarist, pianist and vocalist. A folk influenced country songwriter, whose material has been recorded by Sandy Posey, Leon Russell and Billie Jo Spears. Her song *I Never Loved Anyone Anymore*, has been recorded over forty times. During the late 1970s, Hargrove became a born-again Christian. CHART COMPOSITIONS: *Blue Jean Country Queen* (1974) C&W#98, *I Never Loved Anyone Anymore* (1974) C&W#82, *Love Was (Once Around the Dance Floor)* (1975) C&W#39, *Love, You're the Teacher* (1976) C&W#86, *Fire at First Sight* (1976) C&W#86, *Down to My Pride* (1977) C&W#91, *Mexican Love Songs* (1977) C&W#61, *You Are Still the One* (1978) C&W#93. ALBUMS: **Music Is Your Mistress** (1972), **Blue Jean Country Queen** (1974, both Elektra); **Love, You're the Teacher** (1975), **Just Like You** (1976), **Impressions** (1978, all Capitol). HIT VERSION: *Just Get Up and Close the Door* Johnny Rodriguez (1975) C&W#1.

420. HARLEY, Steve (b. Steven Nice, February 27, 1951, London, England) Pop vocalist. A rock journalist turned pop star who fronted the 1970s group Cockney Rebel. CHART COMPOSITIONS: *Judy Teen* (1974) UK#5, *Mr. Soft* (1974) UK#8, *Make Me Smile (Come Up and See Me)* (1975) US#96 UK#1, re-issued (1992) UK#46, re-issued (1995) UK#33; *Mr. Raffles (Man It Was Mean)* (1975) UK#13, *Love's a Prima Donna* (1976) UK#41. ALBUMS: **Human Menagerie** (1973), **The Psychomodo** (1974) UK#8, **The Best Years of Our Lives** (1975) UK#4, **Timeless Flight** (1976) UK#18, **Love's a Prima Donna** (1976) UK#28, **Face to Face-A Live Recording** (1977, all EMI) UK#40. COMPILATIONS: **Best of Steve Harley and Cockney Rebel** (1979), **Greatest Hits** (1988, both EMI); **Live at the BBC** (1995, Windsong). Since the mid-1970s, Harley has pursued a solo recording and acting career, charting with *Freedom's Prisoner* (1979) UK#58. ALBUMS: **Hobo with a Grin** (1978), **The Candidate** (1979, both EMI); **Yes You Can** (1993, Food for Thought). HIT VERSIONS: *Make Me Smile (Come Up and See Me)* Duran Duran on B-side of *The Reflex* (1984) p US#1 UK#1.

421. HARPER, Roy (b. June 12, 1941, Manchester, England) Folk guitarist and vocalist. A hippie and folk influenced singer-songwriter with a small but devoted following. During the early 1960s Harper was a London street busker, before graduating to the folk circuit and recording contracts with a variety of labels. ALBUMS: **The Sophisticated Beggar** (1966, Strike); **Come Out Fighting Ghengis Smith** (1967, CBS); **Folkjokeopus** (1969, Liberty); **Flat, Baroque and Berserk** (1970), **Stormcock** (1971), **Life Mask** (1973), **Valentine** (1974) UK#27, **H.Q.** (1975, all Harvest) UK#31; **When an Old Cricketer Leaves His Crease** (1975), **One of Those Days in England** (1977, both Chrysalis); **Bullinamingvase** (1977) UK#25, **Commercial Break** (1977), **The Unknown Soldier** (1978, all Harvest); **Born in Captivity** (1985), **Work of Heart** (1986, both Awareness); **Whatever Happened to Jugula?** (1985, Beggar's Banquet) UK#44; **In Between Every Lines** (1986), **Descendants of Smith** (1988, both EMI); **Loony on the Bus** (1988), **Death or Glory?** (1992, both Awareness); **Born in Captivity!! (Live)** (1992), **Live at the BBC, Volumes 1 to 6** (1997, both Hard). COMPILATION: **Flashes from the Archives of Oblivion** (1974, Harvest); **The Early Years** (1977, Embassy); **Roy Harper, 1970–1975** (1978, Harvest).

422. HARPO, Slim (b. James Moore, January 11, 1924, Lobdell; d. January 31, 1970, Baton Rouge, both LA) Blues guitarist, harmonica player and vocalist. Arguably the finest exponent of the blues harmonica, and a significant influence on the playing style of Mick Jagger. Harpo's material contributed greatly to the repertoire of the 1960s British blues boom, his songs *Shake Your Hips* and *Got Love if You Want It* being recorded by the Rolling Stones and the Kinks respectively. Harpo died of a heart attack in 1970. CHART COMPOSITIONS: *Rainin' in My Heart* (1961) R&B#17 US#34, *Baby Scratch My Back* (1966) R&B#1 US#16, *Shake Your Hips* (1966) US#116, *I'm Your Bread Maker, Baby* (1966) US#116, *Tip on In, Part 1* (1967) R&B#37 US#127, *Te-Ni-Nee-Ni-Nu* (1968) R&B#36. ALBUMS: **Baby Scratch My Back** (1960), **Rainin' in My Heart** (1960, both Excello); **A Long Drink of the Blues** with Lightnin' Slim (1965, Stateside); **Tip on In** (1968, President); **He Knew the Blues** (1970), **Trigger Finger** (1970, both Blue Horizon); **Blues Hangover** (1976), **Got Love if You Want It** (1980), **Shake Your Hips** (1983, all Flyright); **Best of Slim Harpo** (1987, Excello); **I'm a King Bee** (1989, Flyright).

423. HARRIS, Charles K. (b. Charles Kassell Harris, May 1, 1867, Poughkeepsie; d. December 22, 1930, New York, both NY) Film and stage composer. Often called the father of Tin Pan Alley, it was Harris who, after receiving less than a dollar in royalties for his first hit *When the Sun Has Set* (1892), became the first known songwriter to publish his own compositions. Harris is also remembered for having hung a sign outside his office that read "Banjoist and song writer, songs written to order," thus becoming the first professional songwriter for hire. Entirely self-taught, and never able to read or write music, Harris' forte was plot oriented sentimental ballads. He paid the performer James Aldrich Libby to sing *After the Ball* (1892), which eventually sold over ten million copies, becoming Tin Pan Alley's first multi-million selling piece of sheet music. Other hits of the period that he wrote include *Always in the Way* for Byron G. Harlan (1903), and his songs were featured in such films as "Wait Till the Sun Shines Nellie" (1952). HIT VERSIONS: *After the Ball* John Yorke Atlee (1893) US#2/George J. Gaskin (1893) US#1/Winifred Atwell in *Make It a Party* (1956) UK#7; *Break the News to Mother* Edison Male Quartette (1898) US#2/George J. Gaskin (1898) US#1/Steve Porter (1898) US#3/Shannon Four (1917) US#6; *For Old Times' Sake* Jere Mahoney (1902) US#3, *Hello Central, Give Me Heaven* Byron G. Harlan (1901) US#1, *'Mid the Green Fields of Virginia* George J. Gaskin (1899) US#4/Harry MacDonough & S.H. Dudley (1899) US#2/Frank Stanley (1899) US#4; *Nobody Knows, Nobody Cares* Harvey Hindermyer (1909) US#10/Will Oakland (1909) US#2.

424. HARRIS, Jimmy "Jam" (b. June 6, 1959, Minneapolis, MN), and **LEWIS, Terry** (b. November 24, 1956, Omaha, NE) Both R&B multi-instrumentalists, producers and vocalists. The most successful R&B songwriting and production partnership since Kenny Gamble and Leon Huff. Like Burt Bacharach and Hal David, Harris and Lewis compose with the production and arrangement as an integral part of the song itself, utilizing modern recording techniques to create entire soundscapes, upon which many of their artists become mere embellishments and finishing touches. Harris and Lewis sometimes work separately on projects, but credit everything as a duo, and have achieved over thirty gold and platinum records. They own their own studio complex, which they use solely for their own in-house team. Harris said of their success in 1993, "any professional production begins with a good song." The Lewis family had moved to Minneapolis during the 1960s, where he played in his father's jazz band while also working as a local club and radio disc jockey. In 1973, he became the bassist in Prince's band Champagne, co-founding the group Flyte Tyme the following year. Harris and Lewis met as teenagers at the University of Minnesota, and first played together in Flyte Tyme, where they first attempted to merge the pop-soul of Motown Records with the funk sound of George Clinton. The group evolved into the Time, Prince's backing during 1978, and released the album **Pandemonium** (1990, Paisley Park) g US#18 UK#66. Harris and Lewis were fired by Prince when they missed a gig, so they set up on their own, writing the songs *When You're Far Away* and *Wild Girls* for the vocal group Klymaxx in

1982. Their work with the studio group Change in the mid-1980s heralded a new era in R&B, creating what became known as techno-funk: a tough, repetitive, drum-heavy urban sound. Harris and Lewis' greatest success has been turning around the career of Janet Jackson, whose lush, punchy, industrial dance sound defined R&B for a number of years. In 1991 they formed their own Perspective label, which was first successful with the Sounds of Blackness, a contemporary gospel group that blended mass vocals with in-vogue studio sounds. Harris and Lewis also made a substantial contribution to the film soundtrack **Mo' Money** (1992, Perspective) p US#6 UK#16. HIT VERSIONS: *Again* [xv] Janet Jackson (1993) p R&B#7 US#1 UK#6, *Alright* [xviii] Janet Jackson (1990) US#4, re-mixed on *Twenty Foreplay* (1996) UK#22; *All True Man* Alexander O'Neal (1991) US#43 UK#18, *Any Time, Any Place/And On and On* [xv] Janet Jackson (1994) R&B#1 US#2 UK#13, *Artificial Heart* Cherrelle (1986) R&B#18, *Because of Love* [xv] Janet Jackson (1994) R&B#9 US#10 UK#19, *Best Things in Life Are Free, The* [v] Luther Vandross & Janet Jackson (1992) R&B#1 US#10 UK#2, re-mixed (1995) UK#7; *Borrowed Love* S.O.S. Band (1986) R&B#14, *Broken Heart Can Mend, A* Alexander O'Neal (1985) R&B#62 UK#53, *Can You Stand the Rain* New Edition (1989) US#44, *Change of Heart* Change (1984) R&B#7 UK#17, *Choose* [vii] Color Me Badd (1994) R&B#106 US#23 UK#65, *Come Back to Me* [xv] Janet Jackson (1990) R&B#1 US#2 UK#20, *Control* [xv] Janet Jackson (1986) R&B#1 US#5 UK#42, *Diamonds* Herb Alpert (1987) R&B#1 US#5 UK#27, *Encore* Cheryl Lynne (1983) R&B#1 US#69 UK#68/Tongue 'n' Cheek (1989) UK#41; *Escapade* [xv] Janet Jackson (1990) R&B#1 US#1 UK#17, *Everything Is Gonna Be Alright* [iii] Sounds of Blackness (1994) R&B#51+, *Fake* Alexander O'Neal (1987) R&B#1 US#25 UK#33, re-mixed (1988) UK#16; *Fidelity* Cheryl Lynn (1985) R&B#25, *Finest, The* S.O.S. Band (1986) R&B#2 US#44 UK#17, *Fishnet* [ix] Morris Day (1988) R&B#1 US#23, *Floor, The* Johnny Gill (1993) R&B#11 US#56, *For Your Love* S.O.S. Band (1984) R&B#34, *Forever Love* [vii] Color Me Badd (1992) US#15, *Fragile* Cherrelle (1984) R&B#37, *Hearsay '89* Alexander O'Neal (1988) UK#56, *Heat of Heat, The* Patti Austin (1986) R&B#13 US#45, *Hitmix (Official Bootleg Mega-Mix)* Alexander O'Neal (1989) UK#19, *Human* Human League (1986) R&B#3 US#1 UK#8, *I Adore You* [xx] Caron Wheeler (1992) R&B#12 US#59, *I Believe* [vi] Sounds of Blackness (1994) R&B#15 US#99 UK#17, *I Didn't Mean to Turn You On* Cherrelle (1984) R&B#8 US#79/Robert Palmer (1986) US#2 UK#9; *I Need Your Loving* [xi] Human League (1986) R&B#52 US#44 UK#72, *I'm in Love* [xvi] Lisa Keith (1994) US#84,

If [xv] Janet Jackson (1993) g R&B#3 US#4 UK#14, *If It Isn't Love* New Edition (1988) US#7, *It Burns Me Up* Change (1984) R&B#61, *Just Be Good to Me* S.O.S. Band (1983) R&B#2 US#55 UK#13/Beats International as *Dub Be Good to Me* [viii] (1990) US#76 UK#1; *Just the Facts* Patti LaBelle (1987) R&B#33, *Just the Way You Like It* S.O.S. Band (1984) R&B#6 US#64 UK#32, *Keep Your Eye on Me* Herb Alpert (1987) R&B#3 US#46 UK#19, *La La Love* [ii] Bobby Ross Avila (1993) R&B#93 US#86, *Let's Wait Awhile* [i] Janet Jackson (1987) R&B#1 US#2 UK#3/Everette Harp (1992) R&B#80; *Love Is All That Matters* Human League (1986) UK#41, *Love Will Never Do (Without You)* Janet Jackson (1990) R&B#1 US#1 UK#34, *Lovers, The* Alexander O'Neal (1988) R&B#41, *Making Love in the Rain* Herb Alpert (1987) R&B#7 US#35, *Miss You Much* Janet Jackson (1989) g R&B#1 US#1 UK#25, *Money Can't Buy You Love* [xix] Ralph Tresvant (1992) R&B#2 US#54, *Nasty* [xv] Janet Jackson (1986) R&B#1 US#3 UK#19, *Never Knew Love Like This Before* Alexander O'Neal & Cherrelle (1988) R&B#2 US#28 UK#26, *No One's Gonna Love You* S.O.S. Band (1984) R&B#15 US#102, *Now I'm Going All the Way* Sounds of Blackness (1993) UK#27, *On Bended Knee* Boyz II Men (1994) p R&B#1 US#1 UK#20, *Optimistic* [xiii] Sounds of Blackness (1991) R&B#59+ UK#28, *Pressure, The* [xii] Sounds of Blackness (1991) R&B#16 UK#71, re-issued (1992) UK#49; *Quiet Time to Play* [xiv] Johnny Gill (1994) R&B#25 US#111, *Renee* [xvii] Lost Boyz (1996) R&B#13+ US#36+, *Rhythm Nation* [xv] Janet Jackson (1990) R&B#1 US#2 UK#23, *Right Kinda Lover, The* [iv] Patti LaBelle (1994) R&B#8 US#61, *Romantic* [xxi] Karyn White (1991) R&B#1 US##1 UK#23, *Rub You the Right Way* Johnny Gill (1991) US#3, *Saturday Love* Cherrelle & Alexander O'Neal (1986) R&B#2 US#26 UK#6, *Sensitivity* Ralph Tresvant (1991) US#4 UK#18, *Sentimental* Alexander O'Neal (1992) UK#53, *Shame on Me* Alexander O'Neal (1991) UK#71, *Slow and Sexy* [x] Shabba Ranks featuring Johnny Gill (1992) R&B#4 US#41 UK#71, *Sunshine* Alexander O'Neal (1987) UK#72, *Tell Me (If You Still Care About Me)* S.O.S. Band (1983) R&B#5 US#65, *Tender Love* Force M.D.'s (1986) US#10 UK#23/Kenny Thomas (1991) UK#26; *Testify* [xii] Sounds of Blackness (1992) R&B#12, *That's the Way Love Goes* [xv] Janet Jackson (1993) p R&B#1 US#1 UK#2/Norman Brown (1994) R&B#93; *What Can I Say to Make You Love Me* Alexander O'Neal (1987) UK#27, *What Have You Done for Me Lately?* [xv] Janet Jackson (1986) R&B#1 US#4 UK#3, *What Is This Thing Called Love* Alexander O'Neal (1991) UK#53, *What's Missing* Alexander O'Neal (1986) R&B#8, *When I Need Somebody* Ralph Tresvant (1994) R&B#45, *When I Think of You* [xv] Janet Jackson (1986) R&B#3 US#1 UK#10, *Where Do U Want Me to Put It* [xiv] Solo (1996) R&B#8 US#50, *Who's the Mack* Ralph Tresvant (1993) R&B#35, *Wrap My Body Tight* Johnny Gill (1991) US#84 UK#57, *You Are My Melody* Change (1984) UK#48, *You Look Good to Me* Cherrelle (1985) R&B#26, *You Used to Hold Me So Tight* Thelma Houston (1984) R&B#13 UK#49, *You're Not My Kind of Girl* New Edition (1988) US#95. Co-writers: [i] Renee Andrews/Janet Jackson (b. Janet Damita Jackson, May 16, 1966, Gary, IN), [ii] Bobby Ross Avila/Bobby Avila, Sr., [iii] Burt Bacharach/Hal David, [iv] A. Bennet-Nesy/J. Wright, [v] M. Bivins/R. Devoe/ Ralph Tresvant (b. May 16, 1968, Boston, MA), [vi] Bonner/Holland/Jones/Morrison/Noland/Webster, [vii] Color Me Badd, [viii] Norman Cook, [ix] Morris Day, [x] C. Dillon/Sly Dunbar/R. Gordon, [xi] D. Eiland/L. Richey/D. Williams, [xii] G. Hines, [xiii] G. Hines/Professor T., [xiv] M. Horton, [xv] Janet Jackson, [xvi] Lisa Keith, [xvii] T. Kelly, [xviii] Terry Lewis only, [xix] Ralph Tresvant, [xx] Caron Wheeler, [xxi] Karyn White (b. October 14, 1965, Los Angeles, CA). (*See also under* Mariah CAREY, Marvin GAYE, Lionel RICHIE.)

425. HARRISON, George, M.B.E. (b. February 25, 1943, Liverpool, England) Rock guitarist, producer and vocalist. A founder member of the Beatles, the most popular group of all time, with which he became a significant songwriter in the late 1960s, penning such classics as *Something*, a BMI five million broadcast performance song, of which there are over one hundred and fifty versions. His compositions *Here Comes the Sun* and *My Sweet Lord* have both become three million radio play songs. Harrison learned the guitar as a teenager and joined the group the Rebels, before linking up with John Lennon and Paul McCartney in the Quarrymen, a skiffle group that ultimately evolved into the Beatles. Harrison's first songwriting efforts were heavily influenced by Lennon and McCartney's style, but he soon developed his own distinctive approach. His first ever song *Don't Bother Me* (1963), was written in a Bournemouth hotel room during a Beatles tour, which Harrison claims only to have attempted in order to see if he could actually compose something. **Rubber Soul** (1965), featured his contributions *If I Needed Someone*, *Taxman* and *I Want To Tell You*, and on **Sergeant Pepper's Lonely Hearts Club Band** (1967), he explored his fascination with Eastern religion on the meditative *Within You, Without You*, written from the sitar with sections in a decidedly un-pop 5/4 time. **The Beatles** (1968), included his magnificent *While My Guitar Gently Weeps*. Harrison also composed the Beatles' chart hits: *Cry for a Shadow* [i] on the B-side of *Ain't She Sweet* as Tony

Sheridan & the Beatles (1964) US#19 UK#29; *Blue Jay Way* on *Magical Mystery Tour EP* (1967) UK#2, *The Inner Light* (1968) US#96, also on the B-side of *Lady Madonna* (1968) US#4 UK#1, re-entry (1988) UK#67; *Old Brown Shoe* on the B-side of *Ballad Of John and Yoko* (1969) US#8 UK#1, *Something* (1969) g US#1 UK#4, *For You Blue* as double A-side with *The Long and Winding Road* (1970) g US#1. Harrison was the first Beatle to record solo projects. His triple set **All Things Must Pass** (1970) sold over three million copies and featured the five million seller *My Sweet Lord*, the melody of which he was adjudged to have "unconsciously" stolen in 1976, when he was sued for infringement of copyright by the publishers of the Chiffons' *He's So Fine*. During the late 1970s, Harrison pursued a variety of film projects with his company Handmade films. In 1988 he partnered Bob Dylan, Jeff Lynne, Tom Petty, and Roy Orbison in the group the Traveling Wilburys. In 1992, Harrison toured Japan with Eric Clapton. CHART COMPOSITIONS: *My Sweet Lord* (1970) g US#1 UK#1, *What Is Life* (1970) US#10, *Bangla Desh* (1971) US#23 UK#10, *Give Me Love (Give Me Peace on Earth)* (1973) US#1 UK#8, *Ding Dong* (1974) US#36 UK#38, *Dark Horse* (1974) US#15, *You* (1975) US#20 UK#38, *This Song* (1976) US#25, *Crackerbox Palace* (1976) US#19, *Blow Away* (1979) US#16 UK#51, *All Those Years Ago* (1981) US#2 UK#13, *Teardrops* (1981) US#102, *Wake Up My Love* (1982) US#53, *When We Was Fab* [ii] (1988) US#23 UK#25, *This Is Love* (1988) UK#55. ALBUMS: **Wonderwall Music** (1968) US#49, **Electronic Sounds** (1969) US#191, **All Things Must Pass** (1970) p US#1 UK#4, **Concert for Bangla Desh** (1972) g US#2 UK#1, **Living in the Material World** (1973) g US#1 UK#2, **Dark Horse** (1974) g US#4, **Extra Texture (Read All About It)** (1975, all Apple) g US#8 UK#16; **Thirty Three and a Third** (1976) g US#11 UK#35, **George Harrison** (1979) g US#14 UK#39, **Somewhere in England** (1981) US#11 UK#13, **Gone Troppo** (1982) US#108, **Cloud Nine** (1987) p US#8 UK#10, **Live in Japan** (1992, all Dark Horse) US#126. COMPILATIONS: **Best of George Harrison** (1976, Parlophone) g US#31; **Best of Dark Horse, 1976–1989** (1989, Dark Horse) US#132. HIT VERSIONS: *Awaiting on You All* Silver Hawk (1971) US#108, *Eagle Laughs at You,* The Jackie Lomax (1968) US#125, *Here Comes the Sun* Richie Havens (1971) US#16/Steve Harley (1976) UK#10/Stars On in *Stars on 45/Stars on Long Play* (1981) g US#6 UK#1; *If I Needed Someone* Hollies (1965) UK#20, *My Sweet Lord* Billy Preston (1971) R&B#23 US#90/Stars On in *Stars on 45/Stars on Long Play* (1981) g US#6 UK#1; *Photograph* [iii] Ringo Starr (1973) g US#1 UK#8, *Something* Shirley Bassey (1970) US#55 UK#4/Booker T. & the MG's (1970)

US#76/Pozo-Seco Singers (1970) US#115/James Brown on B-side of *Think* (1973) R&B#15 US#77/Johnny Rodriquez (1974) C&W#6 US#85; *Sour Milk Sea* Jackie Lomax (1968) US#117, also on *The Apple EP* (1991) UK#60; *Taxman* Stars On in *Stars on 45/Stars on Long Play* (1981) g US#6 UK#1, *Try Some Buy Some* Ronnie Spector (1971) US#77, *What Is Life* Olivia Newton-John (1972) UK#16, *While My Guitar Gently Weeps* Stars On in *Stars on 45/Stars on Long Play* (1981) g US#6 UK#1, *Wrack My Brain* Ringo Starr (1981) US#38. Co-writers: [i] John Lennon, [ii] Jeff Lynne, [iii] Ringo Starr, M.B.E. (b. July 7, 1940, Liverpool, England). (*See also under* Eric CLAPTON, Bob DYLAN, John LENNON and Paul McCARTNEY.)

426. HARRY, Deborah (b. July 1, 1945, Miami, FL) Pop vocalist. A former Playboy bunny girl who first sang in the folk group Wind in the Willows, which released the album **The Wind in the Willows** (1968, Capitol) US#195. In 1976, Harry formed the new wave band Blondie with her husband and guitarist Chris Stein, which enjoyed a substantial chart career during the late 1970s. CHART COMPOSITIONS: *Picture This* [ii] (1978) UK#12, *Heart of Glass* [v] (1979) g US#1 UK#1, re-mixed (1995) UK#15; *One Way or Another* [iii] (1979) US#24, *Dreaming* [v] (1979) US#27 UK#2, *Union City Blue* [iii] (1979) UK#12, re-mixed (1995) UK#31; *The Hardest Part* [v] (1980) US#84, *Atomic* [i] (1980) US#39 UK#1, re-mixed (1994) UK#19, *Call Me* [iv] (1980) g US#1 UK#1, re-mixed (1989) US#61; *Rapture* [v] (1981) g R&B#33 US#1 UK#5, *Island of Lost Souls* [v] (1982) US#37 UK#11, *War Child* (1982) UK#39. ALBUMS: **Blondie** (1976, Private Stock) UK#75; **Plastic Letters** (1977) US#72 UK#10, **Parallel Lines** (1978) p US#6 UK#1, **Eat to the Beat** (1979) p US#17 UK#1, **Autoamerican** (1980) p US#7 UK#3, **The Hunter** (1982, all Chrysalis) US#33 UK#9. COMPILATIONS: **Best Of Blondie** (1981) g US#30 UK#6, **Once More into the Bleach** (1988) UK#50, **The Complete Picture-The Very Best of Deborah Harry and Blondie** (1991) UK#3, **Beautiful-The Remix Album** (1995, all Chrysalis) UK#25. Harry has also recorded as a solo artist and has pursued an acting career. CHART COMPOSITIONS: *Rush, Rush* (1984) US#105, *Free to Fall* (1986) UK#46, *In Love with Love* [v] (1987) US#70 UK#45, *I Want That Man* (1989) UK#13, *Sweet and Low* (1990) UK#57, *I Can See Clearly* (1993) UK#23, *Strike Me Pink* (1993) UK#46. ALBUMS: **Koo Koo** (1980, Chrysalis) US#25 UK#6; **Rockbird** (1986, Geffen) US#97 UK#31; **Def, Dumb and Blonde** (1989) US#123 UK#12, **Debravation** (1993, both Sire) UK#24. HIT VERSION: *Heart of Glass* [v] Associates (1998) UK#56. Co-writers: [i]

James Destri (b. April 13, 1954, Brooklyn, NY), [ii] James Destri/Chris Stein (b. January 5, 1950, Brooklyn, NY), [iii] Nigel Harrison, [iv] Giorgio Moroder, [v] Chris Stein.

427. HART, Bobby (b. 1944, Phoenix, AZ) Pop vocalist. One half of the duo Boyce and Hart, who also charted as a solo artist with *Lovers for the Night* (1980) US#110. HIT VERSIONS: *Keep on Singing* [ii] Austin Roberts (1973) US#50/Helen Reddy (1974) US#15; *Something's Wrong with Me* [iii] Austin Roberts (1972) US#12, *Words (Are Impossible)* [i] Drupi as *Vado Via* (1973) US#88/Margie Joseph (1974) R&B#27 US#91/Donny Gerard (1976) US#87; *You Take My Breath Away* [iv] Rex Smith (1979) g US#10. Co-writers: [i] L. Albortolli/Danny Janssen/E. Riccardi, [ii] Danny Janssen, [iii] Danny Harshman, [iv] Stephen Lawrence. (*See also under* Tommy BOYCE, Teddy RANDAZZO.)

428. HART, Corey (b. Montreal, Canada) Rock keyboard player and vocalist. CHART COMPOSITIONS: *Sunglasses at Night* (1984) US#7, *It Ain't Enough* (1985) US#17, *Never Surrender* (1985) US#3, *Boy in the Box* (1985) US#26, *Everything in My Heart* (1985) US#30, *I Am By Your Side* (1986) US#18, *Dancin' with My Mirror* (1987) US#88, *In Your Soul* (1988) US#38, *Little Love* (1990) US#37. ALBUMS: **First Offense** (1984) g US#31, **Boy in the Box** (1985) g US#20, **Fields of Fire** (1986, all EMI America) g US#55; **Young Man Running** (1988, EMI Manhattan) US#121; **Bang** (1990, EMI) US#134.

429. HART, Lorenz (b. Lorenz Milton Hart, May 2, 1895; d. November 22, 1943, both New York, NY) Film and stage lyricist. The most humorous commentator on the art of love in the history of the popular song, who wrote in a worldly yet cerebral manner, with a polished emphasis on internal rhymes. Witty, intellectual and decidedly urbane, Hart's talent only deserted him during his later years when he became an alcoholic. During the early 1900s, Hart adapted and translated European operettas, before, with composer Richard Rodgers, forming one of the most influential and widely recorded songwriting partnerships of the twentieth century. He only ever collaborated with one other composer, Franz Lehár, on the show "The Merry Widow" (1934), before dying of pneumonia later that year. (*See also under* Franz LEHAR, Richard RODGERS and Lorenz HART.)

430. HARTFORD, John (b. John Harford, December 30, 1937, New York, NY) C&W multi-instrumentalist and vocalist. A former 1960s Nash-ville session player whose best known composition is the fifteen million selling *Gentle on My Mind*, of which there are over two hundred recorded versions. A master of the banjo and fiddle, Hartford recorded an intriguing body of idiosyncratic country-folk albums for RCA Records during the late 1960s. Raised in St. Louis, where he acquired his love of steamboats, Hartford's later albums feature some fine examples of contemporary bluegrass music. CHART COMPOSITION: *Gentle on My Mind* (1967) C&W#60. ALBUMS: **John Hartford Looks at Life** (1967), **Earthwords and Music** (1967), **The Love Album** (1968), **Housing Project** (1968), **Gentle on My Mind** (1968), **John Hartford** (1969) US#137, **Iron Mountain Depot** (1970, all RCA); **Aereo-Plain** (1971) US#193, **Morning Bugle** (1972, both Warner Brothers); **Tennessee Jubilee** (1975), **Mark Twang** (1976), **Nobody Knows What You Do** (1976), **Glitter Grass from Nashwood Hollyville Strings** (1977), **All in the Name of Love** (1977), **Heading into the Mystery Below** (1978), **Slumbering on the Cumberland** (1979), **You and Me at Home** (1981), **Catalogue** (1982), **Gum Tree Canoe** (1989), **Me Oh My, How Time Does Fly** (1989, all Flying Fish); **Annual Waltz** (1988), **John Hartford** (1988, both MCA); **Wild Hog in the Red Bush** (1996, Rounder). HIT VERSIONS: *California Earthquake* Mama Cass (1968) US#67; *Gentle on My Mind* Glen Campbell (1967) C&W#30 US#39/Patti Page (1968) US#66/Aretha Franklin (1969) R&B#50 US#76/Dean Martin (1969) US#103 UK#2.

431. HARTMAN, Dan (b. 1951, Harrisburg, PA; d. March 22, 1994, Westport, CT) Pop multi-instrumentalist and producer. As the bassist in the rock group Edgar Winter Group, Hartman composed the chart singles *Hangin' Around* [iii] (1973) US#65, *Free Ride* (1973) US#14, *River's Risin'* (1974) US#33, and *Easy Street* (1974) US#83, and featured on the albums **They Only Come Out at Night** (1973) p US#3, **Shock Treatment** (1974, both Epic) g US#13; and **The Edgar Winter Group with Rick Derringer** (1975, Blue Sky) US#124. During the mid-1970s, he recorded as a solo artist in a disco style, before becoming an in-demand producer and composer for such films "Fletch" (1985) and "Bull Durham" (1988). Hartman died at the age of forty-three from a brain tumor. CHART COMPOSITIONS: *Instant Replay* (1978) g R&B#44 US#29 UK#8, *Relight My Fire* (1980) US#104, *All I Need* (1981) US#110, *This Is It* (1979) US#91 UK#17, *I Can Dream About You* (1984) R&B#60 US#6 UK#12, *We Are the Young* (1984) R&B#58 US#25, *Second Nature* [ii] (1985) US#39 UK#66. ALBUMS: **Images** (1976), **Instant Replay** (1978) US#80, **Relight My Fire** (1980, all Blue Sky) US#189; **I Can Dream**

About You (1984, MCA) US#55; **New Green/Clear Blue** (1989, Private). HIT VERSIONS: *Free Ride* Tavares (1975) R&B#8 US#52, *Gravity* [ii] James Brown (1986) R&B#26 US#93 UK#65, *How Do You Stop* James Brown (1987) R&B#10, *Instant Replay* Mico Wave (1988) R&B#15/Yell (1990) UK#10; *Living in America* [ii] James Brown (1986) g R&B#10 US#4 UK#5, *Relight My Fire* Take That with Lulu (1993) UK#1, *Ride on Time* [i] Black Box (1989) UK#1, re-mixed (1991) UK#16. Co-writers: [i] Daniel Davoli/Mirko Limoni/Valerio Semplici, [ii] Charles Midnight, [iii] Edgar Winter (b. December 28, 1946, Beaumont, TX).

432. HARVEY, Alexander (b. 1945, Brownsville, TN) C&W guitarist and vocalist. A music graduate who conducted his university symphony orchestra before becoming a much recorded Nashville songwriter in the mid-1960s. Kenny Rogers cut an entire album of Harvey's songs, **The Ballad of Calico** (1972, Reprise) US#118. Harvey also appeared on the television series "Fun Farm," and in the mid-1990s he formed his own Laureate label to profile new singer-songwriters. ALBUMS: **Alex Harvey** (1971), **Souvenirs** (1972), **True Love** (1974, all Capitol); **Preshus Child** (1976, Kama Sutra); **Purple Crush** (1977, Buddah). HIT VERSIONS: *Delta Dawn* [i] Helen Reddy (1972) g C&W#6 US#1, *Hell and High Water* T. Graham Brown (1986) C&W#1, *Molly* Eddie Arnold (1964) C&W#5/Jim Glaser (1969) C&W#53; *Reuben James* Kenny Rogers (1969) C&W#46 US#26, *Rings* [ii] Cymarron (1971) US#17/Tompall & the Glaser Brothers (1971) C&W#7/Reuben Howell (1974) US#86/Lobo (1974) US#43; *School Teacher* Kenny Rogers (1972) US#91, *Someone Who Cares* Kenny Rogers & the First Edition (1971) US#51, *Tell It All Brother* Kenny Rogers (1970) US#17. Co-writers: [i] Larry Collins, [ii] Eddie Reeves.

433. HARVEY, P.J. (b. Polly Jean Harvey, October 9, 1969, Corscombe, England) Pop guitarist, saxophonist and vocalist. A singer-songwriter who initially recorded as the group P.J. Harvey. CHART COMPOSITIONS: *Sheela-Na-Gig* (1992) UK#69, *50 Foot Queenie* (1993) UK#27, *Man-Size* (1993) UK#42, *Down By the Water* (1995) UK#38, *C'mon Billy* (1995) UK#29, *Send His Love to Me* (1995) UK#34, *This Was My Veil* with John Parish (1996) UK#75. ALBUMS: **From a Diva to a Diver** (1992, Big International); **Dry** (1992, Too Pure) UK#11; **Rid of Me** (1993) US#158 UK#3, **4-Track Demos** (1993) UK#19, **To Bring You My Love** (1995) US#40 UK#12, **Dance Hall at Louise Point** with John Parish (1996, all Island).

434. HASTINGS, Pye (b. Julian Hastings, January 21, 1947, Banffshire, Scotland) Rock gui-

tarist and vocalist. The principal songwriter and lead singer in the progressive rock group Caravan. CHART COMPOSITION: *Stuck in a Hole* (1975) US#110. ALBUMS: **Caravan** (1968, Verve); **If I Could Do It All Again, I'd Do It All Over You** (1970, Decca); **In the Land of the Grey and Pink** (1971), **Waterloo Lily** (1972), **For Girls Who Grow Plump in the Night** (1973), **Live Caravan and the New Symphonia** (1974, all Deram); **Cunning Stunts** (1975, Decca) US#124 UK#50; **Blind Dog at St. Dunstan's** (1976, BTM UK#53); **Better By Far** (1977, Arista); **The Album** (1980), **Back to Front** (1982, both Kingdom); **Cool Water** (1994), **The Battle of Hastings** (1995), **All Over You** (1996, all HTD). COMPILATION: **The Canterbury Tales** (1976, Decca).

435. HATCH, Tony (b. June 1939, Pinner, England) Pop producer and orchestra leader. A songwriter and producer, best known for his work with the vocalist Petula Clark. As a teenager, Hatch sung in the London Choir School before becoming head chorister at All Soul's Church in London. After leaving school he became the tea-boy at a music publishers, eventually graduating to A&R and production assistant at Rank Records. Hatch was posted with the Coldstream Guards during his National Service years, where he learned the music arranging that influenced his use of brass in much of his later work. As a songwriter and producer at Pye Records in 1960, Hatch published his first song *Look for a Star*, written for the film "Circus of Horrors" (1960). At Pye, Hatch produced the acts Emile Ford, Lonnie Donegan and the Searchers, before, in 1962, teaming up with Clark, whose second-take recording of the Hatch composition *Downtown* (1964), became a three million seller. Most of his songs were co-written with his wife, the lyricist and vocalist Jackie Trent, the duo later becoming the subject of the television special "Mr. and Mrs. Music" (1969), which they followed with three musicals "Nell," "The Card" and "Rock Nativity." During the 1970s, Hatch also wrote the television soap opera themes to "Crossroads," "Emmerdale Farm" and "Neighbors." Between 1969–1973, Hatch performed concerts and on Australian television, and was a panelist on the British talent show "New Faces." In 1992, Hatch and Trent received the Jimmy Kennedy Award in recognition of their services to the craft of songwriting. Hatch has also written under the pseudonym Mark Anthony. CHART COMPOSITION: *Out of this World* (1962) UK#50. ALBUMS: **Beautiful in the Rain** (1962), **The Card** oc (1963), **Showcase** (1963), **Mr. and Mrs. Music*** (1969), **The Cool Latin Sound** (1968), **Songs of Burt Bacharach and Hal David** (1971, all Pye); **Two for the Show*** (1973,

Columbia); **Opposite Your Smile** (1974), **Tony Hatch with Love Sounds** (1976), **Mr. Nice Guy** (1978), **A Latin Happening** (1979, all Pye); **Quiet Nights In** (1983, Starblend). COMPILATION: **Best of Tony Hatch and His Orchestra** (1997, Sequel). HIT VERSIONS: *American Boys* [ii] Petula Clark (1968) US#59, *Call Me* [ii] Chris Montez (1966) US#22, *Color My World* [ii] Petula Clark (1966) US#16/Barbara Fairchild (1972) C&W#38; *Don't Give Up* [ii] Petula Clark (1968) US#37, *Don't Sleep in the Subway* [ii] Petula Clark (1967) US#5 UK#12, *Downtown* Petula Clark (1964) g US#1 UK#2, re-mixed (1988) UK#10/Mrs. Miller (1966) US#82/Dolly Parton (1984) C&W#36 US#80; *Forget Him* Bobby Rydell (1964) US#4 UK#13, *I Couldn't Live Without Your Love* [ii] Petula Clark (1966) US#9 UK#6, *I Know a Place* Petula Clark (1965) US#3 UK#17, *Joanna* [ii] Scott Walker (1968) UK#7, *Look at Mine* Petula Clark (1969) US#89, *Look for a Star* Dean Hawley (1960) US#29/Garry Miles (1960) US#16/Garry Mills (1960) US#26 UK#7/Billy Vaughn & His Orchestra (1960) US#19; *My Love* Petula Clark (1966) g US#1 UK#4/Sonny James (1970) C&W#1 US#125; *Other Man's Grass Is Always Greener, The* [ii] Petula Clark (1967) UK#20, *'Round Every Corner* Petula Clark (1965) US#21 UK#43, *Sad Sweet Dreamer* Sweet Sensation (1974) R&B#63 US#14 UK#1, *Sign of the Times, A* Petula Clark (1966) US#11 UK#49, *Where Are You Now (My Love)* [ii] Jackie Trent (1965) UK#1, *Who Am I?* [ii] Petula Clark (1966) US#21, *You Better Come Home* Petula Clark (1965) US#22 UK#44, *You're the One* [i] Vogues (1965) US#4 UK#23, *You've Got to Be Loved* Montanas (1968) US#58. With: * Jackie Trent. Co-writers: [i] Petula Clark (b. November 15, 1932, Epsom, England), [ii] Jackie Trent (b. Jacqueline Trent, September, 1940, Newcastle-under-Lyme, England).

436. HATHAWAY, Donny (b. October 1, 1945, Chicago, IL; d. January 13, 1979, New York, NY) R&B keyboard player, producer, arranger and vocalist. A multi-talented musician and composer who recorded a small but influential catalogue of gospel and jazz tinged R&B albums. Hathaway was raised in St. Louis, Missouri, where he first heard gospel music and attended the same high school as Roberta Flack, with whom he would later form a musical partnership. Hathaway first sang and performed at the age of three as Donny Pitts, before majoring in music theory from Howard University, Washington, and playing piano in the Ric Powell Jazz Trio. During the early 1960s, he worked as a session musician, and as a staff producer at Curtis Mayfield's Curtom label, where he contributed highly original string arrangements on the Impressions'

album **The Young Mod's Forgotten Story** (1969). Hathaway's own albums displayed his skill at arranging and his extensive use of tonal colors, particularily on *The Ghetto*, *The Slums* and *Someday We'll All Be Free*. At the age of thirty-three, Hathaway died after falling from a fifteenth floor window of the Essex House hotel in New York. CHART COMPOSITIONS: *The Ghetto (Part 1)* (1970) R&B#23 US#87, *Little Ghetto Boy* (1972) R&B#25 US#109, *Come Back Charleston Blue* [i] with Margie Joseph (1972) US#102, *Come Little Children* (1973) R&B#67, *You Were Meant for Me* (1978) R&B#17. ALBUMS: **Everything Is Everything** (1970) US#73, **Donny Hathaway** (1970) US#89, **Live** (1972) g US#18, **Come Back Charleston Blue** ost (1972, all Atco) US#198; **Roberta Flack and Donny Hathaway** (1972, Atlantic) g US#3; **Extension of a Man** (1973, Atco) US#69. COMPILATIONS: **Best of Donny Hathaway** (1978), **Roberta Flack featuring Donny Hathaway** (1980) g US#25 UK#31, **In Performance** (1980), **A Donny Hathaway Collection** (1990, all Atlantic). HIT VERSIONS: *Someday We'll All Be Free* Bobby Womack (1985) R&B#74/Aretha Franklin (1993) R&B#32; *Song for Donny, A* Whispers (1979) R&B#21. Co-writers: [i] Alfred Cleveland/Quincy Jones. (b. Quincy Delight Jones, Jr. March 14, 1933, Chicago, IL).

437. HAWKINS, Screamin' Jay (b. Jalacy Hawkins, July 18, 1929, Cleveland, OH) R&B vocalist. A former boxer who blended elements of voodooism with R&B on *I Hear Voices*, *Alligator Wine* and *Feast of the Mau Mau*. Hawkins is best known as the composer of the much recorded *I Put a Spell on You* (1956). ALBUMS: **At Home with Screamin' Jay Hawkins** (1957, Epic); **The Night and Day of Screamin' Jay Hawkins** (1966, Planet); **A Nite at the Forbidden City** (1968, Sound of Hawaii); **I Put a Spell on You** (1969, Direction); **What That Is** (1969, Mercury); **Screamin' Jay Hawkins** (1970, Philips); **Portrait of a Man and His Woman** (1972, Hot Line); **Screamin' the Blues** (1979, Red Lightnin'); **Frenzy** (1982, Edsel); **Live** (1986, Midnight); **Feats of the Mau Mau** (1988, Edsel); **Real Life** (1998, Charly); **Somethin' Funny Goin' On** (1994, Demon). HIT VERSIONS: *I Put a Spell on You* Nina Simone (1965) R&B#23 US#120 UK#49, re-issued (1969) UK#28/Alan Price (1966) UK#9/Crazy World of Arthur Brown (1968) US#111.

438. HAY, Colin James (b. June 29, 1953, Scotland) Pop guitarist and vocalist. The lead singer and principal songwriter in the Australian group Men at Work. CHART COMPOSITIONS: *Who Can It Be Now?* (1982) US#1 UK#45, *Down Under* [i] (1982) p US#1 UK#1, *Overkill* (1983) US#3

UK#21, *It's a Mistake* (1983) US#6 UK#33, *Dr. Heckle and Mr. Jive* (1983) US#28 UK#31, *Everything I Need* (1985) US#47. ALBUMS: **Business As Usual** (1982) p US#1 UK#1, **Cargo** (1983) p US#3 UK#8, **Two Hearts** (1985, all Columbia) g US#50. COMPILATION: **Contraband: The Best of Men at Work** (1996, Sony). By the mid-1980s, Hay was recording as a solo artist. CHART COMPOSITION: *Hold Me* (1987) US#99. ALBUMS: **Looking for Jack** (1987, Columbia) US#126; **Wayfaring Sons** (1987), **Peaks and Valleys** (1988, both MCA); **Topanga** (1996, Lazy Eye). Co-writer: [i] Roy Strykert (b. August 18, 1957, Australia).

439. HAYES, Isaac (b. August 20, 1938, Covington, TN) R&B multi-instrumentalist, producer and vocalist. A major R&B talent, who played on most of Otis Redding's prime recordings between 1962–1976, and achieved over thirty R&B hits as a solo performer. Hayes was a backbone of the Stax Records' sound during the 1960s, whose film soundtracks during the early 1970s were a much imitated film scoring style, while his deep, love-man vocals were to influence the singers Barry White and Luther Vandross. Hayes was raised in a rural community by his sharecropping grandparents, and he first sang in his local church. He was schooled in Memphis from the age of seven, where he played in high school bands, and graduated from college in 1962 with seven scholarships in vocal music. Having learned the piano and saxophone, Hayes played in the amateur groups Sir Isaac and the Do-Duds, the Teen Tones, and Sir Calvin Valentine and his Swinging Cats. When his composition *Frog Stomp* was brought to the attention of the owner of Stax, Jim Stewart, Hayes was promptly hired as a session player and staff writer. During his early years at the label, Hayes maintained his day job at a meat packing factory, where he met the life insurance salesman David Porter, with whom he formed a highly successful songwriting partnership, composing over two hundred songs, many of which were recorded by Sam and Dave. Hayes' second solo album **Hot Buttered Soul** (1969), with its mix of extended rap monologues, wah-wah guitars and sultry string arrangements, proved unexpectedly popular, and having struck upon a winning formula he continued with it on most of his subsequent sets. In 1971, Hayes achieved his biggest solo success with the soundtrack to the film "Shaft," his dynamic title theme having been recorded and sampled many times since. By **Live at the Sahara Tahoe** (1973), Hayes' stage act had become somewhat larger than life, and his expensive, lavish concert sets with full orchestral backing, led to his declaration of bankruptcy in 1976. Since the 1980s, Hayes has embraced both the disco

and electro eras, becoming something of an R&B elder statesman. CHART COMPOSITIONS: *Theme from Shaft* (1971) g R&B#2 US#1 UK#4, *Do Your Thing* (1971) R&B#3 US#30, *Ain't That Loving You (For More Reasons Than One)* with David Porter (1972) R&B#37 US#86, *Theme from the Men* [iv] (1972) R&B#19 US#38, *Joy (Part 1)* (1973) R&B#7 US#30, *Wonderful* (1973) R&B#18 US#71, *Rolling Down a Mountainside* (1973) US#104, *Three Tough Guys Title Theme* (1974) R&B#72, *Chocolate Chip* (1975) R&B#13 US#92, *Come Live with Me* (1975) R&B#20, *Disco Connection* (1976) R&B#60 US#10, *Rock Me Easy Baby (Part 1)* (1976) R&B#58, *Juicy Fruit (Disco Freak)* (1976) US#102, *Out of the Ghetto* (1978) R&B#42 US#107, *Moonlight Lovin'* (1978) R&B#96, *Zeke the Freak* (1978) R&B#19, *A Few More Kisses to Go* (1980) R&B#89, *I Ain't Never* (1980) R&B#49, *Ike's Rap* (1987) R&B#9, *Thing for You* (1987) R&B#43. ALBUMS: **Presenting Isaac Hayes** (1967, Enterprise) re-issued as **In the Beginning** (1972, Atlantic) US#102; **Hot Buttered Soul** (1969) g US#8, **The Isaac Hayes Movement** (1970) US#8, **To Be Continued** (1970) US#11, **Shaft** ost (1971) g US#1 UK#17, **Black Moses** (1972) g US#10 UK#38, **Live at the Sahara Tahoe** (1973) g US#14, **Joy** (1973) g US#16, **Tough Guys** ost (1974) US#146, **Truck Turner** ost (1974, all Enterprise) US#156; **Chocolate Chip** (1975) g US#18, **Disco Connection** (1976) US#85, **Groove-A-Thon** (1976) US#45, **Juicy Fruit (Disco Freak)** (1976) US#124, **Memphis Movement** (1977, all Hot Buttered Soul); **A Man and a Woman** with Dionne Warwick (1977, ABC) US#49; **New Horizon** (1977) US#78, **For the Sake of Love** (1978) US#75, **Royal Rappin's** with Millie Jackson (1979) US#80, **Don't Let Go** (1979) g US#39, **And Once Again** (1980) US#59, **Lifetime Thing** (1981, all Polydor); **U-Turn** (1987), **Love Attack** (1987, both Columbia); **Branded** (1995), **Raw and Refined** (1995, both Pointblank). COMPILATIONS: **Best of Isaac Hayes** (1975, Enterprise) US#165; **Hot Bed** (1977), **Enterprise Greatest Hits** (1980, both Stax); **Double Feature** (1993, Stax/Ace). HIT VERSIONS: *B.A.B.Y.* [iii] Carla Thomas (1966) R&B#3 US#14/Rachel Sweet (1976) UK#36; *Baby, Baby Don't Stop Now* [iii] Sam & Dave (1970) US#117, *Born Again* [iii] Sam & Dave (1969) R&B#27 US#92, *Candy* Astors (1965) R&B#12 US#63, *Deja Vu* [i] Dionne Warwick (1979) R&B#25 US#15, *Do Your Thing* James & Bobby Purify (1975) R&B#30 US#101, *Give Everybody Some* [iii] Bar-Kays (1967) R&B#36 US#91, *Hold on, I'm Coming* [iii] Billy Larkin & the Delegates (1966) US#130/Sam & Dave (1966) g R&B#1 US#21, also in *The Sam and Dave Medley* (1985) R&B#92/Chuck Jackson & Maxine Brown (1967) R&B#20 US#91/ Mauds as *Hold On* (1967) US#114/Soul Children

(1970) R&B#48/Waylon Jennings (1983) C&W#20; *How Can You Mistreat the One You Love* [iii] Jean & the Darlings (1967) US#96, *I Got to Love Somebody's Baby* [iii] Johnnie Taylor (1966) R&B#15, *I Had a Dream* [iii] Johnnie Taylor (1966) R&B#19, *I Love Your Love* Donald Byrd (1982) R&B#77, *I Take What I Want* [iii] James & Bobby Purify (1967) R&B#23 US#41, *I Thank You* [iii] Sam & Dave (1968) R&B#4 US#9 UK#34, also in *The Sam and Dave Medley* (1985) R&B#92/Donny Hathaway & June Conquest (1969) R&B#45, re-issued (1972) R&B#41 US#94/ZZ Top (1980) US#34; *I'll Understand* [iii] Soul Children (1969) R&B#29, *Left Over Love* [iii] William Bell & Judy Clay on B-side of *My Baby Specializes* (1969) R&B#45 US#104, *Let Me Be Good to You* [iii] Carla Thomas (1966) R&B#11 US#62, *Love Can't Turn Around* Farley "Jackmaster" Funk (1986) UK#10, *My Baby Specializes* [iii] William Bell & Judy Clay (1969) R&B#45 US#104, *Never Like This Before* [ii] William Bell (1966) R&B#29, *One Part Love-Two Parts Pain* [iii] Sam & Dave (1970) US#123, *Said I Wasn't Gonna Tell Nobody* [iii] Sam & Dave (1966) R&B#8 US#64, *Shaft, Theme from* Eddie & the Soul Band (1985) UK#13/Van Twist (1985) UK#57/S'Express sampled in *Theme from S'Express* (1988) US#91 UK#1, also on *The Brits 1990* (1990) UK#2/Wedding Present on B-side of *Boing!* (1992) UK#19; *Shoot Your Best Shot* Linda Clifford (1980) R&B#43, *Show Me How* [iii] Emotions (1971) R&B#13 US#52, *So I Can Love You* [iii] Emotions (1969) R&B#3 US#39, *Something Good (Is Going to Happen to You)* [iii] Carla Thomas (1967) R&B#29 US#74, *Soul Man* [iii] Ramsey Lewis (1967) US#49/Sam & Dave (1967) g R&B#1 US#2 UK#24, also in *The Sam and Dave Medley* (1985) R&B#92/Blues Brothers (1978) US#14/Lou Reed & Sam Moore (1987) UK#30; *Soul Sister, Brown Sugar* [iii] Sam & Dave (1969) R&B#18 US#41 UK#15, also in *The Sam and Dave Medley* (1985) R&B#92, *Stealin' Love* [iii] Emotions (1969) R&B#40, *Sweeter He Is, The* [iii] Soul Children (1969) R&B#7 US#52, *Tighten Up My Thang* [iii] Soul Children (1969) R&B#49, *When Something Is Wrong with My Baby* [iii] Sam & Dave (1967) R&B#2 US#42/Otis Redding & Carla Thomas (1969) US#109/Sonny James (1976) C&W#6/Stacy Lattisaw & Johnny Gill (1983) R&B#57/Joe Stampley (1985) C&W#67/Linda Ronstadt (1990) US#78; *Wrap It Up* [iii] Archie Bell & the Drells (1970) R&B#33 US#93/Fabulous Thunderbirds (1986) US#50; *You Don't Know Like I Know* [iii] Sam & Dave (1966) R&B#7 US#90, also in *The Sam and Dave Medley* (1985) R&B#92/Genty (1980) R&B#51; *You Got Me Hummin'* [iii] Sam & Dave (1966) R&B#7 US#77/Hassles (1967) US#112/Cold Blood (1969) US#52; *Your Good Thing (Is About to End)* [iii] Lou Rawls (1969) R&B#3 US#18. Co-writers:

[i] Adrienne Anderson, [ii] Booker T. Jones/David Porter, [iii] David Porter, [iv] Ronny Scaife.

440. HAYWARD, Justin (b. David Justin Hayward, October 14, 1946, Swindon, England) Rock guitarist and vocalist. The lead guitarist, vocalist and principal tunesmith in the symphonic and progressive rock influenced Moody Blues, that was initially a 1960s R&B group. CHART COMPOSITIONS: *Nights in White Satin* (1968) US#103 UK#19, re-issued (1972) g US#2 UK#9, re-issued (1979) UK#14; *Voices in the Sky* (1968) UK#27, *Tuesday Afternoon* (1968) US#24, *Ride My See Saw* (1968) US#61 UK#42, *Never Comes the Day* (1969) US#91, *Question* (1970) US#21 UK#2, *The Story in Your Eyes* (1971) US#23, *Driftwood* (1978) US#59, *Gemini Dream* [i] (1981) US#12, *The Voice* (1981) US#15, *Blue World* (1983) US#62 UK#35, *Your Wildest Dreams* (1986) US#9, *The Other Side of Life* (1986) US#58, *I Know You're Out There Somewhere* (1988) US#30 UK#52. ALBUMS: **Days of Future Passed** (1968) p US#3 UK#27, **In Search of the Lost Chord** (1968) g US#23 UK#5; **On the Threshold of a Dream** (1969, all Deram) p US#20 UK#1; **To Our Children's Children's Children** (1969) g US#14 UK#2, **A Question of Balance** (1970) p US#3 UK#1, **Every Good Boy Deserves Favor** (1971) g US#2 UK#1, **Seventh Sojourn** (1972) g US#1 UK#5, **Caught Live + 5** (1977, all Threshold) US#26; **Octave** (1978, Decca) p US#13 UK#6; **Long Distance Voyager** (1981) p US#1 UK#7; **The Present** (1983) US#26 UK#15, **The Other Side of Life** (1986, all Threshold) p US#9 UK#24; **Sur La Mer** (1988, Polydor) US#38 UK#21; **Keys of the Kingdom** (1991, Threshold) US#94 UK#54; **A Night at Red Rocks** with the Colorado Symphony Orchestra (1993, Polydor) US#93. COMPILATIONS: **This Is the Moody Blues** (1974, Threshold) g US#11 UK#14; **Out of This World** (1975, K-Tel) UK#15; **Voices in the Sky/The Best of the Moody Blues** (1985) US#132, **Greatest Hits** (1989, both Threshold) US#113; **The Story of the Moody Blues...Legend of a Band** (1993) p, **Time Traveller** (1994), **Very Best of the Moody Blues** (1996, all PolyGram) UK#13. Since the late 1970s, Hayward has occasionally recorded as a solo performer, charting with the singles *I Dreamed Last Night** (1975) US#47 and *Blue Guitar** (1975) UK#8. ALBUMS: **Blue Jays*** (1975, Threshold) US#16 UK#4; **Songwriter** (1977, Deram) US#37 UK#28; **Night Flight** (1980, Decca) US#166 UK#41; **Moving Mountains** (1985, Towerbell) UK#78; **Classic Blue** (1989, Trax) UK#47; **A View from the Hill** (1996, CMC). HIT VERSIONS: *Nights in White Satin* Dickies (1979) UK#39/Elkie Brooks (1982) UK#33. With: * John Lodge. Co-writer: [i] John Lodge.

441. HAZLEWOOD, Lee (b. July 9, 1929, Mannford, OK) Pop producer and vocalist. An Arizona based disc jockey who became a songwriter, producer and record label owner during the 1960s. Hazlewood produced many of Duane Eddy's biggest hits, and also recorded a series of successful duets with Nancy Sinatra. CHART COMPOSITIONS: *Lady Bird** (1967) US#20 UK#47, *Sand** (1967) US#107, *Some Velvet Morning** (1968) US#26, *Sleep in the Grass* with Ann-Margret (1969) US#113. ALBUMS: **The Very Special World of Lee Hazlewood** (1966), **Hazlewoodism-It's Cause and Cure** (1966, both MGM); **Trouble Is a Lonesome Town** (1968, LHI); **Sweet Ride** ost (1968, 20th Century Fox); **Nancy and Lee*** (1968) g US#13, **Love and Other Crimes** (1968), **Houston** (1968), **Nancy and Lee Again*** (1969, all Reprise); **Poet, Fool or Bum** (1972, Capitol). HIT VERSIONS: *Bonnie Came Back* [i] Duane Eddy (1960) US#26 UK#12, *Boss Guitar* [i] Duane Eddy (1963) US#28 UK#27, *California Sunshine Girl* Shackelfords (1967) US#115, *Cannonball* [i] Duane Eddy (1958) US#15 UK#22, *(Dance with the) Guitar Man* [i] Duane Eddy (1962) US#12 UK#4, *Fool, The* Sanford Clark (1956) US#7, *Forty Miles of Bad Road* [i] Duane Eddy (1959) US#9 UK#11, *Friday's Child* Nancy Sinatra (1966) US#36, *Houston* Dean Martin (1965) US#21, *How Does That Grab You Darlin'?* Nancy Sinatra (1966) US#7 UK#19, *Lightning's Girl* Nancy Sinatra (1967) US#24, *Lonely One, The* [i] Duane Eddy (1959) US#23, *Love Eyes* Nancy Sinatra (1967) US#15, *Not the Lovin' Kind* Dino, Desi & Billy (1965) US#25, *Rebel Rouser* [i] Duane Eddy (1958) US#6 UK#19, *Shazam* [i] Duane Eddy (1960) US#45 UK#4, *Sugar Town* Nancy Sinatra (1966) g US#5 UK#8, *These Boots Are Made for Walkin'* Nancy Sinatra (1965) g US#1 UK#1/Kon Kan (1989) US#58/Billy Ray Cyrus (1992) UK#63. With: * Nancy Sinatra. Co-writer: [i] Duane Eddy (b. April 26, 1938, Corning, NY).

442. HAZZARD, Tony Pop guitarist and vocalist. A British singer-songwriter who composed a number of 1960s hits for other artists. ALBUMS: **Demonstration** (1969, CBS); **Loudwater House** (1971), **Was That Alright Then?** (1973, both Bronze); **Hazzard and Barnes** (1974, Warner Brothers). HIT VERSIONS: *Fox on the Run* Manfred Mann (1969) UK#5 US#97, *Ha Ha Said the Clown* Manfred Mann (1967) UK#4, *Listen to Me* Hollies (1968) UK#11, *Maria Elena* Gene Pitney (1969) UK#25, *Me the Peaceful Heart* Lulu (1968) UK#9.

443. HEATON, Paul (b. May 9, 1962, Birkenhead, England) Pop guitarist and vocalist. The lead singer and principal songwriter in the British group the Housemartins. CHART COMPOSI-

TIONS: *Sheep* (1986) UK#54, *Happy Hour* [i] (1986) UK#3, *Think for a Minute* [i] (1986) UK#18, *Five Get Over Excited* (1987) UK#11, *Me and the Farmer* (1987) UK#15, *Build* (1987) UK#15, *There Is Always Something There to Remind Me* [i] (1988) UK#35. ALBUMS: **London 0 Hull 4** (1986) US#124 UK#3, **The Housemartins' Christmas Singles Box** (1986) UK#84, **The People Who Grinned Themselves to Death** (1987) US#177 UK#9, **Now That's What I Call Quite Good** (1988, all Go! Discs) UK#8. When the Housemartins split up in 1988, Heaton moved on to even greater success with the group the Beautiful South. CHART COMPOSITIONS: *Song for Whoever* [ii] (1989) UK#2, *I'll Sail This Ship Alone* [ii] (1990) UK#31, *A Little Time* [ii] (1990) UK#1, *Love Speak Up Itself* [ii] (1991) UK#51, *Old Red Eyes Is Back* [ii] (1992) UK#22, *We Are Each Other* [ii] (1992) UK#30, *Bell Bottomed Tear* [ii] (1992) UK#16, *36D* [ii] (1992) UK#46, *Good as Gold* [ii] (1994) UK#23, *Prettiest Eyes* [ii] (1994) UK#37, *One Last Love Song* [ii] (1994) UK#14, *Pretenders to the Throne* [ii] (1995) UK#18, *Rotterdam (Or Anywhere)* (1996) UK#5, *Don't Marry Her* (1996) UK#5. ALBUMS: **Welcome to the Beautiful South** (1989) UK#2, **Choke** (1990) UK#2, **0898** (1992) UK#4, **Miaow** (1994) UK#6, **Blue Is the Colour** (1996, Go! Discs) UK#1. COMPILATION: **Carry on Up the Charts-The Best of the Beautiful South** (1994, Go! Discs) UK#1. Co-writers: [i] Stan Cullimore (b. April 6, 1962, Hull, England), [ii] David Rotheray (b. February 9, 1961, Hull, England).

444. HEBB, Bobby (b. July 26, 1941, Nashville, TN) C&W guitarist, pianist and vocalist. One of the first black artists, at the age of twelve, to perform on the Grand Ole Opry, who went on to write over one thousand published songs. Hebb first played the spoons in the Smoky Mountain Boys, before recording for a variety of labels and achieving a worldwide hit with *Sunny* (1963). During the early 1960s, he recorded duets with Sylvia Shemwell as Bobby and Sylvia. Hebb later wrote film incidental music and composed string trios. CHART COMPOSITIONS: *Sunny* (1963) g R&B#3 US#2 UK#12, new version (1976) R&B#94; *Love, Love, Love* (1972) UK#32. ALBUM: **Sunny** (1966, Philips) US#103. HIT VERSIONS: *Natural Man, A* [i] Lou Rawls (1971) R&B#17 US#17, *Sunny* Cher (1966) UK#32/ Georgie Fame (1966) UK#13/Yambu (1976) R&B#36/ Boney M (1977) UK#3; *Where Are You Going* Jerry Butler (1970) R&B#42 US#95. Co-writer: [i] Sandy Barren.

445. HENDERSON, Ray (b. Raymond Brost, December 1, 1896, Buffalo, NY; d. December 31, 1970, Greenwich, CT) Film and stage composer, pianist and producer. A successful composer of the 1930s, who composed the jazz standard *Bye Bye Blackbird* [ix] (1926). After studying at the Chicago Conservatory of Music, Henderson became a dance band pianist, arranger and song-plugger, before embarking on a career as a composer with his first published song *Humming* [i] (1920). In 1922, he formed a songwriting partnership with the lyricist Lew Brown, a duo that became a trio with the addition of Buddy De Sylva in 1926. Henderson's compositions were featured in the shows "The Greenwich Village Follies of 1922," "George White's Scandals of 1931" and "George White's Scandals of 1934," alongside the films "Rainbow 'Round My Shoulder" (1952), "The Eddie Cantor Story" (1954) and "Pete Kelly's Blues" (1955). ALBUMS: **Billy Barnes' L.A.** ost (1962, B.B.); **Turnabout** oc (1975, Pelican). HIT VERSIONS: *Alabamy Bound* [iv] Isham Jones (1925) US#10/Blossom Seeley (1925) US#2/Mulcays (1954) US#24; *Animal Crackers in My Soup* [vi] Don Bestor (1935) US#14, *Bam, Bam, Bamy Shore* [ix] Ted Lewis (1926) US#9, *Bye Bye Blackbird* [ix] Gene Austin (1926) US#1/Benny Krueger (1926) US#7/Nick Lucas (1926) US#4/Leo Reisman (1926) US#11/Russ Morgan (1948) US#20/Winifred Atwell in *Let's Have Another Party* (1954) UK#1; *Don't Bring Lulu* [iii] Ernest Hare & Billy Jones (1925) US#5/Billy Murray (1925) US#5/Dorothy Provine (1961) UK#17; *Don't Tell Her What Happened to Me* Ruth Etting (1930) US#6, *Dummy Song, The* [v] Louis Armstrong (1953) US#30, *Five Foot Two, Eyes of Blue* [xii] Gene Austin (1926) US#1/Ernie Golden (1926) US#15/Art Landry (1926) US#10/Tiny Hill (1940) US#25/Benny Strong (1949) US#30; *Follow the Swallow* [x] Al Jolson (1924) US#3, *Georgette* [ii] Ted Lewis (1922) US#8, *Hold My Hand* [vii] Arthur Lally (1932) US#12/Ray Noble (1932) US#5/Rudy Vallee (1934) US#11; *Humming* [i] Paul Whiteman (1921) US#5, *I Want to Be Bad* Helen Kane (1929) US#18, *I Wonder Who's Dancing with You Tonight?* [x] Benny Krueger (1924) US#10, *(I'm a Dreamer) Aren't We All?* [viii] Paul Whiteman (1929) US#6, *I'm Sitting on Top of the World* [xii] Frank Crumit (1926) US#12/Al Jolson (1926) US#1/Roger Wolfe Kahn (1926) US#9/Les Paul & Mary Ford (1953) US#10/Big Ben Banjo Band in *Let's Get Together Again* (1955) UK#18; *If I Had a Girl Like You* [vi] Benny Krueger (1925) US#5/Hal Kemp (1930) US#14/Rudy Vallee (1930) US#3; *Keep Your Skirts Down, Mary Ann* [xi] Billy Murray & Aileen Stanley (1926) US#10, *Life Is Just a Bowl of Cherries* [ii] Rudy Vallee (1931) US#3/Jaye P. Morgan (1954) US#26; *My Song* [ii] Rudy Vallee (1931) US#10, *Nasty Man* [vii] Rudy Vallee (1934) US#10, *That Old Gang of Mine* [x] Benson Orchestra of Chicago (1923) US#6/Irving & Jack Kaufman (1923) US#11/Benny Krueger (1923) US#3/

Billy Murray & Ed Smalle (1923) US#1/Ernest Hare & Billy Jones (1924) US#6/Dick Robertson (1938) US#14; *That's Why Darkies Were Born* [ii] Kate Smith (1931) US#12, *Thrill Is Gone, The* [ii] Rudy Vallee (1931) US#10/Roy Hawkins (1951) R&B#6; *Why Did I Kiss That Girl?* [iii] Paul Whiteman (1924) US#6. Co-writers: [i] Louis Breau, [ii] Lew Brown, [iii] Lew Brown/Robert King, [iv] Lew Brown/Bud Green, [v] Lew Brown/Billy Rose, [vi] Irving Caesar/Ted Koehler, [vii] Irving Caesar/Jack Yellen, [viii] Buddy De Sylva, [ix] Mort Dixon (b. March 20, 1892, New York, NY; d. March 23, 1956, Bronxville, NY), [x] Mort Dixon/Billy Rose, [xi] Robert King/Andrew Sterling, [xii] Sam M. Lewis/Joe Young. (*See also under* Buddy DE SYLVA, Lew BROWN and Ray HENDERSON.)

446. HENDRICKS, Jon (b. John Carl Hendricks, September 16, 1921, Newark, OH) Jazz drummer and vocalist. A respected jazz vocalist who has also added lyrics to a considerable number of previously composed jazz melodies. At the age of fourteen, Hendricks performed with the pianist Art Tatum, before studying law and literature. During the 1950s, he began writing lyrics for jazz solos that were recorded by such musicians as Art Pepper. In 1957, he performed and recorded as one third of the jazz vocal group Lambert, Hendricks and Ross, with Dave Lambert and Annie Ross. Ross was replaced by Yolanda Bavan in 1963. ALBUMS: **Sing a Song of Basie** (1957, ABC/Paramount); **Sing Along with Basie** (1958, Roulette); **The Swingers!** (1959, World Pacific); **The Hottest New Group in Jazz** (1959), **Lambert, Hendricks and Ross Sing Ellington** (1960), **High Flying** (1961, all Columbia); **Live at Basin Street East** (1963), **Lambert, Hendricks and Bavan at Newport** (1963), **Lambert, Hendricks and Bavan at the Village Gate** (1963, all RCA); **Swingin' Til the Girls Come Home** (1988, Bluebird). Hendricks' best known lyric is the one that he wrote for Manhattan Transfer's version of *Birdland*, a group influenced by the pioneering work of his own trio that also recorded an entire album of his lyrics as **Vocalese** (1985, Atlantic) US#74. Hendricks has also recorded as a solo artist. ALBUMS: **A Good Git-Together** (1959, World Pacific); **Evolution of the Blues** (1961), **Fast Livin' Blues** (1962, both Columbia); **Recorded in Person at the Trident** (1963, Smash); **September Songs** (1976, Stanyan); **Salud!** (1964, Reprise); **Tell Me the Truth** (1979), **Blues for Pablo** (1980, both Arista); **Cloudburst** (1972, Enja); **Love** (1981, Muse). HIT VERSIONS: *I Want You to Be My Baby* Lillian Briggs (1955) US#18/Georgia Gibbs (1955) US#14; *Twilight Zone/Twilight Tone* Manhattan Transfer (1979) US#30 UK#25, *Yeh Yeh* [i] Georgie Fame (1965) US#21 UK#1/Matt Bianco

(1985) UK#13. Co-writers: [i] Roger Grant/Pat Patrick. (*See also under* Antonio Carlos JOBIM.)

447. HENDRIX, Jimi (b. Johnny Allen Hendrix, November 27, 1942, Seattle, WA; d. September 18, 1970, London, England) Rock guitarist and vocalist. The most technically accomplished, innovative and influential blues-rock electric guitarist since the invention of the instrument. Although he only released four albums during his lifetime, posthumous releases have added a further three hundred albums to the Hendrix catalogue over the years. The son of a Cherokee Indian mother, Hendrix learned the guitar in his teens and played in various R&B bands, serving a lengthy apprenticeship as a session musician, before, in 1966, forming the trio the Jimi Hendrix Experience, with bassist Noel Redding and drummer Mitch Mitchell. An influence on just about every rock guitarist since, Hendrix's songs have been recorded by artists as diverse as Gil Evans and the Kronos Quartet, including Rubber Band's **Hendrix Songbook** (1969, GRT) US#116. His pioneering career was cut woefully short in 1970, when he died from inhalation of vomit due to barbiturate intoxication. CHART COMPOSITIONS: *Purple Haze* (1967) US#65 UK#3, *The Wind Cries Mary* (1967) UK#6, *The Burning of the Midnight Lamp* (1967) UK#18, *Foxy Lady* (1968) US#67, *Up from the Skies* (1968) US#82, *Crosstown Traffic* (1968) US#52 UK#37, re-issued (1990) UK#61; *Stone Free* (1969) US#130, *Voodoo Chile* (1970) UK#1, also on *All Along the Watchtower EP* (1990) UK#52; *Freedom* (1971) US#59, *Dolly Dagger* (1971) US#74, *Gypsy Eyes/Remember* (1971) UK#35. ALBUMS: **Are You Experienced?** (1967) p US#5 UK#2, **Axis: Bold as Love** (1967) p US#3 UK#5, **Electric Ladyland** (1968, all Reprise) p US#1 UK#6; **Band of Gypsies** (1970, Capitol) p US#5 UK#6. COMPILATIONS: **Get That Feeling** with Curtis Knight (1967, Capitol) US#75 UK#39; **Smash Hits** (1968) p US#6 UK#4, **Monterey Pop Festival** (1970) g US#16, **The Cry of Love** (1971, all Reprise) g US#3 UK#2; **Two Great Experiences Together** with Lonnie Youngblood (1971, Maple) US#127; **Experience** (1971, Ember) UK#9; **Rainbow Bridge** (1971, Reprise) g US#15 UK#16; **Jimi Hendrix at the Isle of Wight** (1971, Track) UK#17; **Hendrix in the West** (1972, Reprise) g US#12 UK#7; **Rare Hendrix** (1972, Trip) US#82; **War Heroes** (1972) US#48 UK#23, **Soundtrack Recordings from the Film Jimi Hendrix** ost (1973, both Reprise) US#89 UK#37; **Jimi Hendrix** (1975, Polydor) UK#35; **Crash Landing** (1975) g US#5 UK#35, **Midnight Lightning** (1975) US#43 UK#46, **The Essential Jimi Hendrix** (1978) US#114, **The Essential Jimi Hendrix, Volume 2** (1979, all Reprise) US#156; **10th Anniversary Box**

(1980, Polydor); **Nine to the Universe** (1980) US#127, **The Jimi Hendrix Concerts** (1982, both Reprise) US#79 UK#16; **The Singles Album** (1983, Polydor) UK#77; **Kiss the Sky** (1984) US#148, **Jimi Plays Monterey** (1986, both Reprise) US#192; **Radio One** (1989, Rykodisc) US#119 UK#30; **Cornerstones, 1967–1970** (1990, Polydor) UK#5; **Lifelines/The Jimi Hendrix Story** (1991) US#174, **The Ultimate Experience** (1992, both Reprise) US#72 UK#25; **Jamming Live at the Scene Club, NYC** (1994, Realization); **Blues** (1994, MCA) US#45 UK#10; **Woodstock** (1994, Polydor) US#37 UK#32; **Voodoo Soup** (1995) US#66, **First Rays of the New Rising Sun** (1997, both MCA). HIT VERSIONS: *Angel* Rod Stewart (1972) US#40 UK#4, *Purple Haze* Dion (1969) US#63.

448. HENLEY, Don (b. July 22, 1947, Gilmer, TX) Rock drummer and vocalist. The lead vocalist in the rock group the Eagles, whose **Their Greatest Hits, 1971–1975** (1975), has sold over twenty-two million copies. Henley's central theme as a songwriter has been a study of the unfulfilled desires that arise from a disenchanted longing for something better. Influenced by the vocal harmonies of the Kingston Trio and the Beach Boys, but merging a laid-back country sound with the rhythms of rock, the Eagles became one of the most successful groups in the world during the 1970s. Raised in the small rural town of Linden, Texas, Henley grew up listening to such artists as Fats Domino, and as a teenager learned to sing and play the drums. For seven years he was a member of the group Felicity, which evolved into Shilo during the late 1960s and released the album **Shilo** (1970, Amos). After re-locating to California, Henley befriended Glenn Frey and J.D. Souther, a struggling duo called Longbranch Pennywhistle. As habitues of the Troubadour club in Los Angeles, the trio became backing musicians for the vocalist Linda Ronstadt, before leaving to form the Eagles. The pinnacle of the group's career was their fifteen million selling album **Hotel California** (1976), which featured Henley and Frey's classic bible belt parable *The Last Resort*. The group disintegrated in 1980, having sold over eighty million records worldwide, with Henley later saying, "I had an ulcer before I was thirty because of the Eagles." CHART COMPOSITIONS: *Witchy Woman* [xiv] (1972) US#9, *Tequila Sunrise* [v] (1973) US#64, *James Dean* [i] (1974) US#77, *The Best of My Love* [ix] (1974) g US#1, *One of These Nights* [v] (1975) US#1 UK#23, *Lyin' Eyes* [v] (1975) C&W#8 US#2 UK#23, *Take It to the Limit* [vi] (1976) US#4 UK#12, *New Kid in Town* [ix] (1977) g C&W#43 US#1 UK#20, *Hotel California* [iv] (1977) g US#1 UK#8, *Life in the Fast Lane* [x] (1977) US#11, *Funky New*

Year [v] on B-side of *Please Come Home for Christmas* (1978) US#18 UK#30, *Heartache Tonight* [vii] (1979) g US#1 UK#40, *The Long Run* [v] (1979) US#8 UK#66, *I Can't Tell You Why* [vii] (1980) US#8, also on B-side of Ambrosia's *Outside* (1991) US#102; *Get Over It* [v] (1994) US#31. ALBUMS: **The Eagles** (1972) g US#22, **Desperado** (1973) g US#41 UK#39, **On the Border** (1974) g US#17 UK#28, **One of These Nights** (1975) g US#1 UK#8, **Hotel California** (1976) p US#1 UK#2, **The Long Run** (1979) p US#1 UK#4, **Live** (1980, all Asylum) p US#6 UK#24; **Hell Freezes Over** (1994, Geffen) p US#1 UK#28. COMPILATIONS: **Their Greatest Hits, 1971–1975** (1975) p US#1 UK#2, **Greatest Hits, Volume 2** (1982) US#52, **Best of the Eagles** (1985, all Asylum) UK#8; **Very Best of the Eagles** (1994, Elektra) UK#4. Henley pursued a solo career for much of the 1980s, remaining the most successful former band member, and when an Eagles reunion was touted as a possibility in the late 1980s, he infamously remarked, "Nostalgia is an intoxicant. I don't mind walking down memory lane...I just don't want to live there." Henley oversaw the release of **Common Thread** (1993, Giant) p US#3, a three million selling selection of Eagles' songs by contemporary country artists, five of which charted on the country Hot 100 simultaneously. The following year, nostalgia, memory lane and an intoxicating offer of dollars resulted in an Eagles reformation. CHART COMPOSITIONS: *Johnny Can't Read* [xii] (1982) US#42, *Dirty Laundry* [xii] (1982) g US#3 UK#59, *I Can't Stand Still* [xii] (1983) US#48, *The Boys of Summer* [ii] (1984) US#5 UK#12, *Not Enough Love in the World* [xiii] (1985) US#34, *Sunset Grill* [xiii] (1985) US#22, *The End of the Innocence* [xi] (1989) US#8 UK#48, *The Last Worthless Evening* [iii] (1989) US#21, *The Heart of the Matter* (1990) US#21, *How Bad Do You Want It?* (1990) US#48, *New York Minute* (1990) US#48. ALBUMS: **I Can't Stand Still** (1982, Asylum) g US#24; **Building the Perfect Beast** (1984) p US#13 UK#14, **The End of the Innocence** (1989, both Geffen) p US#8 UK#17. COMPILATION: **Actual Miles-Henley's Greatest Hits** (1995, Geffen) g US#48. HIT VERSIONS: *Best of My Love, The* [ix] Aswad on *Too Wicked EP* (1990) UK#61, *Desperado* [v] Johnny Rodriguez (1977) C&W#5/Clint Black (1992) C&W#54; *Heartache Tonight* [vii] Conway Twitty (1983) C&W#6, *Hollywood Waltz* [v] Buck Owens (1976) C&W#44, *I Can't Tell You Why* [vii] Vince Gill (1993) C&W#42, *Lyin' Eyes* [v] Sarah (1987) C&W#81, *Take It to the Limit* [vi] Waylon Jennings & Willie Nelson (1983) C&W#8 US#102, *Tequila Sunrise* [v] Alan Jackson (1992) C&W#64. Co-writers: [i] Jackson Browne/Glenn Frey/J.D. Souther, [ii] Mike Campbell (b. February 1, 1954, Panama City,

FL), [iii] J. Corey/S. Lynch, [iv] Don Felder (b. September 21, 1947, Topanga, CA)/Glenn Frey, [v] Glenn Frey, [vi] Glenn Frey/Randy Meissner (b. March 8, 1946, Scottsbluff, NE), [vii] Glenn Frey/ Timothy B. Schmit (b. October 30, 1947, Sacramento, CA), [viii] Glenn Frey/Bob Seger/J.D. Souther, [ix] Glenn Frey/J.D. Souther, [x] Glenn Frey/Joe Walsh, [xi] Bruce Hornsby, [xii] Danny Kortchmar, [xiii] Danny Kortchmar/Benmont Tench (b. September 7, 1954, Gainesville, FL), [xiv] Bernie Leadon (b. July 19, 1947, Minneapolis, MN).

449. HERBERT, Victor (b. February 1, 1859, Dublin, Ireland; d. May 24, 1924, New York) Film and show composer, cellist. An American citizen since 1902, whose operettas were written in European traditions without ever being influenced by American ragtime or blues styles. Herbert was a cellist who studied at the Stuttgart Conservatory in Germany, before moving to New York in 1886, where he became the leader of the 22nd Army Regimental Band. Shortly after scoring the silent film "The Fall of a Nation," Herbert began composing for the theatre, achieving his first success with "The Wizard of the Nile" (1895), a show that featured his song *Starlight, Star Bright*. Herbert ultimately worked on over forty operettas, and also composed such classical works as the tone poem *Here and Leander*. One of his most popular numbers was *Gypsy Love Song*, from the show "The Fortune Teller" (1898). Herbert conducted the Pittsburgh Symphony Orchestra between 1894 and 1904, and in 1903, produced his biggest Broadway hit, "Babes in Toyland." His longest running show was the comedy "The Red Mill" (1906), and his last major score was "Sweethearts" (1913). Many of Herbert's most successful shows were later filmed by Hollywood, and he was a founder member of ASCAP. Herbert died from a heart attack in 1924. CHART COMPOSITIONS: *March of the Toys* [v] (1911) US#4, *Naughty Marietta Selection* (1911) US#5, *Naughty Marietta Intermezzo* (1912) US#5, *The Toymaker's Shop* (1913) US#10, *Sweethearts* [vii] (1914) US#8, *Dance of the Hours* (1914) US#10, *American Fantasie* (1918) US#8, *Kiss Me Again* [ii] (1919) US#7. ALBUMS: Eileen sc (1917, RCA); **Babes in Toyland** sc (1950), **The Red Mill** ost (1950, both Decca); **Naughty Marietta** sc (1951), **Sweethearts** sc (1951), **The Red Mill** sc (1952), **Mademoiselle Modiste** sc (1953), **Relax with Victor Herbert** (1954, all RCA); **Babes in Toyland** ost (1961, Buena Vista); **Melachrino Presents Immortal Melodies of Victor Herbert** with Sigmund Romberg (1974, Decca); **Babes in Toyland** oc (1979, Bit); **Victor Herbert Souvenir** (1985, Arabesque). HIT VERSIONS: *Ah, Sweet Mystery of Life* [viii] Leo Reisman (1928) US#7/Fred Waring's

Pennsylvanians (1928) US#2/Nelson Eddy (1935) US#5/Bing Crosby (1939) US#12; *Angelus, The* Christine MacDonald & Reinald Werrenrath (1913) US#3/Prince's Orchestra (1913) US#7; *Because You're You* [ii] Harry MacDonough & Elise Stevenson (1907) US#1, *Gypsy Love Song* [vi] William F. Hooley (1899) US#1/Reinald Werrenrath (1922) US#14; *I Can't Do the Sun* Billy Murray (1904) US#4, *I Might Be Your Once-in-a-While* [vii] Olive Kline (1920) US#5, *I Want What I Want When I Want It* [ii] Frank Stanley (1906) US#3, *I'm Falling in Love with Someone* [viii] John McCormack (1911) US#1/Charles Harrison (1912) US#9/Nelson Eddy (35) US#4; *Indian Summer* [iv] Tommy Dorsey (1940) US#1/Glenn Miller (1940) US#8; *Italian Street Song* [viii] Lucy Isabelle Marsh & the Victor Light Opera Co. (1911) US#2, *Kiss in the Dark, A* [iii] Amelia Galli-Curci (1924) US#13/Fritz Kreisler (1913) US#13; *Kiss Me Again* [ii] Olive Kline (1916) US#5, *March of the Toys* [v] Tommy Dorsey (1939) US#14, *Moonbeams* [ii] All-Star Trio (1921) US#5, *Neapolitan Love Song* [ii] Reinald Werrenrath (1916) US#4, *'Neath the Southern Moon* Merle Tillotson (1911) US#7, *Sweethearts* [vii] Grace Kerns (1913) US#6/Christie MacDonald (1913) US#2; *To the Land of My Own Romance (I Have a Dream, By Night, By Day)* [vi] Lucy Isabelle Marsh (1912) US#5, *Toyland* [v] Corrine Morgan & the Hayden Quartet (1904) US#1, *Tramp! Tramp! Tramp!* [viii] Frank Stanley & Byron Harlan (1910) US#1, *When You're Away* [ii] Olive Kline (1915) US#6, *Yesterthoughts* [I] Glenn Miller (1940) US#14. Co-writers: [I] Stanley Adams, [ii] Henry Blossom, [iii] Buddy De Sylva, [iv] Al Dubin, [v] Glen MacDonough, [vi] Harry B. Smith, [vii] Robert B. Smith, [viii] Rida Johnson Young.

450. HERMAN, Jerry (b. July 10, 1932, New York, NY) Film and stage composer, pianist. A former television scriptwriter who became a songwriter in the late 1950s. Herman composed for such shows as "I Feel Wonderful" (1954), "Nightcap," "A to Z" (both 1960); and "Madame Aphrodite" (1961). Herman's biggest success was with "Hello, Dolly!" (1964), the title tune of which the song's publisher initially paid a reluctant Louis Armstrong to record. ALBUMS: **Parade** oc (1960, Kapp); **Milk and Honey** oc (1961) US#10, **Hello Dolly!** oc (1964, both RCA) g US#1; **Opening Night at the Winter Garden-Mame** oc (1966), **Mame** oc (1966) g US#23, **Dear World** oc (1969, all Columbia); **Hello Dolly!** ost (1969, 20th Century–Fox); **An Evening with Jerry Herman** (1974, Laureate); **Mack and Mabel** oc (1974, ABC); **Mame** ost (1974, Warner Brothers) US#196; **Grand Tour** oc (1979, Columbia); **Day in Hollywood/Night in the Ukraine** oc (1980, DRG); **La Cage Aux Folles** oc (1983, RCA) US#52; **Jerry's**

Girls oc (1984, Polydor). HIT VERSIONS: *Hello, Dolly!* Louis Armstrong (1964) US#1 UK#4/Kenny Ball & His Jazzmen (1964) UK#30/Ella Fitzgerald (1964) US#125/Lou Monte (1964) US#131/Frank Sinatra (1964) UK#47/Frankie Vaughan (1964) UK#18/Bachelors (1966) UK#38; *I Am What I Am* Gloria Gaynor (1983) R&B#82 US#102 UK#13, *If He Walked into My Life* Eydie Gorme (1966) US#120.

451. HERON, Mike (b. December 12, 1942, Glasgow, Scotland), and **WILLIAMSON, Robin** (b. November 24, 1943, Glasgow, Scotland) Both folk multi-instrumentalists and vocalists. The masterminds behind the esoteric folk group the Incredible String Band, which blended British and Celtic folk traditions, hippie ideologies, ancient mythology, and pagan rituals with Indian, North African and calypso rhythms, to create a psychedelic canvas of improvisational folk music. Their records verged from the unlistenable to the spiritually enlightening, and their best known song remains the much recorded *First Girl I Ever Loved*. ALBUMS: **The Incredible String Band** (1965), **The 5,000 Spirits or the Layers of the Onion** (1967), **The Hangman's Beautiful Daughter** (1968) US#161, **Wee Tam and the Big Huge** (1968), **Changing Horses** (1969) US#166, **I Looked Up** (1970) US#196, **"U"** (1970, all Elektra) US#183; **Be Glad for the Song Has No Ending** (1970), **Liquid Acrobat as Regards the Air** (1971) US#189, **Earth Span** (1972), **No Ruinous Feud** (1972), **Hard Rope and Silken Twine** (1974), **Seasons They Change** (1976, all Island). COMPILATIONS: **Wee Tam** (1968) US#174, **The Big Huge** (1969) US#180, **Relics of the Incredible String Band** (1970, all Elektra); **On Air** (1992, Band of Joy); **The Chelsea Sessions, 1967** (1997, Pig's Whisker Music). After the group split up, Heron recorded as a solo artist. ALBUMS: **Smiling Men with Bad Reputations** (1971, Island); **Mike Heron's Reputation** (1975, Neighborhood); **Diamond of Dream** (1977, Bronze); **Mike Heron** (1980, Casablanca). Williamson re-located to America, where he recorded in an even more traditional, roots style, often with his Merry Band. ALBUMS: **Myrrh** (1972, Island); **Journey's Edge** (1977), **American Stonehenge** (1978), **A Glint at the Kindling** (1979), **Songs of Love and Parting** (1981), **Music for the Mabinogi** (1982), **Legacy of the Scottish Harpers** (1985, all Flying Fish); **The Dragon Has Two Tongues** (1985, Towerbell); **Winter's Turning** (1987, Flying Fish); **Songs for Children** (1988, Claddagh); **The Merry Band's Farewell Concert** (1997).

452. HEYMAN, Edward (b. 1907, America) Film and stage lyricist. A Tin Pan Alley lyricist who often worked with the composer Victor Young,

210

and occasionally wrote his own melodies as well. Heyman's songs were included in such shows as "Monkey Business" (1931), "Casino De Paris," "Bachelor of Arts" (both 1934); and "Three's a Crowd" (1944). HIT VERSIONS: *Blame It on My Youth* [iv] Jan Garber (1935) US#17, *Body and Soul* [i] Ruth Etting (1930) US#10/Annette Hanshaw (1930) US#12/Libby Holman (1930) US#3/Helen Morgan (1930) US#16/Ozzie Nelson (1930) US#18/Paul Whiteman (1930) US#1/Leo Reisman (1931) US#15/Louis Armstrong (1932) US#7/Henry Allen (1935) US#17/Benny Goodman (1935) US#5/Art Tatum (1937) US#19/Coleman Hawkins (1944) R&B#4/US#13/Ziggy Elman (1947) US#25/Billy Eckstine (1949) US#27/Anita Baker (1994) UK#48; *Boo Hoo!* [v] Mal Hallet (1937) US#3/Guy Lombardo (1937) US#1; *Easy Come, Easy Go* [ii] Eddy Duchin (1934) US#4, *Ho Hum!* [viii] Gus Arnheim (1931) US#6/Ted Lewis (1931) US#6; *I Cover the Waterfront* [ii] Eddy Duchin (1933) US#3/Joe Haymes (1933) US#17/Cars 'n' Jammers (1946) R&B#3/Erroll Garner (1946) R&B#8/Jimmy McGriff (1966) US#135; *I Wanna Be Loved* [iii] Andrews Sisters (1950) US#1/Billy Eckstine (1950) US#7/Jan Garber (1950) US#28/Dottie O'Brien (1950) US#23/Dinah Washington (1950) US#22/Hugo Winterhalter (1950) US#11; *My Darling* [vii] Don Bestor (1933) US#9, *My Silent Love* [viii] Isham Jones (1932) US#4/Roger Wolf Kahn (1932) US#8/Ruby Newman (1932) US#3; *Out of Nowhere* [ii] Bing Crosby (1931) US#1/Leo Reisman (1931) US#6/Frank Ifield (1967) US#132; *They Say* [vi] Sammy Kaye (1938) US#11/Artie Shaw (1939) US#1; *You Oughta Be in Pictures* [viii] Boswell Sisters (1934) US#17/Little Jack Little (1934) US#2/Rudy Vallee (1934) US#5. Co-writers: [i] Frank Eyton/Johnny Green/Robert Sour, [ii] Johnny Green, [iii] Johnny Green/Billy Rose, [iv] Oscar Levant, [v] John Jacob Loeb/Carmen Lombardo, [vi] Paul Mann/Stephen Weiss, [vii] Richard Myers, [viii] Dana Suesse. (*See also under* Harold ARLEN, Vincent YOUMANS, Victor YOUNG.)

453. HEYWARD, Nick (b. May 20, 1961, Beckenham, England) Pop guitarist and vocalist. The principal songwriter and lead vocalist in the briefly popular Haircut 100. CHART COMPOSITIONS: *Favourite Shirts (Boy Meets Girl)* (1981) US#101 UK#4, *Love Plus One* (1982) US#37 UK#3, *Fantastic Day* (1982) UK#9, *Nobody's Fool* (1982) UK#9. ALBUMS: **Pelican West** (1982, Arista) US#31 UK#2. COMPILATION: **Best of Nick Heyward and Haircut 100** (1992, Arista). Heyward left the band in 1983 to pursue a solo career. CHART COMPOSITIONS: *Whistle Down the Wind* (1983) UK#13, *Take That Situation* (1983) UK#11, *Blue Hat for a Blue Day* (1983) UK#14, *On a Sunday* (1983)

UK#52, *Love All Day* (1984) UK#31, *Warning Sign* (1984) UK#25, *Laura* (1984) UK#45, *Over the Weekend* (1986) UK#43, *You're My World* (1988) UK#67, *Kites* (1993) US#107 UK#44, *He Doesn't Love You Like I Do* (1993) UK#58, *The World* (1996) UK#47, *Rollerblade* (1996) UK#37. ALBUMS: **North of a Miracle** (1983) US#178 UK#10, **Postcards from Home** (1986, both Arista); **I Love You Avenue** (1993, Warner Brothers); **From Monday to Sunday** (1993, Columbia); **Tangled** (1995, Epic).

454. HIATT, John (b. August 20, 1952, Indianapolis, IN) Rock guitarist and vocalist. A country and R&B influenced singer-songwriter who continually garners more critical accolades than he does record sales. During the 1960s, Hiatt worked as a staff writer in Nashville, penning material for such singers as Conway Twitty. Hiatt has also contributed songs to the films "American Gigolo," "Cruising" and "The Border" (all 1980), and was a member of the group Little Village, with Ry Cooder and Nick Lowe, which recorded the album **Little Village** (1992, Reprise) US#66 UK#23. ALBUMS: **Hangin' Around the Observatory** (1974), **Overcoats** (1975, both Epic); **Slug Line** (1979), **Two-Bit Monsters** (1980, both MCA); **All of a Sudden** (1982), **Riding with the King** (1983), **Warming Up to the Ice Age** (1985, all Geffen); **Bring the Family** (1987) US#107, **Slow Turning** (1988) US#98, **Stolen Moments** (1990) US#61 UK#72, **Perfectly Good Guitar** (1993) US#47 UK#67, **Hiatt Comes Alive at Budokan** (1995, all A&M); **Walk On** (1995) US#48 UK#74, **Little Head** (1997, both Capitol). HIT VERSIONS: *Angel Eyes* [i] Jeff Healey Band (1989) US#5, *Drive South* Suzy Boguss (1992) C&W#32, *She Don't Love Nobody* Desert Rose Band (1989) *As Sure as I'm Sittin' Here* Three Dog Night (1974) US#16, *True Believer* Ronnie Milsap (1993) C&W#30. Co-writer: [i] F. Koller.

455. HICKS, Dan (b. December 9, 1941, Little Rock, AR) Pop guitarist, drummer and vocalist. A country and jazz influenced jug band artist who performed with his band Hot Licks. ALBUMS: **Original Recordings** (1969, Epic); **Where's the Money?** (1972) US#195, **Striking It Rich** (1972) US#170, **Last Train to Hicksville...the Home of Happy Feet** (1973, all Blue Thumb) US#67; **It Happened One Bite** (1978, Warner Brothers) US#165. HIT VERSION: *I Scare Myself* Thomas Dolby (1984) UK#46.

456. HILL, Andy (b. England) Pop producer. A former jingle writer who was successful with the 1981 Eurovision song contest winner *Making Your Mind Up* [ii], the first of many hits that he wrote for the vocal group Buck Fizz. HIT VERSIONS: *Give a Little Bit More* [iv] Cliff Richard (1981) US#41, *Have You Ever Been in Love* [iii] Leo Sayer (1982) UK#10, *If You Can't Stand the Heat* [i] Bucks Fizz (1983) UK#10, *Land of Make Believe, The* [vi] Bucks Fizz (1982) UK#1, *London Town* Bucks Fizz (1983) UK#34, *Making Your Mind Up* [ii] Bucks Fizz (1981) UK#1, *My Camera Never Lies* [v] Bucks Fizz (1982) UK#1, *Now Those Days Are Gone* [v] Bucks Fizz (1982) UK#8, *Peace in Our Time* [vi] Eddie Money (1989) US#11, *Think Twice* [vi] Celine Dion (1995) US#95 UK#1. Co-writers: [i] Ian Bairson, [ii] John Dantier, [iii] John Dantier/Peter Sinfield, [iv] J. Hodge, [v] Nicola Martin, [vi] Peter Sinfield.

457. HILL, Billy (b. 1899; d. 1940, both America) Film and stage composer. A Tin Pan Alley songwriter whose songs were featured in such shows as "The Ziegfeld Follies of 1934," and the films "Rhythm on the Range" (1936) and "Call of the Canyon" (1941). HIT VERSIONS: *Alone at a Table for Two* [i] Guy Lombardo (1936) US#13, *Call of the Canyon, The* Tommy Dorsey (1940) US#14/Glenn Miller (1940) US#10; *Empty Saddles* Bing Crosby (1936) US#8, *Glory of Love, The* Benny Goodman (1936) US#1, *Have You Ever Been Lonely?* [ii] Ted Lewis (1933) US#8, *In the Chapel in the Moonlight* Shep Fields (1936) US#1/Richard Himber (1936) US#7/Ruth Etting (1937) US#20/Mal Hallet (1937) US#11/Four Knights (1954) US#30/Kitty Kallen (1954) g US#4/Bachelors (1965) UK#27; *Last Round-up, The* Gene Autry (1933) US#12/Don Bestor (1933) US#2/Bing Crosby (1933) US#2/Guy Lombardo (1933) US#1/George Olsen (1933) US#1/Conrad Thibault (1933) US#18/Victor Young (1933) US#3; *Lights Out* Eddy Duchin (1936) US#1/Victor Young (1936) US#13; *Night on the Desert* Leo Reisman (1934) US#10, *Old Spinning Wheel, The* Ray Noble (1934) US#1/Emil Velasco (1934) US#9/Victor Young (1934) US#10; *On a Little Street in Singapore* [ii] Jimmy Dorsey (1940) US#13/Frank Sinatra & Harry James (1944) US#27/Manhattan Transfer (1978) UK#20; *Rain* [ii] Arnold Frank (1927) US#20/Sam Lanin (1928) US#16/Frank Petty Trio (1950) US#17; *Wagon Wheels* [iii] Paul Whiteman (1934) US#1. Co-writers: [i] Ted Fiorito (b. December 20, 1900, Newark, NJ; d. July 22, 1971, Scottsdale, AZ)/Dan Richman, [ii] Peter De Rose, [iii] Peter De Rose/Antonin Dvorak.

458. HILLIARD, Bob (b. 1918; d. 1971, both America) Pop lyricist. A prolific lyricist who worked with a variety of composers. One of Hilliard's most poignant songs was the Frank Sinatra classic *In the Wee Small Hours of the Morning* [viii] (1955). ALBUMS: **Hazel Flag** oc (1953, RCA); **Liv-**

ing It Up st (1954, Capitol). HIT VERSIONS: *Be My Life's Companion* [v] Rosemary Clooney (1952) US#18/Mills Brothers (1952) US#7; *Bouquet of Roses, A* [xii] Eddy Arnold (1948) C&W#1 US#13/Dick Haymes (1949) US#22/Mickey Gilley (1975) C&W#11; *Big Brass Band from Brazil* [xiii] Jack Smith (1948) US#26, *Careless Hands* [xiii] Bob & Jeanne (1949) US#21/Bing Crosby (1949) US#12/Sammy Kaye (1949) US#3/Mel Torme (1949) US#1/Des O'Connor (1967) US#6; *Castles in the Sand* [ix] Little Stevie Wonder (1964) US#52, *Civilization (Bongo, Bongo, Bongo)* [xiii] Ray McKinley (1947) US#8/Louis Prima (1947) US#8/Jack Smith (1947) US#9/Andrews Sisters & Danny Kaye (1948) US#3/Woody Herman (1948) US#15; *Coffee Song, The* [ix] Frank Sinatra (1946) US#6, new version (1961) UK#39; *Dearie* [viii] Ray Bolger (1950) US#12/Lisa Kirk (1950) US#22/Guy Lombardo (1950) US#5/Ethel Merman (1950) US#12/Jo Stafford & Gordon MacRae (1950) US#10/Fran Warren (1950) US#22; *Downhearted* [viii] Eddie Fisher (1953) US#5 UK#3, *English Muffins and Irish Stew* [iv] Sylvia Syms (1956) US#21, *From the Candy Store on the Corner to the Chapel on the Hill* Tony Bennett (1956) US#11, *Gotta Have Something in the Bank, Frank* [vii] Frankie Vaughan & the Kaye Sisters (1957) UK#8, *I'm in Favor of Friendship* [viii] Five Smith Brothers (1955) UK#20, *In the Middle of the House* Alma Cogan (1956) UK#20/Rusty Draper (1956) US#20/Johnston Brothers (1956) UK#27/Vaughn Monroe (1956) US#11/Jimmy Parkinson (1956) UK#20; *Moonlight Gambler, The* [xiv] Frankie Laine (1956) US#3 UK#13, *My Summer Love* [vii] Ruby & the Romantics (1963) US#16, *Only Man on the Island, The* [viii] Vic Damone (1958) UK#24/Tommy Steele (1958) UK#16; *Our Day Will Come* [vii] Ruby & the Romantics (1963) R&B#1 US#1 UK#38/Franki Valli (1975) US#11; *Pancho Maximillian Hernandez* [vi] Woody Herman (1947) US#25, *Poor Man's Roses (Or a Rich Man's Gold)* [v] Patti Page (1957) US#14, *Red Silk Stockings and Green Perfume* [xi] Sammy Kaye (1947) US#8/Ray McKinley (1947) US#10/Tony Pastor (1947) US#8; *Shanghai* [v] Bing Crosby (1951) US#21/Bob Crosby (1951) US#22/Doris Day (1951) US#7/Billy Williams Quartet (1951) US#20; *Somebody Bad Stole De Wedding Bell (Who's Got De Ding Dong)* [viii] Georgia Gibbs (1954) US#18/Eartha Kitt (1954) US#16; *Strawberry Moon (In a Blueberry Sky), A* [x] Blue Barron (1948) US#20, *Till They've All Gone Home* [ii] Joan Regan (1953) US#23, *Zambesi* [iii] Lou Busch (1956) UK#2/Eddie Calvert (1956) UK#13/Piranhas (1982) UK#17. Co-writers: [i] Robert Allen, [ii] Alex Alstone, [iii] Nico Carsten/Anton De Waal, [iv] Moose Charlap, [v] Milton De Lugg, [vi] Al Frisch, [vii] Mort Garson, [viii] Dave Mann, [ix] Dick Miles, [x] Sammy Mysels, [xi]

Sammy Mysels/Dick Sanford, [xii] Steve Nelson, [xiii] Carl Sigman, [xiv] Phil Springer. (*See also under* Burt BACHARACH, Sammy FAIN, Lee POCKRISS, Carl SIGMAN, Jule STYNE.)

459. HILLMAN, Chris (b. December 4, 1944, San Diego, CA) C&W bassist, mandolin player, guitarist and vocalist. A country and bluegrass influenced musician who first performed with the 1960s group the Scottsville Squirrel Barkers, which recorded the album **Bluegrass Favorites** (1961, Crown), and the Hillmen, which released **The Hillmen** (1971, Together). In 1964, Hillman joined the legendary group the Byrds, writing their hit *Have You Seen Her Face?* (1967) US#74, but he left the following year to form, with Gram Parsons, the country-rock band the Flying Burrito Brothers. ALBUMS: **The Gilded Palace of Sin** (1969) US#164, **Burrito Deluxe** (1970), **The Flying Burrito Brothers** (1971) US#176, **Last of the Red Hot Burritos** (1972) US#171, **Close Up the Honky Tonks** (1974, all A&M). Over the years, Hillman has re-united with his former Byrds colleagues for the albums **The Byrds** (1973, Asylum) US#20 UK#31, **McGuinn, Clark and Hillman** (1979) US#39, **City** (1980) US#136, **McGuinn/Hillman** (1980, all Capitol); and **3 Byrds Land in London** (1996, Strange Fruit). After a brief spell in Stephen Stills' Manassas, Hillman formed the short-lived Souther-Hillman-Furay Band with Richie Furay and J.D. Souther, which released the albums **The Souther-Hillman-Furay Band** (1974) g US#11 and **Trouble in Paradise** (1975, both Asylum) US#39. In 1986, he formed the country, rock and bluegrass influenced Desert Rose Band, which gave him his greatest post-Byrds success. CHART COMPOSITIONS: *Ashes of Love* (1987) C&W#26, *Love Re-united* (1987) C&W#6, *One Step Forward* (1987) C&W#2, *He's Back and I'm Blue* (1988) C&W#1, *Summer Wind* (1988) C&W#2, *I Still Believe in You* (1988) C&W#1, *You Can Go Home* [ii] (1991) C&W#53, *Twilight Is Gone* [i] (1992) C&W#67, *What About* [i] (1993) C&W#71. ALBUMS: **The Desert Rose Band** (1987), **Running** (1988), **The Pages of Life** (1990, all MCA/Curb) US#187; **Life Goes On** (1993, Curb). COMPILATION: **A Dozen Roses-Greatest Hits** (1991, Curb). The Desert Rose Band broke up in 1994, by which time Hillman had become a born-again Christian. He has also recorded as a solo artist, charting with *Somebody's Back in Town* (1984) C&W#81 and *Running the Road Blocks* (1985) C&W#77. ALBUMS: **Cherokee** (1971, ABC); **Slippin' Away** (1976) US#153, **Clear Sailin'** (1977, both Asylum) US#188; **Morning Sky** (1982), **Desert Rose** (1984, both Sugar Hill); **Ever Call Ready** (1985, Word); **Bakersfield Bound** (1996, Sugar Hill); **Out of the Woodwork**

with Herb Pederson, Larry Rice and Tony Rice (1996, Rounder). Co-writers: [i] S. Hill, [ii] Jack Tempchin. (*See also under* Roger McGUINN, Stephen STILLS.)

460. HITCHCOCK, Robyn (b. March 3, 1952, London, England) Rock guitarist and vocalist. A singer-songwriter who remains more popular in America than in his home land. Hitchcock first performed in the group the Soft Boys. ALBUMS: **Can of Bees** (1979, Aura); **Underwater Moonlight** (1980), **2 Halfs for the Price of One** (1981), **Near the Soft Boys** (1980, all Armageddon); **Invisible Hits** (1980), **Live at Portland Arms** (1983, both Midnight); **Wading Through a Ventilator** (1984, Delorean). Since 1981, he has pursued a solo career on a variety of labels. ALBUMS: **Black Snake Diamond Role** (1981, Armageddon); **Groovy Decay** (1982, Albion); **I Often Dream of Trains** (1984), **Fegmania** (1985), **Gotta Let This Hen Out** (1985), **Element of Light** (1986), **Exploding in Science** (1986, all Midnight); **Invisible Hitchcock** (1986, Glass Fish); **Globe of Frogs** (1988) US#111, **Queen Elvis** (1989) US#139, **Respect** (1993, all A&M). COMPILATION: **Uncorrected Person** (1997).

461. HODGES, Charles (b. December 28, 1943, London, England) Pop pianist, guitarist and vocalist, and **PEACOCK, Dave** (b. May, 24 1945, London, England) Pop guitarist and vocalist. Hodges first recorded as a member of the group Heads, Hands and Feet, releasing the albums **Heads, Hands and Feet** (1971), **Tracks** (1972, both Island); and **Old Soldiers Never Die** (1973, Atlantic). In the late 1980s, he formed a partnership with Peacock in the Cockney styled, Music Hall revivalists Chas and Dave. CHART COMPOSITIONS: *Strummin'* (1978) UK#52, *Gertcha* (1979) UK#20, *The Sideboard Song (Got My Beer in the Sideboard Here)* (1979) UK#55, *Rabbit* (1980) UK#8, *Stars Over 45* (1981) UK#21, *Ossie's Dream (Spurs Are on Their Way to Wembley)** (1981) UK#5, *Ain't No Pleasing You* (1982) UK#2, *Margate* (1982) UK#46, *Tottenham, Tottenham** (1982) UK#19, *London Girls* (1983) UK#63, *Snooker Loop* with Matchroom Mob (1986) UK#6. ALBUMS: **Chas and Dave's Christmas Jamboree Bag** (1981, Warwick) UK#25; **Mustn't Grumble** (1982) UK#35, **Job Lot** (1983) UK#59, **Chas and Dave's Knees Up-Jamboree Bag #2** (1983) UK#7, **Well Pleased** (1984) UK#27, **Jamboree Bag #3** (1985, all Rockney) UK#15; **Chas and Dave's Christmas Carol Album** (1986) UK#37, **Street Party** (1995, both Telstar) UK#3. COMPILATION: **Greatest Hits** (both 1984, Rockney) UK#16. With: * Tottenham Hotspur F.A. Cup Final Squad.

462. HODGSON, Roger (b. May 21, 1950, Portsmouth, England) Rock guitarist and vocalist. A founder member, with co-writer and keyboard player Richard Davies, of the group Supertramp, which achieved a sixteen million selling album with **Breakfast in America** (1979). CHART COMPOSITIONS: *Dreamer* [i] (1975) UK#13, live version (1980) US#15; *Bloody Well Right* [i] (1975) US#35, *Give a Little Bit* [i] (1977) US#15 UK#29, *The Logical Song* [i] (1979) US#6 UK#7, *Breakfast in America* [i] (1979) UK#9, live version (1980) US#62; *Goodbye Stranger* [i] (1979) US#15 UK#57, *Take the Long Way Home* [i] (1979) US#10, *It's Raining Again* [i] (1982) US#11 UK#26, *My Kind of Lady* [i] (1983) US#31. ALBUMS: **Supertramp** (1970) US#158, **Indelibly Stamped** (1971), **Crime of the Century** (1974) g US#38 UK#4, **Crisis? What Crisis?** (1975) US#44 UK#20, **Even in the Quietest Moments...** (1977) g US#16 UK#12, **Breakfast in America** (1979) p US#1 UK#3, **Paris** (1982) g US#8, **...famous last words...** (1982, all A&M) g US#5 UK#6. COMPILATIONS: **The Autobiography of Supertramp** (1986) UK#9, **Very Best of Supertramp** (1992, both A&M) UK#24. Hodgson departed in 1982 for the obligatory solo career, charting with *Had a Dream* (1984) US#48. ALBUMS: **In the Eye of the Storm** (1984) US#46 UK#70, **Hai Hai** (1987, both A&M) US#163; **Rites of Passage** (1997, Unichord). HIT VERSION: *Topical Song, The* [i] Barron Knights (1979) US#70. Co-writer: [i] Richard Davies (b. July 22, 1944, England).

463. HOFFMAN, Al (b. September 25, 1902, Minsk, Russia; d. July 21, 1960, New York, NY) Film and stage composer. A drummer and bandleader who began writing songs in the late 1920s. Hoffman's family had emigrated to America when he was six years old, shortly after which he began singing in local choirs. In the mid–1930s Hoffman lived in England, where he composed for British films, including the jocular *Everything Stops for Tea* [xi] from "Come Out of the Pantry" (1935), *Everything's in Rhythm with My Heart* [xi] from "First a Girl" (1935), and *Gangway* [viii] from "Gangway" (1937). Hoffman also contributed to the British stage shows "This'll Make You Whistle" (1936) and "Going Greek" (1937). By the 1940s he had returned to America, where he wrote for such films as "Cinderella" (1950) and "Singin' in the Rain" (1952). ALBUM: **Cinderella** ost (1957, Disneyland). HIT VERSIONS: *Allegheny Moon* [xiv] Patti Page (1956) US#2, *Are You Really Mine?* [xv] Jimmie Rodgers (1958) US#10, *Ashby De La Zouch (Castle Abbey)* [vi] Merry Macs (1946) US#21, *Bibbidi-Bobbidi-Boo* [v] Perry Como (1950) US#14/Jo Stafford & Gordon MacRae (1950) US#13/Dinah Shore (1950) US#25/

Ilene Woods (1950) US#22; *Black-Eyed Susan Brown* [xi] Mark Fisher (1933) US#16, *Chi-Baba Chi-Baba* [v] Blue Barron (1947) US#14/Charioteers (1947) US#16/Perry Como (1947) US#1/Peggy Lee (1948) US#10; *Close to You* [xiii] Tommy Dorsey (1936) US#11, *Dennis the Menace* [xiv] Jimmy Boyd (1953) US#25/Rosemary Clooney (1953) US#25; *Don't You Love Me Anymore?* [v] Buddy Clark (1947) US#22/Freddy Martin (1947) US#23/Jose Mellis (1947) US#26; *Fit as a Fiddle* [vii] Fred Waring's Pennsylvanians (1932) US#4/Three Keys (1933) US#16; *Fuzzy-Wuzzy* [vi] Jesters (1945) US#12, *Gilly, Gilly, Ossenfeffer, Katzenellen Bogen By the Sea* [xiv] Four Lads (1954) US#18/Max Bygraves (1954) UK#7; *Hawaiian Wedding Song, The* [xii] Andy Williams (1959) R&B#27 US#11, *Heartaches* [xv] Guy Lombardo (1931) US#12/Jimmy Dorsey (1947) US#11/Eddy Howard (1947) US#11/Harry James (1947) US#4/Ted Weems (1947) g US#1/Marcels (1961) R&B#19 US#7/Patsy Cline (1962) UK#31/Vince Hill (1966) UK#28; *Hot Diggity* [iii] Perry Como (1956) US#1 UK#4/Michael Holliday (1956) UK#14/Stargazers (1956) UK#28; *I Apologize* [x] Bing Crosby (1931) US#3/Nat Shilkret (1931) US#12/Champ Butler (1951) US#29/Billy Eckstine (1951) g R&B#4 US#6/Tony Martin (1951) US#20/P.J. Proby (1965) US#135 UK#11; *I Can't Tell a Waltz from a Tango* [xiv] Alma Cogan (1954) UK#6/Patti Page (1954) US#30, *I Saw Stars* [xi] Freddy Martin (1934) US#1/Paul Whiteman (1934) US#4; *I Ups to Her and She Ups to Me (And the Next Thing I Knows I'm in Love)* Guy Lombardo (1939) US#6, *I'm a Big Girl Now* [vi] Sammy Kaye (1946) US#1, *I'm in a Dancing Mood* [xi] Ambrose (1936) US#16/Tommy Dorsey (1937) US#5/Russ Morgan (1937) US#5; *If I Knew You Were Comin' I'd've Baked a Cake* [xix] Eileen Barton (1950) US#1/Georgia Gibbs (1950) US#5/Ethel Merman & Ray Bolger (1950) US#15/Art Mooney (1950) US#28/Benny Strong (1950) US#11; *Little Man, You've Had a Busy Day* [xx] Emil Coleman (1934) US#2/Isham Jones (1934) US#10; *Mairzy Doats and Dozy Doats* [vi] King Sisters (1944) US#21/Merry Macs (1944) US#1/Pied Pipers (1944) US#8/Al Trace (1944) US#7/Lawrence Welk (1944) US#16; *Mama, Teach Me to Dance* [xiv] Eydie Gorme (1956) US#34, *Moon-Talk* [xiv] Perry Como (1958) US#28 UK#17, *My House Is Your House* [xiv] Perry Como (1957) US#50, *Oh, Oh, I'm Falling in Love Again* [xv] Jimmie Rodgers (1958) US#7 UK#18, *Papa Loves Mambo* [xvii] Perry Como (1954) g US#4 UK#16/Joan Regan (1960) UK#29; *Santo Natale* [xvi] David Whitfield (1954) US#19 UK#2, *Secretly* [xiv] Jimmie Rodgers (1958) C&W#5 R&B#7 US#3/Lettermen (1965) US#64; *Story of a Starry Night, The* [v] Glenn Miller (1942) US#15, *Takes Two to Tango* [xiv] Louis Armstrong (1952) US#19 UK#6/

Pearl Bailey (1952) US#7; *There's No Tomorrow* [ii] Tony Martin (1949) US#2, *Torero* [i] Renato Carosone (1958) US#18/Julius Larosa (1958) US#21 UK#15; *Where Will the Dimple Be* [xviii] Rosemary Clooney (1955) UK#6, *Who Walks in When I Walk Out?* [vii] Ray Noble (1934) US#15, *You Can't Be True to Two* [xiv] Dave King (1956) UK#11. Co-writers: [i] Renato Carosone/Dick Manning/"Nisa," [ii] Leon Carr/Leo Corday, [iii] Chabrier/Dick Manning, [iv] Mann Curtis/Walter Kent, [v] Mann Curtis/Jerry Livingston/Peter Tchaikovsky, [v] Mack David/Jerry Livingston, [vi] Milton Drake/Jerry Livingston, [vii] Arthur Freed/Al Goodhart, [vii] Al Goodhart/Manny Kurtz, [viii] Al Goodhard/Samuel Lerner, [ix] Al Goodhart/Herb Magidson, [x] Al Goodhart/Ed Nelson, [xi] Al Goodhart/Maurice Sigler, [xii] Charles E. King/Dick Manning, [xiii] Carl Lampl/Jerry Livingston, [xiv] Dick Manning, [xv] Dick Manning/Mark Maxwell, [xvi] Dick Manning/Belle Nardone, [xvii] Dick Manning/Bix Reichner, [xviii] Bob Merrill, [xix] Bob Merrill/Clem Watts, [xx] Maurice Sigler/Mabel Wayne. (*See also under* Milton AGER.)

464. HOLDER, Noddy (b. Neville Holder, June 15, 1946, Walsall, England) Pop guitarist and vocalist, and **LEA, Jim** (b. June 14, 1952, Wolverhampton, England) Pop bassist, pianist, producer and vocalist. One of the most successful British songwriting teams of the 1970s, who specialized in rock influenced soccer chants and the occasional dramatic ballad. Holder and Lea first recorded and performed as members of the skinhead group Ambrose Slade, which released the album **Beginnings** (1969, Fontana). The band evolved into the more commercially oriented Slade, and spent much of the 1970s dominating the British singles charts. By 1997, Holder was pursuing an acting career. CHART COMPOSITIONS: *Coz I Luv You* (1971) UK#1, *Look Wot You Dun* [i] (1972) UK#4, *Take Me Bak 'Ome* (1972) US#97 UK#1, *Mama Weer All Crazee Now* (1972) US#76 UK#1, *Gudbuy T'Jane* (1972) US#68 UK#2, *Cum on Feel the Noize* (1973) US#98 UK#1, *Skweeze Me Pleeze Me* (1973) UK#1, *My Friend Stan* (1973) UK#2, *Merry Christmas Everybody* (1973) UK#1, live version (1980) UK#70; re-issued (1981) UK#32, re-issued (1982) UK#67, re-issued (1983) UK#20, re-issued (1984) UK#47, re-issued (1985) UK#48, re-issued (1986) UK#71; *Everyday* (1974) UK#3, *Bangin' Man* (1974) UK#3, *Far Far Away* (1974) UK#2, *How Does It Feel* (1975) UK#15, *Thanks for the Memory (Wham Bam Thank You Man)* (1975) UK#7, *In for a Penny* (1975) UK#11, *Let's Call It Quits* (1976) UK#11, *Gypsy Roadhog* (1977) UK#48, *Slade Alive at Reading '80 EP* (1980) UK#44, *We'll Bring the House Down* (1981) UK#10, *Wheels Are*

Comin' Down (1981) UK#60, *Lock Up Your Daughters* (1981) UK#29, *Ruby Red* (1982) UK#51, *(And Now the Waltz) C'Est La Vie* (1982) UK#50, *My Oh My* (1983) US#37 UK#2, *Run Run Away* (1984) US#20 UK#7, *All Join Hands* (1984) UK#15, *Seven Year Bitch* (1985) UK#60, *Myzsterious Mizter Jones* (1985) UK#50, *Little Sheila* (1985) US#86, *Do You Believe in Miracles* (1985) UK#54, *Still the Same* (1987) US#73, *Radio Wall of Sound* (1991) UK#21. ALBUMS: **Play It Loud** (1970), **Slade Alive** (1972) US#158 UK#2, **Slayed?** (1973) US#69 UK#1, **Sladest** (1973) US#129 UK#1, **Old, New, Borrowed and Blue** (1974) UK#1, **Slade in Flame** ost (1974) US#93 UK#6, **Nobody's Fool** (1976, all Polydor) UK#14; **Slade Alive, Volume 2** (1978, Bam); **Return to Base** (1979, RSO); **We'll Bring the House Down** (1981, Cheapskate) UK#25; **Till Deaf Us Do Part** (1981) UK#68, **On Stage** (1982) UK#58, **The Amazing Kamikaze Syndrome** (1983) UK#49, **Keep Your Hands Off My Power Supply** (1983) US#33, **Rogues Gallery** (1985, all RCA) UK#50; **Crackers: The Slade Christmas Party Album** (1985, Telstar) UK#34, **You Boyz Make Big Noize** (1987, RCA) UK#98. COMPILATIONS: **Stomp Your Hands, Clap Your Feet** (1974) US#168, **Slade Smashes** (1980) UK#21, **Slade's Greats** (1984) UK#89, **Wall of Hits** (1991) UK#34, **Feel the Noize — The Very Best of Slade** (1996, all Polydor) UK#19; **The Slade Collection, 1981–1987** (1986, Castle); **The Genesis of Slade** (1997, TMC). HIT VERSIONS: *Cum on Feel the Noize* Quiet Riot (1983) g US#5 UK#45, *Mama Weer All Crazee Now* Quiet Riot (1984) US#51, *Merry Christmas Everybody* Metal Gurus (1990) UK#55. Co-writer: [i] Donald Powell (b. September 10, 1950, Bilston, England).

465. HOLLAND, Brian (b. February 15, 1941, Detroit, MI), **DOZIER, Lamont**, and **HOLLAND, Edward** (b. October 30, 1939, Detroit, MI) R&B producers and vocalists. The most successful songwriting and production trio of the 1960–1970s. A genuinely collaborative partnership, in which Dozier often initiated a tune to which Eddie would assist lyrically and melodically, with Brian frequently arranging and producing the studio session. They first worked for Motown Records, where, Dozier later commented, "We punched the clock, literally punched a clock." Toiling under such Machiavellian conditions seemed to spark certain creative juices, as they soon became Motown's most lucrative backroom team, creating a pop-soul sound that, like Jerry Leiber and Mike Stoller, took black music out of the R&B market and into the white pop mainstream. Dozier recorded uncredited backing vocals on much of their work, and the first of their many collaboration was the Marvelettes' *Locking Up My Heart*. Writing two or three songs per day, the Holland, Dozier and Holland formula was deceptively simple and uncannily effective. They constructed short, catchy material with hooks and choruses that were often placed at the very start of the song, an approach that clearly influenced John Lennon and Paul McCartney while key phrases were repeated throughout a song. They nearly always used the same melody line for both the verse and chorus, and specialized in girl vocal groups that sang somewhat breathlessly. *Stop! In the Name of Love*, was one of ten million selling number ones that they composed for the Supremes, who also recorded an entire album of their compositions as **The Supremes Sing Holland-Dozier-Holland** (1967, Motown) US#6. Brian had begun his career at Motown as a recording engineer in 1958, graduating to producer on many early Motown classics, including *Please Mr. Postman* [i] by the Marvelettes. His elder brother Eddie started out as a singer on publishing demos for such artists as Jackie Wilson, before recording a version of Berry Gordy, Jr.'s composition *Merry-Go-Round*, which he followed with the hits *Jamie* [xi] (1962) R&B#6 US#30, *Leaving Here* (1964) US#76, *Just Ain't Enough Love* (1964) US#54, and *Candy to Me* (1964) US#58, from the albums **Eddie Holland** (1962, Motown) and **Jamie** (1963, United Artists). In 1969, Holland-Dozier-Holland demanded an accounting of royalties from Motown, painfully aware that they were not receiving anywhere near their share of the money that their song catalogue was generating. A lengthy legal battle resulted in a parting of ways with the label, and with their royalties frozen until the dispute was settled, they formed their own Invictus and Hot Wax labels, which were successful with the acts the Honey Cone, Laura Lee, Chairman of the Board and Freda Payne. As executive producers, they brought in a number of songwriters to provide additional material for their roster, and it remains unclear exactly which songs the trio actually wrote during this period, as they often composed under such pseudonyms as Ronald Dunbar and Edith Wayne. Holland and Dozier also recorded a handful of singles on Invictus, including the anthemic *I Shall Not Be Moved* as the Barrino Brothers. CHART COMPOSITIONS: *Why Can't We Be Lovers* (1972) R&B#9 US#57 UK#29, *Don't Leave Me Starvin' for Your Love* (1972) R&B#13 US#52, *New Kind of Woman* (1973) R&B#61, *Slipping Away* (1973) R&B#46. Dozier later worked as a solo artist and producer. HIT VERSIONS: *Ain't Too Proud to Beg* [x] Temptations (1966) R&B#1 US#13 UK#21/Rolling Stones (1974) US#17/Rick Astley (1989) US#89; *All I Do Is Think of You* Jackson Five (1975) US#50, *All I Need* [ix] Temptations (1967) R&B#2 US#8, *Ask the Lonely* Four Tops (1965) R&B#9 US#24, *Baby, Don't Do It*

Marvin Gaye (1964) US#27/Band (1972) US#34; *Baby, I Need Your Lovin'* Four Tops (1964) US#11/Fourmost (1964) UK#24/Johnny Rivers (1967) US#3/O.C. Smith (1970) R&B#30 US#52/Geraldine Hunt (1972) R&B#47/E.D. Wofford (1978) C&W#77/Eric Carmen (1979) US#62/Carl Carlton (1982) US#103; *Baby Love* Supremes (1964) US#1 UK#1, re-issued (1974) UK#12/Joni Lee (1976) C&W#62/Mother's Finest (1977) R&B#79 US#58/Honey Bane (1981) UK#58/Stars On in *Stars on 45/Long Play, Volume 2* (1981) US#120 UK#18/Aurra (1983) R&B#78/Dannii Minogue (1991) UK#14; *Back in My Arms Again* Supremes (1965) R&B#1 US#1 UK#40/Genya Ravan (1978) US#92/High Energy (1983) US#105/Cynthia Manley (1983) US#109; *Band of Gold* [v] Freda Payne (1970) g R&B#20 US#3 UK#1/Charly McClain (1984) C&W#22; *Beauty Is Only Skin Deep* [x] Temptations (1966) R&B#1 US#3 UK#18/Aswad (1989) UK#31; *Behind a Painted Smile* Isley Brothers (1969) UK#5, *Bernadette* Four Tops (1967) R&B#3 US#4 UK#8, re-issued (1972) UK#23; *Bless You* Martha & the Vandellas (1971) R&B#21 US#53 UK#33; *Can I Get a Witness* Marvin Gaye (1964) US#22/Lee Michaels (1971) US#39/Sam Brown (1989) UK#15; *Chairman of the Board* [v] Chairman of the Board (1971) R&B#10 US#42 UK#48, *Cherish What Is Dear to You (While It's Near to You)* Freda Payne (1971) R&B#11 US#44 UK#46, *Come and Get These Memories* Martha & the Vandellas (1963) R&B#6 US#29/Anna King on B-side of *If Somebody Told You* (1964) US#67; *(Come 'Round Here) I'm the One You Need* Smokey Robinson & the Miracles (1966) R&B#4 US#17 UK#45, re-issued (1971) UK#13; *Come See About Me* Supremes (1965) R&B#3 US#1 UK#27/Junior Walker & the All Stars (1966) R&B#33 US#24/Mitch Ryder & the Detroit Wheels (1967) US#113/Nelia Dodds (1964) US#74; *Crumbs Off the Table* [v] Glass House (1969) R&B#7 US#59, *Darling Baby* Elgins (1966) R&B#4 US#72/Jackie Moore (1972) R&B#22 US#106; *Deeper and Deeper* Freda Payne (1970) R&B#9 US#24 UK#33, *Everybody Needs Love* [x] Gladys Knight & the Pips (1967) R&B#3 US#39, *Everything's Tuesday* [vi] Chairman of the Board (1970) R&B#14 US#38 UK#12, *Forever* Marvelettes (1963) US#78, *Forever Came Today* Diana Ross & the Supremes (1968) R&B#17 US#28 UK#28/Jackson Five (1975) R&B#6 US#60; *Function at the Junction* Shorty Long (1966) R&B#42 US#97/Energy (1974) R&B#66; *Get the Cream Off the Top* [viii] Eddie Kendricks (1975) R&B#7 US#50, *Girl's Alright with Me, The* Undisputed Truth (1972) R&B#43 US#107, *Girls It Ain't Easy* [v] Honey Cone (1969) R&B#8 US#68, *Give Me Just a Little More Time* [v] Chairman of the Board (1970) g R&B#8 US#3 UK#3/Kylie Minogue (1992) UK#2; *Happening, The*

[xiii] Supremes (1967) R&B#12 US#1 UK#6/Herb Alpert & the Tijuana Brass (1967) US#32; *He Was Really Saying Something* [xiv] Velvettes (1965) R&B#21 US#64/Bananarama (1982) US#108 UK#5; *Heaven Must Have Sent You* Elgins (1966) R&B#9 US#50 UK#3/Bonnie Pointer (1979) R&B#52 US#11; *Helpless* Kim Weston (1966) R&B#13 US#56, *How Sweet It Is (To Be Loved By You)* Marvin Gaye (1964) US#6 UK#49/Junior Walker & the All Stars (1966) R&B#3 US#18/James Taylor (1975) US#5; *I Can't Be with You (You Can't Be with Me)* Glass House (1970) R&B#33 US#90, *I Can't Help Myself* Four Tops (1965) R&B#1 US#1 UK#23, re-issued (1970) UK#10/Donnie Elbert (1972) R&B#14 US#22 UK#11/Price Mitchell & Jerri Kelly (1975) C&W#65/ Shalamar in *Uptown Festival* (1977) R&B#10 US#25 UK#30/Bonnie Pointer (1979) R&B#42 US#40; *I Got a Feeling* Barbara Randolph (1967) US#116, *I Gotta Dance to Keep from Cryin'* Smokey Robinson & the Miracles (1963) US#35, *I Guess I'll Always Love You* Isley Brothers (1966) R&B#31 US#61 UK#45, re-issued (1969) UK#11; *I Hear a Symphony* Supremes (1965) R&B#2 US#1 UK#39/Stars On in *Stars on 45/Long Play, Volume 2* (1981) US#120 UK#18; *I Just Can't Walk Away* Four Tops (1983) R&B#36 US#71, *I Just Want to Be Loved* Lee Charles Nealy (1973) R&B#65, *(I Know) I'm Losing You* [vii] Temptations (1966) R&B#1 US#8 UK#19/Rare Earth (1970) R&B#20 US#7/Rod Stewart (1971) US#24/Uptown (1986) US#87; *I Need It Just as Bad as You* Laura Lee (1974) R&B#55, *I'll Catch You When You Fall* Laura Lee (1973) R&B#49, *I'll Turn to Stone* Four Tops (1967) R&B#50 US#76, *(I'm a) Roadrunner* Junior Walker & the All Stars (1966) R&B#4 US#20 UK#12, *I'm Gonna Let My Heart Do the Walking* [iv] Supremes (1976) R&B#25 US#40, *I'm In a Different World* Four Tops (1968) R&B#23 US#51 UK#27, *I'm Not My Brother's Keeper* Flaming Ember (1970) R&B#12 US#34, *I'm Ready for Love* Martha & the Vandellas (1966) R&B#2 US#9 UK#29, *I'm So Glad* Junior Walker & the All Stars (1976) R&B#43, *I'm Your Driving Wheel* Supremes (1977) US#85, *If You Can't Beat Me Rockin' (You Can Have My Chair)* [v] Laura Lee (1972) R&B#31 US#65, *In and Out of Love* Diana Ross & the Supremes (1967) R&B#16 US#9 UK#13/Martha & the Vandellas (1972) R&B#22 US#102; *In My Lonely Room* Martha & the Vandellas (1964) US#44, *It's the Same Old Song* Four Tops (1965) R&B#2 US#5 UK#34/Weathermen (1971) UK#19/Shalamar in *Uptown Festival* (1977) R&B#10 US#25 UK#30/K.C. & the Sunshine Band (1978) R&B#30 US#35 UK#49; *Jimmy Mack* Martha Reeves & the Vandellas (1967) R&B#1 US#10 UK#21, re-issued (1970) UK#21/Stars On in *Stars on 45/Long Play* (1981) g US#9 UK#1/Sheena Easton (1986) US#65; *Just a Lit-*

tle Bit of You [viii] Michael Jackson (1975) R&B#4 US#23, *Keep on Holding On* [viii] Temptations (1975) R&B#3 US#54, *Little Darlin' (I Need You)* Martha & the Vandellas (1964) US#42/Marvin Gaye (1966) US#7 UK#50/Doobie Brothers (1977) US#48; *Locking Up My Heart* Marvelettes (1963) R&B#25 US#44, *(Loneliness Made Me Realize) It's You That I Need* [x] Temptations (1967) R&B#3 US#14, *Love and Liberty* Laura Lee (1971) R&B#23 US#94, *Love Is Here and Now You're Gone* Supremes (1967) R&B#1 US#1 UK#17/Stars On in *Stars on 45/Long Play, Volume 2* (1981) US#120 UK#18; *(Love Is Like a) Heatwave* Martha & the Vandellas (1963) R&B#1 US#4/ Linda Ronstadt (1975) US#5; *Love Is Like an Itching in My Heart* Supremes (1966) R&B#7 US#9, *Love Like Yours (Don't Come Knocking Every Day), A* Ike & Tina Turner (1966) UK#16, *Love (Makes Me Do Foolish Things)* Martha & the Vandellas (1965) R&B#22 US#70, *Love's Gone Bad* Chris Clark (1966) R&B#41 US#105, *Mashed Potato Time* [ii] Dee Dee Sharp (1962) R&B#1 US#2, *Mickey's Monkey* Miracles (1963) R&B#3 US#8, *Mind, Body and Soul* [v] Flaming Ember (1969) US#26, *My World Is Empty Without Me* Supremes (1966) R&B#10 US#5/Jose Feliciano (1969) US#87; *90 Day Freeze* 100 Proof Aged in Soul (1971) R&B#34, *Nothing But Heartaches* Supremes (1965) R&B#6 US#11, *Nowhere to Run* Martha & the Vandellas (1965) R&B#5 US#8 UK#26, re-issued (1969) UK#42, re-issued (1988) UK#52/Dynamic Superiors (1977) R&B#53; *One, Two, Three (1,2,3)* [xii] Len Barry (1965) R&B#11 US#2 UK#2/Jane Morgan (1966) US#135/Ramsey Lewis (1967) US#67; *Playboy* Marvelettes (1961) R&B#4 US#7, *Please Mr. Postman* [i] Marvelettes (1961) R&B#1 US#1/Beatles on *Four By the Beatles EP* (1964) US#92/Carpenters (1971) g US#1 UK#2/ Gentle Persuasion (1983) US#82/Backbeat Band (1994) UK#69; *Put Yourself in My Place* Elgins (1966) US#92 UK#28/Isley Brothers (1967) UK#13; *Quicksand* Martha & the Vandellas (1963) US#8, *Reach Out, I'll Be There* Four Tops (1966) R&B#1 US#1 UK#1, re-mixed (1988) UK#11/Diana Ross (1971) US#29/Gloria Gaynor (1975) R&B#56 US#60 UK#14/Stars On in *Stars on 45/Long Play, Volume 2* (1981) US#120 UK#18/Michael Narada Walden (1983) R&B#40/Michael Bolton (1993) UK#37; *Reflections* Diana Ross & the Supremes (1967) R&B#4 US#2 UK#5/Stars On in *Stars on 45/Long Play, Volume 2* (1981) US#120 UK#18; *Road We Didn't Take, The* Freda Payne (1972) US#100, *Run, Run, Run* Supremes (1964) US#93, *Seven Rooms of Gloom* Four Tops (1967) R&B#10 US#14 UK#12, *Shake Me, Wake Me (When It's Over)* Four Tops (1966) R&B#5 US#18, *She's Not Just Another Woman* 8th Day (1971) g R&B#3 US#11, *Since You've Been Gone* Velvettes on B-side *These Things Will Keep Me Loving You* (1966)

R&B#43 US#102 UK#34, *Something About You* Four Tops (1965) R&B#9 US#19/LeBlanc & Carr (1977) US#48; *Standing in the Shadows of Love* Four Tops (1967) R&B#2 US#6 UK#6/Deborah Washington (1978) R&B#93; *Stop! In the Name of Love* Supremes (1965) R&B#2 US#1 UK#7/Margie Joseph (1971) R&B#38 US#96/Hollies (1983) US#29/Shalamar in *Uptown Festival* (1977) R&B#10 US#25 UK#30/ Stars On in *Stars on 45/Long Play, Volume 2* (1981) US#120 UK#18/Sinitta on *The Supreme EP* (1993) UK#49; *Stop the World (And Let Me Off)* Flaming Ember (1971) R&B#43 US#101, *Strange I Know* Marvelettes (1962) US#49, *Take Me in Your Arms (And Rock Me)* Kim Weston (1965) R&B#4 US#50/ Gladys Knight & the Pips (1967) US#98/Isley Brothers (1968) R&B#22 US#121/Jermaine Jackson on B-side of *Daddy's Home* (1972) US#9/Doobie Brothers (1975) US#11 UK#29; *Take Me with You* Honey Cone (1970) R&B#28 US#108, *Thankyou (For Loving Me)* Stevie Wonder on B-side of *Castles in the Sand* (1964) US#52, *Third Finger, Left Hand* Pearls (1972) UK#31, *This Old Heart of Mine (Is Weak for You)* Isley Brothers (1966) R&B#6 US#12 UK#47, re-issued (1968) UK#3/Tammi Terrell (1969) R&B#31 US#67/Rod Stewart (1975) US#83 UK#4/ Rod Stewart & Ronald Isley (1989) US#10 UK#51; *Too Many Fish in the Sea* [x] Marvelettes (1964) R&B#15 US#25/Mitch Ryder & the Detroit Wheels (1967) US#24; *Twistin' Postman* Marvelettes (1961) R&B#13 US#34, *Two Wrongs Don't Make a Right* Freda Payne (1973) R&B#75, *Unhooked Generation, The* Freda Payne (1969) R&B#43, *We're Almost There* [xiii] Michael Jackson (1975) R&B#7 US#54 UK#46, *Wedlock Is a Padlock* Laura Lee (1971) R&B#37, *Westbound #9* [vi] Flaming Ember (1970) R&B#15 US#24, *What's the Matter with You, Baby* Marvin Gaye (1964) US#17, *When the Lovelight Starts Shining Through His Eyes* Supremes (1964) US#23, *When Will It End* Honey Cone (1970) US#117, *Where Did Our Love Go* Supremes (1964) US#1 UK#3/Donnie Elbert (1971) R&B#6 US#15 UK#8/J. Geils Band (1976) US#68/Manhattan Transfer (1978) UK#40/ Stars On in *Stars on 45/Long Play, Volume 2* (1981) US#120 UK#18/Reddings (1985) R&B#37/Sinitta on *The Supreme EP* (1993) UK#49; *Where Do I Go from Here* Supremes (1975) R&B#93, *While You're Out Looking for Sugar* [v] Honey Cone (1969) R&B#26 US#62, *Whole Lot of Shakin' Goin' on in My Heart (Since I Met You)* Smokey Robinson & the Miracles (1963) R&B#20 US#46, *Without the One You Love (Life Is Not Worthwhile)* Four Tops (1964) US#43, *Woman's Love Rights* Laura Lee (1971) R&B#11 US#36, *Working On a Building of Love* Chairman of the Board (1972) UK#20, *You Brought the Joy* Freda Payne (1971) R&B#21 US#52, *You Can't Hurry Love* Supremes (1966) R&B#1 US#1 UK#3/

Phil Collins (1982) g US#10 UK#1/Sinitta on *The Supreme EP* (1993) UK#49; *You Keep Me Hanging On* Supremes (1966) R&B#1 US#1 UK#8/Joe Simon (1968) R&B#11 US#25/Vanilla Fudge (1968) US#6 UK#18/Wilson Pickett (1969) R&B#16 US#92/ Jackie De Shannon (1970) US#93/Roni Hill (1977) UK#36/Stars On in *Stars on 45/Long Play, Volume 2* (1981) US#120 UK#18/Sam Harris on B-side of *Sugar Don't Bite* (1984) US#36/Kim Wilde (1987) US#1 UK#2; *You Keep Running Away* Four Tops (1967) R&B#7 US#19 UK#26, *You Lost the Sweetest Boy* Mary Wells (1963) US#22, *You're a Wonderful One* Marvin Gaye (1964) US#15, *You're My Driving Wheel* [iii] Supremes (1976) R&B#50 US#85, *You're What's Missing in My Life* G.C. Cameron (1977) R&B#24, *You've Got to Crawl Before You Walk* 8th Day (1971) R&B#3 US#28, *Your Unchanging Love* Marvin Gaye (1967) US#33. All compositions Holland-Dozier-Holland, except: [i] R. Bateman/Frederick C. Gorman/Brian Holland, [ii] R. Bateman/G. Dobbins/ W. Garrett/Frederick C. Gorman/Brian Holland, [iii] H. Beatty/R. Brown/Brian Holland/F. Stafford, [iv] H. Beatty/Brian Holland/Edward Holland, [v] as Ronald Dunbar/Edith Wayne, [vi] as Daphne Dumas/Ronald Dunbar/Edith Wayne, [vii] Cornelius Grant/Norman Whitfield, [viii] Brian Holland/Edward Holland, [ix] Edward Holland/R. Dean Taylor/Frank Wilson, [x] Edward Holland/ Norman Whitfield, [xi] Edward Holland/William Stevenson/Barrett Strong (b. February 5, 1941, Westpoint, MS). Co-writers: [xii] Leonard Borisoff/John Madera/David White, [xiii] Frank Devol, [xiv] William Stevenson/Norman Whitfield. (*See also* under Lamont DOZIER, R. Dean TAYLOR.)

466. HOLLIS, Mark (b. 1955, London, England) Pop guitarist, keyboard player and vocalist. The principal tunesmith in the synthesizer dominated group Talk Talk. CHART COMPOSITIONS: *Talk Talk* [ii] (1982) US#75 UK#23, *Today* (1982) UK#14, *My Foolish Friend* (1983) UK#57, *It's My Life* [i] (1984) US#31 UK#46, re-issued (1990) UK#13; *Such a Shame* (1984) US#49 UK#49, *Dum Dum Girl* (1984) UK#74, *Life's What You Make It* [i] (1986) US#90 UK#16, re-issued (1990) UK#23; *Living in Another World* (1986) UK#48, *Give It Up* (1986) UK#59. ALBUMS: **The Party's Over** (1982) US#132 UK#21, **It's My Life** (1984) US#42 UK#46, **The Color of Spring** (1986, all EMI) US#58 UK#8; **Spirit of Eden** (1988, Parlophone) UK#19; **Laughing Stock** (1991, Verve) UK#26. COMPILATIONS: **It's My Mix** (1984, EMI), **Natural History: The Very Best of Talk Talk** (1990) UK#3, **History Revisited-The Remixes** (1991, both Parlophone) UK#35; **Very Best of Talk Talk** (1997, EMI). Co-writers: [i] Tim Friese-Green, [ii] E. Hollis.

467. HOLLY, Buddy (b. Charles Hardin Holley, September 7, 1936, Lubbock, TX; d. February 2, 1959, Mason City, IA) Pop guitarist and vocalist. The performer that introduced rock and roll to a wide audience, and whose effect on the genre was second only to that of Elvis Presley. Holly composed a small catalogue of frequently recorded songs that merged innocent melodies with teenage melancholy. He was the first singer to overdub his own vocal lines on records, and was one of the earliest artists to blend elements of R&B into a rocking, country sound. Holly not only introduced string arrangements to pop disks, he was also a significant influence on both the Beatles and the Rolling Stones. With his high school friend Bob Montgomery, he first performed as the duo Buddy and Bob, whose 1954 demos were later released as **Holly in the Hills** (1965). Holly's debut single was *Blue Days, Black Nights* (1956), which he followed with sessions as Buddy Holly and the Three Tunes for the Decca label. As the Crickets, Holly linked up with producer Norman Petty and achieved a worldwide million seller with *That'll Be the Day* [i] (1957), a disk that changed the entire sound of rock and roll music. By 1958, Holly had parted company with both Petty and the Crickets in order to record the solo single *It's So Easy* [v], but shortly after the release of *Heartbeat* [iv] (1959), he was killed in a plane crash en route to a concert. His songs were later interpreted by Hank Marvin as **Hank Plays Holly** (1996, PolyGram) UK#39. CHART COMPOSITIONS: *That'll Be the Day* [i] (1957) g R&B#2 US#1 UK#1, *Maybe Baby* [v] (1957) R&B#4 US#17 UK#4, *Peggy Sue* [i] (1958) g R&B#2 US#3 UK#6, re-issued (1968) UK#32; *Listen to Me* [v] (1958) UK#16, re-issued (1962) UK#48; *Think It Over* [i] (1958) US#27, *Fool's Paradise* [v] (1958) US#58, *It's So Easy* [v] (1958) UK#19, *Heartbeat* [iv] (1959) US#82 UK#30, *Midnight Shift* [v] (1959) UK#26, *Peggy Sue Got Married* (1960) UK#13, *True Love Ways* [v] (1960) UK#25, re-issued (1988) UK#65; *Learning the Game* (1960) UK#36, *What to Do* [v] (1961) UK#34, re-issued (1963) UK#27; *Wishing* [iv] (1963) UK#10, *You've Got Love* (1964) UK#40, *Love's Made a Fool Out of You* [iv] (1964) UK#39. ALBUMS: **The Chirping Crickets** (1957, Brunswick); **Buddy Holly** (1958, Coral). COMPILATIONS: **That'll Be the Day** (1958, Decca) UK#5; **The Buddy Holly Story** (1959) g US#11 UK#2, **The Buddy Holly Story, Volume 2** (1960) UK#17, **Reminiscing** (1963) US#40 UK#2, **Holly in the Hills** (1965) UK#13, **Greatest Hits** (1967) UK#9, **Giant** (1969, all Coral) UK#13; **20 Golden Greats** (1978, MCA) g US#55 UK#1; **The Buddy Holly Story** ost (1978, Epic) US#86; **True Love Ways** (1989, Telstar) UK#8; **The Complete Buddy Holly Story** (1993), **Words of Love** (1993, both MCA) UK#1; **Very Best of Buddy Holly** (1996, Dino) UK#24. HIT VERSIONS: *Everyday* [v] Bruce & Terry (1965) US#101/Don McLean (1973) UK#38/Oak Ridge Boys (1984) C&W#1/James Taylor (1985) C&W#26 US#61; *Fool's Paradise* [v] Don McLean (1974) US#107, *Heartbeat* [iv] England Sisters (1960) UK#33/Showaddywaddy (1975) UK#7; *It's So Easy* [v] Denny Laine (1976) US#108/Linda Ronstadt (1977) C&W#81 US#5; *Learning the Game* Hullaballoos (1965) US#121, *Look at Me* Jimmy Gilmer (1964) US#133, *Love's Made a Fool Out of You* [iv] Crickets (1959) UK#26/Bobby Fuller Four (1966) US#26; *Maybe Baby* [v] Crickets (1958) US#17 UK#4/Gallery featuring Jim Gold (1973) US#118/Susan Allanson (1978) C&W#7; *Not Fade Away* [v] Rolling Stones (1964) UK#3 US#48/Tanya Tucker (1978) US#70, also on B-side of *Texas (When I Die)* (1978) C&W#5; *Peggy Sue* [i] Beach Boys (1978) US#59, *That'll Be the Day* [i] Everly Brothers (1965) US#111 UK#30/Kenny Vernon (1972) C&W#56/Pure Prairie League (1976) C&W#98 US#106/Linda Ronstadt (1976) C&W#27 US#11; *True Love Ways* [v] Peter & Gordon (1965) US#14 UK#2/Randy Gurley (1978) C&W#77/Mickey Gilley (1980) C&W#1 US#66/Cliff Richard (1983) UK#8/David Essex & Catherine Zeta Jones (1994) UK#38; *Well...All Right* [iii] Santana (1978) US#69, *Words of Love* Diamonds (1957) R&B#12 US#13, *You're the One* [ii] Billy Swan (1976) C&W#75. Co-writers: [i] Jerry Allison/Norman Petty, [ii] Jerry Allison/Mauldin/Norman Petty, [iii] Waylon Jennings, [iv] Bob Montgomery, [v] Norman Petty.

468. HOLMES, Rupert (b. February 24, 1947, Northwich, England) Pop pianist, producer and vocalist. A 1960s session musician and arranger who also scored such films as "Five Savage Men." Holmes' songs have been recorded by Barry Manilow, Barbra Streisand and Dionne Warwick, and he also wrote the Broadway musical "The Mystery of Edwin Drood" (1986). CHART COMPOSITIONS: *Escape (The Pina Colada Song)* (1979) US#1 UK#23, *Him* (1980) US#6 UK#31, *Answering Machine* (1980) US#32, *I Don't Need You* (1981) US#56. ALBUMS: **Widescreen** (1974, Epic); **Rupert Holmes** (1975), **Singles** (1977), **Pursuit of Happiness** (1978, all MCA); **Partners in Crime** (1979, Infinity) g US#33; **Adventure** (1980, MCA); **Full Circle** (1981, Elektra); **Songwriters for the Stars, Volume 1** (1982), **The Mystery of Edwin Drood** oc (1986, both Polydor) US#150. HIT VERSIONS: *Jennifer Tompkins* Street People (1970 US#36), *Timothy* Buoys (1971) US#17, *You Got It All* Jets (1986) R&B#2 US#3.

469. HOOKER, John Lee (b. August 22, 1917, Clarksdale, MS) Blues guitarist, harmonica player and vocalist. An influential folk-blues artist whose total disregard for time signatures, conventional rhythms or other musical matters of a technical nature, resulted in a unique and much imitated style. Hooker learned the guitar in his teens and performed with various gospel quartets and groups, before making his first recordings for the Modern label in 1948. Throughout the 1940s and early 1950s, Hooker recorded some seventy singles under various pseudonyms in order to avoid contractual disputes. He continues to record and perform well into his late seventies. CHART COMPOSITIONS: *Boogie Chillen'* (1949) R&B#1, *Hobo Blues* (1949) R&B#5, *Hoogie Boogie* (1949) R&B#9, *Crawling King Snake* (1949) R&B#6, *Huckle Up, Baby* (1950) R&B#15, *I'm in the Mood* (1951) R&B#1 US#30, *I Love You Honey* (1958) R&B#29, *No Shoes* (1960) R&B#21, *Boom Boom* (1962) R&B#16 US#60, re-issued (1992) UK#16; *Dimples* (1962) UK#23, *Boogie at Russian Hall* (1993) UK#53, *Chill Out (Things Gonna Change)* (1995) UK#54, *Baby Lee* with Robert Cray (1996) UK#65. ALBUMS: **Alone** (1951), **Goin' Down Highway** (1951, both Speciality); **The Folk Blues of John Lee Hooker** (1959, Riverside); **I'm John Lee Hooker** (1959, Vee-Jay); **That's My Story** (1960, Riverside); **John Lee Hooker Sings the Blues** (1960, King); **Concert at Newport** (1960), **The Folk Lore of John Lee Hooker** (1961), **Burnin'** (1962), **Travellin'** (1962), **Best of John Lee Hooker** (1962, all Vee-Jay); **Tupelo Blues** (1962, Riverside); **I Want to Shout The Blues** (1964); **House of the Blues** (1967, Marble Arch) UK#34; **It Serves You Right to Suffer** (1967), **Live at the Cafe Au Go-Go** (1968), **Urban Blues** (1968), **If You Miss 'Im...I Get 'Im** (1969, all Bluesway); **Hooker 'n' Heat** (1971, Liberty) US#73; **Endless Boogie** (1971) US#126, **Never Get Out of These Blues Alive** (1971, both ABC) US#130; **Detroit Special** (1974), **Don't Turn Me from Your Door** (1974, both Atlantic); **The Cream** (1974, Tomato); **The Healer** (1988, Silvertone) US#62 UK#63; **Mr. Lucky** (1991) US#101 UK#3, **Boom Boom** (1992) UK#15, **Chill Out** (1995, all Pointblank) US#136 UK#32.

470. HOPKINS, Lightnin' (b. Sam Hopkins, March 15, 1912, Centerville; d. January 30, 1982, Houston, both TX) Blues guitarist and vocalist. A songwriter with a reportage and narrative style, whose technique of making up songs on the spot was to influence Bob Dylan. Hopkins learned the guitar in his teens and first recorded for the Aladdin and Gold Star labels in the mid–1940s, during which time he composed such incisive social commentaries such as *Tim Moore's Farm* and *Unsuccessful Blues*. In the 1950s, Hopkins recorded for a variety of labels, but did not release an album until 1959. He appeared in the film "The Blues Accordin' to Lightnin' Hopkins' (1968), and died of cancer in 1982. CHART COMPOSITIONS: *Tim Moore's Farm* (1949) R&B#13, *"T" Model Blues* (1949) R&B#8, *Shotgun Blues* (1950) R&B#5, *Give Me Central 209* (1952) R&B#6, *Coffee Blues* (1952) R&B#6. ALBUMS: **The Roots of Lightnin' Hopkins** (1959, Folkways); **Down South Summit Meetin'** (1960, WP); **Country Blues** (1960), **Autobiography** (1960, both Tradition); **Lightnin' Hopkins Sings the Blues** (1961, Crown); **Mojo Hand** (1961, Fire); **On Stage** (1962, Imperial); **Lightnin' Strikes** (1962, Vee-Jay); **And the Blues** (1963, Imperial); **Goin' Away** (1963), **Blues Hoot** (1964, both Prestige); **First Meeting** (1964, World); **Hootin' the Blues** (1965), **Down Home Blues** (1965, both Prestige): **Lightnin' Hopkins** (1965, Archive Folk); **Lightnin' Hopkins and Barbara Dane** (1965), **Texas Blues Man** (1965, both Arhoolie); **Soul Blues** (1965, Prestige); **Something Blue** (1966), **Roots of Lightnin' Hopkins** (1966, both Verve); **Lightnin' Hopkins** (1966, Saga); **Best** (1968, Tradition); **Free Form Patterns** (1968, Int Artists); **His Greatest Hits** (1968, Bluesville); **Blues in My Bottle** (1968), **Got to Move Your Body** (1968, both Xtra); **Best of Texas Blues Band** (1969, Prestige); **The Great Electric Show and Dance** (1969), **Blue Lightnin'** (1970), **Talking Some Sense** (1970, all Jewel); **In New York** (1970, Barnaby); **Lightnin', Volume 1** (1970, Poppy); **Let's Work Awhile** (1971, Blue Horizon); **Original Folk Blues** (1971, Kent); **King of Dowling Street** (1972, Pathe); **Lonesome Lightnin'** (1972, Carnival); **Lightnin' Hopkins** (1972, Trip); **The Blues** (1973), **Dirty Blues** (1973, both Mainstream); **Legacy of the Blues** (1973, GNP); **Greatest Hits** (1974, Prestige); **The Legacy of the Blues, Volume 12** (1974, Sonet); **In Berkeley** (1975), **Early Recordings** (1975), **Early Recordings 2** (1975, all Arhoolie); **Shake It Baby** (1975, Vogue); **Lowdown Dirty Blues** (1975, Mainstream); **Rooster Crowed in England** (1975, 77); **Legend** (1976, Blue Anthology); **All Them Blues** (1976, DJM); **Legend in His Own Time** (1976, Kent); **Gotta Move Your Baby** (1977, Prestige); **At His Natural Best** (1980, Rhapsody); **Lightnin' Strikes Back** (1981, Charly); **At the Bird Lounge** (1982, Bulldog); **Strums the Blues** (1983, EMI); **Electric Lightnin'** (1984, JSP); **Great Songs of Lightnin' Hopkins** (1984, Astan); **Houston's King of the Blues** (1985, Blues Classics); **The Collection** (1987, Deja Vu); **Move on Out** (1987, Charly); **Bad Boogie** (1988), **Flash Lightnin'** (1988, both Diving Duck); **Herald Material, 1954** (1988, Collectibles); **Lightnin' Hopkins** (1988), **Po' Lightnin'** (1988, both Arhoolie); **Walkin' This Road By Myself** (1988, Ace). HIT VERSIONS: *Feel So Bad* Little Milton (1967) R&B#7 US#91/Ray Charles (1971) R&B#16 US#68.

471. HORNSBY, Bruce (b. Bruce Randall Hornsby, November 23, 1954, Williamsburg, VA) Rock keyboard player and vocalist. A jazz influenced rock pianist who studied music at Miami University and the Berkeley School of Music. In 1970, Hornsby formed the Bruce Hornsby Band, which performed in bars and lounges. In 1980, at the behest of singer Michael McDonald, Hornsby moved to Los Angeles with his brother John Hornsby, where they composed for the publishing arm of 20th Century–Fox. Three years later, Hornsby played in Sheena Easton's backing band, where his refined piano styling was first noticed. Hornsby formed Bruce Hornsby and the Range and charted with the three million selling *The Way It Is* (1985), which he followed with a series of radio friendly rock albums. In 1990, Hornsby split up the Range and undertook a lengthy sabbatical as a stand-in pianist with the Grateful Dead, after which his solo albums became more fluid and improvisational. CHART COMPOSITIONS: *Every Little Kiss* (1986) US#72, re-mixed (1987) US#14; *The Way It Is* (1986) g US#1 UK#15, *Mandolin Rain* [ii] (1986) C&W#38 US#4 UK#70, *The Valley Road* [ii] (1988) US#5 UK#44, *Look Out of Any Window* [ii] (1988) US#35, *Across the River* (1990) US#18, *Lost Soul* (1990) US#84, *Fields of Gray* (1993) US#69, *Rainbow's Cadillac* (1994) US#121, *Walk in the Sun* (1995) US#54. ALBUMS: **The Way It Is** (1986) p US#3 UK#16, **Scenes from the Southside** (1988) p US#5 UK#18, **A Night on the Town** (1990) g US#20 UK#23, **Harbor Lights** (1993) g US#46 UK#32, **Hot House** (1995, all RCA) US#68. HIT VERSION: *Jacob's Ladder* [ii] Huey Lewis & the News (1986) US#1, *Nobody There But Me* Willie Nelson (1988) C&W#82. Co-writers: [i] C. Hayden/John Hornsby, [ii] John Hornsby. (*See also under* Don HENLEY.)

472. HOWARD, Harlan (b. September 8, 1929, Lexington, KY) C&W guitarist and vocalist. A prolific songwriter who once stated that his recipe for a hit was three chords and the truth. Howard has achieved more hits than any other country tunesmith, and his forte is simple, melodramatic story songs, that cleverly manipulate faithful cliches and use amusing aphorisms. Both his *Heartaches By the Number* and *I Fall to Pieces* have received BMI million radio play awards, and Waylon Jennings has recorded over forty of his compositions. There have been over four thousand versions of the one thousand songs that Howard has had recorded, which have collectively given him over one hundred top ten country hits. He set an unbeaten record during the 1960s, when fifteen of his tunes were in the country top forty in the same week. Howard grew up on a farm, but during the depression years he lived in Detroit, where he listened to hillbilly music on the radio. He began writing songs at the age of twelve, and after befriending the country singer Buck Owens, Howard achieved his first hit with *Above and Beyond (The Call of Love)* [iii] (1960). Owens later recorded the album **Buck Owens Sings Harlan Howard** (1965, Capitol). CHART COMPOSITION: *Sunday Morning Christian* (1971) C&W#38. ALBUMS: **Harlan Howard Sings Harlan Howard** (1961, Capitol); **All-Time Favorite Country Songwriter** (1965, Monument); **Mr. Songwriter** (1967), **Down to Earth** (1968, both RCA); **To the Silent Majority with Love** (1971, Nugget). HIT VERSIONS: *All I Can Be (Is a Sweet Memory)* Collin Raye (1991) C&W#41+, *Baby It's You* Janie Frickie (1978) C&W#21, *Blame It on Your Heart* [ii] Patty Loveless (1993) C&W#1 US#112, *Blizzard, The* Jim Reeves (1961) C&W#4 US#62, *Bummin' Around* Jimmy Dean (1953) C&W#5/T. Texas Tyler (1953) C&W#5; *Busted* Johnny Cash (1963) C&W#13/Ray Charles (1963) R&B#3 US#4 UK#21/John Conlee (1982) C&W#6; *California Sunshine* Rusty Draper (1968) C&W#70, *Call Me Mr. In-Between* Burl Ives (1962) C&W#3 US#2, *Chokin' Kind, The* Waylon Jennings (1967) C&W#8/Joe Simon (1969) g R&B#1 US#13/Diana Trask (1971) C&W#59/Z.Z. Hill (1971) R&B#30 US#108/Freddy Fender (1983) C&W#87; *Come with Me* Waylon Jennings (1979) C&W#1, *Everglades, The* Kingston Trio (1960) US#60, *Evil on Your Mind* Jan Howard (1966) C&W#5, *Go Cat Go* Norma Jean (1964) C&W#8 US#134, *Goin' Home* Ron Shaw (1978) C&W#79, *Green River* Waylon Jennings (1967) C&W#11, *He/She Called Me Baby* Patsy Cline (1964) C&W#23/Carl Smith (1965) C&W#32/Dick Curless (1965) C&W#32/Charlie Rich (1974) C&W#1 US#47; *Heartaches By the Number* Ray Price (1959) C&W#2/Guy Mitchell (1959) R&B#19 US#1 UK#5/Jack Reno (1972) C&W#26; *Heartbreak U.S.A.* Kitty Wells (1961) C&W#1, *Heaven Help the Poor Working Girl* Norma Jean (1968) C&W#18, *Honky Tonk Crazy* Tommy Bell (1983) C&W#97/Gene Watson (1987) C&W#43; *Hurtin's All Over, The* Connie Smith (1966) C&W#3, *I Ain't Got Nobody* Dick Curless (1968) C&W#34/Del Reeves (1976) C&W#51/Roy Clark (1980) C&W#60; *I Don't Believe I'll Fall in Love Today* Warren Smith (1960) C&W#5/Gilbert Ortega (1978) C&W#93; *I Don't Know a Thing About Love (The Moon Song)* Conway Twitty (1984) C&W#1, *I Wish I Was Your Friend* Wanda Jackson (1969) C&W#51, *I Wish That I Could Fall in Love Today* Barbara Mandrell (1988) C&W#5, *I Won't Forget You* Jim Reeves (1965) C&W#3 US#93 UK#3, *I Wouldn't Buy a Used Car from Him* Norma Jean (1965) C&W#8, *I'll Catch You When You Fall* Charlie

Walker (1959) C&W#16, *I'm Always on a Mountain When I Fall* Merle Haggard (1978) C&W#2, *I'm Down to My Last Cigarette* K.D. Lang (1988) C&W#21, *I've Cried a Mile (For Every Inch I've Laughed)* Hank Snow (1966) C&W#18/Tari Hensley (1986) C&W#52; *If I Cried Everytime You Hurt Me* Wanda Jackson (1962) C&W#28, *Image of Me, The* Bob Wills (1961) C&W#26/Conway Twitty (1968) C&W#5/Jim Reeves (1984) C&W#70; *It's All Over (But the Crying)* Kitty Wells (1966) C&W#14/ Hank Williams, Jr. (1968) C&W#3; *It's Nothin' to Me* Jim Reeves (1977) C&W#14, *Key's in the Mailbox, The* Freddie Hart (1960) C&W#18/Tony Booth (1972) C&W#15; *Life Turned Her That Way* Mel Tillis (1967) C&W#11 US#129/Ricky Van Shelton (1988) C&W#1; *Look into My Teardrops* Conway Twitty (1966) C&W#36, *Lovable Fool* Goldie Hill Smith (1968) C&W#73, *Lying Again* Freddie Hart (1961) C&W#27, *Mary Ann Regrets* Burl Ives (1963) C&W#12 US#39, *Meanwhile, Down at Joe's* Kitty Wells (1965) C&W#9, *Minute Men (Are Turning in Their Graves), The* Stonewall Jackson (1966) C&W#24, *Mommie for a Day* Kitty Wells (1959) C&W#5, *My Lips Are Sealed* Jim Reeves (1956) C&W#8, *Nashville Women* Hank Locklin (1967) C&W#73, *Never Mind* Nanci Griffith (1987) C&W#58, *No Charge* Melba Montgomery (1974) C&W#1 US#39/Shirley Caesar (1975) US#91/J.J. Barrie (1976) UK#1/Billy Connolly as *No Chance (No Charge)* (1976) UK#24; *Nothing Behind You, Nothing in Sight* John Conlee (1982) C&W#26, *Now Everybody Knows* Charlie Rich (1976) C&W#56, *Odds and Ends (Bits and Pieces)* Warren Smith (1961) C&W#7/Charlie Walker (1974) C&W#66; *One You Slip Around With, The* Jan Howard (1960) C&W#13, *Only the Names Have Been Changed* Penny DeHaven (1983) C&W#74, *Pick Me Up on Your Way Down* Charlie Walker (1958) C&W#2/Hank Thompson (1966) US#134/Carl Smith (1970) C&W#46/Bobby G. Rice (1976) C&W#35; *Pretty Girl, Pretty Clothes, Pretty Sad* Kenny Price (1967) C&W#26, *Pursuing Happiness* Norma Jean (1966) C&W#28, *Second Hand Rose* Roy Drusky (1963) C&W#3/Barbra Streisand (1966) UK#14; *She's a Little Bit Country* George Hamilton, IV (1970) C&W#3, *She's Gone, Gone, Gone* Lefty Frizzell (1965) C&W#12/Carl Jackson (1984) C&W#44; *Somebody Should Leave* Reba McEntire (1985) C&W#1, *Someone's Gotta Cry* Jean Shepard (1965) C&W#30, *Streets of Baltimore* [i] Bobby Bare (1966) C&W#5 US#124, *Three Steps to the Phone (Millions of Miles)* George Hamilton, IV (1961) C&W#9, *Time Out* Bill Anderson & Jan Howard (1966) C&W#44, *Time to Bum Again* Waylon Jennings (1966) C&W#17, *Time to Love Again* Liz Anderson (1973) C&W#72, *Tonight We're Calling It a Day* Hugh X. Lewis (1969) C&W#69, *Too Many*

Rivers Brenda Lee (1965) US#13 UK#22/Forester Sisters (1987) C&W#5; *Wall, The* Freddie Hart (1959) C&W#24, *Watermelon Time in Georgia* Lefty Frizzell (1970) C&W#49, *What Do Lonely People Do* Burch Sisters (1988) C&W#61, *When I Get Thru with You (You'll Love Me Too)* Patsy Cline (1962) C&W#10 US#53, *Why Not Me* Fred Knoblock (1980) C&W#30 US#18/Judds (1984) C&W#1; *You Took Her/Him Off My Hands (Now Please Take Her/Him Off My Mind)* Ray Price (1963) C&W#11/Marion Worth (1964) C&W#33; *You're a Hard Dog (To Keep Under the Porch)* Gail Davies (1983) C&W#18, *You're So Cold (I'm Turning Blue)* Hugh X. Lewis (1967) C&W#38, *Your Heart Turned Left (And I Was on the Right)* George Jones (1964) C&W#5, *Yours Love* Waylon Jennings (1969) C&W#5/Porter Wagoner & Dolly Parton (1969) C&W#9/Jerry Wallace (1979) C&W#67. Co-writer: [i] Tompall Glaser, [ii] Kostas, [iii] Buck Owens. (*See also under* Bill ANDERSON, Bobby BRADDOCK, Hank COCHRAN, Rodney CROWELL, Willie NELSON, Buck OWENS.)

473. HOWARD, Joe (b. Joseph E. Howard, February 12, 1867, New York, NY; d. 1961, Chicago, IL) Vaudeville performer. A pre–Tin Pan Alley songwriter, who ran away from home at the age of eight and survived by selling newspapers and singing for spare change. As a teenager Howard joined a traveling vaudeville act, and developed a song-and-dance routine with Ida Emerson, the duo achieving notoriety in Tony Pastor's Music Hall. Howard subsequently wrote for, and starred in, several Chicago productions between 1905–1915. His most famous song remains *I Wonder Who's Kissing Her Now* [i], from "The Prince of Tonight" (1909), although Harold Orlob later successfully sued that he was sole composer of the song. Howard's life was the subject matter of the film "I Wonder Who's Kissing Her Now" (1947), and he continued to perform well into the radio and television era. He died in 1961, after a performance at the Opera House in Chicago. HIT VERSIONS: *Hello, Ma Baby* [ii] Arthur Collins (1899) US#1/Len Spencer (899) US#1; *Goodbye, My Lady Love* Henry Burr (1904) US#3/Harry MacDonough (1904) US#5; *I Wonder Who's Kissing Her Now* [i] Henry Burr (1909) US#1/Billy Murray (1910) US#4/Manuel Romain (1910) US#6/Perry Como & Ted Weems (1947) US#2/Ray Noble (1947) US#11/ Dinning Sisters (1947) US#12. Co-writers: [i] Frank R. Adams/Will M. Hough, [ii] Ida Emerson.

474. Howlin' Wolf (b. Chester Arthur Burnett, June 10, 1910, West Point, MS; d. January 10, 1976, Hines, IL) Blues harmonica player, guitarist, and vocalist. One of the most influential Chicago bluesmen, who recorded many of Willie Dixon's finest compositions, plus a handful of his own. During the 1940s, Howlin' Wolf performed on Arkansas radio, and during the 1950s he recorded his seminal sides for Chess Records. In the 1970s he experimented with psychedelic influenced material, and lived long enough to perform with many of the artists that his music had influenced, including Eric Clapton and the Rolling Stones. Howlin' Wolf died of complications from kidney disease in 1976. CHART COMPOSITIONS: *Moanin' at Midnight* (1951) R&B#10, *How Many More Years* (1951) R&B#4, *Who Will Be Next* (1955) R&B#14, *Smoke Stack Lightnin'* (1956) R&B#8, re-issued (1964) UK#42, *I Asked for Water* (1956) R&B#8, *Evil* (1969) R&B#43. ALBUMS: **Howlin' Wolf** (1962), **Folk Festival of the Blues** (1963), **Moanin' in the Moonlight** (1964), **Poor Boy** (1965, all Chess); **Big City Blues** (1966, Ember); **Real Folk Blues** (1965, Chess); **The Super Super Blues Band** (1968, Checker); **The Howlin' Wolf Album** (1969, Cadet); **Message to the Young** (1971), **The London Howlin' Wolf Sessions** (1971, both Chess) US#79; **Going Back Home** (1971, Syndicate Chapter); **Howlin' Wolf** (1971, Python); **Live and Cookin' at Alice's Restaurant** (1972), **The Back Door Wolf** (1973), **Chess Masters** (1991, all Chess); **Memphis Days, Volume 1** (1991), **Memphis Days, Volume 2** (1991, both Bear Family); **Ain't Gonna Be Your Dog-Chess Collectibles, Volume 2** (1996), **The Genuine Article** (1997, both Chess).

475. HUCKNALL, Mick (b. June 8, 1960, Manchester, England) Pop vocalist. The distinctive singer and front man of the group Simply Red, who was a former art student and member of the punk group Frantic Elevators. Hucknall specializes in carefully chosen cover versions to supplement his original compositions. Simply Red's album **Stars** (1991), has sold over nine million copies worldwide. CHART COMPOSITIONS: *Come to My Aid* (1985) UK#66, *Holding Back the Years* [iii] (1985) UK#51, re-issued (1986) R&B#29 US#1 UK#2; *Jericho* (1986) UK#53, *Open Up the Red Box* (1986) UK#61, *The Right Thing* (1987) US#27 UK#11, *Infidelity* [i] (1987) UK#31, *I Won't Feel Bad* (1988) UK#68, *A New Flame* (1989) UK#17, *You've Got It* (1989) UK#46, *Something Got Me Started* [ii] (1991) US#23 UK#11, *Stars* (1991) US#44 UK#8, *For Your Babies* (1992) UK#9, *Thrill Me* [i] (1992) UK#33, *Your Mirror* (1992) UK#17, *Montreux EP* (1992) UK#11, *Fairground* (1995) UK#1, *Remembering the First Time* (1995) UK#22, *Never, Never Love* (1996) UK#18, *We're in This Together* (1996) UK#11. ALBUMS: **Picture Book** (1985, Elektra) p US#16 UK#2; **Men and Women** (1987, WEA) US#31 UK#2; **A New Flame** (1989, Elektra) g US#22 UK#1; **Stars** (1991) g US#79

UK#1, **Life** (1995) US#75 UK#1; **Blue** (1998, all East West) UK#1. COMPILATION: **Greatest Hits** (1996, East West) UK#1. Co-writers: [i] Lamont Dozier, [ii] McIntyre, [iii] Neil Moss.

476. HULL, Alan (b. February 20, 1945; d. November 17, 1995, both Newcastle-upon-Tyne, England) Pop guitarist and vocalist. A founder member of the British folk-rock group Lindisfarne. CHART COMPOSITIONS: *Lady Eleanor* (1972) US#82 UK#3, *All Fall Down* (1972) UK#34, *Run for Home* (1978) US#33 UK#10, *Fog on the Tyne* with Gazza (1990) UK#2. ALBUMS: **Nicely Out of Tune** (1970) UK#8, **Fog on the Tyne** (1971) UK#1, **Dingly Dell** (1972) UK#5, **Live** (1973) UK#25, **Roll on Ruby** (1973, all Charisma); **Happy Daze** (1974, Warner Brothers); **Back and Fourth** (1978) UK#22, **The News** (1979), **Magic in the Air** (1978, all Mercury) UK#71; **Sleepless Nights** (1982), **Lindisfarntastic Live** (1984), **Lindisfarntastic, Volume 2** (1984, all LMP); **Dance Your Life Away** (1986, River City); **Amigos** (1989, Black Crow). COMPILATIONS: **Finest Hour** (1975, Charisma) UK#55; **Best of Lindisfarne** (1989, Virgin). Hull also recorded as a solo artist, before dying of heart failure in 1995. ALBUMS: **Pipedream** (1973, Charisma) UK#29; **Squire** (1975, Warner Brothers); **Raditor** (1977), **Phantoms** (1979, both Rocket); **On the Other Side** (1983), **Another Little Adventure** (1988, both Black Crow); **Back to Basics** (1994, Mooncrest); **Statues and Liberties** (1996, Transatlantic).

477. HUNTER, Ian (b. June 3, 1946, Shrewsbury, England) Rock pianist, guitarist and vocalist. The lead vocalist and principal songwriter in the 1970s rock group Mott the Hoople, whose songwriting style displayed an acute but romanticized eye for Americana. Hunter's period with the band was later detailed in his book "The Diary of a Rock and Roll Star" (1974). CHART COMPOSITIONS: *Honaloochie Boogie* (1973) UK#12, *All the Way from Memphis* (1973) UK#10, *Roll Away the Stone* (1973) UK#8, *The Golden Age of Rock 'n' Roll* (1974) US#96 UK#16, *Foxy Foxy* (1974) UK#33, *Saturday Gigs* (1974) UK#41. ALBUMS: **Mott the Hoople** (1969) US#185 UK#66, **Mad Shadows** (1970) UK#48, **Wildlife** (1971) US#44, **Brain Capers** (1971, all Island); **All the Young Dudes** (1972) US#89 UK#21, **Mott** (1973) US#35 UK#7, **The Hoople** (1973) US#28 UK#11, **Live** (1974) US#23 UK#32. COMPILATIONS: **Rock 'n' Roll Queen** (1972, Island) US#112; **The Ballad of Mott: A Retrospective** (1994, Columbia); **Live at the BBC** (1996, Windsong). Hunter left the group in 1974 to record as a solo artist. CHART COMPOSITIONS: *Once Bitten, Twice Shy* (1975) UK#14, *Just Another Night* [i]

(1979) US#68, *When the Daylight Comes* (1979) US#108, *We Gotta Get Out of Here* (1980) US#108. ALBUMS: **Ian Hunter** (1975) US#50 UK#21, **All American Alien Boy** (1976) US#177 UK#29, **Overnight Angels** (1977, all CBS); **You're Never Alone with a Schizophrenic** (1979) US#35 UK#49, **Welcome to the Club** (1980) US#69 UK#61, **Short Back and Sides** (1981, all Chrysalis) US#62 UK#79; **All of the Good Ones Are Taken** (1983, CBS) US#125; **Y U I ORTA*** (1989, Mercury) US#157; **BBC Live in Concert*** (1995, Windsong); **The Artful Dodger** (1997, Citadel). HIT VERSION: *All the Way from Memphis* Contraband (1991) UK#65, *Once Bitten, Twice Shy* Great White (1989) g US#5, *Ships* Barry Manilow (1979) US#9. With: * Mick Ronson. Co-writer: [i] Mick Ronson.

478. HUNTER, Ivory Joe (b. October 10, 1914, Kirbyville, TX; d. November 8, 1974, Memphis, TN) R&B pianist and vocalist. A blues artist who transcended genres, blending soul ballads with country on nearly one thousand compositions. During the 1930s, Hunter performed gospel throughout Texas, and recorded on cylinders for the Library of Congress. During the 1940s he ran his own Ivory label, and achieved twelve R&B hits between 1945–1958. Hunter's material was recorded by Elvis Presley, and he later became a regular Grand Ole Opry star in Nashville. Hunter died of lung cancer in 1974. CHART COMPOSITIONS: *Blues at Sunrise* (1945) R&B#3, *Pretty Mama Blues* (1948) R&B#1, *Don't Fall in Love with Me* (1948) R&B#8, *What You Do to Me* (1948) R&B#9, *I Like It* (1948) R&B#14, *Waiting in Vain* (1949) R&B#5, *Blues at Midnight* (1949) R&B#10, *Guess Who* (1949) R&B#2, *Landlord Blues* (1949) R&B#6, *Jealous Heart* (1949) R&B#2, *I Almost Lost My Mind* (1950) R&B#1, *I Quit My Pretty Mama* (1950) R&B#4, *S.P. Blues* (1950) R&B#9, *I Need You So* (1950) R&B#1, *It's a Sin* (1950) R&B#10, *It May Sound Silly* (1955) R&B#14, *A Tear Fell* (1956) R&B#15, *Since I Met You Baby* [i] (1956) R&B#1 US#12, *Empty Arms* (1957) R&B#2 US#43, *Love's a Hurting Game* (1957) R&B#7, *Yes I Want You* (1958) R&B#13. ALBUMS: **I've Always Been Country** (1974, Paramount); **The Artistry of Ivory Joe Hunter** (1977, Bulldog); **77th Street Boogie** (1980, Route 66); **This Is Ivory Joe Hunter** (1984, Ace); **The Hits** (1988, Official); **Sixteen All-Time Hits** (1989, King). HIT VERSIONS: *Ain't That Loving You Baby* Elvis Presley (1964) US#16 UK#15, re-issued (1987) UK#47; *Empty Arms* Teresa Brewer (1957) US#13/Ace Cannon (1965) US#135/Sonny James (1971) C&W#1 US#93; *I Almost Lost My Mind* Nat "King" Cole (1950) US#26/ Pat Boone (1956) US#1; *It May Sound Silly* McGuire Sisters (1955) US#11, *My Wish Came True* Elvis Pres-

ley (1959) R&B#15 US#12, *Out of Sight, Out of Mind* Five Keys (1956) US#23, *Since I Met You Baby* [i] Mindy Carson (1957) US#34/Bobby Vee (1960) US#81/Ace Cannon (1963) US#130/Sonny James (1969) C&W#1 US#65/Freddy Fender (1975) C&W#10 US#45; *Without You* Aretha Franklin (1974) R&B#6 US#45. Co-writer: [i] Clyde Otis.

479. HUPFELD, Herman, Jr. (b. February 1, 1894; d. June 8, 1951, both Montclair, NJ) Film and stage composer, pianist. The composer of one of the most famous songs in the world, *As Time Goes By*, which was introduced in the show "Everybody's Welcome" (1932), but did not become widely known until it was featured in the film "Casablanca" (1942). HIT VERSIONS: *As Time Goes By* Jacques Renard (1931) US#13, re-issued (1943) US#3/Rudy Vallee (1931) US#15, re-issued (1943) US#1/Ray Anthony (1952) US#10/Richard Allan (1960) UK#44/Mel Carter (1967) US#111/Dooley Wilson (1977) UK#15/ Jason Donovan (1992) UK#26; *Let's Put Out the Lights (And Go to Sleep)* Ben Bernie (1932) US#11/ Rudy Vallee (1932) US#2/Paul Whiteman (1932) US#2; *Sing Something Simple* Jacques Renard (1930) US#6.

480. HUTCHENCE, Michael (b. January 22, 1962; d. November 22, 1997, both Sydney, Australia) Rock vocalist and actor. The lead singer in the Australian rock group INXS, who commited suicide at the age of 35. CHART COMPOSITIONS: *The One Thing* [i] (1983) US#30, *Don't Change* [iii] (1983) US#80, *Original Sin* [i] (1984) US#58, *I Send a Message* [i] (1984) US#77, *What You Need* [i] (1986) US#5 UK#51, *Listen Like Thieves* [iii] (1986) US#54 UK#46, *Kiss the Dirt (Falling Down the Mountain)* [iii] (1986) UK#54, *Need You Tonight* [i] (1987) R&B#73 US#1 UK#58, re-issued (1988) UK#2; *New Sensation* [i] (1988) US#3 UK#25, *Devil Inside* [i] (1988) US#2 UK#47, *Never Tear Us Apart* [i] (1988) US#7 UK#24, *Mystify* [i] (1989) UK#14, *Suicide Blonde* [i] (1990) US#9 UK#11, *Disappear* [ii] (1990) US#8 UK#21, *By My Side* [i] (1991) UK#42, *Bitter Tears* [i] (1991) US#46 UK#30, *Shining Star EP* [iii] (1991) UK#27, *Not Enough Time* [i] (1992) US#28, *Taste It* [i] (1992) UK#21, *Beautiful Girl* [i] (1993) US#46 UK#23, *The Gift* [i] (1993) UK#11, *Please (You Got That...)* [i] (1993) UK#50, *The Strangest Party (These Are the Times)* [i] (1994) UK#15. ALBUMS: **INXS** (1980, Deluxe) US#164; **Underneath the Colors** (1981, RCA); **Shabooh Shoobah** (1982) g US#46, **The Swing** (1984, both Atco) g US#52; **Listen Like Thieves** (1986) p US#11 UK#48, **Kick** (1988) p US#3 UK#9, **X** (1990) p US#5 UK#2, **Live Baby Live** (1991) US#72 UK#8, **Welcome to Wherever You Are** (1992) g US#16

UK#1, **Full Moon, Dirty Hearts** (1993) US#53 UK#3; **Elegantly Wasted** (1997, all Atlantic) UK#16. COMPILATIONS: **Dekadance** (1983, Atco) US#148; **Greatest Hits** (1994, Atlantic) US#112 UK#3. Hutchence also performed in the group Max Q, recording the album **Max Q** (1989, Atlantic) US#182 UK#65. HIT VERSION: *Listen Like Thieves* [iii] Was (Not Was) (1992) UK#48. Co-writers: [i] Andrew Farriss (b. March 27, 1959, Perth, Australia), [ii] Jon Farriss (b. August 10, 1961, Perth, Australia), [iii] Garry Beers (b. June 22, 1957, Sydney, Australia)/Andrew Farriss/Jon Farriss/Tim Farriss (b. August 16, 1957, Perth, Australia)/Kirk Pengilly (b. July 4, 1958, Sydney, Australia).

481. HYNDE, Chrissie (b. September 7, 1951, Akron, OH) Pop guitarist and vocalist. A former New Musical Express journalist who formed the punk influenced quartet the Pretenders in 1978. CHART COMPOSITIONS: *Kid* (1979) UK#33, re-issued (1995) UK#73; *Brass in Pocket* [ii] (1979) US#14 UK#1, *Talk of the Town* (1980) UK#8, *Message of Love* (1981) UK#11, *Day After Day* (1981) UK#45, *Back on the Chain Gang* (1983) US#5 UK#17, *2,000 Miles* (1983) UK#15, *Learning to Crawl* (1984) US#5 UK#11, *Middle of the Road* (1984) US#19, *Show Me* (1984) US#28, *Don't Get Me Wrong* (1986) US#10 UK#10, *My Baby* (1987) US#64, *If There Was a Man* [i] (1987) UK#49, *I'll Stand By You* (1994) US#16 UK#10, *Night in My Veins* [iii] (1994) US#71 UK#25, *977* (1994) UK#66. ALBUMS: **The Pretenders** (1980) p US#9 UK#1, **The Pretenders II** (1981) US#10 UK#7, **Learning to Crawl** (1984, all Real) p US#5 UK#11; **Get Close** (1986) g US#25 UK#6, **Packed** (1990) US#48 UK#19, **Last of the Independents** (1994) g US#41 UK#8, **Live** (1995), **The Isle of View** (1995, all WEA) US#100 UK#23. COMPILATIONS: **Extended Play** (1981, Sire) US#27; **The Singles** (1987, WEA) g US#69 UK#6. HIT VERSIONS: *Private Life* Grace Jones (1980) UK#17. Co-writers: [i] John Barry, [ii] James Honeyman-Scott (b. November 4, 1956, Hereford, England), [iii] Tom Kelly/Billy Steinberg.

482. IAN, Janis (b. Janis Eddy Fink, May 7, 1951, New Jersey, NY). Pop guitarist, pianist and vocalist. A folk influenced singer-songwriter whose compositions have examined, from a female perspective, such themes as self-doubt, success, failure, and peer pressure. Ian's father was a music teacher, and she grew up listening to classical music, Billie Holiday and Edith Piaf. She started writing songs at the age of twelve, and attended New York's High School of Music and Performing Arts, after which she appeared on the New York folk circuit. Ian's first published song was *Hair of Spun Gold* (1963), which fea-

tured in the folk magazine Broadside. In 1967, at the age of sixteen, she charted with her tale of a doomed interracial love affair, *Society's Child*, a song that had been rejected by over twenty record companies due to its controversial lyric. The sudden pressure of stardom had a negative effect on Ian, and after the album **Present Company** (1971), she married and withdrew from music making altogether, only to return in 1974 with a more sophisticated and mature style. Her album **Between the Lines** (1975), topped the American chart after an unprecedented six month climb, but by **Restless Eyes** (1981), her career had once again turned full circle, and she headed back into semi-retirement, dabbling in acting and ballet, before moving to Nashville to write for such artists as Kenny Rogers, Alabama, Amy Grant, and John Mellencamp. In 1993, after a break of twelve years, Ian made her second comeback with the austere **Breaking Silence**, a set that focused on topics as varied as domestic violence and the holocaust. CHART COMPOSITIONS: *Society's Child* (1967) US#14, *Insanity Comes Quietly to the Structured Mind* (1967) US#109, *The Man You Are in Me* (1974) US#104, *At Seventeen* (1975) g US#3, *Fly Too High* [i] (1979) UK#44, *Under the Covers* (1981) US#71. ALBUMS: **Janis Ian** (1967) US#29, **For All the Seasons of the Mind** (1968) US#179, **The Secret Life of J. Eddy Fink** (1968), **Who Really Cares** (1969, all Verve Forecast); **Present Company** (1971, Capitol); **Stars** (1974) US#83, **Between the Lines** (1975) p US#1, **Aftertones** (1975) US#12, **Miracle Row** (1977) US#45, **Janis Ian** (1978) US#120, **Night Rains** (1979), **Restless Eyes** (1981, all Columbia) US#156; **Breaking Silence** (1993, Morgan Creek); **Revenge** (1995, Beacon). COMPILATIONS: **Janis Ian** (1978, Columbia); **Best of Janis Ian** (1980, CBS); **My Favorites** (1980), **At Seventeen** (1990, both Columbia); **Up 'Til Now** (1992, Sony); **Live on the Test, 1976** (1995, Strange Fruit); **Society's Child: The Anthology** (1995, PolyGram). HIT VERSION: *Jesse* Roberta Flack (1973) R&B#19 US#30. Co-writer: [i] Giorgio Moroder.

483. IDOL, Billy (b. William Michael Albert Broad, November 30, 1955, Stanmore, England) Rock vocalist. A successful punk singer turned American stadium rocker, who in 1976, formed and fronted the punk group Generation X. CHART COMPOSITIONS: *Your Generation* (1977) UK#36, *Ready Steady Go* [ii] (1978) UK#47, *King Rocker* [i] (1979) UK#11, *Valley of the Dolls* (1979) UK#23, *Friday's Angels* (1977) UK#62, *Dancing with Myself* (1980) UK#62, re-issued (1981) UK#60, re-issued (1983) US#102. ALBUMS: **Generation X** (1978) UK#29, **Valley of the Dolls** (1979) UK#51, **Kiss Me Deadly** (1981, all Chrysalis). Since re-locating to Los Angeles in the early 1980s, Idol has recorded as a solo artist. CHART COMPOSITIONS: *Hot in the City* (1982) US#23 UK#58, re-mixed (1988) US#48 UK#13; *White Wedding* (1982) US#108, re-issued (1983) US#36, re-issued (1985) UK#6; *Rebel Yell* [ii] (1984) US#46 UK#62, re-issued (1985) UK#6; *Eyes Without a Face* [i] (1984) US#4 UK#18, *Flesh for Fantasy* [i] (1984) US#54 UK#29, *Catch My Fall* (1984) US#50, re-issued (1988) UK#63; *I Don't Need a Gun* (1987) US#37 UK#26, *Sweet Sixteen* (1987) US#20, *Cradle of Love* [iii] (1990) US#2 UK#34, *Prodigle Blue* (1990) UK#47, *Shock to the System* (1993) UK#30, *Speed* (1994) UK#47. ALBUMS: **Don't Stop** (1981) US#71, **Billy Idol** (1982) g US#45, **Rebel Yell** (1983) p US#6 UK#36, **Whiplash Smile** (1986) p US#6 UK#8, **Charmed Life** (1990) p US#11 UK#15, **Cyberpunk** (1993) US#48 UK#20, **Shock to the System** (1993, all Chrysalis) US#105. COMPILATIONS: **Vital Idol** (1985) p US#10 UK#7, **Idol Songs — 11 of the Best** (1988, both Chrysalis) UK#2. Co-writers: [i] Tony James, [ii] Steve Stevens, [iii] D. Werner.

484. INNES, Neil (b. December 9, 1944, Essex, England) Pop pianist, guitarist and vocalist. A musical satirist who first came to prominence in the 1960s group the Bonzo Dog Doo-Dah Band, which charted with his composition *I'm the Urban Spaceman* (1968) UK#5. ALBUMS: **Gorilla** (1966), **The Doughnut in Granny's Greenhouse** (1968) UK#40, **Tadpoles** (1969) UK#36, **Keynsham** (1969), **Let's Make Up and Be Friendly** (1972, all Liberty) US#199. COMPILATIONS: **Best of the Bonzo Dog Doo-Dah Band** (1970, Liberty); **History of the Bonzo Dog Doo-Dah Band** (1974, United Artists) UK#41. The English equivilant of Tom Lehrer and Randy Newman, Innes' art is his ability to write witty, melodic pastiches of any musical genre. He became the resident musician with the British comedy team Monty Python, and, with the former Python, Eric Idle, mocked the Beatles in the spoof group the Rutles, creating an accurate and affectionate parody of John Lennon and Paul McCartney's songwriting on the hits *I Must Be in Love* (1978) UK#39 and *Shangri-La* (1996) UK#68. ALBUMS: **The Rutles** (1978, Warner Brothers) US#63 UK#12; **Archaeology** (1996, Virgin). Innes has also recorded as a solo artist, and contributed to over two hundred children's television shows. ALBUMS: **Lucky Planet***** (1970, Liberty); **Funny Game Football**** (1972, Charisma); **Grimms*** (1973), **Rockin' Duck*** (1973, both Island); **How Sweet to Be an Idiot** (1973, United Artists); **The Rutland Weekend Television Songbook** (1976, BBC); **Sleepers*** (1976, DJM); **Taking Off** (1977, Arista); **The Innes Book of Records** (1979, Polydor); **Off the Record** (1982, MMC); **Eric the Viking** ost

(1989, Sonet); **Re-cycled Vinyl Blues** (1994, EMI). As: * Grimms, ** The Group, *** The World.

485. ISAACS, Gregory (b. June 16, 1950, Kingston, Jamaica) Reggae vocalist. A highly successful lovers-rock and reggae singer, known affectionately as the Cool Ruler, who writes melodic, medium paced material about love and social inequity. Isaacs' first record was for the Success label, *Don't Let Me Suffer* (1970), since which, he has issued over one thousand singles. His hundreds of Jamaican hits include, *My Only Lover, Lonely Soldier, Extra Classic,* and *Mr. Know It All.* ALBUMS: **In Person** (1975, African Musuem); **Best of Gregory Isaacs** (1979, Channel 1); **Cool Ruler** (1979), **Soon Forward** (1979, both Virgin); **For Everyone** (1980, Success); **Lonely Lover** (1980), **More Gregory** (1981) UK#93, **Lovers Rock** (1982, all Pre); **Night Nurse** (1982) UK#32, **Out Deh** (1983, both Island); **Crucial Cuts** (1983, Virgin); **Extra Classic** (1983, Vista Sounds); **In Person** (1983), **The Early Years** (1983), **All I Have Is Love** (1984, all Trojan); **Two Bad Superstars*** (1984, Burning Sounds); **Reggae Greats** (1985, Island); **Judge Not*** (1984), **Private Beach Party** (1985, both Greensleeves); **Live '84** (1984, Rough Trade); **Easy** (1985, Tads); **Double Dose** with Sugar Minot (1987, Blue Trac); **Live at the Academy** (1987), **Encore** (1987, both Kingdom); **Talk Don't Bother Me** (1987, Skengdon); **Mr. Isaacs** (1987, Shanachie); **Reggae, It's Fresh** (1988, Tads); **Best of Gregory Isaacs, Volume 2** (1988, GG's); **Slum Dub** (1988, Burning Sounds); **Sly and Robbie Present Gregory Isaacs** (1988, RAS); **Watchman of the City** (1988, Rohit); **Live** (1988, Mango); **Come Along** (1988, Live and Love); **Experience Vs. Common Sense** (1989, Exodus); **New Dance** (1989, Bun); **Victim** (1989, VP); **Gregory in Red** (1989, Tappa Zukie); **Reserved for Gregory** (1989, EX); **Rock On** (1989, OBS); **The Sensational Gregory Isaacs** (1989), **Live at Reggae Sunsplash** (1989, both Vista Sounds); **I.O.U.** (1989), **Midnight Confidential** (1994, both Greensleeves); **State of Shock** (1995, RAS); **Boom Shot** (1995, Shanachie); **Memories** (1995, Musicdisc); **Work Up a Sweat** (1995, African Musuem); **Set Me Free** (1995, Grapevine); **Private Lesson** (1995, Acid Jazz); **Mr. Love** (1995, Virgin). With: * Dennis Brown.

486. ISAAK, Chris (b. June 26, 1956, Stockton, CA) Pop guitarist and vocalist. A singer-songwriter who first recorded as a member of the rockabilly group Silvertone, releasing the album **Silvertone** (1985, Warner Brothers). Since the late 1980s, Isaak has pursued a solo recording and acting career. CHART COMPOSITIONS: *Wicked Game* (1990) US#6 UK#10, *Blue Hotel* (1991) UK#17, *Can't*

Do a Thing (To Stop Me) (1993) US#105 UK#36, *San Francisco Days* (1993) UK#62, *Somebody's Crying* (1994) US#45. ALBUMS: **Chris Isaak** (1987, Warner Brothers) US#194; **Heart Shaped World/ Wicked Game** (1989) p US#7 UK#3, **San Francisco Days** (1993) US#35 UK#12, **Forever Blue** (1995) US#31 UK#27, **The Baja Sessions** (1996, all Reprise).

487. JACKSON, Alan (b. 1960, Newnan, GA) C&W guitarist and vocalist. A contemporary country artist with a rocky, mainstream sound, who charted twelve consecutive country number ones. CHART COMPOSITIONS: *Here in the Real World* (1990) C&W#3, *Wanted* (1990) C&W#3, *Chasin' That Neon Rainbow* (1990) C&W#2, *I'd Love You All Over Again* (1990) C&W#1, *Don't Rock the Jukebox* [iii] (1991) C&W#2, *Someday* [ii] (1991) C&W#1, *Dallas* [v] (1992) C&W#1, *Midnight in Montgomery* [iv] (1992) C&W#3, *Love's Got a Hold on You* (1992) C&W#1, *She's Got the Rhythm (And I Got the Blues)* [vi] (1992) C&W#1, *Tonight I Climbed the Wall* (1993) C&W#4, *Chattahoochee* [ii] (1993) C&W#1 US#46, *Tropical Depression* [i] (1993) C&W#75, *(Who Says) You Can't Have It All* [iii] (1994) C&W#5, *I'll Try* (1996) C&W#1, *Home* (1996) C&W#67+. ALBUMS: **Here in the Real World** (1990) p US#57, **Don't Rock the Jukebox** (1991) p US#17, **A Lot About Livin' (And a Little 'Bout Love)** (1992) p US#20, **Honky Tonk Christmas** (1993), **Who I Am** (1994) p US#7, **Everything I Love** (1996, all Arista). COMPILATION: **Greatest Hits Collection** (1995, Arista) p US#5. Co-writers: [i] C. Craig/J. McBride, [ii] J. McBride, [iii] Roger Murrah/Keith Stegall, [iv] Don Sampson, [v] Keith Stegall, [vi] Randy Travis. (*See also under* Randy TRAVIS.)

488. JACKSON, Chuck (b. Charles Jackson, Jr., 1945, Greenville, SC), and **YANCY, Marvin, Rev.** (b. 1950, Chicago, IL; d. 1985) Both R&B producers. A songwriting and production duo that first worked together at Jerry Butler's Writer's Workshop in Chicago, and performed as members of the R&B vocal group the Independents. CHART COMPOSITIONS: *Just as Long as You Need Me* (1972) R&B#8 US#84, *I Just Want to Be There* (1972) R&B#38 US#113, *Leaving Me* (1973) g R&B#1 US#21, *Baby I've Been Missing You* (1973) R&B#4 US#41, *It's All Over* (1973) R&B#12 US#65, *The First Time We Meet* (1974) R&B#20 US#103, *Arise and Shine (Let's Get It On)* (1974) R&B#19, *Let This Be a Lesson to You* (1974) R&B#7 US#88. ALBUM: **The First Time We Meet** (1973, Wand) US#127. Jackson and Yancy left the Independents in the mid–1970s, in order to write and produce for

Yancy's wife, the singer Natalie Cole. HIT VERSIONS: *I've Got Love on My Mind* Natalie Cole (1977) g R&B#1 US#5, *Inseparable* Natalie Cole (1975) R&B#1 US#32, *It's Cool* Tymes (1976) R&B#3 US#68, *Mr. Melody* Natalie Cole (1976) R&B#10 US#49, *More You Do It (The More I Like It Done to Me), The* Ronnie Dyson (1976) R&B#6 US#62, *Our Love* Natalie Cole (1978) g R&B#1 US#10, *Same Thing It Took* [ii] Impressions (1975) R&B#3 US#75, *Sophisticated Lady (She's a Different Lady)* Natalie Cole (1976) R&B#1 US#25, *This Will Be* Natalie Cole (1975) R&B#1 US#6 UK#32, *United Together* [i] Aretha Franklin (1980) R&B#3 US#56, *You* Aretha Franklin (1976) R&B#15. Co-writers: [i] Chuck Jackson/P. Perry only, [ii] Ed Townsend.

489. JACKSON, George (b. 1936, Greenville, MS) R&B vocalist. A country influenced R&B songwriter and performer, whose greatest success has been with versions of his compositions by other artists. Jackson first recorded for Prann Records in 1963, before singing with the group the Ovations and charting with *It's Wonderful to Be in Love* (1965) R&B#22 US#61. Jackson wrote many of Candi Staton's highly regarded Fame label recordings during the 1970s, and later worked at Malaco Records, where he produced Z.Z. Hill. Jackson's songs were also featured in the film "Risky Business" (1983). CHART COMPOSITIONS: *That's How Much You Mean to Me* (1970) R&B#48, *Aretha, Sing One for Me* (1972) R&B#38. ALBUM: **Heart to Heart Collect** (1991, Hep' Me). HIT VERSIONS: *Double Lovin'* [i] Spencer Wiggins (1970) R&B#44/Osmonds (1971) US#14; *Find 'Em, Fool 'Em and Forget 'Em* [iv] Dobie Gray (1976) R&B#71 US#94, *I'd Rather Be an Old Man's Sweetheart (Than a Young Man's Fool)* Candi Staton (1969) R&B#9 US#46, *I'm Just a Prisoner (Of Your Good Lovin')* Candi Staton (1970) R&B#13 US#56, *If There Were No Music* Rufus Thomas (1976) R&B#92, *Man and a Half, A* [ii] Wilson Pickett (1968) R&B#20 US#42, *Old Time Rock and Roll* [vi] Bob Seger (1979) US#28, *One Bad Apple* Osmonds (1971) g R&B#6 US#1/ Nolan Thomas (1985) R&B#48 US#105; *Only Way Is Up, The* [v] Yazz & the Plastic Population (1988) US#96 UK#1, *This Is the Way That I Feel* Marie Osmond (1977) US#39, *Too Hurt to Cry* Candi Staton (1971) R&B#20 US#109, *Too Weak to Fight* [iv] Clarence Carter (168) g R&B#3 US#13, *Trying to Live My Life Without You* Otis Clay (1972) R&B#24 US#102/Bob Seger (1981) US#5; *Turn That Beat Around* [v] Vicki Sue Robinson (1976) R&B#73 US#10. Co-writers: [i] Mickey Buckins, [iii] Larry Chambers/Melvin Leakes/Raymond Moore, [iii] Rick Hall, [iv] Clarence Carter (b. 1936, Montgomery, AL)/Rick Hall/John M. Keyes, [v] John Henderson, [vi] P. Jackson, [vii] Thomas Jones, III.

490. JACKSON, Joe (b. August 11, 1955, Burton-on-Trent, England) Pop multi-instrumentalist, vocalist and producer. An idiosyncratic singer-songwriter who has recorded in many different musical styles. Jackson learned music at an early age, studying at the Royal College of Music, and playing saxophone in the National Youth Jazz Orchestra. He directed a musical theatre in Portsmouth, before releasing a series of unsuccessful singles as the group Arms and Legs. Since the late 1970s, Jackson has recorded as a solo artist, ranging in styles from British new wave to jazz and semi-classical. CHART COMPOSITIONS: *Is She Really Going Out with Him?* (1979) US#21 UK#13, *It's Different for Girls* (1980) US#101 UK#5, *Jumpin' Jive* (1981) UK#43, *Steppin' Out* (1983) US#6 UK#6, *Breaking Us in Two* (1983) US#18 UK#59, *Memphis* (1983) US#85, *Happy Ending* (1984) US#57 UK#58, *Be My Number Two* (1984) UK#70, *You Can't Get What You Want* (1984) US#15. ALBUMS: **Look Sharp!** (1978) g US#20 UK#40, **I'm the Man** (1979) US#22 UK#12, **Beat Crazy** (1980) US#41 UK#42, **Jumpin' Jive** (1981) US#42 UK#14, **Night and Day** (1982) g US#4 UK#3, **Mike's Murder** ost (1983) US#64, **Body and Soul** (1984) US#20 UK#14, **Big World** (1986) US#34 UK#41, **Will Power** (1987) US#131, **Live, 1980–1986** (1988) US#91 UK#66, **Blaze of Glory** (1989, all A&M) US#61 UK#36; **Laughter and Lust** (1990) US#116 UK#41, **Tucker-The Man and his Dream** ost (1994), **Night Music** (1994, all Virgin). COMPILATIONS: **Steppin' Out: The Very Best of Joe Jackson** (1991, A&M) UK#7; **This Is It! The A&M Years** (1997, A&M).

491. JACKSON, Michael (b. Michael Joseph Jackson, August 29, 1958, Gary, IN) R&B-pop producer and vocalist. One of the best known and biggest selling entertainers in the world, who revolutionized pop music video when he introduced lengthy dance and dialogue scenes. Jackson's albums **Off the Wall** (1979), **Thriller** (1982) and **Bad** (1987), have, in America, sold over twelve, fifty and twenty-five million copies respectively. Almost as famous for the minutiae of his personal life, Jackson has been a pop star since the age of six, when he and his brothers first performed in the vocal group the Jackson Five. As the more adult oriented disco act the Jacksons, Jackson began co-writing his own material. CHART COMPOSITIONS: *Shake Your Body (Down to the Ground)* [vi] (1979) p R&B#3 US#7 UK#4, *Lovely One* [vi] (1980) R&B#2 US#12 UK#29, *Heartbreak Hotel* (1980) R&B#2 US#22 UK#44, *Walk Right Now* [v] (1981) R&B#50 US#73

UK#7, *Can You Feel It* [iv] (1981) R&B#30 US#77 UK#6, *State of Shock* [iii] with Mick Jagger (1984) g R&B#4 US#3 UK#14. ALBUMS: **Diana Ross Presents the Jackson Five** (1970) US#5 UK#16, **ABC** (1970) US#4 UK#22, **Third Album** (1970) US#4, **Christmas Album** (1970), **Maybe Tomorrow** (1971) US#11, **Goin' Back to Indiana** (1971) US#16, **Lookin' Through the Windows** (1972) US#7 UK#16, **Skywriter** (1973) US#44, **Get It Together** (1973) US#100, **Dancing Machine** (1974) US#16, **Moving Violation** (1975, all Motown) US#36; **The Jacksons** (1977) g US#36 UK#54, **Goin' Places** (1977) US#63 UK#45, **Destiny** (1979) p US#11 UK#33, **Triumph** (1980) p US#10 UK#13, **Jacksons Live** (1981) US#30, **Victory** (1984, all Epic) p US#4 UK#3. COMPILATIONS: **Greatest Hits** (1972) US#12 UK#26, **Anthology** (1976, both Motown) US#84; **18 Greatest Hits** (1983, Telstar) UK#1; **14 Greatest Hits** (1984, Motown) US#168; **Soulsation!** (1995, Motown); **Best of Michael Jackson and the Jackson Five** (1997, PolyGram) UK#7. Since 1971, Jackson has concentrated on his solo career, the peak of which was the album **Thriller** (1982), the biggest selling album in recorded music history. CHART COMPOSITIONS: *Don't Stop 'Til You Get Enough* [ix] (1979) R&B#1 US#1 UK#3, *The Girl Is Mine** (1982) g R&B#1 US#2 UK#8, re-entry (1983) UK#75; *Billie Jean* (1983) g R&B#1 US#1 UK#1, *Beat It* (1983) g R&B#1 US#1 UK#3, *Wanna Be Startin' Somethin'* (1983) R&B#5 US#5 UK#8, *Say, Say, Say* [vii]* (1983) p R&B#2 US#1 UK#2, *I Just Can't Stop Loving You* with Siedah Garrett (1987) g R&B#1 US#1 UK#1, *Bad* (1987) R&B#1 US#1 UK#3, *The Way You Make Me Feel* (1987) R&B#1 US#1 UK#3, *Dirty Diana* (1988) R&B#5 US#1 UK#4, *Another Part of Me* (1988) R&B#1 US#11 UK#15, *Smooth Criminal* (1988) US#7 UK#8, *Leave Me Alone* (1989) UK#2, *Liberian Girl* (1989) UK#13, *Black or White* [ii] (1991) R&B#3 US#1 UK#1, re-mixed (1992) UK#14; *Remember the Time* [i] (1992) R&B#1 US#3 UK#3, *In the Closet* [xi] (1992) R&B#1 US#6 UK#8, *Who Is It* (1992) R&B#6 US#14 UK#10, *Jam* [viii] (1992) R&B#3 US#26 UK#13, *Heal the World* (1992) R&B#62 US#27 UK#2, *Give in to Me* (1993) UK#2, *Will You Be There* (1993) R&B#53 US#7 UK#9, *Gone Too Soon* (1993) R&B#104 UK#23, *Scream* with Janet Jackson (1995) US#5 UK#3, re-mixed (1995) UK#43; *They Don't Care About Us* (1996) UK#4, *Stranger in Moscow* (1996) UK#4. ALBUMS: **Got to Be There** (1972) US#14 UK#37, **Ben** (1972) US#5 UK#17, **Music and Me** (1973) US#92, **Forever, Michael** (1975, all Motown) US#101; **Off the Wall** (1979) p US#3 UK#5, **Thriller** (1982) p US#1 UK#1, **Bad** (1987) p US#1 UK#1, **Dangerous** (1991) p US#1 UK#1, **HIStory-Past, Present and Future, Book 1** (1995, all Epic) p US#1 UK#1. COMPILATIONS: **Best of Michael Jackson** (1975) US#156, **One Day in Your Life** (1981) US#144 UK#29, **Best of Michael Jackson** (1981, all Motown) UK#11; **9 Single Pack** (1983, Epic) UK#66; **Farewell, My Summer Love** (1984, Motown) US#46 UK#9; **Love Songs** (1987, Telstar) UK#15; **The Michael Jackson Mix** (1987, Stylus) UK#27; **Souvenir Singles Pack** (1988, Epic) UK#91; **Motown's Greatest Hits** (1992, Motown) UK#53; **Tour Souvenir Pack** (1992, Epic) UK#32; **Blood on the Dancefloor-HIStory in the Making** (1997, Epic) UK#1. HIT VERSIONS: *Bad* "Weird" Al Yankovic as *Fat* (1988) US#99, *Beat It* "Weird" Al Yankovic as *Eat It* (1984) R&B#84 US#12 UK#36, *Behind the Mask* [ix] Eric Clapton (1987) UK#15, *Billie Jean* Clubhouse (1983) UK#11/Slingshot (1983) R&B#25; *Centipede* Rebbie Jackson (1984) R&B#4 US#24, *Don't Stop 'Til You Get Enough* Ashaye in *Michael Jackson Medley* (1983) UK#45, *Eaten Alive* Diana Ross (1985) US#77 UK#71, *Muscles* Diana Ross (1982) R&B#4 US#10 UK#15, *Shake Your Body (Down to the Ground)* [vi] Ashaye in *Michael Jackson Medley* (1983) UK#45, *Wanna Be Startin' Somethin'* Ashaye in *Michael Jackson Medley* (1983) UK#45, *We Are the World* [x] USA for Africa (1985) p C&W#76 R&B#1 US#1 UK#1. With: * Paul McCartney. Co-writers: [i] B. Belle/Teddy Riley, [ii] B. Bottrell, [iii] Randy Hansen/Mick Jagger, [iv] Jackie Jackson (b. Sigmund Esco Jackson, May 4, 1951, Gary, IN), [v] Jackie Jackson/Randy Jackson (b. Stephen Randall Jackson, October 29, 1962, Gary, IN), [vi] Randy Jackson, [vii] Paul McCartney, [viii] R. Moore/Teddy Riley/Bruce Swedien, [ix] Greg Phillinganes, [x] Lionel Richie, [xi] Teddy Riley.

492. JAFFE, Moe Pop lyricist. A Tin Pan Alley songwriter who worked with the composer Lew Brown. HIT VERSIONS: *Bell-Bottom Trousers* Jerry Colonna (1945) US#9/Jesters (1945) US#11/Kay Kyser (1945) US#3/Guy Lombardo (1945) US#2/Tony Pastor (1945) US#2/Louis Prima (1945) US#6; *Collegiate* [i] Carl Fenton (1925) US#15/Fred Waring's Pennsylvanians (1925) US#3; *I'm My Own Grandpa* [iii] Guy Lombardo (1948) US#10/Jo Stafford (1948) US#21; *If I Had My Life to Live Over* [iv] Larry Vincent & the Fielden Foursome (1947) US#20/Lloyd Price (1965) US#107; *If You Are But a Dream* [ii] Jimmy Dorsey (1942) US#20/Frank Sinatra (1945) US#19. Co-writers: [i] Nat Bonx, [ii] Nat Bonx/Jack Fulton, [iii] Dwight Latam, [iv] Henry Tobias/Larry Vincent. (*See also under* Lew BROWN.)

493. JAGGER, Mick The lead vocalist in the British rock group the Rolling Stones, who has also recorded as a solo artist and acted in films, the best of which remains "Performance" (1969), a vio-

lent juxtaposition of the life of an East End gangster on the run, with that of an ambiguous, reclusive pop star. Jagger also featured on the instrumental album **Jamming with Edward** (1972, Rolling Stones) US#33. CHART COMPOSITIONS: *Memo from Turner* [iv] (1970) UK#32, *State of Shock* [iii] with the Jacksons (1984) g R&B#4 US#3 UK#14, *Just Another Night* (1985) R&B#23 US#12 UK#32, *Lucky in Love* [i] (1985) UK#38, *Ruthless People* [ii] (1986) US#51, *Let's Work* [v] (1987) US#39 UK#31, *Throwaway* (1987) US#67, *Sweet Thing* (1993) US#84 UK#24. ALBUMS: **She's the Boss** (1985) p US#13 UK#6, **Primitive Cool** (1987, both CBS) US#41 UK#26; **Wandering Spirit** (1993, Atlantic) g US#11 UK#12. Co-writers: [i] Carlos Alomar, [ii] Daryl Hall/Dave A. Stewart, [iii] Randy Hansen/Michael Jackson, [iv] Keith Richards, [v] Dave A. Stewart. (*See also under* Mick JAGGER and Keith RICHARDS.)

494. JAGGER, Mick (b. Michael Phillip Jagger, July 26, 1943, Dartford, England) Rock guitarist, harmonica player, producer and vocalist, and **RICHARDS, Keith** (b. December 18, 1943, Dartford, England) Rock guitarist, producer and vocalist. Two primary school friends who formed one of the most successful rock bands of all time, the Rolling Stones. As songwriters, Jagger and Richards developed a unique and authentic hybrid of blues, rock, country and R&B. Their initial songs were generally crafted from Jagger's lyrics and Richards' tunes, but by the 1970s, they often wrote separately and credited songs jointly. Jagger attended the London School of Economics, and Richards the Sidcup Art School. Having lost contact with one another as teenagers, they met again by chance at Dartford train station, where they discovered a mutual love of American blues and R&B. Jagger subsequently invited Richards to join his group Little Boy Blue and the Blue Boys, which played a mixture of skiffle and R&B. Jagger also sang for a while with Alexis Korner's Blues Incorporated. In 1962, Jagger and Richards formed a band with Brian Jones, Ian Stewart, Bill Wyman and Charlie Watts, naming themselves the Rolling Stones, after a Muddy Waters song. They performed their first gig at the Marquee in Wardour Street, London, and by 1963, they held a residency at the Crawdaddy Club in the Station Hotel, Richmond, Surrey. After signing to Decca Records, the group began charting with cover versions of Chuck Berry, Buddy Holly and Bobby Womack material, their B-sides being credited to Jagger and Richards under the pseudonyms Nanker and Phelge. Their first hit composition was Gene Pitney's *That Girl Belongs to Yesterday* (1964), and their first self-composed Rolling Stones' tune to chart was *Tell Me (You're Coming Back)* (1964). By *The Last Time* (1965), Richards was creating unforgettable guitar riffs, over which Jagger would not so much sing as taunt and provoke, with an arrogant and insolent posturing that would become standard fare for many future rock singers. The group's albums **Beggar's Banquet** (1968) through **Exile on Main Street** (1972) remain some of the finest rock music ever recorded. Their subsequent albums have all had highlights, such as the songs *Fingerprint File* and *Time Waits for No One* from **It's Only Rock 'N Roll** (1974). Since the 1980s, the Rolling Stones have tended to coast on their reputation rather than break new ground. In 1988, Richards stated, "After food, air, water and warmth, music is the next necessity of life." Their songs were also recorded by the London Symphony Orchestra as **The Symphonic Music of the Rolling Stones** (1994, RCA) US#196. CHART COMPOSITIONS: *Tell Me (You're Coming Back)* (1964) US#24, *Heart of Stone* (1965) US#19, *The Last Time* (1965) UK#1, *Play with Fire* (1965) US#96, *(I Can't Get No) Satisfaction* (1965) g R&B#19 US#1 UK#1, *Get Off My Cloud* (1965) US#1 UK#1, *As Tears Go By* [i] (1965) US#6, *19th Nervous Breakdown* (1965) R&B#32 US#2 UK#2, *Paint It Black* (1965) US#1 UK#1, re-issued (1990) UK#61; *Mother's Little Helper* (1965) US#8, *Lady Jane* (1965) US#24, *Have You Seen Your Mother, Baby, Standing in the Shadows?* (1965) US#9 UK#5, *What a Shame* (1965) US#125, *Let's Spend the Night Together* (1966) US#55 UK#3, *Ruby Tuesday* (1967) g US#1, live version (1990) UK#59; *We Love You* (1967) US#50 UK#8, *Dandelion* (1967) US#14, *She's a Rainbow* (1967) US#25, *Jumping Jack Flash* (1968) g US#3 UK#1, *Street Fighting Man* (1968) US#48, re-issued (1971) UK#21; *Honky Tonk Women* (1969) g US#1 UK#1, *Brown Sugar* (1971) US#1 UK#2, *Wild Horses* (1971) US#28, *Tumblin' Dice* (1972) US#7 UK#5, *Happy* (1972) US#22, *Angie* (1973) g US#1 UK#5, *You Can't Always Get What You Want* (1973) US#42, *Doo Doo Doo Doo Doo (Heartbreaker)* (1973) US#15, *It's Only Rock and Roll* (1974) US#16 UK#10, *Out of Time* (1975) UK#45, *Fool to Cry* (1976) US#10 UK#6, *Hot Stuff* (1976) R&B#84 US#49, *Miss You* (1978) g R&B#33 US#1 UK#3, *Respectable* (1978) UK#23, *Beast of Burden* (1978) US#8, *Shattered* (1978) US#31, *Emotional Rescue* (1980) US#9 UK#3, *She's So Cold* (1980) US#26 UK#33, *Start Me Up* (1981) US#2 UK#7, *Waiting on a Friend* (1981) US#13 UK#50, *Hang Fire* (1981) US#20, *Undercover of the Night* (1983) US#9 UK#11, *She Was Hot* (1983) US#44 UK#42, *One Hit (To the Body)* [ii] (1986) US#28, *Mixed Emotions* (1989) US#5 UK#36, *Rock and a Hard Place* (1989) US#23 UK#63, *Almost Hear You Sigh* (1989) US#50, *Highwire* (1990) US#57 UK#29, *Love Is Strong* (1994) US#91 UK#14, *You Got Me Rocking* (1994)

UK#23, *Out of Tears* (1994) US#60 UK#36, *I Go Wild* (1995) UK#29. ALBUMS: **The Rolling Stones** (1964) UK#1, **The Rolling Stones 2** (1965) UK#1, **Out of Our Heads** (1965) p US#1 UK#2, **Aftermath** (1966) p US#2 UK#1, **Between the Buttons** (1967) g US#2 UK#3, **Their Satanic Majesties Request** (1967) g US#2 UK#3, **Beggar's Banquet** (1968) p US#3 UK#3, **Let It Bleed** (1969) p US#3 UK#1, **Get Yer Ya Ya's Out** (1970, all Decca) p US#6 UK#1; **Sticky Fingers** (1971) g US#1 UK#1, **Exile on Main Street** (1972) g US#1 UK#1, **Goat's Head Soup** (1973) g US#1 UK#1, **It's Only Rock 'N Roll** (1974) g US#1 UK#2, **Black and Blue** (1976) p US#1 UK#2, **Love You Live** (1977) g US#5 UK#3, **Some Girls** (1978) p US#1 UK#2, **Emotional Rescue** (1980) p US#1 UK#1, **Tattoo You** (1981) p US#1 UK#2, **Still Life (American Concerts 1981)** (1982) g US#5 UK#4, **Undercover** (1983) p US#4 UK#3, **Dirty Work** (1986) p US#4 UK#4, **Steel Wheels** (1989) p US#3 UK#2, **Flashpoint** (1991, all Rolling Stones) g US#16 UK#6; **Voodoo Lounge** (1994) p US#2 UK#1, **Stripped** (1995) p US#9 UK#9, **Babylon Bridge** (1997, all Virgin). COMPILATIONS: **England's Newest Hitmakers-The Rolling Stones** (1964) g US#11, **12 x 5** (1964) g US#3, **The Rolling Stones Now** (1965) g US#5, **December's Children (And Everybody's)** (1965, all London) g US#4; **Big Hits (High Tide and Green Grass)** (1965, Decca) p US#3 UK#4; **Got Live If You Want It** (1966) g US#6, **Flowers** (1966, both London) g US#3; **Through the Past Darkly (Big Hits, Volume 2)** (1969) p US#2 UK#2, **Stone Age** (1971) UK#4, **Gimme Shelter** (1971) UK#19, **Milestones** (1972, all Decca) UK#14; **Hot Rocks, 1964–1971** (1972, London) p US#4 UK#3; **Rock 'n' Rolling Stones** (1972, Decca) UK#41; **More Hot Rocks (Big Hits and Fazed Cookies)** (1972, London) g US#9; **No Stone Unturned** (1973, Decca); **Made in the Shade** (1975, Rolling Stones) g US#6 UK#14; **Metamorphosis** (1975) US#8 UK#45, **Rolled Gold-The Very Best of the Rolling Stones** (1975, both Decca) UK#7; **Get Stoned** (1977, Arcade) UK#8; **Sucking in the Seventies** (1981, Rolling Stones) g US#15; **In Concert** (1982, Decca) UK#94; **The Story of the Stones** (1982, K-Tel) US#24; **Rewind, 1971–1984** (1983, Rolling Stones) US#86 UK#23; **The Singles Collection-The London Years** (1989, Abkco) p US#91; **Jump Back-Best of the Rolling Stones, 1971–1993** (1993, Virgin) UK#16; **Rock 'n' Roll Circus** (1996, Abkco). HIT VERSIONS: *Angie* Tori Amos on *Crucify EP* (1992) UK#15, *As Tears Go By* [i] Marianne Faithfull (1964) US#22 UK#9, *Beast of Burden* Bette Midler (1983) US#71, *Blue Turns to Grey* Cliff Richard (1966) UK#15, *Citadel* Damned on *Friday the 13th EP* (1981) UK#50, *Dead Flowers* New Riders of the Purple Sage (1976) US#105, *Gimme Shelter*

Merry Clayton (1970) US#73/Grand Funk Railroad (1971) US#61/Various Artists on *Gimme Shelter EP* (1993) UK#32; *Honky Tonk Women* Charlie Walker (1970) C&W#56/Big Country on B-side of *Hold the Heart* (1986) UK#55/Pogues (1992) UK#56; *(I Can't Get No) Satisfaction* Otis Redding (1966) R&B#4 US#75 UK#6/Aretha Franklin (1967) UK#37/ Jimmy McGriff (1967) US#130/Bubblerock (1974) UK#29/Eddie & the Hot Rods on *Live at the Marquee EP* (1976) UK#43/Devo (1978) UK#41/Andre Cymone (1986) R&B#75/Vanilla Ice (1991) UK#22; *I'm Free* Soup Dragons (1990) UK#5, *Jumping Jack Flash* Johnny Winter (1971) US#89/Aretha Franklin (1986) R&B#20 US#21 UK#51/Terence Trent D'Arby on B-side of *Sign Your Name* (1988) US#4 UK#2; *Lady Jane* David Garrick (1966) UK#28/ Tony Merrick (1966) UK#49/Plastic Cow (1969) US#113; *Last Time, The* Who (1967) UK#44/ Buchanan Brothers (1969) US#106; *Out of Time* Chris Farlowe (1966) US#122 UK#1, re-issued (1975) UK#44/Dan McCafferty (1975) UK#41; *Paint It Black* Modettes (1980) UK#42, *Ride on Baby* Chris Farlowe (1966) UK#31, *Ruby Tuesday* Melanie (1970) US#33 UK#9/Rod Stewart (1993) UK#11; *She's a Rainbow* World of Twist (1992) UK#62, *Sittin' on a Fence* Twice as Much (1966) US#122 UK#25, *Sympathy for the Devil* Guns n' Roses (1995) US#55 UK#9, *Take It or Leave It* Searchers (1965) UK#31, *That Girl Belongs to Yesterday* Gene Pitney (1964) US#49 UK#7, *Think* Chris Farlowe (1966) UK#37, *Tumblin' Dice* Linda Ronstadt (1977) US#32, *Under My Thumb* Del Shannon (1966) US#128/Who (1967) UK#44/Wayne Gibson (1974) UK#17/Hounds (1979) US#110. Co-writers: [i] Andrew Loog Oldham, [ii] Ron Wood (b. June 1, 1947, Hillingdon, England). (*See also under* Mick JAGGER, Keith RICHARDS.)

495. JAMES, Elmore (b. Elmore Brooks, January 27, 1918, Richland, MS; d. May 24, 1963). Blues guitarist and vocalist. A blues guitarist whose shuffle style was to influence the British group Fleetwood Mac. James died of a heart attack in 1963. CHART COMPOSITIONS: *I Believe* (1953) R&B#9, *The Sky Is Crying* (1960) R&B#15, *It Hurts Me Too* (1965) R&B#25 US#106. ALBUMS: **The Best of Elmore James** (1965), **The Elmore James Memorial Album** (1965, both Sue); **Something Inside of Me** (1968, Bell); **The Late, Fantastically Great Elmore James** (1969, Ember); **The Legend of Elmore James** (1970, United Artists); **To Know a Man** (1970), **Tough** (1970, both Blue Horizon); **Cotton Patch Hotfoots** (1973, Polydor); **All Them Blues** (1975, DJM); **King of the Slide Guitar** (1983, Ace); **The Elmore James Story** (1989, Deja Vu); **The Classic Early Recordings, 1951–1956** (1994, Ace).

496. JAMES, Mark (b. Houston, TX) C&W producer and arranger. A staff writer at Screen Gems-Columbia Music during the 1970s, who had studied the violin from the age of eight, but was drawn to country-blues during his teens. James' songs have been recorded by dozens of artists in a variety of musical genres. HIT VERSIONS: *Always on My Mind* [i] Elvis Presley (1973) UK#9, also on B-side of *Separate Ways* (1973) US#20, new version (1985) UK#59/Willie Nelson (1982) C&W#1 US#5 UK#49/Pet Shop Boys (1987) US#4 UK#1/Michael Ball on *If I Can Dream EP* (1992) UK#51/Stylistics featuring Russell Thompkins, Jr. (1992) R&B#89; *Everyone Loves a Rain Song* [ii] B.J. Thomas (1978) C&W#25 US#43, *Eyes of a New York Woman* B.J. Thomas (1968) US#28, *Hooked on a Feeling* B.J. Thomas (1968) g US#5/Jonathan King (1971) UK#23/Blue Swede (1974) g US#1; *It's Only Love* [iii] Elvis Presley (1971) US#51/B.J. Thomas (1969) US#54; *Moody Blue* Elvis Presley (1977) US#31 UK#6, *Raised on Rock* Elvis Presley (1973) US#41 UK#36, *Sunday Sunrise* Anne Murray (1975) C&W#49 US#98, *Suspicious Minds* Elvis Presley (1969) g US#1 UK#2, also in *The Elvis Medley* (1982) US#71 UK#51/Waylon Jennings & Jessi Colter (1970) C&W#25, re-issued (1976) C&W#2/Dee Dee Warwick (1971) R&B#24 US#80/Fine Young Cannibals (1986) UK#8/Dwight Yoakam (1992) C&W#35. Co-writers: [i] John Christopher/Wayne Thompson, [ii] Chips Moman, [iii] Steve Tyrell. (*See also under* Mac DAVIS.)

497. JAMES, Rick (b. James Johnson, February 1, 1952, Buffalo, NY) R&B guitarist, vocalist and producer. The creator of a brand of street funk that was influenced by James Brown, Sly Stone and George Clinton, who in turn, was to influence both Prince and M.C. Hammer. James first recorded an unreleased album as the group the Mynah Birds with his roommate Neil Young, and he later played in the blues group Main Line. In 1977 he formed the Stone City Band, with which he enjoyed twenty-five R&B hits between 1978–1988. In 1994, James was sentenced to five years in prison for drug and assault offences. CHART COMPOSITIONS: *You and I* (1978) g R&B#1 US#13 UK#46, *Mary Jane* (1978) R&B#3 US#41, *High on Your Love Suite* (1979) R&B#12 US#72, *Bustin' Out* (1979) R&B#8 US#71, *Fool on the Street* (1979) R&B#35, *Love Gun* (1979) R&B#13, *Come into My Life* (1980) R&B#26, *Big Time* (1980) R&B#17 UK#41, *Give It to Me Baby* (1981) R&B#1 US#40 UK#47, *Super Freak* [ii] (1981) R&B#3 US#16, *Ghetto Life* (1981) R&B#38 US#102, *Standing on the Top* with the Temptations (1982) R&B#6 US#66 UK#53, *Dance wit' Me* (1982) R&B#3 US#64 UK#53, *Hard to Get* (1982) R&B#15,

She Blew My Mind (69 Times) (1982) R&B#62, *Cold Blooded* (1983) R&B#1 US#40, *U Bring the Freak Out* (1983) R&B#16 US#101, *Ebony Eyes* with Smokey Robinson (1984) R&B#22 US#43, *17* (1984) R&B#6 US#36, *You Turn Me On* (1984) R&B#31, *Can't Stop* (1985) R&B#10 US#50, *Glow* (1985) R&B#5 US#106, *Spend the Night with Me* (1985) R&B#41, *Sweet and Sexy Thing* (1986) R&B#6, *Lossey's Rap* with Roxanne Shante (1988) R&B#1. ALBUMS: **Come Get It** (1978) g US#13, **Bustin' Out of L-Seven** (1978) US#16, **Fire It Up** (1979) US#34, **In 'n' Out** (1980) US#122, **Garden of Love** (1980) US#83, **Street Songs** (1981) p US#3, **Throwin' Down** (1982) g US#13 UK#93, **Cold Blooded** (1983) g US#16, **Glow** (1985) US#50, **The Flag** (1986) US#95, **Wonderful** (1988, all Gordy) US#148. COMPILATIONS: **Reflections** (1984, Gordy) US#41. HIT VERSIONS: *All Night Long* Mary Jane Girls (1983) R&B#11 US#101 UK#13, *Boys* Mary Jane Girls (1983) R&B#29 US#102, *Bustin' Out (On the Funk)* Doug E. Fresh & the New Get Fresh Crew (1992) R&B#28, *Candy Man* Mary Jane Girls (1983) R&B#23 US#101, *How Could It Be* Eddie Murphy (1986) US#26, *In My House* Mary Jane Girls (1985) R&B#3 US#7, *Jealousy* Mary Jane Girls (1984) R&B#84 US#106, *Party All the Time* Eddie Murphy (1985) g R&B#8 US#2, *Super Freak* [ii] M.C. Hammer sampled in *U Can't Touch This* (1990) R&B#1 US#8 UK#3, *Tonight's Da Night* [iii] Redman (1993) R&B#87, *Wild and Crazy Love* [i] Mary Jane Girls (1985) R&B#10 US#42. Co-writers: [i] K. Hawkins, [ii] A. Miller, [iii] R. Noble/J. Stone.

498. JAMES, Skip (b. Nehemiah James, June 9, 1902, Bentonia, MS; d. October 3, 1969, Philadelphia, PA) Blues guitarist, pianist and vocalist. A former church pianist and organist, who performed the blues throughout the Mississippi area during the 1920s. In 1931, James recorded twenty-six songs for the Paramount label, which, alongside the music of Robert Johnson, remain some of the most authentic blues music ever recorded. In the 1930s, James became a church minister, and after working for many years as a sharecropper, he was tracked down in 1964 and booked to perform at the Newport Folk Festival. His compositions *I'd Rather Be the Devil* and *I'm So Glad* were recorded by John Martyn and Cream respectively. ALBUMS: **Skip James: The Greatest of the Delta Blues Singers** 1964 (Melodeon); **Skip James Today** (1965), **Devil Got My Woman** (1968, both Vanguard); **A Tribute** (1970), **This Old World** (1974), **Early Recordings** (1975, all Biograph); **I'm So Glad** (1978, Vanguard); **1931** (1983, Matchbox); **Skip's Piano Blues** (1997, Edsel).

499. JAMES, Tommy (b. Thomas Gregory Jackson, April 29, 1947, Dayton, OH) Pop vocalist and producer. The lead singer of the 1960s group Tommy James and the Shondells. CHART COMPOSITIONS: *Mony Mony* [i] (1968) US#3 UK#1, *Crimson and Clover* [vi] (1969) g US#1, *Sweet Cherry Wine* [iii] (1969) US#7, *Crystal Blue Persuasion* [iv] (1969) US#2, *Ball of Fire* [vii] (1969) US#19, *She* [ii] (1970) US#23. ALBUMS: **Hanky Panky** (1966) US#46, **I Think We're Alone Now** (1967) US#74, **Mony Mony** (1968) US#193, **Crimson and Clover** (1969) US#8, **Cellophane Symphony** (1969, all Roulette) US#141. COMPILATIONS: **Something Special-The Best of Tommy James and the Shondells** (1968) US#174, **Best of Tommy James and the Shondells** (1970, both Roulette) US#21; **Anthology** (1991, Rhino). James quit the group in 1970 to pursue an intially successful solo career. CHART COMPOSITIONS: *Ball and Chain* (1970) US#57, *Church Street Soul Revival* (1971) US#62, *Adrienne* (1971) US#93, *Draggin' the Line* [v] (1971) g US#4, *I'm Comin' Home* (1971) US#40, *Nothing to Hide* (1971) US#41, *Cat's Eye in the Window* (1972) US#90, *Love Song* (1972) US#95, *Boo, Boo, Don't 'Cha Be Blue* (1973) US#70, *Three Times in Love* [ix] (1980) C&W#93 US#19, *You Got Me* (1980) US#101, *You're So Easy to Love* [viii] (1981) US#58. ALBUMS: **Christian of the World** (1971, Roulette) US#131; **Head, My Bed, My Red Guitar** (1972), **In Touch** (1976), **Midnight Rider** (1977, all Fantasy); **Three Times in Love** (1980, Millennium) US#134; **Hi-Fi** (1991, Aegis). HIT VERSIONS: *Church Street Soul Revival* Exiles (1970) US#104, *Crimson and Clover* [vi] Joan Jett (1982) US#7, *I'm Alive* Johnny Thunder (1969) US#122, *Mony Mony* [i] Billy Idol (1981) US#107, live version (1987) US#1 UK#7/Amazulu (1987) UK#38; *Tighter, Tighter* [v] Alive and Kicking (1970) US#7. Co-writers: [i] Bobby Bloom/Ritchie Cordell/Bo Gentry, [ii] Richie Cordell/Jerry Kasenetz/Jeff Katz/Mike Vale (b. Michael Vacush, July 17, 1949), [iii] Richie Grasso, [iv] Ed Gray (b. February 27, 1948)/Mike Vale, [v] Robert L. King, [vi] Peter Lucas, [vii] Paul Nauman/Bruce Sudano/Mike Vale/Woody Wilson, [viii] J. Roberge, [ix] Rick Serota.

500. JANS, Tom Rock guitarist and vocalist. A folk and country influenced singer-songwriter, whose best known song is the much recorded *Lovin' Arms*. ALBUMS: **Tom Jans and Mimi Farina** * (1971), **Take Heart** * (1972, both A&M); **Eyes of an Only Child** (1975), **Dark Blonde** (1977, both Columbia); **Tom Jans** (1978, A&M). HIT VERSIONS: *Lovin' Arms* Dobie Gray (1973) R&B#81 US#61/Kris Kristofferson & Rita Coolidge (1974) C&W#98 US#86/Sammi Smith (1977) C&W#19/Elvis Presley (1981) C&W#8 UK#47/Livingston Taylor & Leah

Kunkel (1988) C&W#94; *My Mother's Eyes* Bette Midler (1980) US#39, *Old Time Feeling* [i] Johnny Cash & June Carter (1976) C&W#26. With: * Mimi Farina. Co-writer: [i] Waylon Jennings.

501. JARREAU, Al (b. March 12, 1940, Milwaukee, WI) Jazz-R&B vocalist. A former psychologist who was a jazz nightclub performer for many years before he became a recording artist in his late thirties. CHART COMPOSITIONS: *Thinkin' About It Too* [ii] (1978) R&B#55, *Never Givin' Up* [ii] (1980) R&B#26 US#102, *Gimme What You Got* [ii] (1980) R&B#63, *Distracted* (1980) R&B#61, *Breakin' Away* [ii] (1982) R&B#25 US#43, *Mornin'* [iii] (1983) R&B#6 US#21 UK#28, *Boogie Down* [vi] (1983) R&B#9 US#77 UK#63, *After All* [iii] (1984) R&B#26 US#69, *Raging Waters* [i] (1985) R&B#42, *L Is for Lover* (1986) R&B#42, *Tell Me What I Gotta Do* (1986) R&B#37, *Moonlighting* [i] (1987) R&B#32 US#23. ALBUMS: **We Got By** (1975), **Glow** (1976, both Reprise) US#132; **Look to the Rainbow/Live in Europe** (1977) US#49, **All Fly Home** (1978) US#78, **This Time** (1980) g US#27, **Breakin' Away** (1981) p US#9 UK#60, **Jarreau** (1983) g US#13 UK#39, **High Crime** (1984) US#49 UK#81, **In London** (1985) US#125, **L Is for Lover** (1986, all Warner Brothers) US#81 UK#45; **Heart's Horizon** (1988) g US#75, **Heaven and Earth** (1992) US#105, **Tenderness** (1994, all Reprise). Co-writers: [i] Robbie Buchanan/Jay Graydon, [ii] Tom Canning, [iii] Tom Canning/Jay Graydon, [iv] David Foster/Jay Graydon, [v] Lee Holdridge, [vi] Michael Omartian.

502. Jazzie B. (b. Beresford Romeo, January 26, 1963, London, England) R&B-rap producer, arranger and vocalist. A radio disc jockey and clothes shop owner who popularized the swingbeat rhythm with his recording collective Soul II Soul, which blended reggae, hip-hop, rap, dance and pop. CHART COMPOSITIONS: *Fairplay* (1988) UK#63, *Feel Free* (1988) UK#64, *Keep on Movin'* (1989) g R&B#1 US#11 UK#5, re-mixed (1996) UK#31; *Back to Life (However Do You Want Me)* [ii] (1989) R&B# US#4 UK#1, *Get a Life* (1989) US#54 UK#3, *A Dream's a Dream* (1990) US#85 UK#6, *Missing You* (1990) UK#22, *Joy* [iii] (1992) R&B#14 UK#4, *Just Right* [i] (1992) UK#38, *Wish* (1993) UK#24, *Love Enuff* (1995) UK#12, *I Care* (1995) UK#17. ALBUMS: **Club Classics Volume One/Keep on Moving** (1989) p US#14 UK#1, **Volume II: A New Decade** (1990) g US#21 UK#1, **Volume III: Just Right** (1992, all Ten) US#88 UK#3; **Volume IV: The Classic Singles, 1988–1993** (1993) UK#10, **Volume V-Believe** (1995, both Virgin) UK#13. Co-writers: [i] Clarke/Mowatt, [ii] P. Hooper/S. Law/Caron Wheeler, [iii] Mowatt.

503. JEFFERSON, Blind Lemon (b. July, 1897, Couchman, TX; d. December, 1929, probably Chicago, IL) Blues guitarist and vocalist. A blind, singing beggar, who was one of the first to record the blues. Jefferson was a major record seller during his lifetime, recording nearly one hundred sides, including his own compositions *Black Snake Blues*, *Pneumonia Blues*, *See That My Grave Is Kept Clean* and *Mojo Woman Blues*. ALBUMS: **Black Snake Moan** (1981, Joker); **The Remaining Titles** (1984, Matchbox); **King of Country Blues** (1985, Yazoo); **Collection: Blind Lemon Jefferson** (1986, Deja Vu); **Blind Lemon Jefferson and Son House** (1987, Blue Moon); **Blind Lemon Jefferson, Volume 1** (1988), **Blind Lemon Jefferson, Volume 2** (1988), **Blind Lemon Jefferson, Volume 3** (1988, all Roots); **Master of the Blues** (1989, Blue Moon).

504. JEFFREYS, Garland (b. 1944, New York, NY) Pop vocalist. A reggae and pop influenced singer-songwriter who charted with the single *Reelin'* (1978) US#107. ALBUMS: **Grinder's Switch with Garland Jeffreys** (1969); **Garland Jeffreys** (1973, Atlantic); **Ghost Writer** (1977) US#140, **One-Eyed Jack** (1978) US#99, **American Boy and Girl** (1979, all A&M) US#151; **Escape Artist** (1981) US#59, **Rock and Roll Adult** (1982) US#163, **Guts for Love** (1983, Epic) US#176.

505. JENNINGS, Waylon (b. June 15, 1937, Littlefield, TX) C&W guitarist and vocalist. A country music pioneer, whose move away from traditional country values created what became known as the "outlaw movement," influencing such contemporary artists as Steve Earle, Lyle Lovett and Travis Tritt. Jennings' nonchalant, dry and underproduced studio sound, best evidenced on his classic album **Dreaming My Dreams** (1975), was the very antithesis of the Nashville sound, and was an influence on the genre for many years. He learned the guitar as a young boy, and began performing at the age of twelve. Jennings worked as a disc jockey before Buddy Holly produced his first single *Jole Blon* (1955), after which, he became Holly's bassist. It was Jennings who gave up his seat to the Big Bopper on the ill-fated plane flight that killed both Holly and the Big Bopper. He recorded for a variety of record labels before becoming a major star during the 1970s, later featuring alongside his then wife Jessi Colter, on **The Outlaws** (1976, RCA) p US#10, country music's first million selling album. Jennings has charted over ninety singles since 1965. CHART COMPOSITIONS: *You Asked Me Too* [vii] (1973) C&W#8, *Rainy Day Woman* (1975) C&W#2, *Waymore's Blues* [iii] (1975) US#110, *Are You Sure Hank Done It This Way?* (1975) C&W#1 US#60, *Good*

Hearted Woman [v]* (1975) C&W#1 US#25, *Don't You Think This Outlaw Bit's Done Got Out of Hand* (1978) C&W#5, *Theme from the Dukes of Hazzard (Good Ol' Boys)* (1980) g C&W#1 US#21, *Shine* (1981) C&W#5, *Women Do Know How to Carry On* [iv] (1982) C&W#4, *Just to Satisfy You* [ii]* (1982) C&W#1 US#52, *The Conversation* [i] with Hank Williams, Jr. (1983) C&W#15, *How Much Is It Worth to Live in L.A.* (1988) C&W#38. ALBUMS: **At JD's** (1964, Sound); **Folk-Country** (1966), **Leavin' Town** (1966), **Nashville Rebel** ost (1966), **Waylon Jennings Sings Ol' Harlan** (1966), **Love of the Common People** (1967), **Hangin' On** (1968), **Only the Greatest** (1968), **Jewels** (1968), **Just to Satisfy You** (1969, all RCA); **Waylon Jennings** (1969, Vocalion); **Country-Folk** (1969) US#169, **Waylon** (1970, both RCA) US#192; **Don't Think Twice** (1970, A&M); **Ned Kelly** ost (1970, United Artists); **Singer of Sad Songs** (1970), **The Taker/Tulsa** (1970), **Cedartown, Georgia** (1971), **Ladies Love Outlaws** (1971), **Good Hearted Woman** (1972), **Lonesome, On'ry and Mean** (1973), **Honky Tonk Heroes** (1973) US#185, **Only Daddy That'll Walk the Line** (1974), **This Time** (1974), **The Ramblin' Man** (1974) US#105, **Dreaming My Dreams** (1975) g US#49, **Mackintosh and T.J.** ost (1976) US#189, **Are You Ready for the Country** (1976) g US#34, **The Dark Side of Fame** (1976), **Waylon-Live** (1976) g US#46, **Ol' Waylon** (1977) p US#15, **Waylon and Willie*** (1978) p US#12, **I've Always Been Crazy** (1978) g US#48, **What Goes Around Comes Around** (1979) g US#49, **Music Man** (1980) g US#36, **Leather and Lace** with Jessi Colter (1982) g US#43, **The Pursuit of D.P. Cooper** ost (1982), **Black on Black** (1982) US#39, **WWII*** (1982) g US#57, **It's Only Rock and Roll** (1983, all RCA) US#109; **Take It to the Limit*** (1983, Columbia) US#60; **Waylon and Company** (1983), **Never Could Toe the Mark** (1984), **Turn the Page** (1985, all RCA); **Highwayman**** (1985, Columbia) US#92; **Sweet Mother Texas** (1986, RCA); **Heroes** with Johnny Cash (1986, Columbia); **Will the Wolf Survive** (1986), **Hangin' Tough** (1987), **A Man Called Hoss** (1987), **Full Circle** (1988), **New Classic Waylon** (1989, all MCA); **Highwayman 2**** (1990, Columbia); **The Eagle** (1990) US#172, **Clean Shirt*** (1991) US#193, **Too Dumb for New York City, Too Ugly for L.A.** (1992, all Epic); **Waymore's Blues, Part II** (1994, RCA); **The Road Goes on Forever**** (1995, Liberty); **Right for the Time** (1996, Transatlantic). COMPILATIONS: **Best of Waylon Jennings** (1973), **Greatest Hits** (1979) p US#28, **Greatest Hits, Volume 2** (1984, all RCA); **Files, Volumes 1–15** (1985, Bear Family). HIT VERSIONS: *Feelins'* [vi] Conway Twitty & Loretta Lynn (1975) C&W#1, *Julie* Porter Wagoner (1967) C&W#15, *Tryin' to Satisfy You*

Dottsy (1979) C&W#12. With: * Willie Nelson, ** Johnny Cash/Kris Kristofferson/Willie Nelson. Co-writers: [i] R. Albright/Hank Williams, Jr., [ii] Don Bowman, [iii] Curtis Buck, [iv] Bobby Emmons, [v] Willie Nelson, [vi] Troy Seals, [vii] Billy Joe Shaver. (*See also under* Buddy HOLLY, Tom JANS, Billy Joe SHAVER)

506. JENNINGS, Will Pop lyricist. A mainstream pop lyricist who has worked with a variety of composers, and has been particularly successful in collaboration with Steve Winwood. HIT VERSIONS: *Blues Come Over Me, The* [v] B.B. King (1992) R&B#63, *Boys Night Out* [ii] Timothy B. Schmit (1987) US#25, *I'll Never Love This Way Again* [iv] Dionne Warwick (1979) g R&B#1 US#5, *I'm So Glad I'm Standing Here Today* [v] Crusaders with Joe Cocker (1981) R&B#67 US#97 UK#61, *If Love Must Go* Dobie Gray (1976) US#78, *If We Hold on Together* [iii] Diana Ross (1992) UK#11, *Last Night in Danceland* [v] Randy Crawford (1980) R&B#68 UK#61, *Looks Like We Made It* [iv] Barry Manilow (1977) g US#1, *No Night So Long* [iv] Dionne Warwick (1980) R&B#19 US#23, *One Day I'll Fly Away* [v] Randy Crawford (1981) UK#2, *Papa'z Song* [i] 2 Pac with Mopreme (1994) R&B#82 US#87, *Somewhere in the Night* [iv] Batdorf & Rodney (1975) US#69/Barry Manilow (1979) US#9/Helen Reddy (1976) US#19; *Street Life* [v] Crusaders with Randy Crawford (1979) R&B#17 US#36 UK#5/Herb Alpert (1980) R&B#65 US#104; *You and Me, Me and You* [vi] Sharon Vaughn (1975) C&W#99. Co-writers: [i] D. Evans/Tupac Shakur, [ii] Bruce Gaitsch/Timothy B. Schmit, [iii] James Horner, [iv] Richard Kerr, [v] Joe Sample (b. Joseph Leslie Sample, February 1, 1939, Houston, TX), [vi] Troy Seals. (*See also under* Eric CLAPTON, Rodney CROWELL, Michael MASSER, Buffy SAINTE-MARIE, Troy SEALS, Steve WINWOOD.)

507. JOBIM, Antonio Carlos (b. Antonio Carlos Brasieriro de Almeida Jobim, January 25, 1927, Rio de Janeiro, Brazil; d. December 8, 1994, New York, NY) Jazz guitarist, pianist and vocalist. A Brazilian composer who introduced the samba to American audiences during the 1960s. Many of his compositions have since become jazz and supper club standards. His father was a diplomat and poet, who died when Jobim was eight years old. Before his teens, Jobim had learned the guitar, flute and piano, and after studying architecture he achieved his first Brazilian hits in the 1950s. Jobim became closely associated with the Bossa Nova sound that came from the cafes of Rio during the 1950s: Bossa meaning "the knack" and Nova meaning "new." He became the musical director for the Odeon record label in

Brazil, and in 1958, he co-composed the film sound-track "Black Orpheus" with Luiz Bonfa, from which came one of his most popular tunes, *A Felicidade*. After Jobim's music appeared in the jazz film "Co-pacabana Palace," and on the saxophonist Stan Getz's albums **Jazz Samba** (1962), **Big Band Bossa Nova** (1962) and **Jazz Samba Encore!** (1963), Jobim's com-positions attracted the attention of dozens of per-formers, many of which had English words added to them, including *Aqua De Beber (Drinking Water)*, *Aquas De Marco (Waters Of March)*, *Insensatez (How Insensitive)* [iii], *Samba De Uma Nota So (One Note Samba)* [iv], and *Samba Do Aviao (Song of the Jet)* [v]. Shortly before his death, Jobim performed at Verve Records' 50th Anniversary Concert at Carnegie Hall, New York. ALBUMS: **Black Orpheus** ost (1959, Epic); **The Composer of Desafinado, Plays** (1963, Verve); **The Wonderful World of Antonio Carlos Jobim** (1965, Warner Brothers) US#57; **Francis Al-bert Sinatra and Antonio Carlos Jobim** (1967, Reprise) US#19; **Wave** (1967) US#114, **Tide** (1967, both A&M); **Stone Flower** (1970, CTI) US#196; **Cronica Da Casa Assassinada** ost (1972, Brazil); **Elis and Tom** (1974, Philips); **Terra Brasilis** (1980, Warner Brothers); **Um Homem de Aquarious** (1980, Philips); **A Certain Mr. Jobim** (1980, Hallmark); **Antonio Carlos Jobim Plays Jobim** (1984, Verve); **O Tempo e O Vneto** ost (1985, Brazil); **Rio Revis-ited** (1988), **Passarim** (1989), **Compact Jazz** (1989), **Antonio Carlos Jobim and Guests** (1991), **The Art of Antonio Carlos Jobim** (1992, all Verve); **Anto-nio Brasileiro** (1995, Sony); **The Girl from Ipanema** (1996, A&M). HIT VERSIONS: *Corcov-ado (Quiet Nights of Quiet Stars)* [v] Andy Williams (1965) US#92, *Desafinado (Slightly Out of Tune)* [i] Ella Fitzgerald (1962) US#102 UK#38/Stan Getz & Charlie Byrd (1962) US#15 UK#11/Julie London (1962) US#110; *Felicidade, A (Happiness)* Sally Field (1967) US#94, *Garota De Ipanema (Girl/Boy from Ipanema, The)* [ii] Stan Getz, Joao Gilberto & As-trud Gilberto (1964) US#5 UK#29, re-issued (1984) UK#55/Ernie Heckscher & His Orchestra (1964) US#125; *Jazz Carnival* Azymuth (1980) UK#19, *Meditacao (Meditation)* [iii] Charlie Byrd (1963) US#66/Claudine Longet (1967) US#98. Co-writers: [i] Jessie Cavanaugh/Jon Hendricks, [ii] Vincent De Moraes/Norman Gimble, [iii] Norman Gimble, [iv] Jon Hendricks, [v] Gene Lees (b. February 8, 1928, Hamilton, Ontario, Canada).

508. JOEL, Billy (b. William Martin Joel, May 9, 1949, Hicksville, Long Island, NY). Rock pianist, producer and vocalist. One of America's most popular singer-songwriters, whose song *Just the Way You Are* has been recorded over two hundred times. Born to Italian immigrant parents, much of

Joel's early work would examine the lives and strug-gles of first generation Italians in New York during the 1950s. He was raised by his mother in Levittown, New York, and learned the piano at the age of four. After a failed boxing career, Joel worked as a local journalist and performed in his first band the Echoes, which became the Emerald Lords and ultimately the Lost Souls. During the 1960s, Joel recorded a pret-zel commercial with Chubby Checker, before join-ing the Hassles, which recorded the albums **The Hassles** (1967) and **Hour of the Wolf** (1969, both United Artists). After the group split up, Joel dredged oysters for a living and spent three weeks of obser-vation in Meadowbrook Hospital after a suicide at-tempt. In 1970, he formed the short-lived duo At-tila, which released an eponymous album on Epic Records, before he recorded his solo debut set **Cold Spring Harbor** (1971). As Bill Martin, Joel served an ultimately inspiring apprenticeship in Los Angeles piano lounges, an experience which he turned into his first hit song, *Piano Man* (1974). After signing long-term to Columbia Records, Joel became a multi-million selling artist, carving himself a niche somewhere between the melodic pop of Elton John and harder rock of Bruce Springsteen, selling seven million copies of **The Stranger** (1977), six million copies of **52nd Street** (1978), and charting six hit singles from **An Innocent Man** (1983), two of which sold a million each, *Tell Her About It* and *Uptown Girl*. After a lengthy break from recording, Joel re-turned in 1993 with the four million selling **River of Dreams**, about which he said, "I've reached a point in my life where I'm not going to write unless I have something to say." CHART COMPOSI-TIONS: *Piano Man* (1974) US#25, *Worse Comes to Worst* (1974) US#80, *Travelin' Prayer* (1974) US#77, *The Entertainer* (1974) US#34, *Just the Way You Are* (1977) g US#3 UK#19, *Movin' Out (Anthony's Song)* (1978) US#17 UK#35, *Only the Good Die Young* (1978) US#24, *She's Always a Woman* (1978) US#17, *My Life* (1978) g US#3 UK#12, *Big Shot* (1979) US#14, *Until the Night* (1979) UK#50, *Honesty* (1979) US#24, *You May Be Right* (1980) US#7, *All for Lenya* (1980) UK#40, *It's Still Rock and Roll to Me* (1980) g US#1 UK#14, *Don't Ask Me Why* (1980) US#19, *Sometimes a Fantasy* (1980) US#36, *Say Goodbye Hollywood* (1981) US#17, *She's Got Away* (1981) US#23, *Pressure* (1982) US#20, *Allentown* (1982) US#17, *Goodnight Saigon* (1983) US#56, *Tell Her About It* (1983) g US#1, *Uptown Girl* (1983) g US#3 UK#1, *An Innocent Man* (1984) US#10 UK#8, *The Longest Time* (1984) US#14 UK#25, *Leave a Ten-der Moment Alone* (1984) US#27 UK#29, *Keeping the Faith* (1985) US#18, *You're Only Human (Second Wind)* (1985) US#9, *The Night Is Still Young* (1985) US#34, *She's Always a Woman/Just the Way You Are*

(1986) UK#53, *Modern Woman* (1986) US#10, *A Matter of Trust* (1986) US#10 UK#52, *This Is the Time* (1986) US#18, *Baby Grand* with Ray Charles (1987) US#75, *We Didn't Start the Fire* (1989) g US#1 UK#7, *Leningrad* (1989) UK#53, *I Go to Extremes* (1990) US#6 UK#70, *The Downeaster Alexa* (1990) US#57, *That's Not Her Style* (1990) US#77, *And So It Goes* (1990) US#37, *River of Dreams* (1993) US#3 UK#4, *All About Soul* (1993) US#29 UK#32, *No Man's Land* (1994) UK#50, *Lullabye (Goodnight, My Angel)* (1994) US#77. ALBUMS: **Cold Spring Harbor** (1971, Family), re-mixed (1983, Columbia) US#158 UK#95; **Piano Man** (1974) p US#27, **Streetlife Serenade** (1974) g US#35, **Turnstiles** (1976) p US#122, **The Stranger** (1977) p US#2 UK#25, **52nd Street** (1978) p US#1 UK#10, **Glass Houses** (1980) p US#1 UK#9, **Songs in the Attic** (1981) p US#8 UK#57, **The Nylon Curtain** (1982) p US#7 UK#27, **An Innocent Man** (1983) p US#4 UK#2, **The Bridge** (1986) p US#7 UK#38, **Kohuept** (1987) g US#38 UK#92, **Storm Front** (1989) p US#1 UK#5, **River of Dreams** (1993, all Columbia) p US#1 UK#3. COMPILATION: **Greatest Hits, Volumes 1 & 2** (1985, Columbia) p US#6 UK#7. HIT VERSIONS: *Just the Way You Are* Barry White (1978) UK#12, *Shameless* Garth Brooks (1990) C&W#1 UK#71, *You May Be Right* Chipmunks (1980) US#101.

509. JOHN, Sir Elton (b. Reginald Kenneth Dwight, March 25, 1947, Pinner, England) Rock pianist, producer and vocalist. A consistently successful singer-songwriter since the early 1970s, whose songs *Candle in the Wind*, *Your Song* and *Daniel* have received two, four and five million BMI American Radio Broadcast awards respectively. Most of John's songs have been written in collaboration with the lyricist Bernie Taupin, and their compositions have sold over one hundred million records. John's father was a trumpeter, and he grew up listening to his parents' 78 records, taking piano lessons from the age of four. In 1958, he attended the Royal Academy of Music, and during the early 1960s he played in the R&B group Bluesology while working as a gofer for Mills Music publishers in London. His first recorded composition was Bluesology's *Come Back Baby* [i], after which, he hovered around the fringes of the British music business for many years. He linked up with Taupin via a music paper advertisement, and the duo wrote songs through the mail before they eventually met up. In 1968, they signed to Dick James Music as staff writers at a salary of ten pounds a week, but only a few of their songs were ever recorded. James was sufficiently confident in his proteges to set up his own DJM label in 1969, upon which began issuing Elton John discs. By the album

Elton John (1970), John and Taupin's material had begun attracting the attention of such artists as Three Dog Night and Aretha Franklin, the latter recording a superb gospel arrangement of *Border Song*. After his million selling ballad *Your Song*, John's career seldom faltered. **Honky Chateau** (1972) was the first of five consecutive American number one albums. The duo reached an artistic peak on the five million selling **Goodbye Yellow Brick Road** (1974), a double album that flirted with many different musical styles, and contained some of their most crafted material, including *I've Seen That Movie Too*, *Candle in the Wind* and *The Ballad of Danny Bailey, 1909–1934*. **Captain Fantastic and the Dirt Brown Cowboy** (1975), was an autobiographical song cycle written on-board a cruise liner. John later starred in the film "Tommy," and formed his own Rocket label, while his **Greatest Hits** (1977), sold a phenomenal ten million copies. They were also the subject of the tribute album **Two Rooms-The Songs of Elton John and Bernie Taupin** (1991, Mercury) p US#18 UK#1. CHART COMPOSITIONS: *Border Song* (1970) US#92, *Your Song* (1971) US#8 UK#7, *Friends* (1971) US#34, *Levon* (1972) US#24, *Tiny Dancer* (1972) US#41, *Rocket Man* (1972) US#6 UK#2, *Honky Cat* (1972) US#8 UK#31, *Crocodile Rock* (1973) g US#1 UK#5, *Daniel* (1973) g US#2 UK#4, *Saturday Night's Alright for Fighting* (1973) US#12 UK#7, *Goodbye Yellow Brick Road* (1973) g US#2 UK#6, *Step into Christmas* (1973) UK#24, *Candle in the Wind* (1974) UK#11, live version (1988) US#6 UK#5, new version (1997) p US#1 UK#1; *Bennie and the Jets* (1974) g R&B#15 US#1 UK#37, *Don't Let the Sun Go Down on Me* (1974) g US#2 UK#16, live version with George Michael (1991) US#1 UK#1; *The Bitch Is Back* (1974) US#4 UK#15, *Philadelphia Freedom* (1975) g R&B#32 US#1 UK#12, *Island Girl* (1975) g US#1 UK#14, *Grow Some Funk of Your Own* [ii]/*I Feel Like a Bullet (In the Gun of Robert Ford)* (1975) US#14, *Don't Go Breaking My Heart* with Kiki Dee (1975) g US#1 UK#1, new version with Rupaul (1994) US#92 UK#7; *Sorry Seems to Be the Hardest Word* (1976) g US#6 UK#11, *Crazy Water* (1977) UK#27, *Bite Your Lip (Get Up and Dance)* (1977) US#28 UK#28, *Ego* (1978) US#34 UK#34, *Part Time Love* [iv] (1978) US#22 UK#15, *Song for Guy* [iv] (1978) US#110 UK#4, *Little Jeannie* [iv] (1980) g US#3 UK#33, *(Sartorial Eloquence) Don't Ya Wanna Play This Game No More?* [vi] (1980) US#39 UK#44, *Chloe* [iv] (1981) US#34, *Blue Eyes* [iv] (1982) US#12 UK#8, *Empty Garden* (1982) US#13 UK#51, *I Guess That's Why They Call It the Blues* [ii] (1983) US#4 UK#5, *I'm Still Standing* (1983) US#12 UK#4, *Kiss the Bride* (1983) US#25 UK#20, *Cold as Christmas* (1983) UK#33, *Sad Songs (Say So Much)* (1984) US#5 UK#7, *Passengers* [iii] (1984) UK#5, *Who Wears These Shoes?*

(1984) US#16 UK#50, *In Neon* (1984) US#38, *Breaking Hearts (Ain't What It Used to Be)* (1985) UK#59, *Act of War* with Millie Jackson (1985) UK#32, *Nikita* (1985) US#7 UK#3, *Wrap Her Up* [ii] (1985) US#20 UK#12, *Cry to Heaven* (1985) UK#47, *Heartbreak All Over the World* (1986) US#55 UK#45, *Slow Rivers* with Cliff Richard (1986) UK#44, *I Don't Want to Go on with You Like That* (1988) US#2 UK#30, *Town of Plenty* (1988) UK#74, *A Word in Spanish* (1988) US#19, *Healing Hands* (1989) US#13 UK#45, *Sacrifice* (1989) US#18 UK#55, *Healing Hands/Sacrifice* (1990) UK#1, *Club at the End of the Street/Whispers* (1990) US#28 UK#47, *You Gotta Love Someone* (1990) US#43 UK#33, *Easier to Walk Away* (1990) UK#63, *The One* (1992) US#9 UK#10, *Runaway Train* with Eric Clapton (1992) UK#31, *Last Song* (1992) US#23 UK#21, *Simple Life* (1993) US#30 UK#44, *Can You Feel the Love Tonight* [v] (1994) US#4 UK#14, *Circle of Life* (1994) US#18 UK#11, *Believe* (1995) US#13 UK#15, *Made in England* (1995) US#52 UK#18, *Blessed* (1995) US#34, *Please* (1996) UK#33, *Live Like Horses* with Luciano Pavarotti (1996) UK#9. ALBUMS: **Empty Sky** (1969) US#6, **Elton John** (1970) g US#4 UK#11, **Tumbleweed Connection** (1971, all DJM) g US#5 UK#6; **Friends** ost (1971, Paramount) g US#36; **17–11–70** (1971) US#11 UK#20, **Madman Across the Water** (1972) p US#8 UK#41, **Honky Chateau** (1972) g US#1 UK#2, **Don't Shoot Me I'm Only the Piano Player** (1973) p US#1 UK#1, **Goodbye Yellow Brick Road** (1973) p US#1 UK#1, **Caribou** (1974) p US#1 UK#1, **Captain Fantastic and the Brown Dirt Cowboy** (1975) p US#1 UK#2, **Rock of the Westies** (1975) p US#1 UK#5, **Here and There** (1976, all DJM) g US#4 UK#6; **Blue Moves** (1976) p US#3 UK#3, **A Single Man** (1978) p US#15 UK#8, **Victim of Love** (1979) US#35 UK#41, **21 at 33** (1980) g US#13 UK#12, **The Fox** (1981) US#21 UK#12, **Jump Up!** (1982) g US#17 UK#13, **Too Low for Zero** (1983) g US#25 UK#7, **Breaking Hearts** (1984) g US#20 UK#2, **Ice on Fire** (1985) g US#48 UK#3, **Leather Jackets** (1986) US#91 UK#24, **Live in Australia** (1987) g US#24 UK#43, **Reg Strikes Back** (1988) g US#17 UK#18, **Sleeping with the Past** (1989) p US#23 UK#1, **The One** (1992) p US#8 UK#2, **Duets** (1992, all Rocket) p US#25 UK#5; **The Lion King** ost (1994, Mercury) g US#1 UK#4; **Made in England** (1995, Rocket) US#13 UK#3. COMPILATIONS: **Greatest Hits** (1974) p US#1 UK#1, **Greatest Hits, Volume 2** (1977, both DJM) p US#21 UK#6; **The Thom Bell Sessions** (1979, MCA) US#51; **Lady Samantha** (1980, DJM) UK#56; **Very Best of Elton John** (1980, K-Tel) UK#24; **Love Songs** (1982, TV Records) UK#39; **Decade-Greatest Hits, 1976–1986** (1986, MCA) g; **Greatest Hits, Volume 3** (1987, Geffen) p US#84;

Very Best of Elton John (1990) UK#1, **To Be Continued** (1990, both Rocket) g US#82; **Rare Masters** (1992, PolyGram); **Elton John Plays the Siran** (1992), **The Fishing Trip** (1993, both Happenstance); **Reg Dwight's Piano Plays Pop** (1995, RPM); **Love Songs** (1995, Rocket) UK#4. HIT VERSIONS: *Bad Side of the Moon* April Wine (1972) US#106, *Border Song* Aretha Franklin (1970) R&B#5 US#37/Dorothy Morrison (1970) R&B#43 US#114; *Dixie Lily* Roy Drusky (1974) C&W#45, *Don't Let the Sun Go Down on Me* Oleta Adams (1991) UK#33, *Jamaica Jerk-Off* Judge Dread on *5th Anniversary EP* (1977) UK#31, *Man Who Loved to Dance, The* Kiki Dee on B-side of *First Thing in the Morning* (1977) UK#32, *Rocket Man* Kate Bush (1991) UK#12, *Rumour, The* Olivia Newton-John (1988) US#62, *Snookeroo* Ringo Starr (1975) US#3, *Step into Christmas* Wedding Present on B-side of *No Christmas* (1992) UK#25, *Supercool* Kiki Dee (1974) US#108, *Your Song* Rod Stewart (1992) US#48 UK#41. All compositions John/Taupin, except: [i] Elton John only, [ii] Davey Johnstone (b. May 6, 1951, Edinburgh, Scotland)/Bernie Taupin, [iii] Davey Johnstone/Phineas McHize/Bernie Taupin, [iv] Gary Osbourne, [v] Tim Rice, [vi] Tom Robinson.

510. JOHNSON, Charles Leslie (b. December 3, 1876; d. December 28, 1950, both Kansas City, KS) Multi-instrumentalist and arranger. One of the most prolific and versatile composers of Tin Pan Alley, who often published his compositions under such pseudonyms as Raymond Birch. Johnson learned the piano at the age of six, and later studied musical theory and harmony, alongside such instruments as the violin and banjo. He led a variety of theatre and hotel orchestras, and also worked as a song and piano demonstrator before publishing his first rag, *Scandalous Thompson* (1899). After selling a million copies of *Dill Pickles Rag* (1910), he formed his first of many publishing companies, which were successful with the rags *Powder Rag* (1909), *Porcupine Rag* (1909) and *Crazy Bone Rag* (1913). HIT VERSIONS: *Dill Pickles Rag* Arthur Pryor's Band (1910) US#10, *Sweet and Low* Elsie Baker (1920) US#14/Art Hickman (1920) US#2.

511. JOHNSON, General (b. Norman Johnson, May 23, 1944, Norfolk, VA). R&B producer and vocalist. The lead singer of the 1970s soul group Chairman of the Board, which recorded in a gospel-R&B style. Johnson first performed as Boy Wonder at the age of six, and while still in high school he formed Norman Johnson and the Showmen, who, as the Showmen, charted with *It Will Stand* (1961), which was featured on the album **It**

Will Stand (1985, Collectibles). In 1968, Johnson formed the Gentlemen, which became the Chairman of the Board, and enjoyed twelve R&B hits during the 1970s. CHART COMPOSITIONS: *(You've Got Me) Dangling on a String* [viii] (1970) R&B#19 US#38 UK#5, *Pay to the Piper* [vii] (1970) R&B#4 US#13 UK#34, *Try on My Love for Size* (1971) R&B#48 US#103, *Men Are Getting Scarce* [vi] (1971) R&B#33 US#104, *Everybody's Got a Song to Sing* (1972) R&B#30, *Elmo James* [vi] (1972) UK#21, *I'm on My Way to a Better Place* [vi] (1972) UK#38, re-entry (1973) UK#30; *Finder's Keepers* [iii] (1973) R&B#7 US#59 UK#21, *Life and Death* (1974) R&B#52, *Everybody Party All Night* (1974) R&B#80, *Lover Boy* (1986) UK#56. ALBUMS: **Give Me Just a Little More Time** (1970) US#133, **In Session** (1970) US#117, **Bittersweet** (1972) US#178, **The Skin I'm In** (1974, all Invictus). COMPILATIONS: **Greatest Hits** (1973, Invictus); **Salute the General** (1984), **You've Got Me Danglin'** (1984), **AGM** (1985, all HDH); **Soul Agenda** (1992, Demon); **General Johnson's Chairman of the Board** (1997, Castle). Johnson was also a writer-producer at the Invictus and Hot Wax labels, before pursuing a briefly successful solo career. He has continued to perform as Chairman of the Board on the east coast beach music scene, releasing singles on the Surfside label. CHART COMPOSITIONS: *All in the Family* (1976) R&B#22, *We the People* (1976) R&B#36, *Don't Walk Away* (1976) R&B#42, *Let's Fool Around* (1977) R&B#78, *Can't Nobody Love Me Like You Do* (1978) R&B#79. ALBUMS: **Generally Speaking** (1972, Invictus); **General Johnson** (1977, Arista). HIT VERSIONS: *Bring the Boys Home* [ii] Freda Payne (1971) g R&B#3 US#12, *Day I Found Myself, The* Honey Cone (1972) R&B#8 US#23, *Everything Good Is Bad* [ii] 100 Proof Aged in Soul (1972) R&B#15 US#45, *Get the Point* [i] C.E.B. (1993) R&B#88, *If I Could See the Light* 8th Day (1972) R&B#27 US#79, *Innocent 'Til Proven Guilty* Honey Cone (1972) R&B#37 US#101, *One Man's Leftovers (Are Another Man's Feast)* 100 Proof Aged in Soul (1971) R&B#37 US#96, *One Monkey Don't Stop No Show* [vi] Honey Cone (1971) R&B#5 US#15, *Patches* [iv] Clarence Carter (1970) g R&B#2 US#4 UK#2/Roy Griff (1970) C&W#26/ Jerry Reed (1981) C&W#30; *Slipped, Tripped and Fell in Love* Clarence Carter (1971) R&B#25 US#84, *Somebody's Been Sleeping in My Bed* [ii] 100 Proof Aged in Soul (1970) g R&B#6 US#8, *Stick-Up* [vi] Honey Cone (1971) g R&B#1 US#11, *Want Ads* [v] Honey Cone (1971) g R&B#1 US#1/Ullanda (1979) R&B#65/Robin Lee (1984) C&W#63; *(You've Got Me) Dangling on a String* [viii] Donny Osmond (1977) US#109. Co-writers: [i] Angelo Bond/Mc-Glone/Greg Perry/Roney, [ii] Angelo Bond/Greg Perry, [iii] Jeffrey Bowden, [iv] Ronald Dunbar, [v]

Barney Perkins/Greg Perry, [vi] Greg Perry, [vii] Ronald Dunbar/Greg Perry, [viii] Ronald Dunbar/ Edith Wayne. (*See also under* Brian HOLLAND, Lamont DOZIER & Eddie HOLLAND.)

512. JOHNSON, George (b. May 17, 1953, Los Angeles, CA) R&B guitarist and vocalist, and **JOHNSON, Louis A.** (b. April 13, 1955, Los Angeles, CA) R&B bassist and vocalist. Sibling musicians who were session players with Quincy Jones, before they struck out on their own in the mid–1970s as the Brothers Johnson. CHART COMPOSITIONS: *I'll Be Good to You* [v] (1976) g R&B#1 US#3, *Get the Funk Out Ma Face* [iv] (1976) R&B#4 US#30, *Free and Single* (1976) R&B#26 US#103, *Runnin' for Your Lovin'* (1977) R&B#20 US#107, *Love Is* (1978) R&B#50, *Ain't We Funkin' Now* (1978) R&B#45 US#102, *Stomp!* [iii] (1980) R&B#1 US#7 UK#6, *Light Up the Night* (1980) R&B#16, *The Real Thing* (1981) R&B#11 US#67, *Dancin' Free* (1981) R&B#51, *Welcome to the Club* (1982) R&B#13, *I'm Giving You All of My Love* (1983) R&B#75, *You Keep Me Coming Back* (1984) R&B#12 US#102, *Kick It to the Curb* (1988) R&B#52. ALBUMS: **Look Out for #1** (1976) p US#9, **Right on Time** (1977) p US#13, **Blam!!** (1978) p US#7 UK#48, **Light Up the Night** (1980) p US#5 UK#22, **Winners** (1981) US#48 UK#42, **Blast!-The Latest and the Greatest** (1983) US#138, **Out of Control** (1984, all A&M) US#91. HIT VERSIONS: *I'll Be Good to You* [v] Quincy Jones featuring Ray Charles & Chaka Khan (1989) US#18 UK#21, *Is It Love That We're Missin'* [vi] Quincy Jones (1975) R&B#18 US#70, *Sweet Love* [i] Anita Baker (1986) US#8 UK#13. Co-writers: [i] Gary Bias/Anita Baker (b. December 20, 1957, Memphis, TN)/Louis A. Johnson only, [ii] Valerie Johnson, [iii] Valerie Johnson/Rod Temperton, [iv] Quincy Jones, [v] Senora Sam, [vi] D. Smith.

513. JOHNSON, Howard (b. 1887; d. 1941, both America) Film lyricist. A Tin Pan Alley lyricist who worked with a wide variety of composers. HIT VERSIONS: *Am I Wasting My Time on You?* [i] Lewis James (1926) US#5/Ben Selvin (1926) US#5; *Feather Your Nest* [ii] Henry Burr & Albert Campbell (1921) US#2, *I Don't Want to Get Well* [iv] Van & Schenck (1918) US#8, *M-O-T-H-E-R (A Word That Means the World to Me)* [v] Henry Burr (1916) US#1/George Wilton Band (1916) US#7; *Mystery* [iii] Paul Biese Trio (1920) US#4. Co-writers: [i] Irving Bibo, [ii] James Brockman/James Kendis, [iii] Joseph Cirina, [iv] Harry Jentes/Harry Pease, [v] Theodore F. Morse. (*See also under* Walter DONALDSON, Jimmy MONACO, Charles TOBIAS, Harry WOODS.)

514. JOHNSON, Matt (b. August 15, 1961, London, England) Pop keyboard player and vocalist. A synthesizer based solo artist, better known as the fictional group The The. Johnson first recorded two albums as the Gadgets, **Gadgetress** (1979) and **Love, Curiosity, Freckles and Doubt** (1980, both Vinyl Solution), before releasing the solo set **Burning Blue Soul** (1981, 4AD) UK#65. All his future recordings were as the one-man band The The. CHART COMPOSITIONS: *Uncertain Smile* (1982) UK#68, *This Is the Day* (1983) UK#70, *Heartland* (1986) UK#29, *Infected* (1986) UK#48, *Slow Train to Dawn* (1987) UK#64, *Sweet Bird of Youth* (1987) UK#55, *The Beat(en) Generation* (1989) UK#18, *Gravitate to Me* (1989) UK#63, *Armageddon Days Are Here* (1989) UK#70, *Shades of Blue EP* (1991) UK#54, *Dogs of Lust* (1994) UK#25, *Slow Motion Replay* (1993) UK#35, *Love Is Stronger Than Death* (1993) UK#39, *Dis-Infected EP* (1994) UK#17, *I Saw the Light* (1995) UK#31. ALBUMS: **Soul Mining** (1983) UK#27, **Infected** (1986, both Some Bizarre) US#89 UK#14; **Mind Bomb** (1989) US#138 UK#4, **Dusk** (1993) US#142 UK#2, **Hanky Panky** (1995, all Epic) UK#28.

515. JOHNSON, Robert (b. May 8, 1911, either Hazelhurst or Robinsville, MS; d. August 16, 1938, Greenwood, MS) Blues guitarist, harmonica player and vocalist. Arguably the single most important and influential blues songwriter ever to record. Johnson was raised in poverty on a farm, and taught himself the Jews harp and the harmonica before running away from home and playing music throughout the Mississippi delta. In 1930, Johnson lost both his wife and child in childbirth, shortly after which, he seemingly disappeared for a year, returning as a gifted bottleneck guitarist, and thus creating the blues myth that in return for his new found skill, Johnson had sold his soul to the devil at a dusty rural crossroads. The evidence that something remarkable had happened to Johnson was shortly apparent in the series of make-shift studio recordings that he made between 1936–1937 for the Vocalion label. His rough, blues-based country songs were either Johnson originals, or the first recorded versions of material that he had heard and adapted during his travels. Although many of them were big selling 78s at the time, in particular *Terraplane Blues*, after his death by poisoning in 1938, Johnson's music remained almost forgotten until the Chicago blues boom of the 1950s. During the British blues revival of the 1960s, his songs began to appear on albums by the Bluesbreakers, Cream, the Rolling Stones and Led Zeppelin, among them, *Come on in My Kitchen*, *Hellhound on My Trail*, *Love in Vain*, *Malted Milk*, *Ramblin' on My Mind*, *Traveling Riverside Blues*, and *Walking Blues*. Columbia subsequently issued his masters in two volumes **The King of The Delta Blues Singers**, before **The Complete Recordings** (1990) became a million seller. Johnson's tormented recordings remain the most chilling catalogue of blues songs ever recorded, being music haunted by primitive demons, fear, ignorance, poverty and the echoes of slavery. ALBUM: **The Complete Recordings** (1990, Columbia) p US#80. HIT VERSIONS: *Crossroads* Cream (1968) US#28, *I Believe I'll Dust My Broom* Elmore James (1952) R&B#9.

516. JOHNSTON, Arthur (b. Arthur James Johnston, January 10, 1898, New York, NY; d. May 1, 1954, Corona del Mar, CA) Film and stage composer, pianist and conductor. A publisher's staff pianist from the age of sixteen, who learned arranging and became a transcriber for Irving Berlin, before becoming the musical director of some of Berlin's earliest shows. Johnston's own musicals were often written with the lyricist Sam Coslow, their first being "Dixie to Broadway" (1925). A move to Hollywood during the late 1920s, resulted in contributions to the films "Puttin' on the Ritz," "Mammy," "Reaching for the Moon" (all 1929); "College Coach" (1932), "College Humor" and "Hello Everybody" (both 1933); and "Murder at the Vanities" (1934). In collaboration with Gus Khan, Johnston composed the score of "Thanks a Million" (1935), and with Johnny Burke, "Pennies from Heaven" (1936). HIT VERSIONS: *Between a Kiss and a Sigh* [i] Bing Crosby (1939) US#15/Artie Shaw (1939) US#13; *Cocktails for Two* [iii] Duke Ellington (1934) US#1/Johnny Green (1934) US#13/Will Osborne (1934) US#15/Spike Jones (1945) US#4; *Day You Came Along, The* [iii] Bing Crosby (1933) US#3, *Down the Old Ox Road* [iii] Bing Crosby (1933) US#8, *Ebony Rhapsody* [iv] Rosetta Howard (1948) R&B#8 US#21, *Learn to Croon* [iii] Bing Crosby (1933) US#3/Fran Frey (1933) US#15; *I'm Sitting High on a Hilltop* [vii] Guy Lombardo (1935) US#6, *If I Only Had a Match* [vi] Al Jolson (1948) US#26, *It's the Natural Thing to Do* [i] Mildred Bailey (1937) US#14/Bing Crosby (1937) US#2/Hoarce Heidt (1937) US#5; *Just One More Chance* [iii] Bing Crosby (1931) US#1, re-issued (1940) US#16/Abe Lyman (1931) US#6/Ben Selvin (1931) US#20/Les Paul & Mary Ford (1951) US#5; *Learn to Croon* [iii] Bing Crosby (1933) US#3/Fran Frey (1933) US#15; *Let's Call a Heart a Heart* [i] Billie Holiday (1936) US#18/Bing Crosby (1937) US#10; *Mandy, Make Up Your Mind* [ii] Paul Whiteman (1925) US#4/Tommy Dorsey (1943) US#16; *Moon Got in My Eyes, The* [i] Bing Crosby (1937) US#1/Shep Fields (1937) US#11; *Moon Song, The* [iii] Jack Denny (1933) US#5/Art Kassel (1933) US#6/Wayne King (1933) US#3; *My Old Flame* [iii] Guy

Lombardo (1934) US#7/Nino Tempo & April Stevens (1967) US#101; *Oh!* [v] Pee Wee Hunt (1953) US#3, *One, Two, Button Your Shoe* [i] Shep Fields (1936) US#12/Bing Crosby (1937) US#19; *Pennies from Heaven* [i] Bing Crosby (1936) US#1/Jimmy Dorsey (1936) US#19/Hildegarde (1936) US#16/Hal Kemp (1936) US#8/Eddy Duchin (1937) US#2/Teddy Wilson & Billie Holiday (1937) US#3/Frank Sinatra on *Songs for Swinging Lovers LP* (1956) UK#12; *So Do I* [i] Bing Crosby (1936) US#18, *Thanks* [iii] Bing Crosby (1933) US#2, *Thanks a Million* [vii] Paul Pendarvis (1935) US#5/Paul Whiteman (1935) US#11/Louis Armstrong (1936) US#17. Co-writers: [i] Johnny Burke, [ii] Grant Clarke/George W. Meyer/Roy Turk, [iii] Sam Coslow, [iv] Sam Coslow/Franz Liszt (b. Ferencz Liszt, October 22, 1811, Raiding; d. July 31, 1886, Bayreuth, both Hungary), [v] Byron Gay, [vi] Lee Morris, [vii] Gus Kahn.

517. JOHNSTON, Tom (b. August 15, 1948, Visalia, CA) Rock guitarist and vocalist. A founder member of the rock group the Doobie Brothers, which sold over forty million records. After studying graphic design at San Jose University, Johnston formed the group Pud with Patrick Simmons, which evolved into the Doobie Brothers, a group that established a formidable live reputation as the house band at the Chateau Liberte in the Santa Cruz mountains, with its brand of roots and country influenced rock. During the group's 1975 tour, Johnston dropped out due to ill health, and the former Steely Dan keyboard player Michael McDonald was brought in as a replacement. By the 1990s, Johnston was in better form and back at the helm. CHART COMPOSITIONS: *Nobody* (1971) US#122, re-issued (1974) US#5; *Listen to the Music* (1972) US#11 UK#29, re-mixed (1994) UK#37; *Long Train Running* (1973) US#8, re-mixed (1993) UK#7; *China Grove* (1973) US#15, *Another Park, Another Sunday* (1974) US#32, *Eyes of Silver* (1974) US#52, *Sweet Maxine* [ii] (1975) US#40, *The Doctor* [i] (1989) US#9 UK#73. ALBUMS: **The Doobie Brothers** (1971), **Toulouse Street** (1972) p US#21, **The Captain and Me** (1973) p US#7, **What Were Once Vices Are Now Habits** (1974) p US#4 UK#19, **Stampede** (1975) g US#4 UK#14, **Takin' It to the Streets** (1976) p US#8 UK#42, **Livin' on the Fault Line** (1977) g US#10 UK#25, **Minute By Minute** (1978) p US#1, **Farewell Tour** (1983, all Warner Brothers) US#79; **Cycles** (1989) g US#17, **Brotherhood** (1991, both Capitol) US#82; **Rockin' Down the Highway-The Wildlife Concert** (1996, Legacy). COMPILATIONS: **Best of the Doobies** (1976, Warner Brothers) p US#5; **Introducing The Doobie Brothers** (1980, Pickwick); **Best of the Doo-**

bies, **Volume 2** (1981) g US#39, **Listen to the Music-The Very Best of the Doobie Brothers** (1994, both Warner Brothers) UK#37. Johnston has also recorded as a solo artist, charting with the single *Savannah Nights* (1979) US#34. ALBUMS: **Everything You've Heard Is True** (1979) US#100, **Still Feels Good** (1981, both Warner Brothers) US#158. HIT VERSIONS: *Listen to the Music* Candi Staton (1977) R&B#90, *Long Train Running* Bananarama (1991) UK#30. Co-writers: [i] Charlie Midnight/Eddie Schwartz, [ii] Patrick Simmons. (*See also under* Patrick SIMMONS.)

518. JONES, Booker T. (b. December 11, 1944, Memphis, TN) R&B keyboard player and producer. The namesake in the R&B group Booker T. and the M.G.'s, who studied music at Indiana University, before joining Stax Records as a saxophonist in 1960. He first played in the label's house band the Mar-Keys, which became Booker T. and the M.G.'s, the best known backing group in the world. Jones co-wrote many of the group's hits with guitarist Steve Cropper, who left before the singles *Sticky Stuff* (1977) R&B#68 and *I Want You* (1981) R&B#35. ALBUMS: **Green Onions** (1962) US#33 UK#11, **Soul Dressing** (1964), **Hip Hug-Her** (1967) US#35, **Back to Back** (1967) US#98, **Doin' Our Thing** (1968) US#176, **Uptight** ost (1968) US#98, **Soul Limbo** (1968) US#127, **The Booker T. Set** (1969) US#53, **McLemore Avenue** (1970) US#107 UK#70, **Melting Pot** (1971) US#43, **Memphis Sound** (1975), **Union Extended** (1976, all Stax); **Universal Language** (1977, Asylum); **That's the Way It Should Be** (1994, Columbia). COMPILATIONS: **Best of Booker T. and the MG's** (1968, Atlantic) US#167; **Greatest Hits** (1970, Stax) US#132; **And Now** (1992, Rhino). During the 1970s, Jones recorded as a solo artist, and later worked as a producer for Bill Withers and Willie Nelson. ALBUMS: **Booker T. and Priscilla*** (1971) US#106, **Home Grown*** (1972), US#190; **Evergreen** (1975), **Try and Love Again** (1978), **The Best of You** (1980, all A&M). HIT VERSION: *My Whole World Is Falling Down* [i] William Bell (1969) R&B#39. With: * Priscilla Coolidge. Co-writer: [i] Bettye Crutcher. (*See also under* William BELL, Steve CROPPER.)

519. JONES, Howard (b. John Howard Jones, February 23, 1955, Southampton, England) Pop keyboard player and vocalist. A classically trained pianist who played in various semi-professional bands during the 1970s. Since 1980, Jones has performed as a one-man band synthesizer act. CHART COMPOSITIONS: *New Song* (1983) US#27 UK#3, *What Is Love* (1984) US#33 UK#2,

Hide and Seek (1984) UK#12, *Pearl in the Shell* (1984) UK#7, *Like to Get to Know You Well* (1984) US#49 UK#4, *Look Mama* (1985) UK#10, *Things Can Only Get Better* (1985) R&B#54 US#5, *Life in One Day* (1985) US#19 UK#14, *No One Is to Blame* (1986) US#4 UK#16, *All I Want* (1986) US#76 UK#35, *You Know I Love You...Don't You?* (1986) US#17, *A Little Bit of Snow* (1987) UK#70, *Everlasting Love* (1989) US#12 UK#62, *The Prisoner* (1989) US#30, *Lift Me Up* [i] (192) US#32 UK#52. ALBUMS: **Human's Lib** (1984) US#59 UK#1, **Dream into Action** (1985) p US#10 UK#2, **One to One** (1986) US#56 UK#10, **Cross That Line** (1989, all WEA) US#65 UK#64; **In the Running** (1992, East West); **Working in the Backroom** (1994, private pressing); **Live Acoustic America** (1996, Plump). COMPILATIONS: **The Twelve Inch Album** (1984, WEA) UK#15; **Action Replay** (1986, Elektra) US#34; **Best of Howard Jones** (1993, East West) UK#36. Co-writer: [i] R. Cullum.

520. JONES, Isham (b. January 31, 1894, Coalton, OH; d. October 19, 1956, Los Angeles, CA) Multi-instrumentalist, arranger and band leader. The leader and tenor saxophonist of a dance band that was often referred to as the finest pre-swing era orchestra. A composer of considerable merit, Jones was initially a bassist, who, by 1914, had become a dance band leader in Michigan, on account of his original arranging style. He first recorded for Brunswick Records in 1920, and his first published composition was *At That Dixie Jubilee* (1915). His ballad *It Had to Be You* [iii] (1924), was a hit in twelve different versions. Jones composed over two hundred songs and charted seventy-three times between 1920–1938. CHART COMPOSITIONS: *Wabash Blues* (1921) g US#1, *On the Alamo* [iv] (1922) US#1, *Broken Hearted Melody* [iii] (1923) US#2, *Swingin' Down the Lane* [iii] (1923) US#1, *The One I Love Belongs to Somebody Else* [iii] (1924) US#5, *Spain* [iii] (1924) US#1, *It Had to Be You* [iii] (1924) US#1, *Never Again* (1924) US#5, *I'll See You in My Dreams* [iii] (1925) US#1, *Why Couldn't It Be Poor Little Me?* (1925) US#8, *I'm Tired of Everything But You* (1925) US#3, *I'll Never Have to Dream Again* [v] (1932) US#7, *I Can't Believe It's True* [iii] (1932) US#5, *(There Is) No Greater Love* [vii] (1936) US#20. ALBUM: **Isham Jones and His Orchestra** (1979, Fountain). HIT VERSIONS: *Honestly* [v] Eddy Duchin (1939) US#16, *I'll See You in My Dreams* [vii] Ford & Glenn (1925) US#9/Marion Harris (1925) US#4/Lewis James (1925) US#12/Paul Whiteman (1925) US#5/Winifred Atwell in *Piano Party* (1959) UK#10/Pat Boone (1962) US#32 UK#27; *I'm Tired of Everything But You* Ben Selvin (1925) US#11, *Indiana Moon* [ii] Ben Selvin (1923) US#2/Carl Fen-

ton (1923) US#6/John McCormack (1924) US#9; *It Had to Be You* [iii] Cliff Edwards (1924) US#6/Marion Harris (1924) US#3/Sam Lanin (1924) US#10/Billy Murray & Aileen Stanley (1924) US#8/Paul Whiteman (1924) US#8/Red Nichols (1930) US#19/Artie Shaw (1941) US#22, re-issued (1944) US#10/Jimmie Lunceford (1942) R&B#9/Helen Forrest & Dick Haymes (1944) US#4/Earl Hines (1944) US#18/Betty Hutton (1944) US#5; *On the Alamo* [iv] Norman Petty Trio (1954) US#29, *One I Love Belongs to Somebody Else, The* [iii] Al Jolson (1924) US#2/Ray Miller (1924) US#5/Sophie Tucker (1924) US#10/Tommy Dorsey (1938) US#16, re-issued (1940) US#11; *Spain* [iii] Paul Whiteman (1924) US#7, *Swingin' Down the Lane* [iii] Ben Bernie (1923) US#2/Columbians (1923) US#11/Frank Sinatra on *Songs for Swinging Lovers LP* (1956) UK#12; *Wabash Blues* Benson Orchestra (1922) US#6/Dolly Kay (1922) US#13/Ted Lewis (1930) US#16/Russ Morgan (1939) US#17; *Why Couldn't It Be Poor Little Me?* Ray Miller (1925) US#8, *You've Got Me Crying Again* [v] Bing Crosby (1933) US#12/Hal Kemp (1933) US#13, re-issued (1939) US#10. Co-writers: [i] Ben Bernie/Charles Newman, [ii] Benny Davis, [iii] Gus Kahn, [iv] Gilbert Keys/Joe Lyons, [v] Charles Newman, [vi] Marty Symes, [vii] Marty Symes/Peter Tchaikovsky.

521. JONES, Mick (b. December 27, 1944, London, England) Rock guitarist, producer and vocalist. A former musical director for the French singer Johnny Halliday, who became the guitarist in Gary Wright's group Wonderwheel and featured on the album **Foot Print** (1971, A&M). Jones linked up with Wright again as a member of Spooky Tooth, appearing on their albums **You Broke My Heart So I Busted Your Jaw** (1973) US#84, **Witness** (1973) US#99 and **The Mirror** (1974, all Island) US#130; and the compilation **That Was Only Yesterday** (1976, A&M) US#172. In 1976, Jones formed the Anglo-American rock band Foreigner, which sold over twenty-four million albums in America. CHART COMPOSITIONS: *Feels Like the First Time* (1977) US#4 UK#39, *Cold as Ice* [i] (1977) US#6 UK#24, re-mixed (1985) UK#64; *Long Way from Home* [ii] (1978) US#20, *Hot Blooded* [i] (1978) p US#3 UK#42, *Double Vision* [i] (1978) p US#2, *Blue Morning, Blue Day* [i] (1979) US#15 UK#45;, *Dirty White Boy* [i] (1979) US#12, *Head Games* [i] (1979) US#14, *Women* (1980) US#41, *Urgent* (1981) US#4 UK#54, re-issued (1982) UK#45; *Juke Box Hero* [i] (1981) UK#48, re-issued (1982) US#26; *Waiting for a Girl Like You* [i] (1981) p US#2 UK#8, *Break It Up* (1982) US#26, *Luanne* [i] (1982) US#75, *I Want to Know What Love Is* (1985) p R&B#85 US#1 UK#1, *That Was Yesterday* [iii] (1985) US#12 UK#28,

Reaction to Action [i] (1985) US#54, *Down on Love* [i] (1985) US#54, *Say You Will* [i] (1987) US#6 UK#71, *I Don't Want to Live Without You* (1988) US#5, *Heart Turns to Stone* [i] (1988) US#56, *With Heaven on Our Side* (1992) US#117, *White Lie* (1994) UK#58, *Until the End of Time* (1995) US#42. ALBUMS: **Foreigner** (1977) p US#4, **Double Vision** (1978) p US#3 UK#32, **Head Games** (1979) p US#5, **4** (1981) p US#1 UK#5, **Agent Provocateur** (1984) p US#5 UK#1, **Inside Information** (1988) p US#15 UK#64, **Unusual Heat** (1991) US#117 UK#56, **Classic Hits Live** (1993, all Atlantic); **Mr. Moonlight** (1994, Arista) UK#59. COMPILATIONS: **Records** (1982) p US#10 UK#58, **Very Best of Foreigner** (1992) UK#16, **The Very Best...And Beyond** (1992, all Atlantic) US#123. Jones has also worked as a producer, and recorded the solo set **Mick Jones** (1989, Atlantic) US#184. HIT VERSIONS: *Bad Love* Eric Clapton (1989) US#88 UK#25, *I Want to Know What Love Is* New Jersey Mass Choir (1985) R&B#37 US#101, *Yeah, Yeah, Yeah* [iv] Judson Spence (1988) US#32. Co-writers: [i] Lou Grammatico, [ii] Ian MacDonald (b. June 25, 1946, London, England)/Lou Grammatico, [iii] Alex Sadkin, [iv] Judson Spence (b. Pascagoula, MS).

522. JONES, Mick (b. June 26, 1955, London, England) Rock guitarist and vocalist. A co-founder, with Joe Strummer, of the definitive punk-rock group the Clash. Jones left the band in 1984 to form Big Audio Dynamite, one of the earliest acts to use sampling and cut-up musical techniques. CHART COMPOSITIONS: *E=MC2* (1986) UK#11, *Medicine Show* (1986) UK#29, *C'mon Every Beatbox* (1986) UK#51, *V Thirteen* (1987) UK#49, *Badrock City* (1987) R&B#66, *Just Play Music* (1988) UK#51, *Rush* (1991) US#32, *The Globe* [i] (1992) US#72, *Looking for a Song* (1994) UK#68. ALBUMS: **This Is Big Audio Dynamite** (1985) US#103 UK#27, **No. 10 Upping Street** (1986) US#119 UK#11, **Tighten Up, Volume 88** (1988) US#102 UK#33, **Megatop Phoenix** (1989) US#87 UK#26, **Kool-Aid** (1990, all CBS) UK#55; **The Globe** (1991, Columbia) g US#76 UK#63; **Higher Power** (1994, Sony/Columbia); **F-Punk** (1995, Radioactive). COMPILATION: **The Lost Treasure of B.A.D. I and II** (1994, Sony). Co-writer: [i] G. Stonadge. (*See also under* Joe STRUMMER.)

523. JONES, Rickie Lee (b. November 8, 1954, Chicago, IL) Rock guitarist, pianist, producer and vocalist. An engaging, individualistic singer-songwriter, whose songs often examine the American experience of dislocation. Jones uses scattered and transitory images to relay the briefest of communications and she writes in a moody, sketching

style that merges Tin Pan Alley pop, jazz, R&B and beat poetry. Some of her lineage had been in vaudeville, and she wrote her first song *I Wish*, at the age of seven. By 1969, Jones had been thrown out of three schools for insubordination, eventually running away from her home in Phoenix, Arizona, to San Diego, California. By 1973, she was a waitress in Los Angeles who performed her songs in the coffee houses of Venice Beach, to, she claimed, "bikers, degenerates, drunken men and toothless women." Around this time, Jones befriended the vocalist Tom Waits, and submitted a four track demo to Warner Brothers Records, which promptly signed her as a recording artist. Jones' albums for the label were strikingly original, influenced in part by Joni Mitchell and the late Laura Nyro. **Pop Pop** (1991), was an audacious deviation from the increasingly technological albums that everybody else was recording during the early 1990s, being an acoustic set of cover versions, including Sammy Cahn and Jimmy Van Heusen's *Second Time Around*, Fran Landesman and Tommy Wolf's *Spring Can Really Hang You Up the Most*, Jimi Hendrix's *Up from the Skies*, Carolyn Leigh and Mark Chalap's *I Won't Grow Up*, and Marty Balin's *Coming Back to Me*. Jones continues to work in an area quite unrelated to the pop mainstream. CHART COMPOSITIONS: *Chuck E's in Love* (1979) R&B#79 US#4 UK#18, *Young Blood* (1979) US#40, *A Lucky Guy* (1981) US#64, *The Real End* (1984) US#83. ALBUMS: **Rickie Lee Jones** (1979) p US#3 UK#18, **Pirates** (1981) g US#5 UK#37, **Girl at Her Volcano** (1983) US#39 UK#51, **The Magazine** (1984, all Warner Brothers) US#44 UK#40; **Flying Cowboys** (1988) US#39 UK#50, **Pop Pop** (1991) US#121, **Traffic from Paradise** (1993, all Geffen) US#111; **Naked Songs** (1995) US#121, **Ghostyhead** (1997, both Reprise).

524. JORDAN, Louis (b. July 8, 1908, Brinkley, AK; d. February 4, 1975, Los Angeles, CA) R&B saxophonist and vocalist. An innovative performer whose jump band jive was essential to the development of R&B and rock and roll. Jordan was taught the saxophone and clarinet by his father, and during his teens he played with the Rabbit Foot Minstrels. In the 1930s, he sang in Chick Webb's band, before making his first solo recordings for the Brunswick label. In 1938, Jordan formed his Tympany Five, recording such gems as *At the Swing Cats Ball* (1939) and *Five Guys Named Moe* (1942). Jordan charted fifty-seven hits between 1942–1951, including eighteen number ones. He also appeared in the films "Follow the Boys" (1944) and "Reet, Petite and Gone" (1947). A showman and highly competent musician, Jordan died of a heart attack in 1975. CHART COMPOSITIONS: *Ration Blues* (1944)

C&W#1 R&B#1 US#11, *Deacon Jones* (1944) C&W#7, *Is You Is or Is You Ain't (Ma' Baby)* [i] (1944) R&B#3 C&W#1 US#2, *Caldonia Boogie* (1945) g US#6, *You Can't Get That No More* [v] (1945) R&B#2 US#11, *Early in the Mornin'* [ii] (1947) R&B#3, *Reet, Petite and Gone* [iv] (1948) R&B#4, *Saturday Night Fish Fry* [vi] (1949) g R&B#1 US#21, *Blue Light Boogie* [iii] (1950) R&B#1, *Hard Head* (1963) US#128. ALBUMS: **Somebody Up There Digs Me** (1957), **Man We're Wailin'** (1959, both Mercury); **Hallelujah, Louis Jordan Is Back** (1964, HMV); **Let the Good Times Roll** (1965, Ace); **I Believe in Music** (1973, Black & Blue); **Louis Jordan and Chris Barber** (1974), **Choo Choo Ch'Boogie** (1976, both Black Lion); **Best of Louis Jordan** (1981, MCA); **Jumpin' Stuff** (1981, Rarities); **Great Rhythm and Blues, Volume 1** (1982, Bulldog); **Go Blow Your Horn** (1983, EMI); **Look Our Sister** (1983); **Reet Petite and Gone** (1983, both Krazy Kat); **Look Out** (1983, Charly); **1944/5** (1984, Circle); **Collates** (1984), **Good Times** (1984, both Swing House); **Jump and Jive** (1984, JSP); **Prime Cuts** (1984, Swing House); **Golden Greats** (1985, MCA); **Jivin' with Jordan** (1985, Charly); **Hoodoo Man** (1986, Swingtime); **Jivin' 1956–1958, Volume 1** (1986), **Jivin' 1956–1958, Volume 2** (1986), **Rock 'n' Roll Call** (1986, all Bear Family); **Knock Me Out** (1986, Swingtime); **Somebody Done Hoodooed the Hoodoo** (1986, Jukebox); **20 Golden Greats** (1987, Magic); **Cole Slaw** (1987), **G.I. Jive** (1987, both Jukebox); **More, 1944–1945** (1987, Circle); **Louis Jordan and Friends** (1988, MCA); **Louis Jordan and Tympany Five, 1945–1952** (1988, Star Performance); **Live Jive** (1989, A Touch of Magic). HIT VERSIONS: *Caldonia* Erskine Hawkins (1945) US#12/Woody Herman (1945) US#2; *Is You Is or Is You Ain't (Ma' Baby)* [i] Bing Crosby & the Andrews Sisters (1944) US#2/Cootie Williams (1944) R&B#9. Co-writers: [i] Billy Austin, [ii] Dallas Bartley/Leo Hickman, [iii] Jessie Mae Robinson, [iv] Spencer Lee, [v] Sam Thread, [vi] Ellis Walsh.

525. KAEMPFERT, Bert (b. Berthold Kaempfert, October 16, 1923, Hamburg, West Germany; d. June 21, 1980, Zug, Switzerland) Orchestra leader, arranger, producer and multi-instrumentalist. One of Europe's most popular light orchestral arrangers, who was also successful in America during the 1960s. A composer of considerable merit, Kaempfert co-adapted the German folk song *Muss I Denn* as *Wooden Heart* [viii], and composed the original melody to *Spanish Eyes* [vi], which was first recorded as the instrumental *Moon Over Naples*. Kaempfert ultimately composed over two hundred tunes. He learned the piano at the age of six, and

later studied at the Hamburg School of Music, where he learned the saxophone, accordion, trumpet and clarinet. During his tenure with the Hans Busch Dance Band, Kaempfert developed a love of jazz — a decadent sound that was frowned upon by Germany's ruling Nazi Party. During World War II, he performed in the German Navy Band, and while on active service, secretly listened to BBC Radio broadcasts of American jazz. After the war, Kaempfert played in American occupation service clubs. In 1948, he became a professional arranger in Hamburg, an experience that led him to write his first tunes, later saying, "I felt I could compose a better one during breakfast." In 1959, Kaempfert became the house producer for Polydor Records in Germany, where, two years later, he was the first person to produce recordings by the little known Tony Sheridan and the Beatles. Throughout the 1960s, Kaempfert performed around the world with his own sixty piece orchestra. Two of the most successful albums of his songs, were **Al Hirt Plays Bert Kaempfert** (1968, RCA) US#116, and **Johnny Mathis Sings the Music of Bacharach and Kaempfert** (1971, Columbia) US#169. CHART COMPOSITIONS: *Afrikaan Beat* (1962) US#42, *Echo in the Night* (1962) US#108, *That Happy Feeling* (1962) US#67, *Moon Over Naples* (1965) US#59, *Strangers in the Night* [vii] (1966) US#124. ALBUMS: **Wonderland By Night** (1960) g US#1, **Dancing in Wonderland** (1961) US#92, **Afrikaan Beat and Other Favorites** (1962) US#82, **That Happy Feeling** (1962) US#14, **Living It Up** (1963) US#87, **Lights Out, Sweet Dreams** (1963) US#79, **Christmas Wonderland** (1963), **Blue Midnight** (1965) g US#5, **Three O'Clock in the Morning** (1965) US#42, **The Magic of Far Away Places** (1965, all Decca) US#27; **Bye Bye Blues** (1966) US#46 UK#4, **Best of Bert Kaempfert** (1966) UK#27, **Swinging Safari** (1966) UK#20, **Strangers in the Night** (1966, all Polydor) US#39 UK#13; **Greatest Hits** (1966) g US#30, **Terror After Midnight** ost (1966, both Decca); **A Man Could Get Killed** ost (1966), **Relaxing Sound of Bert Kaempfert** (1967) UK#33, **Best Seller** (1967) UK#25, **Hold Me** (1967) US#122 UK#36, **Kaempfert Special** (1967, all Polydor) UK#24; **The World We Knew** (1967) US#136, **My Way of Life** (1968) US#186, **Warm and Wonderful** (1969) US#194, **Traces of Love** (1969) US#153, **The Kaempfert Touch** (1970) US#87, **You Can't Win 'Em All** ost (1970, all Decca); **Orange Colored Sky** (1971, Polydor) US#140 UK#49; **Bert Kaempfert Now** (1971, Decca) US#188, **Very Best of Bert Kaempfert** (1974), **Live in London** (1975), **His Greatest Hits** (1977), **Tropical Sunrise** (1978), **Sounds Sensational** (1980, all Polydor) UK#17; **Images** (1989, Knight). HIT VERSIONS: *Danke Schoen* [iii] Wayne

Newton (1963) US#13, *Lady* Jack Jones (1967) US#39, *L-O-V-E* [i] Nat "King" Cole (1965) US#81, *Maltese Melody, The* [v] Herb Alpert & the Tijuana Brass (1970) US#108, *Over and Over (The World We Knew)* [vi] Frank Sinatra (1967) US#30 UK#35, *Remember When (We Made These Memories)* Wayne Newton (1966) US#69, *Someone* Billy Vaughn (1962) US#115, *Spanish Eyes* [vii] Al Martino (1965) US#15, re-issued (1970) UK#49, re-entry (1973) UK#5/ Charlie Rich (1979) C&W#20; *Strangers in the Night* [vii] Frank Sinatra (1966) US#1 UK#1/Osborne & Giles (1985) R&B#67; *Sweet Maria* Billy Vaughn Singers (1967) US#105, *Swingin' Safari, A* Billy Vaughn (1962) US#13, *Wiederseh'n* [ii] Al Martino (1966) US#57, *Wooden Heart* [viii] Gus Backus (1961) US#102/Joe Dowell (1961) US#1/Elvis Presley (1961) UK#1, re-issued (1964) US#107, re-issued (1965) US#110, re-issued (1977) UK#49, also on B-side of *Puppet on a String* (1965) US#14/Bobby Vinton (1975) US#58; *You Turned My World Around* [iv] Frank Sinatra (1974) US#83. Co-writers: [i] Milt Gabler, [ii] Milt Gabler/Herb Rehbein, [iii] Milt Gabler/Kurt Schwabach, [iv] Herb Rehbein, [v] Herb Rehbein, [vi] Herb Rehbein/Carl Sigman, [vii] Charlie Singleton/Eddie Snyder, [viii] Kay Twomey/ Ben Weisman/Fred Wise.

526. KAHAL, Irving (b. March 5, 1903, Houtzdale, PA; d. February 7, 1942) Film and stage lyricist. A Tin Pan Alley lyricist who wrote almost exclusively with Sammy Fain for seventeen years. HIT VERSIONS: *It Was Only a Sun Shower* [ii] Ted Weems (1927) US#13, *(There Ought to Be a) Moonlight Saving Time* [i] High Hatters (1931) US#6/Hal Kemp (1931) US#2/Guy Lombardo (1931) US#1. Co-writers: [i] Harry Richman, [ii] Francis Wheeler. (*See also under* Sammy FAIN, Billy ROSE, Harry WARREN.)

527. KAHN, Gus (b. November 6, 1886, Koblenz, Germany; d. October 8, 1941, Beverly Hills, CA) Film and stage lyricist. One of the most talented lyricists of the Tin Pan Alley era, who frequently worked with Walter Donaldson. Kahn began writing for vaudeville acts in his youth, and his first significant tunes were *Memories* [xxvi] (1915) and *Pretty Baby* [xv] (1916). Kahn's songs were featured in such films as "Bring on the Girls" (1928), "Flying Down to Rio" (1933) and "A Day at the Races" (1937), alongside the shows "The Passing of 1916" and "Whoopee!" (1928). ALBUM: **Whoopee!** oc (1928, Smithsonian). HIT VERSIONS: *All God's Chillun Got Rhythm* [xvi] Duke Ellington (1937) US#14/Artie Shaw (1937) US#15; *Alone at Last* [ix] Carl Fenton (1925) US#3/Lewis James (1925) US#11/Henry Burr (1926) US#5; *Around the Corner*

and Under the Tree [xviii] Tom Gerun (1930) US#12/ Leo Reisman (1930) US#17/Ben Selvin (1930) US#18; *Blue Love Bird* [xvii] Mitchell Ayres (1940) US#14/ Kay Kyser (1940) US#7; *Charly, My Boy* [ix] Eddie Cantor (1924) US#3/International Novelty Orchestra (1924) US#11/Andrews Sisters (1950) US#15; *Chloe (Song of the Swamp)* [xxii] Paul Whiteman (1928) US#7/Spike Jones (1945) US#5/Louis Armstrong (1953) US#26; *Coquette* [xii] Dorsey Brothers Orchestra (1928) US#20/Guy Lombardo (1928) US#6/Rudy Vallee (1929) US#10/Billy Eckstine (1953) US#26/Fats Domino (1959) R&B#26 US#92; *Dream a Little Dream of Me* [i] Wayne King (1931) US#1/Frankie Laine (1950) US#18/Jack Owens (1950) US#14/Mama Cass (1968) US#12 UK#11/ Anita Harris (1968) UK#33; *Everybody Rag with Me* [xix] George O'Connor (1915) US#8, *Goofus* [xiv] Wayne King (1931) US#10, re-issued (1932) US#16/ Red Nichols (1932) US#15/Dan Russo (1932) US#5/ Les Paul (1950) US#21/Carpenters (1976) US#56; *Hour of Parting, The* [xxiv] Benny Goodman (1940) US#19, *How Strange* [v] Ted Fiorito (1939) US#16, *I Never Knew* [ix] Gene Austin (1926) US#8/Sam Donohue (1947) US#2; *I Wish I Had a Girl* [xix] Billy Murray (1909) US#2/Manuel Romain (1909) US#7/Harry Tally (1909) US#4; *I'll Never Be the Same* [xxi] Guy Lombardo (1932) US#8/Paul Whiteman (1932) US#14; *I'm Through with Love* [xx] Henry Busse (1931) US#7/Bing Crosby (1931) US#3; *Josephine* [ii] Tommy Dorsey (1937) US#3/Sammy Kaye (1937) US#15/Wayne King (1937) US#3/Les Paul (1951) US#12; *Memories* [xxvi] Henry Burr (1916) US#9/John Barnes Wells (1916) US#4; *My Isle of Golden Dreams* [iii] Ben Selvin (1920) US#4/Bing Crosby (1939) US#18/Glenn Miller (1939) US#15; *No, No, Nora* [ix] Eddie Cantor (1923) US#1, *Nobody's Sweetheart* [vi] Isham Jones (1924) US#2/Red Nichols (1928) US#13/Paul Whiteman (130) US#2/ Cab Calloway (1931) US#13/Mills Brothers (1932) US#4/Russ Conway in *More Party Pops* (1958) UK#10; *Now That You're Gone* [ix] Ruth Etting (1931) US#13/Guy Lombardo (1931) US#2; *Pretty Baby* [xv] Billy Murray (1916) US#1, *Ready for the River* [xxii] Coon-Sanders Orchestra (1928) US#20, *San Francisco* [ix] Tommy Dorsey (1936) US#10, *Sometime* [ix] Green Brothers Novelty Band (1925) US#3/Ink Spots (1950) US#26/Mariners (1950) US#16/Jo Stafford (1950) US#27; *Sweetheart Darlin'* [xxv] Ben Selvin (1933) US#8, *Tomorrow Is Another Day* [xvi] Ted Fio Rito (1937) US#10, *Tonight Is Mine* [xiii] Leo Reisman (1934) US#19, *Toot Toot Tootsie (Goodbye)* [viii] Benson Orchestra of Chicago (1923) US#12/ Ernest Hare & Billy Jones (1923) US#9/Al Jolson (1923) US#1/Vincent Lopez (1923) US#11/Mel Blanc (1949) US#26/Art Mooney (1949) US#19; *Waltz You Saved For Me, The* [xi] Wayne King (1931) US#4, re-issued (1934) US#18; *When Lights Are Low* [x] Benson Orchestra of Chicago (1924) US#4, *When You and I Were Seventeen* [xxiii] Marion Harris (1925) US#11, *Your Eyes Have Told Me So* [iv] John McCormack (1920) US#6. Co-writers: [i] Fabian Andre/Wilbur Schwandt, [ii] Bruce Bivens/Wayne King, [iii] Walter Blaufuss, [iv] Walter Blaufuss/Egbert Van Alstyne, [v] Earl K. Brent/Herbert Stothart, [vi] Ernie Erdman/Billy Meyers/Elmer Schoebel, [vii] Ernie Erdman/Ted Fiorito/Robert A. King, [viii] Ernie Erdman/Dan Russo, [ix] Ted Fiorito, [x] Ted Fiorito/Ted Koehler, [xi] Emil Flindt/Wayne King (b. 1901; d. July 16, 1985), [xii] John Green/Carmen Lombardo, [xiii] W. Franke Harling, [xiv] William Harold/Wayne King, [xv] Tony Jackson/Egbert Van Alstyne, [xvi] Walter Jurmann/Bronislaw Kaper, [xvii] Bronislaw Kaper, [xviii] Art Kassel, [xix] Grace Le Boy, [xx] Fud Livingston/Matt Malneck, [xxi] Matt Malneck/Frank Signorelli, [xxii] Neil Moret, [xxiii] Charles Rosoff, [xxiv] Mischa Spoilansky, [xxv] Herbert Stothart, [xxvi] Egbert Van Alstyne. (*See also under* Buddy DE SYLVA, Walter DONALDSON, George GERSHWIN, Arthur JOHNSTON, Isham JONES, Jimmy McHUGH, George W. MEYER, Sigmund ROMBERG, Victor SCHERTZINGER, Richard A. WHITING, Harry WOODS, Vincent YOUMANS.)

528. KALMAR, Bert (b. February 16, 1884, New York, NY; d. September 18, 1947, Los Angeles, CA), and **RUBY, Harry** (b. January 27, 1895, New York, NY; d. February 23, 1974, Los Angeles, CA) Both film and stage composers. A songwriting partnership that created many popular film and show numbers, their most famous being *Who's Sorry Now?* (1923). Kalamar had been a child magician and vaudeville performer before he formed a partnership with the pianist Ruby. The duo created nine Broadway musicals, beginning with "Helen of Troy, NY" (1921), but they were not successful until "The Ramblers" (1926), which they followed with "Good Boy" (1928). For the Marx Brothers, Kalmar and Ruby composed the film theme *Hooray for Captain Spaulding*, and contributed to the comedy teams' films "Animal Crackers" (1930), "Horse Feathers" (1932) and "Duck Soup" (1933). They continued to work together until the 1940s. HIT VERSIONS: *Give Me the Simple Life* [i] Bing Crosby & Jimmy Dorsey (1946) US#16/Benny Goodman (1946) US#13; *I Love You So Much* Bob Haring (1930) US#14/Vicki Young (1953) US#26; *I Wanna Be Loved By You* Helen Kane (1928) US#2/Ben Selvin (1929) US#8; *In the Land of Harmony* American Quartet (1911) US#9/Arthur Collins (1911) US#5; *Three Little Words* Duke Ellington (1930) US#1/Ipana Troubadours (1930) US#10/Jacques Renard

(1930) US#3/Claude Hopkins (1934) US#15/Ethel Waters (1931) US#8; *Who's Sorry Now?* Marion Harris (1923) US#5/Harry James (1923) US#18/Lewis James (1923) US#11/Irving Kaufman (1923) US#11/Isham Jones (1923) US#3/Original Memphis Five (1923) US#8/Johnny Ray (1956) UK#7/Connie Francis (1958) US#4 UK#1/Marie Osmond (1975) C&W#29 US#40. All Kalmar/Ruby, except: [i] Rube Bloom/Harry Ruby. (*See also under* Otto HARBACH, Edgar LESLIE.)

529. KAYE, Buddy Pop saxophonist. A jazz influenced saxophonist and lyricist who recorded as the Buddy Kaye Quintet. CHART COMPOSITIONS: *Toughtless* (1948) US#22, *"A" You're Adorable (The Alphabet Song)* [vii] (1949) US#27. ALBUMS: **That Man in Istanbul** ost (1966, Mainstream); **Man Called Dagger** ost (1967, MGM). HIT VERSIONS: *Boys Cry* [xii] Eden Kane (1964) UK#8, *Christmas Alphabet* [viii] McGuire Sisters (1954) US#25/Dickie Valentine (1955) UK#1; *Don't Be a Baby, Baby* [xiv] Mills Brothers (1946) R&B#3 US#12, *Full Moon and Empty Arms* [x] Ray Noble (1946) US#18/Frank Sinatra (1946) US#17; *Give Up This Day* [iii] Joni James (1956) US#30, *In the Middle of Nowhere* [xv] Dusty Springfield (1965) US#108, *Italian Theme, The* [iv] Cyril Stapleton (1956) US#25 UK#18, *Little By Little* [v] Dusty Springfield (1966) UK#17/Ray Charles Singers (1967) US#135; *Next Time, The* [xiii] Cliff Richard (1963) UK#1, *Old Songs, The* [xi] Barry Manilow (1981) US#15 UK#48; *Penny a Kiss, a Penny a Hug, A* [ii] Andrews Sisters (1951) US#17/Eddy Howard (1951) US#14/Dinah Shore (1951) US#8; *Speedy Gonzales* [vi] Pat Boone (1962) US#6 UK#2, *Till the End of Time* [i] Les Brown (1945) US#3/Perry Como (1945) g US#1/Dick Haymes (1945) US#3; *Time* [xiii] Craig Douglas (1961) UK#9, *Walkin' with My Honey (Soon, Soon, Soon)* [ix] Sammy Kaye (1945) US#10. Co-writers: [i] Frederic Chopin (b. Fryderyk Franciszek Chopin, March 1, 1810, Zelazowa Wola, Poland; d. October 17, 1849, Paris, France)/Ted Mossman, [ii] Ralph Clare, [iii] Bobby Day, [iv] Angleo Giacomazzi/Clyde Hamilton, [v] E. Ginn/Beatrice Verdi, [vi] David Hill/Ethel Lee, [vii] Sidney Lippman, [viii] Jules Loman, [ix] Sam Medoff, [x] Ted Mossman/Sergey Vassilievich Rakhmaninov (b. April 1, 1873, Oneg, Russia; d. March 28, 1943, Beverly Hills, CA), [xi] David Pomeranz, [xii] Tommy Scott, [xiii] Philip Springer, [xiv] Howard Steiner, [xv] Beatrice Verdi. (*See also under* Sidney LIPPMAN.)

530. KAZ, Eric (b. Eric Justin Kaz, January 21, 1946, New York, NY). Rock guitarist, pianist and vocalist. A performer whose various groups have never matched the success that he has had as a songwriter for others. Kaz first played in the band Bear, which released the album **Bear** (1968, Verve), before recording with the Blues Magoos, scoring a handful of quasi-psychedelic minor hits during the late 1960s and issuing the albums **Never Going Back to Georgia** (1969) and **Gulf Coast Bound** (1970, both ABC). After an eponymous album as the group Mud Acres (1972, Rounder), Kaz attempted a country-rock approach in American Flyer, a group that failed to break the stranglehold on the genre held by the Eagles, America and Poco, despite Kaz's excellent compositions *Light of Your Love*, *Love Has No Pride* [v] and the hit *Let Me Down Easy* [ii] (1976) US#80. ALBUMS: **American Flyer** (1976) US#87, **Spirit of a Woman** (1977, both United Artists) US#171. His best ballads have been recorded by Bonnie Raitt, who cut *River of Tears*, *I'm Blowin' Away*, and *Love Has No Pride* [v], and Linda Ronstadt, who covered *Sorrow Lives Here* and *Cry Like a Rainstorm, Howl Like the Wind*. Kaz has also recorded as a solo artist. ALBUMS: **If You're Lonely** (1972), **Cul De Sac** (1973, both Atlantic); **Craig Fuller and Eric Kaz** (1978, Columbia). HIT VERSIONS: *Beast in Me, The* [iv] Bonnie Pointer (1985) R&B#87, *Deep Inside My Heart* [iii] Randy Meisner (1980) US#22, *Gotta Get Away* Randy Meisner (1981) US#104, *Heartbeat* [vi] Don Johnson (1986) US#5, *Hearts on Fire* [iii] Randy Meisner (1981) US#19, *Hypnotize the Moon* [ii] Clay Walker (1996) C&W#2 US#109+, *I Cross My Heart* [i] George Strait (1992) C&W#1, *Love Has No Pride* [v] Linda Ronstadt (1974) US#51. Co-writers: [i] Steve Dorff, [ii] Craig Fuller, [iii] Randy Meisner, [iv] Marvin Morrow, [v] Libby Titus, [vi] Wendy Waldman. (*See also under* Michael BOLTON.)

531. KEEN, Robert Earl (b. January 11, 1956, Houston, TX) C&W guitarist and vocalist. A singer-songwriter in a traditional country style, who co-wrote Lyle Lovett's *This Old Porch*. Keen's songs have also been recorded by Nanci Griffith and Reba McEntire. ALBUMS: **No Kinda Dancer** (1988, Rounder); **Live Album** (1988, Sugar Hill); **West Texas** (1990, Special Delivery); **A Bigger Piece of the Sky** (1993, Sugar Hill); **Picnic** (1997, Arista).

532. KELLER, Jack (b. November 11, 1936, Brooklyn, NY) Pop composer. One of the many successful Brill Building songwriters of the 1960s, whose songs featured in such films as "The Victors" (1963) and "I'd Rather Be Rich" (1964). HIT VERSIONS: *Almost There* [ix] Andy Williams (1965) US#67 UK#2, *Angel Say No* [vi] Tommy Tutone (1980) US#38, *Breakin' in a Brand New Broken Heart* [iv] Connie Francis (1961) US#7 UK#12/Debby Boone (1979) C&W#25; *Easy Come, Easy Go* [vii] Bobby Sherman (1969) g US#9, *867-5309/Jenny* [ii] Tommy

Tutone (1982) US#4, *Everybody's Somebody's Fool* [iv] Connie Francis (1960) R&B#2 US#1 UK#5/Debby Boone (1979) C&W#48; *Forever Kind of Love, A* [v] Bobby Vee (1962) UK#13, *Here Comes Summer* Jerry Keller (1959) US#14 UK#1/Wildfire (1977) US#49; *How Can I Meet Her* [v] Everly Brothers (1962) US#75 UK#12, *It Started All Over Again* [iv] Brenda Lee (1962) US#29 UK#15, *Just Between You and Me* [iii] Chordettes (1957) US#8, *Just for Old Time's Sake* [viii] McGuire Sisters (1961) US#20, *My Heart Has a Mind of Its Own* [iv] Connie Francis (1960) US#1 UK#3/Susan Raye (1972) C&W#10/Debby Boone (1979) C&W#11; *No One Can Make My Sunshine Smile* [v] Everly Brothers (1962) UK#11, also on B-side of *Don't Ask Me to Be Friends* (1962) US#48; *One Way Ticket* [viii] Eruption (1979) UK#9, *Please Don't Ask About Barbara* [i] Bobby Vee (1961) US#15 UK#29, *Run to Her/Him* [v] Bobby Vee (1961) US#2 UK#6/Susie Allanson (1981) C&W#53; *Venus in Blue Jeans* [iv] Jimmy Clanton (1962) US#7/Mark Wynter (1962) UK#4. Co-writers: [i] Bill Buchanon, [ii] A. Call, [iii] Lee Cathy, [iv] Howard Greenfield, [v] Gerry Goffin, [vi] T. Heath, [vii] Diane Hilderbrand, [viii] Hank Hunter, [ix] Gloria Shayne.

533. KELLY, R. (b. Robert Kelly, January 8, 1969, Chicago, IL) R&B keyboard player, producer and vocalist. One of the most successful R&B artists of the 1990s, whose emphasis on soulful, groove laden dance music has been extremely influential. Kelly learned the piano by ear as a child and was a teenage busker, before forming the short-lived group MGM in the late 1980s. CHART COMPOSITIONS: *She's Got That Vibe* (1991) R&B#7 US#59 UK#57, re-issued (1994) UK#3; *Honey Love* (1992) R&B#1 US#39, *Slow Dance (Hey Mr. D.J.)* (1992) R&B#1 US#43, *Dedicated* (1993) US#31, *Sex Me (Parts I and II)* (1993) g R&B#1 US#20 UK#75, *Bump N' Grind* (1994) g R&B#1 US#1 UK#8, *Your Body's Callin'* (1994) g US#13 UK#19, *Summer Bunnies* (1994) US#55 UK#23, *The 4 Plays EPs* (1994) UK#23, *An Angel* (1995) UK#69, *You Remind Me of Something* (1995) p R&B#1 US#4 UK#24, *Down Low (Nobody Has to Know)* (1996) R&B#1 US#4 UK#23, *Thank God It's Friday* (1996) UK#14. ALBUMS: **Born in the '90s** (1992) p US#42 UK#67, **12 Play** (1995) p US#2 UK#20, **R. Kelly** (1995) p US#1 UK#18. HIT VERSIONS: *At Your Best (You Are Love)* Aaliyah (1994) US#6, *Back and Forth* Aaliyah (1994) US#5, *Spend the Night* N-Phase (1994) US#23, *Stroke You Up* Changing Faces (1994) US#3, *You Are Not Alone* Michael Jackson (1995) R&B#1 US#1 UK#1.

534. KELLY, Tom, and **STEINBERG, Billy** Pop composers. American pop composers, who have enjoyed five number one singles. HIT VERSIONS: *Alone* Heart (1987) US#1, *Eternal Flame* [ii] Bangles (1989) g US#1 UK#1, *How Do I Make You* [iv] Linda Ronstadt (1980) US#10, *I Drove All Night* Cyndi Lauper (1989) US#6 UK#7/Roy Orbison (1992)UK#7, re-entry (1993) UK#47; *I Touch Myself* [i] Divinyls (1991) US#4, *I Want You So Bad* Heart (1988) US#49, *In Your Room* [ii] Bangles (1988) US#5 UK#35, *Jackie* Blue Zone U.K. (1988) US#54, *Like a Virgin* Madonna (1984) g R&B#9 US#1 UK#3/"Weird" Al Yankovic as *Like a Surgeon* (1985) US#47; *Lucky Love* [iii] Ace of Base (1996) US#30, *Sex as a Weapon* Pat Benatar (1985) US#28 UK#67, *So Emotional* Whitney Houston (1987) R&B#5 US#1 UK#5, *True Colors* Cyndi Lauper (1986) US#1 UK#12. Co-writers: [i] Amphlett/ McEntee, [ii] Susanna Hoffs, [iii] Joker/Billy Steinberg only, [iv] Billy Steinberg only. (*See also under* Chrissie HYNDE, Cyndi LAUPER.)

535. KEMP, Gary (b. October 16, 1959, London, England) Pop guitarist and vocalist. The songwriter and guitarist in the British "new romantic" group Spandau Ballet. CHART COMPOSITIONS: *To Cut a Long Story Short* (1980) UK#5, *The Freeze* (1981) UK#17, *Musclebound* (1981) UK#10, *Chant #1 (I Don't Need This Pressure On)* (1981) UK#3, *Paint Me Down* (1981) UK#30, *She Loved Like Diamond* (1982) UK#49, *Instinction* (1982) UK#10, *Lifeline* (1982) US#108 UK#7, *Communication* (1983) US#59 UK#12, *True* (1983) R&B#76 US#4 UK#1, *Gold* (1983) US#29 UK#2, *Only When You Leave* (1984) US#34 UK#3, *I'll Fly for You* (1984) UK#9, *Highly Strung* (1984) UK#15, *Round and Round* (1984) UK#18, *Fight for Ourselves* (1986) UK#15, *Through the Barricades* (1986) UK#6, *How Many Lies* (1987) UK#34, *Raw* (1988) UK#47, *Be Free with Your Love* (1989) UK#42. ALBUMS: **Journey to Glory** (1981) UK#5, **Diamond** (1982) UK#15, **True** (1983) US#19 UK#1, **Parade** (1984) UK#2, **Through the Barricades** (1986, all Reformation) UK#7; **Heart Like a Sky** (1989, CBS) UK#31. COMPILATIONS: **The Singles Collection** (1985) UK#3, **Best of Spandau Ballet** (1991, both Chrysalis) UK#44. In 1995, after debuting in the film "The Krays," Kemp recorded his first solo set, **Little Bruises** (1995, Columbia). HIT VERSIONS: *True* PM Dawn sampled in *Set Adrift on Memory Bliss* (1991) g R&B#16 US#1 UK#3.

536. KEMP, Wayne (b. June 1, 1941, Greenwood, AK) C&W vocalist. A teenage auto racer, who wrote and recorded for Dial Records during the late 1950s. CHART COMPOSITIONS: *Won't You Come Home (And Talk to a Stranger)* (1969) C&W#61, *Bar Room Habits* (1969) C&W#73, *Who'll Turn Out*

the Lights (1971) C&W#57, *Award to an Angel* (1971) C&W#52, *Did We have to Come This Far* (1971) C&W#72, *Darlin'* (1972) C&W#53, *Honky Tonk Wine* (1973) C&W#17, *Kentucky Sunshine* (1973) C&W#53, *Listen* (1974) C&W#32, *Harlan County* (1974) C&W#57, *Waiting for the Tables to Turn* (1976) C&W#72, *I Should Have Watched That First Step* (1976) C&W#71, *Leona Don't Live Here Anymore* (1977) C&W#91, *I Love It (When You Love All Over Me)* (1977) C&W#76, *Love Goes to Hell When It Dies* (1980) C&W#62, *I'll Leave This World Loving You* (1980) C&W#47, *Your Wife Is Cheatin' on Us Again* (1981) C&W#35, *Just Got Back from No Man's Land* (1981) C&W#46, *Why Am I Doing Without* (1981) C&W#75, *Sloe Gin and Fast Women* (1982) C&W#78, *She Only Meant to Use Him* (1982) C&W#64, *Don't Send Me No Angels* (1983) C&W#55, *I've Always Wanted To* (1984) C&W#75, *Red Neck and Over Thirty* with Bobby G. Rice (1986) C&W#70. HIT VERSIONS: *Darling You Know I Wouldn't Lie* Conway Twitty (1969) C&W#2, *I'll Leave This World Loving You* Ricky Van Shelton (1988) C&W#1, *Image of Me, The* Conway Twitty (1968) C&W#5/Jim Reeves (1984) C&W#70; *Love Bug* George Jones (1965) C&W#6, *Next in Line* Conway Twitty (1968) C&W#1, *That's When She Started to Stop Loving You* Conway Twitty (1970) C&W#3.

537. KENNEDY, Jimmy (b. James Kennedy, July 20, 1902, Omagh, County Tyrone, Northern Ireland; d. April 10, 1984, London, England) Film and stage lyricist. An occasional composer and frequent lyricist, who graduated from Trinity College, Dublin, before becoming a British Tin Pan Alley songwriter. Kennedy composed *The Teddy Bears Picnic* [iii] (1907), a four million seller for Henry Hall in 1933, *At the Cafe Continental* [vi], *Beside My Caravan* [xii] (both 1934); *Bird on the Wing* [vi] (1936), *Down the Old Spanish Trail* [x] (1947), and *The French Can-Can Polka* [viii] (1950). In 1935, he formed a successful five year alliance with the composer Michael Carr, writing material for the show "Cowboy" (1936), and the theme tune to "South of the Border" (1939), which was recorded over one hundred times. Kennedy's songs were also included in such films as "Little Boy Lost" (1953). During the 1950s, Kennedy became one of the first songwriters to translate or create new English language lyrics for continental hits, before residing in America, where he became the first of very few British songwriters to become a successful country composer. HIT VERSIONS: *An Apple Blossom Wedding* [ix] Buddy Clark (1947) US#14/Eddy Howard (1947) US#9/Sammy Kaye (1947) US#5; *And Mimi* [ix] Frankie Carle (1947) US#24/Dick Haymes (1947) US#15/Art Lund (1947) US#14; *April in Portugal* [iv] Les Baxter (1953)

US#2/Vic Damone (1953) US#10/Richard Hayman (1953) US#12/Freddy Martin (1953) US#15/Tony Martin (1953) US#17; *Down the Trail of Achin' Hearts* [ix] Patti Page (1951) US#17/Hank Snow & Anita Carter (1951) C&W#2; *Harbor Lights* [xiii] Frances Langford (1937) US#6/Claude Thornhill (1937) US#7/Ray Anthony (1950) US#4/Jerry Byrd & Jerry Murad's Harmonicats (1950) US#19/Bing Crosby (1950) US#8/Ralph Flanagan (1950) US#5/Ken Griffin (1950) US#11/Sammy Kaye (1950) US#1/Guy Lombardo (1950) US#2/Dinah Washington (1951) R&B#10/Platters (1960) R&B#15 US#8 UK#11/ Rusty Draper (1980) C&W#87; *Hokey Cokey, The* Judge Dread (1978) UK#59/Snowmen (1981) UK#18/ Black Lace (1985) UK#31/Captain Sensible (1996) UK#71; *Hour Never Passes, An* Jimmy Dorsey (1944) US#20, *Isle of Capri* [vi] Freddy Martin (1935) US#2/Ray Noble (1935) US#1/Lew Stone (1935) US#3/Gaylords (1954) US#14/Jackie Lee (1954) US#17; *Istanbul (Not Constantinople)* [ix] Frankie Vaughan (1954) UK#11/They Might Be Giants (1990) UK#61; *Love Is Like a Violin* [vii] Ken Dodd (1960) UK#8, *My Prayer* [ii] Ink Spots (1939) US#3/Glenn Miller (1939) US#2/Platters (1956) R&B#1 US#1 UK#22/Johnny Thunder (1966) US#106/Gerry Monroe (1970) UK#9/Narvel Felts (1976) C&W#14/Ray, Goodman & Brown (1980) R&B#31 US#47; *Never Goodbye* Karl Denver (1962) UK#9, *Play to Me, Gypsy* [xii] Henry Hall (1934) US#9/Jack Jackson (1934) US#12/Arthur Tracy (1934) US#19; *Red Sails in the Sunset* [xiii] Louis Armstrong (1936) US#15/Bing Crosby (1935) US#1/ Nat "King" Cole (1951) US#24/Fats Domino (1963) R&B#24 US#35 UK#34/Jack Jackson (1935) US#13/ Guy Lombardo (1935) US#1/Mantovani (1935) US#2/Platters (1960) US#36/Johnny Lee (1976) C&W#22; *Red We Want Is the Red We've Got (In the Old Red, White and Blue), The* Ralph Flanagan (1950) US#13, *Romeo* [ii] Petula Clark (1961) UK#3, *Serenade in the Night* [i] Jan Garber (1937) US#12/ Mantovani (1937) US#7; *Ten Pretty Girls* [vi] Jan Garber (1938) US#18. Co-writers: [i] C.A. Bixio/B. Cherubini, [ii] Georges Boulanger, [iii] John Bratton, [iv] Paul Ferrao, [v] Paul Ferrao/Jose Galhardo, [vi] Will Grosz, [vii] Marka Laparcerie, [viii] Jacques Offenbach (b. Jakob Levy Eberst, June 20, 1819, Cologne, Germany; d. October 5, 1880, Paris, France), [ix] Nat Simon, [x] Kenneth Leslie Smith, [xi] Robert Stolz, [xii] Karel Vacek, [xiii] Hugo Williams. (*See also under* Michael CARR, Tommie CONNORS.)

538. KENNERLEY, Paul (b. England) C&W producer. A former advertising executive whose fascination with the American old west resulted in two concept albums, **White Mansions**

(1978) US#181 UK#51 and **The Legend of Jesse James** (1980, both A&M) US#154. In 1983, Kennerley married the country singer Emmylou Harris, moved to Nashville, and became a producer. HIT VERSIONS: *Blue Side of Town* Patty Loveless (1989) C&W#4, *Chains of Gold* Sweethearts of the Rodeo (1987) C&W#4, *Cry Myself to Sleep* Judds (1987) C&W#1, *Have Mercy* Judds (1985) C&W#1, *Hey Baby* [i] Marty Stuart (1992) C&W#38, *In My Dreams* Emmylou Harris (1984) C&W#9, *Looking for Suzanne* Osmond Brothers (1986) C&W#70, *Tempted* [i] Marty Stuart (1991) C&W#5. Co-writer: [i] Marty Stuart (b. 1958, Philadelphia, MS).

539. KENNY, Charles (b. England), and **KENNY, Nick** (b. England) Film composers. A sibling songwriting team whose songs were included in such films as "Ride Tenderfoot, Ride" (1940). HIT VERSIONS: *Carelessly* [ii] Teddy Wilson & Billie Holiday (1937) US#1, *Cathedral in the Pines* Shep Fields (1938) US#1, *Dream Valley* [i] Eddy Duchin (1940) US#17/Sammy Kaye (1941) US#1; *Gone Fishin'* Bing Crosby & Louis Armstrong (1951) US#19, *Leanin' on the Ole Top Rail* Bob Crosby (1940) US#7/ Ozzie Nelson (1940) US#16; *Make Believe Island* [iii] Mitchell Ayres (1940) US#1/Dick Jurgens (1940) US#17/Sammy Kaye (1940) US#19/Jan Savitt (1940) US#8/Dick Todd (1940) US#14; *There's a Gold Mine in the Sky* Bing Crosby (1938) US#6/Hoarce Heidt (1938) US#5/Isham Jones (1938) US#13/Pat Boone (1957) US#20 UK#5; *While a Cigarette Was Burning* Buddy Rogers (1938) US#2/Paul Whiteman (1938) US#17. Co-writers: [i] Joe Burke, [ii] Norman Ellis, [iii] Will Grosz. (*See also under* John F. COOTS, Duke ELLINGTON.)

540. KERN, Jerome (b. January 27, 1885; d. November 11, 1945, both New York, NY) Film and stage composer. One of America's most melodic tunesmiths, who turned Tin Pan Alley songwriting into a genuine art form when he took the essence of European musical drama to the American theatre. An influence on both George Gershwin and Richard Rodgers, Kern re-defined the popular song. His unusual sixteen-measure verses and thirty-two-measure choruses, delicate rhythms and sophisticated key changes, created, for the first time, a development of melody lines within the song itself, the essential ingredient that made many of his compositions future jazz standards. Kern learned the piano at an early age, and began writing songs in the operetta tradition during his teens, later studying at the New York School of Music. After working as a song-plugger and rehearsal pianist, he was successful with *How'd You Like to Spoon with Me* [xiv] from the operetta "The Earl and the Girl" (1905). His first full score was "The Red Petticoat" (1912), which he followed with over one hundred compositions for a total of thirty-seven Broadway shows, including "Mr. Wix of Wickham" (1905), "The Girl from Utah" (1914), "Very Good Eddie" (1915), "Oh, Boy!" (1917), and "She's a Good Fellow" (1922). Kern collaborated with Guy Bolton and P.G. Wodehouse on a series of American comedies, including "Leave It to Jane" (1917) and "Oh Lady! Lady!!" (1918), before composing for the revues "Sally" (1920) and "Sunny" (1925), alongside the shows "Music in the Air" (1932) and "Joy of Living" (1938). In collaboration with the lyricist Oscar Hammerstein, II, Kern wrote "The Three Sisters" (1934) and "Very Warm for May" (1939), the latter introducing the jazz standard *All the Things You Are* [viii]. The duo's finest creation was "Show Boat" (1927), which introduced the black spiritual *Ol' Man River* [viii], and was filmed three times. "Show Boat" heralded a new era of Broadway musicals, as it introduced a firm plot and story line after forty years of little substance between songs. Kern also worked with Otto Harbach on the shows "The Cat and the Fiddle" (1931) and "Roberta" (1932), and his film work included "Lady Be Good" (1941), which featured the Oscar winning ballad *The Last Time I Saw Paris* [viii]. During his later years, Kern wrote increasingly in Hollywood, collaborating with Dorothy Fields on "Swingtime" (1936), and with Ira Gershwin on "Cover Girl" (1944). He died from a cerebral hemorrhage in 1945. ALBUMS: **Show Boat** oc (1946, Columbia); **Roberta** sc (1949, Decca); **Till the Clouds Roll By** ost (1950, MGM); **Music in the Air** sc (1951, RCA); **Show Boat** ost (1951), **Lovely to Look At** st (1952), **Lovely to Look At** ost (1952, all MGM); **The Cat and the Fiddle** sc (1953, RCA); **The Music of Jerome Kern** st (1955, Columbia); **Paris Holiday** st (1958), **An Evening with Jerome Kern** (1959, both United Artists); **Leave It to Jane** oc (1959, Strand); **Oh Boy!** oc (1960, World); **Sally** oc (1960), **Very Warm for May** sc (1960, both Monmouth Evergreen); **Show Boat** sc (1960, HMV) UK#12; **Show Boat** oc (1962, Columbia) US#95; **Show Boat/Annie Get Your Gun** ost (1973, MGM) US#184; **Very Good Eddie** oc (1975, DRG); **Jerome Kern Goes to Hollywood** (1986, Safari). HIT VERSIONS: *All the Things You Are* [viii] Tommy Dorsey (1940) US#1/Frank Masters (1940) US#14/Artie Shaw (1940) US#8; *All Through the Day* [viii] Perry Como (1946) US#8/Frank Sinatra (1946) US#7/Margaret Whiting (1946) US#11; *Babes in the Wood* [vii] Prince's Orchestra (1916) US#5/Gladys Rice & Walter Van Brunt (1916) US#8/Harry MacDonough & Lucy Isabelle Marsh (1917) US#2; *Bill* [xi] Helen Morgan (1928) US#4, *Bojangles of Harlem* [iii] Fred Astaire (1936) US#17, *Can I Forget You* [viii] Henry Allen (1937) US#13/

Bing Crosby (1937) US#8/Guy Lombardo (1937) US#13; *Can't Help Lovin' Dat Man* [viii] Ben Bernie (1928) US#19/Helen Morgan (1928) US#7; *Dearly Beloved* [xv] Alvino Rey (1942) US#21/Dinah Shore (1942) US#10/Glenn Miller (1943) US#4; *Fine Romance, A* [iii] Fred Astaire (1936) US#1/Billie Holiday (1936) US#9/Henry King (1936) US#13/Guy Lombardo (1936) US#13; *Folks Who Live on the Hill, The* [viii] Guy Lombardo (1937) US#17, *Have a Heart* [vii] Conway's Band (1916) US#9/Olive Kline & Lambert Murphy (1916) US#3; *How'd You Like to Spoon with Me?* [xiv] Corrine Morgan & Haydn Quartet (1906) US#1, *I Dream Too Much* [iii] Leo Reisman (1936) US#18, *I Won't Dance* [iv] Eddy Duchin (1935) US#1/Johnny Green (1935) US#6/George Hall (1935) US#20/Leo Reisman (1935) US#9; *I'm Old Fashioned* [xv] Fred Astaire (1943) US#23, *I'm the Echo* [iii] Paul Whiteman (1936) US#20, *I've Told Ev'ry Little Star* [viii] Jack Denny (1933) US#10/Linda Scott (1961) R&B#22 US#3 UK#7; *In Love in Vain* [xvii] Helen Forrest & Dick Haymes (1946) US#12/Margaret Whiting (1946) US#12; *Journey's End* [xix] Paul Whiteman (1923) US#2, *Ka-Lu-A* [i] Elsie Baker & Elliott Shaw (1922) US#3, *Last Time I Saw Paris, The* [viii] Kate Smith (1941) US#8, *Left All Alone Again Blues* [i] Marion Harris (1920) US#5, *Long Ago (And Far Away)* [vii] Perry Como (1944) US#8/Bing Crosby (1944) US#5/Helen Forrest & Dick Haymes (1944) US#2/Guy Lombardo (1944) US#11/Jo Stafford (1944) US#6/Three Suns (1944) US#16; *Look for the Silver Lining* [ii] Elsie Baker (1921) US#7/Marion Harris (1921) US#1/Charles Harrison (1921) US#7/Lewis James (1921) US#12/Isham Jones (1921) US#11/Elizabeth Spencer (1921) US#12; *Lovely to Look At* [v] Eddy Duchin (1935) US#1/Irene Dunne (1935) US#20/Leo Reisman (1935) US#10; *Magic Melody* [vii] Billy Murray (1915) US#9, *Make Believe* [viii] Paul Whiteman (1928) US#7, *More and More* [xiii] Bing Crosby (1945) US#14/Tommy Dorsey (1945) US#10; *Never Gonna Dance* [iii] Fred Astaire (1936) US#5, *Night Was Made for Love, The* [xii] Leo Reisman (1932) US#10, *Ol' Man River* [viii] Al Jolson (1928) US#4/Revelers (1928) US#10/Paul Robeson & Paul Whiteman (1928) US#7/Paul Whiteman (1928) US#1/Luis Russell (1934) US#19/Ravens (1948) R&B#10/Johnny Nash (1962) US#120/Shylo (1976) C&W#86/Mel McDaniel (1983) C&W#22; *Once in a Blue Moon* [i] Bing Crosby (1934) US#11, *Pick Yourself Up* [iii] Fred Astaire (1936) US#7, *Raggedy Ann* [i] Paul Whiteman (1924) US#12, *Reckless* [viii] Freddy Martin (1935) US#16, *Same Sort of Girl, The* [xviii] John Barnes Wells & Inez Babrour (1915) US#9, *She Didn't Say "Yes"* [xii] Leo Reisman (1932) US#13, *Siren's Song, The* [xix] Helen Clark & Gladys Rice (1918) US#8, *Smoke Gets in Your Eyes* [xii] Emil Coleman

(1934) US#4/Ruth Etting (1934) US#15/Leo Reisman (1934) US#3/Paul Whiteman (1934) US#1/ Artie Shaw (1941) US#24/Platters (1959) R&B#3 US#1 UK#1/Blue Haze (1972) US#27 UK#32/Bryan Ferry (1974) UK#17/Penny McLean (1976) US#108/ Narvel Felts (1982) C&W#84/John Alford (1996) UK#13; *Song Is You, The* [viii] Jack Denny (1933) US#12/Frank Sinatra on *Come Dance with Me LP* (1959) UK#30; *Sunny* [ix] Eddie Elkins (1925) US#14/ George Olsen (1926) US#2; *They Didn't Believe Me* [xvi] Harry MacDonough & Olive Kline (1915) US#1/Grace Kerns & Reed Miller (1916) US#8/Walter Van Brunt & Gladys Rice (1916) US#9/Morton Downey (1934) US#15; *Till the Clouds Roll By* [xix] Vernon Dalhart (1917) US#10/Prince's Orchestra (1917) US#2/Anna Wheaton & James Harrod (1917) US#1; *Touch of Your Hand, The* [xii] Leo Reisman (1934) US#10, *Waltz in Swing Time* [iii] Johnny Green (1936) US#16, *Way You Look Tonight, The* [iii] Fred Astaire (1936) US#1/Guy Lombardo (1936) US#3/ Teddy Wilson & Billie Holiday (1936) US#3/Benny Goodman (1942) US#21/Lettermen (1961) US#13 UK#36/Denny Seyton & the Sabres (1964) UK#48/ Edward Woodward (1971) UK#42; *Whip-Poor-Will* [ii] Isham Jones (1921) US#8/Vernon Country Club Band (1921) US#9; *Who?* [ix] Brox Sisters (1925) US#12/George Olson (1926) g US#1/Tommy Dorsey (1937) US#5; *Whose Baby Are You?* [i] Joseph C. Smith's Orchestra (1920) US#10, *Why Do I Love You?* [viii] Nat Shilkret (1928) US#9, *Why Was I Born?* [viii] Libby Holman (1930) US#19/Helen Morgan (1930) US#8/Vic Damone (1949) US#20; *Yesterdays* [xii] Leo Reisman (1933) US#3, *You Are Love* [viii] James Melton (1932) US#20, *You Couldn't Be Cuter* [iii] Tommy Dorsey (1938) US#3/Ray Noble (1938) US#16; *You're Here and I'm Here* [xviii] Harry MacDonogh & Olive Kline (1914) US#10. Co-writers: [i] Anne Caldwell, [ii] Buddy De Sylva, [iii] Dorothy Fields, [iv] Dorothy Fields/Oscar Hammerstein, II/ Otto Harbach/Jimmy McHugh, [v] Dorothy Fields/ Jimmy McHugh, [vi] George Gershwin, [vii] Schuyler Green, [viii] Oscar Hammerstein, II, [ix] Oscar Hammerstein, II/Otto Harbach, [x] Oscar Hammerstein, II/Leo Robin, [xi] Oscar Hammerstein, II/P.G. Wodehouse, [xii] Otto Harbach, [xiii] E.Y. Harburg, [xiv] Edward Laska, [xv] Johnny Mercer, [xvi] Herbert Reynolds, [xvii] Leo Robin, [xviii] Harry B. Smith, [xix] P.G. Wodehouse (b. Pelham G. Wodehouse, 1881, Guildford, England; d. February 14, 1975, America).

541. KERSHAW, Nik (b. March 1, 1958, Bristol, England) Pop keyboard player, producer and vocalist. After singing in the heavy metal group Half Pint Hog, and the jazz-funk act Fusion, Kershaw became a solo synthesizer artist in the 1980s. CHART

COMPOSITIONS: *I Won't Let the Sun Go Down on Me* (1983) UK#47, re-issued (1984) UK#2; *Wouldn't It Be Good* (1984) US#46 UK#4, *Dancing Girls* (1984) UK#13, *Human Racing* (1984) UK#19, *The Riddle* (1985) US#107 UK#3, *Wide Boy* (1985) UK#9, *Don Quixote* (1985) UK#10, *When a Heart Beats* (1985) UK#27, *Nobody Knows* (1986) UK#44, *Radio Musicola* (1986) UK#43, *One Step Ahead* (1989) UK#55. ALBUMS: **Human Racing** (1984) US#70 UK#5, **The Riddle** (1984) US#113 UK#8, **Radio Musicola** (1986, all MCA) UK#47. HIT VERSIONS: *Call My Name* [iii] Orchestral Manoeuvres in the Dark (1991) UK#50, *One and Only, The* Chesney Hawkes (1991) US#10, *Sailing on the Seven Seas* [i] Orchestral Manoeuvres in the Dark (1991) UK#3, *Show Me the Way* Osmond Boys (1992) UK#60, *Then You Turn Away* [ii] Orchestral Manoeuvres in the Dark (1991) UK#50, *Woman I Love, The* Hollies (1993) UK#42. Co-writers: [i] Paul Humphreys (b. February 27, 1960, London, England)/Andy McCluskey (b. June 24, 1959, Wirral, England), [ii] Andy McCluskey/Massett, [iii] Paul Humphreys/Andy McCluskey/Massett.

542. KIHN, Greg (b. 1952, Baltimore, MD) Rock guitarist and vocalist. An occasionally humorous singer-songwriter with a "new wave" sound, who enjoyed a run of American chart entries during the early 1980s. CHART COMPOSITIONS: *Remember* (1978) US#105, *The Girl Most Likely* (1981) US#104, *The Breakup Song (They Don't Write 'Em)* [iii] (1981) US#1, *Happy Man* [iii] (1982) US#62, *Every Love Song* [ii] (1982) US#82, *Jeopardy* [iii] (1983) R&B#48 US#2 UK#63, *Love Never Fails* [i] (1984) US#59, *Re-united* (1984) US#101, *Rock* (1984) US#107, *Boys Won't (Leave the Girls Alone)* (1985) US#110, *Lucky* [iii] (1986) US#30, *Love and Rock and Roll* (1986) US#92. ALBUMS: **Greg Kihn** (1975), **Greg Kihn Again** (1976), **Next of Kihn** (1978) US#145, **With the Naked Eye** (1979) US#114, **Glass House Rock** (1980) US#167, **Rockihnroll** (1981) US#32, **Kihntinued** (1982) US#33, **Kihnspiracy** (1983) US#15, **Kihntagious** (1984, all Beserkley) US#121; **Citizen Kihn** (1985, EMI-America) US#51; **Powerlines** (1990), **Kihn of Hearts** (1990), **Unkihntrollable** (1993, all Rhino); **Mutiny** (1994), **Horrorshow** (1997, both Clean Cut). COMPILATION: **Kihnsolidation: The Best of Greg Kihn** (1989, Rhino). HIT VERSION: *Jeopardy* [iii] "Weird Al" Yankovic as *I Lost on Jeopardy* (1984) US#81. Co-writers: [i] Greg Douglas/Larry Lynch/Gary Phillips/ Steven Wright, [ii] Larry Lynch/Gary Phillips/Steven Wright, [iii] Steven Wright.

543. KILGORE, Merle (b. Wyatt Merle Kilgore, August 9, 1934, Chickasha, OK) C&W

guitarist and vocalist. A former disc jockey and rock-abilly singer, who turned to country music for eight solo hits between 1960–1985. During the 1950s, Kilgore performed regularly on the Louisiana Hayride and the Grand Ole Opry, before moving into films in the 1960s. During the 1980s, he became Hank Williams, Jr.'s manager. CHART COMPOSITIONS: *Dear Mama* (1960) C&W#12, *Love Has Made You Beautiful* (1960) C&W#10, *Gettin' Old Before My Time* (1960) C&W#29, *Fast Talkin' Louisiana Man* (1967) C&W#71, *Montgomery Mable* (1974) C&W#95, *Mister Garfield* with Johnny Cash and Hank Williams, Jr. (1982) C&W#54, *Guilty* (1985) C&W#92. ALBUMS: **Tall Texan** (1963, Mercury); **There's Gold in Them Thar Hills** (1965, London); **Ring of Fire** (1965, Hilltop). HIT VERSIONS: *Folk Singer, The* Tommy Roe (1963) US#84 UK#4, *Johnny Reb* Johnny Horton (1959) C&W#10 US#54, *More and More* Webb Pierce (1954) C&W#1 US#22/ Charley Pride (1983) C&W#7; *Ring of Fire* [i] Johnny Cash (1963) C&W#1 US#17/Eric Burdon & the Animals (1969) UK#35/Randy Howard (1988) C&W#66; *Wolverton Mountain* [ii] Claude King (1962) C&W#1 US#6. Co-writers: [i] June Carter (b. June 23, 1929, Maces Spring, VA), [ii] Claude King (b. February 5, 1933, Shreveport, LA).

544. KING, Carole (b. Carole Klein, February 9, 1942, Brooklyn, NY) Pop pianist, drummer and vocalist. One of popular music's most consistently successful songwriters, who, during the 1960s, partnered the lyricist Gerry Goffin on a series of melodramatic teenage-angst songs that were written in New York's Brill Building. From the age of four, King was given piano lessons by her mother, and during her teens she dated the then struggling songwriter Neil Sedaka, inspiring his composition *Oh Carol!* After studying at Queens College, Brooklyn, where she briefly attempted a songwriting partnership with Paul Simon, King linked up with future husband Goffin as a songwriter at Don Kirshner's Aldon Music. Goffin and King's infectious, R&B influenced pop was aimed directly at white adolescents, and their first million seller was the ballad *Will You Love Me Tomorrow* (1960), a song that virtually defined the sound of American pop music during the early 1960s. The duo broke up on a personal and professional level in 1967, but would write together again in later years. King recorded a handful of solo sides during the 1960s, and also as a member of the groups the Myddle Class, recording the album **The Myddle Class** (1967, Buddah), and the City, which released **Now That Everything's Been Said** (1969, Ode). The phenomenal success of her second solo album, the twenty-four million selling **Tapestry** (1971), was to influence the course of popular music

for half a decade, capturing the mood of a generation and remaining on the chart for six years. Alongside James Taylor, King was a new type of singer-songwriter, who wrote about the environment, personal relationships, politics and spirituality. In 1988, she scored the film "Murphy's Romance," and in 1993, was the subject of the New York theatrical show "Tapestry-The Music of Carole King," which was shortly followed by the album **Tapestry Revisited: A Tribute to Carole King** (1996, Lava/Atlantic) US#88. CHART COMPOSITIONS: *It Might as Well Rain Until September* [i] (1962) US#22 UK#3, re-issued (1972) UK#43, *School Bells Are Ringing* (1962) US#123, *He's a Bad Boy* (1963) US#94, *It's Too Late* [vi]/*I Feel the Earth Move* (1971) g US#1 UK#6, *So Far Away* (1971) US#14, *Sweet Seasons* [iii] (1972) US#9, *Been to Canaan* (1972) US#24, *Believe in Humanity*/*You Light Up My Life* (1973) US#28, *Corazon* (1973) US#37, *Jazzman* [v] (1974) US#2, *Nightingale* [v] (1975) US#9, *Only Love Is Real* (1976) US#28, *High Out of Time* [i] (1976) US#76, *Hard Rock Cafe* (1977) US#30, *One Fine Day* (1980) US#12, *One to One* [vii] (1982) US#45. ALBUMS: **Writer** (1970) US#84, **Tapestry** (1971) p US#1 UK#4, **Music** (1972) g US#1 UK#18, **Rhymes and Reasons** (1972) g US#2 UK#40, **Fantasy** (1973) g US#6, **Wrap Around Joy** (1974) g US#1, **Really Rosie** ost (1975) US#20, **Thoroughbred** (1976, all Ode) g US#3; **Simple Things** (1977) g US#17, **Welcome Home** (1978) US#104, **Touch the Sky** (1979) US#104, **Pearls-The Songs of Goffin and King** (1980, all Capitol) US#44; **One to One** (1982) US#119, **Speeding Time** (1983, both Atlantic); **City Streets** (1989, Capitol) US#111; **Color of Your Dreams** (1993), **In Concert** (1994, both King's X/Rhythm Safari) US#160; **Carnegie Hall Concert, June 18, 1971** (1996, Sony). COMPILATIONS: **Her Greatest Hits** (1978, Ode) g US#47, **The Ode Collection, 1968–1976** (1994, Ode/Epic). HIT VERSIONS: *After All This Time* Merry Clayton (1971) R&B#42 US#71, *Am I the Guy* [i] Tony Orlando on B-side of *Bless You* (1961) US#15 UK#5, *At the Club* [i] Drifters (1964) R&B#10 US#43 UK#35, re-issued (1972) UK#3; *Baby Sittin'* [i] Bobby Angelo (1961) UK#30, *Chains* [i] Cookies (1962) R&B#6 US#17 UK#50/Buddy Alan (1974) C&W#35/Sarah (1988) C&W#81/River Detectives (1989) UK#51; *Corazon* LTG Exchange (1974) R&B#66, *Crying in the Rain* [iv] Everly Brothers (1962) US#6 UK#6/ Sweet Inspirations (1969) R&B#42 US#112/Del Reeves & Penny DeHaven (1972) C&W#54/Tammy Wynette (1981) C&W#18; *Don't Bring Me Down* [i] Animals (1966) US#12 UK#6; *Don't Ever Change* [i] Crickets (1962) UK#5, *Don't Say Nothin' Bad About My Baby* [i] Cookies (1963) R&B#3 US#7, *Every Breath I Take* [i] Gene Pitney (1960) US#42, *Go*

Away, Little Girl [i] Mark Wynter (1962) UK#6/ Steve Lawrence (1963) R&B#14 US#1/Happenings (1966) US#12/Tokens (1969) US#118/Donny Osmond (1971) g US#1; *Goin' Back* [i] Dusty Springfield (1966) UK#10/Byrds (1971) US#89; *Halfway to Paradise* [i] Billy Fury (1961) UK#3/Tony Orlando (1961) US#39/Bobby Vinton (1968) US#23; *He Knows I Love Him Too Much* [i] Paris Sisters (1962) US#34, *He's a Rebel* [i] Crystals (1962) US#1/Vikki Carr (1962) US#115; *He's in Town* [i] Tokens (1964) US#43/Rockin' Berries (1964) UK#3; *Her Royal Majesty* [i] James Darren (1962) US#6 UK#36, *Hey, Girl* [i] Freddie Scott (1963) R&B#10 US#10/Small Faces (1966) UK#10/Mamas & Papas (1967) US#34/ Bobby Vee (1968) US#35/Panhandle (1969) US#122/ Lettermen (1970) US#104/George Kerr (1970) R&B#15 US#124/Donny Osmond (1971) g US#9/ Isaac Hayes (1986) R&B#9/Michael McDonald (1993) R&B#125; *Hi-De-Ho* [i] Blood, Sweat & Tears (1970) US#14, *How Many Tears* [i] Bobby Vee (1961) US#63 UK#10, *Hung on You* [i] Righteous Brothers (1962) US#47, *I Can't Hear You No More* [i] Betty Everett (1964) US#66/Helen Reddy (1976) US#29; *I Can't Make It Alone* [i] P.J. Proby (1966) UK#37, *I Can't Stay Mad at You* [i] Skeeter Davis (1963) C&W#14 US#7, *I Feel the Earth Move* Martika (1989) US#25, *I Need You* [i] Chuck Jackson (1965) R&B#22 US#75, *I Want to Stay Here* [i] Steve Lawrence & Eydie Gorme (1963) US#28, *I'd Never Find Another You* [i] Billy Fury (1961) UK#5, *I'm into Something Good* [i] Earl-Jean (1964) US#38/Herman's Hermits (1964) g US#13 UK#1; *I've Got Bonnie* [i] Bobby Rydell (1961) US#18, *Is This What I Get for Loving You?* [i] Ronettes (1965) US#75/Marianne Faithfull (1967) UK#43; *It's Going to Take Some Time* [vi] Carpenters (1972) US#12, *It's Too Late* [vi] Bill Deal & the Rhondells (1972) US#108/Isley Brothers (1973) R&B#39/Quartz with Dina Carroll (1991) UK#8; *Just Another Fool* [i] Curtis Lee (1962) US#110, *Just Once in My Life* [ii] Righteous Brothers (1965) R&B#26 US#9, *Keep Your Hands Off My Baby* [i] Little Eva (1962) R&B#6 US#12 UK#30, *Let Me Get Close to You* [i] Skeeter Davis (1964) C&W#45 US#106, *Let's Start the Party Again* [i] Little Eva (1963) US#123, *Let's Turkey Trot* [i] Little Eva (1962) R&B#16 US#20 UK#13, *Loco-motion, The* [i] Little Eva (1962) g R&B#1 US#1 UK#2, re-issued (1972) UK#11/Vernons Girls (1962) UK#47/Grand Funk Railroad (1974) g US#1/Dave Stewart & Barbara Gaskin (1986) UK#70/Kylie Minogue (1988) US#3 UK#2; *Lucky 7 Megamix* Mixmasters (1991) UK#43, *No Sad Song* Helen Reddy (1971) US#62, *Oh No, Not My Baby* [i] Maxine Brown (1964) US#24/Manfred Mann (1965) UK#11/Merry Clayton (1972) R&B#30 US#72/Rod Stewart (1973) US#59 UK#6/Deblanc (1976) R&B#70/Cher (1992) UK#33; *One Fine Day*

[i] Chiffons (1963) R&B#6 US#5 UK#29/Julie (1975) US#93/Rita Coolidge (1979) US#66; *Pleasant Valley Sunday* [i] Monkees (1967) g US#3 UK#11/ Wedding Present on B-side of *Come Play with Me* (1992) UK#10; *Point of No Return* [i] Gene McDaniels (1962) R&B#23 US#21, *Poor Little Rich Girl* [i] Steve Lawrence (1963) US#27, *Porpoise Song* Monkees (1968) US#62, *Sharing You* [i] Bobby Vee (1962) US#15 UK#10, *Show Me Girl* [i] Herman's Hermits (1964) UK#19, *So Far Away* Crusaders (1972) US#114, *Some Kind of Wonderful* [i] Drifters (1961) R&B#6 US#32/Soul Brothers Six (1967) US#91/Thee Prophets (1969) US#111/Blow Monkeys (1987) UK#67; *Some of Your Lovin'* [i] Dusty Springfield (1965) UK#8, *Take Good Care of My Baby* [i] Bobby Vee (1961) g US#1 UK#3/Bobby Vinton (1968) US#33; *This Little Girl* [i] Dion (1963) US#21, *Time Don't Run Out on Me* [i] Anne Murray (1985) C&W#2, *Up on the Roof* [i] Drifters (1962) g R&B#4 US#5/Kenny Lynch (1962) UK#10/Julie Grant (1963) UK#33/ Cryan' Shames (1968) US#85/Laura Nyro (1970) US#92/James Taylor (1979) US#28/II D Extreme (1993) R&B#33 US#103/Robson & Jerome (1995) UK#1; *Walk on In* Lou Rawls (1972) US#106, *Walking Proud* [i] Steve Lawrence (1963) US#26, *Walkin' with My Angel* [i] Bobby Vee (1961) US#53, *What a Sweet Thing That Was* [i] Shirelles (1961) US#54, *What I Gotta Do (To Make You Jealous)* [i] Little Eva (1963) US#101, *When My Little Girl Is Smiling* [i] Drifters (1962) US#28 UK#31, re-issued (1976) UK#69/Craig Douglas (1962) UK#9/Jimmy Justice (1962) US#127 UK#9/Steve Alaimo (1971) US#72; *Where You Lead* Barbra Streisand (1971) US#40, re-issued (1972) US#37; *Will You Love Me Tomorrow* [i] Shirelles (1961) g R&B#2 US#1 UK#4/Four Seasons (1968) US#24/Linda Ronstadt (1970) US#111/Roberta Flack (1972) R&B#38 US#76, also on B-side of *The First Time Ever I Saw Your Face* (1972) UK#14/Linda K. Lance (1973) C&W#74/Melanie (1973) US#82 UK#37/Jody Miller (1975) C&W#69/Dana Valery (1976) US#95/Donnie Elbert (1977) R&B#94/ Dave Mason (1978) US#39/Cheryl Handy (1987) C&W#56/Bryan Ferry (1993) UK#23; *(You Make Me Feel Like) A Natural Woman* [iii] Aretha Franklin (1967) R&B#2 US#8/Mary J. Blige (1995) UK#23; *You've Got a Friend* James Taylor (1971) g US#1 UK#4/Roberta Flack & Donny Hathaway (1971) R&B#8 US#29; *Yours Until Tomorrow* [i] Gene Pitney (1968) UK#34. Co-writers; [i] Gerry Goffin, [ii] Gerry Goffin/Phil Spector, [iii] Gerry Goffin/Jerry Wexler, [iv] Howard Greenfield, [v] David Palmer, [vi] Toni Stern, [vii] Cynthia Weil.

545. KING, Pee Wee (b. Julius Frank Kuczynski, February 18, 1914, Abrams, WI) C&W bandleader and multi-instrumentalist. A 1930s bandleader who is noted for his introduction of the electric guitar to western swing music. Many future country stars first performed in King's bands, including Eddy Arnold and Ernest Tubb. King was an exceptional fiddle and accordion player, and first played with the Log Cabin Cowboys between 1935–1936, before forming the Golden West Cowboys in 1936. From 1947, King hosted his own radio and television shows in Louisville, and during the late 1950s, he worked with the singer Minnie Pearl. CHART COMPOSITIONS: *Tennessee Waltz* [ii] (1948) C&W#3 US#30, *Tennessee Tears* (1949) C&W#12, *Tennessee Polka* (1949) C&W#3, *Bonaparte's Retreat* (1950) C&W#6, *Slow Poke* [ii] (1951) g C&W#1 US#1, *Silver and Gold* (1952) C&W#5 US#18, *Busybody* (1952) C&W#8 US#27, *Changing Partners* (1954) C&W#4, *Bimbo* (1954) C&W#9, *Backward, Turn Backward* (1954) C&W#15. ALBUMS: **Ballroom King** (1982, Detour); **Rompin', Stompin', Singin', Swingin'** (1984, Bear Family); **Best of Pee Wee King and Redd Stewart** (1987, Starday); **Hog Wild Too** (1990, Zu Zazz). HIT VERSIONS: *Bimbo* Jim Reeves (1954) C&W#1 US#26/Ruby Wright (1954) UK#7; *Bonaparte's Retreat* Gene Krupa (1950) US#9/Kay Starr (1950) US#4/Glen Campbell (1974) C&W#3; *Slow Poke* [ii] Roberta Lee (1951) US#13/Ralph Flanagan (1952) US#6/Arthur Godfrey (1952) US#12/Hawkshaw Hawkins (1952) C&W#7 US#26/Helen O'-Connell (1952) US#8; *Tennessee Waltz* [ii] Roy Acuff (1948) C&W#12/Cowboy Copas (1948) C&W#3/ Erskine Hawkins (1950)

546. KNIGHT, Holly (b. America) Pop

keyboard player and vocalist. A songwriter who first performed in the American group Spider. CHART COMPOSITIONS: *New Romance (It's a Mystery)* (1980) US#39, *Everything Is Alright* (1980) US#86, *It Didn't Take Long* (1981) US#43. ALBUMS: **Spider** (1980) US#130, **Between the Lines** (1981, both Dreamland) US#185. Knight subsequently formed the group Device, which charted with *Hanging on a Heart Attack* [i] (1986) US#35 and *Who Says?* [i] (1986) US#79, from the album **22B3** (1986, Chrysalis) US#73. After a brief attempt at a solo career, charting with *Heart Don't Fail Me Now* (1988) US#59, Knight became a successful co-writer for other artists. HIT VERSIONS: *Change* John Waite (1985) US#54, *Little Darlin'* [iii] Sheila (1981) US#49, *Never* [iv] Heart (1985) US#4, re-issued (1988) UK#8; *Obsession* [ii] Animotion (1985) US#6, *One of the Living* Tina Turner (1985) US#15 UK#55, *Warrior, The* [v] Scandal featuring Patti Smith (1984) US#7. Co-writers: [i] Mike Chapman, [ii] Michael Des Barres, [iii] A. Blue, [iv] Gene Bloch/Connie, [v] Nick Gilder. (q.v Mike CHAPMAN and Nicky CHINN, Simon CLIMIE, Lou GRAMM, Albert HAMMOND, Paul STANLEY, Steven TYLER, Ann WILSON and Nancy WILSON.)

547. KNOPFLER, Mark (b. August 12,

1949, Glasgow, Scotland) Rock guitarist, vocalist and producer. A former journalist who fronted the group Dire Straits, which became one of the best selling bands of the 1980s, their album **Brothers in Arms** (1985), shifting over twenty million copies worldwide. CHART COMPOSITIONS: *Sultans of Swing* (1979) US#4 UK#8, re-issued (1988) UK#62; *Lady Writer* (1979) US#45 UK#51, *Skateaway* (1981) US#58 UK#37, *Romeo and Juliet* (1981) UK#8, *Tunnel of Love* (1981) UK#54, *Private Investigation* (1982) UK#2, *Industrial Disease* (1983) US#75, *Twisting By the Pool EP* (1983) UK#14, *Love Over Gold/Solid Rock* (1984) UK#50, *So Far Away* (1985) US#19 UK#20, *Money for Nothing* [i] (1985) p US#1 UK#4, *Brothers in Arms* (1985) UK#16, *Walk of Life* (1986) US#7 UK#2, *Your Latest Trick* (1986) UK#26, *Calling Elvis* (1991) UK#21, *Heavy Fuel* (1991) UK#55, *On Every Street* (1992) UK#42, *The Bug* (1992) UK#67, *Encores EP* (1993) UK#31. ALBUMS: **Dire Straits** (1978) p US#2 UK#5, **Communique** (1979) g US#11 UK#5, **Making Movies** (1981) g US#19 UK#4, **Love Over Gold** (1982) g US#19 UK#1, **Alchemy-Dire Straits Live** (1984) US#46 UK#3, **Brothers in Arms** (1985) p US#1 UK#1, **On Every Street** (1991) p US#12 UK#1, **On the Night** (1993, all Vertigo) US#116 UK#4. COMPILATION: **Twisting By the Pool** (1983, Warner Brothers) US#53; **Money for Nothing** (1988, Vertigo) g US#62 UK#1; **Live at the BBC** (1995, Windsong) UK#71. Knopfler has also recorded as a solo artist and written film scores. CHART COMPOSITIONS: *Going Home* (1983) UK#56, *Darling Pretty* (1996) UK#33, *Cannibals* (1996) UK#42. ALBUMS: **Local Hero** ost (1982) UK#14, **Cal** ost (1984, both Vertigo) UK#65; **The Princess Bride** ost (1987, Warner Brothers) US#180; **Missing…Presumed Having a Good Time** as the Notting Hillbillies (1990, Vertigo) US#52 UK#2; **Last Exit to Brooklyn** ost (1990); **Neck and Neck** with Chet Atkins (1990, CBS) US#127 UK#41; **Screenplaying** (1993), **Golden Heart** (1996, both Vertigo) US#105 UK#9. HIT VERSIONS: *Bug, The* Mary Chapin-Carpenter (1993) C&W#18, *Private Dancer* Tina Turner (1985) R&B#3 US#7 UK#26, *Setting Me Up* Highway 101 (1989) C&W#2, *When It Comes to You* John Anderson (1992) C&W#4. Co-writer: [i] Sting.

548. KOEHLER, Ted (b. 1894; d. 1973,

both America) Film and stage lyricist. A Tin Pan Alley composer who collaborated with some of the best known tunesmiths of the day. HIT VERSIONS: *Don't Worry 'Bout Me* [i] Hal Kemp (1939) US#5/

Frank Sinatra (1954) US#17; *Everybody's Twisting* [i] Frank Sinatra (1962) UK#22, *Out in the Cold Again* [i] Glen Gray (1934) US#4/Richard Hayes (1951) US#9; *Some Sunday Morning* [ii] Helen Forrest & Dick Haymes (1945) US#9/Wayne Newton (1965) US#123; *Sweet Dreams, Sweetheart* [iii] Ray Noble (1945) US#14, *Truckin'* [i] Mills Blue Rhythm Band (1935) US#11/Fats Waller (1935) US#1. Co-writers: [i] Rube Bloom, [ii] Ray Heindorf/M.K. Jerome, [iii] M.K. Jerome. (*See also under* Harold ARLEN, Harry BARRIS, Jimmy MONACO, Gus KAHN.)

549. KOTTKE, Leo (b. September 11, 1945, Athens, GA) Folk guitarist and vocalist. A supremely talented 12-string acoustic guitarist, who specializes in blending folk, country, bluegrass and jazz, on improvisational instrumental pieces. Kottke is sometimes a fine songwriter of ironic material, that he delivers in a dry, deadpan baritone. ALBUMS: **12-String Blues: Live at the Scholar Coffee House** (1969, Oblivion) re-issued as **Circle 'Round the Sun** (1970, Symposium); **6 and 12-String Guitar** (1969, Takoma); **Mudlark** (1971) US#168, **Greenhouse** (1972) US#127, **My Feet Are Smiling** (1973) US#108, **Ice Water** (1973) US#69, **Dreams and All That Stuff** (1974) US#45, **Chewing Pine** (1974, all Capitol) US#114; **Leo Kottke** (1976) US#107, **Burnt Lips** (1978) US#143, **Balance** (1979), **Live in Europe** (1980), **Guitar Music** (1982), **Time Step** (1983, all Chrysalis); **Regards from Chuck Pink** (1986), **My Father's Face** (1987), **A Shout Towards Noon** (1989), **That's What** (1990), **Great Big Boy** (1991), **Peculiaroso** (1994), **Live** (1995) **Standing in My Shoes** (1997, all Private). COMPILATIONS: **Leo Kottke, 1971–76: Did You Hear Me?** (1976) US#153, **Best of Leo Kottke** (1979, both Capitol).

550. KRAMER, Alex (b. 1893; d. 1955, both America), and **WHITNEY, Joan** (b. 1914, America) Both film and stage composers. A songwriting duo that composed material for such films as "South of Dixie" (1943) and "Meet Miss Bobby Socks" (1945), alongside the show "High Time" (1946). HIT VERSIONS: *Ain't Nobody Here But Us Chickens* Louis Jordan (1947) R&B#1 US#6, *Candy* [i] King Sisters (1945) US#15/Johnny Long (1945) US#8/Johnny Mercer & Jo Stafford (1945) US#1/ Dinah Shore (1945) US#5/Jerry Wald (1945) US#18; *Far Away Places* Perry Como (1949) US#4/Bing Crosby (1949) US#2/Dinah Shore (1949) US#14/ Margaret Whiting (1949) US#2; *High on a Windy Hill* Will Bradley (1941) US#9/Jimmy Dorsey (1941) US#1/Gene Krupa (1941) US#2/Vaughn Monroe (1941) US#13; *It All Comes Back to Me Now* [ii] Eddy Duchin (1941) US#14/Hal Kemp (1941) US#5/Gene Krupa (1941) US#2/Ted Weems (1941) US#22; *It's*

Love, Love, Love! [i] Guy Lombardo (1944) US#1/ King Sisters (1944) US#4; *Love Somebody* Doris Day & Buddy Clark (1948) g US#1, *Money Is the Root of All Evil* Andrews Sisters (1946) US#9, *My Sister and I* [ii] Bob Chester (1941) US#17/Jimmy Dorsey (1941) US#1/Benny Goodman (1941) US#20/Bea Wain (1941) US#15; *No Other Arms, No Other Lips* [ii] Chordettes (1959) US#27, *That's the Beginning of the End* Perry Como (1947) US#19, *You'll Never Get Away* [ii] Teresa Brewer & Don Cornell (1952) US#17. Co-writers: [i] Mack David, [ii] Hy Zaret.

551. KRAVITZ, Lenny (b. May 26, 1964, New York, NY) Rock-R&B multi-instrumentalist, producer and vocalist. A teenage actor who, heavily influenced by Jimi Hendrix and James Brown, has pursued a musical career since the early 1990s. CHART COMPOSITIONS: *Let Love Rule* (1990) US#89 UK#39, *Mr. Cabdriver* (1990) UK#58, *Always on the Run* (1991) UK#41, *It Ain't Over 'Til It's Over* (1991) R&B#10 US#2 UK#11, *Stand By My Woman* [ii] (1991) US#76 UK#55, *What Goes Around Comes Around* (1991) R&B#38, *Are You Gonna Go My Way* (1993) UK#4, *Believe* [i] (1993) US#60 UK#30, *Heaven Help* (1993) US#80 UK#20, *Is There Any Love in Your Heart* (1993) UK#52, *Rock and Roll Is Dead* (1995) US#75 UK#22, *Circus* (1995) UK#54, *Can't Get You Off My Mind* (1996) US#62 UK#54. ALBUMS: **Let Love Rule** (1989) g US#61 UK#56, **Mama Said** (1991) p US#39 UK#8, **Are You Gonna Go My Way** (1993) p US#12 UK#1, **Circus** (1995) g US#10 UK#5; **5** (1998, all Virgin). HIT VERSION: *Be My Baby* Vanessa Paradis (1992) UK#6. Co-writers: [i] H. Hirsch, [ii] H. Hirsch/A. Krizan/ S. Pasch. (*See also under* Madonna)

552. KRISTOFFERSON, Kris (b. Kristoffer Kristofferson, June 22, 1936, Brownsville, TX) C&W guitarist and vocalist. A periodically brilliant songwriter, whose best songs evoke an element of honesty, warmth and old world Americana. Fellow songwriter Felice Bryant once said of him, "Kris Kristofferson brought the bedroom onto the Opry stage." During his teens, Kristofferson learned the guitar and developed a love of country music, and after publishing some of his short stories in the *Atlantic Monthly* magazine, he studied as a Rhodes Scholar at Oxford University, England, where he also wrote two unpublished novels. As Kit Carson, Kristofferson turned to songwriting and performing, but his musical career was interrupted when he enlisted in the U.S. Army in 1960, serving five years in West Germany as a pilot. After teaching English at West Point, Kristofferson returned to songwriting and headed to Nashville, where his first songs to be recorded were *Viet Nam Blues* by Dave Dudley and

Jody and the Kid by Roy Drusky. After Roger Miller scored a country hit with *Me and Bobby McGee* (1969), Kristofferson began recording his own albums, which were fertile ground for other artists in search of a hit. Between 1973–1979, he was married to the singer Rita Coolidge, and between 1971–1993, he starred in nearly thirty films, including the infamous "Heaven's Gate" (1980). Willie Nelson recorded an entire album of his material, **Willie Nelson Sings Kristofferson** (1979, Columbia) p US#42. CHART COMPOSITIONS: *Loving Her Was Easier (Than Anything I'll Ever Do Again)* (1971) US#26, *Josie* (1972) C&W#70 US#63, *Jesus Was a Capricorn* (1973) US#91, *Why Me* (1973) g C&W#1 US#16, *Prove It to You One More Time Again* (1980) C&W#91, *Nobody Loves Anybody Anymore* (1981) C&W#68, *How Do You Feel About Foolin' Around* [i]*** (1984) C&W#46, *They Killed Him* (1987) C&W#67. ALBUMS: **Kristofferson** (1970) re-issued as **Me and Bobby McGee** (1971) g US#43, **The Silver Tongued Devil and I** (1971) g US#21, **Border Lord** (1972) US#41, **Jesus Was a Capricorn** (1973, all Monument) g US#31; **Full Moon**** (1973, A&M) g US#26; **Spooky Lady's Sideshow** (1974) US#78, **Breakaway**** (1974) US#103, **Who's to Bless and Who's to Blame** (1975) US#105, **Surreal Thing** (1976, all Monument) US#180; **A Star Is Born** with Barbra Streisand ost (1976, Columbia) p US#1 UK#1; **Easter Island** (1978) US#86, **Shake Hands with the Devil** (1979, both Monument); **Natural Act**** (1979, A&M) US#106 UK#35; **To the Bone** (1981), **Music from Songwriter**** ost (1984, both Columbia) US#152; **The Winning Hand** with Brenda Lee, Dolly Parton and Willie Nelson (1983, Monument) US#109; **Highwayman*** (1985, Columbia) g US#92; **Re-possessed** (1987), **Third World Warrior** (1990, both Mercury); **Highwayman 2*** (1990, Columbia) US#79; **The Road Goes on Forever*** (1995, Liberty); **A Moment of Forever** (1995, Justice). COMPILATIONS: **The Songs of Kris Kristofferson** (1977, Monument) g US#45; **Singer/Songwriter** (1991, Columbia). HIT VERSIONS: *Come Sundown* Bobby Bare (1970) C&W#7 US#122, *Enough for You* Brenda Lee (1981) C&W#75, *For the Good Times* Ray Price (1971) g C&W#1 US#11/Perry Como (1973) UK#7/7th Wonder (1973) R&B#51; *Help Me Make It Through the Night* [ii] Joe Simon (1971) R&B#13 US#69/O.C. Smith (1971) R&B#38 US#91/Sammi Smith (1971) g C&W#1 US#8/Gladys Knight & the Pips (1972) R&B#13 US#33 UK#11/John Holt (1974) UK#6/Willie Nelson (1979) C&W#4/Pinkard & Bowden in *Adventures in Parodies* (1984) C&W#64; *I Won't Mention It Again* Ray Price (1971) C&W#1 US#42/Ruby Winters (1978) UK#45; *I'd Rather Be Sorry* Patti Page (1971) C&W#63/Ray Price (1971) C&W#2 US#70; *I've Got to Have You* Peggy Little

(1971) C&W#75/Sammi Smith (1972) C&W#13 US#77; *If It's All the Same to You* Bill Anderson & Jan Howard (1969) C&W#2, *Jody and the Kid* Roy Drusky (1968) C&W#24, *Last Time, The* Johnny Cash (1980) C&W#85, *Loving Gift, The* Johnny Cash & June Carter (1973) C&W#27, *Loving Her Was Easier (Than Anything I'll Ever Do Again)* Roger Miller (1971) C&W#28/Tompall & the Glaser Brothers (1981) C&W#2; *Me and Bobby McGee* Roger Miller (1969) C&W#12 US#122/Janis Joplin (1971) g US#1/Jerry Lee Lewis (1971) C&W#1 US#40; *Nobody Wins* Brenda Lee (1973) C&W#1 US#70, *Once More with Feeling* Jerry Lee Lewis (1970) C&W#2/Willie Nelson (1970) C&W#42; *One Day at a Time* [iii] Don Gibson (1974) C&W#8/Marilyn Sellars (1974) C&W#19 US#37/Lena Martell (1979) UK#1/Christy Lane (1980) C&W#1; *Please Don't Tell Me How the Story Ends* Bobby Bare (1971) C&W#8/Ronnie Milsap (1974) C&W#1 US#95; *Stranger* Johnny Duncan (1976) C&W#4, *Sunday Mornin' Comin' Down* Ray Stevens (1969) C&W#55 US#81/Johnny Cash (1970) C&W#1 US#46; *Taker, The* Waylon Jennings (1970) C&W#5 US#94, *Viet Nam Blues* Dave Dudley (1966) C&W#12 US#127, *You're Gonna Love Yourself (In the Morning)* Wayne Carson (1973) C&W#77/Roy Clark (1975) C&W#35/Charlie Rich (1980) C&W#22/Willie Nelson & Brenda Lee (1983) C&#43. With: * Johnny Cash, Waylon Jennings and Willie Nelson, ** Rita Coolidge, *** Willie Nelson. Co-writers: [i] S.Bruton/Mike Utley, [ii] Fred L. Foster, [iii] Marijon Wilkin.

553. LAKE, Greg (b. November 10, 1948, Bournemouth, England) Rock bassist, guitarist and vocalist. A founder member of the late 1960s progressive-rock group King Crimson, which charted with *In the Court of the Crimson King* [ii] (1969) US#80. Lake featured on the group's albums **In the Court of the Crimson King** (1969) g US#28 UK#5, **In the Wake of Poseidon** (1970, both Island) US#31 UK#4; **A Young Person's Guide to King Crimson** (1976, EG); and **Epitaph: Live in 1969** (1997, Discipline). Lake left King Crimson in 1970 to form the more classically oriented rock trio Emerson, Lake and Palmer, which charted with his compositions *Lucky Man* (1971) US#48, re-issued (1973) US#51; *From the Beginning* (1972) US#39, *C'est La Vie* [iv] (1977) US#91, and *Touch and Go* [i] (1986) US#60. ALBUMS: **Emerson, Lake and Palmer** (1970) g US#18 UK#4, **Tarkus** (1971) g US#9 UK#1, **Pictures at an Exhibition** (1971) g US#10 UK#3, **Trilogy** (1972, all Island) g US#5 UK#2; **Brain Salad Surgery** (1974) g US#11 UK#2, **Welcome Back My Friends to the Show That Never Ends: Ladies and Gentlemen...Emerson, Lake and Palmer** (1974, both Manticore) g US#4 UK#5; **Works** (1977) g US#12 UK#9, **Love Beach** (1978, both Atlantic) g US#55 UK#48; **In Concert** (1979) US#73, **Emerson, Lake and Powell** (1986, both Polydor) US#23 UK#35; **Black Moon** (1992) US#78, **Live at the Royal Albert Hall** (1993), **In the Hot Seat** (1994, all Victory). COMPILATIONS: **Works, Volume 2** (1977) g US#37 UK#20, **Best of Emerson, Lake and Palmer** (1979) US#108, **The Atlantic Years** (1992, all Atlantic); **Return of the Manticore** (1993, Manticore). After a brief stint with the group Asia in 1983, Lake linked up with Keith Emerson as the group 3, releasing the album **To the Power of Three** (1988, Geffen) US#97. He has also recorded as a solo artist. CHART COMPOSITION: *I Believe in Father Christmas* [iii] (1975) US#95 UK#2. ALBUMS: **Greg Lake** (1981) US#62 UK#62, **Manoeuvres** (1983, both Chrysalis). COMPILATION: **From the Beginning** (1997, Rhino). HIT VERSION: *I Talk to the Wind* [ii] Opus III (1992) UK#52. Co-writers: [i] Keith Emerson (b. November 2, 1944, Todmorden, England), [ii] Robert Fripp (b. April 11, 1945, Wimborne, England)/Michael Giles (b. 1942, Bournemouth, England)/Ian MacDonald/Pete Sinfield, [iii] Sergey Sergeyevich Prokofiev (b. April 27, 1891, Sontsovka, Ekaterinoslav; d. March 5, 1953, Moscow, Russia)/Pete Sinfield, [iv] Pete Sinfield.

554. LAMBERT, Dennis Pop producer and vocalist. A successful R&B tinged pop producer, whose first hit was with *Do the Freddie* [iii] by Freddie and the Dreamers in 1965. Lambert was a successful producer during the 1970s, working with the Grass Roots, the Four Tops, the Righteous Brothers and Glen Campbell. He also recorded as a solo artist in the early 1970s. ALBUMS: **At Home*** (1970, A&M); **Bags and Things** (1972, Dunhill); **As You Will*** (1973, 20th Century). HIT VERSIONS: *Ain't No Woman (Like the One I've Got)* [ix] Four Tops (1972) g R&B#2 US#4, *Aphrodisiac (You're My)* Dennis Edwards (1984) R&B#15, *Are You Man Enough* [ix] Four Tops (1973) R&B#2 US#15, *Ashes to Ashes* 5th Dimension (1973) US#52, *Break It to Me Gently* [x] Juice Newton (1982) C&W#2 US#11, *Country Boy (You've Got Your Feet in L.A.)* [ix] Glen Campbell (1975) C&W#3 US#11, *Do the Freddie* [iii] Freddie & the Dreamers (1965) US#18, *Don't Look Any Further* [vi] Dennis Edwards (1983) R&B#2 US#72 UK#45, re-entry (1987) UK#55/Kane Gang (1988) US#64; *Don't Pull Your Love Out* [ix] Glen Campbell (1976) C&W#4 US#27/Hamilton, Joe, Frank & Reynolds (1971) US#4; *Dream On* [ix] Righteous Brothers (1974) US#32/Oak Ridge Boys (1979) C&W#7; *Give It to the People* [ix] Righteous Brothers (1974) US#20, *Goin' to the Bank* [v] Commodores (1986) R&B#2 US#65 UK#43, *Gonna Be*

Alright Now [ix] Gayle McCormick (1971) US#84, *I Just Can't Get You Out of My Mind* [ix] Four Tops (1974) R&B#18 US#62, *If Looks Could Kill* [i] Player (1982) US#48, *It Only Takes a Minute* [ix] Tavares (1975) R&B#1 US#10 UK#46/100 Ton & a Feather (1976) UK#9/Take That (1993) UK#7; *It's a Crying Shame* [ix] Gayle McCormick (1971) US#44, *Keeper of the Castle* [ix] Four Tops (1972) R&B#7 US#10 UK#18, *Look in My Eyes Pretty Woman* [ix] Tony Orlando & Dawn (1974) US#11, *Love I Never Had, The* [ix] Tavares (1976) R&B#11, *Love on My Mind Tonight* [i] Temptations (1983) R&B#17 US#88, *Mama You're Alright with Me* [ix] Four Tops (1976) R&B#72 US#107, *Moment of Truth, The* [ii] Survivor (1984) US#63, *Nightshift* [iv] Commodores (1985) g R&B#1 US#3 UK#3, *Once a Fool* [ix] Kiki Dee (1976) US#82, *One Chain Don't Make No Prison* [ix] Four Tops (1974) R&B#3 US#41/Santana (1979) R&B#68 US#59; *One Tin Soldier* [ix] Coven (1971) US#26/Skeeter Davis (1972) C&W#54; *Put a Little Love Away* [ix] Emotions (1974) R&B#53 US#73, *Remember What I Told You to Forget* [ix] Tavares (1975) R&B#4 US#25, *See You on Sunday* [ix] Glen Campbell (1976) C&W#18, *This Heart* [ix] Gene Redding (1974) US#34, *Too Late* [ix] Tavares (1974) R&B#10 US#59, *Two Divided By Love* [vii] Grass Roots (1972) US#16/Kendalls (1972) C&W#53; *We Built This City* [viii] Starship (1985) g US#1 UK#12, *You Brought the Woman Out of Me* [ix] Evie Sands (1975) US#50/Hot (1978) US#71. With: * Craig Nuttycoombe. Co-writers: [i] P. Beckett, [ii] P. Beckett/Bill Conti, [iii] Lou Courtney, [iv] Frannie Golde/Walter Lee Orange (b. December 10, 1947, FA), [v] Frannie Golde/Andy Goldmark, [vi] Frannie Golde/D. Hitching, [vii] Marty Kupps/Brian Potter, [viii] Martin Page/Bernie Taupin/Peter Wolfe, [ix] Brian Potter, [x] J. Seneca.

555. LAMM, Robert (b. October 13, 1944, New York, NY) Rock keyboard player and vocalist. A founder member of the jazz-rock group Chicago, who composed many of the group's initial hits. CHART COMPOSITIONS: *Questions 67 and 68* (1969) US#71 UK#24, *Twenty Five or Six to Four* [i] (1970) US#4 UK#7, new version (1971) US#48; *Does Anybody Really Know What Time It Is?* (1971) US#7, *Free* (1971) US#20, *Beginnings* (1971) US#7, *Harry Truman* (1975) US#13, *Saturday in the Park* (1972) g US#3, *Another Rainy Day in New York City* (1976) US#32, *Thunder and Lightning* [ii] (1980) US#56. ALBUMS: **Chicago Transit Authority** (1969) p US#17 UK#9, **Chicago II** (1970) g US#4 UK#6, **Chicago III** (1971) p US#2 UK#31, **Chicago at Carnegie Hall** (1971) p US#3, **Chicago V** (1972) p US#1, **Chicago VI** (1973) p US#1, **Live in Japan** (1973), **Chicago VII** (1974) p US#1, **Chicago VIII**

(1975) p US#1, **Chicago X** (1976) p US#3 UK#21, **Chicago XI** (1977) p US#6, **Hot Streets** (1978) p US#12, **Chicago 13** (1979) g US#21, **Chicago XIV** (1980, all Columbia) US#71; **Chicago 16** (1982) p US#9 UK#44, **Chicago 17** (1984, both Full Moon) p US#4 UK#24; **Chicago 18** (1986, Warner Brothers) g US#35, **Chicago 19** (1988) p US#37, **Twenty 1** (1991, both Reprise) US#66; **Night and Day** (1995, Giant) US#90. COMPILATIONS: **Chicago IX-Greatest Hits** (1975) p US#1, **Greatest Hits, Volume 2** (1981, both Columbia) US#171; **Love Songs** (1982, TVR) UK#42; **The Heart of Chicago** (1989, CBS) UK#6; **Greatest Hits, 1982–1989** (1989, Reprise) p US#37; **Chicago-Group Portrait** (1991, Legacy). Lamm has also recorded an album as a solo artist, **Skinny Boy** (1974, Columbia). HIT VERSION: *Does Anybody Really Know What Time It Is?* Copper N' Brass (1970) US#103. Co-writers: [i] James Pankow, [ii] David Seraphine.

556. LANE, Burton (b. February 2, 1912, New York, NY) Film and stage composer, pianist. A staff pianist at the Remick publishing company for twenty years, who was a tunesmith of considerable merit. Lane contributed to the revues "Three's a Crowd" (1930), "Earl Carroll's Vanities of 1931," "Laffing Room Only" (1944), and "Finian's Rainbow" (1947), alongside the films "Dancing Lady" (1933), "Some Like It Hot" (1939) and "Babes on Broadway" (1941). ALBUMS: **On a Clear Day You Can See Forever** oc (1965, RCA) US#59; **Finian's Rainbow** ost (1968, Warner Brothers) US#90; **On a Clear Day You Can See Forever** ost (1970, Columbia) US#108. HIT VERSIONS: *Everything I Have Is Yours* [i] George Olsen (1933) US#17/Rudy Vallee (1934) US#3/Billy Eckstine (1948) R&B#11 US#30/Eddie Fisher (1952) US#23 UK#8; *Feudin' and Fightin'* [iii] Bing Crosby (1947) US#9/Dorothy Shay (1947) US#4/Jo Stafford (1947) US#7; *How About You?* [iv] Tommy Dorsey (1942) US#8/Dick Jurgens (1942) US#21/Frank Sinatra on *Songs for Swinging Lovers LP* (1956) UK#12; *How Are Things in Glocca Morra?* [v] Buddy Clark (1947) US#6/Tommy Dorsey (1947) US#9/Dick Haymes (1947) US#9/Martha Tilton (1947) US#8; *How Could You Believe Me When I Said I Loved You When You Know I've Been a Liar All My Life?* [vi] Fred Astaire (1951) US#30, *How'd Ja Like to Love Me?* [vii] Dolly Dawn (1938) US#17/Jimmy Dorsey (1938) US#4; *I'll Take Tallulah* [v] Tommy Dorsey (1942) US#15, *Lady's in Love with You, The* [vi] Bob Crosby (1939) US#13/Glenn Miller (1939) US#2; *Last Call for Love* [ii] Tommy Dorsey (1942) US#17, *Old Devil Moon* [v] Gene Krupa (1947) US#21/Margaret Whiting (1947) US#11/Frank Sinatra on *Songs for Swinging Lovers LP* (1956) UK#12; *On a Clear Day You Can See Forever*

[vi] Robert Goulet (1965) US#119, *Says My Heart* [vii] Andrews Sisters (1938) US#10/Tommy Dorsey (1938) US#7/George Hall (1938) US#10/Ozzie Nelson (1938) US#5/Red Norvo (1938) US#4; *Swing High, Swing Low* [iv] Dorothy Lamour (1937) US#16/Russ Morgan (1937) US#13; *Tony's Wife* [i] Gertrude Niesen (1933) US#19. Co-writers: [i] Harold Adamson, [ii] Margery Cummings/E.Y. Harburg, [iii] Al Dubin, [iv] Ralph Freed, [v] E.Y. Harburg, [vi] Alan Jay Lerner, [vii] Frank Loesser.

557. LANE, Ronnie (b. April 1, 1946, London, England; d. June 4, 1997, Trinidad, CO) Rock bassist and vocalist. A founder member, with Steve Marriott, of the Small Faces, one of Britain's best loved 1960s groups. Elements of the group later became Rod Stewart's first backing band, a ramshackle but good-time unit that recorded the albums **First Step** (1970) US#119 UK#45, **Long Player** (1971) UK#31, **A Nod's as Good as a Wink…To a Blind Horse** (1971) US#6 UK#2, and **Ooh La La** (1973, all Warner Brothers) US#21 UK#1. COMPILATION: **Best of the Faces** (1977, Warner Brothers) UK#24. Lane left the Faces in 1973, to form his own band Slim Chance, which enjoyed a brief period of chart success during the mid-1970s. From 1982, Lane resided in America, where he suffered, and eventually died from, multiple sclerosis. CHART COMPOSITIONS: *How Come* [i] (1974) UK#11, *The Poacher* (1974) UK#36. ALBUMS: **Anymore for Evermore** (1974, GM) UK#48; **Ronnie Lane's Slim Chance** (1975), **One for the Road** (1976, both Island); **See Me** (1979, Gem); **Rough Mix** with Pete Townshend (1977, Polydor) US#45 UK#44. Co-writer: [i] Clive Westlake. (*See also under* Ronnie LANE and Steve MARRIOTT.)

558. LANE, Ronnie, and MARRIOTT, Steve. The principal songwriting team in the British mod and psychedelic group the Small Faces. CHART COMPOSITIONS: *Hey Girl* (1966) UK#10, *All or Nothing* (1966) UK#1, *My Mind's Eye* (1966) UK#4, *Here Comes the Nice* (1967) UK#12, *Itchycoo Park* (1967) US#16 UK#3, re-issued (1976) UK#9; *Lazy Sunday* (1968) UK#2, re-issued (1976) UK#39; *The Universal* (1968) UK#16. ALBUMS: **The Small Faces** (1966, Decca) UK#3; **The Small Faces** (1967) UK#12, **Ogden's Nut Gone Flake** (1968) US#159 UK#1, **The Autumn Stone** (1971, all Immediate); **Playmates** (1977), **78 in the Shade** (1978, both Atlantic); **For Your Delight** (1980, Virgin). COMPILATIONS: **There Are But Four Small Faces** (1968, Immediate) US#178; **From the Beginning** (1967) UK#17, **Early Faces** (1972, both Decca) US#176; **Greatest Hits** (1978, Immediate); **Live UK, 1969** (1978, Charly); **Boxed: The Definitive An-**

thology (1996, Repertoire); **The Decca Anthology, 1965–1967** (1996, Decca) UK#66. In 1969, Marriott left the group to form Humble Pie with Peter Frampton, although he did re-form the Small Faces without Lane in 1977. HIT VERSIONS: *Itchycoo Park* M People (1995) UK#11. (*See also under* Peter FRAMPTON, Ronnie LANE, Steve MARRIOTT.)

559. LANG, K.D. (b. Kathryn Dawn Lang, November 2, 1961, Consort, Alberta, Canada) C&W pianist, guitarist and vocalist. A country influenced singer-songwriter, whose songs featured in the films "Hiding Out" (1987), "Shag" (1988), "Dick Tracy" (1990), and "Until the End of the World" (1991). CHART COMPOSITIONS: *Constant Crawling* [i] (1992) US#38 UK#52, re-issued (1993) UK#15; *The Mind of Love* (1993) UK#72, *Miss Chatelaine* (1993) UK#68, *Just Keep Me Moving* (1993) UK#59, *If I Were You* (1995) UK#53, *You're O.K.* (1996) UK#44. ALBUMS: **A Truly Western Experience** (1984, Bumstead); **Angel with a Lariat** (1987), **Shadowland** (1988) g US#73, **Absolute Torch and Twang** (1989) g US#69, **Ingenue** (1992) g US#18 UK#3, **Even Cowgirls Get the Blues** ost (1993) US#82 UK#36, **All You Can Eat** (1995) US#37 UK#7, **Drag** (1997, all Sire). Co-writer: [i] B. Mink.

560. LAUDER, Sir Harry (b. August 4, 1870, Portobello; d. February 26, 1950, Strathaven, both Scotland) Vaudeville performer. A music hall performer, comedian and folk singer, who specialized in such emotional ballads as *It's Nice to Get Up in the Morning* (1913), and other self-penned paeans to his native land. Lauder was knighted in 1919 for entertaining troops during World War I. CHART COMPOSITIONS: *I Love a Lassie (My Scotch Bluebell)* [iii] (1907) US#2, *The Wedding of Sandy McNab* (1908) US#10, *When I Get Back to Bonnie Scotland* (1909) US#7, *She Is My Daisy* [iv] (1909) US#2, *He Was Very Kind to Me* (1909) US#7, *Stop Your Ticklin', Jock* (1910) US#4, *The Bounding Bounder, or "On the Bounding Sea"* (1910) US#10, *We Parted on the Shore* (1910) US#7, *The Blarney Stone* (1910) US#7, *Roamin' in the Gloamin'* (1912) US#5, *The Picnic (Every Ladie Loves a Lassie)* (1912) US#8; *She's the Lass for Me* (1913) US#10, *My Bonny Bonny Jean* (1916) US#9. ALBUMS: **I Love a Lassie** (1980, Pearl); **The Golden Age of Harry Lauder** (1983, Golden Age); **We Parted on the Shore** (1988, Seil). Co-writers: [i] Whit Cunliffe/Gerald Grafton/R.F. Morrison, [ii] William Dillon, [iii] Gerald Grafton, [iv] J.D. Harper.

561. LAUPER, Cyndi (b. Cynthia Anne Stephanie Lauper, June 20, 1953, Brooklyn, NY) Pop vocalist. A distinctive singer who first performed as

a member of the group Blue Angel, recording the album **Blue Angel** (1980, Polydor), before pursuing a solo career. CHART COMPOSITIONS: *Time After Time* [iii] (1984) R&B#78 US#1, *She Bop* [ii] (1984) US#3, *The Goonies 'R' Good Enough* [v] (1985) US#10, *Change of Heart* [vi] (1986) US#3, *Boy Blue* [i] (1987) US#71, *My First Night Without You* [iv] (1989) US#62 UK#53, *Heading West* (1989) UK#68, *The World Is Stone* (1992) UK#15, *I'm Gonna Be Strong* (1995) US#37, *Come on Home* [vii] (1995) UK#39. ALBUMS: **She's So Unusual** (1983) p US#4, **True Colors** (1986, both Portrait) p US#4 UK#25; **A Night to Remember** (1989) US#37, **Hat Full of Stars** (1993) UK#56, **Twelve Deadly Cyns… and Then Some** (1995) US#81 UK#2, **Sisters of Avalon** (1997, all Epic). HIT VERSION: *Time After Time* [iii] Everything But the Girl on *Covers EP* (1992) UK#13. Co-writers: [i] J. Bova/Stephen Lunt, [ii] Richard Chertoff/Gary Corbett/Stephen Lunt, [iii] Robert Hyman, [iv] Tom Kelly/Billy Steinberg, [v] Stephen Lunt/Arthur Stead, [vi] Essra Mohawk, [vii] Pulsford. (*See also under* Jules SHEAR.)

562. LAWRENCE, Jack (b. 1912) Film and stage lyricist. A Tin Pan Alley lyricist who occasionally composed his own melodies. Lawrence collaborated with many composers of his era, and his songs were featured in such films as "Weekend Pass" (1943), "Stars on Parade" (1946) and "Susan Slept Here" (1954). He also wrote for the show "I Had a Ball" (1965). ALBUMS: **The Flame and the Flesh** ost (1954, MGM); **I Had a Ball** oc (1965, Mercury) US#126. HIT VERSIONS: *All or Nothing at All* [iii] Frank Sinatra & Harry James (1943) g R&B#8 US#1/Joe Foley (1928) US#54; *Choo Choo Train (Ch-Ch-Foo)* [x] Doris Day (1953) US#20, *Concerto for Two (A Love Song)* [xxii] Claude Thornhill (1941) US#25, *Delicado* [v] Percy Faith (1952) US#1/Ralph Flanagan (1952) US#26/Stan Kenton (1952) US#25/ Dinah Shore (1952) US#28; *Hand in Hand* Sammy Kaye (1947) US#21, *Handful of Stars* [xx] Glenn Miller (1940) US#10, *Hold My Hand* [xv] Don Cornell (1954) US#2 UK#1/Charlie Kunz in *Piano Medley #114* (1954) UK#20; *Huckleberry Duck* [xix] Raymond Scott (1940) US#12, *If I Didn't Care* Ink Spots (1939) US#2/Hilltoppers (1954) US#17/Connie Francis (1959) R&B#29 US#22/Platters (1961) US#30/ David Cassidy (1974) UK#9; *In an Eighteenth Century Drawing Room* [xvii] Guy Lombardo (1939) US#8, *It's Funny to Everyone But Me* Frank Sinatra & Harry James (1944) US#21, *Johnson Rag* [xiv] Larry Clinton (1940) US#16/Jack Teter Trio (1949) US#6/Jimmy Dorsey (1950) US#13/Russ Morgan (1950) US#7/Claude Thornhill (1950) US#24; *Linda* [xviii] Ray Noble & Buddy Clark (1947) US#1/Larry Douglas (1947) US#14/Charlie Spivak (1947) US#5/

Paul Weston (1947) US#8; *Moonlight Masquerade* [i] Jimmy Dorsey (1941) US#25, *No One But You* [vi] Charlie Applewhite (1954) US#26/Billy Eckstine (1954) UK#3; *Play, Fiddle Play* [iv] George Olsen (1932) US#16/Ted Lewis (1933) US#4; *Poor People of Paris, The* [xvi] Winifred Atwell (1956) UK#1/Les Baxter & His Orchestra (1956) US#1/Russ Morgan & His Orchestra (1956) US#19/Lawrence Welk (1956) US#17/Maury Finney (1977) C&W#85; *Sleepy Lagoon* [viii] Harry James (1942) US#1/Dinah Shore (1942) US#12/Platters (1960); *Sunrise Serenade* [vii] Glen Gray (1939) US#1/Glenn Miller (1939) US#7, re-issued (1944) US#23/Roger Williams (1959) US#106; *Symphony* [ii] Bing Crosby (1946) US#3/Benny Goodman (1946) US#2/Guy Lombardo (1946) US#10/Freddy Martin (1946) US#1/Jo Stafford (1946) US#4; *Tenderly* [xiii] Sarah Vaughan (1947) US#27/Lynn Hope Quintet (1950) R&B#8 US#19/Rosemary Clooney (1952) g US#17/Nat "King" Cole (1954) UK#10/Bert Kaempfert (1961) US#31; *Tu-Li Tulip Time* [xii] Andrews Sisters & Jimmy Dorsey (1938) US#9/Dick Barrie (1938) US#19/Henry Busse (1938) US#19/Hoarce Heidt (1938) US#7; *What Will I Tell My Heart?* [xi] Bing Crosby & Jimmy Dorsey (1937) US#5/Dolly Dawn (1937) US#17/Hal Kemp (1937) US#9/Andy Kirk (1937) US#2/Al Hibbler (1950) R&B#9/Fats Domino (1957) R&B#12 US#64/Phil Phillips (1960) US#108; *With the Wind and the Rain in Your Hair* [ix] Bob Chester (1940) US#18/Bob Crosby (1940) US#2/Kay Kyser (1940) US#4; *Yes, My Darling Daughter* [xxi] Glenn Miller (1941) US#9/Dinah Shore (1941) US#10/Fats Domino (1958) R&B#10 US#55/Eydie Gorme (1962) UK#10. Co-writers: [i] Isaac Albeniz/Toots Camarata, [ii] Alex Alstone/Roger Bernstein/Andre Tabert, [iii] Arthur Altman, [iv] Arthur Altman/Emery Deutsch, [v] Waldyr Azevado, [vi] Nicholas Brodszky, [vii] Frankie Carle, [viii] Eric Coates, [ix] Clara Edwards, [x] Marc Fontenoy, [xi] Irving Gordon/Peter Tinturin, [xii] Maria Grever, [xiii] Walter Gross, [xiv] Guy H. Hall/Henry Kleinkauf, [xv] Richard Myers, [xvi] Marguerite Monnot/Rene Rouzaud, [xvii] Wolfgang Amadeus Mozart (b. Johannes Chrysostomus Wolfgangus Theophilus, January 27, 1756, Salzburg; d. December 5, 1791, Vienna, both Austria)/Raymond Scott, [xviii] Ann Ronell, [xix] Raymond Scott, [xx] Ted Shapiro, [xxi] Albert Simay, [xxii] Peter Tchaikovsky. (*See also under* Hoagy CARMICHAEL.)

563. LAYTON, Turner (b. 1890, Washington, DC; d. February 6, 1978, London, England) Film composer, pianist and vocalist. One half of the highly popular 1920s black vocal duo Layton and Johnstone, which recorded for the Columbia label. Layton also composed one of the earliest black mu-

sicals "Strut Miss Lizzie" (1922), and contributed to such films as "For Me and My Gal" (1918), often in collaboration with the lyricist Henry Creamer. HIT VERSIONS: *After You've Gone* [i] Henry Burr & Albert Campbell (1918) US#2/Marion Harris (1919) US#1/Billy Murray & Gladys Rice (1919) US#9/Bessie Smith (1927 US#7/Sophie Tucker (1927) US#10/Paul Whiteman (1930) US#14/Louis Armstrong (1932) US#15/Benny Goodman (1935) US#20/Lionel Hampton (1937) US#6/Quintet of the Hot Club of France (1937) US#20; *Dear Old Southland* [i] Vernon Dalhart (1922) US#12/Paul Whiteman (1922) US#7; *Trees* Isham Jones (1930) US#13/Donald Novis (1933) US#12; *Way Down Yonder in New Orleans* Peerless Quartet (1922) US#9/Blossom Seeley (1923) US#5/Paul Whiteman (1923) US#5/Frankie Laine & Jo Stafford (1953) US#26/Freddy Cannon (1960) R&B#14 US#3 UK#3. Co-writer: [i] Henry Creamer.

564. Leadbelly (b. Huddie Ledbetter, January 29, 1899, Mooringsport, LA; d. December 6, 1949, New York, NY) Folk guitarist, pianist, harmonica player and vocalist. The most important folk singer-songwriter of the second half of the twentieth century. Leadbelly's influence and sound can be heard in the music of Woody Guthrie, Bob Dylan, and nearly every folk artist that came after him. He learned the guitar and harmonica in his teens, and became an itinerant worker and roaming musician across America. Leadbelly was incarcerated between 1918–1925, and again between 1930–1934, where, for Alan Lomax in 1933, he made his first recordings for the Library of Congress. After his release from prison, Leadbelly became something of an ambassador for the black popular song, performing on the 1930s radio series "Folk Songs of America," and making recordings for a variety of record labels. Leadbelly wrote, adapted, or otherwise popularized such standards as *Boll Weevil, The Gallis Pole, Good Mornin' Blues* and *House of the Rising Sun*. ALBUMS: **Leadbelly** (1940, Storyville); **Leadbelly** (1944, Capitol); **Last Session** (1949, Folkways); **Leadbelly Sings Classics in Jazz** (1953, Capitol); **Leadbelly, Volume 1** (1957), **Leadbelly, Volume 2** (1957), **Leadbelly, Volume 3** (1958), **Leadbelly Plays Party Songs** (1958), **The Saga of Leadbelly** (1958), **Leadbelly's Last Sessions, Volume 2, Part 1** (1959), **Leadbelly's Last Sessions, Volume 2, Part 2** (1959, all Melodisc); **A Demon of a Man-Blues Anthology** (1962), **Leadbelly 2-T.B. Blues** (1962, both Storyville); **His Guitar, His Voice and His Piano** (1963, Capitol); **Good Morning Blues** (1963), **The Midnight Special** (1964, both RCA); **Take This Hammer** (1965, Verve); **Leadbelly Plays and Sings** (1965, Society); **The Library of Congress Recordings** (1966, Elek-

tra); **Keep Your Hands Off Her** (1967, Verve); **Leadbelly Sings Folk Songs** (1969), **Shout On** (1969, both Xtra); **In the Evening When the Sun Goes Down** (1969), **Goodnight Irene** (1969, both Storyville); **The Leadbelly Box Set** (1970, Xtra); **Leadbelly** (1970, Ember); **Leadbelly** (1970, CBS); **Legendary** (1988, Demand), **Leadbelly, 1935** (1988, Travelin' Man), **Leadbelly, 1934–1946** (1989, Document); **The Titanic** (1994), **Nobody Knows the Trouble I've Seen** (1994), **Go Down Old Hannah** (1994, all Rounder). HIT VERSIONS: *Black Betty* Ram Jam (1977) US#18 UK#7, re-mixed (1990) UK#13; *Cotton Fields* Highwaymen (1962) US#13/ Beach Boys (1970) UK#5/Creedence Clearwater Revival (1982) C&W#50/Tennessee Express (1983) C&W#65; *Goodnight Irene* [i] Ernest Tubb & Red Foley (1950) C&W#1 US#10/Moon Mullican (1950) C&W#5/Weavers (1950) g US#1; *Have a Drink on Me* Lonnie Donegan (1961) UK#8, *Midnight Special* Weavers (1952) US#30/Paul Evans (1960) US#16 UK#41/Johnny Rivers (1965) US#20; *Pick a Bale of Cotton* [i] (arrangement only) Lonnie Donegan (1962) UK#11, *Rock Island Line* Lonnie Donegan (1956) US#8/Stan Freberg (1956) UK#24/Johnny Cash (1970) C&W#35 US#93; *Sylvie* Weavers (1954) US#27. Co-writer: [i] John Lomax.

565. LEANDER, Mike (b. Michael Farr, June 30, 1941, London; d. April 18, 1996, both England) Pop producer and arranger. A producer who was first successful as an arranger for the vocalist Marianne Faithful during the 1960s. Leander started out performing skiffle while still at school, before studying the law and entering music publishing in the early 1960s. In 1963, Leander became a producer, writer and arranger at Decca Records, where he worked with Billy Fury and Lulu. He co-composed the British television theme *Ready, Steady, Go!* [v], and wrote the film score to "Privilege" (1967), which introduced his first hit, *I've Been a Bad Bad Boy*. In 1969, Leander moved to MCA Records, where he produced John Rowles and toured as the Mike Leander Orchestra, the lead vocalist in which was one Paul Raven. During the early 1970s, Leander re-invented Raven as Gary Glitter, formed him a backing group the Glitter Band, and created a sparse sound with African influenced rhythms and banal, but catchy melodies and lyrics. Glitter epitomized the British "glam rock" movement of the 1970s, and achieved three number one singles. Leander regarded his greatest personal achievement as the arrangement that he created for the Beatles' *She's Leaving Home*. During the 1980s, he worked on audio books, before dying of cancer in 1996. ALBUMS: **Privilege** ost (1967, Uni); **Migration** oc (1969, MCA); **Two a Penny** ost (1971, Light); **Matador** sc (1987 Epic)

UK#26. HIT VERSIONS: *Always Yours* [i] Gary Glitter (1974) UK#1, *All That Glitters* [i] Gary Glitter (1981) UK#48, *And the Leader Rocks On* [i] Gary Glitter (1992) UK#58, *Another Time, Another Place* [vi] Engelbert Humperdinck (1971) US#43 UK#13, *Boy from Nowhere, A* [vi] Tom Jones (1987) UK#2, *Do You Wanna Touch Me (Oh Yeah!)* [i] Gary Glitter (1973) UK#2, also on *Gary Glitter EP* (1980) UK#57/Joan Jett (1982) US#20; *Doin' Alright with the Boys* [i] Gary Glitter (1975) UK#6, *Early in the Morning* [vi] Vanity Fair (1969) US#12 UK#8, *Hello Hello I'm Back Again* [i] Gary Glitter (1973) UK#2, new version (1995) UK#50, also on *Gary Glitter EP* (1980) UK#57; *High Time* [iv] Paul Jones (1966) UK#4, *I Didn't Know I Loved You ('Till I Saw You Rock 'n' Roll)* [i] Gary Glitter (1972) US#35 UK#4/Planet Patrol (1983) R&B#62/Rock Goddess (1984) UK#57; *I Love You Love Me Love* [i] Gary Glitter (1973) UK#1/Joan Jett & the Blackhearts (1984) US#105; *I Was Born to Be Me* [vi] Tom Jones (1987) UK#61, *I'm the Leader of the Gang (I Am!)* [i] Gary Glitter (1973) UK#1, also on *Gary Glitter EP* (1980) UK#57; *I've Been a Bad Bad Boy* Paul Jones (1967) UK#5, *If I Only Had Time* John Rowles (1968) UK#3, *Lady Godiva* [iv] Peter & Gordon (1966) US#6 UK#16, *Little Boogie Woogie (In the Back of My Mind), A* [ii] Gary Glitter (1977) UK#31/Shakin' Stevens (1987) UK#12; *Love Like You and Me, A* [i] Gary Glitter (1975) UK#10, *Oh Yes! You're Beautiful* [i] Gary Glitter (1974) UK#2, *Rock 'n' Roll, Parts 1 and 2* [i] Gary Glitter (1972) US#7 UK#2, also on *Gary Glitter EP* (1980) UK#57/ Timelords sampled in *Doctorin' the Tardis* (1988) UK#1. Co-writers: [i] Gary Glitter (b. Paul Francis Gadd, May 8, 1940, Banbury, England), [ii] Gary Glitter/Edward Seago, [iii] P. Hipps/G. Shepard, [iv] Charles Mills, [v] Andrew Loog Oldham, [vi] Edward Seago.

566. LEE, Arthur (b. Arthur Porter Taylor, March 7, 1945, Memphis, TN) Rock vocalist. The lead singer and principal songwriter in the psychedelic and folk influenced 1960s group Love, which charted with his composition *7 and 7 Is* (1966) US#33. ALBUMS: **Love** (1966) US#57, **Da Capo** (1967) US#80, **Forever Changes** (1967) US#152 UK#24, **Four Sail** (1969, all Elektra) US#102; **Out Here** (1969) US#176 UK#29, **False Start** (1970, both Blue Thumb) US#184; **Reel to Reel** (1974, RSO). COMPILATIONS: **Revisited** (1970, Elektra) US#142; **Best of Love** (1980), **Live** (1982, both Rhino); **Love** (1982, MCA); **Love Story, 1966–1972** (1995, Elektra). From 1972, Lee pursued a fragmented solo career, recording the albums **Vindicator** (1972, A&M) and **Arthur Lee** (1981, Beggar's Banquet), before, in 1995, being given a lengthy prison sentence for firearms offenses. HIT VERSION: *7 and 7 Is* Alice Cooper (1982) UK#62.

567. LEE, Bert (b. June 11, 1880, Ravensthorpe; d. January 27, 1947, London, both England) Film and stage composer, pianist. A former piano-tuner and church organist who is best remembered for his collaborations with the composer R.P. Weston. After Weston's death, Lee continued songwriting with Weston's son, Harris Weston, creating such British pub standards as *Hello! Hello! Who's Your Lady Friend* [ii] (1913) and *Knees Up Mother Brown* [iii] (1938). Lee's songs were featured in the film "The Story of Vernon and Irene Castle" (1914), and one of his biggest pre-chart era songs was *Josh-ua* [i] (1910). HIT VERSIONS: *Knees Up Mother Brown* [iii] Winifred Atwell in *Let's Have a Party* (1953) UK#2/ Lonnie Donegan in *Lonnie's Skiffle Party* (1958) UK#23. Co-writers: [i] George Arthur, [ii] Worton David/Harry Fragson, [iii] Irving Taylor/Harris Weston, [iv] Harris Weston. (*See also under* R.P. WESTON.)

568. LEE, Dickey (b. Dickey Lipscomb, September 21, 1941, Memphis, TN) C&W vocalist. A former boxer who wrote one of he most recorded songs in the country catalogue, *She Still Thinks I Care*. Lee first recorded for the Sun label in 1957, and charted over thirty singles between 1962–1982, including *I Saw Linda Yesterday* [ii] (1962) R&B#12 US#14. ALBUMS: **Dickey Lee** (1979), **Dickey Lee Again** (1980), **Everybody Loves a Winner** (1981, all Mercury). HIT VERSIONS: *Door Is Always Open, The* Dave & Sugar (1976) C&W#1, *Everybody's Reaching Out for Someone* Pat Daisy (1972) C&W#20 US#112, *I'll Be Leaving Alone* Charley Pride (1977) C&W#1, *I've Been Around Enough to Know* [i] John Schneider (1984) C&W#1, *Let's Fall to Pieces Together* George Strait (1984) C&W#1, *She/He Still Thinks I Care* George Jones (1962) C&W#1/Anne Murray (1974) C&W#1, also B-side of *You Won't See Me* (1974) US#8/Elvis Presley on B-side of *Moody Blue* (1977) C&W#1 US#21 UK#6/Pinkard & Bowden as *She Thinks I Steal Cars* (1986) C&W#92; *You're the First Time I've Thought About Leaving* Reba McEntire (1983) C&W#1. Co-writer: [i] Bob McDill, [ii] Allen Reynolds.

569. LEES, John (b. January 13, 1947, Oldham, England) Rock guitarist and vocalist. The lead guitarist and most prolific composer in the progressive rock group Barclay James Harvest, one of Germany's biggest selling acts of the 1980s. CHART COMPOSITIONS: *Barclay James Harvest Live EP* (1977) UK#49, *Life Is for Living* (1980) UK#61, *Just a Day Away* (1981) UK#68, ALBUMS: **Barclay James Harvest** (1970), **Once Again** (1971), **Barclay James Harvest and Other Short Stories** (1971), **Baby James Harvest** (1972, all Harvest); **Live** (1974) UK#40, **Time Honored Ghosts** (1975) UK#32, **Octoberon** (1976) US#174 UK#19, **Gone to Earth** (1977) UK#30, **Harvest XII** (1978) UK#31, **Eyes of the Universe** (1980), **Turn of the Tide** (1981) UK#55, **Concert for the People** (1982) UK#15, **Ring of Changes** (1983) UK#36, **Victims of Circumstance** (1984) UK#33, **Face to Face** (1987) UK#65, **Glasnost (Live)** (1988), **Welcome to the Show** (1990), **Caught in the Light** (1995, all Polydor). COMPILATIONS: **Alone We Fly** (1990, Connoisseur); **The Harvest Years** (1992, Harvest); **Best of Barclay James Harvest** (1992, Polydor). Lees also recorded a solo set in 1972, that was not released for five years, **A Major Fancy** (1977, Harvest).

570. LEGRAND, Michel (b. February 24, 1932, Paris, France) Film and stage composer, multi-instrumentalist, orchestra conductor, arranger, producer and vocalist. An accomplished arranger and jazz pianist who can also play the trombone, trumpet and guitar. Legrand has conducted numerous orchestras around the world, has recorded over one hundred albums, and has scored over one hundred and fifty films, working with artists as diverse as Miles Davis and Barbra Streisand. Legrand has been the recipient of three Oscars, and was the subject of the television shows "Monsanto Night Presents Michel Legrand" and "Michel Legrand in Concert." The son of Raymond Legrand, one of France's best known composer-conductors, Michel learned the piano at an early age, before studying for ten years at the Paris Conservatoire Nationalide Musique under Nadia Boulanger. Legrand conducted and arranged for the singers Maurice Chevalier, Juliette Greco, Lili Jean Marie, and Edith Piaf, and also performed jazz in nightclubs while writing songs and orchestrating for French radio. During the 1950s, Legrand wrote pop songs under the pseudonym Mig Bike, and in 1958, he recorded **I Love Paris**, a million selling album of arrangements of popular and traditional French tunes. His first major film score was "The Umbrellas of Cherbourg" (1964). Many of his title themes have had words set to them by a variety of lyricists, including Hal David, Alan and Marilyn Bergman, Johnny Mercer, Norman Gimbel, and Alan Jay Lerner. Legrand often composes in an impressionistic style, and like fellow countryman Marcel Proust, seems to yearn for some lost, nostalgic, youthful summer—his tunes *Once Upon a Summertime, I Will Wait for You* [ii] and *You Must Believe in Spring*, being prime examples of his orchestral sketching technique. One of Legrand's best known songs is the "The

Thomas Crown Affair" (1968) film theme *The Windmills of Your Mind* [i], which was influenced by the first prelude from Bach's *The Well Tempered Clavier.* His most celebrated score remains "The Summer of "42," a five day semi-autobiographical account of his experiences as a musician in France near the end of World War II. Barbra Streisand recorded an album of his material as **Je m'appelle Barbra** (1966, Columbia) US#5. CHART COMPOSITION: *Brian's Song* [i] (1972) US#56. ALBUMS: **Castles in Spain** (1956) US#9, **Legrand Jazz** (1958), **Legrand Piano** (1958), **Legrand in Rio** (1958), **Scarlet Ribbons** (1959), **I Like Movies** (1959, all Columbia); **Never Say Die** ost (1959, Legends); **Ole Guape** ost (1960, Vox); **Strings on Fire** (1960, Columbia); **Cleo from 5 to 7** ost (1961, Philips); **The Columbia Album of Cole Porter** (1961, Columbia); **Eva** ost (1962), **The Seven Capital Sins** ost (1962), **Michel Legrand Plays for Dancers** (1962), **Bay of Angels** ost (1963), **Love Is a Ball** ost (1963), **Broadway Is My Beat** (1963), **Rendezvous in Paris** (1964), **Rhapsody in Blue** (1965), **The Umbrellas of Cherbourg** ost (1964, all Philips); **Jarry Sur La Butte** oc (1965, PML); **The Umbrellas of Cherbourg** oc (1965, Accord); **I Love Paris** (1955), **Bonjour Paris** (1955), **Holiday in Rome** (1955) US#5, **Vienna Holiday** (1955, all Columbia) US#13; **A Matter of Resistance** ost (1966, Philips); **The Plastic Dome of Norma Jean** ost (1966), **Cinema Legrand** (1966, both MGM); **Legrand Ecran** (1967, Bell); **The Young Girls of Rochefort** ost (1968, Philips); **How to Save a Marriage and Ruin Your Life** ost (1968, Columbia); **Ice Station Zebra** ost (1968, MGM); **A Matter Of Innocence** ost (1968, Decca); **Of Love Remembered** ost (1968), **The Thomas Crown Affair** ost (1968, both United Artists) US#182; **Sweet Murder** ost (1968, Warner Brothers); **Play Dirty/The Swimming Pool** ost (1968), **The Windmills of Your Mind** (1968, both United Artists); **Michel Legrand at Shelley's Manne Hole** (1968, Verve); **L'Amerique Insolite** ost (1969, Barclay); **The Happy Ending** ost (1969, United Artists); **The Magic Garden of Stanley Sweetheart** ost (1970, MGM); **Pieces of Dreams** ost (1970, Bell); **The Lady in the Car with Sunglasses and a Gun** ost (1970, Vogue); **The Picasso Summer/Summer Of '42** ost (1971, Warner Brothers) US#52; **Un Peau De Soleil Dans L'Eau Froide** ost (1971, Bell); **Le Mans** ost (1971), **The Go-Between** ost (1971, both Columbia); **Wuthering Heights** ost (1971, AIR); **Donkey Skin (The Magic Donkey)** ost (1972, Paramount); **Lady Sings the Blues** ost (1972, Motown) US#1 UK#50; **One Is a Lonely Number** ost (1972, Daybreak); **Brian's Song Themes and Variations** (1972, Bell) US#127; **Michel Legrand and Sarah Vaughan** (1972, Mainstream) US#173; **Breezy** ost (1973, MCA); **Twenty Songs of the Century** (1973), **Live in Japan** (1973, both Bell); **Peau D'Ane** (1973, Pathe); **Paris Was Made for Lovers (A Time for Loving)** ost (1973, Audio Fidelity); **A Slightly Pregnant Man** ost (1973), **Cops and Robbers** ost (1973, both Philips); **A Doll's House/The Outside Man/The Impossible Object** ost (1974), **The Three Musketeers** ost (1974, both Bell); **Brainchild** ost (1974, Brainchild); **F for Fake** ost (1974, RCA); **Our Time (Death of Her Innocence)** ost (1974, Centurion); **The Umbrellas of Cherbourg/The Go-Between Symphonic Suites** (1974, Columbia); **Cage Without a Key** ost (1975, RCA); **Monte Christo** oc (1975, Polydor); **Sheila Levine Is** ost (1975), **Lena Horne and Michel Legrand** (1975), **Recorded Live at Jimmy's** (1975, all RCA); **Portrait of Michel Legrand** (1975, Polydor); **Le Sauvage** ost (1976, Barclay); **Gable and Lombard** ost (1976, MCA); **Ode to Billy Joe** ost (1976, Warner Brothers); **The Concert Legrand** (1976, RCA); **The Man and His Music** (1976, MFP); **Michel Legrand and Friends** (1976, RCA); **The Other Side of Midnight** ost (1977, 20th Century); **Special Magic of Michel Legrand** (1977, MGM); **French Leave** ost (1978, Bell); **Routes to the South** ost (1978, Gryphon); **Michel Legrand with Disco Magic Concorde** (1978, Festival); **Lady Oscar** ost (1979, Kitty); **Les Maries De L'An 2** ost (1979, Bell); **La Dame Dans L'Auto** ost (1979, Vogue); **The Most Important Event Since Man Walked on the Moon** ost (1979, Philips); **Les Uns Et Les Autres** ost (1979), **Parking** ost (1979, both RCA); **Three Seats for the 26th** ost (1979, Philips); **Le Jazz Grand** (1979, Gryphon); **Times of Your Life** (1979, RCA); **Pastorales De Noel** (1979, Columbia); **Images** (1979, RCA); **Michel Legrand and the London Symphony Orchestra** (1979, Columbia); **Falling in Love Again** ost (1980, Ota); **Hinotori (The Firebird)** ost (1980, Alfa); **I Love Movies** (1980, Columbia); **Michel Legrand Sings** (1980, Philips); **The Hunter** ost (1981, United Artists); **Michel Legrand** (1981, Bell); **Les Moulins De Mon Coeur** (1981, Philips); **Michel Legrand** (1981, Warner Brothers); **Atlantic City** ost (1982, DRG); **Bolero** ost (1982, RCA); **Michel Legrand, Pedro Paulo and Castro Neves** (1982, Pointer); **The Smurfs and the Magic Flute** ost (1983, Polydor); **What Makes David Run (Qu' Est Ce Qui Fait Courir David?)** ost (1983, Milan); **Yentl** ost (1983, Columbia) p US#9 UK#21; **Never Say Never Again** ost (1983, Seven Seas); **After the Rain** (1983, Pablo); **Slapstick** ost (1984, Varese Sarabande); **Secret Places** ost (1984, Shanachie); **A Love in Germany** ost (1984, Milan); **Michel Legrand** (1984, Audio Fidelity); **Live at Fat Tuesday's** (1984, Verve); **Love Songs** ost (1985, Varese Sarabande); **Sins** ost (1986, Polydor); **Live at the 1986 Montreal**

Jazz Festival with Ginette Reno (1986, Audiogram); Il Fait Une Fois L'Espace ost (1987, RCA); **Palace** ost (1988, Carrere); **Partir Revenir** ost (1989, WEA); **Compact Jazz** (1990, Philips); **Dingo** with Miles Davis ost (1991, Warner Brothers); **The Burning Shore** ost (1991, Mercury); **Musiques De Films De Claude Lelouch** ost (1992, Sony); **Legrand Live Jazz** (1992, Novus); **Paris Was Made for Lovers** (1992, Prestige); **Magic: Kiri Te Kanawa Sings Michel Legrand** (1992, Teldec); **Legrand Plays Legrand** (1994, Laserlight); **Pret-a-Porter** ost (1995). HIT VERSIONS: *Brian's Song* [i] Peter Nero (1972) US#105, *How Do You Keep the Music Playing?* [i] James Ingram (1983) R&B#6 US#45, *I Will Wait for You* [ii] Steve Lawrence (1965) US#113, *Never Say Never Again* Lani Hall (1983) US#103, *Summer Knows, The* aka *Summer of '42* Peter Nero (1971) US#21/Biddu Orchestra (1975) R&B#80 US#57 UK#14; *Watch What Happens* [ii] Lena Horne (1970) US#119, *Way He Makes Me Feel, The* [i] Barbra Streisand (1983) US#40, *Windmills of Your Mind, The* [i] Noel Harrison (1969) UK#8/Jimmy Rodgers (1969) US#123/Dusty Springfield (1969) US#31/ Swing Out Sister on B-side of *Where in the World* (1989) UK#47. Co-writers: [i] Alan Bergman/Marilyn Bergman, [ii] Norman Gimbel.

571. LEHAR, Franz (b. 1870, Komaron, Hungary; d. October 24, 1948, Bad Ischl, Switzerland) Film and stage composer, violinist. The co-composer, with Paul Francis Webster, of the highly influential musical "The Merry Widow" (1905). Lehar studied the violin at the Prague Conservatory, before becoming a bandmaster in his early twenties. He composed his first opera in 1896, "Kukuschka," which was followed by "Land of Smiles" (1929), "Gypsy Love" (1911), "The Three Graces" (1924), "Frederica" (1930), and "Paganini" (1937). The vocalist Richard Tauber recorded much of Lehar's work on the Parlophone label during the 1920s. ALBUMS: **The Merry Widow** sc (1950, Decca); **The Merry Widow** oc (1952, MGM); **The Merry Widow** oc (1964, RCA) US#137. HIT VERSIONS: *Gems from the Merry Widow* [viii] Victor Opera Light Co. (1911) US#6, *Gigolette* [i] Ben Bernie (1925) US#8, *I Love You So (The Merry Widow Waltz)* [vii] Victor Orchestra (1907) US#2/Harry MacDonough & Elise Stevenson (1908) US#3; *Maxim's* [vii] Harry Mac-Donough (1908) US#4, *Say Not Love Is a Dream* [v] Olive Kline (1913) US#4, *Vilia Song* [vii] Helene Noldi (1908) US#9/Elise Stevenson (1908) US#3; *White Dove, The* [iii] Lawrence Tibbett (1930) US#10. Co-writers: [i] William Cary, [ii] Harry Graham, [iii] Clifford Grey, [iv] A.P. Herbert, [v] Basil Hood/ Adrian Ross, [vi] Harry S. Pepper, [vii] Adrian Ross, [viii] Paul Francis Webster.

572. LEHRER, Tom (b. Thomas Andrew Lehrer, April 9, 1928, New York, NY) Pop pianist and vocalist. A Harvard professor of mathematics who, during the late 1950s, became a satirical social commentator, blending darkly humorous lyrics with simple melodies played at jolly tempos. Lehrer delivered his biting material with a debonair aplomb similar to that of Noel Coward, and his rapier wit, perfectly timed delivery, and underlying sense of social concern, were frequently captured on disk. The only American composers to venture anywhere near the same territory since, have been Randy Newman and Warren Zevon. Leher's compositions *Poisoning Pigeons in the Park*, *National Brotherhood Week* and *I Wanna Go Back to Dixie*, were all fine examples of his skill. He ceased writing music during the 1960s, when America entered the Vietnam War, although he did compose some songs for television in 1972. Lehrer's music was also the subject of a London revue, "Tomfoolery" (1980). ALBUMS: **Songs By Tom Lehrer** (1958) UK#7, **More of Tom Lehrer** (1959, both Decca); **That Was the Year That Was** (1965) US#18, **An Evening Wasted with Tom Lehrer** (1966, both Reprise) US#133 UK#7; **Tomfoolery** oc (1980, Multi Media). COMPILATIONS: **Too Many Songs By Tom Lehrer** (1981, Reprise); **In Concert** (1995, Eclipse).

573. LEIBER, Jerry (b. April 25, 1933, Baltimore, MD), and STOLLER, Michael (b. May 13, 1933, Belle Harbor, NY) Both R&B-pop producers and pianists. One of the most important and influential songwriting and production teams since the late 1950s. Leiber and Stoller, two white, Jewish, blues loving New Yorkers, were the most unlikely revolution ever to have happened to black music. They were responsible for introducing R&B to a large white audience in America, and took the concept of the theatre and stage to the three minute pop single. By 1960, over thirty million records of their songs had been sold. Leiber and Stoller replaced the traditional boy-meets-girl theme of pop songs with more life-like story lines, and created characters that were easily identifiable in all walks of life, none more so than the black domestic working for a white household in *I Ain't Here*, the Thomas Mann styled European intellectual in *Is That All There Is?*, and the irrepressible *Charlie Brown*. Leiber and Stoller's complex song structures always sounded deceptively simple, and they successfully masked the regular twelve bar blues mode of repeating the first line of each verse. They were also a considerable influence on the Beatles, and were the first record producers to work independently under contract for a major label, before trying their hand with their own series of record companies. Leiber has likened their early work to

three-minute radio plays, and said of their longevity, "We didn't think we were writing songs that would last." Leiber's parents were Polish immigrants, his father being a Hebrew teacher and his mother running a grocery store in the black neighborhood where he grew up. At the age of nine, he took piano lessons, and from 1945 he lived with his family in Los Angeles, California. After studying music and drama, Leiber became a gofer at the Circle Theatre, and worked in a record store, where he began listening to the blues. In his spare time he began writing lyrics. Stoller's father was an engineer and draftsman, and his mother a former model and dancer. The young Stoller was often taken to see Broadway shows, where he became intoxicated with the power and drama of the popular song. An aunt gave him his first piano lessons, and by the age of fourteen, he was frequenting the speakeasys and bebop clubs along New York's 52nd Street. In 1949, the Stoller family re-located to Los Angeles, where Stoller pursued his interest in music by learning composition and arranging. Leiber and Stoller met in 1950 through a mutual friend, and quickly formed a songwriting partnership. By their early twenties, dozens of their songs had been waxed by the last of the R&B artists still recording on 78s. The marriage of Leiber's witty lyrics and Stoller's tough, street influenced tunes, proved irresistible to such singers as Jimmy Witherspoon, who made the first public performance of a Leiber and Stoller song *Real Ugly Woman*, at a blues jamboree in 1950. Their first published number was *That's What the Good Book Says* by Bobby Nunn and the Robins (1951), after which, their material was recorded by Amos Milburn, Ruth Brown and Floyd Dixon. One of their biggest early hits was Willie Mae "Big Mama" Thornton's million seller *Hound Dog* (1953), a risque record that, three years later, was re-interpreted by Elvis Presley. The six million seller was later described by Leiber as, "a cross between a New Orleans buck dance and a blues-rhumba." Of their early affiliation with black performers, Leiber said, "Actually I think we wanted to be black. Being black was being great. The best musicians in the world were black. The greatest athletes in the world were black, and black people had a better time. As far as we were concerned the worlds that we came from were drab by comparison." By regularly sitting in during the recording sessions of their material, Leiber and Stoller learned record production, and in order to have more control over how their songs were recorded, they began producing their own disks. For the vocal group the Coasters, they penned some of their wittiest material, displaying a love and understanding of 1950s black youth culture. Theirs was a celebration of simple struggles, written with a rhythmic street feel and featuring articulate, amiable char-

acters. In 1955, Leiber and Stoller signed to Atlantic Records as the first independent producers in popular music, for which they wrote many hits in their Brill Building office, sometimes under the pseudonyms Elmo Glick and Lewis Lebish. Their initial Atlantic productions were often cut in three hour sessions, at which, Stoller often played piano. Their revolutionary approach to recording utilized many new methods of studio production, and for the vocal group the Drifters, they embellished their material with Latin percussion, barrio rhythms, castanets and marimbas. Their production of *There Goes My Everything*, was the first known R&B disk to feature strings, while their use of multi-layered guitar lines, percussion and vibes, were all new sounds to R&B. Their production methods were later described by Tom Dowd, "Jerry and Mike would sit down with me and the group by a piano for two or three days and drill the melody and the vocals and the backgrounds. They had lines, counterlines, dialogue, dialect, then they'd come in and fly it live." A three hour recording session with former Drifter Ben E. King resulted in *Stand By Me*, which has since accrued over four million radio plays in America, and *Spanish Harlem*, which has been recorded over one hundred and thirty times. After Presley's success with *Hound Dog*, Leiber and Stoller provided him with a further twenty-four songs, many of which were multi-million sellers, the best being collected on **Elvis Presley Sings Leiber and Stoller** (1988, RCA) UK#32. During the 1960s, Leiber and Stoller built themselves a lucrative publishing empire, and they remained successful producers throughout 1970–1980s, also working on an animated feature "Hound Dog," and a short film of their lives entitled "Yakety Yak." ALBUMS: **Scooby-Doo** (1959, Kapp); **The Leiber and Stoller Big Band** (1961, Atlantic); **Only in America** (1980, Warner Brothers). HIT VERSIONS: *Along Came Jones* Coasters (1959) R&B#14 US#9/Righteous Brothers (1967) US#108/Ray Stevens (1969) US#27; *Baltimore* Drifters on B-side *This Magic Moment* (1960) R&B#4 US#16, *Bazoom (I Need Your Lovin')* Charms (1955) R&B#15, *Best Thing, The* Billy Eckstine (1976) R&B#84, *Bossa Nova Baby* Elvis Presley (1963) g R&B#20 US#8 UK#11, re-issued (1987) UK#47; *Charlie Brown* Coasters (1959) g R&B#2 US#2 UK#6/Compton Brothers (1970) C&W#16; *Chicken and the Hawk (Up Up and Away), The* Joe Turner (1955) R&B#7, *Climb, The* Kingsmen (1965) US#65; *Dance with Me* [viii] Drifters (1959) R&B#2 US#15/Intrigue (1996) R&B#91+ US#122+; *Do Your Own Thing* Brook Benton (1968) US#99, *Don't* Elvis Presley (1957) g C&W#2 R&B#4 US#1 UK#2/Sandy Posey (1973) C&W#39; *Down in Mexico* Coasters (1956) R&B#8, *Drip Drop* Drifters (1958) US#58/Dion (1963) US#6;

D.W. Washburn Monkees (1968) US#19 UK#17, *Fools Fall in Love* Drifters (1957) R&B#10 US#69/Elvis Presley (1967) US#102; *Framed* Cheech & Chong (1976) US#41, *Get Him* Exciters (1963) US#76, *Girls, Girls, Girls* Coasters (1962) US#96/Elvis Presley (1962) g US#3 UK#2/Fourmost (1965) UK#33; *Hard Times* Charles Brown (1952) R&B#7, *His Kiss* Betty Harris (1964) US#89, *Hound Dog* Willie Mae "Big Mama" Thornton (1953) R&B#1/Elvis Presley (1956) g C&W#1 R&B#1 US#1 UK#2, re-issued (1971) UK#10, also in *The Elvis Medley* (1982) US#71 UK#51; *I Keep Forgettin'* Gene McDaniels (1962) US#55/Michael McDonald as *I Keep Forgettin' (Every Time You're Near)* (1982) US#4 UK#43/Warren G. sampled in *Regulate* (1994) g R#&B#7; *I (Who Have Nothing)* [ii] Shirley Bassey (1963) UK#6/Ben E. King (1963) R&B#16 US#29/Terry Knight & the Pack (1966) US#46/Linda Jones (1968) US#116/Tom Jones (1970) US#14 UK#16/Sylvester (1979) R&B#27 US#40 UK#46; *I'm a Woman* Peggy Lee (1963) US#54/Maria Muldaur (1974) US#12; *Idol with the Golden Head* Coasters (1957) US#64, *If It's the Last Thing I Do* Dinah Washington (1955) R&B#13, *If You Don't Come Back* Drifters (1963) US#101, *Is That All There Is?* Peggy Lee (1969) US#11, *Jailhouse Rock* Elvis Presley (1957) g C&W#1 R&B#1 US#1 UK#1, re-issued (1972) UK#42, re-issued (1983) UK#27, also in *The Elvis Medley* (1982) US#71 UK#51; *Just Tell Her Jim Said Hello* Elvis Presley (1962) US#55, *Kansas City* aka *Kansas City Lovin'/K.C. Lovin'* Hank Ballard & the Midnighters (1959) R&B#16 US#72/Wilbert Harrison (1959) g R&B#1 US#1, new version as *Good Bye Kansas City* (1960) US#102/Little Richard (1959) US#95 UK#26/Rocky Olson (1959) US#60/James Brown (1967) US#55/Trini Lopez (1964) US#23/Paul McCartney on B-side of *Once Upon a Long Ago* (1987) UK#10; *King Creole* Elvis Presley (1958) US#2 UK#4, *Little Egypt* Coasters (1961) R&B#16 US#23/Elvis Presley (1969) g US#8 UK#2; *Lorelei* Lonnie Donegan (1960) UK#10, *Love Me* Elvis Presley (1956) C&W#10 R&B#7 US#2, *Love Potion #9* Clovers (1959) R&B#23 US#23/Searchers (1965) g US#3/Coasters (1967) US#76/Tygers of Pan Yang (1982) UK#45; *Lovey Lovey* Clovers (1960) R&B#2, *Loving You* Elvis Presley (1957) US#20 UK#24/Dave Clark Five in medley *More Good Old Rock 'n' Roll* (1969) UK#34; *Lucky Lips* Ruth Brown (1957) US#25/Cliff Richard (1963) UK#4; *On Broadway* [v] Drifters (1963) R&B#7 US#9/George Benson (1978) R&B#2 US#7; *One Kiss Led to Another* Coasters (1956) R&B#11 US#73, *Only in America* [v] Jay & the Americans (1963) US#25, *Past, Present and Future* Shangri-Las (1966) US#59, *Pearl's a Singer* [ii] Elkie Brooks (1977) UK#8, *Poison Ivy* Coasters (1959) g R&B#1 US#7 UK#15/Paramounts (1964) UK#35/Lambretas (1980)

UK#7; *Ruby Baby* Drifters (1955) R&B#10/Dion & the Belmonts (1963) g R&B#5 US#2/Mitch Ryder & the Detroit Wheels (1968) US#106/Billy "Crash" Craddock (1974) C&W#1 US#33; *Run Red Run* Coasters (1959) R&B#29 US#36, *Saved* LaVern Baker (1961) R&B#17 US#37, *Searchin'* Coasters (1957) g R&B#1 US#3 UK#30/Hollies (1963) UK#25, also in *Holliedaze (A Medley)* (1981) UK#51/Johnny Rivers (1973) US#113; *She's Not You* [vi] Elvis Presley (1962) R&B#13 US#5 UK#1, *Smokey Joe's Cafe* Robins (1955) R&B#10 US#79, *Some Other Guy* Big Three (1963) UK#37, *Sorry, But I'm Gonna Have to Pass* Coasters (1994) UK#41, *Spanish Harlem* [iv] Ben E. King (1961) R&B#15 US#10/Jimmy Justice (1962) UK#20/Santo & Johnny (1962) US#101/Sounds Incorporated (1964) UK#35/King Curtis (1965) US#89/Aretha Franklin (1971) g R&B#1 US#2 UK#14; *Stand By Me* Ben E. King (1961) g R&B#1 US#4 UK#50, re-entry (1961) UK#27, re-issued (1987) US#9 UK#1/Little Junior Parker (1961) R&B#11/Cassius Clay (1964) US#102/Kenny Lynch (1964) UK#39/Spyder Turner (1966) R&B#3 US#12/David & Jimmy Ruffin (1970) R&B#24 US#61/John Lennon (1975) UK#30/Mickey Gilley (1980) C&W#1 US#22/Maurice White (1985) R&B#6 US#50; *There Goes My Baby* Drifters (1959) g R&B#1 US#2/Donna Summer (1984) R&B#20 US#21; *Treat Me Nice* Elvis Presley (1957) R&B#7 C&W#11 US#18, *What About Us* Coasters (1960) R&B#17 US#47, *What to Do with Laurie* Mike Clifford (1962) US#98, *Yakety Yak* Coasters (1958) g R&B#1 US#1 UK#12/Sam the Sham (1968) US#110/Eric Weissberg & Deliverance (1975) C&W#91; *You Can't Love 'Em All* Drifters (1964) US#115, *(You're So Square) Baby I Don't Care* Buddy Holly (1958) UK#12/Elvis Presley (1958) R&B#14 UK#61/Joni Mitchell (1982) US#47; *Young Blood* [vi] Coasters (1957) R&B#2 US#8/Bad Company (1976) US#20/UFO (1980) UK#36/Bruce Willis (1987) US#68. Co-writers: [i] Ralph Dino/John Sembello, [ii] C. Donida, [iii] Ben E. King (b. Benjamin Earl Nelson, September 23, 1938, Henderson, NC), [iv] Jerry Leiber/Phil Spector only, [v] Barry Mann/Cynthia Weil, [vi] Doc Pomus, [vii] Phil Spector, [viii] George Treadwell.

574. LEIGH, Fred W. (b. England) Film and show composer. A British Victorian Music Hall songwriter who composed the popular songs *A Little Bit Off the Top* [v] for Reg Grant (1898), *Captain Gingah* [ii] for George Bastow (1910), *The Army of Today's Alright* [iv] for Vesta Tilley (1914), and *The Galloping Major* [ii] for Harry Fay (1906). Leigh's song *Poor John* [vi] was included in the film "Cover Girl" (1906), while *Jolly Good Luck to the Girl Who Loves a Soldier* [iv] appeared in "After the Ball" (1907) and *A Little of What You Fancy* [i] in "Variety Jubilee" (1908). HIT VERSIONS: *Don't Dilly Dally on the Way* [iii] Winifred Atwell in *Make It a Party* (1956) UK#7/Muppets in *The Muppet Show Music Hall EP* (1977) UK#19; *Waiting at the Church (My Wife Won't Let Me)* [vi] Ada Jones (1906) US#2/Vesta Victoria (1907) US#4/Muppets in *The Muppet Show Music Hall EP* (1977) UK#19. Co-writers; [i] George Arthurs, [ii] George Bastow, [iii] Charles Collins, [iv] Kenneth Lyle, [v] Fred Murray, [vi] Henry Pether.

575. LENNON, John A founder member of the British group the Beatles, which broke up in 1970. Lennon's initial solo projects were a series of avante-garde recordings with his future wife, Yoko Ono. Under the collective group name the Plastic Ono Band, Lennon achieved his first solo hit with the anthemic two million seller *Give Peace a Chance* [i] (1969), which had been recorded in a motel room. He followed it with the remarkable *Cold Turkey* (1969), a raw rock and roll record that saw him moving as far away from the sound of the Beatles as fast as he could. Easily his finest solo single was the Phil Spector produced *Instant Karma* (1970), a loose, one-take number recorded live in the studio. After primal scream therapy, Lennon released the album **John Lennon and the Plastic Ono Band** (1970), a collection of intensely personal songs that were bleak and often painful self-examinations of his troubled childhood. The album also contained his classic contemporary folk ballad *Working Class Hero*, and proved something of a catharsis, for it was a mellower, more relaxed Lennon that would emerge on subsequent recordings. On September 3, 1971, Lennon boarded a plane for New York, where he set up residence, never to return to England. After the birth of his second son Sean in 1975, Lennon retired from music for five years, living in an apartment in the Dakota Building in Manhattan. In 1980, Lennon began recording again, releasing the light but catchy **Double Fantasy** (1980), a confident and positive album. On December 8, 1980, after working in the studio on Ono's composition *Walking on Thin Ice*, Lennon was shot dead by Mark Chapman in the lobby of the Dakota Building. His songs were recorded by a variety of artists as **Working Class Hero-A Tribute to John Lennon** (1995) US#94. CHART COMPOSITIONS: *Give Peace a Chance* [i] (1969) g US#14 UK#2, re-issued (1981) UK#33; *Cold Turkey* (1969) US#30 UK#14, *Instant Karma* (1970) g US#3 UK#5, *Mother* (1971) US#43, *Power to the People* (1971) US#11 UK#7, *Imagine* (1971) US#3, re-issued (1976) UK#6, re-issued (1981) UK#1; *Happy Xmas (War Is Over)* [ii] (1972) UK#4, re-issued (1975) UK#48, re-issued (1980) UK#2, re-

issued (1981) UK#28, re-issued (1982) UK#56; *Woman Is the Nigger of the World* (1972) US#57, *Mind Games* (1973) US#18 UK#26, *Whatever Gets You Thru the Night* [ii] (1974) US#1 UK#36, *#9 Dream* (1974) US#9 UK#23, *(Just Like) Starting Over* (1980) g US#1 UK#1, *Woman* (1981) g US#2 UK#1, *I Saw Her Standing There* [i] with Elton John (1981) UK#40, *Watching the Wheels* (1981) US#10 UK#30, *Love* (1982) UK#41, *Nobody Told Me* (1984) US#5 UK#6, *Borrowed Time* (1984) US#108 UK#32, *Jealous Guy* (1985) US#80 UK#65, *I'm Stepping Out* (1984) US#55, *Imagine/Happy Xmas (War Is Over)* [ii]/*Jealous Guy* (1988) UK#45. ALBUMS: **Unfinished Music #1-Two Virgins*** (1968) US#124, **Unfinished Music #2-Life with the Lions*** (1969) US#174, **The Wedding Album*** (1969) US#178, **The Plastic Ono Band-Live Peace in Toronto, 1969*** (1970) g US#10, **John Lennon and the Plastic Ono Band** (1970) g US#6 UK#11, **Imagine** (1971) g US#1 UK#1, **Sometime in New York City** (1972) US#48 UK#11, **Mind Games** (1973) g US#9 UK#13, **Walls and Bridges** (1974) g US#1 UK#6, **Rock 'n' Roll** (1975, all Apple) US#6 UK#6; **Double Fantasy*** (1980, Geffen) p US#1 UK#1. COMPILATIONS: **Roots** (1975, Adam VIII); **Shaved Fish** (1975, Apple) p US#12 UK#8; **The John Lennon Collection** (1982, Parlophone) US#33 UK#1; **Heartplay-Unfinished Dialogue*** (1983) US#94, **Milk and Honey*** (1984, all Polydor) g US#11 UK#3; **Reflections and Poetry** (1984, Silhouette); **Live in New York City** (1986, Parlophone) US#41 UK#55; **Menlove Avenue** (1986, Capitol) US#127; **Imagine — Music from the Motion Picture** ost (1988, Parlophone) p US#31 UK#64; **The Interview** (1990, BBC); **The Ultimate Collection** (1990), **Lennon Legend** (1998, both Parlophone) UK#6+. HIT VERSIONS: *Cold Turkey* Lenny Kravitz on B-side of *Let Love Rule* (1990) US#89 UK#39, *Gimme Some Truth* Generation X on B-side of *King Rocker* (1979) UK#11, *Give Peace a Chance* [i] Peace Choir (1991) US#54, *Imagine* Randy Crawford (1983) R&B#69 US#108 UK#60/Tracie Spencer (1989) US#85; *Instant Karma* Tori Amos on B-side of *Only Saw Today* (1994) UK#48, *(It's All Down To) Goodnight Vienna* Ringo Starr (1975) US#31, *Jealous Guy* Roxy Music (1981) UK#1, *Love* Lettermen (1971) US#42, *Mother* Barbra Streisand (1971) US#79, *Working Class Hero* Tommy Roe (1973) C&W#73 US#97. With: * Yoko Ono. Co-writers: [i] Paul McCartney, [ii] Yoko Ono (b. February 18, 1933, Tokyo, Japan). (*See also under* David BOWIE, George HARRISON, John LENNON and Paul McCARTNEY.)

576. LENNON, John (b. John Winston Lennon, October 9, 1940, Liverpool, England; d. December 8, 1980, New York, NY) Rock guitarist, pianist, producer and vocalist, and **McCART-NEY, Sir Paul** (b. James Paul McCartney, June 18, 1942, Liverpool, England) Rock bassist, pianist, drummer, producer and vocalist. The founder members of the Beatles, the most successful and influential group of all time. The Lennon and McCartney publishing catalogue earns over thirty million dollars a year in mechanical royalties alone, and such was the effect that the Beatles had on songwriting, recording and the music industry itself, that the history of contemporary popular music can be divided into two halves — Before the Beatles and after. Up until the early 1960s, record companies made most of their money from soundtrack and original cast recordings, but after the arrival of the Beatles, pop and rock music became one of the fastest growing industries in the world. Lennon and McCartney's songs eclipsed in sales even those of two of their heroes, Jerry Leiber and Mike Stoller. McCartney's composition *Yesterday*, has achieved over six million radio plays, and has been recorded over two and a half thousand times, while *And I Love Her* has been recorded three hundred and seventy-two times, *Eleanor Rigby* over two hundred times, and *Fool on the Hill* and *With a Little Help from My Friends* over one hundred times each. Lennon and McCartney created songs that live alongside those of Cole Porter and George Gershwin, and will probably be played for as long as music is listened to. They first met at school in 1957, with McCartney subsequently joining Lennon's skiffle group the Quarrymen. By 1958, the group included the guitarist George Harrison, its only known recording being an acetate of Buddy Holly's *That'll Be the Day*. A regular slot at the Casbah coffee house in Liverpool, and several name and line-up changes, resulted in the formation of the Beatles, who, during the late 1950s and early 1960s, developed a formidable rock and roll sound by performing two or more sets a night at the Kaiserkeller Club in Hamburg, Germany, where, as backing musicians for the vocalist Tony Sheridan, they recorded the first inauspicious sides for the producer Bert Kaempfert. The Beatles' earliest musical influences were country and western, the skiffle sound of Lonnie Donegan, and early American rock and roll and rockabilly, in particular Elvis Presley, Carl Perkins, Little Richard, the Everly Brothers and Chuck Berry. They also absorbed the sounds of the black American R&B artists Smokey Robinson, Ben E. King, and the Shirelles, alongside the straighter pop of the Brill Building. In 1961, the Beatles became regulars at the Cavern, an airless, brick basement that was Liverpool's premier music venue for many years. After acquiring the managerial services of Brian Epstein, the Beatles signed to the Parlophone label under the stewardship of record producer Sir George

Martin. Their debut single, the plaintiff *Love Me Do* (1962), reached the British top twenty on account of its Liverpool sales alone, and within a year, the group became a phenomenon, adding a new word to the English language, Beatlemania. Their debut album **Please Please Me** (1962), was recorded in two eight hour sessions at an approximate cost of four hundred pounds, and sold an unprecedented half a million copies in Britain alone, where pop groups hitherto had only ever been successful with singles. With *From Me to You* (1963), the Beatles began an uninterrupted run of eleven consecutive number one singles, all of which sold over a million copies each. The song was also the first Lennon-McCartney composition to appear on the American Hot 100, when, on June 29, 1963, it charted for Del Shannon. The group's American parent company, Capitol Records, were initially reluctant to issue any Beatles material at all, so EMI licensed fourteen tracks to the small Vee-Jay label, which managed to create four albums, six singles and an EP out of their gift horse. Capitol were soon to flood the American market with shortened versions of the Beatles' British album releases, spreading their lucrative wares as thinly as possible until the simultaneous release of **Revolver** (1965). On January 25, 1964, the Beatles entered the American singles chart with *I Want to Hold Your Hand*, a song that eventually sold over fifteen million copies worldwide, and by April 4, 1964, the group occupied the entire top five. With an additional seven other singles in lower positions, the Beatles' share of the American Hot 100 amounted to an unprecedented twelve percent. Their music developed rapidly, and they continually re-defined the boundaries of popular music and culture, as pop ceased to be a mere youthful diversion and became a fully fledged entertainment industry in its own right. By the mid-1960s, Lennon and McCartney's increasingly sophisticated melodies were introducing sounds and instruments never before recorded on pop disks, with **Sergeant Pepper's Lonely Hearts Club Band** (1967), becoming the most influential album of the decade. **Abbey Road** (1969) was the Beatles' final album, **Let It Be** (1970) having been recorded earlier but actually released last. The group went its separate ways in 1970, and despite much repackaging of its catalogue down the years, very little of genuine interest was to surface until the forty million selling **Anthology** series in the mid-1990s. There have been numerous entire albums of their songs by other artists, the most successful being: **Beatlemania** (1964, Top Six) UK#19; the George Martin Orchestra, **Off the Beatle Track** (1964, United Artists) US#111; **The Chipmunks with David Seville Sing the Beatles Hits** (1964, Liberty) US#14; the Hollyridge Strings, **The Beat-**

les' Songbook (1964) US#15 and The New Beatles' Songbook (1966, both Capitol) US#142; Joshua Rifkin, The Baroque Beatles' Songbook (1965, Elektra) US#83; Keely Smith, The Lennon and McCartney Songbook (1965, Reprise) UK#12; the Brothers Four, A Beatles' Songbook (1966, Columbia) US#97; Chet Atkins Picks on the Beatles (1966, RCA) US#112; Ramsey Lewis, Mother Nature's Son (1969, Cadet) US#156; Percy Faith, The Beatles Album (1970, Columbia) US#179; Rostal and Schaefer, Beatles Concerto (1979, Parlophone) UK#61; Stars on Long Play/Stars on 45 (1981, Radio) g US#9 UK#1; James Last Plays the Great Songs of the Beatles (1983, Polydor) UK#52; and Come Together: America Salutes the Beatles (1995) US#90. There were also two R&B recordings of Abbey Road, Booker T. and the M.G.'s McLemore Avenue (1970, Stax) US#107 UK#70, and George Benson's The Other Side of Abbey Road (1976, A&M) US#125. Lennon and McCartney's compositions were also extensively featured on three film soundtracks, Sgt. Pepper's Lonely Heart's Club Band (1978, A&M) p US#5 UK#38; All This and World War II (1976, 20th Century) US#48; and Backbeat (1994, Virgin) US#190. In 1995, the three surviving members of the Beatles, McCartney, George Harrison and Ringo Starr, reassembled to record two unfinished Lennon numbers, Free as a Bird [i] and Real Love [i]. CHART COMPOSITIONS: Love Me Do (1962) g US#1 UK#17, re-issued (1982) UK#4, re-issued (1992) UK#53; Please Please Me (1963) g US#3 UK#2, re-issued (1983) UK#29; From Me to You (1963) US#41 UK#1, re-issued (1983) UK#40; She Loves You (1963) g US#1 UK#1, re-issued (1983) UK#45, also recorded as Sie Liebt Dich (1964) US#97; I Want to Hold Your Hand (1963) g US#1 UK#1, re-entry (1964) UK#48, re-issued (1983) UK#62; I Saw Her Standing There (1964) US#14, Can't Buy Me Love (1964) g US#1 UK#1, re-issued (1984) UK#53; You Can't Do That (1964) US#48, There's a Place (1964) US#74, All My Loving (1964) US#45, Do You Want to Know a Secret (1964) g US#2, P.S. I Love You (1964) US#10, Four By the Beatles EP (1964) US#97, re-entry (1965) US#68; A Hard Days Night (1964) g US#1 UK#1, re-issued (1984) UK#52; I'm Happy Just to Dance with You (1964) US#95, I Should Have Known Better (1964) US#53, I'll Cry Instead (1964) US#25, And I Love Her (1964) US#12, If I Fell (1964) US#53, Thank You Girl (1963) US#35, I Feel Fine (1964) g US#1 UK#1, re-issued (1984) UK#65; She's a Woman (1964) US#4, Eight Days a Week (1965) g US#1, I Don't Want to Spoil the Party (1965) US#39, Ticket to Ride (1965) g US#1 UK#1, re-issued (1984) UK#70; Yes It Is (1965) US#46, Help (1965) g US#1 UK#1, re-issued (1976) UK#37; Boys (1965) US#102,

I'm Down (1965) US#101, Yesterday (1964) g US#1, re-issued (1976) UK#8; Day Tripper/We Can Work It Out (1965) UK#1, Day Tripper (1965) g US#5, We Can Work It Out (1965) g US#1, Nowhere Man (1966) g US#3, What Goes On (1966) US#81, Paperback Writer (1966) g US#1 UK#1, re-issued (1976) UK#23; Rain (1966) US#23, Eleanor Rigby/Yellow Submarine (1966) UK#1, re-issued (1985) UK#63; Yellow Submarine (1966) g US#2, Eleanor Rigby (1966) US#11, Penny Lane/Strawberry Fields Forever (1967) UK#2, re-issued (1976) UK#32, re-issued (1987) UK#65; Penny Lane (1967) g US#1, Strawberry Fields Forever (1967) US#8, All You Need Is Love (1967) g US#1 UK#1, re-issued (1987) UK#47; Baby You're a Rich Man Beatles (1967) US#34, Hello Goodbye (1967) g US#1 UK#1, re-issued (1987) UK#63; I Am the Walrus (1967) US#58, Magical Mystery Tour EP (1967) UK#2, Lady Madonna (1968) g US#4 UK#1, re-issued (1988) UK#67; Hey Jude (1968) g US#1 UK#1, re-issued (1976) UK#12, re-issued (1988) UK#52; Revolution (1968) US#12, Get Back (1969) g US#1 UK#1, re-issued (1976) UK#28, re-issued (1989) UK#74; Don't Let Me Down (1969) US#35, The Ballad of John and Yoko (1969) g US#8 UK#1, Come Together (1969) g US#1, Let It Be (1970) g US#1 UK#2, The Long and Winding Road (1970) g US#1, Back in the U.S.S.R. (1976) UK#19, Got to Get You into My Life (1976) US#7, Ob-La-Di, Ob-La-Da (1976) US#49, Sergeant Pepper's Lonely Hearts Club Band (1978) US#71 UK#63, The Beatles Movie Medley (1982) US#12 UK#10, Free As a Bird [i] (1995) US#6 UK#2, Real Love [i] (1996) US#11 UK#4. ALBUMS: Please Please Me (1963) UK#1, With the Beatles (1963) UK#1, A Hard Day's Night (1964) UK#1, Beatles for Sale (1964) UK#1, Help! (1965) UK#1, Rubber Soul (1965) p US#1 UK#1, Revolver (1966) p US#1 UK#1, Sergeant Pepper's Lonely Hearts Club Band (1967) p US#1 UK#1, Yellow Submarine ost (1967, all Parlophone) p US#2 UK#3; The Beatles (1968) p US#1 UK#1, Abbey Road (1969) p US#1 UK#1, Let It Be (1970, all Apple) g US#1 UK#1. COMPILATIONS: Introducing the Beatles (1963, Vee-Jay) g US#2; Meet the Beatles (1964, Capitol) p US#1; The Beatles First with Tony Sheridan (1964, Polydor); The Beatles with Tony Sheridan and Guests (1964, MGM) US#68; Jolly What! The Beatles and Frank Ifield on Stage (1964, Vee-Jay) US#104; The Beatles Second Album (1964, Capitol) g US#1; The American Tour with Ed Rudy (1964, RP) US#20; Hear the Beatles Tell All (1964, Vee-Jay); A Hard Day's Night ost (1964, United Artists) US#1; Something New By the Beatles (1964, Capitol) p US#2; The Beatles Versus the Four Seasons (1964, Vee-Jay) US#142; Songs, Pictures and Stories of the Fabulous Beatles (1964, Vee-Jay) US#63; The Beatles' Story (1964) g US#7, **Beatles '65** (1965) p US#1, **The Early Beatles** (1965) g US#43, **The Beatles VI** (1965) g US#1, **Yesterday and Today** (1965, all Capitol) g US#1; **Help!** ost (1965, United Artists) g US#1; **A Collection of Beatles' Oldies (But Goodies)** (1966, Parlophone) UK#7; **Magical Mystery Tour** (1967, Capitol) p US#1 UK#31; **Hey Jude** (1969, Apple) p US#2; **In the Beginning** (1970, Polydor) US#117; **The Beatles Christmas Album** (1970), **The Beatles Again** (1970), **The Beatles, 1962–1966** (1973) p US#3 UK#2, **The Beatles, 1967–1970** (1973, all Apple) p US#1 UK#3; **Rock and Roll Music** (1976, Parlophone) p US#2 UK#11; **Beatles Tapes from the David Wigg Interviews** (1976, Polydor) UK#45; **The Beatles at the Hollywood Bowl** (1977, EMI) p US#2 UK#1; **The Beatles Live at the Star Club Hamburg Germany, 1962** (1977, Lingasong) US#111; **Love Songs** (1977) g US#24 UK#7, **Rarities** (1979) US#21 UK#71, **The Beatles Ballads — 20 Original Tracks** (1980) UK#17, **The Beatles EP Collection** (1981), **Reel Music** (1982) g US#19, **20 Greatest Hits** (1982, all Parlophone) p US#50 UK#10; **The Decca Sessions, 1-1-62** (1987 Topline); **Past Masters, Volume 1** (1988) US#149 UK#49, **Past Masters, Volume 2** (1988, both Parlophone) US#121 UK#46; **The Beeb's Lost Beatles Tapes** (1988, BBC); **Live at the BBC** (1994) p US#3 UK#1, **Anthology 1** (1995) p US#1 UK#2, **Anthology 2** (1996) p US#1 UK#1, **Anthology 3** (1996, all Apple) p US#1 UK#4. HIT VERSIONS: *All My Loving* Chipmunks (1964) US#134/Dowlands (1964) UK#33/Jimmy Griffin (1964) US#118/Hollyridge Strings (1964) US#93/Mundo Earwood (1982) C&W#58; *All You Need Is Love* Tom Jones & Dave Stewart (1993) UK#19, *And I Love Her/Him* George Martin (1964) US#105/Esther Phillips (1965) R&B#11 US#54/Vibrations (1966) R&B#47 US#118/Casey Kasem as *Letter from Elaina* (1964) US#103; *Back in the U.S.S.R.* Chubby Checker (1969) US#82, *Bad to Me* Billy J. Kramer & the Dakotas (1963) US#9 UK#1, *Birthday* Underground Sunshine (1969) US#26/Paul McCartney (1990) UK#29; *Can't Buy Me Love* Ella Fitzgerald (1964) UK#34, *Carry That Weight* Trash (1969) US#112 UK#35, *Come Together* Ike & Tina Turner (1970) R&B#50 US#57/Aerosmith (1978) US#23/Michael Jackson on B-side of *Remember the Time* (1992) US#3; *Day Tripper* Ramsey Lewis (1966) US#74/Vontastics (1966) R&B#7 US#100/Otis Redding (1967) UK#43/Anne Murray (1974) US#59; *Dear Prudence* Five Stairsteps (1970) US#66, also on B-side of *Ooh Child* (1970) R&B#14 US#8/Katfish (1975) US#62; *Disco Beatlemania* D.B.M. (1977) UK#45, *Discomania (Beatles Medley)* Cafe Creme (1978) US#105, *Do You Want to Know a Secret* Billy J. Kramer & the Dakotas (1963) UK#2,

Drive My Car Bob Kuban & the In-Men (1966) US#93/Gary Toms Empire (1975) R&B#32 US#69; *Eight Days a Week* Wright Brothers (1984) C&W#57, *Eleanor Rigby* Ray Charles (1968) R&B#30 US#35 UK#36/Aretha Franklin (1969) R&B#5 US#17/El Chicano (1970) US#115; *Fool on the Hill, The* Sergio Mendes & Brazil '66 (1968) US#6/Shirley Bassey (1971) UK#48; *From a Window* Billy J. Kramer & the Dakotas (1963) US#23 UK#10/Chad & Jeremy (1965) US#97; *From Me to You* Del Shannon (1963) US#77, *Get Back* Rod Stewart (1976) UK#11/Billy Preston (1978) US#86; *Girl* St. Louis Union (1966) UK#11/Truth (1966) UK#27/Billy Preston (1977) R&B#44; *Golden Slumbers* Trash (1969) US#112 UK#35, *Good Day Sunshine* Claudine Longet (1967) US#100, *Got to Get You into My Life* Cliff Bennett & the Rebel Rousers (1966) UK#6/Blood, Sweat and Tears (1975) US#62/Earth, Wind and Fire (1978) g R&B#1 US#9 UK#33; *Hard Days Night, A* George Martin Orchestra (1964) US#122/Peter Sellers (1965) UK#14/Ramsey Lewis Trio (1966) R&B#29 US#29; *Hello Little Girl* Fourmost (1962) UK#9, *Help* Peter Sellers on B-side of *A Hard Days Night* (1965) UK#14/Tina Turner (1984) UK#40/Bananarama (1989) UK#3; *Here, There and Everywhere* Fourmost (1964) US#120/Claudine Longet (1967) US#126/Emmylou Harris (1976) US#65 UK#30; *Hey Jude* Terry Knight in *Saint Paul* (1969) US#114/Paul Mauriat (1969) US#119/Wilson Pickett (1969) R&B#13 US#23 UK#16; *I Am the Walrus* Oasis on B-side of *Cigarettes and Alcohol* (1994) UK#7, *I Call Your Name* Billy J. Kramer & the Dakotas on B-side of *Bad to Me* (1963) US#9 UK#1, *I Don't Want to See You Again* Peter & Gordon (1964) US#16, *I Don't Want to Spoil the Party* Rosanne Cash (1989) C&W#1, *I Feel Fine* Penny DeHaven (1970) C&W#59/Sweethearts of the Rodeo (1988) C&W#9/Wet Wet Wet (1990) UK#30; *I Saw Her/Him Standing There* Elton John on B-side *Philadelphia Freedom* (1975) g R&B#32 US#1 UK#12/Elton John & John Lennon (1981) UK#40/Tiffany (1988) US#7 UK#8; *I Should Have Known Better* George Martin Orchestra (1964) US#111/Naturals (1964) UK#24; *I Wanna Be Your Man* Rolling Stones (1963) UK#12, also B-side of *Not Fade Away* (1964) US#48/Rezillos (1979) UK#71/Chaka De Mus & Pliers (1994) UK#19; *I Want to Hold Your Hand* Boston Pops Orchestra (1964) US#55/Homer & Jethro (1964) C&W#49/Dollar (1979) UK#9/Lakeside (1982) R&B#5 US#102; *I'll Cry Instead* Ron Shaw (1979) C&W#68, *I'll Keep You Satisfied* Billy J. Kramer & the Dakotas (1963) US#30 UK#4, *I'm Happy Just To Dance With You* Anne Murray (1980) C&W#23 US#64, *I'm in Love* Fourmost (1964) UK#17, *I'm on My Way* Betty Boo sample (1992) UK#44, *I'm Only Sleeping* Suggs (1995) UK#7, *I've Just Seen a Face* Calamity Jane

(1982) C&W#44, *It's for You* Cilla Black (1964) US#79 UK#7, *It's Only Love* Bryan Ferry on *Extended Play* (1976) UK#7, *Julia* Ramsey Lewis (1969) R&B#37 US#76, *Lady Madonna* Fats Domino (1968) US#100, *Lazy Itis* Happy Mondays as a sample (1990) UK#46, *Let It Be* Joan Baez (1971) US#49/Boys on the Block (1987) R&B#76/Ferry Aid (1987) UK#1; *Like Dreamers Do* Applejacks (1964) UK#20, *Long and Winding Road, The* Ray Morgan (1970) UK#32/New Birth (1976) R&B#91/Melba Moore (1977) R&B#94; *Love Me Do* Hollyridge Strings (1964) US#134, *Love of the Loved* Cilla Black (1963) UK#35, *Lucy in the Sky with Diamonds* Elton John (1974) g US#1 UK#10/Natalie Cole (1978) R&B#53; *Magical Mystery Tour* Ambrosia (1977) US#39, *Michelle* Billy Vaughan (1965) US#77/David & Jonathan (1966) US#16 UK#11/Overlanders (1966) UK#1/Bud Shank (1966) US#65/Spokesmen (1966) US#106; *Nobody I Know* Peter & Gordon (1963) US#12 UK#10, *Norwegian Wood* Sergio Mendes & Brazil '66 (1970) US#107/Alan Copeland Singers (1968) US#120; *Nowhere Man* Alan Copeland Singers (1968) US#120/Three Good Reasons (1966) UK#47; *Ob-La-Di, Ob-La-Da* Bedrocks (1968) UK#20/Arthur Conley (1968) R&B#41 US#51/Marmalade (1968) UK#1/Herb Alpert & the Tijuana Brass (1969) US#118; *Please Please Me* David Cassidy (1974) UK#16/Soft Touch (1987) R&B#83; *Revolution* Thompson Twins(1985) UK#56, *She Came in Through the Bathroom Window* Joe Cocker (1969) US#30, *She's a Woman* Jose Feliciano (1969) US#103/Scritti Politti (1991) UK#20; *She's Leaving Home* David & Jonathan (1967) US#123/Billy Bragg (1988) UK#1; *Step Inside Love* Cilla Black (1968) UK#8, *Strawberry Fields Forever* Pozo-Seco Singers (1970) US#115/Terri Hollowell (1978) C&W#76/Candy Flip (1990) UK#3; *That Means a Lot* P.J. Proby (1965) UK#30, *This Boy* George Martin Orchestra as *Ringo's Theme* (1964) US#53, *Ticket to Ride* Carpenters (1970) US#54, *We Can Work It Out* Stevie Wonder (1971) R&B#3 US#13 UK#27/Four Seasons (1976) US#34/Chaka Khan (1981) R&B#34; *When I'm Sixty-Four* Kenny Ball & His Jazz Men (1967) UK#43; *With a Little Help from My Friends* Joe Brown (1967) UK#32/Young Idea (1967) UK#10/Joe Cocker (1968) US#68 UK#1/Wet Wet Wet (1988) UK#1; *Woman* Peter & Gordon (1966) US#14 UK#28/David Wills (1976) C&W#55; *World Without Love, A* Peter & Gordon (1963) g US#1 UK#1/Bobby Rydell (1964) US#80; *Yesterday* Marianne Faithfull (1965) UK#36/Matt Monroe (1965) UK#8/Ray Charles (1967) R&B#9 US#25 UK#44/Billie Joe Spears (1979) C&W#60; *You Can't Do That* Nilsson (1967) US#122, *You Won't See Me* Anne Murray (1974) US#8, *You've Got to Hide Your Love Away* Silkie (1965) US#10 UK#28.

All compositions Lennon/McCartney, except: [i] John Lennon only.

577. LENNON, Julian (b. John Charles Julian Lennon, April 8, 1963, Liverpool, England) Pop keyboard player and vocalist. John Lennon's first son, who initially seemed on the verge of a successful career. CHART COMPOSITIONS: *Too Late for Goodbyes* (1984) US#5 UK#6, *Valotte* [i] (1984) US#9 UK#55, *Say You're Wrong* (1985) UK#75, *Because* (1985) UK#40, *Stick Around* (1986) US#32, *Now You're in Heaven* [iii] (1989) US#93 UK#59, *Help Yourself* [iii] (1991) UK#53, *Saltwater* [iv] (1991) UK#6, *Get a Life* [ii] (1992) UK#56. ALBUMS: **Valotte** (1984) g US#17 UK#20, **The Secret Value of Daydreaming** (1986, both Charisma) g US#32 UK#93; **Mr. Jordan** (1989) US#87, **Help Yourself** (1991, both Virgin) UK#42; **Photograph Smile** (1998) UK#75+. Co-writers: [i] J. Clayton/C. Morales, [ii] Humphrey/Tilbrook, [iii] J. McCurry, [iv] Spiro/Spiro.

578. LENNOX, Annie (b. December 25, 1954, Aberdeen, Scotland) Pop keyboard player and vocalist. The lead singer in the highly successful duo Eurythmics. Lennox first teamed up with her musical partner Dave Stewart in the 1970s group Catch, which evolved into the punk band the Tourists. CHART COMPOSITIONS: *Blind Among the Flowers* (1979) UK#52, *The Loneliest Man in the World* (1979) UK#32, *So Good to Be Back Home* (1979) UK#8, *Don't Say I Told You So* (1979) UK#40. ALBUMS: **The Tourists** (1979) UK#72, **Reality Affair** (1979, both Gem) UK#23; **Luminous Basement** (1979, RCA) UK#75. After the Tourists split up in 1980, Lennox and Stewart formed the considerably more successful Eurythmics. CHART COMPOSITIONS: *Never Gonna Cry Again* [ii] (1981) UK#63, *Love Is a Stranger* [ii] (1982) UK#54, re-issued (1983) US#23 UK#6, re-issued (1991) UK#46; *Sweet Dreams (Are Made of This)* [i] (1983) US#1 UK#2, re-issued (1991) UK#48; *Who's That Girl?* [ii] (1983) UK#3, re-issued (1984) US#21; *Right By Your Side* [ii] (1983) UK#10, re-issued (1984) US#29; *Here Comes the Rain Again* [ii] (1984) US#4 UK#8, *Sex Crime* [ii] (1984) US#81 UK#4, *Julia* [ii] (1985) UK#44, *Would I Lie to You?* [ii] (1985) US#5 UK#17, *There Must Be an Angel (Playing with My Heart)* [ii] (1985) US#22 UK#1, *Sisters Are Doing It for Themselves* [ii] with Aretha Franklin (1985) US#18 UK#9, *It's Alright (Baby's Coming Back)* [ii] (1986) US#78 UK#12, *When Tomorrow Comes* [ii] (1986) UK#30, *Thorn in My Side* [ii] (1986) US#68 UK#5, *Missionary Man* [ii] (1986) US#14 UK#31, *The Miracle of Love* [ii] (1987 UK#23, *Beethoven (I Love to Listen To)* [ii] (1987) UK#25, *Shame* [ii] (1988)

UK#41, *I Need a Man* (1988) US#46 UK#26, *You Have Placed a Chill in My Heart* [ii] (1988) US#64 UK#16, *Revival* [ii] (1989) UK#26, *Don't Ask Me Why* [ii] (1989) US#40 UK#25, *King and Queen of America* [ii] (1990) UK#29, *Angel* [ii] (1990) UK#23. ALBUMS: **(In the Garden)** (1982), **Sweet Dreams (Are Made of This)** (1983) g US#15 UK#3, **Touch** (1984) p US#7 UK#1, **Touch Dance** (1984) US#115 UK#31, **1984 (For the Love of Big Brother)** ost (1984) UK#23, **Be Yourself Tonight** (1985) p US#9 UK#3, **Revenge** (1986) g US#12 UK#3, **Savage** (1987, all RCA) US#41 UK#7; **We Too Are One** (1989, Arista) US#34 UK#1; **Live, 1983–1989** (1992, RCA) UK#22. COMPILATION: **Greatest Hits** (1991, RCA) g US#72 UK#1. In 1992, Lennox parted company with Stewart and embarked on a solo career. CHART SINGLES: *Why* (1992) US#34 UK#5, *Precious* (1992) UK#23, *Walking on Broken Glass* (1992) US#14 UK#8, *Cold* (1992) UK#26, *Little Bird* (1993) US#49 UK#3. ALBUMS: **Diva** (1992) p US#23 UK#1, **Medusa** (1995) p US#11 UK#1, **Live in Central Park** (1995, all RCA). HIT VERSION: *What Can You Do for Me* Utah Saints (1991) UK#10. Co-writers: [i] Guthrie/Dave A. Stewart/Willis, [ii] Dave A. Stewart.

579. LERNER, Alan Jay (b. August 31, 1918; d. June 14, 1986, both New York, NY) Film and stage lyricist, and **LOEWE, Frederick** (b. June 10, 1904, Vienna, Austria; d. February 14, 1988, Palm Springs, CA) Film and stage composer, pianist. A songwriting partnership that created one of the most successful musicals of all time "My Fair Lady" (1956), which clocked up two thousand seven hundred and seventeen Broadway performances. After studying at the Stern Conservatory in Berlin, Germany, Loewe composed the popular European tune *Kathrin* (1923), before emigrating to America in 1924, where he contributed to the show "Salute to Spring" (1937). Loewe worked as a pianist before meeting and teaming up with Lerner in 1942, a Harvard and Julliard School of Music graduate, who had worked as a radio presenter and script writer. Lerner and Loewe's first revue was "Life of the Party" (1939), which they followed with "What's Up?" (1943), "The Day Before Spring" (1945) and "Brigadoon" (1947), which introduced the song *Almost Like Being in Love*. Their first significant hit was "Paint Your Wagon" (1951), which featured some of their best known compositions, including *Wand'rin' Star* and *They Call the Wind Moriah*. "My Fair Lady" (1956), notable for its five million selling original cast album, introduced the songs *Wouldn't It Be Luverly*, *The Rain in Spain*, *I Could Have Danced All Night*, *Get Me to the Church on Time*, *I've Grown Accustomed to Her Face*, and *On the Street Where You Live*. Lerner and Loewe were

also successful with films of their shows, in particular "Gigi" (1958), which won them two Oscars. Their final Broadway hit was "Camelot" (1960), after which Lerner worked with Andre Previn on "Coco" (1969), and with Burton Lane on the show and subsequent film "On a Clear Day You Can See Forever" (1965). Previn recorded a jazz score of **My Fair Lady** (1964, Columbia) US#147. Lerner collaborated with Kurt Weil on "Love Life" (1948), and in 1987, Jackie and Roy recorded an album of his compositions, **One More Rose** (Audiophile). ALBUMS: **Love Life** sc (1948, Heritage); **Brigadoon** oc (1951, RCA); **Royal Wedding** ost (1951), **Brigadoon** ost (1954, both MGM); **My Fair Lady** oc (1956, Columbia) p US#1 UK#2; **Gigi** ost (1958, MGM) g US#1 UK#2; **An Evening with Lerner and Loewe** sc (1959, RCA); **Camelot** oc (1961) g US#1, **My Fair Lady** ost (1964, both Columbia) g US#4 UK#9; **My Fair Lady** oc (1964) UK#19, **Camelot** oc (1964, both CBS) UK#10; **Camelot** oc (1965, HMV) UK#19; **On a Clear Day You Can See Forever** oc (1965, RCA) US#59; **Camelot** ost (1967, Warner Brothers) p US#11 UK#37; **Coco** oc (1969), **Paint Your Wagon** ost (1969, both Paramount) g US#28 UK#2; **On a Clear Day You Can See Forever** ost (1970, Columbia) US#108; **Gigi** oc (1973, RCA); **Little Prince** ost (1974, ABC); **An Evening with Alan Jay Lerner** oc (1977, Laureate); **Carmelina** oc (1979, Original Cast); **My Fair Lady** sc (1987, Decca) UK#41. HIT VERSIONS: *Almost Like Being in Love* Mildred Bailey (1947) US#21/Mary Martin (1947) US#21/Frank Sinatra (1947) US#20/Michael Johnson (1978) R&B#91 US#32; *Gigi* Les Baxter (1953) US#23/Billy Eckstine (1959) UK#8; *I Could Have Danced All Night* Sylvia Syms (1956) US#20/Frank Sinatra on *Come Dance with Me LP* (1959) UK#30/Ben E. King (1963) US#72/Biddu Orchestra (1976) US#72; *I Talk to the Trees* Clint Eastwood (1970) UK#18, *On the Street Where You Live* Vic Damone (1956) US#4, re-issued (1958) UK#1/Eddie Fisher (1956) US#18/David Whitfield (1958) UK#16/Andy Williams (1964) US#28/Johnny Mathis (1965) US#96; *They Call the Wind Moriah* Mariners (1951) US#30/Jack Barlow (1972) C&W#58; *Wand'rin' Star* Lee Marvin (1970) UK#47. (*See also under* Kurt WEIL.)

580. LESLIE, Edgar (b. December, 31, 1885, Stamford, CT) Film and stage lyricist. A Tin Pan Alley lyricist who contributed to such shows as "The Pleasure Seekers" (1913). HIT VERSIONS: *America, I Love You* [i] American Quartet (1916) US#5/Sam Ash (1916) US#4; *Hello Hawaii, How Are You* [iii] Nora Bayes (1916) US#7/Anna Chandler (1916) US#8/Billy Murray (1916) US#2/Prince's Orchestra (1916) US#1; *Oh! What a Pal Was Mary* [ii] Henry Burr (1919) US#1/Edward Allen (1920)

US#10; *Take Me to the Land of Jazz* [ii] Marion Harris (1919) US#5, *Take Your Girlie to the Movies (If You Can't Make Love at Home)* [ii] Irving Kaufman (1919) US#10/Billy Murray (1919) US#5. Co-writers: [i] Archie Gottler, [ii] Bert Kalmar/Pete Wendling, [iii] Jean Schwartz. (*See also under* Fred AHLERT, Joe BURKE, Grant CLARKE, Lou HANDMAN, Frank LOESSER, Joseph MEYER, Horatio NICHOLS, Jimmy MONACO, Harry WARREN.)

581. LEVINE, Irwin (b. America) Pop composer. The co-composer of the six million selling *Tie a Yellow Ribbon Round the Old Oak Tree* [i], which has been recorded over one thousand times and has become a BMI three million radio performance song. HIT VERSIONS: *Black Pearl* Checkmates, Ltd. featuring Sonny Charles (1969) R&B#8 US#13/Horace Faith (1970) UK#13; *Candida* [ii] Dawn (1970) g US#3 UK#9, *I Woke Up in Love This Morning* [i] Partridge Family (1971) US#13, *It Only Hurts When I Try to Smile* [i] Tony Orlando & Dawn (1974) US#81, *Knock Three Times* [i] Billy "Crash" Craddock (1971) C&W#3 US#113/Dawn (1971) g US#1 UK#1; *Say, Has Anybody Seen My Sweet Gypsy Rose* [i] Dawn (1973) g US#3 UK#12/Terry Stafford (1973) C&W#35; *Steppin' Out (Gonna Boogie Tonight)* [i] Tony Orlando & Dawn (1974) US#7, *Tie a Yellow Ribbon Round the Old Oak Tree* [i] Dawn (1973) g US#1 UK#1, re-entry (1974) UK#41/Johnny Carver (1973) C&W#5; *What Are You Doing Sunday?* [ii] Dawn (1971) US#39, *Your Husband, My Wife* [ii] Brooklyn Bridge (1969) US#46. Co-writers: [i] L. Russell Brown, [ii] Toni Wine. (*See also under* Sandy LINZER.)

582. LEWIS, Al (b. America) Film lyricist. A Tin Pan Alley lyricist whose songs were featured in the films "The Big Pond" (1930), "The Singing Hill" (1940) and "The Eddie Cantor Story" (1954). HIT VERSIONS: *Adoration Waltz, The* [viii] Carl Fenton (1924) US#11/David Whitfield (1957) UK#9; *Blueberry Hill* [ix] Kay Kyser (1940) US#11/Glenn Miller (1940) US#1/Russ Morgan (1940) US#14/ Louis Armstrong (1956) US#29/Fats Domino (1956) R&B#1 US#2 UK#6, re-issued (1976) UK#41/John Barry (1960) UK#34/Dave Clark Five in medley *More Good Old Rock 'n' Roll* (1969) UK#34/Anne J. Morton (1977) C&W#72; *Breeze (That's Bringing My Baby Back to Me), The* [v] Anson Weeks (1934) US#7/Helene Dixon (1953) US#21/Trudy Richards (1953) US#19; *Cincinnati Dancing Pig* [xii] Red Foley (1950) US#7/Vic Damone (1950) US#11; *Every Now and Then* [vii] Ramona (1935) US#11, *Finger of Suspicion, The* Dickie Valentine (1954) UK#1, *Gonna Get a Girl* [i] Larry Green (1948) US#23, *Ninety-*

Nine Out of a Hundred [i] Ben Bernie (1931) US#13, *Livin' in the Sunlight, Loving in the Moonlight* [vi] Bernie Cummins (1930) US#20/Paul Whiteman (1930) US#16; *Now's the Time to Fall in Love* [vi] Ben Selvin (1932) US#17, *Over Somebody Else's Shoulder* [vi] Isham Jones (1934) US#6, *Tears on My Pillow* [ii] Little Anthony & the Imperials (1958) R&B#2 US#4, *Way Back Home* [x] Victor Young (1935) US#6/Bing Crosby & Fred Waring (1949) US#21; *Why Don't You Fall in Love with Me?* [xi] Connee Boswell (1942) US#21/Dick Jurgens (1943) US#4/ Johnny Long (1943) US#10/Dinah Shore (1943) US#3; *You Gotta Be a Football Hero (To Get Along with the Beautiful Girls)* [iii] Ben Bernie (1933) US#10. Co-writers: [i] Paul Ash/Howard Simons, [ii] Sylvester Bradford, [iii] Buddy Fields/Al Sherman, [iv] Paul Mann, [v] Tony Sacco/Richard B. Smith, [vi] Al Sherman, [vii] Al Sherman/Abner Silver, [viii] Larry Stock, [ix] Larry Stock/Vincent Rose, [x] Tom Waring, [xi] Mabel Wayne, [xii] Guy Wood. (*See also under* Joe BURKE.)

583. LEWIS, Huey (b. Hugh Anthony Cregg, III, July 5, 1950, New York, NY) Rock harmonica player and vocalist. A journeyman rock and roller who first recorded as a member of the soft-rock group Clover, releasing the albums **Clover** (1970), **Forty-Niner** (1971, both Fantasy); and **Unavailable** (1976, Vertigo). Lewis finally found major league success with the radio friendly pop-rock of Huey Lewis and the News. CHART COMPOSITIONS: *Workin' for a Livin'* [iv] (1982) US#41, *I Want a New Drug (Called Love)* [iv] (1984) US#6, *The Heart of Rock and Roll* [i] (1984) US#6, re-issued (1986) UK#49, *If This Is It* [i] (1984) US#6 UK#39, *Walking on a Thin Line* (1984) US#18, *The Power of Love* [ii] (1985) g R&B#81 US#1 UK#11, re-issued (1986) UK#9; *Stuck with You* [iv] (1986) US#1 UK#12, *Hip to Be Square* [iii] (1986) US#3 UK#41, *Simple As That* [iv] (1987) UK#47, *I Know What I Like* [iv] (1987) US#9, *Small World* [iv] (1988) US#25, *Give Me the Keys (And I'll Drive You Crazy)* [iii] (1989) US#47, *Couple of Days Off* (1991) US#11, *It Hit Me Like a Hammer* [v] (1991) US#21. ALBUMS: **Huey Lewis and the News** (1980), **Picture This** (1982) g US#13, **Sports** (1984) p US#1 UK#23, **Fore!** (1986) p US#1 UK#8, **Small World** (1988, all Chrysalis) p US#11 UK#12; **Hard at Play** (1991, EMI) g US#27 UK#39; **Four Chords and Several Years Ago** (1994, Elektra) US#55. COMPILATION: **The Heart of Rock and Roll-The Best of Huey Lewis and the News** (1992, Chrysalis) UK#23. HIT VERSIONS: *Don't Make Me Do It* Patrick Simmons (1985) US#75. Co-writers: [i] Johnny Colla (b. July 2, 1952, CA), [ii] Johnny Colla/ Chris Hayes (b. November 24, 1957, CA), [iii] Bill

Gibson/Sean Hopper (b. March 31, 1953, CA), [iv] Chris Hayes, [v] R.J. Lange.

584. LEWIS, Sam M. (b. 1885; d. 1959, both America) Film and stage lyricist. A co-writer of many hit songs during the first half of the twentieth century, who also contributed to the shows "Plantation Revue" (1925) and "Kid Boots" (1926). HIT VERSIONS: *Close to Me* [i] Tommy Dorsey (1936) US#11, *Gloomy Sunday* [iv] Hal Kemp (1936) US#4, *Hello Central, Give Me No Man's Land* [vii] Al Jolson (1918) US#1, *I Kiss Your Hand, Madame* [ii] Smith Ballew (1929) US#12/Leo Reisman (1929) US#13; *In a Little Spanish Town* [viii] Sam Lanin (1927) US#12/Ben Selvin (1927) US#4/Paul Whiteman (1927) US#1/David Carroll (1954) US#29/Bing Crosby (1956) UK#22; *Just a Baby's Prayer at Twilight (For Her Daddy Over There)* [v] Henry Burr (1918) US#1/Charles Hart (1918) US#10/Prince's Orchestra (1918) US#6/Edna White's Trumpet Quartet (1918) US#7; *Just Friends* [vi] Russ Columbo (1932) US#14/Ben Selvin (1932) US#14; *King for a Day* [iii] Ted Lewis (1928) US#5, *Laugh, Clown, Laugh!* [iii] Ted Lewis (1928) US#5/Fred Waring's Pennsylvanians (1928) US#1; *Rock-a-bye Your Baby with a Dixie Melody* [vii] Arthur Fields (1918) US#9/Al Jolson (1918) US#1/Big Ben Banjo Band in *Let's Get Together #1* (1954) UK#6. Co-writers: [i] Peter De Rose, [ii] Ralph Erwin/Fritz Rotter/Joe Young, [iii] Ted Fiorito/Joe Young, [iv] Laszio Javor/ Rezso Seress, [v] M.K. Jerome/Joe Young, [vi] John Klenner, [vii] Jean Schwartz/Joe Young, [viii] Mabel Wayne (b. 1904; d. 1978)/Joe Young. (*See also under* Fred AHLERT, Harry AKST, Con CONRAD, John Frederick COOTS, Walter DONALDSON, Ray HENDERSON, George W. MEYER, Harry WARREN, Victor YOUNG.)

585. LIGHTFOOT, Gordon (b. November 17, 1938, Orillia, Ontario, Canada) Folk guitarist, pianist and vocalist. One of the last singer-songwriters of the 1960s still working in the acoustic folk tradition. Lightfoot has sold over ten million albums, and composed over one hundred and sixty songs, one hundred and thirty of which have been recorded by other artists. His best work is evidenced on such contemporary folk classics as *The Wreck of the Edmund Fitzgerald*, the true story of an ore ship that sank on Lake Superior. Lightfoot learned the piano and guitar as a child, and studied orchestration and harmony at Westlake College in Los Angeles, while supporting himself writing advertising jingles. In 1960, he teamed up with Terry Whelan in the duo the Two-Tones, recording the album **Live at the Village Corner** (1960, Canatal). After a variety of solo singles for small labels during the early

1960s, Lightfoot recorded a series of folk-based albums that were characterized by his distinctive, rich baritone with a tenor top, and his fluid acoustic guitar picking. He also acted in the Bruce Dern film "Harry Tracy" (1984). CHART COMPOSITIONS: *If You Could Read My Mind* (1971) US#5 UK#30, *Talking in Your Sleep* (1971) US#64, *If I Could* (1971) US#111, *Summer Side of Life* (1971) UK#98, *Beautiful* (1972) US#58, *That Same Old Obsession* (1972) US#102, *You Are What I Am* (1973) US#101, *Sundown* (1974) g C&W#13 US#1 UK#33, *Carefree Highway* (1974) C&W#81 US#10, *Rainy Day People* (1975) C&W#47 US#26, *The Wreck of the Edmund Fitzgerald* (1976) g C&W#50 US#2 UK#40, *Race Among the Ruins* (1977) US#65, *The Circle Is Small* (1978) C&W#92 US#33, *Dreamland* (1978) C&W#100, *Daylight Katy* (1978) UK#41, *Dream Street Rose* (1980) C&W#80, *Baby Step Back* (1982) US#50, *Anything for Love* (1986) C&W#71. ALBUMS: **Lightfoot** (1966), **The Way I Feel** (1967), **Did She Mention My Name** (1968), **Back Here on Earth** (1969), **Sunday Concert** (1969, all United Artists) US#143, **Sit Down Young Stranger** (1970) g US#12, **Summer Side of Life** (1971) US#38, **Don Quixote** (1972) US#42 UK#44, **Old Dan's Records** (1972) US#95, **Sundown** (1974) p US#1 UK#45, **Cold on the Shoulder** (1975) US#10, **Summertime Dream** (1976, all Reprise) p US#12; **Endless Wire** (1977) g US#22, **Dream Street Rose** (1980) US#60, **Shadows** (1982) US#87, **Salute** (1983) US#175, **East of Midnight** (1986) US#165, **Waiting for You** (1993, all Warner Brothers). COMPILATIONS: **Best of Gordon Lightfoot** (1971), **Classic Lightfoot — The Best of Gordon Lightfoot, Volume 2** (1973) US#178, **Very Best of Gordon Lightfoot** (1974, all United Artists) US#155; **Gord's Gold** (1975, Reprise) p US#34; **Gord's Gold, Volume 2** (1988), **The Original** (1992, both Warner Brothers). HIT VERSIONS: *Bitter Green* Ronnie Hawkins (1970) US#118, *Cotton Jenny* Anne Murray (1972) C&W#11 US#71, *Early Morning Rain* Peter, Paul & Mary (1965) US#91/George Hamilton, IV (1966) C&W#9/ Oliver (1971) US#124; *For Lovin' Me* Peter, Paul & Mary (1965) US#30, *Last Time I Saw Her, The* Glen Campbell (1971) C&W#21 US#61, *Ribbon of Darkness* Marty Robbins (1965) C&W#1 US#103/Connie Smith (1969) C&W#13; *Steel Rail Blues* George Hamilton, IV (1966) C&W#15, *Wherefore and Why* Glen Campbell (1973) C&W#20 US#111.

586. LIND, Bob (b. November 24, 1942, Baltimore, MD) Pop guitarist and vocalist. A folk influenced singer-songwriter. CHART COMPOSITIONS: *Elusive Butterfly* (1966) US#5 UK#5, *Remember the Rain* (1966) US#64, *Truly Julie's Blues* (1966) US#65 UK#46, *I Just Let It Take Me* (1966)

US#123, *San Francisco Woman* (1966) US#135. AL-BUMS: **Don't Be Concerned** (1966) US#148, **Photographs and Feelings** (1966, both World Pacific); **The Elusive Bob Lind** (1968, Verve Folkways); **Since There Were Circles** (1971, Capitol). HIT VERSIONS: *Cheryl's Goin' Home* Adam Faith (1966) UK#46, *Elusive Butterfly* Val Doonican (1966) UK#5.

587. LINDE, Dennis (b. March 18, 1943, America) C&W guitarist and vocalist. A Nashville based songwriter who played in the Starlighters during the 1960s, before pursuing a brief solo career in the 1970s. Linde's greatest success has been as a songwriter for such artists as Elvis Presley and John Denver. ALBUMS: **Linde Manor** (1968, Intrepid); **Jubal*** (1972), **Dennis Linde** (1973), **Trapped in the Suburbs** (1974, all Elektra); **Surface Noise** (1976, Monument). HIT VERSIONS: *Bubba Shot the Juke Box* Mark Chesnutt (1992) C&W#66, *Burning Love* Elvis Presley (1972) g US#2 UK#7, also in *The Elvis Medley* (1982) US#71 UK#51; *Callin' Baton Rouge* Garth Brooks (1993) C&W#70, *Down to the Station* B.W. Stevenson (1977) US#82, *For the Heart* Elvis Presley (1976) US#28, *Hold On* Elroy Dude Mowrey (1993) C&W#69, *I Could Sure Use the Feeling* Earl Scruggs (1979) C&W#30, *I'm Gonna Get You* Eddy Raven (1988) C&W#1, *It Sure Is Monday* Mark Chesnutt (1993) C&W#1, *John Deere Green* Joe Diffie (1993) C&W#5 US#69, *Letter to You* Eddy Raven (1989) C&W#1/Shakin' Stevens (1984) UK#10; *Tom Green County Fair, The* Roger Miller (1969) C&W#36, *What'll You Do About Me* Forester Sisters (1992) C&W#73, *Wild Love* Joy Lynn White (1994) C&W#73. As: * Jubal. (*See also under* Billy SWAN.)

588. LINZER, Sandy Pop producer. A staff writer for the music publishers Screen Gems, who achieved a considerable number of pop hits during the 1960–1970s. HIT VERSIONS: *Attack* [vii] Toys (1966) US#18 UK#36, *Baby Make Your Own Sweet Music* [vii] Bandwagon (1968) R&B#48/Jay & the Techniques (1968) US#64; *Bon Bon Vie (Gimme Me the Good Life)* [iv] T.S. Monk (1980) R&B#11 US#63, *Breaking Down the Walls of Heartache* [vii] Jimmy James & the Bandwagon (1968) US#115 UK#4, *House of Strangers* [i] Jim Gilstrap (1975) US#64, *If You're Looking for a Way Out* [v] Odyssey (1980) UK#6, *Keep the Ball Rollin'* [vii] Jay & the Techniques (1967) US#14, *Lover's Concerto, A* [iii] Toys (1965) g R&B#4 US#2 UK#5, *Mornin' Beautiful* [ii] Tony Orlando & Dawn (1975) US#14, *Native New Yorker* [vii] Odyssey (1977) R&B#6 US#21 UK#5, *Opus 17 (Don't Worry 'Bout Me)* [vii] Four Seasons (1966) US#13 UK#20, *Pow Wow* [iv] Cory Daye (1979) US#76, *Skiing in the Snow* [vii] Wigans Ova-

tion (1975) UK#12, *Talk It Over* [vi] Grayson Hugh (1989) US#19, *Use It Up, Wear It Out* [iv] Odyssey (1980) UK#1, *Weekend Lover* [vii] Odyssey (1978) R&B#37 US#57, *Working My Way Back to You* [vii] Four Seasons (1966) US#9/Detroit Spinners (1979) g R&B#6 US#2 UK#1; *You Can Do Magic* Limmie & the Family Cooking (1973) R&B#42 US#84 UK#3, *You Keep Me Dancing* [vii] Samantha Sang (1978) US#56. Co-writers: [i] Dave Appell, [ii] Dave Appell/Hank Medress, [iii] Johann Sebastian Bach (b. March 21, 1685, Eisenach; d. July 28, 1750, Leipzig, both Germany)/Denny Randell, [iv] L. Russell Brown, [v] Ralph Kotov, [vi] Irwin Levine, [vii] Denny Randell. (*See also under* Bob CREWE, Bob GAUDIO.)

589. LIPPMAN, Sidney (b. March 1, 1914, Minneapolis, MN) Stage composer and pianist. A former Juilliard scholar who became a manager at the publishers Chappell Music, before working as an arranger at Irving Berlin's publishing company, where he composed his first song, *These Things You Left Me* [iii] (1940). In 1941, Lippman teamed up with the lyricist Sylvia Dee, for a songwriting partnership that lasted sixteen years. They composed one Broadway show, "Barefoot Boy with Cheek" (1947). HIT VERSIONS: *"A" You're Adorable (The Alphabet Song)* [iv] Perry Como (1949) US#1/Buddy Kaye Quintet (1949) US#27/Tony Pastor (1949) US#12/Jo Stafford & Gordon MacRae (1949) US#4; *After Graduation Day* [i] Sammy Kaye (1947) US#22, *Chickery Chick* [i] Sammy Kaye (1945) US#1/Gene Krupa (1945) US#10/George Olsen (1945) US#12/Evelyn Knight (1946) US#10; *I'm Thrilled* [i] Glenn Miller (1941) US#16, *Laroo, Laroo, Lili Bolero* [ii] Perry Como (1948) US#20/Peggy Lee (1948) US#13; *My Sugar Is So Refined* [i] Johnny Mercer (1946) US#11, *These Things You Left Me* [i] Benny Goodman (1941) US#25, *Too Young* [i] Fran Allison (1951) US#20/Patty Andrews (1951) US#19/Toni Arden (1951) US#15/Nat "King" Cole (1951) US#1/Richard Hayes (1951) US#24. Co-writers: [i] Sylvia Dee (b. 1914; d. 1967), [ii] Sylvia Dee/Elizabeth Moore, [iii] Hal Dickenson, [iv] Buddy Kaye/Fred Wise.

590. LIVGREN, Kerry (b. September 18, 1949, KS) Rock guitarist and keyboard player. The principal songwriter in the American rock group Kansas. CHART COMPOSITIONS: *Carry on My Wayward Son* (1977) US#11 UK#51, *Point of Know Return* (1978) US#28, *Dust in the Wind* (1978) g US#6, *Portrait (He Knew)* (1978) US#64, *Lonely Wind* (1979) US#60, *People of the South Wind* (1979) US#23, *Reason to Be* (1979) US#52, *Hold On* (1980) US#40, *Got to Rock On* (1980) US#76, *Play the Game Tonight* [i] (1982) US#17, *Right Away* (1982) US#73,

Fight Fire with Fire (1983) US#58. ALBUMS: **Kansas** (1974) US#174, **Song for America** (1975) g US#57, **Masque** (1975) g US#70, **Leftoverture** (1976) p US#5, **Point of Know Return** (1977) p US#4, **Two for the Show** (1978) p US#32, **Monolith** (1979) g US#10, **Audio-Visions** (1980) g US#26, **Vinyl Confessions** (1982, all Kirshner) US#16; **Drastic Measures** (1983, CBS Associates) US#41. COMPILATIONS: **Best of Kansas** (1984, CBS Associates) p US#154; **The Kansas Box Set** (1995, Sony). Livgren became a born-again Christian in 1980, and left the group shortly afterwards to record contemporary Christian material. ALBUM: **Seeds of Change** (1980). Co-writers: [i] Phil Ehart (b. February 4, 1950, KA)/Danny Flower/Robert Frazier/Richard Williams (b. February 1, 1950, KS).

591. LIVINGSTON, Jerry (b. Jerry Levinson, March 25, 1909, Denver, CO; d. 1987) Film and stage composer, pianist and conductor. A musician who spent many years struggling on Tin Pan Alley until he achieved any degree of success. Livingston worked with a variety of lyricists, and his songs were first included in the Broadway show "Bright Lights of 1934." He worked in Hollywood during the late 1940s, contributing to the films "Those Redheads from Seattle" (1950) and "Cinderella (1959). During the 1970s, Livingston concentrated on television composition. ALBUMS: **Red Garters** ost (1954, Columbia); **Jack and the Beanstalk** sc (1956, RKO/Unique); **Cinderella** sc (1959, RCA); **Hawaiian Eye** tvst (1959), **77 Sunset Strip** tvst (1959, both Warner Brothers); **Follow That Dream** ost (1962, RCA); **Cinderella** ost (1981, Disneyland). HIT VERSIONS: *Baby, Baby, Baby* [ii] Teresa Brewer (1953) US#12, *Blue and Sentimental* [i] Count Basie (1948) US#21, *Hanging Tree, The* [iv] Marty Robbins (1959) C&W#15 US#38, *I've Got an Invitation to a Dance* [iv] Paul Pendarvis (1935) US#8, *It's the Talk of the Town* [iv] Glen Gray (1933) US#6, re-issued (1942) US#22/Fletcher Henderson (1933) US#20; *Sixty Seconds Got Together* [ii] Mills Brothers (1938) US#8, *Thoughtless* [ii] Vic Damone (1948) US#22/Doris Day (1948) US#24/Buddy Kaye Quintet (1948) US#22/Guy Lombardo (1948) US#22/Gordon MacRae (1948) US#28; *Twelth of Never, The* [v] Johnny Mathis (1957) US#9/Cliff Richard (1964) UK#8/Slim Whitman (1966) C&W#17/Chi-Lites (1969) R&B#47 US#122/Donny Osmond (1973) g US#8 UK#1/David Houston (1977) C&W#98/Elvis Presley (1995) UK#21/Carter Twins (1997) UK#61; *Under a Blanket of Blue* [iv] Don Bestor (1933) US#8/Glen Gray (1933) US#6; *Veni-Vidi-Vici (I Came, I Saw, I Conquered)* [v] Gaylords (1954) US#30/Ronnie Hilton (1954) UK#12; *Wake the Town and Tell the People* [iii] Les Baxter & His Orchestra (1955) US#5/Mindy Carson (1955) US#13; *(When It's) Darkness on the Delta* [iv] Chick Bulock (1933) US#19/Ted Fiorito (1933) US#12; *Who Are We* [v] Ronnie Hilton (1956) UK#6/Vera Lynn (1956) UK#30; *Young Emotions* [ii] Ricky Nelson (1960) R&B#28 US#12. Co-writers: [i] William "Count" Basie/Mack David, [ii] Mack David, [iii] Sammy Gallop, [iv] Al Neiburg/Marty Symes, [v] Paul Francis Webster. (*See also under* Al HOFFMAN, Bob MERRILL, Mitchell PARISH.)

592. L.L. Cool J. (b. James Todd Smith, January 14, 1968, Queens, NY) Rapper. An innovative rap artist who was the first to sign to the rap label Def Jam. CHART COMPOSITIONS: *I Can't Live Without My Radio* (1985) R&B#15, *Rock the Bells* (1986) R&B#17, *You'll Rock* (1986) R&B#59, *I'm Bad* [ii] (1987) R&B#4 US#84 UK#71, *I Need Love* [ii] (1987) R&B#1 US#14 UK#8, *Go Cut Creator Go* (1987) UK#66, *Going Back to Cali*/*Jack the Ripper* (1988) R&B#12 US#31 UK#37, *I'm That Type of Guy* [i] (1989) R&B#1 UK#43, *Around the Way Girl* [iii]/*Mama Said Knock You Out* (1990) US#9 UK#41, re-issued (1991) UK#36; *6 Minutes of Pleasure* (1991) US#95, *How I'm Comin'* [vi] (1993) US#57 UK#37, *Pink Cookies in a Plastic Bag Getting Crushed By Buildings* [vi]/*Back Seat of My Jeep* (1993) R&B#24 US#42, *Hey Lover* [v] (1996) p R&B#3 US#3 UK#17, *Doin' It* [iv] featuring Boyz II Men (1996) R&B#7 US#9, *Loungin'* (1996) UK#7. ALBUMS: **Radio** (1985, Columbia) p US#46 UK#71; **Bigger and Deffer** (1987) p US#3 UK#54, **Walking with a Panther** (1989) p US#6 UK#43, **Mama Said Knock You Out** (1990) p US#16 UK#49, **14 Shots to the Dome** (1993) US#5 UK#74, **Mr. Smith** (1996, all Def Jam) p US#20. COMPILATION: **Greatest Hits-All World** (1996, Def Jam) UK#41+. HIT VERSIONS: *Big Ole Butt* TLC sampled in *Hat 2 Da Back* (1993) US#30. Co-writers: [i] Steve Ett, [ii] Bob Erving/Darrly Pierce/Dwayne Simon, [iii] R. James/M. Williams, [iv] J.B.R. Smith, [v] Rod Temperton, [vi] M. Williams.

593. Lobo (b. Roland Kent Lavoie, July 31, 1943, Tallahassee, FL) Pop guitarist, producer and vocalist. A singer-songwriter who achieved sixteen hits between 1971–1979. Lavoie first performed in the groups the Rumors, the Sugar Beats, and the Legends, before taking the stage name Lobo. CHART COMPOSITIONS: *Me and You and a Dog Named Boo* (1971) US#5 UK#4, *I'd Love You to Want Me* (1972) g C&W#40 US#2 UK#5, *It Sure Took a Long, Long Time* (1973) US#27, *How Can I Tell Her* (1973) US#22, *Don't Expect Me to Be Your Friend* (1973) US#8, *There Ain't No Way* (1973) US#68, *Standing at the End of the Line* (1974) US#37, *Don't Tell Me*

Goodnight (1975) US#27. ALBUMS: **Introducing Lobo** (1971) US#163, **Of a Simple Man** (1972) US#37, **Calumet** (1973) US#128, **Just a Singer** (1974) US#183, **A Cowboy Afraid of Horses** (1975, all Big Tree) US#151; **Lobo** (1979, MCA/Curb). HIT VERSIONS: *How Can I Tell Her* Earl Richards (1973) C&W#85, *I'd Love You to Want Me* Narvel Felts (1982) C&W#58, *Me and You and a Dog Named Boo* Stonewall Jackson (1971) C&W#7.

594. LODGE, John (b. July 20, 1945, Birmingham, England) Rock bassist and vocalist. A key member of the Moody Blues, who wrote the hits *Isn't Life Strange* (1972) US#29 UK#13 and *Steppin' in a Slide Zone* (1978) US#39. Lodge also performed in the duo Blue Jays, and recorded the solo album **Natural Avenue** (1977, Threshold) US#121 UK#38. (*See also under* Justin HAYWARD.)

595. LOESSER, Frank (b. June 29, 1910; d. March 28, 1969, both New York, NY) Film and stage composer, pianist. A songwriter of remarkable versatility, who had a nonchalant mastery of the vernacular. Loesser wrote everything from war songs, *Praise the Lord and Pass the Ammunition*, to odes to gambling, *Luck Be a Lady*. The son of German immigrants, Loesser worked as a newspaper reporter before he became a lyricist, his first published song being *In Love with the Memory of You* (1931). After many years of unrewarding toil, Loesser headed to Hollywood, where he achieved his first hit with *Moon of Manakoora* [ix] from the film "The Hurricane" (1937). It was followed by lyrical contributions to the films "Christmas Holiday" (1944), "Variety Girl" (1947) and "Neptune's Daughter" (1949). After World War II, Loesser began composing his own music, and in 1952, he wrote the film score to "Hans Christian Andersen," which introduced the songs *Thumbelina*, *The Ugly Duckling*, *The King's New Clothes*, *Inchworm*, and *Wonderful Copenhagen*. Loesser was finally successful on Broadway with the shows "Where's Charley?" (1948), "Guys and Dolls" (1950), "The Most Happy Fella" (1956), "Greenwillow" (1960), and "How to Succeed in Business Without Really Trying" (1961), which ran for one thousand four hundred and seventeen performances. Loesser died of cancer in 1969. ALBUMS: **Where's Charly?** oc (1948, Monmouth Evergreen); **Guys and Dolls** oc (1951) US#1, **Hans Christian Andersen** ost (1952, both Decca); **Most Happy Fella** oc (1956, Philips) US#11 UK#6; **Greenwillow** oc (1960, RCA); **Most Happy Fella** oc (1960, HMV) UK#19; **How to Succeed in Business Without Really Trying** oc (1961, RCA) US#19; **How to Succeed in Business Without Really Trying** ost (1967, United Artists) US#146; **Guys and Dolls** oc (1992, RCA) US#109.

HIT VERSIONS: *Anywhere I Wander* Mel Torme (1952) US#30/Julius La Rosa (1953) US#4; *Baby, It's Cold Outside* Ella Fitzgerald & Louis Jordan (1949) US#9/Homer & Jethro (1949) US#22/Sammy Kaye (1949) US#12/Johnny Mercer & Margaret Whiting (1949) US#3/Dinah Shore & Buddy Clark (1949) US#4; *Bloop, Bleep!* Danny Kaye (1947) US#21/Alvino Rey (1947) US#13; *Bushel and a Peck, A* Andrews Sisters (1950) US#22/Perry Como & Betty Hutton (1950) US#3/Doris Day (1950) US#16/Johnny Desmond (1950) US#29/Margaret Whiting & Jimmy Wakely (1950) US#6; *Dolores* [i] Bing Crosby (1941) US#2/Tommy Dorsey (1941) US#1; *Fuddy Duddy the Watchmaker* Kay Kyser (1943) US#11, *Have I Stayed Away Too Long?* Perry Como (1944) US#19/Tex Grande (1944) US#28; *Hoop Dee-Doo* [iv] Perry Como (1950) US#1/Doris Day (1950) US#17/Russ Morgan (1950) US#15/Kay Starr (1950) US#2; *I Don't Want to Walk Without You* [xi] Bing Crosby (1942) US#9/Harry James (1942) US#1/Dinah Shore (1942) US#12/Baja Marimba Band (1969) US#121/Barry Manilow (1980) US#36; *I Wish I Didn't Love You So* Dick Farney (1947) US#13/Dick Haymes (1947) US#9/Betty Hutton (1947) US#5/Vaughn Monroe (1947) US#2/Dinah Shore (1947) US#2; *I Wish I Were Twins* [iii] Henry Allen (1934) US#20/Emil Coleman (1934) US#8/Fats Waller (1934) US#8; *If I Were a Bell* Frankie Laine (1950) US#30, *In My Arms* [v] Dick Haymes (1943) US#3, *Jingle, Jangle, Jingle* [viii] Gene Autry (1942) US#14/Kay Kyser (1942) g US#1/Freddy Martin (1942) US#15/Merry Macs (1944) US#4; *Just Another Polka* [iv] Eddie Fisher (1953) US#24/Jo Stafford (1953) US#22; *Leave Us Face It (We're in Love)* [ii] Hildegarde (1944) US#29, *Moon of Manakoora, The* [ix] Bing Crosby (1938) US#10/Ray Noble (1938) US#15; *Moon Over Burma* [vi] Shep Fields (1940) US#26/Gene Krupa (1949) US#23; *My Darling, My Darling* Doris Day & Buddy Clark (1948) US#7/Peter Lind Hayes (1949) US#20/Jack Lathrop & Eve Young (1949) US#26/Jo Stafford & Gordon MacRae (1949) US#1; *No Two People* Doris Day & Donald O'Connor (1952) US#25, *Now That I Need You* Doris Day (1949) US#20/Frankie Laine (1949) US#20; *On a Slow Boat to China* Larry Clinton (1948) US#25/Eddy Howard (1948) US#6/Kay Kyser (1948) g US#2/Snooky Lanson (1948) US#24/Art Lund (1948) US#12/Freddy Martin (1948) US#6/Benny Goodman (1949) US#7/Emile Ford & the Checkmates (1960) UK#3; *Once in Love with Amy* Ray Bolger (1949) US#16, *Praise the Lord and Pass the Ammunition* Merry Macs (1942) US#8/Royal Harmony Quartet (1942) R&B#10/Southern Sons (1942) R&B#7/Kay Kyser (1943) g US#1; *Spring Will Be a Little Late This Year* Morton Downey (1944) US#25, *Standing on the Corner* Four Lads (1956) US#3, re-issued (1960) UK#34/Dean Martin (1956) US#22/ King Brothers (1960) UK#4; *Strange Enchantment* [vi] Dorothy Lamour (1939) US#5/Ozzie Nelson (1939) US#8; *Tallahassee* Bing Crosby & the Andrews Sisters (1947) US#10/Dinah Shore & Woody Herman (1947) US#15; *Thumbelina* Danny Kaye (1952) US#28, *Ugly Duckling, The* Mike Reid (1975) UK#10, *Wave to Me, My Lady* [x] Elton Britt (1946) US#19, *Woman in Love, A* Four Aces (1955) US#14 UK#19/Ronnie Hilton (1956) UK#30/Frankie Laine (1955) US#19 UK#1; *Wonderful Copenhagen* Danny Kaye (1953) UK#5. Co-writers: [i] Louis Alter, [ii] Abe Burroughs, [iii] Eddie De Lange/Joseph Meyer, [iv] Milton De Lugg, [v] Ted Grouya, [vi] Frederick Hollander, [vii] Edgar Leslie/Joseph Meyer, [viii] Joseph J. Lilley, [ix] Alfred Newman, [x] William Stein, [xi] Jules Styne. (*See also under* Hoagy CARMICHAEL, Burton LANE, Jimmy McHUGH, Victor SCHERTZINGER, Arthur SCHWARTZ, Victor YOUNG.)

596. LOFGREN, Nils (b. June 21, 1951, Chicago, IL) Rock guitarist, pianist and vocalist. A former classical music student turned rock guitarist, who played in various high school bands before forming Grin in the late 1960s, which charted with *We All Sung Together* (1970) US#108 and *White Lies* (1972) US#75. ALBUMS: **Grin** (1971) US#192, **1+1** (1972) US#180, **All Out** (1973, all Spindizzy) US#186; **Gone Crazy** (1973, A&M). Lofgren became a sideman for Neil Young during the 1970s, and worked with the group Crazy Horse, before opting for a solo career that has yet to better the classy pop of his eponymous debut album. In 1984, Lofgren toured as a member of Bruce Springsteen's E Street Band. CHART COMPOSITIONS: *Night Fades Away* (1981) US#109, *Secrets in the Street* (1985) UK#53. ALBUMS: **Nils Lofgren** (1975) US#141, **Back It Up** (1976), **Cry Tough** (1976) US#32 UK#8, **I Came to Dance** (1977) US#36 UK#30, **Night After Night** (1977) US#44 UK#38, **Nils** (1979, all A&M) US#54; **Night Fades Away** (1981) US#99 UK#50, **Wonderland** (1983, both Backstreet); **Flip** (1985, Columbia) UK#36; **Code of the Road** (1986, Towerbell) UK#86; **Silver Lining** (1991, Rykodisc) US#153 UK#61; **Crooked Line** (1992, Essential); **Every Breath** ost (1994, Windsong); **Live on the Test** (1994, Windsong); **Damaged Goods** (1995, Transatlantic). COMPILATIONS: **A Rhythm Romance** (1982, A&M) UK#100; **Don't Walk…Rock** (1990, Connoisseur); **Best of Nils Lofgren** (1992, A&M).

597. LOGGINS, Dave (b. October 11, 1947, Mountain City, TN) Pop guitarist and vocalist. The cousin of the singer-songwriter Kenny Loggins, who is a successful Nashville tunesmith. CHART COMPOSITIONS: *Please Come to Boston* (1974) US#5, *Someday* (1974) US#57, *Just as Long as I Have You* with Gus Hardin (1985) C&W#72. ALBUMS: **Personal Belongings** (1972, Vanguard); **Apprentice in a Musical Workshop** (1974) US#54, **Country Suite** (1976), **One Way Ticket to Paradise** (1977), **David Loggins** (1979, all Epic). HIT VERSIONS: *Everything Comes Down to Money and Love* [ii] Hank Williams, Jr. (1993) C&W#62, *If I Had My Wish Tonight* [i] David Lasley (1982) US#36, *Jasper* [iii] Jim Stafford (1976) US#69, *Love Will Find Its Way to You* Reba McIntire (1988) C&W#1, *Morning Desire* Kenny Rogers (1985) C&W#1 US#72, *Pieces of April* Three Dog Night (1972) US#19, *She Is His Only Need* Wynonna (1992) C&W#1, *Til the World Ends* Three Dog Night (1975) US#32. Co-writers: [i] Randy Goodrum, [ii] G. Scrivenor, [iii] Jim Stafford.

598. LOGGINS, Kenny (b. January 7, 1948, Everett, WA) Rock guitarist and vocalist. A singer-songwriter with a clean, clear tenor, who first achieved success as one half of the duo Loggins and Messina. Loggins learned the guitar while still at high school, and by the age of thirteen, was playing in rock bands. In 1967, he majored in music from Pasadena City College, California, and after recording self-titled albums as a member of the groups **Gator Creek** (1970, Mercury) and **Second Helping** (1970, Viva), Loggins obtained a staff writers position with the music publishers Wingate, where his composition *House at Pooh Corner* was recorded by the Nitty Gritty Dirt Band. Loggins signed to Columbia Records in 1971 as a solo artist, where he recorded his debut album with the producer Jim Messina, a project that resulted in the formation of an unplanned, country influenced, soft-rock duo. CHART COMPOSITIONS: *Your Mamma Don't Dance* [viii] (1973) g US#4, *My Music* [viii] (1973) g US#16, *Watching the River Run* [viii] (1973) US#71, *Growin'* [xiii] (1974) US#52. ALBUMS: **Kenny Loggins with Jim Messina Sittin' In** (1971) p US#70, **Loggins and Messina** (1973) p US#16, **Full Sail** (1973) p US#10, **On Stage** (1974) p US#5, **Mother Lode** (1974) g US#8, **So Fine** (1974) US#21, **Native Sons** (1976) g US#16, **Finale** (1977, all Columbia) US#83. COMPILATION: **Best of Friends** (1977, Columbia) p US#61. In 1976, Loggins finally embarked on the solo career that he had originally intended. CHART COMPOSITIONS: *I Believe in Love* [i] (1977) US#66, *Whenever I Call You "Friend"* [vii] (1978) US#5, *This Is It* [vi] (1980) R&B#19 US#11, *Keep the Fire* [v] (1980) US#36, *I'm Alright* (1980) US#7, *Don't Fight It* [x] with Steve Perry (1982) US#17, *Heart to Heart* [iii] (1982) R&B#71 US#15, *Welcome to Heartlight* (1982) US#24, *Foot-*

loose [ix] (1984) g US#1 UK#6, *I'm Free (Heaven Helps the Man)* [ix] (1984) US#22, *Vox Humana* (1985) US#29, *Forever* [ii] (1985) US#40, *I'll Be There* [iii] (1985) US#88, *Playing with the Boys* [xiv] (1986) US#60, *Nobody's Fool* [xii] (1988) US#8, *Conviction of the Heart* [xi] (1991) US#65. ALBUMS: **Celebrate Me Home** (1977) p US#27, **Nightwatch** (1978) p US#7, **Keep the Fire** (1979) p US#16, **Kenny Loggins Alive** (1980) g US#11, **High Adventure** (1982) g US#13, **Vox Humana** (1985) g US#41, **Back to Avalon** (1988) US#69, **Leap of Faith** (1991) g US#71, **Outside-From the Redwoods** (1993) US#60, **Return to Pooh Corner** (1994) g US#65, **The Unimaginable Life** (1997, all Columbia). COMPILATION: **Yesterday, Today, Tomorrow-The Greatest Hits of Kenny Loggins** (1997, Columbia). HIT VERSIONS: *Danny's Song* Anne Murray (1972) C&W#10 US#7, *House at Pooh Corner* Nitty Gritty Dirt Band (1971) US#53, *Love Song, A* [iv] Anne Murray (1974) C&W#5 US#12, *Your Mamma Don't Dance* [viii] Roy Head (1983) C&W#85/Poison (1989) US#10 UK#13. Co-writers: [i] Alan Bergman/Marilyn Bergman, [ii] David Foster, [iii] David Foster/E.E. Loggins, [iv] D.L. George, [v] Eva Loggins, [vi] Michael McDonald, [vii] Melissa Manchester, [viii] Jim Messina, [ix] Dean Pitchford, [x] Dean Pitchford/Steve Perry, [xi] G. Thomas, [xii] M. Towers, [xiii] R. Wilkins, [xiv] I. Wolf/P. Wolf. (*See also under* Michael McDONALD.)

599. LOMAX, Jackie (b. May 10, 1944, Liverpool, England) Pop guitarist and vocalist. One of many artists briefly signed to the Apple label. Lomax had been a member of the group Balls, before recording an album with Badger, **White Lady** (1974, Epic), after which he pursued a brief solo career under the patronage of various former Beatles. ALBUMS: **Is This What You Want?** (1968, Apple) US#145; **Home Is in My Head** (1970), **Three** (1971, both Warner Brothers); **Livin' for Lovin'** (1975), **Did You Ever Have That Feeling?** (1977, both Capitol). HIT VERSION: *Inside Looking Out* Grand Funk Railroad (1971) UK#40.

600. LORDAN, Jerry (b. Jeremiah Patrick Lordan, April 30, 1934; d. July 24, 1995, both London, England) Pop vocalist and producer. A singer who achieved considerably greater success as a composer of 1960s pop instrumentals. Lordan was a self-taught musician who first performed in R.A.F. camp shows, before working as a stand-up comedian. Due to financial problems in the 1970s, he sold many of his copyrights. Lordan died of liver failure in 1995. CHART COMPOSITIONS: *I'll Stay Single* (1959) UK#26, *Who Could Be Bluer?* (1960) UK#17, *Sing Like an Angel* (1960) UK#36. ALBUM: **All My Own Work** (1960, Parlophone). HIT VERSIONS: *Apache* Jorgen Ingmann (1960) R&B#9 US#2/Shadows (1960) UK#1/Bert Weedon (1960) UK#24/Sonny James (1961) US#87/Arrows & Davie Allan (1965) US#64/Sugarhill Gang (1981) R&B#13 US#53; *Atlantis* Shadows (1963) UK#2, *Diamonds* Jet Harris & Tony Meehan (1963) UK#1, *Girl Like You, A* Cliff Richard (1961) UK#3, *I'm a Moody Guy* Shane Fenton (1961) UK#22, *I'm Just a Baby* Louise Cordet (1962) UK#13, *I've Waited So Long* Anthony Newley (1959) UK#3, *Mary Ann* Shadows (1965) UK#17, *Scarlet O'Hara* Bobby Gregg (1963) US#112/Jet Harris & Tony Meehan (1963) UK#2/Lawrence Welk (1963) US#89; *Song of Mexico* Tony Meehan (1964) UK#39, *Walk Away* Shane Fenton (1962) US#38, *Wonderful Land* Shadows (1962) UK#1. (*See also under* Roger COOK.)

601. LOUDERMILK, John D. (b. March 31, 1934, Durham, NC) Pop multi-instrumentalist and vocalist. A highly original country influenced singer-songwriter, with a unique sense of the absurd, who has published over five hundred songs, that have collectively sold over fourteen million records. Loudermilk's albums are bizarre collections of country-blues based story telling, that focus on the minutiae of life as parables of modern living. His best known song *Tobacco Road*— a tale of racial tension in rural southern America — has been recorded over forty times. Loudermilk was raised in a religious family and played the drums in the Salvation Army Band. After learning the guitar, ukelele, trumpet, trombone and saxophone, he made his television debut at the age of twelve, and later had his own radio show under the name of Johnny Dee. During the 1940s he lived in Nashville, where he published his songs and became an assistant to the guitarist Chet Atkins. George Hamilton, IV first popularized a Loudermilk song, when he recorded *A Rose and a Baby Ruth* (1956). Loudermilk recorded for the Colonial label as Ebe Sneezer, before achieving a number of hits under his own name at RCA Records. CHART COMPOSITIONS: *The Language of Love* (1961) US#32 UK#13, *Thou Shalt Not Steal* (1962) US#73, *Callin' Dr. Casey* (1962) US#83, *Road Hog* (1962) US#65, *Bad News* (1963) C&W#23, *Blue Train (Of the Heartbreak Line)* (1964) C&W#44 US#132, *Th' Wife* (1964) C&W#45, *That Ain't All* (1965) C&W#20, *It's My Time* (1967) C&W#51. ALBUMS: **The Language of Love** (1962), **Twelve Sides of John D. Loudermilk** (1963), **John D. Loudermilk Sings a Bizarre Collection of the Most Unusual Songs** (1966), **Suburban Attitudes in Country Verse** (1968), **Country Love Songs** (1968), **The Open Mind of John D. Loudermilk** (1969, all

RCA); **Elloree, Volume 1** (1971, Warner Brothers); **Just Passin' Through** (1978, Mim). COMPILATIONS: **Best of John D. Loudermilk** (1973), **Encores** (1975, both RCA); **Blue Train, 1961–1962** (1989), **It's My Time** (1989, both Bear Family). HIT VERSIONS: *Abilene* [i] George Hamilton, IV (1963) C&W#1 US#15/Sonny James (1977) C&W#24; *Amigo's Guitar* Kitty Wells (1959) C&W#5, *Angela Jones* Johnny Ferguson (1960) US#27/Michael Cox (1960) UK#8; *Bad News* Johnny Cash (1964) C&W#8/Boxcar Willie (1982) C&W#36; *Big Daddy* Sue Thompson (1964) US#132/Boots Randolph (1967) US#105/Browns (1968) C&W#52; *Blue Train (Of the Heartbreak Line)* George Hamilton, IV (1972) C&W#22, *Break My Mind* George Hamilton, IV (1967) C&W#6/Sammy Davis, Jr. (1968) US#106/Bobby Wood (1968) US#110/Vern Gosdin (1978) C&W#6; *Ebony Eyes* Everly Brothers (1961) C&W#25 US#8 UK#17/Orion (1979) C&W#89; *Falling Again* Porter Wagoner (1960) C&W#26/Don Williams (1981) C&W#6; *Fort Worth, Dallas or Houston* George Hamilton, IV (1964) C&W#9, *God Will* Lyle Lovett (1987) C&W#18, *Google Eye* Nashville Teens (1964) US#117 UK#10, *Grin and Bear It* Jimmy Newman (1959) C&W#11, *(He's My) Dreamboat* Connie Francis (1961) US#14, *Hollywood* Connie Francis (1961) US#42, *I Gotta Go ('Cause I Love You)* Brian Hyland (1960) US#101, *I Wanna Live* Glen Campbell (1968) C&W#1 US#36/Eddy Raven (1976) C&W#87, *If the Boy Only Knew* Sue Thompson (1962) US#112, also on B-side of *Have a Good Time* (1962) US#31, *Indian Reservation (The Lament of the Cherokee Reservation Indian)* Raiders (1971) g US#1/Billy Thunderkloud & the Chieftones (1976) C&W#74/Tim McGraw in *Indian Outlaw* (1994) g C&W#8 US#15; *It's My Time* Everly Brothers (1968) US#112 UK#39/George Hamilton, IV (1968) C&W#50; *James (Hold the Ladder Steady)* Sue Thompson (1962) US#17, *Little Bird, The* Nashville Teens (1965) US#123 UK#38, *Little World Girl* George Hamilton, IV (1968) C&W#18, *Mister Jones* Al Downing (1979) C&W#20, *Night Atlanta Burned, The* Atkins-String Company (1975) C&W#77, *Norman* Sue Thompson (1962) US#3/Carol Deene (1962) UK#24; *Paper Tiger* Sue Thompson (1965) US#23, *Sad Movies (Make Me Cry)* Sue Thompson (1961) US#5/Lennon Sisters (1961) US#56/Carol Deene (1961) UK#44; *Sittin' in the Balcony* Eddie Cochran (1957) R&B#7 US#18, *Stayin' In* Bobby Vee (1961) US#33, *Stop Th' Music* Sue Thompson (1965) US#115, *Talk Back Trembling Lips* Eddie Ashworth (1963) C&W#1 US#101/Johnny Tillotson (1964) US#7; *Then You Can Tell Me Goodbye* Casinos (1967) US#6 UK#28/Eddy Arnold (1968) C&W#1 US#84/Glen Campbell (1976) C&W#4 US#27/ Toby Bleau (1979) US#57; *Thou Shalt Not Steal* Dick

& Dee Dee (1964) US#13/Freddie & the Dreamers (1965) UK#44/Newbeats (1969) US#128; *Three Stars* Ruby Wright (1959) US#19, *Tobacco Road* Nashville Teens (1964) US#14 UK#6/Jamul (1970) US#93/Roy Clark (1986) C&W#56; *Torture* Kris Jensen (1962) US#20, *Waterloo* [ii] Stonewall Jackson (1959) C&W#1 R&B#11 US#4 UK#24, *What a Woman in Love Won't Do* Sandy Possey (1967) US#31 UK#48, *What's Wrong Bill* Sue Thompson (1963) US#135. Co-writers: [i] Lester Brown/Bob Gibson/Albert Stanton, [ii] Marijohn Wilkin.

602. LOVETT, Lyle (b. November 1, 1957, Klein, TX) C&W guitarist and vocalist. A contemporary country artist and actor who has been influenced by western swing, rock and jazz. CHART COMPOSITIONS: *Farther Down the Line* (1986) C&W#21, *Cowboy Man* (1986) C&W#10, *God Will* (1987) C&W#18, *Why I Don't Know* (1987) C&W#15, *Give Back My Heart* (1987) C&W#13, *She's No Lady* (1988) C&W#17, *I Loved You Yesterday* (1988) C&W#24, *If I Had a Boat* (1988) C&W#66, *I Married Her Because She Looks Like You* (1988) C&W#45. ALBUMS: **Lyle Lovett** (1986), **Pontiac** (1988, both MCA) US#117; **Lyle Lovett and His Large Band** (1989, MCA/Curb) g US#62; **Joshua Judges Ruth** (1992, Curb) US#57; **I Love Everybody** (1994) US#26 UK#54, **The Road to Ensanada** (1996, both MCA).

603. LOWE, Chris (b. Christopher Sean Lowe, October 4, 1959, Blackpool, England), and **TENNANT, Neil** (b. Neil Francis Tennant, July 10, 1954, Gosforth, England) Both pop keyboard players, producers and vocalists. As the duo the Pet Shop Boys, Lowe and Tennant have become two of the most consistently successful British songwriters since the mid–1980s. Tennant was initially a cellist and pop magazine writer, and Lowe a cabaret pianist who had studied architecture, before they formed their synthesizer dominated group in 1981. CHART COMPOSITIONS: *West End Girls* (1985) R&B#38 US#1 UK#1, *Love Comes Quickly* [i] (1986) US#62 UK#19, *Opportunities (Let's Make Lots of Money)* (1986) US#10 UK#11, *Suburbia* (1986) US#70 UK#8, *It's a Sin* (1987) US#9 UK#1, *What Have I Done to Deserve This* [iii]* (1987) US#2 UK#2, *Rent* (1987) UK#8, *Domino Dancing* (1988) UK#7, *Left to My Own Devices* (1988) US#84 UK#4, *Nothing Has Been Proved** (1989) UK#16, *So Hard* (1990) US#62 UK#4, *Being Boring* (1990) UK#20, *How Can I Expect to Be Taken Seriously?* (1991) US#93 UK#4, *Jealousy* (1991) UK#12, *D.J. Culture* (1991) UK#13, remixed (1991) UK#40; *Was It Worth It?* (1991) UK#24, *Can You Forgive Her?* (1993) US#109 UK#7, *I Wouldn't Normally Do This Kind of Thing* (1993) UK#13, *Lib-*

eration (1994) UK#14, *Yesterday, When I Was Mad* (1994) UK#13, *Paninaro '95* (1995) UK#15, *Before* (1996) UK#7, *Se a Vide E (That's the Way Life Is)* (1996) UK#8, *Single* (1996) UK#14. ALBUMS: **Please** (1986) p US#7 UK#3, **Actually** (1987) g US#25 UK#2, **Introspective** (1988) g US#34 UK#2, **Behaviour** (1990) US#45 UK#2, **Very** (1993) g US#20 UK#1, **Bilingual** (1996, all Parlophone) UK#4. COMPILATIONS: **Disco** (1986) US#95 UK#15, **Discography** (1991) g US#111 UK#3, **Disco 2** (1994) US#75 UK#6, **Alternative** (1995, all Parlophone) US#103 UK#2. Tennant has also recorded as a member of the group Electronic, charting with *Getting Away with It* [ii] (1989) US#38 UK#12 and *Disappointed* [ii] (1992) UK#6, and releasing the album **Electronic** (1991, Warner Brothers) US#109. HIT VERSIONS: *Don't Drop Bombs* Liza Minnelli (1989) UK#46, *I'm Not Scared* Eight Wonder (1988) UK#7, *In Private* Dusty Springfield (1989) UK#14, *Losing My Mind* Liza Minnelli (1989) UK#6, *So Sorry I Said* Liza Minnelli (1989) UK#62, *West End Girls* East 17 (1993) UK#11. With: * Dusty Springfield. Co-writers: [i] S. Hague, [ii] Johnny Marr/Sumner/Neil Tennant only, [iii] Allee Willis.

604. LOWE, Nick (b. March 24, 1949, Woodchurch, England) Pop bassist, producer and vocalist. A performer and producer who was a member of the 1970s group Brinsley Schwarz, which recorded the original version of his song *(What's So Funny 'Bout) Peace Love and Understanding*, that, when recorded by Curtis Stigers, was included on the multi-million selling film soundtrack "The Bodyguard" (1992). ALBUMS: **Brinsley Schwarz** (1970, United Artists); **Despite It All** (1970, Liberty); **Silver Pistol** (1972), **Nervous on the Road** (1972), **Please Don't Ever Change** (1973, all United Artists). COMPILATIONS: **Original Golden Greats** (1974), **New Favorites** (1974), **Fifteen Thoughts of Brinsley Schwartz** (1978, all United Artists). Lowe's cynical solo single *We Love You Bay City Rollers* gave him a Japanese hit in 1975, after which he became the house producer at Stiff Records, where he worked with Elvis Costello. CHART COMPOSITIONS: *I Love the Sound of Breaking Glass* [ii] (1978) UK#7, *So It Goes* (1978) US#109, *Crackin' Up* (1979) UK#34, *Cruel to Be Kind* [iii] (1979) US#12 UK#12, *Switch Board Susan* (1979) US#107, *Half a Boy, Half a Man* (1984) US#110 UK#53, *I Knew the Bride (When She Used to Rock and Roll)* (1986) US#77. ALBUMS: **Jesus of Cool/Pure Pop for Now People** (1978) US#127 UK#22, **Labor of Lust** (1979, both Radar) US#31 UK#43; **Nick the Knife** (1982) US#50 UK#99, **The Abominable Showman** (1983) US#129, **Nick Lowe and His Cowboy Outfit** (1984) US#113, **The Rose of Eng-**

land (1985, all F-Beat); **Pinker and Prouder Than Previous** (1988, Demon); **Party of One** (1990, Reprise) US#182; **The Impossible Bird** (1995, Demon). COMPILATIONS: **Sixteen All-Time Hits** (1984), **Nick's Knack** (1986), **Basher — The Best of Nick Lowe** (1989, both Demon). Lowe has also recorded albums as a member of the groups Little Village, **Little Village** (1992, Reprise) US#66 UK#23, and Rockpile, **Seconds of Pleasure** (1980, F-Beat) US#27 UK#34. HIT SONGS: *I Knew the Bride (When She Used to Rock and Roll)* Dave Edmunds (1977) UK#26, *I Need You* [i] Paul Carrack (1982) US#37, *Milk and Alcohol* [iv] Dr. Feelgood (1979) UK#9. Co-writers: [i] M. Belmont/Paul Carrack, [ii] Andrew Bodnar/Stephen Golding, [iii] Ian Gomm, [iv] John Mayo.

605. LUCAS, Reggie (b. America) R&B guitarist and producer. A frequent collaborator with the percussionist James Mtume, both former Miles Davis sidemen, who wrote and produced for such artists as Randy Crawford. HIT VERSIONS: *Back Together Again* [i] Roberta Flack & Donny Hathaway (1980) US#25 UK#31, *Borderline* Madonna (1984) US#10 UK#56, re-issued (1986) UK#2; *Closer I Get to You, The* [i] Roberta Flack & Donny Hathaway (1978) g R&B#1 US#2 UK#42/For Lovers Only (1994) R&B#87; *Exciting* [i] Marc Sadane (1982) R&B#64, *Never Knew Love Like This Before* [i] Stephanie Mills (1980) g R&B#12 US#6 UK#4, *One Minute from Love* [i] Sadane (1982) R&B#78, *One-Way Love Affair* [i] Sadane (1981) R&B#34, *Sit Up* [i] Sadane (1981) R&B#78, *Super Lover* [i] Rena Scott (1979) R&B#92, *Sweet Sensation* [i] Stephanie Mills (1980) R&B#3 US#52, *Two Hearts* [ii] Stephanie Mills featuring Teddy Pendergrass (1981) R&B#81 US#40 UK#49, *What Cha Gonna Do with My Lovin'* [i] Stephanie Mills (1979) R&B#8 US#22, *You Know How to Love Me* [i] Phyliss Hyman (1979) R&B#12 US#101 UK#47. Co-writers: [i] James Mtume, [ii] James Mtume/T. Mtume.

606. LYDON, Johnny (b. John Lydon, January 31, 1956, London, England) Rock vocalist. As Johnny Rotten, Lydon became a punk icon as the lead singer of the group the Sex Pistols. The group's album **Never Mind the Bollocks, Here's the Sex Pistols** (1977), remains one of the few genuine classics of the punk era. CHART COMPOSITIONS: *Anarchy in the U.K.* [ii] (1976) UK#38, re-issued (1992) UK#33; *God Save the Queen* [ii] (1977) UK#2, *Pretty Vacant* [ii] (1977) UK#6, re-issued (1992) UK#56, live version (1996) UK#18; *Holidays in the Sun* [iii] (1977) UK#8. ALBUM: **Never Mind the Bollocks, Here's the Sex Pistols** (1977, Virgin) p US#106 UK#1. COMPILATIONS: **The Great Rock**

'n' Roll Swindle (1979) UK#7, **Some Product** (1979) UK#6, **Flogging a Dead Horse** (1980) UK#23, **The Great Rock 'n' Roll Swindle** ost (1980) UK#16, **Kiss This** (1992, all Virgin) UK#10; **Filthy Lucre Live** (1996, Quid); **Live at the Winterland, 1978** (1996, When). In 1980, reverting to his given name, Lydon embarked on a solo career with his vaguely avante-garde group Public Image Ltd. CHART COMPOSITIONS: *Public Image* [vii] (1978) UK#9, *Death Disco* (1979) UK#20, *Memories* (1979) UK#60, *Flowers of Romance* (1981) UK#24, *This Is Not a Love Song* [vi] (1983) UK#5, *Bad Life* (1984) UK#71, *Rise* [v] (1986) UK#11, *Home* (1986) UK#75, *Seattle* (1987) UK#47, *Disappointed* (1989) UK#38, *Don't Ask Me* (1990) UK#22, *Cruel* [iv] (1992) UK#49, *Back to Front* [i] with Adamski (1992) UK#63. ALBUMS: **Public Image Ltd.** (1978) UK#22, **Metal Box** (1980) UK#18, re-issued as **Second Edition** (1980) US#171 UK#46; **Paris Au Printemps** (1980) UK#61, **The Flowers of Romance** (1981) US#114 UK#11, **Live in Tokyo** (1983) UK#28, **This Is What You Want...This Is What You Get** (1984) UK#56, **Album** (1986) US#115 UK#14, **Happy?** (1987) US#169 UK#40, **Nine** (1989) US#106 UK#36, **That What Is Not** (1992) UK#46, **Psycho's Path** (1997, all Virgin). COMPILATION: **Greatest Hits...So Far** (1990, Virgin) UK#20. In 1993, Lydon disbanded Public Image to record the solo single *Open Up* with Leftfield (1993) UK#13. HIT VERSIONS: *Anarchy in the U.K.* [ii] Megadeath (188) UK#45/ Green Jelly (1997) UK#27; *World Destruction* Time Zone (1985) UK#44. Co-writers: [i] Adamski/Mike Joyce (b. June 1, 1963, Manchester, England)/Keith Levine/Russell Webb, [ii] Paul Cook (b. July 20, 1956, London, England)/Steve Jones (b. May 3, 1955, London, England)/Glen Matlock (b. August 27, 1956, London, England), [iii] Paul Cook/Steve Jones/Sid Vicious (b. John Simon Ritchie, May 10, 1957, England; d. February 2, 1979, New York, NY), [iv] Mike Joyce/Keith Levine/Russell Webb, [v] William Laswell, [vi] Keith Levine, [vii] Keith Levine/James Walke/Jah Wobble (b. John Wardle, England).

607. LYLE, Graham (b. Largs, Scotland) Pop guitarist and vocalist. One half of the duo Gallagher and Lyle, who became a successful backroom songwriter in the early 1980s. Lyle first recorded with Benny Gallagher in 1967, releasing the single *Trees* [iii], before becoming songwriters at Apple Records in 1969, where they wrote *International* [iii] for Noel Harrison and *Sparrow* [iii] for Mary Hopkin. In 1970, they joined the skiffle influenced McGuinness Flint, charting with *Malt and Barley Blues* [iii] (1970) UK#5 and *When I'm Dead and Gone* [iii] (1971) US#47 UK#2. ALBUMS: **McGuiness Flint** (1971)

US#155 UK#9, **Happy Birthday Ruby Baby** (1971, both Capitol) US#198. COMPILATION: **Greatest Hits** (1973, Sounds Superb). Their second attempt at a duo proved considerably more successful during the mid–1970s. CHART COMPOSITIONS: *I Wanna Stay with You* [iii] (1976) US#49 UK#6, *Heart on My Sleeve* [iii] (1976) US#67 UK#6, *Breakaway* [iii] (1976) UK#35, *Every Little Teardrop* [iii] (1977) US#106 UK#32. ALBUMS: **Gallagher and Lyle** (1973, Capitol); **Willie and the Lap Dog** (1973), **Seeds** (1973), **The Last Cowboy** (1974), **Breakaway** (1976) UK#6, **Love on the Airwaves** (1977) UK#19, **Showdown** (1978, all A&M); **Lonesome No More** (1979, Mercury). COMPILATIONS: **Best of Gallagher and Lyle** (1980, Warwick); **Heart on My Sleeve — The Very Best of Gallagher and Lyle** (1991), **Best of Gallagher and Lyle** (1992, both A&M). Lyle released the solo single *Marley* in 1983, and re-united with Tom McGuinness as the Lyle-McGuinness Band for the album **Acting on Impulse** (1983, Cool King), before writing for such singers as Tina Turner, Anita Baker and Michael Jackson. HIT VERSIONS: *Breakaway* [iii] Art Garfunkel (1975) US#39 UK#35, *Button Off My Shirt* [v] Paul Carrack (1988) US#91, *Heart in New York, A* Art Garfunkel (1981) US#66, *Heart on My Sleeve* [iii] Bryan Ferry (1976) US#86, also on *Extended Play* (1976) UK#7; *I Should Have Known Better* [ii] Jim Diamond (1985) UK#1, *I Wanna Stay with You* [iii] Undercover (1993) UK#28, *I Want You Near Me* [i] Tina Turner (1992) UK#22, *Little Bit of Heaven, A* [iv] Natalie Cole (1985) R&B#28 US#81, *Our Love* Elkie Brooks (1982) UK#43, *Runaway, The* Elkie Brooks (1979) UK#50, *Soul Inspiration* [i] Anita Baker (1990) US#72, *Stay Young* Don Williams (1984) C&W#1, *Straight to the Heart* Crystal Gayle (1987) C&W#1, *Two People* [i] Tina Turner (1986) R&B#18 US#30 UK#43, *Typically Male* [i] Tina Turner (1986) R&B#3 US#2 UK#33, *We Don't Need Another Hero* [i] Tina Turner (1984) R&B#3 US#2 UK#3, *What You Get Is What You See* [i] Tina Turner (1987) US#13, *What's Love Got to Do with It* [i] Tina Turner (1984) g R&B#2 US#1 UK#3/Warren G (1996) UK#2; *When I'm Dead and Gone* [iii] Bob Summers (1971) US#118, *When You Love Somebody (I'm Saving My Love for You)* Patti LaBelle (1992) R&B#70. Co-writers: [i] Terry Britten, [ii] Jim Diamond, [iii] Bernard Gallagher, [iv] Richard Kerr, [v] Billy Livesy. (*See also under* Albert HAMMOND.)

608. LYNNE, Jeff (b. December 12, 1947, Birmingham, England) Pop guitarist, producer and vocalist. The leader of the portentous Electric Light Orchestra, which was a multi-million selling act during the 1970s. Lynne first performed as a member of the 1960s group Idle Race, releasing the albums **The Birthday Party** (1968) and **The Idle Race** (1968, both Liberty). In 1970, he joined Roy Wood's group the Move, composing their hit *Do Ya* (1972) US#93, which was also included on the B-side of Wood's *California Man* (1972) UK#7. Lynne also featured on the Move's album **Message from the Country** (1971, Harvest), before quitting to form the Beatles' influenced, quasi-classical Electric Light Orchestra. CHART COMPOSITIONS: *10538 Overture* (1972) UK#9, *Showdown* (1973) US#53 UK#12, re-issued (1976) US#59; *Ma-Ma-Ma-Belle* (1974) UK#22, *Daybreaker* (1974) US#87, *Can't Get It Out of My Head* (1975) US#9, *Evil Woman* (1976) US#10 UK#10, *Strange Magic* (1976) US#14 UK#38, *Livin' Thing* (1976) US#13 UK#4, *Rockaria!* (1977) UK#9, *Do Ya* (1977) US#24, *Telephone Line* (1977) US#7 UK#8, *Turn to Stone* (1977) US#13 UK#18, *Mr. Blue Sky* (1978) US#35 UK#6, *Sweet Talkin' Woman* (1978) US#17 UK#6, *Wild West Hero* (1978) UK#6, *It's Over* (1978) US#75, *ELO EP* (1978) UK#34, *Shine a Little Love* (1979) US#8 UK#6, *The Diary of Horace Wimp* (1979) UK#8, *Don't Bring Me Down* (1979) US#4 UK#3, *Confusion* (1979) US#37 UK#8, *Last Train to London* (1980) US#39, *Xanadu* with Olivia Newton-John (1980) US#8 UK#1, *All Over the World* (1980) US#13 UK#11, *Don't Walk Away* (1980) UK#21, *Hold on Tight* (1981) US#10 UK#4, *Twilight* (1981) US#38 UK#30, *Rain Is Falling* (1982) US#101, *Ticket to the Moon/Here is the News* (1982) UK#24, *Rock 'n' Roll Is King* (1983) US#19 UK#13, *Secret Messages* (1983) UK#48, *Four Little Diamonds* (1983) US#86, *Stranger* (1983) US#105, *Calling America* (1986) US#18 UK#28. ALBUMS: **Electric Light Orchestra/No Answer** (1972) US#196 UK#32, **ELO II** (1973, both Harvest) US#62 UK#35; **On the Third Day** (1973) US#52, **Eldorado** (1974) g US#16, **The Night the Light Went on in Long Beach** (1974), **Face the Music** (1975) g US#8, **A New World Record** (1976) p US#5 UK#6, **Out of the Blue** (1977, all United Artists) p US#4 UK#4; **Discovery** (1979, Jet) p US#5 UK#1; **Xanadu** ost (1980, MCA) p US#4 UK#2; **Time** (1981) g US#16, **Secret Messages** (1983, both Jet) US#36 UK#4; **Balance of Power** (1986, Epic) US#49 UK#9. COMPILATIONS: **Showdown** (1974, Harvest); **Ole ELO** (1976, Jet) g US#32; **The Light Shines On** (1977, Harvest); **Three Light Years** (1979, Jet) UK#38; **The Light Shines On, Volume 2** (1979, Harvest); **Greatest Hits** (1979, Jet) p US#30 UK#7; **Greatest Hits** (1989, Telstar) UK#23; **Very Best of the Electric Light Orchestra** (1989, Telstar) UK#28; **Very Best of the Electric Light Orchestra** (1994, Dino) UK#4. Since the 1980s Lynne has been a successful producer, and he later participated in the group project the Traveling Wilburys. He has recorded as a solo artist, charting with *Video* (1984) US#85 and *Every Little Thing* (1990) UK#59, the latter taken from the album **Armchair Theatre** (1990, Reprise) US#92 UK#24. HIT VERSIONS: *Showdown* Odia Coates (1975) US#71, *Slipping Away* Dave Edmunds (1983) US#39. (*See also under* Bob DYLAN, Roy ORBISON, Tom PETTY.)

609. LYNOTT, Phil (b. August 20, 1951, Birmingham; d. January 4, 1986, Salisbury, both England) Rock bassist and vocalist. The lead singer and songwriter in the Irish rock group Thin Lizzy, with which he blended hard rock, Americana and rebel Irish romanticism. Lynott was raised in Dublin from the age of three by his grandmother, and first performed as a member of the group Black Eagles, before forming Thin Lizzy in 1970. CHART COMPOSITIONS: *Whiskey in the Jar* [i] (arrangement only) (1973) UK#6, *The Boys Are Back in Town* (1976) US#12 UK#8, re-issued (1991) UK#63; *Jailbreak* (1976) UK#31, *Cowboy Song* [ii] (1976) US#77, *Don't Believe a Word* (1977) UK#12, *Dancin' in the Moonlight (It's Caught Me in the Spotlight)* (1977) UK#14, *Cowgirl's Song* (1978) UK#20, *Waiting for an Alibi* (1979) UK#9, *Do Anything You Want To* (1979) UK#14, *Sarah* (1979) US#24, *Chinatown* (1980) UK#21, *Killer on the Loose* (1980) UK#10, *Killers Live EP* (1981) UK#19, *Trouble Boys* (1981) UK#53, *Hollywood (Down on Your Luck)* (1982) UK#53, *Cold Sweat* (1983) UK#27, *Thunder and Lightning* (1983) UK#39, *The Sun Goes Down* (1983) UK#52, *Dedication* (1991) UK#35. ALBUMS: **Thin Lizzy** (1971), **Shades of a Blue Orphanage** (1972), **Vagabonds of the Western World** (1973, all Decca); **Nightlife** (1974), **Fighting** (1975) UK#60, **Jailbreak** (1976) g US#18 UK#10, **Johnny the Fox** (1976) US#56 UK#11, **Bad Reputation** (1977) US#39 UK#4, **Live and Dangerous** (1978) US#84 UK#2, **Black Rose (A Rock Legend)** (1979) US#81 UK#2, **Chinatown** (1980) US#120 UK#7, **Renegade** (1981) US#157 UK#38, **Thunder and Lightning** (1983) US#159 UK#4, **Life — Live** (1983, all Vertigo) US#185 UK#29. COMPILATIONS: **The Adventures of Thin Lizzy** (1981) UK#6, **Dedication — The Very Best of Thin Lizzy** (1991, both Vertigo) UK#8; **The Peel Sessions** (1994, Strange Fruit); **Wild One — The Very Best of Thin Lizzy** (1996, Vertigo) UK#18. When the group split up in 1983, Lynott embarked on a solo career, that was cut short in 1986 when he died of heart failure and pneumonia, resulting from a drug overdose. CHART COMPOSITIONS: *Dear Miss Lonelyhearts* (1980) UK#32, *King's Call* (1980) UK#35, *Yellow Pearl* (1981) UK#56, re-issued (1982) UK#14. ALBUMS: **Solo in Soho** (1980) UK#28, **The Philip Lynott Album** (1982, both Vertigo). HIT VERSIONS:

Parisienne Walkways [iii] Gary Moore (1979) UK#8. Co-writers: [i] Eric Bell (b. September 3, 1947, Belfast, Northern Ireland)/Brian Donney (b. January 27, 1951, Dublin, Eire), [ii] Brian Donney, [iii] Gary Moore (b. April 4, 1952, Belfast, Northern Ireland).

610. McALOON, Paddy (b. June 7, 1957, Consett, Scotland) Rock multi-instrumentalist, producer and vocalist. The mastermind behind the individualistic group Prefab Sprout, who is a direct descendent of the British songwriting tradition of Ray Davies and Elvis Costello. McAloon grew up in County Durham and studied at Newcastle University, where he formed his band in the early 1980s. After issuing a self-financed single *Lions in My Garden (Exit Someone)* (1982), Prefab Sprout signed to the local independent label Kitchenware, and released an aberrative and frequently charming debut album **Swoon** (1982), which was entirely penned by McAloon in a distinctive, off-beat manner that emphasized enigmatic wordplay, intricate meters, copious internal rhymes and idiosyncratic rhythms. Marrying delphic titles with peculiar melodies, McAloon's songwriting continues to draw accolades from many quarters. CHART COMPOSITIONS: *Don't Sing* (1984) UK#62, *When Love Breaks Down* (1985) UK#25, *Faron Young* (1985) UK#74, *Johnny Johnny* (1985) UK#64, *Cars and Girls* (1988) UK#44, *The King of Rock 'n' Roll* (1988) UK#7, *Hey Manhattan* (1988) UK#72, *Looking for Atlantis* (1988) UK#51, *We Let the Stars Go* (1988) UK#50, *Carnival 2000* (1988) UK#35, *The Sound of Crying* (1992) UK#23, *If You Don't Love Me* (1992) UK#33, *All the World Loves Lovers* (1992) UK#61, *Life of Surprises* (1993) UK#24. ALBUMS: **Swoon** (1984) UK#22, **Steve McQueen/Two Wheels Good** (1985) US#178 UK#21, **From Langley Park to Memphis** (1988) UK#5, **Protest Songs** (1989) UK#18, **Jordan: The Comeback** (1991) UK#7, **Andromeda Heights** (1997, all Kitchenware) UK#7. COMPILATION: **A Life of Surprises—The Best of Prefab Sprout** (1992, Kitchenware) UK#3. HIT VERSION: *Cowboy Dreams* Jimmy Nail (1995) UK#13.

611. McCALL, C.W. (b. William Fries, November 15, 1929, Audubon, IA) C&W vocalist. A former journalist and advertising jingle writer who became the Metz Bread Company character C.W. McCall, for a series of novelty country-trucking hits. His best known song is the seven million selling *Convoy* [i], which later inspired an entire film. CHART COMPOSITIONS: *Old Home Filler-Up and, Keep on-a-Truckin' Cafe* [i] (1974) C&W#19 US#54, *Wolf Creek Pass* [i] (1974) C&W#12 US#40, *Classified* (1975) C&W#13 US#101, *Black Bear Road* (1975)

C&W#24, *Convoy* [i] (1975) C&W#1 US#1 UK#2, *There Won't Be No Country Music (There Won't Be No Rock 'n' Roll)* (1976) C&W#19 US#73, *Crispy Critters* (1976) C&W#32, *Four Wheel Cowboy* (1976) C&W#88, *'Round the World with Rubber Duck* (1976) C&W#40 US#101, *Audubon* (1977) C&W#56, *Roses for Mama* (1977) C&W#2, *Outlaws and Lone Star Beer* (1979) C&W#81. ALBUMS: **Wolf Creek Pass** (1975) US#143, **Black Bear Road** (1976, both MGM) g US#12; **Wilderness** (1976) US#143, **Rubber Duck** (1977), **C.W. McCall and Co.** (1978), **Roses for Mama** (1978, all Polydor). HIT VERSION: *Convoy G.B.* [i] Laurie Lingo & the Dipsticks (1976) UK#4. Co-writer: [i] Louis "Chip" Davis.

612. McCARTHY, Joseph (b. America) Film and stage lyricist. A Tin Pan Alley songwriter whose material was featured in the shows "Irene" (1920) and "Rio Rita" (1929), alongside such films as "The Ziegfeld Girl" (1941) and "The Dolly Sisters" (1945). McCarthy and Percy Wenrich also wrote the popular vaudeville number *Sweet Cider When You Were Mine* (1916). HIT VERSIONS: *Alice Blue Gown* [iii] Edith Day (1920) US#1/Frankie Masters (1940) US#7/Glenn Miller (1940) US#18/Ozzie Nelson (1940) US#16; *I'm Always Chasing Rainbows* [i] Sam Ash (1918) US#9/Harry Fox (1918) US#5/Charles Harrison (1918) US#1/Prince's Orchestra (1918) US#6/Perry Como (1945) g US#5/Helen Forrest & Dick Haymes (1945) US#7/Harry James (1946) US#9; *I'm in the Market for You* [ii] George Olsen (1930) US#9, *Irene* [iii] Edith Day (1920) US#3/Joseph C. Smith's Orchestra (1920) US#6; *Rio Rita* [iii] Ben Selvin (1927) US#4/Nat Shilkret (1927) US#8; *Saw Mill River Road, The* [iii] Isham Jones (1923) US#5, *They Go Wild, Simply Wild, Over Me* [ii] Marion Harris (1917) US#2. Co-writers: [i] Harry Carroll/Frederic Chopin, [ii] James Hanley, [iii] Harry A. Tierney (b. 1890; d. 1965). (*See also under* Joseph BURKE, Fred FISHER.)

613. McCARTNEY, Sir Paul A former Beatle whose first solo recording was a four copy, privately pressed, seasonal album in 1965. While still a member of the group, McCartney had also composed the television soundtrack **The Family Way** (1966, Decca). In 1970, he released **McCartney**, a deliberately low-key selection of material performed and recorded by McCartney in its entirety. It remains his most interesting album, and featured the compositions *Junk*, *Every Night* and *Maybe I'm Amazed*. After forming the group Wings, McCartney reached a post-Beatles creative and commercial peak with the six million selling album **Band on the Run** (1974), and the country waltz *Mull of Kintyre* [iii], which became the biggest selling British single since the Beatles' *She Loves You*. McCartney also composed the title theme for the James Bond film **Live and Let Die** ost (1973, United Artists) US#17, and released a pseudonymous album as Percy "Thrills" Thrillington, **Thrillington** (1977, Regal Zonophone). Always the most commercially successful former Beatle, by 1980, McCartney had written or co-written over one hundred million selling singles, and had sold over one hundred million albums. His orchestral work *Liverpool Oratorio*, was premiered at the Liverpool Cathedral in 1991, and was recorded by Carl Davis and the Royal Liverpool Philharmonic Orchestra as **Paul McCartney's Liverpool Oratorio** (1991, EMI) US#177 UK#36. In 1996, he was knighted. CHART COMPOSITION: *Another Day* [iv] (1971) US#5 UK#2, *Back Seat of My Car* (1971) UK#39, *Uncle Albert/Admiral Halsey* [iv] (1971) g US#1, *Give Ireland Back to the Irish* [iv] (1972) US#21 UK#16, *Mary Had a Little Lamb* [iv] (1972) US#28 UK#9, *Hi Hi Hi* [iv]/*C Moon* (1973) US#10 UK#5, *My Love* [iv] (1973) g US#1 UK#9, *Live and Let Die* [iv] (1973) g US#2 UK#9, *Helen Wheels* [iv] (1973) US#10 UK#12, *Jet* [iv] (1974) US#7 UK#7, *Band on the Run* [iv] (1974) g US#1 UK#3, *Junior's Farm* [iv] (1974) US#3 UK#16, *Sally G* [iv] (1974) C&W#51 US#39, *Listen to What the Man Said* [iv] (1975) g US#1 UK#6, *Letting Go* (1975) US#39 UK#41, *Venus and Mars/Rock Show* (1975) US#12, *Silly Love Songs* [iv] (1976) g US#1 UK#2, *Let 'Em In* [iv] (1976) g US#3 UK#2, *Maybe I'm Amazed* (1977) US#10 UK#28, *Mull of Kintyre* [iii] (1977) UK#1, *Girls School* [iii] (1977) US#33, *With a Little Luck* [iv] (1978) US#1 UK#5, *I've Had Enough* (1978) US#25 UK#42, *London Town* [iii] (1978) US#39 UK#60, *Goodnight Tonight* (1979) g US#5 UK#5, *Old Siam Sir* (1979) UK#35, *Getting Closer/Baby's Request* (1979) US#20 UK#60, *Arrow Through Me* (1979) US#29, *Wonderful Christmas Time* (1979) UK#6, *Coming Up* (1980) g US#1 UK#2, *Waterfalls* (1980) US#106 UK#9, *Ebony and Ivory* with Stevie Wonder (1982) g R&B#8 US#1 UK#1, *Tug of War* (1982) US#53 UK#53, *Take It Away* (1982) US#10 UK#15, *Say, Say, Say* [ii] with Michael Jackson (1983) p R&B#2 US#1 UK#2, *Pipes of Peace* (1983) UK#1, *So Bad* (1983) US#23, *No More Lonely Nights* (1984) US#6 UK#2, *We All Stand Together* (1984) UK#3, re-issued (1985) UK#37; *Spies Like Us* (1985) US#7 UK#13, *Press* (1986) US#21 UK#25, *Stranglehold* [v] (1986) US#81, *Only Love Remains* (1986) UK#34, *Once Upon a Long Ago* (1987) UK#30, *My Brave Face* [i] (1989) US#25 UK#18, *This One* (1989) US#94 UK#18, *Figure of Eight* (1989) US#92 UK#43, *Put It There* (1989) UK#32, *All My Trials* (1990) UK#35, *Hope of Deliverance* (1993) US#83 UK#18, *C'mon People* (1993) UK#41. ALBUMS: **Paul's Christmas Album** (1965, private pressing); **McCartney** (1970) p US#1 UK#2,

Ram (1971) p US#2 UK#1, **Wildlife** (1971) g US#10 UK#11, **Red Rose Speedway** (1973) g US#1 UK#5, **Band on the Run** (1974) p US#1 UK#1, **Venus and Mars** (1975) p US#1 UK#1, **Wings at the Speed of Sound** (1976, all Apple) p US#1 UK#2; **Wings Over America** (1977) p US#1 UK#8, **London Town** (1978) p US#2 UK#4, **Back to the Egg** (1979) p US#8 UK#6, **McCartney II** (1980) p US#3 UK#1, **Tug of War** (1982) p US#1 US#1, **Pipes of Peace** (1983) p US#15 UK#4, **Give My Regards to Broad Street** (1984) g US#21 UK#1, **Press to Play** (1986) US#30 UK#8, **Flowers in the Dirt** (1989) g US#21 UK#1, **Tripping the Live Fantastic** (1990) US#26 UK#17, **Tripping the Live Fantastic — Highlights** (1990) p US#141, **Unplugged — The Official Bootleg** (1991) US#14 UK#7, **Choba B CCCP** (1991) US#109 UK#63, **Off the Ground** (1993, all Parlophone) g US#17 UK#5; **Paul Is Live** (1993, EMI) US#78 UK#34; **Ballad of Skeletons** with Allen Ginsberg (1996), **Flaming Pie** (1997, both Parlophone) UK#2. COMPILATIONS: **Wings' Greatest** (1978, Parlophone) p US#29 UK#5; **The McCartney Interview** (1980, EMI) US#158 UK#34; **All the Best** (1987, Parlophone) p US#62 UK#2. HIT VERSIONS: *Come and Get It* Badfinger (1970) US#7 UK#4, also on *The Apple EP* (1991) UK#60; *Every Night* Billy Joe Royal (1970) US#113/Phoebe Snow (1979) UK#37; *Girlfriend* Michael Jackson (1980) UK#41, *Goodbye* Mary Hopkin (1969) US#13 UK#2, *Let 'Em In* [iv] Billy Paul (1977) R&B#91 UK#26, *Live and Let Die* [iv] Guns 'n' Roses (1991) US#33 UK#5, *Liverpool Lou* Scaffold (1974) UK#7, *Mine for Me* Rod Stewart (1974) US#91, *My Love* [iv] Margie Joseph (1974) R&B#10 US#69, *On the Wings of a Nightingale* Everly Brothers (1984) C&W#49 US#50 UK#4, *Seaside Woman* Suzie & the Red Stripes (1977) US#59. Co-writers: [i] Elvis Costello, [ii] Michael Jackson, [iii] Denny Laine (b. Brian Hines, October 29, 1944, Jersey), [iv] Linda McCartney (b. Linda Eastman, September 24, 1942, Scarsdale, NY), [v] Eric Stewart. (*See also under* Elvis COSTELLO, John LENNON and Paul McCARTNEY.)

614. MacAULEY, Tony (b. Anthony Gordon Instone, April 21, 1944, London, England) Pop producer. The co-composer of six chart toppers during the 1960–1970s, who was also the first British songwriter to be recorded by Elvis Presley. MacAuley grew up listening to skiffle music and playing in amateur groups, before leaving school with the intention of becoming a civil engineer. After joining Essex Music as a song-plugger in the 1960s, he gained his first hit with *Baby, Now That I've Found You* [iii] (1966), after which he became a staff producer at Pye Records, where he produced all of Long John Baldry's hits. MacAuley also fronted a short-lived studio group **The Flying Machine** (1969, Janus) US#179, and during the 1970s, he composed the musicals "Is Your Doctor Really Necessary?" and "Gentlemen Prefer Anything." HIT VERSIONS: *Alibis* [vi] Sergio Mendes (1983) US#29, *Baby Make It Soon* [vii] Marmalade (1969) UK#10/Flying Machine (1970) US#87; *Baby, Now That I've Found You* [iii] Foundations (1966) R&B#33 US#11 UK#1, *Baby, Take Me in Your Arms* [iii] Jefferson (1970) US#23, *Back on My Feet Again* Foundations (1968) US#59 UK#18, *Born to Live and Born to Die* Foundations (1969) UK#46, *Build Me Up, Buttercup* [i] Foundations (1968) UK#2, *By the Devil I Was Tempted* Blue Mink (1973) UK#26, *Can't We Just Sit Down (And Talk It Over)* Donna Summer (1977) R&B#20, *Don't Give Up on Us* David Soul (1977) g US#1 UK#1, *Falling Apart at the Seams* Marmalade (1976) US#49 UK#9, *Going in with My Eyes Open* David Soul (1977) US#54 UK#2, *I Can Take or Leave Your Loving* Herman's Hermits (1968) US#22 UK#11, *I Get a Little Sentimental Over You* [vii] New Seekers (1974) UK#5, *In the Bad, Bad Old Days* [iii] Foundations (1969) US#51 UK#8, *It Sure Brings Out the Love in Your Eyes* [vii] David Soul (1978) UK#12, *It's a Better Than Good Time* Gladys Knight & the Pips (1978) R&B#16 UK#59, *(It's Like a) Sad Old Kinda Movie* Pickettywitch (1970) UK#16, *It's Up to You, Petula* Edison Lighthouse (1971) US#72 UK#49, *Let the Heartaches Begin* [iii] Long John Baldry (1967) UK#1, *Let's Have a Quiet Night In* David Soul (1977) UK#8, *Letter to Lucille, A* Tom Jones (1973) US#60 UK#31, *Lights of Cincinnati, The* [vii] Scott Walker (1969) UK#13, *Love Grows (Where My Rosemary Goes)* [iv] Edison Lighthouse (1970) g US#5 UK#1, *Melody Makes Me Smile* Tony Burrows (1970) US#87, *Mexico* [ii] Long John Baldry (1968) UK#15, *My Little Chickadee* Foundations (1969) US#99, *Our World* Blue Mink (1970) UK#17 US#64, *Play Me Like You Play Your Guitar* [v] Duane Eddy (1975) UK#9, *Silver Lady* [vii] David Soul (1977) US#52 UK#1, *Sing a Simple Song of Freedom* Buckwheat (1972) US#84, *Smile a Little Smile for Me* [vii] Flying Machine (1969) g US#5, *Something Here in My Heart (Keeps a-Tellin' Me No)* [iii] Paper Dolls (1968) UK#11, *Sorry Suzanne* [iii] Hollies (1969) US#56 UK#3, *Sweet Inspiration* Johnny Johnson & the Bandwagon (1970) UK#10, *That Same Old Feeling* [iii] Fortunes (1970) US#62/Pickettywitch (1970) UK#5; *You Won't Find Another Fool Like Me* [vii] New Seekers (1973) UK#1. Co-writers: [i] Mike D'Abo, [ii] John Allen/John MacLeod, [iii] John MacLeod, [iv] Barry Mason, [v] Keith Polger, [vi] Tom Snow, [vii] Geoff Stevens. (*See also under* Roger COOK.)

615. MacCOLL, Ewan (b. William Miller, January 25, 1915, Auchterarder, Scotland; d. October 22, 1989, London, England) Folk guitarist and vocalist. A politically oriented folk artist who penned satire, wrote for radio, acted with the Red Megaphones theatre group, and initiated the Theatre Workshop in the 1940s. MacColl collaborated with his wife Peggy Seeger during the British folk revival of the 1950s, and remained faithful to his traditional folk roots throughout his life. Although his major contribution to music was not as a songwriter, MacColl was responsible for recording the only versions of many long forgotten British folk and popular songs. His best known composition is the love ballad *The First Time Ever I Saw Your Face*. ALBUMS: **Shuttle and Cage** (1957), **Barrack Room Ballads** (1958), **Still I Love Him** (1958), **Streets of Song** (1960), **Chorus from the Gallows** (1961), **Jacobite Songs** (1962), **English and Scottish Folk Ballads** with A.L. Lloyd (1964), **Steam Whistle Ballads*** (1964), **The Ballad of John Axon*** (1965), **The Manchester Angel*** (1967), **The Big Hewer — A Radio Ballad** (1967), **Bundook Ballads** (1967, all Topic); **Sing the Fishing*** (1967), **Solo Flight** (1967, both Argo); **Long Harvest, Volumes 1 to 10*** (all 1967–1968), **The Amorous Muse*** (1968), **The Angry Muse*** (1968), **The Wanton Muse*** (1968), **The Paper Stage, Volumes 1 and 2*** (both 1969), **The Travelling People*** (1970), **On the Edge*** (1971, all Argo); **Classic Scots Ballads** (1974, Tradition); **Streets of Song** with Dominic Behan (1974, Topic); **Blood and Roses, Volumes 1 to 3*** (all 1982), **Hot Blast*** (1982), **Item of News*** (1982), **Kilroy Was Here*** (1982), **Saturday Night at the Bull and Mouth** (1982), **Blood and Roses 5*** (1986, all Blackthorne); **At the Present Moment*** (1988), **Freeborn Man*** (1988, both Rounder). COMPILATIONS: **Best of Ewan MacColl** (1961, Pre); **Folk on 2: Ewan MacColl** (1996, Cooking Vinyl). HIT VERSIONS: *Dirty Old Town* Pogues (1985) UK#62, *First Time Ever I Saw Your Face, The* Roberta Flack (1972) g R&B#4 US#1 UK#14. With: * Charles Parker, ** Charles Parker & Peggy Seeger, *** Peggy Seeger.

616. McCOY, Van (b. January 6, 1944, Washington, DC; d. July 6, 1979) R&B multi-instrumentalist, arranger and producer. A pianist since the age of four, who first recorded with the group the Marylanders, before forming the Starliters in 1959. McCoy ran the Rock 'N Roll and MAXX labels during the 1960s, before becoming a house producer and A&R man at the Sceptor/Wand label between 1961–1964. He was a successful songwriter and performer for over twenty years, and wrote most of Aretha Franklin's album **La Diva** (1979, Atlantic) US#46, and David Ruffin's **Everything's Coming Up Love** (1976, Motown) US#51. McCoy died of a heart attack in 1979. CHART COMPOSITIONS: *Mr. D.J.* (1961) US#104, *Love Is the Answer* (1974) R&B#77, *Boogie Down* (1975) R&B#67, *The Hustle* (1975) g R&B#1 US#1 UK#3, *Change with the Times* (1975) R&B#6 US#46 UK#36, *Night Walk* (1976) R&B#51 US#96, *Party* (1976) R&B#20 US#69, *The Shuffle* (1976) R&B#79 US#105 UK#4, *Soul Cha Cha* (1977) UK#34, *My Favorite Fantasy* (1978) R&B#76. ALBUMS: **Soul Improvisations** (1972), **From Disco to Love** (1972, both Buddah) US#181; **Disco Baby** (1975) US#12 UK#32, **The Disco Kid** (1975, both Avco) US#80; **The Real McCoy** (1976) US#106, **The Hustle and the Best of Van McCoy** (1976) US#193; **Rhythms of the World** (1976, all H&L); **Lonely Dancer** (1977), **My Favorite Fantasy** (1978, both MCA); **Van McCoy and His Magnificent Movie Machine** (1978), **Sweet Rhythm** (1979, both H&L). HIT VERSIONS: *Baby Don't Change Your Mind* Gladys Knight & the Pips (1977) R&B#10 US#52 UK#4, *Baby Don't Take Your Love* Faith, Hope & Charity (1970) R&B#36 US#96, *Baby, I'm Yours* Barbara Lewis (1965) R&B#5 US#11/ Peter & Gordon (1965) UK#19, also on B-side of *Don't Pity Me* (1965) US#83/Debby Boone (1978) US#74; *Before and After* Chad & Jeremy (1965) US#17, *Come Back and Finish What You Started* [i] Gladys Knight & the Pips (1978) UK#15, *5–10–15– 20 (25–30 Years of Love)* Presidents (1970) R&B#5 US#11, *Everything's Coming Up Love* David Ruffin (1976) R&B#8 US#49, *Giving Up* Gladys Knight & the Pips (1964) US#38/Donny Hathaway (1972) R&B#21 US#81; *Heavy Love* [i] David Ruffin (1976) R&B#8 US#47, *I Don't Wanna Lose You, Baby* Chad & Jeremy (1965) US#35, *I Get the Sweetest Feeling* [ii] Jackie Wilson (1968) US#34, re-issued (1972) UK#9, re-issued (1975) UK#25, re-issued (1987) UK#3; *Rat Race* Drifters (1964) US#71/Specials (1980) UK#5; *So Much Love* Faith, Hope & Charity (1970) R&B#14 US#51, *This Is It* Melba Moore (1978) R&B#18 US#91 UK#9/Danni Minogue (1993) UK#10; *To Each His Own* Faith, Hope & Charity (1975) R&B#1 US#50, *Walk Away from Love* David Ruffin (1975) R&B#1 US#9 UK#10, *When You're Young and in Love* Ruby & the Romantics (1964) US#48/Marvelletes (1967) R&B#9 US#23 UK#13/Ralph Carter (1975) R&B#37 US#95/ Choice Four (1975) R&B#45 US#91/Flying Pickets (1984) UK#7. Co-writers: [i] Joe Cobb, [ii] Alicia Evelyn.

617. McDANIELS, Eugene B. (b. February 12, 1935, Kansas City, MO) R&B vocalist. A man of two careers, who, as Gene McDaniels, was a successful interpreter of pop and R&B hits during the 1960s, before becoming a writer and producer under his given name during the 1970s. McDaniels

had studied at Omaha's Conservatory of Music before singing gospel in the 1950s. ALBUMS: **In Times Like These** (1960), **Sometimes I'm Happy (Sometimes I'm Blue)** (1960), **100 lbs of Clay** (1961), **Gene McDaniels Sings Movie Memories** (1962), **Tower of Strength** (1962), **Spanish Lace** (1963), **The Wonderful World of Gene McDaniels** (1963), **Facts of Life** (1968, all Liberty); **Outlaw** (1971, **Natural Juices** (1975), **Headless Horsemen of the Apocalypse** (1971, all Atlantic). COMPILATIONS: **Hit After Hit** (1962), **Another Tear Falls** (1986, both Liberty). HIT VERSIONS: *Feel Like Making Love* Roberta Flack (1974) g US#1 R&B#1 UK#34/Bob James (1974) US#88/Millie Jackson (1976) R&B#71/George Benson (1983) UK#28; *Feelin' That Glow* [i] Roberta Flack (1975) R&B#25 US#76, *Money* Gladys Knight & the Pips (1975) R&B#4 US#50, *River* Joe Simon (1973) R&B#6 US#62, *25th of Last December* Roberta Flack (1977) R&B#52. Co-writers: [i] M. McKinley/L.L. Pendarvis/B. Rusco.

618. MacDERMOT, Galt (b. December 18, 1928, Montreal, Canada) Film and stage composer, conductor. The co-creator of the musical "Hair" (1968), the only known show to spurn an album of songs that did not appear in the original production, **DisinHAIRited** (1970, RCA) US#95. ALBUMS: **Hair** oc (1968, RCA) p US#1 UK#29; **Hair** oc (1968, Polydor) US#186 UK#3; **Cotton Comes to Harlem** ost (1970, United Artists); **Fortune and Men's Eyes** ost (1971, MGM); **Two Gentlemen of Verona** oc (1971, ABC); **Dude** oc (1972), **Via Galactica** sc (1972, both Kilmarnock); **Isabel's a Jezebel** oc (1974, United Artists); **My Fur Lady** oc (1975, McGill); **Hair** ost (1979, RCA) g US#65. HIT VERSIONS: *African Waltz* [iii] Cannonball Adderley (1961) US#41/Johnny Dankworth Orchestra (1961) US#101 UK#9; *Ain't Got No-I Got Life* [iv] Nina Simone (1968) US#94 UK#2, *Aquarius* [iv] Dick Hyman Trio (1969) US#126/Paul Jones (1969) UK#45; *Aquarius/Let the Sunshine In* [iv] 5th Dimension (1969) g R&B#6 US#1 UK#11, *Down with the King* [ii] Run-D.M.C. (1993) R&B#9 US#21 UK#69, *Easy to Be Hard* [iv] Three Dog Night (1969) g US#4/Jennifer Warnes (1969) US#128/ Cheryl Barnes (1979) US#64; *Good Morning Starshine* [iv] C & the Shells (1969) R&B#46, *Hair* [iv] Cowsills (1969) g US#2, *I Got Life/Let the Sunshine In* [iv] Magic Lanterns (1971) US#103, *Where Do I Go* Carla Thomas (1968) R&B#38 US#86, *Written on Ya Kitten* [i] Naughty By Nature (1993) R&B#64 US#93. Co-writers: [i] A. Criss/V. Brown/K. Gist, [ii] Darryl McDaniels (b. May 31, 1964, New York)/P. Phillips/Joseph Simmons (b. November 24, 1966, New York)/James Rado/Gerome Ragni, [iii] Mel

Mitchell/Norman Sachs, [iv] James Rado/Gerome Ragni.

619. McDILL, Bob (b. April 4, 1944, Beaumont, TX) C&W composer. A rock influenced country songwriter who first wrote material for Sam the Sham and the Pharaohs, before becoming a Nashville stalwart during the 1970s, where he worked with Don Williams and many others. McDill has co-written nearly thirty country number ones. HIT VERSIONS: *Amanda* Waylon Jennings (1979) C&W#1, *Baby's Got Her Blue Jeans On* Mel McDaniel (1985) C&W#1, *Be My Angel* [iv] Lionel Cartwright (1992) C&W#63, *Catfish John* Johnny Russell (1973) C&W#12, *Don't Close Your Eyes* Keith Whitley (1988) C&W#1, *Good Ole Boys Like Me* Don Williams (1980) C&W#2, *I Call It Love* Mel McDaniel (1984) C&W#9, *I May Be Used (But Baby I Ain't Used Up)* Waylon Jennings (1984) C&W#4, *I Wish I Was Crazy Again* Johnny Cash & Waylon Jennings (1978) C&W#22, *If Bubba Can Dance (I Can Too)* [v] Shenandoah (1994) C&W#1, *If Only Your Eyes Could Lie* [ii] Earl Thomas Conley (1992) C&W#74, *It Must Be Love* Don Williams (1979) C&W#1, *Just Like Real People* Kendalls (1979) C&W#11, *Lord, Have Mercy on a Country Boy* Don Williams (1991) C&W#34+, *Louisiana Saturday Night* Jimmy Newman (1967) C&W#24/Mel McDaniel (1981) C&W#7; *Nobody Likes Sad Songs* Ronnie Milsap (1979) C&W#1, *On the Road* Lee Roy Parnell (1993) C&W#6, *Rake and Ramblin' Man* Don Williams (1978) C&W#3, *Rednecks, White Socks and Blue Ribbon Beer* Johnny Russell (1973) C&W#4, *Right in the Palm of Your Hand* Mel McDaniel (1981) C&W#10, *Say It Again* Don Williams (1976) C&W#1, *She Don't Know She's Beautiful* [i] Sammy Kershaw (1993) C&W#1 US#119, *Song of the South* Johnny Russell (1981) C&W#57/Tom T. Hall & Earl Scruggs (1982) C&W#72/Alabama (1989) C&W#1; *Standing Knee Deep in a River (Dying of Thirst)* [iii] Kathy Mattea (1993) C&W#19, *(Turn Out the Light) Love Me Tonight* Don Williams (1975) C&W#1, *Why Didn't I Think of That* [i] Doug Stone (1993) C&W#1, *Why Don't You Spend the Night* Ronnie Milsap (1980) C&W#1. Co-writers: [i] Paul Harrison, [ii] J. Jarrad, [iii] B. Jones/D. Lee, [iv] J. Kimball/Dan Seals, [v] Mike McGuire/Marty Raybon. (*See also under* Rodney CROWELL, Dick LEE, Don WILLIAMS.)

620. MacDONALD, Ballard Film and stage lyricist. A Tin Pan Alley lyricist whose songs were featured in such shows as "The Ziegfeld's Midnight Frolics" (1920) and "New York Nights" (1924), alongside the films "With a Song in My Heart" (1952) and "Funny Face" (1957). MacDonald also

co-wrote the much recorded *If I Should Plant a Tiny Seed of Love* [v] (1909) and *Somebody Else, Not Me* [iii] (1920). HIT VERSIONS: *Beautiful Ohio* [ii] Sam Ash (1919) US#8/Henry Burr (1919) US#1/Olive Kline & Marguerite Dunlap (1919) US#5/Fritz Kreisler (1919) US#7/Prince's Orchestra (1919) US#2/Waldorf-Astoria Dance Orchestra (1919) US#1; *Parade of the Wooden Soldiers* [iii] Carl Fenton (1922) US#6/Vincent Lopez (1922) US#3/Paul Whiteman (1923) US#1, re-issued (1928) US#17; *Play That Barbershop Chord* [iv] Bert Williams (1910) US#1/American Quartet (1911) US#2; *There's a Girl in the Heart of Maryland (With a Heart That Belongs to Me)* [i] Henry Burr & Andrea Sarto (1913) US#4/Harry MacDonough (1913) US#2/Walter Van Brunt (1913) US#10; *Trail of the Lonesome Pine, The* [i] Elsie Baker & James F. Harrison (1913) US#9/Henry Burr & Albert Campbell (1913) US#1/Laurel & Hardy with the Avalon Boys (1975) UK#2. Co-writers: [i] Harry Carroll, [ii] Mary Earl, [iii] Leon Jessel, [iv] Lewis Muir/William Tracey, [v] James W. Tate. (*See also under* Billy ROSE.)

621. McDONALD, Country Joe (b. Joseph McDonald, January 1, 1942, El Monte, CA) Rock guitarist and vocalist. A member of the 1960s groups the Berkeley String Quartet and the Instant Action Jug Band, who formed the psychedelic, political-folk act Country Joe McDonald and the Fish in the late 1960s. CHART COMPOSITIONS: *Not So Sweet Martha Lorraine* (1968) US#95, *Who Am I* (1968) US#114, *Here I Go Again* (1969) US#106, *Breakfast for Two* (1975) US#92. ALBUMS: **Electric Music for the Mind and Body** (1967) US#39, **I-Feel-Like-I'm-Fixin'-to-Die** (1967) US#67, **Together** (1968) US#23, **Here We Are Again** (1969) US#48, **C.J. Fish** (1970) US#111, **The Life and Times of Country Joe and the Fish from Haight-Asbury to Woodstock** (1971) US#197, **Thinking of Woody Guthrie** (1969), **Tonight I'm Singing Just for You** (1970), **Hold On — It's Comin'** (1971), **War, War, War** (1971) US#185, **Incredible Live!** (1972) US#179, **Paris Sessions** (1973), **Country Joe** (1975, all Vanguard); **Paradise with an Ocean View** (1975) US#124, **Love Is a Fire** (1977), **Goodbye Blues** (1977), **Rock 'n' Roll Music from Planet Earth** (1978, all Fantasy); **Superstitious Giants** (1992, Rykodisc); **Live! Fillmore West, 1969** (1996, Vanguard). COMPILATIONS: **Greatest Hits** (1970) US#74, **Best of Country Joe and the Fish** (1973, both Vanguard).

622. McDONALD, Michael (b. Michael H. McDonald, December 2, 1952, St. Louis, MO) Rock keyboard player and vocalist. An R&B influenced singer-songwriter who came to prominence as

Tom Johnston's stand-in with the Doobie Brothers. McDonald's traditional approach to the craft of songwriting, with his use of chorus refrains and middle-eights, make him one of very few contemporary songwriters capable of building the tension of a song throughout its performance. Of his music making, he said in 1993, "I'm one of the luckiest that I know. How many people really get to do what they love?" The son of a bus driver, McDonald learned the piano and played in his first band while still at high school. In 1964 he formed Mike and the Majestics, and was later a member of Jerry Jaye and the Sheratons, the Del Rays and Blue. As a solo artist he issued the single *God Knows I Love My Baby* (1972), before cutting further sides for the Bell label. In 1974, McDonald became a member of Steely Dan, contributing to the album **Katy Lied** and augmenting its concert line-up, before, in 1975, he jumped ship to join the Doobie Brothers, learning the band's entire set forty-eight hours before his debut concert, and transforming them into a tight, R&B inflected act. CHART COMPOSITIONS: *Takin' It to the Streets* (1976) R&B#57 US#13, *It Keeps You Runnin'* (1976) US#37, *What a Fool Believes* [iii] (1979) g R&B#72 US#1 UK#31, re-issued (1987) UK#57; *Minute By Minute* [i] (1979) R&B#74 US#14 UK#47, *Dependin' on You* [viii] (1979) US#25, *Real Love* [iv] (1980) R&B#40 US#5 UK#53, *Keep This Train a-Rollin'* (1981) US#62, *Here to Love You* (1982) US#65, *You Belong to Me* [ix] (1983) US#79. ALBUMS: **Takin' It to the Streets** (1976) p US#8 UK#42, **Living on the Fault Line** (1977) g US#10 UK#25, **Minute By Minute** (1978) p US#1, **One Step Closer** (1980) p US#3 UK#53, **Farewell Tour** (1981, all Warner Brothers) US#79, **Rockin' Down the Highway — The Wildlife Concert** (1996, Legacy). COMPILATIONS: **Best of the Doobies** (1976) p US#57, **Best of the Doobies, Volume 2** (1981) g US#39, **Listen to the Music — The Very Best of the Doobie Brothers** (1993, all Warner Brothers). Since 1982, McDonald has pursued a solo career. He also guested as a member of the New York Rock and Soul Revue on the album **Live at the Beacon** (1991, Giant) US#170. CHART COMPOSITIONS: *Let Me Go, Love* [ii] with Nicolette Larson (1980) R&B#96 US#35, *I Keep Forgettin' (Every Time You're Near)* [vi] (1982) R&B#7 US#4 UK#43, *I Gotta Try* [ii] (1982) US#44, *Yah Mo B There* [v] with James Ingram (1984) R&B#5 US#19 UK#44, re-entry (1984) UK#69, re-mixed (1985) UK#12; *No Lookin' Back* [vii] (1985) US#34, *Take It to Heart* [x] (1990) US#98, *Ever Changing Times* with Aretha Franklin (1992) R&B#19, *I Stand for You* (1993) US#114. ALBUMS: **If That's What It Takes** (1982) g US#6, **No Lookin' Back** (1985, both Warner Brothers) US#45; **Take It to Heart** (1990) US#110 UK#35, **Blink of**

an **Eye** (1993, both Reprise). COMPILATIONS: **That Was Then — The Early Recordings of Michael McDonald** (1982, Arista); **Sweet Freedom — The Best of Michael McDonald** (1986, WEA) UK#6. HIT VERSIONS: *I Keep Forgettin' (Every Time You're Near)* [vi] Warren G sampled in *Regulate* (1994) g R&B#7 UK#5, *If You Remember Me* Chris Thompson & Night (1980) US#17 UK#42, *It Keeps You Runnin'* Carly Simon (1976) US#46, *What a Fool Believes* [iii] Aretha Franklin (1981) R&B#17 US#45 UK#46, *You Belong to Me* [ix] Carly Simon (1978) US#6. Co-writers: [i] Lester Abrams, [ii] B.J. Foster, [iii] David Foster/Kenny Loggins, [iv] Patrick Henderson, [v] James Ingram/Quincy Jones/Rod Temperton, [vi] Jerry Leiber/Ed Sanford/Mike Stoller, [vii] Kenny Loggins/Ed Sanford, [viii] Patrick Simmons, [ix] Carly Simon, [x] Diane Warren. (*See also under* Kenny LOGGINS.)

623. MacDONALD, Ralph (b. March 15, 1944, Harlem, NY) R&B percussionist. A performer of disco-fied African and West Indian calypso rhythms, who has also composed many R&B-pop crossover hits. MacDonald's parents were Trinidadian immigrants, and he played congas in his father's carnival band, where he learned the steel drums. Between 1961–1971, MacDonald conducted and arranged for the vocalist Harry Belafonte, before forming a co-writing and production team with William Salter and William Eaton. Between 1970–1975, he backed Roberta Flack, who recorded the best known version of his ten million selling ballad *Where Is the Love* [i], a song that has been covered by over one hundred and fifty artists in nineteen different languages. In 1975, MacDonald formed his own publishing company, Antisia Music, and throughout the 1970s he worked as a session musician. CHART COMPOSITIONS: *Where Is the Love* [i] (1977) R&B#76, *Jam on the Groove* (1977) R&B#42, *The Path (Part 2)* (1978) R&B#90, *In the Name of Love* [iii] with Bill Withers (1984) R&B#13 US#58. ALBUMS: **Sound of a Drum** (1976) US#114, **The Path** (1978) US#57, **Counterpoint** (1979, all Marlin) US#110; **Universal Rhythm** (1984) US#108, **Surprise** (1985, both Polydor). HIT VERSIONS: *Be Mine (Tonight)* [i] Grover Washington, Jr. (1982) R&B#13 US#92/Jammers (1983) R&B#76; *Feel Like Making Love* [i] Roberta Flack (1974) g R&B#1 US#1 UK#34/Bob James (1974) US#88/Millie Jackson (1976) R&B#71/Pauline Henry (1993) UK#12; *I'm the One* [i] Roberta Flack (1982) R&B#24 US#42, *If I'm Still Around Tomorrow* Sadao Watanabe (1984) R&B#79, *In the Name of Love* [iii] Roberta Flack (1982) R&B#80, *Inside Moves* Grover Washington, Jr. (1984) R&B#79, *Mister Magic* [ii] Grover Washington, Jr. (1975) R&B#16 US#54, *No Tears (In the*

End) Grover Washington, Jr. (1972) R&B#49, *Time and Love* Tom Scott (1976) R&B#100, *When You Smile* Leroy Hutson (1973) R&B#81, *Where Is the Love* [i] Roberta Flack & Donny Hathaway (1972) g R&B#1 US#5 UK#29. Co-writers: [i] William Eaton/William Salter, [ii] William Salter, [iii] William Salter/Bill Withers. (*See also under* Nicholas ASHFORD and Valerie SIMPSON, Bill WITHERS.)

624. McDOWELL, "Mississippi" Fred
(b. January 12, 1904, Rossville; d. July 3, 1972, Memphis, both TN) Blues guitarist and vocalist. A self-taught guitarist whose folk-blues style and slide guitar playing was influential on both the Rolling Stones and Bonnie Raitt. ALBUMS: **Delta Blues** (1963, Arhoolie); **My Home Is in the Delta** (1966, Bounty); **Mississippi Delta Blues** (1966, Fontana); **Long Way from Home** (1969, CBS); **Going Down South** (1969, Polydor); **I Do Not Play No Rock 'n' Roll** (1969, (Capitol); **London 1** (1970), **London 2** (1971, both Transatlantic); **Eight Years Ramblin'** with Johnny Woods (1971, Revival); **Mississippi Fred McDowell, 1904–1972** (1974, Xtra); **Standing at the Burying Ground** (1980, Red Lightnin').

625. McFADDEN, Gene, and WHITEHEAD, John
(b. Philadelphia, PA) Both R&B producers and vocalists. Two school friends who performed in the group the Epsilons during the mid–1960s, before recording as Talk of the Town and working at Kenny Gamble and Leon Huff's Philadelphia International label throughout the 1970s. McFadden and Whitehead also recorded briefly as a duo. CHART COMPOSITIONS: *Ain't No Stoppin' Us Now* [ii] (1979) R&B#1 US#13 UK#5, *I've Been Pushed Aside* (1979) R&B#73, *I Heard It in a Love Song* (1980) R&B#23, *One More Time* (1982) R&B#58. ALBUMS: **McFadden and Whitehead** (1979, Philadelphia International) g US#23; **I Heard It in a Love Song** (1980, TSOP) US#153. Whitehead also released the solo album **I Need Money Bad** (1988, Mercury). HIT VERSIONS: *Ain't No Stoppin' Us Now* [ii] Big Daddy Kane (1990) UK#44/Various Artists on *Calibre Cuts* (1980) UK#75/Luther Vandross (1995) UK#22; *Bad Luck* [i] Harold Melvin & the Bluenotes (1975) R&B#4 US#15/Atlanta Disco Band (1976) R&B#38 US#94; *Tell the World How I Feel About 'Cha Baby* [i] Harold Melvin & the Bluenotes (1976) R&B#7 US#94, *Wake Up Everybody* [i] Harold Melvin & the Bluenotes (1976) R&B#1 US#12 UK#23, *Where Are All My Friends* [i] Harold Melvin & the Bluenotes (1974) R&B#8 US#80. Co-writers: [i] Victor Carstarphen, [ii] Jerry Cohen. (*See also under* Kenny GAMBLE and Leon HUFF.)

626. McGARRIGLE, Anna
(b. 1945), and **McGARRIGLE, Kate** (b. 1946, both St. Sauveur-des-Monts, Quebec, Canada) Both folk guitarists and vocalists. A sibling duo who first performed as members of the Mountain City Four during the early 1960s, and composed songs for Canadian television. An English and French language singing duo, their songs *Heart Like a Wheel* and *Mendocino* were both covered by Linda Ronstadt. ALBUMS: **Kate and Anna McGarrigle** (1976), **Dancer with Bruised Knees** (1977) UK#35, **Pronto Monto** (1978, all Warner Brothers); **Entre La Jeunesse et La Sagesse** (1980, Kebec Disc); **Love Over and Over** (1983, Polydor); **Matapoedin** (1996, Rykodisc). HIT VERSION: *Heartbeats Accelerating* Linda Ronstadt (1993) US#112.

627. McGHEE, Wes
(b. October 26, 1948, Lutterworth, England) C&W guitarist and vocalist. One of very few British country artists to achieve any degree of respect and success in America, whose authentic Tex-Mex style sells to an enthusiastic, cult following. ALBUMS: **Long Nights and Banjo Music** (1978), **Airmail** (1980), **Restless Natives** (1981), **Landing Lights** (1983); **Thanks for the Chicken** (1985), **Zacatexas** (1986, all Terrapin); **Freddie "Steady" Krc and Wild Country** (1987, Amazing). COMPILATION: **Heartache Avenue: Classic Recordings, 1978–1992** (Road Goes on Forever).

628. McGUINN, Roger
(b. James Joseph McGuinn III, July 13, 1942, Chicago, IL) Rock guitarist and vocalist. The leader of the seminal 1960s group the Byrds. McGuinn first performed as a member of the Limeliters and the Chad Mitchell Trio. In 1964, he formed the group the Jet Set, which, with the addition of Gene Clark and David Crosby, became the Beefeaters, and ultimately the Byrds. McGuinn's folky, jangly, 12-string guitar playing was pivotal to the group's sound, and he has been the only constant member throughout the band's frequent incarnations. CHART COMPOSITIONS: *It Won't Be Wrong* (1966) US#63, *Eight Miles High* [ii] (1966) US#14 UK#24, *5D (Fifth Dimension)* (1966) US#44, *Mr. Spaceman* (1966) US#36, *So You Want to Be a Rock 'n' Roll Star* [iii] (1967) US#29, *Ballad of Easy Rider* (1969) US#65, *Chestnut Mare* [v] (1970) US#121 UK#19. ALBUMS: **Mr. Tambourine Man** (1965) US#6 UK#7, **Turn! Turn! Turn!** (1966) US#17 UK#11, **Fifth Dimension** (1966) US#24 UK#27, **Younger Than Yesterday** (1967) US#24 UK#37, **The Notorious Byrd Brothers** (1968) US#47 UK#12, **Sweetheart of the Rodeo** (1968) US#77, **Dr. Byrds and Mr. Hyde** (1969) US#153 UK#15, **Ballad of Easy Rider** (1969) US#36 UK#41,

Untitled (1970) US#40 UK#11, **Byrdmaniax** (1971) US#46, **Farther Along** (1971, all Columbia) US#152; **The Byrds** (1973, Asylum) US#20 UK#31. COMPILATIONS: **Greatest Hits** (1967) p US#6, **Preflyte** (1969) US#84, **Best of the Byrds (Greatest Hits, Volume II)** (1972) US#114, **History of the Byrds** (1973) UK#47, **The Byrds** (1990) US#151, **Very Best of the Byrds** (1997, all Columbia). McGuinn has also pursued an intermittent solo career. CHART COMPOSITIONS: *Take Me Away* (1976) US#110, *Don't Write Her Off* [iv]* (1979) US#33, *Surrender to Me* [iv]* (1979) US#104. ALBUMS: **Roger McGuinn** (1973) US#137, **Peace on You** (1974) US#92, **Roger McGuinn Band** (1975) US#16, **Cardiff Rose** (1976), **Thunderbyrd** (1977, all Columbia); **McGuinn, Clark and Hillman*** (1979) US#39, **City*** (1980) US#136, **McGuinn/Hillman**** (1980, all Capitol); **Back from Rio** (1991, Arista) US#44; **Live from Mars** (1996, Hollywood); **3 Byrds Land in London*** (1996, Strange Fruit). HIT VERSIONS: *American Girl* Tom Petty & the Heartbreakers (1994) US#109, *You Showed Me* [i] Turtles (1969) US#6/ Salt-N-Pepa (1991) R&B#68 US#47 UK#15/Lightning Seeds (1996) UK#8. With: * Gene Clark and Chris Hillman, ** Chris Hillman. Co-writers: [i] Gene Clark, [ii] Gene Clark/David Crosby, [iii] Chris Hillman, [iv] R.J. Hippard, [v] Jacques Levy.

629. McHUGH, Jimmy (b. James Francis McHugh, July 10, 1895, Boston, MA; d. May 23, 1969, Beverly Hills, CA) Film and stage composer, pianist. A professionally trained musician who worked as a rehearsal pianist and song-plugger before achieving his first hit with *When My Sugar Walks Down the Street* [iii] (1921). McHugh was a prolific songwriter, and composed songs for seven Cotton Club revues, before writing all the music for "Blackbirds of 1928" in collaboration with the lyricist Dorothy Fields. Their partnership lasted throughout the 1920s, and they contributed to the Broadway shows "Hello, Daddy" (1928) and "The International Revue" (1930). McHugh worked with the lyricist Al Dubin on the shows "Down Argentine Way" (1939) and "Keep Off the Grass" (1940), and with Harold Adamson on "As the Girls Go" (1948). He was also successful in Hollywood, where he composed for over fifty film musicals, including "The Blackbirds of 1928," "The Cuban Love Song" (1930), "Dancing Lady," "Dinner at Eight" (both 1933); "Have a Heart" (1934), "Every Night at Eight," "Hooray for Love," "King of Burlesque" (all 1935); "Higher and Higher," "Follow the Boys," "The Princess and the Pirate," "Four Jills and a Jeep" (all 1944); "Doll Face" (1946), "Calendar Girl" (1947), and "A Date with Judy" (1948). ALBUMS: **Singin' in the Rain** ost (1952, MGM); **Jack the Ripper** ost (1960, RCA);

Blackbirds of 1928 sc (1968, Columbia); **Singin' in the Rain** oc (1983, Rain). HIT VERSIONS: *Bad Humor Man* [xv] Kay Kyser (1940) US#24/Jimmy Dorsey (1941) US#23; *Blue Again* [vi] Duke Ellington (1931) US#12/Red Nichols (1931) US#10; *Can't Get Out of This Mood* [xiii] Johnny Long (1942) US#20/Kay Kyser (1943) US#4; *Comin' in on a Wing and a Prayer* [i] Four Vagabonds (1943) US#24/ Willie Kelly (1943) US#2/Song Spinners (1943) US#1; *Cuban Love Song* [ix] Ruth Etting (1932) US#10/Jacques Renard (1931) US#7/Paul Whiteman (1931) US#13; *Dig You Later (A Hubba-Hubba-Hubba)* [i] Perry Como (1946) US#3, *Diga Diga Doo* [vi] Duke Ellington (1928) US#17, *Dinner at Eight* [vi] Ben Selvin (1933) US#14, *Doin' the New Low-down* [vi] Duke Ellington (1928) US#20, *Don't Believe Everything You Dream* [i] Ink Spots (1944) R&B#6 US#14, *Don't Blame Me* [vi] Charles Agnew (1933) US#13/Nat "King" Cole (1948) US#21/Guy Lombardo (1933) US#9/Ethel Waters (1933) US#6/ Everly Brothers (1961) US#20 UK#20/Frank Ifield (1964) US#128 UK#8; *Dream, Dream, Dream* [xvii] Percy Faith (1954) US#25, *Everything Is Hotsy Totsy Now* [xvi] Gene Austin (1925) US#9, *Exactly Like You* [vi] Ruth Etting (1930) US#11/Sam Lanin (1930) US#19/Harry Richman (1930) US#12/Benny Goodman (1936) US#12/Don Redman (1937) US#14; *Go Home and Tell Your Mother* [vi] Gus Arnheim (1930) US#3/Guy Lombardo (1930) US#8; *Goodbye Blues* [viii] Mills Brothers (1932) US#4, *Here Comes Heaven Again* [i] Perry Como (1945) US#12, *How Blue the Night* [ii] Dick Haymes (1944) US#11, *How Many Times Do I Have to Tell You?* [vi] Dick Haymes (1944) US#27, *I Can't Believe That You're in Love with Me* [x] Roger Wolfe Kahn (1927) US#11/Ames Brothers (1953) US#22; *I Can't Give You Anything But Love* [vi] Cliff Edwards (1928) US#1/Seger Ellis (1928) US#19/Johnny Hamp (1928) US#4/Ben Selvin (1928) US#2/Gene Austin (1929) US#12/Nat Shilkret (1929) US#12/Teddy Wilson & Billie Holiday (1936) US#5/Rose Murray (1948) R&B#3 US#13/Russ Conway in *Even More Party Pops* (1960) UK#27/Fats Domino (1963) US#114/Bert Kaempfert (1966) US#100; *I Couldn't Sleep a Wink Last Night* [i] Frank Sinatra (1944) US#4, *I Don't Care Who Knows It* [i] Harry James (1945) US#8, *I Feel a Song Comin' On* [vi]* Frances Langford (1935) US#15, *I Get the Neck of the Chicken* [xiii] Freddy Martin (1943) US#15, *I Love to Whistle* [i] Fats Waller (1937) US#5, *I Must Have That Man* [vi] Ben Selvin (1928) US#10, *I'd Know You Anywhere* [xv] Glenn Miller (1940) US#24, *I'm in the Mood for Love* [vi] Louis Armstrong (1935) US#3/Frances Langford (1935) US#15/Little Jack Little (1935) US#1/Leo Reisman (1935) US#18/Billy Eckstine (1946) US#12; *I'm Living in a Great Big Way* [vi] Louis Prima (1935) US#13, *I'm Shooting*

High [xii] Jan Garber (1936) US#3/Little Jack Little (193) US#15; *I've Got My Fingers Crossed* [xii] Fats Waller (1936) US#11, *It's a Most Unusual Day* [i] Ray Noble (1948) US#21, *Let's Get Lost* [xiii] Jimmy Dorsey (1943) US#11/Kay Kyser (1943) US#4/ Vaughn Monroe (1943) US#1; *Lonesomest Girl in Town, The* [v] Morton Downey (1926) US#12, *Lost in a Fog* [vi] Dorsey Brothers Orchestra (1934) US#15/Rudy Vallee (1934) US#4; *Love Me as Though There Were No Tomorrow* [i] Nat "King" Cole (1956) UK#11, *Lovely Lady* [xii] Tommy Dorsey (1936) US#12, *Lovely Way to Spend an Evening, A* [i] Ink Spots (1944) US#16/Frank Sinatra (1944) US#11; *Murder, He Says* [xiii] Dinah Shore (1943) US#5, *Music Stopped, The* [i] Woody Herman (1944) US#10, *My Own* [i] Tommy Dorsey (1938) US#5/ George Hall (1938) US#17/Deanna Durbin (1939) US#15; *On the Sunny Side of the Street* [vi] Ted Lewis (1930) US#2/Harry Richman (1930) US#13/Lionel Hampton (1944) R&B#10/Tommy Dorsey (1945) US#16/Jo Stafford (1945) US#17; *Say a Prayer for the Boys Over There* [xiv] Peerless Quartet (1918) US#6, *Say It* [xiii] Isham Jones (1934) US#15/Tommy Dorsey (1940) US#12/Glenn Miller (1940) US#2; *Serenade for a Wealthy Widow* [v] Reginald Foresythe (1934) US#14, *Sing a Tropical Song* [xiii] Andrews Sisters (1944) US#24, *South American Way* [iv] Al Donohue (1939) US#14/Guy Lombardo (1939) US#5; *Thank You for a Lovely Evening* [vi] Don Bestor (1934) US#7, *That Foolish Feeling* [i] Tommy Dorsey (1937) US#15, *There's Something in the Air* [i] Shep Fields (1937) US#5, *Too Young to Go Steady* [i] Nat "King" Cole (1956) US#21 UK#8, *Touch of Texas* [xiii] Freddy Martin (1943) US#12, *When Love Is Young* [i] Fats Waller (1937) US#17, *When My Sugar Walks Down the Street* [iii] Aileen Stanley & Gene Austin (1925) US#3/Warner's Seven Aces (1925) US#14/Ella Fitzgerald (1944) US#27; *Where Are You?* [i] Mildred Bailey (1937) US#5/Gertrude Niesen (1937) US#14/Duprees (1964) US#114; *Where the Lazy River Goes By* [i] Teddy Wilson (1937) US#7, *With All My Heart* [xi] Glen Gray (1936) US#9/Hal Kemp (1936) US#3; *You're a Sweetheart* [i] Dolly Dawn (1938) US#1/Ethel Waters (1938) US#16/Jack Owens (1950) US#29; *You're the One (For Me)* [xv] Orrin Tucker (1941) US#21, *You've Got Me This Way* [xv] Tommy Dorsey (1940) US#14/Kay Kyser (1940) US#12/Glenn Miller (1940) US#12/Jimmy Dorsey (1941) US#19. Co-writers: [i] Harold Adamson, [ii] Harold Arlen, [iii] Gene Austin/Irving Mills, [iv] Al Dubin, [v] Al Dubin/Irving Mills, [vi] Dorothy Fields, [vii] Dorothy Fields/Reginald Foresythe, [viii] Dorothy Fields/Arnold Johnson, [ix] Dorothy Fields/Herbert Stothart, [x] Clarence Gaskill, [xi] Gus Kahn, [xii] Ted Koehler, [xiii] Frank Loesser, [xiv] Herb Magidson, [xv] Johnny Mercer, [xvi] Irving Mills, [xvii] Mitchell Parish. (*See also under* Jerome KERN.)

630. McKEE, Maria (b. August 17, 1964, Los Angeles, CA) Rock guitarist and vocalist. The lead singer and principal songwriter in the group Lone Justice, which charted with *Sweet, Sweet Baby (I'm Falling)* [iii] (1985) US#73 and *Shelter* [iv] (1987) US#47, from the albums **Lone Justice** (1985) US#56 UK#49 and **Shelter** (1986, both Geffen) US#65 UK#84. McKee left the band in 1989 for a solo career. CHART COMPOSITIONS: *Show Me Heaven* [ii] (1990) UK#1, *Sweetest Child* [i] (1992) UK#45. ALBUMS: **Maria McKee** (1989) US#120 UK#49, **You Gotta Sin to Get Saved** (1993) UK#26, **Life Is Sweet** (1996, all Geffen). HIT VERSION: *Good Heart, A* Feargal Sharkey (1985) US#74 UK#1. Co-writers: [i] Brody/Glover, [ii] Eric Rackin/Jay Rifkin, [iii] Benmont Tench/Steve Van Zandt, [iv] Steve Van Zandt.

631. McKUEN, Rod (b. Rodney Marvin McKuen, April 29, 1933, Oakland, CA) Pop vocalist. A successful poet, actor and songwriter. During the 1940s, McKuen worked as a disc jockey, before serving in the Korean War and writing the song *Soldiers Who Want to Be Heroes*. During the 1950s, he composed for films and television, before writing garish lyrics to some of Jacques Brel's finest compositions. Glenn Yarbrough recorded two entire albums of McKuen's material, **Each of Us Alone (The Words and Music of Rod McKuen)** (1968, Warner Brothers) US#188 and **Glenn Yarbrough Sings the Rod McKuen Songbook** (1969, RCA) US#189; and Frank Sinatra recorded **A Man Alone and Other Songs of Rod McKuen** (1969, Reprise) US#30. ALBUMS: **Through European Windows** (1967), **Listen to the Warm** (1968, both RCA) US#178; **Lonesome Cities** (1968) US#175, **At Carnegie Hall** (1969) US#96, **The Earth** (1969, all Warner Brothers); **Joanna** ost with Mike Sarne (1969), **The Prime of Miss Jean Brodie** ost with Mike Redway (1969, both Stateside); **The Sky** (1970), **Home to the Sea** (1970), **New Ballads** (1970) US#126, **Pastorale** (1971) US#182, **Grand Tour** (1971) US#177, **The Rod McKuen Show** (1971, all Warner Brothers); **The Boy Named Charlie Brown** ost (1971, Columbia); **The Single Man** (1972, Reprise). COMPILATIONS: **Greatest Hits** (1969, Warner Brothers) US#149; **Best of Rod McKuen** (1969, RCA) US#175; **Greatest Hits 2** (1970, Warner Brothers) US#148. HIT VERSIONS: *Baby the Rain Must Fall* Glenn Yarbrough (1965) US#12, *I Think of You (Il Faut Trouver Le Temp D'Aimer)* [i] Perry Como (1971) US#53, *It's Raining* Jean Oliver (1969) g US#2, *Mummy, The* Bob McFadden & Dor (1959) US#39,

Sing Boy, Sing [ii] Tommy Sands (1957) US#24. Co-writers: [i] Francis Lai, [ii] Tommy Sands. (*See also under* Jacques BREL.)

632. McLEAN, Don (b. October 2, 1945, New Rochelle, NY). Folk guitarist, banjo player and vocalist. A folk artist with an eclectic interest in all forms of music, who has also composed three modern standards, *And I Love You So, American Pie* and *Vincent.* McLean grew up listening to folk music, and developed a love of rock and roll after hearing Buddy Holly. He learned the guitar while still in high school, and during the 1960s performed in clubs, later saying, "I knew I was going to make a living at music for the simple reason that I couldn't stand to wear a suit or do a day job." In 1969, he toured the Hudson River communities as a member of Pete Seeger's Sloop Singers, an event captured in the television film "The Sloop at Nyack," and contributed to the album **Clearwater** (1974, Clearwater/Soundhouse). McLean later edited a book about the voyage, "Songs and Sketches of the First Clearwater Crew." In 1970, he released the accomplished **Tapestry,** a set of acoustic folk songs that had been rejected by thirty-four record labels. Two years later, McLean sold over four million copies of his composition *American Pie,* a clever documentation of the social, musical and economic changes in America during the 1950–1960s, the theme of which, was, according to the composer, "that commercialism is the death of inspiration." Twenty-five McLean compositions were used in the film "Other Voices" (1971), and his later albums blended elements of folk, country and bluegrass. In 1992, a theatre group in Sheffield, England, staged "Til Tomorrow," a show based around his songs. CHART COMPOSITIONS: *American Pie* (1972) g US#1 UK#2, re-issued (1991) UK#12; *Vincent* (1972) US#12 UK#1, *Dreidel* (1972) US#21, *If We Try* (1973) US#58, *Wonderful Baby* (1975) US#93, *It's Just the Sun* (1981) US#83, *Castles in the Air* (1981) US#36 UK#47, *He's Got You* (1987) US#73, *You Can't Blame the Train* (1987) US#49, *Love in the Heart* (1988) US#65. ALBUMS: **Tapestry** (1971, Media Arts) US#111 UK#16; **American Pie** (1972) g US#1 UK#3, **Don McLean** (1972) US#23, **Playin' Favorites** (1973) UK#42, **Homeless Brother** (1974) US#120, **Solo** (1976, all United Artists); **Prime Time** (1977, Arista); **Chain Lightning** (1978) US#28 UK#19, **Believers** (1981, both Millennium) US#156; **Dominion** (1982), **For the Memories, Volumes 1 and 2** (1986, both Gold Castle); **Love Tracks** (1988, Capitol); **Greatest Hits Live** (1990, Gold Castle); **Headroom** (1991), **Don McLean Christmas** (1991), **Classics** (1992), **River of Love** (1995, all Curb). COMPILATIONS: **Very Best of Don McLean** (1980, United Artists) UK#4; **Greatest Hits — Then and Now** (1987), **Very Best of Don McLean — Favorites and Rarities** (1992, both EMI). HIT VERSIONS: *And I Love You So* Perry Como (1971) US#29 UK#3/Bobby Goldsboro (1971) C&W#48 US#83.

633. McLINTON, O.B. (b. Obie Burnett McClinton, April 25, 1942, Senatobia, MS; d. September 23, 1987, Nashville, TN) C&W vocalist. One of only a few black, R&B based country singers to achieve any degree of commercial success. During the 1960s, McClinton worked as a songwriter for the Stax and Volt labels, before charting fifteen country singles between 1972–1987. McLinton died of abdominal cancer in 1987. CHART COMPOSITION: *Black Speck* (1976) R&B#86. ALBUMS: **Country** (1971, Stax); **Obie from Senatobia** (1973), **Live at Randy's Rodeo** (1973, both Enterprise); **Chocolate Cowboy** (1981, Sunbird). HIT VERSIONS: *Man Needs a Woman, A* James Carr (1968) R&B#16 US#63, *You Got My Mind Messed Up* James Carr (1966) R&B#7 US#63.

634. McNEIR, Ronnie (b. 1951, Camden, AL) R&B pianist and vocalist. A cult R&B artist, whose first single was *Sitting in My Class* (1966). McNeir worked as a musical director and composer for the singer Kim Weston, before recording his own albums whenever he has been able to find a label prepared to release them. CHART COMPOSITIONS: *Wendy Is Gone* (1975) R&B#51, *Sagittarian Affair* (1975) R&B#63, *Come Be with Me* (1984) R&B#76. ALBUMS: **Ronnie McNeir** (1972, RCA); **Ronnie McNeir** (1975, Prodigal); **Love's Comin' Down** (1976, Motown); **The Ronnie McNeir Experience** (1984, Capitol); **Love Suspect** (1987, Setting Sun).

635. McTELL, Blind Willie (b. May 5, 1901, Thomson; d. August 19, 1959, Milledgeville, both GA) Blues guitarist and vocalist. Immortalized in one of Bob Dylan's finest songs, *Blind Willie McTell,* McTell was a highly original yet oddly uninfluential bluesman. During his teens, he worked in traveling shows, before recording his first sides for the Victor label in the 1920s. He also recorded as Blind Sammie and Georgia Bill, and during the 1930s his music became increasingly gospel influenced. In the 1940s, McTell recorded some superb narratives about his own life and the blues for the Library of Congress. His best known song is *Statesboro Blues,* which was made popular by the Allman Brothers Band. ALBUMS: **Last Session** (1956, Prestige/Bluesville); **Blind Willie McTell, 1940** (1967, Storyville); **Atlanta Twelve String Guitar** (1973, Atlantic); **The Legendary Library of Congress Recordings, 1940** (1987, Magnum); **The Early**

Years, 1927–1933 (1988), **Blind Willie McTell, 1927–1935** (1988, both Yazoo); **Remaining Titles, 1927–1949** (1988, Wolf); **Blind Willie McTell, 1933–1935** (1988, Document); **Love Changing Blues** (1989, Magnum).

636. McTELL, Ralph (b. Ralph May, December 3, 1944, Farnborough, England) Folk guitarist and vocalist. A former busker who performed regularly on the 1960s British folk circuit, and who is best known for penning the much recorded *Streets of London*. McTell's finest composition remains *The Hiring Fair*, which was recorded by Fairport Convention. CHART COMPOSITIONS: *Streets of London* (1974) UK#2, *Dreams of You* (1975) UK#36. ALBUMS: **8 Frames a Second** (1968), **Spiral Staircase** (1969, both Transatlantic); **You Well-Meaning Brought Me Here** (1971, Famous); **Not Till Tomorrow** (1972) UK#36, **Easy** (1974, both Reprise) UK#31; **Streets** (1975) UK#13, **Right Side Up** (1976), **Ralph Albert and Sydney** (1977, all Warner Brothers); **Slide Away the Screen** (1979), **Water of Dreams** (1982), **Songs from Alphabet Zoo** (1983), **Bridge of Sighs** (1987, all Mays); **Blue Skies Black Heroes** (1988, Leola); **Sand in Your Shoes** (1995, Transatlantic); **Songs for Six Strings, Volume 2** (1997, OLA). HIT VERSION: *Streets of London* Anti-Nowhere League (1982) UK#48.

637. McVIE, Christine (b. Christine Perfect, July 12, 1943, Birmingham, England) Pop keyboard player and vocalist. A blues singer and pianist with the group Chicken Shack, who joined Fleetwood Mac in 1970, ultimately replacing Peter Green as the band's principal songwriter. CHART COMPOSITIONS: *Over My Head* (1976) US#20, *Say You Love Me* (1976) US#11 UK#40, *Don't Stop* (1977) US#3 UK#32, *You Make Loving Fun* (1977) US#9 UK#45, *Think About Me* (1980) US#20, *Hold Me* [i] (1982) US#4, *Love in Store* [iii] (1983) US#22, *Little Lies* [ii] (1987) US#4 UK#5, *Everywhere* (1988) US#14 UK#4, *As Long as You Follow* [ii] (1989) US#43. ALBUMS: **Mr. Wonderful/English Rose** (1968) US#184 UK#10, **Pious Bird of Good Omen** (1969, both Blue Horizon) UK#18; **Then Play On** (1969) US#109 UK#6, **Kiln House** (1970) US#69 UK#39, **Future Games** (1971) US#91, **Bare Trees** (1972) p US#70, **Penguin** (1973) US#49, **Mystery to Me** (1973) g US#67, **Heroes Are Hard to Find** (1974) US#34, **Fleetwood Mac** (1975, all Reprise) p US#1 UK#23; **Rumours** (1977) p US#1 UK#1, **Tusk** (1979) p US#4 UK#1, **Live** (1980) g US#14 UK#31, **Mirage** (1982) p US#1 UK#5, **Tango in the Night** (1987) p US#7 UK#1, **Behind the Mask** (1990) g US#18 UK#1, **Time** (1995) UK#47, **The Dance** (1997, all Warner Brothers). COMPILATIONS:

Fleetwood Mac in Chicago (1971, Blue Horizon) US#118; **Black Magic Woman** (1971, Epic) US#143; **Greatest Hits** (1972, CBS) US#70 UK#36; **Vintage Years** (1975, Sire) US#138; **Greatest Hits** (1988, Warner Brothers) p US#14 UK#3. McVie has also recorded as a solo artist, charting with the singles *Got a Hold on Me* [iv] (1984) US#10 and *Love Will Show Us How* (1984) US#30, and releasing the albums **The Legendary Christine Perfect Album** (1969, Blue Horizon) US#104 and **Christine McVie** (1984, Warner Brothers) US#26. HIT VERSIONS: *Don't Stop* Status Quo (1996) UK#35, *Say You Love Me* Lynda K. Lance (1976) C&W#93/Stephanie Winslow (1979) C&W#10. Co-writers: [i] Robbie Patton, [ii] Eddy Quintela, [iii] J. Recor, [iv] Todd Sharp.

638. MADDEN, Edward (b. 1878, d. 1952, both America) Film and stage lyricist. A Tin Pan Alley composer, whose best known composition is *By the Light of the Silvery Moon* [i], which was introduced in the show "The Ziegfeld Follies of 1909." HIT VERSIONS: *Blue Bell* [ii] Henry Burr (1904) US#4/Haydn Quartet (1904) US#1/Frank Stanley & Byron G. Harlan (1904) US#1; *By the Light of the Silvery Moon* [i] Ada Jones (1910) US#2/Billy Murray & Haydn Quartet (1910) US#1/Peerless Quartet (1910) US#2/Ray Noble (1942) US#12, re-issued (1944) US#23/Big Ben Banjo Band in *Let's Get Together Again* (1955) UK#18/Joe "Mr. Piano" Henderson in *Sing It with Joe* (1955) UK#14/Russ Conway in *Party Pops* (1957) UK#24/Little Richard (1959) UK#17; *Down in Jungle Town* [ii] Arthur Collins & Byron Harlan (1908) US#4, *Good-by Summer! So Long Fall! Hello, Wintertime!* [iii] Frank Stanley (1906) US#3/Alan Turner (1908) US#5; *I've Got a Feelin' for You* [ii] Arthur Collins (1904) US#2, *Jimmy Valentine* [i] Peerless Quartet (1911) US#3, *Moonlight Bay* [iii] American Quartet (1912) US#1/ Dolly Connolly (1912) US#3/Bing Crosby & Gary Crosby (1951) US#14/Joe "Mr. Piano" Henderson in *Sing It with Joe* (1955) UK#14; *Red Rose Rag* [iii] Dolly Connolly (1911) US#7, *Silver Bell* [iii] Peerless Quartet (1910) US#2/Frank Stanley & Henry Burr (1910) US#5/Ada Jones & Billy Murray (1911) US#7/"That Girl" Quartet (1911) US#9; *Two Little Boys* [ii] Rolf Harris (1969) US#119 UK#1, re-entry (1970) UK#50/Rusty Draper (1970) C&W#73/ Slodgenessabounds (1980) UK#26. Co-writers: [i] Gus Edwards, [ii] Theodore F. Morse, [iii] Percy Wenrich.

639. Madonna (b. Madonna Louise Vernon Ciccone, August 16, 1958, Bay City, MI) Pop vocalist. The most popular female pop singer and actress of the 1980s, whose mildly controversial, publicity oriented antics, and deliberately commercial material, has given her more British number one singles than any other female artist. Madonna first worked as a dancer and drummed for the group the Breakfast Club in 1979, before setting out to conquer the world as a solo performer. CHART COMPOSITIONS: *Everybody* (1982) US#107, *Lucky Star* (1984) R&B#42 US#4, *Angel* [ii] (1985) g R&B#71 US#5 UK#5, *Into the Groove* [ii] (1985) R&B#19 UK#1, *Gambler* (1985) UK#4, re-entry (1986) UK#61; *Live to Tell* [ix] (1986) US#1 UK#2, *Papa Don't Preach* [v] (1986) US#1 UK#1, *True Blue* [ii] (1986) US#3 UK#1, *Open Your Heart* [iii] (1986) US#1 UK#4, *La Isla Bonita* [vii] (1987) US#4 UK#1, *Who's That Girl* [ix] (1987) R&B#78 US#1 UK#1, *Causin' a Commotion* [ii] (1987) US#2 UK#4, *Look of Love* [ix] (1987) UK#9, *Like a Prayer* [ix] (1989) US#1 UK#1, *Express Yourself* [ii] (1989) US#2, *Cherish* [ix] (1989) US#2, *Dear Jessie* [ix] (1989) UK#5, *Oh Father* (1990) US#20, re-issued (1995) UK#16; *Keep It Together* [ii] (1990) US#8, *Vogue* [xi] (1990) US#1 UK#1, *I'm Breathless* (1990) UK#2, *Hanky Panky* [ix] (1990) US#10 UK#2, *Justify My Love* [viii] (1990) US#1 UK#2, *Rescue Me* [xi] (1991) US#9 UK#3, *This Used to Be My Playground* [xi] (1992) g US#1 UK#3, *Erotica* [xi] (1992) US#3 UK#3, *Deeper and Deeper* [xii] (1992) US#7 UK#6, *Bad Girl* [xi] (1993) US#36 UK#10, *Rain* [xi] (1993) US#14 UK#7, *I'll Remember* [x] (1994) g US#2 UK#7, *Secret* (1994) g US#3 UK#5, *Take a Bow* [i] with Babyface (1995) g US#1 UK#16, *Bedtime Story* (1995) US#42 UK#4, *Human Nature* [iv] (1995) US#46 UK#8, *You'll See* [vi] (1995) g US#6 UK#5, *One More Chance* [vi] (1996) UK#11, *You Must Love Me* (1996) UK#10. ALBUMS: **Madonna** (1983) p US#8 UK#6, **Like a Virgin** (1984) p US#1 UK#1, **True Blue** (1986) p US#1 UK#1, **Who's That Girl** ost (1987) p US#7 UK#4, **You Can Dance** (1987) p US#14 UK#5, **Like a Prayer** (1989) p US#1 UK#1, **I'm Breathless** (1990, all Sire) p US#2 UK#2; **Erotica** (1992) p US#2 UK#2, **Bedtime Stories** (1995, both Maverick) p US#3 UK#3; **Evita** ost (1996, Sire); **Ray of Light** (1998, Maverick) US#1 UK#1. COMPILATIONS: **The Immaculate Collection** (1990, Sire) p US#3 UK#1; **Something to Remember** (1995, Maverick) p US#6 UK#3. HIT VERSIONS: *Each Time You Break My Heart* [ii] Nick Kamen (1986) UK#5, *Sidewalk Talk* Jellybean (1985) R&B#51 US#18. Co-writers: [i] Babyface, [ii] Steven Bray, [iii] Gardner Cole/Peter Rafelson, [iv] Deering/Hall/McKenzie/McKenzie, [v] Brian Elliot, [vi] Dave Foster, [vii] Bruce Gaitsch/Patrick Leonard, [viii] Lenny Kravitz, [ix] Patrick Leonard, [x] Patrick Leonard/Richard Page, [xi] Shep Pettibone, [xii] Shep Pettibone/Shimkin.

640. MAEL, Ron (b. August, 1948, Culver City, CA) Pop keyboard player. In partnership with his younger brother, the singer Russell Mael, Ron first performed the groups Urban Renewal Project and Halfnelson, which recorded the album **Halfnelson** (1971, Bearsville). During the 1970s, the duo achieved European chart success with their mock-operatic group Sparks. CHART COMPOSITIONS: *Wonder Girl* [i] (1972) US#112, *This Town Ain't Big Enough for the Both of Us* (1974) UK#2, *Amateur Hour* (1974) UK#7, *Never Turn Your Back on Mother Earth* (1974) UK#13, *Something for the Girl with Everything* (1975) UK#17, *Get in the Swing* (1975) UK#27, *Looks, Looks, Looks* (1975) UK#26, *The Number One Song in Heaven* [i] (1979) UK#14, *Beat the Clock* (1979) UK#10, *Tryouts for the Human Race* (1979) UK#45, *I Predict* [i] (1982) US#60, *Cool Places* [i] with Jane Wiedlin (1983) US#49, *With All My Might* [i] (1984) US#104, *When Do I Get to Sing "My Way"* (1994) UK#38, re-issued (1995) UK#32; *When I Kiss You (I Hear Charlie Parker Playing)* (1995) UK#36, *Now That I Own the BBC* (1996) UK#60. ALBUMS: **Sparks** (1971), **Woofer in Tweeter's Clothing** (1972, both Bearsville); **Kimono My House** (1974) US#101 UK#4, **Propaganda** (1975) US#63 UK#9, **Indiscreet** (1975) US#169 UK#18, **Big Beat** (1976, all Island); **Introducing Sparks** (1977, Epic), **Number One Song in Heaven** (1979) UK#73, **Terminal Jive** (1980, both Virgin); **Whomp That Sucker** (1981, RCA) US#182; **Angst in My Pants** (1982) US#173, **Sparks in Outer Space** (1983, both Atlantic) US#88; **Music That You Can Dance To** (1987, Consolidated Allied); **Interior Design** (1988, Fine Art); **Gratuitous Sax and Senseless Violins** (1994, Logic); **Plagiarism** (1997, Virgin). COMPILATIONS: **Best of Sparks** (1979, Island); **Profile: The Ultimate Collection** (1994, Rhino). HIT VERSION: *Yes or No* [ii] Go-Gos (1984) US#84. Co-writers: [i] Russell Mael (b. October, 1953, Santa Monica, CA), [ii] Russell Mael/Jane Wiedlin.

641. MALONE, Deadric R&B composer. The writer of many of Bobby Bland's biggest hits. HIT VERSIONS: *Ain't Nothing You Can Do* [iv] Bobby Bland (1964) US#20, *Ain't That Loving You* Bobby Bland (1961) R&B#9 US#86, *Call on Me* Bobby Bland (1963) R&B#6 US#22, *Cry Cry Cry* Bobby Bland (1960) R&B#9 US#71, *Do What Ya Set Out to Do* Bobby Bland (1972) R&B#6 US#64, *Goodtime Charlie* [v] Bobby Bland (1966) R&B#6 US#75, *I Pity the Fool* Bobby Bland (1961) R&B#1 US#46, *Rockin' in the Same Boat* [ii] Bobby Bland (1968) R&B#12 US#58, *Share Your Love with Me* [i] Bobby Bland (1964) US#42, *That's the Way Love Is* Bobby Bland (1963) R&B#1 US#33, *This Time I'm Gone for Good* [iii] Bobby Bland (1972) R&B#6 US#64, *Turn on Your Love Light* Bobby Bland (1961)

R&B#2 US#28/Oscar Toney, Jr. (1967) R&B#37. Co-writers: [i] Al Braggs, [ii] V. Morrison, [iii] O. Perry, [iv] Joseph W. Scott, [v] Joseph W. Scott/G. Caple.

642. MANCHESTER, Melissa (b. February 15, 1951, New York, NY) Pop pianist and vocalist. A backing vocalist who became a middle-of-the-road performer and songwriter during the 1970s. CHART COMPOSITIONS: *Midnight Blue* [iii] (1975) US#6, *Just Too Many People* [ii] (1975) US#30, *Just You and I* [iii] (1976) US#27, *Better Days* [iii] (1976) US#71, *Lovers After All* with Peabo Bryson (1981) US#54, *Mathematics* [i] (1985) US#74. ALBUMS: **Home to Myself** (1973) US#156, **Bright Eyes** (1975, both Bell) US#159; **Melissa** (1975) g US#12, **Better Days and Happy Endings** (1976) US#24, **Help Is on the Way** (1976) US#60, **Singin'** (1977) US#60, **Don't Cry Out Loud** (1978) US#33, **Melissa Manchester** (1979) US#63, **For the Working Girl** (1980) US#68, **Hey Ricky** (1982) US#19, **Emergency** (1983, all Arista) US#135; **Mathematics** (1985, MCA) US#144. COMPILATION: **Greatest Hits** (1983, Arista) g US#43. HIT VERSIONS: *Come in from the Rain* [iii] Captain & Tennille (1977) US#61, *Heaven Help Us All* [iii] Beverly Bremers (1972) US#110, *Party Music* [iv] Pat Lundi (1975) US#78. Co-writers: [i] Robbie Nevil/B. Walsh, [ii] Vincent Poncia, [iii] Carole Bayer Sager, [iv] D. Wolfert. (*See also under* Kenny LOGGINS.)

643. MANCINI, Henry (b. Henry Nicole Mancini, April 16, 1924, Cleveland, OH; d. June 14, 1994, Los Angeles, CA) Multi-instrumentalist and orchestral leader. A film composer who worked on nearly six hundred movies, and recorded nearly one hundred albums, eight of which were awarded gold discs. Mancini's best known film theme is *The Pink Panther,* and his best known song is *Moon River* [v], which was introduced in the film "Breakfast at Tiffanys" (1961) by Audrey Hepburn, and has been recorded over five hundred times since. Mancini's scores often manipulated unusual instruments in odd assemblages, and utilized a multitude of compositional techniques, including a distinctive use of slow music against fast paced scenes. He was also one of the first to gain film composers recognition and credit for their work. The son of Italian immigrants, Mancini's father was a proficient flutist, who taught his son the instrument. Mancini grew up in Pennsylvania, where, he learned the piccolo and performed in the group the Sons of Italy, later mastering the piano and developing a love of big band jazz. In 1937, he became the first flute for the Pennsylvania All-State Band, and between 1938–1940, he studied piano, music theory and composition. Mancini sold his first jazz arrangement to the clarinetist Benny Goodman, before attending the Juilliard School of Music in 1942, where he was tutored by the composers Ernst Krenek and Mario Castelnueved-Tedesco. After working as the pianist and arranger in the Glenn Miller Band, he left in 1947 to work as a freelance musician and arranger. In 1952, he was employed by Universal Pictures to write music for a scene in Abbot and Costello's film "Lost in Alaska," a two week contract that ended up lasting six years. Mancini ultimately scored over one hundred films for Universal, including the sophisticated jazz-noire of Orson Welles' "Touch of Evil" (1958). During the 1950s, Mancini also composed for countless television programs, the best known being his *Peter Gunn* theme, which made him the first composer to utilize a jazz arrangement on a television theme. He scored the first rock musical "Rock, Pretty Baby" (1957), and continued to write and perform until his death in 1994, his last work being twenty-five songs written in collaboration with the lyricist Leslie Bricusse for a stage version of "Victor/Victoria." CHART COMPOSITIONS: *Mr. Lucky* (1961) US#21, *Theme from the Great Imposter* (1961) US#90, *Moon River* [v] (1961) US#11 UK#44, *Theme from Hatari* (1962) US#95, *Days of Wine and Roses* [v] (1963) US#33, *Banzai Pipeline* (1963) US#93, *Charade* [v] (1964) US#36, *The Pink Panther Theme* (1964) US#31, *A Shot in the Dark* (1964) US#97, *Dear Heart* [iv] (1964) US#79, *How Soon* [vi] (1964) UK#10, *The Sweetheart Tree* (1965) US#117, *Theme from Z (Life Goes On)* (1970) US#115, *Theme from Cade's County* (1972) UK#42, *Theme from the Thorn Birds* (1984) UK#23. ALBUMS: **The Glenn Miller Story** ost (1954, MGM); **Tarantula** ost (1955), **Congo Crossing** ost (1956, both Coral); **The Benny Goodman Story** ost (1956) US#4, **Rock, Pretty Baby** ost (1957, both Decca) US#16; **Touch of Evil** ost (1958, Fresh Sounds); **Summer Love** ost (1958, Decca); **Music from Peter Gunn** ost (1958) g US#1, **More Music from Peter Gunn** ost (1959) US#7, **The Blues and the Beat** ost (1959), **Music from Mr. Lucky** ost (1960) US#2, **High Time** ost (1960), **Mr. Lucky Goes Latin** ost (1961) US#28, **Breakfast at Tiffany's** ost (1961) g US#1, **Bachelor in Paradise** ost (1961), **Combo** ost (1962) US#28, **Music from High Time** ost (1962), **Experiment in Terror** ost (1962) US#37, **Hatari** ost (1962) US#4, **Charade** ost (1963) US#6, **Our Man in Hollywood** (1963) US#12, **Uniquely Mancini** (1963) US#5, **Best of Henry Mancini** (1963) g US#42, **The Pink Panther** ost (1964) g US#8, **Man's Favorite Sport** ost (1964), **The Concert Sound of Henry Mancini** (1964) US#15, **Dear Heart and Other Songs About Love** (1964) US#11, **The Great Race** ost (1965) US#63, **The Latin Sound of Henry Mancini** (1965) US#46,

Arabesque ost (1966) US#142, **What Did You Do in the War Daddy?** ost (1966) US#148, **A Merry Mancini Christmas** (1966) g, **Music of Hawaii** (1966) US#121, **Two for the Road** ost (1967) US#183, **Gunn** ost (1967), **Encore — More of the Concert Sound of Henry Mancini** (1967) US#126, **Mancini '67** (1967) US#65, **The Party** ost (1968), **A Big Latin Band of Henry Mancini** (1968, all RCA); **Me, Natalie** ost (1969, Columbia); **Six Hours Past Sunset** (1969, RCA) US#91; **Gaily Gaily** ost (1969, United Artists); **A Warm Shade of Ivory** (1969) g US#5, **Darling Lili** ost (1970, both RCA) US#113; **The Sunflower** ost (1970, Avco); **The Molly Maguires** ost (1970, Paramount); **The Hawaiians** ost (1970, United Artists); **Mancini Country** (1970) US#91, **Theme from Z and Other Film Music** (1970) US#111, **This Is Henry Mancini** (1970, all RCA) US#196; **Sometimes a Great Notion** ost (1971, MCA); **Mancini Plays the Theme from Love Story** (1971) US#26, **Mancini Concert** (1971, both RCA) US#85; **The Thief Who Came to Dinner** ost (1972, Warner Brothers); **Brass on Ivory*** (1972) US#74, **Big Screen-Little Screen** (1972) US#109, **The Mancini Generation** (1972) US#195, **In the Pink** (1972), **Visions of Eight** ost (1973), **Oklahoma Crude** ost (1973), **Mancini Salutes Sousa** (1973), **Brass Ivory and Strings*** (1973) US#185, **Country Gentleman** (1973), **The White Dawn** ost (1974), **Hangin' Out with Henry Mancini** (1974), **Academy Award Songs** (1974) US#74, **This Is Henry Mancini, Volume 2** (1974), **Sample Mancini** (1974, all RCA); **The Great Waldo Pepper** ost (1975, MCA); **The Return of the Pink Panther** ost (1976, RCA); **W.C. Fields and Me** ost (1976, MCA); **The Moneychangers** ost (1976, RCA); **The Pink Panther Strikes Again** ost (1976, United Artists); **Symphonic Soul** (1976) US#159, **Film Music Concert** (1976), **Henry Mancini Conducts the London Symphony Orchestra** (1976, all RCA); **Henry Mancini** (1976, Arcade) UK#26; **A Legendary Performer** (1976) US#161, **The Cop Show Themes** (1976), **Moon River, Pink Panther and Other Hits** (1976), **The Mancini Touch** (1976, all RCA); **Forty Greatest** (1976, Arcade); **Mancini's Angels** (1977, RCA) US#126; **The Revenge of the Pink Panther** ost (1978, United Artists); **Who Is Killing the Great Chefs of Europe?** ost (1978, Epic); **Night Visitor** ost (1979, Citadel); **10** ost (1979, Warner Brothers) US#80; **The Theme Scene** (1979), **Best of Henry Mancini, Volume 2** (1979), **Best of Henry Mancini, Volume 3** (1979), **Pure Gold** (1980, all RCA); **The Trail of the Pink Panther** ost (1982 United Artists); **Victor/Victoria** ost (1982, MGM) US#174; **Very Best of Henry Mancini** (1982, RCA); **Hotel** ost (1983, MFP); **A Man and His Music** (1983, Cambra); **Disco De Ouro** (1984, RCA); **The Magic**

of Henry Mancini (1984, WEA); **Mamma** with Luciano Pavarotti (1984, London) US#103 UK#96; **Lifeforce** ost (1985, Varese Sarabande); **Santa Claus — The Movie** ost (1985, EMI); **Mancini Plays Mancini** (1985, Readers Digest); **That's Dancin'** (1985, EMI); **Music from the Films of Blake Edwards** (1985), **Debut — Mancini Conducts the Philadelphia Orchestra Pops** (1985, both RCA); **The Adventures of the Great Mouse Detective** ost (1986, Disneyland); **A Fine Mess** ost (1986, Motown) US#183; **Highway to Hollywood — Big Movie Hits, Volume 2** (1986, Varese Sarabande); **The Hollywood Musicals** with Johnny Mathis (1986, Columbia) US#197 UK#46; **All Time Greatest Hits, Volume 1** (1986, RCA); **At the Movies** (1986, MFP); **The Glass Menagerie** ost (1987, MCA); **Blind Date** ost (1987, Rhino) US#198; **A Touch of Romance** (1987, Readers Digest); **Diamond Series** (1988, Diamond); **Henry Mancini and the Royal Philharmonic Pops Orchestra** (1988), **Mancini Rocks the Pops** (1989, both Denon); **Themes from Classic Science Fiction, Fantasy and Horror Films** (1989, Varese Sarabande); **Born on the Fourth of July** ost (1990, MCA) US#32; **Mancini in Surround — Mostly Monsters, Murders and Mysteries** (1990), **Mancini's Monster Hits** (1990, both RCA); **Switch** ost (1991, MCA); **Mancini Goes to the Movies** (1991), **The Pink Panther and Other Hits** (1992, both RCA); **Film Favorites** (1992, Ariola Express); **Cinema Italiano — Music of Ennio Morricone and Nino Rota** (1992), **Top Hat — Music from the Astaire and Rogers Films** (1992), **As Time Goes By and Other Classic Movie Love Songs** (1992), **In the Pink — The Ultimate Collection** (1996, RCA). HIT VERSIONS: *All His Children* [i] Charlie Pride (1972) C&W#2 US#92, *Baby Elephant Walk* [iii] Miniature Men (1962) US#87/Lawrence Welk (1962) US#48/Donald Jenkins & the Daylighters (1963) US#64; *Charade* [v] Sammy Kaye (1964) US#36/Andy Williams (1964) US#100; *Come to Me* [ii] Johnny Mathis (1957) US#22, *Days of Wine and Roses* [v] Pat Boone (1963) US#117/Andy Williams (1963) US#26; *Dear Heart* [iv] Jack Jones (1965) US#30/Andy Williams (1965) US#24; *(I Love You) Don't You Forget It* [vi] Perry Como (1963) US#39, *In the Arms of Love* [iv] Andy Williams (1966) US#49 UK#33, *Moon River* [v] Andy Williams (1961) UK#1/Jerry Butler (1962) R&B#14 US#11/Greyhound (1972) UK#12; *Peter Gunn, Theme from* Ray Anthony & His Orchestra (1959) R&B#12 US#8/Duane Eddy (1959) US#27 UK#6/Deodata (1977) R&B#96 US#84/Art of Noise & Duane Eddy (1986) US#50 UK#8/Grandmaster Flash as *Style* (1986) R&B#54; *Send a Little Love My Way* [iii] Anne Murray (1973) C&W#79 US#72, *Sweetheart Tree, The* Johnny Mathis (1965) US#108. With: * Doc Severinsen. Co-writers: [i] Alan Bergman/Marilyn Bergman, [ii] Don Black, [iii] Hal David, [iv] Ray Evans/Jay Livingston, [v] Johnny Mercer, [vi] Al Stillman.

644. MANILOW, Barry (b. Barry Alan Pincus, June 17, 1946, Brooklyn, NY) Pop pianist and vocalist. A highly successful middle-of-the-road performer, who has achieved his stated objective: "I wanted to write music that would be played in elevators for ever and ever." Manilow grew up in poverty and learned the piano at the age of thirteen. He studied at the Julliard School in New York, and composed for the off-Broadway show "The Drunkard" (1964), before writing and arranging jingles for television. After a failed nightclub duo with Jeanne Lucas, Manilow arranged for Bette Midler and wrote material for other artists. During the mid–1970s, he became a massively successful solo star in a variety of styles. CHART COMPOSITIONS: *It's a Miracle* [v] (1975) US#12, *Could It Be Magic* [i] (1975) US#6, re-issued (1979) UK#25, re-mixed (1993) UK#36; *This One's for You* (1976) US#29, *Daybreak* [i] (1977) US#23, *Even Now* [v] (1978) US#19, *Copacabana (At the Copa)* [iv] (1978) US#8 UK#42, re-mixed (1993) UK#22; *I Made It Through the Rain* [ii] (1980) US#10, *Some Kind of Friend* [i] (1983) US#26, *I'm Your Man* [vi] (1986) US#86, *Hey Mambo* [iii] with Kid Creole & the Coconuts (1988) US#90. ALBUMS: **Barry Manilow** (1972) g US#28, **Barry Manilow II** (1973, both Bell) p US#9; **Tryin' to Get the Feelin'** (1976) p US#5, **This One's for You** (1977) p US#6, **Live** (1977) p US#1, **Even Now** (1978) p US#3 UK#12, **One Voice** (1979) p US#9 UK#18, **Barry** (1981) p US#15 UK#5, **If I Should Love Again** (1981) g US#14 UK#5, **Oh, Julie** (1982) US#69, **Barry Live in Britain** (1982) UK#1, **I Wanna Do It with You** (1982) UK#7, **Here Comes the Night** (1982) g US#32 US#32, **2.00 A.M. Paradise Cafe** (1984, all Arista) g US#28 UK#28; **Manilow** (1985, RCA) US#40 UK#42; **Grandes Exitos En Espanol** (1986), **Swing Street** (1987) US#70 UK#81, **Songs to Make the Whole World Sing/Barry Manilow** (1989) US#64 UK#20, **Live on Broadway** (1990) US#196 UK#19, **Because It's Christmas** (1990) g US#40, **Showstoppers** (1991) US#68 UK#53, **Hidden Treasures** (1993) UK#36, **Singin' with the Big Bands** (1994) g US#59 UK#54, **Summer of '76** (1996, all Arista) UK#66. COMPILATIONS: **Manilow Magic** (1979) UK#3, **Greatest Hits** (1979) p US#7, **Gift Set** (1981) UK#62, **Greatest Hits** (1982) US#147, **A Touch More Magic** (1983) UK#10, **Greatest Hits, Volume II** (1984) g US#30, **The Manilow Collection — 20 Classic Hits** (1985) g US#100, **The Songs, 1975–1990** (1990) UK#13, **The Complete Collection and Then Some…** (1992) US#182, **The Platinum Col-**

lection (1993, all Arista) UK#37. HIT VERSIONS: *Could It Be Magic* [i] Donna Summer (1976) R&B#21 US#52 UK#40/Take That (1993) UK#3, *Street Singin'* Lady Flash (1976) US#27. Co-writers: [i] Adrienne Anderson, [ii] Jack Feldman/Gerard Kenny/Drey Shepperd/Bruce Sussman, [iii] Jack Feldman/Gerard Kenny/Bruce Sussman, [iv] Jack Feldman/Bruce Sussman, [v] Marty Panzer, [vi] A. Rice/H. Rice.

645. MANN, Barry (b. February 9, 1939, Brooklyn, NY) Pop pianist, producer and vocalist. The composer, often in collaboration with his wife and lyricist Cynthia Weil, of songs that have sold over one hundred and fifty million records. Mann and Weil were the longest serving graduates of the Brill Building, with an uncanny ability to fashion hit material for artists in any musical genre. Mann once said of their success, "We never thought the songs we wrote were going to be standards, or talked about twenty years later." Mann took piano lessons from the age of eleven, after it had been discovered that he could play pop songs from the radio by ear. He began writing songs in his teens, and dropped out of college when he was offered a publishing contract with Aldon Music in the 1950s. His first recorded song was *White Backs and Saddle Shoes* by Bobby Pedrick (1958), which was followed shortly afterward by his first hit *She Say (Oom Dooby Doom)* [i] by the Diamonds (1959). Mann met Weil in the Brill Building, and they charted with their very first collaboration, *Bless You* [xiii] by Tony Orlando (1961). By the 1970s, their compositions had resulted in nearly fifty Hot 100 entries, collectively selling over seventy million records. Their most famous song is *You've Lost That Lovin' Feeling* [xi], which has received over five million American radio plays. In 1968, they composed the film soundtrack "Wild in the Streets." Mann has also recorded as a solo artist. CHART COMPOSITIONS: *Who Put the Bomp (In the Bomp, Bomp, Bomp)?* [iii] (1961) US#7, *Little Miss U.S.A.* (1961) US#109, *Talk to Me Baby* (1964) US#94, *Angelica* [xiii] (1966) US#111, *Feelings* (1970) US#93, *When You Get Right Down to It* (1972) US#105, *The Princess and the Punk* [xiii] (1976) US#78. ALBUMS: **Who Put the Bomp** (1962, ABC/Paramount); **Lay It All Out** (1971, New Design); **Survivor** (1975, RCA); **Barry Mann** (1980, Casablanca); **Songwriters to the Stars, Volume 2** (1983, Polydor). HIT VERSIONS: *All I Need to Know* [x] Bette Midler (1983) US#77, *Baby Come and Get It* Pointer Sisters (1985) R&B#24 US#13, *Blame It on the Bossa Nova* [xiii] Eydie Gorme (1963) US#7 UK#32, *Bless You* [xiii] Tony Orlando (1961) US#15 UK#5, *Born to Be Together* [xiii] Ronettes (1965) US#52, *Brown Eyed Woman* [xiii] Bill Medley (1968) R&B#37 US#43,

Closer Than Close [xiii] Peabo Bryson (1991) R&B#38, *Come Back Silly Girl* [xiii] Lettermen (1962) US#17, *Come on Over to My Place* [xiii] Drifters (1965) US#60 UK#40, re-issued (1972) UK#9; *Conscience* [xiii] James Darren (1962) US#11, *Counting Teardrops* [iv] Emile Ford & the Checkmates (1960) UK#4, *Country Lullaby* Johnny Carver (1974) C&W#27, *Don't Be Afraid, Little Darlin'* [xiii] Steve Lawrence (1963) US#26, *Don't Know Much* [x] Bill Medley (1981) US#89/Linda Ronstadt & Aaron Neville (1989) US#2 UK#2; *Don't Make My Baby Blue* [xiii] Frankie Laine (1963) US#51/Shadows (1965) UK#10; *Feelings* Cherry People (1969) US#134, *Footsteps* [vii] Ronnie Carroll (1960) UK#36/Steve Lawrence (1960) US#7 UK#4/Showaddywaddy (1981) UK#31; *Get Ready* [viii] James Ingram (1992) R&B#59, *Girl Sang the Blues, The* Everly Brothers (1963) UK#25, *Grass Is Greener, The* [i] Brenda Lee (1963) US#17/Teddy Spencer (1988) C&W#82; *He's Sure the Boy I Love* [xiii] Crystals (1962) R&B#18 US#11, *Heart to Heart* [xiii] Erroll Sober (1979) US#65, *Here You Come Again* [xiii] Dolly Parton (1977) g C&W#1 US#3 UK#75, *Hold on to the Night* Hotel (1979) US#80, *Home of the Brave* [xiii] Bonnie & the Treasures (1965) US#77/Jody Miller (1965) US#25 UK#49; *Hungry* [xiii] Paul Revere & the Raiders (1966) US#6, *I Could Have Loved You So Well* Ray Peterson (1961) US#57, *I Just Can't Help Believin'* [xiii] Elvis Presley (1971) UK#6/B.J. Thomas (1970) US#9/David Frizzell (1970) C&W#36/David Rogers (1974) C&W#59; *I Love How You Love Me* [ix] Paris Sisters (1961) US#5/Jimmy Crawford (1961) UK#18/Maureen Evans (1964) UK#34/Paul & Barry Ryan (1966) UK#21/Bobby Vinton (1968) g US#9/Joni Lee (1978) C&W#94/Lynn Anderson (1979) C&W#18/Glen Campbell (1983) C&W#17; *I'll Never Dance Again* [i] Bobby Rydell (1962) US#14, *I'll Take You Home* [xiii] Corsairs (1962) R&B#26 US#68/Drifters (1963) R&B#24 US#25 UK#37; *I'm Gonna Be Strong* [xiii] Gene Pitney (1964) US#9 UK#2, *If a Man Answers (Hang Up the Phone)* Bobby Darin (1962) UK#24/Leroy Van Dyke (1962) C&W#3 US#35; *It's Getting Better* [xiii] Mama Cass (1969) US#30 UK#8, *Johnny Loves Me* [xiii] Shelley Fabares (1962) US#21, *Just Once* [xiii] Quincy Jones (1981) R&B#11 US#17, *Kicks* [xiii] Paul Revere & the Raiders (1966) US#4, *Last Time I Made Love, The* [ii] Joyce Kennedy & Jeffrey Osborne (1984) R&B#2 US#40, *Let the Song Last Forever* [v] Dan Hill (1978) US#91, *Looking Through the Eyes of Love* [xiii] Gene Pitney (1965) US#28 UK#3/Partridge Family (1973) UK#9; *Lost in the Night* [xiv] Peabo Bryson (1992) R&B#45, *Love Her* [xiii] Everly Brothers (1963) UK#25/Walker Brothers (1965) UK#20; *Magic Town* [xiii] Vogues (1966) US#21, *Make Your Own Kind of Music* [xiii] Mama Cass

(1969) US#36/Barbra Streisand (1972) US#94; *Mamacita* [xiii] Grass Roots (1975) US#71, *Mary's Little Lamb* [xiii] James Darren (1962) US#39, *My Dad* [xiii] Paul Peterson (1962) US#6, *Never Gonna Let You Go* [xiii] Sergio Mendes (1983) R&B#28 US#4 UK#45, *Never Saw a Miracle* [xii] Curtis Stigers (1992) UK#34, *New World Coming* [xiii] Mama Cass (1970) US#42, *Olympia* [xiii] Sergio Mendes (1983) US#58, *Patches* [xi] Dicky Lee (1962) g R&B#10 US#6, *Proud* [xiii] Johnny Crawford (1963) US#29, *Right Here and Now* [xiii] Bill Medley (1982) US#58, *Rock and Roll Lullaby* [xiii] B.J. Thomas (1972) US#15, *Saturday Night at the Movies* [xiii] Drifters (1964) US#18, re-issued (1972) UK#3; *Shape of Things to Come, The* [xiii] Max Frost & the Troopers (1968) US#22, *She Say (Oom Dooby Doom)* [i] Diamonds (1959) US#18, *Sometimes When We Touch* [v] Dan Hill (1978) US#3 UK#46/Stephanie Winslow (1981) C&W#39/Mark Gray & Tammy Wynette (1985) C&W#6; *Somewhere Out There* [vi] Linda Ronstadt & James Ingram (1986) US#2 UK#8, *There's No Easy Way* James Ingram (1983) R&B#14 US#58, *Uptown* [xiii] Crystals (1962) R&B#18 US#13, *Walking in the Rain* [xi] Ronettes (1964) R&B#28 US#20/Walker Brothers (1967) UK#26/Jay & the Americans (1969) US#19/Partridge Family (1973) UK#10; *Warpaint* [iv] Brook Brothers (1961) UK#5, *Way of a Clown, The* Teddy Randazzo (1960) US#44, *We Gotta Get Out of This Place* [xiii] Animals (1965) US#13 UK#2/Angelic Upstarts (1980) UK#65; *We're Going all the Way* [xiii] Jeffrey Osbourne (1984) R&B#16 US#48, *When You Get Right Down to It* Delfonics (1970) R&B#70 US#53/Ronnie Dyson (1971) R&B#37 US#94 UK#34; *Where Have You Been all My Life* Arthur Alexander (1962) US#58, *Who Put the Bomp?* [iii] Showaddywaddy (1982) UK#37, *(You're My) Soul and Inspiration* [xiii] Righteous Brothers (1966) g R&B#13 US#1 UK#15, *You've Lost That Lovin' Feeling* [xi] Righteous Brothers (1965) g R&B#3 US#1 UK#1, re-issued (1969) UK#10, re-issued (1977) US#42, re-issued (1990) UK#3, also on B-side of Berlin *Take My Breath Away* (1986) g US#1 UK#1/Cilla Black (1965) UK#2/Vivian Reed (1968) US#115/Dionne Warwick (1969) R&B#13 US#16/Roberta Flack & Donny Hathaway (1971) R&B#30 US#71/Barbara Fairchild (1975) C&W#41/Telly Savalas (1975) UK#47/Long John Baldry (1979) US#89/Daryl Hall & John Oates (1980) US#12 UK#55/Carlette (1987) C&W#57. Co-writers: [i] Michael Anthony, [ii] Jeff Barry/Cynthia Weil, [iii] Gerry Goffin, [iv] Howard Greenfield, [v] Dan Hill, [vi] James Horner/Cynthia Weil, [vii] Hank Hunter, [viii] James Ingram/Cynthia Weil, [ix] Larry Kolber, [x] Tom Snow/Cynthia Weil, [xi] Phil Spector/Cynthia Weil, [xii] Curtis Stigers, [xiii] Cynthia

Weil, [xiv] Cynthia Weil/H. Zimmer. (*See also under* Jerry LEIBER and Mike STOLLER, Leo SAYER.)

646. MANN, Kal Pop producer. The owner of the Cameo and Parkway record labels during the 1960s, who wrote for, and produced, many of the label's acts. HIT VERSIONS: *Bon-Doo-Wah* [i] Orlons (1963) US#55, *Bristol Stomp, The* [i] Dovells (1961) R&B#7 US#2/Late Show (1979) UK#40; *Butterfly* [iv] Charlie Gracie (1957) US#1/Andy Williams (1957) R&B#14 US#1; *Cha-Cha-Cha, The* [i] Bobby Rydell (1962) US#10, *Class, The* Chubby Checker (1959) US#38, *Crossfire* [i] Orlons (1963) R&B#25 US#19, *Dancin' Party* [i] Chubby Checker (1962) US#12 UK#19/Showaddywaddy (1977) UK#4; *Ding-A-Ling* [ii] Bobby Rydell (1960) US#18, *Do the Bird* [i] Dee Dee Sharp (1963) R&B#8 US#10, *Don't Hang Up* [i] Orlons (1962) R&B#3 US#4, *Fish, The* [ii] Bobby Rydell (1961) US#25, *Good Time Baby* [ii] Bobby Rydell (1961) US#11 UK#42, *Gravy (For My Mashed Potatoes)* [i] Dee Dee Sharp (1962) R&B#11 US#9, *Hey, Bobba Needle* [i] Chubby Checker (1964) US#23, *(Let Me Be Your) Teddy Bear* [iv] Elvis Presley (1957) g US#1 UK#3, also in *The Elvis Medley* (1982) US#71 UK#51/Reggie Garner (1971) US#117; *Let's Twist Again* [i] Chubby Checker (1961) R&B#26 US#8 UK#2, re-entry (1962) UK#46, re-issued (1975) UK#5/John Asher (1975) UK#14; *Popeye (The Hitchhiker)* [i] Chubby Checker (1962) R&B#13 US#10, *Remember You're Mine* [iv] Pat Boone (1957) US#6 UK#5, *Rules of Love* [i] Orlons (1964) US#66, *South Street* [i] Orlons (1963) R&B#4 US#3, *Swingin' School* [ii] Bobby Rydell (1960) US#5, *Twenty Miles* [iv] Chubby Checker (1963) US#15, *Wah Watusi, The* [i] Orlons (1962) R&B#5 US#2, *Wandering Eyes* [v] Charlie Gracie (1957) UK#6/Frankie Vaughan (1957) US#6; *We Got Love* [iv] Bobby Rydell (1959) US#6, *Where Did I Go Wrong* [i] Dee De Sharp (1964) R&B#82, *Wild!* [i] Dee Dee Sharp (1963) R&B#25 US#33, *Wild One* [ii] Bobby Rydell (1960) R&B#10 US#2 UK#7, *Wildwood Days* [i] Bobby Rydell (1963) US#17, *You Can't Sit Down* [iii] Philip Upchurch Combo (1961) US#29, re-issued (1966) UK#39/Dovells (1963) R&B#10 US#3. Co-writers: [i] Dave Appell, [ii] Dave Appell/Bernie Lowe, [iii] Dee Clark/Cornell Muldrow, [iv] Bernie Lowe, [v] Bernie Lowe/Hal Norton.

647. MANNING, Dick Film and stage lyricist. A frequent collaborator with Al Hoffman, whose songs were featured in such films as "Love in the Afternoon" (1957). HIT VERSIONS: *Fascination* [ii] Dick Jacobs (1957) US#17/Jane Morgan (1957) US#7/Dinah Shore (1957) US#15; *Jilted* [i] Teresa Brewer (1954) US#6/Red Foley (1954) C&W#7;

Morning Side of the Mountain, The [iii] Tommy Edwards (1951) US#24/Jan Garber (1951) US#29/Merv Griffin (1951) US#27/Paul Weston (1951) US#16/Jimmy Edwards (1959) US#27/Donny & Marie Osmond (1975) US#8 UK#5; *Pussy Cat Song (Nyow! Nyot! Nyow!), The* Patty Andrews (1949) US#12/Perry Como (1949) US#20/Bob Crosby (1949) US#12/Joy Nichols & Benny Lee (1949) US#21/Jo Stafford & Gordon MacRae (1949) US#26; *Three Bells, The* [iv] Browns (1959) US#1 UK#6/Compagnons De La Chanson (1959) UK#21/Dick Flood (1959) US#23. Co-writers: [i] Robert Colby, [ii] F.D. Marchetti, [iii] Larry Stock, [iv] Jean Villard. (*See also under* Al HOFFMAN.)

648. MARESCA, Ernie (April 21, 1939, Bronx, NY) R&B vocalist. An R&B singer-songwriter who composed some of Dion's biggest hits. CHART COMPOSITION: *Shout! Shout! (Knock Yourself Out)* [i] (1962) R&B#25 US#6. ALBUM: **Shout! Shout! (Knock Yourself Out)** (1993, Sequel). HIT VERSIONS: *Lover's Prayer, A* Dion (1959) US#73, also on B-side of *Every Little Thing* (1959) US#48/Wallace Brothers (1964) R&B#97; *Come on Little Angel* Belmonts (1962) US#28, *Donna the Prima Donna* Dion (1964) US#6, *No One Knows* Dion (1958) R&B#12 US#19, *Runaround Sue* Dion (1961) US#1 UK#11/Doug Sheldon (1961) UK#36/Leif Garrett (1978) US#13/Racey (1980) UK#13; *Wanderer, The* Dion (1962) R&B#4 US#2 UK#10, re-issued (1976) UK#16/Status Quo (1984) UK#7. Co-writer: [i] Thomas F. Bogdany.

649. MARIE, Tina (b. Mary Christine Brockert, 1957, Santa Monica, CA) R&B keyboard player, producer and vocalist. A white R&B performer who was discovered by Rick James. CHART COMPOSITIONS: *I'm a Sucker for Your Love* (1979) R&B#8 US#102 UK#43, *Don't Look Back* (1979) R&B#81, *Can It Be Love* (1980) R&B#57, *Behind the Groove* [ii] (1980) R&B#21 UK#6, *I Need Your Lovin'* (1980) R&B#9 US#37 UK#28, *Young Love* (1981) R&B#41, *Square Biz* (1981) R&B#3 US#50, *It Must Be Magic* (1981) R&B#30, *Portuguese Love* (1981) R&B#54, *Fix It (Part 1)* (1983) R&B#21, *Midnight Magnet* (1983) R&B#36, *Dear Lover* (1984) R&B#77, *Lovergirl* (1984) R&B#9 US#4, *Jammin'* (1985) R&B#45 US#81, *Out on a Limb* (1985) R&B#56, *14K* (1985) R&B#87, *Lips to Find You* (1986) R&B#28, *Love Me Down Easy* (1986) R&B#76, *Ooo La La La* [i] (1988) R&B#1 US#85 UK#74, *Work It* (1988) R&B#10, *Since Day One* (1990) UK#69. ALBUMS: **Wild and Peaceful** (1979) US#94, **Lady T.** (1980) US#45, **Irons in the Fire** (1980) US#38, **It Must Be Magic** (1981, all Gordy) g US#23; **Robbery** (1983) US#119, **Starchild** (1984) g US#31, **Emerald City** (1986)

US#81, **Naked to the World** (1988) US#65, **Ivory** (1990, all Epic) US#132. COMPILATIONS: **Greatest Hits** (1986, Motown); **Lovergirl: Tina Marie** (1997, Columbia). Co-writers: [i] A. McGrier, [ii] Richard Rudolph.

650. MARKS, Johnny (b. 1903, Mount Vernon; d. September 3, 1985, New York, both NY)

Pop composer. A mildly obsessive writer of Christmas songs, who composed the one hundred and fifty million selling *Rudolph, the Red-Nosed Reindeer* (1949), the second best seller of all time. HIT VERSIONS: *Rudolph, the Red-Nosed Reindeer* Gene Autry (1949) g C&W#1 US#1, re-issued (1950) C&W#5 US#3, re-issued (1951) US#16, re-issued (1952) US#12, re-issued (1953) US#26/Bing Crosby (1950) US#14/Spike Jones (1950) US#7/Cadillacs (1957) R&B#11/Paul Anka (1960) US#104/Chipmunks (1960) US#21; *Rockin' Around the Christmas Tree* Brenda Lee (1960) US#14, re-issued (1962) UK#6/ Jets (1983) UK#62/Mel & Kim (1987) UK#3.

651. MARLEY, Bob (b. Robert Nester Marley, February 6, 1945, Rhoden Hall, St. Ann's, Jamaica; d. May 11, 1981, Miami, FL)

Reggae guitarist and vocalist. The most widely known and influential reggae artist in the history of the genre. Marley popularized reggae with a white audience, and made it commercially successful outside of Jamaica for the first time, without ever compromising either his musical integrity or his personal beliefs. Marley's songs merged Caribbean rhythms with western pop structures, and his humanitarian lyrics elevated his personal Rastafarian beliefs to a more universal level, while his outspoken stance against injustice, repression, apartheid, racism and greed, has been unrivaled in contemporary music. Marley's success also introduced a wider audience to the music of such reggae acts as Burning Spear, Black Uhuru and Culture. The only child of a Jamaican mother and an English father, Marley was raised by his mother in Trenchtown, Kingston. At the age of fourteen he became an apprentice welder, but after hearing his first American R&B music, in particular Fats Domino, he decided to pursue music. Joining forces with his childhood friend Neville "Bunny" Livingstone, he formed the group the Teenagers, which became the Wailin' Wailers, and eventually the Wailers, as which, he recorded the earliest known ska records, including *Judge Not (Unless You Judge Yourself)* and *Simmer Down*. During the early 1960s, Marley released a vast catalog of Jamaican singles, including seventy-three titles for the producer Clement Seymour Dodd at Studio One, and twenty-six for Tuff Gong. His first compositions emphasized backing vocal arrangements that were clearly influenced by early Motown

records, and the gospel sound of the Impressions, *Mellow Mood* (1966) being a typical example of a Marley song at this time. Chris Blackwell's Island label was the first to issue his recordings in Britain, where they primarily appealed to first and second generation West Indian immigrants. During the mid–1960s, Marley set up his own Wailin' Soul label, and wrote and produced for the singer Johnny Nash. In 1967, Marley wrote over seventy tunes for the Jad label, and two years later recorded ten sides for Trojan Records. Over one hundred Marley singles were released in Britain during the 1960s, but it was not until he signed to Island Records proper in 1971, that he became an enormous success around the world. Marley died of a cancer related brain tumor in 1981. CHART COMPOSITIONS: *No Woman No Cry* (1975) UK#22, re-issued (1981) UK#8; *Roots, Rock, Reggae* (1976) R&B#37 US#51, *Exodus* (1977) R&B#19 US#103 UK#14, *Jamming* (1977) UK#9, *Waiting in Vain* (1977) R&B#38 UK#27, re-issued (1984) UK#31; *Is This Love* (1978) UK#9, *Satisfy My Soul* (1978) UK#21, *So Much Trouble in the World* (1979) UK#56, *Wake Up and Live* (1979) R&B#93, *Could You Be Loved* (1980) R&B#56 UK#5, re-issued (1984) UK#71; *Three Little Birds* (1980) UK#17, *Reggae on Broadway* (1981) R&B#66, *Buffalo Soldier* [ii] (1983) R&B#71 UK#4, *One Love* (1984) UK#5, re-issued (1991) UK#42; *Iron Lion Zion* (1992) UK#5, *Why Should I/Exodus* (1992) UK#42, *Keep on Moving* (1995) UK#17, *What Goes Around Comes Around* (1996) UK#42. ALBUMS: **The Wailing Wailers — Jamaica's Top-Rated Sensation, Accompanied By the Soul Brothers** (1970), **Marley, Tosh, Livingston and Associates** (1971, both Studio One); **Soul Rebels** (1970), **African Herbsman** (1973, both Trojan); **Catch a Fire** (1973) US#171, **Burnin'** (1973) US#151, **Natty Dread** (1974) US#92 UK#43, **Live** (1975) US#90 UK#38, **Rastaman Vibration** (1976) US#8 UK#15, **Exodus** (1977) US#20 UK#8, **Kaya** (1978) US#50 UK#4, **Babylon By Bus** (1978) US#102 UK#40, **Survival** (1979) US#70 UK#20, **Uprising** (1980, all Island) US#45 UK#6. COMPILATIONS: **Best of the Wailers** (1970, Beverley); **Rasta Revolution** (1974, Trojan); **Best of the Wailers** (1974, Studio One); **Birth of a Legend** (1976, Calla); **In the Beginning** (1979, Trojan); **Soul Rebel** (1981, New Cross); **Chances Are** (1981, WEA) US#117; **Confrontation** (1983) US#55 UK#5, **Legend** (1984) p US#54 UK#1, **Rebel Music** (1986, all Island) US#140 UK#54; **The Lee Perry Sessions** (1987, Konnexion); **Soul Revolution 1 & 2** (1988, Trojan); **Talkin' Blues** (1991, Tuff Gong) US#103; **The Upsetter Record Shop, Part 1** (1992), **The Upsetter Record Shop, Part 2** (1992, both Rhino); **Songs of Freedom** (1992, Tuff Gong) p US#86 UK#10; **The Never Ending Wailers** (1994, Ras);

Natural Mystic—The Legend Continues (1995, Tuff Gong) US#67 UK#5; Roots of a Legend (1997, Trojan). HIT VERSIONS: *I Shot the Sheriff* Eric Clapton (1974) g R&B#33 US#1 UK#9/Aswad on *Too Wicked EP* (1990) UK#61; *I Wanna Give You Some Love* Chuck Jackson (1980) R&B#90, *Is This Love* Pat Travers Band (1980) US#50, *Jamming* Grover Washington, Jr. (1982) R&B#65 US#102, *No Woman No Cry* Londonbeat (1991) UK#64/ Naughty By Nature sampled in *Everything's Gonna Be Alright* (1992) R&B#22 US#62/Fugees (1996) UK#2; *Stir It Up* Johnny Nash (1972) US#12 UK#13/Diana King (1994) R&B#53; *Waiting in Vain* Lee Ritenour featuring Maxi Priest (1993) R&B#54, *Why You Treat Me So Bad* [i] Shaggy featuring Grand Puba (1996) R&B#52 US#113+. Co-writers: [i] O. Burrell/M. Dixon/R. Livingston, [ii] Noel Williams.

652. MARRIOTT, Steve (b. January 30, 1947, London; d. April 20, 1991, Arkesden, both England) Rock guitarist and vocalist. The lead vocalist in the British group the Small Faces, who, in 1969, formed Humble Pie with Peter Frampton, which performed a heavy blend of blues and R&B, and charted with *Natural Born Boogie* (1969) UK#4 and *Fool for a Pretty Face (Hurt By Love)* [i] (1980) US#52. ALBUMS: **As Safe as Yesterday Is** (1969) UK#32, **Town and Country** (1969, both Immediate); **Humble Pie** (1970), **Rock On** (1971) US#118, **Performance—Rockin' the Fillmore** (1972) g US#21 UK#32, **Smokin'** (1972) g US#6 UK#28, **Eat It** (1973) US#13 UK#34, **Thunderbox** (1974) US#52, **Street Rats** (1975, all A&M) US#100; **On to Victory** (1980) US#60, **Go for the Throat** (1981, both Atco) US#154. COMPILATION: **Lost and Found** (1972, A&M) US#37. Marriott also recorded as a solo artist, and performed with his group Packet of Three throughout the 1980s. He died from smoke inhalation at a fire in his home in 1991. ALBUM: **Marriott** (1975, A&M); **Dingwalls, 6.7.84** (1992, Mau Mau); **Live at the George Robey** (1996, Zeus). Co-writer: [i] Jerry Shirley (b. February 4, 1952, England). (*See also under* Ronnie LANE and Steve MARRIOTT.)

653. MARSDEN, Gerry (b. Gerard Marsden, September 24, 1942, Liverpool, England) Pop guitarist and vocalist. The lead vocalist in the British beat group Gerry and the Pacemakers, which topped the chart with its first three singles. Marsden's *Ferry 'Cross the Mersey* received a million broadcast BMI award in 1991. CHART COMPOSITIONS: *I'm the One* (1964) US#82 UK#2, *Don't Let the Sun Catch You Crying* [i] (1964) US#4 UK#6, re-issued (1970) US#112; *Ferry 'Cross the Mersey* (1964) US#6 UK#8, re-recorded (1989) UK#1; *It's Gonna Be Al-*

right (1964) US#23 UK#24. ALBUMS: **How Do You Like It?** (1963, Columbia) UK#2; **Don't Let the Sun Catch You Crying** (1964) US#29, **Second Album** (1964, both Laurie) US#129; **Ferry 'Cross the Mersey** ost (1965, Columbia) US#13 UK#19; **I'll Be There** (1965) US#120, **Greatest Hits** (1965, both Laurie) US#44; **20 Year Anniversary** (1983, DEB); **The Collection** (1990, Connoisseur). HIT VERSIONS: *Don't Let the Sun Catch You Crying* [i] Ray Charles (1960) US#95/Steve Alaimo (1963) US#125/ Trini Lopez (1969) US#133. Co-writers: [i] Les Chadwick (b. John Leslie Chadwick, May 11, 1943, Liverpool, England)/Les Maguire (b. December 27, 1941, Wallasey, England)/Fred Marsden (b. November 23, 1940, Liverpool, England).

654. MARTIN, Moon (b. John Moon Martin, 1950, OK) Pop guitarist and vocalist. Initially a member of the group Southwind, which recorded the albums **Ready to Ride** (1969) and **What a Place to Land** (1973, both Blue Thumb), who later recorded as solo artist. CHART COMPOSITIONS: *Rolene* (1979) US#30, *No Chance* (1979) US#50, *Love Gone Bad* (1981) US#105. ALBUMS: **Shots from a Cold Nightmare** (1978), **Escape from Domination** (1979) US#80, **Street Fever** (1980, all Capitol) US#138; **Mystery Ticket** (1982, EMI). HIT VERSION: *Bad Case of Loving You (Doctor Doctor)* Robert Palmer (1979) US#14 UK#61.

655. MARTYN, John (b. 1948, Glasgow, Scotland) Folk guitarist and vocalist. A singer-songwriter who blends British folk music with rock and jazz, and sings in a lazy, laconic style. Some of Martyn's best work has been his intriguing arrangements of more traditional material, as on *Spencer the Rover*. Taught the guitar by the Scottish folk singer Hamish Imluch, Martyn became a regular on the British folk circuit during the 1960s, and a lengthy association with the Island label resulted in a consistent run of albums, such as **Bless the Weather** (1971), which featured the mystical epic *Glistening Glyndebourne*. ALBUMS: **London Conversation** (1967), **The Tumbler** (1968), **Stormbringer*** (1970), **Road to Ruin*** (1970), **Bless the Weather*** (1971), **Solid Air** (1973), **Inside Out** (1973), **Sunday's Child** (1975), **Live at Leeds** (1975), **One World** (1977) UK#54, **Grace and Danger** (1980, all Island) UK#54; **Glorious Fool** (1981, Geffen) UK#25; **Well Kept Secret** (1982, Warner Brothers) UK#20; **Sapphire** (1984) UK#84, **Piece By Piece** (1986, both Island) UK#28; **Philentropy** (1986, Dojo); **Foundations** (1987, Island); **The Apprentice** (1990), **Cool Tide** (1991, both Permanent); **BBC Radio 1 Live in Concert** (1992, Windsong); **Couldn't Love You More** (1992) UK#65, **No Little Boy** (1993), **John Martyn and**

Friends Live at the Shaw Theatre (1995, all Permanent); **And** (1996, Go! Disks). COMPILATIONS: **So Far So Good** (1976), **The Electric John Martyn** (1982), **Sweet Little Mysteries — The Island Anthology** (1996, all Island). With: * Beverly Martyn.

656. MARX, Richard (b. September 16, 1963, Chicago, IL) Rock guitarist, producer and vocalist. A mainstream rock artist who was first successful as a songwriter for such artists as Chicago and Philip Bailey. CHART COMPOSITIONS: *Don't Mean Nothing* [i] (1987) US#3, *Should've Known Better* (1987) US#3 UK#50, *Endless Summer Nights* (1988) UK#50, *Hold on to the Nights* (1988) US#1, *Satisfied* (1989) US#1 UK#52, *Right Here Waiting* (1989) US#1 UK#2, *Angelia* (1989) US#4, *Too Late to Say Goodbye* (1990) US#12 UK#38, *Children of the Night* (1990) US#13 UK#54, *Endless Summer Nights/Hold on to the Nights* (1990) UK#60, *Keep Coming Back* (1991) R&B#71 US#12 UK#55, *Hazard* (1992) US#9 UK#3, *Take This Heart* (1992) US#20 UK#13, *Chains Around My Heart* [iv] (1992) US#44 UK#29, *Now and Forever* (1994) US#7 UK#13, *Silent Scream* (1994) UK#32, *The Way She Loves Me* (1994) US#20 UK#39. ALBUMS: **Richard Marx** (1988, EMI-Manhattan) p US#8 UK#68; **Repeat Offender** (1989, EMI) p US#1 UK#8; **Rush Street** (1991) p US#35 UK#7, **Paid Vacation** (1994) p US#37 UK#11, **Ballads** (1995), **Flesh and Bone** (1996, all Capitol). HIT VERSIONS: *Crazy* [ii] Kenny Rogers (1985) US#79, *Edge of a Broken Heart* [iv] Vixen (1988) US#26, *Nothin' to Hide* [i] Poco (1990) US#39, *Surrender to Me* [iii] Ann Wilson & Robin Zander (1989) US#6. Co-writers: [i] Bruce Gaitsch, [ii] Kenny Rogers, [iii] R. Vannelli, [iv] Fay Waybill. (*See also under* David FOSTER.)

657. MASCHWITZ, Eric (b. June 10, 1901, Birmingham; d. October 27, 1969, London, both England) Film and stage lyricist. A lyricist who contributed to three musicals that ran for over five hundred performances, "Balalaika" (1936), "Zip Goes a Million" (1951) and "Love from Judy" (1952). Maschwitz also wrote under the pseudonym Holt Marvell, and in his later years was a BBC television executive. HIT VERSIONS: *At the Balalaika* [i] Abe Lyman (1940) US#13/Orrin Tucker (1940) US#3; *Nightingale Sang in Berkeley Square, A* [iii] Glenn Miller (1940) US#2/Ray Noble (1940) US#10/Sammy Kaye (1941) US#21/Guy Lombardo (1941) US#3; *Rainy Day Refrain, A* [ii] Mindy Carson (1950) US#24. Co-writers: [i] Chet Forrest/George Posford/Robert B. Wright, [ii] Heino Gaze, [iii] Manning Sherwin/Jack Strachey.

658. MASON, Dave (b. May 10, 1947, Worcester, England) Rock guitarist, producer and vocalist. A founder member, with Steve Winwood, of the British group Traffic, for which he composed the hits *Hole in My Shoe* (1967) UK#2 and *Feelin' Alright* (1968) US#123. Mason quit the group in 1967 for a solo career. CHART COMPOSITIONS: *Only You Know and I Know* (1970) US#42, *Satin Red and Black Velvet Woman* (1970) US#97, *To Be Free* (1972) US#121, *Let It Go, Let It Flow* (1978) US#45. ALBUMS: **Alone Together** (1970) g US#22, **Dave Mason and Cass Elliot** (1971) UK#49, **Headkeeper** (1972) US#51, **Dave Mason Is Alive** (1973, all Blue Thumb) US#116; **It's Like You Never Left** (1973) US#50, **Dave Mason** (1974) g US#25, **Split Coconut** (1975) US#27, **Certified Live** (1976) US#78, **Let It Flow** (1977) g US#37, **Mariposa de Oro** (1978) g US#41, **Old Crest on a New Wave** (1980, all Columbia) US#74. COMPILATIONS: **Best of Dave Mason** (1974) US#183, **At His Best** (1975) US#133, **Very Best of Dave Mason** (1978, all Blue Thumb) US#179. In 1994, Mason joined Fleetwood Mac for the album **Time** (1995, Warner Brothers) UK#47. HIT VERSIONS: *Feelin' Alright* Joe Cocker (1969) US#33/Mongo Santamaria (1970) US#96/Grand Funk Railroad (1971) US#54; *Hole in My Shoe* neil (1967) UK#17, *Only You Know and I Know* Delaney & Bonnie (1970) US#20. (*See also under* Steve WINWOOD.)

659. MASSER, Michael (b. March 24, 1941, Chicago, IL) Pop producer. A successful songwriter-producer for such artists as Diana Ross, whose forte is epic pop-soul ballads. HIT VERSIONS: *Ali Bom-Ba-Ye I* Mandrill (1977) R&B#69, *Didn't We Almost Have It All* [v] Whitney Houston (1987) g R&B#2 US#1 UK#14, *Do You Know Where You're Going To (Theme From Mahogany)* [iii] Diana Ross (1979) g R&B#14 US#1 UK#5, *Greatest Love of All, The* [i] George Benson (1977) R&B#2 US#24 UK#27/Whitney Houston (1985) g US#1 US#3 UK#8; *Hold Me* [i] Whitney Houston & Teddy Pendergrass (1985) US#46 UK#44, *I Thought It Took a Little Time (But Today I Fell in Love)* [viii] Diana Ross (1976) R&B#61 US#47 UK#32, *If Ever You're in My Arms Again* [ix] Peabo Bryson (1983) R&B#6 US#10, *In Your Eyes* [iv] Jeffrey Osbourne (1987) R&B#82, *It's My Turn* [vii] Diana Ross (1980) R&B#14 US#9 UK#16, *Last Time I Saw Him, The* [viii] Diana Ross (1973) R&B#15 US#14 UK#35/Dottie West (1974) C&W#8; *Long and Lasting Love (Once in a Lifetime), A* [iii] Crystal Gayle (1985) C&W#4/Glenn Medeiros (1988) US#68; *Miss You Like Crazy* [ii] Natalie Cole (1989) R&B#1 US#7 UK#2, *Nothing's Gonna Change My Love for You* [iii] Glenn Medeiros (1987) US#12 UK#1, *One More*

Chance [iii] Diana Ross (1981) R&B#54 US#79, *Saving All My Love for You* [iii] Whitney Houston (1985) g R&B#1 US#1 UK#1, *So Sad the Song* [iii] Gladys Knight & the Pips (1976) R&B#12 US#47, *Some Changes Are for Good* [vii] Dionne Warwick (1981) R&B#43 US#65, *Someone That I Used to Love* [iii] Natalie Cole (1980) R&B#21 US#21, *Sorry Doesn't Always Make It Right* Diana Ross (1975) UK#23/ Gladys Knight & the Pips (1977) R&B#24; *Tonight, I Celebrate My Love* [iii] Peabo Bryson & Roberta Flack (1983) R&B#5 US#16 UK#2, *Touch Me in the Morning* [vi] Diana Ross (1973) g R&B#5 US#1 UK#9. Co-writers: [i] Linda Creed, [ii] Preston Glass/Gerry Goffin, [iii] Gerry Goffin, [iv] Daniel Hill, [v] Will Jennings, [vi] Ron Miller, [vii] Carole Bayer Sager, [viii] Pam Sawyer, [ix] Tom Snow/Cynthia Weil.

660. MAYFIELD, Curtis (b. June 3, 1942, Chicago, IL) R&B guitarist, producer and vocalist. One of R&B's greatest talents, who has created some of the most influential soul music since the 1960s. Mayfield merged gospel and R&B with lyrics that emphasized hope, pride and dignity for black Americans, using his music as a forum to discuss the possibilities of social change, which ultimately paved the way for such rap artists as Ice-T. Mayfield said of his songs in 1988, "I wouldn't call them radical, I just spoke my mind." Growing up in poverty in the Cabrini-Green projects of Chicago, he first sang with his mother and grandmother in church. By the age of eleven, Mayfield was composing gospel tunes and had learned the guitar. He sang in the vocal groups the Alphatones and the Northern Jubilee Gospel Singers, where he befriended the singer Jerry Butler. Mayfield dropped out of high school in 1957 (having been told by a teacher that he did not have a future in music) to join Butler's group the Roosters, which performed in clubs and at parties. The Roosters released two unsuccessful singles before re-christening themselves the Impressions, as which they scored a hit with a version of *For Your Precious Love* (1958). An unusual vocal group for their time, the Impressions' spiritual harmonies were quite unlike the doo-wop sound of other black groups. When Butler left to pursue a solo career and follow-up singles failed to chart, the Impressions were dropped by their record label. Mayfield later said of this period, "Went back and starved a bit." After working as a delivery boy for a cigar manufacturer, he became Butler's composer, producer and guitarist, writing such hits as *Need to Belong*, upon which Mayfield introduced the Brazilian baino rhythm to R&B. A re-formed but Butler-less Impressions, now led by Mayfield's sweet falsetto tenor, went on to achieve a series of hits with some of Mayfield's most beautiful compositions, including the cha cha *Gypsy Woman* (1961), and the inspiring ballad *People Get Ready* (1965). In the late 1960s Mayfield formed his own Curtom label, and issued the Impressions' album **This Is My Country** (1968), a concise examination of social and economic issues in America. As the 1960s civil rights movement gained prominence in America, Mayfield became one of the major dissenting voices in popular music, speaking out against racism and injustice. The group reached a creative peak on **The Young Mod's Forgotten Story** (1969), an articulate and accomplished set that was brilliantly arranged by Donny Hathaway and Johnny Pate. CHART COMPOSITIONS: *Come Back My Love* (1958) R&B#29, *Gypsy Woman* (1961) R&B#2 US#20, *Grow Closer Together* (1962) US#99, *Little Young Lover* (1962) US#96, *Minstrel and Queen* (1962) US#113, *Sad, Sad, Girl and Boy* (1963) US#84, *It's All Right* (1963) R&B#1 US#4, *I'm the One Who Loves You* (1963) US#73, *Talkin' 'Bout My Baby* (1964) US#12, *I'm So Proud* (1964) R&B#1 US#10, *Keep on Pushing* (1964) R&B#1 US#10, *You Must Believe Me* (1965) US#15, *Amen* [iii] (1964) R&B#17 US#7, new version (1970) R&B#44 US#110; *Just One Kiss from You* (1965) US#76, *Long, Long Winter* (1965) R&B#35, *People Get Ready* (1965) R&B#3 US#14, *I've Been Trying* (1965) R&B#35 US#133, *Woman's Got Soul* (1965) R&B#9 US#29, *Meeting Over Yonder* (1965) R&B#12 US#48, *I Need You* (1965) R&B#26 US#64, *Never Could You Be* (1965) R&B#35, *You've Been Cheatin'* (1965) R&B#12 US#33, *Since I Lost the One I Love* (1966) US#90, *Too Slow* (1966) US#91, *Can't Satisfy* (1966) R&B#12 US#65, *You Always Hurt Me* (1967) R&B#20 US#96, *You Got Me Running* (1967) R&B#50, *I Can't Stay Away from You* (1967) R&B#34 US#80, *We're a Winner* (1968) R&B#1 US#14, *We're Rolling On* (1968) R&B#17 US#59, *I Loved and I Lost* (1968) R&B#9 US#61, *Fool for You* (1968) R&B#3 US#22, *This Is My Country* (1968) R&B#8 US#25, *Don't Cry My Love* (1968) R&B#44 US#71, *My Deceiving Heart* (1969) R&B#26 US#104, *Seven Years* (1969) R&B#15 US#84, *Choice of Colors* (1969) R&B#1 US#21, *Say You Love Me* (1969) R&B#10 US#58, *Wherever She Leadeth Me* (1970) R&B#31 US#128, *Check Out Your Mind* (1970) R&B#3 US#28, *(Baby) Turn on to Me* (1970) R&B#6 US#56, *Ain't Got Time* (1971) R&B#12 US#53, *Love Me* (1971) R&B#25 US#94, *This Love's for Real* (1972) R&B#41. ALBUMS: **For Your Precious Love** (1958, Vee-Jay); **The Impressions** (1963) US#43, **The Never Ending Impressions** (1964) US#52, **Keep on Pushing** (1964) US#8, **People Get Ready** (1965) US#23, **One By One** (1965) US#104, **Ridin' High** (1966, all ABC/Paramount) U#79; **The Fabulous Impressions** (1967) US#184, **We're a Winner** (1968) US#35, **The Versatile Impressions**

(1968, all ABC); **This Is My Country** (1968) US#107, **The Young Mod's Forgotten Story** (1969) US#104, **Best Impressions** (1969) **Check Out Your Mind** (1969), **Amen** (1970), **Times Have Changed** (1972) US#192, **Preacher Man** (1972, all Curtom). COMPILATIONS: **Greatest Hits** (1965) US#83, **Best of the Impressions** (1968) US#172, **16 Greatest Hits** (1971) US#180, **Curtis Mayfield — His Early Years with the Impressions** (1973, all ABC) US#180; **The Vintage Years** (1976, Sire) US#199. Throughout the 1960s, Mayfield was a prolific songwriter, and he enjoyed a lengthy relationship with the producer Don Davis at OKeh Records, where they created what became known as the "Chicago Sound," a melodic, gospel tinged, soft soul approach, with a particular style of brass arrangements. In 1970, Mayfield quit the Impressions for a solo career, issuing a stunning eponymous debut album that once again pioneered new sounds in R&B, such as wah-wah and echoplex guitars. Some of the highlights of Mayfield's solo career are his film soundtrack to "Superfly" (1972), and his album **Back to the World** (1973), a fascinating song cycle about one black American's return from the Vietnam war. As a producer, Mayfield also worked with Gladys Knight and the Pips on the album **Claudine** ost (1974, Buddah) g US#35; the Staple Singers on **Let's Do It Again** ost (1975, Curtom) US#20 and **Pass It On** (1976, Warner Brothers) US#155; Mavis Staples on **A Piece of the Action** ost (1977, Curtom); and Aretha Franklin on **Sparkle** ost (1976) g US#18 and **Almighty Fire** (1978, both Atlantic) US#63. He has also been the subject of two tribute albums, **People Get Ready** (1993, Shanachie) and **All Men Are Brothers** (1994, Warner Brothers) US#56. In August 1990, Mayfield was paralyzed from the neck down when a lighting rig fell on him during a concert in Brooklyn, New York. Confined to a wheelchair as a quadriplegic, with his son, Todd Mayfield, running most of his affairs, Mayfield continues to make a partial but slow recovery under therapy. At one time it seemed unlikely that he would ever record again, but in 1996, with the assistance of many fellow R&B musicians, Mayfield overcame his handicap to release the dignified and contemplative album **New World Order**. Mayfield remains as positive about his debilitating personal circumstances as he has displayed in all of his music, saying in 1993, "I'm fair now, I'll be better later. I'll be great tomorrow." CHART COMPOSITIONS: *Move on Up* (1970) UK#12, reissued (1988) UK#87; *(Don't Worry) If There's a Hell Below We're All Gonna Go* (1970) R&B#3 US#29, *Get Down* (1971) R&B#13 US#69, *We've Got to Have Peace* (1971) R&B#32 US#115, *Beautiful Brother of Mine* (1972) R&B#45, *Freddie's Dead* (1972) g R&B#2 US#4, *Superfly* (1972) g R&B#5 US#8, new

version with Ice-T (1990) UK#48; *Future Shock* (1973) R&B#11 US#39, *If I Were Only a Child Again* (1973) R&B#22 US#71, *Can't Say Nothin'* (1973) R&B#16 US#88, *Kung Fu* (1974) R&B#3 US#40, *Mother's Son* (1974) R&B#15, *So in Love* (1975) R&B#9 US#67, *Only You Babe* (1976) R&B#8, *Party Night* (1976) R&B#39, *Show Me Your Love* (1977) R&B#41, *Do Do Wop Is Strong in Here* (1977) R&B#29, *No Goodbyes* (1978) UK#65, *You Are, You Are* (1978) R&B#34, *Do It All Night* (1978) R&B#96, *This Year* (1979) R&B#40, *Between You Baby and Me** (1979) R&B#14, *You're So Good to Me* (1979) R&B#46, *Love's Sweet Sensation** (1980) R&B#34, *Love Me, Love Me Now* (1980) R&B#48, *Tripping Out* (1980) R&B#46, *She Don't Let Nobody (But Me)* (1981) R&B#15 US#103, *Toot an' Toot an' Toot* (1981) R&B#22, *Hey Baby (Give It All to Me)* (1982) R&B#68, *Baby It's You* (1985) R&B#69. ALBUMS: **Curtis** (1970) g US#19, **Curtis Live** (1971) US#21, **Roots** (1971) US#40, **Superfly** ost (1972) g US#1 UK#26, **Back to the World** (1973) g US#16, **Curtis in Chicago** (1973) US#135, **Sweet Exorcist** (1973) US#39, **Got to Find a Way** (1974) US#76, **There's No Place Like America Today** (1975) US#120, **Give, Get, Take and Have** (1976) US#171, **Never Say You Can't Survive** (1976) US#173, **Short Eyes** ost (1977), **Do It All Night** (1978, all Curtom); **Heartbeat** (1979) US#42, **The Right Combination** (1980) US#180, **Something to Believe In** (1980, all RSO) US#128; **Love Is the Place** (1981), **Honesty** (1982, both Boardwalk); **We Come in Peace with a Message of Love** (1985), **Take It to the Streets** (1990), **Live in Europe** (1990, all Curtom); **New World Order** (1996, Warner Brothers). COMPILATIONS: **People Get Ready — Live at Ronnie Scott's** (1990, Essential); **Of All Time — The Classic Collection** (1990, Curtom); **The Anthology, 1961–1977** (1992, MCA); **A Man Like Curtis — The Best of Curtis Mayfield** (1992, Music Club); **Hard Times** (1993, ITM); **Love, Peace and Understanding** (1997, Sequel). HIT VERSIONS: *Ain't Gonna Rest Till I Get You* Five Stairsteps (1967) R&B#37 US#87, *Ain't It a Shame* Major Lance (1965) R&B#20 US#91, *Almighty Fire* Aretha Franklin (1978) R&B#12 US#103, *Amen* [iii] Lloyd Price (1964) US#124, *Baby Make Me Feel So Good* Five Stairsteps & Cubie (1969) R&B#12 US#101, *Come Back* Five Stairsteps (1966) R&B#15 US#61, *Come See* Major Lance (1965) R&B#20 US#40, *Danger! She's a Stranger* Five Stairsteps (1967) R&B#16 US#89, *Don't Change Your Love* Five Stairsteps & Cubie (1968) R&B#15 US#59, *Don't Give It Up* Linda Clifford (1979) R&B#15, *Find Another Girl* [i] Jerry Butler (1961) R&B#10 US#27, *Follow the Leader* Major Lance (1969) R&B#28 US#125, *Freddie's Dead* Smoothe Da Hustler sampled in *Hustler's*

Theme (1996) R&B#77+, Future Shock Herbie Hancock (1984) UK#54, Girls Major Lance (1964) US#68, Girls Are Out to Get You Fascinations (1967) R&B#13 US#92 UK#32, Give Me Your Love Barbara Mason (1973) US#31, (Gotta) Get Away Billy Butler & the Enchanters (1964) US#101, Gypsy Woman Rick Nelson (1963) US#62/Brian Hyland (1971) g US#3 UK#41; He Will Break Your Heart [ii] Jerry Butler (1960) R&B#1 US#7/Freddie Scott (1967) US#120/ Johnny Williams (1972) C&W#68 US#104/Tony Orlando & Dawn as He Don't Love You (Like I Do) (1975) g US#1; Hey Little Girl Major Lance (1963) R&B#12 US#13, I Can't Stay Away from You Fascinations (1967) R&B#49, I'm a Tellin' You Jerry Butler (1961) R&B#8 US#25, I'm So Proud Main Ingredient (1970) R&B#13 US#49/Deniece Williams (1983) R&B#28; (I've Got a Feeling) You're Gonna Be Sorry Billy Butler (1965) US#103, It Ain't No Use Major Lance (1964) US#68, It's All Over Walter Jackson (1964) R&B#10 US#67, (It's Gonna Be) A Long, Long Winter Linda Clifford (1974) R&B#75, It's the Beat Major Lance (1966) R&B#37 US#128, Jump Aretha Franklin (1976) R&B#17 US#72, Just Be True Gene Chandler (1964) US#19, Let's Do It Again Staples Singers (1975) g R&B#1 US#1/George Benson (1988) UK#56; Look into Your Heart Aretha Franklin (1977) R&B#10 US#82, Love Is Good News Ava Cherry (1980) R&B#39 US#107, Love Me, Love Me, Love Me Staples Singers (1976) R&B#11, Madame Mary Five Stairsteps (1969) R&B#38, Make Yours a Happy Home Gladys Knight & the Pips (1976) R&B#13, Mama Didn't Lie Fascinations (1961) US#108/Jan Bradley (1963) R&B#8 US#14; Man's Temptation Gene Chandler (1963) R&B#17 US#71, Monkey Time, The Major Lance (1963) g R&B#2 US#8/Tubes (1983) US#68; More Than Just a Joy Aretha Franklin (1978) R&B#51, Move on Up Destination (1979) R&B#68, Must Be Love Coming Down Major Lance (1969) R&B#31 US#119, Need Someone to Love Billy Butler & the Enchanters as I Can't Work No Longer (1965) R&B#6 US#60, Need to Belong to Someone Jerry Butler (1963) US#31/Laura Lee (1968) R&B#44; Nevertheless (I Love You) Billy Butler & the Enchanters (1964) US#102, New Orleans Staple Singers (1975) R&B#4 US#70, Nothing Can Stop Me Gene Chandler (1965) R&B#3 US#18, On and On Gladys Knight & the Pips (1974) g R&B#2 US#5, Ooh, Baby Baby Five Stairsteps (1967) R&B#34 US#63, People Get Ready Bob Marley & the Wailers (1984) UK#5/Jeff Beck & Rod Stewart (1985) US#48 UK#49/Rod Stewart (1993) UK#45; Piece of the Action Mavis Staples (1977) R&B#47, Rainbow Gene Chandler (1963) R&B#11 US#47, live version (1965) R&B#2 US#69; Rhythm Major Lance (1964) US#24, Say It Isn't So Fascinations (1966) R&B#47, Something He Can Feel Aretha Franklin

(1976) R&B#1 US#28/En Vogue (1992) g R&B#1 US#6 UK#16; Something's Missing Five Stairsteps & Cubie (1967) R&B#17 US#88, Sometimes I Wonder Major Lance (1965) R&B#13 US#64, Stay Away from Me (I Love You Too Much) Major Lance (1970) R&B#13 US#67, Superfly S Express in Superfly Guy (1988) UK#5, Sweeter Than the Sweet Staples Singers (1977) R&B#52, Um, Um, Um, Um, Um, Um Wayne Fontana & the Mindbenders (1964) UK#5/Major Lance (1964) US#5 UK#40, new version (1974) R&B#59/Johnny Rivers as Curious Mind (1977) US#41; We Must Be in Love Five Stairsteps & Cubie (1969) R&B#17 US#88, What Now Gene Chandler (1965) R&B#18 US#40, Without a Doubt Major Lance (1968) R&B#49, World of Fantasy Five Stairsteps (1966) R&B#12 US#49, You Can't Hurt Me No More Gene Chandler (1965) R&B#40 US#92, You're Too Good to Me Mary J. Blige sampled in Be Happy (1994) US#29 UK#30. With: * Linda Clifford. Co-writers: [i] Jerry Butler, [ii] Jerry Butler/Calvin Carter, [iii] John W. Pate, Sr.

661. MAYFIELD, Percy (b. August 12, 1920, Minden, LA; d. August 11, 1984, Los Angeles, CA) R&B pianist and vocalist. A much recorded R&B songwriter whose best known composition is Ray Charles' Hit the Road Jack. Mayfield wrote for the Speciality label during the mid–1940s, where he also scored a series of solo hits with his blues oriented material. He died of a heart attack in 1984. CHART COMPOSITIONS: Please Send Me Someone to Love (1950) g R&B#1 US#26, Strange Things Happening (1951) R&B#7, Lost Love (1951) US#2, What a Fool I Was (1951) R&B#8, Prayin' for Your Return (1951) R&B#9, Cry Baby (1952) R&B#9, The Big Question (1952) R&B#6, River's Invitation (1963) R&B#25 US#99, To Live in the Past (1970) R&B#41, I Don't Want to Be President (1974) R&B#64. ALBUMS: **My Jug and I** (1962), **Percy Mayfield** (1969), **Bought Blues** (1969, all Tangerine); **Tightrope** (1969, Brunswick); **Percy Mayfield Sings** (1970), **Weakness Is a Thing Called Man** (1970), **Blues and Then Some** (1971, all RCA). COMPILATIONS: **Best of Percy Mayfield** (1970), **The Incredible Percy Mayfield** (1972, both Speciality); **My Heart Is Always Singing Sad Songs** (1985, Ace); **Hit the Road Again** (1985, Timeless); **The Voice Within** (1987, Route 66); **Memory Pain** (1993, Ace). HIT VERSIONS: Hit the Road Jack Ray Charles (1961) R&B#1 US#1 UK#6/Jerry Lee Lewis (1963) US#103/ Connie Eaton & Dave Peel (1970) C&W#44/Stampeders (1976) US#40; Hide 'Nor Hair Ray Charles (1962) R&B#7 US#20, Please Send Me Someone to Love Moonglows (1957) R&B#5 US#73/Wade Flemons (1961) R&B#20/B.B. King (1968) US#102. (See also under Ray CHARLES.)

662. Melanie (b. Melanie Safka, February 3, 1947, Astoria, Long Island, NY) Pop guitarist and vocalist. A folk and hippie influenced singer-songwriter who studied at the Academy of Dramatic Arts in New York. CHART COMPOSITIONS: *Lay Down (Candles in the Rain)* (1969) US#6, *Peace Will Come (According to Plan)* (1970) US#32, *What Have They Done to My Song, Ma?* (1971) UK#39, *Brand New Key* (1971) g US#1 UK#4, *Nickel Song* (1972) US#35, *Ring the Living Bell* (1972) US#31, *Together Alone* (1972) US#86, *Bitter Bad* (1973) US#36, *Every Breath of the Way* (1983) UK#70. ALBUMS: **Born to Be** (1969), **Affectionately** (1969) US#196, **Candles in the Rain** (1970) g US#17 UK#5, **Leftover Wine** (1970) US#33 UK#22, **All the Right Noises** ost (1970), **The Good Book** (1971, all Buddah) US#80 UK#9; **Gather Me** (1971) g US#15 UK#14, **Stoneground Words** (1972) US#70, **At Carnegie Hall** (1973) US#109, **Madrugada** (1974) US#192, **As I See It Now** (1975), **Sunset and Other Beginnings** (1975, all Neighborhood); **Photograph** (1976, Atlantic); **Phonogenic — Not Just Another Pretty Face** (1978, Midland International); **Ballroom Streets** (1977, Tomato); **Arabesque** (1982, RCA); **Seventh Wave** (1983), **Am I Real or What** (1987, both Neighborhood); **Cowabonga** (1989, Food for Thought); **Precious Cargo** (1991), **Freedom Knows My Name** (1993, both Lonestar); **Silver** (1994), **Old Bitch Warrior** (1996, both Creastars/BMG). COMPILATIONS: **Garden in the City** (1972) US#115 UK#19, **Four Sides of Melanie** (1972) US#103 UK#23, **Very Best of Melanie** (1975, all Buddah). HIT VERSIONS: *Beautiful People* New Seekers (1971) US#67, *Brand New Key* Jeris Ross (1972) C&W#75/Wurzels as *Combine Harvester* (1976) UK#1; *Nickel Song* New Seekers (1971) US#81, *What Have They Done to My Song, Ma?* New Seekers (1970) US#14 UK#44/Ray Charles (1972) US#65.

663. MELLENCAMP, John "Cougar" (b. October 7, 1951, Seymour, IN) Rock guitarist and vocalist. A blue collar rock and roll singer-songwriter in the style of Bob Seger and Bruce Springsteen. In 1992, Mellencamp directed himself in the film "Falling from Grace." CHART COMPOSITIONS: *I Need a Lover* (1979) US#28, *Small Paradise* (1980) US#87, *This Time* (1980) US#27, *A Little Night Dancin'* (1980) US#105, *Ain't Even Done with the Night* (1981) US#17, *Hurt So Good* [i] (1982) g US#2, *Jack and Diane* (1982) US#1 UK#25, *Hand to Hold on To* (1982) US#19, *Crumblin' Down* [i] (1983) US#9, *Pink Houses* (1984) US#8, *Authority Song* (1984) US#15, *Lonely Ol' Night* (1985) US#6, *Small Town* (1985) US#6 UK#53, *R.O.C.K. in the U.S.A.* (1986) US#2 UK#67, *Rain on the Scarecrow* [i] (1986) US#21, *Rumbleseat* (1986) US#28, *Paper in the Fire*

(1987) US#9, *Cherry Bomb* (1987) US#8, *Check It Out* (1988) US#14, *Rooty Toot Toot* (1988) US#61, *Pop Singer* (1989) US#15, *Jackie Brown* (1989) US#48, *Get a Leg Up* (1991) US#14, *Again Tonight* (1992) US#36, *Human Wheels* [i] (1993) US#48, *Dance Naked* (1994) US#41. ALBUMS: **Chestnut Street Incident** (1976, Mainman); **The Kid Inside** (1977, Gulcher); **A Biography** (1978), **John Cougar** (1979) g US#64, **Nothin' Matters and What If It Did** (1980) p US#37, **American Fool** (1982) p US#1 UK#37, **Uh-Huh** (1983) p US#9 UK#92, **Scarecrow** (1985, all Riva) p US#2; **The Lonesome Jubilee** (1987) p US#6 UK#31, **Big Daddy** (1989) p US#7 UK#25, **Whenever We Wanted** (1991) p US#17, **Human Wheels** (1993) US#7 UK#37, **Dance Naked** (1994) p US#13, **Mr. Happy Go Lucky** (1996, all Mercury). HIT VERSIONS: *Sweet Suzanne* Buzzin' Cousins (1992) C&W#68. Co-writer: [i] George Michael Green.

664. MENKEN, Alan (b. America) Film and stage composer. A composer of many Disney animated features during the 1990s, who has frequently worked with the lyricist Harold Ashman. ALBUMS: **Little Shop of Horrors** ost (1987, Geffen) US#47; **The Little Mermaid** ost (1989) p US#32, **Beauty and the Beast** ost (1991) p US#19, **Aladdin** ost (1992) p US#8, **Newsies** ost (1992) US#149, **Pocahontas** ost (1995, all Disney). HIT VERSION: *Beauty and the Beast* [i] Celine Dion & Peabo Bryson (1991) US#9 UK#9, *Whole New World, A (Aladdin's Theme)* [ii] Peabo Bryson & Regina Belle (1992) g R&B#21 US#3 UK#12. Co-writers: [i] Harold Ashman, [ii] Tim Rice.

665. MERCER, Johnny (b. John Herndon Mercer, November 18, 1909, Savannah, GA; d. June 25, 1976, Los Angeles, CA) Film and stage composer, lyricist and vocalist. One of the most successful lyricists in popular music, who was also an occasional composer. Mercer published over one thousand songs, and was a significant influence on the art of lyric writing with his intelligent optimism. A four times Oscar winner for such songs as his and Henry Mancini's *Moon River*, Mercer was also a co-founder of Capitol Records in 1942. He could not read music, but had an intuitive ability to write in any genre, as evidenced by *I'm an Old Cowhand* and several traditional blues numbers. Mercer's first song *Out of Breath and Scared to Death of You*, was performed in "The Garrick Gaieties" (1930). He sung in Paul Whiteman's band during the 1930s, and charted nearly thirty hits between 1938–1952. Mercer even tried his hand at acting, before returning to songwriting for films such as "Rhythm on the Range" (1938) and "The Inspector General" (1949). CHART

COMPOSITIONS: *Mister Meadowlark* [vi] with Bing Crosby (1940) US#18, *Strip Polka* (1942) US#7, *The G.I. Jive* (1944) R&B#1 US#11, *Ac-Cent-Tchu-Ate the Positive* [i] (1945) R&B#4 US#1, *On the Atchison, Topeka, and the Santa Fe* [xviii] (1945) US#1, *The Glow Worm* [xii] (1952) US#30. ALBUMS: **Rhythm on the Range** st (1950, Decca); **Saint Louis Woman** oc (1952), **Top Banana** oc (1952), **Capitol Presents Johnny Mercer** (1953), **Capitol Presents Johnny Mercer, Volume 2** (1954), **Capitol Presents Johnny Mercer, Volume 3** (1954), **Capitol Presents Johnny Mercer, Volume 4** (1954, all Capitol); **Li'l Abner** oc (1956, Columbia) US#19; **Harvey Girls** ost (1957, Decca); **Merry Andrew** ost (1958, Capitol); **Free and Easy** oc (1959, Columbia); **Saratoga** oc (1959, RCA); **Seven Brides for Seven Brothers** ost (1961, MGM) UK#6; **Foxy** oc (1964, SPM); **Robin Hood** ost (1964, Disneyland); **Not with My Wife, You Don't** ost (1966, Warner Brothers); **Swinger** ost (1966), **Darling Lili** ost (1969, both RCA); **An Evening with Johnny Mercer** (1971, Laureate); **Hooray for Hollywood** ost (1975, United Artists); **Texas Li'l Darlin'** oc (1977, Decca); **Hollywood Hotel** ost (1981, Hollywood Soundstage); **Audio Scrap Book** (1984), **Johnny Mercer's Music Shop** (1984, both Submarine); **Don't Fence Me In** (1986, Prism); **Johnny Mercer** (1988, Glendale). HIT VERSIONS: *Ac-Cent-Tchu-Ate the Positive* [i] Bing Crosby & the Andrews Sisters (1945) US#2/Kay Kyser (1945) US#12/Artie Shaw (1945) US#5/Tommy O'Day (1979) C&W#89; *And the Angels Sing* [vii] Count Basie (1939) US#16/Bing Crosby (1939) US#10/Benny Goodman (1939) US#1, re-issued (1944) US#27; *Autumn Leaves* [xi] Steve Allen (1955) US#35/Roger Williams (1955) US#1, new version (1965) US#92; *Bernadine* Pat Boone (1957) US#14, *Bob White (Whatcha Gonna Swing Tonight?)* [ix] Mildred Bailey (1937) US#14/ Bing Crosby & Connee Boswell (1937) US#1/Benny Goodman (1937) US#15; *Day In, Day Out* [iii] Bob Crosby (1939) US#1/Kay Kyser (1939) US#11/Artie Shaw (1939) US#11/Frank Sinatra on *Come Dance with Me LP* (1959) UK#30; *Dixieland Band* [ix] Benny Goodman (1935) US#10, *Dream* Jimmy Dorsey (1945) US#15/Pied Pipers (1945) g US#1/ Freddy Martin (1945) US#9/Frank Sinatra (1945) US#5/Four Aces (1954) US#17/Sajid Khan (1969) US#119; *Early Autumn* [iv] Claude Thornhill (1947) US#22/Woody Herman (1952) US#28/Jo Stafford (1952) US#23; *Eeny Meeny Miney Mo* [xiii] Benny Goodman (1936) US#7, *Fools Rush In (Where Angels Fear to Tread)* [iii] Tommy Dorsey (1940) US#12/ Glenn Miller (1940) US#1/Tony Martin (1940) US#14/Billy Eckstine (1949) R&B#6/Brook Benton (1960) R&B#61 US#24 UK#50/Rick Nelson (1963) R&B#24 US#12 UK#12/Joey Porrello (1976) US#108;

G.I. Jive, The Louis Jordan (1944) US#1, *Glow Worm, The* [xii] Mills Brothers (1952) g US#1 UK#10/Hank Thompson (1972) C&W#53; *Goody Goody* [xiii] Bob Crosby (1936) US#7/Benny Goodman (1936) US#1/Freddy Martin (1936) US#5/Frankie Lymon & the Teenagers (1957) US#20 UK#24/Rebecca Lynn (1979) C&W#83; *I Wanna Be Around* [xvii] Tony Bennett (1959) US#14, *I'm an Old Cowhand* Bing Crosby with Jimmy Dorsey (1936) US#2, *I'm Building Up to an Awful Letdown* [ii] Fred Astaire (1936) US#4, *If I Had a Million Dollars* [xiii] Richard Himber (1934) US#12/Ozzie Nelson (1934) US#17; *Laura* [xvi] Dick Haymes (1945) US#9/Woody Herman (1945) US#4/Johnnie Johnston (1945) US#5/ Freddy Martin (1945) US#6/Jerry Wald (1945) US#8/Stan Kenton (1951) US#12; *Lonesome Polecat* [v] McGuire Sisters (1954) US#28/Freddy Martin (1954) US#27; *Lost* [xv] Jan Garber (1936) US#6/Hal Kemp (1936) US#7/Guy Lombardo (1936) US#5; *On the Atchison, Topeka, and the Santa Fe* [xviii] Bing Crosby (1945) US#3/Tommy Dorsey (1945) US#6/ Judy Garland (1945) US#10/Tommy Tucker (1945) US#10; *Pardon My Southern Accent* [xiii] Irving Aaronson (1934) US#5/Glen Gray (1934) US#13; *P.S. I Love You* [x] Rudy Vallee (1934) US#12/Hilltoppers (1953) US#4/Starlets (1960) US#106/Classics (1963) US#120; *Riffin' the Scotch* Benny Goodman (1934) US#6, *Something's Gotta Give* Sammy Davis, Jr. (1955) US#9 UK#11/McGuire Sisters (1955) US#5/ Frank Sinatra on *Come Dance with Me LP* (1959) UK#30; *Strip Polka* Andrews Sisters (1942) US#6/ Kay Kyser (1942) g US#1/Alvino Rey (1942) US#6; *Summer Wind* [v] Frank Sinatra (1966) US#25 UK#36, *Waiter and the Porter and the Upstairs Maid, The* Bing Crosby, Mary Martin & Jack Teagarden (1941) US#23, *Weekend of a Private Secretary, The* [ix] Red Norvo (1938) US#10, *You Can't Run Away from It* [v] Four Aces (1956) US#20, *You Grow Sweeter as the Years Go By* Artie Shaw (1939) US#15, *You Have Taken My Heart* [x] Len Gray (1934) US#16. Co-writers: [i] Harold Arlen, [ii] Fred Astaire, [iii] Rube Bloom, [iv] Ralph Burns/Woody Herman, [v] Gene De Paul, [vi] Walter Donaldson, [vii] Ziggy Elman, [viii] Philippe Gerard, [ix] Bernie Hanighan, [x] Gordon Jenkins, [xi] Joseph Kosma/ Jacques Prevert, [xii] Paul Lincke/Lilla Cayley Robinson, [xiii] Matty Malneck, [xiv] Henry Mayer, [xv] Phil Ohman/Macy O. Teetor, [xvi] David Raksin, [xvii] Sadie Vimmerstedt, [xviii] Harry Warren. (*See also under* Harold ARLEN, Hoagy CARMICHAEL, Duke ELLINGTON, Jerome KERN, Michel LEGRAND, Henry MANCINI, Victor SCHERTZINGER, Arthur SCHWARTZ, Jimmy VAN HEUSEN, Harry WARREN, Kurt WEIL, Richard WHITING.)

666. MERCURY, Freddie (b. Frederick Bulsara, September 5, 1946, Zanzibar, Tanzania; d. November 24, 1991, London, England) Rock vocalist. The consummate showman and lead singer of the mock-operatic rock group Queen. CHART COMPOSITIONS: *Seven Seas of Rhye* (1974) UK#10, *Killer Queen* (1974) US#12 UK#2, *Bohemian Rhapsody* (1975) US#9 UK#1, re-issued (1991) UK#1, re-issued (1992) US#2; *Somebody to Love* (1976) US#13 UK#2, new version with George Michael (1993) US#30; *Queen's First EP* (1977) UK#17, *We Are the Champions* (1977) p US#4 UK#2, re-issued (1992) US#52; *Bicycle Race* (1978) US#24 UK#11, *Don't Stop Me Now* (1979) US#86 UK#9, *Crazy Little Thing Called Love* (1979) US#1 UK#2, *Play the Game* (1980) US#42 UK#14, *Under Pressure* [i] with David Bowie (1981) US#29 UK#1, *Body Language* (1982) R&B#30 US#11 UK#25, *It's a Hard Life* (1984) US#72 UK#6, *One Vision* [iii] (1985) US#61 UK#7, *Friends Will Be Friends* [ii] (1986) UK#14, *I Want It All* [iii] (1989) US#50 UK#3, *Innuendo* [iii] (1991) UK#1, *I'm Going Slightly Mad* (1991) UK#22, *Headlong* [iii] (1991) UK#14, *The Show Must Go On* [iii] (1991) g UK#16, *A Winter's Tale* [iii] (1995) UK#6, *Too Much Love Will Kill Me* [iii] (1996) UK#15, *Let Me Live* [iii] (1996) UK#9, *You Don't Fool Me* [iii] (1996) UK#17. ALBUMS: **Queen** (1973) g US#83 UK#24, **Queen II** (1974) US#49 UK#5, **Sheer Heart Attack** (1974) g US#12 UK#2, **A Night at the Opera** (1975) g US#4 UK#1, **A Day at the Races** (1977) g US#5 UK#1, **News of the World** (1977) p US#3 UK#4, **Jazz** (1978) p US#6 UK#2, **Live Killers** (1979) g US#16 UK#3, **The Game** (1980) p US#1 UK#1, **Flash Gordon** ost (1980) US#23 UK#10, **Hot Space** (1982) g US#22 UK#4, **The Works** (1984) g US#23 UK#2, **A Kind of Magic** (1986) US#46 UK#1, **Live Magic** (1986, all EMI) UK#3; **The Miracle** (1989) US#24 UK#1, **Innuendo** (1991) g US#30 UK#1, **Live at Wembley '86** (1992) US#53 UK#2, **Made in Heaven** (1995, all Parlophone) US#58 UK#1. COMPILATIONS: **Greatest Hits** (1981, Parlophone) p US#11 UK#1; **The Complete Works** (1985, EMI); **At the Beeb** (1989, Band of Joy) UK#67; **Greatest Hits II** (1991, EMI) UK#1; **Classic Queen** (1992) p US#4, **Greatest Hits** (1992) p US#11, **Five Live** (1993, all Hollywood) US#46; **Greatest Hits 1 + 2** (1995, Parlophone) UK#37. Mercury also recorded as a solo artist, but his career was cut short when he died in 1991 of complications related to AIDS. CHART COMPOSITIONS: *Love Kills* [v] (1984) UK#10, *I Was Born to Love You* (1985) US#76 UK#11, *Living on My Own* (1985) UK#50, re-issued (1993) UK#1; *Time* (1986) UK#32, *Barcelona* [iv]* (1987) UK#8, re-issued (1992) UK#2; *In My Defense* (1992) UK#8. ALBUMS: **Mr. Bad Guy** (1985, CBS) UK#6;

Barcelona* (1988, Polydor) UK#15; **The Freddie Mercury Album** (1992, Parlophone) UK#4; **Remixes** (1996, EMI). HIT VERSIONS: *Bohemian Rhapsody* Bad News (1987) UK#44/Braids (1996) UK#21/Rolf Harris (1996) UK#50; *Crazy Little Thing Called Love* Orion (1981) C&W#79, *Somebody to Love* George Michael (1993) US#30, also on *Five Live EP* (1993) US#46 UK#1; *Too Much Love Will Kill You* [iii] Brian May (1992) UK#5, *We Are the Champions* Hank Marvin featuring Brian May (1992) UK#66. With: * Monserrat Caballe. Co-writers: [i] David Bowie/John Deacon (b. August 19, 1951, Leicester, England)/Brian May (b. July 19, 1947, Twickenham, England)/Roger Taylor (b. Roger Meddows-Taylor, July 26, 1949, King's Lynne, England), [ii] John Deacon, [iii] John Deacon/Brian May/Roger Taylor, [iv] Mike Moran, [v] Giorgio Moroder.

667. MERRILL, Bob (b. Henry Robert Merrill Lavan, May 17, 1921, Atlantic City, NJ; d. February 17, 1998, Beverly Hills, CA) Film and stage composer, producer. A highly successful songwriter who hitchhiked across America before working as an impressionist and compere. Merrill became the director of the Bucks County Playhouse in the early 1940s, before writing shows and sketches while serving in the U.S. Army. In the 1950s, he turned increasingly to songwriting, providing many hits for Guy Mitchell and other crooners. Merrill was successful on Broadway with the shows "New Girl in Town" (1957), "Take Me Along" (1959) and "Carnival" (1961), and he collaborated with the lyricist Jules Styne on "Funny Girl" (1964) and "Sugar" (1972). ALBUMS: **New Girl in Town** oc (1957, RCA) US#17; **Carnival** oc (1961, MGM) US#1; **The Wonderful World of the Brothers Grimm** ost (1962, MGM); **Funny Girl** oc (1964, Capitol); **Funny Girl** ost (1968, Columbia); **Pretty Belle** oc (1982, Original Cast). HIT VERSIONS: *Belle, Belle, My Liberty Belle* Don Cherry (1951) US#25/Guy Mitchell (1951) US#9/Bobby Wayne (1951) US#23/Hugo Winterhalter (1951) US#25; *Butterflies* Patti Page (1953) US#10, *Candy and Cake* [iv] Mindy Carson (1950) US#12/Arthur Godfrey (1950) US#16/Evelyn Knight (1950) US#20; *'Cause I Love You, That's a-Why* Guy Mitchell & Mindy Carson (1952) US#24, *Chick a Boom* Guy Mitchell (1953) UK#4, *Chicken Song (I Ain't Gonna Take It Settin' Down)* [v] Guy Lombardo (1951) US#22, *Christopher Columbus* [iii] Guy Mitchell (1951) US#27, *Cuff of My Shirt, The* Guy Mitchell (1954) UK#9, *Feet Up (Pat Him on the Po-Po)* Guy Mitchell (1952) US#14 UK#2, *Fool's Paradise* Billy Eckstine (1949) US#24, *Honeycomb* Jimmy Rodgers (1957) R&B#1 US#1/Gary Morris (1986) C&W#27; *(How Much Is) That Doggie in the Window* Patti Page (1953) UK#9/Lita Roza (1953)

UK#1; *It's Like Taking Candy from a Baby* [ii] Tony Pastor (1949) US#21, *Kid's Last Fight, The* Frankie Laine (1954) US#20 UK#3, *Let Me In* Blue Barron (1951) US#16/Fontane Sisters & Texas Jim Robertson (1951) US#14/Bobby Wayne (1951) US#26; *Look at That Girl* Guy Mitchell (1953) UK#1, *Love (Makes the World Go 'Round)* Perry Como (1958) US#33 UK#6/Paul Anka (1963) US#26/Deon Jackson (1966) US#11; *Make Yourself Comfortable* Andy Griffith (1955) US#26/Peggy King (1955) US#30/ Sarah Vaughan (1955) US#6; *Mambo Italiano* Rosemary Clooney (1954) UK#1/Dean Martin (1955) UK#14; *Miracle of Love, The* Eileen Rodgers (1956) US#18, *Mustafa* [i] Staiffi & His Mustafas (1960) UK#43, *My Truly, Truly Fair* Ray Anthony (1951) US#28/Vic Damone (1951) US#4/Freddy Martin (1951) US#18/Guy Mitchell (1951) g US#2; *Nairobi* Tommy Steele (1958) UK#3, *Pittsburgh, Pennsylvania* Guy Mitchell (1952) US#4, *She Wears Red Feathers* Guy Mitchell (1953) US#19 UK#1, *Sparrow in the Treetop* Rex Allen (1951) C&W#10 US#28/Bing Crosby & the Andrews Sisters (1951) US#8/Guy Mitchell (1951) US#8; *Sweet Old-Fashioned Girl* Teresa Brewer (1956) US#7 UK#3, *There's Always Room at Our House* Guy Mitchell (1951) US#10, *Walkin' to Missouri* Tony Brent (1952) UK#7/ Sammy Kaye (1952) US#11; *When the Boys Talk About the Girls* Valerie Carr (1959) US#19 UK#28, *You Don't Have to Be a Baby to Cry* [v] Ernest Tubb (1950) C&W#10/Caravelles (1963) UK#6/Ann J. Morton (1977) C&W#63. Co-writers: [i] Bob Azzam, [ii] Joel Cowan/Al Russell, [iii] Terry Gilkyson, [iv] Arthur Godfrey, [v] Terry Shand. (*See also under* Al HOFFMAN, Jules STYNE.)

668. MESSINA, Jim (b. December 5, 1947, Maywood, CA) Rock guitarist, producer and vocalist. As a member of the surf group Jim Messina and the Jesters, Messina recorded the albums **Jim Messina and the Jesters** (1967) and **The Dragsters** (1967, both Audio Fidelity), before joining Buffalo Springfield for **Buffalo Springfield Again** (1967, Atco) US#44. He subsequently co-founded the country-rock group Poco, charting with *You Better Think Twice* (1970) US#72 and *Call It Love* [i] (1989) US#18. ALBUMS: **Pickin' Up the Pieces** (1969) US#63, **Poco** (1970) US#58, **Deliverin'** (1971, all Epic) US#26; **Legacy** (1989, RCA) US#40. COMPILATION: **Very Best of Poco** (1975, Epic) US#90. In 1972, Messina formed an informal duo with Kenny Loggins, writing their hits *Nobody But You* (1972) US#86, *Thinking of You* (1973) US#18 and *Changes* (1975) US#84. He has also recorded as a solo artist. CHART COMPOSITIONS: *Do You Want to Dance* (1980) US#110, *Stay the Night* with Pauline Wilson (1981) US#110. ALBUMS: **Oasis**

(1979, Columbia) US#58; **Messina** (1981) US#95, **One More Mile** (1983, both Warner Brothers). Co-writers: [i] B. Crain/R. Guilbeau/R. Lonow. (*See also under* Kenny LOGGINS.)

669. MEYER, George W. (b. January 1, 1884, Boston, MA; d. August 28, 1959, New York, NY) Film and stage composer. A Tin Pan Alley song-plugger whose first published hit was *Lonesome* (1909). In 1912, Meyer became a successful publisher of rags, before writing his only Broadway show, "Plantation Follies," which became "Dixie to Broadway" (1924). HIT VERSIONS: *Brown Eyes, Why Are You Blue?* [ii] Nick Lucas (1925) US#2/Ben Selvin (1925) US#12/Carl Fenton (1926) US#5/Franklyn Baur (1926) US#11; *For Me and My Gal* [iv] Henry Burr & Albert Campbell (1917) US#7/Billy Murray (1917) US#9/Prince's Orchestra (1917) US#5/Van & Schenck (1917) US#1/Judy Garland (1942) US#3/ Guy Lombardo (1943) US#17/Big Ben Banjo Band in *Let's Get Together #1* (1954) UK#6/Russ Conway in *Party Pops* (1957) UK#24; *I Believe in Miracles* [vii] Dorsey Brothers Orchestra (1935) US#3/Fats Waller (1935) US#10; *I Wonder* [vii] Jane Froman (1955) UK#14/Dickie Valentine (1955) UK#4; *I'm Sure of Everything But You* [ix] Guy Lombardo (1932) US#9, *In a Little Bookshop* [v] Vaughn Monroe (1948) US#21, *In the Land of Beginning Again* [iii] Charles Harrison (1919) US#6/Bing Crosby (1946) US#18; *Lonesome* Haydn Quartet (1909) US#3/ Byron G. Harlan (1909) US#6; *My Song of the Nile* [ii] Melody Three (1929) US#7/Ben Selvin (1929) US#8/Nat Shilkret (1929) US#17; *Someone Is Losin' Susan* Harry Reser's Orchestra (1926) US#10/Phil Spitalny (1927) US#14; *There Are Such Things* [i] Tommy Dorsey (1943) g R&B#2 US#1, *Tuck Me to Sleep (In My Old 'Tucky Home)* [viii] Ernest Hare (1921) US#12/Billy Jones (1921) US#15/Vernon Dalhart (1922) US#2; *When You're a Long, Long Way from Home* [viii] Henry Burr (1914) US#2, *Where Did Robinson Crusoe Go with Friday on Saturday Night?* [viii] Al Jolson (1916) US#6/Ian Whitcomb (1966) US#101. Co-writers: [i] Stanley Adams/Abel Baer, [ii] Alfred Bryan, [iii] Grant Clarke, [iv] E. Ray Goetz/Edgar Leslie, [v] Al Goodhart/Kay Twomey, [vi] Sam M. Lewis, [vii] Sam M. Lewis/ Pete Wending, [viii] Sam M. Lewis/Joe Young, [ix] Charles O'Flynn/Pete Wending. (*See also under* Milton AGER, Arthur JOHNSTON, Carl SIGMAN.)

670. MEYER, Joseph (b. March 12, 1894, Modesto, CA; d. June 22, 1987, New York, NY) Film and stage composer. A composer who worked with a variety of lyricist and tunesmiths, and whose first major hit was *My Honey's Lovin' Arms* [v] (1922). Meyer's songs were featured in such shows as "Gay

Paree" (1925), "Charlotte's Revue of 1926" and "George White's 1935 Scandals," alongside the films "Big Boy" (1925) and "You Were Meant for Me" (1948). HIT VERSIONS: *But I Did* [iv] Dinah Shore (1945) US#16, *Crazy Rhythm* [ii] Roger Wolfe Kahn (1928) US#10/Happenings (1968) US#114; *Idle Gossip* [iii] Perry Como (1953) UK#3, *It's an Old Southern Custom* [vi] Eddy Duchin (1934) US#11, *My Honey's Lovin' Arms* [v] California Ramblers (1922) US#10/Isham Jones (1922) US#4/Benny Goodman (1939) US#14; *Passe* Tex Beneke (1946) US#9/Margaret Whiting (1946) US#12; *Tonight's My Night with Baby* [i] "Whispering" Jack Smith (1926) US#13. Co-writers: [i] Bobby Buttenuth/Irving Caesar, [ii] Irving Caesar/Roger Wolfe Kahn, [iii] Floyd Huddleston, [iv] Al Jacobs/Herb Magidson/Jack Yellen, [v] Herman Ruby, [vi] Jack Yellen. (*See also under* Buddy DE SYLVA, Al DUBIN, Sam M. LEWIS, Frank LOESSER, Ballard MacDONALD, Billy ROSE, Charles TOBIAS.)

671. MICHAEL, George (b. Georgios Kyriacos Panayiotou, June 25, 1963, London, England) Pop multi-instrumentalist, producer and vocalist. A highly successful artist since the early 1980s, who first came to prominence as the lead vocalist and main songwriter in the pop duo Wham! CHART COMPOSITIONS: *Young Guns (Go for It)* (1982) UK#3, *Wham Rap! (Enjoy What You Do)* [ii] (1983) UK#8, *Bad Boys* (1983) US#60 UK#2, *Club Tropicana* [ii] (1983) UK#4, *Club Fantastic Megamix* (1983) UK#15, *Wake Me Up Before You Go Go* (1984) US#1 UK#1, *Last Christmas/Everything She Wants* (1984) UK#2, re-issued (1985) UK#6, re-issued (1986) UK#45; *Everything She Wants* (1985) R&B#12 US#1, *Freedom* (1985) US#3, *I'm Your Man* (1985) R&B#55 US#3 UK#1, *The Edge of Heaven* (1986) UK#1. ALBUMS: **Fantastic** (1983, Inner Vision) g US#83 UK#1; **Make It Big** (1984, Epic) p US#1 UK#1. COMPILATIONS: **The Final** (1986) UK#2, **Music from the Edge of Heaven** (1986, both Epic) p US#10. In 1984, Michael parted company with his Wham! partner Andrew Ridgeley, and embarked upon a more R&B and dance oriented solo career. His album **Faith** (1987), has sold over ten million copies. CHART COMPOSITIONS: *Careless Whisper* [ii] (1984) g R&B#8 US#1 UK#1, *A Different Corner* (1986) US#7 UK#1, *I Want Your Sex* (1987) R&B#43 US#2 UK#3, *Faith* (1987) US#1 UK#2, *Hard Day* (1987) R&B#21, *Father Figure* (1987) R&B#6 US#1 UK#11, *One More Try* (1988) R&B#1 US#1 UK#8, *Monkey* (1988) US#1 UK#13, *Kissing a Fool* (1988) US#5 UK#18, *Praying for Time* (1990) US#1 UK#6, *Waiting for That Day* (1990) US#27 UK#23, *Freedom!* (1990) US#8 UK#28, *Heal the Pain* (1991) UK#31, *Mother's Pride* (1991) US#46,

Cowboys and Angels (1991) UK#45, *Too Funky* (1992) US#10 UK#4, *Five Live EP* (1993) US#46 UK#1, *Jesus to a Child* (1996) g R&B#22 US#7 UK#1, *Fast Love* [iii] (1996) US#8 UK#1, *Spinning the Wheel* (1996) UK#2. ALBUMS: **Faith** (1987) p US#1 UK#1, **Listen Without Prejudice, Volume 1** (1990, both Epic) p US#2 UK#1; **Older** (1996, Creation) p US#6 UK#1. HIT VERSIONS: *Father Figure* PM Dawn in *Looking Through Patient Eyes* (1993) R&B#62 US#6 UK#11, *Heaven Help Me* [i] Deon Estus (1989) US#5 UK#41, *Turn to Gold* David Austin (1984) UK#68. Co-writers: [i] Deon Estus, [ii] Andrew Ridgeley (b. January 26, 1963, Windlesham, England), [iii] Patrice Rushen (b. September 30, 1954, Los Angeles, CA)/Freddie Washington.

672. MILLER, Bob (b. September 20, 1895, Memphis, TN; d. August 26, 1955, New York, NY) C&W pianist and producer. A former riverboat pianist who led his own orchestra and wrote jazz-blues compositions during the 1920s. Miller recorded his own *Eleven Cent Cotton, Forty Cent Meat* (1928), before becoming a prolific songwriter, penning, in one year, over four hundred and fifty hillbilly songs. By the 1950s, he had written over seven thousand compositions. Miller became one of only a few country songwriters to establish offices in New York's Brill Building, and his topics ranged from farm working tales to bank foreclosures, often presented in a journalistic style. The singer Carson Robison was particularly successful with his material during the 1930s, when Miller worked for ARC/Columbia Records, and his song *Seven Years with the Wrong Woman* was included in the musical "On with the Show" (1933). One of the wiser composers of his era, Miller kept control of his own copyrights, and his publishing royalties saw him comfortably into retirement. HIT VERSIONS: *There's a Star-Spangled Banner Waving Somewhere* Elton Britt (1943) US#7/Jimmy Wakely (1943) US#14.

673. MILLER, Ned (b. Henry Ned Miller, April 12, 1925, Raines, UT) C&W vocalist. A country tinged singer-songwriter who scored a run of hits during the 1960s. CHART COMPOSITIONS: *From a Jack to a King* (1962) C&W#2 US#6 UK#2, *One Among the Many* (1963) C&W#27, *Another Fool Like Me* (1963) C&W#28, *Invisible Tears* (1964) C&W#13 US#131, *Do What You Do Well* (1965) C&W#7 US#52 UK#48, *Whistle Walkin'* (1965) C&W#28, *Summer Roses* (1966) C&W#39, *Teardrop Lane* (1966) C&W#44, *Hobo* (1967) C&W#53, *Only a Fool* (1968) C&W#61, *The Lover's Song* (1970) C&W#39. ALBUMS: **From a Jack to a King** (1962, Fabor); **Teardrop Lane** (1966, Capitol). HIT VERSIONS: *Dark Moon* Tony Brent (1957) UK#17/Bonnie Guitar (1957) C&W#14 US#6/Gale Storm (1957) US#4; *From a Jack to a King* Ricky Van Shelton (1989) C&W#1; *Invisible Tears* [i] Ray Conniff Singers (1964) US#57, *Behind the Tear* Sonny James (1965) C&W#1. Co-writer: [i] Sue Miller.

674. MILLER, Roger (b. Roger Dean Miller, January 2, 1936, Fort Worth, TX; d. October 25, 1992, Los Angeles, CA) C&W multi-instrumentalist and vocalist. An influential country star who charted over forty hit singles, and composed over eight hundred songs, many of which were notable for a sardonic, tongue-in-cheek sense of irony. He was also the first vocalist to introduce scatting to country music. Miller's best known song is the two million selling *King of the Road*, a world-weary tribute to a hobo that has been recorded over one hundred and twenty-five times in thirty different languages. Raised by his aunt and uncle in Erick, Oklahoma, Miller grew up in rural poverty, and after leaving school, he held various jobs and learned the guitar, banjo and fiddle. During his U.S. Army service in Korea, he was a member of a country-bluegrass group that entertained other troops, and upon his discharge, he became a fireman in Amarillo, Texas. In Nashville, Miller worked as a hotel bell hop and plugged his songs, one of his earliest successes being *Swiss Maid* by the singer Del Shannon. Miller was Ray Price's bassist, played the fiddle for Minnie Pearl and drums for Faron Young, before his own career as a solo performer took off. Between 1965–1966, Miller starred in various television shows and specials, and in 1985 he composed the musical "Big River: The Adventures of Huckleberry Finn." Miller died of cancer in 1992. He had always been flippant about his achievements, once saying, "No matter how big you get, the size of your funeral depends on the weather." CHART COMPOSITIONS: *You Don't Want My Love* (1960) C&W#14, *When Two Worlds Collide* [i] (1961) C&W#6, *Lock, Stock and Teardrops* (1963) C&W#26, *Dang Me* (1964) g C&W#1 US#7, *Chug-A-Lug* (1964) C&W#3 US#9, *(And You Had A) Do-Wacka-Do* (1964) C&W#15 US#31, *King of the Road* (1965) g C&W#1 US#4 UK#1, *Engine Engine #9* (1965) C&W#2 US#7 UK#33, *One Dyin' and a Buryin'* (1965) C&W#10 US#34, *It Happened Just That Way* (1965) US#105, *Kansas City Star* (1965) C&W#7 US#31 UK#48, *England Swings* (1965) C&W#3 US#8 UK#45, re-entry (1966) UK#13; *Husbands and Wives* (1966) C&W#5 US#26, *I've Been a Long Time Leavin' (But I'll Be a Long Time Gone)* (1966) C&W#13 US#103, *You Can't Roller Skate in a Buffalo Herd* (1966) C&W#35 US#40, *My Uncle Used to Love Me But She Died* (1966) C&W#39 US#58, *Walkin' in the Sunshine* (1967) C&W#7 US#37, *The*

Ballad of Waterhole #3 (1967) C&W#27 US#102, *Vance* (1968) C&W#15 US#80, *Where Have All the Average People Gone* (1969) C&W#14, *Don't We All Have the Right* (1970) C&W#15, *We Found It in Each Other's Arms* (1972) C&W#34, *Rings for Sale* (1972) C&W#41, *Hoppy's Gone* (1972) C&W#42, *Open Up Your Heart* (1973) C&W#14 US#105, *I Believe in Sunshine* (1973) C&W#24, *Whistle Stop* (1974) C&W#86, *Our Love* (1974) C&W#44, *I Love a Rodeo* (1975) C&W#57, *The Hat* (1979) C&W#98, *Everyone Gets Crazy Now and Then* (1981) C&W#36, *Old Friends* with Willie Nelson and Ray Price (1982) C&W#19, *River in the Rain* (1985) C&W#36, *Some Hearts Get All the Breaks* (1986) C&W#81. ALBUMS: **Roger and Out/Dang Me** (1964) g US#37, **The Return of Roger Miller** (1965) g US#4, **The 3rd Time Around** (1965) US#13, **Words and Music By Roger Miller** (1966) US#108, **Walkin' in the Sunshine** (1967) US#118, **A Tender Look at Love** (1968) US#173, **Roger Miller** (1969) US#163, **Roger Miller, 1970** (1970, all Smash) US#200; **A Trip in the Country** (1970, Mercury); **Painted Poetry** (1971, Starday); **Off the Wall** (1972, Windsong); **Sorry I Haven't Written Lately** (1974), **Supersongs** (1975, both Columbia); **Making a Name for Myself** (1979, 20th Century); **Old Friends** with Willie Nelson (1982, Columbia); **Big River** ost (1985, MCA); **The Big Industry** (1988, Fundamental); **Wham on Express** (1990, SST). COMPILATIONS: **Roger Miller** (1964), **The One and Only Roger Miller** (1965, both RCA); **Golden Hits** (1965, Smash) g US#6; **King of the Road-The Best of Roger Miller** (1992, Laserlight); **Best of Roger Miller, Volume 2** (1992), **King of the Road — The Genius of Roger Miller** (1995, both Mercury). HIT VERSIONS: *Billy Bayou* Jim Reeves (1959) C&W#1 US#95, *Don't We All Have the Right* Ricky Van Shelton (1988) C&W#1, *Half a Mind* Ernest Tubb (1958) C&W#8, *Heartache for Keepsake, A* Kitty Wells (1963) C&W#29, *Home* Jim Reeves (1959) C&W#2/Loretta Lynn (1975) C&W#10; *Husbands and Wives* David Frizzell & Shelly West (1981) C&W#16, *I've Been a Long Time Leaving (But I'll Be a Long Time Gone)* Joey Martin (1978) C&W#92, *Invitation to the Blues* Ray Price (1958) C&W#3 UK#92, *It Wasn't God Who Made Honky Tonk Angels* Kitty Wells (1952) C&W#1 US#27/Lynn Anderson (1971) C&W#20/Waylon Jennings & Jessi Colter (1981) C&W#10; *King of the Road* Billy Howard as *King of the Cops* (1976) UK#6/Proclaimers (1990) UK#9; *Last Word in Lonesome Is Me, The* Eddy Arnold (1966) C&W#2 US#40/Terry Bradshaw (1976) C&W#90; *Lock, Stock and Teardrops* Diana Trask (1968) C&W#70/K.D. Lang (1988) C&W#53; *My Ears Should Burn (When Fools Are Talked About)* Claude Gray (1961) C&W#3, *Open Up Your Heart* Buck Owens (1966)

C&W#1, *Private John Q* Glen Campbell (1965) US#114, *Queen of the House* Jody Miller (1965) C&W#5 US#12, *Some Hearts Get All the Breaks* Charly McClain (1984) C&W#25, *Swiss Maid* Del Shannon (1962) UK#2, *That's the Way I Feel* [ii] Faron Young (1958) C&W#9, *There's Nobody Like You* Kin Vassey (1980) C&W#88, *When Two Worlds Collide* [i] Jim Reeves (1969) C&W#6 UK#17/Jerry Lee Lewis (1980) C&W#11; *World So Full of Love, A* Ray Sanders (1960) C&W#18/Faron Young (1961) C&W#28; *You Don't Want My Love (In the Summertime)* Andy Williams (1960) US#64. Co-writers: [i] Bill Anderson, [ii] George Jones.

675. MILLER, Ron Pop producer. An R&B influenced composer and producer who worked at Motown Records during the 1970s. HIT VERSIONS: *Can't We Try* [iii] Teddy Pendergrass (1980) R&B#3 US#52, *Freddie* [iii] Charlene (1977) US#96, *It Ain't Easy Comin' Down* Charlene (1977) US#97, *For Once in My Life* [iv] Tony Bennett (1967) US#91/Jackie Wilson (1968) US#70/Stevie Wonder (1969) R&B#2 US#2 UK#3; *Heaven Help Us All* Stevie Wonder (1970) R&B#2 US#9 UK#29, *I've Never Been to Me* [iii] Charlene (1982) C&W#60 US#3 UK#1, *Place in the Sun, A* Stevie Wonder (1966) R&B#3 US#9 UK#20/Sonny James (1982) C&W#60; *Sleepin'* [ii] Diana Ross (1974) R&B#50 US#70, *Touch Me in the Morning* [i] Diana Ross (1973) R&B#5 US#1 UK#9, *Travelin' Man* [v] Stevie Wonder (1967) R&B#31 US#32, *Used to Be* [iii] Stevie Wonder & Charlene (1982) R&B#35 US#46, *Yester-Me, Yester-You, Yester-Day* [v] Stevie Wonder (1969) R&B#5 US#7 UK#2. Co-writers: [i] Tom Baird, [ii] T. Etlinger, [iii] Ken Hirsch, [iv] Orlando Murden, [v] Bryan Wells. (*See also under* Michael MASSER.)

676. MILLER, Steve (b. October 5, 1943, Milwaukee, WI) Rock guitarist and vocalist. A blues influenced singer-songwriter who has dabbled with psychedelia and country music, and was one of the first rock artists to experiment with electronics and synthesizers. Miller first played in the group the Marksmen Combo with the guitarist Boz Scaggs, which he followed with the Goldberg-Miller Blues Band. In 1966 he formed the Steve Miller Band, which has had many line-up changes over the years. CHART COMPOSITIONS: *Living in the U.S.A.* (1968) US#94, re-issued (1974) US#49; *My Dark Hour* (1969) US#126, *Going to the Country* (1970) US#69, *Steve Miller's Midnight Tango* (1970) US#117, *The Joker* [i] (1974) US#1, re-issued (1990) UK#1; *Take the Money and Run* (1976) US#11, *Rock 'n' Me* (1976) US#1 UK#11, *Fly Like an Eagle* (1977) R&B#20 US#2, *Swingtown* [iii] (1977) US#17, *Heart Like a Wheel* (1981) US#24, *Circle of Love* (1982)

US#55, *Abracadabra* (1982) g R&B#26 US#1 UK#2, *Keeps Me Wondering* (1982) UK#52, *Give It Up* (1983) US#60, *Shangri-La* [ii] (1984) US#57, *Bongo Bongo* [iii] (1985) US#84, *I Want to Turn the World Around* (1986) US#97, *Wide River* [iii] (1992) US#64. ALBUMS: **Children of the Future** (1968) US#134, **Sailor** (1968) US#24, **Brave New World** (1969) US#22, **Your Saving Grace** (1969) US#38, **Number 5** (1970) US#23, **Rock Love** (1971) US#82, **Recall the Beginning-Journey from Eden** (1972) US#109, **The Joker** (1973) p US#2, **Fly Like an Eagle** (1976) p US#3 UK#11, **Book of Dreams** (1977) p US#2 UK#12, **Circle of Love** (1981) g US#26, **Abracadabra** (1982) p US#3 UK#10, **Live** (1983) US#125 UK#79, **Italian X-Rays** (1984) US#101, **Living in the 20th Century** (1986) US#65, **Born 2 B Blue** (1988) US#108, **Wide River** (1992, all Capitol) US#85. COMPILATIONS: **Anthology** (1972) g US#56, **Greatest Hits, 1974–1978** (1978, both Capitol) p US#18; **Greatest Hits, 1976–1986** (1988, Mercury); **Best of Steve Miller, 1968–1973** (1990) UK#34, **The Steve Miller Band Box Set** (1994, all Capitol). HIT VERSION: *Living in the U.S.A.* Wilmer & the Dukes (1969) US#114. Co-writers: [i] Eddie Curtis/Ahmet Ertegun, [ii] Kenny Lee Lewis, [iii] Chris McCarty.

677. MITCHELL, Joni (b. Roberta Joan Anderson, November 7, 1943, Fort McLeod, Alberta, Canada) Folk-rock guitarist, pianist and vocalist. The single most influential female singer-songwriter since the late 1960s, who is also one of the finest vocalists in popular music, and a composer of perspicacious songs that introduced folk music to jazz vocal stylings. Before Mitchell, there were no female songwriters who produced music of such breadth and clarity, and she single-handedly introduced more meaningful themes to female pop songs from a distinctly feminine perspective. Her insights into the human condition, and examinations of weakness, integrity, growth and experience, are quite at odds with much of the machismo posturing of rock. Mitchell's mother was a school teacher, and her father a grocery store manager. She grew up in Saskatoon, Saskatchewan, and as a teenager listened to such jazz-vocal groups as Lambert, Hendricks and Ross. After studying painting at the Alberta College of Art, she taught herself the ukelele from a Pete Seeger instruction disk, and developed her interest in folk music by singing at the Depression Coffeehouse with Peter Albling. In 1965, Mitchell toured as a duo with her husband Chuck Mitchell, but their marriage soon faltered and she headed to New York, where she performed on the folk scene. Her eponymous solo album in 1968 was a frail, poetical and alluring collection of folk based melodies that contrasted city and country living. By **Ladies of the Canyon** (1970), Mitchell's topics included Catholicism in *The Priest*, childhood and growth in *The Circle Game*, and the observation that a death of personality often results in the personal quest for financial success in *The Arrangement*. **Blue** (1971) was a thematic study of a relationship, upon which her use of simile and metaphor became an art in itself, while the jazzy **Hissing of Summer Lawns** (1975), investigated the void at the heart of middle-class Californian lifestyles. **Hejira** (1976) featured lengthy, dreamy material that evoked a landscape of travel imagery, while **Mingus** (1979), originally a collaboration with the jazz bassist Charlie Mingus that Mitchell was left to complete after his death, "hammered the nail into my coffin which said: 'Joni is dead on pop radio, she's a jazzer'." A series of somewhat patchy attempts to grapple with modern recording techniques ultimately resulted in a stunning return to form with the largely acoustic **Night Ride Home** (1991). CHART COMPOSITIONS: *Big Yellow Taxi* (1970) US#67 UK#11, live version (1975) US#24; *Carey* (1971) US#93, *You Turn Me On, I'm a Radio* (1973) US#25, *Raised on Robbery* (1974) US#65, *Help Me* (1974) US#7, *Free Man in Paris* (1974) US#22, *In France They Kiss on Main Street* (1976) US#66, *Good Friends* with Michael McDonald (1986) US#85. ALBUMS: **Joni Mitchell** (1968) US#189, **Clouds** (1969) US#31, **Ladies of the Canyon** (1970) p US#27 UK#8, **Blue** (1971, all Reprise) p US#15 UK#3; **For the Roses** (1972) g US#11, **Court and Spark** (1974) g US#2 UK#14, **Miles of Aisles** (1974) g US#2 UK#34, **The Hissing of Summer Lawns** (1975) g US#4 UK#14, **Hejira** (1976) g US#13 UK#11, **Don Juan's Reckless Daughter** (1977) g US#25 UK#20, **Mingus** (1979) US#17 UK#24, **Shadows and Light** (1980, all Asylum) US#38 UK#63; **Wild Things Run Fast** (1982) US#25 UK#32, **Dog Eat Dog** (1985) US#63 UK#57, **Chalk Mark in a Rainstorm** (1988) US#45 UK#26, **Night Ride Home** (1991, all Geffen) US#41 UK#25; **Turbulent Indigo** (1994) US#47 UK#53, **Facelift** (1997, both Reprise). COMPILATIONS: **Hits** (1996), **Misses** (1996, both Warner Brothers). HIT VERSIONS: *Big Yellow Taxi* Neighborhood (1970) US#29/Amy Grant (1995) US#67 UK#20; *Both Sides Now* Judy Collins (1968) US#8 UK#14/Harper's Bizarre (1968) US#123/Johnstons (1968) US#128/Dion (1969) US#91/Viola Wills (1986) UK#35/Clannad & Paul Young (1991) UK#74; *Case of You, A* Frank Stallone (1980) US#67/Tori Amos on B-side of *Cornflake Girl* (1994) US#111 UK#4; *Chelsea Morning* Judy Collins (1969) US#78, *Circle Game, The* Buffy Sainte-Marie (1970) US#109, *This Flight Tonight* Nazareth (1970) UK#11, also on *Hot Tracks EP* (1975) UK#15; *Urge for Going* George Hamilton,

IV (1967) C&W#7, *Woodstock* Assembled Multitude (1970) US#79/Crosby, Stills, Nash & Young (1970) US#11/Matthews Southern Comfort (1971) US#23 UK#1; *You Turn Me On, I'm a Radio* Gail Davies (1982) C&W#17.

678. MOMAN, Chips (b. Lincoln Moma, 1936, La Grange, GA) Pop guitarist and producer. An R&B and country influenced producer who worked at Stax Records during the early 1960s. Moman had left school to become a session musician in 1957, and worked briefly as Gene Vincent's guitarist during 1959. In 1964, he set up his own studio in Memphis, where he recorded highly regarded sides with such artists as the Box Tops, Elvis Presley, Aretha Franklin, and Bobby Womack. HIT VERSIONS: *Class of '55* Carl Perkins (1987) C&W#83, *(Hey Won't You Play) Another Somebody Done Somebody Wrong Song* [i] B.J. Thomas (1975) g C&W#1 US#1, *Luckenback Texas (Back to the Basics of Love)* [ii] Waylon Jennings (1977) C&W#1 US#25, *This Time* Troy Shondell (1961) US#6/Johnny Lee (1978) C&W#43. Co-writers: [i] Larry Butler, [ii] Bobby Emmons. (*See also under* Mark JAMES, Spooner OLDHAM.)

679. MONACO, Jimmy (b. James V. Monaco, January 13, 1885, Fonia, Italy; d. October 16, 1945, Beverly Hills, CA) Film and stage composer, pianist. A self-taught pianist who emmigrated to America in 1891 with his parents, where he played ragtime piano in the bars and cafes of New York, and published his first song *Oh You Circus Day*, which was introduced in the Broadway revue "Hanky Panky" (1911). Monaco followed with contributions to "Ziegfeld Follies of 1912," "Bombo" (1923) and "Harry Delmar's Revels of 1927", before becoming successful in Hollywood, where he worked for Paramount Pictures, collaborating with a variety of lyricists, including Johnny Burke. His songs were included in the films "Doctor Rhythm," "Sing You Sinners" (both 1938); "Road to Singapore," "If I Had My Way," "Rhythm on the River" (all 1940); "Weekend in Havana" (1941), "Stage Door Canteen" (1943), "Sweet and Lowdown," "Pin-Up Girl" (both 1944); and "The Dolly Sisters" (1945). ALBUMS: **Judy Garland** oc (1951), **Star Maker** st (1951), **The Eddie Cantor Story** ost (1956), **Road Begins** ost (1962, all Decca). HIT VERSIONS: *An Apple for the Teacher* [i] Bing Crosby & Connee Boswell (1939) US#2, *April Played the Fiddle* [i] Bing Crosby (1940) US#10, *Dirty Hands! Dirty Face!* [ii] Marion Harris (1923) US#6/Irving Kaufman (1923) US#6/Ben Selvin (1923) US#12/Al Jolson (1928) US#8; *Don't Let That Moon Get Away* [i] Bing Crosby (1938) US#19, *East Side of Heaven* [i] Bing Crosby (1939) US#6, *Ev'ry*

Night About This Time [vii] Jimmy Dorsey (1942) US#20/Ink Spots (1942) US#17/Kay Kyser (1943) US#18/Fats Domino (1950) R&B#5; *I Can't Begin to Tell You* [iv] Bing Crosby & Carmen Cavallaro (1945) g US#1/Harry James featuring Betty Grable (1946) US#5/Sammy Kaye (1946) US#9/Andy Russell (1946) US#7/Jane Morgan (1959) US#113/Buddy Greco (1965) US#132; *I Haven't Time to Be a Millionaire* [i] Bing Crosby (1940) US#13, *I'll Take Care of Your Cares* [iii] Frankie Laine (1967) US#39, *I'm Making Believe* [iv] Ella Fitzgerald & the Ink Spots (1944) g R&B#2 US#1/Hal McIntyre (1945) US#14; *I've Got a Pocketful of Dreams* [i] Bing Crosby (1938) US#1/Russ Morgan (1938) US#1; *Man and His Dream, A* [i] Bing Crosby (1939) US#4, *Me and the Man in the Moon* [viii] Cliff Edwards (1929) US#19/Helen Kane (1929) US#8/Ted Weems (1929) US#12; *Meet the Sun Half Way* [i] Bing Crosby (1940) US#15, *On the Sentimental Side* [i] Bing Crosby (1938) US#4, *Once Too Often* [iv] Ella Fitzgerald (1944) US#24, *Only Forever* [i] Bing Crosby (1940) US#1/Tommy Dorsey (1940) US#7/Eddy Duchin (1940) US#15; *Row, Row, Row* [v] American Quartet (1913) US#8/Arthur Collins & Byron Harlan (1913) US#7/Ada Jones (1913) US#1/Mitchell Ayres (1940) US#15/Russ Conway in *Party Pops* (1957) UK#24; *Sing a Song of Sunbeams* [i] Bing Crosby (1939) US#8, *Six Lessons from Madame La Zonga* [x] Charlie Barnet (1940) US#11/Jimmy Dorsey (1940) US#4; *Sweet Potato Piper* [i] Bing Crosby (1940) US#11, *That Sly Old Gentleman (From Featherbed Lane)* [i] Bing Crosby (1939) US#10, *That's for Me* [i] Bing Crosby (1940) US#9, *Through (How Can You Say We're Through?)* [ix] Ted Lewis (1929) US#10, *What Do You Want to Make Those Eyes at Me For?* [vi] Ada Jones & Billy Murray (1917) US#3/Betty Hutton (1945) US#15/Ray Peterson (1960) US#104/Emile Ford & the Checkmates (1959) UK#1/Shakin' Stevens (1987) UK#5; *When the Moon Comes Over Madison Square* [i] Bing Crosby (1940) US#27, *You Know You Belong to Somebody Else (So Why Don't You Leave Me Alone)* [xi] Henry Burr (1923) US#5, *You Made Me Love You* [ix] William J. Halley (1913) US#6/Al Jolson (1913) US#1/Bing Crosby (1940) US#25/Harry James (1941) US#5/Aretha Franklin (1965) US#109; *You're Gonna Lose Your Gal* [xii] Jan Garber (1933) US#10/Glen Gray (1934) US#12/Harry Reser's Orchestra (1934) US#13. Co-writers: [i] Johnny Burke, [ii] Grant Clarke/Al Jolson/Edgar Leslie, [iii] Mort Dixon, [iv] Mack Gordon, [v] William Jerome, [vi] Howard Johnson/Joseph McCarthy, [vii] Ted Koeheler, [viii] Edgar Leslie, [ix] Joseph McCarthy, [x] Charles Newman, [xi] Eugene West, [xii] Joe Young.

680. MONCKTON, Lionel (b. December 18, 1861; d. February 15, 1924, both London, England) Music Hall composer. A music critic who gave up the law to write musical theatre. Monckton's first songs were performed at the Gaiety Theatre, and he eventually contributed to nearly twenty shows, including "A Runaway Girl" (1898), "A Toreador" (1901), "A Country Girl" (1902), "The Orchid" (1903), and "The Girls of Gotenberg" (1907). His show "The Arcadians" (1909), which introduced *Arcady Is Ever Young* [ii] and *The Pipes of Pan* [ii], was probably the earliest British musical to fully integrate songs into the plot. Monckton's songs were often recorded by his wife, the singer Gertie Miller. HIT VERSIONS: *Come to the Ball* [i] Henry Burr (1912) US#5. Co-writers: [i] Percy Greenbank/Adrian Ross, [ii] Howard Talbot/Arthur Wimperis.

681. MONROE, Bill (b. September 13, 1911, Rosine, KY; d. September, 1996) C&W mandolin player. One of the most significant bluegrass musicians in America, whose traditional blend of Appalachian mountain music and conventional country rhythms made him a popular Grand Ole Opry star for fifty years. Monroe learned the mandolin as a child and performed with his brothers throughout the 1920–1930s, eventually recording over sixty sides for the Victor label. He began composing in 1934, and performed with the Kentuckyians and the Bluegrass Boys. CHART COMPOSITIONS: *The Kentucky Waltz* (1946) C&W#3, *Footprints in the Snow* (1946) C&W#5, *Sweetheart, You Done Me Wrong* (1948) C&W#11, *Wicked Path of Sin* (1948) C&W#13, *Little Community Church* (1948) C&W#11, *Toy Heart* (1949) C&W#12, *When You're Lonely* (1949) C&W#12, *Scotland* (1958) C&W#27. ALBUMS: **I Saw the Light** (1961), **Bluegrass Ramble** (1963), **Bluegrass Special** (1965, all Brunswick); **Knee Deep in Bluegrass** (1985, Stetson). COMPILATIONS: **Best of Bill Monroe** (1975), **Country Music Hall of Fame** (1980, both MCA); **The Father of Bluegrass** (1987, RCA); **Bluegrass, 1950–1958** (1989), **Bluegrass, 1959–1969** (1991, both Bear Family); **Mule Skinner Blues** (1991, CA); **The Essential Bill Monroe and His Blue Grass Boys** (1992, Columbia); **Live Recordings, 1956–1980** (1994), **Live Duet Recordings, 1963–1980** (1994, both Smithsonian Folkways); **Bluegrass, 1970–1979** (1994, Bear Family). HIT VERSIONS: *Blue Moon of Kentucky* Earl Scruggs Revue (1980) C&W#46, *Kentucky Waltz, The* Eddy Arnold (1951) C&W#1, *Uncle Pen* Porter Wagoner (1956) C&W#14/Ricky Scaggs (1984) C&W#1.

682. MORODER, Giorgio (b. April 26, 1941, Ortisel, Italy) Pop multi-instrumentalist and producer. A European producer of synthesizer based dance music, who frequently worked with the lyricist Peter Bellotte. The duo's *Nachts Schient die Sonne*, became a million seller for Chicory Tip as *Son of My Father* (1972), after which, Moroder worked with Donna Summer on a series of disco era multimillion sellers. Moroder has also recorded as a solo artist and composed film soundtracks. CHART COMPOSITIONS: *Son of My Father* [iii] (1972) US#46, *From Here to Eternity* [i] (1977) US#109 UK#16, *The Chase* (1979) US#33, *Reach Out* with Paul Engeman (1984) US#81, *Together in Electric Dreams* [xi]* (1984) UK#3, *Goodbye Bad Times* [xi]* (1985) UK#44. ALBUMS: **From Here to Eternity** (1977) US#130, **Midnight Express** ost (1978) US#59, **A Whiter Shade of Pale**** (1978) US#190, **E=MC2** (1979, all Casablanca); **American Gigolo** ost (1980, Polydor) g US#7; **Cat People** ost with David Bowie (1982, Backstreet) US#47; **Flashdance** ost (1983, Casablanca) p US#1; **Electric Dreams** ost 1984 (Virgin) US#94 UK#46; **Metropolis** ost (1984, Columbia) US#110; **Philip Oakey and Giorgio Moroder**** (1985, Virgin) UK#52. HIT VERSIONS: *Breakdance* [viii] Irene Cara (1984) R&B#23 US#8, *Crazy World* [xiii] Big Trouble (1987) US#71, *Danger Zone* [xiii] Kenny Loggins (1986) g US#2 UK#45, *Dream (Hold on to Your Dream), The* [ii] Irene Cara (1983) R&B#65 US#37, *Flashdance...What a Feeling* [vi] Irene Cara (1983) g R&B#2 US#1 UK#2/ Bjorn Again (1993) UK#65; *Givin' Up Givin' In* [i] Three Degrees (1978) R&B#39 UK#12, *Good Grief Christina* [i] Chicory Tip (1973) UK#17, *Heaven Knows* [iv] Donna Summer & Brooklyn Dreams (1979) g R&B#10 US#4 UK#34, *Here She Comes* [i] Bonnie Tyler (1984) US#76, *I Feel Love* [v] Donna Summer (1977) g R&B#9 US#6 UK#1, re-mixed (1982) UK#21, new version (1995) UK#8/Marc Almond in *I Feel Love Medley* (1985) UK#3/Messiah & Precious Wilson (1992) UK#19; *I Love You* [v] Donna Summer (1977) R&B#28 US#37 UK#10, *I Remember Yesterday* [v] Donna Summer (1977) UK#14, *Lady, Lady, Lady* [x] Joe "Bean" Esposito (1983) US#86, *Love to Love You Baby* [v] Donna Summer (1975) g R&B#3 US#2 UK#4/Marc Almond in *I Feel Love Medley* (1985) UK#3; *Love's Unkind* [v] Sophie Lawrence (1991) UK#21, *Meet Me Halfway* [xiii] Kenny Loggins (1987) US#11, *Never Ending Story* [x] Limahl (1984) UK#4, *On the Radio* [xii] Donna Summer (1980) g R&B#9 US#5 UK#32, *Runner, The* [ix] Three Degrees (1979) UK#10, *Rumor Has It* [v] Donna Summer (1978) R&B#21 US#53 UK#19, *Son of My Father* [iii] Chicory Tip (1972) US#91 UK#1, *Spring Affair* [v] Donna Summer (1976) R&B#24 US#47, *Seduction, The* James Last Band (1980) US#28, *Take My Breath Away (Love Theme from Top Gun)* [xiii] Berlin (1986) g US#1 UK#1, re-entry (1988) UK#52, re-issued (1990) UK#3; *Try*

Me, I Know We Can Make It [v] Donna Summer (1976) R&B#35 US#80, *Wanderer, The* [xii] Donna Summer (1980) g R&B#13 US#3 UK#48, *What's Your Name?* Chicory Tip (1972) UK#13, *Why Me?* [vii] Irene Cara (1983) R&B#41 US#13, *Winner Takes It All* [xiii] Sammy Hagar (1987) US#54, *Winter Melody* [v] Donna Summer (1977) R&B#21 US#43 UK#27, *You Can* [i] Madleen Kane (1982) US#77. As: ** Munich Machine. With: * Phil Oakey. Co-writers: [i] Pete Bellotte, [ii] Pete Bellotte/Irene Cara (b. March 18, 1959, New York, NY), [iii] Pete Bellotte/Michael Holme, [iv] Pete Bellotte/Gregg Mathieson/Donna Summer (b. Adrian Donna Gaines, December 31, 1948, Dorchester, MA), [v] Pete Bellotte/Donna Summer, [vi] Irene Cara, [vii] Irene Cara/Keith Forsey, [viii] Irene Cara/Bunny Hull, [ix] Sheila Fergus, [x] Keith Forsey, [xi] Phil Oakey, [xii] Donna Summer, [xiii] Tom Whitlock. (Debbie HARRY, Janis IAN, Freddie MERCURY.)

683. MORRISEY (b. Steven Patrick Morrisey, May 22, 1959, Davyhulme, England) Pop vocalist. The lead singer in the angst-ridden, alternative group the Smiths, who composed most of the band's songs in partnership with the guitarist Johnny Marr. CHART COMPOSITIONS: *This Charming Man* [ii] (1983) UK#25, re-issued (1992) UK#8; *What Difference Does It Make* [ii] (1984) UK#12, *Heaven Knows I'm Miserable Now* [ii] (1984) UK#10, *William, It Was Really Nothing* [ii] (1984) UK#17, *How Soon Is Now?* [ii] (1985) UK#24, re-issued (1992) UK#16; *Shakespeare's Sister* [ii] (1985) UK#26, *That Joke Isn't Funny Anymore* [ii] (1985) UK#49, *The Boy with the Thorn in His Side* [ii] (1985) UK#23, *Big Mouth Strikes Again* [ii] (1986) UK#26, *Panic* [ii] (1986) UK#11, *Ask* [ii] (1986) UK#14, *Shoplifters of the World Unite* [ii] (1987) UK#12, *Sheila Take a Bow* [ii] (1987) UK#10, *Girlfriend in a Coma* [ii] (1987) UK#13, *I Started Something I Couldn't Finish* [ii] (1987) UK#23, *Last Night I Dreamed That Somebody Loved Me* [ii] (1987) UK#30, *There Is a Light That Never Goes Out* [ii] (1992) UK#25, *How Does It Feel?* [ii] (1992) UK#27. ALBUMS: **The Smiths** (1984) US#150 UK#2, **Hatful of Hollow** (1984) UK#7, **Meat Is Murder** (1985) US#110 UK#1, **The Queen Is Dead** (1986) g US#70 UK#2, **Strangeways, Here We Come** (1987) g US#55 UK#2, **Rank** (1988, all Rough Trade) US#77 UK#2. COMPILATIONS: **The World Won't Listen** (1987) UK#2, **Louder Than Bombs** (1987, both Rough Trade) g US#63 UK#38; **Best...I** (1992) US#139 UK#1, **Best...II** (1982) UK#29, **The Singles** (1995, all WEA) UK#5. The Smiths broke up in 1988, after which Morrisey recorded as a solo artist. CHART COMPOSITIONS: *Suedehead* [iv] (1988) UK#5, *Everyday Is Like Sunday* [iv] (1988) UK#9, *Last of the Interna-*

tional Playboys (1989) UK#6, *Interesting Drug* (1989) UK#9, *Ouija Board, Ouija Board* (1989) UK#18, *November Spawned a Monster* (1990) UK#12, *Piccadilly Palare* (1990) UK#18, *Our Frank* (1991) UK#26, *Sing Your Life* (1991) UK#33, *Pregnant for the Last Time* [iii] (1991) UK#25, *My Love Life* [iii] (1991) UK#29, *We Hate It When Our Friends Become Successful* [v] (1992) UK#17, *You're the One for Me, Fatty* [iii] (1992) UK#19, *Certain People I Know* (1992) UK#35, *The More You Ignore Me, the Closer I Get* [i] (1994) UK#46 UK#8, *Hold on to Your Friends* (1993) UK#47, *Interlude* (1993) UK#25, *Boxers* (1995) UK#23, *Dagenham Dave* (1995) UK#26, *The Boy Racer* (1995) UK#36, *Sunny* (1995) UK#42. ALBUMS: **Viva Hate** (1988) g US#48 UK#1, **Bona Drag** (1990) US#59 UK#9, **Kill Uncle** (1991) US#52 UK#8, **Your Arsenal** (1992) US#21 UK#4, **Beethoven Was Deaf** (1993, all HMV) UK#13; **Vauxhall and I** (1994) US#18 UK#1, **World of Morrisey** (1995, both Parlophone) US#134 UK#15; **Southpaw Grammar** (1995, RCA) US#66 UK#4; **Maladjusted** (1997, Island). HIT VERSIONS: *Hand in Glove* [ii] Sandie Shaw (1984) UK#27, *How Soon Is Now?* [ii] Soho sampled in *Hippychick* (1990) UK#8. Co-writers: [i] Boorer, [ii] Johnny Marr, [iii] Nevin, [iv] Stephen Street, [v] Whyte.

684. MORRISON, Jim (b. December 8, 1943, Melbourne, FL; d. July 3, 1971, Paris, France) Rock vocalist. The lyricist, vocalist and co-founder member of the 1960s rock group the Doors, which played a blues based blend of psychedelia. Influenced by such writers as William Blake, W.B. Yeats and Aldous Huxley, Morrison became a legendary, iconic rock figure after he died of a heart attack on account of his excessive alcohol and drug consumption. CHART COMPOSITIONS: *Light My Fire* [i] (1967) US#1 UK#49, re-issued (1992) UK#7; *People Are Strange* [i] (1967) US#12, *Break on Through (To the Other Side)* [i] (1967) US#126, re-issued (1992) UK#43; *Love Me Two Times* [i] (1968) US#25, *The Unknown Soldier* [i] (1968) US#39, *Hello, I Love You* [i] (1968) US#1 UK#15, re-issued (1979) UK#71; *Touch Me* [i] (1969) US#3, *Wishful Sinful* [i] (1969) US#44, *Tell All the People* [i] (1969) US#57, *Runnin' Blue* [i] (1969) US#64, *You Make Me Real* [i] (1970) US#50, *Love Her Madly* [i] (1971) US#11, *Riders on the Storm* [i] (1971) US#14 UK#22, re-issued (1976) UK#33, re-issued (1992) UK#68. ALBUMS: **The Doors** (1967) p US#2 UK#43, **Strange Days** (1967) g US#3, **Waiting for the Sun** (1968) p US#1 UK#16, **The Soft Parade** (1969) p US#6, **Morrison Hotel** (1970) g US#4 UK#12, **Absolutely Live** (1970) g US#8 UK#69, **L.A. Woman** (1971, all Elektra) p US#9 UK#28. COMPILATIONS: **13** (1971) p US#25, **Weird Scenes Inside the Gold Mine** (1972)

g US#55 UK#50, **Best of the Doors** (1973) g US#32 UK#17, **An American Prayer** (1979) US#54, **Greatest Hits** (1980) p US#17, **Alive, She Cried** (1983) g US#23 UK#36, **Classics** (1985) US#124, **Live at the Hollywood Bowl** (1987) US#154 UK#51, **The Doors** ost (1992) g US#8 UK#11, **In Concert** (1992, all Elektra) US#50 UK#24; **Stoned But Articulate** (1996, Ozit). HIT VERSIONS: *L.A. Woman* [i] Billy Idol (1990) US#52 UK#70, *Light My Fire* [i] Jose Feliciano (1968) g R&B#29 US#3 UK#6/Rhetta Hughes (1969) R&B#36 US#102/Amii Stewart (1979) R&B#36 US#69 UK#5, re-mixed (1985) UK#7/Mike Flowers Pops (1996) UK#39; *People Are Strange* [i] Echo & the Bunnymen (1988) US#12 UK#29, re-issued (1991) UK#34; *Riders on the Storm* [i] Annabel Lamb (1983) UK#27. Co-writers: [i] John Densmore (b. December 1, 1944, Los Angeles, CA)/Robert Krieger (b. January 8, 1946, Los Angeles, CA)/Ray Manzarek (b. February 12, 1935, Chicago, IL).

685. MORRISON, Van (b. George Ivan Morrison, August 31, 1945, Belfast, Northern Ireland) Rock multi-instrumentalist and vocalist. The performer once described by Bob Seger as, "the master himself." Morrison frequently displays a musical integrity and unclouded vision that has few equals, and his music transcends the normal concept of song, as each new composition is essentially another exploration of his singular, on-going melody. Morrison's coalescence of traditional Irish folk music, American country, R&B, blues, rock, soul and jazz, is incomparable to anything else in rock. He developed a passion for music from an early age, and, encouraged by his parents, he learned the guitar and soprano saxophone before playing in various Belfast groups. In 1963 he fronted the R&B group Them, which charted with two Bert Berns' compositions and Morrison's *Gloria* (1965) US#93 and *Mystic Eyes* (1965) US#33. ALBUMS: **Them** (1965, Parrot) US#54; **The Angry Young Them** (1965), **Them Again** (1966) US#138, **Them featuring Van Morrison** (1972, all Decca) US#154. He quit the group in 1967 and headed to New York for a solo career, where he recorded for the Bang label, before releasing the innovative album **Astral Weeks** (1968), which was an audacious masterpiece of rambling, mystical poetry and acoustic-jazz melodies that were encased in discordant string arrangements. **Astral Weeks** was to influence entire generations of songwriters, from Nick Drake to the Hothouse Flowers. **Saint Dominic's Preview** (1972), was a joyous celebration of R&B that also featured *Listen to the Lion* and *Almost Independence Day*, two lengthy, rap styled tonal works. Backed by his Caledonia Soul Orchestra, Morrison also recorded the finest genuine live album of the rock era, **It's Too Late to Stop Now** (1974). The riveting **Common One** (1980), was a tribute to Irish classical romanticism and poetry, and featured Morrison' best stream-of-consciousness monologues, all of which were contemplative, meditative, multifarious inner-dialogues. An uncompromising artist, Morrison keeps up a heady release schedule with his introspective, spiritual journeys, that pay little attention to any current musical trend. CHART COMPOSITIONS: *Brown Eyed Girl* (1967) US#10, *Ro Ro Rosey* (1967) US#107, *Come Running* (1970) US#39, *Moondance* (1970) US#92, *Domino* (1970) US#9, *Blue Money* (1970) US#23, *Call Me Up in Dreamland* (1970) US#95, *Wild Night* (1971) US#28, *Tupelo Honey* (1971) US#47, *(Straight to Your Heart) Like a Cannonball* (1972) US#119, *Jackie Wilson Said (I'm in Heaven When You Smile)* (1972) US#61, *Redwood Tree* (1972) US#98, *Gypsy* (1973) US#101, *Wavelength* (1978) US#42, *Bright Side of the Road* (1979) US#110 UK#63, *Tore Down a La Rimbaud* (1985) US#101, *Have I Told You Lately* (1989) UK#74, new version with the Chieftans (1995) UK#71; *Whenever God Shines His Light* with Cliff Richard (1989) UK#20, *Gloria* with John Lee Hooker (1993) UK#31, *Days Like These* (1995) UK#65, *No Religion* (1995) UK#54. ALBUMS: **Blowin' Your Mind** (1967, Bang) US#182; **Astral Weeks** (1968), **Moondance** (1970) p US#29 UK#32, **His Band and Street Choir** (1970) US#32, **Tupelo Honey** (1971) g US#27, **Saint Dominic's Preview** (1972) US#15, **Hard Nose the Highway** (1973) US#27 US#22, **It's Too Late to Stop Now** (1974) US#53, **Veedon Fleece** (1974) US#53 UK#41, **A Period of Transition** (1977) US#43 UK#23, **Wavelength** (1978, all Warner Brothers) US#28 UK#27; **Into the Music** (1989, Vertigo) US#43 UK#21; **Common One** (1980) US#73 UK#53, **Beautiful Vision** (1982) US#44 UK#31, **Inarticulate Speech of the Heart** (1983) US#116 UK#14, **Live at the Grand Opera House** (1984) UK#47, **A Sense of Wonder** (1984) US#61 UK#25, **No Guru, No Method, No Teacher** (1986) US#70 UK#27, **Poetic Champions Compose** (1987) US#90 UK#26, **Irish Heartbeat** with the Chieftains (1988, all Mercury) US#102 UK#18; **Avalon Sunset** (1989) US#91 UK#13, **Enlightenment** (1990) US#62 UK#5, **Hymns to the Silence** (1991, all Polydor) g US#99 UK#5; **Too Long in Exile** (1993) US#29 UK#4, **A Night in San Francisco** (1994) US#125 UK#8, **Days Like These** (1995, all Exile/Polydor) US#33 UK#5; **How Long Has This Been Going On** with Georgie Fame (1995) US#55, **Tell Me Something: The Songs of Mose Allison** with Mose Allison, Georgie Fame and Ben Sidran (1996, both Exile/Verve); **The Healing Game** (1997, Exile/Polydor) UK#10. COMPILATIONS: **Best of Van Morrison** (1970), **This Is**

Where I Came In (1970), **T.B. Sheets** (1974, all Bang) US#181; **Chair Fellows** (1978, Impossible); **Best of Van Morrison** (1990, Polydor) p US#41 UK#4; **Cuchulainn** (1991, Moles); **The Bang Masters** (1992, Epic); **The Lost Tapes, Volume 1** (1993), **The Lost Tapes, Volume 2** (1993, both Movieplay); **Best of Van Morrison, Volume 2** (1993) US#176 UK#31, **Very Best of Van Morrison** (1994, both Polydor) UK#15, **Payin' Dues** (1994, Charley); **The New York Sessions, '67** (1997, Burning Airlines). HIT VERSIONS: *Brown Eyed Girl* El Chicano (1972) US#45/Henry Paul Band (1982) US#105/Joe Stampley (1984) C&W#29; *Carrying a Torch* Tom Jones (1991) UK#57, *Crazy Love* Helen Reddy (1971) US#51, *Gloria* Shadows of Knight (1966) US#10/Belfast Gypsies as *Gloria's Dream (Round and Around)* (1966) US#124/Eddie & the Hot Rods on *Live at the Marquee EP* (1976) UK#43/Enchantment (1977) US#25/Doors (1983) US#71; *Have I Told You Lately* Rod Stewart (1993) g US#5 UK#5, *He Ain't Give You None* Freddie Scott (1967) R&B#24 US#100, *I Shall Sing* Art Garfunkel (1973) US#38, *Into the Mystic* Johnny Rivers (1970) US#51, *Jackie Wilson Said (I'm in Heaven When You Smile)* Dexy's Midnight Runners (1982) UK#5, *Moondance* Anita Baker on B-side of *Just Because* (1988) US#14, *Wild Night* John Mellencamp (1994) US#3 UK#34.

686. MORSE, Theodore F. (b. April 13, 1873, Washington, DC; d. May 25, 1924, New York, NY) Tin Pan Alley composer. A former staff composer and song-plugger who had a successful writing partnership with Edward Madden. Morse later worked with his lyricist wife, Theodora Terriss. HIT VERSIONS: *Another Rag (A Raggy Rag)* [ii] American Quartet (1912) US#8, *Hail! Hail! the Gang's All Here* [i] Irving Kaufman (1918) US#1/Shannon Four (1918) US#5; *When Uncle Joe Plays a Rag on His Old Banjo* [ii] Arthur Collins (1912) US#2. Co-writers: [i] Arthur Sullivan/Theodora Terriss, [ii] Theodora Terriss. (*See also under* Howard. JOHNSON, Edward MADDEN.)

687. MOTEN, Patrick (b. Los Angeles, CA) R&B keyboard player and producer. A producer and songwriter who specializes in richly orchestrated, mid-tempo soul ballads. Much of Moten's best work was with Bobby Womack and Johnnie Taylor, for the short-lived Beverly Glen label during the early 1980s. Moten also composed most of Anita Baker's debut set **The Songstress** (1983). HIT VERSIONS: *Angel* Anita Baker (1983) R&B#5, *Feel the Need* Anita Baker (1984) R&B#67, *How Can I Get Next to You* Chapter 8 (1985) R&B#89, *What About My Love* Johnnie Taylor (1982) R&B#24, *Will You Be Mine* Anita Baker (1983) R&B#49, *You're the Best*

Thing Yet [i] Anita Baker (1983) R&B#28. Co-writer: [i] Geronne C. Turner.

688. MOY, Sylvia (b. Detroit, IL) R&B producer and vocalist. A Motown Records staff writer and producer, who co-composed some of Stevie Wonder's earliest hits. In 1972, Moy formed her own Michigan Satellite label, and in 1989 she recorded the solo single *Major Investment*. HIT VERSIONS: *Honey Chile* [iv] Martha & the Vandellas (1968) R&B#5 US#11 UK#30, *It Takes Two* [v] Marvin Gaye & Kim Weston (1967) R&B#4 US#14 UK#16/ Rod Stewart & Tina Turner (1990) UK#5; *Love Bug Leave My Heart Alone* [iv] Martha & the Vandellas (1967) R&B#14 US#25, *My Baby Loves Me* [iii] Martha & the Vandellas (1966) R&B#3 US#22, *Nothing's Too Good for My Baby* [ii] Stevie Wonder (1966) R&B#4 US#20, *With a Child's Heart* [i] Stevie Wonder (1966) R&B#8 US#131/Michael Jackson (1973) R&B#14 US#50. Co-writers: [i] Henry Cosby/Basemore, [ii] Henry Cosby/William Stevenson, [iii] Ivy Hunter/William Stevenson, [iv] Richard Morris, [v] William Stevenson. (*See also under* Stevie WONDER.)

689. MURPHEY, Michael Martin (b. Dallas, TX) C&W guitarist and vocalist. A folk and country influenced singer-songwriter, who began singing while still in high school. Murphey toured in the group the Lewis and Clark Expedition during the 1960s, before becoming a songwriter for Screen Gems and pursuing a solo career. CHART COMPOSITIONS: *Geronimo's Cadillac* [ii] (1972) US#37, *Wildfire* [i] (1975) US#3, *Carolina in the Pines* (1975) US#21, new version (1985) C&W#9; *Renegade* (1976) US#39, *A Mansion on the Hill* (1976) C&W#36, *Cherokee Fiddle* (1977) C&W#58, *Backslider's Wine* (1979) C&W#92, *Take It As It Comes* with Katy Moffatt (1981) C&W#83, *The Two-Step Is Easy* (1982) C&W#44, *Still Taking Chances* (1982) C&W#3 US#76, *Love Affairs* (1983) C&#11, *Don't Count the Rainy Days* (1983) C&W#9, *Will It Be Love By Morning* (1984) C&W#7, *Disenchanted* (1984) C&W#12, *Radio Land* (1984) C&W#19, *What She Wants* (1984) C&W#8, *Tonight We Ride* (1986) C&W#26, *Rollin' Nowhere* (1986) C&W#15, *Fiddlin' Man* (1986) C&W#40, *A Face in the Crowd* with Holly Dunn (1987) C&W#4, *I'm Gonna Miss You, Girl* (1987) C&W#3, *Talkin' to the Wrong Man* with Ryan Murphey (1988) C&W#4, *Pilgrim's on the Way (Matthew's Song)* (1988) C&W#29, *From the Word Go* (1988) C&W#3. ALBUMS: **Geronimo's Cadillac** (1972) US#160, **Cosmic Cowboy Souvenir** (1973, both A&M) US#196; **Michael Murphey** (1973), **Blue Sky-Night Thunder** (1975) g US#18, **Swans Against the Sun** (1976) US#44, **Flowing Free For-**ever (1976) US#130, **Lonewolf** (1977) US#99, **Peaks, Valleys, Honky-Tonks and Alleys** (1979, all Epic); **Hard Country** ost (1981), **Michael Martin Murphey** (1982) US#69, **The Heart Never Lies** (1983, all Liberty) US#187; **Cowboy Songs III — Rhymes of the Renegades** (1993, Warner Brothers). HIT VERSIONS: *Cosmic Cowboy* Nitty Gritty Dirt Band (1973) US#123, *Geronimo's Cadillac* [ii] Jeff Stevens & the Bullets (1987) C&W#53. Co-writers: [i] Larry Cansler, [ii] Charles Quarto.

690. MURPHY, Elliott (b. March 16, 1949, Garden City, NY) Rock guitarist and vocalist. A singer-songwriter who retains a cult following in Europe. ALBUMS: **Aquashow** (1973, Polydor); **Lost Generation** (1975), **Night Lights** (1976, both RCA); **Just a Story from America** (1977, Columbia); **Affairs** (1981), **Murph the Surf** (1982, both Courtesan); **Unreal City** (1993, Razor & Tie). COMPILATION: **Diamonds By the Yard** (1992, Razor & Tie).

691. MURRAY, Mitch (b. January 30, 1940, Hove, England) Pop producer. A songwriter and producer whose first published composition was *Save a Dream for Me* (1962). Murray composed many British television and film themes between 1960–1979, and in 1967 he formed a highly successful partnership with Pete Callender, the duo later forming their own Bus Stop label. During the 1980s, Murray concentrated on advertising jingles. HIT VERSIONS: *Ballad of Bonnie and Clyde, The* [i] Georgie Fame (1968) g US#7 UK#1/New Vaudeville Band (1968) US#122; *Billy, Don't Be a Hero* [i] Bo Donaldson & the Heywoods (1974) US#1/Paper Lace (1974) US#96 UK#1; *Black Eyed Boys, The* [i] Paper Lace (1974) US#41 UK#11, *By the Way* [i] Big Three (1963) UK#22/Tremeloes (1970) UK#35; *Drive Safely Darling* [i] Tony Christie (1976) UK#35, *Even the Bad Times Are Good* [iv] Jerry Wallace (1964) US#114, re-issued (1970) C&W#74, also on B-side of *In the Misty Moonlight* (1964) US#19/Tremeloes (1967) US#36 UK#4; *Goodbye Sam, Hello Samantha* [ii] Cliff Richard (1970) UK#6, *Hitchin' a Ride* [i] Vanity Fair (1969) g US#5 UK#16/Jack Reno (1971) C&W#12/Sinitta (1990) UK#24; *How Do You Do It* Gerry & the Pacemakers (1963) US#9 UK#1, *Hush, Not a Word to Mary* [i] John Rowles (1968) UK#12, *I Did What I Did for Maria* [i] Tony Christie (1971) UK#2, *I Like It* Gerry & the Pacemakers (1963) US#17 UK#1, *I'm Telling You Now* [iii] Freddie & the Dreamers (1963) g US#1 UK#2, *Just for You* Freddie & the Dreamers (1964) UK#41, *Las Vegas* Tony Christie (1971) UK#21, *Man Without Love, A* Engelbert Humperdinck (1968) US#19 UK#2/Kenneth McKellar (1996) UK#30; *Night Chicago Died, The*

[i] Paper Lace (1974) US#1 UK#3, *Primrose Lane* [i] Jerry Wallace (1969) US#8, *Ragamuffin Man* [i] Manfred Mann (1969) UK#8/Donna Fargo (1978) C&W#19; *Tell the Boys* [i] Sandie Shaw on B-side of *Puppet on a String* (1967) UK#1, *You Were Made for Me* Freddie & the Dreamers (1963) US#21 UK#3. Co-writers: [i] Pete Callander, [ii] Pete Callander/Geoff Stevens, [iii] Freddie Garrity (b. November 14, 1936, Manchester, England), [iv] Geoff Stevens.

692. NASH, Graham (b. February 2, 1942, Blackpool, England) Rock guitarist and vocalist. A singer-songwriter, who has been a member of two of the most successful three-part harmony groups since the 1960s, the Hollies, and Crosby, Stills and Nash. Nash co-founded the Hollies in the early 1960s with the lead vocalist Allan Clarke. CHART COMPOSITIONS: *We're Through* [ii] (1964) UK#7, *Stop! Stop! Stop!* [ii] (1966) UK#2, *On a Carousel* [ii] (1967) US#11 UK#4, *Carrie Anne* [ii] (1967) US#9 UK#3, *Pay You Back with Interest* [ii] (1967) US#28, *King Midas in Reverse* [ii] (1967) US#51 UK#18, *Jennifer Eccles* [i] (1968) US#40 UK#7, *Holliedaze (A Medley)* [ii] (1981) UK#29. ALBUMS: **Stay with the Hollies** (1964) UK#2, **In the Hollies Style** (1964), **The Hollies** (1965) UK#8, **Would You Believe** (1966) UK#16, **For Certain Because** (1966) UK#23, **Butterfly** (1967), **Evolution** (1967, all Parlophone) US#43 UK#13; **What Goes Around** (1983, Epic) US#90. COMPILATIONS: **Hear! Hear!** (1966) US#145, **Bus Stop** (1967) US#75, **Stop! Stop! Stop!** (1967) US#91, **Greatest Hits** (1967, all Imperial) US#11; **The Hollies' Greatest** (1968) UK#1, **Greatest Hits** (1973, both Epic) US#157; **20 Golden Greats** (1978) UK#2, **All the Hits and More — The Definitive Collection** (1988) UK#51, **The Air That I Breathe — The Best of the Hollies** (1993) UK#15, **Treasured Hits and Hidden Treasures** (1993, all EMI). He left the group in 1968 to form Crosby, Stills and Nash, with David Crosby and Stephen Stills, writing the hits *Marrakesh Express* (1969) US#28 UK#17, *Teach Your Children* (1970) US#16, *Our House* (1970) US#30, *Out of the Darkness* [iii] (1976) US#89, *Just a Song Before I Go* (1977) US#7, and *Wasted on the Way* (1982) C&W#87 US#9. Nash has also recorded as a solo artist. CHART COMPOSITIONS: *Chicago* (1971) US#35, *Military Madness* (1971) US#73, *Used to Be a King* (1971) US#111. ALBUMS: **Songs for Beginners** (1971) g US#15 UK#13, **Wild Tales** (1974, both Atlantic) US#34; **Earth and Sky** (1980, Capitol) US#117; **Innocent Eyes** (1986, Atlantic) US#136. HIT VERSIONS: *On a Carousel* [ii] Glass Moon (1982) US#50, *Pay You Back with Interest* [ii] Gary O. (1981) US#70. Co-writers: [i] Allan Clarke (b. Harold Allan Clarke, April 5, 1942, Salford, England), [ii] Allan Clarke/Tony Hicks (b. December 16, 1943, Nelson, England), [iii] C. Degree. (*See also under* David CROSBY, Neil YOUNG.)

693. NEIL, Fred (b. 1947, St. Petersburg, FL) Folk guitarist and vocalist. One of the most influential folk and blues artists of the 1960s, whose classic *Everybody's Talkin'*, is one of only a handful of songs to receive a BMI four million radio performance award. As a teenager, Neil performed country on the Grand Ole Opry in Nashville, before developing an interest in folk, and becoming a respected figure on the 1960s Greenwich Village folk scene. His twelve-string guitar playing and world weary vocal style has been much imitated, and his songs were covered by artists ranging from Buddy Holly to Jefferson Airplane. Neil recorded a series of excellent folk-blues albums before retiring gracefully in the 1970s. ALBUMS: **Tear Down the Walls** (1964), **Bleecker and MacDougal** (1965, both Elektra); **Fred Neil** (1966), **Everybody's Talkin'** (1969), **Sessions** (1971), **The Other Side of This Life** (1971, all Capitol). COMPILATION: **Everybody's Talkin' — The Theme from Midnight Cowboy** (1994, Rev-Ola). HIT VERSIONS: *Candy Man* [i] Roy Orbison (1961) US#25, also on B-side of *Cryin'* (1961) g US#2 UK#25/Brian Poole & the Tremeloes (1964) UK#6/Mickey Gilley & Charley McClain (1984) C&W#5; *Everybody's Talkin'* Nilsson (1968) US#122, re-issued (1969) US#6 UK#23/Beautiful South (1994) UK#12; *Other Side of This Life, The* Peter, Paul & Mary (1966) US#100. Co-writer: [i] Beverly Ross.

694. NELSON, Rick(y) (b. Eric Hilliard Nelson, May 8, 1940, Teaneck, NJ; d. December 31, 1985, De Kalb, TX) Pop guitarist and vocalist. A popular performer for nearly thirty years, whose father had been a bandleader. After singing on the radio, Nelson became a 1950s television personality and teen idol, charting fifty-three singles between 1957–1963. He dropped the "y" from his stage name in the late 1960s, and forged a second career with a country-rock sound that he performed with his Stone Canyon Band. Never an innovator, and an influence on nobody, Nelson remained a durable pop commodity until his death in a plane crash. CHART COMPOSITIONS: *Easy to Be Free* (1970) US#48, *Life* (1971) US#109, *Garden Party* (1972) g C&W#44 US#6 UK#41. ALBUMS: **Ricky** (1958) US#1, **Ricky Nelson** (1958) US#7, **Ricky Sings Again** (1959) US#14, **Songs By Ricky** (1959) US#2, **More Songs By Ricky** (1960) US#18, **Rick Is 21** (1961) US#8, **Album Seven By Rick** (1962) US#27, **It's Up to You** (1963, all Imperial) US#128; **For Your Sweet Love**

(1963) US#20, **Rick Nelson Sings for You** (1964) US#14, **Bright Lights and Country Music** (1966), **Country Fever** (1967), **Another Side of Rick Nelson** (1968), **Perspective** (1969), **In Concert** (1970) US#54, **Rick Sings Nelson** (1970) US#196, **Rudy the Fifth** (1971), **Garden Party** (1973, all Decca) US#32; **Windfall** (1974, MCA) US#190; **Intakes** (1977, Epic); **Playing to Win** (1981, Capitol) US#153. COMPILATIONS: **Best Sellers** (1963, Imperial) US#112. HIT VERSION: *Garden Party* Johnny Lee as *Country Party* (1977) C&W#15.

695. NELSON, Willie (b. William Hugh Nelson, April 30, 1933, Abbot, TX) C&W guitarist and vocalist. The composer, according to record producer Jerry Wexler, of "some of the greatest American songs ever written." Nelson has penned over two thousand compositions, has charted over one hundred singles since 1962, and is the most original country artist since Hank Williams. Nelson later became the foremost country interpreter of Tin Pan Alley songs. His distinctive, laconic voice pays little attention to meter, rhythm or any other musical convention, preferring instead to coast along with an intuitive sense of phrasing in a talking-singing style, that is nearer to Frank Sinatra than it is to other country vocalists. The sparsity of Nelson's sound, his rugged individualism, and his craftsman's ear for a great song, have all contributed to a career quite unlike that of any other artist. He was raised by his grandparents and played the guitar from the age of six, which he taught himself by ear from the radio. Nelson worked as a disc jockey and served in the U.S. Air Force in Korea, before, in 1943, joining Johnny Paycheck's Bohemian Polka Band. Before he achieved any success in music, Nelson held numerous day jobs, including that of bible, vacuum cleaner and encyclopedia salesman, a period of his life that he humorously documented in the film "Songwriter" (1984). During the early 1950s Nelson became a staff writer at Pamper Music, where he recorded his first disk, *No Place for Me* (1956). Due to his often dire financial circumstances, he sold the copyrights to some of his later country standards, including *Family Bible*, *Nite Life* and *Funny How Time Slips Away*. Since the 1970s, Nelson has recorded some of country's most consistent albums, such as the bluesy **Phases and Stages** (1974), and the two million selling **Red Headed Stranger** (1975), which remains the definitive country concept album, with its western renegade mythology and bleak, cowboy-loner imagery. Having redefined the country genre, Nelson then introduced it to America's pop mainstream, before, in 1978, turning to the nation's rich heritage of tunes from the 1930s–1940s, on the four million selling **Stardust**, which spent over five hundred weeks

on the country chart. By 1991, Nelson was being pursued by the Internal Revenue Service for a tax demand of some sixteen million dollars, one of the results of which was his amusing and austere mail-order only album, **Who'll Buy My Memories?— The IRS Tapes**. He has continued to record to a high standard well into the 1990s, his album **Spirit** (1996), being easily comparable with his best work. CHART COMPOSITIONS: *Willingly***** (1962) C&W#10, *Touch Me* (1962) C&W#7 US#109, *Half a Man* (1963) C&W#25 US#129, *You Took My Happy Away* (1964) C&W#33, *She's Not for You* (1965) C&W#43, *I Just Can't Let You Say Goodbye* (1965) C&W#48, *One in a Row* (1966) C&W#19, *The Party's Over* (1967) C&W#24, *Blackjack County Chain* (1967) C&W#21, *San Antonio* (1967) C&W#50, *Little Things* (1968) C&W#22, *Good Times* (1968) C&W#44, *I Hope So* (1969) C&W#36, *Laying My Burdens Down* (1970) C&W#68, *I'm a Memory* (1971) C&W#28, re-issued (1977) C&W#22; *Yesterday's Wine* (1971) C&W#62, *The Words Don't Fit the Picture* (1972) C&W#73, *Shotgun Willie* (1973) C&W#60, *After the Fire Is Gone*^^^^ (1974) C&W#17, *Stay All Night (Stay a Little Longer)* (1973) C&W#22, *I Still Can't Believe You're Gone* (1974) C&W#51, *Bloody Mary Morning* (1974) C&W#17, *Sister's Coming Home* (1974) C&W#93, *Good Hearted Woman* [i]++ (1975) C&W#1 US#25, *The Last Letter* (1976) C&W#46, *I Gotta Get Drunk* (1976) C&W#55 US#101, *Uncloudy Day* (arrangement only) (1976) C&W#4, *Lily Dale*^^ (1977) C&W#32, *You Ought to Hear Me Cry* (1977) C&W#16, *Ain't Life Hell**** (1978) C&W#77, *Will You Remember Mine* (1978) C&W#67, *Nite Life****** (1980) C&W#20, *Funny How Time Slips Away****** (1980) C&W#41, *On the Road Again* (1980) C&W#1 US#20, *Family Bible* (1980) C&W#92, *Angel Flying Too Close to the Ground* (1981) C&W#1, *Good Times* (1981) C&W#25, *Mountain Dew* (1981) C&W#23, *Heartaches of a Fool* (1981) C&W#39, *Little Old Fashioned Karma* (1983) C&W#10, *Why Do I Have to Choose*++ (1983) C&W#3, *Forgiving You Was Easy* (1985) C&W#1, *Me and Paul* (1985) C&W#14, *Living in the Promiseland* (1986) C&W#1, *I'm Not Trying to Forget You* (1986) C&W#21, *Partners After All* (1986) C&W#24. ALBUMS: **And Then I Wrote** (1962), **Here's Willie Nelson** (1963, both Liberty); **Country Willie — His Own Songs** (1964), **Country Favorites Willie Nelson Style** (1965), **Country Music Concert** (1966) re-issued as **Willie Nelson Live** (1976) US#149, **Make Way for Willie Nelson** (1967), **The Party's Over** (1967), **Texas in My Soul** (1967), **Good Times** (1968), **My Own Peculiar Way** (1969), **Both Sides Now** (1970), **Laying My Burdens Down** (1970, all RCA); **The Troublemaker** (1970, Atlantic) US#60; **Willie Nelson and Family**

(1971), **Yesterday's Wine** (1971, both RCA); **Shotgun Willie** (1971, Atlantic); **The Words Don't Fit the Picture** (1972), **The Willie Way** (1972, both RCA); **Phases and Stages** (1974, Atlantic) US#187; **Red Headed Stranger** (1975) p US#28, **The Sound in Your Mind** (1976) g US#48, **To Lefty from Willie** (1976, all Columbia) US#91; **Face of a Fighter** (1978, Lone Star); **Waylon and Willie**++ (1978, RCA) p US#12; **Stardust** (1978) p US#30, **Willie and Family Live** (1978) p US#32, **One for the Road**~~~ (1979) g US#25, **Willie Nelson Sings Kris Kristofferson** (1979) p US#42, **Pretty Paper** (1979, all Columbia) p US#73; **The Winning Hand**++++ (1979, Monument) US#109; **San Antonio Rose**~~ (1980) g US#70, **Honeysuckle Rose** ost (1980) p US#11, **The Electric Horseman** ost (1980) g US#52, **Somewhere Over the Rainbow** (1981) p US#31, **Always on My Mind** (1982, all Columbia) p US#2; **WWII**++ (1982, RCA) g US#57; **Old Friends**^^^ (1982, Columbia); **Poncho and Lefty**+ (1982, Epic) p US#37; **Tougher Than Leather** (1983) US#39, **Take It to the Limit**++ (1983) g US#60, **Without a Song** (1983) p US#54, **Angel Eyes**+++ (1984) US#116, **City of New Orleans** (1984) p US#69, **Music from Songwriter** ost (1984) US#152, **Brand on My Heart**~~~~ (1984), **Me and Paul** (1985) US#152, **Highwayman*** (1985) g US#92, **Funny How Time Slips Away**~~~~~ (1985), **In the Jailhouse Now**^^^^^ (1985), **Partners** (1986), **The Promised Land** (1987), **Island in the Sea** (1987), **Seashores of Old Mexico**+ (1987), **What a Wonderful World** (1988), **A Horse Called Music** (1989), **Born for Trouble** (1989), **Highwayman 2*** (1990, all Columbia) US#79; **Who'll Buy My Memories? — The IRS Tapes** (1991, private pressing); **Clean Shirt**++ (1991, Epic) US#193; **Across the Borderline** (1993, Columbia) US#75; **Moonlight Becomes You** (1994, Justice) US#188; **Six Hours in Pedernales** (1994, One Step); **The Healing Hands of Time** (1994) US#103, **Peace in the Valley** (1994), **The Road Goes on Forever*** (1995, all Liberty); **Augusta**** (1995, Semaphore); **Just One Love** (1995, Justice); **Spirit** (1996, Island); **Nowhere Road for the Outlaws: 20th Anniversary**++ (1996, RCA). COMPILATIONS: **What Can You Do to Me Now** (1975) US#196, **Before His Time** (1977) US#78, **Sweet Memories** (1979) US#154, **Willie Nelson and Danny Davis with the Nashville Brass***** (1980) US#150, **The Minstrel Man** (1981, all RCA) US#148; **Greatest Hits and Some That Will Be** (1981, Columbia) p US#27; **My Own Way** (1984, RCA) US#182; **Half-Nelson** (1985, Columbia) g US#178; **Nite Life — Greatest Hits and Rare Tracks, 1959–1971** (1992, Rhino); **45 Original Tracks — The Complete Liberty Recordings** (1993, EMI); **A Classic and Unreleased Col-

lection** (1994, Rhino); **Super Hits** (1995, Columbia) US#193; **Revolutions of Time: The Journey, 1975–1993** (1995, Sony). HIT VERSIONS: *Angel Flying Too Close to the Ground* Bob Dylan on B-side of *Union Sundown* (1983) UK#90, *Congratulations* Faron Young (1961) C&W#28, *Crazy* Patsy Cline (1961) C&W#2 US#9, re-issued (1990) UK#14/Ray Price (1967) C&W#73/Linda Ronstadt (1976) C&W#6; *Family Bible* Claude Gray (1960) C&W#10, *Funny How Time Slips Away* Billy Walker (1961) C&W#23/Jimmy Elledge (1962) US#22/ Johnny Tillotson (1963) US#50/Joe Hinton (1964) US#13/Ace Cannon (1966) US#102/Narvel Felts (1975) C&W#12/Dorothy Moore (1976) R&B#7 US#58/Spinners (1982) R&B#43 US#67; *Hello Walls* Faron Young (1961) C&W#1 US#12/Ben Colder as *Hello Wall #2* (1963) C&W#30 US#131; *I Gotta Get Drunk* Joe Carson (1963) C&W#27, *It's Not Supposed to Be That Way* Steve Young (1977) C&W#84/ Pam Rose (1980) C&W#52; *Nite Life* Ray Price (1963) C&W#28/B.J. Thomas (1986) C&W#59; *Permanently Lonely* Timi Yuro (1964) US#130, *Pretty Paper* Roy Orbison (1963) US#15 UK#6, *Three Days* Faron Young (1962) C&W#7, *Touch Me* Howdy Glenn (1977) C&W#62. With: * Johnny Cash/Waylon Jennings/Kris Kristofferson, ** Don Cherry, *** Hank Cochran, **** Shirley Collie, ***** Danny Davis, + Merle Haggard, ++ Waylon Jennings, +++ Jackie King, ++++ Kris Kristofferson, +++++ Kris Kristofferson/Brenda Lee/Dolly Parton, ^ Brenda Lee, ^^ Darrell McCall, ^^^ Roger Miller, ^^^^ Tracy Nelson, Webb Pierce, ~ Mary Kay Place, ~~ Ray Price, ~~~ Leon Russell, ~~~~ Hank Snow, ~~~~~ Faron Young. Co-writer: [i] Waylon Jennings. (*See also under* Hank COCHRAN, Merle HAGGARD.)

696. NESMITH, Michael (b. December 30, 1942, Houston, TX) Pop guitarist and vocalist. A session musician who came to prominence as a member of the manufactured 1960s pop group the Monkees, composing the band's hit *Listen to the Band* (1969) US#63. ALBUMS: **The Monkees** (1966) g US#1 UK#1; **More of the Monkees** (1967) g US#1 UK#1, **Headquarters** (1967) g US#1 UK#2, **Pisces, Aquarius, Capricorn & Jones Ltd.** (1967) g US#5, **The Birds, the Bees and the Monkees** (1968) g US#3, **Head** ost (1968) US#45, **Instant Replay** (1969) US#32, **The Monkees Present** (1969, all Colpix) US#100; **Justus** (1997). COMPILATIONS: **Greatest Hits** (1969, Colpix) US#89; **Greatest Hits** (1976) p US#8, **Then and Now-The Best of the Monkees** (1986) p US#21, **Hey Hey It's the Monkees' Greatest Hits** (1989, both Arista) UK#12; **The Greatest Hits** (1997, Warner/ESP) UK#15. Nesmith quit the group in 1968, and released solo singles as Michael Blessing, before recording an album as the

Wichita Train Whistle, **Mike Nesmith Presents/ The Wichita Train Whistle Sings** (1968, Dot) US#144. He subsequently formed his country influenced First National Band for a series of solo efforts. CHART COMPOSITIONS: *Joanne* (1970) US#21, *Silver Moon* (1971) US#42, *Nevada Fighter* (1971) US#70, *Rio* (1977) UK#28. ALBUMS: **Magnetic South** (1970) US#143, **Loose Salute** (1971) US#159; **Nevada Fighter** (1971), **Tantamount to Treason** (1972), **And the Hits Just Keep Comin'** (1972), **Pretty Much Your Standard Ranch Stash** (1973, all RCA); **The Prison** (1975), **From an Engine to a Photon Wing** (1977), **Live at the Palais** (1978), **Infinite Rider on the Big Dogma** (1979, all Pacific Arts) US#151. COMPILATIONS: **Best of Michael Nesmith** (1972, RCA); **Compilation** (1977, Pacific Arts); **The Newer Stuff** (1990), **The Older Stuff** (1990, both Awareness), **Complete** (1994, Pacific Arts). HIT VERSIONS: *Different Drum* Stone Poneys (1967) US#13, *Mary, Mary* Run-D.M.C. (1988) US#75, *Some of Shelly's Blues* Nitty Gritty Dirt Band (1971) US#64/Maines Brothers Band (1985) C&W#72.

697. NEWBURY, Mickey (b. Milton S. Newbury Jr., May 19, 1940, Houston, TX) C&W guitarist and vocalist. A country-pop songwriter who first began composing at high school, and sang tenor in various harmony quartets. Newbury's southern influenced ballads have principally appealed to male country singers, and as a recording artist himself, he has never been able to better his quite magnificent *An American Trilogy* (1972), a distinctive arrangement of three traditional American civil war songs, *Dixieland, Battle Hymn of the Republic* and *All My Trials*. CHART COMPOSITIONS: *An American Trilogy* (1972) US#26 UK#42, new version (1988) C&W#93; *Sunshine* (1973) C&W#53 US#87, *Heaven Help the Child* (1973) US#103, *Hand Me Another of Those* (1977) C&W#94, *Gone to Alabama* (1978) C&W#94, *Looking for the Sunshine* (1979) C&W#82, *Blue Sky Shinin'* (1979) C&W#81. ALBUMS: **Harlequin Melodies** (1968, RCA); **Looks Like Rain** (1969, Mercury); **Frisco Mabel Joy** (1971, Elektra) US#58; **Mickey Newbury Sings His Own** (1972, RCA); **Heaven Help the Child** (1973) US#173, **Live at Montezuma/Looks Like Rain** (1973), **I Came to Hear Music** (1974), **Lovers** (1975, all Elektra) US#172; **Rusty Tracks** (1977), **His Eye on the Sparrow** (1978), **The Sailor** (1979, all Hickory); **After All These Years** (1981, Mercury); **In a New Age** (1988, Airborne). COMPILATIONS: **Funny, Familiar, Forgotten Feelings** (1968, RCA); **Sweet Memories** (1986, MCA); **Best of Mickey Newbury** (1992, Collectibles). HIT VERSIONS: *American Trilogy, An* Elvis Presley (1972) US#66

UK#8, *Are My Thoughts with You?* Kenny Rogers & the First Edition (1968) US#119, *Baby's Not Home* Roy Head (1974) C&W#66, *Funny, Familiar, Forgotten Feelings* Don Gibson (1967) C&W#8/Tom Jones (1967) US#49 UK#7; *How I Love Them Old Songs* Jim Ed Brown (1972) C&W#57/Carl Smith (1970) C&W#20/Danny Davis & the Nashville Brass (1977) C&W#91; *I Still Love You (After All These Years)* Tompall & the Glaser Brothers (1982) C&W#28, *If You Ever Get to Houston (Look Me Down)* Don Gibson (1977) C&W#16, *Just Dropped In (To See What Condition My Condition Was In)* First Edition (1968) US#5, *Love Look at Us Now* Johnny Rodriguez (1980) C&W#29, *Mister, Can't You See* [i] Buffy Sainte-Marie (1972) US#38, *She/He Even Woke Me Up to Say Goodbye* Jerry Lee Lewis (1969) C&W#2/Lynn Anderson (1971) C&W#54/Ronnie Milsap (1975) C&W#15; *Sweet Memories* Don Gibson & Dottie West (1969) C&W#32/Willie Nelson (1979) C&W#4/Andy Williams (1968) US#75; *Swiss Cottage Place* Jerry Wallace (1969) C&W#12, *When Do We Stop Starting Over* Don Gibson (1977) C&W#67, *Why You Been Gone So Long* Johnny Darrell (1969) C&W#17/Jerry Lee Lewis (1983) C&W#69/Brenda Lee (1986) C&W#50; *You Only Live Once (In a While)* Glenn Barber (1974) C&W#65. Co-writer: [i] Townes Van Zandt.

698. NEWMAN, Randy (b. Randolph Newman, November 28, 1944, New Orleans, LA) Rock and film pianist, vocalist. The devil's advocate of the popular song, who incorporates aspects of Stephen Foster and Noel Coward in his sardonic, satirical compositions about intense, neurotic characters. Newman once said of his material, "A lot of people I write about are insensitive or a little crazy." The Newman family lived in Louisiana, Mississippi and Alabama, before settling in Los Angeles, California. His three uncles, Alfred, Emil and Lionel Newman, were all successful Oscar winning Hollywood composers, and as a boy, Newman had watched Alfred conducting full orchestras on the 20th Century–Fox sound stage. By the age of seven he had learned the piano, and he began writing songs in his teens, later commenting, "I was always going to be a musician." After graduating in music from UCLA, he released the single *Golden Gridiron Boy* (1962), a typically early example of his peculiar twist on the boy-meets-girl theme. After securing a publishing deal at Metric Music, Newman served the same songwriting apprenticeship as Jackie De Shannon, David Gates and Leon Russell, working as a full-time songwriter on a salary of fifty dollars a week in advance of royalties. In 1964 he contributed to his first film soundtrack, "The Lively Set," and in 1966 he scored the television series "Peyton Place." His compositions were given further prominence when Alan Price recorded half a dozen of them in a clever, mock vaudeville style. As a staff arranger at Warner Brothers Records, Newman embarked on a solo career, his eponymous debut album in 1968 being a wholly uncommercial record, that nevertheless introduced the music of a true innovator. Contrasting gloomy lyrics with jolly tunes, Newman's album **Good Old Boys** (1974), was a loosely based song cycle about the American south. He has described songwriting as hard work, and said, "When I'm walking into a room with the piano in it my legs begin to get heavy and I feel pressure…I've made up schedules for myself since I was eight years old, but I haven't followed one of them." **Little Criminals** (1977), was written on a nine-to-five basis in a rented office in downtown Los Angeles, and became his most commercially successful album, featuring the million selling single *Short People*, a barbed attack on ignorance and prejudice that unfortunately ended up being taken at face value. "Maybe I was right about them all along," quipped Newman at the time, "I'm surprised at the reaction, and am working on an even bigger insult." In 1991, he toured America with the Boston Pops Orchestra performing his film music. There have been three cabarets of his material, "Maybe I'm Doing It Wrong" (1982), "The Middle of Nowhere" (1988), and "Roll with the Punches — The Songs of Randy Newman" (1996), alongside two complete albums of his songs, **Nilsson Sings Newman** (1970, RCA), and Mathilde Santing's **Texas Girl and Pretty Boy — The Songs of Randy Newman** (1993, Sony). CHART COMPOSITIONS: *Short People* (1978) g US#2, *Rider in the Rain* (1978) C&W#78, *The Blues* with Paul Simon (1983) US#54, *I Love L.A.* (1983) US#102, *It's Money That Matters* (1988) US#60. ALBUMS: **Randy Newman** (1968), **12 Songs** (1970), **Live** (1971) US#191, **Sail Away** (1972) US#163, **Good Old Boys** (1974, all Reprise) US#36; **Little Criminals** (1977) g US#9, **Born Again** (1979, all Warner Brothers) US#41; **Ragtime** ost (1981, Elektra) US#134; **Trouble in Paradise** (1983) US#64, **The Natural** ost (1984), **Parenthood** ost (1989), **Awakenings** ost (1991, all Warner Brothers); **Land of Dreams** (1988) US#80, **The Paper** ost (1994), **Faust** (1995, all Reprise). COMPILATION: **Lonely at the Top** (1987, Warner Brothers). HIT VERSIONS: *Anyone Who Knows What Love Is (Will Understand)* Irma Thomas (1964) US#52, *I Don't Want to Hear It Anymore* Jerry Butler (1964) US#95, also on B-side of *I Stand Accused* (1964) US#61/P.J. Proby on B-side *Let the Water Run Down* (1965) UK#19/Dusty Springfield (1969) US#105, also on B-side of *The Windmills of Your Mind* (1969) US#31; *I Think It's Going to Rain Today* UB40 (1980) UK#6, *I'll Be Home*

Vikki Carr (1971) US#96, *I've Been Wrong Before* Cilla Black (1965) UK#17, *Just One Smile* Gene Pitney (1966) US#64 UK#8, *Living Without You* Manfred Mann's Earth Band (1972) US#69, *Love Story* Peggy Lee (1970) US#105, *Mama Told Me Not to Come* Eric Burdon & the Animals on B-side of *Help Me Girl* (1966) US#29 UK#14/Three Dog Night (1970) g US#1 UK#3/Wilson Pickett (1972) R&B#16 US#99; *My Old Kentucky Home* Osborne Brothers (1970) C&W#69/Johnny Cash (1975) C&W#42; *Nobody Needs Your Love* Gene Pitney (1966) UK#2, *Sail Away* Sam Neely (1977) US#84, *Simon Smith and the Amazing Dancing Bear* Alan Price (1967) UK#4, *Somebody's Waiting* Gene McDaniels on B-side of *Spanish Lace* (1962) US#31, *They Tell Me It's Summer* Fleetwoods on B-side of *Lovers By Night, Strangers By Day* (1962) US#36.

699. NICHOLS, Horatio (b. Lawrence Wright, February 15, 1888, Leicester; d. May 19, 1964, London, both England) Stage composer, pianist and arranger. A songwriter and publisher who was the founder of Britain's Tin Pan Alley in Denmark Street, London. Born into the music business, Nichols' father was a music teacher who taught his son the violin, piano and banjo. At the age of seventeen he wrote his first song *Down By the Stream*, after which he performed and sold his compositions from a market stall, while also buying the copyrights to such million sellers as *Don't Go Down the Mine Daddy* (1906). Nichols achieved his first hit with the patriotic *Coronation Waltz* (1910), and thereafter specialized in lovelorn ballads, which he wrote under a number of pseudonyms, ultimately writing over five hundred of them. Aside from his massive publishing empire, Nichols also co-founded the music paper Melody Maker, and produced the annual Blackpool revue "On with the Show" (1924), which ran for thirty-two years. Nichols is famous for once having promoted his song *Sahara* (1924), by riding a camel round Piccadilly Circus in London. Some of his most popular songs were *Blue Eyes* [v] (1916), *Heart of a Rose* [iii] (1918), *Omaha* [iii] (1919), *Playthings* [iii] (1921), *Babette* [ix] and *Bouquet (I Shall Always Think of You)* [ix] (both 1925); *Mistakes* [vi] (1928), *Bathing in the Sunshine* [iv] (1931), *A Bedtime Story* [vii] and *Liszt, Chopin and Mendelssohn* [vii] (both 1932), *Let's All Go to the Music Hall* [i] (1934), *Delyse* [iv] (1937), *The Badge from Your Coat* [viii] and *Down Forget-Me-Not Lane* [ii] (both 1941). HIT VERSIONS: *Among My Souvenirs* [vi] Roger Wolf Khan (1928) US#12/Revelers (1928) US#10/Ben Selvin (1928) US#3/Paul Whiteman (1928) US#1/Connie Francis (1960) R&B#10 US#7 UK#11/Marty Robbins (1976) C&W#1. Co-writers: [i] Ralph Butler/Harry Tilsley, [ii] Charlie Chester/Reg Morgan, [iii] Worton David, [iv] Joseph Gilbert,

[v] Fred Godfrey, [vi] Edgar Leslie, [vii] Harry Leon/ Leo Towers, [viii] Annette Mills, [ix] Ray Morelle.

700. NICKS, Stevie

(b. Stephanie Nicks, May 26, 1948, Phoenix, AZ) Rock vocalist. A singer-songwriter who first recorded with the guitarist Lindsay Buckingham, releasing the album **Buckingham Nicks** (1971, Polydor). As a member of Fleetwood Mac between 1974–1990, Nicks was responsible for the band's hits *Rhiannon* (1976) US#11, re-issued (1978) UK#46; *Dreams* (1977) US#1 UK#24, *Sara* (1980) US#7 UK#37, *Sisters of the Moon* (1980) US#86, *Fireflies* (1981) US#60, *Gypsy* (1982) US#12 UK#46, and *Seven Wonders* [v] (1987) US#19 UK#56. She has also enjoyed the most successful solo career of any former Fleetwood Mac member. CHART COMPOSITIONS: *Leather and Lace* with Don Henley (1982) US#6, *Edge of Seventeen (Just Like the White Winged Dove)* (1982) US#11, *After the Glitter Fades* (1982) C&W#70 US#32, *Stand Back* [iv] (1983) US#5, *If Anyone Falls* [v] (1983) US#14, *Nightbird* [v] (1984) US#33, *I Can't Wait* [ii] (1986) US#16 UK#54, re-issued (1991) UK#47; *Has Anyone Ever Written Anything for You* [iii] (1986) US#60, *Rooms on Fire* [i] (1989) US#16, *Maybe Love Will Change Your Mind* (1994) US#57 UK#42. ALBUMS: **Belladonna** (1981) p US#1 UK#11, **The Wild Heart** (1983) p US#5 UK#28, **Rock a Little** (1985) p US#12 UK#30, **The Other Side of the Mirror** (1989) g US#10, **Street Angel** (1994, all Modern) US#45 UK#16. COMPILATION: **Timespace — The Best of Stevie Nicks** (1991, Modern) g US#30 UK#15. Co-writers: [i] Rick Nowells, [ii] Rick Nowells/Eris Pressly, [iii] Ken Olsen, [iv] Prince, [v] Sandy Stewart. (*See also under* Christine McVIE.)

701. NIELSEN, Rick

(b. December 22, 1946, Rockford, IL) Rock guitarist and vocalist. After performing in the band Fuse, which recorded the album **Fuse** (1969, Epic), Nielsen formed the considerably more successful pop-rock group Cheap Trick. CHART COMPOSITIONS: *I Surrender* (1978) US#62, *I Want You to Want Me* (1979) US#7 UK#29, *Dream Police* (1979) US#26, *Voices* (1980) US#32, *Way of the World* (1980) UK#73, *Everything Works If You Let It* (1980) US#44, *Stop This Game* [iii] (1980) US#48, *If You Want My Love* (1982) US#45 UK#57, *She's Tight* (1982) US#65, *Tonight It's You* [i] (1985) US#44, *Ghost Town* [ii] (1988) US#33, *Can't Stop Falling into Love* (1990) US#12. ALBUMS: **Cheap Trick** (1977), **In Color** (1977) g US#73, **Heaven Tonight** (1978) g US#48, **At Budokan** (1979) p US#4 UK#29, **Dream Police** (1979) p US#6 UK#41, **Found All the Parts** (1980) US#39, **All Shook Up** (1980) g US#24, **One on One** (1982)

p US#39 UK#95, **Next Position Please** (1983) US#61, **Standing on the Edge** (1985) US#35, **The Doctor** (1986) US#115, **Lap of Luxury** (1988) p US#16, **Busted** (1990, all Epic) US#48; **Woke Up with a Monster** (1994, Warner Brothers) US#123; **Cheap Trick** (1997, Red Ant). COMPILATION: **Greatest Hits** (1991, Epic) US#174. Co-writers: [i] J. Brandt/M. Radice/J. Zander/Robin Zander (b. January 23, 1953, Rockford, IL), [ii] Diane Warren, [iii] Robin Zander.

702. Nilsson

(b. Harry Edward Nelson, III, June 15, 1941, Brooklyn, NY; d. January 15, 1994, Los Angeles, CA) Pop vocalist. An esoteric, off-beat composer and song interpreter, who was blessed with a sadly under-utilized three octave voice. Nilsson's career was one of occasional brilliance and serious under-achievement. His own compositions were flippant, charming and nonchalant songs in a style that drew on vaudeville, music hall and Tin Pan Alley. Nilsson's grandparents had been circus performers, and he was raised by his mother in California. In 1967 he worked as a computer programmer for the Security First National Bank, and in his spare time learned the guitar and piano in order to perform in clubs. He issued a number of unsuccessful solo singles during the 1960s, and also sang radio commercials, before the producer Phil Spector selected two of his tunes for the Ronettes and the Modern Folk Quartet, shortly after which, Nilsson signed to RCA Records. When John Lennon heard his versions of the Beatles' *She's Leaving Home* and *You Can't Do That*, he became a fan and eventual friend. Nilsson also composed for a number of films, including "The Telephone" (1988), and the television theme "The Courtship of Eddie's Father." His album **A Little Touch of Schmilsson in the Night** (1973), was a classy selection of sentimental torch songs from the 1930s and 1940s. In his later years, Nilsson headed an unsuccessful television and film company, and published the children's book "The Boy Who Knew Everything" (1988). In 1992, he began rehearsals for his first ever live dates, but was hospitalized in February, 1993, following a heart attack. Nilsson never fully recovered his health, and he died in his sleep the following year, two days after completing the recording of his first album of new material since 1976. He is best remembered for singing two songs that he did not compose, *Everybody's Talkin'* and *Without You*. George Tipton recorded his compositions as **Nilsson By Tipton** (1970, Warner Brothers). CHART COMPOSITIONS: *I Guess the Lord Must Be in New York City* (1969) US#34, *Me and My Arrow* (1971) US#34, *Coconut* (1972) US#8 UK#42, *Jump into the Fire* (1972) US#27, *Spaceman* (1972) US#23, *Remember (Christmas)* (1972) US#53, *Daybreak*

(1974) US#39, *All I Think About Is You* (1977) US#43. ALBUMS: **Pandemonium Shadow Song** (1967), **Aerial Ballet** (1968), **Skidoo** ost (1968), **Harry** (1969) US#120, **The Point** ost (1970) US#25 UK#46, **Nilsson Sings Newman** (1970), **Nilsson Schmilsson** (1972) g US#3 UK#4, **Son of Schmilsson** (1972) g US#12 UK#41, **A Little Touch of Schmilsson in the Night** (1973) US#46 UK#20, **Son of Dracula** ost (1974) US#106, **Pussy Cats** (1974) US#60, **Duit on Mon Dei** (1975) US#141, **Sandman** (1976) US#111, **That's the Way It Is** (1976) US#158, **Knnillssonn** (1977, all RCA) US#108; **The Point** oc (1977, MCA); **Night After Night** (1979, Polydor); **Flash Harry** (1980, Mercury); **Popeye** ost (1980, Boardwalk) US#115. COMPILATIONS: **Spotlight on Nilsson** (1967, Tower); **Aerial Pandemonium Ballet** (1971, RCA) US#149; **Early Tymes** (1977, Springboard); **Greatest Hits** (1978) US#140, **Songwriter** (1987), **A Touch More Schmilsson in the Night** (1988), **Without Her, Without You — The Very Best of Nilsson, Volume 1** (1990), **Lullaby in Ragtime — The Best of Nilsson, Volume 2** (1992), **Personal Best: The Harry Nilsson Anthology** (1995, all RCA); **Nilsson '62 — The Debut Sessions** (1995, Retro). HIT VERSIONS: *Don't Leave Me* Robert John (1968) US#108, *I Guess the Lord Must Be in New York City* Sagittarius (1969) US#135, *One* Three Dog Night (1969) g US#5, *Puppy Song, The* David Cassidy (1973) UK#1, *Story of Rock 'n' Roll, The* Turtles (1968) US#48, *Ten Little Indians* Yardbirds (1967) US#96, *Without Her* Herb Alpert & the Tijuana Brass (1969) US#63 UK#36.

703. NOBLE, Ray (b. Raymond Stanley Noble, December 17, 1903, Brighton; d. April 2, 1978, London, both England) Pop composer, pianist, bandleader and arranger. The leader of the most successful pre-war British dance band and orchestra, who lived in America from 1936, where he charted over fifty singles between 1931–1949. Noble was also the composer of some extremely successful romantic ballads, and he achieved his first success with *Nobody's Fool But Your Own* (1928). After studying the classical piano, Noble became an arranger for Jack Payne during the 1920s, and later the musical director at HMV Records in 1929, where he recorded dance music. During the late 1930s, Noble was a musical director in Hollywood, where he wrote material for such films as "Princess Charming" (1934), "The Big Broadcast of 1936" and "Brewster's Millions" (both 1936). CHART COMPOSITIONS: *Love Is the Sweetest Thing* (1933) US#1, *Love Locked Out* [ii] (1934) US#18, *The Very Thought of You* (1934) US#1, *The Touch of Your Lips* (1936) US#12, *I Hadn't Anyone 'Till You* (1938) US#4. ALBUMS:

Ray Noble Orchestra, 1935–1936 (1978, London); **Ray Noble and Al Bowlly, Volumes 1 to 6** (1979), **Ray Noble's Encores, Volumes 1 to 6** (1979, all Everest); **Ray and Joe Haymes, 1935** (1979, Aircheck); **Dinner Music** (1982, Golden Era); **Goodnight Sweetheart** (1983, President); **The HMV Sessions** (1984, Retrospect); **We Danced All Night** (1984, BMG); **Notable Noble** (1985, Retrospect); **Over on the Sunny Side** (1986, Submarine); **The 1930s, Volume 2** (1988, Aircheck). HIT VERSIONS: *By the Fireside* [i] George Olsen (1932) US#10, *Cherokee* Charlie Barnet (1938) US#15, *Goodnight, Sweetheart, Goodnight* [i] Guy Lombardo (1931) US#1, *I Found You* [i] Frankie Laine (1968) US#118, *I Hadn't Anyone 'Till You* Tommy Dorsey (1938) US#10, *Love Is the Sweetest Thing* Hal Kemp (1933) US#14/Peter Skellern (1978) UK#60; *Love Locked Out* [ii] Ambrose (1934) US#10, *Touch of Your Lips, The* Bing Crosby (1936) US#4/Hal Kemp (1936) US#3; *Very Thought of You, The* Bing Crosby (1934) US#11/Vaughn Monroe (1944) US#19/Luis Russell (1946) R&B#3/Arthur Pryscock (1960) R&B#19/Rick Nelson (1964) US#26/Tony Bennett (1965) UK#21/Albert King (1979) R&B#87/Natalie Cole (1992) UK#71. Co-writers: [i] James Campbell/Reginald Connelly/Rudy Vallee, [ii] Max Kester.

704. NOLAN, Bob (b. Robert Charles Nobles, April 1, 1908, New Brunswick, Canada; d. June 15, 1980, Los Angeles, CA) C&W vocalist. An influential country songwriter, who had been a traveling tent show singer before founding the Rocky Mountaineers, which performed three-part harmony yodels with guitar accompaniment. Nolan is best remembered for his work with the trio the Sons of the Pioneers, of which he was a member until 1949. CHART COMPOSITIONS: *Cool Water* (1941) C&W#4 US#25, new version with Vaughn Monroe (1948) C&W#7 US#9; *Tumblin' Tumbleweeds* (1934) US#13, re-issued (1948) C&W#11. ALBUMS: **Favorite Cowboy Songs** (1956), **Wagons West** (1958), **Lure of the West** (1959), **Down Memory Lane** (1961), **Campfire Favorites** (1963), **South of the Border** (1966, all RCA); **Cowboy Country** (1984, Bear Family); **20 of the Best** (1985, RCA); **Cool Water, Edition 1, 1945–1946** (1987), **A Hundred and Sixty Acres, Edition 3, 1946–1947** (1987), **Riders in the Sky, Edition 4 1947–1949** (1987, all Bear Family); **The Standard Radio Transcriptions, 1934–1935** (1987, Outlaw); **1940** (1988, JEMF). HIT VERSIONS: *Cool Water* Nellie Lutcher (1948) R&B#7/Frankie Laine (1955) UK#2/Jack Scott (1960) US#85/Blue Belles (1963) US#127; *Tumbling Tumbleweeds* Gene Autry (1935) US#10/Glen Gray (1939) US#17/Bing Crosby (1940) US#12/Slim Whitman (1956) UK#9/Billy Vaughn (1958) US#30/

Roger Williams (1957) US#60. (*See also under* Tim SPENCER.)

705. NOVELLO, Ivor (b. David Ivor Davies, January 15, 1893, Cardiff, Wales; d. March 6, 1951, London, England) Film and stage composer, pianist and producer. A composer, actor and author who, in 1947, was a founder member of the Songwriters' Guild. Novello's contribution to popular song has been recognized by a prestigious yearly award for songwriting that was created in his name. He was given piano lessons in his childhood, and later attended Magdalene College, Cambridge, as a choral scholar, where he developed an interest in musical theatre. In 1910, he published his first song *Spring of the Year*. One of his earliest successes was *'Till the Boys Come Home*, which is also known as *Keep the Home Fires Burning* [i] (1914). In collaboration with the lyricist Fred Weatherly, Novello composed material for the musicals "Theodore and Co." (1916), "Arlette" (1917), "Who's Hooper?" (1919), and "A to Z" (1921). Although he principally wrote operetta material, during the 1920–1930s, Novello also worked with the lyricist Christopher Hassall on the musicals "Glamorous Night" (1935) and "The Dancing Years" (1939). In 1945, he composed the show "Perchance to Dream" in its entirety. Some of his best known songs were *And Her Mother Came Too* by Jack Buchanan (1921), *Fold Your Wings, Shine Through My Dreams* [ii] and *Glamorous Night* [ii] from the film "Glamorous Night" (1935), *I Can Give You the Starlight* [ii] from the film "The Dancing Years" (1939), and *Rose of England* [ii] from the show "Crest of the Wave" (1937). Novello died of thrombosis in 1951. ALBUM: **The Dancing Years** (1958, HMV). HIT VERSIONS: *Keep the Home Fires Burning* [i] James F. Harrison (1916) US#1/James F. Harrison & James Reed (1916) US#4/John McCormack (1917) US#4; *We'll Gather Lilacs in the Spring Again* Tommy Dorsey (1946) US#25/Simon May (1977) UK#49. Co-writers: [i] Lena Guilbert-Ford, [ii] Christopher Hassall.

706. NUGENT, Ted (b. December 13, 1948, Detroit, MI) Rock guitarist and vocalist. A heavy-metal stalwart for three decades, who first performed as a member of the group Amboy Dukes, which charted with the single *Journey to the Center of the Mind* [i] (1968) US#16. ALBUMS: **The Amboy Dukes** (1968) US#183, **Journey to the Center of the Mind** (1968) US#74, **Migration** (1969, all Mainstream); **Marriage on the Rocks/Rock Bottom** (1970) US#191, **Survival of the Fittest/Live** (1971, both Polydor) US#129; **Call of the Wild** (1974), **Tooth, Fang and Claw** (1974, both Discreet). Nugent quit the group in the mid–1970s for a solo ca-

reer. CHART COMPOSITIONS: *Dog Eat Dog* (1976) US#91, *Cat Scratch Fever* (1977) US#30, *Home Bound* (1978) US#70, *Yank Me, Crank Me* (1978) US#58, *Need You Bad* (1979) US#84, *Wango Tango* (1980) US#86, *Tied Up in Love* (1984) US#107. ALBUMS: **Ted Nugent** (1975) p US#28 UK#56, **Free for All** (1976) p US#24 UK#33, **Cat Scratch Fever** (1977) p US#17 UK#28, **Double Live Gonzo** (1978) p US#13 UK#47, **Weekend Warriors** (1978) p US#24, **State of Shock** (1979) g US#18, **Scream Dream** (1980) g US#13 UK#37, **Intensities in 10 Cities** (1981, all Epic) US#36 UK#75; **Nugent** (1982) US#51, **Penetrator** (1984) US#56, **Little Miss Dangerous** (1986) US#76, **If You Can't Lick 'Em…Lick 'Em** (1988) US#112, **Spirit of the Wild** (1996 all Atlantic) US#86. COMPILATIONS: **Great Gonzos!— The Best of Ted Nugent** (1982, Epic) US#140; **Out of Control** (1993, Sony). In tandem with his solo career, Nugent concurrently heads the hard rock group Damn Yankees. CHART COMPOSITIONS: *Coming of Age* (1990) US#60, *High Enough* [ii] (1991) US#3, *Come Again* [ii] (1991) US#50, *Where You Goin' Now* [ii] (1992) US#20, *Silence Is Broken* (1993) US#62. ALBUMS: **Damn Yankees** (1990) p US#13, **Don't Tread** (1992, both Warner Brothers) g US#22. Co-writers: [i] Steve Farmer, [ii] Jack and Tom.

707. NUMAN, Gary (b. Gary Anthony James Webb, March 8, 1958, London, England) Pop keyboard player and vocalist. A synthesizer performer who first appeared with his group Tubeway Army. CHART COMPOSITIONS: *Are "Friends" Electric?* (1979) US#105 UK#1, *Cars* (1979) US#9 UK#1, remixed as *Cars E Reg Mix* (1987) UK#16, re-issued (1993) UK#53, re-mixed (1996) UK#17; *Complex* (1979) UK#6, *We Are Glass* (1980) UK#5, *I Die: You Die* (1980) US#102 UK#6, *This Wreckage* (1981) UK#20, *She's Got Claws* (1981) UK#6, *Music for Chameleons* (1982) UK#19, *We Take Mystery (To Bed)* (1982) UK#9, *White Boys and Heroes* (1982) UK#20, *Warriors* (1983) UK#20, *Sister Surprise* (1983) UK#32, *Beserker* (1984) UK#32, *My Dying Machine* (1984) UK#66, *Change Your Mind* (1985) UK#17, *The Live EP* (1985) UK#27, *Your Fascination* (1985) UK#46, *Call Out the Dogs* (1985) UK#49, *Miracles* (1985) UK#49, *This Is Love* (1986) UK#28, *I Can't Stop* (1986) UK#27, *New Thing from London* (1986) UK#52, *I Still Remember* (1986) UK#74, *No More Lies* (1988) UK#34, *New Anger* (1988) UK#46, *America* (1988) UK#49, *I'm on Automatic* (1989) UK#44, *Heart* (1991) UK#43, *The Skin Game* (1992) UK#68, *Machine + Soul* (1992) UK#72. ALBUMS: **Tubeway Army** (1979) UK#14, **Replicas** (1979) US#124 UK#1, **The Pleasure Principal** (1979) US#16 UK#1, **Telekon** (1980) US#64 UK#1, **Living**

Ornaments, 1979–1980 (1981) UK#2, 1979 (1981) UK#47, 1980 (1981) UK#39, Dance (1981) US#167 UK#3, I. Assassin (1982) UK#8, Warriors (1983) UK#12, The Plan (1984, all Beggars Banquet) UK#29; Beserker (1984) UK#45, White Noise Live (1984) UK#29, The Fury (1985) UK#24, Strange Charm (1986, all Numa) UK#59; Metal Rhythm (1988, Illegal) UK#48; Automatic with Sharpe (1989, Polydor) UK#59; Skin Mechanic (1989) UK#55, Outland (1991, IRS) UK#39; Machine + Soul (1993, Numa) UK#42. COMPILATIONS: New Man Numan — The Best of Gary Numan and Tubeway Army (1982, TVR) UK#45; Exhibition (1987) UK#43, Best of Gary Numan, 1979–1983 (1993, both Beggars Banquet) UK#70; The Premier Hits (1996) UK#21, Story So Far (1996, Receiver).

708. NYRO, Laura (b. Laura Nigro, October 18, 1947, Bronx, NY; d. April 8, 1997, Danbury, CT) Rock pianist and vocalist. A singer-songwriter with an unforgettable soprano, whose uniquely feminine perspective resulted in compositions on subjects not normally associated with popular music. Nyro's early material blended folk, R&B and pop, and were often major hits when they were recorded in a more commercial style by other artists, resulting, on November 29, 1969, in three cover versions holding an American top ten position during the same week. Nyro began creating music from the age of eight, and attended Manhattan's High School of Music and Art, where she learned the piano and took opera vocal lessons. In 1965, she released her debut album **More Than a New Discovery**, which featured a selection of mini-melodramas, all of which were sung in a confessional style with an unrestrained passion. Nyro's odd musical meters and sophisticated time changes contrasted fully charged emotional battles with passages of whispered intimacies. **Eli and the Thirteenth Confession** (1968), was a magnificent urban blues song cycle about sin and salvation, and is the definitive study of a young girl's discovery of love and sex, while **New York Tendaberry** (1969), was an ambitious reflection on city life. **Christmas and the Beads of Sweat** (1970), introduced oriental themes on *Upstairs By a Chinese Lamp*, and militant feminism on *When I Was a Freeport and You Were the Main Drag*, but after a rapturous duet of R&B covers with Patti LaBelle on **Gonna Take a Miracle** (1971), Nyro married and retired to a small fishing community on the east coast. She recorded only intermittently thereafter, the highlight of her come-back years being the jazzy **Smile** (1976), which critic Allan Jones succinctly reviewed as "One of the most remarkable achievements of any artist working within the context of contemporary music." Nyro's career was cut dreadfully short when

she died from ovarian cancer at the age of forty-nine. CHART COMPOSITION: *Wedding Bell Blues* (1966) US#103. ALBUMS: **More Than a New Discovery** (1966, Verve Forecast) re-issued as **First Songs** (1973, Columbia) US#92; **Eli and the Thirteenth Confession** (1968) US#181, **New York Tendaberry** (1969) US#32, **Christmas and the Beads of Sweat** (1970) US#51, **Gonna Take a Miracle** (1971) US#46, **Smile** (1976) US#60, **Season of Lights — Laura Nyro in Concert** (1977) US#137, **Nested** (1978), **Mother's Spiritual** (1984, all Columbia) US#182; **Live at the Bottom Line** (1988, Cypress); **Walk the Dog and Light the Light** (1993, Columbia). COMPILATIONS: **Impressions** (1980, CBS); **Classics** (1991, Elite); **Stoned Soul Picnic — The Best of Laura Nyro** (1996, Columbia). HIT VERSIONS: *And When I Die* Blood, Sweat & Tears (1969) g US#2, *Blowing Away* 5th Dimension (1970) US#21, *Eli's Coming* Three Dog Night (1969) US#10, *Flim Flam Man* Barbra Streisand (1971) US#82, *Save the Country* 5th Dimension (1970) R&B#41 US#27/ Thelma Houston (1970) US#74; *Stoned Soul Picnic* 5th Dimension (1968) g R&B#2 US#3, *Stoney End* Peggy Lipton (1968) US#121/Barbra Streisand (1971) US#6 UK#27; *Sweet Blindness* 5th Dimension (1968) R&B#45 US#13, *Time and Love* Barbra Streisand (1971) US#51, *Wedding Bell Blues* 5th Dimension (1969) g R&B#23 US#1 UK#16.

709. OAKEY, Philip (b. October 2, 1955, Sheffield, England) Pop vocalist. The lead singer of the synthesizer based group the Human League. CHART COMPOSITIONS: *Holiday '80* [vi]/*Being Boiled* [vi] (1980) UK#56, *Empire State Human* [vi] (1980) UK#62, *Boys and Girls* (1981) UK#48, *The Sound of the Crowd* (1981) UK#12, *Love Action* [i] (1981) UK#3, *Open Your Heart* [iii] (1981) UK#6, *Don't You Want Me* [iv] (1981) g US#1 UK#1, re-mixed (1995) UK#16; *Being Boiled* [vi] (1982) UK#6, *Holiday '80* [vi] (1982) UK#46, *Mirror Man* [ii] (1982) US#30 UK#2, *(Keep Feeling) Fascination* [iii] (1983) R&B#56 US#8 UK#2, *The Lebanon* [iii] (1984) US#64 UK#11, *Life on Your Own* (1984) UK#16, *Louise* (1984) UK#13, *Heart Like a Wheel* (1990) US#32 UK#29, *Tell Me When* (1995) US#31 UK#6, *One Man in My Heart* (1995) UK#13, *Filling Up with Heaven* (1995) UK#36, *Stay with Me Tonight* (1996) UK#40. ALBUMS: **Reproduction** (1979) UK#49, **Travelogue** (1980) UK#16, **Dare** (1981) US#3 UK#1, **Love and Dancing** (1982) US#135 UK#3, **Hysteria** (1984) US#62 UK#3, **Crash** (1986) US#24 UK#7, **Romantic** (1990, all Virgin) UK#24; **Octopus** (1995, East West) UK#6. COMPILATIONS: **Fascination** (1983) US#30, **Greatest Hits** (1988, both Virgin) UK#3. Oakey has also recorded as a solo artist, in collaboration with Giorgio Moroder. CHART COMPOSITIONS: *Together in Electric Dreams* [v] (1984) UK#3, *Goodbye Bad Times* [v] (1985) UK#44. ALBUM: **Philip Oakey and Giorgio Moroder** (1985) UK#52. HIT VERSIONS: *Don't You Want Me* [iv] Farm (1992) UK#18. Co-writers: [i] Ian Burden (b. December 24, 1957, Sheffield, England), [ii] Ian Burden/Jo Callis (b. May 2, 1955, Glasgow, Scotland), [iii] Jo Callis, [iv] Jo Callis/Adrian Wright (b. Philip Adrian Wright, June 30, 1956, Sheffield, England), [v] Giorgio Moroder, [vi] Martyn Ware (b. May 19, 1956, Sheffield, England)/Ian Craig Marsh (b. November 11, 1956, Sheffield, England).

710. OCASEK, Ric (b. Richard Otcasek, March 23, 1949, Baltimore, MD) Pop guitarist, producer and vocalist. The lead singer and founder member of the new-wave group the Cars. CHART COMPOSITIONS: *Just What I Needed* (1978) US#27 UK#17, *My Best Friend's Girl* (1978) US#35 UK#3, *Good Times Roll* (1979) US#41, *Let's Go* (1979) US#14 UK#51, *It's All I Can Do* (1979) US#41, *Touch and Go* (1980) US#37, *Shake It Up* (1982) US#4, *Since You've Been Gone* (1982) US#41 UK#37, *You Might Think* (1984) US#7, *Magic* (1984) US#12, *Drive* (1984) p US#3 UK#5, re-entry (1985) UK#5; *Hello Again* (1984) US#20, *Why Can't I Have You?* (1985) US#33, *Tonight She Comes* (1986) US#7, *I'm Not the One* (1986) US#32, *You Are the Girl* (1987) US#17, *Strap Me In* (1987) US#85, *Coming Up You* (1988) US#74. ALBUMS: **The Cars** (1978) p US#18 UK#29, **Candy-O** (1979) p US#3 UK#30, **Panorama** (1980) p US#5, **Shake It Up** (1982) p US#9, **Heartbeat City** (1984) p US#3 UK#25, **Door to Door** (1987, all Elektra) g US#26 UK#72. COMPILATIONS: **Greatest Hits** (1985, Elektra) p US#12 UK#27; **Just What I Needed: The Cars Anthology** (1996), **Prototypes: Raw Hits and Rare Tracks** (1996, both Elektra/Rhino). Ocasek has also recorded as a solo artist. CHART COMPOSITIONS: *Something to Grab For* (1983) US#47, *Emotion in Motion* (1986) US#15, *True to You* (1986) US#75. ALBUMS: **Beatitude** (1983) US#28, **This Side of Paradise** (1986, both Geffen) US#31; **Fireball Zone** (1991), **Negative Theatre** (1993, both Warner Brothers). HIT VERSION: *Slip Away* Ian Lloyd (1979) US#50.

711. OCEAN, Billy (b. Leslie Sebastian Charles, January 21, 1950, Trinidad, West Indies) Pop vocalist and producer. A former tailor who was raised in England, and sung in the groups Shades of Midnight and Dry Ice, before recording solo sides as Joshua, Les Charles and Scorched Earth during the 1970s. As Billy Ocean, he enjoyed a decade's worth of R&B flavored pop hits. CHART COMPOSITIONS: *American Hearts* (1979) UK#54, *Are You*

Ready (1980) UK#42, *Night (Feel Like Getting Down)* (1981) R&B#7 US#103, *European/Caribbean Queen (No More Love on the Run)* [v] (1984) g R&B#1 US#1 UK#6, *Suddenly* [v] (1985) R&B#5 US#4 UK#4, *Mystery Lady* [vi] (1985) R&B#10 US#24 UK#49, *When the Going Gets Tough, the Tough Get Going* [iii] (1986) R&B#6 US#2 UK#1, *There'll Be Sad Songs (To Make You Cry)* [ii] (1986) R&B#1 US#1 UK#12, *Love Zone* [ii] (1986) R&B#1 US#10 UK#49, *Bittersweet* [ii] (1986) UK#44, *Love Is Forever* [ii] (1986) R&B#10 US#16 UK#34, *Get Outta My Dreams (Get into My Car)* [viii] (1988) R&B#1 US#1 UK#3, *Calypso Crazy* (1988) UK#35, *The Color of Love* [iv] (1988) R&B#10 US#17 UK#65, *License to Chill* [viii] (1989) US#32, *Everything's So Different Without You* [vii] (1993) R&B#91, *Pressure* (1993) UK#55. ALBUMS: **Nights (I Feel Like Getting Down)** (1981, GTO) US#152; **Inner Feeling** (1982), **Suddenly** (1984) p US#9, **Love Zone** (1986) p US#6 UK#2, **Tear Down These Walls** (1988) p US#18 UK#3, **Time to Move On** (1993, all Jive). COMPILATION: **Greatest Hits** (1989, Jive) p US#77 UK#4. HIT VERSION: *Who's Gonna Rock You* Nolans (1980) UK#12. Co-writers: [i] Wayne Brathwaite, [ii] Wayne Brathwaite/Barry Eastmond, [iii] Wayne Brathwaite/Barry Eastmond/Robert John Lange, [iv] Wayne Brathwaite/Barry Eastmond/J. Skinner, [v] Keith Diamond, [vi] Keith Diamond/James Woodley, [vii] R. Kelly, [viii] Robert John Lange.

712. OCHS, Phil (b. Philip David Ochs, December 19, 1940, El Paso, TX; d. April 9, 1976, Far Rockaway, NY) Folk guitarist and vocalist. A singer-songwriter in the folk-protest tradition, whose highly original compositions and themes of struggle have remained potently contemporary. Ochs' superb vocal diction and satirical, topical, political observations, were performed in a singing journalist style, very much influenced by Woody Guthrie. He attended military academy in Virginia, before studying journalism at Ohio State University in 1958. During the 1950s he developed a love of folk and country music, moving to New York in 1960, where he formed the Sundowners folk duo with Jim Glover. A regular solo performer and political activist on the Greenwich Village folk scene, Ochs' earliest recordings were subject to an unspoken radio ban on account of his left-wing politics. **Pleasures of the Harbor** (1967), was an attempt to create a more commercial album, and although somewhat fussy and over-arranged, it featured some of his best writing. By the deeply melancholic **Rehearsals for Retirement** (1969), Ochs had become increasingly frustrated by his poor record sales, and he returned to journalism for a while, before traveling extensively throughout Chile and Africa. In 1973, while still in

Africa, he was the subject of a mysterious and vicious assault, resulting in permanent damage to his vocal chords. The incident propelled Ochs into a downward spiral of drinking and depression, and in 1976, he took his own life at his sister's home. CHART COMPOSITION: *Outside of a Small Circle of Friends* (1968) US#118. ALBUMS: **All the News That's Fit to Sing** (1964), **I Ain't Marchin' Anymore** (1965), **Phil Ochs in Concert** (1966, all Elektra) US#149; **Pleasures of the Harbor** (1967) US#168, **Tape from California** (1968), **Rehearsals for Retirement** (1969) US#167, **Greatest Hits** (1970) US#194, **Gunfight at Carnegie Hall** (1971, all A&M). COMPILATIONS: **Chords of Fame** (1976, A&M); **Phil Ochs Sings** (1976), **Interviews with Phil Ochs — Broadside Ballads, Volume 11** (1976), **Broadside Tapes — Broadside Ballads, Volume 14** (1976, all Verve Folkways); **A Toast to Those Who Are Gone** (1988), **There and Now — Live in Vancouver, 1968** (1991, both Rhino); **American Troubadour** (1997, Chronicles); **Fantasies and Farewells** (1997, Rhino). HIT VERSIONS: *Flower Lady* Peter & Gordon on B-side of *Knight in Rusty Armor* (1966) US#15, *There But for Fortune* Joan Baez (1965) US#50 UK#8.

713. O'CONNOR, Sinead (b. December 12, 1966, Glenageary, Eire) Pop vocalist. A singer-songwriter with a distinctive vocal style, who has recorded in a variety of styles. CHART COMPOSITIONS: *Mandinka* (1988) UK#17, *The Emperor's New Clothes* (1990) US#60 UK#31, *Three Babies* (1990) UK#42, *My Special Child* (1991) UK#42, *Success Has Made a Failure of Our Home* [i] (1992) UK#18, *You Made Me the Thief of Your Heart* (1994) UK#42, *Thank You for Hearing Me* (1994) UK#13, *Haunted* with Shane McGowan (1995) UK#30, *Famine* (1995) UK#51. ALBUMS: **The Lion and the Cobra** (1988, Chrysalis) g US#36 UK#27; **I Do Not Want What I Haven't Got** (1990) p US#1 UK#1, **Am I Not Your Girl?** (1992) US#27 UK#6, **Universal Mother** (1994, all Ensign) US#36 UK#19. Co-writer: [i] Muins.

714. O'DAY, Alan (b. October 3, 1940, Los Angeles, CA) Pop guitarist and vocalist. A singer-songwriter whose best known composition is *Angie Baby*. CHART COMPOSITIONS: *Undercover Angel* (1977) g US#1 UK#43, *Started Out Dancing, Ended Up Making Love* (1977) US#73. ALBUM: **Appetizers** (1977, Pacific) US#109. HIT VERSIONS: *Angie Baby* Helen Reddy (1974) g US#1 UK#5, *Easy Evil* Travis Wammack (1975) US#72, *Flashback* [ii] 5th Dimension (1973) R&B#75 US#82, *Rock 'n' Roll Heaven* [i] Righteous Brothers (1974) US#3, *Train of Thought* Cher (1974) US#27. Co-writers: [i] J. Stevenson, [ii] A. Wayne.

715. O'DELL, Kenny (b. Kenneth Gist, Jr., c. 1940, OK) C&W guitarist and vocalist. A Nashville based singer-songwriter who has been a successful country tunesmith since the late 1960s. CHART COMPOSITIONS: *Happy with You* (1968) US#118, *You Bet Your Sweet, Sweet Love* (1974) C&W#58, *Soulful Woman* (1975) C&W#18, *My Honky Tonk Ways* (1975) C&W#37 US#105, *Let's Shake Hands and Come Out Lovin'* (1978) C&W#9, *As Long as I Can Wake Up in Your Arms* (1978) C&W#12, *Medicine Woman* (1979) C&W#32. HIT VERSIONS: *Beautiful People* Bobby Vee (1967) US#37, *Behind Closed Doors* Charlie Rich (1973) g C&W#1 US#15 UK#16, *I Take It on Home* Charlie Rich (1972) C&W#6, *Lizzie and the Rainman* Tanya Tucker (1975) C&W#1 US#37.

716. O'KEEFE, Danny (b. 1943, Wenatchee, WA) Rock guitarist and vocalist. A folk influenced singer-songwriter who first recorded for the local Jerden label, before becoming a member of the group Calliope, which released the album **Steamed** (1968, Buddah). Although O'Keefe has always existed on the margins of the pop mainstream, his sometimes excellent songs have been recorded by Jackson Browne and Judy Collins. CHART COMPOSITIONS: *The Road* (1972) US#102, *Good Time Charlie's Got the Blues* (1972) C&W#63 US#9, *Angel, Spread Your Wings* (1973) US#110. ALBUMS: **Introducing Danny O'Keefe** (1966, Panorama); **Danny O'Keefe** (1971, Cotillion); **O'Keefe** (1972, Signpost) US#87; **Breezy Stories** (1973, Atlantic) US#172; **So Long, Harry Truman** (1975, Atco); **American Roulette** (1977), **Global Blues** (1978, both Warner Brothers); **The Seattle Tapes** (1977), **Seattle Tapes, Volume 2** (1978, both FA); **The Day to Day** (1985, Coldwater). HIT VERSIONS: *Good Time Charlie's Got the Blues* Red Steagall (1979) C&W#41/Leon Russell (1984) US#63.

717. OLDHAM, Spooner (b. Lindon Oldham, America) R&B pianist. A country and gospel influenced R&B songwriter, who has often composed with Dan Penn. Oldham first recorded his own composition *Crazy Over You* for the Spar label in 1960, and during the 1960s, he recorded at his own Beautiful Sounds studio. In 1997, Oldham made a rare concert appearance with Penn in Brooklyn. HIT VERSIONS: *Cry Like a Baby* [ii] Aretha Franklin (1966) R&B#27 US#113/Box Tops (1968) g US#2 UK#15/Joe Stampley (1975) C&W#70/Kim Carnes (1980) US#44; *Dark End of the Street* [i] James Carr (1967) R&B#10 US#77/Archie Campbell & Lorene Mann (1968) C&W#24; *Do Right Woman-Do Right Man* [i] Aretha Franklin (1967) R&B#37, also on B-side of *I Never Loved a Man (The Way I Loved You)*

(1967) g R&B#1 US#9/Barbara Mandrell (1971) C&W#17 US#128; *I'm Your Puppet* [ii] James & Bobby Purify (1966) R&B#5 US#6, re-issued (1976) UK#12/Mickey Gilley (1988) C&W#49; *It Tears Me Up* [ii] Percy Sledge (1966) R&B#7 US#20, *Let's Do It Over* [ii] Joe Simon (1965) R&B#13, *Sweet Inspiration* [ii] Sweet Inspirations (1967) R&B#5 US#18, *Wish You Didn't Have to Go* [ii] James & Bobby Purify (1967) R&B#27 US#38. Co-writers: [i] Chips Moman, [ii] Dan Penn.

718. OLMAN, Abe (b. December 20, 1888, Cincinnati, OH; d. January 4, 1984, Rancho Mirage, CA) Tin Pan Alley composer. A successful music publisher and composer of a number of million selling songs. Olman's other contribution to the craft of songwriting was his formation of the National Academy of Popular Music, which created its own Songwriters Hall of Fame in 1969. HIT VERSIONS: *Down Among the Sheltering Palms* [i] Lyric Quartet (1915) US#3/Sammy Kaye (1949) US#14; *Oh Johnny, Oh Johnny, Oh!* [ii] American Quartet (1917) US#1/Elizabeth Brice (1917) US#4/Orrin Tucker (1939) US#2. Co-writers: [i] James Brockman, [ii] Ed Rose. (*See also under* Jack YELLEN.)

719. ORBISON, Roy (b. Roy Kelton Orbison, April 23, 1936, Vernon, TX; d. December 7, 1988, Nashville, TN) Pop guitarist and vocalist. One of the most endearing influences on numerous rock, pop and country artists—Orbison's music can be heard in the early sound of the Beatles and such contemporary country artists as Rodney Crowell. His compositions *Blue Bayou* [iv] and *Crying* [iv], have both garnered BMI three million radio play awards, and of his incredible voice, the ever modest Orbison said in 1988, "It's a gift and a blessing." He grew up in Wink, Texas, and at the age of six was given a guitar by his parents. Two years later, Orbison began performing on a local radio show, while listening to and absorbing the sounds of country, Mexican, flamenco and R&B. After studying geology he worked briefly for the El Paso Natural Oil Company. Orbison's first group was the Wink Westerners, and in 1955, as the Teen Kings, he recorded his songs *Ooby Dooby* and *Trying to Get to You*. A re-recorded *Ooby Dooby* for the Sun label, became Orbison's first hit. In 1957 he moved to Nashville, where he became a writer for the publishers Acuff-Rose, penning *Claudette* (1958) for the Everly Brothers. After signing to Monument Records, he achieved his first million seller with *Only the Lonely* [iv] (1961), an archetypal Orbison number about loneliness and disenchantment, with a powerful, immediate melody and melodramatic production values. Tragedy plagued Orbison during the 1960s, when he lost his first wife in a motorbike accident and two of his three sons in a fire at his home. In 1989, he teamed up with Bob Dylan, George Harrison, Tom Petty and Jeff Lynne as the group the Traveling Wilburys, but his revitalized career was cut short when he died of a heart attack in 1988. CHART COMPOSITIONS: *Ooby Dooby* (1956) C&W#59, *Up Town* (1960) C&W#72, *Only the Lonely* [iv] (1961) g R&B#14 US#2 UK#1, *Blue Angel* [iv] (1961) R&B#23 US#9 UK#11, *I'm Hurtin'* (1961) US#27, *Running Scared* [iv] (1962) g US#1 UK#9, *Crying* [iv] (1962) US#2 UK#25, re-issued (1992) UK#13, new version with K.D. Lang (1987) C&W#42, re-issued (1992) UK#13; *The Crowd* [iv] (1962) US#26 UK#40, *Leah* (1962) US#25, *Working for the Man* (1962) US#33 UK#50, *In Dreams* (1963) R&B#19 US#7 UK#6, new version (1987) C&W#75; *Blue Bayou* [iv] (1963) R&B#26 US#29 UK#5, *Oh, Pretty Woman* (1963) g US#1 UK#1, *Falling* (1963) US#22 UK#9, *It's Over* [i] (1963) US#9 UK#1, *Goodnight* [i] (1965) US#21 UK#14, *(Say) You're My Girl* [i] (1965) US#39 UK#23, *Ride Away* [i] (1965) US#25 UK#34, *Crawling Back* (1966) US#46 UK#19, *Breakin' Up Is Breakin' My Heart* (1966) US#3 UK#22, *Twinkle Toes* (1966) US#39 UK#29, *There Won't Be Many Coming Home* [i] (1966) UK#18, *So Good* (1966) US#132 UK#32, *Communication Breakdown* (1967) US#60, *Cry Softly Lonely One* (1967) US#52, *She* (1967) US#119, *Walk On* (1968) US#121 UK#39, *Heartache* (1968) US#104 UK#44, *My Friend* (1969) UK#35, *So Young* (1970) US#122, *Easy Way Out* (1979) US#109, *That Lovin' You Feelin' Again* [v] with Emmylou Harris (1980) C&W#6 US#15, *You Got It* [iii] (1989) US#9 UK#3, *She's a Mystery to Me* (1989) UK#27. ALBUMS: **Lonely and Blue** (1961) US#15, **Crying** (1962) US#21 UK#17, **In Dreams** (1963, all Monument) g US#35 UK#6; **Oh, Pretty Woman** (1963, London) UK#4; **There Is Only One Roy Orbison** (1964) US#55 UK#10, **The Orbison Way** (1966) US#128 UK#11, **Classic Roy Orbison** (1966) UK#12, **Roy Orbison Sings Don Gibson** (1967), **Cry Softly Lonely One** (1967), **Roy Orbison's Many Moods** (1968), **Hank Williams — The Roy Orbison Way** (1969, all MGM); **The Big O** (1970, London); **Memphis** (1973, MGM); **I'm Still in Love with You** (1976, Mercury); **Laminar Flow** (1979, Elektra); **Problem Child** (1984, Zu Zazz Z); **Class of '55** with Johnny Cash, Jerry Lee Lewis and Carl Perkins (1986, Smash) US#87; **Mystery Girl** (1988, Virgin) p US#5 UK#2. COMPILATIONS: **At the Roundhouse** (1960, Sun); **Greatest Hits** (1962, Monument) g US#13 UK#40; **The Exciting Sounds of Roy Orbison** (1964, Ember) UK#17; **More of Roy Orbison's Greatest Hits** (1964) US#19, **Early Orbison** (1964) US#101, **Orbisongs** (1964) US#136 UK#40, **Very Best of Roy Orbison** (1966) US#94,

Greatest Hits (1967) UK#40, **All-Time Greatest Hits** (1973, all Monument) UK#39; **Best of Roy Orbison** (1975, Arcade) UK#1; **Golden Days** (1981, Monument) UK#63; **In Dreams — The Greatest Hits** (1987, Virgin) US#95 UK#86; **For the Lonely — A Roy Orbison Anthology, 1956–1965** (1988, Rhino) US#110; **The Legendary Roy Orbison** (1988, Telstar) UK#1; **A Black and White Night Live** (1989, Virgin) US#123 UK#51; **Ballads — 22 Classic Songs** (1990, Telstar) UK#38; **King of Hearts** (1992) US#179 UK#23, **Very Best of Roy Orbison** (1996, both Virgin) UK#18. HIT VERSIONS: *As Long As I Can Dream* [vi] Expose (1993) US#55, *Baby's Gone* [ii] Bobby Wright (1974) C&W#55, *Bad Boy* Sue Thompson (1965) US#134, *Blue Bayou* [iv] Linda Ronstadt (1977) g C&W#2 US#3 UK#35, *Claudette* Everly Brothers (1958) C&W#15 US#30, also a double A-side with *All I Have to Do Is Dream* (1958) UK#1/Compton Brothers (1972) C&W#41; *Crying* [iv] Jay & the Americans (1966) US#25/Arlen Harden (1970) C&W#28/Ronnie Milsap (1976) C&W#79/Stephanie Winslow (1980) C&W#14/Don McLean (1981) C&W#6 US#5 UK#1; *Down the Line* Jerry Lee Lewis on B-side of *Breathless* (1958) C&W#4 US#7 UK#7, *It's Over* [i] Jimmie Rodgers (1966) US#37/Eddy Arnold (1968) C&W#4 US#74/Rex Allen, Jr. (1980) C&W#14; *Oh, Pretty Woman* Arlen Harden as *Lovin' Man* (1970) C&W#13/Van Halen (1982) US#12; *Only the Lonely* [iv] Sonny James (1969) C&W#1 US#92, *Running Scared* [iv] Fools (1981) US#50. Co-writers: [i] Bill Dees, [ii] Bobby Goldsboro, [iii] Jeff Lynne/Tom Petty, [iv] Joe Melson, [v] C. Price, [vi] Diane Warren. (*See also under* Johnny CASH, Rodney CROWELL, Bob DYLAN.)

720. ORZABEL, Roland (b. Roland Orzabal de la Quintana, August 22, 1961, Portsmouth, England) Pop guitarist, keyboard player and vocalist. The remaining half of the British synthesizer pop duo Tears for Fears, who first performed as a member of the group Graduate, releasing the album **Acting My Age** (1980, Precision). By 1995, Tears for Fears had sold nearly seventeen million records worldwide. CHART COMPOSITIONS: *Mad World* (1982) UK#3, *Change* (1983) US#73 UK#4, *Pale Shelter* [v] (1983) UK#5, re-issued (1985) UK#73; *The Way You Are* [v] (1983) UK#24, *Mother's Talk* [vi] (1984) UK#14, re-mixed (1986) US#27; *Shout* [vi] (1984) p R&B#56 US#1 UK#4, *Everybody Wants to Rule the World* [iv] (1985) g US#1 UK#2, re-recorded as *Everybody Wants to Run the World* [iv] (1986) UK#5; *Head Over Heels* [v] (1985) US#3 UK#12, *Suffer the Children* [v] (1985) UK#52, *I Believe (A Soulful Re-recording)* [v] (1985) UK#23, *Sowing the Seeds of Love* [ii] (1989) US#2 UK#5,

Woman in Chains (1989) US#36 UK#26, re-issued (1992) UK#57; *Advice for the Young at Heart* (1990) US#89 UK#36, *Johnny Panic and the Bible of Dreams** (1991) UK#70, *Laid So Low (Tears Roll Down)* [i] (1992) UK#17, *Breakdown* (1993) UK#20, *Cold* (1993) UK#72, *Break It Down Again* [iii] (1993) US#25, *Goodnight Song* (1993) US#125, *Raoul and the Kings of Spain* (1995) UK#31, *God's Mistake* (1996) UK#61. ALBUMS: **The Hurting** (1983) g US#73 UK#1, **Songs from the Big Chair** (1985, both Mercury) p US#1 UK#2; **The Seeds of Love** (1989, Fontana) p US#8 UK#1; **Elemental** (1993, Mercury) g US#45 UK#5; **Raoul and the Kings of Spain** (1995, Epic) US#79 UK#41. COMPILATION: **Tears Roll Down (The Hits, 1981–1992)** (1992, Mercury) p US#53 UK#2. As: * Johnny Panic & the Bible of Dreams. Co-writers: [i] David Bascombe, [ii] David Bascombe/Curt Smith (b. June 24, 1961, Bath, England), [iii] A. Griffiths, [iv] Chris Hughes/Ian Stanley, [v] Curt Smith, [vi] Ian Stanley.

721. O'SULLIVAN, Gilbert (b. Raymond Edward O'Sullivan, December 1, 1946, Waterford, Eire) Pop pianist and vocalist. A successful singer-songwriter during the 1970s, whose *Nothing Rhymed* (1970), was later interpreted in a folk style by Martin Carthy. O'Sullivan grew up in Swindon, England, where he learned to play the family piano, and later joined the teenage bands the Doodles and Rick's Blues. After studying graphic design, O'Sullivan began composing songs, two of his earliest efforts being recorded by the Tremeloes, *You* and *Come on Home*, while Mike Smith recorded *Disappear*. In 1970, O'Sullivan signed to Gordon Mills' MAM agency and record label. Mills created for O'Sullivan a Charles Dickens' styled street urchin image, complete with short trousers and a cap, the result of which, was a series of British hits during the early 1970s. In 1973, O'Sullivan hosted his own BBC television special, but a lengthy legal dispute with his record company over unpaid royalties dealt a fatal blow to his career momentum. O'Sullivan remains a popular recording artist in Japan, where he reached number one with *Tomorrow, Today*. CHART COMPOSITIONS: *Nothing Rhymed* (1970) US#114 UK#8, *Underneath the Blanket* (1971) UK#40, *We Will* (1971) UK#16, *No Matter How Hard I Try* (1971) UK#5, *Alone Again (Naturally)* (1972) g US#1 UK#3, *Ooh-Wakka-Doo-Wakka-Day* (1972) UK#8, *Clair* (1972) g US#2 UK#1, *Out of the Question* (1972) US#17, *Get Down* (1973) g US#7 UK#1, *Ooh Baby* (1973) US#25 UK#18, *Why Oh Why Oh Why* (1973) UK#6, *Happiness Is Me and You* (1974) US#62 UK#19, *A Woman's Place* (1974) UK#42, *A Christmas Song* (1974) UK#12, *I Don't Love You But I Think*

I Like You (1975) UK#14, *What's in a Kiss?* (1980) UK#19, *So What* (1989) UK#72. ALBUMS: **Himself** (1971) US#9 UK#5, **Back to Front** (1972) US#48 UK#1, **I'm a Writer Not a Fighter** (1973) US#101 UK#2, **Stranger in My Own Back Yard** (1974) UK#9, **Southpaw** (1977, all MAM); **Off Centre** (1980), **Life and Rhymes** (1982), **Frobisher Drive** (1988, all CBS); **In the Key of G** (1989, Dover); **Nothing But the Best** (1991, Castle) UK#50; **Sounds of the Loop** (1993), **By Larry** (1994), **Every Song Has Its Play** (1995), **The Little Album** (1995, all Park). COMPILATIONS: **Greatest Hits** (1976, MAM) UK#13; **20 Golden Greats** (1981, K-Tel) UK#98; **The Ultimate Collection** (1991, Castle); **Rare Tracks** (1992, Kitty). HIT VERSIONS: *Alone Again (Naturally)* Brush Arbor (1973) C&W#72/ Biz Markie sampled on *I Need a Haircut* (1991) US#113; *Who Was It* Hurricane Smith (1972) US#49 UK#23.

722. OVERSTREET, Paul (b. VanCleave, MS) C&W guitarist and vocalist. A country songwriter who, in 1986, performed in the trio S.K.O., which charted with *You Can't Stop Love* (1986) C&W#9, *Baby's Got a New Baby* (1986) C&W#1, and *American Me* (1987) C&W#16. Overstreet left the group in 1987 to record as a solo artist. CHART COMPOSITIONS: *Beautiful Baby* (1982) C&W#76, *I Won't Take Less Than Your Love* with Tanya Tucker and Paul Davis (1988) C&W#1, *Love Helps Those* (1988) C&W#3, *Seein' My Father in Me* (1990) C&W#2, *Richest Man on Earth* (1990) C&W#3, *Daddy's Come Around* (1990) C&W#1, *Ball and Chain* [iv] (1991) C&W#5, *If I Could Bottle This Thing Up* [i] (1991) C&W#31, *Billy Can't Read* [iii] (1992) C&W#59, *Still Out There Swinging* (1992) C&W#57, *Take Another Run* [iv] (1993) C&W#60. ALBUMS: **Sowin' Love** (1989), **Heroes** (1991) US#163, **Love Is Strong** (1992, all RCA). HIT VERSIONS: *Deeper Than the Holler* [iv] Randy Travis (1988) C&W#1, *Diggin' Up Bones* Randy Travis (1986) C&W#1, *Forever and Ever, Amen* [iv] Randy Travis (1987) C&W#1, *Long Line of Love, A* Michael Martin Murphey (1987) C&W#1, *On the Other Hand* [iv] Randy Travis (1985) C&W#67, re-issued (1986) C&W#1; *Same Ole Me* George Jones (1982) C&W#5, *Somebody's Doin' Me Right* [ii] Keith Whitley (1991) C&W#16, *Still Got a Crush on You* [i] Davis Daniel (1992) C&W#48, *When You Say Nothing at All* Keith Whitely (1988) C&W#1, *You're Still New to Me* Marie Osmond & Paul Davis (1986) C&W#1. Co-writers: [i] D. Dillon, [ii] Fred Knobloch/Dan Tyler, [iii] J. Michael, [iv] Don Schlitz.

723. OWENS, Buck (b. Alvis Edgar Owens, August 12, 1929, Sherman, TX) C&W guitarist and vocalist. One of country music's most successful artists, who charted eighty-six singles between 1959–1988, including twenty number ones. A prolific composer who regularly collaborated with Harlan Howard, Owens retired in 1977, only to start recording again in 1988. He learned the guitar and mandolin as a child, and first performed professionally during his teens. After some early television appearances, Owens joined Bill Woods' 1950s band, and earned himself a reputation as a premier session musician. During the 1960s, he starred in his own television show, "Buck Owens' Ranch House," and cohosted "Hee-Haw" between 1969–1986. CHART COMPOSITIONS: *Under Your Spell Again* [ii] (1959) C&W#4, *Above and Beyond (The Call of Love)* [i] (1960) C&W#3, *Excuse Me (I Think I've Got a Heartache)* [i] (1960) C&W#2, *Foolin' Around* [i] (1961) C&W#2, *Under the Influence of Love* [i] (1961) C&W#2, *Together Again* (1964) C&W#1 US#94, *I've Got a Tiger By the Tail* [i] (1965) C&W#1 US#25, *Only You (Can Break My Heart)* (1965) C&W#1 US#120, *Gonna Have Love* [iii] (1965) C&W#10, *Sam's Place* [iii] (1967) C&W#1 US#92, *Your Tender Loving Care* (1967) C&W#1, *The Kansas City Song* [iii] (1970) C&W#2, *I Wouldn't Live in New York City (If They Gave Me the Whole Dang Town)* (1970) C&W#9 US#110, *You Ain't Gonna Have 'Ol Buck to Kick Around No More* (1972) C&W#13. ALBUMS: **Together Again/My Heart Skips a Beat** (1964) US#88, **I Don't Care** (1964) US#135, **I've Got a Tiger By the Tail** (1965) US#43, **Roll Out the Red Carpet for Buck Owen and His Buckaroos** (1966) US#106, **Carnegie Hall Concert** (1966) US#114, **Dust on Mother's Bible** (1966), **Your Tender Loving Care** (1967) US#177, **It Takes People Like You to Make People Like Me** (1968), **I've Got You on My Mind Again** (1969) US#199, **In London** (1969) US#113, **Tall Dark Stranger** (1969) US#122, **Big in Vegas** (1970) US#141, **Your Mother's Prayers** (1970) US#198, **We're Gonna Get Together** with Susan Raye (1970) US#154, **The Kansas City Song** (1970) US#196, **I Wouldn't Live in New York** (1970) US#190, **Bridge Over Troubled Water** (1972), **Too Old to Cut the Mustard** (1972, all Capitol); **Buck 'Em** (1976), **Our Old Mansion** (1979, both Warner Brothers); **Buck Owens** (1984, Audio Fidelity); **Blue Love** (1987, Sundown); **Hot Dog** (1989), **Act Naturally** (1990, both Capitol). COMPILATIONS: **Best of Buck Owens** (1964) g US#46, **Close-Up** (1969) US#185, **The Stars of Hee-Haw** tvst (1970, all Capitol) US#196. HIT VERSIONS: *Cryin' Time* Lorrie Morgan (1993) C&W#59/Ray Charles (1966) R&B#5 US#6 UK#50; *Number One Heel* Bonnie Owens (1965) C&W#41, *Together Again* Ray Charles (1966) C&W#10 US#19 UK#48/Emmylou Harris (1976) C&W#1; *Under Your Spell Again* [ii] Ray Price

(1959) C&W#5/Johnny Rivers (1966) US#35/Waylon Jennings & Jessi Colter (1971) C&W#39/Barbara Fairchild (1975) C&W#65. Co-writers: [i] Harlan Howard, [ii] Dusty Rhodes, [iii] Red Simpson. (*See also under* Merle HAGGARD.)

724. PAGE, Jimmy (b. James Patrick Page, January 9, 1944, Heston, England) Rock guitarist and producer. A founder member of the influential heavy-rock band Led Zeppelin, Zeppelin's fourth album alone sold over eleven million copies in America, and its combined American album sales has exceeded sixty million. Page first worked as a session musician, before becoming the lead guitarist in the 1960s R&B group the Yardbirds, featuring on its albums **The Yardbirds** (1966, Columbia) UK#20; **Over Under Sideways Down** (1966) US#52, **Greatest Hits** (1967) US#28, and **Little Games** (1967, all Epic) US#80. By 1968, Page had formed the blues-rock group Led Zeppelin, with the vocalist Robert Plant, bassist John Paul Jones and drummer John Bonham. Page co-composed most of the band's material, including the masterpiece *Stairway to Heaven* [iii]. CHART COMPOSITIONS: *Good Times, Bad Times* (1969) US#80, *Whole Lotta Love* [i] (1969) g US#4, *Living Loving Maid (She's Just a Woman)* [iii] (1970) US#65, *Immigrant Song* [i] (1971) US#16, *Black Dog* [ii] (1972) US#15, *Rock and Roll* (1972) US#47, *Over the Hills and Far Away* (1973) US#51, *D'Yer Maker* (1973) US#20, *Trampled Underfoot* [ii] (1975) US#38, *Fool in the Rain* [ii] (1980) US#21. ALBUMS: **Led Zeppelin** (1969) p US#10 UK#6, **Led Zeppelin II** (1969) p US#1 UK#1, **Led Zeppelin III** (1970) p US#1 UK#1, **Led Zeppelin IV** (1971) p US#2 UK#1, **Houses of the Holy** (1973, all Atlantic) p US#1 UK#1; **Physical Graffiti** (1975) p US#1 UK#1, **Presence** (1976) p US#1 UK#1, **The Song Remains the Same** ost (1976) p US#2 UK#1, **In Through the Out Door** (1979, all Swan Song) p US#1 UK#1. COMPILATIONS: **Coda** (1982, Swan Song) p US#6 UK#4; **Led Zeppelin** (1990) p US#18 UK#48, **Re-masters** (1992) g US#47 UK#10, **Boxed Set II** (1993) US#87 UK#56, **The Complete Studio Recordings** (1993, all Atlantic) g. After the band broke up in 1980, Page unsuccessfully spent much of the decade in pursuit of another suitable musical environment, first recording an album as the Honeydrippers, **The Honeydrippers, Volume 1** (1984, Es Paranza) p US#4 UK#56, followed by the Firm, with Paul Rodgers, which charted with *Satisfaction Guaranteed* [iv] (1985) US#73, and released the albums **The Firm** (1985) g US#17 UK#15 and **Mean Business** (1986, both Atlantic) US#22 UK#46. Page has also recorded as a solo artist. CHART COMPOSITIONS: *Take Me for a Little While** (1993) UK#29, *Take a Look at Yourself** (1993) US#115 UK#43, *Gallows Pole*** (1995) UK#35. ALBUMS: **Deathwish II** ost (1982, Swan Song) US#50 UK#40; **Outrider** (1988, Geffen) g US#26 UK#27; **Coverdale/Page*** (1993, EMI) US#5 UK#4; **No Quarter: Jimmy Page and Robert Plant Unleaded**** (1994) p US#4 UK#7; **Walking into Clarksdale**** (1998, both Fontana). Zeppelin's legacy was amusingly sent-up in a reggae style by the group Dread Zeppelin on **Un-Led-Ed** (1990, IRS) US#116 UK#71, and his songs were also the subject of the album **Encomium: A Tribute to Led Zeppelin** (1995, Atlantic) US#17. HIT VERSIONS: *Black Dog* [ii] Newcity Rockers (1987) US#80, *Stairway to Heaven* [iii] Far Corporation (1985) US#89 UK#8/Dread Zeppelin (1991) UK#62/Rolf Harris (1993) UK#7; *Whole Lotta Love* [i] C.C.S. (1969) US#58 UK#13/King Curtis (1971) R&B#43 US#64/Tina Turner (1975) R&B#61/Wonder Band (1979) US#87; *Your Time Is Gonna Come* Dread Zeppelin (1990) UK#59. With: * David Coverdale, ** Robert Plant. Co-writers: [i] John Bonham (b. May 31, 1948, Bromwich, England)/John Paul Jones (b. John Baldwin, June 3, 1946, Sidcup, England)/Robert Plant, [ii] John Paul Jones/Robert Plant, [iii] Robert Plant, [iv] Paul Rodgers. (*See also under* Roy HARPER.)

725. PAICH, David (b. June 25, 1954, Los Angeles, CA) Rock keyboard player and vocalist. The son of the bandleader Marty Paich, who performed in the group Rural Still Life, before becoming a session player for such artists as Boz Scaggs. In 1978, Paich co-founded the slick, radio-friendly rock group Toto. CHART COMPOSITIONS: *Hold the Line* (1978) p US#5 UK#14, *I'll Supply the Love* (1979) US#45, *Georgie Porgy* (1979) R&B#18 US#48, *99* (1979) US#26, *Rosanna* (1982) p US#2, re-issued (1983) UK#12; *Make Believe* (1982) US#30, *Africa* [iii] (1982) p US#1 UK#3, *Stranger in Town* [iii] (1984) US#30, *Holyanna* [iii] (1985) US#71, *Without Your Love* (1986) US#38, *Pamela* [iv] (1988) US#22, *I Will Remember* (1995) UK#64. ALBUMS: **Toto** (1979) p US#9 UK#37, **Hydra** (1979) g US#37, **Turn Back** (1981) US#41, **Toto IV** (1982) p US#4, **Isolation** (1984, all Columbia) g US#42 UK#67; **Dune** ost (1985, Polydor) US#168; **Fahrenheit** (1986) g US#40 UK#99, **The Seventh One** (1988) US#64 UK#73, **Kingdom of Desire** (1992, all Columbia); **Tambu** (1996, Sony). COMPILATION: **Past to Present, 1977–1990** (1990, Columbia) US#153. HIT VERSIONS: *Georgie Porgy* Side Effect (1980) R&B#77, *Got to Be Real* [i] Cheryl Lynn (1978) g R&B#1 US#12, *Houston (I'm Comin' to See You)* Glen Campbell (1974) C&W#20 US#68, *Lady Love Me (One More Time)* [ii] George Benson (1983) R&B#21 US#30 UK#11. Co-writers: [i] David Foster/Cheryl Lynn (b. March 11, 1957, Los Angeles,

CA), [ii] James Howard, [iii] Jeff Porcaro (b. April 1, 1954, Hartford, CT; d. August 5, 1992, Los Angeles, CA), [iv] J. Williams.

726. PALMER, Robert (b. Alan Palmer, January 19, 1949, Batley, England) Rock vocalist. A former graphic designer with an urbane and soulful vocal style, who first performed as a teenager in the Mandrakes, before joining the British blues influenced Alan Bown Set, which recorded the albums **London Swings** (1966, Pye); **Outward Bound** (1967, Music Factory); **The Alan Bown Set** (1968, Deram); **Listen** (1970), **Stretchin' Out** (1971, both Island); and **Kick Me Out** (1985, See for Miles). As a member of Dada, Palmer released the album **Dada** (1970, Atco), which evolved into the R&B influenced Vinegar Joe for the albums **Vinegar Joe** (1972), **Rock 'n' Roll Gypsies** (1972), and **Six Star General** (1973, all Island). Since the mid–1970s, Palmer has pursued an eclectic career as a solo artist, recording in a variety of styles. CHART COMPOSITIONS: *Get Outside* (1976) US#105, *Give Me an Inch Girl* (1976) US#106, *Jealous* (1979) US#106, *Johnny and Mary* (1980) UK#44, *Looking for Clues* (1980) US#105 UK#33, *Addicted to Love* (1986) US#1 UK#5, *Hyperactive* [iv] (1986) US#33, *Sweet Lies* [i] (1988) US#94 UK#58, *Simply Irresistible* (1988) US#2 UK#44, *She Makes My Day* (1988) UK#6, *Change His Ways* (1989) UK#28, *You're Amazing* (1991) US#28, *Girl U Want* (1994) UK#57, *Know By Now* (1994) UK#25, *You Blow Me Away* (1994) UK#29. ALBUMS: **Sneakin' Sally Through the Alley** (1974) US#107, **Pressure Drop** (1975) US#136, **Some People Can Do What They Like** (1976) US#68 UK#46, **Double Fun** (1978) US#45, **Secrets** (1979) US#19 UK#54, **Clues** (1980) US#59 UK#31, **Maybe It's Live** (1982) US#148 UK#32, **Pride** (1983) US#112 UK#37, **Riptide** (1985, all Island) p US#8 UK#5; **Heavy Nova** (1988) p US#13 UK#17, **Don't Explain** (1990) US#88 UK#25, **Ridin' High** (1992) US#173 UK#32, **Honey** (1994, all EMI) UK#25. COMPILATIONS: **Addictions: Volume 1** (1989) g US#79 UK#7, **Addictions: Volume 2** (1992, both Island) UK#12; **Very Best of Robert Palmer** (1995, EMI) UK#4. Palmer has also recorded as a member of the Power Station, charting with *Some Like It Hot* [iii] (1985) US#6 UK#14 and *Communication* [ii] (1985) US#34, from the albums **The Power Station** (1985, Capitol) p US#6 UK#12 and **Living in Fear** (1996, Chrysalis). HIT VERSIONS: *Addicted to Love* Tina Turner (1988) UK#71, *Give Me an Inch* Ian Matthews (1979) US#67, *You're Gonna Get What's Coming* Bonnie Raitt (1980) US#73. Co-writers: [i] F. Blair/D. Wynn, [ii] D. Bramble/Andy Taylor (b. February 16, 1961, Tynemouth, England)/John Taylor (b. Nigel John Taylor, June 20, 1960, Birming-

ham, England), [iii] Andy Taylor/John Taylor, [iv] D. Nelson/T. Haynes.

727. PANKOW, James (b August 20, 1947, Chicago, IL) Rock trombonist. A founder member of the group Chicago, who composed its hits *Make Me Smile* (1970) US#9, *Just You 'N Me* (1973) g US#4, *(I've Been) Searchin' So Long* (1974), *Old Days* (1975) US#5, *Brand New Love Affair (Parts I & II)* (1975) US#61, *You Are on My Mind* (1977) US#49, *Alive Again* (1978) US#14. (*See also under* Pete CETERA, Robert LAMM.)

728. PARISH, Mitchell (b. July 10, 1900, Shreveport, LA; d. March 31, 1993, New York, NY) Film and stage lyricist. A lyricist who frequently wrote words for tunes many years after they had been originally composed, the first of which was *Sweet Lorraine* [iii] (1928). Parish is best remembered as the lyricist on the most recorded popular song ever, Hoagy Carmichael's *Stardust*, which he transformed from a swing tune into a classic ballad. He initially composed for vaudeville artists, and his first published song was *Carolina Rolling Stone* (1921), before contributing to such shows as "Continental Varieties" (1934) and "The Broadway Revue Stardust" (1987). Parish died of a stroke in 1993. HIT VERSIONS: *All My Love* [v] Bing Crosby (1950) US#11/Dennis Day (1950) US#22/Percy Faith (1950) US#7/Guy Lombardo (1950) US#10/Patti Page (1950) US#1; *Blond Sailor, The* [xiii] Andrews Sisters (1945) US#8, *Blue Skirt Waltz* [ii] Guy Lombardo (1949) US#30/Frankie Yankovic (1949) US#12; *Blue Tango* [i] Leroy Anderson (1952) US#1/Les Baxter (1952) US#10/Guy Lombardo (1952) US#9/Hugo Winterhalter (1952) US#6; *Cabin in the Cotton* [xvix] Cab Calloway (1932) US#17/Bing Crosby (1932) US#11; *Cia, Ciao Bambina* [xvii] Jacky Noguez (1959) US#24/Marino Marini (1959) US#24/Domenico Modugno (1959) UK#29; *Deep Purple* [vii] Larry Clinton (1939) US#1/Bing Crosby (1939) US#14/Jimmy Dorsey (1939) US#2/Guy Lombardo (1939) US#9/Artie Shaw (1939) US#17/Paul Weston (1939) US#17/Billy Ward & His Dominos (1957) US#20 UK#30/Nino Tempo & April Stevens (1963) US#1 UK#17/Donny & Marie Osmond (1976) US#14 UK#25; *Does Your Heart Beat for Me?* [xii] Carl Lorch (1940) US#18, *Don't Be That Way* [ix] Chick Webb (1935) US#20/Mildred Bailey (1938) US#9/Benny Goodman (1938) US#1; *Emaline* [xvix] Wayne King (1937) US#14, *Hands Across the Table* [vi] Lucienne Boyer (1934) US#2/Hal Kemp (1934) US#9; *I'm a Hundred Percent for You* [xvii] Benny Goodman (1935) US#8, *Lamp Is Low* [viii] Tommy Dorsey (1939) US#3, *Let Me Love You Tonight* [xxii] Woody Herman (1944) US#18, *Lilacs in the Rain* [vii] Charlie Barnet (1939)

US#8/Bob Crosby (1939) US#3; *Mr. Ghost Goes to Town* [xi] Mills Blue Rhythm Band (1937) US#15, *Moonlight Serenade* [xvi] Glenn Miller (1939) g US#3, re-issued (1954) UK#12, re-issued (1976) UK#13/Bobby Vinton (1976) US#97/Tuxedo Junction (1978) US#103; *Orchids for Remembrance* [vii] Eddy Howard (1940) US#21, *Organ Grinder's Swing, The* [xi] Frank Froeba (1936) US#12/Benny Goodman (1936) US#9/Hudson-DeLange Orchestra (1936) US#9/Tempo King (1936) US#10/Jimmie Lunceford (1936) US#2/Four Aces (1953) US#17; *Ruby* [xxi] Les Baxter (1953) US#7/Les Brown (1953) US#29/ Richard Hayman (1953) US#3/Harry James (1953) US#20/Vaughn Monroe (1953) US#27/Victor Young (1953) US#20; *Sleigh Ride* [i] Boston Pops Orchestra (1949) US#24, *Stairway to the Stars* [xiv] Al Donohue (1939) US#12/Jimmy Dorsey (1939) US#8/ Kay Kyser (1939) US#4/Glenn Miller (1939) US#1; *Starlit Hour, The* [vii] Tommy Dorsey (1940) US#13/ Ella Fitzgerald (1940) US#17/Glenn Miller (1940) US#10; *Stars Fell on Alabama* [xx] Richard Himber (1934) US#2/Guy Lombardo (1934) US#1; *Sweet Lorraine* [iii] Teddy Wilson (1935) US#17, *Syncopated Clock, The* [i] Leroy Anderson (1951) US#12/ Boston Pops Orchestra (1951) US#28; *Tzena, Tzena, Tzena* [x] Vic Damone (1950) US#6/Ralph Flanagan (1950) US#16/Mitch Miller (1950) US#3/Weavers with Gordon Jenkins (1950) g US#2; *Volare* [xv] Charlie Drake (1958) UK#28/Marino Marini (1958) UK#13/Dean Martin (1958) US#12 UK#2/Domenico Modugno (1958) US#1 UK#10/Bobby Rydell (1960) R&B#9 US#4 UK#22/Ace Cannon (1962) US#107/ Al Martino (1975) US#33. Co-writers: [i] Leroy Anderson, [ii] Vaclav Blaha, [iii] Cliff Burwell, [iv] Henri Contet/Paul Durand, [v] Benny Davis/Peter De Rose, [vi] Jean Delettre, [vii] Peter De Rose, [viii] Peter De Rose/Maurice Ravel/Bert Shelter, [ix] Benny Goodman/Edgar Sampson, [x] Julius Grossman/Issach Miron, [xi] Will Hudson/Irving Mills, [xii] Arnold Johnson/Russ Morgan, [xiii] Bell Leib/ Jacob Pfeil, [xiv] Matty Malneck (b. 1904; d. 1981)/ Frank Signorelli, [xv] Franco Migliacci/Domenico Modungo, [xvi] Glenn Miller, [xvii] Irving Mills/ Ben Oakland (b. 1907; d. 1979), [xvii] Domenico Modungo, [xviii] Domenico Modungo/"Verde," [xviv] Frank Perkins, [xx] Ray Perkins, [xxi] Heinz Roemheld, [xxii] Rene Touzet. (*See also under* Hoagy CARMICHAEL, Duke ELLINGTON, Jimmy McHUGH.)

729. PARKER, Graham (b. November 18, 1950, Camberley, England) Rock guitarist and vocalist. An R&B influenced singer-songwriter, who, during the 1960s, had busked and played in the group Way Out, before becoming a solo artist with his group the Rumor. CHART COMPOSITIONS:

The Pink Parker EP (1977) UK#24, *(Let Me Get) Sweet on You* (1977) US#107, *Hey, Lord Don't Ask Me Questions* (1978) UK#32, *Temporary Beauty* (1982) UK#50, *Life Gets Better* (1983) US#94, *Wake Up (Next to You)* (1985) US#39. ALBUMS: **Howlin' Wind** (1976), **Live at Marble Arch** (1976), **Heat Treatment** (1976) US#169, **Stick to Me** (1977) US#125 UK#19, **The Parkerilla** (1978) US#149 UK#14, **Squeezing Out Sparks** (1979) US#40 UK#18, **Live Sparks** (1979, all Vertigo); **The Up Escalator** (1980, Stiff) US#40 UK#11; **Another Grey Area** (1982) UK#40, **The Real Macaw** (1983, both RCA) US#59; **Steady Nerves** (1985, Elektra); **The Mona Lisa's Sister** (1988, Demon) US#77; **Human Soul** (1989) US#165, **Live Alone in America** (1989), **Struck By Lightning** (1991, all RCA) US#131; **Burning Questions** (1992, Capitol); **Live on the Test** (1994, Windsong); **12 Haunted Episodes** (1995, Razor & Tie); **BBC Live in Concert** (1996, Strange Fruit); **Live from New York** (1996, Nectar Masters); **Acid Bubblegum** (1996, When). COMPILATIONS: **Best of Graham Parker** (1980, Mercury); **Passion Is No Ordinary Word: Anthology** (1993, Rhino); **Vertigo (The Very Best of Graham Parker)** (1996, Chronicles); **No Holding Back** (1997, Demon). HIT VERSIONS: *Crawling from the Wreckage* Dave Edmunds (1979) UK#59.

730. PARKER, Ray, Jr. (b. May 1, 1954, Detroit, MI) R&B guitarist, producer and vocalist. A session musician at Motown Records, who, in 1977, formed and fronted the group Raydio. CHART COMPOSITIONS: *Jack and Jill* (1978) g R&B#5 US#8 UK#11, *Is This a Love Thing* (1978) R&B#20 UK#27, *Honey I'm Rich* (1978) R&B#43 US#102, *You Can't Change That* (1979) R&B#3 US#9, *More Than One Way to Love a Woman* (1979) R&B#25 US#103, *Two Places at the Same Time* (1980) R&B#6 US#30, *For Those Who Like to Groove* (1980) R&B#14, *Can't Keep You from Cryin'* (1980) R&B#57, *A Woman Needs Love (Just Like You Do)* (1981) R&B#1 US#4, *That Old Song* (1981) R&B#26 US#21, *It's Your Night* (1981) R&B#73. ALBUMS: **Raydio** (1978) g US#27, **Rock On** (1979) g US#45, **Two Places at the Same Time** (1980) g US#33, **A Woman Needs Love** (1981, all Arista) g US#13. COMPILATION: **Greatest Hits** (1982, Arista) US#51. In 1982, Parker left the group for a solo career. CHART COMPOSITIONS: *The Other Woman* (1982) R&B#2 US#4, *Let Me Go* (1982) R&B#3 US#38, *It's Our Own Affair* (1982) R&B#44 US#106, *Bad Boy* (1983) R&B#6 US#35, *The People Next Door* (1983) R&B#60, *I Still Can't Get Over Losing You* (1984) R&B#12 US#12, *Woman Out of Control* (1984) R&B#71, *In the Heat of the Night*

(1984) R&B#64, *Ghostbusters* (1984) g R&B#1 US#1 UK#2, re-issued (1986) UK#6; *Jamie* (1985) R&B#12 US#14, *Girls Are More Fun* (1986) R&B#21 US#34 UK#46, *I Don't Think a Man Should Sleep Alone* (1987) R&B#5 US#68 UK#13, *Over You* with Natalie Cole (1988) R&B#10 UK#65. ALBUMS: **The Other Woman** (1982) g US#11, **Woman Out of Control** (1984) US#30, **Chartbusters** (1984) g US#60, **Ghostbusters** ost (1984) p US#6, **Sex and the Single Man** (1985) US#65, **After Dark** (1987, all Arista) US#86 UK#40; **I Love You Like You Are** (1991, MCA). HIT VERSIONS: *Bad Girls* Junior Tucker (1983) R&B#61, *Doin' It* Herbie Hancock (1973) R&B#83, *Girl in Me, The* Maxine Nightingale (1979) US#73, *Make Your Body Move* Hamilton Bohannon (1983) R&B#63, *Mr. Telephone Man* New Edition (1985) R&B#1 US#12 UK#19, *Shake It Up Tonight* Cheryl Lynn (1981) R&B#5 US#70, *You Got the Love* [i] Rufus (1974) R&B#1 US#11, *You See the Trouble with Me* Barry White (1976) R&B#14 UK#2. Co-writer: [i] Chaka Khan.

731. PARR-DAVIES, Harry (b. May 24, 1914, Briton Ferry, Wales; d. October 14, 1955, London, England) Film and stage composer, pianist and arranger. One of the most prolific British songwriters of his era, who composed his first musical while still at school, and later became Gracie Field's accompanist. Parr-Davies' first published song was *I Hate You* (1931), and his first success was with Fields' *Happy Ending* and *Mary Rose*, from the film "This Week of Grace" (1933). He also contributed to the films "Sing as We Go" (1934), "Shipyard Sally" (1935) and "We're Going to Be Rich" (1938), alongside such revues and stage shows as "Black Velvet" (1939), "Top of the World" (1940), "Gangway" (1941), "Happidrome" (1942), "The Lisbon Story" (1943), "The Shephard Show" (1946), "Her Excellency" (1949), "Blue for a Boy," and "Dear Miss Phoebe" (both 1950). Parr-Davies also composed for the 1930s radio show "Welsh Rarebit," and wrote the title theme of the film "It's in the Air" (1939). HIT VERSIONS: *Bluebird of Happiness* [i] Art Mooney (1948) US#5/Jan Peerce (1948) US#23/Jo Stafford & Gordon MacRae (1948) US#16. Co-writer: [i] Edward Heyman.

732. PARSONS, Geoffrey (b. England) Film lyricist. A lyricist who often translated European songs into English. Parsons' compositions were also included in such films as "Limelight" and "Night Without Stars" (both 1952). HIT VERSIONS: *Autumn Concerto* [ii] Melachrino Strings (1956) UK#18, *Chee Chee-Oo-Chee (Sang the Little Bird)* [vii] Perry Como & Jaye P. Morgan (1955) US#12, *Eternally (Terry's Theme)* [iv] Vic Damone (1953) US#12/

Jimmy Young (1953) UK#8; *If You Love Me (Really Love Me)* [v] Vera Lynne (1954) US#21/Kay Starr (1954) US#4/Lamar Morris (1971) C&W#27; *Little Serenade* [i] Eddie Calvert (1958) UK#28, *Little Shoemaker, The* [v] Petula Clark (1954) UK#7/Gaylords (1954) US#2/Hugo Winterhalter (1954) US#9; *Mama* [iii] Hoarce Heidt (1941) US#14/David Whitfield (1955) UK#12/Connie Francis (1960) US#8 UK#2/Heintje (1971) US#112; *Smile* [iv] Nat "King" Cole (1954) US#10 UK#2/Sunny Gale (1954) US#19/David Whitfield (1954) US#25/Art Mooney (1959) US#107; *Stars Shine in Your Eyes* [vii] Ronnie Hilton (1955) UK#13. Co-writers: [i] Antonio Amurri/Giovanni Ferrio/John Turner, [ii] Camillo Bargoni/Paul Siegel/John Turner, [iii] C.A. Bixio/R. Cherubini/John Turner, [iv] Charles Chaplin/John Turner, [v] Francis Lemarque/Rudi Revil/John Turner, [vi] Nino Rota/John Turner, [vii] Saverio Serachini/John Turner. (*See also under* Gilbert BECAUD.)

733. PARSONS, Gram (b. Cecil Ingram Connor, November 5, 1946, Winterhaven, FL; d. September 19, 1973, Joshua Tree, CA) C&W guitarist, pianist and vocalist. A country music pioneer in the manner of Merle Haggard, who introduced what later became known as country-rock, but who ultimately squandered his unique musical talent. Parsons introduced country to a mainstream rock music audience, influencing the Eagles, Poco, and ultimately Garth Brooks. His mother was a wealthy orange grove owner and his father died in jail from alcohol poisoning. Parsons grew up listening to soul, country, rock, gospel, and the blues, before playing in such local bands as the Pacers, the Legends and the Shilos. Shortly before graduating from high school, his mother also died from an alcohol related illness. Parsons attended Harvard University in 1965, but dropped out the following year to pursue music with his group the International Submarine Band, which recorded a country-rock version of Bobby Bare's *Truck Driving Man* on its album **Safe at Home** (1968, LHI). After performing as a member of the Byrds on the album **Sweetheart of the Rodeo** (1968, Columbia) US#77, Parsons formed the psychedelic-country influenced Flying Burrito Brothers, with Chris Hillman, releasing the albums **The Gilded Palace of Sin** (1969) US#164, **Burrito Deluxe** (1970) and **Close Up the Honky Tonks** (1974, all A&M) US#158. In the early 1970s, Parsons discovered and teamed up with the country singer Emmylou Harris, who made significant contributions to his classic couplet of solo albums, **GP** (1973), and the posthumously issued **Grievous Angel** (1974), both of which finally realized all that Parsons had hinted at over the years, being glorious mergers of country, white gospel and rock and roll. Sadly, like a character in a Ross McDonald novel, Parsons was doomed to repeat the actions of his ancestors, and at the time of his death he was an alcoholic separated from his wife. Parsons died from drug and alcohol consumption in a Mohave desert motel room in 1973, the second major American songwriter to be lost in two days, Jim Croce having been killed in a plane crash the day before. ALBUMS: **GP** (1973), **Grievous Angel** (1974, both Reprise) US#195. COMPILATIONS: **Sleepless Nights** (1976, A&M) US#185; **Gram Parsons** (1976, Shilo); **The Early Years, 1963–1965** (1979, Sierra); **Luxury Liner** (1979, Shilo); **Gram Parsons and the Fallen Angels Live, 1973** (1982, Sierra); **Warm Evenings, Pale Mornings, Bottled Blues, 1963–1973** (1992, Raven).

734. PARTON, Dolly (b. Dolly Rebecca Parton, January 19, 1946, Locust Ridge, TN) C&W vocalist. After Patsy Cline, Parton is the most famous rags-to-riches female country star in the world, who has charted nearly one hundred singles since 1967, including twenty-one number ones. During the 1980s, Parton hosted her own television show "Dolly," and in 1993, Whitney Houston's version of her composition *I Will Always Love You*, became the second biggest selling single in American chart history. Born into rural poverty, Parton learned the guitar at the age of five, and recorded her first single in 1955. She achieved her first hit as a songwriter when Bill Phillips recorded *Put It Off Until Tomorrow* (1966). During the late 1960s, Parton toured and recorded with Porter Wagoner, later starring in such films as "9 to 5" (1980) and "The Best Little Whorehouse in Texas" (1982). CHART COMPOSITIONS: *Dumb Blonde* (1967) C&W#24, *Something Fishy* (1967) C&W#17, *Just Because I'm a Woman* (1968) C&W#17, *In the Good Old Days (When Times Were Bad)* (1968) C&W#25, *Daddy* (1969) C&W#40, *My Blue Ridge Mountain Boy* (1969) C&W#45, *Daddy Come and Get Me* (1970) C&W#40, *Joshua* (1970) C&W#1 US#108, *Coat of Many Colors* (1971) C&W#4, *Jolene* (1974) C&W#1 US#60 UK#7, *I Will Always Love You* (1974) C&W#1, re-issued (1982) C&W#1 US#53; *Love Is Like a Butterfly* (1974) C&W#1 US#105, *The Bargain Store* (1975) C&W#1, *Say Forever You'll Be Mine*** (1975) C&W#5, *Light of a Clear Blue Morning* (1977) C&W#11 US#87, *Two Doors Down* (1978) C&W#1 US#19, *Baby I'm Burnin'* (1979) C&W#48 US#25, *Old Flames Can't Hold a Candle to You* (1980) C&W#1, *9 to 5* (1980) g C&W#1 US#1 UK#47, *Wildflowers** (1988) C&W#6, *Think About Love* (1985) C&W#1, *Eagle When She Flies* (1991) C&W#33, *Straight Talk* (1992) C&W#64, *Romeo* (1993) C&W#27 US#50, *More Where That Came From*

(1993) C&W#58. ALBUMS: **Just the Two of Us*** (1969) US#184, **Always, Always*** (1969) US#162, **My Blue Ridge Mountain Boy** (1969), **Porter Wayne and Dolly Rebecca*** (1970) US#137, **A Real Live Dolly*** (1970) US#154, **Once More*** (1970) US#191, **Two of a Kind*** (1971) US#142, **Joshua** (1971) US#198, **New Harvest…First Gathering** (1977) US#71, **Here You Come Again** (1978) p US#20, **Heartbreaker** (1978) g US#27, **Great Balls of Fire** (1979, all RCA) g US#40; **Winning Hand** with Kris Kristofferson, Brenda Lee and Willie Nelson (1979, Monument) US#109; **Dolly, Dolly, Dolly** (1980) US#71, **9 to 5 and Other Odd Jobs** (1980) g US#11, **You Are** (1980), **Heartbreak Express** (1982, all RCA) US#106; **The Best Little Whorehouse** ost (1982, MCA) US#63; **Burlap and Satin** (1983) US#127, **The Great Pretender** (1983) US#73, **Rhinestone** ost (1984) US#135, **Once Upon a Christmas** with Kenny Rogers (1984) p US#31, **Real Love** (1985, all RCA), **Trio*** (1987, Warner Brothers) US#6 UK#60; **Rainbow** (1987) US#153, **White Limozeen** (1989) g, **Eagle When She Flies** (1991, all Columbia) p US#24; **Straight Talk** ost (1992, Hollywood) US#138; **Slow Dancing at the Moon** (1993) p US#16, **Honky Tonk Angels** with Loretta Lynn and Tammy Wynette (1993) g US#42, **Heartsongs — Live from Home** (1994) US#87, **Home for Christmas** (1994) g, **Something Special** (1995, all Columbia) US#54. COMPILATIONS: **Best of Dolly Parton** (1975, RCA) g; **Both Sides** (1978, Lotus) UK#45; **Greatest Hits** (1972, RCA) UK#74; **The Dolly Parton Story** (1977, Columbia); **Greatest Hits** (1982) US#77, **Greatest Hits** (1985) UK#74, **The RCA Years, 1967–1986** (1993, all RCA); **The Greatest Hits** (1994, Telstar) UK#65; **I Will Always Love You and Other Greatest Hits** (1996, Columbia); **The Essential Dolly Parton, Volume 2** (1997, RCA). HIT VERSIONS: *Carolina Moonshiner* Porter Wagoner (1974) C&W#19, *Company You Keep, The* Bill Phillips (1966) C&W#8, *Down from Dover* Nancy Sinatra & Lee Hazlewood (1972) US#120, *Kentucky Gambler* Merle Haggard (1974) C&W#1, *Mountain Music* Porter Wagoner (1978) C&W#64, *I Will Always Love You* Jimmie Peters (1978) C&W#84/Whitney Houston (1993) p R&B#1 US#1 UK#1; *I'm in No Condition* Hank Williams, Jr. (1967) C&W#60, *Jolene* Strawberry Switchblade (1985) UK#53, *Last One to Touch Me, The* Porter Wagoner (1971) C&W#18, *Put It Off Until Tomorrow* Bill Phillips (1966) C&W#6/Kendalls (1980) C&W#9; *To Daddy* Emmylou Harris (1978) C&W#3 US#102, *Two Doors Down* Joe Thomas (1978) R&B#70, *Waltz Me to Heaven* Waylon Jennings (1985) C&W#10, *Your Old Handy Man* Priscilla Mitchell (1968) C&W#73. With: * Emmylou Harris and Linda Ronstadt, ** Porter Wagoner.

735. PARTRIDGE, Andy (b. December 11, 1953, Malta) Rock guitarist, producer and vocalist. The lead singer in the British new-wave group XTC. CHART COMPOSITIONS: *Life Begins at the Hop* (1979) UK#54, *Don't Lose Your Temper* (1980) UK#32, *Towers of London* (1980) UK#31, *Sgt. Rock (Is Going to Help Me)* (1981) UK#16, *Generals and Majors* (1981) US#104, *Senses Working Overtime* (1982) UK#10, *Ball and Chain* (1982) UK#58, *Love on a Farmboys Wages* (1983) UK#50, *All You Pretty Girls* (1984) UK#55, *The Mayor of Simpleton* (1989) US#72 UK#46, *The Disappointed* (1992) UK#33, *The Battle of Peter Pumpkinhead* (1992) UK#71. ALBUMS: **White Music** (1978) UK#38, **Go 2** (1978) UK#21, **Drums and Wires** (1979) US#176 UK#34, **Black Sea** (1980) US#41 UK#16, **English Settlement** (1982) US#48 UK#5, **Mummer** (1983) US#145 UK#51, **The Big Express** (1984) US#178 UK#38, **Skylarking** (1986) US#70 UK#90, **Oranges and Lemons** (1989) US#44 UK#28, **Nonsuch** (1992, all Virgin) US#97 UK#28. COMPILATIONS: **Waxworks — Some Singles, 1977–1982** (1982) UK#54, **The Compact XTC** (1986, both Virgin); **Drums and Wireless: BBC Radio Sessions, 1977–1989** (1994, Night Track); **Fossil Fuel: The XTC Singles Collection** (1996, Virgin). Partridge has also recorded as a solo artist. ALBUMS: **25 O'Clock*** (1985), **Psonic Psunspots*** (1987), **Chips from the Chocolate Fireball*** (1987), **Takeaway/The Lure of Salvage** (1980, all Virgin); **The Greatest Living Englishman** (1993, Pipeline); **Through the Hill** with Harold Budd (1994, All Saints). As: *Dukes of Stratosphere.

736. PAXTON, Tom (b. October 31, 1937, Chicago, IL) Folk guitarist and vocalist. A regular performer on the 1960s Greenwich Village folk scene, who specialized in left-wing political material and children's songs. ALBUMS: **Ramblin' Boy** (1964), **Ain't That News** (1965), **Outward Bound** (1966), **Morning Again** (1968), **The Things I Notice Now** (1968) US#155, **Tom Paxton #6** (1970, all Elektra) US#184 UK#23; **How Come the Sun** (1971) US#120, **Peace Will Come** (1972) US#191 UK#47, **New Songs for Old Friends** (1973, all Reprise); **Something in My Life** (1976, Private Stock); **Saturday Night** (1976, MAM); **New Songs from the Briarpatch** (1976), **Heroes** (1978, both Vanguard); **Up and Up** (1980), **The Paxton Report** (1981, both Mountain Railroad); **In the Orchard** (1982, Cherry Lane); **Even a Gray Day** (1983), **One Million Lawyers and Other Disasters** (1985), **And Loving You** (1987, all Flying Fish); **Wearing the Time** (1994), **Live for the Record** (1996, both Sugar Hill). COMPILATIONS: **Compleat** (1971, Elektra) UK#18; **Very Best of Tom Paxton** (1988, Start). HIT

VERSIONS: *Bottle of Wine* Fireballs (1968) US#9/ Doc & Merle Watson (1973) C&W#71; *I Will Love You* Fureys (1982) UK#54, *Marvelous Toy* Chad Mitchell Trio (1963) US#43, *Last Thing on My Mind, The* Neil Diamond (1973) US#9/Porter Wagoner & Dolly Parton (1968) C&W#7; *Wasn't That a Party* Rovers (1981) US#37.

737. PAYNE, Leon (b. June 15, 1917, Alba, TX; d. September 11, 1969) C&W multi-instrumentalist and vocalist. A country musician who was born blind but overcame his handicap to learn the keyboards, trombone and guitar while still at school. Payne played for various Texas bands during the 1930s, recorded for the Bluebird label, and from 1949, fronted his own band, the Lone Star Buddies. During the 1950s he continued to record for a variety of small labels, but he retired after a heart attack in 1965. CHART COMPOSITION: *I Love You Because* (1949) C&W#1. ALBUM: **Living Legend** (1964, Starday). HIT VERSIONS: *Blue Side of Lonesome, The* Jim Reeves (1966) C&W#1 US#59, *Call Her Your Sweetheart* Eddy Arnold (1952) C&W#9/ Frank Ifield (1966) C&W#28 UK#24; *I Love You Because* Clyde Moody (1950) C&W#8/Ernest Tubb (1950) C&W#2/Johnny Cash (1960) C&W#20/Al Martino (1963) US#3 UK#48/Carl Smith (1969) C&W#14/Jim Reeves (1964) UK#5, re-issued (1971) UK#34, re-issued (1976) C&W#54/Don Gibson on B-side of *Oh, Such a Stranger* (1978) C&W#61/Roger Whittaker (1983) C&W#91; *Lost Highway* Hank Williams (1949) C&W#12/Don Gibson (1967) C&W#51/James Storie (1988) C&W#100; *They'll Never Take Her Love from Me* Hank Williams (1950) C&W#5/Johnny Darrell (1970) C&W#74; *Take Me* George Jones (1966) C&W#8/George Jones & Tammy Wynette (1972) C&W#9; *Things Have Gone to Pieces* George Jones (1965) C&W#9.

738. PENN, Dan (b. Wallace Daniel Pennington, November 16, 1941, Vernon, AL) R&B guitarist, producer and vocalist. A country and R&B songwriter who has frequently collaborated with Spooner Oldham. Penn initially performed as a member of Dan Penn and the Pallbearers, and later became a born-again Christian and white gospel artist. ALBUMS: **Nobody's Fool** (1977, Atlantic); **Do Right Man** (1994, Sire). HIT VERSIONS: *I Hate You* Ronnie Milsap (1973) C&W#10, *Out of Left Field* Percy Sledge (1967) R&B#25 US#59, *You Left the Water Running* Barbara Lynn (1966) R&B#42. (*See also under* Spooner OLDHAM.)

739. PERKINS, Carl (b. Carl Lee Perkins, April 9, 1932, Tiptonville, TN) Rockabilly guitarist and vocalist. A rockabilly performer who was a considerable influence on the Beatles, yet, who despite his contribution to the development of rock and roll, insisted, "I don't understand how I ever influenced anybody." Perkins grew up in poverty, his father being a white sharecropper on a cotton plantation. At the age of seven he learned the rudiments of the guitar from a black blues picker, and as a boy he enjoyed listening to the gospel melodies that he heard sung in the cotton fields. After signing to the Sun label in 1955, Perkins was successful with his third single *Blue Suede Shoes*, a song that he wrote from a phrase he had overheard in a dance club. CHART COMPOSITIONS: *Blue Suede Shoes* (1956) C&W#1 US#2 UK#2 UK#10, *Boppin' the Blues* (1956) C&W#7 US#70, *Dixie Fried* [i]/*I'm Sorry I'm Not Sorry* (1956) C&W#10, *Your True Love* (1957) C&W#13 US#67, *Pink Pedal Pushers* (1958) C&W#17 US#91, *Country Boy's Dream* (1966) C&W#22, *Shine, Shine* (1967) C&W#40, *Restless* (1969) C&W#20, *Me Without You* (1971) C&W#65, *Cotton Top* (1971) C&W#53, *High on Love* (1972) C&W#60, *(Let's Get) Dixiefried* [i] new version (1973) C&W#61, *Birth of Rock and Roll* (1986) C&W#31. ALBUMS: **Dance Album "Teenbeat"** (1959, Sun); **Whole Lotta Shakin'** (1959, Columbia); **Country Boy Dreams** (1968, Dollie); **On Top** (1969), **Boppin' the Blues** (1970, both Columbia); **Hilltop** (1971, Hilltop); **The Man Behind Johnny Cash** (1973, Columbia); **My Kind of Country** (1974, Mercury); **The Carl Perkins Show** (1976, Suede); **From Jackson, Tennessee** (1977, Lake County); **Ol' Blue Suedes Is Back** (1978, Jet) UK#38; **Trio Plus** with Jerry Lee Lewis and Charlie Rich (1980, Sun); **The Survivors** with Johnny Cash and Jerry Lee Lewis (1982, Columbia); **Class of '55** with Johnny Cash, Jerry Lee Lewis and Roy Orbison (1986, Smash) US#87; **Live at Austin City Limits** (1982, Suede); **Born to Rock** (1989, Capitol); **Friends, Family and Legends** (1992, Platinum); **706 Reunion** with Scotty Moore (1992); **Carl Perkins and Sons** (1993), **Disciple in Blue** (1994), **Take Me Back** (1994, all BMG); **Go Cat Go!** (1996, Dinosaur). COMPILATIONS: **The Sun Story, Volume 3** (1979, Sun); **Up Through the Years** (1986, Bear Family); **Best of Carl Perkins — Jive After 5, 1958–1978** (1988, Rhino); **Restless — The Columbia Recordings** (1989, Columbia); **Classic** (1990, Bear Family); **The Sun Years** (1990, Sun). HIT VERSIONS: *Blue Suede Shoes* Elvis Presley (1956) US#20 UK#9/Dave Clark Five in medley *Good Old Rock 'n' Roll* (1969) UK#7/Johnny Rivers (1973) US#38/Con Hunley (1986) C&W#49; *Daddy Sang Bass* Johnny Cash (1969) C&W#1 US#42/Pinkard & Bowden in *Adventures in Parodies* (1984) C&W#64; *Honey Don't* Beatles on *4 By the Beatles* EP (1965) US#68/Mac Curtis (1970) C&W#43; *Let*

Me Tell You About Our Love Judds (1989) C&W#1, *(Let's Get) Dixie Fried* [i] Kentucky Headhunters (1993) C&W#74, *Matchbox* Beatles (1964) US#17, *Poor Boy Blues* Bob Luman (1966) C&W#39, *Right String Baby (Wrong Yo-Yo)* Danny Shirley with Piano Red (1985) C&W#93. Co-writer: [i] H. Griffin.

740. PERRETT, Peter (b. England) Rock guitarist and vocalist. An underrated songwriter who first recorded a self-financed album with his band England's Glory in 1973, which was later released as **The Legendary Lost Album** (1994, Anagram). After recording the single *Lovers of Today* as Peter and the Pets, Perrett formed the Only Ones, one of the most significant bands of the punk era. CHART SINGLE: *Another Girl, Another Planet* (1992) UK#57. ALBUMS: **The Only Ones** (1978) UK#56, **Even Serpents Shine** (1979) UK#42, **Baby's Got a Gun** (1980, all CBS) UK#37. COMPILATIONS: **Special View** (1979, Epic); **Remains** (1984, Cherry Red); **Alone in the Night** (1986), **The Immortal Story** (1992, both CBS); **The Peel Sessions Album** (1994, Strange Fruit); **The Big Sleep** (1994, Freud). The Only Ones broke up in 1981, after which, Perret spent much of the 1980s battling a heroin addiction, ultimately returning to record as the group the One, which released the album **Woke Up Sticky** (1996, Demon).

741. PERRY, Steve (b. January 22, 1953, Hanford, CA) Rock vocalist. The lead vocalist in Neal Schon's group Journey from 1978, who wrote the hits *Lovin', Touchin', Squeezin'* (1979) US#16, *Walks Like a Lady* (1980) US#32, *The Party's Over (Hopelessly in Love)* (1981) US#34, *Who's Crying Now* [ii] (1981) US#4, *Separate Ways (World's Apart)* [ii] (1983) US#8, *After the Fall* [ii] (1983) US#23, *Send Her My Love* [ii] (1983) US#23, *Suzanne* [ii] (1986) US#17, and *Why Can't This Night Go on Forever* [ii] (1987) US#60. Perry has also recorded as a solo artist. CHART COMPOSITIONS: *Don't Fight It* [vi] with Kenny Loggins (1982) US#17, *Oh, Sherrie* [iii] (1984) US#3, *She's Mine* [iv] (1984) US#21, *Strung Out* [v] (1984) US#40, *Foolish Heart* [iv] (1985) US#18, *You Better Wait* [i] (1994) US#29, *Missing You* (1994) US#74. ALBUMS: **Street Talk** (1984) p US#12 UK#59, **For the Love of Stranger Medicine** (1994, both Columbia) US#15 UK#64. HIT VERSIONS: *Foolish Heart* [iv] Sharon Bryant (1989) US#90, *Who's Crying Now* [ii] Randy Crawford (1992) R&B#30. Co-writers: [i] L. Brewster/G. Hawkins/ M. Lucas/J. Pierce/P. Taylor, [ii] Jonathan Cain (b. February 26, 1950, Chicago, IL), [iii] Bill Cuomo/ Randy Goodrum/Craig Krampf, [iv] Randy Goodrum, [v] Craig Krampf/B. Steele, [vi] Kenny Loggins/ Dean Pitchford. (*See also under* Neal SCHON.)

742. PETTY, Tom (b. October 20, 1953, Gainesville, FL) Rock guitarist, producer and vocalist. The leader of the Byrds influenced group Tom Petty and the Heartbreakers, who first performed in the band Mudcrutch, which recorded an unreleased album for Shelter Records in 1969. CHART COMPOSITIONS: *Anything That's Rock 'n' Roll* (1977) UK#36, *Breakdown* (1978) US#40, *I Need to Know* (1978) US#41, *Listen to Her Heart* (1978) US#59, *Don't Do Me Like That* (1980) US#10, *Refugee* [i] (1980) US#15, *Here Comes My Girl* [i] (1980) US#59, *The Waiting* (1981) US#19, *Stop Draggin' My Heart Around* [i] with Stevie Nicks (1981) US#3 UK#50, *A Woman in Love (It's Not Me)* [i] (1981) US#79, *You Got Lucky* [i] (1983) US#20, *Change of Heart* (1983) US#21, *Don't Come Around Here No More* [iv] (1985) US#13 UK#50, *Make It Better (Forget About Me)* [vi] (1985) US#54, *Rebels* (1985) US#74, *Jammin' Me* [ii] (1987) US#18, *I Won't Back Down* [v] (1989) US#12 UK#28, *Runnin' Down a Dream* [iii] (1989) US#23 UK#55, *Free Fallin'* [v] (1989) US#7 UK#64, *A Face in the Crowd* (1990) US#46, *Learning to Fly* [v] (1991) US#28 UK#46, *Into the Great Wide Open* [v] (1991) US#92, *Too Good to Be True* (1992) UK#34, *Mary Jane's Last Dance* (1993) US#14 UK#52, *You Don't Know How It Feels* (1995) US#13, *It's Good to Be King* (1995) US#68. ALBUMS: **Tom Petty and the Heartbreakers** (1976) g US#55 UK#24, **You're Gonna Get It** (1978, both Shelter) g US#23 UK#34; **Damn the Torpedoes** (1979) p US#2 UK#57, **Hard Promises** (1981) p US#5 UK#32, **Long After Dark** (1982, all Backstreet) g US#9 UK#45; **Southern Accents** (1985) p US#7 UK#23, **Pack Up the Plantation — Live** (1986) US#22, **Let Me Up (I've Had Enough)** (1987) g US#20 UK#59, **Full Moon Fever** (1989) p US#3 UK#8, **Into the Great Wide Open** (1991, all MCA) p US#13 UK#3; **Wildflowers** (1994) p US#8 UK#36, **She's the One** ost (1996, both Warner Brothers) UK#37. COMPILATIONS: **Greatest Hits** (1993) p US#5 UK#10, **Playback, 1973–1993** (1995, both MCA). Petty also performed as a member of the all-star group the Traveling Wilburys. HIT VERSIONS: *Leave Virginia Alone* Rod Stewart (1995) UK#52, *Lost in Your Eyes* Jeff Healey Band (1993) US#91, *Never Be You* Rosanne Cash (1986) C&W#1, *Thing About You* Southern Pacific (1985) C&W#14, *Ways to Be Wicked* [i] Lone Justice (1985) US#71. Co-writers: [i] Mike Campbell, [ii] Mike Campbell/Bob Dylan, [iii] Mike Campbell/Jeff Lynne, [iv] Jimmy Iovone/Dave A. Stewart, [v] Jeff Lynne, [vi] Dave A. Stewart. (*See also under* Bob DYLAN, Roy ORBISON.)

743. PHILLIPS, John (b. August 30, 1935, Paris Island, SC) Pop guitarist and vocalist. The composer of a couple of the most popular songs of the 1960s, who, after recording three albums for Capitol Records as a member of the trio the Journeymen, formed the vocal group the Mamas and the Papas. The group's two-male, two-female lead vocal style was a format that would not be repeated so successfully until the arrival of Abba in the 1970s. CHART COMPOSITIONS: *California Dreamin'* [iii] (1966) g US#4 UK#23, *Monday Monday* (1966) g US#1 UK#3, *Look Through My Window* (1966) US#24, *Words of Love* (1966) g US#5 UK#47, *I Saw Her Again Last Night* [i] (1966) US#5 UK#11, *Straight Shooter* (1967) US#130, *Creeque Alley* [iii] (1967) US#5 UK#9, *Dancing Bear* (1967) US#51, *Twelve Thirty (Young Girls Are Coming to the Canyon)* (1967) US#20, *Safe in My Garden* (1968) US#53, *For the Love of Ivy* (1968) US#81, *Step Out* (1971) US#81. ALBUMS: **If You Can Believe Your Eyes and Ears** (1966) g US#1 UK#3, **The Mamas and the Papas** (1966) g US#4 UK#24, **Deliver** (1967) g US#2 UK#4, **The Papas and the Mamas** (1968) US#15, **People Like Us** (1971, all Dunhill) US#84. COMPILATIONS: **Farewell to the First Golden Era** (1967) g US#5, **Golden Era, Volume 2** (1968, both Dunhill) US#53; **Hits of Gold** (1969, Stateside) UK#7; **16 of Their Greatest Hits** (1969) US#61, **20 Golden Hits** (1973, both Dunhill) US#186; **Best of the Mamas and the Papas** (1977, Arcade) UK#6; **California Dreamin' — The Very Best of the Mamas and the Papas** (1995, PolyGram) UK#14. Phillips was one of the organizers of the Monterey Pop Festival in 1967, and later that year co-wrote Scott McKenzie's quintessential hippie anthem *San Francisco*. After the Mamas and the Papas split up in 1968, he attempted a solo career with the single *Mississippi* (1970) C&W#58 US#32, from the album **John Phillips (John the Wolfking of L.A.)** (1970, Dunhill) US#181, but he spent much of the 1970s battling a drug dependency. By the 1980s, the partially reformed Mamas and the Papas had become little more than an American oldies circuit act. HIT VERSIONS: *California Dreamin'* [iii] Bobby Womack (1968) R&B#16 US#52/Colorado (1978) UK#45/America (1979) US#56/Beach Boys (1986) US#57/River City People (1990) UK#13; *Go Where You Wanna Go* 5th Dimension (1967) US#16, *Holy Man* Scott McKenzie (1968) US#126, *Kokomo* [ii] Beach Boys (1988) g US#1 UK#25, *Like an Old Time Movie* Scott McKenzie (1967) US#24 UK#50, *San Francisco* Scott McKenzie (1967) g US#4 UK#1/Paul Mauriat (1968) US#103. Co-writers: [i] Dennis Doherty (b. November 29, 1941, Halifax, NS, Canada), [ii] Mike Love (b. March 15, 1941, Baldwin Hills, CA)/Terry Melcher/Scott McKenzie, [iii] Michelle Phillips (b. Holly Michelle Gilliam, April 6, 1944, Long Beach, CA).

744. PHILLIPS, Shawn (b. February 3, 1943, Fort Worth, TX) Pop multi-instrumentalist and vocalist. A singer-songwriter who remains something of a cult artist. CHART COMPOSITION: *We* (1973) US#92. ALBUMS: **I'm a Loner** (1965), **Shawn** (1966, both Columbia); **Contribution** (1970), **Second Contribution** (1971), **Collaboration** (1972), **Faces** (1973) US#57, **Bright White** (1973) US#72, **Furthermore** (1974) US#50, **Do You Wonder** (1975) US#101, **Rumpelstiltskin's Resolve** (1976), **Spaced** (1977, all A&M); **Transcendence** (1978, RCA).

745. PINKARD, Maceo (b. June 27, 1897, Bluefield, WV; d. July 21, 1962, New York, NY) Film and stage composer. The first black composer to work solely with white lyricists, whose job in a theatrical agency led to the publication of his first song *I'm Goin' Back Home* (1915). Pinkard scored a million seller with *Mammy O' Mine* [v] (1919), after which he became successful during the mid–1920s co-writing such jazz standards as *Sweet Georgia Brown* [v] (1925). Pinkard's songs were included in the show "Africana" (1927), and the film "Show Boat" (1929). HIT VERSIONS: *Congratulations* [i] Jack Denny (1929) US#12, *Don't Be Like That* [ii] Helen Kane (1929) US#16, *Gimme a Little Kiss, Will Ya, Huh?* [iv] Billy Jones (1926) US#13/"Whispering" Jack Smith (1926) US#1/April Stevens (1951) US#10; *Mammy O' Mine* [v] Yerkes Jazarimba Orchestra (1919) US#8, *Sugar* [iii] Ethel Waters (1926) US#9/Paul Whiteman (1928) US#19/Vic Damone (1953) US#13; *Sweet Georgia Brown* [v] Ben Bernie (1925) US#1/Isham Jones (1925) US#5/Ethel Waters (1925) US#6/Bing Crosby (1932) US#2/Brothers Bones (1949) US#10; *Them There Eyes* [v] Gus Arnheim (1931) US#7. Co-writers: [i] Coleman Goetz/Bud Green/Sam H. Stept, [ii] Archie Gottler/Charles Tobias, [iii] Sidney Mitchell, [iv] Jack Smith/Roy Turk, [v] William Tracey. (*See also under* Billy ROSE.)

746. PITCHFORD, Dean (b. America) Pop composer. A backroom songwriter who has contributed to such films as "Footloose" (1984) and "Sing" (1989). HIT VERSIONS: *All the Man That I Need* [i] Sister Sledge (1982) R&B#45/Whitney Houston (1991) R&B#1 US#1 UK#13, *Birthday Suit* [iii] Johnny Kemp (1989) US#36, *Blood, The* [ii] Bebe & Cece Winans featuring Hammer (1992) R&B#78, *Dancing in the Sheets* [v] Shalamar (1984) R&B#18 US#17 UK#41, *Fame* [i] Irene Cara (1980) US#4, re-issued (1982) UK#1; *I Still Believe in You* [iv] Cliff Richard (1992) UK#7, *One Sunny Day (From Quicksilver)* [v] Ray Parker, Jr. & Helen Terry (1986) US#96, *Red Light* [i] Linda Clifford (1980) R&B#40 US#41. Co-writers: [i] Michael Gore, [ii]

Hammer/R. Lawrence/Bebe Winans, [iii] R. Lawrence, [iv] Dave Pomeranz, [v] Bill Wolfer. (*See also under* Kenny LOGGINS, Steve PERRY, Tom SNOW.)

747. PLANT, Robert (b. August 20, 1948, West Bromich, England) Rock vocalist. One of the most imitated rock singers of the 1970s, who, with the guitarist Jimmy Page, formed the group Led Zeppelin. When the band broke up in 1980, Plant updated his sound and embarked on a successful solo career. CHART COMPOSITIONS: *Burning Down One Side* [iii] (1982) US#64 UK#73, *Pledge Pin* [i] (1982) US#74, *Big Log* [iii] (1983) US#20 UK#11, *In the Mood* [ii] (1984) US#39, *Little By Little* [v] (1985) US#36, *Too Loud* (1985) US#108, *Heaven Knows* (1988) UK#33, *Tall Cool One* [iv] (1988) US#25, *Ship of Fools* [iv] (1988) US#84, *Hurting Kind (I've Got My Eyes on You)* (1991) US#46 UK#45, *29 Palms* (1993) US#11 UK#21, *I Believe* (1993) UK#64. ALBUMS: **Pictures at Eleven** (1982, Swan Song) p US#5 UK#2; **The Principle of Moments** (1983) p US#8 UK#7, **Shaken 'N' Stirred** (1985) g US#20 UK#19, **Now and Zen** (1988) p US#6 UK#10, **Manic Nirvana** (1991) g US#30 UK#15, **Fate of Nations** (1993, all Es Paranza) g US#34 UK#6. Co-writers: [i] Blunt, [ii] Blunt/Martinez, [iii] Blunt/J. Woodruffe, [iv] P. Johnstone, [v] J. Woodruffe. (*See also under* Jimmy PAGE.)

748. POCKRISS, Lee Film and stage composer. A successful 1960s songwriter, who often worked with Paul J. Vance. Pockriss also worked with the lyricist Anne Croswell, on the Broadway shows "Senior Prom" (1958) and "Tovarich" (1963). ALBUMS: **Ernest in Love** oc (1960, Columbia); **Tovarich** oc (1963, Capitol) US#64. HIT VERSIONS: *Calcutta* [iv] Lawrence Welk (1961) g US#1, *Catch a Falling Star* [vii] Perry Como (1958) g US#1 UK#9, *Four Little Heels* [vii] Avons (1960) UK#45/Brian Hyland (1960) UK#29; *Itsy Witsy Teenie Weeny Polka Dot Bikini* [vii] Brian Hyland (1960) R&B#10 US#1 UK#8/Bombalurina (1990) UK#1; *Jimmy's Girl* [vii] Johnny Tillotson (1961) US#25 UK#43, *Johnny Angel* [iii] Shelly Fabares (1962) US#1 UK#41/Patti Lynn (1962) UK#37; *Kites* [v] Simon Dupree & the Big Sound (1967) UK#9, *Leader of the Laundromat* [vii] Detergents (1965) US#19, *My Heart Is an Open Book* [ii] Glen Gray (1935) US#13, *My Little Corner of the World* [vi] Anita Bryant (1960) UK#48, *Playground in My Mind* [vii] Clint Holmes (1973) g US#2, *Seven Little Girls Sitting in the Back Seat* [vi] Avons (1959) UK#3/Paul Evans (1959) US#9 UK#25/Bombalurina (1990) UK#18; *Starbright* [vii] Johnny Mathis (1960) US#25 UK#47, *Tracy* [vi] Cuff Links (1960) UK#4, re-issued (1969)

US#9; *What Is Love?* [vii] Playmates (1959) US#15, *When Julie Comes Around* [vii] Cuff Links (1969) US#41 UK#10. Co-writers: [i] Anne Crosswell, [ii] Hal David, [iii] Lyn Duddy, [iv] Heino Gaze/Paul J. Vance, [v] Hal Hackady, [vi] Bob Hilliard, [vii] Paul J. Vance.

749. POLLACK, Lew (b. 1895; d. 1946, both America) Film and stage composer.

A Tin Pan Alley composer whose compositions were included in such films as "Street Angel" (1928), "One in a Million" (1936), "Sunset Boulevard" (1950), and "Gentlemen Marry Brunettes" (1955). HIT VERSIONS: *Angela Mia (My Angel)* [iv] Scrappy Lambert (1928) US#16/Vincent Lopez (1928) US#2/Paul Whiteman (1928) US#1/Don, Dick, N'Jimmy (1954) US#23/Ralph Flanagan (1954) US#27; *Charmaine* [iv] Lewis James (1927) US#11/Guy Lombardo (1927) US#1/Frankie Carle (1944) US#25/Harmonicats (1951) US#21/Gordon Jenkins (1951) US#18/Mantovani (1951) US#10/Billy May (1952) US#17/Vaughn Monroe (1952) US#27/Paul Weston (1952) US#8/Bachelors (1963) US#10 UK#6/Four Preps (1963) US#116; *Cheatin' on Me* [v] Ben Bernie (1925) US#8, *Diane (I'm in Heaven When You Smile)* [iv] Franklyn Bauer (1928) US#20/Nathan Glantz (1928) US#19/Nat Shilkret (1928) US#2/Bachelors (1964) UK#1; *Miss Annabelle Lee* [i] Ben Selvin (1927) US#8, *My Yiddishe Momme* [v] Willie Howard (1926) US#7/Sophie Tucker (1928) US#5; *Sing, Baby Sing* [v] Charlie Barnet (1936) US#6/Ruby Newman (1936) US#4/Teddy Wilson (1936) US#12; *Toy Trumpet* [iii] Raymond Scott (1937) US#15, re-issued (1938) US#15; *Who's Afraid of Love?* [ii] Fats Waller (1937) US#8, *You Do the Darndest Things, Baby* [ii] Guy Lombardo (1936) US#11. Co-writers: [i] Sidney Clare/Harry Richman, [ii] Sidney Mitchell, [iii] Sidney Mitchell/Raymond Scott, [iv] Erno Rapee (b. 1981; 1945), [v] Jack Yellen. (*See also under* Paul Francis WEBSTER.)

750. POMUS, Doc (b. Jerome Felder, June 27, 1925, Brooklyn; d. March 14, 1991, New York, both NY), and SHUMAN, Mort (b. Mortimer Shuman, November 12, 1936, New York, NY; d. November 4, 1991, London, England) Both R&B pianists and vocalists.

Two of the most successful R&B influenced songwriters in America, whose compositions defined a certain era of 1960s popular music. Pomus and Shuman's blues based melodies were some of the most authentic ever created by white tunesmiths, and by the end of the 1960s, their compositions had sold over twenty-one million records, with *Save the Last Dance for Me* ultimately earning a BMI four million radio plays award. Pomus began singing at the age of six, and started writing songs in his teens, becoming, during the 1940s, a respected blues singer under the stage name Doc Pomus. His first major composition was *Boogie Woogie Country Girl* by Joe Turner (1956). Shuman had been writing songs since his teens. They became friends in 1958 when they shared an apartment in Greenwich Village, composing together in New York's Brill Building. Their songs were initially a collaborative effort, but they later veered towards Pomus' lyrics and Shuman's tunes. Taking much of their initial inspiration from comic books and *True Confessions* magazine, they penned such gems as *A Teenager in Love* (1959). Elvis Presley recorded some of their best compositions, including the wry *Viva Las Vegas* and the delightful *Little Sister*. By the late 1960s, Shuman had become disenchanted with American popular music, so he emigrated to France, where he produced a one-man show and recorded a series of solo albums, **My Death** (1969, Reprise); **Mort Shuman** (1973), **Voila Comment** (1973), **Imagine** (1976), **My Name Is Mortimer** (1977), **Mort Shuman** (1988, all Philips); and **Distant Drum** (1991, Atlantic). While in Paris, Shuman befriended the Belgium songwriter Jacques Brel, who allowed him to translate some of his songs into English for the show "Jacques Brel Is Alive and Well and Living in Paris" (1968), which ran for seven years off-Broadway. Pomus remained in America and continued to write in a blues vein, releasing the solo albums **Send for the Doctor** (1987, Wine, Women & Song) and **It's Great to Be Young and in Love** (1991, RBB). The singer Johnny Adams also recorded an entire album of his material, **Johnny Adams Sings Doc Pomus — The Real Me** (1992, RND), and he later collaborated with Dr. John on the film "Short Cuts" (1993). In his later years, Pomus became something of a champion for the original blues artists, often helping them out financially and gaining them previously unpaid royalties on their old recordings. Despite the popularity of much of his work, Pomus once said, "every hit song I've ever written has been rejected by ten or fifteen artists." They both died of cancer within seven months of one another. HIT VERSIONS: *Boogie Woogie Country Girl* [i] Big Joe Turner on B-side of *Corrina, Corrina* (1956) R&B#2 US#41, *Can't Get Used to Losing You* Andy Williams (1963) US#2 UK#2/Beat (1983) UK#3; *Clinging Vine* Bobby Vinton (1970) US#17, *Ecstacy* [viii] Ben E. King (1962) US#56, *First Taste of Love* [viii] Ben E. King (1960) US#53 UK#27, *Get It While You Can* [ix] Howard Tate (1967) US#134/Janis Joplin (1971) US#78; *Go, Jimmy, Go* Jimmy Clanton (1960) R&B#19 US#5, *Havin' Fun* Dion (1961) US#42, *Here I Go Again* [x] Hollies (1964) UK#4, *Hopeless* [iii] Andy Williams (1963) US#13, *Hound Dog Man* Fabian (1959) US#9 UK#46, *Hushabye* Jay & the Americans (1969)

US#62/Robert John (1972) US#99; *I Count the Tears* Drifters (1960) R&B#6 US#17 UK#28, *I'm a Man* Fabian (1959) US#31, *(If You Cry) True Love, True Love* Drifters (1959) R&B#5 US#33, *It's a Lonely Town* Gene McDaniels (1963) US#64, *Kiss Me Quick* Elvis Presley (1962) US#34 UK#14, *Little Children* [v] Billy J. Kramer & the Dakotas (1964) g US#7 UK#1, *Little Sister* Elvis Presley (1961) g US#4 UK#1/Dwight Yoakam (1987) C&W#7; *Lonely Avenue* [vi] Ray Charles (1956) R&B#6, *Lonely Winds* Drifters (1960) R&B#9 US#54, *Look at Granny Run Run* Howard Tate (1966) R&B#12 US#67, *Love Roller Coaster* Joe Turner (1957) R&B#12, *Love's Just a Broken Heart* [iv] Cilla Black (1966) UK#5, *(Marie's the Name) His Latest Flame* Elvis Presley (1961) g US#4 UK#1, *Mess of Blues, A* Elvis Presley (1960) US#32 UK#2, *My Baby* Garnet Mimms (1966) US#132, *No One* Connie Francis (1961) US#34/Ray Charles (1963) R&B#9 US#21 UK#35/Brenda Lee (1965) US#98; *Petticoat White (Summer Sky Blue)* Bobby Vinton (1966) US#81, *Plain Jane* Bobby Darin (1959) US#38, *Room Full of Tears* Drifters (1961) US#72, *Save the Last Dance for Me* Drifters (1960) g R&B#1 US#1 UK#2, re-issued (1979) UK#69/Buck Owens (1962) C&W#11/DeFranco Family featuring Tony DeFranco (1974) US#18/Bennie Lindsey (1976) C&W#100/ Jerry Lee Lewis (1978) C&W#26/Ron Shaw (1978) C&W#36/Emmylou Harris (1979) C&W#4/Dolly Parton (1983) C&W#3 US#45/Ben E. King (1987) UK#69; *Seven Day Weekend* Gary "U.S." Bonds (1962) US#27, *Sha La La La Lee* [iv] Small Faces (1966) UK#3, *Spanish Lace* Gene McDaniels (1961) US#31, *Surrender* Elvis Presley (1961) US#1 UK#1, *Suspicion* Terry Stafford (1964) US#3 UK#31/Elvis Presley (1964) US#103 UK#9/Bobby G. Rice (1972) C&W#33/Ronnie McDowell (1988) C&W#27; *Sweets for My Sweet* Drifters (1961) R&B#10 US#16/Searchers (1963) UK#1/Tony Orlando (1979) US#54; *Teenager in Love, A* Dion & the Belmonts (1959) g US#5 UK#28/Craig Douglas (1959) UK#13/Marty Wilde (1959) UK#2; *There Must Be a World Somewhere* [vii] B.B. King (1981) R&B#91, *This Magic Moment* Drifters (1960) R&B#4 US#16/Jay & the Americans (1969) US#6/Richard Roundtree (1976) R&B#90/Sandra Kaye (1978) C&W#52/ Richie Furay (1978) US#101/Rick James (1989) R&B#74; *Time, Time* Ed Ames (1967) US#61, *Turn Me Loose* Fabian (1959) US#9, *Viva Las Vegas* Elvis Presley (1964) US#29 UK#17/ZZ Top (1992) UK#10; *What's It Gonna Be?* [ix] Dusty Springfield (1967) US#49, *Where Have They Gone* [ii] Jimmy Beaumont & the Skyliners (1975) US#100, *World of Broken Hearts, The* Amen Corner (1967) UK#26/Elvis Costello on B-side of *From Head to Toe* (1982) UK#43; *Young Blood* [viii] Coasters (1957) R&B#2 US#8/Bad Company (1976) US#20/UFO (1980)

UK#36/Bruce Willis (1987) US#68; *Young Boy Blues* [viii] Ben E. King (1961) US#66, *Your Other Love* Connie Francis (1963) US#28. All compositions Doc Pomus/Mort Shuman, except: [i] Reginald Ashby/ Doc Pomus, [ii] Ken Hirsh/Doc Pomus, [iii] Alan Jeffreys/Doc Pomus, [iv] Kenny Lynch/Mort Shuman, [v] John Leslie McFarland/Mort Shuman, [vi] Doc Pomus, [vii] Doc Pomus/Mac Rebennack, [viii] Doc Pomus/Mort Shuman/Phil Spector, [ix] Doc Pomus/Mort Shuman/Jerry Ragovoy, [x] Mort Shuman/Clive Westlake. (*See also under* Jacques BREL, Jerry LEIBER & Mike STOLLER.)

751. POP, Iggy (b. James Newell Osterberg, April 21, 1947, Muskegan, MI) Rock vocalist. A rock performer who was a considerable influence on the punk-rock movement of the 1970s. Pop was initially a drummer with the 1960s groups, the Iguanas and the Prime Movers, but from 1969 he fronted the Stooges, which recorded the albums **The Stooges** (1969) US#106, **Fun House** (1970, both Elektra); **Raw Power** (1973, Columbia) US#182 UK#44; **Metallic K.O.** (1973), and **No Fun** (1980, both Elektra). Two of Pop's Stooges compositions, *No Fun* and *I Wanna Be Your Dog*, became punk standards ten years later, but it was not until he linked up with David Bowie during the mid–1970s, that he enjoyed any degree of chart success. CHART COMPOSITIONS: *Living on the Edge* (1990) UK#51, *Candy* (1990) US#28 UK#67, *The Wild America EP* (1993) UK#63, *Beside You* (1994) UK#47, *Lust for Life* (1996) UK#26. ALBUMS: **The Idiot** (1977) US#72 UK#30, **Lust for Life** (1977, both RCA) US#120 UK#28; **Skydog in France** (1978), **Kill City** (1978), **T.V. Eye** (1977), **Live** (1978), **New Values** (1979) US#180 UK#60, **Soldier** (1980) US#125 UK#62, **Party** (1981, all Arista) US#166; **Zombie Birdhouse** (1982, Animal); **Blah-Blah-Blah** (1986) US#75 UK#43, **Instinct** (1988, both A&M) US#110 UK#61; **Brick By Brick** (1990) US#90 UK#50, **American Caesar** (1993) UK#43, **Beside You** (1994) UK#47, **Naughty Little Doggie** (1996, all Virgin); **Best of Iggy Pop...Live!** (1996, Geffen). HIT VERSIONS: *Passenger, The* Siouxsie & the Banshees (1987) UK#41. (*See also under* David BOWIE.)

752. PORTER, Cole (b. June 9, 1891, Peru, IN; d. October 15, 1964, Santa Monica, CA) Film and stage composer, pianist and vocalist. One of the greatest songwriters of the twentieth century, who wrote unforgettable melodies and literate, witty, cosmopolitan lyrics, that blended American colloquialisms with European sophistication. Porter composed over twenty Broadway musicals, although none of them were as remotely engaging as the individual songs that they introduced. After studying law at Harvard and serving in the French Army during World War I, Porter married into wealth and spent much of the early 1920s cavorting around Paris. His first major hit was *I'm in Love Again* (1924), which he followed with the shows "See America First" (1916), "Fifty Million Frenchmen," "Wake Up and Dream" (both 1929); "The New Yorkers" (1930), "The Gay Divorcee" (1932), "Anything Goes" (1934), "Jubilee" (1935), "Red, Hot and Blue" (1936), "You Never Know" (1938), "Leave It to Me" (1938), "DuBarry Was a Lady" (1939), "Panama Hattie" (1940), "Let's Face It" (1941), "Something for the Boys" (1943), "Mexican Hayride," "Seven Lively Arts" (both 1944); "Around the World in Eighty Days" (1946), "The Pirate" (1947), "Kiss Me Kate" (1948), "Out of This World" (1950), "Can-Can" (1954), and "Silk Stockings" (1955). He also composed for such films as "Born to Dance" (1936), "Rosalie" (1937), "Broadway Melody of 1940," "Something to Shout About" (1943), "High Society" (1956), and "Les Girls" (1957). Porter's forte was portraying the rich, socialite circles that he and his wife moved in, frequently in an acerbic manner. He relocated to New York in the early 1930s, where, after a riding accident in 1937, he lost the use of both legs. Numerous singers have recorded albums of his material, but the most successful were **Ella Fitzgerald Sings the Cole Porter Songbook** (1956, Verve) US#15; **Bobby Short Loves Cole Porter** (1972, Atlantic) US#169; **Dionne Warwick Sings Cole Porter** (1990, Arista) US#155; and the various artists selection **Red, Hot and Blue** (1990, Chrysalis) UK#6. CHART COMPOSITION: *You're the Top* (1935) US#10. ALBUMS: **Anything Goes** oc (1934), **Leave It to Me!** oc (1938, both Smithsonian); **Holiday in Manhattan** st (1947, Design); **Kiss Me Kate** oc (1949, Columbia); **Anything Goes** ost (1950), **Mexican Hayride** oc (1950, both Decca); **Out of This World** oc (1950, Columbia); **Cole Porter Review** st (1951, RCA); **Pirate** st (1951, MGM); **Can-Can** oc (1953, Capitol); **Kiss Me Kate** ost (1953, MGM); **Pajama Game** oc (1954, Columbia); **Somebody Bad Stole De Wedding Bell** st (1954, RCA); **Young at Heart** ost (1954, Columbia); **Silk Stockings** oc (1955, RCA) US#9; **High Society** ost (1956, Capitol) US#5 UK#16; **Les Girls** st (1957), **Silk Stockings** ost (1957, both MGM); **Aladdin** tvst (1958, Columbia); **Can-Can** ost (1960, Capitol) US#3 UK#2; **Cole Porter and Me** st (1965, RCA); **Decline and Fall of the Entire World as Seen Through the Eyes of Cole Porter** oc (1965, Columbia); **The Painted Smiles of Cole Porter** oc (1972, Painted Smiles); **Cole** oc (1974, RCA); **Cole Porter in London** (1974, Retrospective); **R.S.V.P. The Cole Porters** oc (1974, Respond); **At Long Last Love** ost (1975, RCA); **The Gay Divorcee** ost (1975, SE); **Let's Face It** oc (1979,

Smithsonian); **Panama Hattie** ost (1981, Sandy Hook). HIT VERSIONS: *All of You* Sammy Davis, Jr. (1956) UK#28/Julio Iglesias (1984) US#19; *All Through the Night* Harry Rosenthal (1935) US#18/Paul Whiteman (1935) US#8; *Allez-Vous-En* Kay Starr (1953) US#11, *Anything Goes* Paul Whiteman (1934) US#5/Frank Sinatra on *Songs for Swinging Lovers LP* (1956) UK#12/Harper's Bizarre (1967) US#43 UK#33; *At Long Last Love* Larry Clinton (1938) US#11/Ozzie Nelson (1938) US#3; *Begin the Beguine* Xavier Cugat (1935) US#13/Artie Shaw (1938) g US#1, re-issued (1942) US#20/Eddie Heywood (1945) US#16/Frank Sinatra (1946) US#23/Julio Iglesias (1981) UK#1; *Blow, Gabriel, Blow* [i] Enric Madriguera (1935) US#13, *C'est Magnifique* Gordon MacRae (1953) US#29, *Ca C'est L'amour* Tony Bennett (1957) US#22, *Do I Love You, Do I?* Leo Reisman (1940) US#7, *Don't Fence Me In* Bing Crosby & the Andrews Sisters (1944) g R&B#9 US#1/Gene Autry (1945) C&W#4/Horace Heidt (1945) US#10/Sammy Kaye (1945) US#4/Kate Smith (1945) US#8/Tommy Edwards (1960) US#74/George Maharis (1963) US#93; *Easy to Love* Shep Fields (1936) US#13/Frances Langford (1936) US#20/Ray Noble (1937) US#7; *Ev'ry Time We Say Goodbye* Benny Goodman (1945) US#12/Simply Red (1987) UK#11; *Ev'rything I Love* Glenn Miller (1942) US#7, *Find Me a Primitive Man* Libby Holman & the Colonial Club Orchestra (1929) US#19, *Friendship* Kay Kyser (1940) US#11, *From Now On* Isham Jones (1934) US#12/Eddy Duchin (1938) US#8; *Get Out of Town* Eddy Duchin (1939) US#7, *I Am in Love* Nat "King" Cole (1953) US#19, *I Concentrate on You* Tommy Dorsey (1940) US#20/Eddy Duchin (1940) US#25; *I Get a Kick Out of You* Ethel Merman (1935) US#12/Leo Reisman (1935) US#20/Paul Whiteman (1935) US#3/Gary Shearston (1974) UK#7; *I Love Paris* Les Baxter (1953) US#13, *I Love You* Tommy Tucker (1943) US#21/Perry Como (1944) US#12/Bing Crosby (1944) US#1/Enric Madriguera (1944) US#7/Jo Stafford (1944) US#8; *I'm in Love Again* April Stevens (1951) US#6, *I've Got My Eyes on You* Bob Crosby (1940) US#8/Tommy Dorsey (1940) US#6; *I've Got You on My Mind* Leo Reisman & Fred Astaire (1933) US#17, *I've Got You Under My Skin* Hal Kemp (1936) US#8/Ray Noble (1936) US#3/Stan Freberg (1951) US#11/Frank Sinatra on *Songs for Swinging Lovers LP* (1956) UK#12/Four Seasons (1966) US#9 UK#12/Neneh Cherry (1990) UK#25/Frank Sinatra & Bono (1993) UK#4; *In the Still of the Night* Tommy Dorsey (1937) US#3/Leo Reisman (1938) US#9/Crests (1960) US#102/Dion & the Belmonts (1960) US#38/Paul Anka (1969) US#64; *It's De-Lovely* Leo Reisman (1936) US#7/Eddy Duchin (1937) US#1/Shep Fields (1937) US#9/Will Osborne (1937) US#14; *Just One of Those Things*

Richard Himber (1935) US#10/Peggy Lee (1952) US#14; *Let's Be Buddies* Connee Boswell (1940) US#25, *Let's Do It (Let's Fall in Love)* Irving Aaronson (1929) US#5/Dorsey Brothers Orchestra (1929) US#9/Paul Whiteman (1929) US#5; *Let's Misbehave* Ben Bernie (1928) US#18, *Little Skipper* Tommy Dorsey (1939) US#4/Ozzie Nelson (1939) US#3; *Love for Sale* Libby Holman (1931) US#5/Fred Waring's Pennsylvanians (1931) US#14/Hal Kemp (1939) US#14/Simply Red on *Montreux EP* (1992) UK#11; *Me and Marie* Johnny Green (1935) US#18, *Miss Otis Regrets (She's Unable to Dine Today)* Ethel Waters (1934) US#19, *My Heart Belongs to Daddy* Larry Clinton (1939) US#4/Mary Martin & Eddy Duchin (1939) US#9/Artie Shaw (1946) US#22; *Night and Day* Leo Reisman & Fred Astaire (1932) US#1/Eddy Duchin (1933) US#2, re-issued (1934) US#13/Charlie Barnet (1940) US#24/Frank Sinatra (1942) US#16, re-issued (1944) US#16/Bing Crosby (1946) US#21/John Davis (1976) R&B#100 US#109; *Nobody's Chasing Me* Dinah Shore (1950) US#18, *Now You Has Jazz* Bing Crosby & Louis Armstrong (1956) US#88, *Rosalie* Sammy Kaye (1938) US#1/Hoarce Heidt (1938) US#6; *So in Love* Gordon MacRae (1949) US#20/Patti Page (1949) US#13/Dinah Shore (1949) US#20/Shirley Bassey on B-side of *As Long as He Needs Me* (1960) UK#2; *True Love* Bing Crosby & Grace Kelly (1965) US#3 UK#4, re-issued (1983) UK#70/Jane Powell (1956) US#15/Terry Lightfoot & His New Orleans Jazzmen (1961) UK#33/Richard Chamberlain (1963) US#98 UK#30/Red Steagall (1973) C&W#51/LeGardes (1978) C&W#88/Shakin' Stevens (1988) UK#23/Elton John & Kiki Dee (1993) US#56 UK#2; *Well, Did You Evah?* Bing Crosby & Frank Sinatra (1956) US#92/Debbie Harry & Iggy Pop (1991) UK#42; *What Is This Thing Called Love* Ben Bernie (1930) US#10/Leo Reisman (1930) US#5/Fred Rich (1930) US#19/Artie Shaw (1939) US#15/Tommy Dorsey (1942) US#13/Les Paul (1948) US#11; *Where Have You Been?* Emil Coleman (1931) US#6, *You Do Something to Me* Leo Reisman (1930) US#13, *You Never Know* Glen Gray (1938) US#19, *You'd Be So Nice to Come Home to* Dinah Shore (1943) R&B#10 US#3/Six Hits & a Miss (1943) US#11; *You're Sensational* Frank Sinatra (1956) US#52, *You're the Top* Dorsey Brothers Orchestra (1934) US#17/Paul Whiteman (1934) US#2/Ethel Merman (1935) US#4; *You've Got That Thing* Ted Lewis (1930) US#4/Leo Reisman (1930) US#11. Co-writer: [i] Ira Gershwin.

753. PORTER, David (b. November 21, 1941, Memphis, TN) R&B vocalist. A staff writer at Stax Records during the 1960s, who is best known for his songwriting partnership with Isaac Hayes. Porter also recorded many solo sides for a variety of small labels during the 1960s. CHART COMPOSITION: *Can't See You When I Want To* (1970) R&B#29 US#105. ALBUMS: **Gritty, Groovy and Gettin' It** (1970) US#163, **Into a Real Thing** (1971) US#104, **Sweet and Love** (1973), **Victim of the Joke?—An Opera** (1974, all Enterprise). (*See also under* Isaac HAYES.)

754. POWELL, Michael J. (b. Detroit, MI) R&B producer, arranger and vocalist. A producer best known for his work with the vocalist Anita Baker, on the albums **The Songstress** (1983), the four million selling **Rapture** (1986), and the three million selling **Giving You the Best That I've Got** (1988). Powell has also recorded with his own group Chapter 8, and written and produced for Regina Belle, Perri, David Peaston, Jimmy Scott, and James Ingram. CHART COMPOSITIONS: *I Just Wanna Be Your Girl* (1979) R&B#81, *Don't You Like It* (1980) R&B#55. ALBUMS: **Chapter 8** (1979, Ariola); **This Love's for Real** (1985, Beverly Glen); **Forever** (1989, Capitol). HIT VERSIONS: *I Think I'm Over You* Mini Curry (1987) R&B#34, *No More Tears* Anita Baker (1983) R&B#49, *Talk to Me* [i] Anita Baker (1990) US#44 UK#68, *Tell Me Where It Hurts* [ii] Guess (1994) US#45, *Where Would I Be* Gladys Knight (1992) R&B#66. Co-writers: [i] Anita Baker (b. January 26, 1958, Toledo, OH)/Vernon Fails, [ii] A. Mason/T. Mason.

755. PRESLEY, Reg (b. Reginald Ball, June 12, 1943, Andover, England) Pop vocalist. The lead singer in the 1960s group the Troggs, who enjoyed revived personal fortunes when Wet Wet Wet recorded his song *Love Is All Around* in 1994. CHART COMPOSITIONS: *With a Girl Like You* (1966) US#29 UK#1, also on B-side of *Wild Thing* (1966) US#1; *I Can't Control Myself* (1966) US#43 UK#2, *Give It to Me* (1967) UK#12, *Night of the Long Grass* (1967) UK#17, *Love Is All Around* (1967) US#7 UK#5. ALBUMS: **From Nowhere...** (1966) UK#6, **Trogglodynamite** (1967, both Page One) UK#10; **Hip Hip Hooray** (1968, Hansa); **Live at Max's Kansas City** (1980, Basement); **Black Bottom** (1981, New Rose); **Athens Andover** (1992, Essential/Page One). COMPILATIONS: **Wild Thing** (1966, Fontana) US#52; **Best of the Troggs** (1967, Page One) UK#24; **Love Is All Around** (1968, Fontana) US#109; **The Troggs Tapes** (1976, Penny Farthing); **Archeology, (1966–1976)** (1993, Fontana); **Greatest Hits** (1994, PolyGram) UK#27; **The EP Collection** (1997, See for Miles). HIT VERSION: *Love Is All Around* Wet Wet Wet (1994) US#41 UK#1/D.J. Bobo (1995) UK#49.

756. PRESTON, Billy (b. September 9, 1946, Houston, TX) R&B keyboard player, producer and vocalist. A session musician who was drafted in by both the Rolling Stones and the Beatles, to add an element of R&B to their respective sounds. Preston first recorded as a solo performer in the 1960s, and he enjoyed a lengthy chart run during the 1970s. CHART COMPOSITIONS: *All That I've Got (I'm Gonna Give to You)* (1970) US#108, *The Bus* (1972) R&B#43, *Outa-Space* [ii] (1972) g R&B#1 US#2, *Slaughter* (1972) R&B#17 US#50, *Will It Go Round in Circles* (1973) g R&B#1 US#1, *Space Race* (1973) g R&B#1 US#4, *You're So Unique* [ii] (1973) R&B#11 US#48, *Nothing from Nothing* [i] (1974) g R&B#8 US#1, *Struttin'* [iii] (1974) R&B#11 US#22, *Fancy Lady* [v] (1975) R&B#23 US#71, *Do It While You Can* (1975) R&B#58, *I've Got the Spirit/Do What You Want* (1977) R&B#48, *Girl* (1977) R&B#44, *Wide Stride* (1977) R&B#33, *I'm Really Gonna Miss You* (1978) R&B#59. ALBUMS: **Gospel in My Soul** (1962, SAR); **The Apple of Their Eye** (1965), **Early Hits of 1965** (1965, both President); **The Most Exciting Organ Ever** (1965) US#143, **Wildest Organ in Town** (1966, both Vee-Jay); **That's the Way God Planned It** (1969) US#127, **Greazee Soul** (1969), **Encouraging Words** (1970, all Apple); **I Wrote a Simple Song** (1971) US#32, **Music Is My Life** (1972) US#32, **Everybody Likes Some Kind of Music** (1973) US#52, **The Kids and Me** (1974) US#17, **Live European Tour** (1974), **It's My Pleasure** (1975, all A&M); **Do What You Want** (1976), **Billy Preston** (1976), **A Whole New Thing** (1977), **Soul'd Out** (1977), **Fast Break** (1979), **Late at Night** (1979, all Motown) US#49; **Behold** (1980), **Universal Love** (1980, Myrrh); **The Way I Am** (1981), **Billy Preston and Syreeta** (1981) US#127, **Pressin' On** (1982, all Motown). COMPILATIONS: **Best of Billy Preston** (1988, A&M). HIT VERSIONS: *Great Gosh A'Mighty! (It's a Matter of Time)* [iv] Little Richard (1986) US#42, *You Are So Beautiful* [i] Joe Cocker (1975) US#5/Ray Stevens (1976) C&W#16 US#101/Tanya Tucker (1977) C&W#40. Co-writers: [i] Bruce Fisher, [ii] Joseph Greene, [iii] George Johnson, [iv] R. Penniman, [v] Syreeta Wright.

757. PREVIN, Dory (b. Dory Langdon, October 22, 1935, Woodbridge, NJ) Pop pianist and vocalist. A dancer who studied at New York's Academy of Dramatic Arts, before performing in vaudeville and night clubs while writing television themes at MGM and United Artists. Previn married the classical pianist Andre Previn in 1959, after which she began setting his and Elmer Bernstein's tunes to her lyrics. Previn's film themes included *You're Gonna Hear from Me* from "Inside Daisy Clover" (1965), *The Faraway Part of Town* from "Pepe" (1960) and the title theme *The Last Tango in Paris* [i] (1973). During the 1970s, Previn recorded a series of some-

what verbose singer-songwriter albums. ALBUMS: **Dory and Andre Previn** (1957, DRG); **Valley of the Dolls** (1968, 20th Century) US#11; **On My Way to Where** (1970), **Mythical Kings and Iguanas** (1972, both Media Arts); **Reflections in a Mud Puddle** (1972), **Mary C Brown and The Hollywood Sign** (1972), **Live at Carnegie Hall** (1973, all United Artists); **Dory Previn** (1974), **We're Children of Coincidence and Harpo Marx** (1976, Warner Brothers); **One A.M. Phone Calls** (1977, United Artists). HIT VERSIONS: *Come Saturday Morning* [ii] Sandpipers (1970) US#17, *Valley Of The Dolls, Theme from* [iii] Dionne Warwick (1968) R&B#13 US#2 UK#28/King Curtis (1968) US#83. Co-writers: [i] Gato Barbieri, [ii] Fred Carlin, [iii] Andre Previn.

758. PRICE, Lloyd (b. March 9, 1933, Kenner, LA) R&B pianist and vocalist. An influential performer on the early development of rock and roll, who achieved twenty-three hits between 1952–1976. CHART COMPOSITIONS: *Lawdy Miss Clawdy* (1952) R&B#1, *Oooh, Oooh, Oooh* (1952) R&B#4, *Restless Heart* (1952) R&B#5, *Tell Me Pretty Baby* (1953) R&B#8, *Ain't It a Shame* (1953) R&B#4, *Just Because* (1957) R&B#3 US#29, *Stagger Lee* [i] arrangement only (1958) R&B#1 US#1 UK#7, *Where Were You (On Our Wedding Day)* (1959) R&B#4 US#23 UK#15, *Personality* [i] (1959) R&B#1 US#2 UK#9, *I'm Gonna Get Married* [i] (1959) R&B#1 US#3 UK#23, *Come into My Heart* [i] (1959) R&B#2 US#20, *Wont'cha Come Home* (1959) R&B#6 US#43, *Lady Luck* [i] (1960) R&B#3 US#14 UK#45, *Never Let Me Go* (1960) R&B#26 US#82, *No If's-No And's* (1960) R&B#16 US#40, *Question* (1960) R&B#5 US#19. ALBUMS: **Lloyd Price** (1959, Speciality); **Mr. Personality** (1959), **The Exciting Lloyd Price** (1959), **Mr. Personality Sings the Blues** (1960), **Mr. Personality's Big 15** (1960), **Lloyd Price Sings the Million Sellers** (1960), **The Fantastic Lloyd Price** (1960), **Cookin'** (1961, all ABC); **Mr. Rhythm and Blues** (1964, Grand Prix); **Stagger Lee** (1965, Joy); **Lloyd Swings for Sammy** (1965, Monument); **Best of Lloyd Price** (1970, Regal Starline); **Misty** (1976, DJM); **Sixteen Greatest Hits** (1976), **The ABC Collection** (1976, both ABC); **Lloyd Price Now** (1968, Jad); **To the Roots and Back** (1972, GSF); **Juke Box Giants** (1981, Audio Fidelity); **Mr. Personality Revisited** (1983, Charly). HIT VERSIONS: *Just Because* MacGuire Sisters (1961) US#99, *Lawdy Miss Clawdy* Elvis Presley (1957) UK#15/Gary Stites (1960) US#49/Buckinghams (1967) US#41; *Stagger Lee* [i] Wilson Pickett (1967) R&B#13 US#22. Co-writers: [i] Harold Logan.

759. PRINCE (b. Prince Rogers Nelson, June 7, 1958, Minneapolis, MN). R&B multi-instrumentalist, producer and vocalist. A virtuoso R&B musician who took the music of his influences, George Clinton, Sly Stone, Jimi Hendrix, the Beatles, David Bowie, and James Brown, and created a unique hybrid of rock, funk, rap and pop. The prolific Prince virtually defined the sound of R&B during the 1980s. Born to musician parents, by the 1970s he had learned the piano, guitar, saxophone, bass and drums, ultimately mastering over twenty instruments. In 1972 he joined the group Grand Central, which was followed by short spells in Champagne and Flyte Tyme, before he learned studio production techniques and signed a long-term recording contract with Warner Brothers in 1977. Prince wrote and performed his debut album in its entirety, and by the thirteen million selling **Purple Rain** (1984), he had become the biggest R&B artist in the world, branching out into films, and forming his own Paisley Park record label. In 1992, Prince collaborated with the Joffrey Ballet troupe on the musical dance piece "Billboards," and the following year he announced that he no longer wished to be known as Prince, naming himself thereafter by the moniker of his 1992 album. In 1993 he collaborated on an interactive CD-ROM, alongside a theatrical production of thirteen new songs entitled "Glam Slam Ulysses," which was premiered in Los Angeles. CHART COMPOSITIONS: *Soft and Wet* (1978) R&B#12 US#92, *Just as Long as We're Together* (1978) R&B#91, *I Wanna Be Your Lover* (1979) g R&B#1 US#11 UK#41, *Why You Wanna Treat Me So Bad?* (1979) R&B#13, *Still Waiting* (1980) R&B#65, *Uptown* (1980) R&B#5 US#101, *Dirty Mind* (1981) R&B#65, *Controversy* (1981) R&B#3 US#70, *Let's Work* (1981) R&B#9 US#104, *1999* (1982) R&B#4 US#44, re-issued (1983) US#12 UK#25; *Little Red Corvette* (1983) R&B#15 US#6 UK#54, re-issued (1983) UK#66; *Delirious* (1983) R&B#18 US#8, *Let's Pretend We're Married/Irresistible Bitch* (1984) R&B#55 US#52, *When Doves Cry* (1984) p R&B#1 US#1 UK#4, *Let's Go Crazy* [ix] (1984) g R&B#1 US#1, *Purple Rain* (1984) g R&B#4 US#2 UK#8, *I Would Die for U* (1984) R&B#11 US#8 UK#58, *Take Me with U* [ix] (1984) R&B#40 US#25 UK#7, *1999/Little Red Corvette* (1985) UK#2, *Paisley Park* [ix] (1985) UK#18, *Raspberry Beret* [ix] (1985) R&B#3 US#2 UK#25, *Pop Life* [ix] (1985) R&B#8 US#7 UK#60, *America* [ix] (1985) R&B#35 US#46, *Kiss* (1986) g R&B#1 US#1 UK#6, *Mountains* [ix] (1986) R&B#15 US#23 UK#45, *Anotherloverholenyohead* [ix] (1986) R&B#18 US#63 UK#36, *Girls and Boys* (1986) UK#11, *Sign O' the Times* (1987) R&B#1 US#3 UK#10, *If I Was Your Girlfriend* (1987) R&B#12 US#67 UK#20, *U Got the Look* (1987) R&B#11 US#2 UK#11, *I Could Never Take the Place of Your Man* (1987) R&B#10 UK#29, *Hot Thing* (1987) R&B#14 UK#63, *Alphabet Street* (1988) R&B#3 US#8 UK#9,

Glam Slam (1988) UK#29, *I Wish U Heaven* (1988) UK#24, *Batdance* (1989) US#1 UK#2, *Partyman* (1989) US#18 UK#14, *The Arms of Orion* with Sheena Easton (1989) US#36 UK#27, *Thieves in the Temple* (1990) US#6, *New Power Generation* (1990) US#64, *Cream* [viii] (1990) US#1 UK#15, *Gett Off* [viii] (1991) US#21 UK#4, *Diamonds and Pearls* [viii] (1992) US#3 UK#25, *Insatiable* [viii] (1992) US#5 UK#77, *Money Don't Matter 2 Night* [viii] (1992) R&B#14 US#23 UK#19, *Thunder* [viii] (1992) UK#28, *Sexy M.F.* [x] (1992) R&B#76 US#66 UK#4, *My Name Is Prince* [xii] (1992) R&B#25 US#36 UK#7, re-mixed (1992) UK#51; *7* [v] (1992) g R&B#61 US#7 UK#27, *Damn U* (1992) R&B#32 US#108, *The Morning Papers* (1993) R&B#70 US#44 UK#52, *Pink Cashmere* (1993) R&B#15 US#50, *Peach* (1993) US#107 UK#14, *Nothing Compares to U* (1993) R&B#62, *Controversy* (1993) UK#5, *The Most Beautiful Girl in the World* (1994) R&B#16+ UK#1, *LetItGo* (1994) UK#30, *The Purple Medley* (1995) UK#33, *Eye Hate U* (1995) UK#20, *Gold* (1995) UK#10, *Dinner with Delores* (1996) UK#36. ALBUMS: **For You** (1978) US#163, **Prince** (1979) p US#22, **Dirty Mind** (1980) g US#45, **Controversy** (1981) p US#21, **1999** (1982) p US#9 UK#30, **Purple Rain** ost (1984, all Warner Brothers) p US#1 UK#7; **Around the World in a Day** (1985) p US#1 UK#5, **Parade** (1986) p US#3 UK#4, **Sign O' the Times** (1987) p US#6 UK#4, **Lovesexy** (1988, all Paisley Park) US#11 UK#1; **Batman** ost (1989, Warner Brothers) p US#1 UK#1; **Graffiti Bridge** ost (1990) g US#6 UK#1, **Diamonds and Pearls** (1991) p US#3 UK#2, ✿ (1992, all Paisley Park) p US#5 UK#1; **Come** (1994) UK#1, **The Black Album** (1994) UK#36, **The Gold Experience** (1995) UK#4, **Exodus** (1995) UK#11, **Music from the Motion Picture Girl 6** ost (1996), **Chaos and Disorder** (1996, all Warner Brothers) UK#14; **Emancipation** (1997, NPG/EMI). COMPILATIONS: **Gett Off** (1991) US#33, **The Hits/The B-Sides** (1993) p US#19 UK#4, **The Hits 1** (1993) g US#46 UK#5, **The Hits 2** (1993, all Paisley Park) US#54 UK#5; **94 East featuring Prince** (1995, Charly). HIT VERSIONS: *Bird, The* Morris Day & the Time (1985) R&B#33 US#36, *Born 2 B.R.E.E.D.* [vi] Monie Love (1993) R&B#56 US#89 UK#18, *Do Me Baby* Meli'sa Morgan (1985) R&B#1 US#46, *Get It Up* Time (1981) R&B#6/TLC (1993) R&B#15 US#42; *Girl* Time (1982) R&B#49, *Girl 6* [ii] New Power Generation (1996) R&B#78+, *Glamorous Life, The* Sheila E. (1984) R&B#9 US#7, *Hold Me* Sheila E. (1987) R&B#3 US#68, *How Come U Don't Call Any More* Stephanie Mills (1983) R&B#12, *I Feel for You* Chaka Khan (1984) g R&B#1 US#3 UK#1, re-mixed (1989) UK#45; *Jungle Love* [iii] Morris Day & the Time (1984) R&B#6 US#20, *Kiss* Art of Noise with Tom

Jones (1988) US#31 UK#5, *Love Bizarre, A* [iv] Sheila E. (1985) R&B#2 US#11, *Love…Thy Will Be Done* [vii] Martika (1991) US#10 UK#9, *Manic Monday* Bangles (1986) US#2 UK#2, *Martika's Kitchen* Martika (1992) US#93 UK#17, *Nothing Compares to U* Sinead O'Connor (1990) g US#1 UK#1, *Oooo This I Need* Eliso Fiorillo (1991) US#90, *Round and Round* Tevin Campbell (1990) US#12, *Sex Shooter* Apollonia 6 (1984) R&B#14 US#85, *She Ain't Worth It* [i] Glenn Medeiros featuring Bobby Brown (1990) US#1, *Sign O' the Times* Simple Minds on *The Amsterdam EP* (1989) UK#18, *Still Waiting* Rainy Davis (1987) R&B#41, *Strut* Sheena Easton (1984) US#7, *Sugar Walls* Sheena Easton (1985) R&B#3 US#9, *Voice, The* Mavis Staples (1993) R&B#110, *When Doves Cry* M.C. Hammer sampled in *Pray* (1990) R&B#1 US#2 UK#8, *When You Were Mine* Mitch Ryder (1983) US#87, *Wouldn't You Love to Love Me?* Taja Sevelle (1988) R&B#61. Co-writers: [i] A. Armato/Bobby Brown, [ii] T. Barbarella, [iii] Morris Day/Jesse Johnson, [iv] Sheila Escovedo (b. December 12, 1959, San Francisco, CA), [v] Fulson/Mc-Cracklin, [vi] Monie Love/L. Seacer Jr., [vii] Martika (b. Martika Marrero, 1970, Los Angeles, CA), [viii] New Power Generation, [ix] Revolution, [x] L. Seacer Jr./Tony M., [xi] Tony M. (*See also under* Stevie NICKS.)

760. PRINE, John (b. October 10, 1946, Maywood, IL) Folk guitarist and vocalist. A country and folk influenced singer-songwriter, whose forte is narrative styled songs that champion off-beat characters. Prine's best known composition is *Angel from Montgomery*, which was recorded by Bonnie Raitt. He learned the guitar at the age of fourteen and started writing songs while still at high school, later working for the post office, before recording his first album in 1971. ALBUMS: **John Prine** (1972) US#154, **Diamonds in the Rough** (1973) US#148, **Sweet Revenge** (1974) US#135, **Common Sense** (1975, all Atlantic) US#66; **Bruised Orange** (1978) US#116, **Pink Cadillac** (1979) US#152, **Storm Windows** (1980, all Asylum) US#144; **Aimless Love** (1984), **German Afternoons** (1986), **Live** (1987), **The Missing Years** (1990), **A John Prine Christmas** (1993), **Lost Dogs and Mixed Blessings** (1995), **Live on Tour** (1997, all Oh Boy). COMPILATIONS: **Prime Prine** (1976, Atlantic) g US#196; **We're Children of Coincidence** (1976, Warner Brothers); **Great Days — The John Prine Anthology** (1993, Rhino). HIT VERSIONS: *Paradise* Jackie DeShannon (1972) US#110. (*See also under* Bobby BRADDOCK, Roger COOK.)

761. RABBIT, Eddie (b. Edward Thomas Rabbit, November 27, 1944, Brooklyn, NY) C&W guitarist and vocalist. A major star, who achieved sixteen number one singles with his brand of rocking country. Rabbit was raised in East Orange, New Jersey, and learned the guitar and banjo as a teenager, before performing in New Jersey bars. In 1967, Rabbit re-located to Nashville, where he struggled to become a songwriter until his material attracted the attention of Elvis Presley, Roy Drusky, Bobby Lewis, and Mel Street. CHART COMPOSITIONS: *You Get to Me* (1974) C&W#34, *Forgive and Forget* (1975) C&W#12, *I Should Have Married You* (1975) C&W#11, *Drinkin' My Baby (Off My Mind)* (1976) C&W#1, *Rocky Mountain Music/Do You Right Tonight* (1976) C&W#5 US#76, *Two Dollars in the Jukebox* (1976) C&W#3, *I Can't Help Myself* [v] (1977) C&W#2 US#77, *We Can't Go on Living Like This* (1977) C&W#6, *Hearts on Fire* (1978) C&W#2, *I Just Want to Love You* (1978) C&W#1, *Suspicions* [ii] (1979) C&W#1 US#13, *Pour Me Another Tequila* (1979) C&W#5, *Gone Too Far* [iv] (1980) C&W#1 US#82, *Drivin' My Life Away* [iv] (1980) g C&W#1 US#5, *I Love a Rainy Night* [iv] (1981) g C&W#1 US#1 UK#53, *Step By Step* [iv] (1981) C&W#1 US#5, *Someone Could Lose a Heart Tonight* [iv] (1981) C&W#1 US#15, *You Can't Run from Love* [iii] (1983) C&W#1 US#55, *Nothing Like Falling in Love* (1983) C&W#10, *B-B-B-Burnin' Up with Love* (1984) C&W#3, *The Best Year of My Life* (1984) C&W#1, *Warning Sign* (1985) C&W#4, *She's Comin' Back to Say Goodbye* (1985) C&W#6, *A World Without Love* (1985) C&W#10, *Repetitive Regret* (1986) C&W#4, *Born to Each Other (Friends and Lovers)* with Juice Newton (1986) C&W#1, *Gotta Have You* (1986) C&W#9, *I Wanna Dance with You* (1988) C&W#1, *The Wanderer* (1988) C&W#1, *We Must Be Doin' Somethin' Right* (1988) C&W#7, *On Second Thoughts* (1990) C&W#1, *Hang Up the Phone* (1991) C&W#50. ALBUMS: **Eddie Rabbit** (1975), **Rocky Mountain Music** (1976), **Rabbit** (1977), **Variations** (1978) US#143, **Loveline** (1979) US#91, **Horizon** (1980) p US#19, **Step By Step** (1981) g US#23, **Radio Romance** (1982, all Elektra) US#31; **Rabbit Trax** (1986), **I Wanna Dance with You** (1988, both RCA); **Ten Rounds** (1991, Liberty); **Jersey Boy** (1992, Capitol). COMPILATIONS: **Best of Eddie Rabbit** (1979) g US#151, **An Autobiography** (1979, both Elektra); **Greatest Hits, Volume 2** (1983) US#131, **Number Ones** (1985, both Warner Brothers); **Ten Years of Greatest Hits** (1989, Capitol). HIT VERSIONS: *Ball and Chain* Tommy James (1970) US#57, *Kentucky Rain* [i] Elvis Presley (1970) C&W#31 US#16 UK#21, *Lovin' on Borrowed Time* Mel Street (1973) C&W#11, *Love Me and Make It All Better* Bobby Lewis (1967) C&W#12, *Loveline* [iv] Dr. Hook (1982) US#60, *Patch It Up* Elvis Presley on B-side of *You Don't Have to Say You Love Me* (1970)

US#11 UK#9, *Pure Love* Ronnie Milsap (1974) C&W#1, *Sign on for the Good Times* Merrilee Rush (1969) US#125. Co-writers: [i] Dick Heard, [ii] Randy McCormick/David Malloy/Even Stevens, [iii] David Malloy, [iv] David Malloy/Even Stevens, [v] Even Stevens.

762. RAFFERTY, Gerry (b. April 16, 1947, Paisley, Scotland) Rock guitarist, producer and vocalist. A folk influenced singer-songwriter who first performed in the 1960s beat groups the Censors and the Mavericks. Rafferty was a member of the Humblebums in the late 1960s, which released the albums **The New Humblebums** (1969) and **Open Up the Door** (1970), later compiled on **The Complete Humblebums** (1974, all Transatlantic). In 1972, Rafferty linked up with the keyboard player Joe Egan to form Stealers Wheel, which charted with *Stuck in the Middle with You* [i] (1973) US#6 UK#8 and *Everything Will Turn Out Fine* [i] (1973) US#49 UK#33, and issued the albums **Stealer's Wheel** (1972) US#50, **Ferguslie Park** (1974) US#181 and **Right or Wrong** (1975, all A&M). The group broke up in 1975, and after a three year hiatus, Rafferty returned as a solo artist. CHART COMPOSITIONS: *Baker Street* (1978) g US#2 UK#3, re-mixed (1990) UK#53; *Right Down the Line* (1978) US#12, *Home and Dry* (1979) US#28, *Night Owl* (1979) UK#5, *Days Gone Down (Still Got the Light in Your Eyes)* (1979) US#17, *Get It Right the Next Time* (1979) US#21 UK#30, *Bring It All Home* (1980) UK#54, *The Royal Mile (Sweet Darlin')* (1980) US#54 UK#67. ALBUMS: **Can I Have My Money Back?** (1971, Transatlantic); **City to City** (1978) p US#1 UK#6, **Night Owl** (1979) g US#29 UK#9, **Snakes and Ladders** (1980, all United Artists) US#61 UK#15; **Sleepwalking** (1982, Liberty) UK#39; **North and South** (1988, London) UK#43; **A Wing and a Prayer** (1993, A&M) UK#73; **Over My Head** (1995, Polydor). COMPILATION: **Right Down the Line — The Best of Gerry Rafferty** (1990, EMI); **One More Dream — The Very Best of Gerry Rafferty** (1995, PolyGram) UK#17. HIT VERSIONS: *Baker Street* Undercover (1992) UK#2, *Blind Faith* [i] Pointer Sisters (1979) US#107. Co-writer: [i] Joe Egan.

763. RAGOVOY, Jerry (b. September 4, 1930, Philadelphia, PA) R&B pianist and producer. A writer and producer of some of the best loved R&B of 1960s, whose songs have attracted the attention of artists well into the 1990s, his *Move Me No Mountain* [iv] becoming a hit for Soul II Soul in 1992, and his and Bert Berns' *Piece of My Heart* topping the country chart for Faith Hill in 1994. Ragovoy's powerful orchestral approach worked best on such raw gospel-soul as *Stay with Me Baby*. The son of Italian immigrants, Ragovoy learned to play and write music from the age of eight. During the 1950s, he listened to doo-wop, and worked in a record store while studying the piano, an instrument he later taught. He formed his own Grand label in 1954, and achieved hits with *My Girl Awaits Me* and *This Silver Ring* by the Castells. As one of the first freelance writer-arranger-producers, Ragovoy worked at Chandler Records with Frankie Avalon and Fabian during the 1950s, and in 1959 he wrote and produced sides for the Majors. After his 1960s successes, Ragovoy worked as a writer and producer on such albums as Dionne Warwick's **Then Came You** (1975). He sometimes wrote under the pseudonym Norman Meade. HIT VERSIONS: *Ain't Nobody Home* Howard Tate (1968) R&B#12 US#63/B.B. King (1972) R&B#28 US#48; *All I Know Is the Way I Feel* [v] Pointer Sisters (1987) R&B#69 US#93, *Baby Don't You Weep* Garnet Mimms & the Enchanters (1963) US#30, *Disappointed* Claudine Clark on B-side of *Party Lights* (1962) US#5, *Look Away* Garnet Mimms (1964) US#73, *Malayisha* Mariam Makeba (1967) US#85, *Mecca* Gene Pitney (1963) US#12/Cheetahs (1964) UK#36; *Move Me No Mountain* [iv] Soul II Soul (1992) R&B#33, *My Baby* Garnet Mimms (1966) US#132, *Pata Pata* [iii] Mariam Makeba (1967) R&B#7 US#12/Osibisa on *Calibre Cuts* (1980) UK#75; *Stay with Me Baby* Lorraine Ellison (1966) R&B#11 US#64/Walker Brothers (1967) UK#26/David Essex (1978) UK#45/Ruby Turner (1994) UK#39; *Stop* Howard Tate (1968) R&B#15 US#76, *Sure Thing* [v] Dionne Warwick (1974) R&B#66, *Take It from Me* Dionne Warwick (1975) R&B#30, *Try (Just a Little Bit)* Janis Joplin (1970) US#103, *What Is Love* Mariam Makeba (1968) US#123, *Wonderful Dream, A* Majors (1962) R&B#23 US#22, *You Got It* Diana Ross (1978) R&B#39 US#49. Co-writers: [i] E. Levitt, [ii] L. Laurie, [iii] Miriam Makeba (b. Zensi Miriam Makeba, March 4, 1932, Johannesburg, South Africa), [iv] Aaron Schroeder, [v] Aaron Schroeder/ George Weiss. (*See also under* Bert BERNS, Doc POMUS and Mort SHUMAN.)

764. RAINGER, Ralph (b. Ralph Reichenthal, October 7, 1901, New York, NY; d. October 23, 1942, Beverly Hills, CA) Film and stage composer, pianist and arranger. A law graduate who took piano lessons from an early age, before performing in local dance bands. Rainger's first published composition was the rag *Piano Puzzle* (1923), which he recorded for the Bell label. After working as a rehearsal pianist, he performed in vaudeville with Edgar Fairchild. Rainger achieved his first hit with *Moanin' Low* [i] (1929), after which he composed in

Hollywood for Paramount Pictures, where he formed a lengthy songwriting partnership with the lyricist Leo Robin, their material being included in the films "The Big Broadcast" (1932), "Here Is My Heart" (1934), "The Big Broadcast of 1936" (1935), "Waikiki Wedding" (1937), "Paris Honeymoon" and "Gulliver's Travels" (both 1939). Rainger died in an air crash in 1942. ALBUMS: **Paris Honeymoon** st (1950), **Waikiki Wedding** st (1951, both Decca). HIT VERSIONS: *Blossoms on Broadway* [iii] Dolly Dawn (1937) US#4/Dick Robertson (1937) US#5; *Blue Hawaii* [iii] Paul Whiteman (1929) US#12/Bing Crosby (1937) US#5/Billy Vaughn & His Orchestra (1959) US#37; *Ebbtide* [iii] Bunny Berigan (1937) US#5/Claude Thornhill (1937) US#15/Frank Chacksfield (1953) g US#2 UK#9; *Faithful Forever* [iii] Glenn Miller (1940) US#4, *Funny Old Hills, The* [iii] Bing Crosby (1939) US#5, *Here Lies Love* [iii] Bing Crosby (1932) US#11, *Here's Love in Your Eyes* [iii] Benny Goodman (1936) US#9/Henry Allen (1937) US#17; *I Don't Want to Make History (I Just Want to Make Love)* [iii] Hal Kemp (1936) US#12, *I Have Eyes* [iii] Benny Goodman (1938) US#6/Artie Shaw (1938) US#10/Bing Crosby (1939) US#4; *I Wished on the Moon* [ii] Bing Crosby (1935) US#2/Little Jack Little (1935) US#13; *I'll Take an Option on You* [iii] Ted Fiorito (1933) US#7, *If I Should Lose You* [iii] Richard Himber (1936) US#15, *In the Park in Paree* [iii] Hotel Bossert Orchestra (1933) US#8, *June in January* [iii] Bing Crosby (1934) US#1/Little Jack Little (1934) US#7/Ted Fiorito (1934) US#10/Guy Lombardo (1935) US#14; *Little Kiss at Twilight* [iii] Benny Goodman (1938) US#7, *Love in Bloom* [iii] Bing Crosby (1934) US#1/Hal Kemp (1934) US#12/Guy Lombardo (1934) US#11/Paul Whiteman (1934) US#4; *Moanin' Low* [i] Charleston Chasers (1929) US#19/Libby Holman (1929) US#5/Teddy Wilson & Billie Holiday (1937) US#11; *Please* [iii] Bing Crosby (1932) US#1, re-issued (1941) US#24/George Olsen (1932) US#5; *Thanks for the Memory* [iii] Mildred Bailey (1938) US#11/Shep Fields (1938) US#1; *What Goes on Here in My Heart* [iii] Benny Goodman (1938) US#3, *What Have You Got That Gets Me?* [iii] Benny Goodman (1938) US#6, *With Every Breath I Take* [iii] Bing Crosby (1935) US#4, *You Started Something* [iii] Tony Pastor (1948) US#16, *You're a Sweet Little Headache* [iii] Bing Crosby (1939) US#3/Benny Goodman (1939) US#6. Co-writers: [i] Howard Dietz, [ii] Dorothy Parker, [iii] Leo Robin.

765. RALPHS, Mick (b. May 31, 1944, Hereford, England) Rock guitarist. A rock guitarist who first recorded as a member of the group Mott the Hoople, which he left in 1973, to form Bad Company with Paul Rodgers, writing its hits *Can't Get* *Enough* (1974) US#5 UK#15, *Movin' On* (1975) US#19 and *Good Lovin' Gone Bad* (1975) US#36 UK#31. ALBUMS: **Bad Company** (1974) p US#1 UK#3, **Straight Shooter** (1975) p US#3 UK#3, **Run with the Pack** (1976) p US#5 UK#4, **Burnin' Sky** (1977, all Island) g US#15 UK#17; **Desolation Angels** (1979) p US#3 UK#10, **Rough Diamonds** (1982, both Swan Song) US#26 UK#15; **Fame and Fortune** (1986) US#106, **Dangerous Age** (1988, both Atlantic) g US#58; **Holy Water** (1990) p US#35, **Here Comes Trouble** (1992, both Atco) g US#40; **Best of Bad Company Live…What You Hear Is What You Get** (1993), **Company of Strangers** (1995, both East West) US#159. COMPILATION: **10 from 6** (1986, Atlantic) p US#137. (*See also under* Ian HUNTER, Paul RODGERS.)

766. RAM, Buck (b. Samuel Ram, December 18, 1908, Chicago, IL; d. January 1, 1991, Las Vegas, NV) Pop pianist, arranger and producer. A law school graduate who became a booking agent and manager, and discovered the doo-wop groups the Penguins and the Platters. HIT VERSIONS: *Afterglow* [vi] Leo Reisman (1936) US#14, *At Your Beck and Call* [ii] Jimmy Dorsey (1938) US#10, *Boog-It* [i] Gene Krupa (1940) US#13/Glenn Miller (1940) US#7; *Chew-Chew-Chew (Your Bubble Gum)* [iv] Ella Fitzgerald & Chick Webb (1939) US#14, *Come Prima (For the First Time)* [vii] Marino Marini (1958) UK#2, *Enchanted* Platters (1959) R&B#9 US#12, *Great Pretender, The* Jimmy Parkinson (1956) UK#9/Platters (1956) R&B#1 US#1 UK#5/Lamar Morris (1968) C&W#46/Freddie Mercury (1987) UK#4; *I'll Be Home for Christmas* [v] Bing Crosby (1943) US#3, re-issued (1944) US#16; *Only You* [viii] Platters (1955) R&B#1 US#5 UK#5/Hilltoppers (1956) UK#3/Frank Pourcel's French Fiddles (1959) R&B#18 US#9/Wayne Newton (1964) US#122/Mark Wynter (1964) UK#38/Jeff Collins (1972) UK#40/Ringo Starr (1974) UK#28/Freddie Hart (1978) C&W#34/Reba McEntire (1981) C&W#13/Statler Brothers (1986) C&W#36/John Alford (1996) UK#9; *Twilight Time* [iii] Three Suns (1944) US#14/Les Brown (1945) US#16/Johnny Maddox (1953) US#21/Platters (1958) R&B#1 US#1 UK#3/Carl Mann (1976) C&W#100; *(You've Got) The Magic Touch* Platters (1956) R&B#4 US#4. Co-writers: [i] Cab Calloway/Jack Palmer, [ii] Edward De Lange, [iii] Artie Dunn/Al Nevins/Morty Nevins, [iv] Ella Fitzgerald/Chick Webb, [v] Kim Gannon/Walter Kent, [vi] Phil Levant/Al Stillman, [vii] V. Di Paola/Taccani, [viii] Ande Rand.

767. RANDAZZO, Terry Pop vocalist. A solo singer who achieved considerably greater success as a songwriter for others. CHART COMPOSITIONS:

Big Wide World [i] (1962) US#61, *Lost Without You* (1964) US#130. HIT VERSIONS: *Goin' Out of My Head* [iv] Little Anthony & the Imperials (1965) R&B#22 US#6, *Have You Looked into Your Heart* [i] Jerry Vale (1964) US#24, *Hurt So Bad* [ii] Little Anthony & the Imperials (1965) R&B#3 US#10/Jackie DeShannon (1970) US#96/Philly Devotions (1976) R&B#94; *I'm on the Outside (Looking In)* [iv] Little Anthony & the Imperials (1964) US#15, *It's Gonna Take a Miracle* [iii] Royalettes (1965) R&B#28/Truth (1981) R&B#80/Deniece Williams (1982) R&B#1 US#10; *Pretty Blue Eyes* [iv] Steve Lawrence (1960) US#9/Craig Douglas (1960) UK#4; *Salty Tears* Mara Lynn Brown (1973) US#118, *Take Me Back* Little Anthony & the Imperials (1965) R&B#15 US#16. Co-writers: [i] Billy Barberis/Bobby Weinstein, [ii] Bobby Hart/Bobby Wilding, [iii] Lou Stallman/Bobby Weinstein, [iv] Bobby Weinstein.

768. RAYE, Don (b. Donald McRae Wilhoite, Jr., March 16, 1909, Washington, DC; d. January, 1985) Stage and film composer. A former child dancer who became a successful Tin Pan Alley songwriter. Raye's material was included in such films as "Buck Privates" (1941), "Swingtime Johnny" and "Broadway Rhythm" (both 1943). HIT VERSIONS: *Beat Me Daddy, Eight to the Bar* [xii] Will Bradley (1940) US#1/Glenn Miller (1940) US#15/Andrews Sisters (1941) US#2; *Boogie Woogie Bugle Boy* [xi] Andrews Sisters (1941) US#6/Bette Midler (1973) US#8; *Cow Cow Boogie* [iii] Freddie Slack (1943) R&B#6 US#9/Ella Fitzgerald & the Ink Spots (1944) R&B#1 US#10; *Daddy-O (I'm Gonna Teach You Some Blues)* [iv] Martha Davis (1948) R&B#9/Louis Jordan (1949) R&B#7; *Domino* [vii] Bing Crosby (1951) US#15/Doris Day (1951) US#21/Tony Martin (1951) US#9; *Down the Road a Piece* Will Bradley (1940) US#10, *For Dancers Only* [x] Jimmie Lunceford (1937) US#7, *He's My Guy* [iv] Harry James (1942) US#7/Dinah Shore (1942) US#20; *House of Blue Lights, The* [xiii] Andrews Sisters (1946) US#15/Freddie Slack (1946) US#8/Chuck Miller (1955) US#9/Earl Richards (1969) C&W#39/Asleep at the Wheel (1987) C&W#17; *I Still Love You All* [viii] Kenny Ball & His Jazzmen (1961) UK#24, *I'll Remember April* [v] Woody Herman (1942) US#23, *Irresistible You* [iv] Ginny Simmons (1944) US#27, *Milkman Keep Those Bottles Quiet* [iv] Woody Herman (1944) US#10/King Sisters (1944) US#13/Ella Mae Morse (1944) US#7; *Mister Five By Five* [iv] Andrews Sisters (1942) US#14/Freddie Slack (1942) US#10/Harry James (1943) US#1; *Music Makers, The* [ix] Harry James (1941) US#9, *Rhumboogie* [xi] Andrews Sisters (1940) US#11, *Scrub Me, Mama, with a Boogie Beat* Andrews Sisters (1941) US#10/Will Bradley (1941) US#2; *Star Eyes* [iv] Jimmy Dorsey (1944) US#3,

Struttin' with Some Barbecue [i] Louis Armstrong (1928) US#14, *They Were Doin' the Mambo* [ii] Vaughn Monroe (1954) US#7, *Well All Right (Tonight's the Night)* [vi] Andrews Sisters (1939) US#5. Co-writers: [i] Lillian Hardin Armstrong, [ii] Sonny Burke, [iii] Benny Carter/Gene De Paul, [iv] Gene De Paul, [v] Gene De Paul/Patricia Johnston, [vi] Francis Faye/Dan Howell, [vii] Louis Ferrari/Jacques Plante, [viii] Norbert Glanzberg, [ix] Harry James, [x] Sy Oliver/Vic Schoen, [xi] Hughie Prince, [xii] Hughie Prince/Eleanor Sheehy, [xiii] Freddie Slack.

769. RAZAF, Andy (b. Andrea Paul Razafkeriefo, December 16, 1895, Washington, DC; d. February 3, 1973, North Hollywood, CA) Film and stage composer, vocalist. A lyricist who occasionally composed, Razaf contributed to the shows "Keep Shufflin'" (1928), "Hot Chocolates" (1929) and "Blackbirds of 1930," alongside the film "The Benny Goodman Story" (1956). He recorded under such pseudonyms as Tommy Thompson, and co-wrote many of Fats Waller's biggest hits. HIT VERSIONS: *Christopher Columbus* [i] Benny Goodman (1936) US#9/Fletcher Henderson (1936) US#10/King Garcia (1936) US#16/Andy Kirk (1936) US#2/Teddy Wilson (1936) US#12; *Dusky Stevedore* [viii] Nat Shilkret (1928) US#10/Frankie Trumbauer (1928) US#17; *Gee Baby, Ain't I Good to You?* [vi] Nat "King" Cole (1944) US#15, *I'm Gonna Move to the Outskirts of Town* [vii] Jimmie Lunceford (1942) US#12/Ray Charles (1961) R&B#25 US#84: *In the Mood* [iv] Glenn Miller (1940) g US#1, re-issued (1943) US#20, re-issued (1976) UK#13/Johnny Maddox (1953) US#16/Ernie Fields (1959) R&B#7 US#4 UK#13/Bette Midler (1974) US#51/Joe Bob's Nashville Sound Company (1975) C&W#84/Sound 9418 (1976) UK#46/Henhouse Five Plus Too (1977) C&W#39 US#40/Ray Stevens (1977) UK#31/Meco in *Big Band Medley* (1982) US#101/Stars on 45 in *The Star Sisters Medley* (1983) US#107/John Anderson Big Band in *The Glenn Miller Medley* (1985) UK#63, re-entry (1986) UK#61; *Knock Me a Kiss* [vi] Gene Krupa (1942) US#24, *Louisiana* [ix] Paul Whiteman (1928) US#12, *Lover's Lullaby, A* [ii] Glen Gray (1940) US#9/Frankie Masters (1940) US#25; *Reefer Man* [xi] Cab Calloway (1932) US#11, *S'posin'* [iii] Rudy Vallee (1929) US#7/Fats Waller (1936) US#5/Don Cornell (1953) US#28; *Stompin' at the Savoy* [v] Chick Webb (1934) US#10, re-issued (1936) US#18/Benny Goodman (1936) US#11, re-issued (1937) US#4/Ozzie Nelson (1936) US#12; *That's What I Like About the South* Phil Harris (1947) US#21. Co-writers: [i] Leon Berry, [ii] Frankie Carle/Larry Wagner, [iii] Paul Denniker, [iv] Joe Garland, [v] Benny Goodman/Edgar Sampson/Chick Webb,

[vi] Mike Jackson, [vii] Roy Jacobs/William Weldon, [viii] J.C. Johnson, [ix] J.C. Johnson/Bob Schafer, [x] Don Redman, [xi] J. Russel Robinson. (*See also under* Eubie BLAKE.)

770. REA, Chris (b. March 4, 1951, Middlesbrough, England) Pop guitarist and vocalist. A singer-songwriter who first performed in the 1970s bands, Magdalene and Beautiful Losers, before becoming a successful solo artist in the late 1970s. CHART COMPOSITIONS: *Fool (If You Think It's Over)* (1978) US#12 UK#30, *Whatever Happened to Benny Santini?* (1978) US#71, *Diamonds* (1979) US#44 UK#44, *Loving You* (1982) US#88 UK#65, *I Can Hear Your Heartbeat* (1983) UK#60, re-issued (1988) UK#74; *I Don't Know What It Is But I Love It* (1984) UK#65, *Stainsby Girls* (1985) UK#27, *Josephine* (1985) UK#67, *It's All Gone* (1986) UK#69, *On the Beach* (1986) UK#57, re-mixed (1988) UK#12; *Let's Dance* (1987) UK#12, *Loving You Again* (1987) US#81 UK#47, *Que Sera* (1988) UK#73, *Driving Home for Christmas* (1988) UK#53, *Working on It* (1989) US#73 UK#53, *The Road to Hell (Part 2)* (1989) UK#10, *Tell Me There's a Heaven* (1990) UK#24, re-issued (1994) UK#70; *Texas* (1990) UK#69, *Auberge* (1991) UK#16, *Heaven* (1991) UK#57, *Looking for Summer* (1991) UK#49, *Winter Song* (1991) UK#27, *Nothing to Fear* (1992) UK#16, *God's Great Banana Skin* (1992) UK#31, *Soft Top, Hard Shoulder* (1993) UK#53, *Julia* (1993) UK#18, *You Can Go Your Own Way* (1994) UK#28, *"Disco" La Passione* with Shirley Bassey (1996) UK#41. ALBUMS: **Whatever Happened to Benny Santini?** (1978) g US#49, **Deltics** (1979) UK#54, **Tennis** (1980) UK#60, **Chris Rea** (1982) UK#52, **Water Sign** (1983) UK#64, **Wired to the Moon** (1984) UK#35, **Shamrock Diaries** (1985) UK#15, **On the Beach** (1986) UK#11, **Dancing with Strangers** (1987, all Magnet) UK#2; **The Road to Hell** (1989) UK#1, **Auberge** (1991, both WEA) US#176 UK#1; **God's Great Banana Skin** (1992) UK#4, **Espresso Logic** (1993) UK#8, **La Passione** ost (1996, all East West) UK#43. COMPILATIONS: **New Light Through Old Windows** (1988, WEA) US#92 UK#5; **Best of Chris Rea** (1994, East West) UK#3. HIT VERSIONS: *Fool (If You Think It's Over)* Elkie Brooks (1982) UK#17.

771. RECORD, Eugene (b. December 23, 1940, Chicago, IL) R&B producer and vocalist. The lead vocalist and songwriter in the R&B vocal group the Chi-Lites. Record first sung with the Chantours, before joining Marshall and the Chi-Lites in 1960. By 1969, the group were recording in a commercial, soft soul style as the Chi-Lites. CHART COMPOSITIONS: *Give It Away* (1969) R&B#19 US#88,

(For God's Sake) Give More Power to the People (1971) R&B#4 US#26 UK#32, *Have You Seen Her?* [i] (1971) R&B#1 US#3 UK#3, new version (1981) R&B#48; *Oh Girl* (1972) R&B#1 US#1 UK#14, *The Coldest Day of My Life* (1972) R&B#8 US#47, *A Lonely Man* (1972) R&B#25 US#57, *We Need Order* (1972) US#61, *A Letter to Myself* (1973) R&B#3 US#33, *My Heart Just Keeps on Breakin'* [iv] (1973) R&B#46 US#92, *Stoned Out of My Mind* [i] (1973) R&B#2 US#30, *I Found Sunshine* (1973) R&B#17 US#47 UK#35, *Homely Girl* [iv] (1974) R&B#3 US#54 UK#5, *Too Good to Be Forgotten* [i] (1974) UK#10, *There Will Never Be Peace (Until God Is Seated at the Conference Table)* (1974) R&B#8 US#63, *You Got to Be the One* [ii] (1974) R&B#15 US#83, *Toby* [i] (1974) R&B#7 US#78, *Have You Seen Her?* [i]/*Oh Girl* (1975) UK#5, *It's Time for Love* (1975) R&B#27 US#94, *You Don't Have to Go* [i] (1976) R&B#50 UK#3, *Heavenly Body* (1980) R&B#36, *Me and You* (1981) R&B#70, *Bottom's Up* (1983) R&B#7, *Changing for You* (1984) UK#61. ALBUMS: **Give It Away** (1969) US#180, **(For God's Sake) Give More Power to the People** (1971) US#70, **A Lonely Man** (1972) R&B#13 US#5, **A Letter to Myself** (1973) US#50, **The Chi-Lites** (1973) US#89, **Toby** (1974) US#181, **Half a Love** (1973, all Brunswick); **Heavenly Body** (1980) US#179, **Me and You** (1981, both Chi-Sound) US#162; **Bottom's Up** (1983, Larc) US#98; **Hard Act to Follow** (1986, Nuance). COMPILATIONS: **Greatest Hits** (1972) US#55, **Greatest Hits, Volume 2** (1976, both Brunswick). Record later held an executive position at Brunswick Records, and recorded as a solo artist, charting with *Laying Beside You* (1977) R&B#24. ALBUMS: **The Eugene Record** (1977), **Trying to Get You** (1978), **Welcome to My Fantasy** (1979, all Warner Brothers). HIT VERSIONS: *Have You Seen Her?* [i] M.C. Hammer (1990) R&B#1 US#4 UK#8, *Homely Girl* [iv] UB40 (1989) UK#6, *Love Makes a Woman* [iii] Barbara Acklin (1968) R&B#3 US#15, *Soulful Strut* [v] Young-Holt Unlimited (1968) g R&B# US#3, *Oh Girl* Con Hunley (1982) C&W#12/Paul Young (1990) US#8 UK#25, *There'll Come a Time* [vi] Betty Everett (1969) R&B#2 US#26, *Too Good to Be Forgotten* [i] Amazulu (1986) UK#5. *You Got Me Walking* Jackie Wilson (1972) US#93. Co-writers: [i] Barbara Acklin (b. February 28, 1944, Chicago, IL), [ii] M. Arrington, [iii] Carl Davis/William Sanders, [iv] Stan McKenny, [v] William Sanders, [vi] Floyd Smith.

772. REDDING, Otis (b. September 9, 1941, Dawson, GA; d. December 10, 1967, Lake Monona, Madison, WI) R&B vocalist. A highly influential vocal stylist who was the most significant

R&B artist after Sam Cooke. Redding learned the drums as a teenager and sang gospel at school, before holding a variety of day jobs and winning his first talent show as a singer in 1957. After developing a style that was influenced by Cooke and Little Richard, Redding became a backing vocalist for the Upsetters and Gladys Williams. By 1958, he was singing with Johnny Jenkins and the Pinetoppers, and two years later he issued his debut solo single, *Shout Bamalama* on the Confederate label. Redding's big break came when, during the spare studio time remaining at the end of a Jenkins recording session for Stax Records, he was given the opportunity to record his composition *These Arms of Mine*. The epic 6/8 time ballad so impressed the label that it was issued as a single in 1963, and became his first hit. With his pleading vocal style, Redding became a major R&B star, releasing a series of innovative ballads and uptempo dance numbers. A magnetic live performer, Redding captured the hearts of the hippie generation at the Monterey Pop Festival in 1967, but his career was cut tragically short when he died in a plane crash four days after recording his composition *(Sittin' On) The Dock of The Bay* [ii], which became a posthumous four million seller. CHART COMPOSITIONS: *These Arms of Mine* (1963) R&B#20 US#85, *That's What My Heart Needs* (1963) R&B#27, *Come to Me* [v] (1964) US#69, *Security* (1964) US#97, *Chained and Bound* (1964) US#70, *Mr. Pitiful* [ii] (1965) R&B#10 US#41, *I've Been Loving You Too Long* [i] (1965) R&B#2 US#21, live version (1971) US#110, *Respect* (1965) R&B#4 US#35, *I Can't Turn You Loose* [ii] (1965) R&B#11 US#85 UK#29, *Just One More Day* [ii] (1965) R&B#15, *My Lover's Prayer* (1966) R&B#10 US#61 UK#37, *Fa-Fa-Fa-Fa-Fa (Sad Song)* [ii] (1966) R&B#12 US#29 UK#23, *I Love You More Than Words Can Say* (1967) R&B#30 US#78, *Let Me Come on Home* (1967) UK#48, *Glory of Love* (1967) R&B#19 US#60, *(Sittin' On) The Dock of the Bay* [ii] (1968) g R&B#1 US#1 UK#3, *The Happy Song (Dum-Dum)* [ii] (1968) R&B#10 US#25 UK#24, *Amen* (arrangement only) (1968) R&B#15 US#36, *Hard to Handle* [iii] (1968) R&B#38 US#51 UK#15, *I've Got Dreams to Remember* [iv] (1968) R&B#6 US#41, *Love Man* (1969) R&B#17 US#72 UK#43, *Free Me* (1969) R&B#30 US#103, *(Your Love Has Lifted Me) Higher and Higher* (1969) US#110, *Demonstration* (1970) US#105. ALBUMS: **Pain in My Heart** (1964, Atco) US#69; **The Great Otis Redding Sings Soul Ballads** (1965) US#147 UK#30, **Otis Blue** (1965) US#75 UK#6, **The Soul Album** (1966) US#54 UK#22, **Complete and Unbelievable — The Otis Redding Dictionary of Soul** (1967, all Volt) US#73 UK#23; **King and Queen*** (1967, Stax) US#36 UK#18; **Live in Europe** (1967, Volt) US#32 UK#14.

COMPILATIONS: **Apollo Saturday Night** (1964, Atco) US#43; **Stax-Volt Revue Live in London** (1967) US#145, **Stax-Volt Revue, Volume 2-Live in Paris** (1967, both Stax); **Soul as Sung By Otis Redding** (1967, Alshire); **History of Otis Redding** (1968) US#9 UK#2, **The Dock of the Bay** (1968, both Volt) US#4 UK#1; **The Immortal Otis Redding** (1968) US#58 UK#19, **Otis Redding in Person at the Whiskey-a-Go-Go** (1968) US#82, **Love Man** (1969, all Atco) US#46; **Monterey International Pop Festival** ost (1970, Reprise) g US#16; **Tell the Truth** (1970) US#200, **Best of Otis Redding** (1972, both Atco) US#76; **Live-Recorded in July 1965** (1991, Traditional Line); **It's Not Just Sentimental** (1992), **Remember Me** (1992, both Stax); **Dock of the Bay — The Definitive Collection** (1992, Atlantic) UK#50; **Good to Me** (1993, Stax/Ace); **Otis! — The Definitive** (1993, Rhino/Atlantic). HIT VERSIONS: *Dreams to Remember* Robert Palmer (1991) UK#68, *Good to Me* Irma Thomas (1968) R&B#42, *Hard to Handle* [iii] Black Crowes (1990) UK#45, re-issued (1991) US#26 UK#39; *I Can't Turn You Loose* Chambers Brothers (1968) US#37/Edgar Winter's White Trash (1972) US#81; *I've Been Loving You Too Long* [i] Billy Vera (1968) US#121/Barbara Mandrell (1969) C&W#55/Ike & Tina Turner (1969) R&B#23 US#68, live version (1971) US#120; *Respect* Aretha Franklin (1967) g R&B#1 US#1 UK#10/Real Roxanne (1988) UK#71/Adeva (1989) UK#17; *(Sittin' On) The Dock of the Bay* [ii] King Curtis (1968) US#84/Dells (1969) US#42/Sergio Mendes & Brazil '66 (1969) US#66/Sammy Hagar (1979) US#65/Waylon Jennings & Willie Nelson (1982) C&W#13/Reddings (1982) R&B#21 US#55/Michael Bolton (1988) R&B#58 US#11. With: * Carla Thomas. Co-writers: [i] Jerry Butler, [ii] Steve Cropper, [iii] Alvertis Isbell/Alan Jones, [iv] Zelma Redding, [v] Phil Walden. (*See also under* Sam COOKE.)

773. REED, Jerry (b. Jerry Reed Hubbard, March 20, 1937, Atlanta, GA) C&W guitarist and vocalist. One of Nashville's most highly regarded session guitarists, who learned the instrument in his childhood. Reed has been a recording artist since the 1950s, and after 1967, he achieved nearly sixty hits. During the 1970s he starred in such movies as "Smokey and the Bandit" (1977), and hosted his own television show "Concrete Cowboys." CHART COMPOSITIONS: *Guitar Man* (1967) C&W#53, *Tupelo Mississippi Flash* (1967) C&W#15, *Remembering* (1968) C&W#14, *Alabama Wild Man* (1968) C&W#48, *Oh What a Woman!* (1969) C&W#60, *There's Better Things in Life* (1969) C&W#20, *Are You from Dixie ('Cause I'm from Dixie Too)* (1969) C&W#11, *Talk About the Good Times* (1970) C&W#14,

Georgia Sunshine (1970) C&W#16, *Amos Moses* (1970) g C&W#16 US#8, *When You're Hot, You're Hot* (1971) C&W#1 US#9, *The Crude Oil Blues* (1974) C&W#13 US#91, *Ballad of Gator McClusky* (1976), *East Bound and Down* [i] (1977) C&W#2 US#103. ALBUMS: **Alabama Wild Man** (1968), **Better Things in Life** (1969), **Jerry Reed Explores Country Guitar** (1970), **Me and Jerry*** (1970), **Cookin'** (1970) US#194, **Georgia Sunshine** (1971) US#102, **Ko-Ko Joe** (1971) US#45, **When You're Hot, You're Hot** (1971), **Nashville Underground** (1971), **The Unbelievable Guitar and Voice of Jerry Reed** (1971), **Oh What a Woman** (1972), **Smell the Flowers** (1972) US#196, **Lord, Mr. Ford** (1973) US#183, **Hot A'Mighty** (1973), **Jerry Reed** (1973), **Tupelo Mississippi Flash** (1974), **A Good Woman's Love** (1974), **The Uptown Poker Club** (1974), **Mind Your Love** (1975), **Red Hot Picker** (1976), **Alabama Woman** (1976), **Both Barrels** (1976), **Eastbound and Down** (1977), **Sweet Love Feelings** (1978), **Half and Half** (1979), **Live at East Inn** (1979), **Jerry Reed Sings Jim Croce** (1980), **Dixie Dreams** (1981, all RCA); **Sneakin' Around*** (1992, Columbia). COMPILATIONS: **Best of Jerry Reed** (1972) US#116, **Hits of Jerry Reed** (1979), **Twenty of the Best** (1982, all RCA); **Guitar Man** (1996, Camden). HIT VERSIONS: *Guitar Man* Elvis Presley (1968) US#43 UK#19, re-mixed (1981) US#28 UK#43; *Misery Loves Company* Porter Wagoner (1962) C&W#1, *That's All You Gotta Do* Brenda Lee (1960) US#6, *U.S. Male* Elvis Presley (1968) US#28 UK#15, *Walkin'* Al Hirt (1964) US#103. With: * Chet Atkins. Co-writer: [i] Dick Feller.

774. REED, Jimmy (b. Mathis James Reed Leland, September 6, 1925, Dunleith, MS; d. August 29, 1976, Oakland, CA) Blues guitarist, harmonica player and vocalist. An influential boogie styled blues artist, who first recorded for the Vee-Jay label in the 1950s. Reed's songs have been recorded by such artists as Steve Miller, the Rolling Stones and the Grateful Dead. He suffered from epilepsy in the late 1950s, and subsequently died from a seizure in 1976. CHART COMPOSITIONS: *You Don't Have to Go* (1955) R&B#5, *I Don't Go for That* (1955) R&B#12, *Ain't That Loving You Baby* (1956) R&B#3, *Can't Stand to See You Go* (1956) R&B#10, *I Love You Baby* (1956) R&B#13, *You've Got Me Dizzy* (1956) R&B#3, *Honey, Where You Going* (1957) R&B#13, *Little Rain* (1957) R&B#7, *The Sun Is Shining* (1957) R&B#12 US#65, *Honest I Do* [i] (1957) R&B#4 US#32, *I'm Gonna Get My Baby* (1958) R&B#5, *Down in Virginia* (1958) US#93, *I Told You Baby* (1959) R&B#19, *Baby What Do You Want Me to Do* (1960) R&B#10 US#37, *Found Love* (1960) R&B#16 US#88, *Hush-Hush* (1960) R&B#18 US#75, *Going

By the River (1960) US#104, *Close Together* (1961) R&B#12 US#68, *Bright Lights Big City* (1961) R&B#3 US#58, *Aw Shucks, Hush Your Mouth* (1962) US#93, *Good Lover* (1962) US#77, *Shame Shame Shame* (1963) US#52 UK#45, *Mary-Mary* (1963) US#119, *Knockin' at Your Door* (1966) R&B#39, *Two Ways to Skin (A Cat)* (1967) US#125. ALBUMS: **I'm Jimmy Reed** (1957), **Rockin' with Jimmy Reed** (1959), **Found Love** (1960), **At Carnegie Hall** (1961) US#46, **Now Appearing** (1962), **Just Jimmy Reed** (1962) US#103, **T'Ain't No Big Thing** (1964), **Jimmy Reed Sings the Best of the Blues** (1964), **Jimmy Reed Plays 12-String Guitar Blues** (1964), **The Boss Man of the Blues** (1964), **At Soul City** (1964, all Vee-Jay); **Things Ain't What They Used to Be** (1965, Fontana); **Down in Virginia** (1969), **The New Jimmy Reed** (1967), **Big Boss Man** (1973), **I Ain't from Chicago** (1973), **The Ultimate Jimmy Reed** (1973), **Soulin'** (1973, all Bluesway); **Cold Chills** (1976, Antilles); **Funky Funky Soul** (1981, Manhattan). COMPILATIONS: **Best of Jimmy Reed** (1961, Vee-Jay); **The Legend — The Man** (1969, Joy); **The History of Jimmy Reed** (1972, Trip); **Big Boss Man (Memorial Album #1)** (1976, DJM); **Very Best of Jimmy Reed** (1974, Buddah); **Upside Your Head** (1980), **High and Lonesome** (1981), **Got Me Dizzy** (1982, all Charly); **Bright Lights, Big City** (1991, Chameleon). HIT VERSIONS: *Ain't That Lovin' You, Baby* Everly Brothers (1964) US#133/David Houston (1977) C&W#68; *Bright Lights, Big City* Sonny James (1971) C&W#1 US#91. Co-writer: [i] Ewart G. Abner, Jr.

775. REED, Les (b. July 24, 1935, Woking, England) Pop multi-instrumentalist, arranger and producer. One of the most successful British songwriters of the 1960–1970s. Reed was taught music by his father, who ran an impresario troupe, and by the age of fifteen he was performing in his own semi-professional group. During his National Service years, Reed played in the military band of the Royal East Kent Regiment, where he also learned the clarinet and studied music theory. Between 1958–1961, he was the pianist in the John Barry Seven, after which he began writing songs and arranging. Reed worked at Decca Records in the 1960s, where he created material with an American R&B slant for Tom Jones, including the three million selling *It's Not Unusual* [vi]. His songs were also recorded by Connie Francis on her album **Connie Francis Sings the Songs of Les Reed** (1970, MGM). During the late 1960s, Reed ran his own record label, Chapter One, and during the 1970s he worked as a television theme writer. He also composed the musical "American Heroes." ALBUMS: **The Girl on a Motorcycle** ost (1968, Tetragrammaton); **The Bespoke Overcoat ost (1969, Golden Guinea); **Les Bicyclettes De Belsize** ost (1969, Polydor); **The Hit Making World of Les Reed** (1975), **The World of Les Reed** (1976), **Focus on Les Reed** (1977, all Decca); **Rhapsody** (1978, Polydor); **You Should Be Dancing** (1979, Warwick). HIT VERSIONS: *Baby I Won't Let You Down* Pickettywitch (1970) UK#27, *Daughter of Darkness* [viii] Tom Jones (1970) US#13 UK#5, *Delilah* [v] Tom Jones (1968) US#15 UK#2, re-issued (1992) UK#68/Sensational Alex Harvey Band (1975) UK#7; *Don't Bring Me Your Heartaches* [ii] Paul & Barry Ryan (1965) UK#13, *Everybody Knows I Still Love You* [v] Steve Lawrence (1964) US#72; *Give Me One More Chance* Donald Peers (1972) UK#36, *Have Pity on the Boy* Paul & Barry Ryan (1966) UK#18, *Hello Happiness* [iii] Drifters (1976) UK#12, *Here It Comes Again* [v] Fortunes (1965) US#27 UK#4, *I Love Her* [i] Paul & Barry Ryan (1966) UK#17, *I Never Said Goodbye* Engelbert Humperdinck (1972) US#61, *I Pretend* [v] Des O'Connor (1968) UK#1, *I'm Coming Home* [v] Tom Jones (1967) US#57 UK#2, *It's Not Unusual* [vi] Tom Jones (1965) R&B#26 US#10 UK#1, re-issued (1987) UK#17; *Kiss Me Goodbye* [v] Petula Clark (1968) US#15 UK#50, *Last Waltz, The* [v] Engelbert Humperdinck (1967) US#25 UK#1, *Leave a Little Love* [ii] Lulu (1964) UK#8, *Leeds, Leeds, Leeds* [viii] Leeds United F.C. (1992) UK#54, *Leeds United* [viii] Leeds United F.C. (1972) UK#10, *Les Bicyclettes De Belsize* [v] Engelbert Humperdinck (1968) US#31 UK#5, *Love Is All* [v] Malcom Roberts (1969) UK#12/Engelbert Humperdinck (1973) US#91 UK#44; *Marry Me* Mike Preston (1961) UK#14, *Please Don't Go* [vii] Donald Peers (1968) UK#3, re-entry (1969) UK#38/Eddy Arnold (1969) C&W#10 US#129; *Tell Me When* [viii] Applejacks (1964) US#135 UK#7, *That's What Life Is All About* Bing Crosby (1975) UK#41, *There's a Kind of Hush* [viii] Herman's Hermits (1967) g US#4 UK#7/Gary & the Hornets (1967) US#127/Brian Collins (1972) C&W#47/Carpenters (1976) US#12 UK#22; *To Make a Big Man Cry* [i] P.J. Proby (1965) UK#34/Roy Head (1966) US#95; *24 Sycamore* [v] Gene Pitney (1973) UK#34, *When There's No You* [vii] Engelbert Humperdinck (1971) US#45, *When We Were Young* Solomon King (1968) UK#21, *Winter World of Love* [v] Engelbert Humperdinck (1969) US#16 UK#7. Co-writers: [i] Pete Callender, [ii] Robin Conrad, [iii] Roger Greenaway, [iv] Tony MacAulay/Barry Mason, [v] Barry Mason, [vi] Gordon Mills, [vii] Jacques Offenbach/Jackie Rae, [viii] Geoff Stevens. (*See also under* Roger COOK.)

776. REED, Lou (b. Lewis Allen Reed, March 2, 1942, Freeport, Long Island, NY) Rock guitarist and vocalist. An inquisitive, sometimes ex-perimental, and frequently witty singer-songwriter, whose self-destructive lyrics of the 1960s have, during the 1990s, evolved into more contemplative and literate observations about the human condition. Reed learned the guitar in his teens and studied at Syracuse University, New York, before playing in a number of 1960s groups and working as an uncredited musician for the Pickwick label. In 1964, Reed and violinist John Cale, formed the avante-garde rock group the Velvet Underground, to record a quartet of influential and frequently magnificent albums, which were highlighted by a primitive and raw sound, and featured Reed's sharply observed compositions *Beginning to See the Light*, *What Goes On*, *Jesus*, *Pale Blue Eyes*, *There She Goes Again*, *Heroin*, *Rock 'n' Roll*, and *Sweet Jane*. CHART COMPOSITION: *Venus in Furs* (1994) UK#71. ALBUMS: **The Velvet Underground and Nico** (1967) US#171, **White Light/White Heat** (1968) US#199, **The Velvet Underground** (1969, all Verve) US#197; **Loaded** (1970, Cotillion); **Live MCMXCIII** (1993, Sire/Warner Brothers) US#180 UK#70. COMPILATIONS: **Andy Warhol's Velvet Underground** (1971, MGM); **Live at Max's Kansas City** (1972, Cotillion); **Live, 1969** (1974, Mercury); **VU** (1985, Verve) US#85 UK#47; **Another View** (1986, Polydor); **What Goes On** (1993, Raven); **Peel Slowly and See** (1995, Polydor); **Best of Lou Reed and the Velvet Underground** (1995, Global) UK#56. After the group split up in 1970, Reed pursued a solo career that has verged from the truly inspired to the vaguely embarrassing. His finest hour remains **Berlin** (1973), the thematic examination of a self-destructive and violent relationship. CHART COMPOSITIONS: *Walk on the Wild Side* (1973) US#16 UK#10, *Satellite of Love* (1973) US#119, *Sally Can't Dance* (1974) US#103. ALBUMS: **Lou Reed** (1972) US#189, **Transformer** (1973) US#29 UK#13, **Berlin** (1973) US#98 UK#7, **Rock 'n' Roll Animal** (1974) g US#5 UK#26, **Sally Can't Dance** (1974) US#10, **Live** (1975) US#41, **Metal Machine Music** (1975), **Coney Island Baby** (1976, all RCA) US#41 UK#52; **Rock and Roll Heart** (1976) US#64, **Street Hassle** (1978) US#89, **Live — Take No Prisoners** (1979), **The Bells** (1979) US#130, **Growing Up in Public** (1980, all Arista) US#158; **The Blue Mask** (1982) US#169, **Legendary Hearts** (1983) US#159, **Live in Italy** (1984), **New Sensations** (1984) US#56 UK#92, **Mistrial** (1986, all RCA) US#47 UK#69; **New York** (1989) US#40 UK#14, **Songs for Drella — A Fiction** with John Cale (1989) US#103 UK#22, **Magic and Loss** (1992, all Sire) US#80 UK#6; **Set the Twilight Reeling** (1996, Warner Brothers) US#110 UK#26. COMPILATIONS: **Walk on the Wild Side — The Best of Lou Reed** (1977, RCA) US#156; **Rock and Roll Diary, 1967–1980** (1980, Arista)

US#178; **Retro** (1989) UK#29, **Between Thought and Expression** (1992, both RCA). HIT SONGS: *All Tomorrow's Parties* Japan (1983) UK#38, *European Son (To Delmore Schwartz)* Japan (1982) UK#31, *Perfect Day* Duran Duran (1995) UK#28/Various Artists (1998) UK#1; *Rock and Roll* Detroit featuring Mitch Ryder (1972) US#107, *Walk on the Wild Side* Marky Mark & the Funky Bunch sampled in *Wildside* (1991) US#10, *White Light/White Heat* David Bowie (1983) UK#46. (*See also under* Paul STANLEY.)

777. REID, Billy (b. William Gordon Reid, September 19, 1902; d. December 12, 1974, both Southampton, England) Stage composer, accordion player and pianist. A self-taught musician who became a popular songwriter in the mid-1940s. After a successful career during the 1930s, as a musical accompanist in a stage duo with the singer Dorothy Squires, Reid began composing songs. His first hit was the multi-million selling *The Gypsy* (1945), the first British composition to top the American charts. Squires recorded a large number of Reid's compositions, including *My First Love, My Last Love for Always* (1947) and *Anything I Dream Is Possible* (1948). HIT VERSIONS: *Bridge of Sighs, The* Georgia Gibbs (1953) US#30/David Whitfield (1953) UK#9; *Gypsy, The* Jan Garber (1946) US#14/Hildegarde & Guy Lombardo (1946) US#7/Ink Spots (1946) R&B#1 US#1/Sammy Kaye (1946) US#3/Hal McIntyre (1946) US#8/Dinah Shore (1946) US#1; *I Still Believe* Ronnie Hilton (1954) UK#3, *I'll Close My Eyes* Andy Russell (1947) US#15, *I'm Walking Behind You* Eddie Fisher (1953) g US#1 UK#1/Frank Sinatra (1953) US#7/Dorothy Squires (1953) UK#12; *Tree in a Meadow, A* Sam Browne (1948) US#22/Paul Fennelly & the Ames Brothers (1948) US#21/Buddy Johnson (1948) US#27/Paul Laurenz (1948) US#18/Monica Lewis (1948) US#21/Joe Loss (1948) US#17/Margaret Whiting (1948) g US#1.

778. REVEL, Harry (b. December 21, 1905, London, England; d. November 3, 1958, New York, NY) Film and stage composer, pianist. A British songwriter who was extremely successful in Hollywood during the 1930s. Revel studied the piano as a teenager, after which he toured Europe in various bands before settling in Berlin, and composing the score to the operetta "Was Frauen Traumen" (1922). In London, he composed the show "Andre Charlot's Revue of 1927," alongside such American influenced compositions as *Westward Bound, I'm Going Back to Old Nebraska* and *Just Give the Southland to Me.* In 1929, Revel emigrated to America, where he formed a lengthy partnership with the lyricist Mack Gordon, working on the shows "Fast and Furious" (1930) and "Ziegfeld Follies of 1931." Revel and Gordon achieved their greatest success in Hollywood, contributing to such films as "Sitting Pretty" (1933), "We're Not Dressing," "Shoot the Works," "College Rhythm" (all 1934); "Love in Bloom," "Two for Tonight" (both 1935); "Collegiate," "Stowaway" (both 1936); "Wake Up and Live" (1937), and "My Lucky Star" (1938). During World War II, they organized troop shows. Revel also worked with the lyricist Paul Francis Webster, composed three symphonic suites, and ran his own publishing company. HIT VERSIONS: *Afraid to Dream* [i] Benny Goodman (1937) US#6, *But Definitely* [i] Ray Noble (1936) US#20, *Did You Ever See a Dream Walking?* [i] Bing Crosby (1933) US#5/Meyer Davis (1933) US#6/Eddy Duchin (1933) US#1/Guy Lombardo (1933) US#2/Pickens Sisters (1934) US#20; *Don't Let It Bother You* [i] Leo Reisman (1934) US#11/Fats Waller (1934) US#10; *From the Top of Your Head (To the Tip of Your Toes)* [i] Bing Crosby (1935) US#10, *Good Morning Glory* [i] Tom Croakley (1934) US#12, *Good Night, Lovely Little Lady* [i] Bing Crosby (1934) US#2/Hal Kemp (1934) US#9; *Goodnight, My Love* [i] Art Kassel (1932) US#14/Shep Fields (1937) US#9/Benny Goodman (1937) US#1/Hal Kemp (1937) US#10/McGuire Sisters (1957) US#32/Fleetwoods (1963) US#32/Paul Anka (1969) US#27/Randy Barlow (1976) C&W#53; *I Feel Like a Feather in the Breeze* [i] Jan Garber (1936) US#3, *I Never Knew Heaven Could Speak* [i] Bob Crosby (1939) US#15, *I Wanna Be in Winchell's Column* [i] Isham Jones (1938) US#13, *I Wish I Were Aladdin* [i] Bing Crosby (1935) US#7, *I've Got a Date with a Dream* [i] Benny Goodman (1938) US#4/George Hall (1938) US#8; *It Was a Night in June* Anson Weeks (1933) US#15, *It's Swell of You* [i] Little Jack Little (1937) US#17/Teddy Wilson (1937) US#18; *Love Thy Neighbor* [i] Bing Crosby (1934) US#2/Raymond Paige (1934) US#19; *Loveliness of You* [i] Russ Morgan (1937) US#17, *May I?* [i] Bing Crosby (1934) US#4/Eddy Duchin (1934) US#16; *May I Have the Next Romance with You?* [i] Tommy Dorsey (1937) US#11/Lud Gluskin (1937) US#9; *Never in a Million Years* [i] Mildred Bailey (1937) US#8/Bing Crosby & Jimmy Dorsey (1937) US#2/Glen Gray (1937) US#7; *Orchid to You, An* [i] Eddy Duchin (1933) US#10, *Paris in the Spring* [i] Freddy Martin (1935) US#9/Ray Noble (1935) US#1; *She Reminds Me of You* [i] Earl Burtnett (1934) US#8/Bing Crosby (1934) US#10/Eddy Duchin (1934) US#7; *Star Fell Out of Heaven, A* [i] Ben Bernie (1936) US#14/Hal Kemp (1936) US#3; *Stay as Sweet as You Are* [i] Jimmie Grier (1934) US#1/Little Jack Little (1934) US#16/Guy Lombardo (1934) US#15/Lanny Ross (1934) US#20; *Straight from the Shoulder* [i] Bing Crosby (1934) US#16, *Sweet as a Song* [i] Glen Gray (1938) US#19/Hoarce Heidt (1938) US#3; *Thanks* for *Everything* [i] Tommy Dorsey (1939) US#7/Artie Shaw (1939) US#1; *There's a Lull in My Life* [i] Duke Ellington (1937) US#12/Alice Faye (1937) US#20/George Hall (1937) US#5/Teddy Wilson (1937) US#2; *To Mary with Love* [i] Tempo King (1936) US#12, *Under the Harlem Moon* [i] Chick Bullock (1932) US#18/Fletcher Henderson (1932) US#19/Don Redman (1932) US#17/Joe Rines (1932) US#6; *Wake Up and Live* [i] Cab Calloway (1937) US#17/Hudson-De Lange Orchestra (1937) US#18/Red Nichols (1937) US#17; *When I'm with You* [i] Hal Kemp (1936) US#1/Ray Noble (1936) US#15; *When There's a Breeze on Lake Louise* [ii] Freddy Martin (1942) US#22, *With My Eyes Wide Open, I'm Dreaming* [i] Isham Jones (1934) US#11/Leo Reisman (1934) US#3/Patti Page (1950) g US#11; *Without a Word of Warning* [i] Bing Crosby (1935) US#5, *You Hit the Spot* [i] Richard Himber (1936) US#9. Co-writers: [i] Mack Gordon, [ii] Mort Greene.

779. REYNOLDS, Malvina (b. August 23, 1900, San Francisco; d. March 17, 1978, Berkeley, both CA) Folk pianist, violinist and vocalist. A topical, humorous folk and children's composer who began writing songs in the mid-1940s. ALBUMS: **Malvina** (1966), **Held Over** (1975), **Mama Lion** (1977), **Magical Songs** (1978, all Cassandra); **Artichokes, Griddleworms, Etc.** (1979), **Funnybugs, Giggleworms, Etc.** (1980, both Pacific Cascades); **Malvina Reynolds Sings the Truth** (198?, Columbia); **Another Country Heard From** (198?, Folkways). HIT VERSIONS: *Little Boxes* Pete Seeger (1964) US#70/Womenfolk (1964) US#83; *Morningtown Ride* Seekers (1967) US#44 UK#2, *What Have They Done to the Rain* Searchers (1965) US#29 UK#13, *Turn Around* Dick & Deedee (1963) US#27.

780. RHODES, Emitt (b. Hawthorne, CA) Pop multi-instrumentalist and vocalist. A singer-songwriter who first recorded as a member of the group the Merry-Go-Round, charting with *Live* (1967) US#63 and *You're a Very Lovely Woman* (1967) US#94, both from the album **The Merry-Go-Round** (1967, A&M) US#190. Rhodes subsequently pursued a briefly successful solo career. CHART COMPOSITION: *Fresh as a Daisy* (1970) US#54. ALBUMS: **Emitt Rhodes** (1970) US#29, **Mirror** (1971, both Dunhill) US#182. COMPILATIONS: **The American Dream** (1971, A&M) US#194; **Listen, Listen — The Best of Emitt Rhodes** (1995, Varese).

781. RICE, Mack (b. Detroit, MI) R&B vocalist. An R&B singer who recorded with the Five Scalders during the 1950s, and the Falcons between 1957–1963, before recording solo sides as Sir Mack Rice, and writing gospel tinged material for a variety of artists at Stax Records. CHART COMPOSITIONS: *Mustang Sally* (1965) R&B#15 US#108, *Coal Man* (1969) R&B#48 US#135. HIT VERSIONS: *Cheaper to Keep Her* Johnnie Taylor (1973) R&B#2 US#15, *Mustang Sally* Wilson Pickett (1967) R&B#6 US#23 UK#28/Commitments (1991) UK#63; *My Main Man* [i] Staple Singers (1974) R&B#18 US#76, *Respect Yourself* [ii] Staple Singers (1971) R&B#2 US#12/Kane Gang (1984) UK#21, re-entry (1985) UK#75/Bruce Willis (1987) R&B#20 US#5 UK#7/Robert Palmer (1995) UK#45. Co-writers: [i] Bettye Crutcher/B. Manuel/L. Nix, [ii] Luther Ingram (b. November 30, 1944, Jackson, TN).

782. RICHARDS, Keith The lead guitarist in the Rolling Stones, who has also recorded as a solo artist. ALBUMS: **Talk Is Cheap** (1988) g US#24 UK#37, **Keith Richards and the X-Pensive Winos Live at the Hollywood Palladium: December 15, 1988** (1991), **Main Offender** (1992, all Virgin) US#99 UK#45. (*See also under* Mick JAGGER and Keith RICHARDS.)

783. RICHIE, Lionel (b. Lionel Brockman Richie, Jr., June 20, 1949, Tuskegee, AL) R&B pianist, producer and vocalist. One of the most successful mainstream R&B artists since the 1970s, whose forte is instantly commercial melodies and somewhat unadventurous rhyming couplets. Richie's father was an army captain and his mother a teacher, and he first sang in his local church choir, before learning the piano and saxophone in his teens. In 1967, Richie played in the group the Mighty Mystics, which evolved into the Commodores, and signed to the Motown label. After polishing up its live act opening for the Jackson Five, the Commodores became one of Motown's biggest selling groups. CHART COMPOSITIONS: *Slippery When Wet* [vi] (1975) R&B#1 US#19, *This Is Your Life* (1975) R&B#13, *Sweet Love* [vi] (1975) R&B#2 US#5 UK#32, *Just to Be Close to You* (1976) R&B#1 US#7 UK#62, *Fancy Dancer* [viii] (1977) R&B#9 US#39, *Easy* (1977) R&B#1 US#4 UK#9, re-issued (1988) UK#15; *Brick House* [vi] (1977) R&B#4 US#5, *Zoom* (1977) UK#38, *Too Hot Ta Trot* [vi] (1977) R&B#1 US#24, *Three Times a Lady* (1978) g R&B#1 US#1 UK#1, *Flying High* [vii] (1978) R&B#21 US#38 UK#37, *Sail On* (1979) R&B#8 US#4 UK#8, *Still* (1979) R&B#1 US#1 UK#4, *Heroes* [v] (1980) R&B#27 US#54, *Jesus Is Love* (1980) R&B#34, *Oh, No* (1981) R&B#5 US#4 UK#44, *Why You Wanna Try Me* [ii] (1982) R&B#42 US#66. ALBUMS: **Machine Gun** (1974) US#138, **Caught in the Act** (1975) US#26, **Movin' On** (1975) US#29, **Hot on the Tracks** (1976) US#12, **The Commodores** (1977) US#3, **Live** (1977) US#3 UK#60, **Natural High** (1978) p US#3 UK#8,

Midnight Magic (1979) US#3 UK#15, **Heroes** (1980) p US#7 UK#50, **In the Pocket** (1981, all Motown) p US#13 UK#69. COMPILATIONS: **Greatest Hits** (1978, Motown) US#23 UK#19; **Love Songs** (1982, K-Tel) UK#5; **All the Great Hits** (1982) UK#37, **Anthology** (1983, both Motown) US#141; **Very Best of the Commodores** (1985, Telstar) UK#25; **Very Best of the Commodores** (1995, Motown) UK#26. Richie quit the group in 1981 for an instantly successful solo career, his album **Can't Slow Down** (1983), selling over ten million copies. He also co-composed the seven million selling charity single *We Are the World* (1985) with Michael Jackson. CHART COMPOSITIONS: *Endless Love* with Diana Ross (1981) p R&B#1 US#1 UK#7, *Truly* (1982) g R&B#2 US#1 UK#6, *You Are* [iii] (1982) R&B#2 US#4 UK#43, *My Love* (1982) R&B#6 US#5 UK#70, *All Night Long (All Night)* (1983) g R&B#1 US#1 UK#2, *Running with the Night* [xii] (1983) R&B#6 US#7 UK#9, *Hello* (1984) g R&B#1 US#1 UK#1, *Stuck on You* (1984) R&B#8 C&W#24 US#3 UK#12, *Penny Lover* [iii] (1984) R&B#8 US#8 UK#18, *Say You, Say Me* (1985) g R&B#1 US#1 UK#8, *Dancing on the Ceiling* [xi] (1986) R&B#6 US#2 UK#7, *Love Will Conquer All* [x] (1986) R&B#2 US#9 UK#45, *Ballerina Girl* (1986) R&B#5 US#7 UK#17, *Deep River Woman* (1986) R&B#10 US#71, *Sela* [ix] (1987) R&B#12 US#20 UK#43, *Do It to Me* (1992) R&B#7 US#21 UK#33, *My Destiny* (1992) R&B#56 UK#7, *Love Oh Love* (1992) UK#52, *Don't Wanna Lose You* [iv] (1996) R&B#18+ US#39 UK#17, *Still in Love* (1996) UK#66. ALBUMS: **Lionel Richie** (1982) p US#3 UK#9, **Can't Slow Down** (1983) p US#1 UK#1, **Dancing on the Ceiling** (1986, all Motown) p US#1 UK#2; **Louder Than Words** (1996, Mercury) US#28 UK#11. COMPILATION: **Back to Front** (1992, Motown) p US#19 UK#1. HIT VERSIONS: *Easy* Barry Kaye (1978) C&W#89/Faith No More (1992) R&B#58; *Endless Love* Mariah Carey & Luther Vandross (1994) p US#2 UK#3, re-entry (1995) UK#55; *Happy People* [i] Temptations (1975) R&B#1 US#40, *I Don't Need Your Love* Kenny Rogers (1981) US#3, *Just to Be Close to You* Originals on B-side of *Down to Love Town* (1976) R&B#93 US#47/Trey Lorenz (1993) R&B#66 US#103; *Lady* Kenny Rogers (1980) g C&W#1 R&B#42 US#1 UK#12, *Love Will Find a Way* George Howard (1985) R&B#80, *Missing You* Diana Ross (1984) R&B#1 US#10, *Oh, No* Randy Parton (1982) C&W#76, *Sail On* Tom Grant (1979) C&W#16, *Share Your Love* Kenny Rogers (1981) US#14, *Three Times a Lady* Nate Harvell (1978) C&W#23/Conway Twitty (1983) C&W#7; *Zoom* Fat Larry's Band (1986) R&B#89. Co-writers: [i] D. Baldwin/J. Bowen, [ii] D. Cochrane, [iii] Brenda Harvey-Richie, [iv] Jimmy Harris, III/Terry Lewis, [v] D.

Jones, [vi] William King (b. January 30, 1949, AL)/ Thomas McClary (b. October 6, 1950, Tuskegee, AL)/Milan Williams (b. March 28, 1948, MS)/Walter Lee Orange (b. December 10, 1947, FA)/Ronald LaPread (b. September 4, 1946, AL), [vii] Thomas McClary, [viii] Ronald LaPread, [ix] Greg Phillinganes, [x] Greg Phillinganes/Cynthia Weil, [xi] Carlos Rios, [xii] Cynthia Weil. (*See also under* Marvin GAYE, Michael JACKSON.)

784. RICHMAN, Jonathan (b. May 16, 1951, Boston, MA) Pop guitarist and vocalist. A founder member of the esoteric new wave group the Modern Lovers. CHART COMPOSITIONS: *Roadrunner* (1977) UK#11, *Egyptian Reggae* (1977) UK#5, *The Morning of Our Lives* (1978) UK#29. ALBUMS: **The Modern Lovers** (1975), **Jonathan Richman and the Modern Lovers** (1976), **Rock and Roll with the Modern Lovers** (1977) UK#50, **Live** (1977), **Back in Your Life** (1979), **The Jonathan Richman Songbook** (1980, all Beserkley); **The Original Modern Lovers** (1981, Bomp); **Jonathan Sings** (1985), **Rockin' and Romance** (1985), **It's Time for Jonathan Richman** (1986, all Sire); **The Modern Lovers '88** (1988), **Jonathan Richman** (1989), **Jonathan Goes Country** (1990), **I, Jonathan, Te Vas a Emocinar** (1993), **You Must Ask the Heart** (1995, all Rounder); **Surrender to Jonathan** (1996, Vapor). COMPILATION: **The Collection** (1995, Castle).

785. ROBBINS, Marty (b. Martin David Robinson, September 26, 1925, Glendale, AZ; d. December 8, 1982) C&W guitarist and vocalist. One of country music's most successful performers, who charted nearly one hundred singles between 1952–1983, including sixteen number ones. Robbins' career embraced numerous styles, including folk, country, rockabilly, rock and roll, Hawaiian, parlor ballads, cajun, 1930s standards, honky-tonk, and Caribbean and Mexican music. He composed over five hundred songs and interpreted hundreds of others, in a career that encompassed the full range of the American popular song. Robbins sung in a delightful falsetto, and his cowboy songs were later an influence on both the outlaw and the country-rock movements of the 1970s, in particular Willie Nelson and Waylon Jennings. The son of Polish immigrants who grew up in poverty, Robbins developed a strong affinity to his maternal grandfather, a former Confederate soldier, Texas Ranger, and medicine show performer, who spellbound his grandson with the old western tales, that, alongside the music and films of Gene Autry, would be a considerable influence on Robbins' music. He saw active service in the U.S. Navy in the South Pacific during 1943, and after a variety of day jobs, including that of truck driver and ranch hand, he began writing songs and performing on a local radio show in Mesa, Arizona. By 1950, Robbins was hosting the radio show "Chuck Wagon Time," and the following year his own television show "Country Caravan." After signing a long-term recording contract with Columbia, Robbins achieved his first chart topper with *I'll Go on Alone* (1952). Under the stewardship of the arranger and orchestrator Ray Conniff, Robbins updated his sound during the late 1950s, and scored his first cowboy influenced hit with the Gary Cooper film theme *The Hanging Tree* (1959). Filling the vacant throne of his deceased hero Autry, Robbins became the Louis L'Amour of country music, pioneering a new breed of gunfighter ballad, that was rich in western mythology on such tunes as *Big Iron* and *El Paso*, many of which were embellished by Grady Martin's Tex-Mex guitar playing. The album **Gunfighter Ballads and Trail Songs** (1959), featured deep characterizations and tragic outcomes, and remains a classic of the genre. Robbins was a Grand Ole Opry star for thirty years, and a frequent performer on the Ed Sullivan Show. He appeared in the film "Buffalo Guns" (1957), and in the television series "The Drifter." Robbins died from heart by-pass complications at the age of fifty-seven, after extensive surgery resulting from one of many heart attacks that had plagued much of his later years. CHART COMPOSITIONS: *I'll Go on Alone* (1952) C&W#1, *I Couldn't Keep from Crying* (1953) C&W#5, *Pretty Words* (1954) C&W#12, *Call Me Up* (1954) C&W#14, *Time Goes By* (1955) C&W#14, *I Can't Quit (I've Gone Too Far)* (1956) C&W#7, *The Same Two Lips* (1957) C&W#14, *A White Sport Coat (And a Pink Carnation)* (1957) C&W#1 US#2, *Please Don't Blame Me* (1957) C&W#11, *Just Married* (1958) C&W#1 US#26, *Stairway of Love* (1958) C&W#2 US#68, *She Was Only Seventeen (He Was One Year More)* (1958) C&W#4 US#27, *El Paso* (1959) C&W#1 US#1 UK#19, re-entry (1960) UK#44; *Big Iron* (1960) C&W#5 US#26 UK#48, *Don't Worry* (1961) C&W#1 US#3, *Jimmy Martinez* (1961) C&W#24 US#51, *It's Your World* (1961) C&W#3 US#51, *Sometimes I'm Tempted* (1962) C&W#12 US#109, *I Told the Brook* (1962) US#81, *Love Can't Wait* (1962) C&W#12 US#69, *Devil Woman* (1962) C&W#1 US#16 UK#5, *Cigarettes and Coffee Blues* (1963) C&W#14 US#93, *Not So Long Ago* (1963) C&W#13 US#115, *Begging to You* (1963) C&W#1 US#74, *Girl from a Spanish Town* (1964) C&W#15 US#106, *The Cowboy in the Continental Suit* (1964) C&W#3 US#103, *One of These Days* (1964) C&W#8 US#105, *Old Red* (1965) C&W#50, *Count Me Out* (1966) C&W#14, *Private Wilson White* (1966) C&W#21, *The Shoe Goes on the Other Foot Tonight*

(1966) C&W#3, *Mr. Shorty* (1966) C&W#16, *No Tears Milady* (1967) C&W#16, *Fly Butterfly Fly* (1967) C&W#34, *Tonight Carmen* (1967) C&W#1 US#114, *I Can't Say Goodbye* (1969) C&W#8, *Camelia* (1969) C&W#10, *My Woman, My Woman, My Wife* (1970) C&W#1 US#42, *Seventeen Years* (1971) C&W#7 US#121, *Early Morning Sunshine* (1971) C&W#9, *The Best Part of Living* (1972) C&W#6, *I've Got a Woman's Love* (1972) C&W#32, *This Much a Man* (1972) C&W#11, *Walking Piece of Heaven* (1973) C&W#6, *A Man and a Train* (1973) C&W#40, *Twentieth Century Drifter* (1974) C&W#10, *Don't You Think* (1974) C&W#12, *Two Gun Daddy* (1974) C&W#39, *Life* (1975) C&W#23, *It Takes Faith* (1975) C&W#76, *Shotgun Rider* (1975) C&W#55, *El Paso City* (1976) C&W#1, *Don't Let Me Touch You* [i] (1977) C&W#6, *Please Don't Play a Love Song* (1978) C&W#17, *Touch Me with Magic* (1979) C&W#15, *All Around Cowboy* (1979) C&W#16, *She's Made of Faith* (1980) C&W#37, *One Man's Trash (Is Another Man's Treasure)* (1980) C&W#72, *An Occasional Rose* (1980) C&W#28, *Completely Out of Love* (1981) C&W#47, *Jumper Cable Man* (1981) C&W#83, *Teardrops in My Heart* (1981) C&W#45, *Tie Your Dream to Mine* (1982) C&W#24, *Honkytonk Man* (1982) C&W#10, *Change of Heart* (1983) C&W#48, *What If I Said I Love You* (1983) C&W#57. ALBUMS: **Rockin, Rollin', Robbins** (1956), **The Song of Robbins** (1957), **Song of the Islands** (1958), **Marty Robbins** (1958), **Gunfighter Ballads and Trail Songs** (1959) p US#6 UK#20, **More Gunfighter Ballads and Trail Songs** (1961) US#21, **After Midnight** (1961), **Just a Little Sentimental** (1962), **Devil Woman** (1962) US#35, **Hawaii's Calling Me** (1962), **Return of the Gunfighter** (1963), **Island Woman** (1963), **R.F.D.** (1964), **Turn the Lights Down Low** (1964), **The Drifter** (1964), **What God Has Done** (1964), **Carl, Lefty and Marty** (1965), **Tonight Carmen** (1967), **I Walk Alone** (1968) US#160, **It's a Sin** (1969) US#194, **My Woman, My Woman, My Wife** (1970) US#117, **El Paso** (1970), **Today** (1971) US#175, **El Paso City** (1977), **Long Time Ago** (1977), **Don't Let Me Touch You** (1977), **All Around Cowboy** (1980), **Come Back to Me** (1982, all Columbia); **Twentieth Century Drifter** (1986, MCA). COMPILATIONS: **Marty's Greatest Hits** (1959), **More Greatest Hits** (1960), **Greatest Hits, Volume 3** (1971) US#143, **All-Time Greatest Hits** (1972, all Columbia) g; **The Marty Robbins Collection** (1979, Lotus) UK#5; **Biggest Hits** (1983) US#170, **A Lifetime of Song, 1951–1982** (1984, both Columbia); **The Marty Robbins Files, 1951–1953, Volume 1** (1984), **The Marty Robbins Files, 1953–1954, Volume 2** (1984), **The Marty Robbins Files, 1954–1956, Volume 3** (1984), **The Marty**

Robbins Files, 1957–1958, Volume 4 (1984), **The Marty Robbins Files, 1959–1962, Volume 5** (1984), **In the Wild West, Part 1** (1985), **In the Wild West, Part 2** (1985), **In the Wild West, Part 3** (1985), **In the Wild West, Part 4** (1985), **In the Wild West, Part 5** (1985, all Bear Family); **The Essential Marty Robbins, 1951–1982** (1991, Columbia). HIT VERSIONS: *Cigarettes and Coffee Blues* Lefty Frizzell (1958) C&W#13, *Don't Worry* Billy Fury (1961) UK#40/Glenda Griffith (1978) C&W#96; *Kate* Johnny Cash (1972) C&W#2 US#75, *My Woman, My Woman, My Wife* Dean Martin (1970) US#110, *White Sport Coat (And a Pink Carnation), A* Max Bygraves on *All Star Hit Parade #2 EP* (1957) UK#15/Terry Dene (1957) UK#18; *You Don't Owe Me a Thing* Johnnie Ray (1957) US#10 UK#12, *You Gave Me a Mountain* Johnny Bush (1969) C&W#7/Frankie Laine (1969) US#24. Co-writer: [i] Billy Sherrill.

786. ROBERTS, Allan Film composer. A lyricist and composer whose songs were included in such films as "Gilda" and "Memory for Two (both 1946). HIT VERSIONS: *Angelina (The Waitress at the Pizzeria)* [iii] Louis Prima (1944) US#14, *Every Single Little Tingle of My Heart* [vi] Dorsey Brothers Orchestra (1935) US#17, *Good, Good, Good (That's You-That's You)* [iii] Xavier Cugat (1945) US#6/Sammy Kaye (1945) US#10; *I Wish* [iii] Mills Brothers (1945) R&B#4 US#6, *Into Each Life Some Rain Must Fall* [iii] Ella Fitzgerald & the Ink Spots (1944) R&B#1 US#1/Teresa Brewer (1953) US#23; *Kissin' Bug Boogie* [i] Jo Stafford (1951) US#20, *Noodlin' Rag* [i] Perry Como (1952) US#23, *Rainbow Rhapsody* [ii] Glenn Miller (1944) US#20, *Sabre Dance* [iv] Andrews Sisters (1948) US#20/Woody Herman (1948) US#3/Love Sculpture (1968) UK#5; *Tampico* [iii] Stan Kenton (1945) g US#3, *That Old Devil Called Love* [iii] Alison Moyet (1985) UK#2, *To Know You (Is to Love You)* [i] Perry Como (1952) US#19, *You Always Hurt the One You Love* [iii] Mills Brothers (1944) g R&B#5 US#1/Sammy Kaye (1945) US#10/Connie Francis (1958) UK#13/Clarence "Frogman" Henry (1961) R&B#11 US#12 UK#6/Fats Domino (1963) US#102; *You Can't See the Sun When You're Cryin'* [iii] Ink Spots (1947) US#19/Vaughn Monroe (1947) US#21. Co-writers: [i] Robert Allen, [ii] Benny Carter, [iii] Doris Fisher, [iv] Aram Ilyich Khachaturian (b. 1903, Tbilisi; d. 1978, Moscow, both Russia)/Lester Lee, [v] Lester Lee, [vi] Jules Loman/Nat Simon.

787. ROBERTS, Bruce Pop vocalist. A singer who has been more successful as a songwriting collaborator for others. ALBUM: **Intimacy** (1995). HIT VERSIONS: *Anyone Can See* [iii] Irene Cara (1981) US#64, *Dynamite* [v] Jermaine Jackson (1984) R&B#8 US#15, *Flames of Paradise* [v] Jennifer Rush & Elton John (1987) US#36 UK#59, *Goldmine* [v] Pointer Sisters (1986) R&B#17 US#33, *Lucky One, The* Laura Branigan (1984) US#20, *Main Event, The* [iv] Barbra Streisand (1979) g US#3, *No More Tears (Enough Is Enough)* [vi] Donna Summer & Barbra Streisand (1979) g R&B#20 US#1 UK#3, *Oh, People* [v] Patti LaBelle (1986) R&B#7 US#29 UK#26, *Shoppin' from A to Z* [i] Toni Basil (1983) US#77, *Sugar Don't Bite* [vii] Sam Harris (1984) US#36, *Twist My Arm* [v] Pointer Sisters (1986) R&B#61 US#83, *Whisper in the Dark* [ii] Dionne Warwick (1986) R&B#49 US#72, *You Should Be Mine (The Woo Woo Song)* [v] Jeffrey Osbourne (1986) R&B#2 US#13. Co-writers: [i] Toni Basil/Allee Willis, [ii] E. Bronfman, Jr., [iii] Irene Cara, [iv] Bob Esty/Paul Jabara, [v] Andy Goldmark, [vi] Paul Jabara, [vii] Donna Weiss. (*See also under* Burt BACHARACH, Carole Bayer SAGER.)

788. ROBERTS, Lucky (b. Charles Luckyeth Roberts, August 7, 1887, Philadelphia, PA; d. February 5, 1968, New York, NY) Film and stage pianist, vocalist. A child vaudeville star and pianist, who wrote his own songs *Junk Man Rag, Pork and Beans, Railroad Blues*, and *Ripples on the Nile*. Although mostly forgotten now, Roberts composed over twelve Broadway shows from 1911, and performed on his own radio show. ALBUM: **Lucky Roberts** (1958, Good Time Jazz). (*See also under* Kim GANNON.)

789. ROBERTS, Paddy Film composer. A British songwriter whose compositions were included in the films "An Alligator Named Daisy" (1955) and "The Good Companions" (1957). HIT VERSIONS: *Book, The* [vi] David Whitfield (1954) UK#5, *Evermore* [viii] Ruby Murray (1955) UK#3, *Heart of a Man* [iii] Frankie Vaughan (1959) UK#5, *Johnny Is the Boy for Me* [xi] Les Paul & Mary Ford (1953) US#15, *Lay Down Your Arms* [v] Chordettes (1956) US#16/Anne Shelton (1956) UK#1; *Meet Me on the Corner* [v] Max Bygraves (1955) UK#2, *Pickin' a Chicken* [i] Eve Boswell (1960) UK#20, *Softly, Softly* [iv] Ruby Murray (1955) UK#1, *You Are My First Love* [x] Ruby Murray (1956) UK#16. Co-writers: [i] Derek Bernfield/Garfield De Mortimer, [ii] Elton Box/Desmond Cox/Ralph Butler, [iii] Peggy Cochrane, [iv] Pierre Dudan/Mark Paul, [v] Ake Gerhard/Leon Land, [vi] Hans Gottwald, [vii] Peter Hart, [viii] Gerry Levine, [ix] Geoffrey Parsons/C.A. Ross, [x] Lester Powell, [xi] Marcel Stellman, [xii] Jack Woodman.

790. ROBERTS, Rick (b. 1950, FL) Rock

vocalist. The country influenced lead vocalist who first recorded with the Flying Burrito Brothers. ALBUMS: **The Flying Burrito Brothers** (1971) US#176, **Last of the Red Hot Burritos** (1972, both A&M) US#171. COMPILATIONS: **Close Up the Honky Tonks** (1974, A&M) US#158; **Live in Amsterdam** (1975, Phonogram); **Bluegrass Special** (1973), **Honky Tonk Heaven** (1973, both Ariola). In 1975, Roberts co-founded the soft-rock group Firefall. CHART COMPOSITIONS: *You Are the Woman* (1976) US#9, *Livin' Ain't Livin'* (1976) US#42, *Cinderella* (1977) US#34, *Just Remember I Love You* (1977) US#11, *Strange Way* (1978) US#11, *So Long* (1978) US#48, *Goodbye, I Love You* (1979) US#43, *Headed for a Fall* (1980) US#35, *Love That Got Away* (1980) US#50, *Staying with It* with Lisa Nemzo (1981) US#37, *Always* (1983) US#59. ALBUMS: **Firefall** (1976) g US#28, **Luna Sea** (1977) g US#27, **Elan** (1978) p US#27, **Undertow** (1980) US#68, **Clouds Across the Sun** (1981) US#102, **Break of Dawn** (1983) US#199, **Mirror of the World** (1983, all Atlantic). COMPILATION: **Best of Firefall** (1981, Atlantic) US#186. Roberts has also recorded as a solo artist. ALBUMS: **Windmills** (1972), **She Is a Song** (1973, both A&M). COMPILATION: **Best of Rick Roberts** (1979, A&M).

791. ROBERTSON, B.A. Pop vocalist. A British singer-songwriter and occasional actor. CHART COMPOSITIONS: *Bang Bang* [i] (1979) UK#2, *Knocked It Off* [i] (1979) UK#8, *Cool in a Kaftan* (1980) UK#17, *To Be or Not to Be* [i] (1980) UK#9, *Hold Me* with Maggie Bell (1981) UK#11, *Time* with Frida (1983) UK#45. ALBUMS: **Wringing Applause** (1973, Ardent); **Initial Success** (1980) UK#32, **Bully for You** (1981) UK#61, **R and Ba** (1982, all Asylum). HIT VERSIONS: *Carrie* [i] Cliff Richard (1980) US#34 UK#4, *We Have a Dream* Scottish World Cup Squad (1982) UK#5. Co-writer: [i] Terry Britten. (*See also under* Mike RUTHERFORD, Alan TARNEY.)

792. ROBERTSON, Don (b. December 5, 1922, Peking, China) C&W pianist and arranger. An influential country pianist and songwriter, who studied composition at the Chicago College of Music during the 1940s. Robertson was a session player for Capitol Records, before writing the frequently recorded *I Really Don't Want to Know* [i]. Many of his songs were featured in Elvis Presley's films between 1961–1963. CHART COMPOSITION: *The Happy Whistler* (1956) US#6 UK#8. ALBUM: **Heart on My Sleeve** (1964, RCA). HIT VERSIONS: *Anything That's Part of You* Elvis Presley (1962) US#31, *Born to Be with You* Chordettes (1956) US#5 UK#8/Echoes (1960) US#101/Capitol Showband

(1965) US#126/Silkie (1966) US#133/Sonny James (1968) C&W#1 US#81/Dion (1976) US#108/Dave Edmunds (1973) UK#5/Sandy Posey (1978) C&W#21; *Happy Whistler, The* Cyril Stapleton (1956) UK#22, *Hummingbird* Les Paul & Mary Ford (1955) US#7/Frankie Laine (1955) US#17 UK#16; *I Don't Hurt Anymore* Hank Snow (1954) g C&W#1 US#22/Linda Cassady (1977) C&W#92/Narvel Felts (1977) C&W#37; *I Love You More and More Each Day* Al Martino (1964) US#9/Sonny James (1973) C&W#4; *I Really Don't Want to Know* [i] Eddy Arnold (1954) C&W#1/Les Paul & Mary Ford (1954) US#11/Tommy Edwards (1960) US#18/Ronnie Dove (1966) US#22/Elvis Presley (1971) C&W#23 US#21/Charlie McCoy (1972) C&W#19; *I'm Counting on You* Kitty Wells on B-side of *Repenting* (1956) C&W#6, *I'm Yours* [ii] Elvis Presley (1965) US#11, *Please Help Me, I'm Falling (In Love with You)* [ii] Hank Locklin (1960) C&W#1 US#8, new version with Danny Davis & the Nashville Brass (1970) C&W#68/Janie Frickie (1978) C&W#12; *Ringo* [ii] Lorne Green (1964) C&W#21 US#1 UK#22. Co-writers: [i] Howard Barnes, [ii] Hal Blair.

793. ROBERTSON, Robbie (b. Jaime Robertson, July 5, 1944, Toronto, Canada) Rock guitarist, producer and vocalist. A songwriter who, as a member of the group the Band, questioned his own musical and personal heritage in a series of semi-mystical songs. Born of a Jewish father, but raised by his mother on a Sioux Indian Reservation near Lake Erie, Canada, Robertson learned the ukelele and guitar in his teens. He grew up listening to R&B and the blues, before playing in local Toronto bands and forming Robbie and the Robots at the age of thirteen. Three years later he was a roadie for Ronnie Hawkins and the Hawks, graduating to bass player and eventually guitarist, and appearing on Hawkins' album **Mojo Man** (1963, Roulette). Hawkins was also the first to record a Robertson song, *Hey Boba Lu*. The hapless Hawkins lost his entire backing band when it quit to perform as Levon Helm and the Hawks, the Canadian Squires, and ultimately the Hawks, as which, they accompanied Bob Dylan on his infamous 1965 world tour, when he so controversially introduced electric instruments to folk music. In 1967, the group signed to Capitol Records as the Crackers, but re-christened itself the Band shortly before the release of the magnificent **Music from Big Pink** (1968), which showcased the group's multi-instrumentalist, three lead vocalist approach. The album was the very antithesis of the then in-vogue heavy rock sound, examining instead the mythology of the Old West and the lifestyle and values of rural America. Between 1968–1972, the Band were one of the most significant live and recording acts in America, its music a wonderfully inconsistent series of paradoxes, and its sound an absorption of every element of American music, including R&B, the blues, ragtime, rock and roll, country, and cajun, the likes of which only the Grateful Dead has matched. By **The Band** (1969), the group had become totally immersed in Americana, adding folk and bluegrass to its sound, and avoiding all studio gadgetry by performing much of the material on traditional instruments. **Cahoots** (1971), was a sweeping look at the dying small towns of America, with songs, such as *The Last of the Blacksmiths*, about skilled craftsmen and their financial struggle for survival. After the ill-judged "The Last Waltz" final concert film, Robertson departed for a solo career. CHART COMPOSITIONS: *The Weight* (1968) US#63 UK#21, *Up on Cripple Creek* (1969) US#25, *Rag Mama Rag* (1969) US#57 UK#16, *Time to Kill* (1970) US#77, *Life Is a Carnival* (1971) US#72, *The Shape I'm In* (1971) US#121, *Ophelia* (1976) US#62. ALBUMS: **Music from Big Pink** (1968) US#30, **The Band** (1969) p US#9 UK#25, **Stage Fright** (1970) g US#5 UK#15, **Cahoots** (1971) US#21 UK#41, **Rock of Ages** (1972) g US#6, **Moondog Matinee** (1974, all Capitol) US#28; **Before the Flood*** (1974, Asylum) g US#3 UK#8; **The Basement Tapes*** (1975, Columbia) US#7 UK#8; **Northern Lights — Southern Cross** (1976) US#26, **Islands** (1977, both Capitol) US#64; **The Last Waltz** ost (1978, Warner Brothers) US#16 UK#39. COMPILATIONS: **Best of the Band** (1976) US#51, **Anthology** (1978), **To Kingdom Come — The Definitive Collection** (1989), **The Great Divide** (1994), **Live at Watkins Gap** (1995, all Capitol). Robertson collaborated with the director Martin Scorsese on a number of film projects, before recording as a solo artist. In 1994, he composed the soundtrack to "Jimmy Hollywood." CHART COMPOSITION: *Somewhere Down the Crazy River* (1987) UK#15. ALBUMS: **Robbie Robertson** (1987) g US#38 UK#23, **Storyville** (1991, both Geffen) US#69 UK#30; **Music for the Native Americans** ost (1994, Capitol) US#149. HIT VERSIONS: *Broken Arrow* Rod Stewart (1991) US#20 UK#54, re-issued (1992) UK#41; *Davy's on the Road Again* [i] Manfred Mann's Earthband (1978) UK#6, *Night They Drove Old Dixie Down, The* Buckaroos (1970) C&W#71/Joan Baez (1971) g US#3 UK#6/Alice Creech (1971) C&W#33; *Weight, The* Jackie DeShannon (1968) US#55/Aretha Franklin (1969) R&B#3 US#19/Diana Ross & the Supremes with the Temptations (1969) R&B#33 US#46. With: * Bob Dylan. Co-writer: [i] John Simon.

794. ROBIN, Leo (b. April 6, 1900, Pittsburgh, PA; d. 1984) Film and stage lyricist. A playwright who turned to songwriting and achieved his first hit with *Hit the Deck* (1927), which he co-wrote with Vincent Youmans. Robin also composed songs for the revue "Ca c'est Paris" (1927), and the film "Playboy of Paris" (1930). In partnership with the composer Ralph Rainger, he provided songs for some forty movies, including "A Bedtime Story" (1932). Robin's last Broadway success was with "The Girl in Pink Tights" (1954). ALBUMS: **Gentlemen Prefer Blondes** oc (1950, Columbia); **Paris Honeymoon** st (1950), **Waikiki Wedding** st (1951, both Decca); **Gentlemen Prefer Blondes** ost (1953, MGM); **Ruggles of Red Gap** tvst (1957, Verve); **The Girl in Pink Tights** oc (1958, Columbia); **Lorelei** oc (1974, Verve); **Hit the Deck** oc (1976, World); **The Gang's All Here** ost (1978, Sandy Hook). HIT VERSIONS: *Love Is Just Around the Corner* [ii] Bing Crosby (1935) US#8, *Moonlight and Shadows* [iii] Bing Crosby (1937) US#10/Eddy Duchin (1937) US#5/Shep Fields (1937) US#3/Dorothy Lamour (1937) US#10; *Paree! (Ca c'est Paris)* [iv] Nat Shilkret (1927) US#9, *Prisoner of Love* [i] Russ Columbo (1932) US#16/Perry Como (1946) US#1/Billy Eckstine (1946) R&B#3 US#10/Ink Spots (1946) R&B#5 US#9/James Brown (1963) R&B#6 US#18/Millie Scott (1986) R&B#78; *Whispers in the Dark* [iii] Connee Boswell (1937) US#9/Bob Crosby (1937) US#1/Hal Kemp (1937) US#11. Co-writers: [i] Russ Columbo/Clarence Gaskill (b. 1892; d. 1947), [ii] Lewis E. Genslar, [iii] Frederick Hollander, [iv] Jose Padilla. (*See also under* Harold ARLEN, Jerome KERN, Ralph RAINGER, Sigmund ROMBERG, Jule STYNE, Albert VON TILZER, Harry WARREN, Richard WHITING, Vincent YOUMANS.)

795. ROBINSON, Christopher (b. December 20, 1966, Atlanta, GA) Rock vocalist, and **ROBINSON, Richard** (b. May 24, 1969, Atlanta, GA) Rock guitarist. Founder members of, and co-writers in, the rock group the Black Crowes. CHART COMPOSITIONS: *Jealous Again* (1990) US#75, *Twice as Hard* (1991) UK#47, *She Talks to Angels* (1991) US#30, *Jealous Again/She Talks to Angels* (1991) UK#70, *Seeing Things* (1991) UK#72, *Remedy* (1992) US#48 UK#24, *Thorn in My Pride* (1992) US#80, *Sting Me* (1992) UK#42, *Hotel Illness* (1992) UK#47, *High Head Blues/A Conspiracy* (1995) UK#25, *Wiser Time* (1995) UK#34. ALBUMS: **Shake Your Money Maker** (1990) p US#4 UK#36, **Southern Harmony and Musical Companion** (1992) p US#1 UK#2, **amorica** (1994, all Def America) g US#11 UK#12.

796. ROBINSON, Earl (b. Earl Hawley Robinson, July 2, 1910, Seattle, WA) R&B guitarist and vocalist. A graduate of music from the University of Washington, who wandered across America with the singers Woody Guthrie and Leadbelly, collecting folk songs for the Library of Congress. Robinson's best known compositions remain the often covered *Joe Hill* and *Black and White* [ii]. In the 1930s, he conducted the American People's Chorus, and during the 1940s he presented his own radio series. Robinson also contributed material to such films as "A Walk in the Sun" (1945), "California" and "Romance of Rosie Ridge" (both 1947), before composing the cantata *The Lonesome Train* (1948). Like Pete Seeger, Robinson was one of the many folk artists to be blacklisted during the McCarthy era, and in 1950, he became a guitar teacher. His later compositions include the orchestral work *To the Northwest Indian* (1974), and *Ballad for Americans* [iii], for the radio program "Pursuit of Happiness" (1940). HIT VERSIONS: *Black and White* [ii] Greyhound (1971) UK#6/Three Dog Night (1972) g US#1; *House I Live In, The* [i] Frank Sinatra (1946) US#22. Co-writers: [i] Lewis Allen, [ii] Dave Arkin, [iii] John Latouche.

797. ROBINSON, J. Russel (b. July 8, 1892, Indianapolis, IN; d. September 30, 1963, Palmdale, CA) Vaudeville pianist and arranger. A vaudeville performer who toured the theatres as one half of the Famous Robinson Brothers, before composing his first songs, *Sapho Rag* (1909) and *Eccentric* (1923). Between 1917–1925, Robinson worked as a demonstrator for piano roll companies, before becoming an arranger for the duo Pace and Handy. He later formed the Dixie Stars, a vaudeville act with Al Bernard. HIT VERSIONS: *Blue Eyed Sally* [i] Ted Weems (1925) US#3, *Mary Lou* Abe Lyman (1926) US#3/Ipana Troubadors (1927) US#7; *Swing, Mr. Charlie* Herbie Kay (1936) US#17. Co-writer: [i] Al Bernard. (*See also under* Con CONRAD, Roy TURK.)

798. ROBINSON, Smokey (b. William Robinson, February 19, 1940, Detroit, MI) R&B vocalist and producer. A stylish and prolific songwriter who was a major hitmaker during the 1960s, and an influence on the songwriting style of the Beatles. Robinson's compositions have been recorded by artists across all musical genres, and his smooth, distinctly sweet voice with a fragrant quiver in the upper register, was used to great effect when he was a member of the group Smokey Robinson and the Miracles. He began singing at an early age, and wrote his first song for a school play at the age of six. By the time he was eighteen, Robinson had written over one hundred songs. In 1954, he sang in the clubs of Detroit in the vocal group the Matadors with Marvin Tarplin, a group, that by 1957, was known as the Miracles, one of Berry Gordy, Jr.'s earliest signings to his fledgling Motown label. CHART COMPOSITIONS: *Bad*

Girl (1959) US#93, *Shop Around* [vii] (1960) R&B#1 US#2, *Ain't It Baby* (1961) R&B#15 US#49, *Mighty Good Lovin'* (1961) R&B#21 US#51, *Everybody's Gotta Pay Some Dues* (1962) R&B#11 US#52, *What's So Good About Goodbye* (1962) R&B#16 US#35, *I'll Try Something New* (1963) R&B#11 US#39, *Way Over There* [vii] (1962) US#94, *I've Been Good to You* (1962) US#103, *You've Really Got a Hold on Me* (1962) R&B#1 US#8, *A Love She Can Count On* (1963) R&B#21 US#31, *(You Can't Let the Boy Overpower) The Man in You* (1964) US#59, *I Like It Like That* (1964) US#27, *That's What Love Is Made Of* (1964) US#35, *Come on Do the Jerk* [xiv] (1964) US#50, *Ooh Baby Baby* [xi] (1965) R&B#4 US#16, *The Tracks of My Tears* [xv] (1965) R&B#2 US#16 UK#9, *My Girl Has Gone* [xvi] (1965) R&B#3 US#14, *Going to a Go Go* [xiii] (1965) R&B#2 US#11 UK#44, *Choosey Beggar* [xi] (1966) R&B#35, *The Love I Saw in You Was Just a Mirage* [xviii] (1967) R&B#10 US#20, *More Love* (1967) R&B#5 US#23, *I Second That Emotion* [ii] (1967) R&B#1 US#4 UK#27, *If You Can Want* (1968) R&B#3 US#11 UK#50, *Yester Love* [ii] (1968) R&B#9 US#31, *Special Occasion* [ii] (1968) R&B#4 US#26, *Baby, Baby Don't Cry* [iii] (1969) R&B#3 US#8, *Doggone Right* [v] (1969) R&B#7 US#33, *Here I Go Again* [v] (1969) R&B#15 US#37, *Point It Out* (1969) R&B#4 US#37, *The Tears of a Clown* [vi] (1970) R&B#1 US#1 UK#1, re-issued (1976) UK#34; *I Don't Blame You at All* (1971) R&B#7 US#18 UK#11, *Crazy About the La La La* (1971) R&B#20 US#56, *Satisfaction* (1971) R&B#20 US#49, *I Can't Stand to See You Cry* (1972) R&B#21 US#45. ALBUMS: **Hi, We're the Miracles** (1961), **Cookin' with the Miracles** (1962), **Shop Around** (1962), **I'll Try Something New** (1962), **Christmas with the Miracles** (1963), **The Fabulous Miracles** (1963) US#118, **The Miracles on Stage** (1963) US#139, **Doin' Mickey's Monkey** (1963) US#113, **Gemini** (1964), **Going to a Go Go** (1965) US#8, **Away We a Go Go** (1966) US#41, **Make It Happen** (1967) US#28, **The Tears of a Clown** (1967) US#143, **Special Occasion** (1968) US#42, **Live** (1969) US#71, **Time Out for Smokey Robinson and the Miracles** (1969) US#25, **Four in Blue** (1969) US#78, **What Love Has Joined Together** (1970) US#97, **A Pocketful of Miracles** (1970) US#56, **The Season for the Miracles** (1970), **One Dozen Roses** (1971) US#92, **Flying High Together** (1972, all Tamla) US#46. COMPILATIONS: **Greatest Hits from the Beginning** (1964) US#21, **Greatest Hits, Volume 2** (1968) US#7, **1957–1972** (1972, all Tamla) US#75; **Anthology** (1974, Motown) US#97. Robinson eventually became a Motown vice-president, a position he maintained until Gordy sold out to MCA Records in 1991. In 1973, Robinson left the Miracles for a solo career, recording in a softer, more mainstream style. CHART COMPOSITIONS:

Sweet Harmony (1973) R&B#31 US#48, *Baby Come Close* [x] (1973) R&B#7 US#27, *It's Her Turn to Live* [xviii] (1974) R&B#29 US#82, *Just My Soul Responding* (1974) UK#35, *Virgin Man* [viii] (1974) R&B#12 US#56, *I Am I Am* (1974) R&B#6 US#56, *Baby That's Backatcha* (1975) R&B#1 US#26, *The Agony and the Ecstasy* (1975) R&B#7 US#36, *Quiet Storm* [viii] (1975) R&B#25 US#61, *Open* [xviii] (1976) R&B#10 US#81, *Vitamin U* (1977) R&B#18 US#101, *Theme from Big Time (Part 1)* (1977) R&B#38, *Daylight and Darkness* [viii] (1978) R&B#9 US#75, *Shoe Soul* (1978) R&B#68, *Get Ready* (1979) R&B#82, *Cruisin'* [viii] (1979) R&B#4 US#4, *Let Me Be the Clock* (1980) R&B#4 US#31, *Heavy on Pride (Light on Love)* (1980) R&B#34, *Being with You* (1981) g R&B#1 US#2 UK#1, *You Are Forever* (1981) R&B#31 US#59, *Who's Sad* (1981) R&B#62, *Yes It's You Lady* (1982) US#107, *I've Made Love to You a Thousand Times* (1983) R&B#8 US#101, *Touch the Sky* (1983) R&B#68 US#110, *Don't Play Another Love Song* (1983) R&B#75 US#103, *And I Don't Love You* (1984) R&B#33 US#106, *I Can't Find* (1984) R&B#41 US#109, *Hold on to Your Love* (1986) R&B#11, *Sleepless Nights* (1986) R&B#51, *What's Too Much* [ix] (1987) R&B#16 US#79, *Love Don't Give No Reason* (1987) R&B#35, *We've Saved the Best for Last* with Kenny G (1989) US#47, *Rewind* (1992) R&B#56, *I Love Your Face* (1993) R&B#57. ALBUMS: **Smokey** (1973) US#70, **Pure Smokey** (1974) US#99, **A Quiet Storm** (1975) US#36, **Smokey's Family Robinson** (1976) US#57, **Deep in My Soul** (1977, all Tamla) US#47; **Big Time** ost (1977, Motown); **Love Breeze** (1978) US#75, **Smokin'** (1978) US#165, **Where There's Smoke** (1979) US#17, **Warm Thoughts** (1980) US#14, **Being with You** (1981) g US#10 UK#17, **Yes It's You Lady** (1982) US#33, **Touch the Sky** (1983) US#50, **Essar** (1984) US#141, **Smoke Signals** (1985, all Tamla) US#104; **One Heartbeat** (1987) g US#26, **Love, Smokey** (1990, both Motown) US#112; **Double Good Everything** (1991, SBK). COMPILATIONS: **Blame It on Love and All the Great Hits** (1983, Tamla) US#124; **Love Songs** with Marvin Gaye (1988, Telstar) UK#69; **The Greatest Hits** (1992, Motown) UK#65. HIT VERSIONS: *Ain't That Peculiar* [xviii] Marvin Gaye (1965) US#8/Ramsey Lewis (1966) US#129, also on B-side of *Wade in the Water* (1966) US#19/George Tindley (1969) R&B#35/Fanny (1972) US#85/Diamond Reo (1975) US#44/Stevie Woods (1983) R&B#54/New Grass Revival (1986) C&W#53; *As Long As I Know He's Mine* Marvelettes (1963) US#47, *As Long As There Is L-O-V-E Love* Jimmy Ruffin (1966) US#120, *Automatically Sunshine* Supremes (1972) R&B#21 US#37 UK#10, *Breathtaking Guy, A* Supremes (1964) US#75, *Composer, The* Diana Ross & the Supremes (1969) R&B#21

US#27, *Day She Needed Me, The* Contours (1965) R&B#37, *Don't Look Back* [xix] Temptations (1965) R&B#15 US#83/Peter Tosh (1978) US#81 UK#43/Teena Marie (1979) R&B#91; *Don't Mess with Bill* Marvelettes (1966) R&B#3 US#7, *First I Look at the Purse* Contours (1964) R&B#12 US#57, *Floy Joy* Supremes (1972) R&B#5 US#16 UK#9, *From Head to Toe* Elvis Costello (1982) UK#43, *Get Ready* Temptations (1966) R&B#1 US#29/Ella Fitzgerald (1969) US#126/King Curtis (1970) R&B#46/Rare Earth (1970) R&B#20 US#4/Stars On *Stars on Long Play 2/On 45 Volume 2* (1981) US#120 UK#18; *Going to a Go Go* [xiii] Shalamar in *Uptown Festival* (1977) R&B#10 US#25/Sharonettes (1975) UK#46/Rolling Stones (1982) US#25 UK#26; *He's a Good Guy (Yes He Is)* Marvelettes (1963) US#55, *Here I Am Baby* Barbara McNair (1967) US#125/Marvelettes (1968) R&B#14 US#44; *Hunter Gets Captured By the Game, The* Marvelettes (1963) R&B#2 US#13/Grace Jones (1980) R&B#87; *I Second That Emotion* [ii] Japan (1982) UK#9, *I'll Be in Trouble* Temptations (1964) US#33, *I'll Try Something New* Diana Ross & the Supremes (1969) R&B#8 UK#25/Temptations (1969) R&B#8 US#25/A Taste of Honey (1982) R&B#9 US#41; *I've Been Good to You* Temptations (1967) US#124; *It's Growing* [xi] Temptations (1965) R&B#3 US#18 UK#45, *Laughing Boy* Mary Wells (1962) R&B#6 US#15, *More Love* Kim Carnes (1980) US#10, *More, More, More of Your Love* Bob Brady & the Con Chords (1967) US#104, *My Baby (Changes with the Weather)* [xii] Temptations (1965) R&B#4 US#13, *My Baby Must Be a Magician* Marvelettes (1963) R&B#8 US#17, *My Girl* [xix] Temptations (1964) g R&B#1 US#1 UK#43, re-issued (1992) UK#2/Otis Redding (1965) UK#11, re-issued (1968) UK#36/Bobby Vee (1968) US#35/Stevie Wonder on B-side of *You Met Your Match* (1968) R&B#2 US#35/Eddie Floyd (1970) R&B#43 US#116/Dale McBride (1977) C&W#73/Rod Stewart (1980) UK#32/Savannah (1984) C&W#73/Hall & Oates (1985) R&B#40 US#20 UK#58/Suave (1988) R&B#3 US#20; *My Girl/My Guy* [xix] Ami Stewart & Johnny Bristol (1980) US#63 UK#39/Ami Stewart & Deon Estus (1986) UK#63; *My Guy* [xix] Mary Wells (1964) US#1 UK#5/Linda K. Lance (1971) C&W#46/Petula Clark (1972) US#70/Margo Smith (1980) C&W#43/Sister Sledge (1982) R&B#14 US#23/Tracy Ullman (1984) UK#23; *One More Heartache* [xiv] Marvin Gaye (1966) US#29, *One Who Really Loves You, The* Mary Wells (1962) R&B#2 US#8, *Ooh Baby Baby* [xi] Linda Ronstadt (1978) C&W#85 R&B#77 US#7, *Operator* Brenda Holloway (1965) R&B#36 US#78, *Quiet Storm* [viii] De La Soul sampled in *Breakadawn* (1993) US#76 UK#39, *Shop Around* [vii] Captain & Tennille (1976) US#4, *Since I Lost My Baby* [xi] Temptations (1965) R&B#4 US#17/Luther Vandross

(1983) R&B#17; *Still Water (Love)* [xx] Four Tops (1970) R&B#4 US#11 UK#10/O'Bryan (1982) R&B#23; *Take This Heart of Mine* Marvin Gaye (1966) US#44, *Tears of a Clown, The* [vi] Beat (1979) UK#6/Stars On *Stars on Long Play 2/On 45 Volume 2* (1981) US#120 UK#18; *This Heart of Mine* Marvin Gaye (1966) US#44, *Too Hurt to Cry, Too Much in Love to Say Goodbye* Darnells (1961) US#117, *Tracks of My Tears, The* [xv] Johnny Rivers (1967) US#10/Aretha Franklin (1969) R&B#21 US#71/Linda Ronstadt (1976) C&W#11 US#25 UK#42/Colin Blunstone (1982) UK#60/Go West (1993) UK#16; *Two Lovers* Mary Wells (1962) R&B#1 US#7, *Way Over There* [vii] Edwin Starr (1968) US#119, *Way You Do the Things You Do, The* [xvii] Temptations (1964) US#11/Stoney & Meat Loaf on B-side of *What You See Is What You Get* (1971) R&B#36 US#71/Rita Coolidge (1977) US#20/Hall & Oates (1985) R&B#40 US#20 UK#58/UB40 (1991) US#6 UK#49; *What's Easy for Two Is Hard for One* Mary Wells (1962) R&B#8 US#29/Marvelettes (1968) US#114, also on B-side of *Destination: Anywhere* (1968) R&B#28 US#63; *What's So Good About Goodbye* Giant Sunflower (1967) US#116, *When I'm Gone* Brenda Holloway (1965) R&B#12 US#25, *Who's Lovin' You* Brenda & the Tabulations (1967) R&B#19 US#66/Jackson 5 (1992) R&B#48, also on B-side of *I Want You Back* (1969) R&B#1 US#1 UK#2; *You Beat Me to the Punch* [xix] Mary Wells (1962) R&B#1 US#9, *(You Can't Let the Boy Overpower) The Man in You* Chuck Jackson (1968) US#94, *You're My Remedy* Marvelettes (1963) US#48, *You're the One for Me, Baby* Marvelettes (1966) R&B#20 US#48, *You've Got to Earn It* Temptations (1965) R&B#22 US#123, *You've Really Got a Hold on Me* Gayle McCormick (1972) US#98/Eddie Money (1978) US#72/Mickey Gilley (1984) C&W#2; *Your Old Stand-By* [i] Mary Wells (1962) R&B#8 US#40, *Your Wonderful, Sweet, Sweet Love* Supremes (1972) R&B#22 US#59. Co-writers: [i] Janie Bradford, [ii] Alfred Cleveland, [iii] Alfred Cleveland/Terry Johnson, [iv] Alfred Cleveland/Terry Johnson/Warren Moore, [v] Alfred Cleveland/Marvin Tarplin, [vi] Henry Cosby/Stevie Wonder, [vii] Berry Gordy, Jr., [viii] R.E. Jones, [ix] L. Kirtz/I. Stone/P. Talbert, [x] Pamela Moffett/Marvin Tarplin, [xi] Warren Moore [xii] Warren Moore/Robert Rogers (b. February 14, 1940, Detroit, MI), [xiii] Warren Moore/Robert Rogers/Marvin Tarplin, [xiv] Warren Moore/Robert Rogers/Marvin Tarplin/Ronald White (b. April 5, 1939, Detroit, MI), [xv] Warren Moore/Marvin Tarplin, [xvi] Warren Moore/Marvin Tarplin/Ronald White, [xvii] Robert Rogers, [xviii] Marvin Tarplin, [xix] Ronald White, [xx] Frank Wilson.

799. **ROBINSON, Tom** (b. July 1, 1950,

Cambridge, England) Pop guitarist and vocalist. One of the most political and outspoken songwriters of the punk era, who had studied various wind instruments at school before becoming a member of the group Café Society, which recorded the album **Café Society** (1975, Konk). In 1976, he formed the short-lived Tom Robinson Band, and from 1983 he has recorded as a solo artist. Robinson's finest compositions is the gay love song *Still Loving You*. CHART COMPOSITIONS: *2–4–6–8 Motorway* (1977) UK#5, *Don't Take No for an Answer* (1978) UK#18, *Up Against the Wall* (1978) UK#33, *Bully for You* [i] (1979) UK#68, *War Baby* (1983) UK#6, *Listen to the Radio: Atmospherics* [i] (1983) UK#39. ALBUMS: **Power in the Darkness** (1978) US#144 UK#4, **TRB2** (1979, both EMI) US#163 UK#18; **Sector 27** (1980, IRS); **North By Northwest** (1982, Panic); **Hope and Glory** (1984) UK#21, **Still Loving You** (1987, both Castaway); **Midnight at the Fringe** (1987, Dojo); **Love Over Rage** (1994), **Having It Both Ways** (1996), **Last Tango** (1977, all Cooking Vinyl). COMPILATION: **Rising Free — The Very Best of the Tom Robinson Band** (1997, EMI). Co-writer: [i] Peter Gabriel. (*See also under* Peter GABRIEL, Elton JOHN.)

800. **ROBISON, Carson J.** (b. August 4, 1890, Chetopa, KS; d. March 24, 1957, Poughkeepsie, NY) C&W guitarist, arranger and vocalist. The composer of a number of country standards, who was a teenage guitarist in various Kansas dance bands during the 1920s, before becoming a radio show host and recording for the Victor label in 1924. In 1932, Robison formed the group the Buckaroos, which became the Carson Robison Trio, and later the Pleasant Valley Boys. Robison was popular in Britain during the 1930s, with record sales comparable to those of Jimmie Rodgers. He dabbled in all manner of musical topics, from *Carry Me Back to the Lone Prairie* from the film "Stars Over Broadway" (1935), to the inanely patriotic and jingoistic *We're Gonna Have to Slap That Dirty Little Jap (And Uncle Sam's the Man That Can Do It)* (1942). CHART COMPOSITIONS: *Whistling the Blues Away**** (1924) US#10, *Way Down Home** (1925) US#9, *My Carolina Home*** (1927) US#7, *A Memory That Time Cannot Erase*** (1928) US#19, *The Utah Trail***** (1929) US#19, *Mussolini's Letter to Hitler* (1942) US#21, *1942 Turkey in the Straw* (1942) US#22, *That Old Grey Mare Is Back Where She Used to Be* (1943) US#21, *Life Gets Tee-Jus, Don't It?* (1948) US#14. HIT VERSIONS: *Barnacle Bill the Sailor* [i] Frank Luther (1929) US#13, *Death of Floyd Collins, The* Vernon Dalhart (1926) US#3, *My Blue Ridge Mountain Home* Vernon Dalhart (1928) US#7, *Life Gets Tee-Jus, Don't It?* Tex Williams (1948) US#27. With: * Gene Austin,

** Vernon Dalhart, *** Wendell Hall, **** Frank Luther. Co-writer: [i] Frank Luther.

801. RODGERS, Jimmie (b. James Charles Rodgers, September 8, 1897, Meridian, MS; d. May 26, 1933, New York, NY) C&W guitarist, banjo player and vocalist. The single most important influence in country music before Hank Williams, and a most exceptional balladeer and composer of railroad and hobo ballads. Rodgers merged hillbilly, southern American folk, and black blues and jazz, to create what became country music as it is known today, and he first popularized the "Blue Yodel" singing style that was to influence Gene Autry, Woody Guthrie and Merle Haggard. Rodgers learned the banjo and guitar as a child, and left school to work on the railroads, where he first heard hillbilly and black music. His first recordings were for the Victor label in 1927, his second session including the million seller *Blue Yodel*. Although only a light baritone with a vocal range of little more than an octave and a third, it was Rodgers' enunciation that made him such a formidable singer. He recorded over one hundred songs in styles that ran the entire breadth of American music at the time. In 1929, he was the subject of the film "The Singing Brakeman," and during the early 1930s he hosted his own radio show in Texas. Rodgers recorded his last sides in 1933, in considerable pain as he wasted away from tuberculosis, having sold some twelve million records during the Great Depression. Merle Haggard recorded a magnificent tribute album to Rodgers, **Same Train, Different Time** (1969, Capitol) US#67. CHART COMPOSITIONS: *The Soldier's Sweetheart* (1927) US#9, *Blue Yodel* (1928) g US#2, *In the Jail House Now* (1928) US#14, new version (1955) C&W#7; *The Brakeman's Blues* (1928) US#7, *Blue Yodel #3* (1928) US#10, *Waiting for a Train (All Around the Watertank)* (1929) US#14, *Anniversary Yodel (Blue Yodel #7)* (1930) US#19, *Roll Along, Kentucky Moon* (1932) US#18. ALBUMS: **Train Whistle Blues** (1959), **Never No Mo' Blues (The Jimmie Rodgers Memorial Album)** (1959), **My Rough and Rowdy Ways** (1961), **Jimmie the Kid** (1961), **Country Music Hall of Fame** (1962), **The Short But Brilliant Life of Jimmie Rodgers** (1963), **My Time Ain't Long** (1964), **Twenty of the Best** (1984, all RCA); **Train Whistle Blues** (1986), **My Old Pal** (1989, both Living Era); **The Singing Brakeman** (1992, Bear Family). HIT VERSIONS: *Blue Yodel #4* Grandpa Jones as *T for Texas* (1962) C&W#5/Redwing as *California Blues* (1971) US#108/Compton Brothers as *California Blues* (1973) C&W#65/Tompall & His Outlaw Band as *T for Texas* (1976) C&W#36; *In the Jailhouse Now* Webb Pierce (1955) C&W#1/Johnny Cash (1962) C&W#8/Sonny James

(1977) C&W#15/Willie Nelson & Webb Pierce (1982) C&W#72; *It's Over* Eddy Arnold (1968) C&W#4/Rex Allen, Jr. (1980) C&W#14; *Lovesick Blues* Red Kirk (1949) C&W#14/Hank Williams (1949) C&W#1 US#24/Sonny James (1957) C&W#15/ Sonny Curtis (1975) C&W#78/Drifting Cowboys (1978) US#97; *Mule Skinner Blues* [i] Fendermen (1960) C&W#16 US#5/Dolly Parton (1970) C&W#3; *Waitin' for a Train (All Around the Watertank)* Jerry Lee Lewis (1970) C&W#11. Co-writer: [i] George Vaughn.

802. RODGERS, Paul (b. December 12, 1949, Middlesbrough, England) Rock vocalist. A blues inspired singer who was a founder member of the notable British rock group Free. CHART COMPOSITIONS: *All Right Now* [iii] (1970) US#4 UK#2, re-issued (1973) UK#15, re-mixed (1991) UK#8; *The Stealer* [iii] (1971) US#49, *My Brother Jake* [iii] (1971) UK#4, *Little Bit of Love* (1972) US#119 UK#13, *Wishing Well* [i] (1973) US#112 UK#7, *The Free EP* [iii] (1978) UK#11, re-issued (1982) UK#57. ALBUMS: **Tons of Sobs** (1968) US#197, **Fire and Water** (1970) US#17 UK#2, **Highway** (1971) US#190 UK#41, **Live** (1971) US#89 UK#4, **Free at Last** (1972) US#69 UK#9, **Heartbreaker** (1973, all Island) US#47 UK#9. COMPILATIONS: **The Free Story** (1974, Island) UK#2; **Best of Free** (1975, A&M) US#120; **Best of Free — All Right Now** (1991, Island) UK#9; **Molten Gold: The Anthology** (1993, PolyGram). After Free broke up in the early 1970s, Rodgers formed the similar, but immeasurably more commercially successful, Bad Company, with guitarist Mick Ralphs, penning its hits *Feel Like Makin' Love* [iv] (1975) US#10 UK#20, *Honey Chile* [ii] (1976) US#59, *Burnin' Sky* (1977) US#78, *Rock 'n' Roll Fantasy* (1979) US#13, and *Electricland* (1982) US#74. After the album **Rough Diamonds** (1982), Rodgers quit to form the Firm, with Jimmy Page, composing the hits *Radioactive* (1985) US#28 and *All the King's Horses* (1986) US#61. He subsequently formed the Law, which released the album **The Law** (1991, Atlantic) US#126 UK#61. Rodgers has also recorded as a solo artist. CHART COMPOSITIONS: *Cut Loose* (1983) US#102, *Muddy Water Blues* (1994) UK#45. ALBUMS: **Cut Loose** (1983, Atlantic) US#135; **Muddy Waters Blues: A Tribute to Muddy Waters** (1993, London) US#91 UK#9; **Now/Live — The Loreley Tapes** (1997, SPV). HIT VERSIONS: *All Right Now* [iii] Lea Roberts (1975) R&B#54 US#92/Rod Stewart (1985) US#72/Pepsi & Shirlie (1988) R&B# US#66 UK#50; *Fire and Water* [iii] Wilson Pickett (1972) R&B#2 US#24. Co-writers: [i] John Bundrick/ Simon Kirke (b. July 28, 1949, Shrewsbury, England)/Paul Kossoff (b. September 14, 1950, London,

England)/Tetsu Yamauchi (b. October 21, 1947, Fukuoka, Japan), [ii] Boz Burrell/Simon Kirke/Mick Ralphs, [iii] Andy Fraser (b. August 7, 1952, London, England), [iv] Mick Ralphs. (*See also under* Jimmy PAGE, Mick RALPHS.)

803. RODGERS, Richard (b. June 28, 1902, Arverne, Long Island, NY; d. December 30, 1979, New York, NY) Film and stage composer, pianist, and **HART, Lorenz** Film and stage lyricist. The most succinct American songwriting partnership of the twentieth century, which composed such classics as *I Wish I Were in Love Again* (1937). Rodgers received music lessons from an early age, and wrote his first songs when he was eleven. During his teens, Rodgers became obsessed with musical theatre, and he was influenced by the pioneering work of the composer Jerome Kern. In 1918, he formed a lengthy partnership with the witty lyricist, Lorenz Hart. Rodgers' use of thirty-two-bar verses with sixteen-bar choruses were an inversion of the then current style of songwriting, and his augmented seventh chords meant his melodies appealed to jazz musicians. Their first published composition was *Any Old Place with You* from the show "A Lonely Romeo" (1919), but they were not successful until they composed for the revue "The Garrick Gaieties" (1925), which featured their first classic, *Manhattan*. They were also successful with the shows "Dearest Enemy," "The Girl Friend" (both 1926); "A Connecticut Yankee" (1927), "Present Arms" (1928), "Spring Is Here" (1929), "Simple Simon" and "Evergreen" (both 1930), "Jumbo" (1935), "On Your Toes" (1936), "Babes in Arms" (1937), "The Boys from Syracuse" (1938), "Too Many Girls" (1939), "Pal Joey" (1940), and "By Jupiter" (1942). During the early 1930s, Rodgers and Hart worked in Hollywood on the film musicals "Love Me Tonight" (1932), "Hallelujah I'm a Bum" (1933) and "Hollywood Party" (1934). Twelve of their Broadway shows were turned into films, and the only song that they ever wrote that was not for a film or musical, was the multi-million selling *Blue Moon* (1934). The most successful albums of their songs were **Ella Fitzgerald Sings the Rodgers and Hart Songbook** (1957, Verve) US#11; **The Supremes Sing Rodgers and Hart** (1967, Motown) US#20; and **Frank Sinatra Sings Rodgers and Hart** (1971, Starline) UK#35. Rodgers also composed the music for the NBC television series "Victory at Sea" (1958). ALBUMS: **Victory at Sea** tvst (1958) UK#12, **Victory at Sea, Volume 2** tvst (1958) US#2, **Victory at Sea, Volume 3** tvst (1961, all RCA) US#7; **No Strings** (1962, Capitol) US#5; **Billy Roses's Jumbo** ost (1963) US#33, **Do I Hear a Waltz?** (1965, both Columbia) US#81. HIT VERSIONS: *Bewitched* Leo Reisman (1941) US#25/Jan August (1950) US#8/

Doris Day (1950) US#9/Larry Green (1950) US#13/Harmonicats (1950) US#8/Gordon Jenkins (1950) US#4/Roy Ross (1950) US#28/Bill Snyder Orchestra (1950) US#3/Mel Torme (1950) US#8; *Blue Moon* Al Bowlly & Ray Noble (1935) US#5/Benny Goodman (1935) US#2/Glen Gray (1935) US#1/Billy Eckstine (1949) R&B#12 US#21/Mel Torme (1949) US#20/Elvis Presley (1956) US#55 UK#9/Herb Lance (1961) US#89/Marcels (1961) R&B#1 US#1 UK#1/Ventures (1961) US#54/Ray Conniff (1964) US#119/Showaddywaddy (1980) UK#32/Meco (1981) US#106/John Alford (1996) UK#9; *Blue Room, The* Sam Lanin (1926) US#9/Melody Sheiks (1926) US#9/Revelers (1926) US#3/Perry Como (1949) US#18; *Bombadier Song, The* Bing Crosby (1942) US#19, *Dancing on the Ceiling* Jack Hylton (1932) US#10, *Do I Hear You Saying "I Love You"?* Vaughn Deleath & Irving Kaufman (1928) US#16, *Down By the River* Bing Crosby (1935) US#17/Guy Lombardo (1935) US#14; *Falling in Love with Love* Frances Langford (1939) US#18, *From Another World* Charlie Barnet (1940) US#14, *Girl Friend, The* George Olsen (1926) US#3, *Glad to Be Unhappy* Mamas & Papas (1967) US#26, *Hallelujah, I'm a Bum* Vernon Dalhart (1928) US#6/Al Jolson (1933) US#19; *Here in My Arms* Jack Shilkret (1926) US#10/Leo Reisman (1926) US#7; *I Could Write a Book* Eddy Duchin (1941) US#26/Jerry Butler (1970) R&B#15 US#70; *I Didn't Know What Time It Was* Jimmy Dorsey (1939) US#13/Benny Goodman (1939) US#6/Ray Charles (1969) US#105; *I Married an Angel* Larry Clinton (1938) US#4/Sammy Kaye (1938) US#17; *I've Got Five Dollars* Emil Coleman (1931) US#14/Ben Pollack (1931) US#19; *In a Great Big Way* Annette Hanshaw (1929) US#19, *Isn't It Romantic?* Harold Stern (1932) US#13, *It's Easy to Remember* Bing Crosby (1935) US#1, *Johnny One-Note* Hal Kemp (1937) US#15/Victor Young (1937) US#17; *Lady Is a Tramp, The* Bernie Cummins (1937) US#16/Tommy Dorsey (1937) US#15/Joe Rines (1937) US#19/Sophie Tucker (1937) US#19/Buddy Greco (1962) UK#26; *Lady Luck* Ted Lewis (1929) US#3, *Little Girl Blue* Margaret Whiting (1947) US#25, *Love Me Tonight* Bing Crosby (1932) US#4/George Olsen (1932) US#14; *Lover* Greta Keller (1933) US#15/Guy Lombardo (1933) US#8/Paul Whiteman (1933) US#3/Les Paul (1948) US#21/Peggy Lee (1952) g US#3; *Manhattan* Ben Selvin (1925) US#1/Paul Whiteman (1925) US#3; *March of the Siamese Children, The** Kenny Ball & His Jazzmen (1962) US#88 UK#4, *Mimi* Paul Biese Trio & Frank Crumit (1921) US#10/Maurice Chevalier (1932) US#9; *Most Beautiful Girl in the World, The* Ted Straeter (1952) US#27/Tommy Dorsey (1953) US#21; *Mountain Greenery* Roger Wolfe Kahn (1926) US#4/Mel Torme (1956) UK#4; *My Funny Valentine*

Hal McIntyre (1945) US#16, *My Heart Stood Still* George Olsen (1928) US#5/Ben Selvin (1928) US#8/Paul Whiteman (1928) US#11; *My Lucky Star* Fred Waring's Pennsylvanians (1929) US#11/Paul Whiteman (1929) US#4; *My Romance* Paul Whiteman (1936) US#18, *On Your Toes* Ruby Newman (1936) US#18, *Sentimental Me* Ben Selvin (1925) US#2/Arden-Ohman Orchestra (1926) US#5; *Slaughter on 10th Avenue** Lennie Hayton (1949) US#19/Ray Anthony (1952) US#21/Ventures (1964) US#35; *Soon (There'll Just Be Two of Us)* Bing Crosby (1935) US#1/Will Osborne (1935) US#20; *Spring Is Here* Buddy Clark (1938) US#19/Leo Reisman (1938) US#14; *Ten Cents a Dance* Ruth Etting (1930) US#5, *There's a Small Hotel* Hal Kemp (1936) US#1/Paul Whiteman (1936) US#19; *This Can't Be Love* Hoarce Heidt (1938) US#6/Benny Goodman (1939) US#2; *Thou Swell* Ben Selvin (1928) US#10, *Tree in the Park, A* Frank Black (1927) US#15/Helen Morgan (1927) US#9; *Where or When?* Hal Kemp (1937) US#1/Guy Lombardo (1943) US#19/Dion & the Belmonts (1960) R&B#19 US#3/Lettermen (1963) US#98; *Where's That Rainbow?* George Olsen (1927) US#12, *With a Song in My Heart* James Melton (1929) US#18/Leo Reisman (1929) US#3; *You Are Too Beautiful* Bob Eberly (1953) US#30, *You Took Advantage of Me* Paul Whiteman (1928) US#9. * Richard Rodgers only. (*See also under* Lorenz HART.)

804. RODGERS, Richard, and HAMMERSTEIN, II, Oscar.

Richard Rodgers' second prolific songwriting partnership, which lasted eighteen years from 1943. Rodgers and Hammerstein's first work together was the deceptively simple, yet ground-breaking "Oklahoma!" (1943), the first show wherein the songs actually advanced the action, the original cast recording of which, became the first ever album to chart. After their masterpiece "South Pacific" (1949), they wrote "The King and I" (1951), "Me and Juliet" (1953), "Pipe Dream" (1955), "Flower Drum Song" (1958), and the mawkish "The Sound of Music" (1959). After Hammerstein's death, Rodgers wrote "No Strings" (1962) in its entirety, before collaborating with the lyricists Stephen Sondheim on "Do I Hear a Waltz" (1965), and Martin Charnin on "Two By Two" (1970). ALBUMS: **Oklahoma!** oc (1943, Decca) g US#9; **South Pacific** ost (1958, RCA) g US#1 UK#1; **The King and I** ost (1956) g US#1 UK#4, **Oklahoma!** ost (1955) p US#1 UK#4, **Carousel** ost (1956, all Capitol) p US#2 UK#8; **Cinderella** tvst (1957, Columbia) US#15; **Pal Joey** ost (1960, Capitol) UK#20; **Flower Drum Song** oc (1959, Columbia) g US#1 UK#2; **Flower Drum Song** oc (1960, HMV) UK#10; **Flower Drum Song** ost (1961, Decca) US#15; **The Sound of Music** oc (1959, Columbia) g US#1 UK#4; **The Sound of**

Music oc (1961, HMV) UK#4; **State Fair** ost (1962, Dot) US#12; **Carousel** oc (1962, Command) US#12; **The Sound of Music** ost (1965, RCA) g US#1 UK#1; **South Pacific** sc (1986, CBS) UK#5; **The King and I** sc (1992, Philips) US#135 UK#57. HIT VERSIONS: *All at Once You Love Her* Perry Como (1955) US#11, *Bali Ha'i* Perry Como (1949) US#5/Bing Crosby (1949) US#12/Peggy Lee (1949) US#13/Frank Sinatra (1949) US#18/Paul Weston (1949) US#10; *Carousel Waltz, The* Ray Martin (1956) UK#24/Dire Straits in *Tunnel of Love* (1981) UK#54; *Climb Ev'ry Mountain* Tony Bennett (1960) US#74/Shirley Bassey (1961) UK#1/Hesitations (1968) US#90; *Edelweiss* Vince Hill (1967) US#119 UK#2, *Everybody's Got a Home But Me* Eddie Fisher (1955) US#20, *Fellow Needs a Girl, A* Bing Crosby (1947) US#25/Frank Sinatra (1947) US#24; *Gentleman Is a Dope, The* Jo Stafford (1947) US#20, *Getting to Know You* Sajid Khan (1968) US#108, *Happy Christmas, Little Friend* Rosemary Clooney (1954) US#30, *Happy Talk* Captain Sensible (1982) UK#1, *Hello, Young Lovers* Perry Como (1951) US#27/Paul Anka (1960) US#23 UK#44; *I Have Dreamed* Chad & Jeremy (1965) US#91, *If I Loved You* Perry Como (1945) US#3/Bing Crosby (1945) US#8/Harry James (1945) US#8/Frank Sinatra (1945) US#7/Roy Hamilton (1954) R&B#4 US#26/Richard Anthony (1964) UK#18/Chad & Jeremy (1965) US#23/Lettermen (1969) US#129; *It Might as Well Be Spring* Dick Haymes (1945) US#5/Paul Weston (1945) US#6/Sammy Kaye (1946) US#4; *It's a Grand Night for Singing* Dick Haymes (1946) US#21, *June Is Bustin' Out All Over* Hildegarde & Guy Lombardo (1945) US#11 1945, *Keep It Gay* Perry Como (1953) US#30, *My Favorite Things* Herb Alpert (1968) US#45/Lorrie Morgan (1994) C&W#64; *No Other Love* Perry Como (1953) US#1/Ronnie Hilton (1956) UK#1/Edmund Hockridge (1956) UK#30/Johnston Brothers (1956) UK#22/Dave King on *All Star Hit Parade EP* (1956) UK#2/Jay & the Americans (1968) US#114; *Oh, What a Beautiful Mornin'* Frank Sinatra (1943) US#12/Bing Crosby (1944) US#4; *People Will Say We're in Love* Bing Crosby (1943) US#2/Hal Goodman (1943) US#11/Frank Sinatra (1943) US#3; *Shall We Dance?* Fred Astaire (1937) US#3, *So Far* Perry Como (1947) US#11/Frank Sinatra (1947) US#8; *Some Enchanted Evening* Perry Como (1949) g US#1/Bing Crosby (1949) US#3/John Laurenz (1949) US#28/Ezio Pinza (1949) g US#7/Frank Sinatra (1949) US#6/Jo Stafford (1949) US#4/Paul Weston (1949) US#9/Jay & the Americans (1965) US#13/Jane Olivor (1977) US#91/Temptations (1996) R&B#11+; *Sound of Music, The* Patti Page (1960) US#90, *Surrey with the Fringe on Top* Alfred Drake (1944) US#22, *That's for Me* Dick Haymes (1945) US#6/Kay Kyser (1945) US#12/Jo Stafford (1945)

US#4; *We Kiss in the Shadows* Frank Sinatra (1951) US#22, *You Are Beautiful* Johnny Mathis (1960) UK#38, *You Are Never Away* Buddy Clark (1948) US#26, *You'll Never Walk Alone* Frank Sinatra (1945) US#9/Judy Garland (1946) US#21/Roy Hamilton (1954) R&B#1 US#21/Gerry & the Pacemakers (1963) UK#1, re-issued (1965) US#48/Patti LaBelle & the Bluebells (1964) US#34/Elvis Presley (1968) US#90 UK#44, re-issued (1982) C&W#73/Brooklyn Bridge (1969) US#51/Liverpool Football Club in *We Can Do It EP* (1977) UK#15/Crowd (1985) UK#1/Robson & Jerome (1996) UK#1; *Younger Than Springtime* Gordon MacRae (1949) US#30. (*See also under* Oscar HAMMERSTEIN, II, Richard RODGERS and Lorenz HART.)

805. RODNEY, Winston (b. 1946, St. Anns, Jamaica) Reggae vocalist. One of reggae's most soulful singers and composers, who vocalizes as if he is ruminating aloud. A solo artist who records as Burning Spear, Rodney first issued sides in Jamaica during the 1960s for such producers as Coxsone Dodd. He achieved a wider audience in Britain when he issued albums on the Island label in the 1970s, many of which were exceptional examples of the genre, featuring elements of gospel, R&B, and unusual brass arrangements. ALBUMS: **Burning Spear** (1969), **Rocking Time** (1970, both Studio One); **Marcus Garvey** (1975), **Garvey's Ghost** (1976), **Man in the Hills** (1976), **Dry and Heavy** (1977), **Live** (1977), **Harder Than the Best** (1979, all Island); **Hail H.I.M.** (1980, Radic); **Social Living** (1980), **Living Dub** (1980, both Island); **Far Over** (1982), **Fittest of the Fittest** (1983, both Radic); **Resistance** (1985), **Revolution** (1985), **People of the World** (1986, all Greensleeves); **Rasta Business** (1996, Heartbeat); **An Appointment with His Majesty** (1997, Hannibal). COMPILATION: **Reggae Greats** (1985, Island).

806. ROE, Tommy (b. Thomas David Roe, May 9, 1942, Atlanta, GA) Pop guitarist, producer and vocalist. A Buddy Holly influenced pop performer whose simple, catchy compositions gave him a series of sizeable hits during the 1960s. Roe later sought refuge in country music, charting eight singles between 1973–1987. CHART COMPOSITIONS: *Sheila* (1962) g R&B#6 US#1 UK#2, *Everybody* (1963) US#3 UK#9, *Come On* (1964) US#36 UK#61, *Party Girl* (1964) US#61, *Sweet Pea* (1966) g US#8, *Hooray for Hazel* (1966) US#6, *It's Now Winter's Day* (1967) US#23, *Sing Along with Me* (1967) US#91, *Little Miss Sunshine* (1967) US#99, *Dizzy* [i] (1969) g US#1 UK#1, *Heather Honey* (1969) US#29 UK#24, *Jack and Jill* (1969) US#53, *Jam Up Jelly Tight* [i] (1969) g US#8, *Stir It Up and Serve* (1970)

US#50, *Pearl* (1970) US#50, *We Can Make Music* (1970) US#49, *Mean Little Woman, Rosalie* (1972) US#92. ALBUMS: **Sheila** (1962) US#110, **Everybody Likes Tommy Roe** (1964), **Ballads and Beat** (1965), **Sweet Pea** (1966, all ABC/Paramount) US#94; **It's Now Winter's Day** (1967) US#159, **Dizzy** (1969) US#25, **We Can Make Music** (1970) US#134, **Beginnings** (1971, all ABC); **Energy** (1976), **Full Bloom** (1976, both Monument), COMPILATIONS: **12 in a Roe: A Collection of Greatest Hits** (1970, ABC) US#21; **Greatest Hits** (1970, Stateside); **Best of Tommy Roe: Yesterday, Today and Tomorrow** (1991, Curb). HIT VERSIONS: *Birmingham* Movers (1968) US#116, *Dizzy* [i] Vic Reeves & the Wonder Stuff (1991) UK#1, *Sheila* Greg Kihn (1981) US#102. Co-writer: [i] Freddy Weller.

807. ROMBERG, Sigmund (b. July 29, 1887, Nagy Kaniza, Hungary; d. November 9, 1951, New York, NY) Film and stage composer, pianist and conductor. The composer of approximately fifty Broadway shows, nearly all of which were hits, and some of which were later filmed. Romberg was the first composer to merge European operetta with the American popular song. After performing in European cafés as a pianist, Romberg emigrated to America in 1909, where he became a staff composer and small orchestral conductor. His first published compositions were *Some Smoke* and *Leg of Mutton* (both 1913), after which, he contributed to the Broadway shows "The Whirl of the World" (1914), "Maytime" (1917), "Sinbad" (1918), and "The New Moon" (1928). His show "Blossom Time" (1921), was based on the life of the composer Franz Schubert, and was one of the most popular ever performed, remaining a favorite among touring companies for over thirty years. Romberg's finest score was "The Student Prince" (1924), which ran for over six hundred performances. He collaborated with a variety of lyricists, and worked in Hollywood on the films "Viennese Nights" (1930), "The Girl of the Golden West," "Broadway Serenade" (both 1938); and "The Night Is Young" (1953). During the 1940s, Romberg performed across America with his own orchestra, and in 1945, he worked with the lyricist Dorothy Fields on the show "Up in Central Park." Romberg was also a founder member of ASCAP. ALBUMS: **New Moon** oc (1928, Monmouth Evergreen); **Maytime** oc (1944, Pelican); **Desert Song** sc (1950), **Student Prince** oc (1950, both Decca); **Deep in My Heart** ost (1955, MGM) US#4; **Girl in Pink Tights** oc (1954, Columbia). HIT VERSIONS: *Auf Wiederseh'n* [vi] Harry MacDonough & Olive Kline (1915) US#2, *Close as Pages in a Book* [ii] Benny Goodman (1945) US#11, *Deep in My Heart* [i] Franklyn Baur (1924) US#5/Benny Krueger (1924) US#5/Victor

Light Opera Co. (1925) US#12; *Desert Song, The* [v] Nat Shilkret (1927) US#19, *Drinking Song, The* [i] Victor Light Opera Co. (1925) US#12, *I Built a Dream One Day* [iv] Ray Noble (1936) US#19, *Lost in Loveliness* [vii] Billy Eckstine (1954) US#24/Dolores Gray (1954) US#29; *Lover, Come Back to Me* [iv] Arden-Ohman Orchestra (1929) US#6/Rudy Vallee (1929) US#9/Paul Whiteman (1929) US#3/ Perry Askam (1930) US#20/Al Hibbler (1949) R&B#9/Nat "King" Cole (1953) US#16; *Marianne* [iv] Arden-Ohman Orchestra (1929) US#15, *One Alone* [v] Nat Shilkret (1927) US#4/Don Voorhees (1927) US#19; *One Kiss* [iv] Nat Shilkret (1929) US#6, *Riff Song, The* [v] Nat Shilkret (1927) US#9, *Serenade, The* [i] Efrem Zimbalist (1921) US#9, *Softly, as in a Morning Sunrise* [iv] Nat Shilkret (1929) US#5, *Song of Love* [i] Edwin Dale (1922) US#5/ Lucy Isabelle Marsh & Royal Dadmun (1922) US#2/ Prince's Orchestra (1922) US#8; *Stout-Hearted Men* [iv] Perry Askam (1930) US#20, *When Hearts Are Young* [iii] Paul Specht (1923) US#7/Paul Whiteman (1923) US#12; *When I Grow Too Old to Dream* [iv] Nelson Eddy (1935) US#8/Glen Gray (1935) US#1/ Rose Murphy (1948) R&B#10; *Will You Remember (Sweetheart)?* [vix] Olive Kline & Lambert Murphy (1918) US#3/Victor Young (1937) US#14, *You Will Remember Vienna, Your Land and My Land* [i] Paul Whiteman (1927) US#6, *Zing Zing-Zoom Zoom* [viii] Perry Como (1951) US#12. Co-writers: [i] Dorothy Donnelly (b. 1880; d. 1928), [ii] Dorothy Fields, [iii] Alfred Goodman/Cyrus Wood, [iv] Oscar Hammerstein, II, [v] Oscar Hammerstein, II/Otto Harbach, [vi] Herbert Reynolds, [vii] Leo Robin, [viii] Charles Tobias, [vix] Rida Johnson Young.

808. ROME, Harold (b. 1908, Hartford, CT; d. October 26, 1993, New York, NY) Film and stage composer, pianist. A Tin Pan Alley songwriter who abandoned a career as an architect to become a band pianist and composer. Rome wrote for the revues "Pins and Needles" (1937), "Sing Out the News" (1938), "Anchors Aweigh" (1945), "Call Me Mister" (1949), "Wish You Were Here" (1952), "Destry Rides Again" (1959), "I Can Get It for You Wholesale" (1962), and "Zulu and the Zayda" (1965). Many of his musicals were later successfully filmed. Rome died from a stroke in 1993. ALBUMS: **Call Me Mister** oc (1950, Decca); **Wish You Were Here** oc (1952), **Fanny** oc (1955, both RCA) US#7; **Destry Rides Again** oc (1959, Decca) US#44; **Fanny** ost (1961, Warner Brothers) US#88; **I Can Get It for You Wholesale** oc (1962) US#125, **Pins and Needles** sc (1962), **Zulu and the Zayda** oc (1965, all Columbia); **Gone with the Wind** ost (1967, MGM); **Gone with the Wind** sc (1973, Chappell); **A Touch of Rome** (1989, Silva Screen). HIT VERSIONS: *Along*

with Me Margaret Whiting (1946) US#13, *(All of a Sudden) My Heart Sings* [i] Johnnie Johnston (1945) US#7/Martha Stewart (1945) US#12/Paul Anka (1959) US#15 UK#10; *F.D.R. Jones* Cab Calloway (1938) US#14/Ella Fitzgerald & Chick Webb (1939) US#8; *Fanny* Eddie Fisher (1954) US#29/Fred Waring's Pennsylvanians (1954) US#29; *Meadowlands* [ii] Tex Beneke (1948) US#21, *South America, Take It Away* Bing Crosby & the Andrews Sisters (1946) US#2/Xavier Cugat (1946) US#6; *Sunday in the Park* Hudson-DeLange Orchestra (1938) US#11, *Wish You Were Here* Eddie Fisher (1952) (1952) US#1/Jane Froman (1952) US#25/Guy Lombardo (1952) US#26. Co-writers: [i] Herpin, [ii] Lev Knipper.

809. ROMEO, Tony (b. America) Pop composer. HIT VERSIONS: *I Am a Clown* David Cassidy (1973) UK#3, *I Think I Love You* Partridge Family (1970) p US#1 UK#18/Voice of the Beehive (1991) UK#25; *I'm Gonna Make You Mine* Lou Christie (1969) US#10 UK#2, *Indian Lake* Cowsills (1968) US#10/Freddy Weller (1971) C&W#3 US#108; *It's One of Those Nights* Partridge Family (1972) US#20 UK#11, *Oh Boy (The Mood I'm In)* Brotherhood of Man (1977) UK#8.

810. RONELL, Ann (b. December 28, 1908, Omaha, NE) Film and stage composer, pianist. A former music teacher who became the first female to compose film music in Hollywood. Ronell was a rehearsal pianist on Broadway during the late 1920s, and worked on such theatrical projects as "The Magic Flute" (1937), "Martha" (1939) and "Oh Susanna" (1947). She also contributed to the films "Three Little Pigs" (1933), "The Story of G.I. Joe" (1945), "One Touch of Venus" (1948), "Love Happy" (1949), and "The Main Street to Broadway" (1953). HIT VERSION: *Willow Weep for Me* Ted Fiorito (1932) US#17/Paul Whiteman (1933) US#2. (*See also under* Frank CHURCHILL.)

811. ROSE, Billy (b. September 6, 1899, New York, NY; d. February 10, 1966, Jamaica) Film and stage lyricist, producer. A New York theatre owner of the 1930s, who wrote the lyrics to many memorable tunes of the era. His songs were featured in such shows as "Andre Charlot's Revue of 1926," "Great Day" (1930) and "Billy Rose's Crazy Quilt" (1931), alongside the films "The King of Jazz" (1930), "Encore" (1952) and "Hit the Deck" (1955). Rose retired from music in the early 1940s. HIT VERSIONS: *Back in Your Own Back Yard* [iv] Ruth Etting (1928) US#5/Patti Page (1950) US#23; *Barbara* Ted Weems (1927) US#11, *Clap Hands! Here Comes Charley* [vii] Johnny Marvin (1926) US#8, *Does the Spearmint Lose Its Flavor on the Bedpost Overnight* [ii]

Ernest Hare & Billy Jones (1924) US#9/Lonnie Donegan as *Does Your Chewing Gum Lose Its Flavor* (1959) UK#3; *Here Comes the Showboat* [viii] Vaughn Deleath (1928) US#20, *House Is Haunted, The* [i] Glen Gray (1934) US#13/Paul Whiteman (1934) US#15; *It Happened in Monterey* [x] Ruth Etting (1930) US#19/George Olsen (1930) US#10/Regent Club Orchestra (1930) US#5/Paul Whiteman (1930) US#2/Frank Sinatra on *Songs for Swinging Lovers* LP (1956) UK#12; *Me and My Shadow* [iv] Johnny Marvin (1927) US#15/Nat Shilkret (1927) US#5/"Whispering" Jack Smith (1927) US#1/Frank Sinatra & Sammy Davis, Jr. (1962) US#64 UK#20, re-entry (1963) UK#47; *Night Is Young and You're So Beautiful, The* [vi] Smith Ballew (1935) US#17/Glen Gray (1935) US#14/Jan Garber (1937) US#5/George Hall (1937) US#5/Wayne King (1937) US#15/Ray Anthony (1951) US#26; *There's a Rainbow 'Round My Shoulder* [iv] Al Jolson (1928) US#1, *Tonight You Belong to Me* [iii] Irving Kaufman (1926) US#11/Gene Austin (1927) US#1/Franklyn Baur (1927) US#5/Roger Wolfe Kahn (1927) US#11/Frankie Laine (1953) US#26/Patience & Prudence (1956) UK#28/Dottie West (1977) C&W#30; *Twelve O'Clock at Night* [v] Ted Lewis (1924) US#6. Co-writers: [i] Basil G. Adlam, [ii] Marty Bloom/Ernest Breuer, [iii] Lee David, [iv] Dave Dreyer (b. 1894; d. 1967)/Al Jolson, [v] Lou Handman/Herman Ruby, [vi] Irving Kahal/Dana Suesse, [vii] Ballard MacDonald/Joseph Meyer, [viii] Maceo Pinkard, [ix] Abner Silver, [x] Mabel Wayne. (*See also under* Harold ARLEN, Con CONRAD, Al DUBIN, Fred FISHER, Ray HENDERSON, Edward HEYMAN, Harry WARREN, Harry WOODS, Vincent YOUMANS.)

812. ROSE, Fred (b. August 24, 1897, Evansville, IN; d. December 1, 1954, Nashville, TN) C&W pianist, arranger, producer and vocalist. The writer of a formidable catalogue of country songs, who also formed the publishing house Acuff-Rose, with Roy Acuff in 1942, and discovered Hank Williams. After performing as a pianist in Chicago honky-tonks, Rose composed a series of jazz tinged hits, including *Sweet Mama (Papa's Gettin' Mad)* (1921), before joining the Paul Whiteman Orchestra. In the 1930s, he moved to Nashville, where he became a hillbilly influenced songwriter and radio performer. Rose occasionally wrote under the pseudonyms Floyd Jenkins and Bart Dawson, and as Rambling Rogue he charted with *Tender-Hearted Sue* (1945) C&W#5. HIT VERSIONS: *Blue Eyes Crying in the Rain* Willie Nelson (1975) C&W#1 US#21/Pinkard & Bowden in *Adventures in Parodies* (1984) C&W#64; *Charleston* [vii] Arthur Gibbs (1924) US#1/Paul Whiteman (1925) US#5; *Crazy Heart* [v] Hank Williams (1951) C&W#4/Guy Lombardo

(1952) US#20; *Deed I Do* [iii] Ruth Etting (1927) US#2/Johnny Marvin (1927) US#4/Lena Horne (1948) US#26; *Flamin' Mamie* [viii] Coon-Sanders Orchestra (1926) US#15, *Home in San Antone* Bob Wills (1943) US#21, *Honest and Truly* [vii] Henry Burr (1925) US#14/Ben Selvin (1928) US#9; *It's a Sin* [vi] Marty Robbins (1969) C&W#5, *No One Will Ever Know* Frank Ifield (1966) C&W#42 UK#25/Gene Watson (1967) US#13; *Red Hot Mama* [i] Sophie Tucker (1924) US#7, *Roly-Poly* Bob Wills (1946) C&W#3/Carl Smith (1975) C&W#97; *Settin' the Woods on Fire* Frankie Laine (1952) US#21/Jo Stafford (1952) US#21/Hank Williams (1952) C&W#2; *Sweet Mama (Papa's Gettin' Mad)* Marion Harris (1921) US#4/Original Dixieland Jazz Band (1921) US#12; *Take These Chains from My Heart* [ii] Hank Williams (1953) C&W#1/Ray Charles (1963) R&B#7 US#8 UK#5/Lee Roy Parnell (1994) C&W#17+; *Texarkana Baby* Eddy Arnold (1948) C&W#1/Bob Wills (1948) C&W#15; *We Live in Two Different Worlds* Rachael Sweet (1976) C&W#96. Co-writers: [i] Bud Cooper/Gilbert Wells, [ii] Hy Heath, [iii] Walter Hirsch, [iv] Clarence Jennings/Billy McCabe, [v] Maurice Murray, [vi] B. Tubert, [vii] Paul Whiteman, [viii] Leo Wood. (*See also under* Gene AUTRY, Hank WILLIAMS.)

813. ROSE, Tim (b. September, 1940, WA) Rock guitarist and vocalist. A former member of the group the Big Three, with Cass Elliott and Denny Doherty, who recorded folk and R&B influenced singer-songwriter material with little success during the 1970s. Rose's best known song is the apocalyptic *Morning Dew*, which became a Grateful Dead stage favorite for many years. ALBUMS: **Tim Rose** (1967), **Through Rose Colored Glasses** (1969, both Columbia); **Love — A Kind of Hate Story** (1970, Capitol); **Tim Rose** (1971, Playboy); **The Musician** (1975, Atlantic). COMPILATION: **Retrospective** (1977, Capitol). HIT VERSION: *Morning Dew* Lulu (1968) US#52/Sound Foundation (1969) US#118.

814. ROSENFELD, Monroe H. (b. April 22, 1862, Richmond, VA; d. December 12, 1918, New York, NY) Vaudeville pianist and arranger. The music industry's first huckster. The man who named Tin Pan Alley was a former journalist, pianist and press agent, before he became a composer and arranger. Rosenfeld's first published song was *She's Sweet as She Can Be* (1882), which he followed with such ballads as *Take Back Your Gold* (1897). He sold song ideas to other composers, and wrote so many himself that he published them under a variety of pseudonyms. A true maverick of his time, Rosenfeld squandered much of his money at the race track

track, and sold many of his copyrights for mere dollars, sometimes to multiple publishers. HIT VERSION: *With All Her Faults, I Love Her Still* Will Oakland (1913) US#6.

815. ROSS, Ricky (b. December 22, 1957, Dundee, Scotland) Pop vocalist. The lead singer and songwriter in the Scottish group Deacon Blue, which, after a formidable debut album, wandered increasingly into the bland, pop mainstream. CHART COMPOSITIONS: *Dignity* (1987) UK#31, re-issued (1994) UK#20; *When Will You Make My Telephone Ring* (1988) UK#34, *Real Gone Kid* (1988) UK#8, *Wages Day* (1989) UK#18, *Fergus Sings the Blues* (1989) UK#14, *Love and Regret* (1989) UK#28, *Queen of the New Year* (1990) UK#21, *Your Swaying Arms* (1991) UK#23, *Twist and Shout* (1991) UK#10, *Closing Time* (1991) UK#42, *Cover from the Sky* (1991) UK#31, *Your Town* (1992) UK#14, *Will We Be Lovers* (1993) UK#31, *Only Tender Love* (1993) UK#22, *Hang Your Head EP* (1993) UK#21, *I Was Right and You Were Wrong* (1994) UK#32. ALBUMS: **Raintown** (1986) UK#14, **When the World Knows Your Name** (1989) UK#1, **Ooh Las Vegas** (1990, all CBS) UK#3; **Fellow Hoodlums** (1991) UK#2, **Whatever You Say, Say Nothing** (1993, both Columbia) UK#4. COMPILATION: **Our Town — Greatest Hits** (1994, Columbia) UK#1. In 1996, Ross quit the group for a solo career, charting with the singles *Radio On* (1996) UK#35 and *Good Evening Philadelphia* (1996) UK#58. ALBUM: **What You Are** (1996, Epic).

816. ROSSELSON, Leon (b. June 22, 1934, London, England) Folk vocalist. An often political songwriter in the folk tradition, who first wrote for the television series "That Was the Week That Was" during the 1960s. Rosselson released the EP *Songs for City Squares* (1962, Topic), before joining the group the Galliards, which recorded the albums **Scottish Choice** (1962), **A-Roving** (1962, both Decca); and **The Galliards** (1963, EMI). In partnership with the guitarist Martin Carthy, Rosselson recorded two albums as 3 City 4, **The Three City Four** (1964) and **Smoke and Dust** (1965, both Decca), and after 1967, he recorded as a solo artist. ALBUMS: **Songs for Sceptical Circles** (1967, Bounty); **A Laugh, a Song and a Hand-Grenade** (1968, Transatlantic); **The Word Is-Hugga Mugga Chugga Lugga Humbugga Boom Chit** (1971, Trailor); **That's Not the Way It's Got to Be** (1975), **Palaces of Gold** (1975), **Love, Loneliness, Laundry** (1977), **If I Knew Who the Enemy Was** (1979, all Acorn); **For the Good of the Nation** (1981), **Temporary Loss of Vision** (1986), **Bringing the News from Nowhere** (1986, all Fuse).

817. ROSSI, Francis (b. Francis Michael Rossi, April 29, 1949, London, England) Pop guitarist and vocalist. The principal songwriter and lead singer in the group Status Quo, which has sold over one hundred million records worldwide, and charted over fifty British hit singles since 1968. CHART COMPOSITIONS: *Pictures of Matchstick Men* (1968) US#12 UK#7, *Are You Growing Tired of My Love* (1969) UK#46, *In My Chair* (1970) UK#21, *Paper Plane* [v] (1973) UK#8, *Mean Girl* [v] (1973) UK#20, *Caroline* [v] (1973) UK#5, live version (1982) UK#13; *Break the Rules* [iii] (1974) UK#8, *Down Down* [v] (1975) UK#1, *Roll Over Lay Down* [iii] (1975) UK#9, *Accident Prone* (1978) UK#36, *What You're Proposing* [iv] (1980) UK#2, *Lies* [iv] (1981) UK#11, *Rock 'n' Roll* [iv] (1981) UK#8, *She Don't Fool Me* [iv] (1982) UK#36, *A Mess of the Blues* [iv] (1983) UK#15, *Marguerita Time* [iv] (1984) UK#3, *Going Down Town Tonight* (1984) UK#20, *Red Sky* (1986) UK#19, *Dreamin'* (1987) UK#15, *Ain't Complaining* (1988) UK#19, *Who Gets the Love* (1988) UK#34, *Burning Bridges (On and Off and on Again)* [i] (1989) UK#5, *Not at All* (1989) UK#50, *Can't Give You More* [v] (1991) UK#37, *Rock 'Til You Drop* (1992) UK#38, *Roadhouse Medley (Anniversary Waltz Part 25)* [ii] (1992) UK#21, *I Didn't Mean It* (1994) UK#21, *Sherri Don't Fail Me Now* (1994) UK#38. ALBUMS: **Picturesque Matchsickable** (1968), **Spare Parts** (1969), **Ma Kelly's Greasy Spoon** (1970), **Dog of Two Head** (1971, all Pye); **Piledriver** (1973) UK#5, **Hello** (1973) UK#1, **Quo** (1974) UK#2, **On the Level** (1975) UK#1, **Blue for You** (1976) UK#1, **Live** (1977) UK#3, **Rockin' All Over the World** (1977) UK#5, **If You Can't Stand the Heat** (1978) UK#3, **Whatever You Want** (1979) UK#3, **Just Supposin'** (1980) UK#4, **Never Too Late** (1981) UK#2, **1982** (1982) UK#1, **From the Makers of...** (1982) UK#4, **Back to Back** (1983) UK#9, **Live at the NEC** (1984) UK#83, **In the Army Now** (1986) UK#7, **Ain't Complaining** (1988) UK#12, **Perfect Remedy** (1989) UK#49, **Rock 'Til You Drop** (1991, all Vertigo) UK#10; **Live Alive Quo** (1992) UK#37, **Thirsty Work** (1994, Polydor) UK#13; **Don't Stop** (1996, all PolyGram) UK#2. COMPILATIONS: **Best of Status Quo** (1973, Pye) UK#32; **Down the Dustpipe** (1975, Golden Hour) UK#20; **Status Quo** (1975, Capitol) US#148; **12 Gold Bars** (1980, Vertigo) UK#3; **Fresh Quota** (1981, PRT) UK#74; **12 Gold Bars, Volume 2** (1984) UK#12, **Rockin' All Over the Years** (1990, both Vertigo) UK#2. Rossi has also recorded as a solo artist. CHART COMPOSITIONS: *Modern Romance (I Want to Fall in Love Again)* (1985) UK#54, *Give Myself to Love* (1996) UK#42. ALBUM: **King of the Doghouse** (1996, Virgin). HIT VERSION: *Burning Bridges (On and Off and on Again)* [i] Manchester

United Football Club as *Come on You Reds* (1994) UK#1. Co-writers: [i] Andy Bown, [ii] Andy Bown/ Bernard Frost/Rick Parfitt (b. Richard Harrison, October 12, 1948, Woking, England)/Supa/Robert Young, [iii] John Coghlan (b. September 19, 1946, Dulwich, England)/Alan Lancaster (b. February 7, 1949, London, England)/Rick Parfitt/Robert Young, [iv] Bernard Frost, [v] Robert Young.

818. ROWLAND, Kevin

(b. August 17, 1953, Wolverhampton, England) Pop vocalist. The lead singer in the R&B influenced group Dexy's Midnight Runners. CHART COMPOSITIONS: *Dance Stance* (1980) UK#40, *Geno* [ii] (1980) UK#1, *There There My Dear* [ii] (1980) UK#7, *Plan B* (1981) UK#58, *Show Me* (1981) UK#16, *The Celtic Soul Brothers* [iii] (1982) UK#45, new version (1983) US#86 UK#20; *Come on Eileen* [i] (1982) US#1 UK#1, *Let's Get This Straight (From the Start)/Old* (1982) UK#17, *Because of You* (1986) UK#13. ALBUMS: **Searching for the Young Soul Rebels** (1980, Parlophone) UK#6; **Too-Rye-Ay** (1982) US#14 UK#2, **Don't Stand Me Down** (1985, both Mercury) UK#22. COMPILATIONS: **Geno** (1983, EMI) UK#79; **Very Best of Dexy's Midnight Runners** (1991, Mercury) UK#12; **It Was Like This** (1996, EMI). In 1987, Rowland attempted a solo career with the albums **The Wanderer** (1988) and **Manhood** (1991), before declaring bankruptcy in 1991. Co-writers: [i] Kevin Adams/James Patterson, [ii] Kevin Archer, [iii] N. Billmingham/James Patterson.

819. RUNDGREN, Todd

(b. June 22, 1948, Upper Darby, PA) Rock multi-instrumentalist, producer and vocalist. A musical maverick whose lucrative production work for such mainstream artists as Meat Loaf, has financed his own increasingly individualistic albums, many of which have explored musical territories that have paid scant regard for commercial considerations. At the age of ten Rundgren attempted to learn the flute, but turned instead to the guitar and joined the high school R&B group Money. He subsequently mastered as many instruments as he could, and learned studio production techniques while playing in the 1960s blues group Woody's Truck Stop. In 1967, he formed the Nazz, which charted with *Hello, It's Me* (1969) US#66 and *Open My Eyes* (1968) US#112, and released the albums **Nazz** (1968) US#118, **Nazz Nazz** (1969) US#80, and **Nazz 3** (1971, all Screen Gems). In 1969, Rundgren joined the Bearsville label as an in-house producer, where he traded studio time in lieu of wages, in order to record his debut solo set **Runt** (1970), which, like all his albums, displayed flashes of true brilliance alongside pure self-indul-

gence. In 1974, he formed Utopia, which became more of a lifestyle than a simple rock band, and toured the world almost continually for ten years, playing a brand of harder, guitar oriented rock. CHART COMPOSITIONS: *Set Me Free* [ii] (1980) US#27, *The Very Last Time* [ii] (1980) US#76, *Feet Don't Fail Me Now* [i] (1982) US#82. ALBUMS: **Todd Rundgren's Utopia** (1974) US#34, **Another Live** (1975) US#66, **Ra** (1977) US#79 UK#27, **Oops! Wrong Planet** (1976) US#73 UK#59, **Adventures in Utopia** (1980) US#32 UK#57, **Deface the Music** (1980) US#65, **Swing to the Right** (1982, all Bearsville) US#102; **Utopia** (1982, Network) US#84; **Oblivion** (1984) US#74, **Pov** (1985) US#161, **Trivia** (1986, all Passport); **Redux '92 — Live in Japan** (1993), **The Individualist** (1995, both Rhino). COMPILATION: **Anthology, 1974–1985** (1985, Rhino). Rundgren's restless solo career has included such esoteric albums as **A Capella** (1985), an electronic, doo-wop experiment that included the beautiful *Pretending to Care*. His **No World Order** (1993), was one of the first inter-active media creations ever released. CHART COMPOSITIONS: *We Gotta Get You a Woman* (1970) US#20, *Be Nice to Me* (1971) US#71, *A Long Time a Long Way to Go* (1971) US#92, *I Saw the Light* (1972) US#16 UK#36, *Hello, It's Me* (1972) US#5, *Couldn't I Just Tell You* (1972) US#92, *A Dream Goes on Forever* (1974) US#69, *Wolfman Jack* with Wolfman Jack (1975) US#105, *Real Man* (1975) US#83, *Good Vibrations* (1976) US#34, *Can We Still Be Friends?* (1978) US#29, *Time Heals* (1981) US#107, *Bang the Drum All Day* (1983) US#63. ALBUMS: **Runt** (1970) US#185, **The Ballad of Todd Rundgren** (1971, Ampex); **Something/Anything** (1972) g US#29, **A Wizard/A True Star** (1973) US#86, **Todd** (1974) US#54, **Initiation** (1975) US#86, **Faithful** (1976) US#54, **Hermit of Mink Hollow** (1978) US#36 UK#42, **Back to the Bars** (1978) US#75, **Healing** (1981) US#48, **The Ever Popular Tortured Artist Effect** (1983, all Bearsville) US#66; **A Capella** (1985) US#128, **Nearly Human** (1989) US#102, **2nd Wind** (1991, Warner Brothers) US#118; **No World Order** (1993, Forward). COMPILATIONS: **Anthology** (1987, Raw Power); **An Elpee's Worth of Productions** (1992, Rhino); **Singles** (1995, Bearsville). HIT VERSIONS: *Can We Still Be Friends* Robert Palmer (1979) US#52, *Love Is the Answer* England Dan & John Ford Coley (1979) US#10, *Mated* Jaki Graham & David Grant (1985) UK#20, *Piece By Piece* [iii] Tubes (1985) US#87. Co-writers: [i] D. Howard/ Roger Powell/Kasim Sulton/John Wilcox, [ii] Roger Powell/Kasim Sulton/John Wilcox, [iii] Rick Anderson/Michael Cotten/Mingo Lewis/Prairie Prince (b. May 7, 1950, Charlotte, NC)/Snow/Re Styles/Bill Spooner/Roger Steen/Fee Waybill/Vince Welnick.

820. RUSHEN, Patrice (b. Patrice Louise Rushen, September 30, 1954, Los Angeles, CA) R&B pianist and vocalist. A classically trained pianist who had studied the instrument from the age of three, becoming a jazz session player for such musicians as Donald Byrd and Stanley Turrentine in the mid–1970s. During the late 1970s, Rushen began recording as a solo artist in a commercial jazz-funk and disco style. CHART COMPOSITIONS: *Hang It Up* (1978) R&B#16, *When I Found You* (1979) R&B#87, *Haven't You Heard* (1979) R&B#7 US#42 UK#62, *Let the Music Take Me* (1980) R&B#50, *Givin' It Up Is Givin' In* with D.J. Rogers (1980) R&B#47, *Look Up* (1980) R&B#13 US#102, *Never Gonna Give You Up (Won't Let You Be)* (1981) R&B#30 UK#66, *Forget Me Nots* [i] (1982) R&B#4 US#23 UK#8, *Breakout!* (1982) R&B#46, *I Was Tired of Being Alone* [i] (1982) R&B#79 UK#39, *Feels So Real (Won't Let Go)* (1984) R&B#3 US#78 UK#51, *Get Off (You Fascinate Me)* (1984) R&B#26, *Watch Out* (1987) R&B#9, *Anything Can Happen* (1987) R&B#51, *Come Back to Me* (1987) R&B#65. ALBUMS: **Traverse** (1974), **Prelusion** (1974), **Before the Dawn** (1975), **Shout It Out** (1977, all Prestige) US#164; **Patrice** (1979) US#98, **Pizzazz** (1979) US#39, **Posh** (1981) US#71, **Straight from the Heart** (1982) US#14, **Now** (1984, all Elektra) US#40; **Watch Out** (1987, Arista) US#77. HIT VERSION: *Forget Me Nots* [i] Tongue 'N' Cheek (1995) UK#26. Co-writer: [i] Freddie Washington. (*See also under* George MICHAEL.)

821. RUSSELL, Bobby (b. 1914; d. 1970, both America) Film lyricist. A lyricist whose songs featured in such films as "Two Girls and a Sailor" (1944) and "The Girl He Left Behind" (1956). Russell also translated European hits into English language versions. HIT VERSIONS: *At the Crossroads* [vi] Jimmy Dorsey (1942) US#21, *Babalu* [vii] Xavier Cugat (1944) US#27, *Brazil* [ii] Xavier Cugat (1943) US#2/Jimmy Dorsey (1943) US#14/Les Paul (1948) US#22; *Circus* [i] Bill Farrell (1949) US#26/Tony Martin (1949) US#24; *Frenesi* [iv] Artie Shaw (1940) g US#1/Woody Herman (1941) US#16/Glenn Miller (1941) US#16; *Full Moon* [viii] Jimmy Dorsey (1942) US#19/Benny Goodman (1942) US#22; *Half a Photograph* [x] Kay Starr (1953) US#7, *No Other Love* [v] Jo Stafford (1950) US#8, *Would I Love You (Love You, Love You)* [ix] Patti Page (1951) g US#4, *You Came a Long Way (From St. Louis)* [iii] Ray McKinley (1948) US#13. Co-writers: [i] Louis Alter, [ii] Ary Barroso, [iii] John Benson Brooks, [iv] Ray Charles/Alberto Dominiguez, [v] Frederic Chopin/Paul Weston, [vi] Ernesto Leucona, [vii] Marguerita Leucona, [viii] Marcelene Odette, [ix] Harold Spina, [x] Hal Stanley. (*See also under* Duke ELLINGTON, Carl SIGMAN.)

822. RUSSELL, Bobby (b. April 19, 1940, Nashville, TN; d. November 19, 1992, Nicholasville, KY) C&W vocalist. A Nashville tunesmith with a whispery baritone, who died of a heart attack in 1992. CHART COMPOSITIONS: *1432 Franklin Pike Circle Hero* (1968) C&W#64 US#36, *Carlie* (1969) C&W#66 US#115, *Better Homes and Gardens* (1969) C&W#34, *Saturday Morning Confusion* (1971) C&W#24 US#28, *Mid-American Manufacturing Tycoon* (1973) C&W#93. ALBUMS: **Words, Music, Laughter and Tears** (1968, Elf); **Saturday Morning Confusion** (1971, United Artists) US#183. HIT VERSIONS: *He Ain't Heavy, He's My Brother* [ii] Hollies (1969) US#7 UK#3, re-issued (1988) UK#1/Olivia Newton-John (1975) US#30/June Neyman (1978) C&W#93; *Honey* Compton Brothers (1968) C&W#64/Bobby Goldsboro (1968) g C&W#1 US#1 UK#2, re-issued (1975) UK#2/Bob Shane (1968) US#104/Orion (1979) C&W#89; *Joker Went Wild, The* Brian Hyland (1966) US#20, *Little Green Apples* O.C. Smith (1968) g R&B#2 US#2/Ben Colder (1969) C&W#65/Roger Miller (1969) UK#39; *Night the Lights Went Out in Georgia, The* Vicki Lawrence (1973) g C&W#36 US#1/Reba McEntire (1992) C&W#12; *Popsicle* [i] Jan & Dean (1966) US#21, *South* Roger Miller (1970) C&W#15, *Sure Gonna Miss Her* Gary Lewis & the Playboys (1966) US#9. Co-writers: [i] Buzz Cason, [ii] Bobby Scott. (*See also under* Carl SIGMAN.)

823. RUSSELL, Brenda (b. Brenda Gordon, Brooklyn, NY) R&B pianist and vocalist. A soul influenced singer-songwriter who was the daughter of two singers, and whose father was once a member of the Ink Spots. At the age of twelve, Russell performed in the Canadian band the Tiaras, and also featured in the Toronto cast of the rock musical "Hair," where she met her future husband Brian Russell. The Russell's hosted the Canadian television series "Music Machine," while also backing the singer Ray Stevens and a variety of other artists on "The Sonny and Cher Show" during the 1960s. A pair of unsuccessful duet albums was followed by a professional and personal separation in 1978, after which, Russell embarked on a solo career. CHART COMPOSITIONS: *That's All Right Too** (1978) R&B#67, *So Good, So Right* (1979) R&B#15 US#30, *In the Thick of It/So Good, So Right* (1980) UK#51, *Way Back When* (1980) R&B#42, *If You Love (The One You Lose)* (1981) R&B#50, *Piano in the Dark* [ii] (1988) R&B#8 US#6 UK#23. ALBUMS: **Word Called Love** * (1976), **Supersonic Lover** * (1977, both Rocket); **Brenda Russell** (1979, Horizon) US#65; **Love Life** (1981, A&M) US#107; **Two Eyes** (1983, Warner Brothers); **Get Here** (1988) US#49 UK#77, **Kiss Me with the Wind** (1990, both A&M); **Soul**

Talkin' (1993, EMI/ERG). COMPILATION: **Greatest Hits** (1992, A&M). HIT VERSIONS: *Dinner with Gershwin* Donna Summer (1987) US#48 UK#13, *Forever* Phil Perry (1991) R&B#35, *Get Here* Oleta Adams (1991) US#5 UK#4/Q featuring Tracy Ackerman (1993) UK#37; *If Only for One Night* Luther Vandross (1986) R&B#59, *Please Pardon Me (You Remind Me of a Friend)* [i] Rufus (1975) R&B#6 US#48, *Think It Over* Cheryl Ladd (1978) US#34. With: * Brian Russell. Co-writers: [i] G. Gordon, [ii] J. Hull/S. Cutler. (*See also under* Maurice WHITE.)

824. RUSSELL, Graham (b. June 1, 1950, Nottingham, England) Pop guitarist and vocalist. The principal songwriter in the Australian soft-rock group Air Supply. CHART COMPOSITIONS: *Lost in Love* (1980) p US#3, *All Out of Love* [i] (1980) p US#2 UK#11, *The One That You Love* (1981) p US#1, *Sweet Dreams* (1982) US#5, *Young Love* (1982) US#38, *The Power of Love (You Are My Lady)* (1985) US#68, *Goodbye* (1993) UK#66. ALBUMS: **Love and Other Bruises** (1980), **Lost in Love** (1980) p US#22, **The One That You Love** (1981) p US#10, **Now and Forever** (1982) p US#25, **Air Supply** (1985) p US#26, **Hearts in Motion** (1986) US#84; **Air Supply: The Christmas Album** (1986, all Arista); **The Earth Is…** (1990), **The Vanishing Race** (1993), **News from Nowhere** (1995), **Now and Forever — Greatest Hits Live** (1995, all Giant). COMPILATION: **Greatest Hits** (1983, Arista) p US#7. HIT VERSION: *Lost in Love* Dickey Lee & Kathy Burdick (1980) C&W#30. Co-writer: [i] Clive Davis.

825. RUSSELL, Leon (b. Hank Wilson, April 2, 1942, Lawton, OK) Rock multi-instrumentalist, producer and vocalist. The first superstar backing musician, who started in the days when supporting players failed to merit even a credit on record sleeves. Russell's own solo career has consisted of interesting and often amusing albums, that have blended most musical styles at one time or another, recordings that have a personality and authenticity that has all but disappeared from contemporary music. From the age of three Russell took classical piano lessons, learning the trumpet at thirteen and forming his first band a year later. He performed in Oklahoma clubs with a forged identity card and played with Ronnie Hawkins and the Hawks, while also sessioning for Jerry Lee Lewis. Russell became a backing musician on America's first pop music show "Shindig," before becoming a highly respected session player and member of Phil Spector's Wall of Sound productions. At Liberty Records, Russell wrote and arranged for Gary Lewis and the Playboys, and his talents became apparent on Joe Cocker's "Mad Dogs and Englishmen" 1970 tour and subsequent film. After building a home recording studio, Russell began recording his own albums, which often served as song demos for other, more commercial artists. By the mid–1980s, Russell had wandered into semi-retirement, returning in 1992 with the Bruce Hornsby produced **Anything Can Happen**, as eclectic an album as anything he had recorded to date. CHART COMPOSITIONS: *Roll Away the Stone* (1970) US#109, *Tryin' to Stay Alive* (1972) US#115, *Tightrope* (1972) US#11, *Queen of the Roller Derby* (1972) US#89, *Lady Blue* (1975) US#14, *Back to the Island* (1975) US#53, *Rainbow in Your Eyes* (1976) US#52. ALBUMS: **Looking Inside — Asylum Choir*** (1968, Smash); **Leon Russell** (1970) US#60, **Leon Russell and the Shelter People** (1971) g US#17 UK#29, **Asylum Choir 2*** (1972) US#70, **Carney** (1972) g US#2, **Leon Live** (1972) g US#9, **Hank Wilson's Back, Volume 1** (1973) US#28, **Stop All That Jazz** (1974) US#34, **Will O' the Wisp** (1975) g US#30, **Live in Japan** (1975, all Shelter); **The Wedding Album**** (1976) US#34, **Make Love to the Music**** (1977) US#142, **Americana** (1978, all Paradise) US#115; **One for the Road** with Willie Nelson (1979, Columbia) g US#25; **Life and Love** (1979), **The Live Album** with the New Grass Revival (1981) US#187, **Solid State** (1984), **Hank Wilson's Back, Volume 2** (1984, all Paradise); **Anything Can Happen** (1992, Virgin). COMPILATIONS: **Looking Back** (1974, Olympic); **Best of Leon** (1976) g US#40, **Gimme Shelter** (1996, both Shelter). HIT VERSIONS: *Bluebird* Helen Reddy (1975) US#35, *Delta Lady* Joe Cocker (1969) US#69 UK#10, *Everybody Loves a Clown* [iv] Gary Lewis & the Playboys (1965) US#4, *Hummingbird* B.B. King (1970) R&B#25 US#48, *Lady Blue* George Benson (1978) R&B#39, *Rainbow in Your Eyes* Al Jarreau (1976) R&B#92/Jan & Malcom (1977) C&W#99; *She's Just My Style* [ii] Gary Lewis & the Playboys (1966) US#3, *Song for You, A* Jaye P. Morgan (1971) US#105/Andy Williams (1971) US#82/Donny Hathaway on B-side of *Love, Love, Love* (1973) R&B#16 US#44/Ray Charles (1993) R&B#57 US#104; *Superstar* [i] Delaney & Bonnie on B-side of *Comin' Home* (1970) US#84 UK#16/ Carpenters (1972) g US#2 UK#18/Luther Vandross (1984) R&B#5 US#87/Sonic Youth (1994) UK#45; *Tennessee* Jan & Dean (1962) US#69, *This Masquerade* George Benson (1976) g R&B#3 US#10, *(You Don't Have to) Paint Me a Picture* [iii] Gary Lewis & the Playboys (1966) US#15. With: * Marc Benno, ** Mary Russell. Co-writers: [i] Bonnie Bramlett (b. Bonnie Lynn O'Farrell, November 8, 1944, Acton, IL), [ii] Al Capps/Gary Lewis (b. Gary Levitch, July 31, 1946, New York, NY)/Thomas Leslie, [iii] Thomas Garrett/Roger Carroll Tillison, [iv] Gary Lewis/ Thomas Leslie. (*See also under* Eric CLAPTON.)

826. RUTHERFORD, Mike (b. October 2, 1950, Guildford, England) Rock guitarist and vocalist. A co-founder of the group Genesis, who has also pursued a concurrent solo career with his band Mike and the Mechanics. CHART COMPOSITIONS: *Silent Running* [ii] (1984) US#6 UK#21, re-issued (1996) UK#61; *All I Need Is a Miracle* [i] (1986) US#5 UK#53, re-mixed (1996) UK#27; *Taken In* [i] (1986) US#32, *Nobody's Perfect* [ii] (1988) US#63, *The Living Years* [ii] (1988) US#1 UK#2, *Seeing Is Believing* [ii] (1989) US#62, *Word of Mouth* (1991) US#78 UK#13, *A Time and a Place* (1991) UK#58, *Everybody Gets a Second Chance* [ii] (1992) UK#56, *Over My Shoulder* (1995) UK#12, *A Beggar on a Beach of Gold* (1995) UK#33, *Another Cup of Coffee* (1994) UK#65. ALBUMS: **Smallcreep's Day** (1980, Charisma) US#163 UK#13; **Acting Very Strange** (1982, WEA) US#145 UK#23; **Mike and the Mechanics** (1986) g US#26 UK#78, **The Living Years** (1988) UK#2, **Word of Mouth** (1991) US#107 UK#11, **Beggar on a Beach of Gold** (1995, all Virgin) UK#9. COMPILATION: **Hits** (1996, Virgin) UK#3. Co-writers: [i] Christopher Neil, [ii] B.A. Robertson. (*See also under* Phil COLLINS, Peter GABRIEL.)

827. Sade (b. Helen Folasade Adu, January 16, 1959, Ibadan, Nigeria) Pop vocalist. A British based, soul influenced singer, whose successful but woefully bland supper club jazz, has sold over ten million records in America. Adu was a fashion student and member of the groups Arriva and Pride during the early 1980s, before forming the group Sade. CHART COMPOSITIONS: *Your Love Is King* [v] (1984) R&B#85 US#54 UK#6, *When Am I Gonna Make a Living* (1984) UK#36, *Hang on to Your Love* (1984) R&B#14 US#102, *Smooth Operator* [v] (1984) R&B#5 US#5 UK#19, *The Sweetest Taboo* [ii] (1985) R&B#3 US#5 UK#31, *Is It a Crime* (1986) R&B#55 UK#49, *Never as Good as the First Time* [iv] (1986) R&B#8 US#20, *Love Is Stronger Than Pride* (1988) UK#44, *Paradise* [i] (1988) R&B#1 UK#29, *No Ordinary Love* [iv] (1992) R&B#11 US#28 UK#26, re-issued (1993) UK#14; *Feel No Pain* [iii] (1992) R&B#59 UK#56, *Kiss of Life* [i] (1993) R&B#10 US#78 UK#44, *Cherish the Day* [iii] (1993) R&B#49 US#109 UK#53. ALBUMS: **Diamond Life** (1984) p US#5 UK#2, **Promise** (1985) p US#1 UK#1, **Stronger Than Pride** (1988) p US#7 UK#3, **Love Deluxe** (1992, all Epic) p US#3 UK#10. COMPILATION: **Best of Sade** (1994, Epic) p US#9 UK#6. Co-writers: [i] Paul Denman/Andrew Hale/Stuart Matthewman, [ii] Ditcham, [iii] Andrew Hale/Stuart Matthewman, [iv] Stuart Matthewman, [v] Ray St. John.

828. SAGER, Carole Bayer (b. August 3, 1946, New York, NY) Pop vocalist. A singer-songwriter whose greatest success has been as a lyricist for other artists. Sager first wrote for the music publisher Screen Gems in the 1960s, and in 1970 she co-composed the musical "Georgy." CHART COMPOSITIONS: *You're Moving Out Today* [ii] (1977) UK#6, *Stronger Than Before* [i] (1981) US#30. ALBUMS: **Carole Bayer Sager** (1977), **Too** (1978, both Elektra); **They're Playing Our Song** oc (1979, Casablanca) US#167; **Sometimes Late at Night** (1981, Boardwalk) US#60. HIT VERSIONS: *Groovy Kind of Love, A* [v] Mindbenders (1966) US#2 UK#2/Les Gray (1977) UK#32/Phil Collins (1988) UK#1; *Fool That I Am* [iii] Rita Coolidge (1980) US#46, *Heartbreaker* [vi] Dolly Parton (1978) C&W#1 US#37, *How Do You Heal a Broken Heart?* [iv] Chris Walker (1994) R&B#87, *I Don't Want to Go* [iii] Joey Travalta (1978) US#43, *Our Night* [iii] Shaun Cassidy (1978) US#80, *Skybird* [iii] Tony Orlando & Dawn (1975) US#49, *You're the Only One* [ii] Dolly Parton (1979) C&W#1 US#59, *You're Moving Out Today* [ii] Bette Midler (1977) US#42. Co-writers: [i] Burt Bacharach/Bruce Roberts, [ii] Bette Midler (b. December 1, 1944, Paterson, NJ)/Bruce Roberts, [iii] Bruce Roberts, [iv] Chris Walker, [v] Toni Wine, [vi] Dave Wolfert. (*See also under* Peter ALLEN, Burt BACHARACH, Neil DIAMOND, Marvin HAMLISCH, Melissa MANCHESTER, Michael MASSER.)

829. SAHM, Doug (b. Douglas Saldana, November 6, 1941, San Antonio, TX) C&W guitarist and vocalist. A country performer who blended Tex-Mex, psychedelia and R&B in the 1960s group Sir Douglas Quintet. CHART COMPOSITIONS: *She's About a Mover* (1965) US#13 UK#15, *The Tracker* (1965) US#105, *The Rains Came* (1966) US#31, *She Digs My Love* (1966) US#132, *Mendocino* (1969) US#27, *It Didn't Even Bring Me Down* (1969) US#108, *Dynamite Woman* (1969) US#83, *At the Crossroads* (1969) US#104. ALBUMS: **The Sir Douglas Quintet** (1966, Tribe); **The Sir Douglas Quintet +2 (Honkey Blues)** (1968), **Mendocino** (1969) US#81, **Together After Five** (1970), **1+1+1+1=4** (1970, all Smash). COMPILATIONS: **Best of Sir Douglas Quintet** (1965, Tribe); **Sir Doug Way Back** (1979, Harlem); **Sir Douglas His First Recordings** (1981, Charly). Since the early 1970s, Sahm has recorded as a solo artist. CHART COMPOSITIONS: *(Is Anybody Going to) San Antone* (1973) US#115, *Cowboy Peyton Place* (1976) C&W#100. ALBUMS: **The Return of Douglas Saldana** (1971), **Rough Edges** (1973, both Smash); **Doug Sahm and Band** (1973, Atlantic) US#125; **Texas Tornado** (1974), **Groover's Paradise** (1974, both Warner Brothers); **Texas Rock for Country Rollers** (1976

ABC/Dot); **Live Love** (1977, Texas); **Hell of a Spell** (1980), **Border Wave** (1981, both Takoma) US#184; **Quintessence** (1982, Varrick); **Rio Medina** (1984, Sonet); **Juke Box Music** (1988), **Very Much Alive/Love Ya, Europe** (1990), **Texas Tornados*** (1990, all Reprise) US#154; **Day Dreaming at Midnight** (1994, Elektra Nonesuch); **The Last Real Texas Blues Band** (1995, Antone's Ant). HIT VERSIONS: *Day the Rains Came, The* Freddy Fender (1977) C&W#4, *She's About a Mover* Otis Clay (1968) R&B#47. As: * the Texas Tornados.

830. SAINTE-MARIE, Buffy (b. February 20, 1941, Piapot Indian Reservation, Saskatchewan, Canada) Folk guitarist, dulcimer player and vocalist. A native American protest singer-songwriter, who cleverly merged her cultural heritage with that of folk and pop music. Sainte-Marie sings in an eerie vibrato, and her wide-ranging style has encompassed self-composed and traditional material that wanders across the boundaries of country, folk, blues and gospel. She was born to Cree Indians, but was adopted as a child, and learned the guitar before graduating in Oriental Philosophy and Education. During the 1960s, Sainte-Marie performed on the Greenwich Village folk scene, and recorded a series of intriguing albums that featured such classics as *Now That the Buffalo's Gone* — the first contemporary folk song to speak out against the genocide committed by the first Europeans on north American soil. It was a theme that she would return to with ever more incisiveness on such later material as *My Country 'Tis of Thy People You're Dying*, which she described as, "a condensation of native American history," and her film theme, the Indian prayer to the approaching U.S. Cavalry, *Soldier Blue* (1971). During the 1970s, Sainte-Marie withdrew from music for fourteen years in order to work in television, although she did co-write *Up Where We Belong*, the Oscar winning film theme to "An Officer and a Gentleman" (1983). Sainte-Marie updated her sound and returned to recording in 1992, with the sometimes excellent album **Coincidence and Likely Stories**, a literate cry for the disenfranchised and disenchanted. CHART COMPOSITIONS: *Soldier Blue* (1971) UK#7, *I'm Gonna Be a Country Girl Again* (1971) US#98 UK#34, *He's an Indian Cowboy in the Rodeo* (1972) US#98, *The Big Ones Get Away* (1992) UK#39, *Fallen Angels* (1992) UK#57. ALBUMS: **It's My Way** (1965), **Many a Mile** (1966), **Little Wheel Spin and Spin** (1967) US#97, **Fire and Fleet and Candlelight** (1968) US#126, **I'm Going to Be a Country Girl Again** (1969) US#171, **At Carnegie Hall** (1969), **Illuminations** (1970), **She Used to Wanna Be a Ballerina** (1971) US#182, **Moonshot** (1972) US#134, **Quiet Places** (1973), **Native North**

American Child (An Odyssey) (1974, all Vanguard); **Buffy** (1974), **Changing Woman** (1975, both MCA); **Sweet America** (1976, ABC); **Coincidence and Likely Stories** (1992, Chrysalis) UK#39; **Up Where We Belong** (1996, EMI). COMPILATIONS: **Best of Buffy Sainte-Marie** (1970) US#142, **Best of Buffy Sainte-Marie, Volume 2** (1974, both Vanguard). HIT VERSIONS: *Universal Soldier* Glen Campbell (1965) US#45/Donovan (1965) US#53; *Until It's Time for You to Go* Four Pennies (1965) UK#19/Neil Diamond (1970) US#53/Elvis Presley (1972) C&W#68 US#40 UK#5/New Birth (1973) R&B#21 US#97; *Up Where We Belong* [i] Joe Cocker & Jennifer Warnes (1983) US#1 UK#7. Co-writers: [i] Will Jennings/Jack Nitzsche (b. Bernard Nitzsche, April 22, 1937, Chicago, IL)

831. SAMWELL, Ian (b. England) Pop bassist. An original member of Cliff Richard and the Drifters, who composed and performed on Richard's first hit *Move It* (1958). Samwell left the group shortly afterwards to concentrate on his songwriting. HIT VERSIONS: *Dynamite* Cliff Richard (1959) UK#16, *Fall in Love with You* Cliff Richard (1960) UK#2, *Gee Whizz, It's You* [i] Cliff Richard (1961) UK#4, *High Class Baby* Cliff Richard (1958) UK#7, *Move It* Cliff Richard (1958) UK#2, *Mean Streak* Cliff Richard (1959) UK#10, *Never Mind* Cliff Richard (1959) UK#21, *Whatcha Gonna Do About It* Small Faces (1965) UK#14, *You Can Never Stop Me Loving You* [ii] Kenny Lynch (1962) UK#10/Johnny Tillotson (1963) US#18. Co-writers: [i] Hank B. Marvin, [ii] Jean Slater.

832. SAWYER, Pam R&B composer. A staff-writer at Motown Records throughout the 1970s. HIT VERSIONS: *I Ain't Gonna Eat Out My Heart Anymore* [ii] Young Rascals (1966) US#52/Angel (1978) US#44; *If I Were Your Woman* [v] Gladys Knight & the Pips (1970) R&B#1 US#9, *Let Me Tickle Your Fancy* [iii] Jermaine Jackson (1982) R&B#5 US#18, *Love Hangover* [vi] 5th Dimension (1976) US#80/Diana Ross (1976) R&B#1 US#1 UK#10, re-mixed (1988) UK#75/Associates (1982) UK#21/Scarlet (1995) UK#54; *My Mistake (Was to Love You)* [iv] Diana Ross & Marvin Gaye (1974) R&B#15 US#19, *Pops We Love You* [vi] Diana Ross, Marvin Gaye, Smokey Robinson & Stevie Wonder (1979) R&B#26 US#59 UK#66, *Yesterday's Dreams* [i] Four Tops (1968) R&B#31 US#49 UK#23, *You Can't Turn Me Off (In the Middle of Turning Me On)* [vi] High Energy (1977) R&B#2 US#12. Co-writers: [i] Vernon Bullock/Jack Goga/Ivy Hunter, [ii] L. Burton, [iii] Jermaine Jackson/Paul M. Jackson, Jr./Marilyn McLeod, [iv] Gloria Jones, [v] Gloria Jones/Clay McMurray, [vi] Marilyn McLeod. (*See* *also under* Johnny BRISTOL, Berry GORDY, Jr., Michael MASSER, R. Dean TAYLOR, Leon WARE.)

833. SAYER, Leo (b. Gerard Hugh Sayer, May 21, 1948, Shoreham-by-Sea, England) Pop vocalist. A former busker who, as a member of the group Patches, recorded the album **Patches** (1970, Warner Brothers). After teaming up with the drummer and co-writer David Courtney, Sayer composed Roger Daltrey's album **Daltrey** (1973, Track) US#43, before embarking on a solo career, that was initially characterized by his performing in a clown outfit. CHART COMPOSITIONS: *The Show Must Go On* [i] (1974) UK#2, *One Man Band* [i] (1974) US#96 UK#6, *Long Tall Glasses* [i] (1974) US#9 UK#4, *Moonlighting* [ii] (1975) UK#2, *You Make Me Feel Like Dancing* [vi] (1976) g R&B#43 US#1 UK#2, *How Much Love* [iv] (1977) US#17 UK#10, *Thunder in My Heart* [vii] (1977) US#38 UK#22, *Easy to Love* [iii] (1978) US#36, *Living in a Fantasy* [viii] (1981) US#23, *Orchard Road* (1983) UK#16, *Till You Come Back to Me* (1983) UK#51. ALBUMS: **Silver Bird** (1973) UK#2, **Just a Boy** (1974) US#16 UK#4, **Another Year** (1975) US#125 UK#8, **Endless Flight** (1977) p US#10 UK#4, **Thunder in My Heart** (1977) US#37 UK#8, **Leo Sayer** (1978) US#101 UK#15, **Here** (1979) UK#44, **Living in a Fantasy** (1980) US#36 UK#15, **World Radio** (1982) UK#30, **Have You Ever Been in Love** (1983, all Chrysalis) UK#15; **Cool Touch** (1990, EMI). COMPILATIONS: **Very Best of Leo Sayer** (1979) UK#1, **All the Best** (1993, both Chrysalis) UK#26; **The Show Must Go On: The Anthology** (1996, Rhino). HIT VERSIONS: *Dreamin'* [viii] Cliff Richard (1980) US#10 UK#8, *Fool for Your Love* [v] Jimmy Hall (1982) US#77, *Giving It All Away* [i] Roger Daltrey (1973) US#83 UK#5, *The Show Must Go On* [i] Three Dog Night (1974) g US#4. Co-writers: [i] David Courtney, [ii] Frank Farrell, [iii] Albert Hammond, [iv] Barry Mann, [v] Michael Omartian, [vi] Vincent Poncia, [vii] Tom Snow, [viii] Alan Tarney.

834. SCAGGS, Boz (b. William Royce Scaggs, June 8, 1944, OH) Rock guitarist, keyboard player and vocalist. A blues influenced guitarist who grew up in Dallas, Texas, before joining the fellow blues aficionado Steve Miller's group, the Marksmen, in 1958. The pair later performed in a variety of 1960s R&B bands, including the Ardells, the Knightrains and the Fabulous Night Train. In 1965, Scaggs recorded a solo set for Polydor Records in Sweden, before returning to America and joining the Steve Miller Band for two albums. Since the early 1970s, Scaggs has recorded as a solo artist. In 1974, the producer Johnny Bristol introduced him to a more soulful sound on the album **Slow Dancer** (1974), which became the blueprint for his five million selling **Silk Degrees** (1976). Scaggs retired to San Francisco in 1981, where he opened a restaurant, and has performed only rarely since. CHART COMPOSITIONS: *We Were Always Sweethearts* (1971) US#61, *Near You* (1971) US#96, *Dinah Flo* (1972) US#86, *You Make It So Hard (To Say No)* (1975) US#107, *It's Over* (1976) US#38, *Lowdown* [iv] (1976) g R&B#5 US#3 UK#28, *What Can I Say?* [iv] (1976) R&B#68 US#42 UK#10, *Lido Shuffle* [iv] (1976) R&B#11 US#13, *Hard Times* (1977) R&B#58, *Hollywood* [iii] (1977) R&B#49 US#33, *Breakdown Dead Ahead* [i] (1980) US#15, *Jo Jo* [ii] (1980) R&B#17 US#17, *Look What You've Done to Me* [i] (1980) US#14, *Miss Sun* [iv] (1980) US#14. ALBUMS: **Boz** (1965, Polydor); **Boz Scaggs** (1969, Atlantic) US#171; **Moments** (1971) US#124, **Boz Scaggs and Band** (1971) US#198, **My Time** (1972) US#138, **Slow Dancer** (1974) g US#81, **Silk Degrees** (1976) p US#2 UK#20, **Down Two Then Left** (1977) p US#11 UK#55, **Middle Man** (1980) p US#8 UK#52, **Other Roads** (1988, all Columbia) US#47; **Some Change** (1994), **Come on Home** (1997, both Virgin). COMPILATION: **Hits** (1981, Columbia) p US#24. HIT VERSIONS: *We're All Alone* Franki Valli (1976) US#78/Rita Coolidge (1977) g C&W#82 US#7 UK#6/La Costa (1977) C&W#75. Co-writers: [i] David Foster, [ii] David Foster/D. Lasley, [iii] Michael Omartian, [iv] David Paich. (*See also under* Steve MILLER.)

835. SCARBOROUGH, Skip (b. Los Angeles, CA) R&B producer. A member of the R&B act Creative Source during the mid–1970s, who later became a producer and songwriter for such groups as the Emotions. CHART COMPOSITION: *Can't Hide Love* (1973) R&B#48 US#114. ALBUMS: **Creative Source** (1974) US#152, **Migration** (1975, both Sussex); **Pass the Feelin' On** (1975, Polydor). HIT VERSIONS: *Can't Hide Love* Earth, Wind & Fire (1976) R&B#11 US#39, *Don't Ask My Neighbors* Emotions (1977) R&B#7 US#44/Ahmad Jamal (1980) R&B#79; *Giving You the Best That I Got* [i] Anita Baker (1988) R&B#1 US#3 UK#55, *Love Ballad* L.T.D. (1976) R&B#1 US#20/Gary Bartz (1977) R&B#95/George Benson (1979) R&B#3 US#18 UK#29; *Love Changes* Mother's Finest (1979) R&B#26/O.C. Smith (1982) R&B#68/Kashif & Meli'sa Morgan (1988) R&B#2; *Love or Let Me Be Lonely* [ii] Friends of Distinction (1970) R&B#13 US#6/Paul Davis (1982) US#40; *Love Music* Regal Dewy (1977) R&B#86, *No One Can Love You More* Phyliss Hyman (1977) R&B#58. Co-writers: [i] Anita Baker/Randy Holland, [ii] J. Peters/Anita Poree. (*See also under* Bill WITHERS.)

836. SCHERTZINGER, Victor (b. April 8, 1880, Mahony City, PA; d. October 26, 1941, Hollywood, CA) Film composer and violinist. A European concert violinist who, in the early 1930s, also wrote and directed movies. As soon as talkies arrived, Schertzinger was quick to produce Hollywood musicals, and he contributed to such successes as "The Love Parade (1930)," "One Night of Love" (1934), "Follow Your Heart" (1937), and "The Fleet's In" (1942). ALBUM: **The Road Begins** st (1962, Decca). HIT VERSIONS: *Arthur Murray Taught Me Dancing in a Hurry* [iv] Jimmy Dorsey (1942) US#18/King Sisters (1942) US#21; *I Remember You* [iv] Jimmy Dorsey (1942) US#9/Harry James (1942) US#24/Frank Ifield (1962) US#5 UK#1/Slim Whitman (1966) C&W#49 US#134, new version (1981) C&W#44/Glen Campbell (1988) C&W#32; *If You Build a Better Mousetrap* [iv] Jimmy Dorsey (1942) US#23, *Kiss the Boys Goodbye* [iii] Tommy Dorsey (1941) US#8/Bea Wain (1941) US#8; *Love Me Forever* [ii] Russ Morgan (1935) US#7/Four Esquires (1957) US#25 UK#23/Eydie Gorme (1957) US#24 UK#21/Roger Williams (1967) US#60; *Marcheta* Olive Kline & Elsie Baker (1922) US#5/Isham Jones (1923) US#8/John McCormack (1924) US#12/Karl Denver (1961) UK#8; *My Love Parade* [i] Maurice Chevalier (1930) US#15, *Nobody's Using It Now* [i] Marion Harris (1930) US#20, *Not Mine* [iv] Jimmy Dorsey (1942) US#22, *One Night of Love* [ii] Grace Moore (1934) US#1, *Sand in My Shoes* [iii] Connee Boswell (1941) US#24, *Tangerine* [iv] Jimmy Dorsey (1942) US#1/Vaughn Monroe (1942) US#11/Salsoul Orchestra (1976) R&B#36 US#18. Co-writers: [i] Clifford Grey, [ii] Gus Kahn, [iii] Frank Loesser, [iv] Johnny Mercer.

837. SCHLITZ, Don (b. August 29, 1952, Durham, NC) C&W guitarist and vocalist. A country singer-songwriter, whose compositions are regularly included on country artists' albums. CHART COMPOSITIONS: *The Gambler* (1978) C&W#65, *You're the One Who Re-wrote My Life Story* (1979) C&W#91. HIT VERSIONS: *Gambler, The* Kenny Rogers (1978) C&W#1 US#16, *No Easy Horses* Schuyler, Knobloch & Bickhardt (1987) C&W#19. (*See also under* Paul OVERSTREET.)

838. SCHOEBEL, Elmer (b. September 8, 1896, St. Louis, IL; d. December 15, St. Petersburg, FL) Jazz pianist, organist and arranger. An accomplished jazz pianist who was a movie house accompanist, before recording with the Friar's Society Orchestra in 1922. Schoebel's first published compositions were *Blue Grass Blues* and *Bugle Call Rag* [ii] (both 1923), after which he joined the Isham Jones Orchestra in 1925, for whom he composed *Everybody Stomp*. During the 1930s, Schoebel became the chief musical arranger for the Music Publishers Holding Corporation. HIT VERSIONS: *Bugle Call Rag* [ii] Fran Westphal (1923) US#15/Red Nichols (1927) US#14/Sophie Tucker (1927) US#10/Mills Brothers (1932) US#2/Benny Goodman (1934) US#5, re-issued (1936) US#13; *Farewell Blues* [i] Isham Jones (1923) US#8/Ted Lewis (1929) US#2; *Spanish Shawl* Blossom Seeley (1926) US#10. Co-writers: [i] Paul Mares/Leon Rappolo, [ii] Billy Meyers. (*See also under* Gus KAHN.)

839. SCHOLZ, Tom (b. March 10, 1947, Toledo, OH) Rock multi-instrumentalist, producer and vocalist. The mastermind behind the rock band Boston, which Scholz only assembled as a group once he had recorded an entire album in his home studio. Boston has sold over forty million records in America. CHART COMPOSITIONS: *More Than a Feeling* (1976) US#5 UK#22, *Long Time* (1977) US#22, *Peace of Mind* (1977) US#38, *Don't Look Back* (1978) US#4 UK#43, *The Man I'll Never Be* (1979) US#31, *Feelin' Satisfied* (1979) US#46, *Amanda* (1987) US#1, *We're Ready* (1987) US#9, *Can'tcha Say (You Believe in Me)* [i]/*Still in Love* [i] (1987) US#20, *I Need Your Love* [ii] (1994) US#51. ALBUMS: **Boston** (1976) p US#3 UK#11, **Don't Look Back** (1978, both Epic) p US#1 UK#9; **Third Stage** (1986) p US#1 UK#37, **Walk On** (1994, both MCA) US#7 UK#56. COMPILATION: **Greatest Hits** (1997, Epic). Co-writers: [i] Brad Delp (b. June 12, 1951, Boston, MA)/J. Green, [ii] Fran Sampson (b. March 26, 1949, Boston, MA).

840. SCHON, Neal (b. February 27, 1954, San Mateo, CA) Rock guitarist. A lead guitarist who initially recorded at the age of fifteen as a member of the latin influenced Santana, featuring on its albums **Santana III** (1971) g US#1 UK#6, **Carlos Santana and Buddy Miles, Live!** (1972) p US#8 UK#29, **Caravanserai** (1972) p US#8 UK#6, **Greatest Hits** (1974, all Columbia) US#17 UK#14; **Viva! Santana — The Very Best** (1986, K-Tel) UK#50; and **Dance of the Rainbow Serpent** (1995, Columbia). Schon left Santana in the mid–1970s, in order to form the slick rock group Journey, which has sold nearly thirty million albums in America. CHART COMPOSITIONS: *Wheel in the Sky* [iv] (1978) US#57, *Anytime* [iii] (1978) US#83, *Lights* [v] (1978) US#68, re-issued (1993) US#74; *Just the Same Way* [ii] (1979) US#58, *Too Late* [v] (1980) US#70, *Any Way You Want It* [v] (1980) US#23, *Good Morning Girl/Stay Awhile* [v] (1980) US#55, *Don't Stop Believin'* [ii] (1981) US#9, *Open Arms* [ii] (1981) US#2, *Still They Ride* [ii] (1982) US#19, *Only the Young* [ii] (1985) US#9, *Be Good to Yourself* [ii] (1986) US#9,

Girl Can't Help It [ii] (1986) US#17, *I'll Be Alright Without You* [ii] (1986) US#14. ALBUMS: **Journey** (1975) US#138, **Look into the Future** (1976) US#100, **Next** (1977) US#85, **Infinity** (1978) p US#21, **Evolution** (1979) p US#20 UK#100, **Departure** (1980) p US#8, **Captured** (1980) p US#9, **Escape** (1981) p US#1 UK#32, **Frontiers** (1983) p US#2 UK#6, **Raised on Radio** (1986) p US#4 UK#22, **Trial By Fire** (1996, all Columbia) p US#3. COMPILATIONS: **In the Beginning** (1980) US#152, **Greatest Hits** (1989) p US#10, **Time** (1993, all Columbia) US#90. Schon has also recorded as a solo artist. ALBUMS: **Untold Passion**** (1981) US#115, **Here to Stay**** (1983, both Columbia) US#122; **Through the Fire*** (1984, Geffen) US#42 UK#92; **Beyond the Thunder** (1995), **Electric World** (1997, both Higher Octave). In 1988, he also sidelined as a member of John Waite's group Bad English, and in 1992 he formed the band Hardline. HIT VERSIONS: *Open Arms* [ii] Mariah Carey (1996) US#2 UK#4, *Too Much Ain't Enough Love* [i] Jimmy Barnes (1988) US#91. As: * Hagar, Schon, Aaronson, Shrieve. With: ** Jan Hammer. Co-writers: [i] Jimmy Barnes/Brock/Jonathan Cain/Randy Jackson, [ii] Jonathan Cain/Steve Perry, [iii] Robert Fleischman/Greg Rolie (b. June 17, 1947)/R. Silver, [iv] Robert Fleischman/Ross Valory (b. February 2, 1949, San Francisco, CA), [v] Steve Perry, [vi] Greg Rolie. (*See also under* John WAITE.)

841. SCHROEDER, Aaron Pop lyricist. A successful lyricist and music publisher since the late 1950s, whose songs were often recorded by Elvis Presley. HIT VERSIONS: *Any Way You Want Me* [xii] Elvis Presley (1956) R&B#12 US#20, also on B-side of *Love Me Tender* (1956) C&W#3 R&B#3 US#1 UK#11; *Because They're Young* [ii] James Darren (1960) UK#29/Duane Eddy (1960) US#4 UK#2; *Big Hunk O' Love, A* [xv] Elvis Presley (1959) R&B#10 US#1 UK#4, *First Name Initial* [ix] Annette (1960) US#20, *Fools Hall of Fame* [vi] Pat Boone (1959) US#29/Paul Anka (1962) US#103; *French Foreign Legion* [xiv] Frank Sinatra (1959) US#61 UK#18, *Good Luck Charm* [vi] Elvis Presley (1962) US#1 UK#1, *Half Heaven-Half Heartache* Gene Pitney (1963) US#12, *I Got Stung* [viii] Elvis Presley (1958) g US#8 UK#1, *I Was the One* [i] Elvis Presley (1956) C&W#8 US#19, *I'm Gonna Knock on Your Door* [xiii] Eddie Hodges (1961) US#12/Billy "Crash" Craddock (1972) C&W#5/Little Jimmie Osmond (1974) UK#11; *It's Now or Never* [iv] Elvis Presley (1960) g R&B#7 US#1 UK#1, re-issued (1977) UK#39/John Schneider (1981) US#14; *Rubber Ball* [xi] Avons (1961) UK#30/Bobby Vee (1961) US#6 UK#4/Marty Wilde (1961) UK#9; *Santa Bring My Baby Back to Me* [iii] Elvis Presley (1957) UK#7,

Stuck on You [x] Elvis Presley (1960) C&W#27 R&B#6 R&B#6 US#1 UK#3, re-issued (1988) UK#58; *'Twixt Twelve and Twenty* [v] Pat Boone (1959) US#17 UK#18, *Wild Cat* [vi] Gene Vincent (1960) UK#21. Co-writers: [i] Hal Blair/Claude Demetrius/Bill Peppers, [ii] Don Costa/Wally Gold, [iii] Claud Demetrius, [iv] Eduardo Di Capua/Wally Gold, [v] Fredda Gold, [vi] Wally Gold, [vii] Wally Gold/Martin Kalmanoff, [viii] David Hill, [ix] Martin Kalmanoff, [x] Leslie MacFarland, [xi] Anne Orlowski, [xii] Cliff Owens, [xiii] Sid Wayne, [xiv] Guy Wood, [xv] Sid Wyche. (*See also under* Abner SILVER, George David WEISS, Barry WHITE.)

842. SCHROEDER, John (b. England) Pop producer and orchestra leader. A producer and arranger at EMI Records during the 1960s, who worked closely with the singer Helen Shapiro. He also recorded versions of current hits as the John Schroeder Orchestra. ALBUMS: **John Schroeder's Working in the Soulmine** (1966), **The Dolly Catcher!** (1967, both Piccadilly); **Witchi-Tai-To** (1971, Pye); **Dylan Vibrations** (1971), **T.V. Vibrations** (1972, both Polydor). HIT VERSIONS: *Don't Treat Me Like a Child* [i] Helen Shapiro (1961) UK#3, *Little Miss Lonely* [i] Helen Shapiro (1962) UK#8, *You Don't Know* [i] Helen Shapiro (1961) UK#1, *Walking Back to Happiness* Helen Shapiro (1961) US#100 UK#1. Co-writer: [i] Mike Hawker.

843. SCHWARTZ, Arthur (b. November 25, 1900, Brooklyn, NY; d. September 3, 1984, Kintnersville, PA) Film and stage composer, vocalist. A law student who became a songwriter after publishing the song *Baltimore MD, You're the Only Doctor for Me*, from the revue "The Grand Street Follies" (1925). Schwartz subsequently formed a lengthy songwriting partnership with the lyricist Howard Dietz, two of their earliest songs being *Dancing in the Dark* [ii] and *I Might as Well Be Miserable with You* [ii] for the film "The Band Wagon" (1931). Throughout the 1930s, Dietz and Schwartz were regular contributors to Broadway shows, including "The Co-optimists of 1930," "Flying Colors" (1932), "Revenge with Music" (1934), "At Home Abroad" (1935), and "Between the Devil" (1937), after which, they parted company for ten years, but re-united for "Inside U.S.A." (1946), "The Gay Life" (1961) and "Jennie" (1963). Schwartz also worked in Hollywood on the films "Thank Your Lucky Stars" (1943), "Cover Girl" and "The Time, the Place and the Girl" (both 1946); "A Tree Grows in Brooklyn" (1951), and "By the Beautiful Sea" (1954). He was the featured vocalist with the Leo Reisman Orchestra during the 1930s, charting with *Louisiana Hayride* [i] (1932) US#10. After retiring to England in the 1960s,

Schwartz recorded an album of his own compositions. ALBUMS: **A Tree Grows in Brooklyn** oc (1951, Columbia); **By the Beautiful Sea** oc (1954, Capitol); **High Tor** tvst (1956, Decca); **The Gay Life** oc (1962, Capitol) US#81, **Jennie** oc (1964, RCA) US#87, **From the Pen of Arthur Schwartz** (1975, RCA). HIT VERSIONS: *Alone Together* [ii] Leo Reisman (1932) US#9, *Alone Too Long* [iii] Nat "King" Cole (1954) US#25, *Dancing in the Dark* [ii] Bing Crosby (1931) US#3/Jacques Renard (1931) US#20/Ben Selvin (1931) US#10/Fred Waring's Pennsylvanians (1931) US#3/Artie Shaw (1941) g US#9, re-issued (1944) US#25/Frank Sinatra on *Come Dance with Me LP* (1959) UK#30; *Dreamer, The* [vi] Kay Armen (1944) US#7, *Gal in Calico, A* [vii] Johnny Mercer (1946) US#5/Tex Beneke (1947) US#6/Bing Crosby (1947) US#8/Benny Goodman (1947) US#6; *Goodbye, Jonah* [ix] Russ Morgan (1937) US#14, *Haunted Heart* [ii] Perry Como (1948) US#20/Jo Stafford (1948) US#23; *High and Low* [i] Fred Waring's Pennsylvanians (1931) US#12, *How Sweet You Are* [vi] Kay Armen (1944) US#10/Jo Stafford (1944) US#14; *I Guess I'll Have to Change My Plan (The Blue Pajama Song)* [ii] Guy Lombardo (1932) US#11/Rudy Vallee (1932) US#2; *I Love Louisa* [ii] Leo Reisman & Fred Astaire (1931) US#4, *I See Your Face Before Me* [ii] Glen Gray (1938) US#13/Guy Lombardo (1938) US#12; *If There Is Someone Lovelier Than You* [ii] Enric Madriguera (1935) US#17, *New Sun in the Sky, A* [ii] Leo Reisman & Fred Astaire (1931) US#10, *Oh, But I Do* [vii] Tex Beneke (1947) US#11/Harry James (1947) US#12/Margaret Whiting (1947) US#7; *Rainy Night in Rio, A* [vii] Sam Donohue (1947) US#7, *Shine on Your Shoes, A* [ii] Roger Wolfe Kahn (1932) US#12, *Something to Remember You By* [ii] Libby Holman (1931) US#6/Dinah Shore (1943) US#18; *Tennessee Fish Fry* [v] Kay Kyser (1940) US#9, *Then I'll Be Tired of You* [iv] Freddy Martin (1934) US#12/Fats Waller (1934) US#9; *They're Either Too Young or Too Old* [vi] Jimmy Dorsey (1944) US#2, *You and I Know* [viii] Tommy Dorsey (1937) US#11, *You and the Night and the Music* [ii] Libby Holman (1935) US#11/Leo Reisman (1935) US#18. Co-writers: [i] Desmond Carter/Howard Dietz, [ii] Howard Dietz, [iii] Dorothy Fields, [iv] E.Y. Harburg, [v] Oscar Hammerstein, II, [vi] Frank Loesser, [vii] Leo Robin, [viii] Laurence Stallings/Al Stillman, [ix] Al Stillman.

844. SCHWARTZ, Jean (b. November 4, 1878; d. November 30, 1956, Los Angeles, CA) Stage composer and pianist. An American immigrant, who, from the age of thirteen, studied the piano. Schwartz's first job was as a department store sheet music demonstrator, after which he became a staff pianist and song-plugger for the music publishers Shapiro, Bernstein and Von Tilzer. His first published song was *Dusky Dudes* (1899), after which he teamed up with the lyricist William Jerome to compose such hits as the three million selling *Bedelia* [i] (1904). Many of Schwartz's songs were interpolated into Broadway shows, and in 1904 he composed his first actual Broadway score, "Piff, Paff, Pouf." HIT VERSIONS: *Au Revoir, Pleasant Dreams* [ii] Ben Bernie (1930) US#15, *Bedelia* [i] George J. Gaskin (1904) US#3/Haydn Quartet (1904) US#1/Billy Murray (1904) US#1/Arthur Pryor's Band (1904) US#3/Jan Garber (1948) US#22; *Chinatown, My Chinatown* [i] American Quartet (1915) US#1/Grace Kerns & John Barnes Wells (1915) US#3/Prince's Orchestra (1915) US#8/Louis Armstrong (1932) US#5/Mills Brothers (1932) US#10/Ray Noble (1935) US#14/Bobby Maxwell (1952) US#24; *Meet Me in Rose-Time, Rosie* [i] Billy Murray & Haydn Quartet (1909) US#6/Frank Stanley & Byron Harlan (1909) US#3; *When Mister Shakespeare Comes to Town* [i] Dan Quinn (1901) US#4. Co-writers: [i] William Jerome, [ii] Jack Meskill. (*See also under* Milton AGER, Sam M. LEWIS.)

845. SCOTT, Jack (b. Jack Scafone, Jr., January 24, 1936, Windsor, Ontario, Canada) Pop guitarist and vocalist. A country influenced pop performer who learned the guitar at the age of eight, before forming the group the Southern Drifters in 1957. Scott recorded as a solo artist after 1958. CHART COMPOSITIONS: *My True Love* (1958) R&B#5 US#3 UK#9, *Leroy* (1958) R&B#25, *The Way I Walk* (1959) UK#30, *What in the Wold's Come Over You?* (1960) R&B#7 US#5 UK#11, *You're Just Gettin' Better* (1974) C&W#92. ALBUMS: **Jack Scott** (1958, Carlton); **Great Scott** (1959, Jade); **What Am I Living For** (1960, Carlton); **What in the World's Come Over You** (1960) UK#11, **I Remember Hank Williams** (1960) UK#7, **The Spirit Moves Me** (1961), **Old Time Religion** (1962, all Top Rank); **Burning Bridges** (1964, Capitol). COMPILATIONS: **Greatest Hits** (1976, Ponie); **The Legendary Jack Scott** (1982, Rockstar); **Scott on Groove** (1984, Bear Family); **Collector's Series** (1992, Capitol). HIT VERSIONS: *What in the World's Come Over You?* Sonny James (1975) C&W#10/Tom Jones (1981) C&W#25 US#109.

846. SCOTT, Mike (b. December 14, 1958, Edinburgh, Scotland) Pop guitarist and vocalist. The lead singer in the folk influenced group the Waterboys. CHART COMPOSITIONS: *The Whole of the Moon* (1985) UK#26, re-issued (1991) UK#3; *Fisherman's Blues* [i] (1989) UK#32, re-issued (1991) UK#75; *And a Bang on the Ear* (1989) UK#51, *The*

Return of Pan (1993) UK#24, *Glastonbury Song* (1993) UK#29. ALBUMS: **The Waterboys** (1983), **A Pagan Place** (1984) UK#100, **This Is the Sea** (1985) UK#37, **Fisherman's Blues** (1988) US#76 UK#13, **Room to Roam** (1990, all Ensign) US#180 UK#5; **Dream Harder** (1993, Geffen) US#171 UK#5. COMPILATIONS: **Best of the Waterboys, '81–'90** (1991, Ensign) UK#2. Since 1995, Scott has recorded as a solo artist. CHART COMPOSITIONS: *Bring 'Em All In* (1995) UK#56, *Building the City of Lights* (1995) UK#60. ALBUMS: **Bring 'Em All In** (1995) UK#23, **Still Burning** (1997, both Chrysalis). HIT VERSION: *The Whole of the Moon* Little Caesar (1990) UK#68. Co-writer: [i] Steve Wickham.

847. SCOTT-HERON, Gil (b. April 1, 1949, Chicago, IL) R&B pianist and vocalist. A published author and poet who became one of the most acerbic satirists in contemporary popular music, examining greed, racism and the follies of elected government, while mixing elements of soul, funk, rock, and jazz. Scott-Heron employs tragic humor in a modern Afro-American Griot style, while his seminal influence on rap music has been acknowledged on many occasions by such artists as the Beatnigs, Hiphoprisy and Two Kings in a Cipher. Initially raised by his grandmother in Jackson, Tennessee, after her death, Scott-Heron lived with his mother in the Bronx, New York, where, as a teenager, he became an avid reader of detective stories and Langston Hughes, and listened to the singer Paul Robeson. He studied composition and attended Lincoln University in Pennsylvania, where he first became interested in black politics, and linked up with the musician Brian Jackson. The duo began composing music for some of Scott-Heron's invective poems, which were featured on a series of albums for the Flying Dutchman label in the 1970s. One of his earliest compositions was *Home Is Where the Hatred Is*, the definitive anti-drug song that was later given a monumental reading by the late Esther Phillips. By **Winter in America** (1975), Scott-Heron had surrounded himself with an accomplished collective of musicians called the Midnight Band, performing material that raged against the destruction of the environment, the genocide of native Americans, alcoholism, and political skullduggery. Scott-Heron seldom missed his mark, and his majestic rap-poems *B-Movie* and *Black History/The World* remain essential items of the genre. He all but disappeared from music making for a decade, returning with **Spirits** (1994), an album that featured two new classic raps, *Work for Peace* and *Message to the Messengers*. CHART COMPOSITIONS: *Johannesburg** (1975) R&B#29, *The Bottle (Part 1)** (1977) R&B#98, *Angel Dust**

(1978) R&B#15, *Show Bizness** (1979) R&B#83, *Shut 'Em Down** (1980) R&B#68, *A Legend in His Own Mind* (1981) R&B#86, *B-Movie* (1981) R&B#49, *Re-Ron* (1984) R&B#72. ALBUMS: **Small Talk at 125th and Lennox** (1972), **Free Will** (1972), **Pieces of a Man** (1971, all Flying Dutchman); **Winter in America** (1975, Strata East); **The First Minute of a New Day** (1975) US#30, **From South Africa to South Carolina** (1975) US#103, **It's Your World** (1976) US#168, **Bridges** (1977) US#130, **Secrets** (1978) US#61, **1980** (1980) US#82, **Real Eyes** (1980) US#159, **Reflections** (1981) US#106, **Moving Target** (1982, all Arista) US#123; **Tales of Gil Scott-Heron** (1990, Essential); **Spirits** (1994, TVT). COMPILATIONS: **The Revolution Will Not Be Televized** (1975, Flying Dutchman); **The Mind of Gil Scott-Heron: A Collection of Poetry and Music** (1978), **Glory-The Gil Scott-Heron Collection** (1990, both Arista). HIT VERSIONS: *Bottle, The* Brother to Brother as *In the Bottle* (1974) R&B#9 US#46/Bataan as *La Botella* (1975) R&B#59 US#102; *Home Is Where the Hatred Is* Esther Phillips (1972) R&B#40 US#122. With: * Brian Jackson.

848. Seal (b. Henry Samuel, February 19, 1963, London, England) R&B vocalist. A soul and dance singer who utilizes contemporary studio sounds. Born of mixed Nigerian, Brazilian and West Indian ancestry, Seal joined his first group Stay Brave, at the age of fifteen. CHART COMPOSITIONS: *Crazy* (1990) US#7 UK#2, *Future Love EP* (1991) UK#12, *The Beginning* [iii] (1991) UK#24, *Killer* [iv] (1991) US#100 UK#8, *Violet: The Acoustic EP* [iii] (1992) UK#39, *Prayer for the Dying* [i] (1994) US#21 UK#14, *Kiss from a Rose* (1994) UK#20, *Newborn Friend* (1994) UK#45, *Kiss from a Rose/I'm Alive* [ii] (1995) US#1 UK#4, *Don't Cry* (1996) R&B#71 US#33 UK#51. ALBUMS: **Seal** (1991) g US#24 UK#1, **Seal** (1995, both ZTT) p US#15 UK#9. HIT VERSIONS: *Killer* [iv] Adamski (1990) UK#1/ George Michael (1993) R&B#88 US#69, also on *Five Live EP* (1993) UK#1. Co-writers: [i] Isidore, [ii] A. Seal, [iii] Sigsworth, [iv] Adam Tinley.

849. SEALS, Dan (b. February 8, 1948, Mc-Camey, TX) C&W guitarist and vocalist. The brother of James Seals, who first performed as a member of the group Southwest F.O.B. on the album **Smell of Incense** (1968, Hip). As one half of the duo England Dan & John Ford Coley, Seals recorded in a mainstream pop-vocal style during the 1970s, charting with *What Can I Do with This Broken Heart* [i] (1979) US#50. ALBUMS: **England Dan and John Ford Coley** (1971), **Fables** (1971), **I Hear Music** (1976, all A&M); **Nights Are Forever** (1976) g US#17, **Dowdy Ferry Road** (1977) US#80, **Some**

Things Don't Come Easy (1978) US#61, **Dr. Heckle and Mr. Jive** (1979, all Big Tree) US#106; **Just Tell Me You Love Me** (1980, MCA). COMPILATION: **Best of England Dan and John Ford Coley** (1980, Big Tree) US#194. Seals' greatest success has been as a solo country artist, charting eleven number ones since 1985. CHART COMPOSITIONS: *Everybody's Dream Girl* (1983) C&W#18, *After You* (1983) C&W#28, *You Really Go for the Heart* (1983) C&W#37, *God Must Be a Cowboy* (1984) C&W#10, *(You Bring Out) The Wild Side of Me* (1984) C&W#9, *My Baby's Got Good Timing* (1984) C&W#2, *My Old Yellow Car* (1985) C&W#9, *Everything That Glitters (Is Not Gold)* (1986) C&W#1, *You Still Move Me* (1986) C&W#1, *I Will Be There* (1987) C&W#1, *Three Time Loser* (1987) C&W#1, *One Friend* (1987) C&W#1, *Addicted* (1988) C&W#1, *Big Wheels in the Moonlight* (1988) C&W#1, *They Rage On* (1989) C&W#1, *Good Times* (1990) C&W#1, *Love on Arrival* (1990) C&W#1, *Mason Dixon Line* (1992) C&W#43. ALBUMS: **Stones** (1980), **Habinger** (1982, both Atlantic); **Rebel Heart** (1983), **San Antone** (1984, both Liberty); **Won't Be Blue Anymore** (1985) g US#59, **On the Front Line** (1987), **San Antone** (1987, both EMI America); **Rage On** (1988), **On Arrival** (1990, both Capitol); **Walking the Wire** (1992, Warner Brothers). COMPILATIONS: **Best of Dan Seals** (1987, Capitol); **The Best** (1992, Liberty). Co-writers: [i] John Ford Coley (b. October 13, 1948, TX)/B. Gundry. (*See also under* Bob McDILL.)

850. SEALS, James (b. October 17, 1941, Sidney, TX), and **CROFTS, Dash** (b. August 14, 1940, Cisco, TX) Both pop multi-instrumentalists and vocalists. Originally members of the American group the Champs, the duo left in 1971 to form Seals and Crofts. CHART COMPOSITIONS: *When I Meet Them* (1971) US#104, *Summer Breeze* (1972) US#6, *Hummingbird* (1973) US#20, *Diamond Girl* (1973) US#6, *We May Never Pass This Way Again* (1973) US#21, *Unborn Child* (1974) US#66, *King of Nothing* (1974) US#60, *I'll Play for You* (1975) US#18, *Get Closer* (1975) US#6, *Baby, I'll Give It to You* [ii] (1976) US#58. ALBUMS: **Seals and Crofts** (1970), **Down Home** (1970, both TA) US#122; **Year of Sunday** (1972) US#133, **Summer Breeze** (1972) g US#7, **Diamond Girl** (1973) g US#4, **Unborn Child** (1974) g US#14, **I'll Play for You** (1975) g US#30, **Get Closer** (1976) g US#37, **Sudan Village** (1977) US#73, **One on One** ost (1977) US#118, **Takin' It Easy** (1978, all Warner Brothers) US#78. COMPILATIONS: **Seals and Crofts I & II** (1974) US#86, **Greatest Hits** (1975, both Warner Brothers) p US#11. HIT VERSIONS: *Summer Breeze* Isley Brothers (1974) R&B#10 US#60 UK#16/Geoffrey

Williams (1992) UK#56. All compositions Dash Crofts/James Seals, except: [i] Louise Bogan/James Seals.

851. SEALS, Troy (b. November 16, 1938, Big Hill, KY) C&W guitarist and vocalist. A cousin of the songwriters Dan Seals and James Seals, who, since the 1970s, has been a regular Nashville session player and songwriter. Seals first recorded during the 1960s in partnership with his wife Jo Ann Campbell, before going solo in the 1970s. CHART COMPOSITIONS: *Star of the Bar* (1974) C&W#78, *Grand Ole Blues* (1977) C&W#93, *One Night Honeymoon* (1980) C&W#85. ALBUMS: **Now Presenting Troy Seals** (1973, Atlantic); **Troy Seals** (1976, Columbia). HIT VERSIONS: *American Waltz* Merle Haggard (1985) C&W#60, *Boogie Woogie Country Man* Jerry Lee Lewis (1975) C&W#24, *But I Will* [viii] Faith Hill (1994) C&W#35, *Call Home* [vii] Mike Reid (1992) C&W#43, *Country Girls* John Schneider (1985) C&W#1, *Don't Take It Away* Conway Twitty (1979) C&W#1; *Drinkin' and Dreamin'* Waylon Jennings (1985) C&W#2, *Every Time I Roll the Dice* [i] Chris LeDoux (1993) C&W#61, *From Seven Till Ten* Conway Twitty & Loretta Lynn (1978) C&W#6, *Heartbreak Radio* [v] Roy Orbison (1992) UK#36, *I Can't Love You Enough* Conway Twitty & Loretta Lynn (1977) C&W#2, *I Won't Need You Anymore (Always and Forever)* Randy Travis (1987) C&W#1, *I've Got a Rock 'n' Roll Heart* [iii] Eric Clapton (1983) US#18, *Lost in the Fifties Tonight (In the Still of the Night)* Ronnie Milsap (1985) C&W#1, *Play, Ruby, Play* [ii] Clinton Gregory (1992) C&W#25, *Red Neckin' Love Makin' Night* Conway Twitty (1982) C&W#1, *Standing on the Edge of Love* [vi] Clinton Gregory (1993) C&W#52, *Ten Feet Away* Keith Whitley (1986) C&W#9, *There's a Honky Tonk Angel (Who'll Take Me In)* Conway Twitty (1974) C&W#1, *We Had It All* [iv] Waylon Jennings (1973) C&W#28/Conway Twitty (1983) C&W#44/Dolly Parton (1986) C&W#31; *When We Make Love* [ix] Alabama (1984) C&W#1 US#72, *Who's Gonna Fill Their Shoes* George Jones (1985) C&W#3, *You Almost Slipped My Mind* Kenny Price (1972) C&W#44/Charley Pride (1980) C&W#4. Co-writers: [i] Max D. Barnes, [ii] T. Brown, [iii] Steve Diamond/Eddie Setser, [iv] Donnie Fritts, [v] Miller, [vi] J.P. Pennington, [vii] Mike Reid, [viii] Eddie Setser/L. Stewart, [ix] M. Williams. (*See also under* Waylon JENNINGS, Will JENNINGS, Travis TRITT.)

852. SEBASTIAN, John (b. John Benson Sebastian, May 17, 1944, New York, NY) Pop guitarist, harmonica player and vocalist. A folk influenced singer-songwriter best known for his good-time group the Lovin' Spoonful. Sebastian first performed in the

Even Dozen Jug Band, releasing the albums **Even Dozen Jug Band** (1964, Elektra); **Jug Band Songs of the Southern Mountains** (1965, Legacy); and **The Even Dozen Jug Band** (1966, Bounty), before, in 1965, forming the Mugwumps for the single *Jug Band Music* (1966) US#127. The Mugwumps evolved into the Lovin' Spoonful, which had a significant chart run between 1966–1968. CHART COMPOSITIONS: *Do You Believe in Magic?* (1965) US#9, *You Didn't Have to Be So Nice* [i] (1965) US#10, *Daydream* (1966) g US#2 UK#2, *Did You Ever Have to Make Up Your Mind?* (1966) US#2, *Summer in the City* [ii] (1966) g US#1 UK#8, *Rain on the Roof* (1966) US#10, *Nashville Cats* (1967) US#8 UK#26, *Full Measure* (1967) US#87, *Darling Be Home Soon* (1967) US#15 UK#44, *Six O'Clock* (1967) US#18, *She Is Still a Mystery* (1967) US#27, *Money* (1968) US#48, *('Til I) Run with You* (1968) US#128. ALBUMS: **Do You Believe in Magic?** (1965) US#32, **Daydream** (1966) US#10 UK#8, **Hums of the Lovin' Spoonful** (1966) US#14, **What's Up Tiger Lily?** ost (1966) US#126, **You're a Big Boy Now** ost (1967) US#160, **Everything Playing** (1968, all Kama Sutra) US#118. COMPILATIONS: **Best of the Lovin' Spoonful** (1967) g US#3, **Best of the Lovin' Spoonful, Volume 2** (1968) US#156, **The Best** (1976, all Kama Sutra) US#183. Sebastian quit the group in 1968 for an increasingly sporadic solo career. CHART COMPOSITIONS: *She's a Lady* (1969) US#84, *Welcome Back* (1976) g C&W#93 US#1, *Hideaway* (1976) US#95. ALBUMS: **John B. Sebastian** (1970) US#20, **Live** (1970, both MGM) US#129; **Cheapo Cheapo Productions Presents Real Live John Sebastian** (1971) US#75, **The Four of Us** (1971) US#93, **Tarzana Kid** (1974), **Welcome Back** (1976, all Reprise) US#79; **Tar Beach** (1993, Shanachie); **I Want My Roots** (1996, Musicmasters). COMPILATION: **Best of John Sebastian** (1980, Rhino). HIT VERSIONS: *Darling Be Home Soon* Bobby Darin (1967) US#93/Association (1972) US#104/Let Loose (1996) UK#65; *Daydream* Jon & Lynn (1982) C&W#86/Right Said Fred (1992) UK#29; *Do You Believe in Magic?* Shaun Cassidy (1978) US#31, *Lovin' You* Bobby Darin (1967) US#32, *Nashville Cats* Flatt & Scruggs (1967) C&W#54, *Summer in the City* [ii] Quincy Jones (1973) US#102, *Younger Girl* Critters (1966) US#42/Hondells (1966) US#52. Co-writers: [i] Steve Boone (b. September 23, 1943, Camp Lejeune, NC), [ii] Steve Boone/Mike Sebastian.

853. SEDAKA, Neil (b. March 13, 1939, Brooklyn, NY) Pop pianist and vocalist. One of the most consistently successful songwriters since the late 1950s, who started out as a teen idol before enjoying a second career in a maturer, singer-songwriter style during the 1970s. Sedaka has written over one thousand songs, charted over forty hit singles, and, between 1959–1963, sold over twenty-five million records of his compositions. Both of Sedaka's parents and his grandmother were trained pianists, and he grew up listening to the radio and his aunt's record collection. At the age of seven, Sedaka sang in his school choir, and, encouraged by a school teacher to develop his musical talents, he ultimately studied at the Julliard Preparatory School. During the 1950s, Sedaka dated another struggling songwriter, Carole King, with whom he shared a love of rock and roll and street corner doo-wop, and about whom he would compose one of his biggest hits, *Oh Carol* [iii]. With his school friend Howard Greenfield, Sedaka formed a songwriting partnership, shortly after which, Sedaka formed the vocal group the Tokens, which released the mid–1950s single *I Love My Baby*. Sedaka's first song to be recorded by another artist was *Never Again* by Dinah Washington, after which, he and Greenfield wrote for five hours a day at Don Kirshner's Aldon Music, at 1650 Broadway, New York-one half of the two locations that were collectively known as the Brill Building. A series of unsuccessful singles followed, until Connie Francis gave him his first number one with her version of *Stupid Cupid* (1958). After signing to RCA Records, Sedaka enjoyed a procession of hits, all of which emphasized his cute, double-tracked tenor, over rumbling piano lines and highly commercial backing tracks. When *The Answer to My Prayer* (1966) failed to chart, Sedaka retired from recording and live performances to become a songwriter for others, but with his loss of pop star status, he initially found that, "I couldn't give a song away." In 1970, he wrote most of the music to the cartoon television series "The Globetrotters," after which he moved to England in order to perform an oldies show on the northern club circuit. During the early 1970s, Sedaka's career picked up again, as he found a new and receptive market for his maturer material. **Neil Sedaka: A Solo Concert** (1977), was an on-stage, one-man musical autobiography, and in 1992, he was reported to be working on a film about his early years as a songwriter, alongside a Broadway show to be entitled "An Evening with Neil Sedaka." CHART COMPOSITIONS: *The Diary* [iii] (1959) R&B#25 US#14, *I Go Ape* [iii] (1959) US#42 UK#9, *Crying My Heart Out for You* [iii] (1959) US#111, *Oh Carol* [iii] (1959 RCA R&B#27 US#9 UK#3, *Stairway to Heaven* [iii] (1960) R&B#16 US#9 UK#8, *You Mean Everything to Me* [iii] (1960) R&B#17 US#45, *Samson Run* [iii] (1960) US#28, *Calendar Girl* [iii] (1961) R&B#22 US#4 UK#8, *Little Devil* [iii] (1961) US#11 UK#9, *Happy Birthday, Sweet Sixteen* [iii] (1962) US#6 UK#3, *King of Clowns* [iii] (1962) US#45 UK#23, *Breaking Up Is Hard to Do* [iii] (1962) R&B#12 US#1

UK#7, new version (1974) US#8; *Next Door to an Angel* [iii] (1962) R&B#19 US#5 UK#29, *Alice in Wonderland* [iii] (1963) US#17, *Let's Go Steady Again* [iii] (1963) R&B#21 US#26 UK#42, *The Dreamer* [iii] (1963) US#47, *Bad Girl* [iii] (1963) US#33, *Sunny* [iii] (1964) US#86, *The Closest Thing to Heaven* [iii] (1964) US#107, *I Hope He Breaks Your Heart* [iii] (1964) US#104, *The World Through a Tear* [iii] (1965) US#76, *Let the People Talk* [iii] (1965) US#107, *We Can Make It if We Try* [iii] (1967) US#121, *Oh Carol* [iii]/*Breaking Up Is Hard to Do* [iii]/*Little Devil* [iii] (1972) UK#19, *Beautiful You* [ii] (1972) UK#43, *That's When the Music Takes Me* (1972) UK#18, re-issued (1975) US#27; *Standing on the Inside* (1973) UK#26, *Our Last Song Together* [iii] (1973) UK#31, *A Little Lovin'* [ii] (1974) UK#34, *Laughter in the Rain* [ii] (1974) US#1 UK#15, *The Queen of 1964* [iii] (1974) UK#35, *The Immigrant* [ii] (1975) US#22, *Bad Blood* [ii] with Elton John (1974) g US#1, *You Gotta Make Your Own Sunshine* [iii] (1976) US#53, *Steppin' Out* [ii] (1976) US#36, *Love in the Shadows* [ii] (1976) US#16, *Is This the Way to Amarillo* [iii] (1977) US#44, *Alone at Last* [ii] (1977) US#104, *Should've Never Let You Go* [ii] with Dara Sedaka (1980) US#19, *Letting Go* [ii] (1980) US#107. ALBUMS: **Neil Sedaka and the Tokens** (1958, Guest Star); **Neil Sedaka, the Tokens and the Coins** (1958, Crown); **Rock with Neil Sedaka** (1959), **On Stage** (1970), **Circulate** (1961, all RCA); **Emergence** (1971), **Solitaire** (1972, both Kirshner) US#159; **The Tra-La Days Are Over** (1973, MGM) UK#13; **Laughter in the Rain** (1973) g US#1 UK#17, **Live at the Royal Festival Hall** (1974) UK#48, **Overnight Success** (1975, both Polydor) UK#31; **Live in Australia** (1976, RCA); **Steppin' Out** (1976) US#26, **Neil Sedaka: A Solo Concert** (1977, both Polydor); **A Song** (1977) US#59, **All You Need Is the Music** (1978), **In the Pocket** (1980) US#135, **Now** (1981, all Elektra); **Come See About Me** (1984, MCA); **Classically Sedaka** (1995, Vision) UK#23; **Tune Weaver** (1995, Varese Sarabande). COMPILATIONS: **Neil Sedaka Sings His Greatest Hits** (1963, RCA) US#55; **Sedaka's Back** (1974) g US#23, **The Hungry Years** (1975, both Rocket) g US#16; **24 Rock 'n' Roll Hits** (1975), **Neil Sedaka Sings His Greatest Hits** (1975, both RCA) US#161; **Laughter and Tears — The Best of Neil Sedaka Today** (1976, Polydor) UK#2; **Greatest Hits** (1977, Rocket) US#143; **Timeless — The Very Best of Neil Sedaka** (1991, Polydor) UK#10. HIT VERSIONS: *Another Sleepless Night* [iii] Jimmy Clanton (1960) US#22 UK#50, *Breaking Up Is Hard to Do* [iii] Happenings (1968) US#67/Lenny Welch (1970) R&B#27 US#34/Heaven Bound with Tony Scotti (1972) US#101/Partridge Family (1972) US#28 UK#3/Jimmy Bee & the Ernie Fields Junior Orchestra (1976) R&B#91/

American Comedy Network as *Breaking Up Is Hard on You* (1983) US#70; *Don't Let It Mess Your Mind* Donny Gerrard (1975) R&B#65 US#104, *Fallin'* [iii] Connie Francis (1958) US#30 UK#20, *Frankie* [iii] Connie Francis (1959) US#9, *Hungry Years, The* [iii] Wayne Newton (1976) US#82, *I Waited Too Long* [iii] LaVern Baker (1959) R&B#5 US#33, *Is This The Way to Amarillo* [iii] Tony Christie (1972) US#121 UK#18, *Kissin' My Life Away* Hondells (1966) US#118, *Laughter in the Rain* [ii] Lea Roberts (1974) R&B#69 US#109, *Lonely Night (Angel Face)* Captain & Tennille (1976) US#3, *Love Will Keep Us Together* [iii] Captain & Tennille (1975) g US#1 UK#32, also as *Por Amor Vivivemos* (1975) US#49/Wilson Pickett (1976) R&B#69/JTQ featuring Alison Limerick (1995) UK#63; *Other Side of Me, The* Andy Williams (1976) UK#42, *Our Last Song Together* [iii] Bo Donaldson & the Heywoods (1975) US#95, *Puppet Man* [iii] 5th Dimension (1969) US#24/Tom Jones (1971) US#26 UK#49; *Rainy Jane* Davey Jones (1971) US#52, *Solitaire* [ii] Andy Williams (1973) UK#4/Carpenters (1975) US#17 UK#32/Elvis Presley on B-side of *Are You Sincere* (1979) C&W#10 US#105; *Stayin' Power* Barbi Benton (1976) US#108, *Stupid Cupid* [iii] Connie Francis (1958) g US#14 UK#1, *What Am I Gonna Do?* Jimmy Clanton (1961) US#50/Emile Ford & the Checkmates (1961) UK#33; *Where the Boys Are* [iii] Connie Francis (1961) g US#4 UK#5, *Workin' on a Groovy Thing* [i] Patti Drew (1968) R&B#34 US#62/5th Dimension (1969) R&B#15 US#20; *You Never Done It Like That* [iii] Captain & Tennille (1978) US#10 UK#63. Co-writers: [i] Roger Atkins, [ii] Phil Cody, [iii] Howard Greenfield. (*See also under* Benny ANDERSSON and Bjorn ULVAEUS.)

854. SEEGER, Pete (b. May 3, 1919, New York, NY) Folk guitarist, banjo player and vocalist. A significant contributor and major influence on many aspects of the folk idiom, who championed such new folk singers as Woody Guthrie, Bob Dylan and Don McLean. Seeger traced the similarities in African and European folk music traditions long before Paul Simon was to explore them on his album **Graceland**, and he was one of the instigators of the singer-songwriter movement of the early 1970s. Seeger also contributed to, standardized, or co-wrote, some of the most popular folk melodies of the 1960s. An idealist and optimist, he is a raconteur in the troubadour tradition who has recorded over sixty albums, including music for children and banjo instructional disks. Born into a musical family, Seeger's father was a musicologist and his mother a violin teacher. He learned to play several instruments in his youth, but never learned to read music. He attended Harvard University in the 1930s, but left before graduation as he had become engrossed in the music of early America, which resulted in him traveling the rural areas of the country listening to and collating folk songs. Seeger's pioneering work forged a path into the remote areas of traditional American music that only Ry Cooder was ever to follow. Between 1939–1940, Seeger appeared on Alan Lomax's radio show, while also working with the Vagabond Puppets Music and Theatre Show. He performed at union meetings and radical political groups with Guthrie, and during the late 1940s joined the Communist Party, remaining a member until 1951. After performing in the Almanac Singers with Guthrie in 1948, recordings later collected on the album **Talking Union and Other Union Songs** (1980, Folkways), Seeger formed the seminal folk group the Weavers, with Fred Hellerman, Ronnie Gilbert and Lee Hays. The Weavers revived the fortunes of folk music during the 1950s, with Seeger's compositions and arrangements of old folk songs, and their triumphant 1955 Carnegie Hall concert sowed the seeds of the folk protest movement. CHART COMPOSITIONS: *Goodnight Irene* (arrangement only) (1950) g US#2, *On Top of Old Smokey* (arrangement only) (1951) g US#2, *Kisses Sweeter Than Wine* [iv] (adaptation only) (1951) US#19, *Wimoweh* (arrangement only) (1952) US#14. ALBUMS: **Folksongs of America and Other Lands** (1955, Decca); **The Weavers at Home** (1958), **Best of the Weavers** (1959), **Folksongs Around the World** (1959), **Travellin' On** (1960), **The Weavers at Carnegie Hall** (1961) US#24, **The Weavers at Carnegie Hall, Volume 2** (1961) US#126, **Almanac** (1962), **Re-union at Carnegie Hall, 1963** (1963), **Re-union at Carnegie Hall, Volume 2** (1963), **Songbag** (1967), **Wasn't That a Time** (1993, all Vanguard). In 1950, Seeger began publishing his "Sing Out" folk magazine, but during the communist witch hunts of the McCarthy era, the Weavers lost their recording contract, effectively blacklisted by their own industry. Seeger wisely refused to testify before the House Of Un–American Activities Committee in 1955, citing the Fifth Constitutional Amendment. The hopelessly backward political events of the 1950s did bring about an unexpected result, as Seeger headed to Britain, where he became an integral part of the blossoming folk movement, singing at schools, colleges and in coffee houses, making British folk music more popular than at any time prior to the 1940s. When the dark ages of the 1950s were over, Seeger signed to Columbia Records in 1961, and co-founded the magazine "Broadside" to promote folk music in general. He remained closely associated with the Civil Rights movement throughout the 1960s, and always spoke out against commercialism in folk music. In 1969, he launched a campaign to clean up the heavily polluted Hudson River, and in 1981, he sang at a Solidarity trade union rally in Poland. ALBUMS: **Darling Corey** (195?), **America's Favorite Folk Songs** (195?), **Goofing-Off Suite** (195?), **Champlain Valley Songbag** (195?), **Frontier Ballads, Volumes 1 & 2** (195?), **Pete Seeger and Sonny Terry** (195?), **Newport Folk Festival** (195?), **German Folk Songs** (195?), **Guitar: Folksingers Guide** (195?), **Hootenany at Carnegie Hall** (195?), **Lonesome Valley** (195?), **Love Song for Friends and Foe** (1958), **America's Favorite Ballads, Volumes 1 to 5** (all 1959), **Pete Seeger at the Village Gate** (1960), **Pete Seeger Sampler** (1960), **Rainbow Quest** (1960), **Broadside Ballads** (1960), **Indian Summer** (1961), **Songs of Struggle and Protest** (1961), **America's Folk Songs for Children** (1961), **Birds, Beats, Bugs and Little Fishes** (1962), **Camp Songs** (1962), **American Game and Activity Songs for Children** (1962), **How to Play the Five String Banjo** (1962), **Pete Seeger on Campus** (1962), **Little Boxes and Other Broadsides** (1962), **Pete Seeger Sings Leadbelly** (1962), **Abiyoyo and Other Songs for Children** (1962, all Folkways); **The Bitter and the Sweet** (1962), **Pete Seeger Story Songs** (1962), **Strangers and Cousins** (1963), **We Shall Overcome** (1963) US#42, **I Can See a New Day** (1964), **God Bless the Grass** (1964), **Pete Seeger Now** (1964), **Complete Carnegie Hall Concert, June 8, 1963** (1964, all Columbia); **In Concert** with Big Bill Broonzy (1964, Verve Folkways); **Pete Seeger, Folk Music** (1965), **Children's Concert at Carnegie Hall** (1965), **God Bless the Grass** (1966), **Dangerous Songs** (1966), **Waist Deep in the Big Muddy** (1967), **Greatest Hits** (1968), **American Industrial Ballads** (1964), **Pete Seeger in Person at the Bitter End** (1964), **Freight Train** (1964), **Pete Seeger Sings Leadbelly** (1967), **3 Saints, 4 Sinners and 6 Other People** (1968, all Columbia); **Pete Seeger** (1968, Ember); **Young Vs. Old** (1969, Columbia); **Best of Pete Seeger** (1973, CBS); **Pete Seeger and Arlo Guthrie Together in Concert** (1975, Reprise) US#181; **The Essential Pete Seeger** (1976, Vanguard); **Pete Seeger Sings Woody Guthrie** (1977), **Banks of Marble** (1978), **Nativity** (1979), **Sing-a-Long Live at Sanders Theatre, 1980** (1980, all Folkways); **20 Golden Pieces of Pete Seeger** (1980, BDG); **Family Concert** (1991, Sony); **Children's Concert at Town Hall** (1992), **Folk Music of the World** (1992, both Columbia); **Live at Newport** (1993, Vanguard); **A Link in the Chain** (1996, Columbia). HIT VERSIONS: *Gotta Travel On* [ii] Billy Grammer (1959) C&W#5 R&B#14 US#4/Bill Monroe (1959) C&W#15/Timi Yuro (1963) US#64/Shylo (1978) C&W#91; *Guantanamera* [i] Sandpipers (1966) US#9 UK#7, *If I Had a Hammer* [iii] Peter, Paul & Mary (1962) US#10/Trini

Lopez (1963) R&B#12 US#3 UK#4/Wanda Jackson (1969) C&W#41; *Kisses Sweeter Than Wine* [iv] (adaptation only) Jimmie Rodgers (1957) R&B#8 US#3 UK#7/Frankie Vaughan (1957) UK#8; *Lion Sleeps Tonight, The* aka *Wimoweh* (arrangement only) Tokens (1961) g R&B#7 US#1 UK#11, new version (1994) US#51/Karl Denver (1962) UK#4/Robert John (1972) g US#3/Tight Fit (1982) UK#1; *On Top of Old Smokey* (arrangement only) Percy Faith (1951) US#10/Vaughn Monroe (1951) US#8/Lonnie Donegan in *Lonnie's Skiffle Party* (1958) UK#23; *Turn! Turn! Turn!* Byrds (1965) US#1 UK#26/Judy Collins (1969) US#69; *Where Have All the Flowers Gone* Kingston Trio (1962) US#21/Johnny Rivers (1965) US#26/Wes Montgomery (1968) US#119. Co-writers: [i] Hector Angulo/Jose Marti, [ii] Paul Clayton/Larry Ehrlich/Dave Lazer/Lee Hayes (b. 1914, Little Rock, AK; d. August 26, 1981, NY)/Fred Hellerman (b. May 13, 1927, New York, NY)/Ronnie Gilbert, [iii] Lee Hayes, [iv] Joel Newman.

855. SEGER, Bob (b. Bob Clark Seger, May 6, 1945, Ann Arbor, MI) Rock guitarist and vocalist. A rock performer whose tenacity and perseverance eventually paid off, and his many years of struggle can be heard in almost every world weary tune and enervated lyric that he has written. Seger excels at mid-tempo ballads and gritty, R&B influenced rock and roll, and is an observer and commentator on everyday American aspirations. Seger once said of his songwriting, "What I try to do is to dig in and try to find the truth in an idea." His father was a factory worker who played clarinet, but Seger was raised solely by his mother from the age of ten. After learning the guitar in his teens, Seger played in the local bands the Decibels, the Town Criers and Doug Brown's Omens. In 1961, he cut an acetate of *The Lonely One*, and recorded various demos with the group the Mushrooms, including his song *Such a Lovely Child*. As the Beach Bums, Seger cut the single *The Ballad of the Yellow Beret* (1966), and as Bob Seger and the Last Heard, he recorded for the East Side Story and Cameo labels during the mid–1960s. Seger finally cracked the top twenty with *Ramblin' Gamblin' Man* (1968), but it was not until his in-concert set **Live Bullet** (1976), that he was finally able to capture the energy of his Silver Bullet Band, and the album ultimately sold over four million copies, rather ironically winning him a best new vocalist Grammy award after over a decade of music making. The five million selling **Night Moves** (1977), was a masterful portrait of ordinary working lives and small town America, wherein economic strains often destroyed relationships and alienated teenagers. Seger's output slowed considerably in the late 1980s, and after a lengthy break from recording, he returned

with **The Fire Inside** (1991), an album threaded together by a succession of pianists, including Roy Bittan, Bruce Hornsby and Bill Payne. HIT VERSIONS: *Heavy Music* (1967) US#103, *Ramblin' Gamblin' Man* (1969) US#17, *Ivory* (1969) US#97, *Noah* (1969) US#103, *Lucifer* (1970) US#84, *Lookin' Back* (1971) US#96, *Get Out of Denver* (1974) US#80, *Katmandu* (1975) US#43, *Beautiful Loser* (1975) US#103, *Night Moves* (1977) US#4, re-issued (1995) UK#45; *Mainstreet* (1977) US#24, *Rock and Roll Never Forgets* (1977) US#41, *Still the Same* (1978) US#4, *Hollywood Nights* (1978) US#12 UK#42, re-issued (1995) UK#52; *We've Got Tonite* (1979) US#13 UK#41, re-issued (1983) US#48, re-issued (1995) UK#22; *Fire Lake* (1980) US#6, *Against the Wind* (1980) US#5, *You'll Accompany Me* (1980) US#14, *The Horizontal Bop* (1980) US#42, *Feel Like a Number* (1982) US#48, *Even Now* (1983) US#12 UK#73, *Roll Me Away* (1983) US#27, *Understanding* (1985) US#11, *American Storm* (1986) US#12 UK#77, *Like a Rock* (1986) US#12, *It's You* (1986) US#52, *Miami* (1986) US#63, *Shakedown* [i] (1987) US#1 UK#88, *The Real Love* (1991) US#24, *Lock and Load* (1996) UK#57. ALBUMS: **Ramblin' Gamblin' Man** (1969) US#62, **Noah** (1969), **Mongrel** (1970) US#171, **Brand New Morning** (1971, all Capitol); **Smokin' O.P.'s** (1972) US#180, **Back in '72** (1973, both Palladium) US#188; **Seven** (1974, Reprise); **Beautiful Loser** (1975) p US#131, **Live Bullet** (1976) p US#34, **Night Moves** (1976) p US#8, **Stranger in Town** (1978) p US#4 UK#31, **Against the Wind** (1980) p US#1 UK#26, **Nine Tonight** (1981) p US#3 UK#24, **The Distance** (1982) p US#5 UK#45, **Like a Rock** (1986) p US#3 UK#90, **The Fire Inside** (1991) p US#7 UK#54, **It's a Mystery** (1995, all Capitol) g US#27. COMPILATION: **Greatest Hits** (1995, Capitol) p US#8 UK#6. HIT VERSIONS: *Get Out of Denver* Eddie & the Hot Rods on *Live at the Marquee EP* (1976) UK#43, *Rosalie* Thin Lizzy (1978) UK#20, *We've Got Tonight* Kenny Rogers & Sheena Easton (1983) C&W#1 US#6 UK#28/Elkie Brooks (1987) UK#69. Co-writers: [i] Harold Faltermeyer (b. West Germany)/Keith Forsey. (*See also under* Don HENLEY.)

856. SETZER, Brian (b. April 10, 1960, New York, NY) Rock guitarist and vocalist. A founder member of the rockabilly trio the Stray Cats. CHART COMPOSITIONS: *Runaway Boys* (1980) UK#9, *Rock This Town* (1981) UK#9, re-issued (1982) US#9; *Stray Cat Strut* (1981) UK#11, re-issued (1983) US#3; *You Don't Believe in Me* (1981) UK#57, *(She's) Sexy and 17* (1983) US#5 UK#29, *I Won't Stand in Your Way* (1983) US#35, *Look at That Cadillac* (1984) US#68. ALBUMS: **The Stray Cats** (1981) UK#6, **Gonna Ball** (1981, both Arista) UK#48;

Rock Therapy (1986) US#122, **Blast Off** (1989, both EMI) US#111; **Original Cool** (1993, Toshiba/EMI). COMPILATIONS: **Built for Speed** (1982, EMI America) p US#2; **Rant 'N' Rave with the Stray Cats** (1983, Arista) g US#14 UK#51; **Back to the Alley — The Best of the Stray Cats** (1996, EMI). Setzer broke up the Stray Cats in 1984, in order to pursue a solo career, charting with *The Knife Feels Like Justice* (1986) US#45. ALBUMS: **The Knife Feels Like Justice** (1984, EMI America) US#45; **Live Nude Guitars** (1988, EMI Manhattan) US#140; **The Brian Setzer Orchestra** (1994) US#158, **Guitar Slinger** (1996, both Hollywood).

857. SEVILLE, David (b. Ross Bagdasarian, January 27, 1919, Fresno; d. January 16, 1972, Beverly Hills, both CA) Pop producer and vocalist. The comedy tunesmith who created the novelty act the Chipmunks, which sang in speeded-up voices and sold over thirty million records. CHART COMPOSITIONS: *The Chipmunk Song* (1958) R&B#5 US#1, re-issued (1962) US#39; *Alvin's Harmonica* (1959) US#3, *Alvin's Orchestra* (1960) US#33, *The Alvin Twist* (1962) US#40. ALBUMS: **Let's All Sing with the Chipmunks** (1959) US#4, **Sing Again with the Chipmunks** (1960) US#31, **Christmas with the Chipmunks** (1962) US#84, **The Chipmunks Sing the Beatles' Hits** (1964, all Liberty) US#14. Seville also recorded as a solo artist, charting with *Witch Doctor* (1958) R&B#1 US#1, from the album **The Witch Doctor Presents David Seville and His Friends** (1959, Liberty). HIT VERSIONS: *Come On-a My House* [i] Rosemary Clooney (1951) US#1/Richard Hayes (1951) US#14/Mickey Katz (1951) US#22/Kay Starr (1951) US#8. Co-writer: [i] William Saroyan.

858. SHAND, Terry Tin Pan Alley composer. HIT VERSIONS: *Cry, Baby, Cry* [ii] Larry Clinton (1938) US#1/Kay Kyser (1938) US#3/Dick Robertson (1938) US#9; *Dance with a Dolly (With a Hole in Her Stocking)* [iii] Evelyn Knight (1944) US#6/Russ Morgan (1944) US#3/Tony Pastor (1944) US#6/Damita Jo (1961) US#105; *I Double Dare You* [ii] Woody Herman (1937) US#18/Louis Armstrong (1938) US#18/Larry Clinton (1938) US#6/Russ Morgan (1938) US#2; *I'm Gonna Lock Away My Heart and Throw Away the Key* [ii] Henry Busse (1938) US#7/Billie Holiday (1938) US#2; *I'm So Right Tonight* [i] Jo Stafford (1947) US#21. Co-writers: [i] By Dunham, [ii] Jimmy Eaton, [iii] Jimmy Eaton/Mickey Leader.

859. SHANNON, Del (b. Charles Westover, December 30, 1934, Coopersville, MI; d. February 8, 1990, Santa Clarita Valley, CA) Pop vocal-ist. One of only a few vocalists of his era to write most of his own hits, whose million seller *Runaway* [i] has been recorded over two hundred times. Shannon committed suicide in 1990. CHART COMPOSITIONS: *Runaway* [i] (1961) R&B#3 US#1 UK#1, live version (1967) US#112; *Hats Off to Larry* (1961) US#5 UK#6, *So Long Baby* (1961) US#28 UK#10, *Hey! Little Girl* (1961) US#38 UK#2, *Cry Myself to Sleep* (1962) US#99 UK#29, *Little Town Flirt* [iii] (1963) US#12 UK#4, *Two Kinds of Teardrops* [iii] (1963) US#50 UK#5, *Two Silhouettes* (1963) UK#23, *Sue's Gotta Be Mine* (1963) US#71 UK#21, *Mary Jane* (1964) UK#35, *Keep Searchin' (We'll Follow the Sun)* (1965) US#9 UK#3, *Stranger in Town* (1965) US#30 UK#40, *Break Up* (1965) US#95, *Comin' Back to Me* [ii] (1969) US#127, *In My Arms Again* (1985) C&W#56. ALBUMS: **Runaway with Del Shannon** (1961, London); **Hats Off to Del Shannon** (1963) UK#9, **Little Town Flirt** (1963, both Big Top) US#12 UK#15; **Handy Man** (1965), **Del Shannon Sings Hank Williams** (1965), **One Thousand Six Hundred and Sixty-One Seconds with Del Shannon** (1965, all Stateside); **This Is My Bag** (1966), **Total Commitment** (1966), **The Further Adventures of Charles Westover** (1968, all Liberty); **Live in England** (1973, United Artists); **Drop Down and Get Me** (1982, Elektra) US#123; **Rock On** (1991). COMPILATIONS: **Best of Del Shannon** (1967, Dot); **Vintage Years** (1975, Sire); **Very Best of Del Shannon** (1975, Contempo); **Runaway Hits** (1984, Edsel). HIT VERSIONS: *Cheap Love* Juice Newton (1986) C&W#9, *I Go to Pieces* Peter & Gordon (1965) US#9/Cotton, Lloyd & Christian (1975) US#66/Tammy Jo (1980) C&W#88/Trisha Lynn (1988) C&W#76; *Runaway* [i] Charlie Kulis (1975) US#46/Rhodes Kids (1975) US#107/Narvel Felts (1978) C&W#30/Bonnie Raitt (1978) US#57/Luis Cardenas (1986) US#83/Bonnie Leigh (1986) C&W#76. Co-writers: [i] Max Crook, [ii] Brian Hyland, [iii] Marion McKenzie.

860. SHAVER, Billy Joe (b. September 15, 1941, Corsicana, TX) C&W guitarist and vocalist. A country tunesmith who has written material for, among others, Tom T. Hall, Dottie West, Jerry Reed and Tex Ritter. Waylon Jennings recorded an entire album of his compositions as **Honky Tonk Heroes** (1973, RCA). CHART COMPOSITIONS: *I Been to Georgia on a Fast Train* (1973) C&W#88, *You Asked Me To* [i] (1978) C&W#80. ALBUMS: **Old Five and Dimers Like Me** (1974, Monument); **When I Get My Wings** (1976), **Gypsy Boy** (1977, both Capricorn); **I'm Just a Chunk of Old Coal** (1981), **Salt of the Earth** (1987), **Hell Raisers** (1987, all Columbia). HIT VERSIONS: *I Couldn't Be Me Without You* Johnny Rodriguez (1976) C&W#3, *I'm*

Just an Old Chunk of Coal John Anderson (1981) C&W#4. Co-writer: [i] Waylon Jennings. (*See also under* Waylon JENNINGS.)

861. SHEAR, Jules (b. March 7, 1952, Pittsburgh, PA) Rock guitarist and vocalist. A singer-songwriter who first performed as a member of Jack Tempchin's group the Funky Kings, before forming Jules and the Polar Bears for the albums **Got No Breeding** (1978) and **Phonetics** (1979, both Columbia). In 1988, under the band name Reckless Sleepers, Shear recorded the album **Big Boss Sounds**. Ian Matthews recorded an album of Shear's material as **Walking a Changing Line** (1988, Windham Hill). Since the early 1980s, Shear has recorded as a solo artist. CHART COMPOSITION: *Steady* [i] (1985) US#57. ALBUMS: **Watch Dog** (1983), **The Eternal Return** (1985, both EMI America); **Demo-Itis** (1986, Enigma); **The Third Party** (1989, IRS); **The Great Puzzle** (1992, Polydor); **Entre Nous** (1997). HIT VERSIONS: *All Through the Night* Cyndi Lauper (1984) US#5 UK#64, *(Believed You Were) Lucky* [ii] 'Til Tuesday (1989) US#95, *If She Knew What She Wants* Bangles (1986) US#29 UK#31, *If We Never Meet Again* Tommy Conwell & Young Ramblers (1988) US#48. Co-writers: [i] Cyndi Lauper, [ii] Aimee Mann. (*See also under* Jack TEMPCHIN.)

862. SHELLEY, Pete (b. Peter McNeish, April 17, 1955, Bolton, England) Pop guitarist and vocalist. The lead vocalist and principal songwriter in angst-ridden, punk-rock group the Buzzcocks. CHART COMPOSITIONS: *What Do I Get* (1978) UK#37, *I Don't Mind* (1978) UK#55, *Love You More* (1978) UK#34, *Ever Fallen in Love (With Someone You Shouldn't Have)* (1978) UK#12, *Promises* (1978) UK#20, *Everybody's Happy Nowadays* (1979) UK#29, *Spiral Scratch EP* (1979) UK#31, *Are Everything/ Why She's a Girl from the Chainstore* (1980) UK#61. ALBUMS: **Another Music in a Different Kitchen** (1978) UK#15, **Love Bites** (1978) UK#13, **A Different Kind of Tension** (1979) UK#26, **Entertaining Friends** (1980, all United Artists); **Trade Test Transmissions** (1993, Essential); **The Peel Sessions Album** (1994, Strange Fruit); **French** (1995, Dojo); **Entertaining Friends** (1996, Live). COMPILATIONS: **Singles-Going Steady** (1987), **Product** (1979), **Chronology** (1997, all EMI). Shelley has also recorded as a solo artist, charting with *Telephone Operator* (1986) UK#66. ALBUMS: **Homosapien** (1986, Island) US#121; **XL-1** (1983, Genetic) US#151 UK#42; **Heaven and Sea** (1986). HIT VERSION: *Ever Fallen in Love (With Someone You Shouldn't Have)* Fine Young Cannibals (1987) UK#9.

863. SHERLEY, Glen (d. November 5, 1978, America) C&W guitarist and vocalist. A former migrant worker and country singer-songwriter of considerable promise, who was championed by Johnny Cash. Sherley's sole album was recorded while he was incarcerated, and it included his classic country-gospel hit *Greystone Chapel* (1971) C&W#63. Sherley died of self-inflicted gunshot wounds in 1978. ALBUM: **Glen Sherley** (1971, Mega).

864. SHERMAN, Al (b. September 7, 1897, Kiev, Russia; d. September 15, 1973, Los Angeles, CA) Pop composer. A Tin Pan Alley composer who collaborated with a number of his peers for a series of hits during the 1930s. HIT VERSIONS: *Comes A-Long A-Love* Kay Starr (1952) US#9 UK#1, *Mood That I'm In, The* [iii] Lionel Hampton (1937) US#20/Teddy Wilson & Billie Holiday (1937) US#8; *On a Little Bamboo Bridge* [i] Shep Fields (1937) US#10, *On the Beach at Bali Bali* [ii] Henry Allen (1936) US#18/Connee Boswell (1936) US#3/ Tommy Dorsey (1936) US#9/Shep Fields (1936) US#17/Leo Reisman (1936) US#6; *Pretending* [iv] Rudy Vallee (1929) US#10/Andy Russell (1946) US#10; *When the Organ Played "Oh Promise Me"* [ii] Emery Deutsch (1937) US#19/Guy Lombardo (1937) US#14/Bing Crosby (1938) US#5. Co-writers: [i] Archie Fletcher, [ii] Jack Meskill/Abner Silver, [iii] Abner Silver, [iv] Marty Symes. (*See also under* Joe BURKE, Buddy DE SYLVA, Al LEWIS, Charles TOBIAS.)

865. SHERMAN, Richard (b. Richard Morton Sherman, June 12, 1928, New York, NY), and **SHERMAN, Robert** (b. Robert Bernard Sherman, December 19, 1925, New York, NY) Both film and stage composers, multi-instrumentalists. Two of the most successful film theme writers in Hollywood, who have published over five hundred songs, some one hundred and fifty of which have been for the Disney studio. Richard said of their songwriting in 1992, "We're from the old school...We write the song and then hope that some wonderful, talented voice will come along and give wings to it." Born into a musical family, both were recipients of a classical music education, Robert studying the violin and Richard the piano and flute. They attended Bard College in New York, where Richard began writing music and lyrics, and composed the show score "The Primitive Angel" (1950). The Shermans were first successful with recordings of their songs by the singer Annette Funicello, and during the 1960s they became staff writers at Disney in Burbank, California, where their first hit score was the Oscar winning "Mary Poppins" (1964), the soundtrack of which sold over seven million copies, and featured *Chim Chim Cheer-ee, Feed the Birds (Tuppence a Bag)* and *Spoonful of Sugar*. They followed their initial success with other witty and melodic themes, including *The Wonderful Thing About Tiggers, Fortuosity, I Wanna Be Like You*, and *The Ugly Bug Ball*. Their short tune *It's a Small, Small World*, is played over a quarter of a million times a year at Disney's theme parks, making it the most performed composition in the world. The Shermans have also contributed to various screenplays, and produced and wrote the television special "Goldilocks" (1970), alongside the stage show "Over Here!" (1974). Their songs were also featured on the various artists albums **Stay Awake** (1988, A&M) US#119 and **Very Best of Disney** (1993, Pickwick) UK#4. ALBUMS: **Goldilocks** ost (1958, Columbia); **The Absent-Minded Professor** ost (1961), **Greyfriars Bobby** ost (1961, both Disneyland); **The Parent Trap** ost (1961, Buena Vista); **The Story of Big Red** ost (1962), **In Search of the Castaways** ost (1962, both Disneyland); **Summer Magic** ost (1963, Buena Vista); **The Sword in the Stone** ost (1963), **Hector, the Stowaway Pup** ost (1964, both Disneyland); **Mary Poppins** ost (1964, Buena Vista) g US#1 UK#2; **Story and Songs from Walt Disney's Mary Poppins** (1964, Disneyland) g; **That Darn Cat** ost (1965, Buena Vista); **Winnie the Pooh and the Honey Tree** ost (1965), **Ugly Dachshund** ost (1966), **The Story of the Gnome-Mobile** ost (1967), **The Adventures of Bullwhip Griffin** ost (1967, all Disneyland); **Chitty Chitty Bang Bang** ost (1968, United Artists) US#58 UK#10; **The One and Only, Genuine, Original Family Band** ost (1968, Buena Vista); **The Jungle Book** ost (1968, Disneyland) g US#19 UK#5; **The Happiest Millionaire** ost (1968, Buena Vista) US#166; **The Aristocats** ost (1971), **Orange Bird** ost (1971, both Disneyland); **Bedknobs and Broomsticks** ost (1971, Buena Vista); **Snoopy Come Home** ost (1972, Columbia); **Tom Sawyer** oc (1972, RD/United Artists); **Charlotte's Web** ost (1973, Paramount); **Tom Sawyer** ost (1973), **Huckleberry Finn** ost (1974, both United Artists); **Over Here!** oc (1974, Columbia) US#137; **The Slipper and the Rose (The Story of Cinderella)** ost (1976, MCA); **The Magic of Lassie** ost (1978, Peter Pan); **The Sherman Brothers — Walt Disney's Supercalifragilistic Songwriting Team** (1992, Disney). HIT VERSIONS: *Chim Chim Cheer-ee* Dick Van Dyke (1965) US#123/Burl Ives (1965) US#120/New Christy Minstrels (1965) US#81; *Chitty Chitty Bang Bang* Paul Mauriat (1969) US#76/New Christy Minstrels (1969) US#114; *It's a Small, Small World* Mike Curb Congregation (1973) US#108, *Let's Get Together* Hayley Mills (1961) US#8 UK#17, *Pineapple Princess* Annette (1960) US#11, *Supercalifragilisticexpialidocious* Julie Andrews & Dick Van Dyke (1964) US#66, *Tall Paul* [i] Annette (1959) US#7, *To the Ends of the Earth* Nat "King" Cole (1956) US#25, *You're Sixteen* Johnny Burnette (1960) US#8 UK#3/Ringo Starr (1973) g US#1 UK#4. Co-writer: [i] Dick Sherman.

866. SHERRILL, Billy (b. Philip Campbell, November 5, 1936, Winston, AL) C&W pianist, saxophonist and producer. A producer notable for his imaginative use of steel guitar and orchestral backing, whose country-pop sound made him one of the most consistently successful country producers of the 1970s. Sherrill played rockabilly during the 1950s, before forming the white soul act the Fairlanes. He wrote his first songs in Nashville in 1960, and worked as a producer for Sun Records. During the 1980s, Sherrill became head of Columbia Records' country music division. HIT VERSIONS: *Aching, Breaking Heart* George Jones (1962) C&W#5, *Almost Persuaded* [viii] David Houston (1966) C&W#1 US#24/Ben Colder as *Almost Persuaded #2* (1966) C&W#6 US#58/Etta James (1969) R&B#32 US#79/ Sherri King (1976) C&W#95/Maury Finney (1977) C&W#85/Merle Haggard (1987) C&W#58; *Apartment #9* Tammy Wynette (1966) C&W#44, *Baron, The* [vii] Dick Curless (1966) C&W#63/Johnny Cash (1981) C&W#10; *Every Time You Touch Me (I Get High)* [vi] Charlie Rich (1975) C&W#3 US#19/ Johnny Mathis on B-side of *When a Child Is Born* (1976) UK#1; *Good Things* [viii] David Houston (1973) C&W#2, *I Don't Wanna Play House* [viii] Tammy Wynette (1967) C&W#1, *I Love My Friend* [ix] Charlie Rich (1974) C&W#1 US#24, *If the World Don't End Tomorrow (I'm Comin' After You)* Doug Warren & the Rays (1960) US#107, *Kiss Away* [viii] Ronnie Dove (1978) US#25/Jody Miller (1978) C&W#65; *Let's Wait a Little Longer* [iv] Canadian Sweethearts (1968) C&W#51, *Livin' in a House Full of Love* [iv] David Houston (1965) C&W#3, *Most Beautiful Girl, The* [i] Charlie Rich (1973) g C&W#1 US#1 UK#2, *My Elusive Dreams* [iv] David Houston & Tammy Wynette (1967) C&W#1 US#89/ Charlie Rich (1975) C&W#3 US#49; *Set Me Free* [iv] Curly Putman (1967) C&W#67/Charlie Rich (1968) C&W#44/Ray Price (1969) C&W#51; *Southtown U.S.A.* Dixiebells (1964) US#15, *Stand By Your Man* [x] Tammy Wynette (1968) C&W#1 US#19, re-issued (1975) UK#1/Patti Page (1968) US#121; *Sugar Lips* [iii] Al Hirt (1964) US#30, *Sweet and Innocent* [ii] Donny Osmond (1971) g US#7, *Take Me to Your World* [viii] Tammy Wynette (1968) C&W#1, *Too Far Gone* Lucille Starr (1967) C&W#72/Joe Stampley (1973) C&W#12/Emmylou Harris (1973) C&W#73, re-issued (1979) C&W#13; *Very Special Love Song, A* [ix] Charlie Rich (1974) C&W#1 US#11, *With One Exception* David Houston (1967) C&W#1, *Your Good Girl's Gonna Go Bad* [viii] Tammy Wynette

(1967) C&W#3. Co-writers: [i] Rory Bourke/Norris Wilson, [ii] Rick Hall, [iii] Buddy Killen, [iv] Claude Putnam, [v] G. Richey/Tammy Wynette (b. Virginia Wynette Pugh, May 5, 1942, Itawamba County, MS; d. 1998), [vi] Charlie Rich (b. December 14, 1932, Colt, AK; d. 1996), [vii] P. Richey/J. Taylor, [viii] Glenn Sutton, [ix] Norris Wilson, [x] Tammy Wynette. (*See also under* Marty ROBBINS.)

867. SHOCKED, Michelle (b. Karen Michelle Johnson, 1962, USA) Pop guitarist and vocalist. A folk influenced singer-songwriter in a contemporary protest style, whose first album was recorded on a portable tape recorder. CHART COMPOSITION: *Anchorage* (1988) US#66. ALBUMS: **Texas Campfire Tapes** (1987), **Short Sharp Shocked** (1988) US#73 UK#33, **Captain Swing** (1989, all Cooking Vinyl) US#95 UK#31; **Arkansas Traveller** (1992, London) UK#46; **Kind Hearted Woman** (1996, Private). COMPILATION: **Mercury Poise: 1988–1995** (1996, Mercury).

868. SIBERRY, Jane (b. 1956, Toronto, Canada) Pop pianist, guitarist and vocalist. A self-taught musician who has experimented with different styles on each successive album. Siberry has also contributed to a number of film soundtracks, including "Until the End of the World" (1991) and "Faraway, So Close" (1993). ALBUMS: **Jane Siberry** (1981, Street); **No Borders Here** (1984), **The Speckless Sky** (1985, both Open Air) US#149; **The Walking** (1987, Duke Street); **Bound By the Beauty** (1989), **When I Was a Boy** (1993), **Maria** (1995, all Reprise); **Teenager** (1997, Sheeba). COMPILATIONS: **Summer in the Yukon** (1992, Reprise); **A Collection, 1984–1989** (1993, Duke Street).

869. SIEBEL, Paul (b. America) Folk guitarist and vocalist. A folk based singer-songwriter whose songs have been recorded by the singers Emmylou Harris, Bonnie Raitt and Jerry Jeff Walker. ALBUMS: **Woodsmoke and Oranges** (1970), **Jack-Knife Gypsy** (1971, both Elektra); **Live** with David Bromberg and Gary White (1981, Rag Baby).

870. SIFFRE, Labi (b. London, England) Pop guitarist and vocalist. A former cab driver whose folk and soul influenced material was briefly popular during the early 1970s. HIT COMPOSITIONS: *It Must Be Love* (1971) UK#14, *Crying, Laughing, Loving, Lying* (1972) UK#11, *Watch Me* (1972) UK#29, *(Something Inside) So Strong* (1987) R&B#49 UK#4, *Nothin's Gonna Change* (1987) UK#52. ALBUMS: **The Singer and the Song** (1971) UK#47, **Crying, Laughing, Loving, Lying** (1972, both Pye) UK#42; **So Strong** (1988, Polydor). COMPILA-

TIONS: **The Labi Siffre Collection** (1986, Conifer); **Make My Day** (1989), **Labi Siffre** (1989, both Connoisseur); **It Must Be Love — The Classic Songs** (1994, Music Club). HIT VERSION: *It Must Be Love* Madness (1982) UK#4.

871. SIGLER, Bunny (b. Walter Sigler, March 27, 1941, Philadelphia, PA) R&B multi-instrumentalist, producer and vocalist. After singing in the 1950s group the Opals, Sigler became a solo artist in the mid–1960s, later working at Kenny Gamble and Leon Huff's Philadelphia International label as a writer and producer. CHART COMPOSITIONS: *Keep Smilin'* [vi] (1974) R&B#46, *That's How Long I'll Be Loving You* (1975) US#102, *Let Me Party with You (Party, Party, Party) (Part 1)* [iii] (1978) R&B#8 US#43, *Only You* with Loleatta Holloway (1978) R&B#11 US#87. ALBUMS: **Let the Good Times Roll** (1965, Cameo Parkway); **That's How Long I'll Be Loving You** (1974), **Keep Smilin'** (1974), **My Music** (1977, all Philadelphia International); **Let Me Party with You** (1978) US#77, **I've Always Wanted to Sing…Not Just Write Songs** (1979) US#119, **Let It Snow** (1980, all Gold Mind). HIT VERSIONS: *Don't Take Your Love* [vi] Manhattans (1974) R&B#7 US#37, *Free Man* South Shore Commission (1975) R&B#9 US#61, *Good Things Don't Last Forever* [v] Ecstacy, Passion & Pain (1974) R&B#14 US#93, *Keep Smilin'* [iv] Gabor Szabo (1976) R&B#77, *Let Me Make Love to You* [iv] O'Jays (1975) R&B#10 US#75, *Mother for My Children, A* [i] Whispers (1974) R&B#32 US#92, *Say It Again* [ii] Jermaine Stewart (1988) R&B#15 US#27 UK#7, *Sunshine (Part 2)* [vii] O'Jays (1974) R&B#17 US#48, *Sweet Charlie Babe* [vii] Jackie Moore (1973) R&B#15 US#42, *Train Called Freedom* [viii] South Shore Commission (1976) R&B#35 US#86. Co-writers: [i] Ron Baker/Norman Harris, [ii] Carol Davis, [iii] R. Earl/K. Miller/S. Miller, [iv] Alan Felder, [v] Alan Felder/Norman Harris, [vi] Alan Felder/R. Kensey, [vii] Phil Hurtt, [viii] R. Tyson.

872. SIGMAN, Carl (b. 1909, England) Film and stage lyricist. A songwriter who specialized in translating European hits into English. Sigman's compositions were also featured in such films as "The Seven Hills of Rome" (1956) and "Love Story" (1971), alongside the show "Angel in the Wings" (1948). HIT VERSIONS: *Answer Me (My Love)* [xxi] Frankie Laine (1953) US#24 UK#1/David Whitfield (1953) UK#1/Nat "King" Cole (1954) US#6/Ray Peterson (1960) UK#47/Barbara Dickson (1976) UK#9; *Arrivederci Darling (Arrivederci Roma)* [x] Anne Shelton (1955) UK#17/Edna Savage (1956) UK#19/Roger Williams (1958) US#55; *Ballerina* [xxii] Vaughn Monroe (1947) g US#1/Buddy Clark (1948) US#5/

Bing Crosby (1948) US#10/Jimmy Dorsey (1948) US#10/Nat "King" Cole (1957) US#18; *Buona Sera* [viii] Louis Prima (1958) UK#25/Acker Bilk (1960) UK#7; *Creep, The* [v] Stan Kenton (1954) US#28/Ken MacKintosh (1954) UK#10/Ralph Marterie (1954) US#25/Three Suns (1954) US#22; *Day in the Life of a Fool, A* [iii] Jack Jones (1966) US#62, *Dream Along with Me (I'm on My Way to a Star)* Perry Como (1955) US#85, *Ebb Tide* [xix] Frank Chacksfield (1953) US#2 UK#9/Vic Damone (1953) US#10/Roy Hamilton (1954) R&B#5 US#30, re-issued (1959) US#105/Platters (1960) US#56/Lenny Welch (1964) US#25/Righteous Brothers (1965) R&B#13 US#5, re-issued (1990) UK#3; *11th Hour Melody* [xviii] Lou Busch (1956) US#35/Al Hibbler (1956) US#21; *Enjoy Yourself (It's Later Than You Think)* [xv] Doris Day (1950) US#24/Guy Lombardo (1950) US#10; *Fool* [xiv] Elvis Presley (1973), *Funny Thing* [xxiii] Tony Bennett (1954) US#24, *Hop-Scotch Polka* [xix] Guy Lombardo (1949) US#16/Art Mooney (1949) US#16; *It's All in the Game* [vi] Tommy Edwards (1951) US#18, re-issued (1958) C&W#1 R&B#1 US#1 UK#1/Cliff Richard (1963) US#25 UK#2/Jackie DeShannon (1967) US#110/Four Tops (1970) R&B#6 US#24 UK#5/Jerry Jaye (1975) C&W#53/Tom T. Hall (1977) C&W#12/Isaac Hayes (1980) R&B#86 US#107; *Losing You* [xx] Brenda Lee (1963) US#6 UK#10/Dusty Springfield (1964) UK#9; *Love Lies* [xi] Tommy Dorsey (1940) US#17, *Marshmellow World* [viii] Bing Crosby (1951) US#24, *Matinee* [xxii] Buddy Clark (1948) US#22/Vaughn Monroe (1948) US#20; *My Heart Cries for You* [ix] Vic Damone (1951) US#4/Bill Farrell (1951) US#18/Red Foley & Evelyn Knight (1951) C&W#6 US#28/Guy Mitchell (1951) g US#2/Al Morgan (1951) US#24/Dinah Shore (1951) US#3/Jimmy Wakely (1951) C&W#7 US#12/Victor Young (1951) US#29/Ray Charles (1964) US#38/Connie Francis (1967) US#118/Dolly Holly (1972) C&W#63/Margo Smith (1981) C&W#72; *Pennsylvania 6-5000* [xii] Glenn Miller (1940) US#5, *Right Now* [xvii] Herbie Mann (1962) US#111/Creatures (1983) UK#14; *Robin Hood* Dick James (1956) UK#14/Gary Miller (1956) UK#10; *Shangri-La* [xvi] Four Coins (1957) US#11/Vic Dana (1964) US#27/Robert Maxwell, His Harp & Orchestra (1964) US#15/Lettermen (1969) US#64; *Till* [vii] Roger Williams (1957) US#22/Tony Bennett (1961) UK#35/Angels (1962) US#14/Vogues (1968) US#27/Dorothy Squires (1970) UK#25/Tom Jones (1971) UK#2; *Twenty-Four Hours of Sunshine* [viii] Art Mooney (1949) US#13, *Where Do I Begin (Theme from Love Story)* [xiii] Henry Mancini (1971) US#13/Francis Lai (1971) US#31/Shirley Bassey (1971) UK#34/Andy Williams (1971) US#9 UK#4; *Willingly* [iv] Malcolm Vaughan (1959) UK#28, *World Outside, The* [i] Four Coins (1958) US#21/Russ Conway (1959) UK#24/Four Aces

(1959) UK#18/Ronnie Hilton (1959) UK#18/Roger Williams (1960) US#71; *You're My World* [ii] Cilla Black (1964) US#26 UK#1/Helen Reddy (1977) US#17. Co-writers: [i] Richard Addinsell, [ii] Umberto Bindi/Gino Paoli, [iii] Luis Bonfa, [iv] Jean Brousolle/Hubert Giraud, [v] Andy Burton, [vi] Charles Dawes, [vii] Charles Danvers, [viii] Peter DeRose, [ix] Percy Faith, [x] Jack Fishman/S. Giovannini/Renato Rascel, [xi] Ralph Freed/Joseph Meyer, [xii] Jerry Gray, [xiii] Francis Lai, [xiv] James Last, [xv] Herb Magidson, [xvi] Matty Malneck/Robert Maxwell, [xvii] Herbie Mann, [xix] Robert Maxwell, [xviii] King Palmer, [xix] Gene Rayburn/William Whitlock, [xx] Jean Renard, [xxi] Fred Rouch/Gerhard Winkler, [xxii] Bob Russell, [xxiii] Arthur Williams. (*See also under* Gilbert BECAUD, Bob HILLIARD, Bert KAEMPFERT.)

873. SILVER, Abner (b. 1899; d. 1966) Tin Pan Alley composer. A consistently successful collaborator with many composers of his day, who also wrote the Vera Lynne favorite *How Green Was My Valley* [iv] (1942). Silver's songs were included in the musicals "Kid Boots" (1921) and "Spice of Life" (1922). HIT VERSIONS: *Angel Child* [ii] Al Jolson (1922) US#1/Ben Selvin (1922) US#7; *C'est Vous (It's You)* [v] Harry Richman (1927) US#11, *Chasing Shadows* [iv] Dorsey Brothers Orchestra (1935) US#1/Henry King (1935) US#7/Enric Madriguera (1935) US#11/Louis Prima (1935) US#14; *My Love for You* [vi] Johnny Mathis (1960) US#47 UK#9, *Puh-Leeze, Mr. Hemingway* [iii] Guy Lombardo (1932) US#5, *Say It While Dancing* [i] Benson Orchestra of Chicago (1922) US#4/Isham Jones (1922) US#10; *There Goes My Heart* [i] Enric Madriguera (1934) US#13, *With These Hands* [i] Eddie Fisher (1953) US#7/Johnnie Ray (1953) US#29/Shirley Bassey (1960) UK#41/Tom Jones (1965) US#27 UK#13. Co-writers: [i] Benny Davis, [ii] Benny Davis/George Price, [iii] Milton Drake/Walter Kent, [iv] Benny Green, [v] Abner Greenberg/Harry Richman, [vi] Sid Wayne. (*See also under* Sam COSLOW, Billy ROSE, Al SHERMAN, Harry WOODS, Alex WRUBEL.)

874. SILVERSTEIN, Shel (b. 1932, Chicago, IL) Pop guitarist and vocalist. A country influenced composer of comedy material, who wrote many of Dr. Hook and the Medicine Show's biggest hits. During the 1960s Silverstein played with the Red Onion Jazz Band, worked as a cartoonist for the magazine *Village Voice*, and wrote the books *Where the Sidewalk Ends* and *A Light in the Attic*. Throughout the 1960s, he was the bald-headed, resident hippie at Hugh Hefner's Playboy mansion, and a regular contributor to the magazine. Silverstein achieved his first big hit when Johnny Cash recorded *A Boy Named Sue* (1969). Two entire albums of Silverstein songs have been recorded, **Bobby Bare Sings Lullabies, Legends, and Lies, Singing in the Kitchen** (1974, RCA), and Tompall Glaser's **The Songs of Shel Silverstein** (1977, MGM). CHART COMPOSITION: *Sarah Cynthia Sylvia Stout (Would Not Take the Garbage Out)* (1973) US#107. ALBUMS: **Hairy Jazz** (1961, Elektra); **Inside Folk Music** (1962, Atlantic); **I'm So Good I Don't Have to Brag** (1966), **Drain My Brain** (1966, both Cadet); **A Boy Named Sue** (1968, RCA); **Freakin' at the Freakers Ball** (1969) US#155, **Where the Sidewalk Ends** (1970), **Who Is Harry Kellerman and Why Is He Saying Those Terrible Things About Me?** (1971, all Columbia); **Crouching on the Outside** (1971, Janus); **Inside Shel Silverstein** (1970, Atlantic); **Great Conch Train Robbery** (1980, Flying Fish); **Songs and Stories** (1972, Parachute). HIT VERSIONS: *All the Time in the World* Dr. Hook (1978) C&W#82 US#54, *Ballad of Lucy Jordan, The* Marianne Faithfull (1980) UK#48, *Boy Named Sue, A* Johnny Cash (1969) C&W#1 UK#3, *Couple More Years, A* Dr. Hook (1976) C&W#51, *Cover of the Rolling Stone, The* Dr. Hook & the Medicine Show (1973) g US#6/Buck Owens as *On the Cover of the Music City News* (1974) C&W#9; *Daddy What If* Bobby Bare (1973) US#41, *Here I Am Again* Loretta Lynn (1972) C&W#3, *Hey Loretta* Loretta Lynn (1974) C&W#3, *Life Ain't Easy* [i] Dr. Hook (1973) US#68, *Marie Lavaux* Bobby Bare (1974) C&W#1, *More Like the Movies* Dr. Hook (1977) UK#14, *One's on the Way* Loretta Lynn (1972) C&W#1, *Penicillin Penny* Dr. Hook (1973) US#68, *Queen of the Silver Dollar* Doyle Holly (1973) C&W#29/Dave & Sugar (1975) C&W#25; *Radio, The* Dr. Hook (1977) UK#14, *Roland the Roadie and Gertrude the Groupie* Dr. Hook & the Medicine Show (1973) US#83, *Singin' in the Kitchen* Bobby Bare (1974) C&W#29, *Sylvia's Mother* Bobby Bare (1972) C&W#12/Dr. Hook & the Medicine Show (1972) g US#5 UK#2; *Tequila Sheila* Bobby Bare (1980) C&W#31, *Unicorn, The* Irish Rovers (1968) US#7. Co-writer: [i] Ray Sawyer (b. February 1, 1937, Chickasaw, AL).

875. SIMMONS, Patrick (b. January 23, 1950, Aberdeen, WA) Rock guitarist and vocalist. A founder member of the rock group the Doobie Brothers, which charted with his compositions *Black Water* (1974) g US#1, *I Cheat the Hangman* (1975) US#60, *Wheels of Fortune* [i] (1976) US#87, and *Echoes of Love* [ii] (1977) US#66. Simmons also charted as a solo artist with the single *So Wrong* [iii] (1983) US#66, from the album **Arcade** (1983, Elektra) US#52. Co-writers: [i] Jeff Baxter (b. December 13, 1948, Washington, DC)/John Hartman (b. March 18, 1950, Falls Church, VA), [ii] Willie Mitchell/Earl Randle, [iii] C. Thompson. (*See also under* Tom JOHNSTON, Michael McDONALD.)

876. SIMON, Carly (b. June 25, 1945, New York, NY) Pop vocalist. A singer-songwriter whose light, mid-tempo ballads often investigate middle-class domesticity from a strangely unimpassioned distance. The daughter of the co-founder of the publishing house Simon and Schuster, Simon first sang with her sister Lucy as the Simon Sisters. Between 1972–1982, she was married to the singer James Taylor. Simon has also contributed to the films "The Spy Who Loved Me" (1977), "Soup for One" (1982), "Nothing in Common" (1986), and "Sleepless in Seattle" (1993). CHART COMPOSITIONS: *That's The Way I've Always Heard It Should Be* (1971) US#10, *Anticipation* (1972) US#13, *Legend in His Own Time* (1972) US#50, *You're So Vain* (1972) g US#1 UK#3, re-issued (1991) UK#41; *The Right Thing to Do* (1973) US#17 UK#17, *Haven't Got Time for the Pain* [i] (1974) US#14, *Attitude Dancing* [i] (1975) US#21, *Waterfall* (1975) US#78, *You Belong to Me* [iv] (1978) US#6, *Vengeance* (1979) US#48, *Jesse* [vi] (1980) g US#11, *Take Me as I Am* (1980) US#102, *Hurt* (1981) US#106, *You Know What to Do* [iii] (1983) US#83, *Coming Round Again* (1986) US#18 UK#10, *Give Me All Night* [v] (1987) US#61, *All I Want Is You* [ii] (1986) US#54, *Let the River Run* (1989) US#49. ALBUMS: **Cuddlebug*** (1964, Kapp); **The Simon Sisters Sing the Lobster Quadrille and Other Children's Songs*** (1969, Columbia); **Carly Simon** (1971) US#30, **Anticipation** (1971) g US#30, **No Secrets** (1972) g US#1 UK#3, **Hot Cakes** (1974) g US#3 UK#19, **Playing Possum** (1975) US#10, **Another Passenger** (1976) US#29, **Boys in the Trees** (1978) p US#10, **Spy** (1979, all Elektra) US#45; **Come Upstairs** (1980) US#36, **Torch** (1981) US#50, **Hello Big Man** (1983, all Warner Brothers) US#69; **Spoiled Girl** (1985, Epic) US#88; **Coming Round Again** (1987) p US#25 UK#25, **Greatest Hits Live** (1988) g US#87 UK#49, **My Romance** (1990) US#46, **Have You Seen Me Lately?** (1991, all Arista) US#60; **This Is My Life** ost (1992, Qwest); **Romulus — A Family Opera** (1992, Angel); **Letters Never Sent** (1994, Arista) US#129. COMPILATIONS: **Best of Carly Simon** (1975, Elektra) g US#17; **Clouds in My Coffee, 1965–1995** (1995, Arista). With: * Lucy Simon. Co-writers: [i] Jacob Brackman, [ii] Jacob Brackman/Andy Goldmark, [iii] Jacob Brackman/Mike Mainieri (b. July 24, 1938, New York, NY)/P. Wood, [iv] Michael McDonald, [v] McMahon, [vi] Mike Mainieri. (*See also under* Michael McDONALD.)

877. **SIMON, Paul** (b. Paul Frederick Simon, October 13, 1941, Newark, NJ) Pop guitarist, producer and vocalist. One of very few singer-songwriters to have genuinely developed the popular song of the late 1950s into a valid art form. Simon's compositions are literate, honest and perceptive evaluations of the human condition, and have sold over sixty million records. Simon's parents were of Hungarian and Jewish decent, and his father was a bass player and session musician. He grew up in Queens, New York, where he befriended the singer Art Garfunkel at high school after performing in a school production of "Alice in Wonderland." Simon began writing songs in 1955, his first copyright being *The Girl Is for Me*. In 1957, he and Garfunkel formed the duo Tom and Jerry, but their chart career was short-lived and the pair eventually drifted apart, after which, Simon issued a number of pseudonymous solo singles before studying English at Queens College, where he and Carole King once recorded demo tapes as the Cosines. Inspired by the growing folk movement, Simon began performing in the folk clubs of Greenwich Village, before visiting England in 1964, where he met, and was influenced by, the folk guitarist Martin Carthy. A since disowned solo album **The Paul Simon Songbook** (1965), was followed by a re-formation with Garfunkel as Simon and Garfunkel, whose early recordings were clearly influenced by the Everly Brothers. When their record label added an electrified backing to Simon's song *The Sound of Silence*, Simon and Garfunkel scored their first major hit. The duo peaked with the eleven million selling **Bridge Over Troubled Water** (1970), an album that featured three million selling singles and displayed Simon's increasing interest in worldwide traditional sounds, as evidenced by his arrangement of the Peruvian folk tune *El Condor Pasa*. The recording of the album proved such a strain on their friendship and musical relationship, that Simon and Garfunkel subsequently split up. In 1993, Simon said of his initial feelings about going solo, "I thought, if Simon and Garfunkel is all about the voices and not the songs, so much for my career." As a solo artist, Simon set about exploring reggae, blues, ragtime, gospel, dixieland and jazz, over a succession of fine albums. By **Hearts and Bones** (1983), he had moved away from structured songs to a more sketch-like approach, working in dialogues and a delineating style. In 1984, a friend gave Simon an unlabeled tape cassette that contained a selection of South African musical pieces. They so captured his imagination that he visited the country in order to discover more of the music, which ultimately resulted in him being invited to Johannesburg to record with some of the musicians on the mystery tape. The move brought him into conflict with the United Na-

tions and various anti-apartheid groups, and at first it seemed that Simon was jeopardizing both his integrity and credibility, but the results of the musical union between American pop and South African township jive and its native rhythms, unwittingly became one of the first in a rapid series of events that led to the dismantling of South African apartheid entirely. Simon's resultant ten million seller **Graceland** (1986), was a landmark release, a headlong meeting of the sounds and rhythms of two continents. **Graceland** altered the course of popular music and introduced, to a new audience, music that had rarely been heard outside of South Africa, and in the final analysis, the album displayed just how far ahead musicians and much of their audience were of self-serving governments and political leaders. Simon subsequently toured behind the record, creating the first genuinely international pop group, that included the South African exiles Mariam Makeba and Hugh Masekela. His follow up **Rhythm of the Saints** (1990), explored the rhythms of South America in a brooding selection of tone poems. Simon's live set **Concert in Central Park** (1991), was highlighted by the track *The Cool, Cool Water*, a quiet revolution in the development of the contemporary song, that was a philosophical ramble over a panoramic soundscape in 9/8 time, set to a West African fighting rhythm in a Joseph Conrad-styled journey back in time. Simon has recorded very little during the 1990s, although he was reported to be collaborating with the writer Derek Walcott on a musical. The Boston Pops Orchestra recorded an orchestral set of Simon arrangements as **The Music of Paul Simon** (1972, Polydor) US#196. CHART COMPOSITIONS: *Hey Schoolgirl* [i]* as Tom and Jerry (1957) US#49, *Motor-cycle* as Tico and the Triumphs (1963) US#99, *Lone Teen Ranger* as Jerry Landis (1963) US#97, *The Sound of Silence* * (1965) g US#1, *Homeward Bound* * (1966) US#5 UK#9, *That's My Story* * as Tom and Jerry (1966) US#123, *I am a Rock* * (1966) US#3 UK#17, *The Dangling Conversation* * (1967) US#25, *A Hazy Shade of Winter* * (1967) US#13, *At the Zoo* * (1967) US#16, *Fakin' It* * (1967) US#23, *Scarborough Fair/Canticle* * (arrangement and counter melody only) (1968) US#11, *Mrs. Robinson* * (1968) g US#1 UK#4, *Mrs. Robinson/Scarborough Fair/Canticle/ The Sound of Silence/April Come She Will* * (1969) UK#9, *The Boxer* * (1969) US#7 UK#6, re-issued (1992) UK##75; *Baby Driver* * (1969) US#101, *Bridge Over Troubled Water* * (1969) g US#1 UK#1, re-entry (1970) UK#45; *Cecilia* * (1970) g US#4, *For Emily, Wherever I May Find Her* * (1972) US#53, *America* * (1972) US#97 UK#25, *Mother and Child Re-union* (1972) US#4 UK#5, *Me and Julio Down By the Schoolyard* (1972) US#22 UK#15, *Duncan* (1972) US#52, *Kodachrome* (1973) g US#2, *Take Me to the Mardi Gras*

(1973) UK#7, *Love Me Like a Rock* (1973) US#2 UK#39, *American Tune* (1974) US#35, *Gone at Last* with Phoebe Snow (1975) US#23, *My Little Town** (1975) US#9, *50 Ways to Leave Your Lover* (1976) g US#1 UK#23, *Still Crazy After All These Years* (1976) US#40, *Slip Slidin' Away* (1977) US#5 UK#36, *Late in the Evening* (1980) US#6 UK#58, *One Trick Pony* (1980) US#40, *Allergies* (1983) US#44, *You Can Call Me Al* (1986) US#44 UK#4, re-issued (1987) US#23; *The Boy in the Bubble* [ii] (1987) US#86 UK#26, *Graceland* (1987) US#81, *The Obvious Child* (1990) US#92 UK#15, *A Hazy Shade of Winter/Seven O'-Clock News** (1991) UK#30, *Something So Right* with Annie Lennox (1995) UK#44. ALBUMS: **The Paul Simon Songbook** (1965, CBS); **Wednesday Morning, 3: A.M.*** (1965) g US#30 UK#24, **Sounds of Silence*** (1966) g US#21 UK#13, **Parsley, Sage, Rosemary and Thyme*** (1966) p US#4 UK#13, **Bookends*** (1968) p US#1 UK#1, **The Graduate** ost* (1968) g US#1 UK#3, **Bridge Over Troubled Water*** (1970) p US#1 UK#1, **Paul Simon** (1972) p US#4 UK#1, **There Goes Rhymin' Simon** (1973) p US#2 UK#4, **Live Rhymin'** (1974) g US#33, **Still Crazy After All These Years** (1975, all Columbia) p US#1 UK#11; **One Trick Pony** ost (1980) g US#12 UK#17, **The Concert in Central Park*** (1982) p US#6 US#6, **Hearts and Bones** (1983) US#35 UK#34, **Graceland** (1986) p US#3 US#1, **The Rhythm of the Saints** (1990) p US#4 UK#1, **The Concert in the Park** (1991, all Warner Brothers) US#74 UK#60. COMPILATIONS: **Early Songs** (1965, Crest); **Simon and Garfunkel*** (1967, Allegro); **Greatest Hits*** (1972, Columbia) p US#5 UK#2; **The Simon and Garfunkel Collection** (1981, CBS) UK#4; **Greatest Hits, Etc.** (1977, Columbia) p US#18 UK#6; **Negotiations and Love Songs, 1971–1986** (1988, Warner Brothers) p US#110 UK#17; **The Definitive Simon and Garfunkel*** (1991) UK#8, **Collected Works** (1992, both Columbia) g; **Paul Simon, 1964–1993*** (1993) g US#173, **Anthology** (1993, both Warner Brothers). HIT VERSIONS: *America* Yes (1975) US#46, *Boxer, The* Emmylou Harris (1980) C&W#13, *Bridge Over Troubled Water* Aretha Franklin (1971) g R&B#1 US#6/Buck Owens (1971) C&W#9 US#119/Linda Clifford (1979) R&B#49 US#41 UK#28/PJB (1991) UK#21; *Cecilia* Times Two (1988) US#79/Suggs featuring Louchie Lou & Michie One (1996) UK#4; *El Condor Pasa* (English lyric only) Julie Felix (1970) UK#19, *59th Street Bridge Song (Feelin' Groovy)* Harper's Bizarre (1967) US#13 UK#34/Southwest F.O.B. (1970) US#115; *50 Ways to Leave Your Lover* Bob Yarbrough (1976) C&W#85/Sonny Curtis (1980) C&W#70; *Gone at Last* Johnny Paycheck & Charnissa (1976) C&W#49, *Graceland* Willie Nelson (1993) C&W#70, *Hazy Shade of Winter, A* Ban-

gles (1987) US#2 UK#11, *Homeward Bound* Quiet Five (1966) UK#44/Brenda Bers (1970) C&W#66; *I Wish You Could Be Here* Cyrkle (1967) US#70, *Keep the Customer Satisfied* Marsha Hunt (1970) US#41/Gary Puckett (1971) US#71; *Loves Me Like a Rock* Dixie Hummingbirds (1973) R&B#72, *Mrs. Robinson* Booker T. & the M.G.'s (1969) US#37, also on B-side of *Soul Clap '69* (1969) UK#35/Lemonheads (1992) US#118 UK#19; *Only Living Boy in New York, The* Everything But the Girl (1993) UK#42, *Red Rubber Ball* [iii] Cyrkle (1966) US#2, *Scarborough Fair/Canticle* (arrangement and counter melody only) Sergio Mendes & Brazil '66 (1968) US#16/Alan Copeland Singers (1969) US#123; *Someday, One Day* Seekers (1966) UK#44, *Sound of Silence, The* Bachelors (1966) UK#3/Peaches & Herb (1971) US#100; *Take Me to the Mardi Gras* TLC sampled in *Ain't 2 Proud 2 Beg* (1992) p R&B#1 US#6 UK#13. With: * Art Garfunkel. Co-writers: [i] Art Garfunkel (b. Arthur Garfunkel, November 5, 1941, Forest Hills, NY), [ii] Forere Montloheloa, [iii] Bruce Woodley.

878. SINFIELD, Pete (b. England) Rock producer and vocalist. A former King Crimson road manager who wrote J.R.R. Tolkien–styled lyrics on the group's albums **In the Court of the Crimson King** (1969) US#28 UK#5, **In the Wake of Poseidon** (1970) US#31 UK#4, **Lizard** (1970) US#113 UK#30, and **Islands** (1971, all Island) US#76 UK#30. Sinfield recorded as a solo artist before becoming a successful mainstream pop writer. ALBUM: **Still** (1973, Manticore) US#190. HIT VERSION: *Rain or Shine* [i] Five Star (1986) UK#2. Co-writer: [i] Bill Livesy. (*See also under* Andy HILL, Greg LAKE.)

879. SISSLE, Noble (b. Noble Lee Sissle, July 10, 1889, Indianapolis, IN; d. December 17, 1975, Tampa, FL) Jazz bandleader and vocalist. A vaudeville performer who partnered Eubie Blake. Sissle also worked in France in 1927, where he presided over the twelve-piece Orchestra O Belgium. Sissle led other bands throughout the 1930s, and later became a publisher. ALBUM: **Basement Blues** (1931, Brunswick). (*See also under* Eubie BLAKE.)

880. SKELLERN, Peter (b. 1947, Bury, England) Pop pianist and vocalist. A graduate of the Guildhall College of Music, London, who performed as a pianist before joining the rock group Harlan County. Skellern's solo career was essentially an affectionate pastiche of Hoagy Carmichael. CHART COMPOSITIONS: *You're a Lady* (1972) UK#3, *Hold on to Love* (1975) US#106 UK#14. ALBUMS: **Not Without a Friend** (1973), **Holding My Own** (1974, both Decca); **Hard Times** (1975, Island);

Kissing in the Cactus (1977), **Skellern** (1978) UK#48, **Astaire** (1979) UK#23, **A String of Pearls** (1982, all Mercury) UK#67; **Stardust Memories** (1995, WEA) UK#50. HIT VERSION: *You're a Lady* Dawn (1973) US#70.

881. SKY, Patrick (b. October 2, 1940, Liveoak Gardens, GA) Folk guitarist and vocalist. A native American singer-songwriter, whose composition *Many a Mile* was recorded by Buffy Sainte-Marie. ALBUMS: **Patrick Sky** (1965), **A Harvest Of Gentle Clang** (1966, both Vanguard); **Reality Is Bad Enough** (1968), **Photographs** (1969, both Verve); **Songs That Made America Famous** (1973, Adelphi); **Two Steps Forward, One Step Back** (1975, Leviathan).

882. SKYLAR, Sunny Film composer. A Tin Pan Alley tunesmith whose songs were included in such films as "Broadway Rhythm" (1943). HIT VERSIONS: *Amor* [xi] Bing Crosby (1944) US#2/ Xavier Cugat (1944) US#10/Andy Russell (1944) US#5/Four Aces (1954) US#21/Roger Williams (1962) US#88; *And So to Sleep Again* [viii] Dick Haymes (1951) US#28/Patti Page (1951) US#4/April Stevens (1951) US#27/Paul Weston (1951) US#30; *Ask Me* [iv] Nat "King" Cole (1956) US#18, *Atlanta, G.A.* [xii] Woody Herman (1946) US#11/Sammy Kaye (1946) US#6; *Be Mine* [vii] Anne Shelton (1949) US#25, *Besame Mucho (Kiss Me)* [xiii] Jimmy Dorsey (1944) g US#1/Abe Lyman (1944) US#21/Andy Russell (1944) US#10/Jet Harris (1962) US#22; *Don't Wait Too Long* Tony Bennett (1963) US#54, *Fifteen Minute Intermission* [ii] Cab Calloway (1940) US#23, *Gotta Be This or That* Benny Goodman (1945) US#2/ Glen Gray (1945) US#9/Sammy Kaye (1945) US#6; *Hair of Gold, Eyes of Blue* Bob Eberly (1948) US#25/ Jack Emerson (1948) US#18/Harmonicats (1948) US#15/Jack Lathrop (1948) US#19/John Laurenz (1948) US#22/Art Lund (1948) US#20/Gordon MacRae (1948) US#7; *It Must Be Jelly ('Cause Jam Don't Shake Like That)* [ix] Glenn Miller (1944) US#12, *It's All Over Now* [x] Frankie Carle (1946) US#6/Peggy Lee (1946) US#10; *Just a Little Bit South of North Carolina* [iii] Mitchell Ayres (1941) US#11/ Gene Krupa (1941) US#4; *Pussy Cat* [vi] Ames Brothers (1958) US#17, *Ruby-Du-Du* [xiv] Tobin Matthews & Co. (1960) US#30, *Waitin' for the Train to Come In* [i] Harry James (1945) US#6/Peggy Lee (1945) US#4/Johnny Long (1945) US#7; *You're Breaking My Heart* [v] Russ Case (1949) US#26/Buddy Clarke (1949) US#4/Vic Damone (1949) g US#1/Ralph Flanagan (1949) US#14/Jan Garber (1949) US#19/ Ink Spots (1949) US#9. Co-writers: [i] Martin Block, [ii] Bette Cannon, [iii] Bette Cannon/Arthur Shaftel, [iv] Heino Gaze, [v] Pat Genaro, [vi] Tom Glazer, [vii] Maria Teresa Lara, [viii] Joe Marsala, [ix] J.C. McGregor/George Williams, [x] Don Marcotte, [xi] Ricardo Mendez/Gabriel Ruiz, [xii] Arthur Shaftel, [xiii] Consuelo Velasquez, [xiv] Charles Wolcott.

883. SLOAN, P.F. (b. Phillip Sloan, 1947, Los Angles, CA) Pop guitarist, producer and vocalist. A writer and producer, alongside Steve Barri, at the ABC/Dunhill label during the 1960s, specializing in electrified folk protest songs and the occasional surf number. The duo also recorded as the group the Fantastic Baggies, releasing the album **Tell 'Em I'm Surfin'** (1964, Imperial), and the compilations **Surfin' Craze** (1983, Edsel) and **Best of the Fantastic Baggies** (1990, EMI). Sloan has also recorded as a solo artist. CHART COMPOSITIONS: *The Sins of a Family* (1965) US#87 UK#38, *From a Distance* (1966) US#109. ALBUMS: **Songs of Our Time** (1965), **12 More Times** (1966, both Dunhill); **Measure of Pleasure** (1968, Atco); **Raised on Records** (1972, Mums); **Serenade of the Seven Sisters** (1993, Japan). COMPILATION: **Precious Times — The Best of P.F. Sloan, 1965–1966** (1990, Rhino); **The Rincon Surfside Band** (1995, Varese Sarabande); **P.F. Sloan (Still on the) Eve of Destruction** (1997, All the Best). HIT VERSIONS: *Another Day, Another Heartache* [i] 5th Dimension (1967) US#45, *Eve of Destruction* [i] Barry McGuire (1965) US#1 UK#3/Turtles (1970) US#100/Stars On in *Stars on 45, Volume 2* (1981) UK#18; *(Here They Come) From All Over the World* [i] Jan & Dean (1965) US#56, *I Found a Girl* [i] Jan & Dean (1965) US#30, *Let Me Be* [i] Turtles (1965) US#29, *Must to Avoid, A* [i] Herman's Hermits (1966) US#8 UK#6, *Only When You're Lonely* [i] Grass Roots (1966) US#96, *Take Me for What I'm Worth* [i] Searchers (1966) US#76 UK#20, *Things I Should Have Said* [i] Grass Roots (1967) US#23, *Where Were You When I Needed You* [i] Grass Roots (1966) US#28/Jerry Vale (1965) US#99, *You, Baby (Nobody But You)* [i] Turtles (1966) US#20. Co-writer: [i] Steve Barri.

884. SMITH, Chris (b. October 12, 1879, Charleston, SC; d. October 4, 1949, New York, NY) Stage composer and performer. A black medicine show performer who formed a lifelong vaudeville partnership with Elmer Bowman in the 1900s. Smith was a composer of ballads, comedy numbers and rags, and his songs were included in such shows as "Marrying Mary" (1906), "Bandana Land" (1908) and "The Girl from Utah" (1914). HIT VERSIONS: *Ballin' the Jack* [i] Prince's Orchestra (1914) US#1, *Good Morning, Carrie* [ii] Bert Williams & George Walker (1902) US#1, *He's a Cousin of Mine* [ii] Bob Roberts (1907) US#7/Bert Williams (1907) US#1.

Co-writers; [i] Jim Burris, [ii] Cecil Mack. (*See also under* Bert WILLIAMS, Clarence WILLIAMS.)

885. SMITH, Howard Russell (b Lafayette, TN) Rock guitarist and vocalist. A former disc jockey, who became the principle songwriter in the country-rock group the Amazing Rhythm Aces. CHART COMPOSITIONS: *Third Rate Romance* (1975) C&W#11 US#14, *Amazing Grace (Used to Be Her Favorite Song)* (1975) C&W#9 US#72, *The End Is Not in Sight (The Cowboy Tune)* (1976) C&W#12 US#42, *Ashes of Love* (1978) C&W#100, *I Musta Died and Gone to Texas* (1980) C&W#77. ALBUMS: **Stacked Deck** (1975) US#120, **Too Stuffed to Jump** (1976) US#157, **Toucan Do It** (1977) US#114, **Burning the Ballroom Down** (1978) US#116, **The Amazing Rhythm Aces** (1979, all ABC) US#144; **How the Hell Do You Spell Rythum?** (1980, Warner Brothers) US#175. COMPILATIONS: **Full House — Aces High** (1981), **4 You 4 Ever** (1982, both MSS). After the group broke up in 1980, Smith pursued a brief solo career. CHART COMPOSITIONS: *Where Did We Go Right* (1984) C&W#74, *Three Piece Suit* (1988) C&W#53, *Betty Jean* (1988) C&W#49. ALBUM: **Russell Smith** (1984, Capitol).

886. SMITH, Mark E. (b. Mark Edward Smith, March 5, 1957, Manchester, England) Rock vocalist. The lead vocalist in the punk and avante-garde influenced group the Fall. CHART COMPOSITIONS: *Mr. Pharmacist* (1986) UK#75, *Hey! Luciani* (1986) UK#59, *Hit the North* (1987) UK#57, *Victoria* (1988) UK#35, *Big New Prinz/Jerusalem* (1988) UK#59, *Telephone Thing* (1990) UK#58, *White Lightning* (1990) UK#56, *Free Range* [i] (1992) UK#40, *Why Are People Grudgeful* (1993) UK#43, *Behind the Counter* (1993) UK#75, *15 Ways* (1994) UK#65, *The Chiselers* (1996) UK#60. ALBUMS: **Live at the Witch Trials** (1979), **Dragnet** (1979, both Step Forward); **Totale's Turns (It's Now Or Never)** (1980), **Grotesque (After the Gramme)** (1980, both Rough Trade); **Live in London, 1980** (1980, Chaos); **Slates** (1981, Rough Trade); **Hex Enduction Hour** (1982) UK#71, **Room to Live** (1982, both Kamera); **Perverted By Language** (1983, Rough Trade); **The Wonderful and Frightening World of The Fall** (1984) UK#62, **The Nation's Saving Grace** (1985) UK#54, **Bend Sinister** (1986) UK#36, **The Frenz Experiment** (1988) UK#19, **I Am Kurious, Oranj** (1988) UK#54, **Seminal Live** (1989, all Beggars Banquet) UK#40; **Extricate** (1990) UK#31, **Shift-Work** (1991) UK#17, **Code: Selfish** (1991, all Cog Sinister) UK#21; **The Infotainment Scan** (1993, Permanent) UK#9; **BBC Radio One Live in Concert** (1993, Windsong); **Middle Class Revolt** (1994, Permanent) UK#48; **Cerebral Caus-**tic (1995, Permanent) UK#67; **The Light User Syndrome** (1996, Jet). COMPILATIONS: **77-Early Years-79** (1981, Step Forward); **In: Palace of Swords Reversed** (1987, Cog Sinister); **Hip Priest and Kamerads** (1989, Situation Two); **458489 A-Sides** (1990) UK#44, **458489 B-Sides** (1990, both Beggar's Banquet); **The Collection** (1993, Castle); **The Twenty-Seven Points** (1995, Permanent); **The Other Side of the Fall** (1996, Receiver). Co-writer: [i] Wolstencroft.

887. SMITH, Patti (b. Patti Lee Smith, December 30, 1946, Chicago, IL) Rock vocalist. A published poet who became a punk influenced songwriter and performer in the 1970s. CHART COMPOSITIONS: *Because the Night* [i] (1978) US#13 UK#5, *Privelege (Set Me Free)* (1978) UK#72, *Frederick* (1979) US#90 UK#63. ALBUMS: **Horses** (1975) US#47, **Radio Ethiopia** (1976) US#122, **Easter** (1978) US#20 UK#16, **Wave** (1979) US#18 UK#41, **Dream of Life** (1988) US#65, **Gone Again** (1996, all Arista). HIT VERSION: *Because the Night* [i] Coro featuring Tarlisa (1992) UK#61/10,000 Maniacs (1993) US#11 UK#65. Co-writer: [i] Bruce Springsteen.

888. SNOW, Hank (b. Clarence Eugene Snow, May 9, 1914, Liverpool, Nova Scotia, Canada) C&W guitarist and vocalist. One of the most successful all-round country music entertainers in the history of the genre. Snow merged traditional country with outlandish commercialism, charting eighty-five hits between 1949–1980, including seven number ones. He also recorded over one hundred albums. Snow grew up in poverty and sang in local clubs, before signing to the Victor label in 1934. During the 1940s he re-located to America. CHART COMPOSITIONS: *I'm Movin' On* (1950) C&W#1 US#27, *The Golden Rocket* (1950) C&W#1, *I'm Still Movin' On* (1977) C&W#80. ALBUMS: **When Tragedy Struck** (1959), **Southern Cannonball** (1962), **The One and Only Hank Snow** (1963), **Railroad Man** (1963), **I've Been Everywhere** (1964), **Songs of Tragedy** (1964), **The Old and Great Songs** (1965), **Hank Snow Sings Your Favorite Country Hits** (1966), **Gospel Train** (1967), **Hank in Hawaii** (1968), **Hits Covered By Snow** (1969), **Hank Snow Sings Jimmie Rodgers** (1969), **Award Winners** (1971), **Opry Favorites** (1971), **Hello Love** (1971), **No. 104** (1977), **Still Movin' On** (1977), **The Mysterious Lady** (1979), **20 of the Best** (1979) **Country Music Hall of Fame** (1981), **Diamond Series** (1988, all RCA); **The Swinging Ranger** (1990, Bear Family); **The Essential Hank Snow** (1997, RCA). HIT VERSIONS: *Golden Rocket, The* Jim & Jesse (1970) C&W#38, *I'm Movin' On* Don Gibson (1959)

C&W#14/Ray Charles (1959) R&B#11 US#40/John Kay (1972) US#52/Emmylou Harris (1983) C&W#5.

889. SNOW, Tom Pop producer. A journeyman producer of such artists as Jennifer Warnes, whose songs have featured in the films "About Last Night" (1986) and "Chances Are" (1989). HIT VERSIONS: *After All* [iv] Cher & Peter Cetera (1989) g US#6, *All the Right Moves* [i] Jennifer Warnes & Chris Thompson (1983) US#85, *Deeper Than the Night* [vi] Olivia Newton-John (1979) US#11 UK#64, *He's So Shy* [vii] Pointer Sister (1980) g R&B#10 US#3, *Livin' in Desperate Times* [i] Olivia Newton-John (1984) US#31, *Love Sneakin' Up on You* [v] Bonnie Raitt (1994) US#19, *So Far So Good* [vii] Sheena Easton (1986) US#43, *Somebody's Eyes* [iv] Karla Bonoff (1984) US#109, *Somewhere Down the Road* [vii] Barry Manilow (1982) US#21, *Stayin' with It* [iii] Firefall (1981) US#37, *You Might Need Somebody* [ii] Randy Crawford (1980) UK#11, *You Should Hear How She Talks About You* [iv] Melissa Manchester (1982) US#5. Co-writers: [i] Barry Alfonso, [ii] N. O'Bryne, [iii] J.L. Parker, [iv] Dean Pitchford, [v] J. Scott, [vi] John Vastano, [vii] Cynthia Weil. (*See also under* John FARRAR, Amy GRANT, Tony MacAULEY, Barry MANN, Michael MASSER.)

890. SNYDER, Ted (b. 1881; d. 1965, both America) Stage pianist. A former staff pianist and song-plugger who became a Tin Pan Alley composer and publisher in the early 1900s. Snyder was the first publisher to hire Irving Berlin as a songwriter. HIT VERSIONS: *Dancing Fool* [i] Club Royal Orchestra (1922) US#8, *Sheik of Araby* [i] Club Royal Orchestra (1922) US#3/Ray Miller (1922) US#3/Jack Teagarden (1939) US#14/Spike Jones (1943) US#19/Super-Sonics (1953) US#22/Winifred Atwell in *Let's Have Another Party* (1954) UK#1/Johnston Brothers in *Join in and Sing Again* (1955) UK#9/Russ Conway in *More and More Party Pops* (1959) UK#5/Mrs. Mills in *Mrs. Mills' Medley* (1961) UK#18. Co-writers: [i] Harry B. Smith/Francis Wheeler. (*See also under* Irving BERLIN, Harry RUBY.)

891. SONDHEIM, Stephen (b. Stephen Joshua Sondheim, March 22, 1930, New York, NY) Stage composer and lyricist. An influential writer of conceptually based musical theatre, who uses songs to advance the plot. Sondheim was given piano lessons by Oscar Hammerstein, II, and he studied with the avante-garde composer Milton Babbit. He began writing musicals while studying composition at Williams College, and after composing incidental music for a number of Broadway shows during the 1950s, Sondheim achieved success with his lyrics

to Leonard Bernstein's "Candide" (1956) and "West Side Story" (1957). Sondheim composed and wrote "A Funny Thing Happened on the Way to the Forum" (1962) in its entirety, but "Anyone Can Whistle" (1964) and "Do I Hear a Waltz?" (1965) were unsuccessful, as was his television play "Evening Primrose" (1966). "Company" (1970), a wry study of the sexual mores of the period, was a big hit, and remains a good example of his internal rhyming technique. Sondheim followed it with "Follies" (1971), "A Little Night Music" (1973), "Pacific Overtures" (1976), "Side By Side By Sondheim" (1976), "Sweeney Todd (The Demon Barber of Fleet Street)" (1979), "Merrily We Roll Along" (1981), "Sunday in the Park with George" (1984), and "Into the Woods" (1987). He has also composed for films, and Barbra Streisand recorded eight of his songs on **The Broadway Album** (1985, Columbia) p US#1 UK#3. ALBUMS: **Candide** oc (1956), **West Side Story** oc (1958) g US#5 UK#3, **Gypsy** oc (1959, all Columbia) US#13, **West Side Story** oc (1960, Philips) UK#14; **West Side Story** ost (1961, Columbia) p US#1 UK#1; **Gypsy** ost (1962, Warner Brothers) US#10; **A Funny Thing Happened on the Way to the Forum** oc (1962, Capitol) US#60; **Anyone Can Whistle** oc (1964), **Do I Hear a Waltz?** (1965) US#81, **Mad Show** oc (1965), **Company** oc (1970, all Columbia) US#178; **Follies** oc (1971, Capitol) US#172; **A Little Night Music** oc (1973, Columbia) US#94; **Sondheim: A Musical Tribute** (1973, Warner Brothers); **Stavisky** ost (1974), **Pacific Overtures** oc (1976), **Side By Side By Sondheim** oc (1977), **Sweeney Todd — The Demon Barber of Fleet Street** oc (1979) US#78, **Marry Me a Little** oc (1981, all RCA); **Reds** ost (1981, Columbia); **Candide** oc (1982, New World); **Merrily We Roll Along** oc (1982, RCA); **A Collector's Sondheim, Sondheim '83** (1983, Book of the Month Club); **A Stephen Sondheim Evening** oc (1983), **Sunday in the Park with George** oc (1984) US#149, **West Side Story** sc (1985) US#70 UK#11, **Follies — In Concert** (1986, all RCA) US#181; **West Side Story — Highlights** sc (1986, both DG) UK#72; **Into the Woods** oc (1988, RCA) US#126; **West Side Story** sc (1993, IMG) UK#33; **Color and Light-Jazz Sketches on Sondheim** (1995, Sony). HIT VERSION: *Send in the Clowns* Judy Collins (1975) US#36 UK#6. (*See also under* Leonard BERNSTEIN, Oscar HAMMERSTEIN, II, Jules STYNE.)

892. SOUTH, Joe (b. February 28, 1942, Atlanta, GA) Pop multi-instrumentalist and vocalist. A session musician and composer who also recorded in a gospel-folk style as a solo performer. South's best tunes featured strong melodies and memorable hooks, and his *Games People Play* has been recorded by over one hundred and twenty-five artists. South once said of songwriting, "You can put something in people's minds that they will never forget. It's like writing a three minute book." He learned the guitar at the age of eleven and grew up listening to country music, before, as a twelve year old, performing on a country radio station in Covington, Georgia. South's first solo hit was *The Purple People Eater Meets the Witch Doctor* (1958), an answer song to Sheb Wooley's novelty tune *Purple People Eater*. During the 1960s, he became an in-demand session musician, performing on over three hundred albums, including Bob Dylan's **Blonde on Blonde**. South also wrote and produced a series of hits for the vocalist Billy Joe Royal, before signing as a solo artist to Capitol Records in 1968, saying, "No one listened to what I wanted to say so I had to go out and do my own thing, write the material, sing the song, and produce the record." During the 1970s, he withdrew from music making completely. CHART COMPOSITIONS: *The Purple People Eater Meets the Witch Doctor* (1958) US#47, *You're the Reason* (1961) C&W#16 US#87, *Birds of a Feather* (1968) US#106, re-issued (1969) US#96; *Games People Play* (1969) US#12 UK#6, *Don't It Make You Want to Go Home* (1969) C&W#27 US#41, *Leanin' on You* (1969) US#104, *Walk a Mile in My Shoes* (1970) C&W#56 US#12, *Children* (1970) US#51, *Why Does a Man Do What He Has to Do* (1970) US#118, *Fool Me* (1971) US#78. ALBUMS: **Introspect** (1968) US#117, **Don't It Make You Want to Go Home** (1969) US#60, **So the Seeds Are Growing** (1971), **Joe South** (1972, all Capitol); **Midnight Rainbow** (1975), **To Have, to Hold and to Let Go** (1995, both Island). COMPILATIONS: **Games People Play** (1969), **Greatest Hits, Volume 1** (1969, both Capitol) US#125; **The Joe South Story** (1977, Mine); **Best of Joe South** (1990, Rhino); **Best of Joe South** (1992, Capitol). HIT VERSIONS: *All My Hard Times* Roy Drusky (1970) C&W#9, *Be Young, Be Foolish, Be Happy* Tams (1968) R&B#26 US#61/Sonia (1991) UK#22; *Birds of a Feather* Raiders (1971) US#23/Almost Brothers (1986) C&W#63; *Children* Diana Trask (1969) C&W#58, *Don't It Make You Want to Go Home* Brook Benton (1970) US#45/Butch Baker (1987) C&W#51; *Down in the Boondocks* Billy Joe Royal (1965) US#9 UK#38/Penny DeHaven (1969) C&W#37/Freddy Weller (1969) C&W#25; *Fool Me* Lynn Anderson (1972) C&W#4 US#101, *Games People Play* King Curtis (1969) US#116/Donald Height (1969) R&B#47/Freddy Weller (1969) C&W#2/Della Reese (1970) US#121; *Greatest Love, The* Billy Joe Royal (1967) US#117/Dorsey Burnette (1969) US#67; *Hitchhike Back to Georgia* Buddy Knox & the Rhythm Orchids (1964) US#114, *How Can I Unlove You* Lynn Ander-

son (1971) C&W#1 US#63, *Hush* Billy Joe Royal (1967) US#52/Deep Purple (1968) g US#4, new version (1988) UK#62/Merrilee Rush (1968) US#7/Jeannie C. Riley (1973) C&W#51/Blue Swede (1975) US#61/Kula Shaker (1997) UK#2; *I Beg Your Pardon* [i] Kon Kan (1989) UK#5, *I've Got to Be Somebody* Billy Joe Royal (1965) US#38, *I Knew You When* Billy Joe Royal (1965) US#14/Donny Osmond (1971) g US#10/Jerry Foster (1976) C&W#86/Linda Ronstadt (1982) C&W#84 US#37; *If Love Is in Your Heart* Friend & Lover (1968) US#86, *It's a Good Time* Billy Joe Royal (1966) US#104, *Old Bridges Burn Slow* Billy Joe Royal (1987) C&W#11, *Party People* Ray Stevens (1965) US#130/Butch Baker (1988) C&W#68; *Reach Out of the Darkness* Friend & Lover (1968) US#10, *Rose Garden* Dobie Gray (1969) US#119/Lynn Anderson (1971) g C&W#1 US#3 UK#3/New World (1971) UK#15; *She's Almost You* Billy Harper (1969) US#121, *These Are Not My People* Billy Joe Royal (1967) US#113/Johnny Rivers (1969) US#55/Freddy Weller (1969) C&W#5 US#113; *Untie Me* Tams (1962) R&B#12 US#60, *Walk a Mile in My Shoes* Willie Hightower (1970) R&B#26 US#107, *Yo Yo* Billy Joe Royal (1966) US#117/Osmonds (1971) g US#3. Co-writer: [i] Barry Harris.

893. SOUTHER, J.D. (b. John David Souther, November 2, 1945, Detroit, MI) Rock multi-instrumentalist, producer and vocalist. One of California's venerable sidemen, co-writers and backing vocalists, who has contributed to nearly every Eagles album, but whose solo career faltered in the early 1980s. Raised in Amarillo, Texas, Souther learned the drums, guitar and piano in his teens, before playing in local bands. He became part of the country-rock scene during the late 1960s, first recording with Glenn Frey as the duo Longbranch Pennywhistle, followed by an ill-fated attempt at a Crosby, Stills and Nash–styled supergroup, the Souther-Hillman-Furay Band. Souther also contributed to the film soundtracks "Urban Cowboy" (1980) and "About Last Night" (1986). CHART COMPOSITIONS: *You're Only Lonely* (1979) C&W#60 US#7, *White Rhythm and Blues* (1980) US#105, *Her Town Too* [ii] with James Taylor (1981) US#11, *Sometimes You Just Can't Win* with Linda Ronstadt (1982) US#27, *Go Ahead and Rain* (1984) US#104. ALBUMS: **John David Souther** (1972), **Black Rose** (1976, both Asylum) US#85; **You're Only Lonely** (1979, Columbia) US#41; **Home By Dawn** (1984, Warner Brothers). HIT VERSIONS: *Faithless Love* Glen Campbell (1984) C&W#10, *If Anybody Had a Heart* [i] John Hiatt (1986) US#76. Co-writers: [i] Danny Kortchmar, [ii] James Taylor/Waddy Wachtel. (*See also under* Glenn FREY, Don HENLEY, Chris HILLMAN.)

894. SOVINE, Red (b. Woodrow Wilson Sovine, July 17, 1918, Charleston, WV; d. April 4, 1980, Nashville, TN) C&W guitarist and vocalist. A country performer best known for his spoken narrative truck-driving songs, none better than *Phantom 309*, which was superbly interpreted by Tom Waits. Sovine first sang with Jim Pike's Carolina Tar Heels on local radio shows in the 1930s, before forming his own group, the Echo Valley Boys, during the 1940s. He became Hank Williams' replacement on the radio show "Louisiana Hayride" in 1949, and in the late 1950s, Sovine became a Grand Ole spry performer. He died of a heart attack in 1980. CHART COMPOSITIONS: *Are You Mine?* with Goldie Hill (1955) C&W#14, *What Would You Do if Jesus Came to Your House?* (1956) C&W#15, *Dream House for Sale* (1964) C&W#22, *Giddyup Go* (1965) C&W#1 US#82, *Long Night* (1966) C&W#47, *Class of '49* (1966) C&W#44, *I Didn't Jump the Fence* (1967) C&W#17, *In Your Heart* (1967) C&W#33, *Phantom 309* (1967) C&W#9, re-issued (1975) C&W#47; *Tell Maude I Slipped* (1967) C&W#33, *Loser Making Good* (1968) C&W#63, *Normally, Norma Loves Me* (1968) C&W#61, *Who Am I* (1969) C&W#62, *Freightliner Fever* (1970) C&W#54, *It'll Come Back* (1974) C&W#16, re-issued (1980) C&W#89; *Can I Keep Him Daddy* (1974) C&W#58, *Daddy's Girl* (1975) C&W#91, *Teddy Bear* [i] (1976) g C&W#1 US#40, re-issued (1981) UK#4; *Little Joe* (1976) C&W#45 US#102, *Last Goodbye* (1976) C&W#96, *Just Gettin' By* (1977) C&W#98, *Woman Behind the Man Behind the Wheel* (1977) C&W#92, *The Days of Me and You* (1978) C&W#77, *The Little Family Soldier* (1980) C&W#74. ALBUMS: **Country Music Time** (1957, Decca); **Town and Country Action** (1966), **I Didn't Jump the Fence** (1967), **I Know You're Married** (1970), **Teddy Bear** (1976) US#119, **Woodrow Wilson Sovine** (1977, all Starday); **16 New Gospel Songs** (1980), **Phantom 309** (1981, both Starday/Gusto); **Best of Red Sovine** (1987), **Classic Narrations** (1987), **Greatest Hits** (1987), **Super Collection** (1987, all Starday); **The One and Only** (1988, Official); **Best of the Best of Red Sovine** (1991, Highland). HIT VERSIONS: *Bye Bye Love* Webb Pierce (1957) C&W#7 US#73, *Missing You* Webb Pierce (1957) C&W#7. Co-writers: [i] Billy Burnett/Tommy Hill/Dale Royal.

895. SPECTOR, Phil (b. Philip Harvey Spector, December 26, 1940, Bronx, NY) Pop producer. A maverick producer and composer who created what became known as the Wall of Sound, an exciting production style, that made frequently corny source material sound like some of the most important music ever recorded. Spector first performed in a group with Kim Fowley, and at the age of seventeen penned the Teddy Bears' hit *To Know Him Is to Love Him* (1958). After working in the Brill Building alongside such songwriters as Jerry Leiber and Mike Stoller, Spector became successful with his own Philles label during the 1960s. Although something of a recluse since the 1970s, Spector remains an influential producer. ALBUMS: **Phil Spector's Christmas Album** (1972, Apple) UK#21; **Echoes of the '60s** (1977, Phil Spector International) UK#21; **Greatest Hits/Phil Spector's Christmas Album** (1983, Impression) UK#19; **Back to Mono** (1990, Phil Spector). HIT VERSIONS: *(Best Part of, The) Breaking Up* Ronettes (1964) US#39 UK#43, *Black Pearl* [iii] Checkmates, Ltd., featuring Sonny Charles (1969) R&B#8 US#13/Horace Faith (1970) UK#13; *Do I Love You* Ronettes (1964) US#34 UK#35, *Second Hand Love* [ii] Connie Francis (1962) US#7, *Some of Your Lovin'* Johnny Nash (1961) US#104, *To Know Him Is to Love Him* Teddy Bears (1958) R&B#10 US#1 UK#2, re-issued (1979) UK#66/Peter & Gordon as *To Know You Is to Love You* (1965) US#24 UK#5/Bobby Vincent (1969) US#43/Jody Miller (1972) C&W#18/Emmylou Harris, Dolly Parton & Linda Ronstadt (1987) C&W#1; *There's No Other (Like My Baby)* [i] Crystals (1961) US#20. Co-writers: [i] Leroy Bates, [ii] Hank Hunter, [iii] Irwin Levine/Toni Wine. (*See also under* Ellie GREENWICH, Carole KING, Barry MANN, Doc POMUS and Mort SHUMAN.)

896. SPENCER, Tim (b. July 13, 1908, Webb City, MO; d. April 26, 1974) C&W vocalist. A founder member of the Sons of the Pioneers, with Bob Nolan, who remained in the group until 1950, composing its hits *Cigareetes, Whuskey and Wild, Wild Women* (1947) C&W#5 and *Room Full of Roses* (1949) C&W#10 US#26. HIT VERSIONS: *Careless Kisses* Russ Morgan (1950) US#24, *Cigareetes, Whuskey and Wild, Wild Women* Red Ingle (1948) US#15/Red Foley (1950) C&W#8; *Room Full of Roses* Dick Haymes (1949) US#6/Eddy Howard (1949) US#4/Sammy Kaye (1949) US#2/George Morgan (1949) C&W#4 US#25/Starlighters (1949) US#21/Jerry Wayne (1949) US#6/Mickey Gilley (1974) C&W#1 US#50. (*See also under* Bob NOLAN.)

897. SPRINGFIELD, Rick (b. Richard Springthorpe, August 23, 1949, Sydney, Australia) Pop guitarist and vocalist. A teen pop idol in the Australian group Zoot during the early 1970s, who became a popular American solo star and actor during the 1970s. CHART COMPOSITIONS: *Speak to the Sky* (1972) US#14, *What Would the Children Think* (1972) US#70, *American Girls* (1974) US#98, *Take a Hand* (1976) US#41, *Jessie's Girl* (1981) g US#1 UK#43, *I've Done Everything for You* (1981) US#8,

Love Is Alright Tonight (1982) US#20, *Don't Talk to Strangers* (1982) US#2, *What Kind of Fool Am I* (1982) US#21, *I Get Excited* (1982) US#32, *Affair of the Heart* [iii] (1983) US#9, *Human Touch* (1983) US#18 UK#23, *Souls* (1983) US#23, *Love Somebody* [i] (1984) US#5, *Hard to Hold Is Love Somebody* (1984) US#5, *Don't Walk Away* (1984) US#26, *Bop 'Til You Drop* (1984) US#20, *Taxi Dancing* (1984) US#59, *Bruce* (1985) US#27, *Celebrate Youth* (1985) US#26, *State of the Heart* [ii] (1985) US#22, *Rock of Life* (1988) US#22. ALBUMS: **Beginnings** (1972, Capitol) US#35; **Comic Book Heroes** (1974, Columbia); **Wait for the Night** (1976, Chelsea) US#159; **Working Class Dog** (1981) p US#7, **Success Hasn't Spoiled Me Yet** (1982) p US#2, **Living in Oz** (1983) p US#12 UK#41, **Hard to Hold** ost (1984) p US#16, **Tao** (1985) g US#21 UK#68, **Rock of Life** (1988, all RCA) US#55 UK#80. COMPILATIONS: **Beautiful Feelings** (1985, Mercury) US#78; **Best of Rick Springfield** (1996, Camden). Co-writers: [i] B. Drescher, [ii] E. McCusker/T. Pierce, [iii] Danny Tate/Blaise Tosti.

898. SPRINGFIELD, Tom (b. Tom O'Brien, July 2, 1934, London, England) Pop guitarist and vocalist. A founder member, in 1960, of the folk influenced vocal harmony group the Springfields, which also featured his sister, Dusty Springfield. CHART COMPOSITIONS: *Breakaway* (1961) UK#31, *Bambino* (1961) UK#16, *Island of Dreams* (1963) US#129 UK#5, *Say I Won't Be There* (1963) UK#5, *Come on Home* (1963) UK#31. ALBUM: **Silver Threads and Golden Needles** (1962, Philips) US#91. Springfield also recorded two albums as the Tom Springfield Orchestra, **Kinda Folksy** (1961) and **Love's Philosophy By the Tom Springfield Orchestra** (1969, both Decca). HIT VERSIONS: *Carnival Is Over, The* Seekers (1965) US#105 UK#1, *Georgy Girl* [i] Seekers (1967) g US#2 UK#3/Baja Marimba Band (1967) US#98; *I'll Never Find Another You* Seekers (1965) US#4 UK#1/Sonny James (1967) C&W#1 US#97; *Just Loving You* Anita Harris (1967) US#120 UK#6, *Losing You* [iii] Dusty Springfield (1964) US#91 UK#9, *Promises* [ii] Ken Dodd (1966) UK#6, *Walk with Me* Seekers (1966) UK#10, *World of Our Own, A* Seekers (1965) US#67 UK#3/Sonny James (1968) C&W#1 US#118. Co-writers: [i] Jim Dale, [ii] Norman Newell, [iii] Clive Westlake.

899. SPRINGSTEEN, Bruce (b. Bruce Frederick Joseph Springsteen, September 23, 1949, Freehold, NJ) Rock guitarist, harmonica player and vocalist. One of the most popular performing artists in the world during the 1980s, whose working man's image and recurring theme of individuals searching for a sense of identity, has proven highly durable. Influenced by Woody Guthrie and Bob Dylan, Springsteen's exacting eye for detail, perfectly captures the pay-off between deeds enacted and the failure to act at all. When asked where he saw his own roots and home, Springsteen replied, "I always felt most at home when I was, like, in the car or on the road, which is why, I guess, I always wrote about it." He became a guitarist after failing as a drummer, learning to play by ear from the radio listening to Chuck Berry and Elvis Presley. Springsteen first played in the teen group the Castiles in 1965, before joining Earth. During the mid–1960s he resided in the Asbury Park district of New York, an experience he later turned into a grandiose, mythical soundscape for many of his early compositions. As his various groups evolved into the formidable E Street Band, Springsteen became one of the hottest live acts in America. His album **Born to Run** (1975) catapulted him into the big league, and featured songs such as *Thunder Road* and *Jungleland*— enormous musical landscapes in which his many characters sought refuge and redemption in escape. Springsteen's tour-de-force was **Darkness on the Edge of Town** (1978), an introspective and harsh examination of the realities facing many of those still in pursuit of the tarnished American dream. Songs such as *Something in the Night* were riddled with an inherent atmosphere of desperation, "You're born with nothing and better off that way," while *Racing in the Street* ruminated about dissonant reality and the open highways that offered a romantic optimism that something better might just lay ahead. Springsteen described the album as, "A collision that happens between this guy and the real world. He ends up very alone and real stripped down." The bleak **Nebraska** (1982), was recorded on a four-track home tape machine, and was, according to its creator, "about that American isolation: what happens to people when they're alienated from their friends and their community and their government and their job." Springsteen's commercial peak was the twenty million selling **Born in the U.S.A.** (1984), an amiable set of foot-stomping stadium rockers that sired seven hit singles. HIT COMPOSITIONS: *Born to Run* (1975) US#23, live version (1987) UK#16; *Tenth Avenue Freeze Out* (1978) US#83, *Prove It All Night* (1978) US#33, *Badlands* (1978) US#42, *Hungry Heart* (1980) US#5 UK#44, re-issued (1995) UK#28; *The River* (1981) UK#35, *Fade Away* (1981) US#20, *Dancing in the Dark* (1984) p US#2 UK#28, re-issued (1985) UK#4; *Cover Me* (1984) US#7 UK#38, re-issued (1984) UK#16; *Born in the U.S.A.* (1985) US#9, *I'm on Fire* (1985) US#6, *I'm on Fire/Born in the U.S.A.* (1985) UK#5, *Glory Days* (1985) US#5 UK#17, *Goin' Down* (1985) US#9,

My Hometown (1985) g US#6 UK#9, *Fire* (1987) US#46 UK#52, *Brilliant Disguise* (1987) US#5 UK#20, *Tunnel of Love* (1988) US#20 UK#45, *Tougher Than the Rest* (1988) UK#13, *Spare Parts* (1988) UK#32, *One Step Up* (1989) UK#13, *Human Touch* (1992) US#16 UK#11, *Better Days* (1992) UK#34, *57 Channels* (1992) US#68 UK#32, *Leap of Faith* (1992) UK#46, *Lucky Town* live version (1993) UK#48, *Streets of Philadelphia* (1994) g US#9 UK#2, *Secret Garden* (1995) UK#44, *The Ghost of Tom Joad* (1996) UK#26. ALBUMS: **Greetings from Asbury Park, New Jersey** (1973) p US#60 UK#41, **The Wild, the Innocent and the E Street Shuffle** (1973) p US#59 UK#33, **Born to Run** (1975) p US#3 UK#17, **Darkness on the Edge of Town** (1978) p US#5 UK#16, **The River** (1980) p US#1 UK#2, **Nebraska** (1982) p US#3 UK#3, **Born in the U.S.A.** (1984) p US#1 UK#1, **Live, 1975–1985** (1986) p US#1 UK#4, **Tunnel of Love** (1987) p US#1 UK#1, **Human Touch** (1992) p US#2 UK#1, **Lucky Town** (1992) p US#3 UK#2, **In Concert — MTV Plugged** (1993) UK#4, **The Ghost of Tom Joad** (1995, all Columbia) US#11 UK#16. COMPILATION: **Greatest Hits** (1995, Columbia) US#1 UK#1. HIT VERSIONS: *Blinded By the Light* Manfred Mann's Earthband (1976) g US#1 UK#6, *Born in the U.S.A.* Cheech & Chong as *Born in East L.A.* (1985) US#48/ Stanley Clarke Band (1985) R&B#52/2 Live Crew sampled in *Banned in the U.S.A.* (1990) US#20; *Born to Run* Emmylou Harris (1982) C&W#3, *Dancing in the Dark* Big Daddy (1985) UK#21, *Darlington County* Jeff Stevens & the Bullets (1986) C&W#69, *Fire* Pointer Sisters (1978) g R&B#14 US#2 UK#34/ Stars On in *Stars on Long Play 2/On 45, Volume 2* (1981) US#120 UK#18; *For You* Manfred Mann's Earthband (1981) US#106, *Light of Day* Barbusters (1987) US#33, *Out of Work* Gary "U.S." Bonds (1982) R&B#82 US#21, *Pink Cadillac* Natalie Cole (1988) R&B#9 US#5 UK#5, *Sandy* Hollies as *Fourth of July, Asbury Park (Sandy)* (1975) US#85, *Spirit in the Night* Manfred Mann's Earth Band (1977) US#97, *Stand on It* Mel McDaniel (1986) C&W#12, *This Little Girl* Gary "U.S." Bonds (1981) US#11 UK#43, *Tougher Than the Rest* Everything But the Girl on *Covers EP* (1992) UK#13. (*See also under* Patti SMITH.)

900. SQUIRE, Billy (b. May 12, 1950, Wellesley Hills, MA) Rock guitarist and vocalist. A singer-songwriter whose career petered out in the early 1990s. CHART COMPOSITIONS: *The Stroke* (1981) US#17 UK#52, *In the Dark* (1981) US#35, *My Kinda Lover* (1981) US#45, *Emotions in Motion* (1982) US#68, *Everybody Wants You* (1982) US#32, *She's a Runner* (1983) US#75, *Rock Me Tonite* (1984) US#15, *Love Is the Hero* (1986) US#80, *Don't Say You Love Me* (1989) US#58. ALBUMS: **The Tale of the**

Tape (1980) US#169, **Don't Say No** (1981) p US#5, **Emotions in Motion** (1982) p US#5, **Signs of Life** (1984) p US#11, **Enough Is Enough** (1986) US#61, **Hear and Now** (1989) US#64, **Creatures of Habit** (1991, all Capitol) US#117.

901. STANLEY, Paul (b. Paul Stanley Eisen, January 20, 1952, New York, NY) Rock guitarist and vocalist. The lead guitarist and principal songwriter in the flamboyant rock band Kiss. The group's songs were also recorded on the various artists tribute **Kiss My Ass: Classic Kiss Re-grooved** (1994, Mercury) US#19. CHART COMPOSITIONS: *Rock 'n' Roll All Nite* [xi] (1975) US#68, live version (1975) US#12; *Flaming Youth* [viii] (1976) US#74, *Detroit Rock City* [v] (1976) US#7, *Hard Luck Woman* (1976) US#15, *Love Gun* (1977) US#61, *Shout It Out Loud* [vi] (1976) US#54, *I Was Made for Lovin' You* [iv] (1979) US#11 UK#50, *Sure Know Something* [x] (1979) US#47, *Shandi* [x] (1980) US#47, *A World Without Heroes* [vii] (1981) US#56 UK#55, *Lick It Up* [xii] (1983) US#66 UK#31, *Heaven's on Fire* [ii] (1984) US#49 UK#43, *Tears Are Falling* (1985) US#51 UK#57, *Crazy, Crazy Nights* [ix] (1987) US#65 UK#4, *Reason to Live* [ii] (1987) US#68 UK#33, *Turn on the Night* (1988) UK#41, *Let's Put the X in Sex* [ii] (1989) US#97, *Hide Your Heart* [iii] (1989) US#22 UK#59, *Forever* [i] (1990) US#8 UK#65. ALBUMS: **Kiss** (1974) g US#87, **Hotter Than Hell** (1974) g US#100, **Dressed to Kill** (1975) g US#32, **Alive!** (1975) g US#9 UK#49, **Destroyer** (1976) p US#11 UK#22, **Rock and Roll Over** (1976) p US#11, **Love Gun** (1977) p US#7 UK#60, **Alive II** (1977) p US#7 UK#60, **Dynasty** (1979) p US#9 UK#50, **Kiss Unmasked** (1980) g US#35 UK#48, **Music from the Elder** ost (1981) US#75 UK#51, **Creatures of the Night** (1982, all Casablanca) US#45 UK#22; **Lick It Up** (1983) p US#24 UK#7, **Animalize** (1984) p US#19 UK#11, **Asylum** (1985) g US#20 UK#12, **Crazy Nights** (1987) p US#18 UK#4, **Hot in the Shade** (1989) g US#29 UK#35, **Revenge** (1992) g US#6 UK#10, **Alive III** (1993) US#9 UK#24, **MTV Unplugged** (1996, all Mercury) US#15 UK#74. COMPILATIONS: **The Originals** (1976) US#36, **Double Platinum** (1978) p US#24, **Killers** (1982, all Casablanca) UK#42; **Smashes, Thrashes and Hits** (1988) p US#21 UK#62, **Greatest Hits** (1996, both Mercury). Stanley has also recorded as a solo artist, charting with *Hold Me, Touch Me* (1978) US#46, from the album **Paul Stanley** (1978, Casablanca) p US#40. HIT VERSION: *Hard Luck Woman* Garth Brooks (1994) C&W#67+. Co-writers: [i] Michael Bolton, [ii] Desmond Child, [iii] Desmond Child/Holly Knight, [iv] Desmond Child/ Vincent Poncia, [v] Bob Ezrin, [vi] Bob Ezrin/Gene Simmons (b. Chaim Witz, August 25, 1949, Haifa,

Israel), [vii] Bob Ezrin/Gene Simmons/Lou Reed, [viii] Ace Frehley (b. Paul Frehley, April 22, 1951, Bronx, NY)/Gene Simmons, [ix] A. Mitchell, [x] Vincent Poncia, [xi] Gene Simmons, [xii] Vinnie Vincent (b. Vincent Cusano).

902. STANSFIELD, Lisa (b. April 11, 1966, Rochdale, England) Pop vocalist. An R&B styled pop singer who, with songwriting partners Andrew Morris and Ian Devaney, first recorded as the group Blue Zone, releasing the album **Big Thing** (1986, Arista). Stansfield has been a successful solo singer since 1989. CHART COMPOSITIONS: *This Is the Right Time* (1989) US#21 UK#13, *All Around the World* [ii] (1989) R&B#1 US#3 UK#1, *Live Together* [ii] (1990) UK#10, *What Did I Do to You* [ii] (1990) UK#25, *You Can't Deny It* [ii] (1990) US#14, *Change* [ii] (1991) R&B#12 US#27 UK#10, *All Woman* [ii] (1992) R&B#1 US#56 UK#20, *A Little More Love* [ii] (1992) R&B#30, *Time to Make You Mine* [ii] (1992) UK#14, *Set Your Loving Free* [ii] (1992) UK#28, *Someday (I'm Coming Back)* [ii] (1993) UK#10, *In All the Right Places* [ii] (1993) UK#8, *So Natural* [ii] (1993) UK#15, *Little Bit of Heaven* [ii] (1993) UK#32. ALBUMS: **Affection** (1989) p US#9 UK#2, **Real Love** (1992) g US#43 UK#3, **So Natural** (1993) UK#6, **Lisa Stansfield** (1997, all Arista) UK#2. HIT VERSION: *People Hold On* [i] Coldcut (1989) UK#11. Co-writers: [i] Matthew Black/Jonathan More, [ii] Ian Devaney/Andrew Morris.

903. STARR, Maurice Pop producer and vocalist. The Svengali-like manager of the 1980s teenage vocal group New Edition, which he initially molded along the lines of the Jackson Five. Starr later scored even greater success when he created an all-white, pop-rap act New Kids on the Block. Starr has also recorded as a solo artist. ALBUMS: **Flaming Starr** (1983), **Spicey Lady** (1984, both RCA). HIT VERSIONS: *Baby, I Believe in You* George Lamond (1992) US#66, *Call It What You Want* New Kids on the Block (1991) UK#12, *Candy Girl* [i] New Edition (1983) US#46 UK#1, *Cover Girl* New Kids on the Block (1989) US#2, re-issued (1990) UK#4; *Don't Forget About Me* Lady Soul (1992) R&B#77, *Games* [iii] New Kids on the Block (1991) UK#14, *Hangin' Tough* New Kids on the Block (1989) g US#1 UK#52, re-issued (1990) UK#1; *I'll Be Loving You (Forever)* New Kids on the Block (1989) g US#1, *Is This the End* [i] New Edition (1983) US#85, *Jealous Girl* [i] Another Bad Creation (1991) R&B#25, *Popcorn Love* [i] New Edition (1983) UK#45, *Step By Step* New Kids on the Block (1990) US#1 UK#2, *This One's for the Children* New Kids on the Block (1989) US#7, re-issued (1990) UK#9; *Tonight* [ii] New Kids on the Block (1990) US#7 UK#3, *You Got It (The Right*

Stuff) New Kids on the Block (1989) g US#3 UK#1. Co-writers: [i] Michael Jonzun, [ii] Alfredo Lancelloti, [iii] Mark Wahlberg.

904. STEINER, Max (b. Maximilian Raoul Steiner, May 10, 1888, Vienna, Austria; d. December 28, 1971, Los Angeles, CA) Film composer and conductor. A composer and the orchestral conductor of over three hundred films, who led the RKO Studio Orchestra during the 1930s. Steiner's compositions were included in such films as "Santa Fe Trail" (1941), "Life with Father" (1947) and "Come Next Spring" (1956). ALBUMS: **The Adventures of Don Juan** ost (1948, Tony Thomas); **Caine Mutiny** ost (1954), **Max Steiner — Great Love Themes from Motion Pictures** st (1955), **Death of a Scoundrel** st (1956), **Band of Angels** ost (1957), **Marjorie Morningstar** ost (1958, all RCA); **John Paul Jones** ost (1959, Warner Brothers); **Gone with the Wind** ost (1961, RCA) US#64; **Gone with the Wind** st (1961) US#50, **Parrish** ost (1961) US#45, **Rome Adventure** ost (1962, all Warner Brothers) US#5; **Gone with the Wind** ost (1967, MGM) US#24; **Now Voyager: The Classic Film Scores of Max Steiner** st (1973, RCA); **Helen of Troy** ost (1974, Elmer Bernstein); **A Star Is Born** ost (1975), **King Kong** ost (1976, United Artists); **Since You Went Away** ost (1976, Citadel); **Film Music of Max Steiner** st (1979, ML); **Bird of Paradise** ost (1980, Medallion); **Come Next Spring** ost (1980, Citadel); **Letter** st (1982, Tony Thomas). HIT VERSIONS: *Come Next Spring* [i] Tony Bennett (1956) UK#29, *Honey Babe* [iii] Art Mooney (1955) US#6, *Theme from a Summer Place, The* [ii] Percy Faith & His Orchestra (1960) g US#1 UK#2/Norrie Paramor (1960) UK#36/Lettermen (1965) US#16. Co-writers: [i] Lenny Adelson, [ii] Mack Discant, [iii] Paul Francis Webster. (*See also under* Mack DAVID, Kim GANNON, Ray EVANS.)

905. STEINMAN, Jim (b. New York, NY) Rock producer. A grandiose rock producer with operatic pretensions, whose recurring theme is the death of teenage dreams during the process of growing up. Steinman is the composer of Meat Loaf's twenty-six million selling album **Bat Out of Hell** (1977) p US#14 UK#9, the million selling **Deadringer** (1981, both Cleveland International) p US#45 UK#1; and the ten million selling **Bat Out of Hell II: Back into Hell** (1993, MCA) p US#1 UK#1. The pair first worked together on the musical "More Than You Deserve" (1974). Steinman created the group Pandora's Box for the conceptual album **Original Sin** (1989, Virgin), and has also recorded as a solo artist. CHART COMPOSITIONS: *Rock 'n' Roll Dreams Come Through* (1981) US#32, *Tonight Is What It Means to Be Young* with Fire, Inc. (1984)

US#80 UK#67. ALBUM: **Bad for Good** (1981, Cleveland International) US#63 UK#7. HIT VERSIONS: *Bat Out of Hell* Meat Loaf (1979) UK#15, re-issued (1993) UK#8; *Dead Ringer for Love* Meat Loaf & Cher (1982) UK#5, re-issued (1991) UK#53; *Faster Than the Speed of Night* Bonnie Tyler (1983) UK#43, *Holding Out for a Hero* [i] Bonnie Tyler (1984) US#34 UK#2, re-issued (1991) UK#69; *I'd Do Anything for Love (But I Won't Do That)* Meat Loaf (1993) p US#1 UK#1, *I'm Gonna Love Her for Both of Us* Meat Loaf (1981) US#84 UK#62, *Left in the Dark* Barbra Streisand (1984) US#50, *Loving You's a Dirty Job (But Someone's Gotta Do It)* Bonnie Tyler & Todd Rundgren (1985) UK#73, *Making Love Out of Nothing at All* Air Supply (1983) p US#2/Bonnie Tyler (1996) UK#45; *Objects in the Rear View Mirror May Appear Closer Than They Are* Meat Loaf (1994) US#38 UK#26, *Paradise by the Dashboard Light* Meat Loaf (1978) US#39, *Read 'Em and Weep* Barry Manilow (1984) US#18 UK#17, *Rock 'n' Roll Dreams Come Through* Meat Loaf (1994) US#13, *Total Eclipse of the Heart* Bonnie Tyler (1983) US#1 UK#1/Nicki French (1995) US#2 UK#54; *Two Out of Three Ain't Bad* Meat Loaf (1978) US#11 UK#32, re-issued (1992) UK#69; *You Took the Words Right Out of My Mouth* Meat Loaf (1978) US#39 UK#33. Co-writer: [i] Dean Pitchford.

906. STEPHENSON, Martin (b. 1965, Durham, England) Pop guitarist and vocalist. The leader of the cult group the Daintees. CHART COMPOSITIONS: *Boat to Bolivia* (1986) UK#70, *Trouble Town* (1987) UK#58, *Big Sky New Light* [i] (1992) UK#71. ALBUMS: **Boat to Bolivia** (1986) UK#85, **Gladsome, Humor and Blue** (1988) UK#39, **Salutation Road** (1990) UK#35, **The Boy's Heart** (1992) UK#68, **High Bells Ring True** (1993, all Kitchenware); **Yogi in My Name** (1995), **Sweet Misdeamor** (1995, both Demon). Co-writers: [i] Dunn/Dunn.

907. STEPT, Samuel H. (b. 1897; d. 1964, both America) Film composer. A contributor of songs to such films as "Laughing Irish Eyes" (1936), "Nothing But the Truth" (1941) and "Syncopation" (1942). HIT VERSIONS: *All My Life* [v] Ted Fiorito (1936) US#15/Fats Waller (1936) US#1/Teddy Wilson (1936) US#13; *Do Something* [iii] Helen Kane (1929) US#12, *I Fall in Love with You Every Day* Jimmy Dorsey (1938) US#3, *I'll Always Be in Love with You* [iv] Morton Downey (1929) US#9/Fred Waring's Pennsylvanians (1929) US#3; *Please Don't Talk About Me When I'm Gone* [i] Gene Austin (1931) US#3/Bert Lown (1931) US#10/Johnnie Ray (1953) US#29/Ray Price (1986) C&W#86; *That's My Weakness Now* [iii] Helen Kane (1928) US#5/Russ Mor-

gan (1949) US#17/Winifred Atwell in *Let's Have a Party* (1953) UK#2; *This Is Worth Fighting For* [ii] Jimmy Dorsey (1942) US#13/Ink Spots (1942) R&B#9; *Tiny Little Fingerprints* [vi] Dorsey Brothers Orchestra (1935) US#10, *When They Ask About You* Jimmy Dorsey (1944) US#4. Co-writers: [i] Sidney Clare, [ii] Eddie De Lange, [iii] Bud Green (b. 1897; d. 1981), [iv] Bud Green/Herman Ruby, [v] Sidney Mitchell, [vi] Charles Newman/Charles Tobias.

908. STEVENS, Cat (b. Steven Georgiou, July 21, 1947, London, England) Pop guitarist, pianist and vocalist. A contemplative singer-songwriter of the 1970s, who started out as a bubblegum pop artist, and became the key link between the British folk boom of the 1960s and the singer-songwriter era a decade later. Stevens is also the only performer to introduce the instruments and rhythms of traditional Greek music to mainstream pop. The son of a restauranteur, Stevens grew up listening to Greek folk songs, before learning the guitar in his teens and performing in London folk clubs and coffeehouses. After a series of mid–1960s hits, Stevens was hospitalized in 1968 with tuberculosis. He returned to recording as a considerably maturer songwriter, and after the album **Mona Bone Jakon** (1970), his music seemed to take on a restless, spiritual searching. **Tea for the Tillerman** (1970), with its general theme of a man setting out on an incorporeal journey, and **Teaser and the Firecat** (1971), were contemporary folk music at its very best. **Buddah and the Chocolate Box** (1974) investigated Islamic religious teachings, and after **Back to Earth** (1979), Stevens retired from music making altogether, adopted the Muslim faith, and changed his name to Yusuf Islam. During the 1980s, he financed and taught at a north London Muslim school. Auctioning off all his gold disks and music related possessions, Stevens rejected his Anglo-Greek heritage in favor of the teachings of the Koran. CHART COMPOSITIONS: *I Love My Dog* (1966) US#118 UK#28, *Matthew and Son* (1967) US#115 UK#2, *I'm Gonna Get Me a Gun* (1967) UK#6, *A Bad Night* (1967) UK#20, *Kitty* (1967) UK#47, *Lady D'Arbanville* (1970) UK#8, *Wild World* (1970) US#11, *Moon Shadow* (1971) US#30 UK#22, *Morning Has Broken* [ii] (1971) US#6 UK#9, *Peace Train* (1971) US#7, *Can't Keep It In* (1972) UK#13, *Sitting* (1972) US#16, *The Hurt* (1973) US#31, *Oh Very Young* (1974) US#10, *Ready* (1974) US#26, *Two Fine People* (1975) US#33, *Banapple Gas* (1976) US#41, *(Remember the Days of the) Old School Yard* (1977) US#33 UK#44, *Was Dog a Doughnut* [iii] (1978) R&B#53 US#70, *Bad Brakes* [i] (1979) US#84. ALBUMS: **Matthew and Son** (1967) UK#7, **New Masters** (1967, both Deram); **Mona Bone**

Jakon (1970) US#164 UK#63, **Tea for the Tiller-man** (1970) g US#8 UK#20, **Teaser and the Fire-cat** (1971) g US#2 UK#3, **Catch Bull at Four** (1972) g US#1 UK#2, **Foreigner** (1973) g US#3 UK#3, **Buddah and the Chocolate Box** (1974) g US#2 UK#3, **Numbers** (1976) g US#13, **Izitso** (1977) g US#7 UK#18, **Back to Earth** (1978, all Island) US#33; **The Life of the Last Prophet** (1995, Mountain of Light). COMPILATIONS: **Matthew and Son/New Masters** (1971) US#173, **Very Young and Early Songs** (1972, both Deram) US#94; **Greatest Hits** (1975, Island) p US#6 UK#2; **Footsteps in the Dark — Greatest Hits, Volume 2** (1985, A&M) US#165; **Very Best of Cat Stevens** (1990, Island) UK#4. HIT VERSIONS: *First Cut Is the Deepest, The* P.P. Arnold (1967) UK#18/Keith Hampshire (1973) US#70/Rod Stewart (1977) US#21 UK#1/ Ride the River (1987) C&W#55; *Here Comes My Baby* Tremeloes (1967) US#13 UK#4, *Morning Has Broken* [ii] Neil Diamond (1992) UK#36, *Wild World* Jimmy Cliff (1970) UK#8/Mike Wells (1976) C&W#77/Maxi Priest (1988) US#25 UK#5/Mr. Big (1993) US#30. Co-writers: [i] Alun Davies, [ii] Eleanor Farjeon, [iii] Jean Rousell.

909. STEVENS, Ray (b. Ray Ragsdale, January 24, 1941, Clarkdale, GA) Pop vocalist. A former disc jockey, who studied music theory and composition at Georgia State University, before becoming a pop opportunist with novelty and parody songs during the 1970s. Stevens also hosted his own television show in 1970. CHART COMPOSITIONS: *Sergeant Preston of the Yukon* (1960) US#108, *Ahab, the Arab* (1962) R&B#9 US#5, *Harry the Hairy Ape* (1963) R&B#14 US#17, *Speed Ball* (1963) R&B#29 US#59, *Funny Man* (1963) US#81, re-issued (1968) US#122; *The Great Escape* (1968) US#114, *Mr. Businessman* (1968) US#28, *Gitarzan* [i] (1969) g C&W#1 US#8, *Have a Little Talk with Myself* (1969) C&W#63 US#123, *Everything Is Beautiful* (1970) g C&W#39 US#1 UK#6, *Shriner's Convention* (1980) C&W#7 US#101, *Turn Your Radio On* (1971) C&W#17 US#63, *Nashville* (1973) C&W#37, *The Streak* (1974) g C&W#3 US#1 UK#1, *Everybody Needs a Rainbow* (1974) C&W#37, *Honky Tonk Waltz* (1976) C&W#27. ALBUMS: **1,837 Seconds of Humor** (1962, Mercury) US#135; **Gitarzan** (1969, Monument) US#57; **Everything Is Beautiful** (1970) US#35 UK#62, **Unreal** (1970) US#141, **Turn Your Radio On** (1972) US#175, **Boogity Boogity** (1974) US#159, **Misty** (1975, all Barnaby) US#106 UK#23; **Just for the Record** (1976, Warner Brothers); **Shriner's Convention** (1980, RCA) US#132; **I Have Returned** (1985) g, **He Thinks He's Ray Stevens** (1985) g US#118, **Surely You Joust** (1986 all MCA). COMPILATIONS: **Greatest Hits** (1971) US#95, **Very Best of Ray Stevens** (1975, both Barnaby) US#173. HIT VERSIONS: *Can't Stop Dancin'* [iii] Captain & Tennille (1977) US#13. Co-writers: [i] Bill Everette, [ii] Bill Justis, [iii] John Pritchard, Jr.

910. STEWART, Al (b. September 5, 1945, Glasgow, Scotland) Rock guitarist and vocalist. A literate, folky, singer-songwriter, who was heavily influenced by Bob Dylan during the 1960s, before developing a style of his own. Stewart became a regular on the London folk circuit in the 1960s, and his early albums veered between the profound and the inane. He peaked commercially with his album **Year of the Cat** (1977), at which time he was writing mini-travelogues and extremely original, film-like lyrics, none more so than *Running Man*. CHART COMPOSITIONS: *Year of the Cat* [i] (1977) US#8 UK#31, *On the Border* (1977) US#42, *Time Passages* [i] (1978) US#7, *Song on the Radio* (1979) US#29, *Midnight Rocks* [i] (1980) US#24. ALBUMS: **Bed-sitter Images** (1967), **Love Chronicles** (1969), **Zero She Flies** (1970) UK#40, **Orange** (1972), **Past, Present and Future** (1974) US#133, **Modern Times** (1975, all CBS) US#30; **Year of the Cat** (1977) p US#5 UK#37, **Time Passages** (1978) p US#10 UK#38, **24 Carrots** (1980) US#37 UK#55, **Live/Indian Summer** (1981) US#110, **Russians and Americans** (1984, all RCA) UK#83; **Last Days of the Century** (1988, Enigma); **License to Steal** (1988), **Rhymes in Rooms — Live featuring Peter White** (1993), **Famous Last Words** (1994), **Between the Wars** (1995, all Permanent). COMPILATION: **Chronicles…The Best of Al Stewart** (1991, EMI). Co-writer: [i] Peter White.

911. STEWART, Dave A. (b. September 9, 1952, Sunderland, England) Pop multi-instrumentalist, producer and vocalist. A former member of the pop group Longdancer, which released the albums **If It Was So Simple** (1973) and **Trailer for a Good Life** (1974, both Rocket). In 1971, Stewart joined Annie Lennox in the punk influenced band the Tourists, before they left to form the highly successful duo Eurythmics. In 1992, Stewart formed the short-lived group Vegas with Terry Hall, charting with *Possessed* (1992) UK#32 and *Walk into the Wind* (1992) UK#65, from the album **Vegas** (1992, BMG). He has also recorded as a solo artist and worked as a producer. CHART COMPOSITIONS: *Lily Was Here** (1990) UK#6, *Jack Talking** (1990) UK#69, *Heart of Stone* (1994) UK#36. ALBUMS: **De Kassiere/Lily Was Here** (1990, Anxious) UK#35; **Dave Stewart and the Spiritual Cowboys** (1990, RCA) UK#38; **Jute City** ost (1992, Anxious); **Greetings from the Gutter** (1995, East West). With: * Candy Dulfer. (*See also under* Mick JAGGER, Annie LENNOX, Tom PETTY.)

912. STEWART, Gary (b. May 28, 1945, Letcher County, KY) C&W guitarist, pianist and vocalist. A country and honky tonk performer with rock overtones, who achieved twenty-nine hits between 1973–1988. Stewart first recorded for the Cory label in 1964, and also fronted the 1960s rock group the Amps. His songs have been recorded by numerous artists, including Kenny Price and Hank Snow. CHART COMPOSITIONS: *You're Not the Woman You Used to Be* [ii] (1975) C&W#15, *Ten Years of This* [i] (1977) C&W#16. ALBUMS: **Out of Hand** (1975), **You're Not the Woman You Used to Be** (1975, both MCA); **Steppin' Out** (1976), **Your Place or Mine** (1977), **Little Junior** (1978), **Gary** (1979), **Cactus and a Rose** (1980, all RCA) US#165; **Brotherly Love** (1982), **Those Were the Days** (1983), **Brand New** (1988, all Hightone). COMPILATIONS: **Greatest Hits** (1981), **20 of the Best** (1984, both RCA). HIT VERSION: *Sweet Thang and Cisco* Nat Stuckey (1969) C&W#8. Co-writers: [i] Wayne Carson, [ii] Bill Eldrige.

913. STEWART, John (b. September 5, 1939, San Diego, CA) Pop guitarist and vocalist. The composer of the Monkees' million seller *Daydream Believer* (1967), who, as a singer-songwriter, has toiled for over twenty years in relative obscurity while retaining a cult audience. Stewart first recorded as a member of the Cumberland Three, releasing the album **Folk Scene**, which was followed by two volumes of Civil War songs for Roulette Records in 1960. In 1961, Stewart joined the influential vocal harmony group the Kingston Trio. ALBUMS: **Close-Up** (1961) US#3, **College Concert** (1962) US#3, **Something Special** (1962) US#7, **New Frontier** (1962) US#16, **#16** (1963) US#4, **Sunny Side** (1963) US#7, **Sing a Song with the Kingston Trio** (1964) US#69, **Time to Think** (1964) US#18, **Back in Town** (1964) US#22, **The Kingston Trio (Nick-Bob-John)** (1965) US#53, **Stay Awhile** (1965) US#126, **Once Upon a Time** (1969, all Capitol) US#163. COMPILATION: **Best of the Kingston Trio** (1962, Capitol) g US#7. During the late 1960s, Stewart began recording as a country influenced solo artist. CHART COMPOSITIONS: *Armstrong* (1969) US#74, *Gold* (1979) US#5 UK#43, *Midnight Wind* (1979) US#28, *Lost Her in the Sun* (1980) US#34. ALBUMS: **John Stewart** (1968), **Buffy Ford** (1968), **California Bloodlines** (1969) US#193, **Willard** (1971, all Capitol); **The Lonesome Picker Rides Again** (1971) US#195, **Sunstorm** (1972, both Warner Brothers); **Cannons in the Rain** (1973), **The Phoenix Concerts — Live** (1974) US#195, **Wingless Angels** (1975, all RCA) US#150; **Fire in the Wind** (1978) US#126, **Bombs Away Dream Babies** (1979) US#10, **Dream Babies Go to Hollywood** (1980, all

RSO) US#85; **Revenge of the Budgie** (1982, Takoma); **Trancas** (1984), **Centennial** (1985), **The Last Campaign** (1985), **The Secret Tapes** (1985), **The Trio Years** (1986, all Homecoming); **Punch the Big Guy** (1987, Cypress); **Bullets in the Hour Glass** (1993, Shanachie); **American Journey** (1996, Laserlight). COMPILATIONS: **In Concert** (1980), **Forgotten Songs of Old Yesterday** (1980, both RCA); **Airdream Believer** (1995, Shanachie). HIT VERSIONS: *Daydream Believer* Monkees (1967) g US#1 UK#5, re-issued (1986) US#79/Anne Murray (1980) C&W#3 US#12 UK#61/Simply Red & White (1996) UK#41; *July, You're a Woman* Pat Boone (1969) US#100, *Never Going Back* Lovin' Spoonful (1968) US#73.

914. STEWART, Rod (b. Roderick David Stewart, January 10, 1945, London, England) Rock vocalist. A folk, R&B and blues influenced singer, whose recordings with the group the Faces during the early 1970s, were some of Britain's most unpretentious rock and roll of period. Stewart's first solo recordings were generally excellent examples of folk influenced pop, but he lost the plot in the late 1970s, and his distinctive voice has been largely wasted on flirtations with every passing musical fashion. Stewart first recorded in the R&B group Steampacket in 1965, their recordings later being collected on the albums **Places and Faces** (1971, Byg), and **First of the Supergroups** (1977, Charly). As lead vocalist in the Jeff Beck Group, Stewart recorded the albums **Truth** (1968) US#15 and **Beckola** (1969, both Columbia) US#15 UK#39, before, in 1969, linking up with former members of the Small Faces as the Faces. CHART COMPOSITIONS: *Stay with Me* [x] (1972) US#17 UK#6, *Cindy Incidentally* [xiv] (1973) US#48 UK#2, *Pool Hall Richard* [xviii] (1974) UK#8, *You Can Make Me Dance Sing or Anything* [xiii] (1974) UK#12, *The Faces EP* [xviii] (1977) UK#41. ALBUMS: **First Step** (1970) US#119 UK#45, **Long Player** (1971) UK#31, **A Nod's as Good as a Wink...To a Blind Horse** (1971) g US#6 UK#2, **Ooh La La** (1973, all Warner Brothers) US#21 UK#1; **Coast to Coast: Overture and Beginners** (1974, Mercury) US#63 UK#3. COMPILATION: **Best of the Faces** (1977, Riva) UK#24. Stewart broke the group up in 1974 in order to concentrate on his solo career. CHART COMPOSITIONS: *Maggie May* [xv] (1971) US#1 UK#1, re-issued (1976) UK#31; *You Wear It Well* [xv] (1972) US#13 UK#1, *Farewell* [xv] (1974) UK#7, *Tonight's the Night (Gonna Be Alright)* (1976) US#1 UK#5, *The Killing of Georgie (Parts 1 and 2)* (1976) US#30 UK#2, *You're in My Heart* (1977) US#4 UK#3, *Ole Ola (Muhler Brasileira)* [ii] with the Scotland World Cup Squad (1978) UK#4, *Hotlegs* [xi] (1978) US#28

UK#5, *I Was Only Joking* [xi] (1978) US#22, *D'Ya Think I'm Sexy* [iii] (1978) p R&B#5 US#1 UK#1, *Ain't Love a Bitch* [xi] (1979) US#22 UK#11, *Blondes (Have More Fun)* (1979) UK#63, *Passion* [vi] (1980) R&B#65 US#5 UK#17, *Somebody Special* [vii] (1981) US#71, *Tonight I'm Yours (Don't Hurt Me)* [ix] (1981) US#20 UK#8, *Young Turks* [iv] (1981) US#5 UK#11, *Baby Jane* [x] (1983) US#14 UK#1, *What Am I Gonna Do (I'm So in Love with You)* [v] (1983) US#35 UK#3, *Sweet Surrender* (1983) UK#23, *Infatuation* [xii] (1984) US#6 UK#27, *Every Beat of My Heart* [xvi] (1986) US#83 UK#2, *Another Heartache* [i] (1986) US#52 UK#54, *Lost in You* [xvii] (1988) US#12 UK#21, *Forever Young* [ix] (1988) US#12 UK#57, *Crazy About Her* [viii] (1989) US#11, *You're the Star* (1995) UK#19, *Lady Luck* (1995) UK#56, *If We Fall in Love Tonight* (1996) UK#58. ALBUMS: **An Old Raincoat Won't Ever Let You Down/The Rod Stewart Album** (1969) US#139, **Gasoline Alley** (1970, both Vertigo) US#27 UK#62; **Every Picture Tells a Story** (1971, Mercury) p US#1 UK#1; **Never a Dull Moment** (1972, Philips) g US#2 UK#1; **Smiler** (1974, Mercury) US#13 UK#1; **Atlantic Crossing** (1975, Warner Brothers) g US#9 UK#1; **A Night on the Town** (1976) p US#2 UK#1, **Foot Loose and Fancy Free** (1977) p US#2 UK#3, **Blondes Have More Fun** (1978) p US#1 UK#3, **Foolish Behavior** (1980) p US#12 UK#4, **Tonight I'm Yours** (1981) p US#11 UK#8, **Absolutely Live** (1982, all Riva) US#46 UK#35; **Body Wishes** (1983) US#30 UK#5, **Camouflage** (1984) g US#18 UK#8, **Love Touch/Rod Stewart** (1986) US#28 UK#5, **Out of Order** (1988) p US#20 UK#11, **Vagabond Heart** (1991) p US#10 UK#2, **Lead Vocalist** (1993) UK#3, **Unplugged...and Seated** (1993) US#2 UK#2, **A Spanner in the Works** (1995) g US#35 UK#4, **If We Fall in Love Tonight** (1996, all Warner Brothers) UK#8. COMPILATIONS: **Sing It Again, Rod** (1973) g US#31 UK#1, **Best of Rod Stewart** (1976, both Mercury) g US#90 UK#18; **Greatest Hits** (1979, Riva) p US#22 UK#1; **Best of Rod Stewart** (1989) UK#3, **Storyteller/The Complete Anthology: 1964–1990** (1989) g US#54, **Downtown Train/Selections from Storyteller** (1990, all Warner Brothers) p US#20; **Best of Rod Stewart and the Faces, 1971–1975** (1992, Mercury) UK#58. HIT VERSIONS: *D'Ya Think I'm Sexy* [iii] Steve Dahl as *Do You Think I'm Disco* (1979) US#58, *Gasoline Alley* Elkie Brooks (1983) UK#52, *Tonight's the Night (Gonna Be Alright)* Roy Head (1978) C&W#28. Co-writers: [i] Bryan Adams/Jim Vallance/R. Wayne, [ii] Jair Amorim/Philip Chen/Evaldo Gouveia, [iii] Carmine Appice, [iv] Carmine Appice/Duane Hitchings/Kevin Savigar, [v] Tony Brock/Jay David, [vi] Philip Chen/Jim Cregan/Gary Grainer/Kevin Savigar, [vii] Philip Chen/Jim Cregan/Gary Grainer/

Harley/Kevin Savigar, [viii] Jim Cregan/Duane Hitchings, [ix] Jim Cregan/Kevin Savigar, [x] Jay Davis, [xi] Gary Grainer, [xii] Duane Hitchings/Michael Omartian, [xiii] Kenny Jones (b. September 16, 1948, London, England)/Ian McLagan (b. May 12, 1945, Hounslow, England)/Ron Wood (b. June 1, 1947, Hillingdon, England)/Tetsu Yamauchi, [xiv] Ian McLagan/Ron Wood, [xv] Martin Quittenton, [xvi] Kevin Savigar, [xvii] A. Taylor, [xviii] Ron Wood.

915. STILLMAN, Al Film and show lyricist. A Tin Pan Alley lyricist who often worked with the composer Robert Allen. Stillman's songs were included in the shows "Earl Carroll's Vanities" (1940) and "Stars on Ice" (1942), and the films "Cuban Pete" (1940) and "Happy Anniversary" (1959). HIT VERSIONS: *Bless 'Em All* [viii] King Sisters (1941) US#25, *Breeze and I, The* [iv] Xavier Cugat (1940) US#13/Jimmy Dorsey (1940) US#1/Vic Damone (1954) US#21/Fentones (1962) UK#48/Caterina Valente (1955) US#8 UK#5/Santo & Johnny (1960) US#109; *Can You Find It in Your Heart* [i] Tony Bennett (1956) US#16, *Chances Are* [i] Johnny Mathis (1957) R&B#12 US#1, *Enchanted Island* [i] Four Lads (1958) US#12, *Every Step of the Way* [i] Johnny Mathis (1963) US#30, *Happy Anniversary* [i] Four Lads (1959)/Joan Regan (1960) UK#29, *Home for the Holidays* [i] Perry Como (1955) US#8, *I Believe* [vii] Jane Froman (1953) US#11/Frankie Laine (1953) g US#2 UK#1/David Whitfield (1960) UK#49/Bachelors (1964) US#33 UK#2/Robson Greene & Jerome Flynn (1995) UK#1; *If Dreams Came True* [i] Pat Boone (1958) US#7 UK#16, *In My Little Red Book* [iii] Guy Lombardo (1938) US#14, *It's Not for Me to Say* [i] Johnny Mathis (1957) US#5, *Juke Box Saturday Night* [x] Glenn Miller (1942) US#7/Modernaires & Paula Kelly (1953) US#23; *Mama Yo Quiero (I Want My Mama)* [xi] Isham Jones (1924) US#8, *Moments to Remember* [i] Four Lads (1955) US#2/Vogues (1969) US#47; *My One and Only Heart* [i] Perry Como (1953) US#11, *No, Not Much!* [i] Four Lads (1956) US#2/Vogues (1969) US#34; *Now and Forever* [xii] Bert Kaempfert (1961) US#48, *Room with a View, A* [xiii] Tommy Dorsey (1939) US#13, *Say "Si Si"* [ix] Xavier Cugat (1936) US#19/Andrews Sisters (1940) US#4/Glenn Miller (1940) US#15/Eugenie Baird (1953) US#26/Mills Brothers (1953) US#12; *Teacher, Teacher* [i] Johnny Mathis (1958) US#21 UK#27, *Tell Me That You Love Me* [ii] Freddy Martin (1935) US#7, *There's Only One of You* [i] Four Lads (1958) US#10, *Way of Love, The* [v] Cher (1972) US#7, *Who Needs You?* [i] Four Lads (1957) US#9, *You Alone* [i] Perry Como (1953) US#9. Co-writers: [i] Robert Allen, [ii] C.A. Bixio, [iii] Ray Bloch/Nat Simon, [iv] Tutti Camarata/Ernesto Leucona, [v]

Jacques Dieval/Mariano Ruiz, [vi] Ervin Drake, [vii] Ervin Drake/Irvin Graham/Jimmy Shirl, [viii] Jimmie Hughes/Frank Lake, [ix] Ernesto Leucona/Francia Luban, [x] Paul McGrane, [xi] Jararaca Paiva/Vincente Paiva, [xii] Jan Savitt/Peter Tchaikovsky, [xiii] Einer Swan. (*See also under* Henry MANCINI, Buck RAM, Arthur SCHWARTZ.)

916. STILLS, Stephen (b January 3, 1945, Dallas, TX) Rock multi-instrumentalist and vocalist. A highly respected former session guitarist, who once failed an audition to join the Monkees. Stills first came to prominence in the seminal folk-rock group Buffalo Springfield, alongside Richie Furay and Neil Young. CHART COMPOSITIONS: *For What It's Worth* (1967) US#7, *Bluebird* (1967) US#58, *Un-Mondo* (1968) US#105, *Special Care* (1968) US#107, *Rock 'n' Roll Woman* (1968) US#44. ALBUMS: **Buffalo Springfield** (1967) US#80, **Buffalo Springfield Again** (1967) US#44, **Last Time Around** (1968, all Atco) US#42. COMPILATIONS: **Retrospective** (1969) p US#42, **Buffalo Springfield** (1973, both Atco) US#104. As a member of Crosby, Stills and Nash, Stills wrote the hits *Suite: Judy Blue Eyes* (1969) US#21, *Fair Game* (1977) US#43, *Southern Cross* [i] (1982) US#18, *Too Much Love to Hide* [iv] (1983) US#69, and *War Games* (1983) US#43. Since the early 1970s, he has also recorded as a solo artist. CHART COMPOSITIONS: *Love the One You're With* (1971) US#14 UK#37, *Sit Yourself Down* (1971) US#37, *Change Partners* (1971) US#43, *Marianne* (1971) US#42, *It Doesn't Matter** (1972) US#72, *Rock 'n' Roll Crazies** (1972) US#92, *Isn't It About Time** (1973) US#56, *Turn Back the Pages* [ii] (1975) US#84, *Stranger* [iii] (1984) US#61. ALBUMS: **Supersession** with Mike Bloomfield and Al Kooper (1968, Columbia) g US#12; **Stephen Stills** (1970) g US#3 UK#30, **Stephen Stills 2** (1971) g US#8 UK#22, **Manassas*** (1972) g US#4 UK#30, **Down the Road*** (1973, all Atlantic) US#26 UK#33; **Stills** (1975, Columbia) US#19 UK#31; **Live** (1975, Atlantic) US#42 UK#31; **Illegal Stills** (1976, Columbia) US#31 UK#54; **Long May You Run** with Neil Young (1976, Reprise) g US#26 UK#12; **Thoroughfare Gap** (1978, Columbia) US#83; **Right By You** (1984, Atlantic) US#75. COMPILATION: **Still Stills — The Best of Stephen Stills** (1977, Atlantic) US#127. HIT VERSIONS: *For What It's Worth* King Curtis (1967) US#87/Cher (1969) US#125/Sergio Mendes & Brasil '66 (1970) US#101; *Love the One You're With* Isley Brothers (1971) R&B#3 US#18/Brentwood (1983) C&W#96/Bucks Fizz (1986) UK#47/Luther Vandross (1994) US#95 UK#31. As: * Manassas. Co-writers: [i] Michael Curtis/Richard Curtis, [ii] D. Dacus, [iii] Chris Stills, [iv] G. Tolman. (*See also under* David CROSBY.)

917. Sting (b. Gordon Matthew Sumner, October 2, 1951, Wallsend, England) Rock bassist, producer and vocalist. The lead singer in the new wave trio the Police, who later pursued a highly successful solo career. Sting first played bass guitar with the Ronnie Pierson Trio on a cruise liner, and performed during the early 1970s with the groups Earthrise, the Phoenix Jazz Band, and the River City Jazz Band. While working as a teacher in 1972, he recorded an eponymous album with the Newcastle Big Band (1972, Impulse), before joining the jazz-rock group Last Exit. In 1975 he formed the Police, which created a punk-rock influenced sound that was based around Stewart Copeland's inverted reggae drumming. The group enjoyed a meteoric rise to fame on the back of Sting's melodramatic compositions, which grew increasingly pretentious, with the album **Ghost in the Machine** (1981), being titled after a work by the author Arthur Koestler, and the four million selling **Synchronicity** (1983), being thematically influenced by Carl Jung's psychology. CHART COMPOSITIONS: *Can't Stand Losing You* (1978) UK#42, re-entry (1979) UK#2, live version (1995) UK#27; *Roxanne* (1979) US#32 UK#12, *Message in a Bottle* (1979) US#74 UK#1, *Fall Out* (1979) UK#47, *Walking on the Moon* (1979) UK#1, *So Lonely* (1980) UK#6, *Six Pack* (1980) UK#17, *Don't Stand So Close to Me* (1980) US#10 UK#1, new version (1986) US#46 UK#24; *De Do Do Do De Da Da Da* (1980) US#10 UK#5, *Invisible Sun* (1981) UK#2, *Every Little Thing She Does Is Magic* (1981) US#3 UK#1, *Spirits in the Material World* (1981) US#11 UK#12, *Secret Journey* (1982) US#46, *Every Breath You Take* (1983) g US#1 UK#1, *Wrapped Around Your Finger* (1983) US#8 UK#7, *King of Pain* (1984) US#3 UK#17, *Synchronicity II* (1983) US#16 UK#17. ALBUMS: **Outlandos D'Amour** (1979) p US#23 UK#6, **Reggata De Blanc** (1979) g US#25 UK#1, **Zenyatta Mondatta** (1980) p US#5 UK#1, **Ghost in the Machine** (1981) p US#2 UK#1, **Synchronicity** (1983, all A&M) p US#1 UK#1. COMPILATIONS: **Every Breath You Take — The Singles** (1986) p US#7 UK#1, **Greatest Hits** (1992) UK#10, **Message in a Box — The Complete Recordings** (1993) g US#79, **Live** (1995, all A&M) US#86 UK#25. After the group broke up in the early 1980s, Sting embarked upon a solo career, taking in jazz and world music influences, but all too often borrowing liberally from literature, naming the album **...Nothing Like the Sun** after a quote from Shakespeare, copping the title of *Tea in the Sahara* from Paul Bowles' novel "The Sheltering Sky," and quoting Frederick Nietzsche in *History Will Teach Us Nothing* and T.S. Eliot in *Bring on the Night*. Sting has also released the CD-ROM "All This Time" (1995). HIT VERSIONS: *If You Love Somebody Set Them Free* (1985)

R&B#17 US#3 UK#24, *Love Is the Seventh Wave* (1985) US#17 UK#41, *Fortress Around Your Heart* (1985) US#8 UK#49, *Russians* (1985) US#16 UK#2, re-entry (1986) UK#71; *Moon Over Bourbon Street* (1986) UK#44, *We'll Be Together* (1987) R&B#39 US#7 UK#41, *Be Still My Beating Heart* (1988) US#15, *Englishman in New York* (1988) US#84 UK#51, re-mixed (1990) UK#15; *Fragile* (1988) UK#70, *All This Time* (1990) US#5 UK#22, *Mad About You* (1991) UK#56, *The Soul Cages* (1991) UK#57, *It's Probably Me* [i] with Eric Clapton (1993) UK#30, *If I Ever Lose My Faith in You* (1993) US#17 UK#14, *Seven Days* (1993) UK#25, *Fields of Gold* (1993) US#24 UK#16, *Shape of My Heart* (1993) UK#57, *Nothing 'Bout Me* (1993) US#57 UK#32, *Demolition Man* (1993) US#162 UK#21, *When We Dance* (1994) US#38 UK#9, *This Cowboy Song* (1995) UK#15, *Spirits in the Material World* with Pato Banton (1996) UK#36, *Let Your Soul Be Your Pilot* (1996) US#86 UK#15, *You Still Touch Me* (1996) US#89 UK#27, *Live at TFI Friday EP* (1996) UK#53, *I Was Brought to My Senses* (1996) UK#31, *I'm So Happy I Can't Stop Crying* (1996) UK#54. ALBUMS: **The Dream of Blue Turtles** (1985) p US#2 UK#3, **Bring on the Night** (1986) UK#16, **...Nothing Like the Sun** (1987) p US#9 UK#1, **The Soul Cages** (1991) p US#2 UK#1, **Acoustic Live in Newcastle** (1991), **Ten Summoner's Tales** (1993) p US#2 UK#2, **Mercury Falling** (1996, all A&M) p US#5 UK#4. COMPILATION: **Fields of Gold — The Best of Sting, 1984–1994** (1995, A&M) p US#7 UK#2. HIT VERSIONS: *Bed's Too Big Without You, The* Sheila Hylton (1981) UK#35, *Every Breath You Take* Mason Dixon (1983) C&W#69/Rich Landers (1983) C&W#68/Puff Daddy (1997) p R&B#1 US#1 UK#1; *Every Little Thing He Does Is Magic* Shawn Colvin (1994) UK#65, *King of Pain* "Weird" Al Yankovic as *King of Suede* (1984) US#62, *Message in a Bottle* Dance Floor Virus (1995) UK#49. Co-writers: [i] Eric Clapton/Michael Kamen. (*See also under* Mark KNOPFLER.)

918. STOCK, Mike (b. December 3, 1951), **AITKEN, Matt** (b. August 25, 1956), and **WATERMAN, Peter** (b. January 15, 1947, all England) All pop multi-instrumentalists and producers. The most successful British writing and production team of the 1980s, which emulated the hit factory principals of Motown Records on their own PWL label, charting over fifty compositions and producing over one hundred and twenty top forty hits. Stock, Aitken and Waterman masterminded the singing careers of the former Australian soap opera stars, Kylie Minogue and Jason Donovan. Waterman was a disc jockey before he became a producer, co-writing *Alright Baby* for the group Stevenson's Rocket, before

linking up with the keyboard players Aitken and Stock. As a trio, they began producing dance oriented records and cutting their own occasional singles, charting with *Roadblock* (1987) UK#13, *Mr. Sleaze* (1987) UK#3, *Packjammed (With the Party Posse)* (1987) UK#41, and *SS Paparazzi* (1988) UK#68. By the mid–1990s, it had all turned sour, and their partnership disintegrated into a series of legal disputes over royalty payments. HIT VERSIONS: *Alright Baby* Stevenson's Rocket (1975) UK#37, *Better the Devil You Know* Kylie Minogue (1990) UK#2, *Beyond Your Wildest Dreams* Sybil (1993) R&B#90 UK#41, *Can't Shake the Feeling* Big Fun (1989) UK#8, *Cross My Broken Heart* Sinitta (1988) UK#6, *Especially for You* Jason Donovan & Kylie Minogue (1989) UK#1, *Every Day (I Love You More)* Jason Donovan (1989) UK#2, *Finer Feelings* [viii] Kylie Minogue (1992) UK#11, *F.L.M.* Mel & Kim (1987) UK#7, *Good Times with Bad Boys* [i] Boy Krazy (1993) US#59, *Got to Be Certain* Kylie Minogue (1988) UK#2, *G.T.O.* Sinitta (1987) UK#15, *Hand on Your Heart* Kylie Minogue (1989) UK#1, *Hang on to Your Love* (1990) Jason Donovan UK#8, *Happenin' All Over Again* Lonnie Gordon (1990) US#98 UK#4, *Harder I Try, The* Brother Beyond (1988) UK#2, *He Ain't No Competition* Brother Beyond (1988) UK#6, *I Can't Help It* [ii] Bananarama (1987) US#47 UK#20, *I Don't Wanna Get Hurt* Donna Summer (1989) UK#7, *I Heard a Rumor* [ii] Bananarama (1987) US#4 UK#14, *I Just Don't Have the Heart* Cliff Richard (1989) UK#3, *I Should Be So Lucky* Kylie Minogue (1988) US#28 UK#1, *I Want You Back* [ii] Bananarama (1988) UK#5, *I'd Rather Jack* Reynolds Girls (1989) UK#8, *If You Were with Me Now* [vi] Kylie Minogue & Keith Washington (1991) UK#4, *It Would Take à Strong Man* Rick Astley (1988) US#10, *It's No Secret* Kylie Minogue (1989) US#37, *Je Ne Sais Pas, Pourquoi* Kylie Minogue (1988) UK#2, *Last Thing on My Mind* [iv] Bananarama (1992) UK#71, *Let's All Chant* Pat & Mick (1988) UK#11, *Love in the First Degree* [ii] Bananarama (1987) UK#3, *Love, Truth and Honesty* [iii] Bananarama (1988) US#89 UK#23, *Love's About to Change My Mind* Donna Summer (1989) US#85 UK#20, *Magic's Back* Malcom McLaren & Alison Limerick (1991) UK#42, *More Than Physical* [ii] Bananarama (1986) US#73 UK#41, *Movin' On* [iv] Bananarama (1992) UK#24, *Never Gonna Give You Up* Rick Astley (1987) US#1 UK#1, *Never Too Late* Kylie Minogue (1989) UK#4, *Nothing Can Divide Us* Jason Donovan (1988) UK#5, *Nothing's Gonna Stop Me Now* Samantha Fox (1987) US#80 UK#8, *Respectable* Mel & Kim (1987) UK#1, *R.S.V.P.* Jason Donovan (1991) UK#17, *Say I'm Your Number One* Princess (1985) R&B#20 UK#7, *Shocked* Kylie Minogue (1991) UK#6, *Showing Out (Get Fresh at the Weekend)* Mel

& Kim (1987) R&B#23 US#78 UK#3, *Step Back in Time* Kylie Minogue (1990) UK#4, *Take Me to Your Heart* Rick Astley (1988) UK#8, *Tears on My Pillow* Kylie Minogue (1990) UK#1, *That's the Way It Is* Mel & Kim (1988) UK#10, *That's What Love Can Do* Boy Krazy (1993) US#18, *This Time I Know It's for Real* [ix] Donna Summer (1989) g US#7 UK#3, *Together Forever* Rick Astley (1988) US#1 UK#2, *Too Many Broken Hearts in the World* Jason Donovan (1989) UK#1, *Toy Boy* Sinitta (1987) UK#4, *What Do I Have to Do* Kylie Minogue (1991) UK#6, *What Kind of Fool* [vii] Kylie Minogue (1992) UK#14, *Whatever I Do (Wherever I Go)* [i] Hazel Dean (1984) UK#4, *When Love Takes Over You* Donna Summer (1989) UK#72, *When You Come Back to Me* Jason Donovan (1989) UK#2, *Whenever You Need Somebody* Rick Astley (1987) UK#3, *Who's Leaving Who* Hazel Dean (1988) UK#4, *Word Is Out* [i] Kylie Minogue (1991) UK#16, *Wouldn't Change a Thing* Kylie Minogue (1989) UK#2, *You'll Never Stop Me Loving You* Sonia (1989) UK#1. All compositions Stock/Aitken/Waterman, except: [i] Matt Aitken/Mike Stock, [ii] Sarah Dallin (b. December 17, 1961, Bristol, England)/Siobhan Fahey (b. September 10, 1957, London, England)/Karen Woodward (b. April 2, 1961, Bristol, England), [iii] Sarah Dallin/Jacqui O'Sullivan/Karen Woodward, [iv] Sarah Dallin/Mike Stock/Peter Waterman/Karen Woodward, [v] Malcom McLaren, [vi] Kylie Minogue (b. May 28, 1968, Melbourne, Australia)/Keith Washington, [vii] Kylie Minogue/Mike Stock/Peter Waterman, [viii] Mike Stock/Peter Waterman, [ix] Donna Summer.

919. STONE, Jesse (b. November 16, 1901, Atchison, KS) R&B pianist, arranger and vocalist. An influential R&B songwriter, who was raised in Missouri and first performed in vaudeville. As Jesse Stone and His Blues Serenaders he recorded the single *Starvation Blues* (1926), and during the 1930s he worked as an arranger for George E. Lee, later recording such solo sides as *Shakey Feelings* (1937). In the 1940s, Stone worked at Atlantic Records, and during the 1950s he worked as a freelance A&R man. HIT VERSIONS: *As Long as I'm Moving* Ruth Brown (1955) R&B#4, *Cole Slaw* Frank Culley (1949) R&B#11/Louis Jordan (1949) R&B#7; *Don't Let Go* Roy Hamilton (1958) R&B#2 US#13/Mel Tillis (1974) C&W#11; *Flip Flop and Fly* Joe Turner (1955) R&B#2, *Idaho* Benny Goodman (1942) US#4/Alvino Rey (1942) US#3; *It Should Have Been Me* Ray Charles (1954) R&B#4, *Lipstick-a-Powder-'n Paint* Gisele MacKenzie & Helen O'Connell (1953) US#25/Shakin' Stevens (1985) UK#11; *Money Honey* Drifters (1953) R&B#1/Elvis Presley (1956) US#76, *Shake, Rattle and Roll* Joe Turner (1954) R&B#1 US#22/Bill Haley & His Comets (1954)

UK#4/Arthur Conley (1967) R&B#20 US#31/Billy Swan (1976) C&W#95; *Sorghum Switch* Jimmy Dorsey (1942) US#21, *Your Cash Ain't Nothin' But Trash* Clovers (1954) R&B#6. (*See also under* Ahmed ERTEGUN.)

920. STONE, Sly (b. Sylvester Stewart, March 15, 1944, Dallas, TX) R&B multi-instrumentalist and vocalist. An R&B innovator who recorded a small but conspicuous legacy of psychedelic and rock influenced soul music. Stone was also the first R&B artist to utilize a drum machine on record. He sang gospel from the age of four in the family group the Stewart Four, which also released the single *On the Battlefield for My Lord*. Stone learned the drums, keyboards and guitar, before playing with various local doo-wop groups in his teens. After majoring in music at Vallejo Junior College, Stone played in numerous 1960s bar bands and recorded unsuccessful solo singles. He also worked as an arranger and producer for Grace Slick's group the Great Society. In 1966, Stone was a disc jockey in San Francisco, where he became a radio celebrity and formed the Stoners, which became the Family Stone, a judiciously talented, inter-racial collective of R&B-hippies that were to influence the future funk stars, George Clinton and Prince. By 1967, Sly and the Family Stone had merged rock, funk, psychedelia and R&B, for a series of splendid dance records. A memorable performance at the Woodstock Festival in 1970 introduced the group to a white rock audience, and its album **Stand** (1969), was a masterpiece of the era, creating a widely imitated pop-funk sound that emphasized heavy guitar riffs, mesmeric rhythms, and the completely new style of slap bass playing by Larry Graham. **There's a Riot Goin' On** (1971), was a politically strident, militant collection that focused on civil rights, economics and government corruption. Riddled with post–1960s paranoia, it defined the death of the hippie dream, and the harsh realities of Vietnam and the ensuing Nixon years. By 1973, Stone had probably ruffled too many establishment feathers, and he became the regular subject of police visits and drug arrests. Although many of the charges against him were subsequently dropped, the harassment exasperated his declining mental and physical health, and he became a promotor's nightmare when he regularly failed to appear for concerts. Stone has recorded very little since the late 1970s. CHART COMPOSITIONS: *Dance to the Music* [ii] (1968) R&B#9 US#8 UK#7, *M'Lady* (1968) UK#32, *Everyday People* [ii] (1968) g R&B#1 US#1 UK#36, *Sing a Simple Song* [ii] (1969) R&B#28 US#89, *Stand!* [ii] (1969) R&B#14 US#22, *I Want to Take You Higher* [ii] (1969) R&B#24 US#60, *Hot Fun in the Summertime*

[ii] (1969) R&B#3 US#2, *Thank You (Falettinme Be Mice Elf Agin)* [ii] (1970) g R&B#1 US#1, *Family Affair* [ii] (1971) g R&B#1 US#1 UK#15, *Runnin' Away* [ii] (1972) R&B#15 US#23 UK#17, *Smilin'* [ii] (1972) B#21 US#42, *If You Want Me to Stay* [ii] (1973) g R&B#3 UK#12, *Frisky* [ii] (1973) R&B#28 US#79, *If It Were Left Up to Me* [ii] (1974) R&B#57, *Time for Livin'* [ii] (1974) R&B#10 US#32, *Loose Booty* [ii] (1974) R&B#22 US#84, *Le Lo Li* (1975) R&B#75, *Family Again* [ii] (1977) R&B#85, *I Get High on You* (1975) R&B#3 US#52, *Remember Who You Are* [ii] (1979) R&B#38 US#104, *Crazay* with Jesse Johnson (1986) R&B#2 US#53. ALBUMS: **Dance to the Music** (1968) US#142, **Life** (1968) US#195, **Stand** (1969) p US#13, **A Whole New Thing** (1970), **There's a Riot Goin' On** (1971) g US#1 UK#31, **Fresh** (1973) g US#7, **Small Talk** (1974) g US#15, **High on You** (1975) US#45, **Heard You Missed Me** (1976, all Epic); **Back on the Right Track** (1979) US#152, **Ain't But the One Way** (1983, both Warner Brothers). COMPILATIONS: **Greatest Hits** (1970) p US#2, **Best of Sly and the Family Stone** (1992), **Ten Years Too Soon** (1979, all Epic); **Takin' You Higher — The Best of Sly and the Family Stone** (1992, Sony). HIT VERSIONS: *C'mon and Swim* [i] Bobby Freeman (1964) US#5, *Dance to the Music* [ii] Muscle Shoals Horns (1977) R&B#57/Stars On in *Stars on Long Play 2/On 45, Volume 2* (1981) US#120 UK#18; *Everyday People* [ii] Joan Jett & the Blackhearts (1983) US#37/Aretha Franklin (1991) UK#69; *Family Affair* [ii] S'Xpress in *Hey Music Lover* (1989) UK#6/B.E.F. featuring Lala Hathaway (1991) UK#37/Shabba Ranks (1993) R&B#16 US#84 UK#18; *Hot Fun in the Summertime* [ii] David T. Walker (1972) US#104/Dayton (1982) R&B#17 US#58; *I Want to Take You Higher* [ii] Ike & Tina Turner (1970) R&B#25 US#34/Kool & the Gang (1971) R&B#35 US#105; *I'll Never Fall in Love Again* Bobby Freeman (1965) US#131, *Life and Death in G & A* Abaco Dream (1969) R&B#25 US#74, *Sing a Simple Song* [ii] Noble Knights (1969) US#132/West Street Mob (1982) R&B#44 US#89; *Somebody's Watching You* Little Sister (1970) US#32. Co-writers: [i] Thomas Coman, [ii] Todd Thomas.

921. STRAYHORN, Billy (b. William Strayhorn, November 29, 1915, Dayton, OH; d. May 31, 1967, New York, NY) Jazz pianist and arranger. One of the finest composers and arrangers of his era. Strayhorn was a classically trained musician who, in 1938, submitted one of his compositions to Duke Ellington, who was sufficiently impressed by it to form a working partnership that resulted in approximately two hundred songs. Strayhorn was Ellington's pianist for nearly three decades, and their compositions and arrangements feature some of the most sophisticated harmonic structures in jazz. Strayhorn also composed melodies on his own, the best known being the standard *Lush Life*. There have been many tribute albums to him, none better than Ellington's **...And His Mother Called Him Bill** (1967, RCA). Strayhorn died of cancer in 1967. ALBUMS: **Billy Strayhorn Trio** (1951), **Billy Strayhorn and All Stars** (1951, both Mercer); **Billy Strayhorn Septet** (1958), **Cue for Saxophone** (1959, both Felsted), **Live** (1960, Roulette); **The Peaceful Side of Billy Strayhorn** (1961, United Artists). HIT VERSION: *Take the "A" Train* Duke Ellington (1941) US#11, re-issued (1943) US#19. (*See also under* Duke ELLINGTON.)

922. STRUMMER, Joe (b. John Mellors, August 21, 1952, Ankara, Turkey) Rock guitarist, producer and vocalist. The co-founder, with the guitarist Mick Jones, of the Clash, the most literate and political punk group of the 1970s. Strummer and Jones were blessed with a melodic sensibility not normally associated with the genre, and the group's album **London Calling** (1979), stands alongside the Sex Pistols' debut set as punk's finest hour. CHART COMPOSITIONS: *White Riot* [i] (1977) UK#38, *Complete Control* [i] (1977) UK#28, *Clash City Rockers* [i] (1978) UK#35, *(White Man) In Hammersmith Palais* [i] (1978) UK#32, *Tommy Gun* [i] (1979) UK#19, *English Civil War (Johnny Comes Marching Home)* [i] (1979) UK#25, *The Cost of Living EP* [i] (1979) UK#22, *London Calling* [i] (1979) UK#11, re-issued (1988) UK#46, re-issued (1991) UK#64; *Train in Vain (Stand By Me)* [i] (1980) US#23, *Bankrobber* [i] (1980) UK#12, *The Call Up* [i] (1980) UK#40, *Hitsville U.K.* [i] (1981) UK#56, *The Magnificent Seven* [i] (1981) UK#34, *This Is Radio Clash* [i] (1981) UK#47, *Know Your Rights* [i] (1982) UK#43, *Rock the Casbah* [ii] (1982) US#8 UK#30, re-issued (1991) UK#15; *Should I Stay or Should I Go?* [i]/*Straight to Hell* [i] (1982) US#45 UK#17, re-issued (1983) US#50, re-issued (1991) UK#1; *This Is England* (1985) UK#24. ALBUMS: **The Clash** (1977) US#126 UK#12, **Give 'Em Enough Rope** (1978) US#128 UK#2, **London Calling** (1979) g US#27 UK#9, **Sandinista!** (1980) US#24 UK#19, **Combat Rock** (1982) p US#7 UK#2, **Cut the Crap** (1985, all CBS) US#88 UK#16. COMPILATIONS: **Black Market Clash** (1980, Columbia) US#74, **The Story of the Clash, Volume 1** (1988, CBS) US#142 UK#7; **The Singles** (1991) UK#68, **The Clash on Broadway** (1995, Columbia). The group split up in 1985, after which Strummer pursued a solo recording and acting career. Throughout 1991, he became Shane MacGowan's replacement in the group the Pogues. CHART COMPOSITIONS: *Love Kills* (1986) UK#69, *Just the One* (1995) UK#12. ALBUMS:

Walker ost (1988, Virgin); **Permanent Record** ost (1988), **Earthquake Weather** (1989, both Epic) UK#58. Co-writers: [i] Mick Jones, [ii] Mick Jones/Topper Headon (b. May 30, 1955, Bromley, England)/Paul Simonon (b. December 15, 1955, London, England).

923. STUART, Leslie (b. Thomas Augustine Barrett, March 15, 1864, Southport; d. March 27, 1928, Richmond, both England) Film and stage composer, organist. A teenage church organist who began writing musical comedies at the turn of the nineteenth century. Stuart's first success was with "Florodora" (1899), which he followed with "The Silver Slipper" (1901), "The Belle of Mayfair" (1906), "Havana" (1908), "The Slim Princess" and "Peggy" (both 1911). He also recorded his own material, such as *Little Dolly Daydream*, while his song *Lily of Laguna* was featured in the film "Lilacs in the Spring" (1955). Stuart's biggest hits were all written in the black-face "coon" tradition, and remained popular well into the 1950s, in particular with the singer G.H. Elliott. HIT VERSIONS: *I May Be Crazy, But I Ain't No Fool* Bob Roberts (1904) US#3, *Lily of Laguna* Winifred Atwell in *Let's Have Another Party* (1954) UK#1, *Tell Me, Pretty Maiden* [i] Byron G. Harlan, Joe Belmont & the Florodora Girls (1901) US#1/ Harry MacDonough & Grace Spencer (1901) US#1. Co-writer: [i] Owen Hall.

924. STYNE, Jule (b. Julius Kerwin Stein, December 31, 1905, London, England) Film and stage composer, arranger, producer, and pianist. A British composer who had a particularly successful partnership with the American lyricist Sammy Cahn. Styne's family emigrated to America in 1913, where, as a child prodigy, he studied at the Chicago Musical College. He became a piano soloist with the Chicago Symphony Orchestra at the age of nine, and led his own dance band in his teens. Styne began writing songs in 1927, scoring his first hit with *Sunday* [iii] by Gene Austin (1927). In Hollywood he worked as a vocal coach and staff composer at 20th Century-Fox, where he contributed to the films "Sailors on Leave" (1941), "Sweater Girl" (1942), "Carolina Blues" (1944), "Step Lively" (1944), and "Anchors Aweigh" (1946). Styne was also successful on Broadway with "High Button Shoes" (1947) and "Gentlemen Prefer Blondes" (1949). During the 1950s, he worked with the lyricists Betty Comden and Adolph Green, the trio first being successful with their Leonard Bernstein collaboration "On the Town" (1944), which they followed with "Two on the Aisle" (1951) "Peter Pan" (1955), and "The Bells Are Ringing" (1956). Styne's last major hit was with

"Funny Girl" (1964). ALBUMS: **Gentlemen Prefer Blondes** ost (1943, MGM); **It Happened in Brooklyn** (1947, Hollywood Soundstage); **Gentlemen Prefer Blondes** oc (1950, Columbia); **Two on the Aisle** oc (1951, Decca); **Hazel Flagg** oc (1953, RCA); **Living It Up** st (1954, Capitol); **Peter Pan** oc (1955, RCA) US#4; **Bells Are Ringing** oc (1957, Columbia) US#20; **Ruggles of Red Gap** tvst (1957, Verve); **High Button Shoes** oc (1958), **Say Darling** oc (1958, both RCA); **Gypsy** oc (1959, Columbia) US#13; **Do Re Mi** (1961, RCA) US#12; **Gypsy** ost (1962, Warner Brothers) US#10; **Subways Are for Sleeping** oc (1962, Columbia) US#81; **Fade Out — Fade In** oc (1964, ABC/Paramount) US#96; **What a Way to Go!** ost (1964, 20th Century–Fox); **Dangerous Christmas of Red Riding Hood** (1965, ABC/Paramount); **Funny Girl** oc (1966, Capitol) UK#19; **Hallelujah Baby!** oc (1967, Columbia); **Darling of the Day** oc (1968, RCA); **Funny Girl** ost (1969, Columbia) p US#12 UK#11; **Sugar** oc (1972, United Artists); **Lorelei** oc (1974, MGM); **Words and Music** sc (1974, World); **Anchors Aweigh** ost (1979, Sandy Hook); **One Night Stand** oc (1980), **Pretty Belle** oc (1982, both Original Cast). HIT VERSIONS: *Barrelhouse Bessie from Basin Street* [vi] Bob Crosby (1942) US#23, *Bye Bye Baby* [viii] Charlie Barnet (1936) US#16/Fats Waller (1936) US#4; *Can't You Read Between the Lines?* [i] Jimmy Dorsey (1945) US#8/Kay Kyser (1945) US#10; *Diamonds Are a Girl's Best Friend* [viii] Jo Stafford (1950) US#30, *Ev'ry Day I Love You (Just a Little Bit More)* [i] Dick Haymes (1948) US#24/Vaughn Monroe (1948) US#22/Jo Stafford (1948) US#25; *Everything's Coming Up Roses* [ix] Jack Wild (1971) UK#107, *Five Minutes More* [i] Tex Beneke (1946) US#4/Bob Crosby (1946) US#12/Skitch Henderson (1946) US#9/Frank Sinatra (1946) US#1/Three Sons (1946) US#7; *Funny Girl* [vii] Barbra Streisand (1968) US#44, *Guess I'll Hang My Tears Out to Dry* [i] Harry James (1945) US#16, *How Do You Speak to an Angel?* [iv] Eddie Fisher (1953) US#14/Gordon MacRae (1953) US#30; *I Believe* [i] Frank Sinatra (1947) US#5, *I Fall in Love Too Easily* [i] Eugenie Baird & Mel Torme (1945) US#20, *I Said No!* [v] Jimmy Dorsey (1942) US#10/Alvino Rey (1942) US#2; *I Still Get Jealous* [i] Harry James (1947) US#23/Gordon MacRae (1947) US#25/Three Suns (1947) US#21; *I'll Walk Alone* [i] Louis Prima (1944) R&B#9/Mary Martin (1944) US#6/Dinah Shore (1944) R&B#10 US#1/Martha Tilton (1944) US#6/Don Cornell (1952) US#4/Jane Froman (1952) US#14/Richard Hayes (1952) US#24/Margaret Whiting (1952) US#29; *I've Heard That Song Before* [i] Harry James (1943) g R&B#1 US#1, *It's Been a Long, Long Time* [i] Bing Crosby & Les Paul (1945) US#1/Harry James (1945) US#1/Stan Kenton (1945) US#6/Charlie Spivak (1945) US#4/

Les Paul & Mary Ford (1961) US#105; *It's Magic* Vic Damone (1948) US#24/Doris Day (1948) g US#2/ Dick Haymes (1948) US#9/Gordon MacRae (1948) US#9/Tony Martin (1948) US#11/Sarah Vaughan (1948) US#11; *It's the Same Old Dream* [i] Tommy Dorsey (1947) US#21, *Just in Time* [ii] Tony Bennett (1963) US#46/Frank Sinatra on *Come Dance with Me LP* (1959) UK#30; *Let It Snow! Let It Snow! Let It Snow!* [i] Connee Boswell (1946) US#9/Bob Crosby (1946) US#14/Woody Herman (1946) US#7/Vaughn Monroe (1946) US#1; *Money Burns a Hole in My Pocket* [ii] Dean Martin (1954) US#23, *Papa Won't You Dance with Me?* [i] Doris Day (1947) US#21/ Skitch Henderson (1947) US#27; *Party's Over, The* [ii] Lonnie Donegan (1962) UK#9, *People* [vii] Nat "King" Cole (1964) US#100/Barbra Streisand (1964) US#5/Tymes (1968) R&B#33 US#39 UK#16; *Poor Little Rhode Island* [i] Guy Lombardo (1945) US#11, *Put 'Em in a Box, Tie It with a Ribbon (And Throw 'Em in the Deep Blue Sea)* [i] Doris Day (1948) US#27/Nat "King" Cole (1948) US#30/Eddy Howard (1948) US#23; *Small World* [ix] Johnny Mathis (1959) US#20, *Saturday Night (Is the Loneliest Night of the Week)* [i] Frankie Carle (1945) US#8/Woody Herman (1945) US#15/Sammy Kaye (1945) US#6/King Sisters (1945) US#15/Frank Sinatra (1945) US#2, also on *Come Dance with Me LP* (1959) UK#30; *Sunday* [iii] Gene Austin (1927) UK#11/Cliff Edwards (1927) US#3/Jean Goldkette (1927) US#11; *That's What I Like* [iv] Don, Dick & Jimmy (1954) US#14, *There Goes That Song Again* [i] Billy Butterfield (1945) US#10/Sammy Kaye (1945) US#8/Kay Kyser (1945) US#7/Russ Morgan (1945) US#4/Kate Smith (1945) US#12/Gary Miller (1961) UK#29; *Things We Did Last Summer, The* [i] Vaughn Monroe (1946) US#13/Frank Sinatra (1946) US#8/Jo Stafford (1946) US#10; *Three Coins in the Fountain* [i] Four Aces (1954) g US#1 UK#5/Julius LaRosa (1954) US#21/Frank Sinatra (1954) US#4 UK#1; *Time After Time* [i] Henry Burr (1922) US#11/Frank Sinatra (1947) US#16/Chris Montez (1966) US#36; *Victory Polka* [i] Bing Crosby & the Andrews Sisters (1944) US#5, *What Makes the Sun Set* [i] Frank Sinatra (1945) US#13, *You're My Girl* [i] Frank Sinatra (1948) US#23. Co-writers: [i] Sammy Cahn, [ii] Betty Comden (b. May 3, 1917, Brooklyn, NY)/ Adolph Green (b. 1915), [iii] Chester Conn/Bennie Kreuger/Ned Miller, [iv] Bob Hilliard, [v] Frank Loesser, [vi] Herb Magidson, [vii] Bob Merrill, [viii] Leo Robin, [ix] Stephen Sondheim.

925. SWAN, Billy (b. May 12, 1942, Cape Giradeau, MI) C&W keyboard player, producer and vocalist. A Nashville session player who wrote the hit *Lover, Please* for Clyde McPhatter in 1962. Swann produced many of Tony Joe White's finest sides dur-

ing the 1970s, and as a member of the group Black Tie, he recorded the album **When the Night Falls** (1986, Bench). As a solo performer, Swan was never able to repeat the enormous success of his initial hit *I Can Help*. CHART COMPOSITIONS: *I Can Help* (1974) g C&W#1 US#1 UK#6, *I'm Her Fool* [i] (1975) US#53, *Everything's the Same (Ain't Nothing Changed)* (1975) C&W#17 US#91. ALBUMS: **I Can Help** (1974) US#21, **Rock 'n' Roll Moon** (1975), **Billy Swan** (1976, all Monument); **You're OK, I'm OK** (1978, A&M); **I'm into Loving You** (1981, Epic); **Bop to Be** (1995, Bench). COMPILATIONS: **At His Best** (1976, Monument); **Golden Classics** (1997, CLT). HIT VERSIONS: *I Can Help* Elvis Presley (1984) UK#30, *Lover, Please* Clyde McPhatter (1962) US#7/Vernons Girls (1962) UK#16/Bobby G. Rice (1971) C&W#46. Co-writer: [i] Dennis Linde.

926. TARNEY, Alan (b. Australia) Pop keyboard player, guitarist and producer. A songwriter and producer whose greatest success has been as a composer for others. Tarney performed on the Shadows' album **Rockin' with Curly Leads** (1974, EMI) UK#45, before forming his own short-lived Tarney-Spencer Band, with the drummer Trevor Spencer. CHART COMPOSITIONS: *It's Really You* [ii] (1978) US#86, *No Time to Lose* [ii] (1981) US#74. ALBUMS: **Tarney-Spencer** (1976, Bradleys); **Three's a Crowd** (1978) US#174, **Run for Your Life** (1979, both A&M) US#181. HIT VERSIONS: *January, February* Barbara Dickson (1980) UK#11, *Last Kiss, The* [i] David Cassidy (1985) UK#6, *Little in Love, A* Cliff Richard (1981) US#17 UK#15, *Living in Harmony* [ii] Cliff Richard (1972) UK#12, *My Pretty One* Cliff Richard (1987) UK#6, *Some People* Cliff Richard (1987) UK#3, *We Don't Talk Anymore* Cliff Richard (1979) US#7 UK#1, *Wired for Sound* [iii] Cliff Richard (1981) US#71 UK#4. Co-writers: [i] David Cassidy (b. April 12, 1950, New York, NY), [ii] Trevor Spencer, [iii] B.A. Robertson. (*See also under* Leo SAYER.)

927. TAUPIN, Bernie (b. May 22, 1950, Sleaford, England) Pop lyricist and producer. A teenage poet who became Elton John's lyricist. Taupin has also recorded as a solo artist, and occasionally produced for others, his most notable work being David Ackles' album **American Gothic** (1972). ALBUMS: **Bernie Taupin** (1971, Elektra); **Taupin** (1971, DJM); **He Who Rides the Tiger** (1980, Asylum). HIT VERSION: *These Dreams* [i] Heart (1986) US#1, re-issued (1988) UK#8. Co-writer: [i] Martin Page. (*See also under* Alice COOPER, Elton JOHN, Holly KNIGHT, Dennis LAMBERT.)

928. TAYLOR, Carmol (b. September 5, 1931, Brilliant, AL; d. December 5, 1986) C&W producer and vocalist. A teenage square dancer who charted eight country singles between 1975–1977. Taylor later worked as a producer for the Country International label, before dying of lung cancer in 1986. CHART COMPOSITIONS: *Who Will I Be Loving Now* (1975) C&W#91, *Play the Saddest Song on the Juke Box* (1976) C&W#35, *I Really Had a Ball Last Night* (1976) C&W#23, *That Little Difference* (1976) C&W#53, *Neon Women* (1977) C&W#87, *What Would I Do Then** (1977) C&W#100, *Good Cheatin' Songs** (1977) C&W#80. HIT VERSIONS: *Grand Tour* George Jones (1974) C&W#1, *He Loves Me All the Way* Tammy Wynette (1970) C&W#1, *There's a Song on the Jukebox* David Wills (1975) C&W#10, *Wild as a Wildcat* Charlie Walker (1965) C&W#8. With: * Stella Parton

929. TAYLOR, Chip (b. James Wesley Voigt, 1940, Yonkers, NY) C&W guitarist, producer and vocalist. The younger brother of the actor Jon Voigt, who, as Chip Taylor, became a successful pop producer and songwriter during the 1960s, and later a country recording artist. Taylor's best known composition is the rock standard *Wild Thing*. During the 1950s, he recorded rockabilly sides for the King label, and in 1968 he added a notable Nashville sound to Neil Diamond's album **Velvet Gloves and Spit**. In 1992, Taylor took part in the "In Our Own Words" American tour of singer-songwriters. CHART COMPOSITIONS: *Here I Am* (1962) US#113, *Me as I Am* (1975) C&W#80, *Early Sunday Morning* (1975) C&W#28, *Big River* (1975) C&W#61, *Circle of Tears* (1976) C&W#92, *Hello Atlanta* (1977) C&W#93. ALBUMS: **Gorgoni, Martin and Taylor*** (1971), **Gotta Get Back to Cisco*** (1972), **Gasoline** (1972, all Buddah); **Chip Taylor's Last Chance** (1974), **Some of Us** (1974), **This Side of the Big River** (1975, all Warner Brothers); **Angel of the Morning** (1975, Buddah); **Somebody Shoot Out the Jukebox** (1976, Columbia); **Saint Sebastian** (1978, Capitol); **Living Room Tapes** (1997, Gad). HIT VERSIONS: *Angel of the Morning* P.P. Arnold (1968) UK#29/Merrilee Rush (1968) US#7/Bettye Swann (1969) US#109/Connie Eaton (1970) C&W#34/Mary Mason (1977) UK#27/Melba Montgomery (1977) C&W#22/Juice Newton (1981) g C&W#22 US#4 UK#43; *Any Way That You Want Me* Liverpool Five (1966) US#98/Troggs (1966) UK#8/American Breed (1968) US#88/Evie Sands (1969) US#53; *Baby, The* Hollies (1972) UK#26, *Country Girl-City Man* [i] Billy Vera & Judy Clay (1968) R&B#41 US#36, *Hello Operator* Joe Stampley (1972) C&W#75, *I Can Make It with You* Jackie DeShannon (1966) US#68/Pozo-Seco Singers (1967) US#32;

I Can't Let Go [ii] Hollies (1966) US#42 UK#2/Linda Ronstadt (1980) US#31; *If You Touch Me (You've Got to Love Me)* Joe Stampley (1972) C&W#9, *Make Me Belong to You* [iii] Barbara Lewis (1966) R&B#36 US#28, *On My Word* Cliff Richard (1965) UK#12, *Son of a Rotten Gambler* Anne Murray (1974) C&W#5, *Step Out of Your Mind* [ii] American Breed (1967) US#24, *Storybook Children* Billy Vera & Judy Clay (1967) R&B#20 US#54/Billy Joe Royal (1968) US#117/Virgil Warner & Suzi Jane Hokum (1968) C&W#65/Sam Dees (1976) R&B#84; *Sweet Dream Woman* [ii] Waylon Jennings (1972) C&W#7, *Take Me for a Little While* Patti LaBelle & the Bluebelles (1967) US#36 US#89/Vanilla Fudge (1968) US#38; *Wild Thing* Troggs (1966) US#1 UK#1, new version (1994) UK#69/Ventures (1966) US#116/Senator Bobby (1967) US#20/Fancy (1974) US#14/Goodies (1975) UK#21. With: * Al Gorgoni and Trade Martin. Co-writers: [i] Ted Daryll, [ii] Al Gorgoni, [iii] Billy Vera (b. William McCord, Jr., May 28, 1944, Riverside, CA).

930. TAYLOR, James (b. James Vernon Taylor, May 12, 1948, Boston, MA) Rock guitarist, banjo player and vocalist. One of America's most gifted and influential singer-songwriters since the 1970s, whose simple melodies and skillful vernacular is distinguished by tight, interior rhymes and an easy intimacy. Taylor is also a distinctive acoustic guitarist, who grew up listening to the music of Woody Guthrie, Leadbelly, and his older brother Alex's blues records. Taylor first teamed up with Danny Kortchmar in the group the Flying Machine, but during the mid-1960s, he was treated at the McLean Psychiatric Hospital, Massachusetts, for severe depression, where, as an inmate, he started writing songs. After discharging himself, and in an attempt to break a heroin dependency, Taylor headed to London, England, where A&R man Peter Asher was sufficiently impressed by Taylor's song demos to sign him to the Beatles' Apple label for an impressive debut album, that was unfortunately marred by unsuitable, baroque string arrangements. In 1969, Asher encouraged Taylor to move to California, where he signed to Warner Brothers and released **Sweet Baby James** (1970), an album that enjoyed a two year chart run, and which, alongside Carole King's **Tapestry**, heralded the era of the laid-back, singer-songwriter. Taylor's bitter-sweet amalgam of folk, country and blues, which he sang in his warm but melancholy tenor, created a style that was copied by many a young hopeful with an acoustic guitar. **Mud Slide Slim and the Blue Horizon** (1971), featured Taylor's million selling version of King's *You've Got a Friend*, and drew on rural country, R&B, rock and jazz. In 1971, he made a convincing film debut in Monte Hellman's existential road movie "Two-Lane Blacktop," and the following year he married the singer Carly Simon. In 1979, he contributed three songs to the Broadway show "Working," but after his divorce from Simon, he took a four year sabbatical from recording. Taylor's two most recent studio albums, **New Moon Shine** (1991) and **Hourglass** (1997), compare favorably with his best work, and display an ever maturing sense of melody and word-play, the former featuring an exceptional arrangement of the traditional *The Water Is Wide*. One of the best of many versions of Taylor's songs, is the Average White Band's soulful rendition of *Daddy's All Gone*. CHART COMPOSITIONS: *Carolina in My Mind* (1969) US#118, re-issued (1970) US#67; *Fire and Rain* (1970) US#3 UK#42, *Country Road* (1971) US#37, *Long Ago and Far Away* (1971) US#31, *Don't Let Me Be Lonely Tonight* (1973) US#14, *One Man Parade* (1973) US#67, *Mexico* (1975) US#49, *Shower the People* (1976) US#22, *Your Smiling Face* (1977) US#20, *Bartender's Blues* (1977) C&W#88, *Honey Don't Leave L.A.* (1978) US#61, *Her Town Too* [i] with J.D. Souther (1981) US#11, *Hard Times* (1981) US#72, *Only One* (1986) US#80. ALBUMS: **James Taylor** (1968, Apple) US#62; **Sweet Baby James** (1970) p US#3 UK#7, **Mud Slide Slim and the Blue Horizon** (1971) p US#2 UK#4, **One Man Dog** (1972) g US#4 UK#27, **Walking Man** (1974) US#13, **Gorilla** (1975) g US#6, **In the Pocket** (1976, all Warner Brothers) g US#16; **JT** (1977) p US#4, **Flag** (1979) p US#10, **Dad Loves His Work** (1981) g US#10, **That's Why I'm Here** (1985) p US#34, **Live in Rio** (1986), **Never Die Young** (1988) p US#25, **New Moon Shine** (1991) p US#37, **James Taylor Live** (1993) p US#20, **Hourglass** (1997, all Columbia). COMPILATIONS: **James Taylor and the Original Flying Machine** (1971, Euphoria) US#74; **Greatest Hits** (1976, Warner Brothers) p US#23; **Classic Songs** (1987, CBS/WEA) UK#53. HIT VERSIONS: *Bartender's Blues* George Jones (1978) C&W#6, *Carolina in My Mind* Crystal Mansion (1970) US#73, *Country Road* Merry Clayton (1970) US#103, *Don't Let Me Be Lonely Tonight* Isley Brothers on B-side of *Highways of My Life* (1974) UK#25/Nancy Wilson (1975) R&B#54; *Fire and Rain* R.B. Greaves (1970) US#82/Johnny Rivers (1970) US#94/Willie Nelson (1975) C&W#29; *Steamroller Blues* Elvis Presley (1973) C&W#31 US#17, also on B-side of *Polk Salad Annie* (1973) UK#23. Co-writers: [i] John David Souther/Waddy Wachtel.

931. TAYLOR, Livingston (b. November 21, 1951, Boston, MA) Rock guitarist and vocalist. A folk influenced singer-songwriter who is the younger brother of James Taylor, and who is an extremely popular performer in Japan. CHART COMPOSI-

TIONS: *Carolina Day* (1971) US#93, *Get Out of Bed* (1972) US#97, *I'll Come Running* (1979) US#82. ALBUMS: **Livingston Taylor** (1970, Atco) US#82; **Liv** (1971) US#147, **Over the Rainbow** (1973) US#189, **Echoes** (1979, all Capricorn); **Three-Way Mirror** (1979), **Man's Best Friend** (1980, both Epic); **Life Is Good** (1988, Critique); **Our Turn to Dance** (1991, Pony Canyon); **Good Friends** (1993, Chesky).

932. TAYLOR, R. Dean (b. 1939, Toronto, Canada) R&B producer and vocalist. A pop and country influenced R&B artist who first recorded for the Parry label in 1960. Taylor was one of the first white singers to record for the Motown organization. CHART COMPOSITIONS: *Indiana Wants Me* (1970) US#5 UK#2, *Gotta See Jane* [i] (1968) US#67 UK#17, re-issued (1974) UK#41; *Candy Apple Red* (1971) US#104, *There's a Ghost in My House* [i] (1974) UK#3, *Window Shopping* (1974) UK#36, *Let's Talk It Over* (1983) C&W#90. ALBUMS: **I Think, Therefore I Am** (1971, Rare Earth) US#198; **Indiana Wants Me** (1971, Motown); **L.A. Sunset** (1975, Polydor). HIT VERSIONS: *All I Need* [iii] Temptations (1967) R&B#2 US#8, *Love Child* [ii] Diana Ross & the Supremes (1968) R&B#2 US#1 UK#15/Stars On in *Stars on 45/Long Play, Volume 2* (1981) US#120 UK#18; *There's a Ghost in My House* [i] Fall (1987) UK#30, *Window Shopping* Messengers (1967) US#132. Co-writers: [i] Brian Holland/Lamont Dozier/Eddie Holland, [ii] Deke Richards/Pam Sawyer/Frank Wilson, [iii] Frank Wilson. (*See also under* Berry GORDY, Jr., HOLLAND, Brian, DOZIER, Lamont and HOLLAND, Eddie.)

933. TEMPCHIN, Jack (b. America) Pop guitarist and vocalist. A songwriter of hit material for such groups as the Eagles. Tempchin's early years were spent as a performer in various San Diego clubs and coffee houses, before he teamed up with Jules Shear in the group the Funky Kings, charting with *(Swayin' to the Music) Slow Dancin'* (1976) US#61, from the country-rock album **The Funky Kings** (1976, Arista). Tempchin is a frequent collaborator with the former Eagle Glenn Frey. He also composed the Pepsi Cola theme *Better in the U.S.A.* ALBUM: **Jack Tempchin** (1978, Arista). HIT VERSIONS: *Already Gone* [i] Eagles (1974) US#32/Tanya Tucker (1993) C&W#75; *Peaceful Easy Livin'* Eagles (1973) US#22/Little Texas (1993) C&W#73; *(Swayin' to the Music) Slow Dancin'* Johnny Duncan (1979) C&W#6/Johnny Rivers (1977) US#10. Co-writer: [i] Rod Strandlund. (*See also under* Glenn FREY, Chris HILLMAN.)

934. TEMPERTON, Rodney (b. Hull, England) R&B keyboard player and producer. A member of the British disco group Heatwave, which was formed in Germany in 1975, and scored a two million seller with *Boogie Nights*, and a ten million seller with the ballad *Always and Forever*. CHART COMPOSITIONS: *Boogie Nights* (1977) p R&B#5 US#2 UK#2, *Too Hot to Handle* (1977) UK#15, *The Groove Line* (1978) p R&B#3 US#7 UK#12, *Always and Forever* (1978) g R&B#2 US#18 UK#9, *Razzle Dazzle* (1979) UK#43, *Jitterbuggin'* (1980) UK#34, *Gangsters of the Groove* (1980) R&B#21 US#110 UK#19, *Lettin' It Loose* (1982) R&B#54. ALBUMS: **Too Hot to Handle** (1977) p US#11 UK#46, **Central Heating** (1978) p US#10 UK#26, **Hot Property** (1979) g US#38, **Candles** (1980, all GTO) US#71 UK#29; **Current** (1982) US#156, **Power Cuts** (1982, both Epic). COMPILATIONS: **Greatest Hits** (1984, Epic); **Gangsters of the Groove — The '90s Mix** (1991, Telstar) UK#56. Temperton went on to compose for Michael Jackson, who included four Temperton songs on the twelve million selling album **Off the Wall** (1979), and three more on **Thriller** (1982), the biggest selling album of all time. HIT VERSIONS: *Always and Forever* Luther Vandross (1995) US#58 UK#20, *Baby, Come to Me* Patti Austin & James Ingram (1982) g R&B#9 US#1/ Stephanie Winslow (1984) C&W#42; *Boogie Nights* Stars On in *Stars on Long Play/On 45* (1981) g US#9 UK#1/La Fleur (1983) UK#51/Sonia (1992) UK#30; *Give Me the Night* George Benson (1980) R&B#1 US#4 UK#7/Randy Crawford (1996) R&B#47; *Givin' in to Love* Patti Austin (1992) R&B#55, *Love Is in Control (Finger on the Trigger)* [iv] Donna Summer (1982) R&B#4 US#10 UK#18, *Love X Love* George Benson (1980) R&B#9 US#61 UK#10, *Man Size Love* Klymaxx (1986) R&B#43 US#15, *Mystery* Manhattan Transfer (1984) R&B#80 US#102, *Never Do You Wrong* [i] Stephanie Mills (1993) R&B#33, *Off the Wall* Michael Jackson (1980) R&B#5 US#10 UK#7, *Razzamatazz* Quincy Jones (1981) R&B#17 UK#11, *Rock with You* Michael Jackson (1979) g R&B#1 US#1 UK#7, *Say You Really Want Me* Kim Wilde (1983) US#44 UK#29, *Secret Garden, The* [iii] Quincy Jones (1990) US#31 UK#67, *Slow Jams* Quincy Jones featuring Babyface, Tamia with Portrait & Barry White (1996) R&B#25+ US#72+, *Spice of Life* [ii] Manhattan Transfer (1983) US#40 UK#19, *Sweet Freedom* Michael McDonald (1986) R&B#17 US#7 UK#12, *Thriller* Michael Jackson (1982) R&B#3 US#4 UK#10, also in *9 Singles* (1985) UK#66; *Treasure* Brothers Johnson (1980) R&B#36 US#73, *Turn Out the Lamplight* George Benson (1980) R&B#33 US#109. Co-writers: [i] V. Benford/ C. Duboc/R. Spearman, [ii] David Bramble, [iii] Quincy Jones, [iv] Quincy Jones/Maria Ross. (*See also under* George and Louis JOHNSON, L.L. Cool J, Michael McDONALD.)

935. TEPPER, Sid (b. 1918) Pop composer. A writer of songs for such Elvis Presley films as "Spinout" (1966). HIT VERSIONS: *All That I Am* [i] Elvis Presley (1966) US#41 UK#18, *If I Had a Girl* [i] Rod Lauren (1960) US#31, *Kewpie Doll* [i] Perry Como (1958) US#6 UK#9/Frankie Vaughan (1958) UK#10; *My Bonnie Lassie* [ii] Ames Brothers (1955) US#11, *Naughty Lady of Shady Lane, The* [i] Ames Brothers (1955) US#3 UK#6/Archie Bleyer (1955) US#17; *Puppet on a String* [i] Elvis Presley (1965) US#14, re-issued (1978) C&W#78; *Red Roses for a Blue Lady* [iii] Vaughn Monroe (1939) US#3/John Laurenz (1949) US#21/Guy Lombardo (1949) US#8/ Bert Kaempfert (1965) US#11/Eddy Arnold (1975) C&W#60; *Stairway of Love* [i] Terry Dene (1958) UK#16/Michael Holliday (1958) UK#3; *Travellin' Light* [i] Cliff Richard (1959) UK#1, *Twenty Tiny Fingers* [i] Alma Cogan (1955) UK#17/Coronets (1955) UK#20/Stargazers (1955) UK#4; *When the Boy/Girl in Your Arms Is the Boy/Girl in Your Dreams* [i] Cliff Richard (1961) UK#3/Connie Francis (1962) US#10; *Wonderful World of the Young, The* [i] Danny Williams (1962) UK#8/Andy Williams (1962) US#99; *Young Ones, The* [i] Cliff Richard (1962) UK#1. Co-writers; [i] Roy C. Bennett (b. 1918), [ii] Roy C. Bennett/Marion McClurg, [iii] Roy Brodsky.

936. TEX, Joe (b. Joseph Arrington, Jr., August 8, 1933, Rogers, TX; d. August 13, 1982) R&B vocalist. One of R&B's most consistent performers, and an early exponent of a rap style. Tex started out singing gospel, and won an Apollo Theatre talent contest in 1954. He recorded his first sides the following year, and between 1965–1978, charted thirty-three R&B hits, including three number ones. In 1972 he converted to the Muslim faith, re-naming himself Joseph Hazziez. Tex died of a heart attack in 1982. CHART COMPOSITIONS: *Hold What You've Got* (1965) R&B#2 US#5, *You Got What It Takes* (1965) R&B#10 US#51, *You Better Get It* (1965) R&B#15 US#46, *A Woman Can Change a Man* (1965) R&B#12 US#56, *One Monkey Don't Stop No Show* (1965) R&B#20 US#65, *I Want to (Do Everything for You)* (1965) R&B#1 US#23, *A Sweet Woman Like You* (1965) R&B#1 US#29, *The Love You Save (May Be Your Own)* (1966) R&B#2 US#56, *S.Y.S.L.J.F.M. (The Letter Song)* (1966) R&B#9 US#39, *I Believe I'm Gonna Make It* (1966) R&B#8 US#67, *I've Got to Do a Little Bit Better* (1966) R&B#20 US#64, *Papa Was Too* (1966) R&B#15 US#44, *Show Me* (1967) R&B#24 US#35, *Woman Like That, Yeah* (1967) R&B#24 US#54, *A Woman's Hands* (1967) R&B#24 US#63, *Skinny Legs and All* (1968) g R&B#2 US#10, *Men Are Gettin' Scarce* (1968) R&B#7 US#33, *I'll Never Do You Wrong* (1968) R&B#26 US#59, *Keep the One You Got* (1968)

R&B#13 US#52, *You Need Me, Baby* (1968) R&B#29 US#81, *Buying a Book* (1969) R&B#10 US#47, *That's the Way* (1969) R&B#46 US#94, *Give the Baby Anything the Baby Wants* (1971) R&B#20 US#102, *I Gotcha* (1972) g R&B#1 US#2, *You Said a Bad Word* (1972) R&B#12 US#41, *Woman Stealer* (1973) R&B#41 US#103, *Under Your Powerful Love* (1975) R&B#27, *Have You Ever* (1976) R&B#74, *Hungry for Your Love* (1977) R&B#84, *Rub Down* (1978) R&B#70, *Loose Caboose* (1978) R&B#48. ALBUMS: **Hold On** (1965, Checker); **Hold What You've Got** (1965) US#124, **The New Boss** (1965) US#142, **The Love You Save** (1966) US#108, **Show Me** (1966), **I've Got to Do a Little Better** (1966), **Live and Lively** (1968) US#84, **Soul Country** (1968) US#154, **Happy Soul** (1969), **You Better Get It** (1969), **Buying a Book** (1969) US#190, **Joe Tex Sings with Strings** (1969), **From the Roots Came the Rapper** (1971, all Atlantic); **I Gotcha** (1972) US#17, **Joe Tex Spills the Beans** (1972), **He Who Is Without Funk** (1973, all Dial); **Another Man's Woman** (1977, Powerpak); **Bumps and Bruises** (1977) US#108, **Rub Down** (1978, both Epic). COMPILATIONS: **Best of Joe Tex** (1965, King); **Best of Joe Tex** (1967) US#168, **Greatest Hits** (1967, both Atlantic), **History of Joe Tex** (1973, Pride). HIT VERSIONS: *I Want to (Do Everything for You)* Raelettes (1970) R&B#30 US#96.

937. THOMAS, Rufus (b. March 17, Cayce, MS) R&B vocalist. A former disc jockey who became a writer of novelty hits at Stax Records during the 1960s. Thomas is the father of the R&B singers Carla Thomas and Vaneese Thomas. CHART COMPOSITIONS: *Bear Cat* (1953) R&B#3, *The Dog* (1963) R&B#22 US#87, *Walking the Dog* (1963) R&B#5 US#10, *Can Your Monkey Do the Dog* (1964) US#48, *Somebody Stole My Dog* (1964) US#86, *Do the Funky Chicken* (1970) R&B#5 US#28 UK#18, *(Do the) Push and Pull* (1970) R&B#1 US#25, *Do the Funky Penguin* (1971) R&B#11 US#44, *Itch and Scratch* (1972) US#103, *Do the Double Bump* (1975) R&B#74. ALBUMS: **Walking the Dog** (1963), **Do the Funky Chicken** (1970), **Live at P.J.'s — Doin' the Push and Pull** (1970), **Did You Heard Me?** (1972), **Crown Prince of Dance** (1973, all Stax); **Blues in the Basement** (1976), **If There Were No Music** (1977), **I Ain't Gettin' Older, I'm Gettin' Better** (1978, all Artists of America); **Rufus Thomas** (1980, Gusto); **Rappin' Rufus** (1986, Ichiban); **That Woman Is Poison** (1989, Alligator); **Blues Thang** (1996, Sequel). COMPILATIONS: **Chronicle** (1979), **Best of Rufus Thomas** (1993, both Stax).

938. THOMPSON, Richard (b. April 3, 1949, London, England) Folk guitarist and vocalist.

Britain's finest electric folk guitarist, and a frequently excellent composer. Thompson first came to prominence as a member of the folk stalwarts Fairport Convention, which recorded such Thompson gems as *Sloth* and *Genesis Hall*. ALBUMS: **Fairport Convention** (1968, Polydor); **What We Did on Our Holidays** (1969), **Unhalfbricking** (1969) UK#12, **Liege and Lief** (1970) UK#17, **Full House** (1970) UK#13, **Angel Delight** (1971), **Live at the Troubadour** (1977, all Island). COMPILATION: **History of Fairport Convention** (1972, Island). Thompson also recorded an album as a member of the Bunch, **Rock On** (1972, Island), before pursuing a solo career. A much recorded composer, his songs have attracted the attention of Martin Carthy, Julie Covington, Elvis Costello, and the Pointer Sisters. ALBUMS: **Henry the Human Fly** (1972), **I Want to See the Bright Lights Tonight** (1974), **Hokey Pokey** (1975), **Pour Down Like Silver** (1976), **Guitar/Vocal** (1976), **Almost Live (More or Less)** (1976, all Island); **First Light** (1978), **Sunnyvista** (1979, both Chrysalis); **Strict Tempo** (1981, Elixir); **Shoot Out the Lights** (1982), **Small Town Romance** (1982), **Hand of Kindness** (1983, all Hannibal) US#186; **Across a Crowded Room** (1985) US#102 UK#80, **Daring Adventures** (1986, both Polydor) US#142 UK#92; **The Marksman** ost (1987, BBC); **Live, Love, Larf and Loaf** with Fred Frith and Henry Kaiser (1988, Rhino); **Amnesia** (1988) US#182 UK#89, **Rumor and Sigh** (1991) UK#32, **Street Talker** (1992), **Mirror Blue** (1994, all Capitol) US#109 UK#23; **Live at Crawley, 1993** (1995, Flypaper); **You? Me? Us?** (1996, Capitol) US#97 UK#32; **Industry** with Danny Thompson (1997, Parlophone). COMPILATIONS: **Watching the Dark: The History of Richard Thompson** (1993), **Doom and Gloom from the Tomb** (1995, both Rykodisc). With: * Linda Thompson.

939. THORNTON, James (b. December 5, 1861, Liverpool, England; July 27, 1938, New York, NY) Vaudeville performer. An American immigrant from the age of eight, who began his musical career in New York as a singing waiter, before graduating to the vaudeville circuit. Thornton's first hit was *My Sweetheart's the Man in the Moon* (1892), after which he specialized in sentimental ballads, none more famous than *When You Were Sixteen* (1898), which he sold outright to two separate publishers for fifteen dollars each. The song was a hit for seven different singers and a number one on two occasions. Thornton's last vaudeville appearance was in 1929. HIT VERSIONS: *Bridge of Sighs* Georgia Gibbs (1953) US#30, *My Sweetheart's the Man in the Moon* F.F. Burnham (1892) US#2, *She May Have Seen Better Days* George J. Gaskin (1896) US#1, *When*

You Were Sixteen George J. Gaskin (1900) US#1/Jere Mahoney (1900) US#1/Harry MacDonough (1901) US#3/J.W. Myers (1901) US#3/Perry Como (1947) US#2/Dick Jurgens (1947) US#17/Mills Brothers (1947) US#15.

940. THUNDERS, Johnny (b. John Genzale, July 15, 1954; d. April 23, 1991) Rock guitarist and vocalist. The lead guitarist in the rock group the New York Dolls, which was highly influential on the British punk movement in the late 1970s, with its albums **New York Dolls** (1973) US#116, **In Too Much Too Soon** (1974, both Mercury) US#167; **Lipstick Killers — Mercer St. Sessions** (1981, Reach Out); **Night of the Living Dolls** (1985, Mercury). Thunders left to form the Heartbreakers in 1977. ALBUMS: **L.A.M.F.** (1977, Track) UK#55; **Live at Max's Kansas City** (1979, Max's Kansas City); **D.T.K. — Live at the Speakeasy** (1982, Jungle); **Live at the Lyceum** (1984, ABC). In 1990, he performed as a member of Gang War, recording the album **Gang War** (Zodiac), but died the following year from longstanding drug related problems. His sometimes compelling songs were the subject of the various artists album **I Only Wrote This Song for You — A Tribute to Johnny Thunders** (1994, Castle). ALBUMS: **So Alone** (1978, Real); **In Cold Blood** (1983, New Rose); **Diary of a Lover** (1983, PVC); **Too Much Junkie Business** (1983 ROIR); **Hurt Me** (1984, New Rose); **Que Sera Sera** (1985, Jungle); **Stations of the Cross** (1987, ROIR); **Copy Cats** (1988), **Bootlegging the Boot Leggers** (1990, both Jungle); **The Studio Bootlegs** (1996, Dojo); **Have Faith** (1997), **Vive La Revolution Live Paris** (1997, both Disco).

941. TIKARAM, Tanita (b. December 8, 1969, Munster, West Germany) Pop guitarist and vocalist. A singer-songwriter who enjoyed ever diminishing chart success since the late 1980s. CHART SINGLES: *Good Tradition* (1988) UK#10, *Twist in My Sobriety* (1988) UK#22, *Cathedral Song* (1989) UK#48, *World Outside Your Window* (1989) UK#58, *We Almost Got It Together* (1990) UK#52, *Only the Ones We Love* (1991) UK#69. ALBUMS: **Ancient Heart** (1988, WEA) US#59 UK#3; **The Sweet Keeper** (1990) US#124 UK#3, **Everybody's Angel** (1991) US#142 UK#19, **Eleven Kinds of Loneliness** (1992), **Lovers in the City** (1995, all East West) UK#75. COMPILATION: **Best of Tanita Tikaram** (1997, East West).

942. TILLIS, Mel (b. Lonnie Melvin Tillis, August 8, 1932, Pahokee, FL) C&W guitarist and vocalist. A country performer and prolific tunesmith, who learned the drums and violin while still at high

school. Tillis intended to become a football player, but moved to Nashville and ended up becoming a hit songwriter, one of his earliest successes being the much recorded melodrama *Ruby, Don't Take Your Love to Town*. He charted seventy-five country hits between 1958–1988, and later pursued an acting career in such films as "Smokey and the Bandit" (1979). CHART COMPOSITIONS: *Stateside* (1966) C&W#17, *Goodbye Wheeling* (1967) C&W#20, *All Right (I'll Sign the Papers)* (1968) C&W#26, *Old Faithful* (1969) C&W#15, *Heart Over Mind* (1970) C&W#3, *Commercial Affection* (1970) C&W#8, *I Ain't Never* (1972) C&W#1, *Burning Memories* (1977) C&W#9. ALBUMS: **Stateside** (1965), **Life Turned Her That Way** (1967), **Mr. Mel** (1967), **Let Me Talk to You** (1968), **Something Special** (1968), **Who's Julie** (1969), **Old Faithful** (1969), **She'll Be Hanging 'Round Somewhere** (1970), **Mel Tillis and Bob Wills in Person** (1971, all Kapp); **One More Time** (1970), **The Arms of a Fool/Commercial Affection** (1971), **Live at the Sam Houston Coliseum** (1971), **Living and Learning** with Sherry Bryce (1971), **Would You Want the World to End** (1972), **I Ain't Never** (1973), **Sawmill** (1973), **Let's Go All the Way Tonight** (1974), **Stomp Them Grapes** (1974), **M-M-Mel** (1976), **Welcome to Mel Tillis Country** (1976, all MGM); **Love Revival** (1976), **Heart Healer** (1977), **Love's Troubled Waters** (1977), **I Believe in You** (1978), **Are You Sincere?** (1979), **Mr. Entertainer** (1979), **M-M-Mel Live** (1980, all MCA); **Me and Pepper** (1979), **Your Body is an Outlaw** (1980), **Southern Rain** (1981), **Mel and Nancy** (1981), **It's a Long Way to Daytona** (1982, all Elektra); **After All This Time** (1983), **New Patches** (1984, both MCA). COMPILATIONS: **Very Best of Mel Tillis** (1986, MCA); **The Great Mel** (1988, Gusto). HIT VERSIONS: *All Right (I'll Sign the Papers)* George Morgan (1964) C&W#45, *Burning Memories* Ray Price (1964) C&W#2, *Detroit City* [i] Bobby Bare (1963) C&W#6/Ben Colder (1963) US#90/Billy Grammer as *I Wanna Go Home* (1963) C&W#18/Solomon Burke (1967) R&B#47 US#104/ Tom Jones (1967) US#27 UK#8/Dean Martin (1970) US#101; *Emotions* [ii] Brenda Lee (1960) US#7, *Heart Over Mind* Ray Price (1961) C&W#5, *Honky-Tonk Memories* Mickey Gilley (1977) C&W#4, *Honky-Tonk Song* Webb Pierce (1957) C&W#1, *I Ain't Never* [iii] Webb Pierce (1959) C&W#2/Lowes (1987) C&W#70; *I'm Gonna Act Right* Nat Stuckey (1971) C&W#17, *I'm Tired* Webb Pierce (1957) C&W#3/ Ricky Scaggs (1988) C&W#18; *Lonely Girl* Jimmy Newman (1959) C&W#30/Carl Smith (1964) C&W#14; *Mary Don't You Weep* Stonewall Jackson (1960) C&W#12, *No Love Have I* Webb Pierce (1960) C&W#4/Gail Davies (1978) C&W#26/Holly Dunn (1992) C&W#67; *Old Faithful* Tony Booth (1973)

C&W#49, *One More Time* Ray Price (1960) C&W#2/ Ferlin Husky (1971) C&W#28/Joanne Heel (1972) C&W#44/Skeeter Davis (1974) C&W#65/Sandra Kaye (1978) C&W#80; *Ruby, Don't Take Your Love to Town* Johnny Darrell (1967) C&W#9/Kenny Rogers & the First Edition (1969) C&W#39 US#6 UK#2; *Thousand Miles Ago, A* Webb Pierce (1959) C&W#6, *Tupleo County Jail* Webb Pierce (1958) C&W#7/Stonemans (1966) C&W#40. Co-writers: [i] Danny Hill, [ii] Ramsey Kearney, [iii] Webb Pierce.

943. TILLMAN, Floyd (b. December 8, 1914, Ryan, OK) C&W guitarist and vocalist. The songwriter who virtually established the cheating song genre in country music, with his compositions *It Makes No Difference Now* and *Slippin' Around*. During the 1930s, Tillman played in a variety of groups, and sang lead in Cliff Bruner's Texas Wanderers, before pursuing a solo career between 1944–1960. CHART COMPOSITIONS: *They Took the Stars Out of Heaven* (1944) C&W#1, *Each Night at Nine* (1944) C&W#4, *Drivin' Nails in My Coffin* (1946) C&W#2, *I Love You So Much, It Hurts* (1948) C&W#5, *Slippin' Around* (1949) C&W#5. ALBUMS: **Floyd Tillman and Friends** (197?, Gilleys). HIT VERSIONS: *I Love You So Much, It Hurts* Jimmy Wakely (1948) US#21/Buddy Clark (1949) US#24/Reggie Goff (1949) US#13/Mills Brothers (1949) US#8; *It Makes No Difference Now* [i] Cliff Bruner's Texas Wanderers (1938) US#16/Bing Crosby (1941) US#23; *Slippin' Around* Ernest Tubb (1949) C&W#1 US#17/Margaret Whiting & Jimmy Wakely (1949) g C&W#1 US#1/Texas Jim Robertson (1950) C&W#13/Marion Worth & George Morgan (1964) C&W#23/Roy Drusky & Priscilla Mitchell (1965) C&W#45/Betty Johnson (1960) US#109/Mack Abernathy (1988) C&W#98. Co-writer: [i] Jimmy Davis.

944. TIOMKIN, Dimitri (b. May 10, 1899, St. Petersburg, Russia; d. November 11, 1979, London, England) Film composer, pianist and conductor. The master of the western film score and melodramatic theme tune. Tiomkin graduated from the St. Petersburg Conservatory of Music before performing as a concert pianist and conductor. He emigrated to America in 1925, where he was successful in Hollywood composing music for over one hundred and fifty films, including, "Alice in Wonderland" (1933), "Lost Horizon" (1937), "Only Angels Have Wings" (1938), "Duel in the Sun" (1946), "Red River" (1948), "Strangers on a Train" (1950), "Giant" (1956), "Rio Bravo" (1959), "The Alamo" (1960), "The High and the Mighty" (1954), "55 Days at Peking" (1963), "The Fall of the Roman Empire"

(1964), and "The War Wagon" (1967). CHART COMPOSITION: *The High and the Mighty* [i] (1954) US#29. ALBUMS: **The Great Waltz** ost (1936, Private); **Duel in the Sun** ost (1946, Sound Stage); **Return to Paradise** ost (1953, Decca); **The High and the Mighty** ost (1954), **The Land of the Pharaohs** ost (1955, both Elmer Bernstein Film Music Collection); **The Court Martial of Billy Mitchell** sc (1955, Mark); **Friendly Persuasion** ost (1956, Dot); **Giant** ost (1956, Capitol); **The Search for Paradise** ost (1957, RCA); **Wild Is the Wind** ost (1957), **The Old Man and the Sea** ost (1958, both Columbia); **Rhapsody of Steel** ost (1958, U.S. Steel); **Impact** ost (1959, RCA); **Rio Bravo** ost (1959, Capitol); **The Alamo** ost (1960, Columbia) US#7; **The Sundowners** ost (1960, Cinema); **The Unforgiven** ost (1960, United Artists); **The Guns of Navarone** ost (1961) US#48, **55 Days at Peking** ost (1963, both Columbia); **Circus World** ost (1964, MGM); **The Fall of the Roman Empire** ost (1964, Columbia) US#147; **36 Hours** ost (1964, Vee-Jay); **The Lost Horizon: The Classic Film Scores of Dimitri Tiompkin** (1976, RCA); **It's a Wonderful Life** st (1988, Telarc). HIT VERSIONS: *Ballad of the Alamo* [ii] Marty Robbins (1960) US#34, *Blowing Wild (The Ballad of Black Gold)* [i] Frankie Laine (1953) US#21 UK#2, *Friendly Persuasion (Thee I Love)* [i] Pat Boone (1956) US#5 UK#3/Four Aces (1957) UK#29; *Green Leaves of Summer, The* [ii] Brothers Four (1960) US#65/Kenny Ball & His Jazzmen (1962) UK#7; *Guns of Navarone, The* [ii] Joe Reisman (1961) US#96/Skatalites (1967) UK#36; *Hajji Baba (Persian Lament)* [i] Nat "King" Cole (1954) US#14, *High and the Mighty, The* [i] Les Baxter (1954) US#4/ Johnny Desmond (1954) US#17/Leroy Holmes (1954) US#9/Victor Young (1954) US#6; *High Noon (Do Not Forsake Me)* [i] Frankie Laine (1952) US#5 UK#7/Tex Ritter (1952) US#12; *Rawhide* [i] Frankie Laine (1959) UK#6/Link Wray & His Ray Men (1959) US#23; *Return to Paradise* [i] Camarata (1953) US#27/Nat "King" Cole (1953) US#15/Percy Faith (1953) US#19; *Town Without Pity* [i] Gene Pitney (1962) US#13 UK#32/Eddi Reader (1996) UK#26; *Sundowners, Theme from the* Mantovani (1960) US#93/Felix Slatkin (1960) US#70/Billy Vaughn (1960) US#51; *Unforgiven (The Need for Love)* [i] Don Costa (1960) US#74, *Wild Is the Wind* [i] David Bowie (1981) UK#24. Co-writers: [i] Ned Washington, [ii] Paul Francis Webster.

945. TOBIAS, Charles (b. August 15, 1898, New York, NY; d. 1970) Film and stage lyricist. A Broadway lyricist who often worked with his siblings Harry and Henry Tobias, on such musicals as "Earl Carroll's Vanities" (1932) and "Earl Carroll's Sketch Book" (1935). The Tobias brothers founded a family publishing firm in 1923, and Charles' songs later featured in such films as "Kid Millions" (1935). HIT VERSIONS: *After My Laughter Came Tears* [xxiv] Cliff Edwards (1928) US#11, *All Over the World* [ix] Nat "King" Cole (1962) US#42/Francoise Hardy (1965) UK#16; *Broken Record, The* [ii] Guy Lombardo (1936) US#3/Freddy Martin (1936) US#4; *Cloud Lucky Seven* [vi] Guy Mitchell (1953) UK#2, *Coax Me a Little Bit* [xx] Andrews Sisters (1946) US#24, *Don't Sweetheart Me* [vii] Lawrence Welk (1944) US#2, *For the First Time (I've Fallen in Love)* [xiii] Dick Haymes (1943) US#13, *Flowers for Madame* [xvii] Bob Crosby (1935) US#12/Ray Noble (1935) US#11; *Gee! But You're Swell* [i] Benny Goodman (1937) US#14/Russ Morgan (1937) US#17; *Get Out and Get Under the Moon* [x] Helen Kane (1928) US#7/Paul Whiteman (1928) US#4; *Good Night, Little Girl of My Dreams* [iii] Henry King (1933) US#7, *(Ho-Die-Ay) Start the Day Right* [xvi] Bing Crosby & Connee Boswell (1939) US#12, *If I Knew Then (What I Know Now)* [xxii] Dick Jurgens (1939) US#15/Ray Conniff Singers (1964) US#126/Val Doonican (1968) UK#14; *In the Valley of the Moon* [iii] Joe Green (1933) US#4, *Just a Prayer Away* [xiii] Bing Crosby (1945) US#4/Sammy Kaye (1945) US#10; *Just Another Wasted Away (Waiting for You)* [xxiv] Fred Waring's Pennsylvanians (1927) US#3, *Kathy-O* [xi] Diamonds (1958) US#16, *Little Curly Hair in a High Chair* [xx] Jimmy Dorsey (1940) US#16/Fats Waller (1940) US#6; *Little Lady Make Believe* [xx] Guy Lombardo (1938) US#9, *Mama Doll Song, The* [xx] Patti Page (1954) US#24, *May I Have the Next Dream with You* [xxii] Malcom Roberts (1968) UK#8, *Mickey Mouse's Birthday Party* [xix] Wayne King (1936) US#19, *Miss You* [xxii] Bing Crosby (1942) US#9/Eddy Howard (1942) US#21/Freddy Martin (1942) US#22/Dinah Shore (1942) US#8/Jimmie Young (1963) US#15; *No Can Do* [xx] Guy Lombardo (1945) US#8, *Old Lamplighter, The* [xx] Hal Derwin (1946) US#5/Morton Downey (1946) US#16/Sammy Kaye (1946) US#1/Kenny Baker (1947) US#11/Kay Kyser (1947) US#3/Browns (1960) C&W#20 R&B#17 US#5; *Rose O'Day (The Filla-Da-Gusha Song)* [xv] Woody Herman (1942) US#17/King Sisters (1942) US#18/Freddy Martin (1942) US#1/Kate Smith (1942) US#8; *Somebody Loves You* [vi] Ted Lewis (1932) US#2/Peter Van Steeden (1932) US#12; *Those Lazy-Hazy-Crazy Days of Summer* [iv] Nat "King" Cole (1963) US#6, *Throw Another Log on the Fire* [xviii] Don Bestor (1934) US#9/George Olsen (1934) US#12; *Time Waits for No One* [vii] Helen Forrest (1944) US#2/Johnny Long (1944) US#8/Hilltoppers (1954) US#25; *Trade Winds* [vii] Bing Crosby (1940) US#1/Tommy Dorsey (1940) US#10; *Wait for Me, Mary* [xxi] Dick Haymes (1943) US#6, *Wake Up and Sing* [viii] Bob Howard

(1936) US#15, *We Did It Before (And We Can Do It Again)* [vii] Dick Robertson (1942) US#22, *(What Do We Do) On a Dew-Dew-Dewy Day* [xii] Ruth Etting (1927) US#4, *When Your Hair Has Turned to Silver* [vi] Frank Luther & Carson Robison (1931) US#4. Co-writers: [i] Abel Baer, [ii] Boyd Bunch/Clifford Friend, [iii] Joe Burke, [iv] Hans Carste, [v] Sidney Clare/Murray Mencher, [vi] Peter De Rose, [vii] Clifford Friend, [viii] Clifford Friend/Guy Lombardo, [ix] Al Frisch, [x] William Jerome/Larry Shay, [xi] Ray Joseph/Jack Sher, [xii] Howard Johnson/Al Sherman, [xiii] David Kapp, [xiv] Ernesto Lecuona, [xv] Al Lewis, [xvi] Al Lewis/Maurice Spitainy, [xvii] Murray Mencher/Charles Newman, [xviii] Murray Mencher/Jack Scholl, [xix] Joseph Meyer/Bob Rothberg, [xx] Nat Simon, [xxi] Nat Simon/Harry Tobias, [xxii] Harry Tobias/Henry Tobias, [xxiii] Harry Tobias, [xxiv] Roy Turk. (*See also under* Lew BROWN, Maceo PINKARD, Sigmund ROMBERG, Samuel H. STEPT.)

946. TOBIAS, Harry (b. September 11, 1895, New York, NY) Film and stage composer, pianist. A Tin Pan Alley composer who often worked with his brothers Charles and Henry Tobias. Harry is best known for his work on Hollywood musicals during the 1930s, his songs later being featured in such films as "It's a Date" (1940). HIT VERSIONS: *At Your Command* [ii] Bing Crosby (1931) US#1, *It's a Lonesome Old Town (When You're Not Around)* [iv] Ben Bernie (1930) US#16, *No Regrets* [iii] Tommy Dorsey (1936) US#4/Billie Holiday (1936) US#9; *Sail Along, Silvery Moon* [v] Bing Crosby (1937) US#4/Billy Vaughn (1958) US#5; *Sweet and Lovely* [i] Gus Arnheim (1931) US#1/Ben Bernie (1931) US#12/Russ Columbo (1931) US#19/Bing Crosby (1931) US#9, re-issued (1944) US#27/Guy Lombardo (1931) US#2. Co-writers: [i] Gus Arnheim/Jules Lemare, [ii] Harry Barris/Bing Crosby, [iii] Roy Ingraham, [iv] Charles Kisco, [v] Percy Wenrich. (*See also under* Charles TOBIAS.)

947. TOUSSAINT, Allen (b. January 14, 1938, New Orleans, LA) R&B pianist, producer, arranger and vocalist. A backroom mastermind who has sold over thirty million records of his songs and productions. Toussaint's blend of soul and funk is R&B's principal link to the black classical music that is otherwise known as jazz. Toussaint's mother Naomi Neville was a pianist, and it was under her name that he would later write some of his songs. After teaching her son the piano at the age of seven, Toussaint studied classical music and began listening to the music of New Orleans' Professor Longhair. By the age of thirteen, Toussaint was playing regular local gigs, and in the 1950s, he became the tour pianist for the vocal duo Shirley and Lee. Toussaint sessioned for Fats Domino in 1957, after which his distinguished musical arrangements were very much in demand by such artists as Alvin "Red" Tyler and Lee Allen. As house producer and arranger at Minit Records, Toussaint received, for the first time in R&B music, a royalty for each of his productions, later saying, "I was personally involved with every artist we had." His unusual arrangements often deployed instruments not normally associated with R&B, such as the distinctive trombone passages on Benny Spellman's *Lipstick Traces*. Toussaint's *Mother-in-Law* (1961), a million seller for Ernie K-Doe, was allegedly retrieved by the singer from Toussaint's waste basket. After spells at the labels Instant, Ace and Alston, Toussaint was drafted in 1963, although he spent much of his time in the army playing in the group the Stokes. In 1966, he produced Aaron Neville's million selling *Tell It Like It Is*, a tune and arrangement that influenced the style of soul ballads for many years. Toussaint also worked closely with Neville's group the Meters, which blended syncopated R&B with dixieland jazz, and which eventually evolved into the Neville Brothers. During the 1970s, Toussaint ran his own Sea-Saint studio complex in New Orleans, before becoming a born-again Christian and recording an unreleased gospel set. In 1992, he directed and starred in the New York musical revue "The High Rollers Social and Pleasure Club." ALBUMS: **The Wild Sounds of New Orleans** (1958, RCA); **The Stokes with Allen Toussaint** (1959, Bandy); **Toussaint** (1971, Tiffany); **Life, Love and Faith** (1972), **Southern Nights** (1975, both Reprise); **Bomp City** (1976), **Motion** (1978, both Warner Brothers); **The Ultimate Session** (1994, Rhino). COMPILATIONS: **Allen Toussaint Sings** (1960, Bandy); **From a Whisper to a Scream-Retro, 1985–1988** (1985, Kent); **The Allen Toussaint Collection** (1991, Reprise); **The Complete Tuosan Sessions** (1992, Bear Family). HIT VERSIONS: *Certain Girl, A* Ernie K-Doe (1961) US#71/Warren Zevon (1980) US#57; *Confusion* Lee Dorsey (1965) UK#38, *Do-Re-Mi* Lee Dorsey (1965) R&B#22 US#27, *Everything I Do Gonna Be Funky from Now On* Lee Dorsey (1969) R&B#33 US#95, *Fortune Teller* Hardtimes (1966) US#97, *Freedom for the Stallion* Hues Corporation (1973) US#63, *Fun Time* Joe Cocker (1978) US#43, *Get Out of My Life, Woman* [ii] Lee Dorsey (1965) R&B#5 US#44 UK#22, *Go-Go Girl* Lee Dorsey (1967) R&B#31 US#62, *Going Down Slowly* Pointer Sisters (1975) R&B#16 US#61, *Happiness* Pointer Sisters (1979) R&B#20 US#30, *Holy Cow* Lee Dorsey (1965) R&B#10 US#23 UK#6, *I Like It Like That* [iv] Chris Kenner (1961) R&B#2 US#2, *It Will Stand* Showmen (1961) US#61, re-issued (1964) US#80; *It's Rain-*

ing Shakin' Stevens (1981) UK#10, *Java* [iii] Al Hirt (1963) US#4/Donna Lynn (1964) US#129; *Life* Betty Wright (1977) R&B#64, *Lipstick Traces (On a Cigarette)* Benny Spellman (1962) R&B#28 US#80, *Love Lots of Lovin'* Lee Dorsey & Betty Harris (1967) US#110, *Mother-in-Law* Ernie K-Doe (1961) R&B#1 US#1/Jim Nesbitt (1964) C&W#20/Clarence Carter (1973) R&B#17 US#65; *My Old Car* Lee Dorsey (1967) US#113, *Night People* Lee Dorsey (1978) R&B#93, *Over You* Aaron Neville (1960) R&B#21 US#111, *Pain in My Heart* Otis Redding (1963) US#61, *Play Something Sweet (Brickyard Blues)* Three Dog Night (1974) US#33, *Rain, Rain Go Away* Lee Dorsey (1967) US#105, *Ride Your Pony* [ii] Lee Dorsey (1965) R&B#7 US#28, *Shoorah, Shoorah* Betty Wright (1974) R&B#28 UK#27, *Southern Nights* Glen Campbell (1977) g C&W#1 US#1 UK#28, *There Should Be a Book* Lee Dorsey on B-side of *Everything I Do Gonna Be Funky from Now On* (1969) R&B#33 US#95, *We Got It* [i] Immature featuring Smooth (1996) R&B#11 US#37, *Whipped Cream* Herb Alpert & the Tijuana Brass (1965) US#68, *Whoever's Thrilling You (Is Killing Me)* Rufus (1973) R&B#40, *Work, Work, Work* Lee Dorsey (1965) US#121, *Working in a Coal Mine* [ii] Lee Dorsey (1965) R&B#5 US#8 UK#8/Devo (1981) US#43/Bob Jenkins (1983) C&W#86; *Yes We Can* Lee Dorsey (1970) R&B#46/Pointer Sisters (1973) R&B#12 US#11. Co-writers: [i] J. Carter/S. Mather/C. Stokes, [ii] Lee Dorsey (b. Irving Lee Dorsey, December 24, 1926, New Orleans, LA; d. December 2, 1986, Portland, OR), [iii] Freddy Friday/Alvin Tyler, [iv] Chris Kenner.

948. TOWNSHEND, Pete (b. Peter Blandford Townshend, May 19, 1945, London, England) Rock guitarist, producer and vocalist. The leader of the influential rock group the Who, who is a uniquely British songwriter in outlook and style. Townshend's father played saxophone and his mother was a singer, but he grew up in a disharmonious family environment, the tensions and hidden aggression of which later surfaced in some of his music. Townshend was given his first guitar by his grandmother, and in 1961, he left school to attend art college, where he joined Roger Daltrey and John Entwistle in the covers group the Detours. The band's manager and publicist Pete Meadon, began molding them into a mod band, re-naming them the High Numbers and introducing the flamboyant drummer Keith Moon. The group released only one single *I'm the Face* (1964), re-issued (1980) UK#49. The High Numbers became the Who, and performed regularly at the Railway Hotel in Richmond, Surrey, and at the Marquee in London. The group became a formidable singles band during the 1960s, and they soon established their own niche alongside the Beatles, the Rolling Stones and the Kinks. In 1968, Townshend turned to the teachings of Meher Baba, which would influence the lyrics of many of his future songs. The following year, the Who premiered Townshend's rock opera "Tommy" at Ronnie Scott's jazz club in Soho, London. The subsequent double album, film and show, have proven immensely popular, and the song cycle was also recorded as **Tommy** ost (1972, Ode) g US#5; **Tommy** ost (1975, Track) g US#2 UK#21; and **The Who's Tommy** oc (1993, RCA) US#114. The Who's creative peak was the album **Who's Next** (1971), which was followed by a second rock opera, "Quadrophenia" (1973). CHART COMPOSITIONS: *I Can't Explain* (1965) US#93 UK#8, *Anyway, Anyhow, Anywhere* [i] (1965) UK#10, *My Generation* (1965) US#74 UK#2, re-issued (1988) UK#68, re-issued (1996) UK#31; *Substitute* (1966) UK#5, re-issued (1976) UK#7; *A Legal Matter* (1966) UK#32, *The Kids Are Alright* (1966) US#106 UK#41, re-entry (1966) UK#48; *I'm a Boy* (1966) UK#2, *Happy Jack* (1967) US#24 UK#3, *Pictures of Lily* (1967) US#51 UK#4, *I Can See for Miles* (1967) US#9 UK#10, *Call Me Lightning* (1968) US#40, *Dogs* (1968) UK#25, *Magic Bus* (1968) US#25 UK#26, *Pinball Wizard* (1969) US#19 UK#4, *I'm Free* (1969) US#37, *The Seeker* (1970) US#44 UK#19, *See Me, Feel Me* (1970) US#12, *Won't Get Fooled Again* (1971) US#15 UK#9, *Let's See Action* (1971) UK#16, *Join Together* (1972) US#17 UK#9, *Relay* (1973) US#39 UK#21, *5.15* (1973) US#45 UK#20, *Love, Reign O'er Me* (1973) US#76, *The Real Me* (1974) US#92, *Squeeze Box* (1975) US#16 UK#10, *Who Are You* (1978) US#14 UK#18, *Long Live Rock* (1979) US#54 UK#48, *Trick of the Light* (1979) US#107, *You Better You Bet* (1981) US#18 UK#9, *Don't Let Go the Coat* (1981) US#84 UK#47, *Athena* (1982) US#28 UK#40, *Eminence Front* (1982) US#68, *Ready, Steady, Who EP* (1983) UK#58. ALBUMS: **My Generation** (1965) UK#5, **A Quick One** (1966, both Brunswick) UK#4; **The Who Sell Out** (1968) US#48 UK#13, **Tommy** (1969) p US#4 UK#2, **Live at Leeds** (1970) p US#4 UK#3, **Who's Next** (1971) p US#4 UK#1, **Quadrophenia** (1973) p US#2 UK#2, **Odds and Sods** (1974, all Track) g US#15 UK#10; **The Who By Numbers** (1975) g US#8 UK#7, **Who Are You** (1978) p US#2 UK#6, **The Kids Are Alright** ost (1979) p US#8 UK#26, **Face Dances** (1981) p US#4 UK#2, **It's Hard** (1982, all Polydor) g US#8 UK#11; **Who's Last** (1984, MCA) US#81 UK#48; **Join Together** (1990, Virgin) US#188 UK#59. COMPILATIONS: **Happy Jack** (1966) US#67, **Magic Bus — The Who on Tour** (1968, both Decca) US#39; **Meaty, Beaty, Big and Bouncy** (1971) p US#11 UK#9, **A Quick One/The Who Sell Out** (1974, both Track) US#185; **The Story of the Who** (1976)

UK#2; **Quadrophenia** ost (1979, both Polydor) US#46 UK#23; **Hooligans** (1981, MCA) g US#52; **Rarities** (1982, Track); **The Who's Greatest Hits** (1983, MCA) p US#94; **The Who Collection** (1985, Impression) UK#44; **Who's Missing** (1985) US#116, **Who's Better, Who's Best** (1988, both Polydor) g UK#10; **The Who Collection** (1988, Stylus) UK#71; **30 Years of Maximum R&B** (1994, Polydor) US#170 UK#48; **My Generation — The Best of the Who** (1996, Polydor) UK#11; **Isle of Wight Live** (1996, Essential). By the early 1980s, the Who had taken heavy casualties. Their two former managers, Meadon and Kit Lambert, and drummer Moon, had all died as a direct result of the excesses of the rock and roll lifestyle, while Townshend himself battled with drug and alcohol addiction. In 1994, Daltrey presented the stage show "Daltrey Sings Townshend" at Carnegie Hall, New York, while Townshend issued the CD-ROM "Pete Townshend Presents Tommy-The Interactive Adventure" (1996). CHART COMPOSITIONS: *Rough Boys* (1980) US#89 UK#39, *Let Love Open Your Door* (1980) US#9 UK#46, *A Little Is Enough* (1980) US#72, *Uniforms (Corps D'Esprit)* (1982) UK#48, *Face Dances (Part 2)* (1982) US#105, *Face the Face* (1986) US#26. ALBUMS: **Who Came First** (1972, Track) US#69 UK#30; **Rough Mix** with Ronnie Lane (1977, Polydor) US#45 UK#44; **Empty Glass** (1980) g US#5 UK#11, **All the Best Cowboys Have Chinese Eyes** (1982) US#26 UK#32; **Scoop** (1983) US#35, **White City** (1985) g US#26 UK#70, **Pete Townshend's Deep End Live** (1986, all Atco) US#98; **Another Scoop** (1987, Polydor) US#198; **The Iron Man** (1989, Virgin) US#58; **Psycho-Derelict** (1993, Atlantic) US#118. COMPILATION: **Best of Pete Townshend** (1996, Atlantic). HIT VERSIONS: *After the Fire* Roger Daltrey (1985) US#48, *Baba O'Reilly* Big Audio Dynamite sampled in *Rush* (1991) US#32, *Overture (Tommy)* Assembled Multitude (1970) US#16/Stars On in *Stars on Long Play 2/On 45, Volume 2* (1981) US#120 UK#18; *Pinball Wizard* New Seekers (1973) US#29 UK#16/Elton John (1976) UK#7; *See Me, Feel Me* New Seekers (1973) US#29 UK#16, *Squeeze Box* Freddy Fender (1979) C&W#61. Co-writer: [i] Roger Daltrey (b. Roger Harry Daltrey, March 1, 1944, London, England).

949. Toyah (b. Toyah Ann Wilcox, May 18 1958, Birmingham, England) Pop vocalist. A drama school graduate who, during the 1980s, was briefly a successful punkette. Since the 1990s, Toyah has concentrated on her acting career. CHART COMPOSITIONS: *Four from Toyah EP* (1981) UK#4, *I Want to Be Free* [i] (1981) UK#8, *Thunder in the Mountains* [ii] (1981) UK#4, *Four More from Toyah EP* (1981) UK#14, *Brave New World* (1982) UK#21,

Ieya (1982) UK#48, *Be Loud Be Proud (Be Heard)* (1982) UK#30, *Rebel Run* (1983) UK#24, *The Vow* (1983) UK#50, *Don't Fall in Love (I Said)* (1985) UK#22, *Soul Passing Through Soul* (1985) UK#57. ALBUMS: **Sheep Farming in Barnet** (1979), **The Blue Meaning** (1980) UK#40, **Toyah Toyah Toyah** (1981) UK#22, **Anthem** (1981) UK#2, **The Changeling** (1982) UK#6, **Warrior Rock — Toyah on Tour** (1982) UK#20, **Love Is the Law** (1983, all Safari) UK#28; **Minx** (1985, Portrait) UK#24; **Desire** (1987), **The Lady and the Tiger** (1987), **Prostitute** (1988, all EG); **Dreamchild** (1994, Cryptic); **Phoenix** (1997, Receiver). COMPILATIONS: **Toyah! Toyah! Toyah!** (1984, K-Tel) UK#43; **Best of Toyah** (1997, Pinnacle). Co-writers: [i] Joel Bogen, [ii] Nigel Glockler/Adrian Lee.

950. TRAVIS, Merle (b. November 29, 1917, Rosewood, KY; d. October 20, 1983, Tahlequah, OK) C&W guitarist and vocalist. The son of a coal miner who learned the banjo as a boy, before becoming one of country music's most distinctive and influential guitar pickers. Throughout the 1930–1940s, Travis performed regularly on the radio with such groups as the Tennessee Tomcats and the Georgia Wildcats. He sung with the Delmore Brothers, and first recorded for the King label in 1943 as the Sheppard Boys. After serving in World War II, Travis played in various western swing bands before charting with his own, often witty, solo material. He is often credited with having built the first solid body electric guitar in 1940s, and he later became an actor in Hollywood. CHART COMPOSITIONS: *Cincinnati Lou* (1946) C&W#2, *No Vacancy* (1946) C&W#3, *Divorce Me C.O.D.* (1946) C&W#1 US#25, *So Round, So Firm, So Fully Packed* (1947) C&W#1 US#21, *Merle's Boogie Woogie* (1948) C&W#7. ALBUMS: **Folk Songs of the Hills** (1947, Capitol); **Walkin' the Strings** (1959); **Country Guitar Giants** with Joe Maphis (1979), **The Merle Travis Story** (1980), **Travis Pickin'** (1982), **Rough, Rowdy and Blue** (1985, all CMH); **Back Home** (1987), **Travis** (1988), **The Great Songs of the Delmore Brothers** (1989, all Stetson); **Merle Travis, 1944–1946** (1990, Country Routes); **Merle Travis** (1993, Capitol). HIT VERSIONS: *Muskrat* [i] Everly Brothers (1961) US#82, *Sixteen Tons* Tennessee Ernie Ford (1955) C&W#1 US#1/Don Harrison Band (1976) US#47; *Dark as a Dungeon* (1964) C&W#49 US#119, *Smoke! Smoke! Smoke! (That Cigarette)* [ii] Phil Harris (1947) US#8/Tex Williams (1947) g C&W#1 US#1, new version (1968) C&W#32/Commander Cody & His Lost Planet Airmen (1973) C&W#97 US#94/Tom Bresh (1978) C&W#78/Sammy Davis, Jr. (1982) C&W#89. Co-writers: [i] Tex Ann/Harold Hensley, [ii] Tex Williams.

951. TRAVIS, Randy (b. Randy Bruce Traywick, May 4, 1959, Marshville, NC) C&W guitarist and vocalist. A contemporary country singer-songwriter in a mainstream style, who first performed at the age of ten, and initially recorded for the Paula label in 1979, before signing to Warner Brothers and achieving ten country number ones. CHART COMPOSITIONS: *She's My Woman* (1979) C&W#91, *1982* (1986) C&W#6, *No Place Like Home* (1987) C&W#2, *Honky Tonk Moon* (1988) C&W#1, *Forever Together* [i] (1991) C&W#1, *Better Class of Losers* [i] (1991) C&W#2, *I'd Surrender All* [i] (1992) C&W#2+. ALBUMS: **Randy Ray Live at the Nashville Palace** (1981, Paula); **Storms of Life** (1986) p US#85, **Always and Forever** (1987) p US#19, **Old 8 x 10** (1988) p US#35 UK#64, **No Holdin' Back** (1989) p US#33, **An Old Time Christmas** (1989) g US#70, **Heroes and Friends** (1990) p US#31, **High Lonesome** (1991) g US#43, **Wind in the Wire** ost (1993) US#121, **This Is Me** (1994, all Warner Brothers) g US#59. COMPILATIONS: **Greatest Hits, Volume 1** (1992) p US#44, **Greatest Hits, Volume 2** (1992, both Warner Brothers) p US#67. Co-writer: [i] Alan Jackson. (*See also under* Alan JACKSON.)

952. TRENET, Charles (b. 1913, Narbonne, France) Film and stage composer, vocalist. One of France's most celebrated songwriter-performers, who specialized in sentimental ballads, ultimately composing over three hundred and fifty songs. Trenet was first successful as one half of the vocal duo Charles and Johnny, before recording for Columbia Records during the 1950s, and achieving major European hits with *Boum!!* [iii] (1939) and *At Last! At Last!* [ii] (1952). Trenet has also written for films and for the stage. In 1994, Les Halles theatre in France staged "Le Marathon Trenet," a three night celebration of over two hundred of his compositions. ALBUMS: **Disque d'Or** (1983), **J'Ai Ta Main** (1983, both EMI); **Florilege '86** (1986, CBS); **Charles Trenet** (1986), **Chansons** (1988), **Special Compilation** (1988), **Top Sixteen** (1988, all Pathe Marconi); **Mon Coeur S'envole** (1992, WEA). HIT VERSIONS: *I Wish You Love(Que Reste-t-il de nos Amours)* [iv] Gloria Lynne (1964) US#28, *La Mer (Beyond the Sea)* [i] Benny Goodman (1948) US#26/Roger Williams (1956) US#37/Bobby Darin (1960) R&B#15 US#6 UK#8/George Benson (1985) UK#60. Co-writers: [i] Jack Lawrence, [ii] Florence Mills, [iii] Roma Campbell-Hunter, [iv] Lee Wilson.

953. TRITT, Travis (b. Marietta, GA) C&W guitarist and vocalist. A former trucking company manager who returned to his teenage love of music and became a major country star in the 1990s.

CHART COMPOSITIONS: *Help Me Hold On* [iv] (1990) C&W#1, *I'm Gonna Be Somebody* (1990) C&W#2, *Drift Off to Dream* (1991) C&W#3, *The Whiskey Ain't Workin'* with Marty Stuart (1991) C&W#2, *Here's a Quarter (Call Someone Who Cares)* (1991) C&W#27, *Anymore* [i] (1991) C&W#1, *Bible Belt* (1992) C&W#72, *Can I Trust You with My Heart* [ii] (1992) C&W#1, *Looking Out for Number One* [iii] (1993) C&W#11, *Worth Every Mile* (1993) C&W#30, *Foolish Pride* (1994) C&W#1 US#112, *Ten Feet Tall and Bullet Proof* (1994) C&W#73. ALBUMS: **Country Club** (1990) p US#70, **It's All About to Change** (1991) p US#27, **T-R-O-U-B-L-E** (1992) g US#27, **A Travis Tritt Christmas — Loving Time of the Year** (1992) US#75, **Ten Feet Tall and Bulletproof** (1994, all Warner Brothers) g US#20. COMPILATION: **Greatest Hits — From the Beginning** (1996, Warner Brothers) US#21. Co-writers: [i] J. Colucci, [ii] S. Harris, [iii] Troy Seals, [iv] P. Terry.

954. TROUP, Bobby

(b. Robert William Troup, Jr., October 18, 1918, Harrisburg, PA) Pop pianist, producer and vocalist. A staff songwriter who, under Tommy Dorsey, composed Frank Sinatra's *(You're a) Snootie Little Cutie*. Troup performed in his own jazz influenced trio, before producing many of his wife Julie London's recordings during the 1950s. He wrote *Girl Talk* [i] from the film "Harlow" (1966), and the title theme to "Rock Pretty Baby" (1956). Troup's best known composition remains his tribute to the mythical strip of American asphalt, *Route 66*. ALBUMS: **Bobby Troup** (1954), **Bobby Troup Plays Johnny Mercer** (1955, both Capitol). HIT VERSIONS: *Baby, Baby All the Time* Superbs (1964) R&B#83, *Daddy* Sammy Kaye (1941) US#1/Frankie Masters (1941) US#21/Joan Merrill (1941) US#13; *Girl Can't Help It, The* Little Richard (1957) R&B#7 US#49 UK#9/Darts (1977) UK#6; *Route 66* Nat "King" Cole (1946) US#11/Bing Crosby & the Andrews Sisters (1946) US#14/Nelson Riddle (1962) US#30/Depeche Mode (1988) US#61. Co-writer: [i] Neil Hefti (b. October 29, 1922, Hasting, NE)

955. TROUTMAN, Roger

(b. Hamilton, OH) R&B multi-instrumentalist, producer and vocalist. An electro-influenced R&B artist who first achieved success in the group Zapp. CHART COMPOSITIONS: *More Bounce to the Ounce* (1980) R&B#2 US#86, *Be Alright* (1980) R&B#26, *Dance Floor* (1982) R&B#1 US#101, *Do Wa Ditty (Blow That Thing)* (1982) R&B#10 US#103, *I Can Make You Dance* (1983) R&B#4 US#102, *Heartbreaker* (1983) R&B#15 US#107, *Spend My Whole Life* (1984) R&B#77, *It Doesn't Really Matter* (1985) R&B#41,

Computer Love [vx] (1986) R&B#8, *Itchin' for Your Twitchin'* (1986) R&B#81, *(Everybody) Get Up* [viii] (1991) R&B#19, *Take Me Back* [viii] (1992) R&B#37, *Mega Medley* [vxiv] (1993) R&B#30 US#54, *Slow and Easy* [vxii] (1993) R&B#18 US#43, *Computer Love '94* [vxii] (1994) R&B#65 US#108. ALBUMS: **Zapp** (1980) g US#19, **Zapp II** (1982) g US#25, **Zapp III** (1983) US#39, **The New Zapp IV** (1985, all Warner Brothers) US#110; **Zapp V** (1989, Reprise) US#154. Troutman has also been successful as the solo artist Roger, becoming, during the 1990s, a heavily sampled artist amongs rappers. CHART COMPOSITIONS: *Do It Roger* (1981) R&B#24, *In the Mix* (1984) R&B#10, *Midnight Hour* (1984) R&B#34, *Girl, Cut It Out* (1985) R&B#79, *I Want to Be Your Man* (1987) R&B#1 US#3, *Thrill Seekers* (1988) R&B#27, *How Do U Want It* with 2 Pac & Dr. Dre (1996) R&B#1 US#1. ALBUMS: **The Many Facets of Roger** (1981) g US#26, **The Saga Continues** (1984, both Warner Brothers) US#64; **Unlimited** (1987, Reprise) g US#35. COMPILATION: **All the Greatest Hits** (1993, Warner Brothers). HIT VERSIONS: *Brooklyn Bounce* [v] Daddy-O (1993) R&B#69, *Computer Love* [vx] NKRU (1993) R&B#55, *Ditty* [iv] Paperboy (1993) R&B#17, *I Get Around/ Keep Ya Head Up* [i] 2 Pac (1993) R&B#5 US#45, *It's a Shame* [vi] Kriss Kross (1993) R&B#55 US#120, *Keep Ya Head Up* [ii] 2 Pac (1993) g R&B#7 US#13, *Pump* [vix] Volume 10 (1994) R&B#64, *Scandalous* [vxi] Click (1996) R&B#49+ US#101+, *Stay Real* [vxiii] Erick Sermon (1993) R&B#54 US#92, *Stay with Me Tonight* [iii] Shirley Murdock (1991) R&B#34, *Time 4 Sum Aksion* [vii] Redman (1993) R&B#63. Co-writers: [i] D. Anderson/Shirley Murdock/Tupac Amaru Shakur (b. 1971, New York, NY; d. September 13, 1996, Las Vegas, NV)/L. Troutman, [ii] D. Anderson/Tupac Amaru Shakur, [iii] B. Beck/L. Troutman/Z. Troutman, [iv] Clark/Ferguson/Ferguson/Johnson, [v] Daddy-O, [vi] J. Dupri/M. Mauldin, [vii] Fulson/McCracklin/Muggerud/Noble, [viii] David Gamson, [vix] D. Hawkins/A. Miller/E. Vidal/N. Vidal, [vx] Hennings/Shirley Murdock/L. Troutman, [vxi] B. Jones/Shirley Murdock/D. Stevens/E. Stevens/T. Stevens/L. Troutman, [vxii] Shirley Murdock/L. Troutman, [vxiii] Erick Sermon/L. Troutman, [vxiv] Barrett Strong/Norman Whitfield.

956. TUBB, Ernest

(b. Ernest Dale Tubb, February 9, 1914, Crisp, TX; d. September 6, 1984, Nashville, TN) C&W guitarist and vocalist. A major selling artist who charted nearly one hundred country hits between 1944–1969, and who was the owner of the legendary Ernest Tubb's Record Shop in Nashville. He first performed on the radio in San Antonio during the 1930s, before recording for the

Bluebird label in 1936. During the 1940s he became a major Grand Ole Opry star, actor and broadcaster. Tubb died of emphysema in 1984. CHART COMPOSITIONS: *Try Me One More Time* (1944) C&W#2 US#18, *Soldier's Last Letter* [ii] (1944) C&W#1 US#16, *Yesterday's Tears* (1944) C&W#4 US#29, *Don't Rob Another Man's Castle* with the Andrews Sisters (1949) C&W#6. ALBUMS: **Country Double Date*** (1955), **Jimmie Rodgers' Songs** (1956), **Favorites** (1957), **Red and Ernie*** (1957); **The Daddy of 'Em All** (1958), **The Importance of Being Earnest** (1959), **The Ernest Tubb Story, Volume One** (1960), **The Ernest Tubb Story, Volume Two** (1960), **The Ernest Tubb Record Shop** (1960), **My Pick of the Hits** (1966, all Brunswick); **The Legend and the Legacy** (1997, Edsel). HIT VERSIONS: *Soldier's Last Letter* [ii] Merle Haggard (1971) C&W#3 US#90, *Tomorrow Never Comes* [i] Glen Campbell (1965) US#118, *Walking the Floor Over You* George Hamilton, IV (1965) C&W#18. With: * Red Foley. Co-writers: [i] Johnny Bond, [ii] H. Stewart.

957. TURK, Roy (b. 1892; d. 1934) Tin Pan Alley lyricist. A versatile lyricist who worked with a variety of composers during the 1920s. HIT VERSIONS: *Aggravatin' Papa* [i] Marion Harris (1923) US#3/Bessie Smith (1923) US#12/Sophie Tucker (1923) US#10; *My Sweetie Went Away* [i] Dolly Kay (1923) US#10/Billy Murray & Ed Smalle (1923) US#8/"Whispering" Jack Smith (1926) US#1/April Stevens (1951) US#10; *Oh! How I Laugh When I Think That I Cried Over You* [ii] Nora Bayes (1920) US#6/Billy Murray & Gladys Rice (1920) US#14. Co-writers: [i] Andy Britt/J. Russel Robinson, [ii] George Jessel/Willy White. (*See also under* Fred AHLERT, Lou HANDMAN, Arthur JOHNSTON, Maceo PINKARD, Charles TOBIAS.)

958. TYLER, Steve (b. Steven Tallarico, March 26, 1948, New York, NY) Rock vocalist. The lead vocalist in the heavy rock group Aerosmith, which by 1990, had sold over twenty-five million records. CHART COMPOSITIONS: *Dream On* (1973) US#59, re-issued (1976) g US#6; *Sweet Emotion* [iii] (1975) US#36, re-issued (1994) UK#74; *Last Child* [vx] (1976) US#21, *Home Tonight* (1976) US#71, *Walk This Way* [vii] (1976) US#10, *Back in the Saddle* [vii] (1977) US#38, *Draw the Line* [vii] (1977) US#42, *Kings and Queens* [iv] (1978) US#70, *Chip Away the Stone* (1979) US#77, *Dude (Looks Like a Lady)* [ii] (1987) US#14 UK#45, re-issued (1990) UK#20; *Angel* [i] (1987) US#3 UK#69, *Rag Doll* [vi] (1988) US#17, re-issued (1990) UK#42; *Love in an Elevator* [vii] (1989) US#5 UK#13, *Janie's Got a Gun* [iii] (1989) US#4, *What It Takes* [ii] (1990) US#9, *The Other Side of Me* (1990) US#22 UK#46, *Livin'*

on the Edge [v] (1993) US#18 UK#19, *Eat the Rich* (1993) UK#34, *Cryin'* [viii] (1993) g US#12 UK#17, *Amazing* [vix] (1993) US#24 UK#57, *Shut Up and Dance* (1994) UK#24, *Crazy* [ii] (1994) US#17 UK#23, *Blind Man* (1994) US#48. ALBUMS: **Aerosmith** (1973) p US#21, **Get Your Wings** (1974) p US#74, **Toys in the Attic** (1975) p US#11, **Rocks** (1976) p US#3, **Draw the Line** (1978) p US#11, **Live! Bootleg** (1979) p US#13, **Night in the Ruts** (1980) p US#14, **Rock in a Hard Place** (1982, all Columbia) g US#32; **Done with Mirrors** (1985) US#36, **Classics Live!** (1986) g US#84, **Permanent Vacation** (1987) p US#11 UK#37, **Pump** (1989) p US#5 UK#3, **Get a Grip** (1993) p US#1 UK#2, **Classics Live! II** (1993, all Geffen) g; **Nine Lives** (1997, Columbia). COMPILATIONS: **Greatest Hits** (1981) p US#53, **Gems** (1988) US#133, **Pandora's Box** (1992, all Columbia) g US#45; **Big Ones** (1995) US#6 UK#7, **Box of Fire** (1995, both Geffen) g. HIT VERSION: *Walk This Way* [vii] Run-D.M.C. (1986) R&B#8 US#4 UK#8. Co-writers: [i] Desmond Child, [ii] Desmond Child/Joe Perry (b. Anthony Joseph Perry, September 10, 1950, Boston, MA), [iii] Tom Hamilton (b. December 31, 1951, Colorado Springs, CO), [iv] Tom Hamilton/Joey Kramer (b. June 21, 1950, New York, NY), [v] M. Hudson/Joe Perry, [vi] Holly Knight/Joe Perry/Jim Vallance, [vii] Joe Perry, [viii] Joe Perry/T. Rhodes, [vix] R. Supa, [vx] Brad Whitford.

959. TYSON, Ian (b. September 25, 1933, Victoria, British Columbia, Canada) Folk guitarist and vocalist. One half, with his wife Sylvia Fricker, of the 1960s folk duo Ian and Sylvia. ALBUMS: **Ian and Sylvia** (1962), **Four Strong Winds** (1963) US#115, **Northern Journey** (1964) US#70, **Early Morning Rain** (1965) US#77, **Play One More** (1966) US#142, **So Much For Dreaming** (1967, all Vanguard) US#130; **Lovin' Sound** (1967) US#148, **Full Circle** (1968, both MGM); **Nashville** (1970, Vanguard); **Ian and Sylvia** (1970), **You Were on My Mind** (1972, both Columbia). COMPILATIONS: **Best of Ian and Sylvia** (1967), **Greatest Hits, Volume 1** (1970), **Greatest Hits, Volume 2** (1972, all Vanguard); **Best of Ian and Sylvia** (1973, Columbia). Tyson has also recorded as a solo artist, releasing the albums **Ol'Eon** (1975, A&M); **One Jump Ahead of the Devil** (1979, Boot) and **Cowboyography** (1986). HIT VERSIONS: *Four Strong Winds* Brothers Four (1963) US#114/Bobby Bare (1964) C&W#3 US#60/Neil Young (1975) US#61 UK#57; *Someday Soon* Judy Collins (1969) US#55/Suzy Bogguss (1991) C&W#12.

960. TZUKE, Judi (b. 1955, London, England) Pop vocalist. A singer-songwriter with a cult following, who charted with the single *Stay with Me Till Dawn* (1979) UK#16. ALBUMS: **Welcome to the Cruise** (1979) UK#14, **Sports Car** (1980) UK#7, **I am Phoenix** (1982, all Rocket) UK#17; **Shoot the Moon** (1982) UK#19, **Road Noise — The Official Bootleg** (1982) UK#39, all Chrysalis) UK#26; **The Cat Is Out** (1985, Legacy) UK#35; **Turning Stones** (1989, Polydor) UK#57, **BBC in Concert** (1995, Windsong); **Under the Angels** (1996, Big Moon).

961. URE, Midge (b. James Ure, October 10, 1953, Gambusland, Scotland) Pop guitarist, producer and vocalist. A pop journeyman who first performed in the teenybop group Slik, which released the album **Slik** (1976, Bell) UK#58, followed by the acts Visage and the Rich Kids. In 1979, Ure joined the synthesizer group Ultravox. CHART COMPOSITIONS: *Vienna* [i] (1980) UK#2, re-issued (1993) UK#13; *All Stood Still* [i] (1981) UK#8, *The Thin Wall* [i] (1981) UK#14, *The Voice* [i] (1981) UK#16, *Reap the Wild Wind* [i] (1982) US#71 UK#12, *Hymn* [i] (1982) UK#11, *Visions in Blue* [i] (1983) UK#15, *We Came to Dance* [i] (1983) UK#18, *One Small Day* [i] (1984) UK#27, *Dancing with Tears in My Eyes* [i] (1984) US#108 UK#3, *Lament* [i] (1984) UK#22, *Love's Great Adventure* [i] (1984) UK#12, *Same Old Story* [i] (1986) UK#31, *All Fall Down* [i] (1986) UK#30. ALBUMS: **Vienna** (1980) US#164 UK#3, **Rage in Eden** (1981) US#144 UK#4, **Quartet** (1982) US#61 UK#6, **Monument — The Soundtrack** (1983) UK#9, **Lament** (1984) US#115 UK#8, **U-Vox** (1986, all Chrysalis) UK#9. COMPILATIONS: **The Collection** (1984) UK#2, **If I Was — The Very Best of Ultravox and Midge Ure** (1993) UK#10; **Dancing with Tears in My Eyes** (1997, all Chrysalis). Ure has also recorded as a solo artist. CHART COMPOSITIONS: *After a Fashion* (1983) UK#39, *If I Was* [iii] (1985) UK#1, *That Certain Smile* (1985) UK#28, *Wastelands* (1986) UK#46, *Call of the Wild* (1986) UK#27, *Answers to Nothing* (1988) US#95 UK#49, *Dear God* (1988) UK#55, *Cold, Cold Heart* (1991) UK#17, *Breathe* (1996) UK#70. ALBUMS: **The Gift** (1985) UK#2, **Answers to Nothing** (1988, both Chrysalis) US#88 UK#30; **Pure** (1991) UK#36, **Breathe** (1996, both Arista). HIT VERSIONS: *Fade to Grey* Visage (1980) UK#8. Co-writers: [i] Warren Cann (b. May 20, 1952, Victoria, British Columbia, Canada)/Christopher Cross (b. Christopher St. John, July 14, 1952, London, England)/William Currie (b. April 1, 1952, Huddersfield, England), [ii] William Currie/Christopher Payne, [iii] Daniel Mitchell. (*See also under* Bob GELDOF, Phil LYNOTT.)

962. VALENTI, Dino (b. November 7, 1943, New York, NY) Rock guitarist and vocalist. A founder member of the 1960s San Francisco band Quicksilver Messenger Service, who, due to imprisonment on drugs charges, did not actually record as a member until 1970, when it charted with the singles *Fresh Air* (1970) US#49 and *What About Me* (1971) US#100. ALBUMS: **Just for Love** (1970) US#27, **What About Me** (1971) US#26, **Quicksilver** (1972) US#114, **Comin' Thru** (1972) US#134, **Anthology** (1973) US#108, **Solid Silver** (1975, all Capitol) US#89. Valenti worked in a carnival during his early years, and penned two of the most recorded songs of the 1960s, *Hey Joe* and *Get Together*, the publishing rights of which he allegedly sold outright. Valenti's solo career was scotched when he underwent extensive brain surgery. ALBUM: **Dino Valenti** (1977, Columbia); **Dino** (1997, Koch). HIT VERSIONS: *Get Together* We Five (1965) US#31/Youngbloods (1967) US#62, re-issued (1969) g US#5/Sunshine Company (1968) US#112/Dave Clark Five (1970) UK#8/Gwen & Jerry Collins (1970) C&W#34/Skeeter Davis & George Hamilton, IV (1970) C&W#65; *Hey Joe* Leaves (1966) US#31/Jimi Hendrix (1967) UK#6, also on *All Along the Watchtower EP* (1990) UK#52/Cher (1967) US#94/Wilson Pickett (1970) R&B#29 US#59/Seal on *Killer EP* (1991) UK#8.

963. VAN ALSTYNE, Egbert Anson (b. March 5, 1882; d. July 9, 1951, both Chicago, IL) Tin Pan Alley composer and keyboard player. A former sunday school organist who studied at the Chicago Musical College. After forming a songwriting partnership with Harry H. Williams, Van Alstyne created a series of ragtime influenced hits, including the multi-million selling *In the Shade of the Old Apple Tree* [ii] (1905). HIT VERSIONS: *I'm Afraid to Come Home in the Dark* [ii] Billy Murray (1908) US#3, *In the Shade of the Old Apple Tree* [ii] Henry Burr (1905) US#1/Albert Campbell (1905) US#2/Haydn Quartet (1905) US#2/Arthur Pryor's Band (1905) US#9/Duke Ellington (1933) US#13; *Navajo* [ii] Harry MacDonogh (1904) US#3/Billy Murray (1904) US#1/J.W. Myers (1904) US#3; *Oh That Navajo Rag* [i] American Quartet (1912) US#9, *San Antonio (Cowboy Song)* [ii] Billy Murray (1907) US#3, *What's the Matter with Father?* [i] Billy Murray (1910) US#2, *Won't You Come Over to My House?* [ii] Henry Burr (1907) US#8/Byron G. Harlan (1907) US#7. Co-writers: [i] Benjamin Hapgood Burt, [ii] Harry H. Williams (b. 1879; d. 1922). (*See also under* Gus KAHN.)

964. VANDA, Harry (b. Harry Wandon, March 22, 1947, The Hague, Holland), and **YOUNG, George** (b. November 6, 1947, Glasgow, Scotland) Both pop guitarists, producers and vocalists. Founder members of the 1960s Australian vocal group the Easybeats, who composed the band's An-dolupian hits *She's Doing Fine*, *Sad and Lonely and Blue* and *In My Book*, alongside its best known song *Friday on My Mind* (1966) US#16 UK#6. ALBUMS: **Friday on My Mind** (1967, United Artists) US#180; **Their Music Goes 'Round Our Heads** (1993, Sony); **Aussie Beat That Shook the World** (1996, Repertoire). Vanda and Young left the Easybeats in 1970 to become producer-writers, later working with AC/DC and forming such studio groups as Paint-box, the Marcus Hook Roll Band, and Flash and the Pan, as which, they charted with *And the Band Played On (Down Among the Dead Men)* (1978) UK#54, *Hey, St. Peter* (1979) US#76 and *Waiting for a Train* (1983) UK#7. ALBUMS: **Flash and the Pan** (1979) US#80, **Lights in the Night** (1980, both Epic) US#159. HIT VERSIONS: *Love Is in the Air* [i] John Paul Young (1978) US#7 UK#5, *Yesterday's Hero* [i] John Paul Young (1975) US#42/Bay City Rollers (1977) US#54. [i] Harry Vanda/John Paul Young only.

965. VANDROSS, Luther (b. Luther Ron-zoni Vandross, April 20, 1951, New York, NY) R&B producer and vocalist. One of R&B's most popular cross-over artists, who has sold over forty million records. Vandross grew up in the lower Manhattan projects, where his father and mother were both gospel singers, and his sisters performed in the 1950s vocal group the Crests. Vandross took piano lessons from the age of three, before studying music and forming his first high school group Listen My Brother, which also featured the guitarist Carlos Alomar. In 1974, Vandross arranged the vocal tracks for David Bowie's album **Young Americans**, which featured *Fascination*, Bowie's re-write of the Vandross original *Funky Music (Is a Part of Me)*. After composing *Everybody Rejoice (A Brand New Day)* for the film "The Wiz" (1975) — which was later used in a Kodak commercial — Vandross became an in-demand session vocalist and arranger. He also recorded as the group Luther, before singing lead on the Change hits *Searchin'*, *A Lover's Holiday* and *The Glow of Love*. Having served a lengthy musical apprenticeship, Vandross finally achieved solo success when he formed a writing and production partnership with Miles Davis' bassist Marcus Miller, in the early 1980s. Their tight, funky sound contained many of the best elements of soul music while appealing to mainstream record buyers as well. Vandross has also worked with the female vocalists Dionne Warwick and Aretha Franklin. His most successful solo album remains **Give Me the Reason** (1986), which featured nine tracks, seven of which were British hit singles. A much imitated song stylist, Vandross has filled the void left by the death of Marvin Gaye, with a distinctive brand of cerebral bedroom ballads and rhythmic dance tracks. CHART COMPOSITIONS: *It's Good for the Soul (Part 1)* (1976) R&B#28 US#102, *Funky Music (Is a Part of Me)/The Second Time Around* (1976) R&B#34, *This Close to You* (1977) R&B#93, *Never Too Much* (1981) R&B#1 US#33 UK#44, re-mixed (1989) UK#13; *Don't You Know That?* (1981) R&B#10 US#107, *Sugar and Spice (I Found Me a Girl)* (1982) R&B#72, *Bad Boy* [v] (1982) R&B##3 US#33, *Promise Me* (1983) R&B#72, *I'll Let You Slide* [v] (1983) R&B#9 US#102, *Make Me a Believer* [i] (1984) R&B#48, *'Til My Baby Comes Home* [v] (1985) R&B#4 US#29, *It's Over Now* [v] (1985) R&B#4 US#101, *Wait for Love* [i] (1985) R&B#11, *Give Me the Reason* [i] (1986) R&B#3 US#57 UK#60, re-issued (1987) UK#71, re-issued (1988) UK#26; *Stop to Love* [i] (1986) R&B#1 US#15 UK#24, *There's Nothing Better Than Love* [ii] with Gregory Hines (1987) R&B#1 US#50 UK#72, *I Really Didn't Mean It* [v] (1987) R&B#6 UK#16, *So Amazing* (1987) R&B#94 UK#33, *See Me* [v] (1987) UK#60, *I Gave It Up (When I Fell in Love)* [v] (1987) UK#28, *She Won't Talk to Me* [iii] (1988) US#30 UK#34, *Come Back* [iv] (1988) UK#53, *Any Love* [v] (1988) R&B#1 US#44 UK#31, *Power of Love/Love Power* [vi] (1991) R&B#3 US#4 UK#46, re-issued (1995) UK#31; *Don't Want to Be a Fool* [v] (1992) R&B#4 US#9, *The Rush* [v] (1992) R&B#6 US#73 UK#53, *Sometimes It's Only Love* [ii] (1992) US#9, *Little Miracles (Happen Every Day)* [v] (1993) R&B#10 US#62 UK#28, *Heaven Knows* [vii] (1993) R&B#24 US#94 UK#34, *Love Is on the Way* (1993) UK#38, *Every Year, Every Christmas* (1995) UK#43. ALBUMS: **Luther** (1976), **This Close to You** (1977, both Cotillion); **Never Too Much** (1981) p US#19 UK#41, **Forever, For Always, For Love** (1982) p US#20 UK#23, **Busy Body** (1983) p US#32 UK#42, **The Night I Fell in Love** (1985) p US#19 UK#19, **Give Me the Reason** (1986) p US#14 UK#9, **Any Love** (1988) p US#9 UK#3, **Power of Love** (1991) p US#7 UK#9, **Never Let Me Go** (1993) p US#6 UK#11, **Songs** (1994) p US#5 UK#1, **This Is Christmas** (1995) US#28, **Your Secret Love** (1996, all Epic) UK#14. COMPILATIONS: **Best of Luther Vandross — The Best of Love** (1989, Epic) p US#26 UK#14; **The 12" Mixes** (1992, Sony); **Greatest Hits, 1981–1995** (1995, Epic) UK#12. HIT VERSIONS: *Do You Really Love Your Baby* [v] Temptations (1986) R&B#14, *Every Girl (Wants My Guy)* Aretha Franklin (1983) R&B#7, *Get It Right* [v] Aretha Franklin (1983) R&B#1 US#61 UK#74, *Got a Date* [v] Dionne Warwick (1984) R&B#45, *Instant Love* Cheryl Lynn (1982) R&B#16 US#105, *Jump to It* [v] Aretha Franklin (1982) R&B#1 US#24 UK#42, *Love Me Right* Aretha Franklin (1982) R&B#22, *So Amazing*

Gerald Albright (1987) R&B#12, *That Girl Wants to Dance with Me* Gregory Hines (1988) R&B#6, *This Is for Real* Aretha Franklin (1983) R&B#63, *You Stopped Loving Me* Roberta Flack (1981) R&B#32 US#108, *You're My Choice Tonight (Choose Me)* Teddy Pendergrass (1984) R&B#15 US#38. Co-writers: [i] Nat Adderley, Jr., [ii] J. Anderson, [iii] Hubert Eaves, III, [iv] David Gamsun, [v] Marcus Miller (b. 1960, Brooklyn, NY), [vi] Marcus Miller/Teddy Vann, [vii] R. Vertelney.

966. VANDYKE, Les (b. Johnny Worth, England) Pop composer. A songwriter who was successful during the 1960s, in particular with a series of hits that he composed for the vocalist Adam Faith. HIT VERSIONS: *Ain't That Funny* Jimmy Justice (1962) UK#8, *Applejack* Jet Harris & Tony Meehan (1963) UK#4, *As You Like It* Adam Faith (1962) UK#5, *Cupboard Love* John Leyton (1963) UK#22, *Don't That Beat All* Adam Faith (1962) UK#8, *Don't You Know It* Adam Faith (1961) UK#12, *Forget Me Not* Eden Kane (1962) UK#3, *Get Lost* Eden Kane (1961) UK#10, *How About That* Adam Faith (1960) UK#4, *Lonely Pup (In a Christmas Shop)* Adam Faith (1960) UK#4, *Poor Me* Adam Faith (1960) UK#1, *Someone Else's Baby* [i] Adam Faith (1960) UK#2, *Time Has Come, The* Adam Faith (1961) UK#4, *Well I Ask Ya* Eden Kane (1961) US#119 UK#1, *What Do You Want* Adam Faith (1959) UK#1/Bobby Vee (1960) US#93; *Who Am I* Adam Faith (1961) UK#5. Co-writer: [i] Perry Ford.

967. VAN HEUSEN, Jimmy (b. Edward Chester Babcock, January 26, 1913, Syracuse, NY; d. February 7, 1990, Rancho Mirage, CA) Film and stage composer, pianist. One of the most highly regarded and regularly recorded American popular songwriters of all time, whose innovative approach and unconventional song structures was to influence many songwriters who came after him. Van Heusen was a former radio announcer and demonstration pianist, who adopted a pseudonym for radio and songwriting purposes. His first success was with Jimmy Dorsey's *It's the Dreamer in Me* [iii] (1938), after which, he composed the music for the Broadway show "Swingin' the Dream" (1939). In partnership with the lyricist Sammy Cahn, Van Heusen became one of Frank Sinatra's most revered composers, writing such material as *Come Fly with Me* [iii], *My Kind of Town* [iii] and *The September of My Years* [iii]. From 1940, Van Heusen often collaborated with the lyricist Johnny Burke, and their compositions appeared in eighteen Bing Crosby films, including "Going My Way" (1944) and "Road to Rio" (1947). Two of Crosby's best loved recordings were Van Heusen numbers, *Ain't Got a Dime to My Name* [ii]

(1943) and *Busy Doing Nothing* [ii] (1949). One of Burke and Van Heusen's finest ballads, although not a major hit, was *Here's That Rainy Day* [ii], from the show "Carnival in Flanders" (1954). During World War II, Van Heusen served as a test pilot for the Lockheed corporation. ALBUMS: **Going My Way** ost (1944, Decca); **Les Poupees de Paris** oc (1964, RCA); **Swinging on a Star** st (1944), **The Emperor Waltz** ost (1949), **Sunshine Cake** st (1950), **Zing a Little Zong** st (1952), **Anything Goes** ost (1956, all Decca); **Our Town** tvst (1956), **Pardners** tvst (1956), **Some Came Running** ost (1958, all Capitol); **Say One for Me** ost (1959, Columbia); **High Time** ost (1960), **The World of Susie Wong** ost (1960, both RCA); **Road to Hong Kong** ost (1962, Liberty); **Come Blow Your Horn** ost (1963, Reprise); **The Pleasure Seeker** ost (1964, RCA); **Robin and the 7 Hoods** ost (1964, Reprise) US#56; **Skyscraper** oc (1966, Capitol) US#128; **Jack and the Beanstalk** tvst (1967, HBR); **Thoroughly Modern Millie** ost (1967, Brunswick) UK#9. HIT VERSIONS: *All I Remember Is You* [iv] Tommy Dorsey (1939) US#11, *All the Way* [ii] Frank Sinatra (1957) US#2 UK#3/Ray Price (1986) C&W#73; *All This and Heaven Too* [iv] Charlie Barnet (1940) US#14/Jimmy Dorsey (1940) US#9/Tommy Dorsey (1940) US#12/Jack Leonard (1940) US#24/Dick Todd (1940) US#20; *Aren't You Glad You're You?* [ii] Pied Pipers (1945) US#18/Les Brown (1946) US#11/Bing Crosby (1946) US#8/Tommy Dorsey (1946) US#14; *As Long as I'm Dreaming* [ii] Tex Beneke (1947) US#21, *Blue Rain* [vii] Glenn Miller (1943) US#8, *Boys' Night Out* [iii] Patti Page (1962) US#49, *But Beautiful* [ii] Bing Crosby (1948) US#20/Art Lund (1948) US#25/Frank Sinatra (1948) US#14/Margaret Whiting (1948) US#21; *Call Me Irresponsible* [iii] Jack Jones (1963) US#75/Frank Sinatra (1963) US#78; *Constantly* [ii] Bing Crosby (1943) US#13, *Darn That Dream* [iv] Blue Barron (1940) US#14/Tommy Dorsey (1940) US#16/Benny Goodman (1940) US#1; *Day After Forever, The* [ii] Bing Crosby (1944) US#15, *Deep in a Dream* [iv] Bob Crosby (1938) US#10/Artie Shaw (1938) US#3; *Do You Wanna Jump, Chillun?* [i] Erskine Hawkins (1939) US#16, *Friend of Yours, A* [ii] Tommy Dorsey (1945) US#9, *Going My Way* [ii] Bing Crosby (1944) US#15, *Good for Nothin' But Love* [iv] Fats Waller (1939) US#7, *Got the Moon in My Pocket* [ii] Kay Kyser (1942) US#17, *Harmony* [ii] Johnny Mercer & the King Cole Trio (1947) US#12, *Heaven Can Wait* [iv] Glen Gray (1939) US#1/Kay Kyser (1939) US#14; *His Rocking Horse Ran Away* [ii] Betty Hutton (1944) US#7, *High Hopes* [iii] Frank Sinatra (1959) R&B#20 US#30 UK#42, *Humpty Dumpty Heart* [ii] Glenn Miller (1942) US#23, *I Thought About You* [vii] Benny Goodman (1940) US#17/Frank Sinatra on *Songs for*

Swinging Lovers LP (1956) UK#12; *If You Please* [ii] Bing Crosby (1943) US#5, *If You Stub Your Toe on the Moon* [ii] Bing Crosby (1949) US#27/Tony Martin (1949) US#17; *Imagination* [ii] Tommy Dorsey (1940) US#8/Ella Fitzgerald (1940) US#15/Glenn Miller (1940) US#1/Ted Straeter (1940) US#29/Quotations (1962) US#105; *It Could Happen to You* [ii] Bing Crosby (1944) US#18/Jo Stafford (1944) US#10/Robert Palmer (1989) UK#71; *It's Always You* [ii] Tommy Dorsey (1943) US#3, *It's the Dreamer in Me* [v] Jimmy Dorsey (1938) US#9, *Just Plain Lonesome* [ii] Freddy Martin (1942) US#24, *Like Someone in Love* [ii] Bing Crosby (1945) US#15, *Looking for Yesterday* [iv] Woody Herman (1940) US#15, *Love and Marriage* [iii] Dinah Shore (1955) US#20/Frank Sinatra (1955) US#5 UK#3; *Moonlight Becomes You* [ii] Bing Crosby (1943) US#1/Harry James (1943) US#15/Glenn Miller (1943) US#5; *My Heart Is a Hobo* [ii] Tex Beneke (1947) US#22, *Nancy (With the Laughing Face)* [viii] Frank Sinatra (1945) US#10, *Not as a Stranger* Tony Bennett (1954) US#27, *Oh, You Crazy Moon* [ii] Tommy Dorsey (1939) US#2, *Once and for Always* [ii] Jo Stafford (1949) US#16, *Personality* [ii] Bing Crosby (1946) US#9/Johnny Mercer (1946) US#1/Dinah Shore (1946) US#10; *Polka Dots and Moonbeams* [ii] Tommy Dorsey (1940) US#18, *Pocketful of Miracles* [iii] Frank Sinatra (1962) US#34, *Road to Morocco, The* [ii] Bing Crosby & Bob Hope (1945) US#21, *Shake Down the Stars* [iv] Ella Fitzgerald (1940) US#18/Glenn Miller (1940) US#4; *So Help Me* [iv] Mildred Bailey (1938) US#2, *Suddenly, It's Spring* [ii] Glen Gray (1944) US#12/Hildegarde (1944) US#15; *Sunday, Monday or Always* [ii] Bing Crosby (1943) g R&B#3 US#1/Frank Sinatra (1943) US#9; *Swinging on a Star* [ii] Bing Crosby (1944) g US#1/Gray Rains (1944) US#28/Big Dee Irwin (1963) US#38 UK#7; *Tender Trap, The* [iii] Frank Sinatra (1956) US#7 UK#2, *Yah-Ta-Ta, Yah-Ta-Ta (Talk, Talk, Talk)* [ii] Bing Crosby & Judy Garland (1945) US#5/Harry James (1945) US#11; *You Don't Have to Know the Language* [ii] Bing Crosby & the Andrews Sisters (1948) US#21. Co-writers: [i] Willie Bryant/Al Donahue/Victor Selsman, [ii] Johnny Burke, [iii] Sammy Cahn, [iv] Eddie De Lange, [v] Jimmy Dorsey, [vi] Buddy Kaye, [vii] Johnny Mercer, [viii] Phil Silvers.

968. VAN ZANDT, Townes (b. 1944, Fort Worth, TX; d. January 1, 1997, Nashville, TN) Country-folk guitarist and vocalist. A poetic composer whose songs were completely untainted by commercial considerations. An alcoholic and somewhat self-destructive personality, Van Zandt was nevertheless the most authentic American folk and country songwriter since Bob Dylan. Throughout his career, he remained close to his country-blues roots,

and said of his songs in 1991, "Most of them are just about being a human being and getting through life." After learning the guitar in his teens, Van Zandt pursued a nomadic lifestyle and listened to the music of Lightnin' Hopkins, Woody Guthrie and Ramblin' Jack Elliot. He played briefly in the group the Delta Momma Boys during the 1960s, before composing his own traditional based material in a talking blues style. Van Zandt lived out of a pickup truck and a trailer in Austin, Texas, before graduating to various rented shacks in the Tennessee hills and the Colorado Rockies, where, a solitary poet, he wrote much of his best material. Many of his early albums are fine examples of melancholic songwriting at its very best, upon which, Van Zandt's rough but lurid voice convey a permanent mood of insight and resignation. **The Late Great Townes Van Zandt** (1973), featured his most recorded tune *Poncho and Lefty*, while **Live at the Old Quarter, Houston, Texas** (1977), remains one of the most authentic live recordings ever made. Van Zandt continued to record and perform until his death, at the age of fifty-two, from a heart attack following surgery for a broken hip. ALBUMS: **For the Sake of the Song** (1968), **Our Mother the Mountain** (1969), **Delta Momma Blues** (1971), **High, Low and Inbetween** (1971), **The Late Great Townes Van Zandt** (1973, all Poppy); **Live At the Old Quarter, Houston, Texas** (1977), **Flyin' Shoes** (1978, both Tomato); **At My Window** (1987), **Live and Obscure** (1987, both Heartland); **Rain on a Conga Drum** (1991, Exile), **Live in the Latin Quarter** (1991, Charly), **Nashville Sessions** (1993, Exile); **Road Songs** (1994), **No Deeper Blue** (1995), **The Highway Kind** (1997, all Sugarhill). HIT VERSIONS: *If I Needed You* Emmylou Harris & Don Williams (1981) C&W#3, *Poncho and Lefty* Merle Haggard & Willie Nelson (1983) C&W#1 US#37, *White Freightliner Blues* Jimmie Dale Gilmore (1988) C&W#72. (*See also under* Mickey NEWBURY.)

969. VEGA, Suzanne (b. August 12, 1959, Santa Monica, CA) Rock guitarist and vocalist. A folk influenced singer-songwriter who grew up in New York, where she studied dance at the High School of Performing Arts in 1975. After learning the guitar, Vega began writing songs and performing in East Coast folk clubs, while working during the daytime as an office receptionist. In 1983, she secured a publishing deal, and after increasingly favorable live reviews, was signed by A&M Records the following year. Her eponymous debut album was issued at a time when singer-songwriters were enjoying an in-vogue backlash against 1980s electro-pop. By **99.9 Degrees F** (1992), Vega had moved away from her folk beginnings in the direction of modern dance and ambiant music. CHART COM-

POSITIONS: *Small Blue Thing* (1986) UK#65, *Marlene on the Wall* (1986) UK#21, *Left of Center* (1986) UK#32, *Gypsy* (1986) UK#77, *Luka* (1987) US#3 UK#23, *Tom's Dinner* (1987) UK#58, *Solitude Standing* [i] (1987) US#94 UK#79, *Book of Dreams* (1990) UK#66, *In Liverpool* (1992) UK#52, *99.9 Degrees F* (1992) UK#46, *Blood Makes Noise* (1992) UK#60, *When Heroes Go Down* (1993) UK#58. ALBUMS: **Suzanne Vega** (1985) US#91 UK#11, **Solitude Standing** (1987) g US#11 UK#2, **Days of Open Hand** (1990) US#50 UK#7, **99.9 Degrees F** (1992) US#86 UK#20, **Nine Objects of Desire** (1997, all A&M). HIT VERSIONS: *Tom's Diner* DNA (1990) UK#2. Co-writers: [i] S. Ferrera/A. Sanko/M. Shulman/M. Visceglia.

970. VON TILZER, Albert

(b. Albert Gumm, March 29, 1878, Indianapolis, IN; d. October 1, 1956, Los Angeles, CA) Film and stage composer, vaudeville performer. The younger brother of the songwriter Harry Von Tilzer, who worked as a song-plugger, before founding his own publishing company with his brother Jack. Von Tilzer first co-wrote for vaudeville, often with the lyricist Lew Brown, and his songs featured in such shows as "The Ziegfeld Follies of 1916," "Hullo America" (1917), "A to Z" (1921), and "The Midnight Rounders" (1921), alongside such films as "Buck Privates" (1941), "The Dolly Sisters" and "The Naughty Nineties" (both 1945). After the bankruptcy of his Broadway Music Corporation in 1922, Von Tilzer became a vaudeville performer and worked in Hollywood as a film composer. HIT VERSIONS: *Chili Bean* [i] Paul Biese Trio & Frank Crumit (1920) US#4, *Dapper Dan* [i] Frank Crumit (1922) US#5, *Give Me the Moonlight, Give Me the Girl (And Leave the Rest to Me)* [i] Sam Ash (1918) US#10, *Honey Boy* [ii] Peerless Quartet (1907) US#2/Billy Murray (1907) US#5; *I Used to Love You, But It's All Over Now* [i] Frank Crumit (1921) US#7/Peerless Quartet (1921) US#8; *I'll Be with You in Apple Blossom Time* [iii] Henry Burr & Albert Campbell (1920) US#5/Charles Harrison (1920) US#2/Reed Miller (1920) US#11/Andrews Sisters (1941) US#5/Winifred Atwell in *Piano Party* (1959) UK#10/Platters (1960) US#102; *Nora Malone (Call Me By Phone)* [v] Blanche Ring (1911) US#9/Teresa Brewer (1957) UK#26; *Oh! By Jingo! Oh! By Gee!* [i] Frank Crumit (1920) US#3/Billy Murray (1920) US#12/Spike Jones (1943) US#20; *Oh How She Could Yacki Hacki Wicki Wacki Woo (That's Love in Honolulu)* [iv] Arthur Collins & Byron Harlan (1916) US#1, *Put Your Arms Around Me, Honey* [v] Arthur Collins & Byron Harlan (1911) US#1/Ada Jones (1911) US#5/Joe "Mr. Piano' Henderson in *Sing It Again with Joe* (1955) UK#18/Winifred Atwell in *Piano Party* (1959) UK#10; *Roll Along Prairie Moon*

[ii] Smith Ballew (1935) US#10, *Smarty* [vii] Ada Jones & Billy Murray (1908) US#2, *Take Me Out to the Ball Game* [vii] Harvey Hindermyer (1908) US#3/Edward Meeker (1908) US#5/Billy Murray & Haydn Quartet (1908) US#1; *Teasing (I Was Only Teasing You)* [vi] Billy Murray (1904) US#2/Bob Roberts (1904) US#3. Co-writers: [i] Lew Brown, [ii] Ted Fiorito/Harry MacPherson, [iii] Neville Fleeson, [iv] Charles McCarron/Stanley Murphy, [v] Junie McRee, [vi] Cecil Mack, [vii] Jack Norworth, [viii] Leo Robin.

971. VON TILZER, Harry

(b. Harry Gumm, July 8, 1872, Detroit, MI; d. January 10, 1946, New York, NY) Tin Pan Alley composer and pianist. A prolific composer of over three thousand songs, and in all probability, the most successful songwriter of the early twentieth century, as it is estimated that he composed and published over one hundred half-million selling songs. One of three musical siblings, Von Tilzer founded the first publishing company in 1902 on what later became known as Tin Pan Alley. A former circus tumbler who had run away from home at the age of fourteen to join the Cole Brothers Circus, Von Tilzer subsequently performed in vaudeville, where he adopted his stage name and wrote his first compositions. He sold many of his copyrights for two dollars each, and achieved his first success with *I Love You Both* (1892), which was followed by such melancholy ballads as *The Little Wooden Whistle Wouldn't Whistle* [ii] (1924). *My Old New Hampshire Home* [vii] (1898) and *I'd Leave My Happy Home for You* (1899), which collectively sold over three million copies, and *A Bird in a Gilded Cage* [iv], which sold over two million. One of his best known songs is the Cockney public house favorite *Down at the Old Bull and Bush* [vi] (1903). Von Tilzer was an originator in his time, able to write in all musical styles, but like so many songwriters and musicians that were to follow, the times soon changed around him, and he never fully adjusted to the changing music business of the 1920s and 1930s, and retired instead to a New York hotel. HIT VERSIONS: *Alexander* [vii] Billy Murray (1904) US#1, *All Aboard for Blanket Bay* Ada Jones (1911) US#4, *All Alone* [iii] Ada Jones & Billy Murray (1911) US#2/Ada Jones & Walter Van Brunt (1911) US#6; *And the Green Grass Grew All Around* [v] Walter Van Brunt (1913) US#4, *Bird in a Gilded Cage, A* [vii] Jere Mahony (1900) US#1/Steve Porter (1900) US#1/Harry MacDonough (1900) US#2; *Cubanola Glide, The* Arthur Collins & Byron Harlan (1910) US#3/Billy Murray (1910) US#6/Prince's Orchestra (1910) US#10; *Down at the Old Bull and Bush* [iv] Winifred Atwell in *Make It a Party* (1956) UK#7, *Down Where the Wurzburger Flows* Arthur Collins

(1903) US#4/Arthur Collins & Byron Harlan (1903) US#1; *I Love My Wife, But Oh You Kid!* Arthur Collins (1909) US#2/Edward M. Favor (1909) US#9/ Bob Roberts (1909) US#5; *I Want a Girl Just Like the Girl That Married Dear Old Dad* [iii] American Quartet (1911) US#2/Walter Van Brunt & the Peerless Quartet (1911) US#2; *I'd Leave My Happy Home for You* Arthur Collins (1899) US#1/Edward M. Favor (1900) US#4; *In the Sweet Bye and Bye* [i] Haydn Quartet (1902) US#3/John Bieling (1903) US#1/J. Aldrich Libbey (1903) US#2/Harry MacDonough (1903) US#1/Peerless Quartet (1905) US#7; *Just Around the Corner* Revelers (1926) US#11, *Mansion of Aching Hearts, The* [vi] Byron G. Harlan (1902) US#1/Harry MacDonough (1902) US#1/J.W. Myers (1902) US#2; *Under the Anheuser Bush* Arthur Collins & Byron Harlan (1904) US#2/Billy Murray (1904) US#2; *Under the Yum Yum Tree* [vii] Arthur Collins & Byron Harlan (1911) US#1, *Wait Till the Sun Shines, Nellie* [vii] Byron G. Harlan (1906) US#1/ Harry Tally (1906) US#1/Prince's Orchestra (1906) US#5; *What You Goin' to Do When De Rent Comes 'Round?* [vii] Arthur Collins (1905) US#2. Co-writers: [i] Vincent P. Bryan, [ii] Billy Curtis, [iii] William Dillon, [iv] Russell Hunting/Percy Krone/Andrew Sterling, [v] William Jerome, [vi] Arthur J. Lamb, [vii] Andrew B. Sterling.

972. WAAKTAAR, Pal (b. September 6, 1961, Oslo, Norway) Pop guitarist and vocalist. The principal songwriter in the group A-ha. CHART COMPOSITIONS: *Take on Me* [iii] (1985) US#1 UK#2, *The Sun Always Shines on T.V.* [iii] (1986) US#20 UK#1, *Train of Thought* [iii] (1986) UK#8, *Hunting High and Low* [iii] (1986) UK#5, *I've Been Losing You* [iii] (1986) UK#8, *Cry Wolf* [ii] (1987) US#50 UK#5, *Manhattan Skyline* [ii] (1987) UK#13, *The Living Daylights* [i] (1987) UK#5, *Stay on These Roads* [iii] (1988) UK#5, *The Blood That Moves the Body* [ii] (1988) UK#25, *Touchy!* [ii] (1988) UK#11, *You Are the One* [ii] (1989) UK#13, *I Call Your Name* [ii] (1990) UK#44, *Move to Memphis* [ii] (1991) UK#47, *Dark Is the Night* [ii] (1993) US#111 UK#19, *Angel* [ii] (1993) UK#41, *Shapes That Go Together* [ii] (1993) UK#27. ALBUMS: **Hunting High and Low** (1985) g US#15 UK#2, **Scoundrel Days** (1986) US#74 UK#2, **Stay on These Roads** (1988) US#148 UK#2, **East of the Sun** (1990) UK#12, **Memorial Beach** (1993, all WEA) UK#17. COMPILATION: **Headlines and Deadlines — The Hits of A-ha** (1991, WEA) UK#12. HIT VERSION: *The Sun Always Shines on T.V.* [iii] Diva (1995) UK#53. Co-writers: [i] John Barry/Magne Furuholmen (b. November 1, 1962, Oslo, Norway), [ii] Magne Furuholmen, [iii] Magne Furuholmen/Morten Harket (b. September 14, 1959, Konigsberg, Norway).

973. WAGONER, Porter (b. August 12, 1930, West Plains, MI) C&W guitarist and vocalist. A former farmer who originally broadcasted from a grocery store during the 1940s, before, in 1951, starring in his own radio show. Wagoner signed to RCA Records in 1955, where he charted nearly eighty solo hits and twenty duets with Dolly Parton between 1954–1980. During the 1960s, he hosted a long-running television syndication "The Porter Wagoner Show," and he was a consistently popular live act in America, with his particular blend of white gospel, commercial country, bluegrass and honky tonk. CHART COMPOSITIONS: *Company's Comin'* (1955) C&W#7, *A Satisfied Mind* (1955) C&W#1, *What Would You Do (If Jesus Came to Your House)* (1956) C&W#8, *Ole Slew-Foot* (1966) C&W#48, re-issued (1978) C&W#31; *A World Without Music* (1972) C&W#14, *Katy Did* (1972) C&W#16, *Is Forever Longer Than Always* with Dolly Parton (1976) C&W#8, *Tore Down* (1974) C&W#46. ALBUMS: **Grand Ole Gospel** (1966), **More Grand Ole Gospel** (1967), **In Gospel Country** (1969), **Porter Wagoner Sings His Own Songs** (1971), **What Ain't to Be, Just Might Happen** (1972), **Best of Porter Wagoner** (1974), **Hits of Porter Wagoner** (19780, **20 of the Best** (1984, all RCA); **Porter Wagoner** (1986, MCA); **Porter Wagoner** (1986, Dot); **A Satisfied Mind** (1988), **Thin Man from West Plains** (1989), **Bluegrass Story** (1989, all Stetson). HIT VERSIONS: *Lonely Coming Down* Keith Bradford (1979) C&W#86, *Satisfied Mind, A* Red Foley & Betty Foley (1955) C&W#3/Jean Shepard (1955) C&W#4/ Bobby Hebb (1966) US#39/Roy Drusky (1973) C&W#25/Bob Luman (1976) C&W#41/Con Hunley (1983) C&W#84; *Trademark* Carl Smith (1953) C&W#2, *What Would You Do (If Jesus Came to Your House)* Red Sovine (1956) C&W#15. (*See also under* Dolly PARTON.)

974. WAINWRIGHT, Loudon, III (b. September 5, 1946, Chapel Hill, NC) Pop guitarist and vocalist. A folk tinged satirist in the singer-songwriter tradition. CHART COMPOSITIONS: *Dead Skunk* (1973) US#16. ALBUMS: **Loudon Wainwright, III** (1971), **Album II** (1972, both Atlantic); **Album III** (1973) US#102, **Attempted Mustache** (1974), **Un-reunited** (1975, all Columbia) US#156; **T-Shirt** (1976) US#188, **Final Exam** (1978, both Arista); **A Live One** (1980), **Wealth and Fame** (1983), **I'm Alright** (1985, all Rounder); **More Love Songs** (1986, Demon); **Therapy** (1989, Silvertone); **Grown Man** (1995, Virgin).

975. WAITE, John (b. July 4, 1954, Lancaster, England) Rock bassist and vocalist. A vocalist who first achieved success in the group the Babys.

CHART COMPOSITIONS: *If You've Got the Time* [ii] (1977) US#88, *Isn't It Time* (1977) US#13 UK#45, *Silver Dreams* [i] (1978) US#53, *Head First* [iii] (1979) US#77, *Back on My Feet Again* [iv] (1980) US#33, *Midnight Rendezvous* [v] (1980) US#72, *Turn Around and Walk Away* [v] (1980) US#42. ALBUMS: **The Babys** (1977) US#133, **Broken Heart** (1977) US#34, **Head First** (1979) US#22, **Union Jacks** (1980) US#42, **On the Edge** (1980) US#71, **Anthology** (1981, all Chrysalis) US#138. After the group split up in 1981, Waite embarked on a solo career. CHART COMPOSITIONS: *Missing You* [ix] (1984) US#1 UK#9, re-issued (1995) UK#56; *Tears* (1984) US#37, *Restless Heart* (1985) US#59, *Every Step of the Way* [viii] (1985) US#25, *Welcome to Paradise* (1985) US#85, *These Times Are Hard for Lovers* [vii] (1987) US#53, *In Dreams* (1993) US#103. ALBUMS: **Ignition** (1982, Chrysalis) US#68; **No Brakes** (1984) g US#10 UK#64, **Mask of Smiles** (1985) US#38, **Rover's Return** (1987, all EMI America) US#77; **Temple Bar** (1995). When his solo career faltered, he sought sanctuary in the contrived, radio-oriented group Bad English, which charted with *Forget Me Not* [vi] (1989) US#45, *Price of Love* [v] (1990) US#5, *Heaven Is a Four Letter Word* [vi] (1990) US#66, *Possession* [vi] (1990) US#21, and *Straight to Your Heart* [vi] (1991) US#42. ALBUMS: **Bad English** (1989) p US#21 UK#74, **Backlash** (1991, both Epic) US#72 UK#91. Co-writers: [i] Tony Brock, [ii] Tony Brock/ Corby/W. Stocker, [iii] Tony Brock/W. Stocker, [iv] Bugatti/Musker, [v] Jonathan Cain, [vi] Jonathan Cain/M. Spiro, [vii] Desmond Child, [viii] Kral/ Sidqwick, [ix] Mark Leonard/Charles Sanford. (*See also under* Neal SCHON.)

976. WAITS, Tom (Thomas Alan Waits, December 7, 1949, Pomona, CA) Rock pianist and vocalist. One of the most original songwriters and performers in popular music, who is a champion of society's oddballs and losers. Waits' early work was an amalgamation of torch songs and supper club tunes, which have, in more recent times, mutated into a primitive form of jazz influenced street sounds. He cleverly off-sets sentimentality against the harsh realities of life, embellishing his fascinating anti-heroes with a nonchalant romance, making him the 1970s musical Raymond Chandler. When questioned as to where he found inspiration for his songs, Waits replied, "It's all out there. If you're stuck for words, just look out the window." Born, allegedly, in the back of a taxi cab in a maternity hospital parking lot, Waits grew up in East Whittier, California, where he listened to his parents' record collection, which contained Bing Crosby, Perry Como, Cole Porter, George Gershwin, and Harry Belafonte. Waits was a member of the high school soul group the Systems,

and in his teens he learned the accordion and sung in the bars and clubs of San Diego and Los Angeles. Influenced in part by Dr. John and Professor Longhair, Waits blended his love of jazz and popular songs from the 1920s, 1930s and 1940s, into a unique narrative style. A variety of dead end day jobs turned him, like the author Graham Greene, into one of the great listeners and observers, and he uses snippets of conversations to create complete characterizations. After a year of intensive songwriting, Waits debuted with the album **Closing Time** (1973), which was sung in a tobacco stained voice. Waits' carefully crafted melodies often attracted cover versions, his songs always being bigger hits for other singers than himself. **The Heart of Saturday Night** (1974), was a sleazy examination of nocturnal low-lifes, coming closer to the writing of Charles Bukowski than any other rock artist. As if a character in one of his own songs, Waits lived in the Tropicana Motor Hotel in West Hollywood, where he had an upright piano installed in the kitchen. His live set **Nighthawks at the Diner** (1975), was a series of monologues, dirty jokes and amusing one-liners, his clever use of street slang and hip colloquialisms being set to the music of a small, meandering, acoustic jazz combo. The album opened with *Emotional Weather Report*, an early example of jazz-rap. In 1978, Waits began a sideline career when he debuted as an actor in the film "Paradise Alley." In 1981, he married his occasional co-writer Kathleen Brennan, and the following year scored the film "One from the Heart." His conceptual trilogy **Swordfishtrombone** (1983), **Rain Dogs** (1985) and **Frank's Wild Years** (1987), introduced a tougher, more urban sound that had clearly been influenced by his re-location to New York, and by the European theatre of Bertolt Brecht and Kurt Weil. The essence of the trilogy was, according to Waits, "a story about a disturbing ten years in the life of a very disappointing accordion player who ends up in Las Vegas, despondent and penniless, in East St. Louis." More recently, his bizarre rhythms have been performed on all manner of non-musical instruments, including household implements and megaphones. His vocal style has increasingly resembled that of an old time music hall impresario, as his music fell somewhere between the comedy of Spike Jones and industrial noise. Waits' compositions were recorded by Holly Cole on **Temptation** (1995, Metro Blue), and on the various artists collection **Step Right Up: The Songs of Tom Waits** (1995, Virgin). ALBUMS: **Closing Time** (1973), **The Heart of Saturday Night** (1974), **Nighthawks at the Diner** (1975) US#164, **Small Change** (1976) US#89, **Foreign Affairs** (1977) US#113, **Blue Valentine** (1978) US#181, **Heartattack and Vine** (1980, all Asylum) US#96; **One from the Heart** ost (1982, Columbia);

Swordfishtrombone (1983) US#167 UK#62, **Rain Dogs** (1985) US#193 UK#29, **Frank's Wild Years** (1987) US#115 UK#20, **Big Time** (1988) US#152 UK#84, **Night on Earth** ost (1992), **Bone Machine** (1992) US#176 UK#26, **The Black Rider** ost (1993, all Island) US#130 UK#47. COMPILATIONS: **Bounced Cheques** (1981), **The Asylum Years** (1983, both Asylum) US#82; **The Early Years** (1990), **The Early Years, Volume 2** (1992, both Edsel). HIT VERSIONS: *Downtown Train* Patty Smyth (1987) US#95/Rod Stewart (1990) US#3 UK#10; *Heartattack and Vine* Screamin' Jay Hawkins (1993) UK#42, *Jersey Girl* Bruce Springsteen on B-side of *Cover Me* (1984) US#7 UK#16, *Tom Traubert's Blues* Rod Stewart (1992) UK#6.

977. WALDEN, Narada Michael (b. Michael Anthony Walden, April 23, 1952, Kalamazoo, MI) R&B drummer, producer and vocalist. A jazz-rock drummer who, after a disco oriented solo career, became a major 1980s R&B writer and producer. Walden first came to prominence as a member of the jazz-fusion group the Mahavishnu Orchestra, featuring on the albums **Apocalypse** (1974) US#43, **Visions of the Emerald Beyond** (1975) US#68 and **Inner Worlds** (1976, all Columbia) US#118. Walden subsequently worked as a session drummer and recorded as a solo artist. CHART COMPOSITIONS: *Delightful* (1977) R&B#81, *I Don't Want Nobody Else (To Dance with You)* (1979) R&B#9 US#47, *Give Your Love a Chance* (1979) R&B#80, *I Shoulda Loved Ya* [xxvi] (1979) R&B#4 US#66 UK#8, *Tonight I'm Alright* (1980) R&B#35 UK#34, *The Real Thang* (1980) R&B#22, *I Want You* (1980) R&B#46, *You're #1* (1982) R&B#19, *Summer Lady* (1982) R&B#39, *Gimme, Gimme, Gimme* with Patti Austin (1985) R&B#39 US#106, *The Nature of Things* (1985) R&B#82, *Divine Emotions* [ix] (1988) R&B#21 UK#8. ALBUMS: **Garden of Love Light** (1977), **I Cry I Smile** (1978), **I Don't Want Nobody Else** (1979), **Awakening** (1979) US#103, **The Dance of Life** (1979) US#74, **Victory** (1980) US#103, **Confidence** (1982, all Atlantic) US#135; **Divine Emotions** (1988, Reprise) UK#60. COMPILATION: **Extacys-The Best of Michael Narada Walden** (1997, WEA). HIT VERSIONS: *All American Girls* [xxv] Sister Sledge (1981) R&B#3 US#79 UK#41, *Another Night* Aretha Franklin (1986) US#22 UK#54, *Attack of the Name Game* [ix] Stacy Lattisaw (1982) R&B#14 US#70, *Baby Come to Me* [ix] Regina Belle (1989) R&B#60, *Blue Angel* [xxiii] Al Jarreau (1992) R&B#74, *Don't Make Me Wait for Love* Kenny G. (1987) US#15, *Freeway of Love* [ix] Aretha Franklin (1985) R&B#1 US#3 UK#51, *Happy Just to Be with You* [xix] Michelle Gayle (1995) UK#15, *How Will I Know* [xxiv] Whitney Houston (1985) R&B#1 US#1 UK#5, *I Love Your Smile* [iii] Shanice (1991) R&B#1 US#2 UK#55, re-mixed (1992) UK#2; *I Wanna Hold on to You* [xv] Mica Paris (1993) R&B#46, *I'm Cryin'* [xvi] Shanice (1992) R&B#11, *I'm on Your Side* [vi] Jennifer Holiday (1991) R&B#10, *It's Not Hard to Love You* [xiv] Al Jarreau (1992) R&B#36, *Jimmy Lee* [xi] Aretha Franklin (1986) R&B#2 US#28 UK#46, *Jody* [xii] Jermaine Stewart (1986) R&B#18 US#42, *Jump to the Beat* [xxvii] Stacy Lattisaw (1980) UK#3/Danni Minogue (1991) UK#8; *Let Me Be Your Angel* [xxii] Stacy Lattisaw (1980) R&B#8 US#21, *Licence to Kill* [i] Gladys Knight (1989) UK#6, *Never in My Life* [v] Cherrelle (1991) R&B#42, *Next Time You'll Know* [xxviii] Sister Sledge (1981) R&B#28 US#82, *One Man Woman* [ix] Milira (1992) R&B#49, *Perfect Combination* [xx] Stacy Lattisaw & Johnny Gill (1984) R&B#10 US#75, *Put Your Mouth on Me* [x] Eddie Murphy (1989) US#27, *Rock-a-Lott* [xxi] Aretha Franklin (1987) R&B#25 US#82, *Save Me* [xvii] Lisa Fisher (1991) R&B#7 US#74, *Save Your Sex for Me* [xxiii] Howard Hewett (1992) R&B#67, *Silent Prayer* [ix] Shanice (1992) R&B#4 US#31, *So Far So Good* Sheena Easton (1986) US#43, *So Intense* [viii] Lisa Fisher (1991) R&B#19, *Still in Love with You* [iv] Cherrelle (1992) R&B#86, *Tell Me What You Want Me to Do* [vii] Tevin Campbell (1991) g R&B#1 US#6, *We Don't Have to Take Our Clothes Off* [xx] Jermaine Stewart (1986) R&B#64 US#5 UK#2, *Who's Zooming Who* [xviii] Aretha Franklin (1985) R&B#2 US#7 UK#11, *You're a Friend of Mine* Clarence Clemons & Jackson Browne (1985) US#18. Co-writers: [i] Walter Afanasieff/Jeffrey Cohen, [ii] Walter Afanasieff/Preston Glass, [iii] J. Baker/S. Jackson/S. Wilson, [iv] L. Biancaniello, [v] L. Biancaniello/Allee Willis, [vi] Angela Bofill/Jeffrey Cohen, [vii] Tevin Campbell/S.J. Dakota, [viii] R. Cantor/C. Richardson, [ix] Jeffrey Cohen, [x] Jeffrey Cohen/Eddie Murphy, [xi] Jeffrey Cohen/Preston Glass/A.L. Walden, [xii] Jeffrey Cohen/Jermaine Stewart, [xiii] S.J. Dakota/Howard Hewett/M. Mani/Nia Peebles, [xiv] S.J. Dakota/S. Jett/K. Walden, [xv] S.J. Dakota/Mica Paris, [xvi] S.J. Dakota/Shanice Wilson, [xvii] Lisa Fisher, [xviii] Aretha Franklin/Preston Glass, [xix] Michelle Gayle/Preston Glass, [xx] Preston Glass, [xxi] Preston Glass/Johnson, [xxii] B. Hill, [xxiii] S. Jett/J. Miro, [xxiv] George Merrill/Sharon Rubicam, [xxv] J. Sledge/Lisa Walden/Allee Willis, [xxvi] T.M. Stevens/Allee Willis, [xxvii] Lisa Walden, [xxviii] Allee Willis. (*See also under* Mariah CAREY.)

978. WALDMAN, Wendy (b. America) Pop vocalist. A female singer-songwriter who has had more success as a writer for others than with her own recordings. Waldman first recorded as a member of the group Bryndle, before pursuing a solo career.

CHART COMPOSITION: *Long Hot Summer Nights* (1978) US#76. ALBUMS: **Love Has Got Me** (1973), **Gypsy Symphony** (1974), **Wendy Waldman** (1975), **Main Refrain** (1976), **Strange Company** (1978, all Warner Brothers); **Which Way to Main Street** (1982, Epic). HIT VERSIONS: *Baby, What About You* [ii] Crystal Gayle (1983) C&W#1 US#83, *Half Enough* [iii] Lorrie Morgan (1993) C&W#8, *Save the Best for Last* [i] Vanessa Williams (1992) g R&B#1 US#1 UK#3. Co-writers: [i] Phil Galdston/John Lind, [ii] J. Leo, [iii] R. Nielsen. (*See also under* Karla BONOFF.)

979. WALKER, Jerry Jeff (b. Paul Crosby, March 16, 1942, Oneonta, NY) C&W guitarist and vocalist. A folk and country-blues influenced singer-songwriter, best known as the composer of the much recorded *Mr. Bojangles*, a song about an old street performer that Walker met in prison. During the late 1950s, Walker was a regular performer on the east coast folk scene, later playing in the groups the Lost Sea Dreamers, and the psychedelic-rock act Circus Maximus, which released the albums **Circus Maximus** (1967) and **Neverland Revisited** (1968, both Vanguard). Walker has long been a champion of new songwriters, recording versions of material by Butch Hancock and Guy Clark. He has never been afraid to experiment, as evidenced by his album **Cowjazz** (1982), which was an intriguing attempt to mix jazz and country. CHART COMPOSITIONS: *Mr. Bojangles* (1968) US#77, live version (1977) C&W#93; *Got Lucky Last Night* (1981) C&W#82. ALBUMS: **Mr. Bojangles** (1968, Atco); **Driftin' Way of Life** (1969, Vanguard); **Five Years Gone** (1969), **Bein' Free** (1970, both Atco); **Jerry Jeff Walker** (1972), **Viva Terlingua** (1973) g US#160, **Walker's Collectibles** (1974) US#141, **Ridin' High** (1975) US#119, **It's a Good Night for Singin'** (1976) US#109, **A Man Must Carry On** (1977) US#60, **Contrary to Ordinary** (1978, all MCA) US#111; **Jerry Jeff** (1978), **Too Old to Change** (1979, both Elektra); **Re-union** (1981) US#188, **Cowjazz** (1982, both South Coast); **Live at Gruene Hall** (1989), **Gypsy Songman** (1990), **Navajo Rug** (1991), **Hill Country Rain** (1992, all Ryko). COMPILATION: **Best of Jerry Jeff Walker** (1980, MCA) US#185. HIT VERSIONS: *Mr. Bojangles* Bobby Cole (1968) US#79/Nitty Gritty Dirt Band (1971) US#9; *Railroad Lady* [i] Lefty Frizzell (1974) C&W#52. Co-writer: [i] Jimmy Buffett.

980. WALKER, Scott (b. Noel Scott Engel, January 9, 1943, Hamilton, OH) Pop vocalist. The lead vocalist in the 1960s vocal trio the Walker Brothers, who later developed into a highly original songwriter, and the definitive English language in-terpreter of the Flemish composer Jacques Brel. After performing as the bassist in the 1960s group the Routers, and working as a session musician, Walker recorded a number of unsuccessful solo singles as Scott Engel. As lead singer in the Walker Brothers, he recorded the albums **Take It Easy with the Walker Brothers** (1966) UK#4, **Portrait** (1966) UK#3, **Images** (1967, all Philips) UK#6; **No Regrets** (1976) UK#49, **Lines** (1976), **Nite Flights** (1978, all GTO). COMPILATIONS: **The Walker Brothers' Story** (1967, Philips) UK#9; **Live in Japan** (1987, Bam Caruso); **After the Lights Go Out — The Best of the Walker Brothers, 1965–1967** (1990), **No Regrets — The Best of the Walker Brothers, 1965–1976** (1992, both Fontana) UK#4. In 1967, Walker embarked on a solo career that was clearly influenced by the work of Brel and Kurt Weill, and concentrated primarily on his own compositions, a quartet of albums that remain some of the most influential and original works of the era. Walker's career nosedived during the early 1970s when he was marketed as a ballad crooner, but he has occasionally re-surfaced with such highly original recordings as **Climate of Hunter** (1984) and **Tilt** (1995), upon which he has clearly dispensed with the formal structure of song in favor of a highly stylized version of lieder. ALBUMS: **Scott** (1967) UK#3, **Scott 2** (1968) UK#1, **Scott 3** (1969) UK#3, **Scott Walker Sings Songs from His T.V. Series** (1969) UK#7, **Scott 4** (1970), **'Til the Band Comes In** (1970), **The Moviegoer** (1972), **Any Day Now** (1973, all Philips); **Stretch** (1974), **We Had It All** (1974, both CBS); **Climate of Hunter** (1984, Virgin) UK#60; **Tilt** (1995, Fontana) UK#27. COMPILATIONS: **Looking Back with Scott Walker** (1967, Ember); **Scott Engel and John Stewart: I Only Came to Dance with You** (1966, Tower); **Fire Escape in the Sky: The Godlike Genius of Scott Walker** (1981, Zoo); **Scott Walker Sings Jacques Brel** (1981, Philips); **Boy Child — The Best of Scott Walker** (1990, Fontana).

981. WALKER, T-Bone (b. Aaron Thibeaux Walker, May 28, 1910, Linden, TX; d. March 16, 1975, Los Angeles, CA) Blues guitarist, pianist and vocalist. A highly rhythmic, self-taught, jazz influenced guitarist, who was a significant influence on future blues artists. Walker had toured with medicine shows during the 1920s, before making his first recordings for Columbia Records in 1929. He died of pneumonia in 1975. CHART COMPOSITIONS: *Bobby Sox Blues* (1947) R&B#3, *Call It Stormy Monday (But Tuesday Is Just as Bad)* (1948) R&B#5, *Long Skirt Baby Blues* (1948) R&B#10, *I'm Waiting for Your Call* (1948) R&B#8, *Midnight Blues* (1948) R&B#11, *West Side Baby* (1948) R&B#8, *Description Blues*

(1949) R&B#13, *T-Bone Shuffle* (1949) R&B#7, *Go Back to the One You Love* (1950) R&B#15. ALBUMS: **T-Bone Blues** (1960, Atlantic); **Stormy Monday Blues** (1967), **Funky Town** (1968, both Bluesway); **Feeling the Blues** (1969, Black and Blue); **Good Feelin'** (1970, Polydor); **Very Rare** (1973, Reprise); **His Original 45–50 Performances** (1983, Capitol); **Plain Ole Blues** (1982), **The Natural Blues** (1983, both Charly); **Hot Leftovers** (1985), **I Get So Weary** (1985, both Pathe Marconi); **The Collection** (1985, Deja Vu); **T-Bone Jumps Again** (1985), **Low Down Blues** (1986, both Charly); **I Don't Be Jivin'** (1987, Bear Family); **The Inventor of the Electric Guitar Blues** (1987, Blues Boy); **The Bluesway Sessions** (1988, Charly); **I Want a Little Girl** (1988, Delmark).

982. WALLER, Fats (b. Thomas Wright Waller, May 21, 1904, New York, NY; d. December 15, 1943, Kansas City, MO) Jazz pianist, organist, bandleader and vocalist. A songwriting genius and one of the most influential artists in popular music, who charted over sixty hit singles between 1929–1943. The number of tunes composed by Waller is inestimable, as he even sold arrangements of his material for the price of a hamburger, and whenever in need of additional funds he often knocked off a handful of melodies which he would sell, under different titles, to dozens of publishers. Contemporary standards that are attributed to Waller include *What Did I Do to Be So Black and Blue* [i] (1933), *Keepin' Out of Mischief Now* [v] (1932) and *Honeysuckle Rose* [v] (1935). He learned the piano at the age of six, and played the organ in his father's church, before becoming an accompanist for a variety of jazz singers. In 1920, Waller recorded his first piano rolls for the OKeh label. He was one of the few organists to make the instrument swing, and in 1925 he published his first tune *Squeeze Me*, shortly after which he formed a partnership with the lyricist Andy Razoff, and contributed to the shows "Keep Shufflin'" (1928) and "Hot Chocolates" (1929). Waller later worked with George Marion, Jr., on the show "Early to Bed" (1943). The Broadway musical about his life "Ain't Misbehavin'" (1978), was revived in London in 1994. Waller died from complications as a result of pneumonia in 1943. CHART COMPOSITIONS: *Ain't Misbehavin'* [i] (1929) US#17, *How Can You Face Me?* (1934) US#16, *Honeysuckle Rose* [v] (1935) US#17, new version (1937) US#4; *The Joint Is Jumpin'* [iii] (1937) US#17, *Jitterbug Waltz* (1942) R&B#6. ALBUMS: **Ain't Misbehavin'** oc (1978, RCA) US#161; **Fine Arabian Stuff** (1981, Deluxe); **Best of Fats Waller** (1981), **1939: Fats Waller** (1981), **Fats Waller and Morris Hot Babies** (1981, all Joker); **Fats at the Organ** (1981, Living Era); **1943** (1981,

Jazz Live); **The Young Fats Waller** (1981, Joker); **20 Golden Pieces** (1982, Bulldog); **Bouncin' on V Disk** (1983, Swaggie): **The Indispensable Fats Waller, Volumes 1 to 10** (1983), **Masters of Jazz** (1983), **Piano Solos, 1929–1941** (1983, all RCA); **Rare Fats Waller, 1927–1942** (1983), **That Old Feeling** (1983, both Swaggie); **African Ripples** (1984), **Ain't Misbehavin'** (1984), **Rare Piano Boogie** (1984, both RCA); **Live at the Yacht Club** (1984, Giants of Jazz); **Fats Waller, His Piano and His Rhythm, Volume 3** (1985, Vogue); **Honeysuckle Rose** (1985, Recollections); **Live: Fats Waller, Volume 2** (1985, Giants of Jazz); **Handful of Keys** (1986, RCA); **Chronological, Volume 1** (1986, JSP); **The Collection** (1986, Deja Vu); **Fats Waller Live, Volume 1** (1986), **Juggling Jive of Fats Waller** (1986, both Giants of Jazz); **Honey on the Moon** (1986, Meteor); **My Very Good Friend, the Milkman** (1986, President); **Magic Moments** (1986, RCA); **That's Fats** (1986, Vogue); **The Vocal Fats** (1986, RCA); **You Rascal, You** (1986, Living Era); **Complete Early Band Works, 1927–1929** with Morriss Hot Babies (1987, Swaggie); **Armful O' Sweetness** (1987), **Dust Off That Piano** (1987, both Saville); **Fats Waller** (1987, Giants of Jazz); **Friends of Fats, Volume 2** (1987, Collectors); **From the Beginning, Volume 2** (1987, JSP); **Diamond Series** (1988, Diamond); **Fats Waller** (1988), **Fats Waller, 1934–1941** (1988, both Joker); **Fats Waller, 1935–1943** (1988, Collector's Classics); **Fats Waller and His Rhythm, 1934–1936** (1988), **Fats Waller and His Rhythm, Volume 1, 1934** (1988, both BBC); **Fats Waller — Piano and Rhythm, 1939** (1988, Vogue); **From the Beginning, Volume 3** (1988, JSP); **Hallelujah, I'm a Bum** (1988, Starline); **Jazz Time, Volume 17** (1988, Vogue); **The Joint Is Jumpin'** (1988, Bluebird); **Take It Easy** (1988, Saville); **Thomas Fats Waller, Volumes 1 and 2** (1988, both Vogue); **On the Air** (1988, Collector's Choice); **Oh Mercy, Looka Here** (1988, Honeysuckle Rose); **Our Very Good Friend, Fats** (1988, Dance Band Days); **Rare Piano Solos, 1923–1927** (1988, Delta); **Fascinatin' Fats** (1989, Starline); **Fats Waller in London** (1989, Retrospective); **The Most Important Recordings of Fats Waller** (1989, Official); **Ragtime Piano Entertainer** (1989, Vogue); **Spreadin' Rhythm Around** (1989, Saville). HIT VERSIONS: *Ain't Cha Glad* [v] Benny Goodman (1934) US#6, *Ain't Misbehavin'* [i] Louis Armstrong (1929) US#7/Gene Austin (1929) US#9/Ruth Etting (1929) US#16/Leo Reisman (1929) US#2/Bill Robinson & Irving Mills (1929) US#8/Teddy Wilson (1937) US#6/Dinah Washington (1946) R&B#8/Johnnie Ray (1956) UK#17/Tommy Bruce (1960) UK#3/Hank Williams, Jr. (1986) C&W#1; *Honeysuckle Rose* [v] Fletcher Henderson (1933) US#18/Dorsey Brothers Orchestra (1935)

US#19/Red Norvo (1935) US#9; *I've Got a Feeling I'm Falling* [iv] Gene Austin (1929) US#10, *Keepin' Out of Mischief Now* [v] Louis Armstrong (1932) US#17/Coon-Sanders Orchestra (1932) US#20; *My Fate Is in Your Hands* [v] Gene Austin (1929) US#20. Co-writers: [i] Harry Brooks/Andy Razaf, [ii] Alexander Hill, [iii] James C. Johnson/Andy Razaf, [iv] Harry Link/Billy Rose, [v] Andy Razaf.

983. WALSH, Joe (b. November 20, 1947, New York, NY) Rock guitarist, producer and vocalist. A guitarist who first recorded as a member of the band the James Gang, which charted with *Funk #48* (1969) US#126, *Funk #49* (1970) US#59, *Walk Away* (1971) US#51, and *Midnight Man* (1971) US#80. ALBUMS: **Yer' Album** (1969, Bluesway) US#83; **The James Gang Rides Again** (1970) g US#20, **Thirds** (1971) g US#27, **Live in Concert** (1971, all ABC) g US#24. COMPILATIONS: **Best of the James Gang** (1973) US#79, **16 Greatest Hits** (1973, both ABC) US#181. In 1972, Walsh left the group for a solo career, the highlight of which remains his wry observation on stardom, *Life's Been Good*. Walsh was also an unsuccessful presidential candidate in 1979. CHART COMPOSITIONS: *Rocky Mountain Way* [i] (1973) US#23 UK#39, *Meadows* (1974) US#89, *Turn to Stone* (1975) US#93, re-issued (1979) US#109; *Walk Away* (1976) US#105, *Rocky Mountain Way* [i]/*Turn to Stone*/*Meadows*/*Walk Away* EP (1977) UK#39, *Life's Been Good* (1978) US#12 UK#14, *Over and Over* (1978) US#106, *All Night Long* (1980) US#19, *A Life of Illusion* [ii] (1981) US#34, *Space Age Whizz Kids* [iii] (1983) US#52. ALBUMS: **Barnstorm** (1972) US#79, **The Smoker You Drink, The Player You Get** (1973) g US#6, **So What** (1975, all Dunhill) g US#11; **You Can't Argue with a Sick Mind** (1976, ABC) US#20 UK#28; **But Seriously, Folks...** (1978) p US#8 UK#16, **There Goes the Neighborhood** (1982, both Asylum) US#20; **You Bought It — You Name It** (1983) US#48, **The Confessor** (1985) US#65, **Got Any Gum?** (1987, all Warner Brothers) US#113; **Ordinary Average Guy** (1991, Pyramid) US#112. COMPILATION: **Best of Joe Walsh** (1978, ABC) US#71. In 1975, Walsh became a member of the Eagles, featuring on its classic album **Hotel California**. Co-writers: [i] Roche Grace/Kenny Passarelli/Joe Vitale, [ii] Kenny Passarelli, [iii] Joe Vitale. (*See also under* Don HENLEY.)

984. WARD, Clifford T. (b. February 10, 1946, Kidderminster, England) Pop guitarist and vocalist. A former school teacher who became a singer-songwriter during the 1970s. Ward has suffered from multiple sclerosis since the 1980s. CHART COMPOSITIONS: *Gaye* (1973) UK#8, *Scullery* (1974)

UK#37. ALBUMS: **Singer-Songwriter** (1972, Dandelion); **Home Thoughts** (1973) UK#40, **Mantle Pieces** (1974) UK#42, **Escalator** (1975, all Charisma); **No More Rock 'n' Roll** (1975), **Waves** (1975, both Philips); **New England Days** (1977, Mercury); **Both of Us** (1984, Philips); **Sometime Next Year** (1986, Tempo); **Laugh It Off** (1992, Aimless); **Julia and Other New Stories** (1994, Graduate).

985. WARE, Leon (b. Detroit, MI) R&B producer and vocalist. An R&B artist who grew up listening to doo-wop, before singing in the Romeos during the 1950s. Ware's first recorded song was *Got to Have You Back* by the Isley Brothers (1965), and one of his earliest productions was the *(I Wanna) Testify* by the Parliaments (1967). In 1967, Ware co-wrote five tracks on the Righteous Brothers' album **Souled Out**, before securing a publishing contract at Jobette, where his songs were recorded by a variety of Motown acts. He has also recorded as a solo singer. CHART COMPOSITIONS: *What's Your Name* (1979) R&B#42, *Baby Don't Stop Me* (1981) R&B#66, *Rockin' You Eternally* (1981) R&B#74. ALBUMS: **Education of Johnny Carson** (1969, Paramount); **Leon Ware** (1972, United Artists); **Musical Massage** (1976, Gordy); **Inside Is Love** (1979, Fabulous); **Rockin' You Eternally** (1981), **Leon Ware** (1982, Elektra); **Undercover** (1987, Slingshot); **Taste the Love** (1995, Expansion). HIT VERSIONS: *Got to Have You Back* Isley Brothers (1965) R&B#47 US#93, *I Wanna Be Where You Are* [iii] Michael Jackson (1972) R&B#2 US#16/Jose Feliciano (1982) R&B#63; *I Want You* [iii] Gato Barbieri (1976) US#110/Marvin Gaye (1976) R&B#1 US#15/Wilson Pickett (1979) R&B#41/Tamiko Jones (1986) R&B#81/Marc Nelson (1991) R&B#26/Robert Palmer (1991) US#16 UK#9; *If I Ever Lose This Heaven* [iv] Quincy Jones (1974) R&B#71/Average White Band (1975) R&B#25 US#39; *In the City* Mica Paris on B-side of *Breath Life into Me* (1986) UK#26, *Inside My Love* [ii] Minnie Riperton (1975) R&B#26 US#76, *Rolling Down the Mountainside* [i] Main Ingredient (1975) R&B#7 US#92, *You Make Me Want (To Love Again)* Vesta Williams (1987) R&B#90. Co-writers: [i] J.D. Hilliard, [ii] Minnie Riperton/Richard Rudolph, [iii] Arthur Ross, [iv] Pam Sawyer. (*See also under* Johnny BRISTOL, Marvin GAYE, Melissa MANCHESTER, Bobby WOMACK.)

986. WARREN, Diane (b. Los Angeles, CA) Pop composer. A prolific songwriter who has become one of the most successful hit makers in America. Although Warren's name is hardly known outside the music industry, she was the number one American singles publisher in 1991, who had achieved fifty American top ten hits by 1995, including five number ones. Warren writes to order from her offices in Los Angeles, and has said that she is "in love with the concept of the three-and-a-half-minute pop song." During one week in 1989, Warren had seven compositions on the American Hot 100, including the number one and the number two spot, with *Blame It on the Rain* and *When I See You Smile*. Warren was writing three songs a day by the age of fourteen, has become something of a songwriter-aholic. Although one of the last genuine examples of the Tin Pan Alley approach, Warren's songs are little more than power-ballad factory fodder, aimed at production-line artists. HIT VERSIONS: *All I Want Is Forever* Regina Belle & J.T. Taylor (1989) R&B#2, *And the Night Still Stood* Dion (1989) US#75, *Because You Loved Me* Celine Dion (1996) US#1 UK#10, *Blame It on the Rain* Milli Vanilli (1989) g US#1 UK#52, *Chasin' the Wind* Chicago (1991) US#39, *Commitment of the Heart* Clive Griffin (1993) US#96, *Don't Lose Any Sleep* John Waite (1987) US#81, *Don't Take Away My Heaven* Aaron Neville (1993) US#56, *Every Road Leads Back to You* Bette Midler (1991) US#78, *Everything Changes* Kathy Troccoli (1992) US#14, *Heart Is Not So Smart, The* El Debarge with Debarge (1985) R&B#29 US#75, *I Get Weak* Belinda Carlisle (1988) US#2 UK#10, *I Will Be Here for You* [ii] Michael W. Smith (1992) US#27, *I'll Be Your Shelter* Taylor Dayne (1990) US#4, *I'll Never Get Over You (Getting Over Me)* Expose (1993) g US#8, *If I Could Turn Back Time* Cher (1989) US#18, *If You Asked Me To (Theme from License to Kill)* Patti LaBelle (1989) US#79/Celine Dion (1992) US#4 UK#60; *In Walked Love* Expose (1994) US#84, *Look Away* Chicago (1988) US#1, *Love and Understanding* Cher (1991) US#17 UK#10, *Love Can Move Mountains* Celine Dion (1992) US#50 UK#46, *Love Will Lead You Back* Taylor Dayne (1990) US#1, *Nothing Broken But My Heart* Celine Dion (1992) US#29, *Rhythm of the Night* DeBarge (1985) R&B#1 US#3 UK#4, *Same Love, The* Jets (1989) US#87, *Saving Forever for You* Shanice (1992) R&B#20 US#4, *Set the Night to Music* Roberta Flack & Maxi Priest (1991) R&B#45 US#6, *Solitaire* [i] Laura Branigan (1983) US#7, *Tell Me Where It Hurts* Kathy Troccoli (1994) US#88, *Time Alone with You, The* Michael Bolton (1991) US#7 UK#28, *What Are You Doing with a Fool Like Me* Joe Cocker (1990) US#96, *When I See You Smile* Bad English (1989) US#1 UK#61, *When I'm Back on My Feet Again* Michael Bolton (1989) US#7 UK#44, *Wherever Would I Be* Cheap Trick (1990) US#50/Daryl Hall & Dusty Springfield (1995) UK#44; *Who Will You Run To* Heart (1987) US#7 UK#30. Co-writers: [i] Martine Clemenceau, [ii] Michael W. Smith. (*See also under* Bryan ADAMS, Michael BOLTON, Desmond CHILD, Gloria ESTEFAN, Albert HAMMOND, Michael McDONALD, Rick NIELSEN, Roy ORBISON.)

987. WARREN, Harry (b. Salvatore Guarangna, December 24, 1893, Brooklyn, NY; d. December 22, 1981, Los Angeles, CA) Film and stage composer, pianist. One of the most successful, prolific and widely recorded tunesmiths of the first half of the twentieth century. The son of Italian immigrants, Warren was a self-taught pianist who first worked as a stage hand, and as a pianist on silent movies and in a carnival show, before becoming a rehearsal pianist and song-plugger. He began writing songs while serving in the U.S. Navy during World War I, first publishing *Rose of the Rio Grande* [xviii] (1922). Some of Warren's earliest songs were used in the revues "Sweet and Low" (1930) and "The Laugh Parade" (1931). Many of his greatest successes were those that he wrote in collaboration with the lyricist Al Dubin, for the film musicals "42nd Street" (1932), "Gold Diggers of 1933" and "Roman Scandals" (both 1933); "Moulin Rouge," "Twenty Million Sweethearts," "Dames" and "Wonder Bar" (all 1934); "Gold Diggers of 1935," "Go into Your Dance" and "Broadway Gondolier" (all 1935); and "Melody for Two" (1937). Warren also worked with Johnny Mercer on the films "Goin' Places" and "Hard to Get" (both 1938), and with Mack Gordon on "Springtime in the Rockies" (1939). The film "Hello Frisco, Hello" (1943), featured his Oscar winning composition *You'll Never Know* [xv], one of three that he was awarded, prompting him to remark to fellow songwriter Harold Arlen, "From now on, you walk two Oscars behind me." Other lyricists that Warren collaborated with include Arthur Freed and Ira Gershwin. In 1932, Warren and Dubin wrote the complete score to the film "Forty-Second Street" (1933), which became a prototype Hollywood musical for many years. ALBUMS: **The Gang's All Here** ost (1943, Sandy Hook); **The Harvey Girls** ost (1946, Decca); **Pagan Love Song** ost (1950), **Summer Stock** ost (1950, both MGM); **Tea for Two** st (1950, Columbia); **The Belle of New York** ost (1952, MGM); **Sun Valley Serenade** ost (1954, RCA); **Artists and Models** ost (1955, Capitol); **An Affair to Remember** ost (1957, Columbia); **Cinderfella** ost (1960, Dot); **Shangri-La** tvst (1960, Sound of Broadway); **Hooray for Hollywood** ost (1975, United Artists); **Death on the Nile** ost (1978, Capitol); **42nd Street** oc (1981, RCA) US#120. HIT VERSIONS: *About a Quarter to Nine* [xi] Johnny Green (1935) US#5/Ozzie Nelson (1935) US#3/Victor Young (1935) US#3; *Absence Makes the Heart Grow Fonder (For Somebody Else)* [xxii] Bernie Cummins (1930) US#7, *Affair to Remember, An* [i] Vic Damone (1957) US#16 UK#29, *At Last* [xvii] Glenn Miller

(1942) US#9/Ray Anthony (1952) US#2/Etta James (1961) R&B#2 US#47; *Baby Doll* Barbara Fairchild (1947) C&W#6/Sons of Pioneers (1947) C&W#5/ Andy Williams (1956) US#33/Marvin & Johnny (1953) R&B#9/Carlo (1963) US#123; *Birds and the Bees, The* [xxv] Alma Cogan (1956) UK#25, *Boulevard of Broken Dreams, The* [xi] Jan Garber (1934) US#6, *By the River Saint Marie* [xxi] Guy Lombardo (1931) US#1, *Chattanooga Choo-Choo* [xvii] Glenn Miller (1941) g US#1/Modernaires & Paula Kelly in *Salute to Glenn Miller* (1946) US#18/Floyd Cramer (1962) US#36/Harpers Bizarre (1967) US#45/ Tuxedo Junction (1978) US#32; *Cheerful Little Earful* [xvi] Tom Gerun (1930) US#7, *Chica, Chica, Boom, Chic* [xvii] Xavier Cugat (1941) US#26, *Coffee in the Morning (Kisses in the Night)* [xi] Boswell Sisters (1934) US#13, *Crying for the Carolines* [xxii] Ben Bernie (1930) US#13/Ruth Etting (1930) US#15/Guy Lombardo (1930) US#6/Fred Waring's Pennsylvanians (1930) US#3; *Dames* [xi] Eddy Duchin (1934) US#12, *Day Dreaming* [xxiv] Rudy Vallee (1938) US#8, *Devil May Care* [v] Glenn Miller (1940) US#7, *Don't Give Up the Ship* [xi] Tommy Dorsey (1935) US#9, *Down Argentina Way* [xvii] Eddy Duchin (1940) US#15/Shep Fields (1940) US#18/Gene Krupa (1940) US#15/Leo Reisman (1940) US#7/Bob Crosby (1941) US#2; *Fair and Warmer* [xi] Dick Powell (1934) US#19, *Forty-Second Street* [xi] Don Bestor (1933) US#1/Hal Kemp (1933) US#7; *Garden of the Moon* [xiii] Red Norvo (1938) US#6, *Girl Friend of the Whirling a Whirling Dervish, The* [xii] Guy Lombardo (1938) US#20, *Go into Your Dance* [xi] Johnny Green (1935) US#20, *Have a Little Faith in Me* [xxii] Guy Lombardo (1930) US#3, *Home in Pasadena* [vi] Billy Murray & Ed Smalle (1924) US#15, *Honeymoon Hotel* [xi] Leo Reisman (1933) US#13, *Honolulu* [xx] Tommy Dorsey (1939) US#10, *How Could You?* [xi] Anson Weeks (1937) US#7/ Teddy Wilson & Billie Holiday (1937) US#12; *I Found a Million Dollar Baby (In a Five-and-Ten Cent Store)* [ix] Ben Selvin (1927) US#17/Boswell Sisters (1931) US#3/Bing Crosby (1931) US#2/Fred Waring's Pennsylvanians (1931) US#1; *I Had the Craziest Dream* [xi] Harry James (1943) g R&B#4 US#1/Skylarks (1953) US#28; *I Know Now* [xi] Lennie Hayton (1937) US#19/Guy Lombardo (1937) US#2/Dick Powell (1937) US#14; *I Know Why* [xvii] Richard Himber (1941) US#24/Glenn Miller (1941) US#18; *I Love My Baby (My Baby Loves Me)* [xix] Aileen Stanley (1926) US#10/Fred Waring's Pennsylvanians (1926) US#6; *I Only Have Eyes for You* [xi] Eddy Duchin (1934) US#4/Jane Froman (1934) US#20/ Ben Selvin (1934) US#2/Flamingos (1959) R&B#3 US#11/Cliff Richard (1964) US#109/Lettermen (1966) US#72/Jerry Butler (1972) R&B#20 US#85/ Mel Carter (1974) US#104/Art Garfunkel (1975)

US#18 UK#1/Heaven & Earth (1979) R&B#63/ Funky Poets (1994) R&B#81; *I Wish I Knew* [xvii] Dick Haymes (1945) US#6, *I Yi Yi Yi Yi (I Like You Very Much)* [xvii] Andrews Sisters (1941) US#11, *I'd Rather Listen to Your Eyes* [xi] Jacques Renard (1935) US#14, *I'll Sing You a Thousand Love Songs* [xi] Eddy Duchin (1936) US#1/Tempo King (1936) US#2; *I'll String Along with You* [xi] Tom Coakley (1934) US#17/Ted Fiorito (1934) US#1; *I'm Goin' Shoppin' with You* [xi] Little Jack Little (1935) US#16/Dick Powell (1935) US#20; *I'm Happy About the Whole Thing* [xv] Lawrence Welk (1939) US#18, *(I've Got a Gal in) Kalamazoo* [xvii] Glenn Miller (1942) g US#1/Meco in *Big Band Medley* (1982) US#101; *I've Got to Sing a Torch Song* [xi] Bing Crosby (1933) US#9/Hal Kemp (1933) US#13/Rudy Vallee (1933) US#18; *Inamorata* [iii] Dean Martin (1956) US#27 UK#21/Jerry Vale (1956) US#30; *It Happened in Sun Valley* [xvii] Glenn Miller (1941) US#18, *Jeeper's Creepers* [xxiv] Louis Armstrong (1939) US#12/Larry Clinton (1939) US#12/Al Donohue (1939) US#1; *Journey to a Star, A* [xxiv] Judy Garland (1944) US#25, *Keep Young and Beautiful* [xi] Abe Lyman (1934) US#19, *Lullaby of Broadway* [xi] Chick Bullock (1935) US#19/Dorsey Brothers Orchestra (1935) US#1/Reginald Foresythe (1935) US#11/Hal Kemp (1935) US#14/Little Jack Little (1935) US#5/ Winifred Shaw (1976) UK#42; *Lulu's Back in Town* [xi] Fats Waller (1935) US#8, *More I See You, The* [xvii] Dick Haymes (1945) US#7/Harry James (1945) US#12/Marcy Jo & Eddie Rambeau (1963) US#132/Richard "Groove" Holmes (1966) US#131/ Joy Marshall (1966) UK#34/Chris Montez (1966) US#16 UK#3/Peter Allen (1976) US#108; *My Heart Tells Me* [xvii] Glen Gray (1944) R&B#7 US#1/Jan Garber (1944) US#14; *Nagasaki* [xix] Ipana Troubadors (1928) US#13, *No Love, No Nothin'* [xxv] Jan Garber (1944) US#5/Johnny Long (1944) US#5/Ella Mae Morse (1944) US#4; *One Sweet Letter from You* [iv] Gene Austin (1927) US#13/Charleston Chasers (1927) US#14/Ted Lewis (1927) US#8/Kate Smith (1927) US#14; *Ooh! That Kiss* [x] Arden-Ohman Orchestra (1931) US#10/Dorsey Brothers Orchestra (1932) US#18; *Page Miss Glory* [xi] Hal Kemp (1935) US#6, *Remember Me?* [xi] Bing Crosby (1937) US#1/Teddy Wilson (1937) US#2; *Rose in Her Hair, The* [i] Russ Morgan (1935) US#9, *Rose of the Rio Grande* [xviii] Marion Harris (1923) US#3, *Rose, Rose, I Love You* [iii] Gordon Jenkins & Cisco Houston (1951) US#21/Frankie Laine (1951) US#3/Buddy Morrow (1951) US#8; *September in the Rain* [xi] James Melton (1937) US#16/Guy Lombardo (1937) US#1/Rhythm Wreckers (1937) US#19/Sam Donohue (1948) US#26/George Shearing (1949) US#25/ Dinah Washington (1961) R&B#5 US#23 UK#35; *Serenade in Blue* [xi] Benny Goodman (1942) US#17/

Glenn Miller (1942) US#2; *Shadow Waltz* [xi] Bing Crosby (1933) US#1/Guy Lombardo (1933) US#11/ Rudy Vallee (1933) US#6; *She's a Latin from Manhattan* [xi] Johnny Green (1935) US#4/Ozzie Nelson (1935) US#15/Victor Young (1935) US#1; *Shuffle Off to Buffalo* [xi] Don Bestor (1933) US#2/Hal Kemp (1933) US#2; *Stanley Steamer, The* [ii] Jo Stafford (1947) US#11, *That's Amore* [iii] Dean Martin (1953) g US#2 UK#2, *There Will Never Be Another You* [xvii] Woody Herman (1942) US#23/ Sammy Kaye (1943) US#20/Chris Montez (1966) US#33; *This Heart of Mine* [xiv] Judy Garland (1945) US#22, *This Is Always* [xvii] Harry James (1946) US#10/Jo Stafford (1946) US#11; *Three's a Crowd* [xii] Tom Gerun (1932) US#11, *Too Many Tears* [xi] Guy Lombardo (1932) US#1, *Two Dreams Met* [xvii] Mitchell Ayres (1940) US#9/Tommy Dorsey (1940) US#12/Eddy Duchin (1940) US#22; *Wait and See* [xxiv] Judy Garland (1945) US#24, *We're in the Money (The Gold-Digger's Song)* [xi] Hal Kemp (1933) US#16/Ted Lewis (1933) US#5/Dick Powell (1933) US#18; *Where Am I? (Am I in Heaven?)* [xi] Little Jack Little (1935) US#7/Hal Kemp (1936) US#12/Ray Noble (1936) US#16; *Where Do You Work-A, John?* [xxiii] Fred Waring's Pennsylvanians (1927) US#6, *Where the Shy Little Violets Grow* [xx] Guy Lombardo (1929) US#4, *Why Do I Dream These Dreams?* [xi] Bob Causer (1934) US#18/Eddy Duchin (1934) US#8; *With Plenty of Money and You* [xi] Henry Busse (1937) US#1/George Hamilton (1937) US#12/Hal Kemp (1937) US#8; *Wonder Bar* [xi] Emil Coleman (1934) US#20, *Would You Like to Take a Walk?* [ix] Rudy Vallee (1931) US#4, *You Let Me Down* [i] Jimmy Dorsey (1935) US#19/Teddy Wilson & Billie Holiday (1936) US#18; *You Must Have Been a Beautiful Baby* [xxiv] Bing Crosby (1938) US#1/Tommy Dorsey (1938) US#8/Bobby Darin (1961) US#5 UK#10; *You'll Never Know* [xvii] Dick Haymes (1943) R&B#1 US#1/Willie Kelly (1943) US#6/Frank Sinatra (1943) US#2/Rosemary Clooney & Harry James (1953) US#18/Platters (1956) R&B#9 US#11, re-issued (1961) US#109/Shirley Bassey (1961) UK#6/Jim Reeves (1975) C&W#71/Lew DeWitt (1985) C&W#77; *You're Getting to Be a Habit with Me* [xi] Bing Crosby & Guy Lombardo (1933) US#1/Fred Waring's Pennsylvanians (1933) US#15/ Frank Sinatra on *Songs for Swinging Lovers LP* (1956) UK#12; *You're My Everything* [xi] Arden-Ohman Orchestra (1931) US#10/Russ Columbo (1932) US#12/ Ben Selvin (1932) US#12; *Young and Healthy* [xi] Bing Crosby & Guy Lombardo (1933) US#2, *Zing a Little Zong* [xxv] Bing Crosby & Jane Wyman (1952) US#18. Co-writers: [i] Harold Adamson/Leo McCarey, [ii] Ralph Blane, [iii] Jack Brooks, [iv] Lew Brown/Sidney Clare, [v] Johnny Burke, [vi] Grant Clarke/Edgar Leslie, [vii] Mack David, [viii] Mort Dixon, [ix] Mort Dixon/Billy Rose, [x] Mort Dixon/ Joe Young, [xi] Al Dubin, [xii] Al Dubin/Irving Kahal, [xiii] Al Dubin/Johnny Mercer, [xiv] Arthur Freed, [xv] Ira Gershwin, [xvi] Ira Gershwin/Billy Rose, [xvii] Mack Gordon, [xviii] Ross Gorman/ Edgar Leslie, [xix] Bud Green, [xx] Gus Kahn, [xxi] Edgar Leslie, [xxii] Sam M. Lewis/Joe Young, [xxiii] Charley Marks/Mortimer Weinberg, [xxiv] Johnny Mercer, [xxv] Leo Robin. (*See also under* Johnny MERCER.)

988. WASHINGTON, Ned (b. August 15, 1901, Scranton, PA; d. December 20, 1976, Beverly Hills, CA) Film lyricist. A lyricist who worked with a variety of composers on material that was featured in such films as "Du Barry Was a Lady" (1943), "An Affair in Trinidad" (1952) and "Fire Down Below" (1957). Washington also wrote such memorable children's songs as *I've Got No Strings* [iii], from the film "Pinocchio" (1940), and *When I See an Elephant Fly* [vi], from "Dumbo" (1941). ALBUMS: **Miss Sadie Thompson** ost (1953, Mercury); **Pinocchio** ost (1956, Disneyland); **Search for Paradise** ost (1957, RCA). HIT VERSIONS: *Fire Down Below* Shirley Bassey (1957) UK#30/Jeri Southern (1957) UK#22; *Give a Little Whistle* [iii] Cliff Edwards (1940) US#16, *I'm Gettin' Sentimental Over You* [i] Dorsey Brothers Orchestra (1934) US#20/Tommy Dorsey (1936) US#8/Ink Spots (1940) US#26/Jack Leonard (1941) US#21; *Man from Laramie, The* [v] Al Martino (1955) UK#19/Jimmy Young (1955) UK#1; *On Green Dolphin Street* [iv] Jimmy Dorsey (1948) US#25, *Prize of Gold* [v] Joan Regan (1955) UK#6, *Smoke Rings* [ii] Clyde McCoy (1933) US#8/Glen Gray (1937) US#15/Les Paul & Mary Ford (1952) US#14; *When You Wish Upon a Star* [iii] Cliff Edwards (1940) US#10/Hoarce Heidt (1940) US#12/ Guy Lombardo (1940) US#5/Glenn Miller (1940) US#1. Co-writers: [i] George Bassman, [ii] Gene Gifford, [iii] Leigh Harline, [iv] Bronislau Kaper, [v] Lester Lee, [vi] Oliver Wallace. (*See also under* Hoagy CARMICHAEL, Frank CHURCHILL, Dimitri TIOMKIN, Alex WRUBEL, Victor YOUNG.)

989. WATERS, Muddy (b. McKinley Morganfield, April 4, 1915, Rolling Fork, MS; d. April 30, 1983, Chicago, IL) Blues harmonica player, guitarist and vocalist. An elder statesman of the blues when he died from a heart attack in 1983, who was the composer of a number of blues perennials, including *Can't Lose What You Never Had*, *I Can't Be Satisfied* and *Screamin' and Cryin'*. Waters' much copied urban country blues style was a considerable influence on the Rolling Stones, and his stately, boastful vocals and raunchy harmonica style was instantly identifiable. After growing up on a share cropping farm, Waters began singing in church choirs, learning the harmonica at the age of nine and playing in local groups during the depression years. In the early 1940s, he toured with Silas Green of the New Orleans Minstrel and Carnival Show, before recording his first solo sides for the Library of Congress. In 1942, Waters moved to Chicago, where he participated in the development of what was to become known as the Chicago blues sound, as he always recorded with talented sidemen, such as James Cotton, Junior Wells, Buddy Guy and Otis Spann. In 1947, he formed a formidable blues trio with Little Walter and Jimmie Rodgers, and in 1963 recorded the album **Folk Singer**, one of the definitive mergers of blues and folk. During the 1970s, Waters released a series of high quality albums under the guiding hand of the guitarist and producer Johnny Winters. Paul Rodgers interpreted some of his best known compositions on **Muddy Water Blues** (1993, Victory) US#91 UK#9. CHART COMPOSITIONS: *(I Feel Like) Going Home* (1948) R&B#11, *Louisiana Blues* (1951) R&B#10, *Long Distance Call* (1951) R&B#8, *Honey Bee* (1951) R&B#10, *Still a Fool* (1951) R&B#9, *She Moves Me* (1952) R&B#10, *Mad Love* (1953) R&B#6, *Mannish Boy* [i] (1955) R&B#5, new version (1988) UK#51; *Sugar Sweet* (1955) R&B#11, *Trouble No More* (1956) R&B#7. ALBUMS: **Live at Newport** (1960), **Muddy Waters** (1964), **Folk Singer** (1964), **Muddy Waters Sings Big Bill Broonzy** (1964), **Real Folk Blues** (1966), **More Real Folk Blues** (1966), **Muddy, Brass and the Blues** (1967, all Chess); **The Super Super Blues Band** (1968, Checker); **Electric Mud** (1968, Cadet) US#127; **Down on Stovall's Plantation** (1968, Testament); **Sail On** (1969, Chess); **After the Rain** (1969, Cadet); **Fathers and Sons** (1969) US#70, **They Call Me Muddy Waters** (1971), **McKinley Morganfield AKA Muddy Waters** (1971), **The London Sessions** (1972), **Live** (1972), **Can't Get No Grindin'** (1973, all Chess); **Mud in Your Ear** (1973, Muse); **London Revised** (1974), **'Unk in Funk** (1974), **Woodstock Album** (1976, all Chess); **Hard Again** (1977) US#143, **I'm Ready** (1977) US#157, **Mississippi Muddy Waters Live** (1978), **King Bee** (1981, all Blue Sky) US#192; **In Europe with the Muddy Waters Blues Band** with Willie Mae Thornton (1982, Arhoolie); **Live in Antibes, Switzerland, 1976** (1990, JV); **Goin' Home — Live in Paris, 1970** (1992, New Rose). COMPILATIONS: **Best of Muddy Waters** (1959, London Jazz); **Rare Live Recordings, Volume 1** (1972), **Rare Live Recordings, Volume 2** (1972), **Rare Live Recordings, Volume 3** (1972, all Black Bear); **Rare and Unissued** (1985), **Trouble No More — The Singles, 1955–1959** (1989, both Chess); **The Complete Muddy Waters, 1947–1967** (1992, Charly); **The Complete**

Plantation Recordings (1997, Chess). HIT VERSIONS: *Got My Mojo Working* Jimmy Smith (1966) R&B#17, *Key to the Highway* Little Walter (1958) R&B#6, *Rollin' and Tumblin'* Johnny Winter (1969) US#129, *Rollin' Stone* Marigolds (1955) R&B#8. Co-writers: Bo Diddley/M. London.

990. WATERS, Roger (b. George Roger Waters, September 6, 1944, Great Bookham, England) Rock bassist and vocalist. A founder member, alongside Syd Barrett, of the influential psychedelic and progressive rock group Pink Floyd. After Barrett quit the band in 1968, Waters became the dominant songwriter, ultimately creating a series of conceptual albums such as the twenty million selling **Dark Side of the Moon** (1973), which, at seven hundred and forty-one weeks, is the longest charting album ever in America. Waters' increasingly harsh indictments of late twentieth century life, continued with the eight million selling **The Wall** (1979), but after the nihilist **The Final Cut** (1983), he left the group somewhat acrimoniously. CHART COMPOSITIONS: *Money* (1973) US#13, *Us and Them* (1974) US#101, *Another Brick in the Wall* (1979) US#1 UK#1, *Run Like Hell* [i] (1980) US#53, *When the Tigers Break Free* (1982) UK#39, *Not Now John* (1983) UK#30. ALBUMS: **The Piper at the Gates of Dawn** (1967) g UK#6, **A Saucerful of Secrets** (1968) g UK#9, **More** ost (1969, all Columbia) US#153 UK#9; **Ummagumma** (1969) p US#74 UK#5, **Atom Heart Mother** (1970) g US#55 UK#1, **Meddle** (1971) p US#70 UK#3, **Obscured By Clouds** ost (1972) g US#46 UK#6, **Dark Side of the Moon** (1973) p US#1 UK#2, **Wish You Were Here** (1975) p US#1 UK#1, **Animals** (1976) p US#3 UK#2, **The Wall** (1979) p US#1 UK#3, **The Final Cut** (1983, all Harvest) p US#6 UK#1. COMPILATIONS: **Pink Floyd** (1967, Tower) US#131; **Relics** (1971, Regal-Starline) US#152 UK#32; **A Nice Pair** (1974) g US#36 UK#21, **A Collection of Great Dance Songs** (1981, both Harvest) p US#31 UK#37; **Works** (1983, Capitol) US#68; **Shine On** (1992, Harvest) g; **London '66–'67** (1995, See for Miles). Since 1984, Waters has continued his conceptual themes as a solo artist. CHART COMPOSITIONS: *5:01 A.M. (The Pros and Cons of Hitch Hiking)* (1984) US#110, *Radio Waves* (1987) UK#74, *The Tide Is Turning* (1988) UK#54, *What God Wants, Part 1* (1992) UK#35. ALBUMS: **Music from the Body** ost (1970), **The Pros and Cons of Hitch Hiking** (1984, both Harvest) US#31 UK#13; **Radio K.A.O.S.** (1987, EMI) US#50 UK#25; **The Wall — Live in Berlin** (1990, Mercury) US#56 UK#27; **Amused to Death** (1992, Columbia) US#21 UK#8. Co-writer: [i] Dave Gilmour. (*See also under* Syd BARRETT.)

991. WEATHERLY, Frederick Edward (b. 1848; d. 1929) Tin Pan Alley lyricist. A professional lyricist who worked with a variety of partners, and who is best known for writing the words to the traditional Irish lament *Danny Boy* (1912). Some of Weatherley's most popular pre-chart era compositions were: *The Old Brigade* [ii] by Peter Dawson (1881), *Nirvana* [i] by John McCormack (1900), *A May Morning* [iii] by Ernest Pike (1907), *Mifanwy* [iv] by Alice Wilna (1910), and *At Santa Barbara* [v] (1912) and *Friend O'Mine* [vi] (1913), both of which were recorded by Dennis Noble. HIT VERSIONS: *Danny Boy* Ernestine Schumann-Heink (1918) US#5/Glenn Miller (1940) US#17/Al Hibbler (1950) R&B#9/Conway Twitty (1959) R&B#18 US#10/Patti LaBelle & the Bluebells (1964) US#76/Jackie Wilson (1965) R&B#25 US#94/Ray Price (1967) C&W#9 US#60/Andy Williams (1961) US#64; *Holy City, The* [i] Haydn Quartet (1905) US#10/Harry MacDonough (1900) US#2; *Roses of Picardy* [vii] Lambert Murphy (1918) US#3/John McCormack (1919) US#9/Paul Specht (1923) US#6/Vince Hill (1967) UK#13. Co-writers: [i] Stephen Adams, [ii] Odoardo Barri, [iii] Luigi Denza, [iv] Dorothy Foster, [v] Kennedy Russell, [vi] Wilfred Sanderson, [vii] Haydn Wood.

992. WEATHERLY, Jim (b. March 17, 1943, Pontotoc, MS) C&W guitarist and vocalist. A singer-songwriter who composed mid-western, white gospel influenced country melodies, many of which were brilliantly interpreted by Gladys Knight and the Pips. By the late 1970s, over three hundred and fifty different versions of Weatherley's songs had been recorded, and he once said of his songwriting, "I am always re-working and trying to get the best possible song to go down on wax and hope that it will be around forever." Weatherly plied his trade and performed in Los Angeles clubs during the 1960s, one of many scuffling songwriters who eventually landed a job as a staff writer on Jim Nabors' television show, of which he later said, "That was a great experience for me because it taught me discipline in writing." In 1972, he signed to RCA Records for a series of soft, country tinged albums, the first of which **Weatherly** (1973), featured *Midnight Plane to Houston*, a song, that as *Midnight Train to Georgia*, became a million seller for Gladys Knight and the Pips. The country singer Ray Price has recorded over thirty Weatherly songs. CHART COMPOSITIONS: *Loving You Is Just an Old Habit* (1973) US#116, *The Need to Be* (1974) US#11, *I'll Still Love You* (1974) C&W#9 US#87, *It Must Have Been the Rain* (1975) C&W#58, *All That Keeps Me Going* (1977) C&W#27, *Smooth Sailin'* (1979) C&W#32, *Gift from Missouri* (1979) C&W#34, *Safe in the Arms of Your Love (Cold in the Streets)* (1980) C&W#82. ALBUMS: **Weatherly** (1972), **A Gentler Time** (1973), **Jim Weatherly** (1973, all RCA); **The Songs of Jim Weatherly** (1974) US#94, **Magnolias and Misfits** (1975, both Buddah); **The People Some People Choose to Love** (1976), **Pictures and Rhymes** (1976, both ABC). HIT VERSIONS: *Best Thing That Ever Happened to Me, The* Ray Price (1973) C&W#1 US#85/Gladys Knight & the Pips (1974) g R&B#1 US#3 UK#7/Persuaders (1974) R&B#29 US#85; *Between Her Goodbye and My Hello* Gladys Knight & the Pips (1974) R&B#45 US#57, *Farthest Thing from My Mind* Ray Price (1975) C&W#17, *If You Ever Change Your Mind* Ray Price (1975) C&W#31, *Just Enough to Make Me Stay* Bob Luman (1974) C&W#23, *Lady Like You, A* Glen Campbell (1984) C&W#4, *Like a First Time Thing* Ray Price (1974) C&W#15, *Like Old Times Again* Ray Price (1974) C&W#4, *Love Finds Its Own Way* Gladys Knight & the Pips (1975) US#47, *Midnight Train to Georgia* Gladys Knight & the Pips (1973) g R&B#1 US#1 UK#10/Eddie Middleton (1977) C&W#87; *My First Day Without Her* Dennis Yost & the Classics IV (1975) US#94, *Neither One of Us (Wants to Be the First to Say Goodbye)* Gladys Knight & the Pips (1973) R&B#1 US#2 UK#31/Bob Luman (1973) C&W#7/David Sanborn (1983) R&B#56; *Roses and Love Songs* Ray Price (1975) C&W#3, *Say I Do* Ray Price (1975) C&W#40, *Storms of Troubled Times* Ray Price (1974) C&W#25, *This Is a Love Song* Bill Anderson (1979) C&W#20, *Where Do I Put Her Memory* Charley Pride (1979) C&W#1, *Where Peaceful Waters Flow* Gladys Knight & the Pips (1973) R&B#6 US#28, *You Are a Song* Batdorf & Rodney (1975) US#87.

993. WEBB, Jimmy (b. Jimmy Layne Webb, August 15, 1946, Elk City, OK) Pop keyboard player, arranger, producer and vocalist. A singularly inventive songwriter who, like Burt Bacharach, conceives of compositions wherein the melody, lyrics and arrangements are integral elements of an entire song. Webb's use of unusual melodic chordings brought a new maturity to the contemporary popular song during the 1960s, and his orchestral arrangements and intensely personal lyrics were a significant departure from the girl-meets-boy norm. His particular emphasis on large voicings, alternate basses, variable tonalities, and thirty-two bar measures, made him the natural successor to Jimmy Van Heusen. Webb once said of his lyrics, "If people get the feeling, then the lyric is successful, whether they know what I'm talking about or not." His father was a baptist minister who taught him the piano at the age of six. Webb grew up listening to country music, white gospel and pop, and began writing songs at the age of thirteen, moving to California in 1964, where he wrote his first recorded song, the Contessas' *This Is Where I Came In*. Webb's first major success came when the vocal group the 5th Dimension recorded his three million BMI radio performance title track to the album **Up, Up and Away** (1967, Soul City) g US#8, a stylish, refreshing and deftly arranged set of close harmony pop-soul. Webb subsequently wrote, arranged and conducted the group's psychedelic influenced **The Magic Garden** (1968, Soul City) US#105, and later worked with them on **Earthbound** (1975, ABC) US#136. One of his earliest ballads *By the Time I Get to Phoenix*, became a million seller when it was recorded by Glen Campbell, and has since become the third most performed tune in the world, with over five million radio plays in America to date. Between 1967–1970, Webb achieved sixteen hits with versions of his songs, including Campbell's magnificent million seller *Wichita Lineman*, a song inspired by a lineman that Webb had seen working along a deserted Kansas highway, "I wondered what he was listening to, what he was thinking about." Campbell and Webb later collaborated on the albums **Reunion — The Songs of Jimmy Webb** (1974) US#166, and **Live in London at the Royal Festival Hall** (1977, both Capitol) US#171. Webb also wrote and produced a pair of conceptual albums for the actor Richard Harris, **A Tramp Shining** (1968) US#4 and **The Yard Went on Forever** (1968, both Dunhill) US#27, and later Thelma Houston's **Sunflower** (1969, Motown), and the Supremes' **The Supremes** (1972, Tamla) US#129. During the 1970s, Webb recorded a series of frequently excellent solo albums, all of which were crammed with crafted songs, such as his allegorical tale of reincarnation *The Highwayman*, which won a Grammy in 1986 when it was recorded by the country group Highwayman. Art Garfunkel has been one of the most consistent interpreters of Webb's material over the years, their collaborations including the elegant **Watermark** (1978) g US#19 UK#25, and the children's work **The Animal's Christmas** (1986, both Columbia). Garfunkel has described Webb as, "The best songwriter since Paul Simon." Linda Ronstadt included three of his best songs on **Cry Like a Rainstorm, Howl Like the Wind** (1989, Elektra) p US#7 UK#43, and during the 1990s, Webb returned to recording his own, passionately sung albums. ALBUMS: **Jimmy L. Webb: Words and Music** (1970), **And So…On** (1971), **Letters** (1972, all Reprise); **Land's End** (1974, Asylum); **El Mirage** (1977, Atlantic); **Angel Heart** (1982, Columbia/Lorimar); **Suspending Disbelief** (1993, Elektra); **10 Easy Pieces** (1996, Guardian). COMPILATIONS: **Jim Webb Sings Jim Webb** (1966, Epic); **Naked Ape** ost (1973, Playboy); **Voices** ost (1979, Planet); **A Jimmy**

Webb Collection (1982, Columbia/Lorimar); **Songwriters to the Stars, Volume 1** (1983, Polydor); **Archive** (1993, WEA). HIT VERSIONS: *All I Know* Art Garfunkel (1973) US#9, *All My Love's Laughter* Ed Ames (1968) US#122, *By the Time I Get to Phoenix* Glen Campbell (1967) C&W#2 US#26/Ace Cannon (1968) US#110/Del Irwin & Mamie Galore (1968) US#114/Isaac Hayes (1969) R&B#37 US#37/Mad Lads (1969) R&B#29 US#84/Glen Campbell & Anne Murray (1971) US#81/Isaac Hayes & Dionne Warwick (1977) R&B#65; *Carpet Man* 5th Dimension (1968) US#29, *Didn't We* Richard Harris (1969) US#63/Barbra Streisand (1972) US#82; *Do What You Gotta Do* Nina Simone (1968) R&B#43 US#83 UK#2/Bobby Vee (1968) US#83/Al Wilson (1968) R&B#39 US#102/Four Tops (1969) UK#11/Roberta Flack (1971) US#117; *Easy for You to Say* Linda Ronstadt (1982) US#54, *First Hymn from Grand Terrace* Mark Lindsay (1969) US#81, *Galveston* Glen Campbell (1969) g C&W#1 US#4 UK#14/Roger Williams (1969) US#99; *Girl's Song, The* 5th Dimension (1968) US#43, *Highwayman, The* Highwayman (1985) C&W#1, *Honey Come Back* Chuck Jackson (1969) R&B#43/Glen Campbell (1970) C&W#2 US#19 UK#4; *It's a Sin* Glen Campbell (1974) C&W#16/Joe Cocker on B-side of *You Are So Beautiful* (1974) US#5; *Light Years* Glen Campbell (1988) C&W#35, *MacArthur Park* Richard Harris (1968) g US#2 UK#4, re-issued (1972) UK#38/Waylon Jennings & the Kimberleys (1969) C&W#23 US#93/Four Tops (1971) R&B#27 US#38/Andy Williams (1972) US#102/Donna Summer (1978) g R&B#8 US#1 UK#5; *Montage from How Sweet It Is (I Knew You When)* Love Generation (1968) US#86, *Paper Cup* 5th Dimension (1968) US#34, *Song Seller* Paul Revere & the Raiders (1972) US#96, *Still Within the Sound of My Voice* Glen Campbell (1987) C&W#5, *Tell 'Em Willie Boy's a Comin'* Tommy James (1972) US#89, *Up, Up and Away* 5th Dimension (1967) US#7/Johnny Mann Singers (1967) US#91 UK#6/Hugh Masekela (1967) R&B#47 US#71/Al Hirt (1968) US#129; *Where's the Playground Susie?* Glen Campbell (1968) C&W#28 US#26/Everything But the Girl on *Don't Leave Me Behind EP* (1986) UK#72; *Wichita Lineman* Glen Campbell (1969) g C&W#1 US#3 UK#7/Sergio Mendes & Brazil '66 (1969) US#95; *Worst That Could Happen, The* Brooklyn Bridge (1969) g US#3, *Yard Went on Forever, The* Richard Harris (1968) US#64.

994. WEBBER, Lord Andrew Lloyd (b.

March 22, 1948, London, England) Film and stage composer, pianist and arranger. The dominant force in British musical theatre since the mid–1970s, who once had four different shows running consecutively in London. Webber's "Cats" is the most performed show ever on both Broadway and in the West End, and introduced the song *Memory* [iii], which has been recorded over one hundred times, and has received over one million American radio plays. The son of the composer William Lloyd Webber, he studied at the Royal Academy of Music, before composing his first classical piece *The Toy Theatre Suite* (1959). In collaboration with the lyricist Tim Rice, Webber created the much staged, and later filmed, pop oratorio "Joseph and the Technicolor Dream Coat" (1968), which they followed with "Jesus Christ Superstar" (1969) and "Evita" (1976). Webber has only been unsuccessful with one production, his and Alan Ayckbourne's "Jeeves" (1975). His other successful musicals include "Song and Dance" (1982), which was recorded on album by Marti Webb as **Tell Me on a Sunday** (1980, Polydor) UK#2, "Starlight Express" (1984), "The Phantom of the Opera" (1986), and "Aspects of Love" (1989). Despite his phenomenal success, Webber has often been accused of writing clumsy, populist songs, with cloying melodies that have been purloined from the classical repertoire. He also composed for the films "Gumshoe" (1971) and "The Odessa File" (1974), and his songs were recorded on the albums **Festival Evita** (1980, RSO) US#50; **Jose Carreras Sings Andrew Lloyd Webber** (1989, WEA) UK#42; Richard Clayderman's **The Love Songs of Andrew Lloyd Webber** (1989, Decca) UK#18; **Michael Crawford Performs Andrew Lloyd Webber** (1991, Telstar) g US#54 UK#3; **Shirley Bassey Sings Andrew Lloyd Webber** (1993, Premier) UK#56; **James Last Plays Andrew Lloyd Webber** (1993, Polydor) UK#12; and the London Symphony Orchestra's **The Works of Rice and Webber** (1994, Vision) UK#55. In 1996, Webber was made a life peer. ALBUMS: **Jesus Christ Superstar** sc (1970, Decca) g US#1; **Joseph and the Amazing Technicolor Dreamcoat** sc (1971, Scepter) US#84; **Jesus Christ Superstar** sc (1972) US#31 UK#6, **Jesus Christ Superstar** ost (1973) g US#21 UK#23, **Evita** sc (1977) UK#4, **Evita** oc (1978) p US#105 UK#24, **Variations** (1978, all MCA) UK#2; **Cats** oc (1981, Polydor) US#86 UK#6; **Cats** oc (1983, Geffen) p US#113; **Starlight Express** oc (1984, Polydor) UK#21; **Requiem** (1985, HMV) UK#4, **The Phantom of the Opera** oc (1987) p US#33 UK#1, **Aspects of Love** oc (1989, all Polydor) UK#1; **The Premier Collection** (1991, MCA) p US#130; **Joseph and the Amazing Technicolor Dreamcoat** oc (1991) UK#1, **The Phantom of the Opera Highlights** oc (1990) p US#46, **The New Starlight Express** oc (1993) UK#42, **Sunset Boulevard** oc (1993, all Really Useful) US#170 UK#11; **The Premier Collection Encore** (1993, Polydor) US#191; **Evita** ost (1996, Warner Brothers) UK#10. HIT VERSIONS: *All I Ask of You* [iv] Cliff Richard &

Sarah Brightman (1986) UK#3, *Another Suitcase in Another Hall* [v] Barbara Dickson (1977) UK#18, *Any Dream Will Do* [v] Jason Donovan (1991) UK#1, *As if We Never Said Goodbye* Barbra Streisand (1994) UK#20, *Christmas Dream* [v] Perry Como (1974) US#92, *Close Every Door* [v] Phillip Schofield (1992) UK#27, *Don't Cry for Me Argentina* [v] Julie Covington (1976) UK#1/Shadows (1979) UK#5/Festival (1980) US#72/Sinead O'Connor (1992) UK#53/Mike Flowers Pops (1996) UK#30/Madonna (1996) UK#3; *I Don't Know How to Love Him* [v] Helen Reddy (1971) US#13/Yvonne Elliman (1972) US#28 UK#47/Petula Clark (1972) UK#47; *I Only Want to Say (Gethsemane)* [v] Jose Feliciano (1971) US#122, *Joseph Mega-Re-mix* [v] Jason Donovan (1992) UK#13, *Love Changes Everything* [ii] Michael Ball (1989) UK#2, *Memory* [iii] Elaine Paige (1981) UK#6/Barbra Streisand (1982) UK#34/Barry Manilow (1983) US#39/Aled Jones (1985) UK#42; *Music of the Night* [iv] Michael Crawford (1987) UK#7, *Oh What a Circus* [v] David Essex (1978) UK#3, *Phantom of the Opera, The* [iv] Sarah Brightman & Steve Harley (1986) UK#7, *Pie Jesu* Sarah Brightman & Paul Miles-Kingston (1985) UK#3, *Superstar* [v] Murray Head (1971) US#14 UK#42, *Take That Look Off Your Face* [i] Marti Webb (1980) UK#3, *Tell Me on a Sunday* Marti Webb (1980) UK#67, *Wishing You Were Here Again Somehow* [iv] Sarah Brightman (1987) UK#7. Co-writers: [i] Don Black, [ii] Don Black/Charles Hart, [iii] T.S. Eliot/Trevor Nunn, [iv] Charles Hart/Richard Stilgoe, [v] Tim Rice.

995. WEBSTER, Paul Francis (b. December 20, 1907, New York, NY; d. 1984) Film lyricist. Although primarily Sammy Fain's lyricist, Webster also collaborated with a number of other composers on material that was included in such films as "Anastasia" (1956) and "Airport" (1970). ALBUMS: **The Merry Widow** sc (1950, Decca); **April Love** ost (1957, Dot); **Let's Be Happy** ost (1957, RCA); **Mardi Grass** st (1958, Bell); **Rio Bravo** ost (1959, Warner Brothers). HIT VERSIONS: *Airport Love Theme* [x] Vincent Bell (1970) US#31, *Anastasia* [x] Pat Boone (1957) US#37, *Black Coffee* [iv] Sarah Vaughan (1948) US#13, *Got the Jitters* [viii] Ben Pollack (1934) US#9, *How It Lies, How It Lies, How It Lies!* [iv] Connie Haines (1949) US#19/Kay Starr (1949) US#28; *Loveliest Night of the Year* [i] Mario Lanza (1951) g US#3/Slim Whitman (1971) C&W#56, *Masquerade* [vii] Ben Selvin (1928) US#12/Ted Black (1932) US#3; *My Moonlight Madonna* [v] Paul Whiteman (1933) US#11, *Padre* [xiii] Toni Arden (1958) US#13/Marty Robbins (1970) C&W#5 US#113/Judy Lynn (1975) C&W#92; *Rainbow on the River* [ii] Guy Lombardo (1937) US#15, *Shadow of Your Smile, The* [ix] Tony Bennett (1965)

US#95/Boots Randolph (1966) US#93/Lou Rawls (1966) R&B#33; *Somewhere, My Love (Lara's Theme)* [vi] Brass Ring (1966) US#126/Ray Coniff (1966) US#9/Manuel & the Music of the Mountains (1966) UK#42/Red Steagall (1972) C&W#22; *Too Beautiful to Last* [iii] Engelbert Humperdinck (1972) US#86 UK#14, *Two Cigarettes in the Dark* [xii] Bing Crosby (1934) US#5/Glen Gray (1934) US#10/ Johnny Green (1934) US#2/Jerry Johnson (1934) US#6/Frank Parker (1934) US#6. Co-writers: [i] Irving Aaronson/Juventino Rosas, [ii] Louis Alter, [iii] Richard Rodney Bennett, [iv] Sonny Burke, [v] Zdenek Fibich/William Scott, [vi] Maurice Jarre, [vii] John Jacob Loeb, [viii] John Jacob Loeb/Billy Rose, [ix] Johnny Mandel, [x] Alfred Newman, [xii] Lew Pollock, [xiii] Alain Romans. (*See also under* Hoagy CARMICHAEL, Duke ELLINGTON, Sammy FAIN, Jerry LIVINGSTON, Max STEINER, Dimitri TIOMKIN.)

996. WEILL, Cynthia (b. October 18, 1937, New York, NY) Pop lyricist. A former actress, dancer and singer, who teamed up with her future husband Barry Mann, to become one of the Brill Building's greatest success stories. HIT VERSIONS: *All of You* [ii] Julio Iglesias & Diana Ross (1984) R&B#38 US#19, *Just for Tonight* [iii] Vanessa Williams (1992) R&B#11 US#26, *Let Me In* [i] Rick Derringer (1976) US#86. Co-writers: [i] Rick Derringer, [ii] Julio Iglesias/Tony Renis, [iii] K. Thomas. (*See also under* David FOSTER, Frank LOESSER, Brian MANN, Michael MASSER, Tom SNOW.)

997. WEILL, Kurt (b. March 2, 1900, Dessau, Germany; d. April 3, 1950, New York, NY) Film and stage composer, pianist. A highly original and influential composer who blended traditional European musical cabaret, jazz and opera, with American popular songs. Weill studied classical music, and wrote modern symphonic pieces while serving as director of the Luchenscheid Opera Company in the 1920s. After co-writing the one-act opera "Der Protagonist" (1925), he teamed up with the lyricist and poet Bertolt Brecht for "Aufstieg und Fall der Stadt Mahagonny" (1927) and "Die Dreigroschenoper" (1928). Weill and Brecht's most famous work is "The Threepenny Opera" (1954), which introduced the universally performed *Mack the Knife* [ii]. Shortly after writing the shows "Happy End" (1929) and "Der Silbersee" (1933), Weill fled Germany for America, where he achieved further theatrical successes with "The Seven Deadly Sins" (1933), "A Kingdom for a Cow" (1935), "Johnny Johnson" (1936), "Knickerbocker Holiday" (1938), "Railroads on Parade" (1939), and "One Touch of Venus" (1943). A frequent collaborator with the lyri-

cist Ira Gershwin, the duo composed for the shows "Lady in the Dark" (1941) and "The Firebrand of Florence" (1945), alongside the film "Where Do We Go from Here" (1945). Weill's later theatrical works include "Street Scene" (1947), "Love Life" (1948) and "Lost in the Stars" (1949). The best performances of his work were often those by his wife Lotte Lenya, which she recorded on the albums **Berlin Theatre Songs by Kurt Weill** (1955), **The Seven Deadly Sins** (1956, both Columbia); and **Johnny Johnson** (1957, MGM). Weill's songs have also worked well in the British folk medium, *The Black Freighter* and *The Wife of the Soldier* being recorded by Steeleye Span in 1977. Other albums of his songs include **The Bitter Mirror** by Bettina Jonic (1975, Transatlantic) and **Supply and Demand** by Dagmar Krause (1986, Hannibal). ALBUMS: **Street Scene** oc (1947, Columbia); **Love Life** sc (1948, Heritage); **Lost in the Stars** oc (1949, Decca); **Down in the Valley** tvst (1950, RCA); **The Threepenny Opera** oc (1954, Telefunken); **Johnny Johnson** sc (1955, MGM); **Knickerbocker Holiday** rc (1956, Mark); **Down in the Valley** oc (1962, Decca); **Kurt Weill Cabaret** oc (1963, MGM); **Lady in the Dark** oc sc (1963, Columbia); **The Threepenny Opera** ost (1964, RCA); **One Touch of Venus** oc (1965, Decca); **The Rise and Fall of the City of Mahogany** sc (1970), **Seven Deadly Sins** sc (1971, both Columbia); **Berlin to Broadway with Kurt Weill** oc (1972, Paramount); **Happy End** oc (1977, Columbia); **Silver Lake** oc (1980, Nonesuch); **Lost in the Stars** (1985, A&M). HIT VERSIONS: *Alabama Song* [iii] David Bowie (1980) UK#23, *Baals' Hymn* [iii] David Bowie (1982) UK#29, *Bilbao Song, The* [v] Andy Williams (1961) UK#37, *Here I'll Stay* [iv] Jo Stafford (1949) US#28, *Mack the Knife* [ii] Louis Armstrong (1956) US#20 UK#8, re-issued (1959) UK#24, also on *Take It Satch EP* (1956) UK#29/Winifred Atwell on *All Star Hit Parade EP* (1956) UK#2/Richard Hayman & Jan August (1956) US#11/Dick Hyman Trio (1956) US#8 UK#9/Billy Vaughn & His Orchestra (1956) US#37/ Lawrence Welk (1956) US#17/Bobby Darin (1959) R&B#6 US#1 UK#1, re-entry (1960) UK#30, re-issued (1979) UK#64/Ella Fitzgerald (1960) R&B#6 US#27 UK#19/King Kurt (1984) UK#55; *Moon-Faced, Starry-Eyed* Benny Goodman & Johnny Spencer (1947) US#21/Freddy Martin (1947) US#14; *September Song* [i] Walter Huston (1938) US#12/ Dardanelle Trio (1946) US#11/Frank Sinatra (1946) US#8/Don Byas (1948) R&B#14/Stan Kenton (1951) US#17/Liberace (1952) US#27/Jimmy Durante (1963) US#51/Roy Clark (1969) C&W#40 US#103/ Willie Nelson (1979) C&W#15/Ian McCullogh (1984) UK#51; *Speak Low (When You Speak, Love)* [vi] Guy Lombardo (1944) US#5. Co-writers: [i] Maxwell Anderson, [ii] Mark Blitzstein/Bertholt

Brecht, [iii] Bertholt Brecht, [iv] Alan Jay Lerner, [v] Johnny Mercer, [vi] Ogden Nash.

998. WEIR, Bob (b. Robert Hall, October 16, 1947, San Francisco, CA) Rock guitarist and vocalist. The rhythm guitarist in the legendary group the Grateful Dead, who, with the lyricist John Barlow, was the band's second songwriting team after Jerry Garcia and Robert Hunter. Weir co-wrote the group's hit *The Music Never Stopped* [i] (1975) US#81, and has also recorded as a solo artist. CHART COMPOSITION: *Bombs Away* [i] (1978) US#70. ALBUMS: **Ace** (1972, Warner Brothers) US#68; **Kingfish**** (1976, Round) US#50; **Heaven Help the Fool** (1978) US#69, **Bobby and the Midnites*** (1981, both Arista) US#158; **Where the Beat Meets the Street*** (1984, Columbia) US#166. When the Grateful Dead retired in 1995, Weir began performing with his new group Ratdog. As: * Bobby and the Midnites, ** Kingfish. Co-writer: [i] John Barlow. (*See also under* Jerry GARCIA.)

999. WEISS, George David Pop composer. A highly successful pop songwriter whose compositions also featured in the show "Mr. Wonderful" (1956). HIT VERSIONS: *Can Anyone Explain? (No! No! No!)* [ii] Ames Brothers (1950) US#5/Ray Anthony (1950) US#5/Louis Armstrong (1950) US#30/Vic Damone (1950) US#25/Ella Fitzgerald (1950) US#30/Larry Green (1950) US#28/Dick Haymes (1950) US#23/Dinah Shore (1950) US#29; *Confess* [ii] Doris Day & Buddy Clark (1948) US#16/Tony Martin (1948) US#25/Patti Page (1948) US#12; *Cross Over the Bridge* [ii] Patti Page (1954) g US#2, *Dancin' with Someone (Longin' for You)* [i] Teresa Brewer (1953) US#17, *Don't Call My Name* [ii] Helene Dixon (1953) US#27, *Echoes* [ii] Ink Spots (1950) US#24/Jo Stafford & Gordon MacRae (1950) US#18; *How Important Can It Be?* [ii] Joni James (1955) US#2/Sarah Vaughan (1955) US#12; *I Don't See Me in Your Eyes Anymore* [ii] Perry Como (1949) US#11/Gordon Jenkins (1949) US#5/Charlie Rich (1974) C&W#1 US#47; *I Ran All the Way Home* [ii] Buddy Greco (1951) US#30/Sarah Vaughan (1951) US#18; *I Want to Thank Your Folks* [ii] Perry Como (1947) US#21, *I'll Keep the Lovelight Burning* [ii] Patti Page (1949) US#26, *I'll Never Be Free* [ii] Ella Fitzgerald & Louis Jordan (1950) R&B#7/Paul Gayten (1950) R&B#4; *Jet* Nat "King" Cole (1951) US#20, *Let Me Cry on Your Shoulder* [vii] Georgia Gibbs (1965) US#132/Ken Dodd (1967) UK#11; *Mandolins in the Moonlight* [vi] Perry Como (1958) UK#13, *Mister Wonderful* [iv] Teddie King (1956) US#18/Peggy Lee (1956) US#14 UK#5/Sarah Vaughan (1956) US#13; *Oh! What It Seemed to Be* [iii] Frankie Carle (1946) US#1/Helen Forrest & Dick Haymes

(1946) US#4/Frank Sinatra (1946) US#1/Charlie Spivak (1946) US#5; *Pianissimo* [ii] Perry Como (1948) US#21, *Rumors Are Flying* [ii] Andrews Sisters (1946) US#4/Billy Butterfield (1946) US#6/Frankie Carle (1946) US#1/Harry Cool & Mindy Carson (1946) US#12/Tony Martin (1946) US#9/Les Paul (1946) US#1/Betty Jane Rhodes (1946) US#5/Three Suns (1946) US#7; *Surrender* [ii] Perry Como (1946) US#1/Woody Herman (1946) US#8; *That Sunday (That Summer)* [vii] Nat "King" Cole (1963) US#12, *To Think You've Chosen Me* [ii] Eddy Howard (1950) US#9, *Too Close for Comfort* [iv] Eddie Gorme (1956) US#39/Frank Sinatra on *Come Dance with Me LP* (1959) UK#30; *What a Wonderful World* [v] Louis Armstrong (1968) US#116 UK#1/Shane MacGowan & Nick Cave (1992) UK#72; *Wheel of Fortune, The* [ii] Bell Sisters (1952) US#10/Cardinals (1952) R&B#6/Kay Starr (1952) g US#1/Dinah Washington (1952) R&B#3/Bobby Wayne (1952) US#6/Eddie Wilcox & Sunny Gale (1952) R&B#2 US#13/Susan Raye (1972) C&W#16. Co-writers: [i] Alex Alstone/Bennie Benjamin, [ii] Bennie Benjamin, [iii] Bennie Benjamin/Frankie Carle, [iv] Jerry Bock/Larry Holofcener, [v] George Douglas, [vi] Aaron Schroeder, [vii] Joe Sherman. (*See also under* Luigi CREATORE & Hugo PERETI.)

1000. WELCH, Bruce (b. Bruce Cripps, November 2, 1941, Bognor Regis, England) Pop guitarist. A founder member of the British instrumental group the Shadows. Welch first performed as a member of the Railroaders in 1958, before joining the Geordie Boys with guitarist Hank Marvin. As the Drifters, they became Cliff Richard's backing group in the late 1950s, and re-named the Shadows, became one of the most successful British instrumental acts of the 1960s. CHART COMPOSITIONS: *F.B.I.* [vi] (1961) UK#4, *Foot Tapper* [iv] (1963) UK#1, *Shindig* [iv] (1963) UK#6, *The Rise and Fall of Flingle Bunt* [ii] (1964) UK#5, *Theme for Young Lovers* (1964) UK#12, *Genie with the Light Brown Lamp* [ii] (1965) UK#17. ALBUMS: **The Shadows** (1961) UK#1, **Out of the Shadows** (1962) UK#1, **Dance with the Shadows** (1964) UK#2, **The Sound of the Shadows** (1965) UK#4, **Shadow Music** (1966) UK#5, **Jigsaw** (1967) UK#8, **From Hank, Bruce, Brian and John** (1967), **Established 1958** (1968, all Columbia); **Marvin, Welch and Farrar** (1971, Regal Zonophone) UK#30; **Second Opinion** (1971), **Rockin' with Curly Leads** (1974) UK#45, **Specs Appeal** (1975), **Live at the Paris Olympia** (1975), **Tasty** (1977), **Thank You Very Much** with Cliff Richard (1978, all EMI); **Change of Address** (1980) UK#17, **Life in the Jungle/Live at Abbey Road** (1982) UK#24, **XXV** (1983) UK#34, **Guardian Angel** (1983) UK#98, **Moonlight Shad-**

ows (1986) UK#6, **Simply Shadows** (1986) UK#11, **Steppin' to the Shadows** (1994, all Polydor) UK#11; **Reflection** (1995), **Themes and Dreams** (1995), **Shadows in the Night** (1995, all Rollover) UK#22. COMPILATIONS: **Greatest Hits** (1993) UK#2, **More Hits** (1965, both Columbia); **20 Golden Greats** (1977) UK#1, **String of Hits** (1980) UK#1, **Another String of Hits** (1980, all EMI) UK#16; **Hits Right Up Your Street** (1981) UK#15, **At Their Very Best** (1994, both Polydor) UK#12; **Best of Hank Marvin and the Shadows** (1994, PolyGram) UK#19. HIT VERSIONS: *Bachelor Boy* [vii] Cliff Richard (1962) UK#1, *Don't Talk to Him* [vii] Cliff Richard (1963) UK#2, *I Could Easily Fall* [ii] Cliff Richard (1964) UK#9, *I Love You* Cliff Richard (1960) UK#1, *In the Country* [ii] Cliff Richard (1966) UK#6, *Let Me Be There* [viii] Olivia Newton-John (1973) g US#6, *On the Beach* [vi] Cliff Richard (1964) UK#7, *Please Don't Tease* [iii] Cliff Richard (1960) UK#1, *Please, Mr. Please* [viii] Olivia Newton-John (1975) g US#3, *Summer Holiday* [i] Cliff Richard (1963) UK#1, *Time Drags On* [ii] Cliff Richard (1966) UK#10. Co-writers: [i] Brian Bennett (b. February 9, 1940, London, England), [ii] Brian Bennett/Hank B. Marvin (b. Brian Rankin, October 28, 1941, Newcastle, England)/John Rostill, [iii] Peter Chester, [iv] Hank B. Marvin, [v] Hank B. Marvin/Jet Harris (b. Terence Harris, July 6, 1939, London, England), [vi] Hank B. Marvin/Cliff Richard (b. Harry Rodger Webb, October 14, 1940, Lucknow, India), [vii] Cliff Richard, [viii] John Rostill.

1001. WELLER, Paul (b. Paul John William Weller, May 25, 1958, Woking, England) Rock guitarist, pianist and vocalist. One of the most consistently successful punk-rock songwriters during the 1970s, who led the mod influenced trio the Jam. CHART COMPOSITIONS: *In the City* (1977) UK#40, re-issued (1980) UK#40; *All Around the World* (1977) UK#13, re-issued (1980) UK#43; *This Is the Modern World* (1977) UK#36, re-issued (1980) UK#52; *News of the World* (1978) UK#27, re-issued (1980) UK#53; *"A" Bomb in Wardour Street* (1978) UK#25, re-issued (1980) UK#54; *Down in the Tube Station at Midnight* (1978) UK#15, *Strange Town* (1979) UK#15, re-issued (1980) UK#44; *When You're Young* (1979) UK#17, *The Eton Rifles* (1979) UK#3, *Going Underground* (1980) UK#1, *Start* (1980) UK#1, *That's Entertainment* (1981) UK#21, re-issued (1983) UK#60, re-issued (1991) UK#57; *Funeral Pyre* [i] (1981) UK#4, *Absolute Beginners* (1981) UK#4, *Town Called Malice/Precious* (1982) UK#1, *Just Who Is the Five O'Clock Hero* (1982) UK#8, *The Bitterest Pill (I Ever Had to Swallow)* (1982) UK#2, *Beat Surrender* (1982) UK#1, *Live Jam* (1993) UK#28. ALBUMS: **In the City** (1977) UK#20, **This Is the Modern World**

(1977) UK#22, **All Mod Cons** (1978) UK#6, **Setting Sons** (1979) US#137 UK#4, **Sound Effects** (1980) US#72 UK#2, **The Gift** (1982) US#82 UK#1, **Dig the New Breed** (1982) US#131 UK#2. COMPILATIONS: **The Jam** (1982) US#172, **The Bitterest Pill (I Ever Had to Swallow)** (1982) US#135, **Beat Surrender** (1983) US#171, **Snap!** (1983) UK#2, **Greatest Hits** (1991) UK#2, **Extras** (1992) UK#15, **Live** (1993) UK#28, **Direction, Reaction, Creation** (1997, all Polydor) UK#8. In 1982, Weller split the group to form the soul influenced Style Council. CHART COMPOSITIONS: *Speak Like a Child* (1983) UK#4, *The Money-Go-Round* (1983) UK#11, *Paris EP* (1983) UK#3, *Solid Bond in Your Heart* (1983) UK#11, *My Ever Changing Moods* (1984) R&B#88 US#29 UK#5, *Groovin' EP* [ii] (1984) UK#5, *You're the Best Thing* (1984) US#76, *Shout to the Top* (1984) UK#7, *Soul Deep* (1984) UK#24, *The Walls Come Tumbling Down* (1985) UK#6, *Come to Milton Keynes* (1985) UK#23, *The Lodgers* (1985) UK#13, *Have You Ever Had It Blue* (1986) UK#14, *It Didn't Matter* [ii] (1987) UK#9, *Waiting* (1987) UK#52, *Wanted* (1987) UK#11, *Life at a Top People's Health Farm* (1988) UK#28, *How She Threw It All Away* (1988) UK#41, *Long Hot Summer '89* (1989) UK#48. ALBUMS: **Café Bleu** (1984) UK#2, **Our Favorite Shop** (1985) UK#1, **Home and Abroad** (1986) UK#8, **The Cost of Loving** (1987) US#122 UK#2, **Confessions of a Pop Group** (1988, all Polydor) US#174 UK#15. COMPILATIONS: **Introducing the Style Council** (1983) US#172, **My Ever Changing Moods** (1984) US#56, **Internationalists** (1985, all Geffen) US#123; **The Singular Adventures of the Style Council** (1989) UK#3, **Here's Some That Got Away** (1993) UK#16, **The Style Council Collection** (1996, all Polydor) UK#60. Since 1991, Weller has recorded as a solo artist. CHART COMPOSITIONS: *Into Tomorrow* (1991) UK#36, *Uh Huh Oh Yeh* (1992) UK#18, *Above the Clouds* (1992) UK#71, *Sunflower* (1993) UK#16, *Wild Wood* (1993) UK#14, *The Weaver EP* (1993) UK#18, *Hung Up EP* (1994) UK#11, *Out of the Sinking* (1994) UK#20, new version (1996) UK#16; *The Changing Man EP* (1995) UK#7, *You Do Something to Me* (1995) UK#9, *Broken Stones* (1995) UK#20, *Peacock Suit* (1996) UK#5. ALBUMS: **Paul Weller** (1992) UK#8, **Wild Wood** (1993) UK#2, **Live Wood** (1994) UK#13, **Stanley Road** (1995, all Go! Disks) UK#1; **Heavy Soul** (1997, Island) UK#2. COMPILATION: **More Wood** (1994, Pony Canyon). Co-writers: [i] Rick Buckler (b. Paul Richard Buckler, December 6, 1955, Woking, England)/Bruce Foxton (b. September 1, 1955, Woking, England), [ii] Michael Talbot (b. September 11, 1958, London).

1002. WENDLING, Pete (b. June 6, 1888; d. April 8, 1974, both New York, NY) Film and stage composer, pianist. A self-taught ragtime pianist who became a staff piano player at F.A. Mills' publishing house, before becoming a piano roll artist in 1914. During the 1920s, Wendling was the vaudeville artist Lewis F. Muir's accompanist. His first composition was *Soup and Fish Rag* (1913), shortly after which he sold over a million copies of *Yaaka Hula Hickey Dula* [i] by Al Jolson, from Jolson's show "Robinson Crusoe, Jr." (1916). Wendling recorded over a thousand piano rolls, and also cut sides for the record label Cameo. His songs were featured in such films as "Puttin' on the Ritz" (1929). HIT VERSIONS: *By the Sycamore Tree* [i] Bob Roberts (1903) US#2/Harry MacDonough (1904) US#3/Paul Whiteman (1932) US#12; *Oh How I Wish I Could Sleep Until My Daddy Comes Back Home* [iv] Henry Burr (1919) US#3, *On the Street of Regret* [iii] Sammy Kaye (1942) US#21, *Swingin' in a Hammock* [vi] Guy Lombardo (1930) US#3, *There's Danger in Your Eyes, Cherie* [v] Harry Richman (1930) US#4/Fred Waring's Pennsylvanians (1930) US#13; *Yaaka Hula Hickey Dula* [ii] Arthur Collins & Byron Harlan (1916) US#7/Al Jolson (1916) US#2. Co-writers: [i] Haven Gillespie, [ii] E. Ray Goetz/Joe Young, [iii] John Klenner, [iv] Lewis/Joe Young, [v] Jack Meskill, [vi] Charles O'Flynn/Tot Seymour. (*See also under* Edgar LESLIE, George W. MEYER.)

1003. WENRICH, Percy (b. January 23, 1880, Joplin, MO; d. March 17, 1952, New York, NY) Tin Pan Alley composer and pianist. A Chicago Musical College graduate who first composed melodies for a publishing house that consisted of the usual array of rags and waltzes. Wenrich's first big success was with *Peaches and Cream* (1906), which he followed with the two million selling *Put on Your Old Gray Bonnet* [iv] (1909). He enjoyed a lengthy partnership with the lyricist Edward Madden, and from 1914, accompanied his wife Dolly Connolly in vaudeville. HIT VERSIONS: *Kentucky Days* [ii] Peerless Quartet (1912) US#3, *Peaches and Cream* Len Spencer & Ada Jones (1906) US#3, *Put on Your Old Gray Bonnet* [iv] Haydn Quartet (1909) US#1/Arthur Clough (1910) US#3/Byron G. Harlan (1910) US#6/Jimmie Lunceford (1937) US#11; *Rainbow* [i] Billy Murray & Haydn Quartet (1908) US#7/Frank Stanley & Henry Burr (1908) US#4; *Smiler, The* Vess Ossman (1911) US#10, *When You Wore a Tulip and I Wore a Big Red Rose* [iii] American Quartet (1915) US#19/Judy Garland & Gene Kelly (1942) US#19/Johnston Brothers in *Join in and Sing Again #3* (1956) UK#24/Russ Conway in *Party Pops* (1957) UK#24. Co-writers: [i] Alfred Bryan, [ii] Homer Howard, [iii] Jack Mahoney, [iv] Stanley Murphy.

(*See also under* Joe McCARTHY, Edward MADDEN.)

1004. WESTON, Robert P. (b. 1878; d. November 6, 1936, both London, England) Film and stage composer. The songwriting partner of Bert Lee, with whom Weston was one of the most important stylistic developers of the British popular song during the first half of the twentieth century. Weston was a music hall writer in the comic tradition, who in 1905, was one half of the comedy duo Conway and Weston. He also collaborated with Fred Murray on material for such cockney singers as Harry Champion. Weston was fired from his first job when he was discovered composing on the firm's time, shortly after which, he published his first song, *Boys of the Chelsea School*. In 1915, he teamed up with Lee for a twenty year partnership that resulted in some three thousand songs, many of which were featured in seventeen films and seventy-five stage shows. Always able to adapt to the ever changing music scene, Weston and Lee moved on from music hall through variety, revue, musical comedy and film, composing some of the most memorable post World War I songs of the period, including *Any Complaints? No!* [iv], *The Brave Old Contemptibles* [iv] and *In a Land Fit for Heroes* [iv]. Lee and Weston pre-dated the Brill Building era by some thirty years, and initially worked on a nine to five basis with the ambition of completing at least one song per day. They later penned sketches for music hall and revue, and during the 1920s contributed to a number of stage productions, including "A to Z," "Pot Luck," "You'd Be Surprised," and "Leap Year." The duo also adapted various American shows for the British theatre, and in partnership with Jack Waller and Joe Tunbridge, they wrote and composed the musical comedies "Tell Her the Truth" (1926), "He Wanted Adventure" (1927) and "Yes, Madam" (1928). Weston and Lee were masters at reflecting the passions, trends or moods of their times, and to a certain degree, songs such as *We'll Have a Woolworth Wedding* [iv] and *Stop and Shop at the Co-op Shop* [iv] (both 1930), are astute sociological satires and historical documents. Some of Weston's biggest pre-chart era hits were: *What a Mouth* by Harry Champion (1906), *The Hobnailed Boots That Farver Wore* [i] by Billy Williams (1907), *The End of Me Old Cigar* by Harry Champion (1914), *Paddy McGinty's Goat* [iv] by David McAlpin (1917), *My Word You Do Look Queer* [iv] (1922) and *With Her Head Tucked Underneath Her Arm* [iv] (1934), both by Stanley Holloway (1934); *Olga Pulloffski (The Beautiful Spy)* [iv] by Jack Hylton (1935), and *And the Great Big Saw Came Near* by Leslie Sarony (1936). HIT VERSIONS: *Goodbye-ee* [iv] Peter Cook & Dudley Moore (1965) UK#18, *I'm 'Enery* *the Eighth, I Am* [vi] Herman's Hermits (1965) g US#1, *I've Got Rings on My Fingers* [ii] Blanche Ring (1909) US#1/Ada Jones (1909) US#1/Billy Murray (1910) US#9/Dick Kuhn (1943) US#20; *Sister Susie's Sewing Shirts for Soldiers* [iii] Al Jolson (1915) US#6/Billy Murray (1915) US#7. Co-writers: [i] Fred J. Barnes, [ii] Fred J. Barnes/Maurice Scott, [iii] Herman Darewski, [iv] Bert Lee, [v] Bert Lee/E.H. Weston, [vi] Fred Murray.

1005. WHEELER, Billy Edd (b. December 9, 1932, Whitesville, WV) C&W guitarist and vocalist. A country and folk tinged singer-songwriter whose songs were widely recorded, arguably the best interpretation of all being *Coming of the Roads* by Judy Collins. CHART COMPOSITIONS: *Ode to the Little Brown Shack Out Back* (1964) C&W#3 US#50, *I Ain't the Worryin' Kind* (1968) C&W#63, *West Virginia Woman* (1969) C&W#51, *Fried Chicken and a Country Tune* (1969) C&W#62, *200 Lbs. O' Slingin' Hound* (1972) C&W#71, *Duel Under the Snow* (1979) C&W#94, *Daddy* (1981) C&W#55. ALBUM: **Memories of America/Ode to The Little Brown Shack Out Back** (1965, Kapp) US#132. HIT VERSIONS: *Blistered* Johnny Cash (1969) C&W#4 US#50, *Coward of the County* [i] Kenny Rogers (1979) g C&W#1 US#3 UK#1, *Jackson* [ii] Johnny Cash & June Carter (1967) C&W#2/Nancy Sinatra & Lee Hazlewood (1967) US#14 UK#11; *Reverend Mr. Black* Kingston Trio (1963) US#8/Johnny Cash (1982) C&W#71. Co-writers: [i] Roger Bowling, [ii] Gaby Roders.

1006. WHITE, Barry (b. September 12, 1944, Galveston, TX) R&B multi-instrumentalist, producer and vocalist. A major R&B star during the 1970s, whose songs and productions have generated an estimated one hundred million record sales worldwide. White has also acquired nearly one hundred and fifty gold and platinum disks, with his lush, orchestral style, that was an influence on such later vocalists as Luther Vandross. White grew up in Los Angeles, where he first sang in church choirs and learned various musical instruments. In his teens he played in the Upfronts, which recorded a number of singles for Lummtone Records, after which, White scuffled around on the fringes of the music business for most of the 1960s, later saying, "You could hear me coming two blocks away. That's how badly my shoes flapped." White claims to have co-written and arranged, despite being uncredited, Bob and Earl's hit *Harlem Shuffle* (1963), after which he sessioned as a keyboard player on numerous R&B disks. In 1965 he arranged *The Duck* for Jackie Lee, and later became Lee's road manager, before touring as Earl Nelson's drummer and recording as Barry Lee for Veep Records. White became an A&R man for Mustang-Bronco Records during the mid–1960s, where he wrote *It May Be Winter Outside (But in My Heart It's Spring)* [iii] for Felice Taylor (1967). When the label went bankrupt, White concluded that the only way he would ever record the kind of music that he wanted, would be to make the records himself. He thus learned studio engineering and as many musical instruments as he could master. In 1968, he discovered the girl vocal trio Love Unlimited, which scored a million seller with his light soul number *Walkin' in the Rain with the One I Love*. White subsequently formed his own production company Soul Unlimited, and signed a solo deal at 20th Century Records, where he would spend most of the 1970s dominating the pop and R&B charts. In 1978, White created his own Unlimited Gold label, but during the 1980s his record sales began a steady decline, resulting in his complete withdrawal from recording and performance. After updating his home recording studio in Sherman Oaks, California, White launched a successful come-back during the late 1980s. He once said of his songs, "You can tell a great song from a good one by what you throw away." CHART COMPOSITIONS: *I'm Gonna Love You Just a Little More Baby* (1973) g R&B#1 US#3 UK#23, *I've Got So Much Love to Give* (1973) R&B#5 US#32, *Never, Never Gonna Give You Up* (1974) g R&B#2 US#7 UK#14, re-mixed (1987) UK#63; *Honey Please, Can't You See* (1974) R&B#6 US#44, *Can't Get Enough of Your Love, Babe* (1974) g R&B#1 US#1 UK#8, *You're the First, the Last, My Everything* [iv] (1974) g R&B#1 US#2 UK#1, *What Am I Gonna Do with You?* (1975) R&B#1 US#8 UK#5, *I'll Do for You Anything You Want Me To* (1975) R&B#4 US#40 UK#20, *Let the Music Play* (1976) R&B#4 US#32 UK#9, *Baby, We Better Try to Get It Together* (1976) R&B#29 US#92 UK#15, *Don't Make Me Wait Too Long* (1976) R&B#20 US#105, *I'm Qualified to Satisfy You* (1976) R&B#25, *Playing Your Game, Baby* (1978) R&B#8 US#101, *Oh What a Night for Dancing* [vi] (1978) R&B#13 US#24, *Your Sweetness Is My Weakness* (1978) R&B#2 US#60, *Sha La La Means I Love You* (1978) UK#55, *Any Fool Could See (You Were Meant for Me)* (1979) R&B#37, *It Ain't Love, Babe (Until You Give It)* (1979) R&B#58, *I Love to Sing the Songs I Sing* (1979) R&B#53, *How Did You Know It Was Me?* (1979) R&B#64, *Love Ain't Easy* (1980) R&B#75, *Sheet Music* (1980) R&B#43, *I Love Makin' Music* (1980) R&B#25, *I Believe in Love* (1980) R&B#71, *Didn't We Make It Happen, Baby** (1981) R&B#78, *I Want You** (1981) R&B#79, *Beware* (1981) R&B#49, *Change* (1982) R&B#12, *Passion* (1982) R&B#65, *Sho' You Right* (1987) R&B#17 UK#14, *For Your Love (I'll Do Most Anything)* (1987) R&B#27, *Super Love* (1988) R&B#34, *Put Me in*

Your Mix [ii] (1991) R&B#8, *Dark and Lovely (You Over There)* with Isaac Hayes (1992) R&B#30, *Practice What You Preach* (1994) g US#18 UK#20, *I Only Want to Be with You* (1995) UK#36, *Come On* (1995) US#87. ALBUMS: **I've Got So Much to Give** (1973) g US#16, **Stone Gon'** (1973) g US#20 UK#18, **Together Brothers** ost (1974) US#96, **Can't Get Enough** (1974) g US#1 UK#4, **Just Another Way to Say I Love You** (1975) g US#17 UK#12, **Let the Music Play** (1976) US#42 UK#22, **Is This Whatcha Wont?** (1976) US#125, **Barry White Sings for Someone You Love** (1977) p US#8, **Barry White Is the Man** (1978, all 20th Century) p US#36 UK#46; **The Message Is Love** (1979, Unlimited Gold) g US#27; **I Love The Songs I Sing** (1979, 20th Century) US#132; **Sheet Music** (1980) US#85, **Barry and Glodean*** (1981), **Change** (1982) US#148, **Dedicated** (1983), **Beware** (1984, all Unlimited Gold); **The Right Night and Barry White** (1987) US#159 UK#74, **The Man Is Back** (1988) US#148, **Put Me in Your Mix** (1991) US#96, **The Icon Is Love** (1995, all A&M) p US#20 UK#44. COMPILATIONS: **No Limit on Love** (1974, Supremacy); **Greatest Hits** (1975) g US#23 UK#18, **Greatest Hits, Volume 2** (1977, both 20th Century) UK#17; **Heart and Soul** (1985, K-Tel) UK#34; **Best of Barry White** (1988, Casablanca); **The Collection** (1990, Mercury) UK#5; **Just for You** (1993, PolyGram). HIT VERSIONS: *Baby Blues* Love Unlimited Orchestra (1974) US#102, *Can't Get Enough of Your Love, Babe* Taylor Dayne (1993) US#20 UK#14, *Forever in Love* Love Unlimited Orchestra (1975) R&B#22, *High Steppin', Hip Dressin' Fella (You Got It Together)* Love Unlimited (1979) R&B#45, *I Belong to You* Love Unlimited (1974) g R&B#1 US#27, *I Did It for Love* Love Unlimited (1977) R&B#66, *I Feel Love Comin' On* Felice Taylor (1967) UK#11, *I'm So Glad I'm a Woman* Love Unlimited (1980) R&B#96, *I'm Under the Influence of Love* Love Unlimited (1974) R&B#70 US#76, *If You Want Me, Say It* Love Unlimited (1980) R&B#71, *Is It Really True Boy, Is It Really Me* Love Unlimited (1972) US#101, *It May Be Winter Outside (But in My Heart It's Spring)* [iii] Felice Taylor (1967) R&B#44 US#42/Love Unlimited (1973) R&B#35 US#83 UK#11; *Just as Long as We're Together (In My Life There Will Never Be Another)* Gloria Scott (1975) R&B#14, *Love's Theme* [v] Love Unlimited Orchestra (1974) g R&B#10 US#1 UK#10, *Mary Hartman Theme, The* Deadly Nightshade (1976) US#79, *Midnight Groove* Love Unlimited Orchestra (1976) R&B#91 US#108, *Music Maestro Please* Love Unlimited Orchestra (1974) US#92, *My Sweet Summer Suite* Love Unlimited Orchestra (1976) R&B#28 US#48, *Rhapsody in White* Love Unlimited Orchestra (1974) R&B#48 US#63, *Satin Soul* Love Unlimited Orchestra (1974) R&B#23

US#22, *Share a Little Love in Your Heart* Love Unlimited Orchestra (1975) R&B#21, *Walkin' in the Rain with the One I Love* Love Unlimited (1972) g R&B#6 US#14 UK#14, *What Am I Gonna Do with You* Gloria Scott (1974) R&B#74, *Yes, We Finally Made It* Love Unlimited (1973) R&B#70 US#101, *You and Your Baby Blues* [i] Solomon Burke (1975) R&B#19 US#96, *You're the First, the Last, My Everything* [iv] O.C. Smith (1986) R&B#52. With: * Glodean White. Co-writers: [i] M. Brooks/Tony Sepe, [ii] H. Johnson, [iii] P. Politi, [iv] Peter Radcliffe/Tony Sepe, [v] Aaron Schroeder, [vi] Vance Wilson.

1007. WHITE, Dave (b. David White Tricker, September, 1940, Philadelphia, PA) Doo-wop vocalist. An original member of the vocal group Danny and the Juniors, for which he co-wrote one of the most famous songs of the era *At the Hop* [ii] (1957) p US#1 UK#3, re-issued (1976) UK#39, and the follow-up *Rock and Roll Is Here to Stay* (1958) US#19. ALBUMS: **Rock and Roll Is Here to Stay** (1987, Singular); **Rockin' with Danny and the Juniors** (1988, MCA). White also recorded the solo album **David White Tricker** (1971, Bell). HIT VERSIONS: *Fly, The* [i] Chubby Checker (1961) R&B#11 US#7, *Like a Baby* [i] Len Barry (1966) US#27 UK#10, *You Don't Own Me* [i] Lesley Gore (1964) US#2. Co-writers: [i] John Madera, [ii] John Madera/ Artie Singer. (*See also under* Brian HOLLAND, Lamont DOZIER and Eddie HOLLAND.)

1008. WHITE, Maurice (b. December 19, 1941, Memphis, TN) R&B percussionist, producer and vocalist. A Chicago Conservatory of Music graduate, who studied composition and percussion before becoming a session drummer at Chess Records, where he joined the Ramsey Lewis Trio in 1966. ALBUMS: **Swingin'** (1966), **Wade in the Water** (1966) US#16, **The Movie Album** (1967) US#124, **Goin' Latin** (1967) US#95, **Dancing in the Street** (1968) US#59, **Up Pops Ramsey Lewis** (1969) US#52, **Maiden Voyage** (1968) US#55, **Mother Nature's Son** (1969) US#156, **Another Voyage** (1969) US#139, **Best of Ramsey Lewis** (1970, all Cadet). White subsequently formed the unsuccessful group the Salty Peppers, before, in 1971, creating Earth, Wind and Fire, which became one of the most successful R&B bands of the 1970s, blending a potent mix of Latin, funk, jazz, rock, disco, gospel and Egyptology. In 1994, White composed the music to the animated television series "Gatchaman." CHART COMPOSITIONS: *Love Is Life* (1971) R&B#43 US#93, *I Think About Lovin' You* (1972) R&B#44, *Evil* [ii] (1973) R&B#25 US#50, *Keep Your Head to the Sky* (1973) R&B#23 US#52, *Mighty Mighty* [xviii] (1974) R&B#4 US#29, *Kalimba Story* [xviii] (1974) R&B#6 US#55, *Devotion* [ii] (1974) R&B#23 US#33, *Hot Dawgit* [xviii]* (1975) R&B#61 US#50, *Shining Star* [ii] (1975) g R&B#1 US#1, *Sun Goddess* [xi]* (1975) R&B#20 US#44, *That's the Way of the World* [xvi] (1975) R&B#5 US#12, *Sing a Song* [xii] (1975) p R&B#1 US#5, *Saturday Nite* [xii] (1976) R&B#4 US#21 UK#17, *Serpentine Fire* [iv] (1977) R&B#1 US#13, *Fantasy* [v] (1978) R&B#12 US#32, *Jupiter* [iii] (1978) UK#41, *Magic Mind* [iii] (1978) UK#54, *September* [xiii] (1978) g R&B#1 US#8 UK#3, *In the Stone* [ix] (1979) R&B#23 US#58 UK#53, *Star* [vi] (1979) R&B#47 US#64 UK#16, *Let Me Talk* [iii] (1980) R&B#8 US#44 UK#29, *You* [viii] (1981) R&B#10 US#48, *Back on the Road* [xii] (1980) UK#63, *And Love Goes On* [vii] (1981) R&B#15 US#59, *Let's Groove* [xvii] (1981) p R&B#1 US#3 UK#3, *Wanna Be with You* [xvii] (1982) R&B#15 US#51, *I've Had Enough* (1982) UK#29, *Fall in Love with Me* [xvii] (1983) R&B#4 US#17 UK#47, *Side By Side* [xii] (1983) R&B#15 US#76, *Spread Your Love* (1983) R&B#57, *Magnetic* (1983) R&B#10 US#57, *Touch* (1984) R&B#23 US#103, *Moonwalk* (1984) R&B#67, *System of Survival* (1987) R&B#1 US#60 UK#54, *Thinking of You* [xvii] (1988) R&B#3 US#67, *Sunday Morning* [x] (1993) R&B#20 US#53, *Two Hearts* [i] (1994) R&B#88. ALBUMS: **Earth, Wind and Fire** (1971) US#172, **The Need of Love** (1972, both Warner Brothers) US#89; **Last Days and Time** (1972) US#87, **Head to the Sky** (1973) g US#27, **Open Our Eyes** (1974) p US#15, **That's the Way of the World** ost (1975) p US#1, **Gratitude** (1975) p US#1, **Spirit** (1976) p US#2, **All 'N All** (1978) p US#3 UK#13, **I Am** (1979) p US#3 UK#5, **Faces** (1980) g US#10 UK#10, **Raise!** (1981) p US#5 UK#14, **Powerlight** (1983) g US#12 UK#22, **Electric Universe** (1983) US#40, **Touch the World** (1987) p US#33, **Heritage** (1990, all Columbia) US#70; **Millenium** (1993, Warner Brothers) US#39; **The Revolution** (1997, Eagle). COMPILATIONS: **Another Time** (1974, Warner Brothers) US#97; **Best of Earth, Wind and Fire, Volume 1** (1979, Columbia) p US#6 UK#6; **The Collection** (1986, K-Tel) UK#5; **Very Best of Earth, Wind and Fire** (1992, Telstar) UK#40; **The Eternal Dance** (1992, Columbia). White has also produced other acts and recorded as a solo artist, charting with *I Need You* (1985) R&B#30 US#95 and *Lady Is Love* (1986) R&B#89, from the album **Maurice White** (1985, ARC) US#61. HIT VERSIONS: *Best of My Love* [xii] Emotions (1977) g R&B#1 US#1 UK#4, *Fantasy* [v] Black Box (1990) UK#5, *Flowers* [xii] Emotions (1977) R&B#16 US#87, *I Am Love* [ix] Jennifer Holliday (1983) R&B#2 US#49, *Skat Strut* [xiv] MC Skat & Stray Mob (1991) R&B#94 US#80, *3-2-1 Pump* [x] Redhead Kingpin & F.B.I. (1992) US#52.

With: * Ramsey Lewis. Co-writers: [i] Burt Bacharach/Philip Bailey (b. May 8, 1951, Denver, CO), [ii] Philip Bailey, [iii] Philip Bailey/Larry Dunn (b. June 19, 1953, CO)/Ralph Johnson (b. July 4, 1951, CA)/Albert McKay (b. February 2, 1948, LA)/Vernon White (b. July 25, 1951), [iv] S. Burke/Vernon White, [v] Eddie De Barrio/Verdine White, [vi] Eddie De Barrio/Allee Willis, [vii] Larry Dunn/ David Foster/Brenda Russell/Vernon White, [viii] David Foster/Brenda Russell, [ix] David Foster/Allee Willis, [x] D. Guppy/Wayne Vaughn, [xi] T. Lind, [xii] Albert McKay, [xiii] Albert McKay/Allee Willis, [xiv] R. Malco/Wayne Vaughn, [xv] Reynolds/Allee Willis, [xvi] C. Stepney, [xvii] Wayne Vaughn, [xviii] Vernon White.

1009. WHITE, Tony Joe (b. July 23, 1943, Oak Grove, LA) Rock guitarist and vocalist. A folk and country influenced singer-songwriter with a deep, laconic southern drawl and laid-back sound. White's finely sketched characters examine the customs, prejudices and injustices of southern American life with wit and verve. He grew up in rural surroundings, where he listened to the blues, folk, country and cajun, and after learning the guitar in his teens, he performed as Tony and the Mojos and as Tony and the Twilights. Seven years on the Texas nightclub scene, and a spell as a staff writer at Combine Music during the 1960s, finally resulted in a record contract and a series of albums that were an intriguing mix of blues, country, white gospel, funk and psychedelic wah-wah guitar. White's songs were often hits for other artists, his ballad *Rainy Night in Georgia* becoming a million seller for Brook Benton. White has also worked as a session player and writer for such artists as Waylon Jennings and Tina Turner. In 1974, he composed the score to "Catch My Soul," a black musical version of Shakespeare's "Othello." CHART COMPOSITIONS: *Polk Salad Annie* (1968) US#8, *Roosevelt and Ida Lee* (1969) US#44, *High Sheriff of Calhoun County* (1970) US#112, *Save Your Sugar for Me* (1970) US#94, *Groupie Girl* (1970) UK#22, *Scratch My Back* (1970) US#117, *It Must Be Love* (1976) US#108, *I Can Get Off on You* (1980) US#79, *Mama Don't Let Your Cowboys Grow Up to Be Babies* (1980) C&W#91, *The Lady in My Life* (1983) C&W#55, *We Belong Together* (1984) C&W#85. ALBUMS: **Black and White** (1968) US#51, **Continued** (1969) US#183, **Tony Joe** (1970, all Monument) UK#63; **Tony Joe White** (1971) US#167, **The Train I'm On** (1972), **Home Made Ice Cream** (1973, all Warner Brothers); **Catch My Soul** ost (1974, Metromedia); **Eyes** (1976), **Tony Joe White** (1977, both 20th Century); **The Real Thang** (1980, Casablanca); **Dangerous** (1983, Columbia); **Live in Europe, 1971** (1990, Dixie Frog); **Closer to the Truth**

(1992), **The Path of a Decent Groove** (1993), **Lake Placid Blues** (1995, all Polydor). COMPILATION: **Best of Tony Joe White** (1975, Warner Brothers). HIT VERSIONS: *For Ol' Times Sake* Elvis Presley (1973) C&W#42 US#41, *I've Got a Thing About You Baby* Troy Seals (1973) C&W#93/Elvis Presley (1974) C&W#4 US#39; *Polk Salad Annie* Elvis Presley (1973) UK#23, *Rainy Night in Georgia* Brook Benton (1970) g R&B#1 US#4/Hank Williams, Jr. (1974) C&W#13/Randy Crawford (1981) UK#18; *Steamy Windows* Tina Turner (1989) US#39 UK#13, *Willie and Laura Mae Jones* Dusty Springfield (1969) US#78.

1010. WHITFIELD, Norman (b. 1943, New York, NY). R&B producer. One of the most innovative R&B songwriter-producers of the 1960–1970s, whose work with the vocal group the Temptations is unsurpassed in the genre. Whitfield brought a maturer sound to Motown Records during the early 1970s, and, frequently in collaboration with Barrett Strong, was one of the label's most prolific composers. In 1964, Whitfield replaced Smokey Robinson as the Temptations' producer, and proceeded to re-define the group's sound completely, with tighter production that vigorously emphasized the full tonal versatility of the group. Whitfield's later albums with the group were Motown's first conceptual works, and introduced socially concerned lyrical themes and dramatic string arrangements, all of which were later to influence Sly Stone, George Clinton and Prince. The pinnacle of his achievements with the Temptations was the brooding, meticulously arranged *Papa Was a Rolling Stone* [viii] (1972), a masterpiece of modern recording techniques and contemporary R&B. Between 1967–1970, Whitfield also worked with Gladys Knight and the Pips, for which he employed a more gospel influenced sound. The group were the first to record one of the best known songs of the late twentieth century, *I Heard It Through the Grapevine* [viii], different versions of which have topped the R&B charts an unprecedented three times. Whitfield later worked with the group the Undisputed Truth, before forming his own Whitfield label in the early 1970s, upon which he produced the vocal act Rose Royce. HIT VERSIONS: *Ball of Confusion (That's What the World Is Today)* [viii] Temptations (1970) R&B#2 US#3 UK#7, *Car Wash* Rose Royce (1976) p R&B#1 US#1 UK#9, re-issued (1988) UK#20/Gwen Dickey (1990) UK#72; *Cloud Nine* [viii] Temptations (1969) R&B#2 US#6 UK#15/Mongo Santamaria (1969) R&B#33 US#32; *Do Your Dance* [ix] Rose Royce (1977) R&B#4 US#39 UK#30, *Don't Let Him Take Your Love from Me* [viii] Jimmy Ruffin (1968) US#113/ Four Tops (1969) US#45; *Don't Let The Jones's Get*

You Down [viii] Temptations (1969) R&B#2 US#20, *Don't You Miss Me a Little Bit, Baby* Jimmy Ruffin (1967) R&B#27 US#68, *End of Our Road, The* [vi] Gladys Knight & the Pips (1968) R&B#5 US#15/ Marvin Gaye (1970) US#40; *Friendship Train* [viii] Gladys Knight & the Pips (1969) R&B#2 US#17, *Funky Music Sho' Nuff Turns Me On* [viii] Edwin Starr (1971) R&B#6 US#64/Temptations (1972) R&B#27 US#92/Yvonne Fair (1974) R&B#32; *Girl (Why You Wanna Make Me Blue)* [viii] Temptations (1964) US#26, *Girl You're Alright* Undisputed Truth (1972) R&B#43 US#107, *Gonna Give Her All the Love I've Got* [viii] Jimmy Ruffin (1967) R&B#14 US#29, *Heavenly* Temptations (1974) R&B#8 US#43, *Help Yourself* Undisputed Truth (1974) R&B#19 US#63, *Hey Girl (I Like Your Style)* Temptations (1973) R&B#2 US#35, *How Can I Forget You* Marvin Gaye (1970) R&B#18 US#41, *Hum Along and Dance* Rare Earth (1973) R&B#95 US#110, *I Can't Get Next to You* [viii] Temptations (1969) R&B#1 US#1 UK#13/Al Green (1970) R&B#11 US#60; *I Could Never Love Another (After Loving You)* [vi] Temptations (1968) R&B#1 US#13 UK#47, *I Gotta Let You Go* Martha & the Vandellas (1970) R&B#43 US#93, *I Heard It Through the Grapevine* [viii] Gladys Knight & the Pips (1967) R&B#1 US#2 UK#47/Marvin Gaye (1968) US#1 UK#1, re-issued (1986) UK#8/King Curtis (1968) US#83/Creedence Clearwater Revival (1976) US#43/Slits (1979) UK#60/ Elton John on B-side of *Who Wears These Shoes?* (1984) UK#50/Roger (1981) R&B#1 US#79/California Raisins (1988) US#84; *I Truly, Truly Believe* [viii] Temptations (1968) R&B#41 US#116, *I Wanna Get Next to You* Rose Royce (1977) R&B#3 US#10 UK#14, *I Wish It Would Rain* [vi] Gladys Knight & the Pips (1968) R&B#15 US#41/Temptations (1968) R&B#1 US#4 UK#45/Faces (1973) UK#8/O.B. McClinton (1973) C&W#67; *I'm Going Down* Rose Royce (1977) R&B#10 US#70, *I'm in Love (And I Love the Feeling)* Rose Royce (1978) R&B#5 UK#51, *It Makes You Feel Like Dancin'* Rose Royce (1977) UK#16, *It Should Have Been Me* [vii] Gladys Knight & the Pips (1968) R&B#9 US#40/Yvonne Fair (1976) US#85 UK#5/Adeva (1991) UK#48; *It's Summer* Temptations (1971) R&B#29 US#51, *Just My Imagination (Running Away with Me)* [viii] Temptations (1971) R&B#1 US#1 UK#8, *Law of the Land* Temptations (1973) UK#41/Undisputed Truth (1973) R&B#40; *Let Your Hair Down* Temptations (1973) R&B#1 US#27, *Ma* Rare Earth (1973) US#108, *Mama I Gotta Brand New Thing (Don't Say No)* Undisputed Truth (1973) R&B#46 US#109, *Masterpiece* Temptations (1973) R&B#1 US#7, *Mother Nature* Temptations (1972) US#92, *Needle in a Haystack* Velvettes (1964) R&B#45 US#45, *On a Sunday Afternoon* [i] A Lighter Shade of Brown (1991)

US#43, *Ooh Boy* Rose Royce (1977) R&B#3 US#72 UK#46, *Papa Was a Rolling Stone* [viii] Temptations (1972) R&B#5 US#1 UK#14, re-mixed (1987) UK#31/ Undisputed Truth (1972) R&B#24 US#63/Stars On in *Stars On Long Play 2/On 45 Volume 2* (1981) US#120 UK#18/Bill Wolfer (1982) R&B#47 US#55/ Was (Not Was) (1990) UK#12/George Michael & Queen (1993) R&B#88 US#69, also on *Five Live EP* (1993) US#46 UK#1; *Plastic Man* Temptations (1973) R&B#8 US#40, *Please Return Your Love to Me* [viii] Temptations (1968) R&B#4 US#26, *Pop Your Fingers* Rose Royce (1980) R&B#60, *Psychedelic Shack* [viii] Temptations (1970) R&B#2 US#7 UK#33, *Put Your Money Where Your Mouth Is* Rose Royce (1977) UK#44, *Rose Royce Express* Rose Royce (1981) UK#52, *Runaway Child, Running Wild* [viii] Temptations (1969) R&B#1 US#6/Earl Van Dyke (1969) US#114; *Sail Away* [ii] Temptations (1983) US#54, *Save My Love for a Rainy Day* Undisputed Truth (1971) R&B#43, *Smiling Faces Sometimes* Undisputed Truth (1971) R&B#2 US#3, *Stop the War Now* Edwin Starr (1970) R&B#5 US#26, *Superstar (Remember How You Got Where You Are)* [viii] Temptations (1972) R&B#8 US#18 UK#32, *Take a Look Around* [viii] Temptations (1972) R&B#10 US#30 UK#13, *That's the Way Love Is* [viii] Isley Brothers (1967) US#125/Marvin Gaye (1969) US#7; *Too Busy Thinking 'Bout My Baby* [iv] Marvin Gaye (1969) US#4 UK#5/Billy Mitchell Group (1969) R&B#49/ Young Vandals (1970) R&B#41/Orbit featuring Carol Hall (1984) R&B#66; *Ungena Za Ulimwengu (Unite the World)* Temptations (1970) R&B#8 US#33, *War* [viii] Edwin Starr (1970) R&B#3 US#1 UK#3/ Bruce Springsteen (1986) US#8 UK#18; *What It Is* Undisputed Truth (1972) R&B#35 US#71, *Which Way Is Up* Starguard (1977) R&B#1 US#21 UK#19, *You Gotta Believe* Pointer Sisters (1977) R&B#14 US#103, *You Make Your Own Heaven and Earth Right Here on Earth* Undisputed Truth (1971) R&B#24 US#72, *You Need Love Like I Do (Don't You?)* Gladys Knight & the Pips (1970) R&B#3 US#25, *You + Me = Love* Undisputed Truth (1977) R&B#37 US#48 UK#43, *You're My Everything* [v] Temptations (1967) R&B#3 US#6 UK#26, *You've Got My Soul on Fire* [viii] Edwin Starr (1973) R&B#40/Temptations (1974) R&B#8 US#72. Co-writers: [i] Blouin/Carter/Chulo/Gutierrez/Ramirez/ Barrett Strong, [ii] Angelo Bond, [iii] Janie Bradford, [iv] Janie Bradford/Barrett Strong, [v] Cornelius Grant/Roger Penzabene, [vi] Roger Penzabene/Barrett Strong, [vii] William Stevenson, [viii] Barrett Strong, [ix] D. Turner. (*See also under* George CLINTON, Marvin GAYE, Brian HOLLAND, Lamont DOZIER and Eddie HOLLAND, Roger TROUTMAN.)

1011. WHITING, Richard A. (b. November 12, 1891, Peoria, IL; d. February 10, 1938, Beverly Hills, CA) Film and stage composer, pianist. A graduate of Harvard Military Academy, Whiting worked as a song-plugger and hotel pianist, before composing the one and a half million seller *It's Tulip Time in Holland* (1915). In 1916, he formed a lengthy songwriting partnership with the lyricist Raymond Egan, their five million selling '*Till We Meet Again* [viii], being a composition that their publisher had retrieved from Whiting's waste bin. His songs were also featured in the Broadway revues "George White's Scandals" and "Toot Sweet" (both 1919); "Satires of 1920," "Free for All" (1931), and "Take a Chance" (1932). Two of Whiting's best known songs are *On the Good Ship Lollipop* [iv] from the film "Bright Eyes" (1935), and the delightful *Hooray for Hollywood* [xvi] (1937), Jack Benny's theme tune for two decades. Whiting contributed material to some of the earliest talkies, and worked for Paramount Pictures on the scores "Innocents of Paris" and "The Dance of Life" (both 1929); "Monte Carlo" and "Playboy of Paris" (both 1930); "Take a Chance" (1933), "The Big Broadcast of 1936," and "Hollywood Hotel" (1937). He died of a heart attack in 1938. ALBUM: **Hollywood Hotel** ost (1981, Hollywood Soundstage). HIT VERSIONS: *Adorable* [xv] Wayne King (1933) US#11, *Ain't We Got Fun* [ix] Benson Orchestra of Chicago (1921) US#9/Van & Schenck (1921) US#1/Billy Jones (1922) US#12; *Beyond the Blue Horizon* [xii] Jeanette MacDonald (1930) US#9/George Olsen (1930) US#5/Phil Spitalny (1930) US#18/Hugo Winterhalter (1951) US#23/ Lou Christie (1974) US#80; *Bimini Bay* [ix] Benson Orchestra of Chicago (1922) US#4, *Breezin' Along with the Breeze* [xi] Abe Lyman (1926) US#11/Johnny Marvin (1926) US#1/Revelers (1927) US#17/Hoosier Hot Shots (1937) US#13; *Double Trouble* [xix] Ray Noble (1935) US#12, *Guilty* [i] Russ Columbo (1931) US#13/Ruth Etting (1931) US#4/Wayne King (1931) US#11/Johnny Desmond (1947) US#12/Ella Fitzgerald (1947) US#11/Margaret Whiting (1947) US#4; *Have You Got Any Castles Baby?* [xvi] Gus Arnheim (1937) US#11/Dolly Dawn (1937) US#8/Tommy Dorsey (1937) US#2; *Honey* [xi] Ben Selvin (1929) US#10/Rudy Vallee (1929) US#1; *Horses* [x] Georgians (1926) US#13/George Olsen (1926) US#2; *I Can't Escape from You* [xx] Bing Crosby & Jimmy Dorsey (1936) US#7, *I'll Dream Tonight* [xvi] Tommy Dorsey (1938) US#14, *I've Hitched My Wagon to a Star* [xvi] Jan Garber (1938) US#14, *It's Tulip Time in Holland* Henry Burr (1915) US#5, *Japanese Sandman, The* [viii] Paul Whiteman (1920) US#1/Nora Bayes (1921) US#7/Ben Selvin (1921) US#15/Benny Goodman (1935) US#10; *Louise* [xx] Maurice Chevalier (1929) US#3/Paul Whiteman (1929) US#6;

Mammy's Little Coal Black Rose [viii] Orpheus Quartet (1917) US#5, *My Future Just Passed* [xv] High Hatters (1930) US#6, *My Ideal* [iv] Maurice Chevalier (1931) US#12/Billy Butterfield (1943) US#12/Jimmy Dorsey (1944) US#5/Maxine Sullivan (1944) US#11; *On the Good Ship Lollipop* [iv] Ted Fio Rito (1935) US#16/Rudy Vallee (1935) US#4; *One Hour with You* [xx] Jimmie Grier (1932) US#2, *She's Funny That Way* [vii] Gene Austin (1929) US#3/Ted Lewis (1929) US#15; *Sleepy Time Gal* [ii] Gene Austin (1926) US#3/Ben Bernie (1926) US#1/Lewis James (1926) US#21/Nick Lucas (1926) US#3/Art Landry (1926) US#10/Ben Selvin (1926) US#11/Harry James (1944) US#21; *Some Sunday Morning* [ix] Ada Jones & M.J. O'Connell (1917) US#4/Joseph C. Smith's Orchestra (1918) US#9; *Sorry* [xvii] Frank Sinatra (1950) US#28, *Sweet Child (I'm Wild About You)* [xiv] Gene Austin (1926) US#13, *They Made It Twice as Nice as Paradise (And They Called It Dixieland)* [viii] Geoffrey O'Hara (1916) US#5, *'Till We Meet Again* [viii] Henry Burr & Albert Campbell (1919) US#1/Vernon Dalhart & Gladys Rice (1919) US#9/Charles Hart & Lewis James (1919) US#1/Nicholas Orlando's Orchestra (1919) US#1/Prince's Orchestra (1919) US#10; *Too Marvelous for Words* [xvi] Bing Crosby & Jimmy Dorsey (1937) US#1/Leo Reisman (1937) US#16/Frank Sinatra on *Songs for Swinging Lovers* LP (1956) UK#12; *True Blue Lou* [vi] Ethel Waters (1929) US#15, *Ukelele Lady* [xiii] Vaughn Deleath (1925) US#6, *Wait 'Till You See Ma Cherie* [xx] Maurice Chevalier (1929) US#9, *Waitin' at the Gate for Katy* [xiii] Don Bestor (1934) US#17, *When Did You Leave Heaven?* [iii] Henry Allen (1936) US#16/Ben Bernie (1936) US#6/Guy Lombardo (1936) US#1; *When Shall We Meet Again?* [viii] Prince's Orchestra (1922) US#12, *Where the Black-Eyed Susans Grow* [xviii] Henry Burr & Albert Campbell (1917) US#5, *Where the Morning Glories Grow* [ix] Elizabeth Spencer & the Spencer Trio (1918) US#3. Co-writers: [i] Harry Akst/Gus Kahn, [ii] Joseph Alden/Raymond Egan/Ange Lorenzo, [iii] Walter Bullock, [iv] Newell Chase/Leo Robin, [v] Sidney Clare, [vi] Sam Coslow, [vii] Charles N. Daniels, [viii] Raymond Egan, [ix] Raymond Egan/Gus Kahn, [x] Byron Gay, [xi] Haven Gillespie/Seymour Simons, [xii] W. Franke Harling/Leo Robin, [xiii] Gus Kahn, [xiv] Al Lewis/Howard Simons, [xv] George Marion, Jr., [xvi] Johnny Mercer, [xvii] Buddy Pepper, [xviii] Dave Radford, [xix] Ralph Rainger/Leo Robin, [xx] Leo Robin. (*See also under* Nacio Herb BROWN.)

1012. WHITTAKER, Roger (b. March 22, 1936, Nairobi, Kenya) Pop guitarist and vocalist. A middle-of-the-road, singer-songwriter and song interpreter. CHART COMPOSITIONS: *Durham Town (The Leavin')* (1969) UK#12, *I Don't Believe in*

if Anymore (1970) UK#8, *New World in the Morning* (1970) UK#17, *The Last Farewell* [ii] US#19 UK#2, *The Skye Boat Song* [i] (arrangement only) with Des O'Connor (1986) UK#10. ALBUMS: **I Don't Believe in if Anymore** (1970) UK#23, **New World in the Morning** (1971, both Columbia) UK#45; **The Last Farewell and Other Hits** (1975, RCA) g US#31; **Roger Whittaker Sings the Hits** (1978, Columbia) UK#52; **When I Need You** (1979) US#115, **Mirrors of My Mind** (1979) US#157, **Voyager** (1980) US#154, **With Love** (1980) US#175, **Live in Concert** (1981, all RCA) US#177; **The Skye Boat Song and Other Great Songs** (1986) UK#89, **Home Lovin' Man** (1989, both Tembo) UK#20. COMPILATIONS: **Very Best of Roger Whittaker** (1975, Columbia) UK#5; **The Second Album of the Very Best of Roger Whittaker** (1976, EMI) UK#27; **20 All Time Greats** (1979, Polydor) UK#24, **The Roger Whittaker Album** (1981, K-Tel) UK#18; **His Finest Collection** (1987, Tembo) UK#15. HIT VERSION: *Last Farewell, The* [ii] Ship's Company & the Royal Marine Band of H.M.S. Ark Royal (1978) UK#46/Elvis Presley (1984) UK#48. Co-writers: [i] Colin Keyes, [ii] Ronald A. Webster.

1013. WILDER, Alec (b. Alexander LaFayette Chew Wilder, February 16, 1907, Gainesville, FL) Film and stage composer. The writer of many jazz influenced songs and classical works, who lived for over fifty years in New York hotels. Wilder also co-wrote material for such revues as "Three's a Crowd" (1930), and the films "Make Mine Music" (1945), "Open the Door and See All the People" (1964) and "The Flight of the Phoenix" (1965). He was a particular favorite of Frank Sinatra, who recorded his songs *The Long Night* and *One More Road*, and the album **Frank Sinatra Conducts the Music of Alec Wilder** (1955, Columbia). ALBUMS: **Alec Wilder and His Octet** (1949, Mercury); **Peter Pan** oc (1950), **Alec Wilder Octet** (1951), **Pinocchio** tvst (1957, all Columbia); **Alice's Adventures in Wonderland** sc (1958, Riverside); **Hansel and Gretel** tvst (1958, MGM); **Sand Castle** ost (1960, Columbia); **Clues to a Life** oc (19?, Original Cast): **Kittiwake Island** oc (19?, Blue Pear). HIT VERSIONS: *I'll Be Around* Mills Brothers (1943) US#17, *If She Should Come to You (La Montana)* [i] Anthony Newley (1960) UK#6, *It's So Peaceful in the Country* Mildred Bailey (1940) US#24, *Phoenix Love Theme* [ii] Brass Ring featuring Phil Bodner (1966) US#32. Co-writers: [i] Augusto Alguero/Georges Moreu, [ii] Gino Paoli.

1014. WILLIAMS, Bert (b. Egbert Austin Williams, November 12, 1874, New Providence, Nassau, West Indies; d. March 4, 1922, New York,

NY) Vaudeville performer. An exceptionally talented comedian and singer who became the first successful black entertainer on Broadway. Of the racial prejudice that he encountered throughout his career, Williams said in 1917, "I have never been able to discover that there was anything disgraceful in being a colored man." After emigrating to California with his parents, Williams first began performing as a solo vocalist with banjo accompaniment. He formed a vaudeville duo with George Walker in the 1890s, and debuted on Broadway in "The Gold Bug" (1896), which they followed with "The Policy Players" and "Sons of Ham" (both 1990). Their "In Dahomey" (1903), was the first full-length, all-black musical to be performed on Broadway, and was also a success in London, England, where they performed in front of King Edward, VII. Walker and Williams' last show together was "Bandana Land" (1908). After Walker's death in 1911, Williams starred in a number of Ziegfeld Follies between 1911–1919, and last performed on Broadway in "Broadway Brevities of 1920." He co-wrote many of his own songs, some of which were to influence the development of dixieland jazz, in particular his theme tune *Nobody* [iv] (1905). CHART COMPOSITIONS: *I Don't Like That Face You Wear* (1902) US#3, *Nobody* [iv] (1906) US#1, new version (1913) US#4; *Let It Alone* (1906) US#1, *Constantly* [ii] (1910) US#2, *The Darktown Poker Club* [iii] (1914) US#3, *Everybody Wants the Key to My Cellar* (1919) US#2. HIT VERSIONS: *Darktown Poker Club, The* [iii] Phil Harris (1946) US#10, re-issued (1947) US#27; *I Don't Like No Cheap Man* [v] Len Spencer (1898) US#1, *Nobody* [iv] Johnny "Guitar" Watson & Larry Williams (1968) R&B#40, *That's A-Plenty* [i] Prince's Orchestra (1914) US#8/Jan Savitt (1938) US#19. Co-writers: [i] Henry Creamer, [ii] James Henry Burris/Chris Smith, [iii] Jean Havez/Will Vodery, [iv] Alex Rogers, [v] George Walker.

1015. WILLIAMS, Clarence (b. October 8, 1898, Plaquemine, LA; d. November 6, 1965, Queens, NY) R&B-jazz pianist, bandleader, producer, arranger and vocalist. A musical all-rounder who recorded over three hundred sides during the 1920s. Williams was one of the first successful black music publishers, and many of his songs were recorded by Bessie Smith. He also composed the music for the unsuccessful Broadway show "Bottomland" (1927). Williams traveled as a minstrel show singer and dancer in 1911, before returning to New Orleans in the mid–1900s to start his own publishing company. After re-locating to New York, he organized recording sessions for the OKeh label between 1923–1930. His most famous recording ensemble was the Blue Five, and he was also the first

to promote the composers Fats Waller and Spencer Williams. Williams' jazz-blues standards include *Jailhouse Blues* [v] (1923) and *I Ain't Gonna Give Nobody None O'This Jelly Roll* [vii] (1919). CHART COMPOSITIONS: *T'ain't Nobody's Bus'ness if I Do* [iii] (1924) US#9, *Cake Walking Babies from Home* [vi] (1925) US#13, *Baby Won't You Please Come Home* [vii] (1927) US#13. ALBUMS: **Clarence Williams Jazz Kings, 1927–1929** (1979), **Clarence Williams Jazz Kings, 1929–1931** (1986, both Vintage Jazz); **WNYC Jazz Festival** (1986, Jazz Unlimited); **Clarence Williams and His Washboard Band, Volume 4** (1987, Classic Jazz); **Wild Cat Blues, 1923–1935** (1987, Rhapsody); **Clarence Williams and His Orchestra** (1988, Classic Jazz Masters); **Piano Album** (1988, Meritt); **Clarence Williams Jug and Washboard Bands** ((1988, Keyhole); **Clarence Williams Jug Bands** (1988), **Clarence Williams, 1924(–1930, Volume 2** (1988), **Clarence Williams and the Washboard Band, 1933–1935, Volumes 1–5** (1988), **Clarence Williams and Eva Taylor, 1925–1926** (1988, all Swaggie); **Jazz Classics in Digital Stereo** (1989, BBC). HIT VERSIONS: *Baby Won't You Please Come Home* [vii] Bessie Smith (1923) US#6/Mills Brothers (1932) US#20; *Gulf Coast Blues* Fletcher Henderson (1923) US#10/Bessie Smith (1923) US#5; *I Can't Dance (I Got Ants in My Pants)* [ii] Chick Webb (1934) US#20, *Royal Garden Blues* [vii] Original Dixieland Jazz Band (1921) US#3/Mamie Smith (1921) US#13; *Sugar Blues* [i] Clyde McCoy (1931) US#2, re-issued (1935) US#6/Ella Fitzgerald (1940) US#27/Johnny Mercer (1947) US#4/Don Costa (1962) US#112; *T'ain't Nobody's Bus'ness if I Do* [iii] Bessie Smith (1923) US#9, *West End Blues* [iv] Louis Armstrong (1928) US#8 re-issued (1939) US#13. Co-writers: [i] Lucy Fletcher, [ii] Charles Gaines, [iii] Porter Granger/Graham Prince, [iv] Joe "King" Oliver, [v] Bessie Smith, [vi] Chris Smith/Henry Troy, [vii] Charles Warfield, [viii] Spencer Williams. (*See also under* Fats WALLER.)

1016. WILLIAMS, Don (b. May 27, 1939, Floydada, TX) C&W guitarist and vocalist. A laid-back, country artist, who has topped the charts on fifteen occasions. During the 1960s, Williams was a member of the group the Strangers Two, which became the Pozo-Seco Singers and recorded for Columbia Records. In 1971, Williams went solo, recording his own songs and cover versions for some forty-six hits between 1972–1988. He is also one of a handful of country stars to make any serious inroads into the British market. CHART COMPOSITIONS: *The Shelter of Your Eyes* (1972) C&W#14, *We Should Be Together* (1974) C&W#5, *You're My Best Friend* (1975) C&W#1, re-issued (1976) UK#35; *I Recall a Gypsy Woman* (1976) UK#13, *'Til the Rivers*

All Run Dry (1976) C&W#1, *Tulsa Time* (1978) C&W#1 US#106, *Back in My Younger Days* (1990) C&W#2. ALBUMS: **Don Williams, Volume 1** (1973), **Don Williams, Volume 2** (1974, both JMI); **Visions** (1977) UK#13, **Country Boy** (1977) UK#27, **You're My Best Friend** (1978) UK#58, **Expressions** (1978, all ABC) US#161 UK#28; **Portrait** (1979) UK#58, **I Believe in You** (1980) p US#57 UK#36, **Especially for You** (1981) US#109 UK#33, **Listen to the Radio** (1982) US#166 UK#69, **Yellow Moon** (1983) UK#52, **Café Carolina** (1984, all MCA) UK#65; **New Moves** (1986), **Traces** (1987, both Capitol); **Lovers and Best Friends** (1987, MCA); **As Long as I Have You** (1989), **True Love** (1990), **Currents** (1992, all RCA). COMPILATIONS: **Greatest Hits, Volume 1** (1976, ABC) UK#29; **Images** (1978) UK#2, **Best of Don Williams** (1979, both MCA) g; **New Horizons** (1979) UK#29, **Love Stories** (1983, both K-Tel) UK#22. HIT VERSIONS: *I Recall a Gypsy Woman* Tommy Cash (1973) C&W#16/B.J. Thomas (1981) C&W#22.

1017. WILLIAMS, Hank (b. Hiram Hank Williams, September 17, 1923, Mount Olive West, AL; d. January 1, 1953, Oak Hill, VA) C&W guitarist and vocalist. The most famous, influential and recorded country songwriter in the history of the genre. There are elements of Williams' music in nearly every country artist that has come after him, and his short, ill-fated life created the very legend that country stars are made of. A gifted songwriter, Williams blended exquisite melodies with some of the most mournful, self-pitying lyrics ever conceived. He grew up poor in the rural south and began singing in the 1930s, his early affiliation with the blues later influencing his own sound. With his backing band the Drifting Cowboys, Williams toured frequently, and in 1946, he signed a publishing deal with Acuff-Rose, where his compositions immediately attracted the attention of other artists, *Your Cheatin' Heart* alone being recorded over three hundred times. Williams first recorded for the Sterling label in 1946, and from 1950, he became successful in the mainstream pop market. Williams died at the age of twenty-nine from heart failure, due to alcohol abuse and over-consumption of pain killers, leaving a legacy of one hundred and twenty-five compositions. In 1992, his song catalogue was estimated to be producing one million dollars a year in royalties. Jack Scott recorded his songs as **I Remember Hank Williams** (1960, Top Rank) UK#7. CHART COMPOSITIONS: *Move It on Over* (1947) C&W#4, *Honky Tonkin'* (1948) C&W#14, *I'm a Long Gone Daddy* (1948) C&W#6, *Never Again* (1949) C&W#6, *Mansion on the Hill* [iii] (1949) C&W#12, *Mind Your Own Business* (1949) C&W#5, *You're*

Gonna Change (1949) C&W#4, *My Bucket's Got a Hole in It* (1949) C&W#2, *I Just Don't Like This Kind of Livin'* (1950) C&W#5, *Long Gone Lonesome Blues* (1950) C&W#1, *My Son Calls Another Man Daddy* [i] (1950) C&W#9, *Why Don't You Love Me* (1950) C&W#1, re-issued (1976) C&W#61; *Why Should We Try Anymore* (1950) C&W#9, *Moanin' the Blues* (1950) C&W#1, *Nobody's Lonesome for Me* (1950) C&W#9, *Cold, Cold Heart* (1951) C&W#1 US#27, *I Can't Help It (If I'm Still in Love with You)* (1951) C&W#2, *Howlin' at the Moon* (1951) C&W#3, *Hey Good Lookin'* (1951) g C&W#1 US#29, *Lonesome Whistle* (1951) C&W#9, *Baby, We're Really in Love* (1951) C&W#4, *Honky Tonk Blues* (1952) C&W#2, *Jambalaya (On the Bayou)* (1952) g C&W#1 US#20, *You Win Again* (1962) C&W#10, *I'll Never Get Out of This World Alive* (1952) C&W#1, *Kaw-Liga* [iii] (1953) g C&W#1 US#23, *Your Cheatin' Heart* (1953) C&W#1 US#25, *I Won't Be Home No More* (1953) C&W#4, *Weary Blues from Waitin'* (1953) C&W#7, *Please Don't Let Me Love You* (1955) C&W#9, *I'm So Lonesome I Could Cry* (1966) C&W#43 US#109. ALBUMS: **Hank Williams Sings** (1952), **Hank Williams as Luke the Drifter** (1953), **The Hank Williams Memorial Album** (1955), **Moanin' the Blues** (1956), **Sing Me a Blue Song** (1958), **The Immortal Hank Williams** (1958), **The Unforgettable Hank Williams** (1959), **Wait for the Light to Shine** (1960), **On Stage** (1962), **The Spirit of Hank Williams** (1963), **May You Never Be Alone** (1966), **In Memory of Hank Williams** (1966), **I'm Blue Inside** (1966), **The Many Moods of Hank Williams** (1966), **The Legend Lives Anew** (1967), **More Hank Williams and Strings** (1967), **Love Songs, Comedy and Hymns** (1967), **I Won't Be Home No More** (1968), **Hank Williams and Strings, Volume 3** (1968), **The Essential Hank Williams** (1970), **On Stage Volumes 1 and 2** (1974), **Live at the Grand Ol' Opry** (1976, all MGM): **The Legendary Hank Williams** (1979, World Records); **Greatest Hits** (1963) g, **Father and Son** (1965) US#139, **24 Greatest Hits** (1971, all MGM) p; **Lost Highway** (1986), **Lovesick Blues** (1986), **On the Air** (1986, all Polydor); **Hank Williams and the Drifting Cowboys** (1987, Flyright); **I'm So Lonesome I Could Cry** (1987), **Let's Turn Back the Years** (1987), **Long Gone Lonesome Blues** (1987), **Beyond the Sunset** (1988), **Rare Takes and Radio Cuts** (1988), **I Ain't Got Nothing But Time** (1988), **The Original Singles Collection...Plus** (1990), **Long Gone Lonesome Blues, August, 1949–December, 1950, Volume 5** (1993), **Hey Good Lookin', December, 1950–July, 1951, Volume 6** (1993), **Let's Turn Back the Years, July, 1951–June, 1952, Volume 7** (1993, all Polydor); **Best of Hank and Hank** (1993) US#179, **Health and Happiness Shows** (1993, both

PolyGram); **Hank Williams — The Collector's Edition** (1995, Mercury). HIT VERSIONS: *Cold, Cold Heart* Tony Bennett (1951) US#1/Tony Fontane (1951) US#28/Fontane Sisters (1951) US#16/Dinah Washington (1951) R&B#3/Eileen Wilson (1951) US#19/Jerry Lee Lewis (1961) C&W#22, re-issued (1979) C&W#84; *Dear John* Status Quo (1982) UK#10, *Half as Much* Rosemary Clooney (1952) US#1/Guy Lombardo (1952) US#20; *Hey Good Lookin'* Frankie Laine & Jo Stafford (1951) US#9/Tommy Zang (1961) UK#45/Connie Stevens (1962) US#104/Bill Black's Combo (1966) US#124/Mavericks (1992) C&W#74; *Honky Tonk Blues* Charley Pride (1980) C&W#1, *Honky Tonkin'* Hank Williams, Jr. (1982) C&W#1, *I Can't Help It (If I'm Still in Love with You)* Johnny Tillotson (1962) US#24 UK#41/Guy Mitchell (1951) US#28/Linda Ronstadt (1974) C&W#2, also on B-side of *You're No Good* (1974) US#1; *I'm So Lonesome I Could Cry* Johnny Tillotson (1962) US#89/Terry Bradshaw (1976) C&W#17 US#91; *I'm Sorry for You, My Friend* Moe Bandy (1977) C&W#9, *Jambalya (On the Bayou)* Jo Stafford (1952) g US#3 UK#11/Bobby Comstock & the Counts (1960) US#90/Fats Domino (1962) US#30 UK#41/Blue Ridge Rangers (1973) C&W#66/Nitty Gritty Dirt Band (1972) US#84/Carpenters (1974) UK#12/Saskia & Serge (1978) C&W#88; *Kaw-Liga* [iii] Dolores Gray (1953) US#23/Charley Pride (1969) C&W#3/Hank Williams, Jr. (1980) C&W#12; *Long Gone Lonesome Blues* Hank Williams, Jr. (1964) C&W#5 US#67, *Mind Your Own Business* Jimmy Dean (1964) C&W#35/Hank Williams, Jr. (1986) C&W#1; *There'll Be No Teardrops Tonight* [ii] Tony Bennett (1954) US#7/Adam Wade (1962) US#104/Willie Nelson (1978) C&W#86/Vassar Clements (1980) C&W#70; *You Win Again* Tommy Edwards (1952) US#13/Jerry Lee Lewis (1958) C&W#2 US#95/Fats Domino (1962) US#22/Charley Pride (1980) C&W#1/Jeris Ross (1980) US#75; *Your Cheatin' Heart* Joni James (1953) g US#2/Frankie Laine (1953) US#18/Ray Charles (1962) R&B#23 US#29 UK#13/Fats Domino (1964) US#112. Co-writers: [i] House, [ii] Nelson King, [iii] Fred Rose, [iv] Curly Williams.

1018. WILLIAMS, Hank, Jr. (b. Randall Hank Williams, May 26, 1949, Shreveport, LA) C&W guitarist and vocalist. The son of the legendary country star Hank Williams, who, despite living in the shadow of his father's legacy, has carved a creditable career for himself selling over thirteen million albums. From the age of thirteen, Williams toured with the Caravan of Stars, and later starred in the film of his father's life "Your Cheatin' Heart" (1964). He has achieved nearly one hundred country hits since 1964. CHART COMPOSITIONS: *Standing in the Shadows* (1966) C&W#5, *I Was with Red Foley (The Night He Passed Away)* (1968) C&W#39, *I'd Rather Be Gone* [i] (1969) C&W#4, *Stoned at the Jukebox* (1975) C&W#19, *Living Proof* (1976) C&W#38, *Cajun Baby* (1969) C&W#3 US#107, new version with Doug Kershaw (1988) C&W#52; *Hank* (1973) C&W#12, *Angels Are Hard to Find* (1991) C&W#59, *Hotel Whiskey* (1992) C&W#54, *Come on Over to the Country* (1992) C&W#56. ALBUMS: **Songs of Hank Williams** (1964), **Your Cheatin' Heart** ost (1965) g US#16, **Ballads of the Hills and Plains** (1965), **Father and Son** with Hank Williams (1965) US#139, **Blues Is My Name** (1966), **Standing in the Shadows** (1966), **My Own Way** (1967), **My Songs** (1968), **A Time to Sing** ost (1968) US#189, **Luke the Drifter, Jr.** (1969), **Songs My Father Left Me** (1969) US#164, **Live at Cobo Hall** (1969) US#187, **Songs of Johnny Cash** (1970), **Removing the Shadow** (1970), **Eleven Roses** (1972), **Just Picking** (1973), **Bocephus** (1975), **Hank Williams, Jr. and Friends** (1975, all MGM); **New South** (1977, Warner Brothers); **Family Tradition** (1979) g, **Whiskey Bent and Hell Bound** (1979) g, **Habits Old and New** (1980) US#154, **Rowdy** (1981) g US#82, **The Pressure Is On** (1981) p US#76, **High Notes** (1982) g US#123, **Strong Stuff** (1983, all Elektra/Curb) g US#64; **Man of Steel** (1983) g US#116, **Major Moves** (1984, both Warner Brothers) g US#100; **Five-O** (1985) g US#72, **Montana Cafe** (1986) g US#93, **Hank Live** (1987) g US#71, **Born to Boogie** (1987) p US#28, **Wild Streak** (1988) g US#55, **Lone Wolf** (1990) g US#71, **America (The Way I See It)** (1990) US#116, **Pure Hank** (1991, all Warner Brothers/Curb) US#50; **Maverick** (1992, Curb/Capri) US#55; **Out of Left Field** (1993, Capricorn) US#121; **Hog Wild** (1995), **Men with Broken Hearts** (1996, both Curb). COMPILATIONS: **Greatest Hits** (1984, Elektra) p US#107; **Greatest Hits, Volume 2** (1986) p US#183, **Greatest Hits III** (1989) g US#61, **Best of Hank Williams, Jr.** (1989, all Warner Brothers); **Best of Hank and Hank** (1992, Curb); **Best of Hank Williams, Jr.** (1992, Polydor); **Greatest Hits, Volume 1** (1994, Curb). HIT VERSION: *Homesick* Bobby Bare (1966) C&W#38. Co-writer: [i] Merle Haggard.

1019. WILLIAMS, Larry (b. Lawrence E. Williams, May 10, 1935, New Orleans, LA; d. January 2, 1980, Los Angeles, CA) R&B pianist and vocalist. A rock and roll influenced R&B vocalist whose small body of work was a considerable influence on John Lennon, who recorded his songs *Bad Boy* and *Dizzy Miss Lizzie* in the Beatles. During the 1950s Williams played in the group the Lemon Drops, and sessioned for a variety of R&B artists, before scoring a series of hits under his own name. Williams committed suicide in 1980. CHART COMPOSITIONS: *Just Because* (1957) R&B#11, *Short Fat Fannie* (1957) R&B#1 US#5 UK#21, *Bony Moronie* (1957) R&B#4 US#14 UK#11. ALBUMS: **The Larry Williams Show** (1964, Decca); **Two for the Price of One** (1967, OKeh); **That Larry Williams** (1978, Fantasy). HIT VERSIONS: *Bony Moronie* Cheeks (1980) US#110, *Slow Down* Beatles (1964) US#25.

1020. WILLIAMS, Lucinda (b. Lake Charles, LA) Folk guitarist and vocalist. A country and folk influenced singer-songwriter. ALBUMS: **Ramblin' on My Mind** (1979), **Happy Woman Blues** (1980, both Folkways); **Lucinda Williams** (1989, Rough Trade); **Sweet Old World** (1992, Warner Brothers).

1021. WILLIAMS, Paul (b. Paul Hamilton Williams, September 19, 1940, Omaha, NE) Pop pianist and vocalist. A former child actor and comedy sketch writer who became a successful songwriter during the 1970s, with his melodic and individualistic love songs. Williams' own recordings were influenced by Tin Pan Alley, vaudeville and music hall. After failing an audition to join the Monkees, Williams linked up with folk singer Biff Rose, and later Roger Nichols, to write songs for Claudette Longet and Harper's Bizarre. In the mid–1960s, he recorded an album as a member of the group the Holy Mackerel, with his brother Mentor Williams, **The Holy Mackerel** (1967, Reprise). After contributing to Michel Columbier's lavish pop symphony **Wings** (1970, A&M), Williams began recording a series of high caliber pop albums that were crammed with songs that were often hits for others. In 1974, he starred in the pastiche rock movie "Phantom of the Opera," and later won an Oscar for *Evergreen* [vi], his and Barbra Streisand's theme tune for the third film version of "A Star Is Born" (1977). CHART COMPOSITIONS: *Waking Up Alone* (1972) US#60, *I Won't Last a Day Without You* [v] (1973) US#106, *Inspiration* (1973) US#108, *Making Believe* (1981) C&W#93. ALBUMS: **Someday Man** (1970, Reprise); **Just an Old Fashioned Love Song** (1971) US#141, **Life Goes On** (1972) US#159, **Here Comes Inspiration** (1974) US#165, **Phantom of the Paradise** ost (1974) US#194, **A Little Bit of Love** (1975) US#95, **Ordinary Fool** (1976, all A&M) US#146; **Bugsy Malone** ost (1976, Polydor); **A Little on the Windy Side** (1979, Portrait); **The Muppet Movie** ost (1979, Atlantic) g US#32. COMPILATIONS: **Songwriter** (1974), **Best of Paul Williams** (1975), **Classics** (1977, all A&M) US#155. HIT VERSIONS: *Cried Like a Baby* [iii] Bobby

Sherman (1971) US#16, *Evergreen* [vi] Barbra Streisand (1977) g US#1 UK#3/Hazel Dean (1984) UK#63; *Family of Man* [ii] Three Dog Night (1972) US#12, *Fill Your Heart* Tiny Tim on B-side of *Tip-Toe Thru' the Tulips with Me* (1968) US#17, *I Won't Last a Day Without You* [v] Carpenters (1972) US#11 UK#9/Maureen McGovern (1973) US#89/Diana Ross on B-side of *Touch Me in the Morning* (1973) R&B#5 US#1 UK#9/Al Wilson (1974) R&B#18 US#70; *Let Me Be the One* Al Wilson (1974) R&B#18 US#70, *My Fair Share (The Love Theme)* [iv] Seals & Crofts (1977) US#28, *Old Fashioned Love Song, An* Three Dog Night (1971) g US#4/Jeris Ross (1972) C&W#58; *Out in the Country* [v] Three Dog Night (1970) US#15, *Rainbow Connection, The* [i] Kermit (1979) US#25, *Rainy Days and Mondays* [v] Carpenters (1971) g US#2/Intruders (1975) R&B#81/Benet (1993) R&B#116; *Someday Man* [v] Monkees (1969) UK#47, *That's What Friends Are For* B.J. Thomas (1972) US#74/Barbra Mandrell (1976) C&W#16; *Traveling Boy* [v] Art Garfunkel (1974) US#102, *Watch Closely Now* [i] Kris Kristofferson (1977) US#52, *We've Only Just Begun* [v] Carpenters (1970) g US#2 UK#28, *You and Me Against the World* [i] Helen Reddy (1974) US#9. Co-writers: [i] Ken Ascher, [ii] Jack S. Conrad, [iii] Craig Doerge, [iv] Charles Fox, [v] Roger Nichols, [vi] Barbra Streisand.

1022. WILLIAMS, Spencer (b. October 14, 1889, New Orleans, LA; d. July 14, 1965, Flushing, NY) Jazz pianist and vocalist. A co-writer and performer of many jazz and pop standards. After performing in New York in 1916, Williams re-located to Paris, France, where he composed for Josephine Baker. He lived in England in the 1940s. HIT VERSIONS: *Basin Street Blues* Charleston Chasers (1931) US#14/Benny Goodman (1934) US#14/Bing Crosby & Connee Boswell (1937) US#12/Louis Armstrong (1938) US#20; *Everybody Loves My Baby (But My Baby Don't Love Nobody But Me)* [ii] Aileen Stanley (1925) US#5/Clarence Williams' Blue Five (1925) US#10/Jimmy Smith (1962) US#107/King Richard's Fluegel Knights (1967) US#126; *I Ain't Got Nobody* [i] Marion Harris (1921) US#3/Sophie Tucker (1924) US#12/Bessie Smith (1926) US#8/David Lee Roth (1985) US#12; *I've Found a New Baby* [ii] Mills Brothers (1934) US#19/Harry James (1939) US#14. Co-writers: [i] Roger Graham/Dave Peyton, [ii] Jack Palmer. (*See also under* W.C. HANDY, Clarence WILLIAMS.)

1023. WILLIS, Chuck (b. January 31, 1928, Atlanta; d. April 10, 1958) R&B vocalist. An R&B artist who was famous for dressing on stage in a turban. Willis first sang with the Red McAlister Band. He died of peritonitis in 1958. CHART

COMPOSITIONS: *My Story* (1952) R&B#2, *Don't Deceive Me* (1953) R&B#6, *You're Still My Baby* (1954) R&B#4, *I Feel So Bad* (1954) R&B#8, *It's Too Late* (1956) R&B#3, *Juanita* (1956) R&B#7, *Whatch Gonna Do When Your Baby Leaves You* (1956) R&B#11, *C.C. Rider* (1957) R&B#1 US#12, *Betty and Dupree* (1958) R&B#15 US#33, *Hang Up My Rock and Roll Shoes* (1958) R&B#9 US#24, *My Life* (1958) R&B#12 US#46, *Keep-a Driving* (1958) R&B#19. ALBUMS: **I Remember Chuck Willis** (1965, Atlantic); **Stoop Down Baby, Let Your Daddy See** (1972, Laval); **Be Good or Be Gone** (1986, Edsel); **Keep-a Drivin'** (1988, Charly). HIT VERSIONS: *Close Your Eyes* Herb Lance & the Classics (1949) R&B#4/Tony Bennett (1955) UK#18/Five Keys (1955) R&B#5/Peaches & Herb (1967) R&B#4 US#8/Three Degrees (1965) US#126; *Door Is Still Open to My Heart, The* Cardinals (1955) R&B#4/ Dean Martin (1964) US#6 UK#42; *Hang Up My Rock and Roll Shoes* Band (1972) US#113, *I Feel So Bad* Elvis Presley (1961) R&B#15 US#5, *Stroll, The* Diamonds (1957) R&B#5, *What a Dream* Ruth Brown (1954) R&B#1/Patti Page (1954) US#10/Conway Twitty (1960) US#106, re-issued (1971) US#50.

1024. WILLS, Bob (b. James Robert Wills, March 6, 1905, near Kosse; d. May 13, 1975, Fort Worth, both TX) C&W violinist and band leader. The best known exponent of western swing, a form of country music that Wills mixed with elements of jazz, ragtime and early R&B during the 1930s. Wills began playing at farmhouse dances in his teens, and created many country classics with his group the Texas Playboys, with which he recorded over two hundred and fifty sides for a variety of record labels. His group appeared in thirteen films, and charted twenty-six country hits between 1944–1976. CHART COMPOSITIONS: *San Antonio Rose* (1939) US#15, *New San Antonio Rose* (1940) g US#2, re-issued (1944) C&W#3 US#11; *Ten Years* (1942) US#21, *We Might as Well Forget It* (1944) C&W#2 US#11, *You're from Texas* (1944) C&W#2 US#14, *New Spanish Two-Step* (1946) C&W#1 US#20, *Bob Wills' Boogie* (1947) C&W#4. ALBUMS: **Very Best of Bob Wills** (1984, Liberty); **Time Changes Everything** (1986, Stetson); **Best of Bob Wills, Volumes 1 and 2** (1986, MCA); **Papa's Jumpin'** (1987, Bear Family); **Bob Wills and His Texas Playboys** (1988, Charly); **Golden Era** (1988, Columbia); **Best of the Tiffanys** (1990), **Tiffany Transcriptions, Volumes 1 to 8** (1990, both Edsel). HIT VERSIONS: *Cherokee Maiden* Merle Haggard (1976) C&W#1, *Faded Love* [i] Willie Nelson & Ray Price (1980) C&W#3, *San Antonio Rose* Bing Crosby (1940) US#1/Floyd Cramer (1961) C&W#8 US#8 UK#36/Ray Price (1983) C&W#70. Co-writer: [i] J. Wills.

1025. WILSON, Ann (b. June 19, 1951) Rock guitarist and vocalist, and **WILSON, Nancy** (b. March 16, 1954, both San Diego, CA) Rock guitarist, keyboard player and vocalist. The principal songwriting sisters in the rock group Heart. CHART COMPOSITIONS: *Crazy on You* [vii] (1975) US#35, re-issued (1978) US#62; *Magic Man* (1976) US#9, *Dreamboat Annie* (1977) US#42, *Barracuda* [iv] (1977) US#11, *Little Queen* [v] (1977) US#62, *Kick It Out* [viii] (1977) US#79, *Heartless* (1978) US#24, *Straight On* [vi] (1978) US#15, *Dog and Butterfly* [vi] (1979) US#34, *Even It Up* [vi] (1980) US#34, *This Man Is Mine* [vi] (1982) US#33, *How Can I Refuse* [i] (1983) US#44, *Never* [iii] (1985) US#4, *There's the Girl* [ix] (1987) US#12 UK#34, *I Don't Want to Need You* (1990) US#23 UK#47, *Stranded* (1990) US#13 UK#60, *Secret* (1991) US#64, *You're the Voice* (1991) UK#56, *Will You Be There (In the Morning)* (1993) US#39 UK#19. ALBUMS: **Dreamboat Annie** (1975, Mushroom) p US#7 UK#36; **Little Queen** (1977, Portrait) p US#9 UK#34; **Magazine** (1978, Mushroom) p US#17; **Dog and Butterfly** (1978) p US#17, **Bebe Le Strange** (1980) p US#5, **Greatest Hits/Live** (1980) p US#13, **Private Audition** (1982) US#25 UK#77, **Passionworks** (1983, all Epic) US#39; **Heart** (1985) p US#1 UK#19, **Bad Animals** (1987) p US#2 UK#7, **Brigade** (1990) p US#3 UK#3, **Rock the House Live!** (1991) US#107 UK#45, **Desire Walks On** (1993) US#48 UK#32, **The Road Home** (1995, all Capitol) US#87. COMPILATIONS: **With Love from Heart** (1988), **These Dreams: Greatest Hits** (1997, both Capitol) UK#35. Ann Wilson has also recorded as a solo artist, charting with *The Best Man in the World* [ii] (1986) US#61. Co-writers: [i] Mark Andes/D. Carmassi/H. Leese, [ii] John Barry/ Sue Ennis, [iii] Walter Bloch/Holly Knight/Ann Wilson, [iv] Michael Derosier (b. August 24, 1951, Canada)/Roger Fisher (b. February 14, 1950), [v] Michael Derosier/Roger Fisher/S. Fossen/H. Leese, [vi] S. Ennis, [vii] Roger Fisher, [viii] Ann Wilson only, [ix] Nancy Wilson/Holly Knight.

1026. WILSON, Brian (b. Brian Douglas Wilson, June 20, 1942, Inglewood, CA) Rock multi-instrumentalist, producer and vocalist. A musical genius whose compositions are some of the most original and endearing American popular music of the late twentieth century. As the leader of the sophisticated vocal group the Beach Boys, Wilson's songwriting developed from simple three chord pop songs into some of the most visionary music of the 1960s. Wilson grew up in Hawthorne, California, with his two brothers, Carl and Dennis Wilson. Their father Murray Wilson, was a shop owner. None of the Wilson's received any formal music training, but Brian displayed an interest in singing at the age of three, influenced by such vocal groups as the Four Fresh-men. As a teenager, he used to record his own four-part harmony arrangements into a portable tape recorder, and influenced by the optimistic, sunny sound of the Kingston Trio, the Wilson brothers formed the Pendletones with their relatives, Alan Jardine and Mike Love. As the Beach Boys, the group released the single *Surfin'* on the local Candix label, which reached the national chart in 1961 due to its California sales alone. By 1962, the Beach Boys had become regular hit makers with Wilson's surf and hot rod songs, and in conjunction with Jan and Dean, they were responsible for a new sound that focused attention on Californian youth obsessions. A phenomenal singles writer from the outset, Wilson's ballads *Surfer Girl* and *In My Room* [viii] displayed a vocal sophistication never before heard on non-folk records, and songs such as the million selling *I Get Around* utilized Wilson's falsetto to sterling effect. By the mid–1960s, Wilson had already withdrawn from live performances with the group in order to concentrate on recording and writing, and in 1966 he claimed that he was working on, "The greatest rock album ever made." It was a prophesy very nearly fulfilled with the album **Pet Sounds**, which employed the spaciousness of Phil Spector's production techniques and the tight song styling of the Beatles. In November 1966, after six months of recording sessions, at a cost of an estimated fifty thousand dollars, Wilson finally unleashed the masterpiece of a single *Good Vibrations* [vi], which he described as, "a pocket symphony." His next project was the unrealized "Smile," bits and pieces of which turned up on the future albums **Smiley Smile** (1967), **Wild Honey** (1968) and **Surf's Up** (1971). After a series of poor selling albums during the 1980s, the group returned to the top of the charts with *Kokomo*, a song from the film "Cocktail" (1987), although by this time, Wilson was no longer recording with it. His songs were also recorded by the Hollyridge Strings on **The Beach Boys Songbook** (1964, Capitol) US#82, while his work with other artists was collected on **Brian Wilson Productions** (1980, World Records). CHART COMPOSITIONS: *Surfin'* (1961) US#75, *Surfin' Safari* [viii] (1962) US#14, *409* (1962) US#76, *Ten Little Indians* (1962) US#49, *Surfin' U.S.A.* [iii] (1963) g R&B#20 US#3 UK#34, *Shut Down* [iv] (1963) US#23, *Surfer Girl* (1963) R&B#18 US#7, *Little Deuce Coup* [iv] (1963) R&B#28 US#15, *Be True to Your School* (1963) R&B#27 US#6, *In My Room* [viii] (1963) US#23, *Fun Fun Fun* [vi] (1964) US#5, new version with Status Quo (1996) UK#24; *I Get Around* (1964) g US#1, *Don't Worry Baby* [iv] (1964) US#24, *When I Grow Up (To Be a Man)* (1964) US#9 UK#27, *Wendy* (1964) US#44, *Little Honda* (1964) US#65, *Dance,*

Dance, Dance [ix] (1965) US#8 UK#24, *She Knows Me Too Well* (1964) US#101, *Please Let Me Wonder* (1965) US#52, *Help Me, Rhonda* (1965) g US#1 UK#27, *California Girls* (1965) US#3 UK#26, *Little Girl I Once Knew, The* (1965) US#20, *Sloop John B.* (arrangement only) (1966) g US#3 UK#2, *God Only Knows* [ii] (1966) US#39 UK#2, *Wouldn't It Be Nice* [ii] (1966) US#8, re-issued (1975) US#103, re-issued (1990) UK#58; *Good Vibrations* [vi] (1966) g US#1 UK#1, re-issued (1976) UK#18; *Heroes and Villains* [vii] (1967) US#12 UK#8, *Darlin'* [vi] (1968) US#19 UK#12, *Wild Honey* [vi] (1968) US#31 UK#29, *Friends* (1968) US#47 UK#25, *Do It Again* [vi] (1968) US#20 UK#1, re-issued (1991) UK#61, *Break Away* [vi] (1969) US#63 UK#6, *Add Some Music to Your Day* (1970) US#64, *Marcella* (1972) US#110, *Sail on Sailor* [i] (1973) US#79 UK#49, *It's O.K.* [vi] (1976) US#29, *Here Comes the Night* [vi] (1979) US#44 UK#37, *Good Timin'* [ix] (1979) US#40, *Goin' On* (1980) US#83, *Beach Boys Medley* (1981) US#12 UK#47. ALBUMS: **Surfin' Safari** (1962) US#32, **Surfin' U.S.A.** (1963) g US#2 UK#17, **Surfer Girl** (1963) g US#7 UK#13, **Little Deuce Coup** (1963) p US#4, **Shut Down, Volume 2** (1964) g US#13, **All Summer Long** (1964) g US#4 UK#8, **The Beach Boys' Christmas Album** (1964) g, **The Beach Boys Concert** (1964) g US#1, **The Beach Boys Today** (1965) g US#4 UK#6, **Summer Days (And Summer Nights)** (1965) g US#2 UK#4, **The Beach Boys' Party** (1965) US#6 UK#3, **Pet Sounds** (1966) US#10 UK#2, **Smiley Smile** (1967) US#41 UK#9; **Wild Honey** (1967) US#24 UK#7, **Friends** (1968) US#126 UK#13, **20/20** (1969) US#68 UK#3, **Live in London** (1970) re-issued as **The Beach Boys '69** (1976, all Capitol) US#75; **Sunflower** (1970) US#151 UK#29, **Surf's Up** (1971) US#29 UK#15, **Carl and the Passions — So Tough/Pet Sounds** (1972) US#50 UK#25, **Holland** (1973), **The Beach Boys in Concert** (1973) g US#25, **15 Big Ones** (1976) g US#8 UK#31, **The Beach Boys Love You** (1977) US#53 UK#28, **M.I.U. Album** (1978, all Brother) US#151; **L.A. (Light Album)** (1979) US#100 UK#32, **Keepin' the Summer Alive** (1980) US#75 UK#54, **The Beach Boys** (1985, all Caribou) US#52 UK#60; **Still Cruisin'** (1989, Capitol) g US#8 UK#49; **Summer in Paradise** (1992, Brother). COMPILATIONS: **Best of the Beach Boys** (1966) p US#8, **Best of the Beach Boys** (1966) UK#2, **Best of the Beach Boys, Volume 2** (1966) UK#3, **Best of the Beach Boys, Volume 2** (1967) p US#50, **Best of the Beach Boys, Volume 3** (1968) US#153 UK#9, **Stack O' Tracks** (1968), **Greatest Hits** (1970) UK#5, **Endless Summer** (1974, all Capitol) g US#1; **Wild Honey/20/20** (1974) US#50, **Friends/Smiley Smile** (1974, both Brother) US#125; **Spirit of America** (1975, Capitol) g US#8; **Good**

Vibrations — The Best of the Beach Boys (1975, Brother) US#25; **20 Golden Greats** (1976, Capitol) UK#1; **The Beach Boys Interviews** (1980), **Ten Years of Harmony, 1970–1980** (1981, Caribou) US#156; **Sunshine Dream** (1982) US#180, **Rarities** (1983), **Very Best of the Beach Boys** (1983) UK#1, **Made in the U.S.A.** (1986) g US#96, **Summer Dreams** (1990) UK#1, **Good Vibrations — 30 Years of the Beach Boys** (1993) g; **Best of the Beach Boys** (1995) UK#25; **Greatest Hits** (1996) US#198, **The Pet Sounds Sessions** (1996, all Capitol). Wilson's declining mental and physical health had seemingly destroyed his music making capabilities by the 1980s, but controversial treatment by the therapist, Eugene Landy, at least returned him to the recording studio, resulting in the album **Brian Wilson** (1988), a flawed work that nevertheless contained at least three new Wilson classics, *Love and Mercy, Melt Away* and *One for the Boys*. His two 1995 projects, **I Just Wasn't Made for These Times** and **Orange Crate Art**, were every bit as good as anything he had recorded since the 1960s. CHART COMPOSITION: *Caroline No* [ii] (1966) US#32. ALBUMS: **Brian Wilson** (1988, Sire) US#54; **I Just Wasn't Made for These Times** (1995, MCA) UK#59: **Orange Crate Art** with Van Dyke Parks (1995, Warner Brothers). HIT VERSIONS: *Almost Summer* [vi] Celebration (1978) US#28, *Beach Boy Gold* Gidea Park (1981) UK#11, *California Girls* David Lee Roth (1985) US#3 UK#68, *Darlin'* [vi] David Cassidy (1975) UK#16/ Paul Davis (1978) US#51/Yipes (1980) US#68; *Dead Man's Curve* Jan & Dean (1963) US#8, *Don't Worry Baby* [iv] Tokens (1970) US#95/B.J. Thomas (1977) US#17/Los Lobos (1985) UK#57; *God Only Knows* [ii] Vogues (1970) US#101/Marilyn Scott (1977) US#61/Diesel Park West (1992) UK#57; *Good Vibrations* [vi] Hugh Montenegro (1969) US#112/ Troggs (1975) US#102/Todd Rundgren (1976) US#34/ Psychic T.V. (1986) UK#65; *Help Me, Rhonda* Johnny Rivers (1975) US#22, *In My Room* [viii] Sagittarius (1969) US#86, *Little Honda* Hondells (1964) US#9, *My Buddy Seat* Hondells (1964) US#87, *New Girl in School, The* Jan & Dean (1964) US#37, *People and Me* New Colony Six (1970) US#116, *Ride the Wild Surf* Jan & Dean (1964) US#16, *Seasons of Gold* Gidea Park (1981) UK#28, *Sidewalk Surfin'* Jan & Dean (1964) US#25, *Surf City* Jan & Dean (1963) g R&B#3 US#1 UK#26, *Surfin' U.S.A.* [iii] Leif Garrett (1977) US#20. Co-writers: [i] T. Almer/R. Kennedy/J. Riley, [ii] Tony Asher, [iii] Chuck Berry, [iv] Roger Christian (d. 1991), [v] Reggie Dunbar, [vi] Mike Love (b. March 15, 1941, Baldwin Hills, CA), [vii] Van Dyke Parks (b. January 3, 1941, MS), [viii] Gary Usher, [ix] Carl Wilson (b. December 21, 1946, Hawthorne, CA; d. 1998, CA). (*See also under* Jan BERRY.)

1027. WILSON, Frank E. R&B producer. A former solo singer who became a respected Motown writer and producer during the 1970s, working with nearly all of the label's acts. HIT VERSIONS: *Boogie Down* [i] Eddie Kendricks (1974) R&B#1 US#2 UK#39, *Chained* Marvin Gaye (1968) R&B#8 US#32, *Darling Come Back Home* [iii] Eddie Kendricks (1973) R&B#26 US#67, *Keep on Truckin'* [i] Eddie Kendricks (1973) R&B#1 US#1 UK#18, *Look What You've Done to My Heart* [iv] Marilyn McCoo & Billy Davis, Jr. (1977) R&B#27 US#51, *Son of Sagittarius* [i] Eddie Kendricks (1974) R&B#5 US#28, *Stoned Love* [v] Supremes (1970) R&B#1 US#7 UK#3, *Up the Ladder to the Roof* [ii] Supremes (1970) R&B#5 US#10 UK#6. Co-writers: [i] Leonard Caston/Anita Poree, [ii] Vincent Dimirco, [iii] King Errisson/K. Wakefield, [iv] J. Footman/T. McFaddin, [v] Yennik Somoht. (*See also under* Berry GORDY, Jr., Smokey ROBINSON, R. Dean TAYLOR.)

1028. WILSON, Norro (b. Norris D. Wilson, April 4, 1938, Scottsville, KY) C&W vocalist. A country performer who charted ten hits between 1969–1977, but one who has been considerably more successful as a songwriter for others. HIT VERSIONS: *Baby, Baby (I Know You're a Lady)* David Houston (1970) C&W#1, *I'll See Him Through* Tammy Wynette (1970) C&W#2 US#100, *Soul Song* Joe Stampley (1973) C&W#1. (*See also under* Billy SHERRILL.)

1029. WINBUSH, Angela (b. St. Louis, MO) R&B producer and vocalist. A former backing singer for Dolly Parton and Jean Carne, who was successful as one half of the vocal duo Rene and Angela between 1978–1986. CHART COMPOSITIONS: *Do You Really Love Me* [ii] (1980) R&B#43, *Everything We Do* [ii] (1980) R&B#39, *I Love You More* [ii] (1981) R&B#14, *Wall to Wall* [ii] (1981) R&B#37, *Imaginary Playmates* [ii] (1982) R&B#26, *Banging the Boogie* [ii] (1983) R&B#33, *My First Love* [ii] (1983) R&B#12, *Save Your Love (For Number 1)* [ii] featuring Kurtis Blow (1985) R&B#1 US#101 UK#66, *I'll Be Good* [ii] (1985) R&B#4 US#47 UK#22, *Secret Rendezvous* [ii] (1985) UK#54, *Your Smile* [ii] (1986) R&B#1 US#62, *You Don't Have to Cry* [ii] (1986) R&B#2 US#75, *No How-No Way* (1986) R&B#26. ALBUMS: **Wall to Wall** (1981, Capitol) US#100; **Street Called Desire** (1985, Mercury) g US#64. Winbush also recorded as a solo artist, before moving into record production. CHART COMPOSITIONS: *Angel* (1987) R&B#1, *Run to Me* (1987) R&B#4, *C'Est Toi (It's You)* (1988) R&B#47. ALBUMS: **Sharp** (1987) US#81, **The Real Thing** (1989, both Mercury) US#113; **Angela Winbush** (1994, Elektra) US#96. HIT VERSIONS:

Baby Don't Cry Lalah Hathaway (1991) UK#54, *Sensitive Lover* [i] Isley Brothers featuring Ronald Isley (1992) R&B#24, *Smooth Sailin' Tonight* Isley Brothers (1987) R&B#3, *Whatever Turns You On* [i] Isley Brothers featuring Ronald Isley (1992) R&B#46, *Young Love* [ii] Janet Jackson (1982) R&B#6 US#64. Co-writers: [i] Ronald Isley, [ii] Rene Moore.

1030. WINCHESTER, Jessi (b. James R. Winchester, May 17, 1944, Shreveport, LA) Rock guitarist and vocalist. A folk influenced singer-songwriter who studied in Germany, and emigrated to Canada in 1967 in order to avoid the Vietnam draft. Winchester's material has been recorded by a variety of artists, including Joan Baez and Ian Matthews. CHART COMPOSITIONS: *Nothing But a Breeze* (1977) US#86, *Say What* (1981) US#32. ALBUMS: **Jesse Winchester** (1971, Ampex); **Third Down, 110 to Go** (1972) US#193, **Learn to Love It** (1974), **Let the Rough Side Drag** (1976), **Nothing But a Breeze** (1977) US#115, **A Touch on the Rainy Side** (1978) US#156, **Talk Memphis** (1981) US#188, **Live at the Bijou Cafe** (1975, all Bearsville). HIT VERSIONS: *Let's Make a Baby King* Wynnona (1993) C&W#61, *Mississippi You're on My Mind* Stoney Edwards (1975) C&W#20, *O What a Thrill* Mavericks (1994) C&W#38+, *Rhumba Girl* Nicolette Larson (1979) US#47, *Sweet Little Shoe* Dan Seals (1991) C&W#62, *Thanks to You* Emmylou Harris (1994) C&W#65.

1031. WINWOOD, Steve (b. Stephen Philip Winwood, May 12, 1948, Birmingham, England) Rock multi-instrumentalist and vocalist. A co-founder of the R&B influenced Spencer Davis Group, which charted with his compositions *Gimme Some Loving* [iii] (1966) UK#2, re-mixed (1967) US#7; and *I'm a Man* [vi] (1967) R&B#48 US#10 UK#9. ALBUMS: **Their First LP** (1965) UK#6, **The Second Album** (1966) UK#3, **Autumn '66** (1966, all Fontana) UK#12. COMPILATIONS: **Gimme Some Lovin'** (1967) US#54, **I'm a Man** (1967) US#83, **Greatest Hits** (1968, all United Artists) US#195. In 1967, Winwood left the group to form the folk, jazz and rock influenced Traffic. CHART COMPOSITIONS: *Paper Sun* [i] (1967) US#94 UK#5, *Here We Go Round the Mulberry Bush* [ii] (1967) UK#8, *Empty Page* (1970) US#74, *Gimme Some Lovin'* [iii] (1971) US#68. ALBUMS: **Mr. Fantasy** (1968) US#88 UK#8, **Traffic** (1968) US#17 UK#9, **Last Exit** (1969) US#19, **John Barleycorn Must Die** (1970) g US#5 UK#11, **Welcome to the Canteen** (1971) US#26, **The Low Spark of the High Heeled Boys** (1972) g US#7, **Shoot-Out at the Fantasy Factory** (1973) g US#6, **Traffic — On the Road** (1973) US#29 UK#40, **When the Eagle Flies** (1974, all Island) g US#9 UK#31; **Far from Home** (1994,

Virgin) US#33 UK#29. COMPILATIONS: **Best of Traffic** (1970) US#48, **Heavy Traffic** (1975) US#155, **More Heavy Traffic** (1975, all United Artists) US#193. In 1969, he linked up with Eric Clapton to record as Blind Faith, and during the mid–1970s, he worked with the percussionist Stomu Yamashta on the album **Go** (1976, Island) US#60. Winwood's solo recordings have merged a more commercial sound with his R&B roots. CHART COMPOSITIONS: *While You See a Chance* [v] (1981) US#7 UK#45, *Arc of a Diver* [vii] (1981) US#48, *Night Train* [v] (1981) US#104, *Still in the Game* [v] (1982) US#47, *Valerie* [v] (1982) US#70 UK#51, re-mixed (1987) US#9 UK#19; *Higher Love* [v] (1986) US#1 UK#13, *Freedom Overspill* [iv] (1986) US#20 UK#69, *The Finer Things* [v] (1987) US#8, *Back in the High Life Again* [v] (1987) US#13 UK#53, *Talking Back to the Night* [v] (1988) US#57, *Roll with It* [v] (1988) R&B#30 US#1 UK#53, *Don't You Know What the Night Can Do?* [v] (1988) US#6, *Holding On* [v] (1988) US#11, *Hearts on Fire* [i] (1989) US#53, *One and Only Man* (1990) US#18. ALBUMS: **Steve Winwood** (1977) US#22 UK#12, **Arc of a Diver** (1981) g US#3 UK#13, **Talking Back to the Night** (1982) US#28 UK#6, **Back in the High Life** (1986, all Island) p US#3 UK#8; **Roll with It** (1988) p US#1 UK#4, **Refugees of the Heart** (1990) g US#27, **Junction Seven** (1997, all Virgin). COMPILATIONS: **Winwood** (1971, United Artists) US#93; **Chronicles** (1987) p US#26 UK#12, **The Finer Things** (1995, both Island). HIT VERSIONS: *Gimme Some Loving* [iii] Jordan Brothers (1967) US#129/Kongas (1978) US#84/Blues Brothers (1980) US#18; *I'm a Man* [vi] Chicago (1971) US#49/Yellow Payges (1970) US#102; *Low Spark of High Heeled Boys* EMF (1992) UK#29. Co-writers: [i] Jim Capaldi, [ii] Jim Capaldi/Dave Mason/Chris Wood, [iii] Spencer Davis/Muff Winwood, [iv] George Fleming/Jake Hooker, [v] Will Jennings, [vi] Jimmy Miller, [vii] Vivian Stanshall. (*See also under* Eric CLAPTON, Dave MASON.)

1032. WISE, Fred Film lyricist. A lyricist who is best known for the material that he co-wrote for the Elvis Presley films "King Creole" (1958), "G.I. Blues" (1960), "Blue Hawaii" (1961), "Kid Galahad" (1962), "Fun in Acapulco" and "It Happened at the World's Fair" (both 1963); "Kissin' Cousins" and "Roustabout" (both 1964); "Tickle Me" (1965), "Frankie and Johnny," "Paradise, Hawaiian Style" and "Spinout" (all 1966). HIT VERSIONS: *Bells of San Raquel* [ii] Dick Jurgens (1941) US#7, *Best Man, The* [i] Les Brown (1946) US#15/Nat "King" Cole (1946) US#14; *Don't Ask Me Why* [x] Elvis Presley (1958) R&B#9 US#25, *Fame and Fortune* [x] Elvis Presley (1960) US#17, *Follow That Dream* [x] Elvis

Presley (1962) US#15 UK#34, *I Won't Cry Anymore* [v] Tony Bennett (1951) US#12, *Kissin' Cousins* [viii] Elvis Presley (1964) US#12 UK#10, *Let's Walk That-a-Way* [ix] Doris Day & Johnnie Ray (1953) UK#4, *Misirlou* [vii] Harry James (1941) US#22/Jan August (1946) US#7/Leon Berry (1953) US#26; *Mother Nature and Father Time* [ix] Nat "King" Cole (1953) UK#7/Brook Benton (1965) R&B#26 US#53, *Oo! What You Do to Me* [ix] Patti Page (1953) US#16, *Pretty Little Black Eyed Susie* [ix] Guy Mitchell (1953) UK#2, *Rock-a-Hula Baby* [vi] Elvis Presley (1962) US#23 UK#1, *Roses in the Rain* [iii] Frankie Carle (1947) US#9, *You, You, You Are the One* [iv] Ames Brothers (1949) US#23/Ken Griffin (1949) US#29/Russ Morgan (1949) US#17/Three Suns (1949) US#21. Co-writers: [i] Roy Alfred, [ii] Lorenzo Barcelata/Milton Leeds, [iii] Frankie Carle/Al Frisch, [iv] Tetos Demey/Milton Leeds, [v] Al Frisch, [vi] Dolores Fuller/Ben Wiseman, [vii] Milton Leeds/N. Roubanis/S.K. Russell, [viii] Randy Starr, [ix] Kay Twomey/Ben Wiseman, [x] Ben Wiseman.

1033. WITHERS, Bill (b. July 4, 1938, Slab Fork, WV) R&B guitarist and vocalist. A late starter in popular music, who did not begin performing professionally until he was thirty-three years old, when he became an almost overnight star with his million selling single *Ain't No Sunshine* (1971). Withers' debut album **Just as I Am** (1971) remains one of the most accomplished singer-songwriter efforts of the decade. During the 1980s, his music took on a lusher sound, but he has remained in semi-retirement for much of the 1990s. CHART COMPOSITIONS: *Ain't No Sunshine* (1971) g R&B#6 US#3, re-issued (1988) US#82; *Grandma's Hands* (1971) R&B#18 US#42, *Lean on Me* (1972) g R&B#1 US#1 UK#18, *Use Me* (1972) g R&B#2 US#2, *Let Us Love* (1972) R&B#17 US#47, *Kissing My Love* (1973) R&B#12 US#31, *Friend of Mine* (1973) R&B#25 US#80, *The Same Love That Made Me Laugh* (1974) R&B#10 US#50, *You* (1974) R&B#15, *Heartbreak Road* (1974) R&B#13 US#89, *Make Love to Your Mind* (1975) R&B#10 US#76, *I Wish You Well* (1976) R&B#54, *If I Didn't Mean You Well* (1976) R&B#74, *Close to Me* (1977) R&B#88, *Lovely Day* [iii] (1977) R&B#6 US#30 UK#7, re-mixed (1988) UK#4; *Lovely Night for Dancing* (1978) R&B#75, *Don't It Make It Better* (1979) R&B#30, *You Got the Stuff (Part 1)* (1979) R&B#85, *Just the Two of Us* [ii] with Grover Washington, Jr. (1981) g R&B#3 US#2 UK#34, *U.S.A.* (1981) R&B#83, *In the Name of Love* [ii] with Ralph MacDonald (1984) R&B#13 US#58, *Oh Yeah!* (1985) R&B#22 US#106 UK#60, *Something That Turns You On* (1985) R&B#46. ALBUMS: **Just as I Am** (1971) US#39, **Still Bill** (1972) g US#4, **Live at Carnegie Hall** (1973) US#63, +

'Justments (1974, all Sussex) US#67; **Making Music** (1975) US#81, **Naked and Warm** (1976) US#169, **Menagerie** (1977) g US#39 UK#27, **'Bout Love** (1978) US#134, **Watching You Watching Me** (1985, all Columbia) US#143 UK#60. COMPILATIONS: **Best of Bill Withers** (1975, Sussex) US#182; **Greatest Hits** (1981, Columbia) US#183 UK#90. HIT VERSIONS: *Ain't No Sunshine* Michael Jackson (1972) UK#8/Lyn Collins on B-side of *Think (About It)* (1972) R&B#9 US#66/Sivuca (1984) UK#56/Kid Frost as *No Sunshine* (1992) US#95; *Grandma's Hands* Simply Red on *Montreux EP* (1992) UK#11, *Harlem* 5th Dimension (1974) R&B#87, *In the Name of Love* [ii] Roberta Flack (1982) R&B#80, *Lean on Me* Paul Delicato (1975) C&W#91/Mud (1976) UK#7/Jack Grayson (1984) C&W#77/Club Nouveau (1987) g R&B#2 US#1 UK#3/Michael Bolton (1994) UK#14; *Lovely Day* [iii] S.O.U.L. S.Y.S.T.E.M. introducing Michelle Visage (1992) R&B#44 US#43 UK#17, *Really into You* [i] Around the Way (1992) US#89, *Soul Shadows* Crusaders (1980) R&B#41. Co-writers: [i] K. Diaz/Ralph MacDonald/William Salter, [ii] Ralph MacDonald/William Salter, [iii] Skip Scarborough.

1034. WOLF, Kate (b. Kathryn Louise Allen, January 27, 1942; d. December 10, 1986, both CA) C&W guitarist and vocalist. A country influenced singer-songwriter, who recorded a small catalogue of highly individualistic albums, before dying of leukemia at the age of forty-four. ALBUMS: **Back Roads** (1976), **Lines on Paper** (1977), **Safe at Anchor** (1979), **Close to You** (1981), **Give Yourself to Love** (1982), **Looking Back at You** (1983), **Poet's Heart** (1984), **Wind Blows Wild** (1985), **Evening in Austin** (1990, all Kaleidoscope). COMPILATION: **Gold in California** (1988, Kaleidoscope).

1035. WOLF, Peter (b. Peter Blankfield, March 7, 1946, New York, NY) Rock vocalist. After a brief period as a member of the 1960s group the Hallucinations, Wolf joined the R&B influenced rock act the J. Geils Band as lead vocalist. CHART COMPOSITIONS: *Give It to Me* [iv] (1973) US#30, *Make Up Your Mind* [iv] (1973) US#98, *Must of Got Lost* [iv] (1974) US#12, *You're the Only One* [iv] (1977) US#83, *One Last Kiss* [iv] (1978) US#35 UK#74, *Take It Back* [iv] (1979) US#67, *Come Back* [iv] (1980) US#32, *Love Stinks* [iv] (1980) US#38, *Just Can't Wait* [iv] (1980) US#78, *Freeze-Frame* [iv] (1982) p R&B#25 US#4. ALBUMS: **J. Geils Band** (1971) US#195, **The Morning After** (1971) US#64, **Live — Full House** (1972) g US#54, **Bloodshot** (1973) g US#10, **Nightmares...and Other Tales from the Vinyl Jungle** (1974) US#26, **Hotline** (1975) US#36, **Blow Your Face Out** (1975)

US#40, **Monkey Island** (1977, all Atlantic) US#51; **Sanctuary** (1979) g US#49, **Love Stinks** (1980) g US#18, **Freeze-Frame** (1982) p US#1 UK#12, **Showtime!** (1983, all EMI America) g US#23. COMPILATIONS: **Best of the J. Geils Band** (1979, Atlantic) US#129; **Flashback** (1987, EMI America); **Anthology — House Party** (1994, Rhino). Since leaving the group in 1982, Wolf has pursued a solo career. CHART COMPOSITIONS: *Lights Out* [ii] (1984) US#12, *I Need You Tonight* [i] (1984) US#36, *Oo-Ee-Diddley-Bop* [iii] (1985) US#61, *Come as You Are* [v] (1987) US#15, *Can't Get Started* (1987) US#75. ALBUMS: **Lights Out** (1984) US#24, **Come as You Are** (1987, both EMI America) US#53; **Up to No Good** (1989, MCA); **Long Line** (1994, Reprise). Co-writers: [i] Paul Bliss, [ii] Don Covay, [iii] Michael Jonzun/G. Worthy, [iv] Seth Justman, [v] Mayer.

1036. WOMACK, Bobby (b. March 4, 1944, Cleveland, OH) R&B guitarist and vocalist. One of the defining artists in R&B, who followed in a gospel-soul tradition that began with Sam Cooke. Womack has charted over forty hits since 1968, and his underrated guitar playing graced many of Atlantic Records' finest sides during the 1960s. He grew up listening to country and blues music before mastering the guitar in his early teens. In 1957, he performed in the gospel vocal group the Five Blind Boys, before forming the Womack Brothers, and playing guitar in Sam Cooke's Soul Stirrers. The Womack Brothers first recorded for Cooke's Sar label, before changing their name to the Valentinos, to perform a stunning blend of gospel influenced R&B on the hits *I'll Make It Alright* (1962) US#97, *It's All Over Now* [xiii] (1964) US#94 and *I Can Understand It* (1973) US#109. ALBUMS: **The Valentinos and the Sims Twins** (1968, Soul City); **The Chess Masters, 1965–1966** (1984, Chess). Womack's solo recordings for the short-lived Beverly Glen label are among the last genuine soul music ever recorded. CHART COMPOSITIONS: *What Is This* (1968) R&B#33, *It's Gonna Rain* [i] (1969) R&B#43, *How I Miss You Baby* [i] (1969) R&B#14 US#93, *More Than I Can Stand* [i] (1970) R&B#23 US#90, *The Preacher (Part 2)* [viii]/*More Than I Can Stand* [i] (1971) R&B#30 US#111, *Breezin'** (1971) R&B#43, *Communication* (1971) R&B#40, *That's the Way I Feel 'Bout Cha* (1972) R&B#2 US#27, *Woman's Gotta Have It* [ii] (1972) R&B#1 US#60, *Across 110th Street* [vi] (1973) R&B#19 US#56, *I'm Through Trying to Prove My Love to You* (1973) R&B#80 US#101, *You're Welcome, Stop on By* [xi] (1974) R&B#5 US#59, *I Don't Know* [xi] (1974) R&B#18, *Check It Out* (1975) R&B#6 US#91, *It's All Over Now* [xiii] with Bill Withers (1975) R&B#68, *Where There's a Will, There's a Way*

(1976) R&B#13, *Daylight* [ix] (1976) R&B#5, *Standing in the Safety Zone* [ix] (1977) R&B#90, *Trust Your Heart* [iii] (1978) R&B#47, *How Could You Break My Heart* [vii] (1979) R&B#40, *If You Think You're Lonely Now* [iv] (1982) R&B#3 US#101, *Secrets* [iv] (1982) R&B#55, *Where Do We Go from Here* [iv] (1982) R&B#26, *Love Has Finally Come at Last* [vii] with Patti LaBelle (1984) R&B#3 US#88, *Tell Me Why* [iv] (1984) R&B#54 UK#60, *Let Me Kiss It Where It Hurts* (1985) R&B#50, *I'm Back for More* with Lulu (1993) US#108 UK#27. ALBUMS: **Fly Me to the Moon** (1968) US#174, **My Prescription** (1969, both Minit); **The Womack Live** (1971, Liberty) US#188; **High Contrast*** (1971, Blue Thumb); **Communication** (1972) US#83, **Understanding** (1972) US#43, **Across 110th Street** ost (1973) US#50, **Facts of Life** (1973) US#37, **Lookin' For a Love Again** (1974) US#85, **I Don't Know What the World Is Coming To** (1975) US#126, **Safety Zone** (1976) US#147, **Bobby Womack Goes C&W** (1976, all United Artists); **Home Is Where the Heart Is** (1976), **Pieces** (1978, both Columbia); **Roads of Life** (1979, Arista); **The Poet** (1981) US#29, **The Poet II** (1984, both Beverly Glen) US#60 UK#31; **So Many Rivers** (1985) US#66 UK#28, **Womagic** (1986), **The Last Soul Man** (1987, both MCA); **Save the Children** (1990, Solar); **Soul Seduction Supreme** (1991, Castle). COMPILATIONS: **Greatest Hits** (1974) US#142, **A Portrait of Bobby Womack** (1979, both United Artists); **Someday We'll All Be Free** (1985, Beverly Glen); **Lookin' for a Love — The Best of Bobby Womack, 1968–1975** (1993, Razor & Tie). HIT VERSIONS: *Baby, Help Me* Percy Sledge (1967) R&B#44 US#87, *Breezin'* George Benson (1976) R&B#55 US#63, *Daylight* [ix] Vicki Sue Robinson (1976) R&B#91 US#63, *I Can Understand It* New Birth (1973) R&B#4 US#35/Kokomo (1975) US#101; *I Found a True Love* Wilson Pickett (1968) R&B#11 US#42, *I'm a Midnight Mover* [x] Wilson Pickett (1968) R&B#6 US#24 UK#38, *I'm in Love* Wilson Pickett (1967) R&B#4 US#45/Aretha Franklin (1974) R&B#1 US#19; *I'm Through Trying to Prove My Love to You* Millie Jackson (1975) R&B#58, *I've Come a Long Way* Wilson Pickett (1968) R&B#46 US#101, *(If You Don't Want My Love) Give It Back* Lea Roberts (1973) US#94, *It's All Over Now* [xiii] Rolling Stones (1964) US#26 UK#1/Rod Stewart (1970) US#126/John Anderson (1985) C&W#15; *Jealous Love* [xii] Wilson Pickett (1968) R&B#18 US#50, *People Make the World (What It Is Today)* Roosevelt Grier (1968) US#126, *She's Lookin' Good* Wilson Pickett (1968) R&B#7 US#15, *Trust in Me* Vicki Sue Robinson (1978) US#110, *You're Welcome, Stop on By* [xi] Rufus featuring Chaka Khan on B-side of *Ain't Nobody* (1984) US#22 UK#8. With: * Gabor Szabo. Co-writers: [i] Darryl Carter, [ii] Darryl Carter/Linda Womack, [iii] Don Davis/Leon Ware, [iv] Jim Ford, [v] Richard Griffin/Patrick Moten, [vi] J.J. Johnson, [vii] Patrick Moten, [viii] D. Patterson, [ix] Harold Payne, [x] Wilson Pickett, [xi] Truman Thomas, [xii] Cecil Womack, [xiii] Shirley Womack. (*See also under* Cecil WOMACK.)

1037. WOMACK, Cecil (b. 1947, Cleveland, OH) R&B producer and vocalist. A younger brother of Bobby Womack, who first sang as a member of the Womack Brothers during the 1950s. In the 1960s, Womack managed his first wife, the singer Mary Wells, for whom he wrote *The Doctor*. During the 1970s, he wrote and produced at Philadelphia International Records. In 1976, he married his second wife, Sam Cooke's daughter Linda Cooke, with whom he began writing and performing together as Womack and Womack, a group concept that has become a large extended family. CHART COMPOSITIONS: *Love T.K.O.* [i] (1984) R&B#87, *Love Wars* [iii] (1984) UK#14, *Baby I'm Scared of You* [iii] (1984) R&B#25 UK#72, *Strange and Funny* [ii] (1985) R&B#44, *Soul Love-Soul Man* [iii] (1986) UK#58, *Teardrops* [iii] (1988) UK#3, *Life's Just a Ballgame* [iii] (1988) UK#32, *Celebrate the World* [iii] (1989) UK#19, *Secret Star* (1994) UK#46. ALBUMS: **Love Wars** (1984) UK#45, **Radio M.U.S.I.C. Man** (1985, both Elektra) UK#56; **Starbright** (1988, EMI Manhattan); **Conscience** (1988, both Fourth & Broadway) UK#4; **Free Spirit** (1990, RCA); **Transformed into the House of Zekkeriyas** (1993, both Warner Brothers). HIT VERSIONS: *Doctor, The* Mary Wells (1968) R&B#22 US#65, *I Just Want to Satisfy* O'Jays (1982) R&B#15 US#101, *I'm So Proud* Johnnie Taylor (1983) R&B#55, *It's My Party* Chaka Khan (1988) US#71, *Love T.K.O.* [i] David Oliver (1980) R&B#77/Teddy Pendergrass (1980) R&B#2 US#44. Co-writers: [i] Eddie Nobel/Linda Womack (b. Linda Cooke, 1952), [ii] Bobby Womack/Linda Womack, [iii] Linda Womack. (*See also under* Bobby WOMACK.)

1038. WONDER, Stevie (b. Steveland Morris, May 13, 1950, Saginau, MN) R&B multi-instrumentalist, producer and vocalist. One of the most successful and popular artists in contemporary music, who has seldom followed musical trends, and has frequently been an influence on other performers. Wonder is capable of writing proficiently in any style, from the reggae of *Masterblaster (Jammin')* to the light samba of *Golden Lady*, often creating rhythm arrangements and melody as a single entity. He has sold over one hundred million albums, and much of his early 1970s work is regarded as classic R&B. Born blind, Wonder first sang in the church choir, and overcame his handicap through his love

of music, quickly mastering many instruments, including the drums, piano and harmonica. At the age of ten, Wonder was introduced to Berry Gordy, Jr. by Ronald White of the Miracles, who signed the talented youngster to Motown Records. Marketed as Little Stevie Wonder, he did not display his musical genius until the mid–1960s, when he had matured into a gifted tunesmith. During the early 1970s, Wonder studied music theory and composition at the University of Carolina, where he added harmonic skills to his formidable instrumental talents. In 1971, at the age of twenty-one, he became entitled to his childhood royalties, with which he formed his own production and publishing companies, and re-signed, to Motown under one of the first ever contracts to give an artist total control over his recordings and releases. Wonder's first album under the new arrangement was the significantly advanced **Where I'm Coming From** (1971), which featured over-layered vocals, structured key and time changes, and his lazy, distinctive, behind the beat drumming. Making extensive use of synthesizers in collaboration with two of its earliest pioneers, Malcom Cecil and Robert Margouleff, Wonder recorded a quartet of albums that changed the sound and course of R&B, **Music of My Mind** (1972), **Talking Book** and **Innervisions** (both 1973); and **Fulfillingness' First Finale** (1974), all of which mixed funk and rock with socially concerned lyrics and delightful love ballads. Wonder's masterpiece **Songs in the Key of Life** (1976), blended jazz, funk, rock and pop, and spent fourteen weeks at the top of the American chart. He has continued to update his sound well into the 1990s, but looks unlikely to top the creative peak that he achieved in the 1970s. CHART COMPOSITIONS: *Uptight (Everything's Alright)* [iii] (1966) R&B#1 US#3 UK#14, *Hey Love* [i] (1967) R&B#9 US#90, *I Was Made to Love Her* [iv] (1967) R&B#1 US#2 UK#5, *I'm Wondering* [iii] (1967) R&B#4 US#12 UK#22, *Shoo-Be-Doo-Be-Doo-Da-Day* [iv] (1968) R&B#1 US#9 UK#46, *You Met Your Match* [ix] (1969) R&B#2 US#35, *I Don't Know Why I Love You Girl* [x] (1969) R&B#16 US#39 UK#14, *My Cherie Amour* [iii] (1969) R&B#4 US#4 UK#44, *Never Had a Dream Come True* [iii] (1970) R&B#11 US#26 UK#6, *Signed, Sealed, Delivered, I'm Yours* [iv] (1970) R&B#1 US#3 UK#15, *Never Dreamed You'd Leave in Summer* [xvi] (1971) US#78, *If You Really Love Me* [xvi] (1971) R&B#4 US#8 UK#20, *Superwoman (Where Were You When I Needed You)* (1972) R&B#13 US#33, *Keep on Running* (1972) R&B#36 US#90, *Superstition* (1973) R&B#1 US#1 UK#11, *You Are The Sunshine of My Life* (1973) R&B#3 US#1 UK#7, *Higher Ground* (1973) R&B#1 US#4 UK#29, *Living for the City* (1973) R&B#1 US#8 UK#15, *He's Mistra Know It All* (1973) UK#10,

Don't You Worry 'Bout a Thing (1973) R&B#2 US#16, *You Haven't Done Nothin'* (1974) R&B#1 US#1 UK#30, *Boogie on Reggae Woman* (1974) R&B#1 US#3 UK#12, *I Wish* (1976) R&B#1 US#1 UK#5, *Sir Duke* (1977) R&B#1 US#1 UK#2, *Another Star* (1977) R&B#18 US#32 UK#29, *As* (1977) R&B#36 US#36, *Send One Your Love* (1979) R&B#5 US#4 UK#52, *Black Orchid* (1979) UK#63, *Outside My Window* (1979) R&B#56 US#52 UK#52, *Masterblaster (Jammin')* (1980) R&B#1 US#5 UK#2, *I Ain't Gonna Stand for It* (1980) R&B#4 US#11 UK#10, *Happy Birthday* (1980) UK#2, *Lately* (1981) R&B#29 US#64 UK#3, *Did I Hear You Say You Love Me* (1981) R&B#74, *That Girl* (1982) R&B#1 US#4 UK#39, *Do I Do* (1982) R&B#2 US#13 UK#10, *Ribbon in the Sky* (1982) R&B#10 US#54 UK#45, *Frontline* (1982) UK#94, *I Just Called to Say I Love You* (1984) g R&B#1 US#1 UK#1, re-entry (1985) UK#64; *Love Light in Flight* (1984) R&B#4 US#17 UK#4, *Don't Drive Drunk* (1984) UK#71, re-entry (1985) UK#62, *Part-Time Lover* (1985) R&B#1 US#1 UK#3, *Go Home* (1985) R&B#2 US#10 UK#67, *Overjoyed* (1986) R&B#8 US#24 UK#17, *Land of La La* (1986) R&B#19 US#86, *Stranger on the Shore of Love* (1987) UK#55, *Skeletons* (1987) R&B#1 US#19 UK#59, *You Will Know* (1987) R&B#1 US#77, *Free* (1987) UK#49, *Get It* with Michael Jackson (1988) R&B#4 US#80 UK#37, *My Love* with Julio Iglesias (1988) R&B#88 US#80 UK#6, *With Each Beat of My Heart* (1989) R&B#28, *Fun Day* (1991) UK#63, *Gotta Have You* (1991) US#92, *You Will Know* (1991) US#77, *These Three Words* (1992) US#7, *We Didn't Know* with Whitney Houston (1992) R&B#20, *For Your Love* (1995) US#53 UK#23, *Tomorrow Robins Will Sing* (1995) UK#71. ALBUMS: **Tribute to Uncle Ray** (1962), **The Jazz Soul of Little Stevie** (1963), **The 12 Year Old Genius Recorded Live** (1963) US#1, **With a Song in My Heart** (1964), **Stevie at the Beach** (1965), **Uptight** (1966) US#33, **Down to Earth** (1966) US#92, **I Was Made to Love Her** (1967) US#45, **Someday at Christmas** (1967), **For Once in My Life** (1969, all Tamla) US#50; **Eivets Rednow** (1969, Gordy); **My Cherie Amour** (1969) US#34 UK#17, **Live** (1970, both Tamla) US#81; **Live at the Talk of the Town** (1970, Motown); **Signed, Sealed, Delivered** (1970) US#25, **Where I'm Coming From** (1971) US#62, **Music of My Mind** (1972) US#21, **Talking Book** (1973) US#3 UK#16, **Innervisions** (1973) US#4 UK#8, **Fulfillingness' First Finale** (1974) US#1 UK#5, **Songs in the Key of Life** (1976) US#1 UK#2, **Journey Through the Secret Life of Plants** (1979) US#4 UK#8, **Hotter Than July** (1980) p US#3 UK#2, **The Woman in Red** ost (1984) p US#4 UK#2, **In Square Circle** (1985, all Tamla) p US#5 UK#5; **Characters** (1987) p US#17 UK#33, **Music from the**

Movie Jungle Fever ost (1991) g US#24 UK#56, **Conversation Peace** (1995) g US#16 UK#8, **Natural Wonder** (1996, all Motown). COMPILATIONS: **Greatest Hits** (1968) US#37 UK#25, **Greatest Hits, Volume 2** (1971) US#69 UK#30, **Looking Back** (1977) US#34, **Stevie Wonder's Original Musiquarium I** (1982, all Tamla) g US#4 UK#8; **Love Songs—16 Classic Hits** (1984, Telstar) UK#20; **Diana Ross/Michael Jackson/Gladys Knight/Stevie Wonder—Their Greatest Hits Back to Back** (1986, Priority) UK#21; **Song Review** (1996, Motown) UK#19. HIT VERSIONS: *All Day Sucker* Liz Anderson (1970) C&W#64, *All in Love Is Fair* Barbra Streisand (1974) US#63, *As* Jean-Luc Ponty (1982) US#108, *Bad Weather* [xvi] Supremes (1973) US#37, *Breakadawn* [xi] De La Soul (1993) R&B#30 US#76 UK#39, *Crown, The* [ii] Gary Byrd & the G.B. Experience (1983) R&B#69 UK#6, *Don't Make Me Wait Too Long* Roberta Flack (1980) R&B#67 US#104, *Don't You Worry 'Bout a Thing* Stars On in *Stars on Long Play 3/Stars Medley* (1982) US#163 UK#94/Incognito (1992) UK#19; *Force Behind the Power, The* Diana Ross (1992) UK#27, *Gansta's Paradise* Coolio featuring L.V. (1996) p US#1, *Girl Blue* Main Ingredient (1973) R&B#51 US#119, *Golden Lady* Three Degrees (1979) UK#36, *Happier Than the Morning Sun* B.J. Thomas (1972) US#100, *Harbor Love* [xvi] Syreeta (1975) R&B#75 UK#32, *Here We Go Again* Portrait (1993) US#12, *Hey Love* [i] Mr. Lee featuring R. Kelly (1992) R&B#23, *I Believe (When I Fall in Love It Will Be Forever)* George Michael on *Don't Let the Sun Go Down on Me* EP (1991) US#1 UK#1, *I Can't Help It* Michael Jackson on B-side of *Don't Stop 'Til You Get Enough* (1979) g R&B#1 US#1 UK#3, *I Do Love You* Beach Boys (1985) US#52 UK#60, *I Don't Know Why I Love You Girl* [x] Rolling Stones (1975) US#42, *I Think It's Love* [xiii] Jermaine Jackson (1986) R&B#14 US#16, *I Was Made to Love Him* [iv] King Curtis (1967) R&B#49 US#76/Stars On in *Stars on Long Play 3/Stars Medley* (1982) US#163 UK#94, *I Wish* Stars On in *Stars on Long Play 3/Stars Medley* (1982) US#163 UK#94, *If You Were My Woman* George Michael on B-side of *Praying for Time* (1990) US#1 UK#6, *Isn't She Lovely* David Parton (1977) US#105 UK#4/Stars On in *Stars on Long Play 3/Stars Medley* (1982) US#163 UK#94; *It's a Shame* [viii] Spinners (1970) R&B#70 US#14 UK#20/Monie Love & True Image (1990) US#26 UK#12; *Just a Little Misunderstanding* [i] Contours (1965) R&B#18 US#85, *Lately* Jodeci (1993) g R&B#1 US#4, *Let's Get Serious* [v] Jermaine Jackson (1980) R&B#1 US#9 UK#8, *Living for the City* Ray Charles (1975) R&B#22 US#91/Gillan (1982) UK#50; *Love's in Need of Love Today* George Michael on B-side of *Father Figure* (1988) US#1 UK#11, *Loving You Is Sweeter Than Ever* [xii] Four

Tops (1966) US#45 UK#21/Nick Kamen (1987) UK#16; *Masterblaster (Jammin')* Stars On in *Stars on Long Play 3/Stars Medley* (1982) US#163 UK#94, *My Cherie Amour* [iii] Soul Train Gang (1977) US#92/ Stars On in *Stars on Long Play 3/Stars Medley* (1982) US#163 UK#94; *Pastime Paradise* Coolio (1995) R&B#1 US#1/"Weird Al" Yankovic sampled in *Amish Paradise* (1996) US#53+; *Pop Goes the Weasel* 3rd Bass (1991) US#29 UK#64, *Ribbon in the Sky* Intro (1994) R&B#11+ US#107+, *She's So Beautiful* Cliff Richard (1985) UK#17, *Signed, Sealed, Delivered, I'm Yours* [vi] Peter Frampton (1977) US#18/Boystown Gang (1982) UK#50; *Sir Duke* Stars On in *Stars on Long Play 3/Stars Medley* (1982) US#163 UK#94, *Spinnin' and Spinnin'* [xvi] Syreeta (1974) UK#49, *Superstition* Stars On in *Stars on Long Play 3/Stars Medley* (1982) US#163 UK#94/Clubhouse (1983) UK#59; *Tell Me Something Good* Rufus (1973) g R&B#3 US#3, *To Know You Is to Love You* [xv] B.B. King (1973) R&B#12 US#38, *Try Jah Love* Third World (1982) R&B#23 US#101, *Until You Come Back to Me* [i] Aretha Franklin (1973) g R&B#1 US#3/Luther Vandross (1984) R&B#5 US#87/Miki Howard (1990) UK#67/Adeva (1992) UK#45; *Uptight (Everything's Alright)* [iii] Jazz Crusaders (1966) US#95/ Ramsey Lewis (1966) R&B#30 US#49/Nancy Wilson (1966) US#84/Bill Crosby as *Little Ole Man* (1967) US#4/Shalamar in *Uptown Festival* (1977) R&B#10 US#25/Stars On in *Stars on Long Play 3/Stars Medley* (1982) US#163 UK#94; *We'll Have It Made* Spinners (1970) R&B#20 US#89, *You Are My Heaven* [xiv] Roberta Flack & Donny Hathaway (1979) R&B#8 US#47, *You Are the Sunshine of My Life* Marty Mitchell (1978) C&W#34/Stars On in *Stars on Long Play 3/Stars Medley* (1982) US#163 UK#94; *You Can't Judge a Book By Its Cover* Yvonne Fair on B-side of *It Should Have Been Me* (1976) UK#5, *You're Supposed to Keep Your Love for Me* Jermaine Stewart (1980) R&B#32 US#34, *Your Kiss Is Sweet* [xvi] Syreeta (1974) UK#12. Co-writers: [i] Maurice Broadnaux/Clarence Paul, [ii] Gary Byrd, [iii] Henry Cosby/Sylvia Moy, [iv] Henry Cosby/ Lula Hardaway/Sylvia Moy, [v] Lee Garrett, [vi] Lee Garrett/Lula Hardaway/Syreeta Wright, [viii] Lee Garrett/Syreeta Wright, [ix] Lula Hardaway/Don Hunter, [x] Lula Hardaway/Don Hunter/Paul Riser, [xi] P. Houston/D. Jolicouer/V. Mason/K. Mercer, [xii] Ivy Hunter, [xiii] Jermaine Jackson/Michael Omartian, [xiv] Eric Mercury, [xv] I. Tucker, Jr., [xvi] Syreeta Wright. (*See also under* Smokey ROBINSON.)

1039. WOOD, Roy (b. Roy Oliver Ulysses Wood, November 8, 1946, Birmingham, England) Pop multi-instrumentalist, producer and vocalist. A successful songwriter during the 1960–1970s, who

fronted the groups the Move and Wizzard. A former art school student, Wood played in numerous bands before forming the psychedelic and classically influenced the Move, in 1965. CHART COMPOSITIONS: *Night of Fear* [i] (1967) UK#2, *I Can Hear the Grass Grow* (1967) UK#5, *Flowers in the Rain* (1967) UK#2, *Fire Brigade* (1968) UK#3, *Blackberry Way* (1969) UK#1, *Curly* (1969) UK#12, *Brontosaurus* (1970) UK#7, *Tonight* (1971) UK#11, *Chinatown* (1971) UK#23, *California Man* (1972) UK#7. ALBUMS: **The Move** (1968) UK#15; **Shazam** (1970), **Looking On** (1970), **Message from the Country** (1971, all Regal Zonophone). COMPILATIONS: **Split Ends** (1973, United Artists) US#172; **Great Move: The Best of The Move** (1993, EMI). In 1970, with guitarist Jeff Lynne, Wood formed the Electric Light Orchestra, but he only remained a member for the album **Electric Light Orchestra** (1971, Harvest) US#196 UK#32, before leaving to form Wizzard, with which he emulated the rock and roll style of the 1950s, with a large, Phil Spector–type sound. CHART COMPOSITIONS: *Ball Park Incident* (1972) UK#6, *See My Baby Jive* (1973) UK#1, *Angel Fingers* (1973) UK#1, *I Wish It Could Be Christmas Every Day* (1973) UK#4, re-issued (1981) UK#41, re-issued (1984) UK#23, new version (1993) UK#53; *Rock 'n' Roll Winter (Looney's Tune)* (1974) UK#6, *This Is the Story of My Love (Baby)* (1974) UK#34, *Are You Ready to Rock* (1975) UK#8. ALBUMS: **Wizzard Brew** (1973, Harvest) UK#29; **Introducing Eddy Falcon and the Falcons** (1974, Warner Brothers) UK#19. After recording briefly as Wizzo, and as the Helicopters, Wood cut solo sides before retiring to his home in Shropshire, to compose television incidental music. CHART COMPOSITIONS: *Dear Elaine* (1973) UK#18, *Forever* (1973) UK#8, *Going Down the Road* (1974) UK#13. ALBUMS: **Boulders** (1973) US#176 UK#15, **Mustard** (1975, both Harvest); **On the Road Again** (1977), **Super Active Wizzo** (1977, both Warner Brothers); **Starting Up** (1987, Legacy). COMPILATIONS: **The Singles** (1982, Speed) UK#37; **Best of Roy Wood and Wizzard** (1990, Action Replay). HIT VERSION: *Hello Suzie* Amen Corner (1969) UK#4. Co-writer: [i] Peter Tchaikovsky.

1040. WOODS, Harry (b. Harold MacGregor Woods, November 4, 1896, North Chelmsford, MS; d. January 7, 1970, Glendale, AZ) Film and stage composer. A Tin Pan Alley composer who, despite having no fingers on his left hand, developed a one-handed piano technique and became a highly successful songwriter. Woods' first published song was *Paddlin' Madeline Home* (1923), and he achieved his first major hit with the million selling *When the Red, Red Robin Comes Bob-Bob-Bobbin' Along* (1926).

His material was included in the show "Sunny" (1925), after which he spent three years in England, where he composed for the Gaumont Pictures' films "Jack Ahoy" and "Evergreen" (both 1935), and "It's Love Again" (1936). Woods effectively retired from songwriting after 1945. HIT VERSIONS: *Dancin' with My Shadow* Henry King (1935) US#9, *Here Comes the Sun* [vii] Bert Lown (1930) US#14, *I'll Never Say "Never Again" Again* Dorsey Brothers Orchestra (1935) US#14/Ozzie Nelson (1935) US#4/Benny Goodman (1953) US#30/Dinah Shore (1957) US#24/Winifred Atwell in *Piano Party* (1959) UK#10; *I'm Goin' South* [xiii] Al Jolson (1924) US#2/Paul Whiteman (1924) US#8; *I'm Looking Over a Four-Leaf Clover* [vi] Ben Bernie (1927) US#3/Jean Goldkette (1927) US#10/Nick Lucas (1927) US#2/Arthur Godfrey (1948) US#14/Art Mooney (1948) g US#1/Russ Morgan (1948) US#6/Alvino Rey (1948) US#6/Three Suns (1948) US#10/Uptown String Band (1948) US#11/Big Ben Banjo Band in *Let's Get Together Again* (1955) UK#18/Russ Conway in *Party Pops* (1957) UK#24/Wayne Newton (1964) US#123; *Just an Echo in the Valley* [iv] Bing Crosby (1933) US#2/Rudy Vallee (1933) US#3; *Just Like a Butterfly That's Caught in the Rain* [vi] Ipana Troubadors (1927) US#8/Vincent Lopez (1927) US#16; *Linger a Little Longer in the Twilight* [iv] Rudy Vallee (1933) US#11, *Little Kiss Each Morning (A Little Kiss Each Night), A* Guy Lombardo (1930) US#11/Rudy Vallee (1930) US#3; *Man from the South* [ii] Ted Weems (1930) US#1, *My Hat's on the Side of My Head* [viii] Ray Noble (1934) US#12, *Paddlin' Madelin' Home* Cliff Edwards (1925) US#3/Ipana Troubadors (1926) US#8; *Pink Elephants* [vi] Guy Lombardo (1932) US#10/George Olsen (1932) US#8; *Poor Papa (He's Got Nothing at All)* [xii] "Whispering" Jack Smith (1926) US#10, *River Stay 'Way from My Door* [vi] Ethel Waters (1931) US#18/Kate Smith & Guy Lombardo (1932) US#1/Frank Sinatra (1960) US#82 UK#18; *She's a Great, Great Girl* Roger Wolfe Kahn (1928) US#14, *Side By Side* Cliff Edwards (1927) US#12/Nick Lucas (1927) US#3/Aileen Stanley & Johnny Marvin (1927) US#7/Paul Whiteman (1927) US#3/Kay Starr (1953) US#3 UK#7/Russ Conway in *Party Pops* (1957) UK#24; *So Many Memories* Frances Langford (1937) US#17/Russ Organ (1937) US#8; *Stay Out of the South (If You Want to Miss a Heaven on Earth)* [vi] Earl Burtnett (1928) US#20, *Try a Little Tenderness* [iv] Ruth Etting (1933) US#16/Ted Lewis (1933) US#6/Aretha Franklin (1962) US#100/Otis Redding (1967) R&B#4 US#25 UK#46/Three Dog Night (1969) US#29/Billy Thundercloud & the Chieftones (1976) C&W#47/Commitments (1991) US#67; *Voice in the Old Village Choir, The* [x] Paul Whiteman (1932) US#10, *Walk Right In* [v] Rooftop Singers (1963) R&B#4

US#1 UK#10, *We Just Couldn't Say Goodbye* Guy Lombardo (1932) US#1/Paul Whiteman (1932) US#3; *What a Little Moonlight Can Do* Jack Jackson (1935) US#16/Teddy Wilson & Billie Holiday (1935) US#12; *When the Moon Comes Over the Mountain* [ix] Nick Lucas (1931) US#7/Radiolites (1931) US#15/Leo Reisman (1931) US#12/Kate Smith (1931) US#1; *When the Red, Red Robin Comes Bob-Bob-Bobbin' Along* Cliff Edwards (1926) US#12/Ipana Troubadors (1926) US#12/Al Jolson (1926) US#1/"Whispering" Jack Smith (1926) US#9/Paul Whiteman (1926) US#7/Doris Day (1953) US#29/Winifred Atwell in *Let's Have Another Party* (1954) UK#1. Co-writers: [i] Irving Bibo/Con Conrad, [ii] Rube Bloom (b. 1902; d. 1976), [iii] George Brown, [iv] James Campbell/Reginald Connelly, [v] Gus Cannon, [vi] Mort Dixon, [vii] Arthur Freed, [viii] Claude Hulbert, [ix] Howard Johnson/Kate Smith, [x] Gus Kahn, [xi] Billy Moll, [xii] Billy Rose, [xiii] Abner Silver.

1041. WRIGHT, Gary (b. April 26, 1945, Creskill, NJ) Rock keyboard player and vocalist. A former child actor who became the principal songwriter in the R&B influenced rock group Spooky Tooth, composing its hit *Feelin' Bad* (1969) US#132. ALBUMS: **Spooky Tooth** (1968), **Spooky Two** (1969) US#44, **Ceremony** (1970) US#92, **You Broke My Heart So I Busted Your Jaw** (1973) US#84, **Witness** (1973) US#99, **The Mirror** (1974, all Island) US#130. COMPILATION: **That Was Only Yesterday** (1976, A&M) US#172. Wright quit Spooky Tooth in 1974, and formed the short-lived Wonderwheel, before achieving success as a solo artist during the mid–1970s with his synthesizer dominated sound. CHART COMPOSITIONS: *The Dream Weaver* (1975) US#2, *Love Is Alive* (1976) R&B#98 US#2, *Made to Love You* (1976) US#79, *Phantom Writer* (1977) US#43, *Touch and Gone* (1978) US#73, *Really Wanna Know You* [ii] (1981) US#16. ALBUMS: **Extraction** (1970), **Foot Print** (1971), **Ring of Changes** (1972, all A&M); **The Dream Weaver** (1975) p US#7, **The Light of Smiles** (1977) US#23, **Touch and Gone** (1977) US#117, **Headin' Home** (1979) US#147, **The Right Place** (1981, all Warner Brothers) US#79; **Who Am I** (1988, Cypress). Co-writers: [i] R. Reichey, [ii] Ali Thompson.

1042. WRUBEL, Allie (b. January 15, 1905, Middleton, CT; d. December 13, 1973, Los Angeles, CA) Film composer and pianist. A Tin Pan Alley composer who was born into a musical family. Wrubel played in the Paul Whiteman Orchestra in 1924, before publishing his first song *Now You're in My Arms* (1934). After a handful of 1930s hits, he headed to Hollywood, where he worked for Warner

Brothers Pictures on such films as "As You Desire Me" (1932), "Go into Your Dance" (1935) and "I Walk Alone" (1947). Wrubel retired from music in the 1960s. ALBUM: **Uncle Remus** ost (1946, Disneyland). HIT VERSIONS: *As You Desire Me* Russ Columbo (1932) US#6/Donald Novis (1932) US#17; *At the Flying "W"* Elliot Lawrence (1948) US#21, *Don't Call It Love* [x] Freddy Martin (1948) US#23, *Fare Thee Well, Annabelle* [i] Guy Lombardo (1934) US#8/Glen Gray (1935) US#2; *Farewell to Arms* [ix] Paul Whiteman (1933) US#4, *First Time I Saw You, The* [viii] Bunny Berigan (1937) US#8/Jimmie Lunceford (1937) US#8; *Flirtation Walk* [i] Victor Young (1934) US#10, *Gone with the Wind* [v] Hoarce Heidt (1937) US#1/Guy Lombardo (1937) US#16/Claude Thornhill (1937) US#19; *Goodnight Angel* [v] Artie Shaw (1938) US#2, *I Can't Love You Anymore (Any More Than I Do)* [v] Mitchell Ayres (1940) US#16/Benny Goodman (1940) US#5/Terry Shand (1940) US#16; *I Met Her on Monday* [vii] Freddy Martin (1942) US#8, *I'll Buy That Dream* [v] Helen Forrest & Dick Haymes (1945) US#2/Harry James (1945) US#2/Hal McIntyre (1945) US#8; *I'm Stepping Out with a Memory Tonight* [v] Henry Burr (1918) US#1/Fats Waller (1937) US#3; *Lady from 29 Palms, The* Andrews Sisters (1947) US#7/Freddy Martin (1947) US#5/Tony Pastor (1947) US#10; *Lady in Red, The* [i] Xavier Cugat (1935) US#3/Joe Haymes (1935) US#20/Louis Prima (1935) US#8; *Little Things You Used to Do, The* [ii] Johnny Green (1935) US#2, *Masquerade Is Over, The* [v] Larry Clinton (1939) US#5/Jimmy Dorsey (1939) US#4/Five Satins (1962) US#102; *Mr. and Mrs. Is the Name* [i] Dick Powell (1935) US#19/Victor Young (1934) US#17; *Music, Maestro, Please* [v] Tommy Dorsey (1938) US#1/Art Kassel (1938)/Kay Kyser (1938) US#5/Frankie Laine (1950) US#13; *Why Does It Get So Late So Early?* [iv] Helen Forrest & Dick Haymes (1946) US#22, *Why Don't We Do This More Often?* [vi] Kay Kyser (1941) US#8/Freddy Martin (1941) US#14; *Zip-a-Dee-Doo-Dah* [iii] Sammy Kaye (1947) US#11/Johnny Mercer (1947) US#8/Modernaires & Paula Kelly (1947) US#11/Bob B. Soxx & the Blue Jeans (1963) R&B#7 US#8 UK#45. Co-writers: [i] Mort Dixon, [ii] Al Dubin, [iii] Ray Gilbert (b. 1912; d. 1976, both England), [iv] Johnny Lehman, [v] Herb Magidson, [vi] Charles Newman, [vii] Lionel Newman, [viii] Nat Shilkret, [ix] Abner Silver, [x] Ned Washington.

1043. WYLIE, Pete (b. March 22, 1958, Liverpool, England) Rock vocalist. A performer who has recorded under a variety of group names, including Wah, Wah Heat and Mighty Wah. CHART COMPOSITIONS: *The Story of the Blues* (1982) UK#3, *Hope (I Wish You'd Believe Me)* (1983)

UK#37, *Come Back* (1984) UK#20, *Sinful* (1986) UK#13, new version with the Farm (1991) UK#36; *Diamond Girl* (1986) UK#57. ALBUMS: **Nah-Poo = The Art of Bluff** (1981, Eternal) UK#33; **A Word to the Wise Guy** (1984, Beggars Banquet) UK#28.

1044. YELLEN, Jack (b. July 6, 1892, Poland; d. 1991, America) Film and stage lyricist. An American emigrant who, after attending the University of Michigan, became a songwriter. Yellen's first success was in partnership with George L. Cobb on the show "High Jinks" (1914), after which he teamed up with the composer Milton Ager. Yellen also worked with Harold Arlen. HIT VERSIONS: *Alabama Jubilee* [i] Arthur Collins & Byron Harlan (1915) US#2/Red Foley (1951) C&W#3 US#28/Ferko String Band (1955) US#14 UK#20; *All Aboard for Dixieland* [i] Ada Jones & the Peerless Quartet (1911) US#3/American Quartet (1914) US#5; *Down By the O-HI-O* [ii] Al Jolson (1921) US#1/Billy Murray & Billy Jones (1921) US#2/Andrews Sisters (1940) US#21/Smoothies (1940) US#29. Co-writers: [i] George Leo Cobb (b. August 31, 1886, Mexico, NY; d. December 25, 1942, Brookline, MA), [ii] Abe Olman. (*See also under* Milton AGER, Harold ARLEN, Sammy FAIN, Joseph MEYER, Lew POLLACK.)

1045. YOAKAM, Dwight (b. October 23, 1956, Pikesville, KY) C&W guitarist and vocalist. A contemporary honky-tonk country artist with rock affections. CHART COMPOSITIONS: *Guitars, Cadillacs* (1986) C&W#4, *I Sand Dixie* (1989) C&W#1, *Nothing's Changed Here* [i] (1991) C&W#15, *It Only Hurts When I Cry* [ii] (1991) C&W#7, *The Heart That You Own* (1992) C&W#18, *Fast as You Can* (1993) C&W#3 US#70, *A Thousand Miles from Nowhere* (1993) C&W#3, *Try Not to Look So Pretty* [i] (1994) C&W#14, *Pocket of a Clown* (1994) C&W#35+, *Sorry You Asked?* (1996) C&W#69+. ALBUMS: **Guitars, Cadillacs, Etc., Etc.** (1987) p US#61 UK#51, **Hillbilly Deluxe** (1987) p US#55, **Buenas Noches from a Lonely Room** (1988) g US#68 UK#87, **Just Lookin' for a Hit** (1989) p US#68, **If There Was a Way** (1990) p US#96, **This Time** (1993) p US#25, **Dwight Live** (1995) US#56, **Gone** (1996) US#30, **Things We Said Today** (1997, all Reprise). COMPILATION: **La Croix de L'Amour** (1992, Reprise). Co-writers: [i] Kostas, [ii] R. Miller.

1046. YOUMANS, Vincent (b. Vincent Miller Youmans, September 27, 1898, New York, NY; d. April 5, 1946, Denver, CO) Film and stage composer, pianist and producer. The composer of the standard *Tea for Two* [v] (1925), who, like George Gershwin, wrote songs that captured the mood of an era. A former Wall Street broker who began writing songs on U.S. Navy service during World War I, Youmans later worked as a song-plugger and orchestrator before becoming Victor Herbert's rehearsal pianist. His first published song was *The Country Cousin* (1920), after which he contributed to the Broadway musical "Two Little Girls in Blue" (1921). The four hundred and seventy-seven performance "Wildflower" (1923), was written with Otto Harbach and Oscar Hammerstein, II, which the trio followed with "No, No Nanette" (1925). Other Youmans shows include "Lollipop" (1924), "A Night Out" (1925), "Oh, Please!" (1926), and "One Girl" (1933). He also worked in Hollywood, where he composed the score to "Flying Down to Rio" (1933), a film notable for being one of the earliest to contain Latin American music. His Broadway show "The Vincent Youmans Ballet Revue" (1943), was not well received, and in 1935 he was declared a bankrupt. Youmans spent his later years fighting tuberculosis, from which he died in 1946. ALBUMS: **Salute to Vincent Youmans** st (1954, RCA); **Hit the Deck** ost (1955, MGM); **No, No Nanette** oc (1971, Columbia) US#61. HIT VERSIONS: *Bambolina* [xiii] Ray Miller (1923) US#9/Paul Whiteman (1923) US#1; *Carioca, The* [viii] Castillian Troubadors (1934) US#4/Enric Madriguera (1934) US#1/RKO Studio Orchestra (1934) US#13/Harry Sosnik (1934) US#2/Les Paul (1952) US#14; *Drums in My Heart* [xv] Leo Reisman (1932) US#16, *Flying Down to Rio* [viii] Fred Astaire (1934) US#6/Rudy Vallee (1934) US#6; *Great Day* [ix] Paul Whiteman (1929) US#1, *Hallelujah* [xi] Cass Hagan (1927) US#20/Revelers (1927) US#11/Nat Schilkret (1927) US#3; *I Know That You Know* [vi] Nat Shilkret (1927) US#5/Benny Goodman (1936) US#14; *I Want to Be Happy* [v] Carl Fenton (1924) US#5/Jan Garber (1925) US#5/Vincent Lopez (1925) US#2/Shannon Four (1925) US#13/Red Nichols (1930) US#19/Benny Goodman (1937) US#17/Mrs. Mills in *Mrs. Mills' Medley* (1961) UK#18; *More Than You Know* [ix] Ruth Etting (1930) US#9/Mildred Bailey (1937) US#15/Perry Como (1946) US#19; *Music Makes Me* [viii] Emil Coleman (1934) US#15/Fred Astaire (1934) US#14; *Oh Me! Oh My!* [x] Frank Crumit (1921) US#14, *Orchids in the Moonlight* [viii] Enric Madriguera (1934) US#6/Rudy Vallee (1934) US#4; *Rise 'N' Shine* [vii] Paul Whiteman (1933) US#16, *Sometimes I'm Happy* [iv] Charles King & Louise Groody (1927) US#9/Roger Wolfe Kahn (1927) US#5/Benny Goodman (1935) US#12/Sammy Kaye (1938) US#18/Lester Young (1944) R&B#5; *Tea for Two* [v] Benson Orchestra of Chicago (1925) US#5/Ben Bernie (1925) US#10/Marion Harris (1925) US#1/Ipana Troubadors (1930) US#15/Teddy Wilson (1937) US#18/Art Tatum (1939) US#18/Tommy Dorsey Orchestra starring Warren Coving-

ton (1958) R&B#19 US#7 UK#3; *Time on My Hands* [ii] Smith Ballew (1931) US#6/Leo Reisman (1931) US#6; *Wildflower* [xiii] Ben Bernie (1923) US#3, *Without a Song* [ix] Paul Whiteman (1930) US#6/Ray Charles (1965) US#112/James Cleveland (1966) US#129/Willie Nelson (1984) C&W#11. Co-writers: [i] Harold Adamson, [ii] Harold Adamson/Mack Gordon, [iii] Irving Caesar, [iv] Irving Caesar/Clifford Grey, [v] Irving Caesar/Otto Harbach, [vi] Anne Caldwell, [vii] Buddy De Sylva, [viii] Edward Eliscu/Gus Khan, [ix] Edward Eliscu/Billy Rose, [x] Arthur Francis, [xi] Clifford Grey/Leo Robin, [xii] Oscar Hammerstein, II/Otto Harbach, [xiii] Oscar Hammerstein, II/Otto Harbach/Herbert Stothart, [xiv] Otto Harbach, [xv] Edward Heyman.

1047. YOUNG, Jesse Colin (b. Perry Miller, November 11, 1944, New York, NY) Rock guitarist and vocalist. The lead singer in the folk influenced group the Youngbloods. ALBUMS: **The Youngbloods** (1967) US#131, **Earth Music** (1967), **Elephant Mountain** (1969, all RCA) US#118; **Rock Festival** (1970) US#80, **Ride the Wind** (1971) US#157, **Good 'n' Dusty** (1971) US#160, **High on a Ridgetop** (1972, all Raccoon) US#185. COMPILATIONS: **Best of the Youngbloods** (1970) US#144, **Two Trips** (1970, Mercury); **Sunlight** (1971, RCA) US#186. Since the early 1970s, Young has recorded in a soft-rock style as a solo artist. ALBUMS: **The Soul of a City Boy** (1964, Capitol) US#172; **Youngblood** (1965, Mercury); **Together** (1972, Raccoon) US#157; **Song for Julie** (1973) US#51, **Light Shine** (1974) US#37, **Songbird** (1975) US#26, **On the Road** (1976) US#34, **Love on the Wing** (1977, all Warner Brothers) US#64; **American Dreams** (1978) US#165, **The Perfect Stranger** (1982, both Elektra); **The Highway Is for Heroes** (1987, Cypress).

1048. YOUNG, Kenny Pop composer. HIT VERSIONS: *Ai No Corrida* [iii] Quincy Jones (1981) R&B#10 US#28 UK#14, *Arizona* Mark Lindsay (1969) g US#10, *Captain of Your Ship, The* [v] Reparta & the Delrons (1968) US#127 UK#13, *Come Back and Shake Me* Clodah Rodgers (1969) UK#3, *Doin' the Do* Betty Boo (1990) UK#7, *Don't Go Out in the Rain (You're Going to Melt)* Herman's Hermits (1966) US#18, *Goodnight Midnight* Clodah Rodgers (1969) UK#4, *Just a Little Bit Better* Herman's Hermits (1965) US#7 UK#15, *Just One More Night* Yellow Dog (1978) UK#8, *Little Bit of Heaven, A* [iv] Ronnie Dove (1966) US#16, *One Kiss for Old Times' Sake* [iv] Ronnie Dove (1965) US#14, *Only You Can* Fox (1975) UK#3, *S-S-S-Single Bed* Fox (1976) UK#4, *Under the Boardwalk* [iv] Drifters (1964) US#4 UK#45/Tom Tom Club (1982) UK#22/Bruce Willis (1987) R&B#72 US#59 UK#2/Lynn Anderson (1988) C&W#24; *When Liking Turns to Loving* [ii] Ronnie Dove (1965) US#16. Co-writers: [i] Alison Clarkson, [ii] Jay Fishman, [iii] Chas Jankel, [iv] Arthur Resnick, [v] B. Yardley.

1049. YOUNG, Neil (b. November 12, 1945, Toronto, Canada) Rock guitarist, pianist and vocalist. A consistently influential singer-songwriter who coherently blends country, blues, rock and R&B. Young's music is driven by an intense passion to communicate. He grew up in Winnipeg, Canada, and taught himself the ukelele and guitar before performing on the Canadian folk circuit as Neil Young and the Squires. In 1966, Young recorded unreleased tracks with Rick James for Motown Records as the Mynah Birds, before moving to California and linking up with Stephen Stills in the folk-rock group Buffalo Springfield, writing the hits *Nowadays Clancy Can't Even Sing* (1967) US#110, *On the Way Home* (1968) US#82, and *Expecting to Fly* (1968) US#98. ALBUMS: **Buffalo Springfield** (1967) US#80, **Buffalo Springfield Again** (1967) US#44, **Last Time Around** (1968, all Atco) US#42. COMPILATIONS: **Retrospective — The Best of Buffalo Springfield** (1969) p US#42, **Buffalo Springfield** (1973, both Atco) US#104. Young has also recorded over the years as a member of the vocal group Crosby, Stills, Nash, and Young, penning its hits *Ohio* (1970) US#14, *American Dream* (1989) UK#55 and *Got It Made* (1989) US#69. ALBUMS: **Deja Vu** (1970) p US#1 UK#5, **4-Way Street** (1971) p US#1 UK#5, **American Dream** (1988, all Atlantic) p US#16. COMPILATIONS: **So Far** (1974) p US#1 UK#25, **CSN** (1992, both Atlantic) US#109. Young has often recorded with his semi-permanent backing band Crazy Horse. CHART COMPOSITIONS: *Cinnamon Girl* (1970) US#55, *Only Love Can Break Your Heart* (1970) US#33, *When You Dance I Can Really Love* (1971) US#93, *Heart of Gold* (1972) g US#1 UK#10, *Old Man* (1972) US#31, *War Song** (1972) US#61, *Time Fades Away* (1973) US#108, *Walk On* (1974) US#69, *Midnight on the Bay*** (1976) US#105, *Hey Hey My My (Into the Black)* (1979) US#79, *Southern Pacific* (1982) US#70, *Little Thing Called Love* (1983) US#71, *Get Back to the Country* (1985) C&W#33, *Harvest Moon* (1993) UK#36, *The Needle and the Damage Done* (1993) UK#75, *Long May You Run* (1993) UK#71, *Philadelphia* (1994) UK#62. ALBUMS: **Neil Young** (1969), **Everybody Knows This Is Nowhere** (1969) p US#34, **After the Goldrush** (1970) p US#8 UK#7, **Harvest** (1972) p US#1 UK#1, **Journey Through the Past** ost (1972) US#45, **Time Fades Away** (1973) g US#22 UK#20, **On the Beach** (1974) g US#16 UK#42, **Tonight's the Night** (1975) US#25 UK#48, **Zuma** (1975) US#25 UK#44, **Long May You Run*** (1976) g

US#26 UK#12, **American Stars 'n' Bars** (1977) g US#21 UK#17, **Comes a Time** (1978) g US#7 UK#42, **Rust Never Sleeps** (1979) p US#8 UK#13, **Live Rust** (1979) p US#15 UK#55, **Hawks and Doves** (1980) US#30 UK#34, **Re-Ac-Tor** (1981, all Reprise) US#27 UK#69; **Trans** (1983) US#19 UK#29, **Everybody's Rockin'** (1983) US#46 UK#50, **Old Ways** (1985) US#75 UK#39, **Landing on Water** (1986) US#46 UK#52, **Life** (1987, all Geffen) US#75 UK#71; **This Note's for You** (1988) US#61 UK#56, **Freedom** (1989) g US#35 UK#17, **Ragged Glory** (1990) US#31 UK#15, **Weld/Arc** (1991) US#154 UK#20, **Harvest Moon** (1992) p US#16 UK#9, **Unplugged** (1993) g US#23 UK#4, **Sleeps with Angels** (1994) US#9 UK#2, **Mirror Ball** (1995) g US#5 UK#4, **Dead Man** ost (1996), **Broken Arrow** (1996), **Year of the Horse** (1997, all Reprise). COMPILATIONS: **Decade** (1977, Reprise) p US#43 UK#46; **Lucky Thirteen** (1992, Geffen) UK#69. HIT VERSIONS: *After the Goldrush* Prelude (1974) US#22 UK#21, new version (1978) UK#28; *Are You Ready for the Country* Waylon Jennings (1976) C&W#7, *Cinnamon Girl* Gentrys (1970) US#52, *Dance, Dance, Dance* New Seekers (1972) US#84, *Don't Cry No Tears Around Me* Wedding Present on B-side of *Go-Go Dancer* (1992) UK#20, *Down By the River* Brooklyn Bridge (1970) US#91/ Buddy Miles & the Freedom Express (1970) US#68/ Joey Gregorash (1971) US#113; *Down to the Wire* Yellow Hand (1970) US#120, *Heart of Gold* Willie Nelson (1987) C&W#44, *Like a Hurricane* Mission (1986) UK#50, *Lotta Love* Nicolette Larson (1979) US#8, *Love Is a Rose* Linda Ronstadt (1975) C&W#5 US#63, *Only Love Can Break Your Heart* Elkie Brooks (1978) UK#43/Saint Etienne (1991) UK#39; *Tell Me Why* Matthews Southern Comfort (1971) US#98. With: * Graham Nash, ** Stephen Stills.

1050. YOUNG, Steve (b. July 12, 1942, Noonan, GA) C&W guitarist and vocalist. A country and bluegrass influenced singer-songwriter who learned the guitar in his teens, and performed in southern bars and honky tonks. Since 1969, Young has recorded sadly neglected solo sets that feature strong ballad material, which he sings in a deep, warm voice. ALBUMS: **Rock, Salt and Nails** (1969, A&M); **Seven Bridges Road** (1972, Reprise); **Honky Tonk Man** (1976, Mountain Railroad); **Renegade Picker** (1976), **No Place to Fall** (1977, both RCA); **To Satisfy You** (1981, Rounder); **Look Homeward Angel** (1986, Mill); **Long Time Rider** (1990, Voodoo); **Solo-Live** (1991), **Switchblades of Love** (1993, both Watermelon). COMPILATION: **Old Memories** (1983, Country Tracks). HIT VERSION: *Seven Bridges Road* Eagles (1981) C&W#55 US#21.

1051. YOUNG, Victor (b. August 8, 1900, Chicago, IL; d. November 11, 1956, Palm Springs, CA) Film and stage composer, violinist and arranger. An extremely popular orchestral leader and composer, who charted twenty-five hits between 1931–1954. Young studied at the Warsaw Conservatory in Poland in 1910, and performed in the Warsaw Philharmonic, before returning to America in the 1920s. He arranged and conducted his own dance bands throughout the 1930s, and recorded with his own orchestra for Brunswick Records. After 1935, Young composed material for Hollywood, ultimately collaborating on over three hundred films and scores, and frequently working with the lyricist Ned Washington. Young won an Oscar for his score to "Around the World in Eighty Days" (1956), and his work was also featured in such shows as "Blackbirds of 1933" and "Blackbirds of 1934." His theme song to the film "High Noon" (1952), won him another Oscar, as did his score to "Pinocchio" (1940). The soundtrack to "Around the World in 80 Days" was also recorded in its entirety by the New World Theatre Orchestra (1957, Stereo-Fidelity) US#8. Many of Young's tunes have since become jazz standards. CHART COMPOSITION: *Around the World* [i] (1957) US#13. ALBUMS: **The Snow Goose** sc (1949, Decca); **Christmas Carol** sc (1950, MCA); **The Count of Monte Christo** cs (1950), **Golden Earrings** sc (1950), **For Whom the Bell Tolls** ost (1950), **Pinocchio** st (1950, all Decca); **The Greatest Show on Earth** ost (1952, RCA); **The Quiet Man** ost (1952), **Samson and Delilah** st (1952), **Seventh Heaven** oc (1955), **The Brave One** ost (1956), **Written on the Wind** st (1956), **Around the World in 80 Days** ost (1957, all Decca) US#1; **Omar Khayyam** ost (1957, Filmusic); **Run of the Arrow** ost (1957, Decca); **The Seven Hills of Rome** ost (1958, RCA: **Moby Dick** sc (1959), **Ichabod (The Legend of Sleepy Hollow)** ost (1961), **But Beautiful** ost (1962, all Decca); **Rio Grande** ost (1979, Varese Sarabande); **Johnny Guitar** ost (1981), **The Sands of Iwo Jima** st (1981, Citadel). HIT VERSIONS: *Around the World* [i] Bing Crosby (1957) US#25 UK#5/Gracie Fields (1957) UK#8/Ronnie Hilton (1957) UK#4/Johnston Brothers on *All Star Hit Parade #2 EP* (1957) UK#15/ Mantovani (1957) US#12 UK#20/Buddy Greco (1961) US#109; *Blue Star (The Medic Theme)* [vii] Charles Applewhite (1955) UK#20/Ron Goodwin (1955) UK#20/Felicia Saunders (1955) US#29/Cyril Stapleton (1955) UK#2/Ventures (1966) US#120; *Can't We Talk It Over* [viii] Bing Crosby & the Mills Brothers (1932) US#10/Andrews Sisters (1950) US#22; *Golden Earrings* [iv] Dinah Shore (1947) US#25/ Peggy Lee (1948) US#2; *Hundred Years from Today, A* [x] Ethel Waters (1933) US#7, *(I Don't Stand) A Ghost of a Chance with You* [ii] Bing Crosby (1933)

US#5/Ted Fiorito (1933) US#12; *Lawd, You Made the Night Too Long* [ix] Louis Armstrong (1932) US#15/Guy Lombardo (1923) US#4; *Love Letters* [vii] Ketty Lester (1962) R&B#2 US#5 UK#4/Dick Haymes (1945) US#11/Elvis Presley (1966) US#11 UK#6/Debi Hawkins (1977) C&W#57/Hazard (1983) C&W#69/Alison Moyet (1987) UK#4; *Love Me* [x] Glen Gray (1934) US#15, *Love Me Tonight* [ii] Bing Crosby (1932) US#4/George Olsen (1932) US#14; *My Foolish Heart* [x] Gene Ammons (1950) R&B#9/Billy Eckstine (1950) g US#6; *Our Very Own* [iii] Sarah Vaughan (1950) US#15, *Stella By Starlight* [x] Harry James (1947) US#21/Frank Sinatra (1947) US#21; *Street of Dreams* [ix] Bing Crosby (1933) US#13/Guy Lombardo (1933) US#5/Ben Selvin (1933) US#5/Tommy Dorsey (1942) US#17; *Sweet Sue-Just You* [vi] Earl Burtnett (1928) US#3/ Ben Pollack (1928) US#3/Mills Brothers (1932) US#8/Tommy Dorsey (1939) US#13/Johnny Long (1949) US#19/Johnston Brothers in *Join in and Sing Again #3* (1956) UK#24; *Waltzing in a Dream* [ii] Bing Crosby (1932) US#6/Guy Lombardo (1932) US#9; *When I Fall in Love* [vii] Doris Day (1952) US#20/Nat "King" Cole (1957) UK#2, re-issued (1987) UK#4/Jimmy Young on *All Star Hit Parade #2 EP* (1957) UK#15/Lettermen (1962) US#7/Marcy Jo & Eddie Rambeau (1963) US#132/Donny Osmond (1973) UK#4/Rick Astley (1987) UK#2/Natalie Cole (1988) R&B#31 US#95/Celine Dion & Clive Griffin (1993) US#23; *Where Can I Go Without You?* [viii] Peggy Lee (1954) US#28. Co-writers: [i] Harold Adamson, [ii] Bing Crosby/Ned Washington, [iii] Jack Elliot, [iv] Ray Evans/Jay Livingston, [v] Mack David, [vi] Will J. Harris, [vii] Edward Heyman, [viii] Peggy Lee, [ix] Sam M. Lewis, [x] Ned Washington.

1052. ZAPPA, Frank (b. December 21, 1940, Baltimore, MD; d. December 4, 1993, Los Angeles, CA) Rock guitarist, producer and vocalist. A satirical and eclectic musician whose career encompassed the avante-garde, jazz, R&B, rock and roll, stand-up comedy, and even orchestral suites. Zappa was nearer to the classical music tradition than he was to rock music, and he paid no heed to commercial considerations whatsoever, and at the time of his death from prostate cancer, he was working on an extensive release schedule from his lifetime of recordings. Zappa played his first music at high school, and wrote the doo-wop hit *Memories of El Monte* by the Penguins (1962), before scoring the obscure film soundtracks "The World's Greatest Singer" (1960) and "Run Home Slow" (1963). Zappa used his earnings from these ventures to pay for his first home recording equipment, and during the mid–1960s he recorded with his group the Mothers of Invention.

Zappa devoted much of his life to either recording or performing. CHART COMPOSITIONS: *Don't Eat the Yellow Snow** (1974) US#86, *Disco Boy* (1977) US#105, *Dancin' Fool* (1979) US#45, *I Don't Wanna Get Drafted* (1980) US#103, *Valley Girl* [i] with Moon Zappa (1982) US#32. ALBUMS: **Freak Out!*** (1966) US#130, **Absolutely Free*** (1967) US#41, **We're Only in It for the Money*** (1968) US#30 UK#32, **Lumpy Gravy** (1968) US#159, **Cruising with Ruben and the Jets*** (1969) US#110, **Mothermania/The Best of the Mothers of Invention*** (1969, all Verve) US#151; **Uncle Meat*** (1969) US#43, **Hot Rats** (1969) US#173 UK#9, **Burnt Weeny Sandwich*** (1970) US#94 UK#17, **200 Motels*** (1970), **Weasels Ripped My Flesh*** (1970) US#189 UK#28, **Chunga's Revenge** (1970) US#119 UK#43, **Live the Mothers/Fillmore East, June, 1971** (1971, all Bizarre) US#38; **Frank Zappa's 200 Motels** ost* (1971, United Artists) US#59; **Just Another Band from L.A.*** (1972, Bizarre) US#85; **Waka/Jawaka — Hot Rats** (1972, Reprise) US#152; **Over-Nite Sensation*** (1973) g US#32, **Apostrophe** (1974) g US#10, **Roxy and Elsewhere*** (1974) US#27, **One Size Fits All** (1975) US#26, **Bongo Fury*** (1975, all Discreet) US#66; **Zoot Allures** (1976, Warner Brothers) US#61; **Zappa in New York** (1978) US#57 UK#55, **Studio Tan** (1978) US#147, **Sleep Dirt** (1979, all Discreet) US#175; **Sheik Yerbouti** (1979, Zappa) US#21 UK#32; **Orchestral Favorites** (1979, Discreet) US#169; **Joe's Garage, Act I** (1979) US#27 UK#62, **Joe's Garage, Acts II and III** (1980, both Zappa) US#53 UK#75, **Tinsel Town Rebellion** (1981) US#66 UK#55, **Shut Up 'n Play Yer Guitar** (1981), **You Are What You Is** (1981) US#93 UK#51, **Ship Arriving Too Late to Save a Drowning Witch** (1982) US#23 UK#61, **Man from Utopia** (1983) US#153 UK#87, **Them or Us** (1984, all Barking Pumpkin) UK#53; **Francesco** (1985), **The Perfect Stranger and Other Works** (1985, both EMI); **Frank Zappa Meets the Mothers of Prevention** (1986) US#152, **London Symphony Orchestra, Volume 22** (1987, both Barking Pumpkin); **Guitar** (1988, Zappa) UK#82; **Jazz from Hell** (1988), **The Hard Way** (1988), **You Can't Do That on Stage Anymore, Volume 1** (1988), **You Can't Do That on Stage Anymore, Volume 2 — The Helsinki Concert** (1988), **Broadway the Hard Way** (1989), **You Can't Do That on Stage Anymore, Volume 3** (1989, all Ryko); **The Best Band You Never Heard in Your Life** (1991), **Make a Jazz Noise Here** (1991, both Barking Pumpkin); **You Can't Do That on Stage Anymore, Volume 4** (1991, Ryko); **Beat the Boots** (1991), **Beat the Boots #2** (1992, Foo-Eee); **You Can't Do That on Stage Anymore, Volume 5** (1992), **You Can't Do That on Stage Anymore, Volume 6** (1992, both Ryko); **Playground Psychotics**

(1992, Barking Pumpkin); **Cucamonga Years** (1992, MSI); **Rare Beefheart/Vintage Zappa** (1992, Disky); **Ahead of Their Time** (1993), **The Yellow Shark** (1993, both Barking Pumpkin); **Zappa's Universe** (1993, Verve); **For Real~** (1994), **Con Safos~** (1994, both Mercury); **An Evening with Wild Man Fischer*** (1995, Reprise); **Civilization Phaze III** (1995, Zappa-Barking Pumpkin); **Strictly Commercial — The Best of Frank Zappa** (1995) UK#45, **Lather** (1996), **Have I Offended Someone?** (1997), **Strictly Genteel** (1997, all Ryko). HIT VERSION: *Dancin' Fool* Guess Who (1974) US#28. As: * the Mothers of Invention, ~ Ruben and the Jets. Co-writer: [i] Moon Zappa.

1053. ZARET, Hy Pop composer and lyricist. The co-composer of the unforgettable *One Meat Ball* [ii], and one of the most widely recorded songs of recent times *Unchained Melody* [i]. HIT VERSIONS: *One Meat Ball* [ii] Andrews Sisters (1945) US#15; *Unchained Melody* [i] Les Baxter (1955) US#1 UK#10/Roy Hamilton (1955) US#6/Al Hibbler (1955) US#3 UK#2/Liberace (1955) UK#20/June Valli (1955) US#29/Jimmy Young (1955) UK#1/Righteous Brothers (1964) R&B#6 US#4 UK#14, re-issued (1990) US#13 UK#1, new version (1990) US#19/Sweet Inspirations (1968) R&B#41 US#73/Heart (1981) US#83/Leo Sayer (1986) UK#54/Robson & Jerome (1995) UK#1; *Young and Warm and Wonderful* [ii] Tony Bennett (1958) US#23. Co-writers: [i] Alex North, [ii] Lou Singer. (*See also under* Sammy CAHN, Alex KRAMER.)

1054. ZEVON, Warren (b. Warren Livotovsky, January 24, 1947, Chicago, IL) Rock guitarist, pianist and vocalist. A perpetually jaded minstrel and composer of amusing material, who humorously investigates the foibles of humanity in conjunction with his own personal frustrations. Zevon excels on characters who fail to fit into what he sees as an increasingly homogenous society, and he was once called the Sam Peckinpah of rock music. Zevon's cast of losers, loners and the slightly insane, are often hopelessly optimistic individuals vigorously in pursuit of the American Dream. His parents were Russian immigrants and his father was a professional gambler. Zevon grew up in Arizona and California, learned classical piano, and once met the composer Igor Stravinsky, an event that was to influence some of his later music. In his teens he formed a group that, "Finally broke up because of dramatic lack of potential." A failed duo with Tule Livingston called Lyme and Cybelle, was followed by a spell writing jingles and working as the musical director for the Everly Brothers, before he embarked on a solo career. During the 1980s, Zevon battled with writer's block and alcoholism, events that contributed to his often scintillating album **Sentimental Hygiene** (1987). He has also recorded as a member of the group Hindu Love Gods, **Hindu Love Gods** (1990, Giant) US#168. CHART COMPOSITION: *Werewolves of London* [i] (1978) US#21. ALBUMS: **Wanted Dead or Alive** (1969, Imperial); **Warren Zevon** (1976) US#189, **Excitable Boy** (1977) g US#8, **Bad Luck Streak at Dancing School** (1980) US#20, **Stand in the Fire** (1980) US#80, **The Envoy** (1982, all Asylum) US#93; **Sentimental Hygiene** (1987) US#63, **Transverse City** (1987, both Virgin); **Mr. Bad Example** (1991), **Learning to Flinch** (1993) US#198, **Mutineer** (1995, all Giant). COMPILATIONS: **A Quiet Normal Life** (1986, Asylum); **I'll Sleep When I'm Dead (An Anthology)** (1996, Elektra/Rhino). HIT VERSION: *Poor, Poor, Pitiful Me* Linda Ronstadt (1978) C&W#46 US#31. Co-writers: [i] Leroy Marinell/Waddy Watchel.

Bibliography

ASCAP Biographical Dictionary (1966, Jaques Cattel Press)

Berry, Chuck; *The Chuck Berry Autobiography* (1987, Faber)

Blom, Eric, revised by Cummings, David; *The New Everyman Dictionary of Music* (96th edition) (1988, Everyman)

Bloom, Ken; *American Song—The Complete Musical Theatre Companion, 1900–1984, Volumes 1 & 2* (1985, Facts on File)

Bonds, Ray, editor; *The Encyclopedia of Black Music* (1980, Salamander/Harmony)

British Hit Singles, 11th Edition (1997, Guinness)

Carr, Roy, and Taylor, Tony; *The Beatles—An Illustrated Record* (1975, New English Library)

Clarke, Donald, editor; *The Penguin Encyclopedia of Popular Music* (1989, Penguin)

Cohen-Stratyner, Barbara, editor; *Popular Music, 1900–1919* (1988, Gale Research)

Cook, Richard, and Morton, Brian; *The Penguin Guide to Jazz on CD, LP and Cassette* (1992, Penguin)

Coryell, Julie, and Friedman, Laura; *Jazz-Rock Fusion: The People, The Music* (1978, Marion Boyars)

Crosby, David, and Gottlieb, Carl; *Long Time Gone—The Autobiography of David Crosby* (1989, William Heinemann)

Cummings, Tony; *The Sound of Philadelphia* (1977, Methuen)

Davis, Clive; *Inside the Record Business* (1974, Ballantine)

DiMartino, Dave; *Singer-Songwriters: Pop Music's Performer-Composers, from A to Zevon* (1994, Billboard)

Dixon, Willie, & Snowden, Don; *I Am the Blues—The Willie Dixon Story* (1989, Quartet)

Dorman, L.S., and Rawling, C.L.; *Leonard Cohen—Prophet of the Heart* (1990, Omnibus Press)

Editors of Country Music; *The Complete Country Music Encyclopedia* (1995, Boxtree)

Editors of Rolling Stone; *Neil Young: The Rolling Stones Files* (1994, Hyperion)

Editors of Time-Life; *As You Remember Them—The Men and the Music* (1972, Time-Life)

80 Years of American Song Hits, 1892–1972 (1972, Chappell)

Eliot, Marc; *Death of a Rebel* (revised edition) (1989, Franklin Watts)

Eliot, Marc, with Appel, Mike; *Down Thunder Road* (1992, Simon & Schuster)

Elliott, Brad; *Surf's Up!—The Beach Boys on Record, 1961–1981* (1982, Pierian Press)

Ewen, David; *American Songwriters* (1979, H.W. Wilson)

____. *Popular American Composers* (1962, H.W. Wilson)

The Faber Companion to Popular Music (1990, Faber)

Fawcett, Anthony; *California Rock, California Sound* (1984, Reed)

Feather, Leonard; *The Encyclopedia of Jazz* (1960, Bonanza)

Freeman, Scott; *Midnight Riders—The Story of the Allman Brothers Band* (1995, Little, Brown)

Furin, Phillip; *The Poets of Tin Pan Alley* (1990, Oxford University Press)

Gambaccini, Paul, Rice, Tim, and Rice, Jonathan; *British Hit Albums 7* (1996, Guinness, 1996)

Ganzl, Kurt; *The Encyclopedia of the Musical Theatre* (1994, Blackwell)

Gargan, William, and Sharma, Sue, editors; *Find That Tune* (1984, Neal-Schuman)

Giuliano, Geoffrey; *Dark Horse—The Private Life of George Harrison* (1989, E.P. Dutton)

Green, Stanley; *Broadway Musicals Show By Show* (1991, Hal Leonard)

____. *Encyclopedia of the Musical Theatre* (1976, Dodd, Mead)

Gregory, Hugh; *1,000 Great Guitarists* (1994, Balafon)

____. *Soul A to Z* (1991, Weidenfeld & Nicholson)

____. *Who's Who in Country* (1993, Weidenfeld & Nicholson)

Grieg, Charlotte; *Will You Still Love Me Tomorrow? —Girl Groups from the '50s On...* (1989, Virago)

Guralnich, Peter; *Sweet Soul Music* (1990, Harper & Row)

Halliwell, Leslie; *Halliwell's Film Guide* (9th Edition) (Scribner's, 1988)

Harris, Sam; *Blues Who's Who* (1977, Arlington House)

Hart, Dorothy; *Thou Swell, Thou Witty: The Life and Lyrics of Lorenz Hart* (1976, Harper & Row)

Havlice, Patricia Pate; *Popular Song Index* (1984, Scarecrow Press)

Helm, Levon, with Davis, Stephen; *This Wheel's on Fire: Levon Helm and the Story of the Band* (1993, William Morrow)

Hounsome, Terry; *Rock Record 4* (1991, Record Researcher Publications)

Howe, Leslie; *Directory of Popular Music* (3rd edition) (1992, Waterlow)

Humphries, John; *Music Master Catalogue* (annually, John Humphries Publishing, Ltd.)

____. *Music Master Tracks Catalogue* (John Humphries Publishing, Ltd.)

Jablonski, Edward; *Gershwin* (1987, Simon & Schuster)

____. *Harold Arlen—Happy with the Blues* (1961, Doubleday)

Jacobs, Dick, and Jacobs, Harriet; *Who Wrote That Song?* (1994, Writer's Digest)

Jasen, David A.; *Tin Pan Alley* (1988, Donald I. Fine, Inc.)

Jones, Leroi; *Black Music* (1968, Morrow)

Kennedy, Michael; *The Concise Oxford Dictionary of Music* (1980, Oxford University Press)

Kernfeld, Barry, editor; *The New Grove Dictionary of Jazz* (1995, Macmillan)

Lablanc, Michael L.; *Contemporary Musicians, Volume 1* (1989, Gale Research)

Landon, Grellun, and Irwin Stambler; *The Encyclopedia of Folk, Country and Western Music* (1985, St. Martin's Press)

Larkin, Colin, editor; *The Guinness Encyclopedia of Popular Music* (1992, Guinness)

Lax, Roger, and Smith, Frederick; *The Great Song Thesaurus* (2nd edition) (1989, Oxford University Press)

Leaf, David; *The Bee Gees—The Authorised Biography* (1980, Octopus)

McNeel, Kent, and Luther, Mark; *Songwriters with a Touch of Gold* (1976, Will Martin Publishing)

Mancini, Henry, with Lees, Gene; *Did They Mention the Music?* (1983, Contemporary)

Marcus, Greil; *Mystery Train* (1975, E.P. Dutton)

Mingus, Charlie; *Beneath the Underdog* (1971, Alfred Knopf)

O'Grady, Terence J.; *The Beatles: A Musical Evolution* (1983, G.K. Hall & Co.)

Oliver, Paul, editor; *The Blackwell Guide to Recorded Blues* (1991, Blackwell)

Osborne, John; *Movie and TV Soundtracks—The Official Price Guide* (1991, House of Collectibles)

Park, James, *Icons* (1994, Collier)

Phillips, John, with Jerome, Jim; *Papa John* (186, Dolphin Doubleday)

Phonolog (updated weekly by Trade Service Corporation)

Picardi, Justin, and Wade, Dorothy; *Music Man* (1990, W.W. Norton)

Pleasants, Henry; *The Great American Popular Singers* (1974, Gollancz)

Pollock, Bruce; *In Their Own Words* (1975, MacMillan)

Record Collector; *Rare Record Guide 1997/98* (1997, Diamond Publishing)

Rees, Dafydd, and Crampton, Luke, with Lazell, Barry; *The Guinness Book of Rock Stars* (1989, Guinness)

Rees, Dafydd, and Crampton, Luke; *The Guinness Book of Rock Stars* (2nd Edition) (1991, Guinness)

____. *The Guinness Book of Rock Stars* (3rd edition) (1994, Guinness)

____. *Q Encyclopedia of Rock Stars* (1996, Dorling Kindersley)

Ritz, David; *Divided Soul—The Life of Marvin Gaye* (1985, McGraw-Hill)

Robinson, Fred; *The Billboard Book of Number One Hits* (1990, Billboard)

Roxon, Lillian; *Rock Encyclopedia* (1969, Grosset & Dunlap)

Russell, Jeff; *The Beatles Album File and Complete Discography* (1982, Blandford Press)

Sandahl, Linda J.; *The Encyclopedia of Rock Music on Film* (1984, Blandford Press)

Santelli, Robert; *The Big Book of the Blues* (1994, Pavillion)

Scheuer, Steven H.; *Movies on T.V., 1982–1983 Edition* (1981, Bantam)

Shapiro, Marc; *The Story of the Eagles: The Long Run* (1995, Omnibus)

Shapiro, Nat, and Pollack, Bruce; *Popular Music, Volumes 1 and 2, 1920–1979* (1985, Gale Research)

____. *Popular Music, Volume 9, 1980–1984* (1986, Gale Research)

____. *Popular Music, Volume 10, 1985* (1986, Gale Research)

____. *Popular Music, Volume 11, 1986* (1987, Gale Research)

____. *Popular Music, Volume 12, 1987* (1989, Gale Research)

Shestack, Melvin; *Country Music Encyclopedia* (1979, Omnibus)

Spector, Ronnie, with Waldron, Vince; *Be My Baby* (1990, Macmillan)

Stambler, Irwin; *The Encyclopedia of Pop, Rock and Soul* (1989, Macmillan)

Station, Observer; *Bob Marley — The Illustrated Disco/Biography* (1982, Omnibus Press)

Steveacre, Tony; *The Songwriters* (1970, BBC)

Suskin, Steven; *Berlin, Kern, Rodgers, Hart, and Hammerstein: A Complete Song Catalogue* (1990, McFarland)

____. *Show Tunes, 1905–1985* (1986, Dodd, Mead)

Swan, Mike; *How Many Roads? — A History and Guide of American Singer/Songwriters* (1989, Temple House Books)

Tee, Ralph; *Who's Who in Soul Music* (1991, Weidenfeld & Nicholson)

Umphred, Neal; *Goldmine's Price Guide to Collectible Jazz Albums, 1949–1969* (1994, Krause, 1994)

Watkinson, Mike, and Anderson, Pete; *Scott Walker: A Deep Shade of Blue* (1994, Virgin)

Wexler, Jerry, and Ritz, David; *Rhythm and Blues: A Life in American Music* (1994, Cape)

Whitburn, Joel; *The Billboard Book of USA Top 40 Hits* (1985, Billboard)

____. *The Billboard Hot 100 Charts: The Sixties* (1991, Record Research)

____. *The Billboard Hot 100 Charts: The Seventies* (1991, Record Research)

____. *The Billboard Hot 100 Charts: The Eighties* (1991, Record Research)

____. *Bubbling Under the Hot 100, 1959–1985* (1992, Record Research)

____. *Pop Memories, 1890–1954: The History of American Popular Music* (1986, Record Research)

____. *Top Country Singles, 1944–1988* (1989, Record Research)

____. *Top 40 Hits* (1985, Billboard)

____. *Top Pop Albums, 1955–1992* (1993, Record Research)

____. *Top R&B Singles, 1942–1988* (1989, Record Research)

White, Adam; *The Billboard Book of Gold and Platinum Records* (1990, Billboard/Omnibus Press, 1990)

White, Mark; *You Must Remember This...Popular Songwriters, 1900–1980* (1983, Warne)

White, Timothy; *Catch a Fire — The Life of Bob Marley* (1983, Henry Holt & Company)

Wilder, Alec; *American Popular Song: The Great Innovators, 1900–1950* (1972, Oxford University Press)

Wilk, Max; *They're Playing Our Song* (1973, Atheneum)

Williams, Paul; *Bob Dylan — Performing Artist* (1990, Xanadu)

Wood, Phil, editor; *Artists of American Folk Music* (1970, GPI Books)

Reference was also made to numerous record company catalogues, television programs, video cassettes, and a variety of editions of the following newspapers and periodicals:

American Songwriter, Bam, Billboard, Blackmail mail order catalogue, Blitz, Blues and Soul, Cashbox, City Limits, Dark Star, Down Beat, Entertainment Weekly, Esquire, The Face, Friends, Goldmine, House of Lords mail order catalogue, The L.A. Weekly, The London Observer, The London Times, The Los Angeles Times, The Manchester Guardian, Magpie mail order catalogue, Melody Maker, Metal Leg, Mojo, Music Week, New Musical Express, The New York Times, Newsweek, Playboy, Premier, Q, Record Collector, Record Mirror, Record Retailer, Rolling Stone, The San Francisco Bay Guardian, The San Francisco Chronicle, See for Miles catalogue, Select, Smash Hits, Songwriter, Soundtrack — The Collector's Quarterly, Spin, Strange Fruit, Strange Things Magazine, Street Life, Time Out, Uncut, USA Today, Vox, Zig-Zag.

Index

References are to entry numbers. Where there is more than one entry with the same title or name, these are listed separately. Names in **CAPS** have their own entries.

Q

X